THE UN WORKING GROUP ON ARBITRARY DETENTION

The United Nations Working Group on Arbitrary Detention is the first comprehensive review of the contributions of this important institution to understanding arbitrary detention today. The Working Group is a body of five independent human rights experts that considers individual complaints of arbitrary detention, adopting legal opinions as to whether a detention is compatible with states' obligations under international law. Since its establishment in 1991, it has adopted more than 1,200 case opinions and conducted more than 50 country missions. But much more than a jurisprudential review, these cases are presented in the book in the style of a treatise, where the widest array of issues on arbitrary detention are placed in the context of the requirements of multilateral treaties and other relevant international standards. Written for both practitioners and serious scholars alike, this book includes five case studies and a foreword by Archbishop Desmond M. Tutu.

Jared Genser is Managing Director of Perseus Strategies, a public interest law firm, and an adjunct professor of Law at Georgetown University Law Center. He also founded Freedom Now, an independent nongovernmental organization, and has been referred to by the *New York Times* as "The Extractor" for his work freeing political prisoners around the world. Previously, he was a partner in the government affairs practice of the global law firm DLA Piper LLP and a management consultant with McKinsey & Company. Genser is a recipient of the American Bar Association's International Human Rights Award.

Reviews and Endorsements for *The UN Working Group on Arbitrary Detention:*

Commentary and Guide to Practice

Jared Genser is the leading attorney in the world on arbitrary detention in international law and established this reputation during the years I was a Member and Chair-Rapporteur of the UN Working Group on Arbitrary Detention. His book makes an important contribution to understanding international law on arbitrary detention and offers a wealth of materials and clear and convincing analysis of the law and the major challenges that arbitrary detention poses to the international community today.

Mads Andenas Q.C.
Professor, University of Oslo and Institute of Advanced Legal Studies,
School of Advanced Study, University of London
Member and Chair-Rapporteur, UN Working Group on Arbitrary Detention (2009–2015)
Director, British Institute of International and Comparative Law, London (1999–2006)

I have a rather unusual perspective on arbitrary detention because having been subjected to it by various authoritarian rulers of The Maldives has been a central and defining set of experiences in my life. Indeed, I've been arrested more than twenty times, repeatedly tortured, and have served more than three years in prison over various periods of arbitrary detention. . . . [A]t that point in 2015, [when I had been convicted on manufactured terrorism charges], I hired this book's author, Jared Genser, to serve as my pro bono counsel, alongside Amal Clooney and Ben Emmerson. The story of their extraordinary efforts is described in a compelling case study chapter in this book. The team submitted my case to the Working Group in April 2015 and in October 2015 it issued Opinion No. 33/2015, a scathing twenty-page judgment that rejected the Government's arguments on every point and demanded my immediate release. Hundreds marched in the streets of Malé supporting the Working Group's decision. With my team's relentless advocacy, the Government could not withstand the political pressure and it was forced to release me. I was greeted by Amal and Jared when I arrived in London on January 21, 2016. But that was not the end of the story . . . in September 2018 our country succeeded in defeating Yameen in a democratic election. My close friend and co-founder of our political party Ibrahim Mohamed Solih was elected President. I returned to The Maldives in November 2018 and was especially pleased that Jared was with me in our Supreme Court on the day it reversed my conviction and acquitted me on all charges, citing to the opinion of the Working Group as a key reason for its decision. In April 2019, I was elected to our Parliament, the People's Majlis, and in May 2019, I was elected and sworn in to be its new Speaker. . . . The greatest fear of any political prisoner is that they will be forgotten. This exceptional and meticulous work of scholarship will be an invaluable tool for advocates to make sure that doesn't happen.

The Honorable Mohamed Nasheed
Speaker of the People's Majlis, The Maldives (2019–Present)
President of The Maldives (2008–2012)

We have seen substantial progress in reducing the phenomenon of arbitrary detention in the Americas but there still remain too many countries in our region with serious challenges to the rule of law and where especially repressive governments stubbornly persist in imprisoning their opponents against the tide of history. While the Inter-American Commission and Court of Human Rights have taken up many of these cases, the UN Working Group on Arbitrary Detention has also highlighted some of the worst. This impressive book, authored by Jared Genser, who over the years has represented prominent political prisoners in countries like Bolivia, Colombia, Cuba, Nicaragua, and Venezuela, shines an important spotlight on a major gap between the commitments of states in the American Convention on Human Rights to end the practice of arbitrary arrest and imprisonment and their implementation in practice.

The Honorable Luis Almagro
Secretary General, Organization of American States

Kudos to Jared Genser for bringing to life the inner workings and substantial accomplishments of one of the key UN human rights bodies – the Working Group on Arbitrary Detention. . . . Genser not only presents an analysis of the legal significance of its jurisprudence over the past twenty seven years, but then reveals to his reader what it really means to submit a case for a decision, to fight for the unjustly imprisoned, and to succeed in securing their freedom. . . . It's easy to criticize "the UN" and its member states for its inconsistent defense of human rights in its politicized forums; but the real achievements of the UN human rights system lie in the norms it has adopted and the independent mechanisms like the Working Group that fight independently to uphold these standards in real world situations, for real people. Genser opens our eyes to what's needed to make a good case – and how to fight for individual freedom, successfully.

Felice D. Gaer
Director, Jacob Blaustein Institute for Human Rights
Vice-Chairperson, UN Committee against Torture

Having spent over a decade in solitary confinement as a political prisoner, I have come to appreciate with great intensity that the subtle aspects of freedom – to read, to walk about, and to sleep – are actions that can easily be taken for granted. The persistent denial of access to family, to information and to human interaction induces a profound loneliness in the prisoner, coupled with the dreadful feeling as though your life's contributions are slowly being excised from public consciousness. This is why, when a sympathetic prison guard tapped on my cell gate one morning and whispered to me with hushed excitement that "the UN just called for your release!," I felt a renewed sense of hope that the wheels of justice were still churning. I learned a short time later that my international lawyer Jared Genser, the book's author, had just made public Opinion No. 22/2015. In a detailed decision, the Working Group unanimously agreed I was being held in violation of international law and it urged my immediate release . . . for the United Nations to have spoken out in this unequivocal way had struck an irrecoverable blow to the former prime minister's efforts to try to justify my detention. . . . Jared Genser is a pioneer in the area of human rights law and a courageous and indefatigable representative of political prisoners around the world. This book represents his singular expertise in this area and should be required reading for all who seek a deeper understanding of the Working Group's activities and inner mechanisms.

Dato' Seri Anwar Ibrahim
President of the People's Justice Party and Member of Parliament (2018–Present)
Deputy Prime Minister of Malaysia (1993–1998)

There are those for whom words have meaning and those who issue hollow promises. This is as true of people as it is of states. . . . It is precisely to ensure that these words were not empty that France, with Robert Badinter and Louis Joinet, has played a leading role in the establishment of an original mechanism to ensure concretely the proper application of the intentions proclaimed by these nations. . . . It is in this spirit that Jared Genser has produced this exceptional work, so rigorous in both legal and methodological terms. This book will surely become an indispensable tool for all those who believe that human rights are nothing if they are not concretely applied to individual situations. . . . Thanks to the author for allowing us to better defend those persecuted around the world by so usefully assisting their advocates, without whom the universality of fundamental rights would be a vain hope.

The Honorable François Zimeray
Ambassador of France for Human Rights (2008–2013)
Lawyer

As someone engaged in the defense of political prisoners over the years, I regard *The United Nations Working Group on Arbitrary Detention* as a tour de force and seminal scholarly work, which makes an enormous contribution to understanding the phenomenon of arbitrary detention in our world today. In particular, it is also a comprehensive and practical guide for freeing the arbitrarily detained, infused with the author's experiences as an international lawyer in this complex, interdisciplinary, and specialist field, where his exceptional work is widely known and respected for its unique and effective contributions.

The Honorable Irwin Cotler, P.C., O.C.
Chairman, Raoul Wallenberg Centre for Human Rights
Minister of Justice and Attorney General of Canada (2003–2006)

Up until the Working Group adopted Opinion No. 2/2003 on my case, I had been detained with total impunity and incommunicado by China for more than fourteen months. Within a day of this decision being made public, I was finally given access to my local lawyer and my hope was restored, learning the world had not forgotten my plight. Despite still having faced a potential death sentence on spurious charges of endangering national security, this invaluable opinion from the United Nations combined with the relentless advocacy of this book's author Jared Genser resulted in my early release, enabling me to dedicate the balance of my life pursuing freedom, democracy, and human rights for the Chinese people.

Yang Jianli
President, Initiatives for China

The UN Working Group on Arbitrary Detention

COMMENTARY AND GUIDE TO PRACTICE

Jared Genser
Perseus Strategies *and* Georgetown University Law Center

CAMBRIDGE UNIVERSITY PRESS

CAMBRIDGE
UNIVERSITY PRESS

University Printing House, Cambridge CB2 8BS, United Kingdom

One Liberty Plaza, 20th Floor, New York, NY 10006, USA

477 Williamstown Road, Port Melbourne, VIC 3207, Australia

314–321, 3rd Floor, Plot 3, Splendor Forum, Jasola District Centre, New Delhi – 110025, India

79 Anson Road, #06–04/06, Singapore 079906

Cambridge University Press is part of the University of Cambridge.

It furthers the University's mission by disseminating knowledge in the pursuit of education, learning, and research at the highest international levels of excellence.

www.cambridge.org
Information on this title: www.cambridge.org/9781107034457
DOI: 10.1017/9781139540711

First published 2020

A catalogue record for this publication is available from the British Library.

Library of Congress Cataloging-in-Publication Data
NAMES: Genser, Jared, author.
TITLE: The UN Working Group on Arbitrary Detention : commentary and guide to practice / Jared Genser.
DESCRIPTION: New York : Cambridge University Press, 2019.
IDENTIFIERS: LCCN 2019014858 | ISBN 9781107034457 (hardback)
SUBJECTS: LCSH: United Nations. Working Group on Arbitrary Detention. | Detention of persons–Government policy. | Due process of law. | Human rights–International cooperation. | BISAC: LAW / International.
CLASSIFICATION: LCC K3241 .G46 2019 | DDC 345/.0527–dc23
LC record available at https://lccn.loc.gov/2019014858

ISBN 978-1-107-03445-7 Hardback

Contents

Figures

About the Author

Jared Genser is Managing Director of Perseus Strategies, a public interest law firm. He also founded Freedom Now, an independent nongovernmental organization, and has been referred to by the *New York Times* as "The Extractor" for his work freeing political prisoners around the world. Although past success is no guarantee of future performance, over the course of his career Genser has taken more than forty-five cases to the UN Working Group on Arbitrary Detention and never lost. Those cases have been brought against many governments, including those of Bolivia, China, Cuba, Egypt, Iran, Iraq, Kazakhstan, Myanmar, Nicaragua, North Korea, Pakistan, Russian Federation, South Sudan, Sudan, Malaysia, Maldives, Turkey, and Viet Nam. The cases were filed on behalf of a total of 309 detainees, of whom 300 have had their cases resolved.

Before founding Perseus Strategies, Genser was a partner in the government affairs practice of the global law firm DLA Piper LLP and a management consultant with McKinsey & Company. He has taught semester-long seminars about the UN Security Council at Georgetown University Law Center and the University of Michigan and University of Pennsylvania law schools. He was an associate of the Carr Center for Human Rights Policy at Harvard University from 2014 to 2016, a visiting fellow with the National Endowment for Democracy from 2006 to 2007, and earlier in his career was named by the *National Law Journal* as one of "40 Under 40: Washington's Rising Stars."

Genser's pro bono clients have included former Czech Republic President Václav Havel and Nobel Peace Prize Laureates Liu Xiaobo, Aung San Suu Kyi, Desmond M. Tutu, and Elie Wiesel. He holds a BS from Cornell University, an MPP from Harvard University's John F. Kennedy School of Government, where he was an Alumni Public Service Fellow, and a JD cum laude from the University of Michigan Law School.

He is coeditor of *The UN Security Council in the Age of Human Rights* (Cambridge University Press, 2016) and *The Responsibility to Protect: The Promise of Stopping Mass Atrocities in Our Time* (2011).

Genser is the recipient of the American Bar Association's International Human Rights Award, Liberty in North Korea's Freedom Fighter Award, and the Charles Bronfman Prize. He is a member of the Council on Foreign Relations and Fellow of the Royal Society of the Arts. In addition to being qualified to practice law in Maryland and the District of Columbia in the United States, he is also a Solicitor of England and Wales.

Foreword

Dear Friends,

Since the beginning of recorded history, people in positions of political and economic power have wielded detention and imprisonment as weapons – often arbitrarily and brutally – to reduce the influence of those who disagree with them. Depending on prevailing environmental circumstances, these "dissenters" are sometimes labeled political detainees, political prisoners, or prisoners of war.

Power can prove more fleeting than we think. As the Reverend Martin Luther King observed, "The arc of the moral universe is long, but it bends towards justice." Yet powerful people keep committing the same mistakes. They keep locking up those who hold different views to their own, hoping that the prison bars will make their problems go away, and proving over and over the truth of Spanish philosopher George Santayana's point: "Those who cannot remember the past are condemned to repeat it."

Two of the people widely regarded as among the brightest lights of the twentieth century, Winston Churchill and Nelson Mandela, have in common that their journeys to the helm of their countries were defined by their confinements in South Africa. Churchill was not held for long, but his derring-do escape from a prisoner-of-war camp during the second Anglo–Boer War was regarded as heroic and a turning point in his career. Mandela, on the other hand, absorbed the pressures of his twenty-seven-year incarceration in apartheid prisons to emerge fully formed, a giant sparkling diamond of humanity – virtually without flaws.

Suffering embitters some people, while ennobling others. But this does not detract from the fact that, whatever the eventual outcome, society must hold those who abuse power to account.

I am not a pacifist; nor do I believe that in situations of wrongfulness claiming neutral ground is morally defensible. I have long said that if you are neutral in situations of injustice then you have chosen the side of the oppressor.

To its enormous credit, since its establishment in 1991, the United Nations Working Group on Arbitrary Detention has been a candle in the darkness, relentlessly shining a bright light on the grave injustice of the arbitrary deprivation of liberty around the world. It has issued more than 1,000 legal opinions regarding the detentions of more than 5,000 people. In many cases these opinions, when combined with effective advocacy, have proved key factors in helping secure freedom for the arbitrarily detained. The group has also conducted more than fifty field visits to nations around the world to better understand the situation of deprivations of liberty and the underlying reasons for arbitrary detentions.

This book is both the first comprehensive review of the Working Group's jurisprudence and activities and a practical guide designed to assist advocates for the arbitrarily detained to be more effective in their efforts. I am especially pleased to recommend it to you because I worked with its author, the tenacious human rights lawyer Jared Genser, on political prisoner cases for more than a dozen years.

If you are reading this foreword, it probably means that you can put the information in the book to good use – in your own way – to contribute to securing the release from prison of someone who has been arbitrarily deprived of their liberty. The greatest fear of any political prisoner is that they will be forgotten. By taking up this cause you can ensure the world will remember.

God bless you.

Archbishop Emeritus Desmond M. Tutu
Cape Town, South Africa
January 2019

Acknowledgments

The research and writing of this book took three years and an enormous amount of effort. That is because it is much more than a treatise about the jurisprudence of the UN Working Group on Arbitrary Detention. It was also written to serve as a guide to how to most effectively address the phenomenon of arbitrary detention in our world today, grounded in my personal experiences helping the courageous detainees who I have had the privilege to represent. Although the Working Group remains a little-known quasi-judicial body overseen by the United Nations Human Rights Council, its opinions, country missions, and broader efforts serve an invaluable function in assisting advocates for the arbitrarily detained in securing their ultimate release and helping governments improve their adherence to their obligations under international law. The Working Group's volunteer expert members and professional staff deserve enormous credit for performing small miracles every day, despite the small budget, that often help save people's lives.

This book would not have been possible without the superb research, drafting, and editorial assistance that I have received from numerous staff, interns, externs, and part-time consultants to my public interest law firm Perseus Strategies, including Emad Ansari, Elise Baranouski, Maraya Best, Sara Birkenthal, Mary Brooks, Michael Cullen, Phoebe Dantoin, Sara Deibler, Skylar Gleason, Csaba Gondola, Anli Jiao, William Juhn, Claire Lynch, Ashley McLaughlin-Leen, Luladay Mengistie, Juan Miramontes, Laura Notess, George O'Connor, Charles Orta, Samuel Ritholtz, Nicole Santiago, Brian Tronic, and Daniel Wassim. And I have also been truly blessed to have extraordinary mentors who inspired and challenged me over the course of my career, including Jerome A. Cohen, Irwin Cotler, Lawrence Levinson, Kathleen Kennedy Townsend, and Desmond M. Tutu, among others.

I would like to dedicate this book to the clients and their families that I have been honored to represent, going back to my time as a law student. Their resilience in the face of adversity, their suffering, and their willingness to put their lives in my hands have been both a sacred trust and enormous responsibility.

I would also like to dedicate this book to my parents, Lyne Taylor Genser and Sander Genser, who inspired my commitment to public service. And I would also like to dedicate it to my children, Alexandra and Zachary, who bring such joy and inspiration to my life. It is for them that I have sought as best I could to leave the world a little better off than how I found it. I also want to extend my profound thanks to my wife, Elaine, whose unyielding love and support truly make everything possible.

And, finally, I would like to thank my editor, John Berger at Cambridge University Press, for his patience and support for this important project.

Abbreviations

ACHPR	African Charter on Human and Peoples' Rights
ACHR	American Convention on Human Rights
AKP	Justice and Development Party ("Adalet ve Kalkınma Partisi," Turkey)
BHRC	Bar Human Rights Committee of England and Wales
CAT	Convention against Torture and other Cruel, Inhuman or Degrading Treatment or Punishment
CERD	Convention on the Elimination of Racial Discrimination
CRC	Convention on the Rights of the Child
CSRT	Combatant Status Review Tribunal
DEA	Drug Enforcement Administration
DPRK	Democratic People's Republic of Korea
ECHR	European Convention on Human Rights
ECOSOC	Economic and Social Council
ECtHR	European Court of Human Rights
ETA	Basque Homeland and Liberty ("Euskadi Ta Askatasuna," Spain/France)
EU	European Union
FIDH	International Federation for Human Rights
HR Committee	UN Human Rights Committee
HRC	UN Human Rights Council
IACHR	Inter-American Commission on Human Rights
ICC	International Criminal Court
ICCPR	International Covenant on Civil and Political Rights
ICJ	International Court of Justice
ICRC	International Committee of the Red Cross
ICTY	International Criminal Tribunal for the Former Yugoslavia
ILO	International Labor Organization
KEGOC	Kazakhstan Electricity Grid Operating Company
LTTE	Liberation Tigers of Tamil Eelam
MDP	Maldivian Democratic Party
MNDF	Maldives National Defence Force
NGO	Non-Governmental Organization
NLD	National League for Democracy
OAS	Organization of American States

OHCHR	UN Office of the High Commissioner for Human Rights
PJAK	Kurdish Free Life Party ("Partiya Jiyana Azad a Kurdistanê," Iran)
TICC	"Títulos de Interés y Capital Cubiertos," Venezuela
TÜBITAK	Scientific and Technological Research Council of Turkey ("Türkiye Bilimsel ve Teknolojik Araştırma Kurumu," Turkey)
UAE	United Arab Emirates
UDHR	Universal Declaration of Human Rights
UN	United Nations
UNCHR	UN Commission on Human Rights
UNGA	UN General Assembly
UNHCR	UN High Commissioner for Refugees
UNOG	UN Office at Geneva
UPR	Universal Periodic Review
VCCR	Vienna Convention on Consular Relations
WGAD	UN Working Group on Arbitrary Detention

Part I. Background

Introduction

There is arbitrary detention in every country in the world today. It knows no boundaries and countless people are subjected to arbitrary detention every year. But what is detention and what makes it arbitrary? The *Universal Declaration of Human Rights* (UDHR) declares that "[n]o one shall be subjected to arbitrary arrest, detention or exile."[1] The *International Covenant on Civil and Political Rights* (ICCPR), a multilateral treaty, goes further: "[e]veryone has the right to liberty and security of the person. No one shall be subjected to arbitrary arrest or detention. No one shall be deprived of his liberty except on such grounds and in accordance with such procedure as are establishment by law."[2]

I What Is Detention?

As originally established by UN Commission on Human Rights (UNCHR) Resolution 1991/42, the five-member UN Working Group on Arbitrary Detention (WGAD) focuses on adjudicating and issuing individual legal opinions as to whether the deprivation of liberty of detainees is or is not in violation of international law. But it did not at the outset define the term "detention," which led to differing interpretations of the term. Ultimately, this was corrected in UNCHR Resolution 1997/50, where it noted the WGAD was "entrusted with the task of investigating cases of *deprivation of liberty* imposed arbitrarily ... "[3]

The deprivation of liberty of a person charged with or convicted of a serious crime may be legitimate. In certain cases, a person may be deprived of liberty by administrative authorities, such as a person with serious mental illness. Personal liberty may also be limited during states of emergency. There are certain categories of deprivation of liberty that are illegal, such as imprisoning a person for failing to pay their debt. The reality is that international instruments used differing terminology and it can be challenging to discern differences between them. Varying terms can include "arrest," "apprehension," "detention," "incarceration," "imprisonment," and "custody," among others.[4]

---

[1] *Universal Declaration of Human Rights*, G.A. Res. 217A (III), U.N. Doc. A/810, at Art. 9 (1948).

[2] *International Covenant on Civil and Political Rights*, G.A. Res 2200A (XXI), 21 U.N. GAOR Supp. (No. 16), at 52, U.N. Doc. A/6316 (1966), 999 U.N.T.S. 171, *entered into force* Mar. 23, 1976, at Art. 9(1).

[3] Resolution 1997/50 (Arbitrary Detention), Commission on Human Rights, E.CN.4/1997/50, Adopted Apr. 15, 1997, at ¶ 15 (emphasis added).

[4] *Revised Fact Sheet No. 26, The Working Group on Arbitrary Detention*, Office of the High Commissioner for Human Rights, Feb. 8, 2019.

With regards to the WGAD, the terms "arbitrary detention" and "deprivation of liberty" were chosen, however, because it is instructed to act for the protection of all individuals deprived of their liberties in all their forms. Its mandate extends to the deprivation of liberty before, during, or after a trial, or in the absence of a trial at all. It also extends to other types of deprivation of liberty such as house arrest, rehabilitation through labor, and involuntary psychiatric hospitalization when accompanied by serious restrictions on freedom of movement.[5]

II What Makes a Deprivation of Liberty Arbitrary?

What makes the deprivation of liberty in a particular case arbitrary is the focus of this book. But prior to examining the concept of arbitrary detention, it is useful to look at arbitrariness generally and in the context of international law. In this regard, the WGAD in its jurisprudence[6] has referred to Judge Cançado Trindade's discussions of arbitrariness in customary international law in his judgment in the International Court of Justice in *Ahmadou Sadio Diallo* (*Republic of Guinea* v. *Democratic Republic of Congo*). In speaking of the notion of arbitrariness, Judge Trindade explained:

> 108. The adjective "arbitrary," derived from the Latin "*arbitrarius*," originally meant that which depended on the authority or will of the arbitrator, of a legally recognized authority. With the passing of time, however, it gradually acquired a different connotation; already in the mid-seventeenth century, it had been taken to mean that which appeared uncontrolled (arbitrary) in the exercise of will, amounting to capriciousness or despotism. The qualification "arbitrary" came thus to be used in order to characterize decisions grounded on simple preference or prejudice, defying any test of "foresee-ability," ensuing from the entirely *free will* of the authority concerned, rather than based on *reason*, on the conception of the rule of law in a democratic society, on the criterion of reasonableness and the imperatives of justice, on the fundamental principle of equality and non-discrimination.

> 109. As human rights treaties and instruments conform a *law of protection* (a *droit de protection*), oriented towards the safeguard of the ostensibly weaker party, the victim, it is not at all surprising that the prohibition of *arbitrariness* (in its modern and contemporary sense) covers arrests and detentions, as well as other acts of the public power, such as expulsions. Bearing in mind the hermeneutics of human rights treaties, as outlined above, a merely exegetical or literal interpretation of treaty provisions would be wholly unwarranted.[7]

Judge Trindade then proceeded to explain the position of the UN Human Rights Committee (HR Committee) as it has interpreted the term "arbitrary." In *Mukong* v. *Cameroon*, the HR Committee interpreted "arbitrary" in the broadest sense, as

---

[5] *Id.*

[6] Liu Xiaobo v. China, WGAD Opinion No. 15/2011, Adopted May 5, 2011, ¶ 20. The author began representing Liu Xiaobo as pro bono counsel through Freedom Now in mid-2010, a few months before he was announced as the recipient of the 2010 Nobel Peace Prize.

[7] Ahmadou Sadio Diallo (Republic of Guinea v. Democratic Republic of Congo), Judgment, Nov. 30, 2010, Separate Opinion of Judge Cançado Trindade, at p. 128, ¶¶ 108–109.

meaning inappropriate, unjust, unpredictable, and inconsistent with legality.[8] As such, arbitrariness was not simply "against the law," but had to be interpreted "more broadly to include elements of inappropriateness, injustice, lack of predictability and due process of law."[9] And in *Jalloh v. The Netherlands*, it said "arbitrary," should be understood as covering "unreasonable action," such that the way a state acted should be appropriate and proportional in the circumstances of the case at issue.[10]

For its part, the WGAD has been unequivocal in its views, which were explained in detail in its Deliberation No. 9 Concerning the Definition and Scope of Arbitrary Deprivation of Liberty under Customary International Law. It stated: "The prohibition of the arbitrary deprivation of liberty is part of treaty law, customary international law, and constitutes a *jus cogens*[11] norm. Its specific content, as laid out in this deliberation, remains fully applicable in all situations."[12]

The WGAD has further explained that it considers a deprivation of liberty as arbitrary if a person is detained in a way that is incompatible with a state's international legal obligations. By definition, if a person is convicted in violation of domestic law and due process rights, their detention is also arbitrary. The WGAD's focus, however, is on violations of international law, though it will consider violations of domestic law to inform whether international law was violated as well.

According to its Methods of Work, when discharging its mandate to assess if specific deprivations of liberty are arbitrary, the WGAD refers to five legal categories of cases:

(a) When it is clearly impossible to invoke any legal basis justifying the deprivation of liberty, as when a person is kept in detention after the completion of his or her sentence or despite an amnesty law applicable to him or her (category I);

(b) When the deprivation of liberty results from the exercise of the rights or freedoms guaranteed by articles 7, 13–14 and 18–21 of the Universal Declaration of Human Rights and, insofar as States parties are concerned, by articles 12, 18–19, 21–22, and 25–27 of the International Covenant on Civil and Political Rights (category II);

(c) When the total or partial nonobservance of the international norms relating to the right to a fair trial, established in the Universal Declaration of Human Rights and in the relevant international instruments accepted by the States concerned, is of such gravity as to give the deprivation of liberty an arbitrary character (category III);

(d) When asylum seekers, immigrants, or refugees are subjected to prolonged administrative custody without the possibility of administrative or judicial review or remedy (category IV);

(e) When the deprivation of liberty constitutes a violation of international law on the grounds of discrimination based on birth, national, ethnic or social origin, language, religion, economic condition, political or other opinion, gender, sexual

---

[8] Mukong v. Cameroon, Communication No. 458/1991, Human Rights Committee, CCPR/C/51/D/458/1991, July 21, 1994, at ¶ 9.8.

[9] *Id.*

[10] Jalloh v. The Netherlands, Communication No. 794/1998, Human Rights Committee, CCPR/C/74/D/794/1998, Mar. 26, 2002, at ¶ 8.2.

[11] *Jus cogens*, from Latin for "compelling law," is a peremptory norm, which is a fundamental, overriding principle of international law, from which no derogation is ever permitted.

[12] *Report of the Working Group on Arbitrary Detention*, Human Rights Council, A/HRC/22/44, Dec. 24, 2012, at ¶¶ 50–51.

orientation, disability, or any other status, that aims toward or can result in ignoring the equality of human beings (category V).[13]

In its annual report published in 2017, the WGAD provided further explanation of what it described as "irregular forms of deprivation of liberty":

50. The right to liberty of person is not an absolute right and limitations to that right may be justified. However, any deprivation of liberty, irrespective of the context in which it occurs, must not be arbitrary and must be carried out with respect to the rule of law.

51. The Working Group wishes to recall that the deprivation of personal liberty occurs when a person is being held without his or her free consent. Individuals who, for example, go voluntarily to a police station to participate in an investigation and who know that they are free to leave at any time are not in fact deprived of their liberty. It is, however, paramount that the element of voluntariness is not abused and that any claim that an individual is at a certain place at his or her own free will is indeed the case.

52. The Working Group is conscious of the increasing number of new regimes of deprivation of liberty that arise in different situations and contexts around the world. While prisons and police stations remain the most common places where an individual may be deprived of his or her liberty, there are a number of different places which an individual is not free to leave at will and which raise a question of de facto deprivation of liberty. It is paramount that, irrespective of what such places are called, the circumstances in which an individual is detained are examined so as to determine whether he or she is in fact at liberty to leave such a place at will. If not, it is paramount that all the safeguards applicable to situations of deprivation of liberty are in place so as to guard against any arbitrariness.

53. The Working Group has come across such examples in the context of immigration detention. There is an increasing number of countries that hold irregular migrants in various temporary or permanent settings, such as holding rooms, reception centers, and shelters. While not officially called "detention centers," those places are in fact closed institutions and individuals kept in them are not at liberty to leave, which makes such places de facto detention places. Therefore, all the safeguards that are in place, or should be in place, to guard against arbitrary deprivation of liberty must be respected in relation to every person held in such a setting.

54. Equally, the Working Group is mindful that some countries have introduced and continue to introduce stringent counter-terrorism measures, of which so-called anti-radicalization measures form an important part. Such measures may include establishing dedicated units within prisons or even separate establishments, such as anti-radicalization centers, to hold not only those suspected or convicted of terrorist offences but also those considered to be "radicalized" or "at risk of radicalization." It is sometimes presumed that people would commit themselves voluntarily to such centers, which would seemingly exclude such places from the scope of the places of deprivation of liberty. However, in most cases, there may be adverse consequences for individuals who do not commit themselves voluntarily and therefore questions surrounding what constitutes "voluntary commitment," the consequences for those who do not volunteer to be committed, or the options to leave become paramount.

---

[13] *Methods of Work of the Working Group*, Human Rights Council, A/HRC/36/38, July 13, 2017, at ¶ 8.

55. The Working Group is aware that there are a variety of health-care and social care settings that are increasingly used for different health-related conditions. They include but are not limited to social care homes for older persons, care facilities for those with dementia, and private institutions for people with psychosocial disabilities. It is increasingly aware of persons with disabilities being detained in psychiatric hospitals, nursing homes, and other institutional settings, or forced treatment in prayer camps to "cure" disability, and of persons subject to physical and chemical restraint in the community. The Working Group reiterates that it is contrary to the provisions of the Convention on the Rights of Persons with Disabilities to deprive a person of his or her liberty on the basis of disability (art. 14). It also reiterates that every State retains a positive duty of care in relation to those on its territory and under its jurisdiction and that a State cannot absolve itself of this responsibility in relation to those in privately run institutions.

56. The Working Group wishes to emphasize that the deprivation of liberty is not only a question of legal definition but also of fact. If the person concerned is not at liberty to leave, then all the appropriate safeguards that are in place to guard against arbitrary detention must be respected and the right to challenge the lawfulness of detention before a court afforded to the individual.[14]

III The Case of *Ayub Masih v. Pakistan*

To understand the importance of the WGAD as an institution, even before understanding how it functions and operates, it is instructive to examine how an actual case brought before it developed and how the opinion adopted in the case was used strategically to help secure the release of a detainee.

Ayub Masih was a twenty-six-year-old Pakistani Christian who was sentenced to death by hanging under Pakistan's draconian blasphemy law. Under Pakistan Penal Code § 295C, the sentence of death is imposed on persons who "directly or indirectly defile[] the sacred name of the Holy Prophet." Masih's Muslim neighbor complained that Masih had purportedly stated that Christianity was "right" and suggested he read Salman Rushdie's *Satanic Verses*. Masih was initially arrested on October 14, 1996, and was held in solitary confinement in Multan, Pakistan, about 200 miles southwest of Lahore, where the daytime temperature in his small cell often exceeded 120 degrees Fahrenheit (49 degrees Celsius). He denied the charges against him.[15]

Masih's trial began more than a year after his arrest. During the trial, the same neighbor who accused him of blasphemy shot and injured Masih in the courtroom but was never charged with any crime. On the day the verdict was to be issued, extremists in the courtroom threatened the lives of Masih and his lawyers if the court ruled in Masih's favor. On April 20, 1998, Masih was sentenced to death. Masih immediately appealed the sentence to the Lahore High Court but the appeal was not heard until more than three years later. Again, extremists crowded the court, threatening Masih, his lawyers, and the court with reprisal if Masih's appeal succeeded. On July 24, 2001, the High Court affirmed the lower court's judgment.[16]

---

[14] *Report of the Working Group on Arbitrary Detention*, Human Rights Council, A/HRC/36/37, at ¶¶ 50–56.
[15] Petition to UN Working Group on Arbitrary Detention, Freedom Now, Oct. 8, 2001.
[16] *Id.*

In September 2001, just before the 9/11 attacks on the United States, Masih's family retained the author to serve as his international counsel.[17] On October 8, 2001, the author submitted a Petition to the WGAD under its "urgent action" procedure. This meant that the WGAD would immediately write to the Government of Pakistan noting the source (under its procedures, whoever sends a communication to the WGAD is kept anonymous and referred to as the "source") had expressed concern about Masih's health and welfare. Without prejudging the merits of the case, the WGAD would request in the first instance that the Government ensure he remain protected. The Petition asserted two sets of violations of international law. First, it argued and presented evidence that Masih was arrested because he was a religious minority in violation of Article 18 of the UDHR, which protects freedom of thought, conscience, and religion. And second, it presented a range of evidence that Masih's due process rights were not upheld in violation of Articles 9 and 10 of the UDHR.[18]

On November 30, 2001, the WGAD issued its Opinion finding "[t]he deprivation of liberty of Ayub Masih is arbitrary" and in violation of Articles 9 and 10 of the UDHR. While noting the cooperation of the Government, it held that "the procedure conducted against Ayub Masih did not respect the fundamental rights of a person charged." It noted the Government had failed to provide Masih with evidence against him and the verdict "was based on the testimony of a … biased witness," and the trial environment was hostile. The requirements under the blasphemy law of having a Muslim judge also contributed to a lack of procedural safeguards to ensure fairness. The WGAD then called for the Government to remedy the situation by either retrying Masih or pardoning him and recommended it consider ratifying the ICCPR.[19]

After the WGAD issued its Opinion, the author requested a meeting with the Ambassador of Pakistan to the United States. She declined, stating her country's Supreme Court was considering the case. Subsequently, working with another nongovernmental organization, Jubilee Campaign, the author secured private letters to then-President Pervez Musharraf from twelve US Senators urging Ayub Masih be pardoned. Intentionally on the part of Masih's advocates, many of these Senators served in influential positions on the appropriations subcommittee that provided foreign assistance to Pakistan.[20] In response to the pressure, the Government accelerated the review of the case. On August 16, 2002, a three-judge panel on the Supreme Court heard the appeal, acquitted Masih of the charges, and ordered his immediate release.[21] The judges' oral judgment echoed the WGAD Opinion, stating that the arrest, conviction, and sentencing violated Masih's fundamental guarantees of due process. Shortly, therefore, Masih was freed from prison and the author and the Jubilee Campaign arranged for his safe exit from Pakistan. He arrived in the United States on September 4, 2002, where he

---

[17] In May 2001, the author had founded a then all-volunteer organization called Freedom Now, whose mission was to free prisoners of conscience through focused legal, political, and public relations advocacy efforts.

[18] Id.

[19] Ayub Masih v. Pakistan, WGAD Opinion No. 25/2001, Adopted Nov. 30, 2001.

[20] Letter from 11 US Senators to President Pervez Musharraf, July 2, 2002 (Nov. 2018), www.freedom-now.org/wp-content/uploads/2010/09/Masih-Senate-Letter-7.2.02.pdf (an additional letter was sent under separate cover).

[21] *Past Campaigns: Ayub Masih*, Freedom Now (Nov. 2018), www.freedom-now.org/campaign/ayub-masih/.

was met at the airport by his advocates. He spoke little English but thanked them saying "God bless you." He was later granted political asylum in the United States.[22]

IV Lessons from Ayub Masih's Case

Ayub Masih's case is instructive as a case study because a closer examination of the role of the WGAD in securing his release from prison demonstrates many of the key features of the institution. This book is focused on explaining how the WGAD functions and operates so as to maximize its value as a tool for practitioners seeking to secure the release of people arbitrarily deprived of their liberty. Examples of these key features, which will be explored in great depth in subsequent chapters include:

- **Speed.** This case was submitted to the WGAD on October 8, 2001, and a written opinion was issued on November 30, 2001. Cases do not ordinarily move that fast – in this instance it was helped along by a swift response from the Government and a fortuitously timed session of the WGAD. But compared to other UN mechanisms and regional human rights courts, the WGAD is much faster. By paying careful attention to the WGAD's schedule, a typical case can generally be decided within six months to one year.
- **Adversarial.** Under the WGAD's procedures, the Government was given an opportunity to respond to the original petition. In addition, the source was then able to reply to the response. This adversarial process enables more objective results to be obtained by the WGAD. If a government fails to respond, by its ordinary practice, the WGAD assumes as fact allegations presented by the source.
- **Soft Law Applied.** The WGAD found the Government had violated Articles 9 and 10 of the UDHR. Pakistan was not a party to the ICCPR, but despite the fact that the UDHR is not generally viewed as binding, it was applied to Masih's case.
- **Narrow Reasoning.** Given its willingness to apply soft law, the WGAD may find the right result but sometimes do so on narrower grounds than requested by sources. In this case, there were egregious abuses of fair trial rights, which made finding Masih's detention in violation of international law very easy. While the focus of the blasphemy laws in Pakistan only targets blasphemy of Islam and judges on such cases are required to be Muslim, the WGAD declined to find a violation of Article 18 of the UDHR relating to freedom of thought, conscience, or religion. Instead, it interpreted the requirement of a Muslim judge to be part of the due process violations in this case. As a matter of international law, Pakistan's blasphemy laws contravene any established right to freedom of religion. But finding Masih's detention to be in violation of international law did not require a practical invalidation of Pakistan's blasphemy laws, which is what finding a violation of Article 18 could have been interpreted to mean. Thus, the WGAD demurred on that question.
- **Recommendations Issued.** As per its standard practices, the WGAD made recommendations to resolve the case. It specifically urged Masih's pardon or retrial. And, as it does with non-state parties, it urged Pakistan to sign and ratify the ICCPR.

---

[22] *Id.*

- **Legal Opinion.** There is immense power in having an independent and impartial group of five experts of a United Nations quasi-judicial body render an opinion that a person's detention is an arbitrary deprivation of liberty in violation of international law. Securing enforcement of an opinion to leverage a detainee's release often requires using it as a tool to mobilize political and public relations pressure on a detaining government. In this instance, the Opinion was sufficient for an influential group of US Senators to write privately to then-President Musharraf, who found a way to resolve the case through the courts.

V Background on UN Human Rights System

The UN Human Rights Council (HRC) is an inter-governmental body within the United Nations systems that is responsible for protecting and promoting human rights around the world. It comprises forty-seven United Nations Member States, which are elected annually by the UN General Assembly (UNGA). The HRC was created by the UNGA on March 15, 2006, through the adoption of Resolution 60/251. The HRC replaced the UN Commission on Human Rights (UNCHR), which itself had been established on December 10, 1946, as one of two functional commissions of the United Nations as a subsidiary body of the UN Economic and Social Council. The HRC is responsible for "promoting universal respect for the protection of human rights and fundamental freedoms for all, without distinction of any kind and in a fair and equal manner." To that end, the HRC should be "guided by the principles of universality, impartiality, objectivity and non-selectivity, constructive international dialogue and cooperation, with a view to enhance the promotion and protection of all human rights … "[23]

The "special procedures" of the HRC are independent volunteer human rights experts appointed by the HRC, who report and advise on a thematic or country-specific perspective. As of 2018, the HRC has forty-four thematic and twelve country mandates. Among the thematic mandate holders, that includes thirty-two "special rapporteurs," six "independent experts," and six "working groups." The roles and functions of the UN Special Procedures are defined in resolutions adopted by the HRC. With the support of the Office of the High Commissioner for Human Rights (OHCHR), they engage in a range of activities to fulfill their mandates. These include country visits; acting on individual cases or broader concerns through communications with relevant Member States; conducting thematic studies; and advocating and raising awareness about issues relating to their mandate. They all report annually to the HRC and many also report to the UNGA as well.[24]

---

[23] Resolution 60/251, General Assembly, A/RES/60/250, Adopted Mar. 15, 2006.
[24] Special Procedures of the Human Rights Council (July 2018), www.ohchr.org/EN/HRBodies/SP/Pages/Welcomepage.aspx.

UNITED NATIONS SPECIAL PROCEDURES

Working Groups	Thematic Rapporteurs/ Independent Experts	Cont'd	Country Rapporteurs/ Independent Experts
• Arbitrary Detention • Discrimination against Women in Law and in Practice • Enforced or Involuntary Disappearances • Human Rights and Transnational Corporations and Other Business Enterprises • People of African Descent • Use of Mercenaries	• Adequate Housing • Effects of Foreign Debt • Enjoyment of Human Rights by Persons with Albinism (IE) • Enjoyment of Safe, Clean, Healthy, and Sustainable Environment • Extrajudicial, Summary, or Arbitrary Execution • Extreme Poverty • Field of Cultural Rights • Freedom of Opinion and Expression • Freedom of Peaceful Assembly and Association • Hazardous Substances • Human Rights Defenders • Independence of Judges and Lawyers • International Solidarity • Indigenous Peoples • Internally Displaced Persons • Migrants • Minority Issues • Older Persons • Privacy • Promotion of a Democratic and Equitable International Order (IE)	• Promotion of Human Rights While Countering Terrorism • Racism • Religion or Belief • Right to Development • Right to Education • Right to Food • Right to Health • Safe Drinking Water and Sanitation • Sale and Sexual Exploitation of Children • Sexual Orientation and Gender Identity (IE) • Slavery, Its Causes and Consequences • Torture, Cruel, Inhuman, or Degrading Treatment or Punishment • Trafficking in Persons • Truth, Justice,, Reparations, and Non-Recurrence • Unilateral Coercive Measures • Violence against Women, Its Causes and Consequences	• Belarus • Cambodia • Central African Republic • Democratic People's Republic of Korea • Islamic Republic of Iran • Mali • Myanmar • Somalia (IE) • Sudan (IE) • Syrian Arab Republic • Palestinian Territories Occupied since 1967

Source: UN Human Rights Council, Summer 2018

Figure 1: List of UN special procedures

1   Overview of the Working Group

The UN Commission for Human Rights (UNCHR) created the WGAD in 1991 after a long investigation by the Sub-Commission on the Prevention of Discrimination and Protection of Minorities into the practice of administrative detention. In his final report to the sub-commission, prominent French lawyer Louis Joinet emphasized the need for "suitable machinery ... to prevent and report violations" of international law regarding detention and recommended the UNCHR create either a special thematic rapporteur or a five-person working group. He thought the latter option "might be more effective, by being able to deal with the variety of categories of detention."

In response, the UNCHR created "for a three-year period, a working group comprised of five independent experts, with the task of investigating cases of detention imposed arbitrarily or otherwise inconsistently with the relevant international standards set forth in the UDHR or in the relevant international legal instruments accepted by the states concerned."[1] It mandated the group to "seek and receive information"[2] about cases and to "present a comprehensive report to the Commission [on Human Rights]" at its annual meeting.[3] This mandate was both broad and vague, leaving the WGAD to draft its own working methods and determine its objectives. The UNCHR made the establishment of the WGAD permanent and renewed its mandate at periodic intervals.

When it was established to replace the UNCHR, the Human Rights Council (HRC) adopted the mandate of the WGAD in accordance with Decision 2006/102 and extended the mandate through the adoption of Resolutions 6/4, 15/18, 24/7, and 33/30. The WGAD's mandate is reviewed every three years and will next be considered for renewal in July 2019. Proud of the role that Louis Joinet played in sparking its creation and strongly supportive of its mandate, the Government of France has been a core financial supporter of the WGAD since it was established.

To get a sense of the range of its activities today, in 2017, the WGAD under its regular procedure adopted 94 opinions concerning the detention of 225 persons in 48 countries. It transmitted 98 urgent appeals to 45 governments concerning 311 individuals and 41 letters of allegation and other letters to 32 governments. It also conducted country missions to Argentina and Sri Lanka.[4]

---

[1] Resolution 1991/42 (Arbitrary Detention), Commission on Human Rights, E.CN.4/1991/91, Mar. 5, 1991, at ¶ 2.
[2] *Id.*, at ¶ 3.
[3] *Id.*, at ¶ 5.
[4] *Report of the Working Group on Arbitrary Detention*, Human Rights Council, A/HRC/39/45, July 2, 2018.

Six key features are identified in the WGAD's first report to the UNCHR,[5] and they still form the guiding approach of the body to this day: (1) independent experts make up the adjudicatory panel, giving it a high level of prima facie credibility; (2) flexible standing and rules of evidence ensure the broadest range of complaints can be considered; (3) an adversarial process that can be conducted by correspondence provides the opportunity for the source, other special procedures, and the government involved to be heard; (4) all available law – from treaties to aspirational soft law – are applied to cases, positioning the WGAD as a place to welcome all complaints about arbitrary detention; (5) nonbinding opinions, with some limited appreciation for diplomatic concerns, reduce direct confrontation with governments; and (6) a flexible mandate, with considerable discretion as to its internal methods and procedures, enables the group to evolve to meet new situations and to build cumulative expertise. Each of these features is examined briefly in the following discussion.

I Consists of Independent Experts

The five members of the WGAD are selected by the President of the HRC, representing each of the five regions of the world. According to HRC Resolution 5/1 (Annex), special procedures mandate holders should be selected based on their expertise, experience, independence, impartiality, personal integrity, and objectivity. The experts are selected from all regions to reflect the geographical distribution requirement for diversity of representation of UN organs.[6]

Members of the UN Working Group on Arbitrary Detention[7]

Regional Group	Current Member	Prior Members
African States	Sètondji Roland Jean-Baptiste Adjovi (Benin), May 8, 2014–September 2020	Malick El Hadji Sow (Senegal), 2008–2014 Leila Zerrougui (Algeria), 2001–2008 Laity Kama (Senegal), 1992–2001
Asia Pacific	Seong-Phil Hong (South Korea), June 2014–March 2021	Shaheen Sardar Ali (Pakistan), 2008–2014 Seyyed Mahammad Hashemi (Islamic Republic of Iran), 2002–2008 Kapil Sibal (India), 1992–2001
Eastern European Group	Elina Steinerte (Latvia) (Vice Chair on Follow-Up), September 2016–September 2022	Vladimir Tochilovsky (Ukraine), March 2010–October 2016 Aslan Abashidze (Russian Federation), 2008–2010 Tamas Ban (Hungary), 2001–2008 Petr Uhl (Czech Republic), 1992–2001

---

[5] *Report of the Working Group on Arbitrary Detention*, Commission on Human Rights, E/CN.4/1992/20, Jan. 21, 1992.

[6] Resolution 5/1 (Annex), Human Rights Council, A/HRC/RES/5/1, June 18, 2007.

[7] *Current and Former Mandate-Holders for Existing Mandates*, Office of the High Commissioner for Human Rights, Dec. 31, 2017.

(*cont.*)

Regional Group	Current Member	Prior Members
Group of Latin America and the Caribbean (GRULAC)	José Guevara Bermúdez (Mexico) (Chair-Rapporteur), May 8, 2014–September 2020	Roberto Garretón (Chile), 2008–2014 Soledad Villagra de Biedermann (Paraguay), 2002–2008 Roberto Garretón (Chile), 1992–2002
Western Europe and Other Group (WEOG)	Leigh Toomey (Australia) (Vice-Chair on Communications), June 2015–March 2022	Mads Andenas (Norway), 2009–2015 Manuela Carmena Castrillo (Spain), 2004–2009 Louis Joinet (France), 1992–2003

In recent years, the HRC has substantially improved the transparency of the appointments process for all mandate holders, including the experts who serve on the WGAD. Specifically, under HRC Resolution 16/21, all candidates for mandates, whether self-nominated or nominated by other institutions, have to submit a written application, which includes biographical data and a motivation letter. These application materials are made publicly available on the website of the HRC.[8]

The "Consultative Group," which consists of the ambassadors of five member states of the HRC from each regional grouping and rotates every six months, reviews the applications and reference letters of all candidates for each open position, interviews a short-list of candidates, and then recommends to the HRC its top three choices for the position. After consultations with council members, the president presents the selected choice to the council for its approval.[9] Originally, special procedures were able to extend their terms indefinitely, but in 2008, the council adopted a new policy limiting a special procedure mandate holder's tenure to six years in a particular position (two terms of three years for thematic procedures).[10] Experts are not remunerated for their work, and in the case of the WGAD, they may not participate in decisions involving their own countries.[11] The WGAD meets three times per year, for roughly five to nine days at a time, to discuss and decide cases, write opinions, and finalize reports.

---

[8] Resolution 16/21 (Annex), Human Rights Council, A/HRC/RES/16/21, Mar. 25, 2011.

[9] Nomination, Selection, and Appointment of Mandate Holders (Nov. 2018), https://www.ohchr.org/EN/HRBodies/HRC/SP/Pages/Nominations.aspx.

[10] *Terms of Office of Special Procedure Mandate Holders*, Presidential Statement, Human Rights Council, 8/PRST/2, June 18, 2008. Four of the current WGAD members have terms that are more than six years. This has occurred only on a one-time basis. This is because in 2015 the Human Rights Council decided to reorganize the appointments of the Special Procedures to spread out their appointments across its cycles. In June 2015, the President of the Human Rights Council issued a Presidential Statement asking for recommendations from the Office of the High Commissioner for Human Rights "to make recommendations and identify modalities to adjust the terms of mandate holders on an exceptional one-time basis, in order to better spread the appointment process over time." *Enhancing the Efficiency of the Human Rights Council*, Statement by the President, Human Rights Council, A/HRC/PRST/29/1, Adopted July 3, 2015. In response to recommendations received, the Human Rights Council adopted a decision on October 2015, where it "extended the term of all Working Group mandate holders for two regular sessions of the Human Rights Council." *Decision Adopted by the Human Rights Council*, Follow-Up to President's Statement PRST 29/1, Human Rights Council, A/HRC/DEC/30/115, Adopted Oct. 1, 2015, at ¶ 2(a).

[11] *Report of the Working Group on Arbitrary Detention*, Commission on Human Rights, E/CN.4/1992/20, Jan. 21, 1992.

II Flexible Standing and Rules of Evidence

The WGAD's mandate grants wide standing to "governments and intergovernmental and non-governmental organizations, and ... the individuals concerned, their families, or their representatives" to bring a case before the WGAD.[12] While the WGAD requires communications to contain certain essential facts, it developed its procedures with the expectation that not all of its sources would have legal experience. It also noted that "[f]ailure to comply with all the formalities ... shall not directly or indirectly result in the inadmissibility of the communication."[13]

Most importantly, the WGAD does not require the exhaustion of domestic remedies to file a case,[14] offering the broadest possible jurisdiction to hear individual cases. This flexible approach signals the WGAD's intention to make its procedures available to the maximum number of arbitrarily detained persons and those advocating on their behalf. Moreover, it allows the WGAD to circumvent national courts that are merely stalling to continue detaining a person. Importantly, the approach of the WGAD differs from the procedures of other prospective international venues that can hear arbitrary detention cases, such as the Human Rights Committee (HR Committee) of the ICCPR (Optional Protocol), African Commission and Court for Human and Peoples' Rights, European Court of Human Rights, and Inter-American Commission and Court of Human Rights. While, as will be discussed further, taking a case to the WGAD will later preclude admissibility to some other venues, in many arbitrary detention cases governments intentionally extend the waiting time to a final judgment. Thus, taking a complaint to the WGAD is often the only swift route to an international legal opinion being issued on an arbitrary detention case. That said, however, by taking this approach, the WGAD risks getting involved in cases prematurely. This may draw hostility from governments that view the WGAD as meddling in their sovereign affairs, and a premature WGAD opinion may have less impact as it can be rendered moot by subsequent government action.

The WGAD's flexible admissibility requirements also create other disadvantages. Petitions submitted by inexperienced or unsophisticated sources may be carelessly drafted or contain inaccuracies. Such communications may be easier for the WGAD to overlook or governments to disregard, even though they may contain substantial information about serious human rights violations. Moreover, since the WGAD relies on evidence provided in written communications to make its findings, carelessly drafted communications can also lead to errors in written opinions.

While its original mandate permitted the WGAD to review a broad spectrum of cases, the WGAD lamented early on its inability to initiate its own investigations and its need to rely entirely on its sources.[15] In response to this concern, the UNCHR expanded the WGAD's jurisdiction, resolving "the Working Group, within the framework of its

---

[12] Resolution 1991/42 (Arbitrary Detention), Commission on Human Rights, E.CN.4/1991/91, Mar. 5, 1991, at ¶ 3.

[13] *Revised Fact Sheet No. 26, The Working Group on Arbitrary Detention*, Office of the High Commissioner for Human Rights, Feb. 8, 2019.

[14] *Report of the Working Group on Arbitrary Detention*, Commission on Human Rights, E/CN.4/1993/24, Jan. 12, 1993, at ¶ 20.

[15] *Id.*, at ¶¶ 28–29.

mandate, and aiming still at objectivity, could take up cases on its own initiative."[16] Nevertheless, it rarely does.

III Engages in an Adversarial Process

The WGAD has adopted an adversarial procedure for investigating cases. After reviewing a communication from a petitioner, referred to as "the source," the WGAD transmits the communication to the relevant government, requesting comments on the allegations to be submitted within sixty days; the government can also ask for up to a one-month extension. If the government does not respond, the WGAD may consider the case and make its recommendations. However, if the government does respond, the WGAD sends the reply to the source of the allegations, requesting more information before ultimately adopting an opinion about the case.[17]

This adversarial procedure is meant to help the WGAD remain neutral in its information-gathering process.[18] The exchange of information not only initiates a dialogue among the source, the government, and the WGAD but it also facilitates international coordination and cooperation by "shar[ing] the information at its disposal with any United Nations organ wishing to have the information."[19]

Despite the fact that governments have no legal obligation to respond to a WGAD request for information, since its founding, governments have responded approximately half the time.[20] This is likely the case because governments like to be viewed as cooperating with the United Nations, and the failure to respond, by the practice of the WGAD, results in an opinion being issued that presumes the accuracy of the allegations contained in the source's communication.

When the WGAD considers a case ripe for the issuance of an opinion, it takes one of the following measures: (a) if a person has been released, "filing" the case, either with or without rendering an opinion as to whether the person's detention had been arbitrary; (b) if the person's detention is considered not arbitrary, rendering a written opinion to that effect; (c) if it is determined that more information is required from the government or source, it may keep the case pending until the additional information is received; or (d) if the person's detention is found to be arbitrary, rendering a written opinion to that effect and making recommendations to the government.[21]

IV Uses All Available Law and Principles

As the only thematic special procedure of the HRC to adopt an adjudicatory function with respect to individual cases, the WGAD had to formulate a clear framework to evaluate claims. Until 2011, the WGAD had three legal categories of cases, but in

---

[16] Resolution 1993/36, Commission on Human Rights, E.CN.4/1993/36, Mar. 5, 1993, at ¶ 4.
[17] *Methods of Work of the Working Group*, Human Rights Council, A/HRC/36/38, July 13, 2017, at ¶¶ 15–16.
[18] *Report of the Working Group on Arbitrary Detention*, Commission on Human Rights, E/CN.4/1993/24, Jan. 12, 1993, at ¶ 3 (noting the WGAD considered that the adversarial approach was the only option that would enable it to comply with the objectivity requirement imposed by UNCHR).
[19] *Report of the Working Group on Arbitrary Detention*, Commission on Human Rights, E/CN.4/1992/20, Jan. 21, 1992, at ¶ 20.
[20] Based on author's analysis of WGAD annual reports.
[21] *Methods of Work of the Working Group*, Human Rights Council, A/HRC/36/38, July 13, 2017, at ¶ 17.

amending its Methods of Work, it added on two additional legal categories. While these categories are comprehensively exhaustive, they are not mutually exclusive – in other words, a person can be arbitrarily deprived of their liberty under multiple legal categories at the same time. The five legal categories of cases include:

(a) When it is clearly impossible to invoke any legal basis justifying the deprivation of liberty, as when a person is kept in detention after the completion of his or her sentence or despite an amnesty law applicable to him or her (category I);

(b) When the deprivation of liberty results from the exercise of the rights or freedoms guaranteed by articles 7, 13–14 and 18–21 of the Universal Declaration of Human Rights and, insofar as States parties are concerned, by articles 12, 18–19, 21–22 and 25–27 of the International Covenant on Civil and Political Rights (category II);

(c) When the total or partial non-observance of the international norms relating to the right to a fair trial, established in the Universal Declaration of Human Rights and in the relevant international instruments accepted by the States concerned, is of such gravity as to give the deprivation of liberty an arbitrary character (category III);

(d) When asylum seekers, immigrants or refugees are subjected to prolonged administrative custody without the possibility of administrative or judicial review or remedy (category IV);

(e) When the deprivation of liberty constitutes a violation of international law on the grounds of discrimination based on birth, national, ethnic or social origin, language, religion, economic condition, political or other opinion, gender, sexual orientation, disability, or any other status, that aims towards or can result in ignoring the equality of human beings (category V).[22]

From its founding, the WGAD decided it was prepared to rely on "soft" international legal principles to adjudicate individual cases. The UDHR is not considered, *in toto*, binding as international law, and the legal status of its various provisions are debated. On the one hand, some scholars argue that the UDHR, or at least certain core provisions of it, reflect widely accepted norms, which over time have become universally recognized as customary international law.[23] To the extent that certain provisions of the UDHR have become customary international law, it is binding on all states. On the other hand, the UDHR generally does not constitute a binding legal obligation as it is a resolution of the General Assembly.[24]

The ICCPR, a treaty signed and ratified by state parties, however, is legally binding. Initially, the WGAD chose to invoke the ICCPR in all cases, even where the state in question had not ratified the ICCPR. However, in 1996, in response to strong government objections, the UNCHR expressly requested the WGAD to apply the ICCPR only to those states that were parties to it.[25] This limitation was criticized as unduly restricting the WGAD's "essentially flexible and pragmatic character: these are not jurisdictional

---

[22] *Id.*, at ¶ 8.

[23] Filartiga v. Pena-Irala, 630 F.2d 876, 883 (2d Cir. 1980).

[24] MARK W. JANIS, AN INTRODUCTION TO INTERNATIONAL LAW 259–260 (4th ed. 2003).

[25] Resolution 1996/28 (Arbitrary Detention), Commission on Human Rights, E.CN.4/1996/28, Apr. 19, 1996, at ¶ 5.

organs, but hybrid mechanisms, partly political, partly legal."[26] Some argue that "[i]t would seriously compromise their usefulness if they were forbidden to function as a catalyst vis-à-vis states by clarifying the common principles of an emerging international community."[27]

Beyond the ICCPR and UDHR, the WGAD looks for interpretive guidance from a wide array of treaties and other soft law sources.[28] The WGAD's analysis is further complicated because not all cases of alleged detention are prohibited by domestic law. Unlike other special procedures, such as the Special Rapporteur on Torture, and Other Cruel, Inhuman or Degrading Treatment, whose mandate is to investigate non-derogable rights, the WGAD must sometimes make tough choices. Since detention is a permissible punishment in some cases, the WGAD must weigh the evidence to determine first "whether internal law has been respected and, [if] in the affirmative, whether this internal law conforms to international standards."[29]

Therefore, in some cases the WGAD reviews both an individual case of detention and, more generally, a country's domestic laws to determine whether they violate international law. While some violations of fair trial rights may make a detention arbitrary, other violations may not. The WGAD has reserved for itself the authority to draw this distinction. By evaluating all cases of detention, irrespective of domestic law, the WGAD is aiming to create a uniform body of international human rights law relating to detention. By repeatedly questioning the same domestic laws in multiple opinions, the WGAD has also drawn attention to particular laws that need to be changed.[30]

The WGAD's ability to use all available law and principles is not unlimited. Indeed, there are some aspects of detention the WGAD will not consider. For example, its mandate does not permit the group to review the evidence presented in a trial, evaluate the merits of a case, or otherwise "substitute itself for domestic appellate tribunals."[31] The WGAD will not "examine complaints about instances of detention and subsequent disappearance of individuals, about alleged torture, or inhuman conditions of detention."[32] These matters will be referred to another body, such as the Working Group on Enforced and Involuntary Disappearances or the Special Rapporteur on Torture. The WGAD has also stated it "will not deal with situations of international armed conflict . . . [if] they are covered by the Geneva Conventions of August 12, 1949, and their Additional Protocols, particularly when the International Committee of the Red Cross (ICRC) has competence."[33]

---

[26] Jeroen Gutter, *Thematic Procedures of the United Nations Commission on Human Rights and International Law: In Search of a Sense of Community*, 21 SCHOOL HUMAN RIGHTS SERIES 100 (2006), at 180 n. 468.

[27] *Id.*

[28] *Methods of Work of the Working Group*, Human Rights Council, A/HRC/36/38, July 13, 2017, at ¶ 7.

[29] *Report of the Working Group on Arbitrary Detention*, Commission on Human Rights, E/CN.4/1992/20, Jan. 21, 1992, at ¶ 22.

[30] James Mawdsley v. Myanmar, WGAD Opinion No. 25/2000, Adopted Nov. 9, 2000 (stating that the law under which the defendant was convicted, the country's printing and publishing law that require pre-approval of all written documents, was inconsistent with Myanmar's international law obligations) (litigated by the author as a law student).

[31] *Revised Fact Sheet No. 26, The Working Group on Arbitrary Detention*, Office of the High Commissioner for Human Rights, Feb. 8, 2019, pt. IV.B.

[32] *Id.*

[33] *Report of the Working Group on Arbitrary Detention*, Commission on Human Rights, E/CN.4/1992/20, Jan. 21, 1992, at ¶ 13.

V Issues Legal Opinions

The WGAD issues legal opinions on individual cases and recommends steps to remedy violations of international law. The formal status of these legal opinions has been subject to debate over the years. The WGAD and other commentators[34] have taken the strong position that its opinions are legally binding on states for the following reasons. First, it has a strong mandate from the United Nations, beginning with UNCHR Resolution 1991/42 through HRC Resolution 33/30, to investigate and issue legal opinions on individual cases. Second, it is applying international law that is binding on states, to the facts of these specific cases, and has emphasized "The prohibition of the arbitrary deprivation of liberty is part of treaty law, customary international law, and constitutes a *jus cogens* norm."[35] Therefore, the WGAD is interpreting binding international law applicable to state conduct. Third, it is an expert body that applies international law to an independent and exacting standard of review. Fourth, the WGAD has been recognized as a procedure of international investigation or settlement that otherwise can preclude detainees from taking their cases to regional human rights mechanisms, including the European Court of Human Rights and Inter-American Commission and Court of Human Rights. And fifth, by the long history of states engaging with the WGAD, they clearly acknowledge its authority to examine individual cases.

Others have argued that the opinions of the WGAD are not legally binding.[36] Those expressing this perspective argue first that the WGAD's mandate was extended by the HRC, which was created by the UNGA, whose resolutions are not legally binding. And it was the UNHCR that created the WGAD and other UN Special Procedures (and the HRC that renewed them). Thus, as the UNGA cannot render binding legal resolutions, nothing it does can exceed its limited powers. Second, since governments do not need to accept the WGAD's competence to have their practices reviewed, they are not legally compelled to respond to its communications or recommendations. Third, under pressure from states, the WGAD decided in 1997 to rename its judgments "opinions," dropping the previous description of these judgments as "decisions."[37] And finally, even "Views" of the HR Committee, which are adjudications of individual cases brought under the *Optional Protocol to the ICCPR*, are not

---

[34] *See, e.g.*, Liora Lazarus, *United Nations Working Group on Arbitrary Detention on Assange: The Balanced View*, OPINION JURIS, Mar. 1, 2016 (rejecting those who deny the authority of the WGAD saying "[t]his strict formalistic reading of international law discredits the UN human rights system as a whole, which depends almost entirely on bodies like the WGAD.")

[35] *Report of the Working Group on Arbitrary Detention*, Human Rights Council, A/HRC/22/44, Dec. 24, 2012, at ¶¶ 50–51.

[36] *See, e.g.*, Matthew Happold, *Julian Assange and the UN Working Group on Arbitrary Detention*, EUROPEAN JOURNAL OF INTERNATIONAL LAW, Feb. 5, 2016 (arguing "[T]he Working Group cannot issue binding decisions ... hence their description as 'opinions.' Nor can it provide authoritative interpretations of any human rights treaty (having not been granted that role by parties to any such treaty). The most that can be said is that States are under a duty to take 'due consideration' to the Working Group's recommendations, which is a rather weak obligation.")

[37] Resolution 1997/50 (Arbitrary Detention), Commission on Human Rights, E.CN.4/1997/50, Apr. 15, 1997, at ¶ 15. For the sake of consistency and to avoid confusion, all WGAD decisions and opinions are referenced as opinions in this book.

legally binding and those are definitive interpretations of a state's obligations under the treaty body created by a legally binding treaty itself.[38]

While the debate over the effect of WGAD opinions is interesting, practically, the author has never found these diverging perspectives to interfere substantially with the indisputable value of the WGAD issuing an opinion about a case, regardless of whether the government involved has responded to a communication. This is because when the WGAD issues an opinion finding a deprivation of liberty to be arbitrary, it speaks with a singularly powerful voice from the United Nations that a person is being held illegally and in violation of international law. Such opinions provide crucial independent and impartial validation for advocates and family members that a person's detention is illegal. And these opinions open the door for much stronger political and public relations pressure to be brought on the detaining government to resolve the case.

As a matter of general practice, states act in a self-interested manner and choose when it is in their interest to abide by their obligations under international law. They operate in a world that is never exclusively legal; they always look at the political implications of decisions to abide by or ignore international law. Thus, some states respond to an unfavorable WGAD opinion by releasing those found to be arbitrarily detained. Others attack the WGAD's legitimacy and their authority. And others simply ignore the opinion. But in the author's experience, how states respond is primarily driven by other factors beyond an assessment as to the legal status of the opinion. Nonetheless, regardless of the legal status of its opinions, the WGAD *will* cite to prior opinions as persuasive authority.[39]

States are not always consistent in how they view opinions of the WGAD. Unsurprisingly, many states will refer to opinions or reports of the WGAD when to do so advances their geostrategic interests, but they will also attack the WGAD when they disagree with its opinions strenuously. As one illustration of this phenomenon, the United States has referred to WGAD opinions when it has advanced its interest. For example, on May 26, 2009, then-President Barack Obama issued a strong statement responding to an opinion on *Aung San Suu Kyi* v. *Myanmar* that had been secured by the author, saying:

> I call on the Burmese government to release National League for Democracy Secretary General and Nobel Peace Prize winner Aung San Suu Kyi from detention immediately and unconditionally. I strongly condemn her house arrest and detention, which have also been condemned around the world. The United Nations Working Group on Arbitrary Detention has issued opinions affirming that the detention of Aung San Suu Kyi dating back to 2003 is arbitrary, unjustified, and in contravention of Burma's own law, and the United Nations Security Council reaffirmed on May 22 their concern about the situation and called for the release of all political prisoners.

---

[38] *See, e.g.,* Thomas Buergenthal, *The UN Human Rights Committee,* 5 MAX PLANCK YEARBOOK OF UNITED NATIONS LAW 341–398 (Vol. 5, 2001), at 376 (noting "[T]he Optional Protocol does not make Views binding on State Parties to it. Some states consequently do not feel obliged to give effect to them." He further observed that the HR Committee submitted a proposal to the 1993 Vienna World Conference on Human Rights to add a new paragraph to the Optional Protocol saying "States Parties undertake to comply with the Committee's Views").

[39] Aung San Suu Kyi v. Myanmar, WGAD Opinion No. 2/2007, Adopted May 8, 2007, at ¶ 17 (citing earlier WGAD opinions referencing house arrest as an arbitrary deprivation of liberty equivalent to house arrest) (litigated by author through Freedom Now).

Aung San Suu Kyi's continued detention, isolation, and show trial based on spurious charges cast serious doubt on the Burmese regime's willingness to be a responsible member of the international community. This is an important opportunity for the government in Burma to demonstrate that it respects its own laws and its own people, is ready to work with the National League for Democracy and other ethnic and opposition groups, and is prepared to move toward reconciliation.[40]

But when the WGAD and other UN Special Procedures issued a blistering report urging the United States to close its detention facility in Guantanamo Bay, Cuba, and arguing many of the interrogation and detention practices used there amounted to torture, the report was rejected out of hand. White House spokesman Scott McClellan for then-President George W. Bush remarked:

I think what we are seeing is a rehash of allegations that have been made by lawyers representing some of the detainees. We know that Al Qaeda detainees are trained in trying to disseminate false allegations. These are dangerous terrorists that we are talking about who are there. Nothing has changed in terms of our views.[41]

Once the WGAD renders its decision on a case, it sends the opinion to the government in question. Forty-eight hours later, the opinion is transmitted to the source, which can do what it chooses with the information, and it is posted on the WGAD web site.[42] While the WGAD cannot compel governments to respond to communications, many governments do respond, even to the issuance of the written opinion. For example, when the delay between an opinion being conveyed to a government and then to a source was previously two weeks, the Cuban government announced at a press conference it had lost a case and rejected the WGAD's Opinion – before the source even received the opinion.[43] This was a remarkable development because it underscored that regardless of the debate over their legal status, its opinions may serve to catalyze the source, detaining state, other states, and international bodies to take action.

VI Updates Its Working Methods and Procedures

Although the UNCHR instructed the WGAD to carry out its task "with discretion,"[44] the mandate's wording is broad, allowing the WGAD flexibility to adopt its own procedures.[45] In its first report to the UNCHR, the WGAD established its own working methods, the principles it would apply to individual cases, and a model questionnaire to help petitioners submit their cases for review. It also reserved the authority to "update

---

[40] *Statement by the President on Aung San Suu Kyi's House Arrest and Detention*, The White House, Office of the Press Secretary, May 26, 2009.

[41] Warren Hoge, *Investigators for UN Urge US to Close Guantanamo*, NEW YORK TIMES, Feb. 17, 2016.

[42] *Methods of Work of the Working Group*, Human Rights Council, A/HRC/36/38, July 13, 2017, at ¶ 18.

[43] Paul Haven, *Alan Gross Cancer Reports: Cuba Accuses US of Lying about Jailed America's Health*, ASSOCIATED PRESS, Dec. 5, 2012 (author represented Alan Gross).

[44] Resolution 1991/42 (Arbitrary Detention), Commission on Human Rights, E.CN.4/1991/42, Adopted Mar. 5, 1991, at ¶ 4.

[45] *Report of the Working Group on Arbitrary Detention*, Commission on Human Rights, E/CN.4/1992/20, Jan. 21, 1992, at ¶ 5.

these documents if this is deemed necessary, in light of experience acquired while discharging its mandate."[46] In response to UNCHR's invitation to "make any suggestions and recommendations which would enable it to discharge its task in the best way possible," the WGAD reviewed and updated its methods in subsequent reports to the UNCHR.[47] For example, in 1993, the WGAD introduced "deliberations," a category of decisions adopted in connection with individual cases but applied generally to all subsequent cases.[48] In its 1996 and 1997 reports, the WGAD stated that it could review cases involving pretrial detention as well as cases involving mid- or post-trial detention where the right to a fair trial had not been satisfied.[49] The WGAD published a highly detailed "Fact Sheet" in 2000, which provided greater clarity on its operations and procedures and was revised in 2019.[50]

In 2011, the WGAD fully updated and re-published its methods of work.[51] The updates to its procedures added the two additional legal categories of detention, explained more fully how it assessed whether a detention was arbitrary, and shortened several timeframes for governments (the time to respond to the original petition was reduced to sixty days from ninety days and the period for the government to see the written opinion before the petitioner was reduced to two weeks from one month and even later to forty-eight hours). In addition, the WGAD explained that at the beginning of each three-year mandate, its members elect their Chair-Rapporteur and Vice-Chair for the term of the renewed mandate. It also noted that it meets at least three times a year, for at least five to eight working days, generally in Geneva.[52]

---

[46] *Id.*, at ¶ 2.

[47] Resolution 1996/28 (Arbitrary Detention), Commission on Human Rights, E.CN.4/1996/28, Mar. 5, 1991, at ¶ 5.

[48] *Report of the Working Group on Arbitrary Detention*, Commission on Human Rights, E/CN.4/1993/24, Jan. 12, 1993, at ¶¶ 4, 19.

[49] *Report of the Working Group on Arbitrary Detention*, Commission on Human Rights, E/CN.4/1997/4, Dec. 17. 1996, at ¶ 96.

[50] *Fact Sheet No. 26, The Working Group on Arbitrary Detention*, Office of the High Commissioner for Human Rights, May 26, 2000. *Revised Fact Sheet No. 26, The Working Group on Arbitrary Detention*, Office of the High Commissioner for Human Rights, Feb. 8, 2019.

[51] *Revised Methods of Work of the Working Group*, Human Rights Council, A/HRC/16/47 (Annex), Jan. 19, 2011. There were further technical updates made in 2017. *Methods of Work of the Working Group*, Human Rights Council, A/HRC/36/38, July 13, 2017.

[52] *Id.*, at ¶¶ 15, 18.

2   Deliberations of the Working Group

In its first report to the Commission on Human Rights (UNCHR), the WGAD identified a number of situations involving questions of principle, which required special consideration.[1] In its third session, the WGAD decided it would consider such questions and adopt decisions about them (referred to as "deliberations") not in the abstract but in connection with the consideration of individual cases submitted to it.[2] Over its history, the WGAD has adopted nine Deliberations and a commentary on drug policies, which will each be examined in turn.

A review of these nine Deliberations and the commentary together provide a window into how the WGAD's collective thinking has evolved over time. Some of its Deliberations are especially thoughtful and well-reasoned, such as the most recent Deliberation No. 9 on the Definition and Scope of Arbitrary Deprivation of Liberty under Customary International Law. Others are focused on defining the scope of the challenge with respect to particular kinds of detention such as House Arrest (Deliberation No. 1), Rehabilitation through Labour (Deliberation No. 4), Immigrants and Asylum Seekers (Deliberation No. 5), and Psychiatric Detention (Deliberation No. 7). But Deliberation No. 8 on Deprivation of Liberty Linked to/Resulting from the Use of the Internet appears to be of less value as it fails to explain why one should even really distinguish individuals arbitrarily detained because of their use of the Internet as compared to others who express their views through different channels of communication.

Until the creation of an online database of WGAD jurisprudence, it was very difficult to research the prior cases and annual reports.[3] Thus, many petitioners were unaware of the Deliberations and would not usually cite to them in their petitions. Similarly, WGAD members themselves also typically have not focused on the existence of the Deliberations or ensuring their consistent invocation and application across similar situations. Given their value to demonstrating the deprivation of liberty in a relevant case is arbitrary, petitioners should definitely reference any deliberations that apply to their case. In addition, the WGAD should ensure that Deliberations are

---

[1] *Report of the Working Group on Arbitrary Detention*, Commission on Human Rights, E/CN.4/1992/20, Chapter IV, Jan. 21, 1992.

[2] *Report of the Working Group on Arbitrary Detention*, Commission on Human Rights, E/CN.4/1993/24, Jan. 12, 1993, at ¶ 19.

[3] This was of special concern to the author, who consequently worked through Freedom Now to facilitate a partnership between the UN Working Group on Arbitrary Detention, Thomson Reuters Foundation, and Freedom Now to build and maintain the now publicly available database: www.unwgaddatabase.org.

referenced, wherever relevant, to enhance the consistency, coherence, and uniformity of its opinions.

I Deliberation No. 1 on House Arrest

Without prejudging the arbitrary character or otherwise of the measure, house arrest may be compared to deprivation of liberty provided that it is carried out in closed premises which the person is not allowed to leave. In all other situations, it will devolve on the Working Group to decide, on a case-by-case basis, whether the case in question constitutes a form of detention, and if so, whether it has an arbitrary character.[4]

In its first Deliberation, the WGAD noted that house arrest is often a measure imposed on a person in ways that are equivalent to a deprivation of liberty in an ordinary prison context. In addition, it acknowledged that there are greater and lesser forms of house arrest, but that it could only pass immediate judgment as being arbitrary situations where a person is in "closed premises" and "not allowed to leave."

Despite having just adopted this deliberation "in connection with the consideration of cases in Myanmar" (Burma), the WGAD then failed to reference Deliberation No. 1 in those cases. In Decision No. 8/1992, the WGAD found both Nobel Peace Prize Laureate and democracy leader Aung San Suu Kyi and former Burmese Prime Minister U Nu had been held under house arrest. It explained that Aung San Suu Kyi and U Nu "have been placed under house arrest for having criticized the Government of Myanmar." It went on to note that neither "have resorted to violence, or have incited violence, or that they have threatened, in any way whatsoever, the national security or public order. It therefore appears that the measure applied to them is based solely on the fact they had freely and peacefully exercised their rights to freedom of opinion, expression and association . . . ."[5]

The WGAD observed they were held "without charge or trial, that they never had access to counsel, that they could never challenge their deprivation of liberty before a court, and that they have been held in almost complete isolation from the outside world."[6] Notwithstanding the claims of the Government that they were being held under the provisions of the 1975 State Protection Law, which authorized the detention of individuals deemed to be a danger to the state, the WGAD found "that the measure of house arrest applied, particularly with regard to Daw Aung San Suu Kyi, who is restricted to her family home, which she cannot leave due to the constant presence of an armed guard, is a deprivation of liberty equivalent to detention." It concluded by finding their detention fell within Categories II and III of cases examined by the WGAD.[7] Interestingly, in these early days of drafting WGAD opinions, it claimed the detention was not only in contravention of Articles 9, 10, 11, 19, and 20 of the UDHR but also of Articles 9, 14, 19, and 21 of the ICCPR. Although this practice was later (and appropriately) abolished, in its earliest days the WGAD would apply the ICCPR to non-party states as indicative of customary international law.

---

[4] *Report of the Working Group on Arbitrary Detention*, Commission on Human Rights, E/CN.4/1993/24, Jan. 12, 1993, at ¶ 19.
[5] Aung San Suu Kyi and U Nu v. Myanmar, WGAD Opinion No. 8/1992, Adopted Session No. 4.
[6] *Id.*
[7] *Id.*

Since this first case involving the situation of persons under house arrest, the WGAD has invoked and applied Deliberation No. 1 in a broad range of other cases, including with regards to a political prisoner in Cuba,[8] the founder of an Islamic association of Morocco,[9] the captain and crew of a Singaporean vessel towed to Indonesia and detained without charges,[10] two Buddhist monks in Viet Nam,[11] two professors in Algeria,[12] and several additional opinions involving Aung San Suu Kyi in Burma.[13] But the WGAD failed to note Deliberation No. 1 in two further opinions regarding renewed terms of Aung San Suu Kyi's house arrest, which happened to be secured by this author, though it did reference past cases where it had ruled similarly.[14]

Over the years the WGAD's precise definition of house arrest has varied, with some inconsistencies. For instance, in *Thich Huyen Quang v. Viet Nam*, although the WGAD cited Deliberation No. 1, they described house arrest as a deprivation of liberty only "if the person concerned is placed in closed *and locked* premises which he cannot leave *without being authorized to do so*" (emphasis added).[15] However, in *Pham Hong Son v. Viet Nam*, the WGAD employed this definition to find that a human rights advocate had not been placed under house arrest, even though he was required to request (and did not receive) permission to travel to a destination two kilometers from his house, was constantly surveilled by plainclothes agents, had his communications restricted, and was denied access to the Internet.[16] And in *Concerning a Minor Whose Name is Known to the Working Group v. Malaysia*, the WGAD found its jurisprudential definition of house arrest, which requires "closed premises which the person is not allowed to leave," had not been met in a situation where the minor was currently required to wear an electronic monitor, report to police regularly, and obtain written approval before leaving his locality.[17] Since Son's case, the WGAD has reverted to its original definition of house arrest.[18]

Pham Hong Son stands in contrast to *Julian Assange v. Sweden and the United Kingdom*, a contentious case that produced the only non-unanimous decision in the WGAD's history.[19] Among other issues, the WGAD considered whether Assange had

---

[8] Esteban González González, et al. v. Cuba, Decision No. 21/1992, Adopted Session No. 4.

[9] Abdesalam Yassin v. Morocco, Decision No. 41/1993, Adopted Sept. 29, 1993.

[10] Shauket Ali Akhtar and Crew of the Kota Indah v. Indonesia, WGAD Opinion No. 3/2001, Adopted May 16, 2001.

[11] Thich Huyen Quang v. Viet Nam, WGAD Opinion No. 4/2001, Adopted May 17, 2001; Thich Quang Do v. Viet Nam, WGAD Opinion No. 11/2001, Adopted Sept. 12, 2001.

[12] Abassi Madani and Ali Benhadj v. Algeria, WGAD Opinion No. 28/2001, Adopted Dec. 3, 2001.

[13] Aung San Suu Kyi v. Myanmar, WGAD Opinion No. 2/2002, Adopted June 19, 2002; Aung San Suu Kyi v. Myanmar, WGAD Opinion No. 2/2007, Adopted May 8, 2007 (Litigated by author through Freedom Now).

[14] Aung San Suu Kyi v. Myanmar, WGAD Opinion No. 46/2008, Adopted Nov. 28, 2008 (Litigated by author through Freedom Now); Aung San Suu Kyi v. Myanmar, WGAD Opinion No. 12/2010, Adopted May 7, 2010 (Litigated by author through Freedom Now).

[15] Thich Huyen Quang v. Viet Nam, WGAD Opinion No. 4/2001, Adopted May 17, 2001, at ¶ 8.

[16] Pham Hong Son v. Viet Nam, WGAD Opinion No. 13/2007, Adopted May 11, 2007, at ¶¶ 19–20, 24.

[17] Concerning a Minor Whose Name is Known to the Working Group v. Malaysia, WGAD Opinion No. 37/2018, Apr. 26, 2018, at ¶ 25.

[18] See, e.g., Hossein Mossavi, et al. v. Iran, WGAD Opinion No. 30/2012, Adopted Aug. 29, 2012, at ¶ 23 (a subsequent case citing the original definition of house arrest as "closed premises which the person is not allowed to leave").

[19] Julian Assange v. Sweden and the United Kingdom, WGAD Opinion No. 54/2015, Adopted Dec. 4, 2015.

been under house arrest in the 550 days before his flight to the Ecuadorian Embassy. Although Assange was able to leave his place of residence during the day (his bail requirements dictated he return at night, and report to police daily), the WGAD nonetheless found that his situation constituted house arrest.[20] This does not align with the definition in Deliberation No. 1, as Assange could leave his house every day. The dissenting Opinion pointed out that where a person is allowed to leave their house, their situation constitutes a restriction of liberty rather than a deprivation, which places the case outside of the WGAD's competence.[21]

In a more recent opinion, also secured by the author, the WGAD found that Liu Xia, the wife of 2010 Nobel Peace Prize Laureate Liu Xiaobo, was being held under house arrest in China.[22] This Opinion is notable in several important respects. First, in a rather unusual development, despite widespread reports by human rights groups and independent media, the Government claimed in its response to our petition on behalf of Liu Xia that "no legal enforcement measure" had been taken against her.[23] It is not often a government denies the detention of a person widely known to be detained. Technically, that might have been an accurate, albeit cynical reply. Nevertheless, the WGAD dismissed this claim swiftly, noting that the Government had failed to dispute the evidence that put forward by the petitioner. Second, the WGAD is improving the quality of its opinions. In this case in the discussion, the WGAD references the prohibition on arbitrary detention both as customary international law and as a preemptory norm of international law, *jus cogens*. It also references related jurisprudence from the International Court of Justice and International Criminal Tribunal for the Former Yugoslavia. And finally, the WGAD referenced its past jurisprudence as persuasive authority, citing to one of its prior Opinions on Aung San Suu Kyi's case.[24]

II Deliberation No. 2 on Admissibility of Communications, National Legislation, and Documents of a Declaratory Nature[25]

In the first of a number of attempts over the years by governments to challenge the WGAD on its work, this Deliberation was adopted in response to a letter from the Government of Cuba on December 24, 1991, where the Government requested the WGAD to "publicly communicate to Member States for their comments" its views on the following points:

(a) The juridical standards which the Working Group has formally established for the admissibility of the communications it receives; under the procedure laid down by Economic and Social Council resolution 1503 (XLVIII), the exhaustion of all

---

[20] *Id.*, at ¶ 82.
[21] Annex to Julian Assange v. Sweden and the United Kingdom, WGAD Opinion No. 54/2015, Adopted Dec. 4, 2015, at ¶ 4.
[22] Liu Xia v. China, WGAD Opinion No. 16/2011, Adopted May 5, 2011 (Litigated by Author through Freedom Now).
[23] *Id.*
[24] *Id.*
[25] *Report of the Working Group on Arbitrary Detention*, Commission on Human Rights, E/CN.4/1993/24, Jan. 12, 1993.

available means at the national level should be a sine qua non for accepting and taking action on each communication.

(b) The Working Group's opinion of the value to be attached to the national legislation in force in the Member States; this is an essential element for determining whether detention, arrest, preventive imprisonment or jailing is or is not arbitrary (that is to say, contrary to the legal order existing in the country in question, including international obligations acquired under treaties freely entered into).

(c) The legal grounds on which the Working Group bases its consideration of the provisions contained in documents of a merely declaratory nature (for example, the principles set out in General Assembly resolution 43/173), or in juridical instruments which cannot be applied to an "accused" State that is not party to them (as would be the case of Cuba with respect to the International Covenant on Civil and Political Rights), as appropriate criteria to be used for determining prima facie whether a case of detention or imprisonment is "arbitrary."[26]

Like most governments, Cuba was not happy about the opinions that were being adopted finding that it was holding people arbitrarily and in violation of its obligations under international law.

To its credit, the WGAD took the criticisms of Cuba seriously and provided a point by point response.

Admissibility of Communications

The WGAD began its response by noting that in establishing the original UN special procedures, the UNCHR in Economic and Social Council Resolution 1503 (XLVIII) of May 27, 1970, made clear there was no requirement that domestic remedies be exhausted for a communication to be admissible for consideration. And it also pointed out that of the sixty-seven countries that had been examined under the 1503 procedure, where there had been allegations of gross patterns of human rights abuses, the exhaustion of domestic remedies had never been a condition of admissibility.

Beyond these general observations, the WGAD emphasized that if the exhaustion of domestic remedies were to be required then the instrument establishing a process for examining complaints should state this clearly. For example, Article 41(1)(c) of the ICCPR says that states can give the Human Rights Committee (HR Committee) competence to hear complaints against it by other states. But that provision makes clear "[t]he Committee shall deal with a matter referred to it only after it has ascertained that all available domestic remedies have been invoked and exhausted in the matter, in conformity with generally recognized principles of international law."[27] The WGAD observed there was no such provision included in Resolution 1991/42 of the Commission on Human Rights, which established the Working Group and defined its mandate and scope of operations.

---

[26] *Id.*, at ¶¶ 2(a)–(c).
[27] ICCPR, at Art. 41(1)(c).

National Legislation

In beginning its response to the question posed by the Government of Cuba, the WGAD observed that Resolution 1991/42 expressly refers to international standards and did not appear to provide for national law to be taken into consideration when determining if a detention is arbitrary. That said, however, the WGAD also noted that while national standards could be examined, international law supersedes national law. To address the specific question more directly, the Working Group decided to adopt a paragraph in its annual report entitled "The Mandate and Legal Framework of the Working Group," which stated:

> 10. The legal framework within which the Working Group will have to carry out its mandate is made up primarily of international standards and legal instruments, but in certain instances of domestic legislation as well. The Working Group will thus have to look into domestic legislation in investigating individual cases, where it will have to determine whether internal law has been respected and, in the affirmative, whether this internal law conforms to international standards. It may thus have to consider, in certain cases where there are alleged practices of arbitrary detention, whether they have not been made possible as a result of laws which may be in contradiction with international standards.[28]

In short, the WGAD concluded that in performing its work it will consider both the national and international standards ensuring, where necessary, that the former conforms to the latter.

Documents of Declaratory Nature

According to Resolution 1991/42, the WGAD's mandate was to apply "international legal instruments accepted by the States concerned," beyond the UDHR. The specific question raised by the Government of Cuba regarding the *Body of Principles for the Protection of All Persons under Any Form of Detention or Imprisonment* was whether it was such an "instrument," because it was "declaratory" as a resolution of the General Assembly and if it could be considered to have been "accepted" by Member States.

In a detailed analysis of more academic interest rather than practical implication, the WGAD concluded that the Body of Principles is an instrument, that it is an instrument declaratory of pre-existing rights recognizable under customary international law, and that when it comes to how the WGAD makes decisions, it will consider the Body of Principles but also consider the ICCPR even regarding a non-state party, "in view of the tenacity of the declaratory effect of the quasi-totality of its provisions."[29] With regards to "accepted" instruments, the WGAD referenced *Nicaragua* v. *United States* of the International Court of Justice, which in its judgment of June 27, 1986, held that "consent" of UN members to the text of declaratory resolutions describing customary international law may be "understood as an acceptance of the validity of the rule or set of

---

[28] *The Mandate and Legal Framework of the Working Group*, cited in *Report of the Working Group on Arbitrary Detention*, Commission on Human Rights, E/CN.4/1993/24, Jan. 12, 1993, at ¶ 13.

[29] *Report of the Working Group on Arbitrary Detention*, Commission on Human Rights, E/CN.4/1993/24, Jan. 12, 1993. Later, under pressure from numerous states, the WGAD dropped its practice of applying the ICCPR to non-state parties.

rules declared by the resolution by themselves." In the case of the Body of Principles, the WGAD concluded, approval was given by all states because the General Assembly resolution was adopted by consensus.

III Deliberation No. 3 on Deprivation of Liberty Subsequent to a Conviction, Quality of Information on Which Decisions are Based, 90-Day Deadline for Replies, and "Urgent Action"[30]

This deliberation was developed in response to a letter sent by the Government of Cuba to the WGAD with questions relating to the four aforementioned issues.

Deprivation of Liberty Subsequent to a Conviction

In its correspondence with the WGAD, the Government indicated its views that once a person had been convicted, it should not consider itself competent to render an opinion about a case. In response to this assertion, the WGAD noted that neither Resolution 1991/42 nor the discussions that led up to its adoption justified a view that communications made post-conviction should be inadmissible. It further referenced language in Resolution 1991/42, which explained that the WGAD's task is to investigate cases where detention "is imposed arbitrarily or otherwise inconsistently with the relevant international standards." In examining both the UDHR and ICCPR, the language about arbitrary detention also makes no distinction between a detention pre- or post-conviction in terms of whether or not such detentions can be considered arbitrary. As a result, the WGAD concluded that the interpretation put forward by the Government would "respect neither the letter nor the spirit of the above-mentioned Resolution 1991/42." It lastly noted that the UNCHR, in adopting Resolution 1992/28, thanked the WGAD for its diligence in devising its Methods of Work and the rigor with which the members had discharged their task. With this implicit endorsement of its efforts, the WGAD decided there was no necessity to review the provisions that it had adopted in relation to its Methods of Work.

Quality of Information on Which Decisions Are Based

It has been and remains absolutely essential that the WGAD receive high-quality information about prospective opinions it is going to adopt. This is because if poor or inaccurate information is provided to it, then the basis on which the WGAD subsequently issues an opinion may be flawed. It was therefore eminently reasonable for the Government to raise the question as to how the WGAD would work to ensure it receives the highest quality information possible.

In its response, the WGAD noted that since its creation, one major amendment to its Methods of Work that helped improve the accuracy of information it received was the adoption of a model questionnaire. In addition, the staff to the WGAD, in coordination with its Chair, was enabled to seek additional information from the source to place before the WGAD.

[30] Id.

With respect to the veracity of the information placed before it, the WGAD considered that the establishment of an adversarial procedure as the foundation of its working methods was "sufficiently effective." The WGAD pointed out that because of such a procedure in the case of communications with the Government of Cuba, for example, certain inaccuracies or errors including non-existent persons, name confusion, nonexistent places of detention, and persons not in detention came to its attention.

90-Day Deadline for Replies

In creating a 90-day deadline for receiving a response from governments, the Working Group stated that it based its decision on the experience of other thematic mandates and rapporteurs. It also noted that under its Methods of Work, if a government's reply has not been received by the deadline, the WGAD may or may not take a decision based on all the information received. This does not, it noted, imply any "presumption as to the veracity of the allegation made."[31] The WGAD substantially revised its Methods of Work in its 2011 annual report and reduced the time limit for a government's response to sixty days. The new Methods of Work state that in requesting a government's reply, the WGAD will inform the government that it is "authorized to render an Opinion determining whether the reported deprivation of liberty was arbitrary or not, if a reply is not received by the Government within the time limit . . . ."[32]

"Urgent Action"

The "urgent action" procedure has become an important part of the Methods of Work of the WGAD. In short, it enables a source to trigger faster engagement by the WGAD to reach out to the detaining government and say that without prejudging the merits of the case it would request that the government ensure the person's health and safety. In response to the request from the Cuban government to clarify when and how its "urgent action" procedure could be invoked, the WGAD referred back to its first annual report, where it stated there were only two circumstances where it would apply the procedure:

(a) in cases in which there are sufficiently reliable allegations that a person is being detained arbitrarily and that the continuation of the detention constitutes a serious danger to that person's health or even life. In such cases, between the Working Group's sessions, the Working Group authorizes its Chairman, or, in his absence, the Vice-Chairman, to transmit the communication by the most rapid means to the Minister for Foreign Affairs of the country concerned, stating that this urgent action in no way prejudges the Working Group's final assessment of whether the detention is arbitrary or not;

(b) in other cases, where the detention may not constitute a danger to a person's health or life, but where the particular circumstances of the situation warrant urgent action. In such cases, between the Working Group's sessions, the Chairman or the Vice-Chairman in consultation with two other members of the

---

[31] Id.
[32] Report of the Working Group on Arbitrary Detention, Human Rights Council, A/HRC/16/47, Jan. 19, 2011.

Working Group, may also decide to transmit the communication by the most rapid means to the Minister for Foreign Affairs of the country concerned.[33]

In practice, when the "urgent action" procedure is invoked, the WGAD now conveys its concerns to the country's permanent representative to the United Nations in Geneva, expecting it will then be conveyed back to the country's Minister of Foreign Affairs.

IV Deliberation No. 4 on Rehabilitation through Labour[34]

At its fifth session, in conjunction with a number of cases that came before it, the WGAD adopted a deliberation which stated that the WGAD "will have to determine whether measures taken most often in the form of administrative detention and generally designed to encourage an individual to change or even renounce his opinions, using methods resembling coercion, constitute, by definition, arbitrary detention under Category II . . . ."[35]

The WGAD further clarified that in deciding if a deprivation of liberty accompanied by compulsory labor is arbitrary, after having determined if the decision involved was judicial or administrative, it would consider the role played by:

- The economic and juridical status of the person deprived of freedom and whether they must perform compulsory labour;[36]
- The determination as to whether there were adequate safeguards to ensure there are no violations of the right to a fair trial of such gravity as to place the deprivation of liberty within the WGAD's Category III cases;[37] and
- The purpose of the measure, whatever it may be called – reform, rehabilitation, readjustment, reintegration, reintegration into society. The key question is whether the measure is in conformity with international norms relating to freedom of opinion and expression, especially Article 18 of the ICCPR, which provides "[n]o one shall be subject to coercion which would impair his freedom to have or to adopt a religion or belief of his choice."[38]

It then sought to explain further considerations under each of these areas that would assist an assessment of when rehabilitation through labor is arbitrary.

Compulsory Labor

The WGAD began by noting that compulsory labor can emanate from either criminal penalty or administrative measure. With regards to criminal penalties, the WGAD observed almost all prison systems include a period of work in the daily schedule of

---

[33] *Report of the Working Group on Arbitrary Detention*, Human Rights Council, E/CN.4/1992/20, Jan. 21, 1992.

[34] *Report of the Working Group on Arbitrary Detention*, Commission on Human Rights, E/CN.4/1993/24, Jan. 12, 1993.

[35] *Id.*

[36] *Id.*, at ¶ I (Introduction).

[37] *Id.*, at ¶ II (Introduction).

[38] *Id.*, at ¶ III (Introduction).

detainees and such work is almost always compulsory after conviction. Such compulsory labor, in the view of the WGAD, is consistent with international norms. With respect to administrative detention, however, even if there is a legal basis for compulsory labor, it is often executed in a manner similar to the execution of criminal penalties. In such cases, the labor is coercive, which makes it possible to exploit the detainee's working capacity. The characteristics that enable an observer to render a conclusion about the coercive nature of the labor includes well-organized camps engaged in planned production, high production norms implying long hours, rapid working tempos, and minimal, if any, remuneration.

The Right to a Fair Trial

With regard to individuals charged and convicted of specific crimes before courts of law, assessing whether international due process requirements have been met is relatively straightforward. With respect to labor imposed through administrative measures, however, the situation is more complex.

First, forced labor is less likely to be considered arbitrary if there is a judicial means to challenge the detention. Specifically, the key question is what safeguards are provided by the remedy and how effective is that remedy?

Second, if the remedy is purely administrative, further inquiry must be made into the laws and regulations that created the remedy, who renders decisions about challenges to forced labor, whether witnesses can be examined and cross-examined, whether counsel is provided to the accused, and how much time elapses between the person's arrest and appearance before the administrative remedy.

Third, one must look differently at forced labor of a limited or unlimited duration. Even in cases where the duration of the forced labor is limited, the deprivation of liberty may be arbitrary if credit is not given to the detainee toward the overall sentence imposed on them. In the cases of forced labor of unlimited duration, the WGAD observed there were four specific situations where such detention has a totally or partially arbitrary character:

- Where the unspecified duration is provided by law;
- Where lifting of forced labor is dependent on the arbitrary views of the authorities as to whether the detainee has been rehabilitated;
- Where a time-limited period of forced labor may be continually reimposed; and
- Where the person can continue to be detained after the measure expires.[39]

Purpose of Deprivation of Freedom

The WGAD began by noting that when the main purpose of forced labor is political and/or cultural rehabilitation through self-criticism, the detention is inherently arbitrary. This is because under the ICCPR Article 14(3)(g) no one can be compelled to testify against himself or to confess guilt and under Article 18 no one may be coerced in a way to impair his freedom to have or to adopt a religion or belief of his choice.

---

[39] *Id.*, at ¶ II.B.3(b).

In conclusion, the WGAD emphasized that there were three cases where forced labor should not be considered arbitrary:

- Cases where forced labor is one aspect of the execution of a penalty of the deprivation of freedom where there were not serious violations of the right to a fair trial.
- Cases of administratively imposed forced labor where the judicial remedies to challenge the detention are sufficient to ensure there are no serious violations of the right to a fair trial.
- Cases where administratively imposed forced labor does not have judicial safeguards, but where alternative safeguards exist that ensure a level of protection comparable to those provided in the right to a fair trial.[40]

The WGAD then examined cases of forced labor where the deprivation of freedom may be considered arbitrary:

- Cases where criminal penalties are imposed in a manner involving serious violations of the right to a fair trial (Category III).
- Cases of administrative measures where the judicial remedy also includes serious violations of the right to a fair trial (Category III).
- Cases of administrative measures where alternatives to a judicial remedy are of less value than a judicial remedy with the rights of a fair trial (Category III).
- Cases where administrative measures whose duration is specified, but not at the time of the decision because the detainee cannot be given credit for time served.[41]

Finally, the WGAD examined cases of forced labor where the deprivation of freedom is inherently arbitrary:

- Cases of administrative measures of indefinite duration where the authorities determine if sufficient progress has been made to release the person, where detention may be continuously renewed, or where a person can be kept to use their working capacity after the period of detention expires.
- Cases of administrative measures whose purpose is not only occupational rehabilitation, but mainly political and cultural rehabilitation through self-criticism.[42]

Despite the WGAD having made substantial efforts to elucidate a clearer understanding of when and how rehabilitation through labor can be considered arbitrary detention, it has only rendered two opinions where Deliberation No. 04 has been cited as justification for an opinion, both in relation to China.[43]

---

[40] *Id.*, at ¶ I.A-C (Conclusion).
[41] *Id.*, at ¶ II.A-D (Conclusion).
[42] *Id.*, at ¶ III.A-B (Conclusion).
[43] Zhou Lunyou, et al. v. China, WGAD Opinion No. 66/1993, Adopted Dec. 9, 1993.

V Deliberation No. 5 on the Situation Regarding Immigrants and Asylum-Seekers[44] and Revision

In adopting Resolution 1997/50 regarding the WGAD's ongoing work, the UNCHR specifically requested that it 'devote all necessary attention to reports concerning the situation of immigrants and asylum seekers who are allegedly being held in prolonged administrative custody without the possibility of administrative or judicial remedy, and to include observations on this question in its report to the next session of the Commission on Human Rights."[45]

In response to this specific request and in consultation with the Office of the UN High Commissioner for Refugees, the WGAD responded through its development of the original Deliberation No. 5 on the Situation Regarding Immigrants and Asylum-Seekers. With respect to the specific situation of asylum-seekers and immigrants, the WGAD began by clarifying several important terms. It noted that it defined "judicial or other authority" as articulated by the Body of Principles as being duly empowered by law and having a status and length of mandate to afford sufficient guarantees of competence, impartiality, and independence.[46] It also observed that with respect to this specific population that house arrest and "confinement on board a ship, aircraft, road vehicle or train" are assimilated with the custody of immigrants and asylum-seekers.[47] And it said places of the deprivation of liberty of these populations could include custody in border areas, on police premises, in prisons, in ad hoc detention centers, in "international" or "transit" zones in ports or airports, or in gathering centers or even hospital premises. Subsequently, it set forth ten principles regarding the treatment of immigrants and asylum-seekers.

In 2018, the WGAD undertook to revise Deliberation No. 5, as it was "concerned by the rising prevalence of deprivation of liberty of immigrants and asylum-seekers in recent years, recognizing the need to consolidate the developments in its own jurisprudence."[48] The revised Deliberation No. 5 on the deprivation of liberty of migrants expanded the scope of concerned persons beyond simply "immigrants and asylum-seekers." In the now-current Revised Deliberation, the term "migrant" is defined to mean:

> Any person who is moving or has moved across an international border away from his or her habitual place of residence, regardless of: (a) the person's legal status; (b) whether the movement is voluntary or involuntary; (c) the cause of the movement; or (d) the duration of stay. The term shall be taken to include asylum seekers, refugees, and stateless persons.[49]

---

[44] *Report of the Working Group on Arbitrary Detention*, Commission on Human Rights, E/CN.4/2000/4, Dec. 28, 1999.

[45] Resolution 1997/50, Commission on Human Rights, E.CN.4/1997/50, Apr. 15, 1997, at ¶ 4.

[46] Yu Shiwen v. People's Republic of China, WGAD Opinion No. 11/2016, Adopted Apr. 20, 2016, at ¶ 31.

[47] *Report of the Working Group on Arbitrary Detention*, Commission on Human Rights, E/CN.4/2000/4, Dec. 28, 1999.

[48] *Revised Deliberation No. 5 on the Deprivation of Liberty of Migrants*, Working Group on Arbitrary Detention, Human Rights Council, Feb. 7, 2018, at ¶ 3 (Advanced Edited Version has been published, but without a UN document number).

[49] *Id.*, at ¶ 6.

The ten principles in the original deliberation were greatly expanded on to create eleven sections encompassing the right to seek asylum, the exceptionality and standards of migrant detention, and the rights to be observed in migrant proceedings. The WGAD emphasized that these apply to states regardless of factors such as an influx of large numbers of migrants.

Detention of Migrants

Article 14 of the UDHR states that any person has the right to seek asylum, the exercise of which cannot be criminalized. The WGAD specifies that irregular entry may not be treated as a crime, or migrants as criminals. Nor are migrants to be viewed from a perspective of national security or public health, with their rights contingent on being aligned with the interests of the state.[50] Thus, any form of detention or custody must be an exception or a last resort, rather than a general rule or default and for a legitimate purpose such as documenting entry or verifying identity.[51] Less restrictive alternatives must be considered.[52] Detention of children, unaccompanied or otherwise, is forbidden, and cannot be justified on the basis of parents' migration status. If accompanied, a child's alternative to detention must be applied to their entire family.[53] Likewise, detention may not be applied to migrants in "other situations of vulnerability or risk" such as pregnant or breastfeeding women, the elderly, persons with disabilities, LGBT persons, or survivors of trafficking or other violent crimes. The determining factor of a detention center (given that some might be labelled "guest houses," "shelters," or "transit centers") is whether a migrant is free to leave the facility in which they are housed.[54]

The decision to detain a migrant should be based on an individual assessment and subject to periodic review.[55] Any detention during migrant proceedings must be prescribed by law and non-punitive, as well as reasonable, necessary, and proportionate.[56] To ensure the detention is reasonable, necessary, and proportionate, it must (a) be in pursuance of a legitimate purpose; (b) be absolutely essential for achieving this purpose; and (c) strike a balance between this purpose and the gravity of deprivation of liberty.[57] A maximum period of detention must be specified by law, after which the detainee must be released.[58] Indefinite detention of migrants is always arbitrary.[59]

During detention, migrants retain certain rights, including those provided within the criminal justice system. The UN Body of Principles still applies in deprivations of liberty pertaining to migrant proceedings, as does the Basic Principles and Guidelines. As such, anyone detained during migrant proceedings has the right to be brought promptly before

[50] *Id.*, at ¶ 10.
[51] *Id.*, at ¶ 12.
[52] *Id.*, at ¶ 16.
[53] *Id.*, at ¶ 40.
[54] *Id.*, at ¶ 45.
[55] *Id.*, at ¶¶ 13, 19.
[56] *Id.*, at ¶¶ 14, 20.
[57] *Id.*, at ¶¶ 22–24.
[58] *Id.*, at ¶ 25.
[59] *Id.*, at ¶ 26.

a judicial authority to determine the lawfulness of their detention, and who must consider possible alternatives to detention.[60] If the methods of detention render this impossible, that detention is arbitrary.[61] The detainee must be informed of the decision in writing and in a language they understand, as well as their right to seek asylum and ability to file an asylum application.[62]

Additionally, detained migrants have the right to:

- Access legal advice, representation, and interpreters (free, if necessary) to challenge detention orders, appeal deportations, or prevent refoulement;[63]
- Contact their consular representative and have this contact facilitated by detaining authorities if necessary;[64]
- Communicate with relatives and the outside world, including by telephone and email;[65]
- Be treated humanely, in appropriate and respectful detention conditions that reflect the non-punitive nature of the detention;[66]
- Free access to appropriate medical care, which includes mental health care;[67] and
- Be detained separately from those held under the criminal justice system, in facilities other than those designed for criminal detainees.[68]

Lastly, a state that outsources migrant detention to private contractors remains responsible for ensuring they operate in accordance with these principles. The United Nations High Commissioner for Refugees, as well as the Red Cross and other relevant NGOs, must be allowed free access to migrant detention facilities.

Despite the broad scope of the global problem of detention of immigrants and asylum-seekers, the WGAD has only adopted eight opinions invoking Deliberation No. 5 since the original deliberation was published.[69] This is not likely a reflection of the scope of the problem, but rather an indication that detained immigrants and asylum-seekers and their counsel have not known about or understood the value of bringing their claims to the WGAD.

---

[60] *Id.*, at ¶¶ 13, 18.

[61] *Id.*, at ¶ 30.

[62] *Id.*, at ¶¶ 33–34.

[63] *Id.*, at ¶ 35.

[64] *Id.*, at ¶ 36.

[65] *Id.*, at ¶ 37.

[66] *Id.*, at ¶ 38.

[67] *Id.*, at ¶ 39.

[68] *Id.*, at ¶ 44.

[69] Pedro Katunda Kambangu v. Lithuania, WGAD Opinion No. 24/2000, Adopted Sept. 14, 2000; Vatcharee Pronsivakulchai v. United States, WGAD Opinion No. 35/2007, Adopted Nov. 30, 2006; Alaa Kasem Lefte, et al. v. Lebanon, Opinion No. 5/2009; Zaza Yambala v. Switzerland, WGAD Opinion No. 4/2011, Adopted May 3, 2011; Mohammad Khairallah Hamid Ali v. Lebanon, WGAD Opinion No. 56/2011, Adopted Nov. 17, 2011; Jawad Kazem Mhabes Mohammed Al Jabouri v. Lebanon, WGAD Opinion No. 55/2011, Adopted Nov. 17, 2011; Mehdi Abedi, et al. v. Iraq, WGAD Opinion No. 32/2012, Adopted Aug. 30, 2012 (Litigated by Author through Perseus Strategies); Reza Raeesi v. Australia and Papua New Guinea, WGAD Opinion No. 52/2014, Adopted Nov. 21, 2014.

VI Deliberation No. 6 on Legal Analysis of Allegations against the International Criminal Tribunal for the Former Yugoslavia[70]

In this rather unusual deliberation, the WGAD considered a communication from General Momir Talić, a Bosnian Serb who was arrested in Vienna on August 23, 1999, under a warrant issued by the International Criminal Tribunal for the Former Yugoslavia (ICTY). After being transferred to the ICTY's Detention Unit, General Talić made a submission to the WGAD, alleging that his pretrial detention is based on provisions of the ICTY's Statute and Rules of Procedure and Evidence that he claimed were inconsistent with various provisions of Article 9 of the ICCPR, which relate to arbitrary detention.[71]

At the outset, the WGAD noted that the examination of this particular case fell outside its usual Methods of Work as it does not contain a complaint against a state but rather against a subsidiary body of the Security Council. Nevertheless, the WGAD noted that beyond this specific case, this issue is one of legal interpretation of the norms of international law and, therefore, it may state a view in the form of a deliberation to which it can refer if it receives further communications concerning the administration of justice by an international criminal tribunal, based on similar reasoning.[72]

According to the communication, there are four specific ways that the Statute and Rules of Procedure and Evidence of the ICTY breach the ICCPR:

- Detention is the rule and release the exception (Article 9(3));
- No grounds are given in the arrest warrants and detention orders (Article 9(1));
- The period of detention is indefinite (Article 9(3));
- There is no compensation for a person unlawfully arrested or detained (Article 9(5));[73]

The WGAD noted at the outset that the fourth allegation is a consequence and not a cause of arbitrariness that can characterize detention and it therefore decided it was inadmissible as it fell outside its mandate.[74]

Before delving into the substance of the specific complaint, the WGAD stopped at a preliminary comment made in the communication that "the rules applied by the Tribunal, at least those that relate to the detention, do not meet international standards for guaranteeing the rights of the accused to a fair trial." It stopped at this comment because it wished to question the assumption made in the communication that the international norms in question must be applicable in the case of international justice in the same way they are applied in a national criminal court.[75]

The WGAD then sought to identify the major features that distinguish an international criminal court from a national criminal court. In so doing, it looked to an

---

[70] *Report of the Working Group on Arbitrary Detention*, Commission on Human Rights, E/CN.4/2001, Dec. 20, 2000.
[71] *Id.*, at ¶ 12.
[72] *Id.*, at ¶ 13.
[73] *Id.*, at ¶ 14.
[74] *Id.*, at ¶ 15.
[75] *Id.*, at ¶¶ 16–17.

expert report that had been commissioned by the UN General Assembly. The key features identified in that report included:

- Hybrid characteristics of the Tribunal's procedures, including common law and civil law systems;
- Rules of procedure and evidence that embrace a broader range of complex matters found in comparable national legal systems;
- Lack of coercive powers or injunction in relation to a Tribunal's arrest warrants, rendering it dependent on cooperation from national governments and international forces;
- Dependence on states for witness and victim testimony and evidence gathering;
- Existence of victims as direct witnesses, whose security must be provided so they will consider it safe to testify; and
- Establishment of victims and witnesses sections within the Tribunal.[76]

Beyond these differences, the WGAD also noted that the ICTY tries international crimes and that national courts rarely try violations of the Geneva Conventions, war crimes, crimes against humanity, and genocide. In addition, the WGAD noted a range of treaties, including the ICCPR, which limit some of the rules protecting an accused person in order to prevent the abuse of those rules to abet impunity for international crimes.[77]

Having examined these preliminary matters, the WGAD then turned to examining the allegations put forward by the petitioner on the merits.

With regards to the first allegation, that detention is the rule and release the exception, it is correct that the Statute contains no specific measures applicable to pretrial detention. That said, however, the WGAD observed that the *Rules of Procedure and Evidence* contain Rule 64 (Detention on Remand) and Rule 65 (Provisional Release), which are similar to those found in national systems when defendants charged with extremely grave crimes are charged. In short, once the accused is indicted and the defendant is held in the Tribunal's detention facilities, the defendant cannot be released except by order of the Tribunal. It is worth noting that the grounds most frequently cited to by national legislation for placing or maintaining a person in detention are the gravity of the breach and corresponding penalty or the lack of ties in the country. Thus, the WGAD noted that with regards to international crimes or in national legal systems where extremely grave crimes are being examined, most countries use similar criteria to determine when a judge may release a defendant pending trial. Those criteria are, in order of importance: (1) preventing flight; (2) preventing pressure on witnesses and victims; and (3) preventing collusion or collaboration between perpetrators and accomplices. In this case, the WGAD determined that the first allegation was unfounded given the nature and

---

[76] *Report of the Expert Group to Conduct a Review of the Effective Operation and Functioning of the International Tribunal for the Former Yugoslavia and International Criminal Tribunal for Rwanda,* Commission on Human Rights, A/54/634, Nov. 22, 1999.

[77] *Report of the Working Group on Arbitrary Detention,* Commission on Human Rights, E/CN.4/2001, Dec. 20, 2000, at ¶ 19.

gravity of the crimes and constraints arising from their international dimension and the need to prevent the release of the accused to help the oppressor to the detriment of the victim.[78]

In regard to the second allegation, that the arrest warrants and detention orders are not sufficiently detailed, the WGAD found these claims to be unfounded. Specifically, the WGAD found that the procedures in the Statute and *Rules of Procedure and Evidence* provided sufficient due process guarantees for the defendant. In this case, the indictment provides both de facto and de jure grounds for the charges. The indictment then must be submitted to a judge of the Tribunal who determines if the charges are sufficient. And lastly, the Prosecutor issues an arrest warrant that requires describing in detail the crimes with which the defendant has been accused. Once the defendant is detained, and at the time of detention, the judge cites to the arrest warrant in ordering the ongoing detention. In this case, the defendant claims that the communication is not precise enough. In response to this claim, the WGAD notes that while this might be a reasonable response to ordinary crimes, the prosecution of international crimes does not necessarily require each victim to be identified individually as long as groups of victims can be identified and their whereabouts be tied to specific mass graves. Furthermore, international criminal law does not require the defendants to have personally and directly participated in every crime so long as it can be proven they had command responsibility for their commission.[79]

Finally, with regards to the length of the detention being indefinite or too long prior to conviction, the WGAD noted that the ICCPR only requires the length of pretrial detention to be "reasonable" and not that it have a fixed end date. In his communication, the petitioner argued that the phrase "reasonable time" be interpreted rigidly and without distinction between the administration of national and international justice. The WGAD noted that it disagrees with such an interpretation, as do the experts who prepared the report for the General Assembly, who observed that defendants have extensive procedural guarantees that affect the length of the proceedings because accused persons make improper use of all forms of motions and each must be considered by a judge. As an illustration, during 1997–1998, the ICTY received over 500 pretrial motions, orders, and applications. In addition, the complex nature of the evidence also prolongs the proceedings because of the burden of collecting material evidence, including the exhumation of mass graves, the gathering of extensive witness testimony, and the organization and deployment of on-site fact finding missions in other countries with language challenges, administrative formality, and coordination required with local authorities.[80]

Ultimately, the WGAD determined that the legal guarantees of a fair trial such as those provided by the Statute and *Rules of Procedure and Evidence* of the ICTY are consistent with relevant international norms.[81]

---

[78] *Id.*, at ¶¶ 21–28.
[79] *Id.*, at ¶ 29.
[80] *Id.*, at ¶ 30.
[81] *Id.*, at ¶ 31.

VII Deliberation No. 7 on Issues Relating to Psychiatric Detention[82]

In its 2003 annual report the WGAD expressed concern for the situation of vulnerable persons such as the disabled, drug addicts, and people suffering from HIV/AIDS, who are held in detention on health grounds.[83] It noted that all persons held for health grounds "must have a judicial means of challenging their detention."[84] In this Deliberation, the WGAD found that persons held in detention because of a mental disability should be included in the broader category of vulnerable people about which it has commented because they are forcibly held in psychiatric hospitals, institutions, or places raising similar concerns.[85]

As noted previously, when the WGAD was initially established in 1991, it deliberately refrained from taking a position in the abstract but decided that it would adopt specific deliberations as warranted by cases being brought to it for consideration. It noted that it had received over the years several individual communications involving the deprivation of liberty of persons of allegedly unsound mind from a range of sources, including non-governmental organizations.[86]

In preparing this Deliberation, the WGAD relied on the following documents:

- *Declaration on the Rights of Disabled Persons* (General Assembly Resolution 3447 (XXX));
- *Principles for the Protection of Persons with Mental Illnesses and the Improvement of Mental Health Care* (General Assembly Resolution 46/199);
- *Declaration of the Rights of Mentally Retarded Persons* (General Assembly Resolution 2856 (XXVI); and
- *Principles, Guidelines, and Guarantees for the Protection of Persons Detained on the Grounds of Mental Ill-Health or Suffering from Mental Disorder.*[87]

The WGAD noted that the phenomenon of mental issues "is an age-old problem for humanity." Even though treatment has improved substantially over time, one aspect of treatment that has gone unchanged in more serious circumstances is isolation from society. The determination of whether isolation in a particular case amounts to a deprivation of liberty cannot be decided in the abstract. But it is important to begin the analysis by understanding that the holding of persons with mental disabilities against their will may, in principle, amount to a deprivation of liberty. Ultimately, it is up to the WGAD to assess, on a case-by-case basis, if the deprivation of liberty in a particular case constitutes detention and, if so, whether that detention is arbitrary.[88]

At the outset, the WGAD reaffirmed that Article 9 of the ICCPR, which prohibits arbitrary arrest or detention as well as deprivation of liberty except in accordance with

---

[82] *Report of the Working Group on Arbitrary Detention*, Commission on Human Rights, E/CN.4/2005/6, Dec. 1, 2004.
[83] *Report of the Working Group on Arbitrary Detention*, Commission on Human Rights, E/CN.4/2004/3, Dec. 15, 2003, at ¶ 74.
[84] *Id.*, at ¶ 87.
[85] *Report of the Working Group on Arbitrary Detention*, Commission on Human Rights, E/CN.4/2005/6, Dec. 1, 2004, at ¶ 47.
[86] *Id.*, at ¶ 49.
[87] *Id.*, at ¶ 50.
[88] *Id.*, at ¶ 51.

law, reflects customary international law, which is binding on all states, including those that have not ratified it. While the deprivation of liberty itself is not prohibited, it follows from Article 9 that detention is only permissible when it is lawful and not arbitrary. To meet these standards, the law under which a person is detained must be clear and describe all permissible restrictions and conditions under which they may be imposed. Furthermore, for a detention to not be arbitrary, it must not be manifestly "disproportionate, unjust, unpredictable or discriminatory." Any detention would be manifestly arbitrary if a person's liberty is deprived on the pretext of an alleged mental disability, but it is obvious they are detained on account of their political, ideological, or religious views or on their opinions, convictions, or activities.[89]

The WGAD indicated that it understood that people with mental disabilities require special attention and mental illness may require measures to be taken to deprive a person of their liberty for their own or society's interest. But, when assessing whether these measures are "taken in compliance with international standards, the vulnerable position of the person affected by his (alleged) illness has to be duly taken into consideration."[90]

In considering individual communications under its mandate, the WGAD decided to apply the following criteria going forward:

- Psychiatric detention constitutes a deprivation of liberty when the person is placed in a closed establishment, which they may not leave freely. Whether such a deprivation of liberty is or is not arbitrary will be assessed by the WGAD on a case-by-case basis.
- Similarly, the WGAD also considers it to be a deprivation of liberty when suspected criminals are detained pending a medical examination, observation, and diagnosis of a presumed mental illness, which may also impact their criminal accountability. Whether such a deprivation of liberty is or is not arbitrary will be assessed by the WGAD on a case-by-case basis.
- The law must provide the conditions of the deprivation of liberty of persons with mental illness as well as procedural guarantees against arbitrariness.
- Article 9(3) of the ICCPR, which protects the right to be brought promptly before a judge on a criminal matter, should also be applied to persons with mental illness. But that a person's vulnerable position and ensuing diminished capacity to argue against detention should be considered, including receiving assistance of their own or family's choosing.
- Article 9(4) of the ICCPR, which provides a person detained the right to challenge the lawfulness of their detention, shall apply to anyone confined by court order, administrative decision, or otherwise in a psychiatric hospital or similar institution on account of mental illness. In addition, the lawfulness of a detention "shall be reviewed regularly at reasonable intervals by a court or competent independent and impartial organ and the patient shall be released if the grounds for his detention do not exist any longer."
- There should be genuine adversarial procedures conducted where a patient can challenge the reports of mental health professionals. Decisions should avoid automatically following the expert opinion of the institution where the patient is held, or the report and recommendations of attending mental health professionals.

---

[89] *Id.*, at ¶ 54.
[90] *Id.*, at ¶ 57.

- Psychiatric detention cannot be used to curtail a person's freedom of expression or to punish, deter, or discredit them on account of their internationally protected rights to freedom of expression, association, and religion.[91]

Although the WGAD has rendered about a dozen opinions that relate to the deprivation of liberty of individuals in psychiatric detention, most were prior to the adoption of this Deliberation. The more recent opinions of the WGAD have only broadly referred to its concerns about people under psychiatric detention and not referenced the Deliberation itself.

VIII Deliberation No. 8 on Deprivation of Liberty Linked to/Resulting from the Use of the Internet[92]

In implementing its mandate, the WGAD observed it had received many communications that, in some way or another, connected to the use of the Internet. The WGAD also noted that in parallel, the Internet was being increasingly used to prepare and bring about terrorist acts. Some states, the WGAD explained, have been inclined to deprive people of their liberty by asserting that the use of the Internet in a particular case served terrorist purposes; however, these types of accusations have often proven to be a pretext to restrict freedom of expression and repress political opponents. In its experience so far, the WGAD explained that not all deprivation of liberty connected to the use of the Internet is arbitrary and indeed in some cases it might be justified. But in examining individual cases, the WGAD has found the deprivation of liberty in most cases to be arbitrary because the individual detained had been punished merely or predominantly for having exercised their right to freedom of expression.[93] Given the complexity of the issue, the WGAD decided to give the use of the Internet as a means of communication further consideration.

The WGAD observed the Internet was similar in many respects to the use of traditional means of information dissemination, including the content of books, newspapers, and letters or messages sent through the mail, telephone, radio, or television. Communication through the Internet, compared to through these other means of information dissemination, is much wider and quicker, accessible to anyone, and operates on a global scale. These differences, however, are technical and "do[] not exert a decisive influence on the meaning and substance of the freedom of expression. In short, the freedom to impart, receive, and seek information through the Internet is protected in the same way by international law as any other form of expression of opinions, ideas, and convictions."[94]

Detention of Internet users for the content or use of this medium of communication is a restriction on the exercise of freedom of expression, and unless such a detention is not arbitrary, it is unlawful. In looking at individual cases, the WGAD found governments often asserted their right to protect the community as a whole or to protect the rights and reputations of others. A source often disagrees with this interpretation. To assess whether

---

[91] *Id.*, at ¶ 58.
[92] *Report of the Working Group on Arbitrary Detention,* Commission on Human Rights, E/CN.4/2006/7, Dec. 12, 2005.
[93] *Id.*, at ¶¶ 32–34.
[94] *Id.*, at ¶¶ 36–38.

a specific deprivation of liberty is consistent with international standards, the WGAD stated it would examine each case on a case-by-case basis.[95]

In its experience, the Working Group has found that restrictions on freedom of expression are only justifiable when done in accordance with domestic and international law, are necessary to ensure the respect of the rights or reputation of others, or for the protection of national security, public order, public health or morale, and are proportionate to the pursued legitimate aims. A vague and general reference to these interests, without being properly explained or documented, is not sufficient to convince the WGAD that restrictions on freedom of expression are necessary. The WGAD also does not accept that the interference of public authorities with an individual's privacy is necessary under an unsubstantiated pretext of protecting public order or the community.[96]

The WGAD noted that opinions expressed by individuals punished are usually critical of the government and cover a broad range of views including: publicly denouncing government policies, participating in an opposition movement, organizing public demonstrations, publicly manifesting a religious view or promoting others to do the same, discussing corruption, encouraging people to vote for opposition candidates, and listening to foreign media broadcasts, among others. It is the WGAD's view, however, that "peaceful, non-violent expression or manifestation of one's opinion, or reception of information, even via the Internet, if it does not constitute incitement to national, racial or religious hatred or violence, remains within the boundaries of the freedom of expression. Hence, deprivation of liberty applied on the sole ground of having committed such actions is arbitrary."[97]

Given that terrorism has become a major threat, the Internet is a powerful tool of communications for terrorists. Thus, the WGAD recognizes that states' actions to prevent and punish the use of the Internet for terrorist purposes are justifiable and legitimate. Beyond these threats, there are a range of other behaviors considered criminal, including illegal access, illegal interception, data interference, system interference, forgery, fraud, infringement of copyright, and offenses relating to the sale of children, sexual abuses against children, and child pornography. Persons suspected of all these offenses may not invoke freedom of expression to justify unlawful or criminal actions. And, as a general rule, the WGAD will not consider arbitrary the deprivation of liberty applied against common criminals on the sole basis that the offense is somehow related to their use of the Internet.[98]

IX Deliberation No. 9 Concerning the Definition and Scope of Arbitrary Deprivation of Liberty under Customary International Law[99]

In recent years, the WGAD has begun more wide-ranging consultations in the process of furthering its own work. Currently, for example, the WGAD has been responding to the Human Rights Council, which requested in 2011 that the WGAD "draft basic principles and guidelines on remedies and procedures on the right of anyone deprived of his or her liberty" and that it "seek the views of States, relevant UN agencies, intergovernmental

---

[95] Id., at ¶¶ 39–41.
[96] Id., at ¶¶ 41–42.
[97] Id., at ¶¶ 46–47.
[98] Id., at ¶¶ 50–52.
[99] Report of the Working Group on Arbitrary Detention, Human Rights Council, A/HRC/22/44, Dec. 24, 2012.

organizations, UN treaty bodies and, in particular, the Human Rights Committee, other special procedures, national human rights institutions, non-governmental organizations and other relevant stakeholders."[100] In this particular case, as a preface for its Deliberation, the WGAD described its consultation with states and civil society. Specifically, it sent a note verbale to all states asking them to respond to two questions: (1) is the prohibition of arbitrary deprivation of liberty expressly contained in your country's legislation? If so, please refer to the specific legislation; and (2) what elements are taken into account by national judges to qualify the deprivation of liberty as arbitrary. If possible, please provide concrete examples of the judgments. It received twenty-nine responses from states and two submissions from non-governmental organizations. The WGAD also held a public consultation on November 22, 2011.[101]

Based on "reviewing its own jurisprudence, international and regional mechanisms, consultations and the submissions to the note verbale," the WGAD adopted Deliberation No. 9 on the definition and scope of the arbitrary deprivation of liberty under customary international law.[102]

Prohibition of Arbitrary Deprivation of Liberty in International Law

The WGAD began its analysis by noting that this prohibition is recognized in all major international and regional instruments for the promotion and protection of human rights, including the UDHR (Article 9), ICCPR (Article 9), *African Charter for Human and Peoples' Rights* (Article 6), *American Convention on Human Rights* (Article 7(1)), *Arab Charter on Human Rights* (Article 14), and the *European Convention for the Protection of Human Rights and Fundamental Freedoms* (Article 5(1)). At the time of adoption of this Deliberation, the WGAD observed that 167 states had ratified the ICCPR and the prohibition of arbitrary deprivation of liberty had been widely enshrined in national constitutions and legislation. Collectively, this "constitute[s] a nearly universal State practice evidencing the customary nature of the arbitrary detention of liberty prohibition." Furthermore, there is also widespread *opinio juris* supporting the customary nature of these rules. This includes both resolutions speaking about states that were not bound at the time by a treaty obligation forbidding arbitrary detention and resolutions discussing the general nature of rules relating to arbitrary detention for all states, without distinction based on treaty obligations. Furthermore, the rights of anyone deprived of their liberty to bring proceedings before a court to challenge the legality of the detention, known as *habeas corpus*, are non-derogable under treaty law and customary international law.[103]

In addition, the WGAD noted that a state can never claim that illegal, unjust, or unpredictable deprivation of liberty is necessary for the protection of a vital interest or proportionate to that end. Consequently, the WGAD concluded: "the prohibition of the arbitrary deprivation of liberty is part of treaty law, customary international law, and

---

[100] Resolution 20/16, Human Rights Council, A/HRC/20/L.5, July 6, 2012, at ¶¶ 10, 11(a).
[101] *Report of the Working Group on Arbitrary Detention*, Human Rights Council, A/HRC/22/44, Dec. 24, 2012, at ¶¶ 39–40.
[102] *Id.*, at ¶ 41.
[103] *Id.*, at ¶¶ 42–43, 46.

constitutions a *jus cogens* norm." Its specific content, as described in this Deliberation, applies to all situations.[104]

Qualifications of Particular Situations as Deprivation of Liberty

In 1964, a committee established by the UNCHR studied the right of everyone to be free from arbitrary arrest, detention, and exile. It remains the one and only multilateral study on the issue. According to this study, detention is "the act of confining a person to a certain place, whether or not in continuation of arrest, and under restraints which prevent him from living with his family or carrying out his normal occupational or social activities." The study defined arrest as "the act of taking a person into custody under the authority of the law or by compulsion of another kind and includes the period from the moment he is placed under restraint up to the time he is brought before an authority competent to order his continued custody or to release him."[105]

Perhaps somewhat ironically, when the WGAD was established in 1991, the term "detention" was not expressly described. It was only when the UNCHR adopted Resolution 1997/50 that it affirmed the WGAD is entrusted "to investigat[e] cases of deprivation of liberty imposed arbitrarily, provided that no final decision has been taken in such cases by domestic courts in conformity with domestic law, with the relevant international standards set forth in the Universal Declaration of Human Rights and with the relevant international instruments accepted by the States concerned."[106] In this regard, the focus of the UNCHR is on the word "arbitrary," and the WGAD has always defined its mandate as looking at the full range of detentions that can occur either pretrial or post-trial. While placing individuals in temporary custody in stations, ports, airports, or places where they remain under constant surveillance may restrict their freedom of movement, they can also constitute a de facto deprivation of liberty. Such an interpretation has been reconfirmed in prior deliberations on house arrest, rehabilitation through labor, retention in centers for migrants or asylum seekers, psychiatric facilities, and so-called international or transit zones. In this regard, "secret and/or incommunicado detention constitutes the most heinous violation of the norm protecting the right to liberty of human beings under customary international law. The arbitrariness is inherent in these forms of deprivation of liberty as the individual is left outside the cloak of any legal protection."[107]

The Notion of "Arbitrary" and Its Constituent Elements

The notion of a detention being "arbitrary" includes both the requirement that a particular form of the deprivation of liberty is taken in accordance with applicable law and procedure and that it is proportional to the aim sought, reasonable, and necessary.

---

[104] *Id.*, at ¶¶ 50–51.

[105] *Study on the Right of Everyone to Be Free from Arbitrary Arrest, Detention, and Exile*, Department of Economics and Social Affairs, UN Publication No. 65.XIV.2, at ¶ 21.

[106] Resolution 1997/50 (Arbitrary Detention), Commission on Human Rights, E.CN.4/1997/50, Apr. 15, 1997, at ¶ 15.

[107] *Report of the Working Group on Arbitrary Detention*, Human Rights Council, A/HRC/22/44, Dec. 24, 2012, at ¶¶ 56–60.

For a detention to be "arbitrary," it "isn't merely that it is against the law, but must be interpreted more broadly to include elements of inappropriateness, injustice, lack of predictability, and due process of law."[108] The HR Committee has reaffirmed that the legal basis justifying a detention must be accessible, understandable, non-retroactive, and applied in a consistent and predictable way to everyone equally. Another key safeguard against arbitrary arrest is the "reasonableness" of the suspicion on which the arrest is made or, as noted by the European Court of Human Rights, it "presupposes the existence of facts or information which would satisfy an objective observer that the person concerned may have committed the offense."[109]

The notion of "arbitrary detention," in the widest sense can arise from a law itself or the acts of government officials. Thus, a detention, even if authorized by law, may be arbitrary if it is based on an arbitrary piece of legislation or is inherently unjust, relying on discriminatory grounds. An overly broad statute, authorizing automatic and indefinite detention without any standards or review, is by implication arbitrary. And the ongoing detention of conscientious objectors to military service may be arbitrary if there is no guarantee of judicial oversight.

The WGAD has also observed that the notion of promptness set out in Article 9(3) of the ICCPR is one key element that might render a detention arbitrary. This right need not be asserted by the detainee, and applies even before formal charges are asserted.[110] It noted that the HR Committee found consistently delays of even a few days to be brought before a judge could render a detention arbitrary.[111] In *Yara Sallam* v. *Egypt*, the case of a women's rights activist held for her internationally recognized work in the field of transitional justice, the WGAD noted that the authorities' delay of eight days before presenting the applicant before a competent judge for a ruling violated the "promptness" requirement, under which a delay of more than forty-eight (48) hours is considered exceptional and warrants justification.[112] The importance of providing a "prompt" inquiry is heightened in the case of minors, though the standard may equally hold for other persons in vulnerable situations.[113]

The WGAD expressed its special concern about the increased reliance of states on administrative detention, in particular preventative detention, detention in emergency or exceptional situations, detention on counter-terrorism grounds, immigration detention, and administrative penal law detention. Since its establishment, the WGAD has handled

---

[108] Mukong v. Cameroon, Communication No. 458/1991, Human Rights Committee, CCPR/C/51/D/458/1991, July 21, 1994.

[109] Fox, Campbell, and Hartley v. United Kingdom, Applications Nos. 12244/86, 12245/86, and 12383/86, Judgment, European Court of Human Rights, at ¶ 32.

[110] Concerning a Minor (Whose Named is Known to the Working Group) v. Egypt, WGAD Opinion No. 17/2015, Adopted Apr. 28, 2015, at ¶ 27.

[111] *Report of the Working Group on Arbitrary Detention*, Human Rights Council, A/HRC/22/44, Dec. 24, 2012, at ¶¶ 63–64.

[112] Yara Sallam v. Egypt, WGAD Opinion No. 52/2015, Adopted Dec. 4, 2015, at ¶ 46.

[113] Concerning a Minor (Whose Named is Known to the Working Group) v. Egypt, WGAD Opinion No. 14/2015, Adopted Apr. 27, 2015, at ¶ 29. The WGAD, referring to HR Committee guidance on the matter, noted that an "especially strict standard of promptness" applies to cases concerning juvenile prisoners. An appropriate period in such cases, the WGAD opined, would be twenty-four hours from the time of arrest to when the detainee should be brought to trial.

an "overwhelming" number of such cases, finding violations of various provisions in Articles 9 and 14 of the ICCPR. In most such cases, the underlying national legislation does not provide for criminal charges or trial. Consequently, the administrative rather than judicial basis for such a detention "poses particular risks that such detention will be unjust, unreasonable, unnecessary, or disproportionate, with no possibility of judicial review."[114] While the WGAD acknowledged that counter-terrorism measures might require some limiting of guarantees, it has repeatedly stressed that "in all circumstances deprivation of liberty must remain consistent with the norms of international law."[115] Furthermore, such detentions often allow secret evidence to be the basis for indefinite detention. No person should be deprived of their liberty on the sole basis of evidence to which they cannot respond. Although administrative detention is not tantamount to arbitrary detention, its application in practice has been overly broad and its compliance with minimum guarantees of due process is in the majority of cases inadequate.[116]

Therefore, in concluding this Deliberation, the WGAD found that all forms of arbitrary deprivation of liberty, including its five categories of cases, are prohibited under customary international law and that the arbitrary deprivation of liberty constitutes a preemptory or *jus cogens* norm.[117]

X Drug Policies and Arbitrary Detention[118]

In its annual report from 2015, the WGAD observed that both from country visits and communications it had received information that drug control laws and policies have triggered arbitrary detentions. Although it did not formally adopt a deliberation, the WGAD did proceed to describe its concerns in substantial detail, both putting states on notice about these issues and signaling to potential sources that this is an area of new focus.

The WGAD initially observed that arbitrary detention for drug offenses can occur either in criminal or administrative settings, particularly absent procedural safeguards. The WGAD also noted that these detentions have a "disproportionate impact on vulnerable groups, such as women, children, minorities groups and people who use drugs."[119]

Further, the WGAD is especially concerned about the administrative detentions that restrict fundamental rights when they are often framed as health interventions. In such circumstances, this "can lead to involuntary commitment or compulsory drug treatment that is unsupported by international drug control conventions or international human rights law."[120] It explained that "[c]ompulsory detention regimes for purposes of drug

---

[114] *Id.*, at ¶¶ 68–70.
[115] *Id.*, at ¶ 71.
[116] *Id.*, at ¶ 72–74.
[117] *Id.*, at ¶ 72–74.
[118] *Report of the Working Group on Arbitrary Detention*, Human Rights Council, A/HRC/30/436, July 15, 2015, at ¶¶ 57–62.
[119] *Id.*, at ¶ 58.
[120] *Id.*, at ¶ 59.

'rehabilitation' through confinement or forced labour are contrary to scientific evidence and inherently arbitrary."[121] The WGAD added that drug consumption or dependence is not sufficient justification for detention.

In addition, it also expressed concern about criminal detention of those charged with drug use, possession, production, and trafficking. In its view, criminal laws of these kinds are often punitive and "raise important questions of legality, proportionality, necessity, and appropriateness."[122]

[121] *Id.*
[122] *Id.*, at ¶ 61.

Part II. Individual Case Procedure

3   Process for Taking a Case to the Working Group

I General Overview

A *Summary of Process*

As a quasi-judicial body, the WGAD operates without a formal set of rules but is instead guided in implementing its mandate by its Methods of Work, which explain the overall process by which to submit a case for consideration.[1] That said, however, the WGAD

REGULAR PROCEDURE FOR TAKING A CASE TO THE WORKING GROUP ON ARBITRARY DETENTION

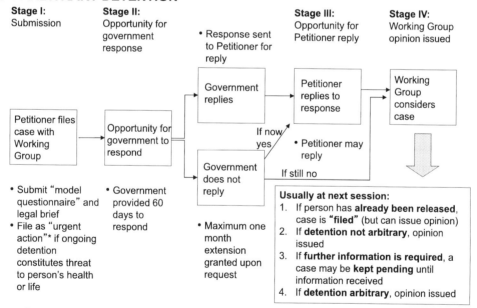

Figure 2 Overview of regular procedure

[1] *Methods of Work of the Working Group*, Human Rights Council, A/HRC/36/38, July 13, 2017.

considers individual cases brought to it in closed sessions of its members and staff. And the day-to-day operations of the WGAD are run by a small secretariat of staff of the Office of the UN High Commissioner for Human Rights (OHCHR) in its Special Procedures Branch, led by its Secretary. This chapter will illuminate and elucidate how an individual case can most effectively be brought to the WGAD, supplementing the procedures described in the Methods of Work with the author's practical experience gained from having taken more than forty-five cases to the WGAD and having interviewed many current and former WGAD members and staff.

B Important Implications of Submitting a Case

To protect those making submissions, when communications are conveyed to the detaining government, the authors of those complaints are identified by the WGAD as "the source." Similarly, when adopting opinions, the WGAD refers to information as having been provided by the source as well. While the WGAD and its staff scrupulously protect confidentiality of the person or organization making a submission, a petitioner should assume that the government detaining a person will, fairly or not, presume a connection between the detainee and the petitioner. This is why the WGAD asks for evidence of consent from the detainee or their family. In short, this means discussing with the families of those who are wrongly detained the opportunities and risks of making a submission to the WGAD and making sure they understand them fully. Typically, a submission is made on behalf of one person, but a submission can be made on behalf of multiple people at the same time, if the facts and circumstances of their arrests, detentions, or deprivations of liberty coincide.

In addition, prior to filing a case to the WGAD, an advocate needs to understand that although the WGAD is likely the fastest international body capable of rendering an opinion on whether a person is detained arbitrarily and in violation of international law, its opinions are non-binding and filing a case does affect several other prospective options.

Specifically, taking a case to the WGAD precludes as inadmissible the simultaneous consideration of the case by the Human Rights Committee (HR Committee) of the ICCPR.[2] That generally is not a concern given that the WGAD does not require a petitioner to have even had a verdict issued in their domestic case, let alone exhaust domestic remedies, which is why it is often the first international venue asked to examine a claim of arbitrary detention. The HR Committee will consider a case later if domestic remedies are later exhausted and the process at the WGAD has been completed. Typically, a petitioner would take a case to the WGAD, which is a faster mechanism narrowly focused on their detention, and then later to the HR Committee, if there is a good reason to do so.

As an example of this kind of strategic approach, in *Mohamed Nasheed* v. *The Maldives*, the WGAD found the arrest, trial, conviction, and sentencing of the former

---

[2] Rule 96(e) of the Rules of Procedure of the HR Committee states that with regards to an individual case submitted for consideration under the Optional Protocol that it must ascertain "[t]hat the same matter is not being examined under another procedure of international investigation or settlement." If the case is being examined at the WGAD, then it will be found inadmissible by the HR Committee. *Rules of Procedure, Human Rights Committee*, CCPR/C/3/Rev.8, Sept. 22, 2005.

President of the Maldives to fourteen years' imprisonment on bogus terrorism charges arbitrary and in violation of international law.[3] From start to finish, the litigation process at the WGAD took a little more than five months. After mobilizing substantial international pressure, built on the strong opinion of the WGAD, the Government ultimately caved and allowed Nasheed to travel abroad for medical treatment in January 2016. That said, however, the illegal conviction had a secondary effect of disqualifying Nasheed from being able to run for President in the country's 2018 elections. To challenge that arbitrary disqualification, he filed his case before the HR Committee under the Optional Protocol explaining that because the disqualification to run for political office emanated from an arbitrary detention, this disqualification was equally arbitrary. The HR Committee agreed in a view adopted on April 4, 2018.[4]

Taking a case to the WGAD precludes taking a case to the European Court of Human Rights, which has consistently interpreted the *European Convention of Human Rights* to deem inadmissible cases brought after the adoption of an opinion where the parties, facts, and general legal violations are the same or similar.[5] Similarly, it also precludes taking a case to the Inter-American Commission and Court of Human Rights, unless issues beyond the detention are the focus of the petition.[6] And it also precludes taking a case to the African Commission or Court on Human and Peoples' Rights, which considers the special procedures of the Human Rights Council (HRC) to be settlement mechanisms for international disputes that might otherwise render a communication inadmissible. And it also precludes taking a case to the African Commission or Court on Human and

---

[3] Mohamed Nasheed v. The Maldives, WGAD Opinion No. 33/2015, Adopted Sept. 4, 2015 (Litigated by Author through Freedom Now with Co-Counsel Amal Clooney and Ben Emmerson QC).

[4] Nasheed v. The Maldives, Communication Nos. 2270/2013 and 2851/2016, Human Rights Committee, CCPR/C/122/D/2851/2016, Apr. 4, 2018 (Litigated by Author through Perseus Strategies).

[5] *See, e.g.,* Peraldi v. France, Application No. 2096/95, Decision on Admissibility, European Court of Human Rights, Apr. 7, 2009; Illiu & Others v. Belgium, Decision on Admissibility, Application No. 14301/08, European Court of Human Rights, May 19, 2009. These judgments, and others, have found the WGAD is "another procedure of international investigation or settlement" under Article 35(2)(b) of the European Convention of Human Rights. This means that if the submission to the WGAD was "substantially the same" and contains "no new information," then the European Court of Human Rights will declare the petition it has received inadmissible.

[6] Under Article 33(1) of the Rules of Procedure of the Inter-American Commission on Human Rights, consideration of a submission is precluded if its subject matter is "pending settlement pursuant to another procedure before an international governmental organization of which the State concerned is a member" or "essentially duplicates a petition pending or already examined and settled … by another international governmental organization of which the State concerned is a member." In one case before the Commission where the WGAD had found the individuals to be held arbitrarily, it concluded "the Commission finds that this case does not refer only to the arbitrary detention of the alleged victims, but also to the alleged violation of other rights. The Working Group was unable to pronounce on these alleged violations, as they fall outside its competence. In addition, the Commission considers that possible violations of due process were not subject to review by the Working Group, since some of the decisions questioned were issued after the Working Group's pronouncement. Indeed, the Working Group issued its opinion in Apr. 2007, one year and a half before the final decision that ordered the immediate release of the alleged victims (Oct. 2008). During this period, as alleged by the petitioner, the reported violations to judicial protection, fair trial and humane treatment of the alleged victims persisted, in addition to the continuing arbitrary detention." It concluded "the present petition has a distinct purpose and intent as compared to the one presented before the Working Group on Arbitrary Detention. In this regard, the Commission considers that there are no grounds for considering the petition inadmissible based on Articles 46(1)(c) and 47(d) of the Convention and Article 33 of the IACHR Rules of Procedure." Jorge Marcial Tzompaxtle Tecpile, et. al v. Mexico, Inter-American Commission on Human Rights, Admissibility, Report No. 67/15 Petition 211-07, Oct. 27, 2015.

Peoples' Rights, which considers the special procedures of the Human Rights Council (HRC) to be settlement mechanisms for international disputes that might otherwise render a communication inadmissible.[7]

C Identifying Detainees for Submission

A source may file a petition regarding an alleged arbitrary deprivation of liberty to the WGAD on one or more individual cases of detainees. If filing on behalf of more than one person, it is most effective to file a petition on behalf of a group of detainees whose detentions share a common set of facts.

This can mean two different things. First, facts can be common where multiple people were arrested in relation to the same event or on the same day in relation to a common investigation. For example, the author filed a joint petition to the WGAD on behalf of 250 detainees in the *Balyoz or "Sledgehammer" Cases* v. *Turkey*.[8] In that case, the defendants were Turkish military officers who had been falsely accused of planning a coup in an alleged common plot against the Government of Turkey.[9] Or second, facts can be common if people are detained in similar circumstances where there are serious questions about the means of detention being incompatible with international law. Thus, for example, the WGAD has rendered general opinions about mass detention situations, such as the situation of detainees being held by the United States in Guantanamo Bay, Cuba, which have been relied on to find a series of Guantanamo detainees to be held in violation of international law.[10]

---

[7] Under Article 56(7) of the African Charter on Human and Peoples' Rights, a case brought before the African Commission or Court cannot "deal with cases which have been settled by those States involved in accordance with the principles of the Charter of the United Nations." But this provision applies "not only to instances of settlement but also to instances where the matter is under consideration before another supranational human rights-based adjudicatory body." Admissibility of Complaints Before the African Court: Practical Guide, FIDH, June 2016, at 29. That said, in Sudan Human Rights Organisation and Centre on Housing Rights and Evictions v. Sudan, the African Commission observed "while recognizing the important role played by the United Nations Security Council, the Human Rights Council (and its predecessor, the Commission on Human Rights) and other UN organs and agencies on the Darfur crisis, [the Commission] is of the firm view that these organs are not the mechanisms envisaged under Article 56 (7). The mechanisms envisaged under Article 56(7) of the Charter must be capable of granting declaratory or compensatory relief to victims, not mere political resolutions and declarations." App. Nos. 279/03-296/ 05, African Commission on Human and People's Rights, May 27, 2009, at ¶ 105. Later, the African Commission unequivocally ruled that a communication is considered settled "if it has been dealt with by any of the human rights treaty bodies or the Charter bodies of the United Nations system." Haregewoin Gabre-Selassie and IHRDA (on Behalf of Former Dergue Officials) v. Ethiopia, Communication 301/O5, Oct. 12, 2013, at ¶ 114. The Commission explained that UN treaty bodies are "bodies created under international human rights treaties," such as the Human Rights Committee, which is the treaty body for the ICCPR. Id., at ¶ 115. And Charter bodies are those "created under the UN Charter and include the . . . [s]pecial procedures of the Human Rights Council . . . ." Id., at ¶ 116. Finally, the Commission explained more precisely that "[t]o be settled also requires that the treaty or Charter body dealing with the matter has taken a decision which addresses the concerns, including the relief being sought by the Complainant. It is not enough for matters to be discussed by these bodies." Id., at ¶ 117.

[8] Balyoz or Sledgehammer Cases v. Turkey, WGAD Opinion No. 6/2013, Adopted May 1, 2013 (Litigated by Author through Perseus Strategies).

[9] Id.

[10] *Report of the Working Group on Arbitrary Detention*, Commission on Human Rights, E/CN./4/2003/8, Dec. 16, 2002, at ¶¶ 61–64.

While about two-thirds of the petitions filed to the WGAD over the years have been on behalf of one person, the remaining one-third have been made on behalf of multiple people.

DISTRIBUTION OF NUMBERS OF PEOPLE INCLUDED PER CASE, 1992–2017

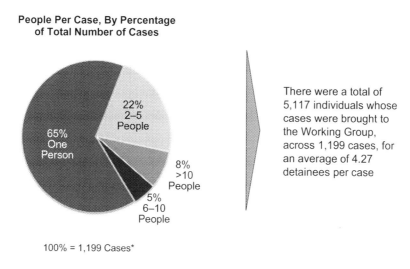

People Per Case, By Percentage of Total Number of Cases

22%
2–5
People

65%
One
Person

8%
>10
People

5%
6–10
People

There were a total of 5,117 individuals whose cases were brought to the Working Group, across 1,199 cases, for an average of 4.27 detainees per case

100% = 1,199 Cases*

* A case can involve one or more individuals; includes all reported cases, regardless of whether an opinion was issued, excludes cases without data

Source: Author's analysis of case data from UN Working Group on Arbitrary Detention

Figure 3 Average number of detainees submitted per case

Unfortunately, the WGAD has not consistently reported the gender of detainees that were the subject of its opinions over time. A review of its 1,199 cases showed that of 5,117 individuals, 3,870 (76 percent) were identifiably male, 391 (8 percent) identifiably female, and 856 (14 percent) unknown. Although the WGAD has asked for the gender of detainees in its Model Questionnaire from its establishment, it would be useful going forward for it to consistently report on the gender of detainees who are the subject of its opinions.

D Adverse State(s) and Detentions by Non-State Actors

In the vast majority of cases, the government of a single state is holding a detainee, which is the adverse party in the petition filed to the WGAD. It is therefore straightforward, on receiving a petition, for the WGAD to send its communication to the government about the petition it has received. Under its Methods of Work: "In the interest of ensuring mutual cooperation, communications shall be brought to the attention of the Govern-ment and the reply of the latter shall be brought to the attention of the source of the communication for its further comments."[11]

---

[11] *Methods of Work of the Working Group*, Human Rights Council, A/HRC/36/38, July 13, 2017, at ¶ 15.

That said, however, it is important to understand, although it is never explicitly stated in the Methods of Work, that the WGAD has the discretion to convey a communication about a petition it has received to any government it believes might have useful information to provide about the case.

Over the years, for example, the WGAD has handled a number of cases where a detainee is imprisoned by one government, but that government's detention center is on the foreign sovereign territory of a second government. Thus, in *Laçin Akhmadjanov v. Afghanistan and the United States*, an Uzbek national was detained by the United States at the Bagram Theatre Internment Facility in Afghanistan.[12] The WGAD conveyed its communication to the governments of both Afghanistan and the United States. But in a series of cases regarding the detentions of inmates at Guantanamo Bay, Cuba, by the United States, the WGAD conveyed its communication only to the United States.[13] The WGAD has not explained this distinction in its approach, but it may practically be that in Cuba, the United States has a perpetual lease for Guantanamo Bay, but in Afghanistan, the US presence is temporary.

There have also been two other highly unusual WGAD cases, where it is not intuitively obvious why communications were sent to particular states.

First, in *Julian Assange v. Sweden and the United Kingdom*, the Wikileaks founder was in the United Kingdom fighting a request for extradition to Sweden. After being released from prison on bail, he fled to the Embassy of Ecuador, where he took up residence. Despite his having voluntarily entered the embassy, he alleged to the WGAD that both Sweden and the United Kingdom were responsible for his being arbitrarily detained there. The WGAD sent the communication to both governments and, ultimately, as discussed in greater detail later in the book, found his detention to be arbitrary and in violation of international law.[14]

And second, in *Mukhtar Ablyazov v. France*, a Kazakhstan citizen was facing extradition from France to either Russia or Ukraine, based on two different extradition requests.[15] Importantly, as was conveyed by the petitioner to the WGAD, he previously had been granted political asylum by the United Kingdom. Given Ablyazov was being detained in France by the Government of France, however, and the allegations of his arbitrary detention related exclusively to the Government's violations of its obligations under international law, it would make sense that France alone should have received the communication. Even though the cases were indirectly connected to Russia and Ukraine, neither Government would have been in a position to comment on whether or not the Government of France was abiding by its obligations under international law when neither were even a party to the proceedings in France. Yet not only did the WGAD convey the communication about the petition to France but it also sent it for comment to the Governments of Russia, Ukraine, *and* Kazakhstan. It was especially

---

[12] Laçin Akhmadjanov v. Afghanistan & The United States, WGAD Opinion No. 53/2016, Adopted Nov. 23, 2016, at ¶ 44.

[13] *See, e.g.*, Mohammed Abdul Rahman Al-Shimrani v. United States, WGAD Opinion No. 2/2009, Adopted May 6, 2009.

[14] Julian Assange v. Sweden and the United Kingdom, WGAD Opinion No. 54/2015, Adopted Dec. 4, 2015.

[15] Mukhtar Ablyazov v. France, WGAD Opinion No. 49/2016, Adopted Nov. 23, 2016 (Litigated by Author through Perseus Strategies).

surprising to see this communication was sent to Kazakhstan, the Government that had been formally recognized by the United Kingdom as persecuting him.

Finally, there is the situation where non-state actors are detaining people. The WGAD has found the adverse party to be a state and have held governments responsible for arbitrary detentions by non-state actors where it concludes its actions were tolerated by[16] or funded or controlled by a state.[17] However, where a government has outlawed the non-state actor, the case is considered a hostage-taking or kidnapping and falls outside the competence of the WGAD, which can only address the conduct of states.[18]

E Approach to Evidence

The mandate of the WGAD is to investigate cases of the deprivation of liberty imposed arbitrarily. It has said repeatedly in its opinions over the years that its role is not to substitute itself for a domestic fact-finder in any given case – e.g., it will not consider or render an opinion on the weight of the evidence that was presented to a domestic tribunal – but rather its function is to ascertain if the process that resulted in the person's detention has been carried out in full compliance with a country's obligations under international law.

After years of customary practice in its jurisprudence, the WGAD presented its approach to evidentiary issues in its annual report presented to the HRC in 2011. It explained:

> [The WGAD's] approach is in line with the ruling of the International Court of Justice in *Ahmadou Sadio Diallo (Republic of Guinea v. Democratic Republic of the Congo)*, which establishes the evidentiary position for claims to succeed in human rights cases, a position which this Working Group has adopted on previous occasions for its own Opinions in individual cases.[19]

The WGAD began by explaining that its approach begins with the assumption that it is very difficult for human rights victims to prove they were denied rights guaranteed to them under international law:

> Where it is alleged that a person has not been afforded, by a public authority, certain procedural guarantees to which he or she was entitled, it may be difficult to establish the negative fact that is asserted.[20]

In light of this reality and that governments that adhere to the rule of law should be able to document their actions, the WGAD has placed the burden on governments to show that the rights of detainees have been respected:

> A public authority is generally able to demonstrate that it has followed the appropriate procedures and applied the guarantees required by law – if such was the case – by producing

---

16 Volodymyr Timchenk, et al. v. Nigeria, WGAD Opinion No. 30/1999, Adopted Nov. 30, 1999, at ¶ 18(b).

17 Abdu Ahmed Abdel Salam v. Libya, WGAD Opinion No. 39/2018, Adopted Apr. 26, 2018, at ¶¶ 31–32.

18 Olga Rodas, et al. v. Colombia, WGAD Opinion No. 25/1999, Adopted Nov. 26, 1999, at ¶ 5.

19 *Report of the Working Group on Arbitrary Detention*, Human Rights Council, A/HRC/19/57, Dec. 26, 2011, at ¶ 68.

20 *Id.*

documentary evidence of the actions that were carried out. In general the burden rests with the Government: it is for the Government to produce the necessary proof.[21]

That said, the burden is not shifted to the government by a petitioner unless they first present a prima facie case that it has violated its obligations under international law with regards to how it has treated a detainee:

> More generally, the matter of the evidentiary burden arises where the source has established a prima facie case for breach of international requirements constituting arbitrary detention.[22]

While governments can decide whether or not to respond to a communication from the WGAD, it has made clear that a response is not required for it to be able to adopt an opinion in a specific case:

> Regrettably, in some cases, Governments have not responded to the request from the Working Group to provide it with information. In the absence of such information, the Working Group must base its Opinion on the prima facie case as made out by the source.[23]

Such an approach was clearly a prerequisite from its establishment for the WGAD to fulfill its mandate. Few governments would reply if not responding extinguished the WGAD's ability to examine any allegation of arbitrary detention.

Importantly, the WGAD has always emphasized in its Methods of Work the importance of the adversarial process in receiving complaints from sources, giving governments an opportunity to respond to communications, and then giving the sources the opportunity to reply to that response. For this process to enable the WGAD to get to the truth, however, it requires governments to provide detailed rebuttals to allegations that have been presented to it. The WGAD has emphasized repeatedly:

> [M]ere assertions that lawful procedures have been followed will not be sufficient to rebut the source's allegations; that follows from the nature of the prohibition of arbitrary detention.[24]

In its jurisprudence, the WGAD often describes its approach to evidence like it did in *Thamki Gyatso, Tseltem Gyatso and Kalsang Gyatso v. China*:

> Where there is a prima facie restriction on human rights, the Working Group looks to the Government's communication to determine whether there is a restriction and whether it can be justified or falls within a derogation which may apply. This reflects general human rights principles where the burden similarly falls on the State where there is a prima facie restriction on human rights.[25]

---

[21] *Id.*
[22] *Id.*
[23] *Id.*
[24] *Id.*
[25] Tseltem Gyatso & Kalsang Gyatso v. China, WGAD Opinion No. 29/2010, Adopted Nov. 24, 2010, at ¶ 25; *see also* Nasrin Sotoudeh v. Iran, WGAD Opinion No. 21/2011, Adopted May 5, 2011, at ¶ 5.

Said in a slightly different way:

> The Working Group has in its jurisprudence established the ways in which it deals with evidentiary issues. If the source has established a prima facie case for breach of international requirements constituting arbitrary detention, the burden of proof should be understood to rest upon the Government if it wishes to refute the allegations.[26]

F Languages

The official languages of OHCHR are English, French, and Spanish, and the WGAD has the capacity to handle cases submitted in those three languages. It will also issue opinions in those three languages. If a case is submitted in another language, the WGAD will ask the source to resubmit in one of the three languages.

It is therefore essential to make submissions in one of the three working languages of OHCHR. In addition, if responses to communications from the WGAD are likely to come back in a language other than one of the three working languages (e.g., when a submission is made in English alleging violations by China, where the Government will respond in Chinese), then it is important to inform the WGAD that it can convey the *original* response back to the source, rather than sending it out for translation.

G Categories of Cases

According to its Methods of Work, when discharging its mandate to deal with situations regarding deprivations of liberty, the WGAD refers to five legal categories of cases:

(a) When it is clearly impossible to invoke any legal basis justifying the deprivation of liberty, as when a person is kept in detention after the completion of his or her sentence or despite an amnesty law applicable to him or her (category I);

(b) When the deprivation of liberty results from the exercise of the rights or freedoms guaranteed by articles 7, 13–14 and 18–21 of the Universal Declaration of Human Rights and, insofar as States parties are concerned, by articles 12, 18–19, 21–22, and 25–27 of the International Covenant on Civil and Political Rights (category II);

(c) When the total or partial non-observance of the international norms relating to the right to a fair trial, established in the Universal Declaration of Human Rights and in the relevant international instruments accepted by the States concerned, is of such gravity as to give the deprivation of liberty an arbitrary character (category III);

(d) When asylum seekers, immigrants, or refugees are subjected to prolonged administrative custody without the possibility of administrative or judicial review or remedy (category IV);

(e) When the deprivation of liberty constitutes a violation of international law on the grounds of discrimination based on birth, national, ethnic or social origin, language, religion, economic condition, political or other opinion, gender, sexual

---

[26] Rebii Metin Görgeç v. Turkey, WGAD Opinion No. 1/2017, Adopted Apr. 19, 2017, at ¶ 42 (Litigated by Author through Perseus Strategies).

orientation, disability, or any other status, that aims toward or can result in ignoring the equality of human beings (category V).[27]

As noted previously, these are not mutually exclusive categories. The WGAD can issue opinions finding a deprivation of liberty falls within more than one of these legal categories. When taking a case to the WGAD, it is important to explain how violations of international law regarding the alleged deprivation of liberty of a detainee fall within one or more of these categories.

H Working Group's Basic Principles and Guidelines, Prior Opinions, and Annual Reports

In July 2012, the HRC specifically requested the WGAD to "prepare draft basic principles and guidelines on remedies and procedures on the right of anyone deprived of his or her liberty."[28] It further explained that in preparing this draft, it was responsible:

(a) To seek the views of States, relevant United Nations agencies, intergovernmental organizations, United Nations treaty bodies, and, in particular, the Human Rights Committee, other special procedures, national human rights institutions, non-governmental organizations, and other relevant stakeholders;

(b) To submit a specific report to the Human Rights Council on national, regional and international laws, regulations, and practices on the right as stated in paragraph 6 (d);

(c) To hold subsequently a consultation with stakeholders in relation to the preparation of the first draft basic principles and guidelines;

(d) To present the draft basic principles and guidelines to the Human Rights Council before the end of 2015, in accordance with its annual programme of work;[29]

After extensive consultations with governments and civil society organizations, the WGAD adopted the *Basic Principles and Guidelines on Remedies and Procedures on the Right of Anyone Deprived of His or Her Liberty by Arrest or Detention to Bring Proceedings Before Court* in April 2015 and it was presented to the HRC in July 2015.[30] Consisting of twenty-one principles and twenty-two guidelines, as described by the WGAD, they are "based on international law, standards and recognized good practice, and are intended to provide [s]tates with guidance on fulfilling, in compliance with international law, their obligation to avoid the arbitrary deprivation of liberty."[31]

Where relevant, reference to these principles and guidelines should be cited in communications to the WGAD as they are grounded in its jurisprudence and now are regularly cited in its opinions. They are also incorporated into the analysis of the WGAD's jurisprudence in Section III.

---

[27] *Methods of Work of the Working Group*, Human Rights Council, A/HRC/36/38, July 13, 2017, at ¶ 8.

[28] Resolution 20/16 (Arbitrary Detention), Human Rights Council, A/HRC/RES/20/16, July 17, 2012, at ¶ 10.

[29] *Id.*

[30] *Basic Principles and Guidelines on Remedies and Procedures on the Right of Anyone Deprived of His or Her Liberty by Arrest or Detention to Bring Proceedings Before Court*, Human Rights Council, Working Group on Arbitrary Detention, Human Rights Council, A/HRC/30/37, July 6, 2015.

[31] *Id.*, at summary.

In addition, prior WGAD deliberations, opinions, and annual reports may be cited in communications as persuasive authority. This means that the WGAD may consult those past cases and refer to them, but they are not binding precedent. In 2011, the WGAD launched its database of prior cases, making publicly available for the first time its jurisprudence in an online and easily searchable form.[32] The database has enabled WGAD members themselves during their sessions to find relevant cases on point as they consider the adoption of new opinions. Today, prior opinions of relevance are frequently referenced in new opinions, improving the coherence, consistency, and reliability of the WGAD's jurisprudence.

I Working Group Country Mission Reports

Throughout its history, the WGAD has conducted forty-five country visits and six preparatory or follow-up visits.[33] As described in its Methods of Work, the WGAD "frequently pays visits on official mission ... in collaboration with the Government, United Nations agencies in the field and civil society representatives ... [which are] an opportunity for the Working Group to engage in direct dialogue ... with the aim of better understanding the situation of deprivation of liberty in the country and the underlying reasons for arbitrary detention."[34] Specifically, the WGAD is seeking to enhance its "understanding of the evolution, state application, and implementation of national legislation from the perspective of international human rights norms, taking into account the social, political and historical context of each country."[35] It typically conducts two country visits per year. It makes requests to governments to visit but can only conduct a country visit after a formal invitation from a government itself.

For the WGAD to agree to visit a country, its government must "assure the Working Group that, during the visit, the Working Group will have the opportunity to conduct

---

[32] As noted earlier, this was of special concern to the Author, who consequently worked through Freedom Now to facilitate a partnership between the UN Working Group on Arbitrary Detention, Thomson Reuters Foundation, and Freedom Now to build and maintain the now publicly-available database: www.unwgaddatabase.org.

[33] The WGAD has issued reports about missions to Angola (2007), Argentina (2003, 2017), Armenia (2010), Australia (2002), Azerbaijan (2016), Bahrain (2001), Belarus (2004), Bhutan (1994, 1996), Brazil (2013), Canada (2005), China (1996, 1997, 2004), Colombia (2008), Ecuador (2006), El Salvador (2013), Equatorial Guinea (2007), Georgia (2012), Germany (2012), Germany (2015), Greece (2014), Honduras (2006), Hungary (2013, 2018), Indonesia (1999), Iran (2003), Italy (2008), Italy (2015), Latvia (2004), Malaysia (2010), Malta (2009), Malta (2015), Mauritania (2008), Mexico (2002), Morocco (2013), Nicaragua (2006), Nepal (1996), New Zealand (2015), Norway (2007), Peru (1998), Romania (1998), Senegal (2009), South Africa (2005), Sri Lanka (2017), Turkey (2006), Ukraine (2008), United Kingdom (1988), and Viet Nam (1994). It has requested the opportunity to visit Algeria, China (follow-up visit), Democratic People's Republic of Korea, Egypt, Ethiopia, Guinea-Bissau, India, Japan, Kenya, Malaysia (follow-up visit), Mexico (follow-up visit), Morocco, Nauru, Nicaragua (follow-up visit), Papua New Guinea, Republic of Korea, Russian Federation, Rwanda, Saudi Arabia, Sierra Leone, Singapore, Thailand, Turkmenistan, Uganda, Uzbekistan, Venezuela, and Viet Nam (follow-up visit). See Country Visits – Working Group on Arbitrary Detention (Nov. 2018), www.ohchr.org/EN/Issues/Detention/Pages/Visits.aspx.

[34] Methods of Work of the Working Group on Arbitrary Detention, Human Rights Council, A/HRC/36/38, July 13, 2017, at ¶ 26.

[35] Country Visits – Working Group on Arbitrary Detention, Office of the High Commissioner for Human Rights (July 2018), www.ohchr.org/en/issues/detention/pages/visits.aspx.

meetings with the highest authorities of the branches of the State (political, administrative, legislative and judicial authorities), that it will be able to visit penitentiaries,
prisons, police stations, immigration detention centers, military prisons, detention centers
for juveniles and psychiatric hospitals and that it will be able to meet with all the
authorities and officials who affect the personal liberty of persons subjected to the
jurisdiction of the host State."[36] In addition, the WGAD also meets "international bodies
and agencies as well as with non-governmental organizations, lawyers, bar associations
and other professional associations of interest, national human rights institutions, diplomatic and consular representatives and religious authorities."[37] The WGAD demands it
be provided absolute confidentiality for interviews it conducts with detainees and that no
reprisals will be taken against those it interviews.

On completing a country visit, the WGAD provides a "preliminary statement" to the
government with its preliminary findings. It then holds a press conference to inform the public
of its findings after debriefing the government. Later, the WGAD adopts a report about its visit,
which is first conveyed to the government in order to receive its observations on any factual or
legal errors and it then publishes that report as an addendum to its annual report.[38]

In April 2014, the WGAD adopted a formal set of "Terms of Reference" to govern its
conducting of country visits. It elaborates on how visits are conducted, as described more
briefly in the Methods of Work. It explains that the purpose of country visits is "to better
understand the situation of the deprivation of liberty in a country and the underlying
reasons for arbitrary detention" and that visits are to "take place in the context of a
collaborative and constructive dialogue."[39]

In terms of how country missions are conducted, the WGAD emphasizes that it can
use "all available information on the country in relation to [its] mandate" as "the basis
of background documentation and country assessment for its members."[40] It also
explains that to build trust with detainees that "due consideration shall be given, to
the extent possible, to avoid working with local interpreters or with interpreters who
reside in the host country."[41] And then it explains in greater detail who it seeks to meet,
visits it conducts to places of detention, and how it conducts the presentation of its
findings through a statement in country, its press conference, the adoption of its report
later, in consultation with the government, and requesting a follow-up visit two years
later.[42]

The country mission reports of the WGAD are highly substantive, detailed, and a
rich source of information on the situation of arbitrary detention in countries it has
visited and should be cited to in petitions to the WGAD regarding complaints of
arbitrary detention by those countries, if there were relevant observations made in its
country mission report. A review of these reports demonstrates that there are common
themes frequently addressed during these visits, beyond the description of the program

---

[36] Methods of Work, at ¶ 27.

[37] Id.

[38] Id., at ¶¶ 29–30.

[39] *Terms of Reference for Country Visits by the Working Group on Arbitrary Detention*, Human Rights
Council, Apr. 2014, at ¶¶ 4, 7.

[40] Id., at ¶ 9.

[41] Id., at ¶ 11.

[42] Id., at ¶¶ 16–41.

of the visit and the country's institutional and legal framework. These themes often include topics such as:

- Arrests without Warrant
- The Right to Be Brought Promptly Before a Judge
- Excessive Use of Pretrial Detention
- Preventative and Administrative Detention
- Absence of Effective Legal Assistance
- Juvenile Justice
- Detentions of Refugees, Asylum Seekers, and Migrants
- Detentions on Grounds of Disability and Health
- Detentions Involving Terrorism or Threats against National Security
- Detentions in Violation of Rights to Freedom of Opinion and Expression and Peaceful Assembly
- Disproportionate Detentions of Minority Groups
- States of Emergency
- Torture and Other Cruel, Inhuman, or Degrading Treatment or Punishment of Detainees

J Applicable Law

1 Law Explicitly Identified under Methods of Work

In addition to assisting advocates by providing five legal categories of cases where it considers arbitrary detention, the WGAD also explains in its Methods of Work what it considers to be the most relevant international legal standards that it applies in individual cases. Specifically, it says:

In the discharge of its mandate, the Working Group refers to the relevant international standards set forth in the Universal Declaration of Human Rights, as well as to the relevant international instruments accepted by the States concerned, in particular the International Covenant on Civil and Political Rights, the Convention relating to the Status of Refugees of 1951 and the Protocol relating to the Status of Refugees of 1967, the International Convention on the Elimination of All Forms of Racial Discrimination and, when appropriate, any other relevant standards, including the following:

(a) *The Convention on the Rights of the Child;*
(b) *The Convention against Torture and Other Cruel, Inhuman or Degrading Treatment or Punishment;*
(c) *The International Convention on the Protection of the Rights of All Migrant Workers and Members of Their Families;*
(d) *The Convention on the Rights of Persons with Disabilities;*
(e) *The Body of Principles for the Protection of All Persons under Any Form of Detention or Imprisonment;*
(f) *The United Nations Standard Minimum Rules for the Treatment of Prisoners* (the Nelson Mandela Rules);
(g) *The United Nations Rules for the Protection of Juveniles Deprived of Their Liberty;*
(h) *The United Nations Standard Minimum Rules for the Administration of Juvenile Justice* (the Beijing Rules);

(i) *The United Nations Basic Principles and Guidelines on Remedies and Procedures on the Right of Anyone Deprived of Their Liberty to Bring Proceedings Before a Court.*[43]

While treaty law has the greatest weight as binding on states parties, customary international law is also binding. And as is clear from its non-exhaustive list of relevant international legal standards and its general practice, the WGAD will also apply soft law such as relevant resolutions from the UN General Assembly.

2 Special Case of Detention of Foreigners or Dual Nationals

The *Vienna Convention on Consular Relations* (VCCR) is an international treaty for diplomatic and consular interactions between countries.[44] Although the WGAD's Methods of Work do not explicitly list the VCCR as one of a number of the human rights instruments it considers, they do allow the WGAD to consider, "when appropriate, any other relevant standards."[45] In multiple opinions, the WGAD has referred to the VCCR. Both the detaining county and the home country of the detained national must be parties to the treaty for the WGAD to apply it to the detention at hand. As of 2018, there are 179 state parties to the VCCR, meaning the right to consular access will often be a relevant and enforceable right.

Article 36(1)(b) of the VCCR provides that when a nonnational is detained:

> If he so requests, the competent authorities of the receiving State shall, without delay, inform the consular post of the sending State if, within its consular district, a national of that State is arrested or committed to prison or to custody pending trial or is detained in any other manner.[46]

The VCCR also requires that authorities inform detained nonnationals of their right to contact a consular official, and that they facilitate communications by forwarding messages to the appropriate official without delay.[47] Under Article 36(1)(c), consular officials must remain able to contact the detainee and arrange legal assistance if necessary.[48]

The *Body of Principles for the Protection of All Persons under Any Form of Detention or Imprisonment* likewise supports the right to consular contact, and provides further protection for persons who may be without an effective consulate:

> If a detained or imprisoned person is a foreigner, he shall also be promptly informed of his right to communicate by appropriate means with a consular post or the diplomatic mission of the State of which he is a national or which is otherwise entitled to receive such communication in accordance with international law or with the representative of the competent international organization, if he is a refugee or is otherwise under the protection of an intergovernmental organization.[49]

---

[43] Methods of Work, at ¶ 7.

[44] *Vienna Convention on Consular Relations*, 596 U.N.T.S. 261, Apr. 24, 1963, *entered into force* Mar. 19, 1967.

[45] Methods of Work, ¶ 7.

[46] Vienna Convention on Consular Relations, at Art. 36(1)(b).

[47] Id.

[48] Id., at Art. 36(1)(c).

[49] *Body of Principles for the Protection of All Persons under Any Form of Detention or Imprisonment*, UN General Assembly, A/RES/43/173, Dec. 9, 1988, at Principle 16(2).

In its most recent annual report, the WGAD addressed comprehensively for the first time the issue of consular assistance and diplomatic protection of foreigners deprived of their liberty.[50] It explained:

> [C]onsular assistance or consular protection is primarily a preventive mechanism, which constitutes an important safeguard for individuals who are arrested and detained in a foreign State to ensure that international standards are being complied with. It provides detainees, as well as consular officials of the detainee's nationality (of the sending State), with certain consular rights, such as the right for consular officials to freely communicate with and have access to their detained nationals and to be informed about the arrest without delay.[51]

And it added:

> Diplomatic protection, on the other hand, is only engaged in the event of an internationally wrongful act committed by the detaining State, for example one that has caused injury to a national of the sending State (i.e. the State of nationality). It is a remedial mechanism that can be invoked where there is an inter-State dispute surrounding the internationally wrongful act. It is a right of the State to exercise diplomatic protection on behalf of its nationals, rather than a duty. A State may, however, have a limited duty to consider whether or not to exercise diplomatic protection in any given case. Although diplomatic protection is not codified, it is a principle of customary international law and is vital for the protection of human rights.[52]

The WGAD explained that consular assistance helps protect detainees from torture and ill-treatment and it is especially needed where detainees may not understand the language, have no contacts, and not be familiar with the country's legal system and traditions. It also explained that nonnational defendants and detainees are especially vulnerable to violations of the right to a fair trial.[53]

In its jurisprudence, the WGAD has found denials of consular contact to be due process violations which contribute to a potential arbitrary detention under Category III.[54] Opinions include several sources of international law to support this right. The International Court of Justice has ruled that Article 36(1) of the VCCR creates individual enforceable rights, and the WGAD has followed this approach.[55] The WGAD considers a breach of the right to contact consular officials to be violations of Article 9 of both the UDHR and ICCPR, which prohibit arbitrary arrest and detention. In addition to the VCCR and the Body of Principles, the WGAD has also cited the *United Nations Standard Minimum Rules for the Treatment of Prisoners* and the *International*

---

[50] *Report of the Working Group on Arbitrary Detention*, Human Rights Council, A/HRC/39/45, July 2, 2018, at ¶¶ 50–58.

[51] *Id.*, at ¶ 51.

[52] *Id.*, at ¶ 52.

[53] *Id.*, at ¶¶ 55–57.

[54] Taysir Hasan Mahmoud Salman v. United Arab Emirates, WGAD Opinion No. 58/2017, Adopted Aug. 24, 2017, at ¶ 67; Ola Yusuf al-Qaradawi & Hossam al-Din Khalaf v. Egypt, WGAD Opinion No. 26/2018, Adopted Apr. 23, 2018, at ¶ 75 (Litigated by Author through Perseus Strategies).

[55] LaGrand Case (Germany v. United States), 2001 I.C.J. Rep. 466, ¶¶65–78, June 27, 2001; Boniface Muriuki Chuma, et al. v. South Sudan, WGAD Opinion No. 18/2016, Adopted Apr. 27, 2016, at ¶ 29.

Convention for the Protection of Migrant Workers and Members of Their Families in support of this right.[56]

The right to contact a consular official also applies to dual nationals detained in one of their countries of citizenship. In *Nazanin Zaghari-Ratcliffe v. Iran*, the WGAD noted that a British-Iranian dual national had been denied access to British consular officials, and that this "violated international standards" of detention.[57] *Gunasundaram Jayasundaram v. Sri Lanka* affirmed that not informing a dual Sri Lankan-Irish citizen about his right to contact Irish consular officials was a violation of the ICCPR Article 14 right to a fair trial.[58] In *Jason Rezaian v. Iran*, the Government refused to recognize the US citizenship of an American-Iranian dual national, maintaining the United States had no interest in his detention and denying an envoy from Switzerland acting as an intermediary and protecting power for US interests in Iran.[59] The source alleged this violated the right to consular access. However, the WGAD made no comment on these facts in a brief opinion finding other violations of the right to a fair trial.

This is not uncommon, since denial of consular access is typically one in a list of fair trial violations. In most cases, the WGAD devotes little discussion to the right to consular access, even if sources provide detailed accounts of denials.[60] As such, it is difficult to tell whether an arrest and trial conducted otherwise fairly would be deemed arbitrary by the WGAD for violating Article 36(1)(b) alone. For instance, in *Boniface Muriuki Chuma, et al. v. South Sudan*, the WGAD found that the "arbitrariness of the deprivation of liberty of the five men has become exacerbated by the denial of their consular rights, thereby depriving them of their right to a fair trial."[61] This acknowledges that denial of consular access is a violation of the right to a fair trial, but the word "exacerbates" seems to imply that this violation is not the basis of the WGAD's findings, and on its own may not be of sufficient gravity to render a detention arbitrary.

Taysir Hasan Mahmoud Salman v. United Arab Emirates and *Ola Yusuf al-Qaradawi and Hosam al-Din Khalaf v. Egypt* explain the reasoning for incorporating consular assistance into the requirements of a fair trial. The first case involved a Jordanian national detained in the United Arab Emirates for online criticism of the Government, and the second involved the wife in a couple being a dual Egypt-Qatari national detained for alleged familial connections to the Muslim Brotherhood. Denied access to consular officials as well as his family and lawyers, Salman had no consular assistance until the

---

[56] Ola Yusuf al-Qaradawi & Hossam al-Din Khalaf v. Egypt, WGAD Opinion No. 26/2018, Adopted Apr. 23, 2018, at ¶¶ 68, 72 (citing Article 16(7) of the International Convention and rule 62, paragraph 1 of the Nelson Mandela Rules).

[57] Nazanin Zaghari-Ratcliffe v. Iran, WGAD Opinion No. 28/2016, Adopted Aug. 23, 2016, at ¶ 51.

[58] Gunasundaram Jayasundaram v. Sri Lanka, WGAD Opinion No. 30/2008, Adopted Sept. 12, 2008, at ¶ 23.

[59] Jason Rezaian v. Iran, WGAD Opinion No. 44/2015, Adopted Dec. 3, 2015, at ¶ 11.

[60] Marcus Haldon Hodge Libya Philippines, WGAD Opinion No. Adopted Aug. 28, 2012, at ¶ 10 (where the initial denial and eventual recording of contact with a consular official was not discussed in the WGAD's opinion); Yuri Korepanov v. Uzbekistan, WGAD Opinion No. 30/2013, Adopted Aug. 30, 2013, at ¶ 13 (where complaints that Russian officials were not allowed to attend court hearings went unaddressed by the WGAD); Jason Rezaian v. Iran, WGAD Opinion No. 44/2015, Adopted Dec. 3, 2015, at ¶ 11 (where alleged denial of US citizenship and visits from a US envoy went unaddressed); Phan (Sandy) Phan-Gillis v. China, WGAD Opinion 12/2016, Adopted Apr. 20, 2016, at ¶ 16 (where the WGAD seemed to accept the Government's late assertion that twelve consular visits had been permitted without further discussion).

[61] Boniface Muriuki Chuma, et al. v. South Sudan, WGAD Opinion No. 18/2016, Adopted Apr. 27, 2016, at ¶ 29.

Jordanian embassy exerted "strong efforts to convince the Emirati authorities" to allow them access.[62] Al-Qaradawi never received consular access.[63] For nonnationals disadvantaged by an unfamiliarity with local law, procedure, and perhaps language, the WGAD discussed in both cases that consular access affords an "invaluable protection" and ensures fairness in their proceedings.[64] This right benefits the international community as well by "reducing the potential for friction between States over the treatment of their nationals."[65] A further benefit of consular access was demonstrated in *Mohamed Hajib v. Morocco*, where German officials were able to confirm and report allegations of torture.[66] This recent increase in elaboration suggests that the WGAD may be beginning to take more notice of consular access cases, and that further analysis may be forthcoming.

3 Most Common Law Cited

Regardless of the explicitly listed applicable legal instruments in the Methods of Work, these are the most cited to sources both by petitioners and by the WGAD in its opinions:

- *International Covenant on Civil and Political Rights*
- General Comments of the Human Rights Committee to the ICCPR
- Views of the Human Rights Committee Adopted under the *Optional Protocol to the ICCPR*
- *Universal Declaration of Human Rights*
- *Body of Principles for the Protection of All Persons under Any Form of Detention or Imprisonment*
- *United Nations Basic Principles and Guidelines on Remedies and Procedures on the Right of Anyone Deprived of Their Liberty to Bring Proceedings before a Court*
- Resolutions of the UN Human Rights Council
- Prior Opinions, Annual Reports, and Country Mission Reports of the WGAD
- Reports of Other UN Special Procedures

That said, the reference to the WGAD applying "any other relevant standards" in its Methods of Work really does mean just that. As just one of many such examples of lesser known but previously applied standards, in *Thulani Rudolf Maseko v. Swaziland*, the WGAD addressed a case of a human rights lawyer who was imprisoned on a contempt of court charge by the Chief Justice of the Supreme Court of Swaziland, who the detainee had personally criticized. In that case the WGAD observed:

---

[62] Taysir Hasan Mahmoud Salman v. United Arab Emirates, WGAD Opinion No. 58/2017, Adopted Aug. 24, 2017, at ¶ 65.

[63] Ola Yusuf al-Qaradawi & Hossam al-Din Khalaf v. Egypt, WGAD Opinion No. 26/2018, Adopted Apr. 23, 2018, at ¶ 61.

[64] Taysir Hasan Mahmoud Salman v. United Arab Emirates, WGAD Opinion No. 58/2017, Adopted Aug. 24, 2017, at ¶ 64; Ola Yusuf al-Qaradawi & Hossam al-Din Khalaf v. Egypt, WGAD Opinion No. 26/2018, Adopted Apr. 23, 2018, at ¶ 73.

[65] Taysir Hasan Mahmoud Salman v. United Arab Emirates, WGAD Opinion No. 58/2017, Adopted Aug. 24, 2017, at ¶ 64.

[66] Mohamed Hajib v. Morocco, WGAD Opinion No. 40/2012, Adopted Aug. 31, 2012, at ¶ 50.

[A]ccording to the Latimer House Guidelines for the Commonwealth, applicable to Swaziland as a Commonwealth country, "the criminal law and contempt proceedings are not appropriate mechanisms for restricting legitimate criticism of the courts" and "the criminal law and contempt proceedings should not be used to restrict legitimate criticism of the performance of judicial functions."[67]

K States of Emergency

Although it is important when filing a petition to the WGAD to make reference to the relevant aforementioned treaties and related legal instruments, there are occasions where governments will refer to a declared state of emergency to try and justify a person's detention. Under Article 4 of the ICCPR:

1. In time of public emergency which threatens the life of the nation and the existence of which is officially proclaimed, the States Parties to the present Covenant may take measures derogating from their obligations under the present Covenant to the extent strictly required by the exigencies of the situation, provided that such measures are not inconsistent with their other obligations under international law and do not involve discrimination solely on the ground of race, colour, sex, language, religion or social origin.

2. No derogation from articles 6, 7, 8 (paragraphs I and 2), 11, 15, 16 and 18 may be made under this provision.

3. Any State Party to the present Covenant availing itself of the right of derogation shall immediately inform the other States Parties to the present Covenant, through the intermediary of the Secretary-General of the United Nations, of the provisions from which it has derogated and of the reasons by which it was actuated. A further communication shall be made, through the same intermediary, on the date on which it terminates such derogation.[68]

It is important to note at the outset that this provision does theoretically allow states to justify derogations from Articles 9 and 14 of the ICCPR in detaining individuals in ways that might, outside of a state of emergency, be arbitrary and in violation of international law. That said, however, there are limits to a state's conduct.

Specifically, in its General Comment No. 29 on states of emergency, the HR Committee explains:

The enumeration of non-derogable provisions in article 4 is related to, but not identical with, the question whether certain human rights obligations bear the nature of peremptory norms of international law. The proclamation of certain provisions of the Covenant as being of a non-derogable nature, in article 4, paragraph 2, is to be seen partly as recognition of the peremptory nature of some fundamental rights ensured in treaty form in the Covenant (e.g., articles 6 and 7). However, it is apparent that some other provisions of the Covenant were included in the list of non-derogable provisions

---

[67] Thulani Rudolf Maseko v. Swaziland, WGAD Opinion No. 6/2015, Adopted Apr. 22, 2015, at ¶ 29, *citing* John Hatchard and Peter Slinn, *Parliamentary Supremacy and Judicial Independence: A Commonwealth Approach: Proceedings of the Latimer House Joint Colloquium*, June 1998, at ¶ VI.1(b).

[68] ICCPR, at Art. 4.

because it can never become necessary to derogate from these rights during a state of emergency (e.g., articles 11 and 18). Furthermore, the category of peremptory norms extends beyond the list of non-derogable provisions as given in article 4, paragraph 2. States parties may in no circumstances invoke article 4 of the Covenant as justification for acting in violation of humanitarian law or peremptory norms of international law, for instance by taking hostages, by imposing collective punishments, *through arbitrary deprivations of liberty or by deviating from fundamental principles of fair trial, including the presumption of innocence.*[69]

The WGAD has further emphasized "the prohibition of arbitrary detention is customary international law, authoritatively recognized as a peremptory norm of international law or jus cogens."[70]

II Submitting a Case

A Authorization for Submission

According to its Methods of Work, cases can be brought to the WGAD from "the individuals concerned, their families or their representatives ... [and they] may also be transmitted by Governments and intergovernmental and non-governmental organizations as well as by national institutions for the promotion and protection of human rights."[71] Submissions do not need to be made by lawyers, but having competent counsel with a strong international law background can strengthen the quality of a communication.

That said, however, in practice the WGAD now consistently requests that petitioners provide "evidence of the explicit consent of the individuals (or their family in order to pursue the case)." In addition, it requests that the petitioner "confirm that they have agreed to (a) their names being mentioned in a letter to the Government and (b) their names being published in an official opinion of the Working Group."[72] It makes eminent sense for the WGAD to seek such confirmation in light of the direct engagement a petition will have with the detaining government and its desire to, at the barest minimum, do no harm through its consideration of a case.

The WGAD is not formalistic in how it receives this information. In the email conveying a petition to the WGAD, a petitioner can simply attach an email from a member of the detainee's immediate family explaining: (1) their relationship to the detainee; (2) explicitly stating that the petitioner is authorized to make the submission to the WGAD; and (3) on behalf of the detainee, the family member has agreed to have that person's name mentioned in a letter to the government and to have their name published in an official opinion.

---

[69] *General Comment No. 29, States of Emergency (Article 4),* Human Rights Committee, CCPR/C/21/Add. 11, Aug. 31, 2001, at ¶ 11 (emphasis added).

[70] Liu Xiaobo v. China, WGAD Opinion No. 15/2011, Adopted May 5, 2011, at ¶ 20 (Litigated by Author through Freedom Now).

[71] *Methods of Work of the Working Group,* Human Rights Council, A/HRC/36/38, July 13, 2017, at ¶ 12.

[72] *See, e.g.,* Email from Secretary of the WGAD to Author, Jan. 11, 2018 (following up on a previously submitted Petition).

The WGAD also has the authority from Resolution 1993/36 of the former UN Commission for Human Rights (UNCHR) to take up cases that might constitute arbitrary deprivation of liberty.[73]

B Timing of Submission

There are two issues relating to the timing of a submission. The first issue relates to at what stage in a domestic proceeding should an advocate file a petition to the WGAD alleging an arbitrary deprivation of liberty, and the second relates to being mindful of the timeframe in which the WGAD will consider a specific case.

A petition to the WGAD must be made when a detainee is actually imprisoned as its mandate narrowly allows it to make determinations as to whether a deprivation of liberty is arbitrary. The WGAD, however, does not require a case to have reached a verdict, let alone show that domestic remedies have been exhausted. In *"Balyoz" or Sledgehammer Cases* v. *Turkey*, the Government argued the WGAD could not consider the case before an initial verdict was rendered by the domestic tribunal. In response, the WGAD explained:

> The Government claims that the communication should be dismissed by the Working Group because the case is *sub judice*, or still under judicial consideration. It suffices to note that the Working Group is not bound by any such *sub judice* rule ... . The Working Group does not follow such doctrines ... Otherwise, the Working Group would not be able to fulfil its mandate to consider cases of violations of the right of the accused to be tried within a reasonable time or to be released.[74]

That said, for the WGAD to conclude that a deprivation of liberty is arbitrary, it needs sufficient facts and violations of international law to reach this conclusion. For example, in *Saddam Hussein al-Tikriti* v. *Iraq and United States*, the case of the former Iraqi president, the WGAD decided to remain apprised of further developments in the course of ongoing criminal proceedings to determine if the apparent and concerning procedural flaws persisted.[75] The length of time an advocate should wait before filing a petition to ensure the WGAD will not simply defer consideration of the case is highly fact-specific – the more egregious the violations, the sooner a case might be appropriately submitted. The author has generally waited at least several months after an initial detention before filing a petition on any given case.

With respect to timing a petition to maximize speed in the WGAD considering a case, it is important to note at the outset that according to its Methods of Work, it meets at least three times a year, for at least five to eight working days, in Geneva, Switzerland. On taking up a case, it is very important to look at the timing for the next two sessions of the WGAD.[76] This is because on the sending of a communication to a government, it has 60 days to respond and can request up to a maximum of an additional one month extension. It is important to appreciate it can take several weeks for a communication to be conveyed to a government.

---

[73] *Methods of Work of the Working Group*, Human Rights Council, A/HRC/36/38, July 13, 2017, at ¶ 13.

[74] Balyoz or Sledgehammer Cases v. Turkey, WGAD Opinion No. 6/2013, Adopted May 1, 2013, at ¶ 69.

[75] Saddam Hussein al-Tikriti, at ¶ 37; Aleksandr Nikitin v. Russian Federation, WGAD Opinion No. 14/1997, Adopted Sept. 18, 1997 (finding the WGAD waiting until the trial had been completed so that it could rule on the basis of compiled and final information).

[76] The calendar of meetings and events at the United Nations in Geneva can be viewed online: www.ohchr .org/EN/NewsEvents/Pages/Meetings.aspx.

Thus, it is ideal to submit a case more than 120 days prior to a forthcoming WGAD session to maximize the likelihood it will be heard during that session. If timed well, a case can be filed and an opinion issued in as little as four to five months.

C Contents of Submission

The WGAD explains in its Methods of Work that communications must be submitted in writing and sent to its secretariat. It summarizes the critical information that it requests be provided as follows:

> As far as possible, each case shall form the subject of a presentation indicating the circumstances of the arrest or detention and the family name, first name and any other information making it possible to identify the person detained, as well as the latter's legal status, particularly:
>
> (a) The date and place of the arrest or detention or of any other form of deprivation of liberty and the identity of those presumed to have carried it out, together with any other information shedding light on the circumstances in which the person was deprived of liberty;
>
> (b) The reasons given by the authorities for the arrest, detention or deprivation of liberty;
>
> (c) The legislation applied in the case;
>
> (d) The action taken, including investigatory action or the exercise of internal remedies, by the administrative and judicial authorities, as well as the steps taken at the international or regional levels, and the results of such action or the reasons why such measures were ineffective or were not taken;
>
> (e) An account of the reasons why the deprivation of liberty is deemed arbitrary;
>
> (f) A report of all elements presented by the source that aim to inform the Working Group on the full status of the reported situation, such as the beginning of a trial; the granting of provisional or definitive release; and changes of incarceration conditions or venue or of any other similar circumstances. An absence of information or an absence of a response by the source may lead the Working Group to terminate its consideration of the case.[77]

It adds that it hopes that communications are submitted using its model questionnaire, described in detail in this section. It also says "[c]ommunications *shall not exceed 20 pages*, including annexes, exceeding that limit may not be taken into account by the Working Group."[78]

There is no required form for making a submission to the WGAD. But a strong, clear, and well-organized petition to the WGAD generally contains the following elements:

> (1) a cover page identifying the case and name and contact details of the petitioner's representative; (2) the aforementioned model questionnaire, and (3) a factual and legal brief synthesizing, summarizing, and analyzing the facts of the case and explaining why the deprivation of liberty of the person detained is arbitrary and in violation of international law. As noted earlier, this submission should be sent to the WGAD along with the authorization from the detainee's family member.

---

[77] *Methods of Work of the Working Group*, Human Rights Council, A/HRC/36/38, July 13, 2017, at ¶ 10.
[78] *Id.*, at ¶ 11 (emphasis added).

1 Cover Page

The first step to preparing a petition to the WGAD is completing a cover page, which makes clear on whose behalf a case is being submitted and the best way to be in touch with the petitioner. Figure 4 is an example of a simple cover page:

PETITION TO:

UNITED NATIONS
WORKING GROUP ON ARBITRARY DETENTION

Chairman/Rapporteur: Mr. José Guevara (Mexico)
Vice-Chairperson: Ms. Leigh Toomey (Australia)
Vice-Chairperson: Ms. Elina Steinerte (Latvia)
Mr. Sètondji Roland Adjovi (Benin)
Mr. Seong-Phil Hong (Republic of Korea)

HUMAN RIGHTS COUNCIL
UNITED NATIONS GENERAL ASSEMBLY

In the Matter of

OLA YUSEF AL-QARADAWI	**HOSAM AL-DIN KHALAF**
Citizen of Qatar and	Citizen of Egypt and
Legal Permanent Resident of the United States	Legal Permanent Resident of the United States

v.

Government of the Arab Republic of Egypt

URGENT ACTION REQUESTED

And Petition for Relief Pursuant to Resolutions 1997/50, 2000/36, 2003/31, 6/4, 15/18, 20/16, 24/7, and 33/30.[1]

Submitted By:
Jared Genser and Nicole Santiago
Perseus Strategies, LLC
1700 K St. NW, Suite 825
Washington, DC 20006
+1.202.466.3069
jgenser@perseus-strategies.org

October 2, 2017

---

[1] Resolutions 1997/50, 2000/36, and 2003/31 were adopted by the UN Commission on Human Rights extending the mandate of the Working Group on Arbitrary Detention. The Human Rights Council, which "assume[d]... all mandates, mechanisms, functions and responsibilities of the Commission on Human Rights..." pursuant to UN General Assembly Resolution 60/251, G.A. Res. 60/251, ¶ 6 (Mar. 15, 2006), has further extended the mandate through Resolution 6/4, 15/18, 20/16, 24/7, and 33/30.

1

Figure 4 Cover page of a WGAD petition

In completing the cover page, advocates need to decide if a case is being submitted under its "urgent action" procedure. According to its Methods of Work, a petitioner may invoke "urgent action" in the following cases:

(a) In cases in which there are sufficiently reliable allegations that a person is being arbitrarily deprived of his liberty and that the continuation of such deprivation constitutes a serious threat to that person's health, physical, or psychological integrity or even to her or his life;

(b) In cases in which, even when no such threat is alleged to exist, there are particular circumstances that warrant an urgent action.[79]

Invoking the "urgent action" procedure can be a good way to send a clear message to a detaining government that a detainee now has representation and intends to defend their rights vigorously. In a usual petition, the justification for urgent action is usually not more than one page and explains the relevant circumstances that justify the concern, including relevant information where applicable such as the prominence of the person detained, past experiences of being tortured by the government, history of any health problems, and record of the government in mistreating detainees.

That said, however, in recent years the WGAD has had a large backlog of cases and in practice it is often unable to proceed with both an urgent action communication and then a subsequent communication under the regular procedure. Therefore, it is advisable not to invoke urgent action when such a communication will not result in the issuance of an opinion by the WGAD.

2 Model Questionnaire

The next section of a petition to the WGAD is filling out the "Model Questionnaire." According to the Methods of Work, it is "hoped" that communications to the WGAD will be submitted in this manner.[80] Given the intense workload of the Secretariat, however, the failure to respond to many of the questions provided in the questionnaire can seriously delay its ability to act. Thus, one should practically consider the submission of the questionnaire obligatory. It is worth reproducing the questionnaire in full to appreciate the areas of inquiry for which information is requested:

Model Questionnaire to be Completed by Persons Alleging Arbitrary Arrest or Detention

I. IDENTITY
1. Family Name:
2. First Name:
3. Sex: Male/Female

---

[79] *Methods of Work of the Working Group*, Human Rights Council, A/HRC/36/38, July 13, 2017, at ¶ 22.

[80] *Model Questionnaire*, Working Group on Arbitrary Detention, Human Rights Council (Nov. 2018), www.ohchr.org/Documents/Issues/Detention/WGADQuestionnaire_en.pdf.

4. Birth Date or Age (at time of detention):
5. Nationality/Nationalities:
6. (a) Identity document (if any):
   (b) Issued by:
   (c) On (date):
   (d) No.:
7. Profession and/or activity (if believed to be relevant to the arrest/detention):
8. Address of usual residence:

II. ARREST

1. Date of arrest:
2. Place of arrest (as detailed as possible):
3. Forces who carried out the arrest or are believed to have carried it out:
4. Did they show a warrant or other decision by a public authority? Yes/No
5. Authority who issued the warrant or decision:
6. Relevant legislation applied (if known):

III. DETENTION

1. Date of detention:
2. Duration of detention (if not known, probable duration):
3. Forces holding the detainee under custody:
4. Places of detention (indicate any transfer and present place of detention):
5. Authorities that ordered the detention:
6. Reasons for the detention imputed by authorities:
7. Relevant legislation applied (if known):

IV. Describe the circumstances of the arrest and/or the detention and indicate precise reasons why you consider the arrest or detention to be arbitrary.

V. Indicate internal steps, including domestic remedies, taken especially with the legal and administrative authorities, particularly for the purpose of establishing the detention and, as appropriate, their results or the reasons why such steps or remedies were ineffective or why they were not taken.

VI. Full name and address of the person(s) submitting the information (telephone and fax number, if possible).

Date:
Signature:

The questionnaire also states in a footnote "a separate questionnaire must be completed for each case of alleged arbitrary arrest or detention. As far as possible, all details requested should be given. Nevertheless, failure to do so will not necessarily result in the inadmissibility of the communication."[81] In short, while the WGAD would like all the information, it is prepared to engage on cases where not all the information is available, but where sufficient information allows for the specificity required to reach out to a government.

---

[81] *Id.*, at fn. 1.

3 Factual and Legal Brief

Before describing the usual contents of a legal brief to the WGAD, it is important to recall at the outset the situation that it finds itself in. Specifically, the WGAD members are five expert volunteers, appointed by the HRC, who gather three times a year to consider individual cases. All of them have other full-time jobs. In addition, the WGAD only has four full-time staff. Currently, it is estimated that the WGAD receives on average 100 requests for action every month or about 1,200 annually. Most of these submissions do not have sufficient information for the WGAD to convey to a government allegedly detaining a person and most of the individuals or groups who receive requests for further information do not respond to those requests, leaving the case "filed," or not considered.

But the implication of this situation is clear – it is one's job as an advocate for an arbitrarily detained person to present a clear and compelling explanation of both the facts of a case and the legal analysis applicable to the situation. Failing to do so can easily result in the WGAD misunderstanding the situation and deriving inaccurate conclusions of fact and of law. In the author's experience, the most compelling legal briefs to the WGAD are clear and efficient and generally include the following elements:

- Executive Summary (two pages)
- Model Questionnaire (two to three pages)
- Country Background (if useful) (one to two pages)
- Biographical Information of Detainee (one page)
- Description of Facts (three to five pages)
- Legal Analysis (seven to nine pages)
- Conclusion and Recommendations (one page)

A strong executive summary includes a written summary of the key facts of the case and violations of international law being alleged, with a special focus on violations of the ICCPR, if applicable, and UDHR. It should also state which of the WGAD's five categories of cases it falls within as well as provide the specific remedies that are being requested, as will be discussed further.

It is often helpful to provide the WGAD with a few pages of background on the country against whom the petitioner is filing their case. Such background is especially useful when the situation in the country is lesser known. Beyond explaining the contours of the country's general political system, special attention should be paid to discussing the state of the country's judicial system as well as the more specific context for the type of person who has been detained.

Therefore, if one is making a submission on behalf of an imprisoned journalist, it will be useful to explain in the country background section the status of freedom of the press in the country and how frequently journalists have been detained for their activities. Such information provides important background for the facts of the specific case being submitted to the WGAD. These country background sections are most effective when they are descriptive and non-polemical and cite to credible independent news organizations, nongovernmental organizations, regional intergovernmental bodies, and UN sources to support in footnotes assertions being made about the country situation. There is no special format required for footnotes, but it is useful to be consistent in how one cites to sources and to provide a URL if the source is available online.

The next section of the petition should provide basic biographical information about the detainee. In situations where a person's profession has no relationship to why they were detained, the biographical information can be quite limited. When the detainee has a long history of an antagonistic relationship with the detaining government, it is generally useful to provide a more detailed description of that relationship because it provides important context for understanding the current detention.

Next a petition should present a description of the facts of the case, beginning with whatever activities were undertaken by the detainee, if any, that led to the government detention. It is important to provide as complete a narrative as possible – but this narrative should be focused on material facts that have a bearing on the specific violations of law that will be alleged in the legal analysis. Thus, for example, when describing a person's arrest, it is worth noting if a state or non-state actor made the arrest, whether an arrest warrant was presented, and how the person was treated as they were being arrested. As much as possible, footnotes to reputable international news organizations, nongovernmental organizations, regional intergovernmental bodies, and UN sources will enhance the credibility to the WGAD of the factual narrative being presented. Even if there are no such independent sources, however, a strong narrative should be presented with whatever information is available to explain what happened.

Looking at this from a different perspective, it can be useful to see an example of how the WGAD analyzed what was ultimately a successful presentation of the facts in a specific case, which enabled it to agree with the source that the charges against the detainee were politically motivated. In *Anwar Ibrahim v. Malaysia*, the WGAD reasoned as follows:

> Turning to the source's claims in relation to category II, the Working Group has analysed: (i) the information provided by the source, (ii) the history of the proceedings brought against Mr. Ibrahim, particularly the pattern of persecution of Mr. Ibrahim in previous proceedings on sodomy charges which were later overturned on appeal, and (iii) the statements issued by prominent and respected human rights organisations in relation to Mr. Ibrahim's most recent trial, including the Office of the UN High Commissioner for Human Rights. Taken together, these factors provide a persuasive body of evidence, which was not contested by the Government, that Mr. Ibrahim has been specifically targeted by the Malaysian authorities. Further, the violations of Mr. Ibrahim's right to a fair trial discussed above are so serious as to lead the Working Group to conclude that the current sodomy charges against Mr. Ibrahim were politically motivated.[82]

Having presented a factual narrative, a petition will next provide a legal analysis of the situation. The legal analysis should begin by summarizing both the categories of WGAD cases being invoked to explain the detention as arbitrary and the specific violations of at least the ICCPR (if the detainee is held in a country that is a state party) and UDHR. Typically, a petition will have a different subsection of legal analysis for each category of case being invoked.

The final section of the petition is the conclusion and recommendations. In this section, the petition should reaffirm and summarize the key reasons why the WGAD should conclude that the deprivation of liberty of the petitioner is arbitrary and in violation of international law. It should also ask the WGAD to make specific recommendations to the detaining government, which would usually include:

---

[82] Anwar Ibrahim v. Malaysia, WGAD Opinion No. 22/2015, Adopted Sept. 1, 2015, at ¶ 35 (Litigated by Author through Perseus Strategies).

- Pressing it to conclude that the appropriate remedy in the case would be the detainee's immediate release;
- Asking for the detainee to be provided an enforceable right of compensation and other reparations; and
- Urging it to ensure a full and independent investigation of the circumstances surrounding the arbitrary deprivation of liberty of the detainee and to take appropriate measures against those responsible for the violation of their rights.

Having completed the petition, the full package, including the family authorization, should be transmitted to the WGAD offices in Geneva. It is best to convey the submission through email to wgad@ohchr.org – and while a submission can be in PDF form, the petition should also be conveyed in Microsoft Word or another widely used word processing format. This makes it easier for the WGAD to extract key elements of the submission to place in its summary of the case that will be provided to the government. It is important to receive a confirmation of receipt from a specific member of the WGAD staff; one cannot rely on an autoreply as, unfortunately, although not recently, the WGAD staff has occasionally lost or misplaced submissions. Indeed, in all cases, it is essential to maintain a written record of correspondence with the WGAD staff in relation to procedural developments relating to specific cases.

III Conveying the Case to the Government

Prior to sending either an "urgent action" communication or one under its regular procedure, the WGAD staff reviews the submission to be sure that it complies with Articles 9, 10, and 14 of the *Code of Conduct for Special Procedures Mandate-Holders* of the HRC.[83]

Article 9 describes the procedures for handling letters of allegation. Specifically, it states:

(a) The communication should not be manifestly unfounded or politically motivated;
(b) The communication should contain a factual description of the alleged violations of human rights;
(c) The language in the communication should not be abusive;
(d) The communication should be submitted by a person or group of persons claiming to be victims of violations or by any person or group of persons, including non-governmental organizations, acting in good faith in accordance with principles of human rights, and free from politically motivated stands or contrary to, the provisions of the Charter of the United Nations, and claiming to have direct or reliable knowledge of those violations substantiated by clear information;
(e) The communication should not be exclusively based on reports disseminated by mass media.[84]

Article 10 of the Code of Conduct addresses the justification for the sending of urgent appeals. It states:

---

[83] *Methods of Work of the Working Group*, Human Rights Council, A/HRC/36/38, July 13, 2017, at ¶ 12.
[84] *Code of Conduct for Special Procedures Mandate-Holders of the Human Rights Council*, A/HRC/RES/5/2, Adopted June 18, 2007, at Annex.

Mandate-holders may resort to urgent appeals in cases where the alleged violations are time-sensitive in terms of involving loss of life, life-threatening situations or either imminent or ongoing damage of a very grave nature to victims that cannot be addressed in a timely manner by the procedure under article 9 of the present Code.[85]

Finally, Article 14 relates to communications with governments. It says "[m]andate-holders shall address all their communications to concerned Governments through diplomatic channels unless agreed otherwise between individual Government and the Office of the High Commissioner for Human Rights."

A "Urgent Action"

When the WGAD receives a submission under the "urgent action" procedure, the secretariat works on an expedited basis to draft a communication to the country detaining the person explaining that while the UN has not prejudged the merits of the specific case, it urges the government to ensure the person's health, safety, and welfare.

Once the draft communication is completed, it is provided to the Rapid Response Desk within OHCHR who assists all the special procedures. Other special procedures are invited to join in the communication. Thus, if the person is detained in a country where there is a country rapporteur, that person will be asked to join. If there are allegations of torture or other cruel, inhuman, or degrading treatment, then that special rapporteur will be given the opportunity to join as well. And thematic rapporteurs whose work covers the area in which the detainee might have been acting when detained will also be asked to consider joining.

The Rapid Response Desk will revise and incorporate suggestions being made to improve the text of the letter and provide the final text to WGAD staff, to be signed by the WGAD Vice-Chair on Communications. The communication will then be sent to the permanent representative of the country in either Geneva or New York, with a request that it be conveyed urgently to that country's foreign minister. An "urgent action" from the WGAD is typically conveyed within several days of such a communication being received, depending on whether the other special procedures have changes they wish to suggest for inclusion in the draft. From there, as explained by the WGAD in its Methods of Work:

> After having transmitted an urgent appeal to the Government, the Working Group may transmit the case through its regular procedure in order to render an opinion on whether the deprivation of liberty was arbitrary or not. Such appeals, which are of a purely humanitarian nature, in no way prejudge any opinion the Working Group may render. The Government is required to respond separately for the urgent action procedure and the regular procedure.[86]

There can sometimes be confusion by governments in relation to urgent appeals and they may respond not only to the appeal but also to the allegation that the person is arbitrarily detained. The petitioner should indicate whether an "urgent action" *or* an opinion under its regular procedure is requested.

As has been noted previously, the special procedures report their activities to the HRC annually. At the 15th annual meeting of special procedures in 2008, mandate holders

---

[85] *Id.*
[86] *Id.*, at ¶ 22.

decided to issue a joint communications report to prevent inconsistencies reporting the same communication, avoid duplication, and ensure the content of communications and follow-up would more effectively support the Universal Periodic Review (UPR) process.[87]

Since September 2011, the special procedures have submitted a joint report to each regular session of the HRC. These periodic reports include short summaries of allegations conveyed to the respective state or other entity. With respect to the WGAD and Working Group on Enforced and Involuntary Disappearances, the reports are exclusively "urgent appeals" sent by the groups by themselves or with other mandates – they do not include communications sent through their usual working methods, which are reported by the Working Groups in separate reports appended to their annual reports.

For example, for the 38th HRC session, which began in June 2018, the report covered communications sent between December 1, 2017, through February 28, 2018, and included replies received through April 30, 2018. For this reporting period, the WGAD stated it had sent forty-seven urgent action communications, with twenty-six responses, for a response rate of 55 percent. The communications report also aggregated reporting for the WGAD showing urgent action communications from June 1, 2006, through April 30, 2018, going back twelve years[88]:

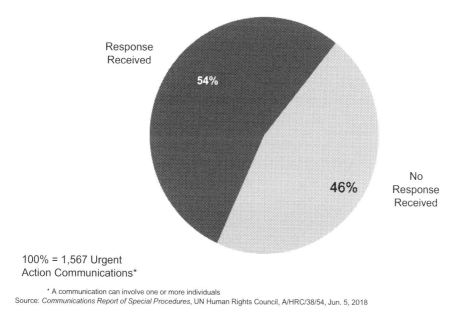

URGENT ACTION APPEALS AND GOVERNMENT RESPONSE JUNE 1, 2006 THROUGH APRIL 30, 2018

Response Received

54%

No Response Received

46%

100% = 1,567 Urgent Action Communications*

* A communication can involve one or more individuals
Source: *Communications Report of Special Procedures*, UN Human Rights Council, A/HRC/38/54, Jun. 5, 2018

Figure 5 Government response rate to urgent action appeals

---

[87] *Report on the Fifteenth Meeting of Special Rapporteurs, Representatives, Independent Experts, and Chairpersons of Working Groups of the Special Procedures of the Human Rights Council*, A/HRC/10/24, June 23–27, 2008, ¶¶ 34–35.
[88] *Communications Report of Special Procedures*, Human Rights Council, A/HRC/38/54, June 5, 2018.

B Regular Procedure

If there is sufficient information in a petition to put forward a case and it meets the requirements under Articles 9, 10, and 14 of the Code of Conduct, the WGAD will typically formally communicate a case to the government detaining the person within a few weeks, and generally under the practice of first in, first out. It is worth noting, however, that the WGAD regularly receives communications from individuals alleging arbitrary detention without sufficient information. In such circumstances, the WGAD staff will send its model questionnaire to the person requesting a response. But it only usually receives a response from the original petitioner in a quarter of those situations. This troubles the WGAD and its staff because though it cannot be sure a detained person even received back the correspondence, it cannot operate without sufficient information to put forward a credible set of allegations to the government detaining the person. In addition, given the quasi-judicial nature of the WGAD and the lack of rules governing its day-to-day operations, sometimes especially sensitive cases are sent out more quickly, even if they were not received first.

Operating under its regular procedure, the WGAD acts alone. The Methods of Work make clear: "In the interest of ensuring mutual cooperation, communications shall be brought to the attention of the Government and the reply of the latter shall be brought to the attention of the source of the communication for its further comments."[89]

A letter to the country's Permanent Representative to the United Nations in Geneva is transmitted by the Chair-Rapporteur of the WGAD or Vice Chairs. In practice, the letter includes a detailed summary of the factual and legal allegations made by the source. It requests to government to respond within sixty days "after having carried out such inquiries as may be appropriate so as to furnish the Working Group with the fullest possible information."[90] The letter also informs the government that the WGAD is authorized to render an opinion determining whether the reported deprivation of liberty was arbitrary or not, if a response is not received "within the time limit." And it explains that responses may not exceed twenty pages and materials provided that exceed that limit may not be taken into account by the WGAD.[91]

If the government wants an extension of the time limit, it "shall inform the Working Group of the reasons for requesting one, so that it may be granted a further period of a maximum of one month in which to reply."[92] While the language of the Working Methods appears unambiguous – a "maximum of one month" for an extension – in practice, for reasons that are unclear, the WGAD has occasionally accepted late responses despite the unambiguous language, which the author has argued is prejudicial to the petitioner as it can delay at what session a case will be considered for the adoption of an opinion. That said, however, when the Government of Libya requested a sixty-day extension because of the transfer of power from the Libyan Transitional Council to the Libyan General National Congress, the WGAD rejected the request. It said the WGAD prior opinions "have emphasized that not only do human rights apply in periods of transition but so do the international system of supervision and international law on state

---

[89] *Methods of Work of the Working Group*, Human Rights Council, A/HRC/36/38, July 13, 2017, at ¶ 15.
[90] *Id.*
[91] *Id.*
[92] *Id.*, at ¶ 16.

responsibility."[93] It further explained that the WGAD had also expressly rejected requests for an extension based on similar reasons from Syria[94] and Egypt.[95]

Given these considerations, it is important to remain vigilant on the issue of deadlines. First, a petitioner must be sure that a case – both "urgent action" and petition under the normal procedure – has been conveyed to the government in a timely manner. It is also very important to know the date a petition was sent under the regular procedure because that is the date from which to begin counting the sixty days for the government to respond. Second, it is important once the sixty-day deadline for the government to respond has expired to confirm with the WGAD whether a response or request for an extension of time has been received. And finally, even once a response has been received and a reply has been submitted as will be discussed later in this chapter, it is important to reconfirm that the reply has been received and that the case will be considered during the next session of the WGAD.

IV Receiving and Replying to a Response from the Government

With regards to responses to the normal procedure, the WGAD reports in its opinions whether or not the government has responded and a summary of the content of the response if one has been received. Historically, governments respond a little more than half the time.

GOVERNMENTS RESPOND TO COMMUNICATIONS FROM THE WORKING GROUP ABOUT HALF THE TIME, DOWN IN LAST DECADE

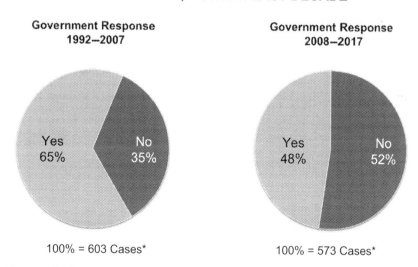

Government Response
1992–2007

Yes 65%   No 35%

Government Response
2008–2017

Yes 48%   No 52%

100% = 603 Cases*   100% = 573 Cases*

* A case can involve one or more individuals; includes all reported cases, including where no opinion adopted
and where there is clear indication if government did or did not respond
Source: Author's analysis of case data from UN Working Group on Arbitrary Detention

Figure 6 Government response rate to regular communications

[93] Sayad Qaddaf Dam v. Libya, WGAD Opinion No. 60/2012, Adopted Nov. 20, 2012, at ¶ 12.
[94] Muhannad Al-Hassani v. Syria, WGAD Opinion No. 26/2011, Adopted Aug. 30, 2011.
[95] Maikel Nabil Sanad v. Egypt, WGAD Opinion No. 50/2011, Adopted Sept. 2, 2011.

It is important to recall the delays that can be caused by the requirements of translation. Thus, as noted previously, if a response is expected in a language other than English, French, or Spanish, the petitioner should proactively inform the WGAD that it would be pleased to receive the response in whatever language it has been conveyed to the WGAD. This is a request the author regularly makes, for example, on cases that he has taken against China, which provides its responses in Chinese when it responds.

It is also worth noting the different response rates for the top countries against which cases have been brought to the WGAD:

FOR TOP COUNTRIES, SHOWING FOR EACH PERCENTAGE OF CASES RESPONDED TO BY THE GOVERNMENT, 1992–2017

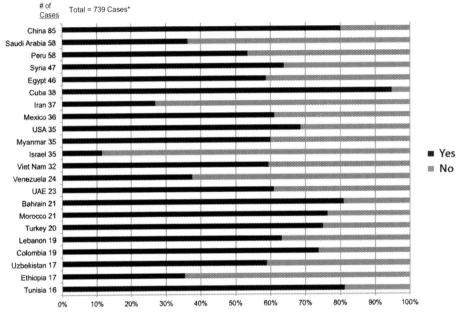

* A case can involve one or more individuals; includes all reported cases, including where no opinion adopted
<u>and</u> where there is clear indication if government did or did not respond

Source: Author's analysis of case data from UN Working Group on Arbitrary Detention

Figure 7 Response rate for Governments with most cases

For example, China has responded to 80 percent of the eighty-five cases brought to the WGAD, Cuba has responded to 95 percent of thirty-eight cases brought to the WGAD, while Israel has only responded to 11 percent of the thirty-five cases brought to the WGAD. It is also interesting to note that when governments respond to communications, they can influence the outcome of a case.

Typically within a week, the Secretary will convey the government response to the petitioner with a cover letter requesting a reply be received in time for consideration during its next session, which is noted in the communication. It is ideal, however, for a reply to the response to be submitted at least a few weeks prior to the beginning of the next session given the way the WGAD considers and adopts opinions, as will be described in further detail in this chapter.

It is also important to emphasize that the standard cover letter to a petitioner accompanying a government response states "[p]lease note that all information given to you by the Working Group on this matter should be treated with discretion." In practice, although there is no mention of this requirement in its Methods of Work, the WGAD expects that the government response will be kept confidential to enable it to carry out its responsibilities with discretion. Thus, a petitioner may not share the response to anyone other than their immediate team. The author has learned through experience that there is a great temptation on the part of nonlegal team members to release the government's response to the media. Thus, instructions provided to anyone who receives the response that will help prepare the reply should make unequivocally clear that it may not be used for any purpose other than in helping formulate a reply to the government.

Having reviewed and replied to dozens of government responses to the WGAD, the author can observe that in most cases the responses received are typically brief – no more than a few pages and often only a few paragraphs. They also frequently do not address the key facts or violations of law that were alleged in the original petition. Based on discussions with WGAD members and staff, the author's experience can also be generalized to the broader set of responses received to WGAD petitions. That said, in a half dozen cases handled by the author, governments have responded with detailed legal briefs that can even be prepared by outside counsel. Such responses have more frequently, in part, tried to justify the detainee's ongoing imprisonment with references to the facts presented to the domestic tribunal. It is important to again recall that the WGAD will not substitute its judgment for a domestic fact finder and in such cases will typically acknowledge a lot of information was submitted but that its inquiry is narrowly focused on alleged violations of international law in the case.

This approach by the WGAD was best summarized in *Yang Jianli* v. *China*, where it observed:

> Bearing in mind the criminal procedure in the case of Mr. Yang Jianli is ongoing, the Working Group points out that its task is not to evaluate the facts and evidence in a particular case; this would be tantamount to substituting itself for the domestic tribunals, which falls outside of the Working Group's remit. The Working Group is called upon to assess, whether or not the international norms and standards have been observed in the criminal procedure during which Mr. Yang Jianli has been and is being deprived of his liberty.[96]

As another example of this phenomenon presented in shorter form, the WGAD stated in *Alan Phillip Gross* v. *Cuba*:

> The Working Group has repeatedly maintained in its Opinions that it does not constitute an additional instance to those established by each country's domestic law for resolving a conflict in which one person has been imprisoned. Its mandate consists of opining on whether the detention is or is not arbitrary.[97]

---

[96] Yang Jianli v. China, WGAD Opinion No. 2/2003, Adopted May 7, 2003, ¶ 8 (Litigated by Author through Freedom Now).

[97] Alan Gross v. Cuba, WGAD Opinion No. 69/2012, Adopted Nov. 23, 2012, ¶ 40 (Litigated by Author through Perseus Strategies).

A strong reply to a government response will address, in turn, each of the material factual and legal claims made by the government to the original petition. Interestingly, however, the first component of an effective reply is actually not a direct response to the government's claims, but rather a clear description of the material facts from the original petition that the government did not reference or dispute in its response. This is because in practice, the WGAD will treat as admissions all cases where material facts were presented by a petitioner and were not disputed by the government. As noted earlier in the discussion of how the WGAD approaches evidence, it is not sufficient for the government to provide general denials to claims by a petitioner. It must address material facts that it disputes and provide direct rebuttals to each claim if it hopes to persuade the WGAD that the detention has not occurred in the way described by the petitioner. Thus, after stating with precision the various facts that were not addressed by the government in its response, a petitioner can then reference any of a large number of past WGAD cases as persuasive authority to reaffirm that it should accept as admissions all such undisputed facts. In *Yang Jianli v. China*, the WGAD applied this principle very clearly, where it stated:

> In light of the allegations made, the Working Group welcomes the cooperation of the Government. The Working Group regrets, however, that the Government has not addressed all the important issues raised by the source. The Working Group transmitted the reply provided by the Government to the source, which provided the Working Group with its Comments. The Working Group believes it is in a position to render an opinion based on the facts and circumstances of the case, in the context of the allegations made and the response of the Government thereto.[98]

After reviewing the facts of the case in detail, the WGAD then presented its analysis of the case:

> 8. Bearing in mind the criminal procedure in the case of Mr. Yang Jianli is ongoing, the Working Group points out that its task is not to evaluate facts and evidence in a particular case; this would be tantamount to substituting itself for domestic tribunals, which falls outside the Working Groups remit. The Working Group is called upon to assess, whether or not the international norms and standards have been observed in the criminal procedure during which Mr. Yang Jianli has been and is being deprived of his liberty . . .
>
> 9. In this respect, the Working Group found that the Government did not contest or refute [several material facts, which it goes on to describe] . . .
>
> 10. Therefore, the Working Group cannot but conclude that to keep Mr. Yang Jianli in detention for more than two months without an arrest warrant and without enabling his family to hire a lawyer to defend Yang constitute the infringement of the basic international norms relating to the right to a fair trial.[99]

---

[98] Yang Jianli v. China, WGAD Opinion No. 2/2003, Adopted May 7, 2003, ¶ 4. This approach has been taken by the WGAD going back to its earliest cases. In Driss Achebrak v. Morocco, the WGAD noted that the Government reply was "limited to vague statements, since it merely indicates that 'the cases of the soldiers imprisoned following the events of 1972 have been settled and all the soldiers who were imprisoned have been released.' It is therefore incomplete and insufficient." It then went on to find that nineteen of twenty-four petitioners had been beyond their sentence in an unofficial prison. Driss Achebrak v. Morocco, WGAD Decision No. 38/1992, Adopted Session No. 4, at ¶ 5.

[99] Id., at ¶¶ 8–10.

Having presented a recitation of material facts that were not disputed by the government in its response, an effective reply will next present and analyze material facts that were disputed by the government. Again, it is important to understand and indeed reaffirm in the response that the petitioner is not going to ask the WGAD to substitute itself for a domestic fact finder. Thus, for example, if the core facts of a case revolve around contradictory eyewitness testimony and experts or what a petitioner believes is a poor assessment of specific facts, it will be very difficult to prevail before the WGAD. That said, however, both in cases of violations of fundamental human rights as well as where there are serious allegations of violations of due process, there is often a creative and appropriate way to demonstrate that the government's perspective on the facts is flawed and that there actually is not a genuine factual dispute.

The easiest way to dispute the government's contested claims on the facts is when there are independent United Nations, media, or credible nongovernmental organization reports that contradict the government's claims. In such cases, one can explain that this is not a case of a mere direct conflict on the allegations between the government and petitioner, where the WGAD will not substitute its judgment for a domestic fact finder, but rather a different situation where one or more independent parties have contradicted the government's allegations. In such cases, it is much easier for the WGAD to discount or ignore the response made by the government, concluding that there is not actually a legitimate dispute on the facts, but rather one that the government is attempting to create without evidentiary basis.

As a high-profile example of the WGAD's willingness to put aside claims of an alleged factual dispute by a government, one can look to the case of *Liu Xia* v. *China*. She was the wife of 2010 Nobel Peace Prize Laureate Liu Xiaobo, who was placed under house arrest by the Government shortly after the Norwegian Nobel Committee announced her husband had been awarded the Prize. The reality of her house arrest had been widely documented by governments, NGOs, and media. As noted previously, in its response to the petition presented on her behalf asking that her house arrest be declared arbitrary, the Government responded by claiming "no legal enforcement measure" had been taken against her. The WGAD succinctly summarized the petitioner's reply to this claim:

> 10. The source points out that the Government has confirmed that there are no charges against Ms. Liu Xia who has not been informed of any reasons justifying her detention. The source replies that the statement of Government that it has taken no legal enforcement measures against Ms. Liu Xia is either an admission of the illegality of her detention – as there would be no legal basis for her continued house arrest – or incorrect. In either event, she should be immediately and unconditionally released from detention.[100]

The WGAD then proceeded to analyze the case, beginning with the fundamental question allegedly in dispute as to whether Liu Xia was under house arrest. The WGAD concluded:

---

[100] Liu Xia v. China, WGAD Opinion No. 16/2011, Adopted May 5, 2011, ¶ 10 (Litigated by Author through Freedom Now).

13. According to the information we have received, and where the Government has not provided us with any further assistance, Ms. Liu Xia is under a house arrest with limitations on her physical movements, visits from others and communications of different kinds.[101]

Although the petitioner had provided the WGAD, in an extended footnote, with dozens of references to independent reports from media and NGOs discussing Liu Xia's house arrest, it did not feel it was even necessary to explain its reasoning. Not unusually and very diplomatically, the WGAD merely presented the simple conclusion that it required, rather than confronting the government more directly by explaining that its claims were disputed by a broad range of independent news sources.

Once all the unaddressed and addressed facts have been presented, the petitioner can then turn to responding to disputes to the legal analysis presented by the government. Given that most government responses are brief, it is highly unusual for a government to present much if any legal analysis, let alone a legal analysis that is compelling and well-grounded in international law.

Often governments are not even very familiar with the WGAD or its Methods of Work. This conclusion is easy to reach when one sees governments arguing that the WGAD is interfering in its internal affairs, that it has no jurisdiction or competence to examine the case at hand, or that it believes that the petitioner should first be required to exhaust domestic remedies before taking a case to the WGAD. Replies to such responses are easily and briefly dismissed by referencing the most recent resolution of the HRC that reaffirmed the jurisdiction of the WGAD and citing to its Working Methods. Beyond such legal claims that are easily dismissed, according to WGAD members and staff, it is also highly unusual for governments to present compelling legal arguments in response to an alleged arbitrary detention.

As one illustration of this phenomenon, the author has worked on numerous cases before the WGAD alleging violations of Article 19 of the ICCPR, which is the right to freedom of opinion and expression. Contrary to popular belief, this right is not absolute. Indeed, governments can subject the exercise of this right to certain restrictions that are provided by law and are necessary to respect the rights and reputations of others, for the protection of national security or public order, and for public health and morals. The author has been surprised that in the cases he has presented to the WGAD that no government has ever tried to respond to claims of violations of Article 19 – even where there might have been a colorable argument – by claiming the exceptions to this provision might apply.

Finally, it is worth observing that when governments respond to communications from the WGAD, they can influence whether an opinion is adopted and whether the opinions find the detentions in question to be arbitrary. It is not surprising that the outcomes of cases where governments do not respond are dramatically in favor of petitioners, given the WGAD does not require a government response to issue an opinion and presumes the accuracy of information presented by a source if not disputed by a government:

---

[101] *Id.*, at ¶ 13.

IF A GOVERNMENT RESPONDS TO COMMUNICATION, IT CAN INFLUENCE THE OUTCOME OF A CASE, 1992–2017

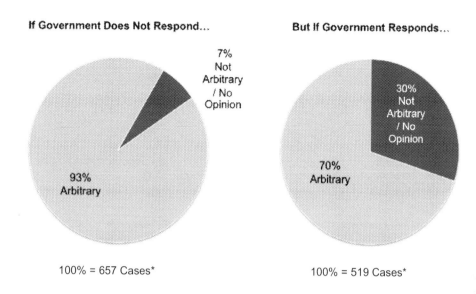

If Government Does Not Respond...

7%
Not
Arbitrary
/ No
Opinion

93%
Arbitrary

100% = 657 Cases*

But If Government Responds...

30%
Not
Arbitrary
/ No
Opinion

70%
Arbitrary

100% = 519 Cases*

* A case can involve one or more individuals; includes all reported cases, including where no opinion adopted _and_ where there is clear indication if government did or did not respond
Source: Author's analysis of case data from UN Working Group on Arbitrary Detention

Figure 8 Impact of Government response on outcome

V Consideration of the Case

A Background on Individual Case Consideration in Methods of Work

Today, after a case is ready for consideration by the WGAD, having received a submission, a response of a government, if any, and a reply to the government's response, it then considers the case. The process by which the WGAD actually considers and takes action on individual cases, however, is private. There are only three narrow references to this process in the Methods of Work.

First, there is the explanation that "opinions of the Working Group are the result of consensus; where consensus is not reached, the view of a majority of the members of the Working Group is adopted as the view of the Working Group."[102] In practice, however, there have only been two cases in the WGAD's history where there was a dissenting opinion one of which was _Julian Assange v. Sweden and the United Kingdom._[103]

Second, there is a description of how WGAD members are automatically precluded from participation in discussions because of potential conflicts of interest:

When the case under consideration or the country visit concerns a country of which one of the members of the Working Group is a national, or in other situations where there

---

[102] _Methods of Work of the Working Group_, Human Rights Council, A/HRC/36/38, July 13, 2017, at ¶ 6.
[103] Julian Assange v. Sweden and the United Kingdom, WGAD Opinion No. 54/2015, Adopted Dec. 4, 2015, at Appendix I (dissenting opinion of WGAD Member Vladimir Tochilovsky).

may be a conflict of interest, that member shall not participate in the discussion of the case, in the visit or in the preparation of the report on the visit.[104]

And finally, the Methods of Work describe the options available to the WGAD on considering a case:

> In the light of the information obtained, the Working Group shall take one of the following measures:
>
> (a) If the person has been released, for whatever reason, following the referral of the case to the Working Group, the case is filed. The Working Group reserves the right to render an opinion, on a case-by-case basis, whether or not the deprivation of liberty was arbitrary, notwithstanding the release of the person concerned;
>
> (b) If the Working Group considers that the case is not one of arbitrary detention, it shall render an opinion to that effect. The Working Group can also make recommendations in this case if it considers it necessary;
>
> (c) If the Working Group considers that further information is required from the Government or from the source, it may keep the case pending until that information is received;
>
> (d) If the Working Group considers that the arbitrary nature of the detention is established, it shall render an opinion to that effect and make recommendations to the Government.[105]

B Process for Reaching Opinions

From interviews with current and former WGAD members and staff and in relation to cases that are ripe for consideration and on which there is an expectation that an opinion will be adopted in a forthcoming session of the WGAD, the process is as follows:

First, a case rapporteur is assigned by the Chairperson/Rapporteur, in consultation with the Secretary, to be the lead WGAD member on a case. Case rapporteurs are generally just assigned on the basis of sharing the workload across all WGAD members, but if communications are in a specific language that is only understood by a specific WGAD member, that person is assigned to the case. Prior to the forthcoming session, the case rapporteur reviews all of the written submissions in the case and, based on their analysis, prepares a working draft of an opinion for discussion with the full WGAD.

Second, the secretariat prepares and makes available to all WGAD members in advance of the session a set of materials for each case under consideration, which includes the written submissions and draft opinion.

Third, at the WGAD session itself, members take turns presenting their cases in detail as well as their draft opinion. The secretariat can supplement the presented information. WGAD members typically ask a lot of questions of the case rapporteur and they debate and discuss the case and proposed opinion. Through the discussions, a consensus emerges as to how to proceed.

Most often, the WGAD members agree with the general substance of the proposed opinion, whether to find a detention arbitrary or not arbitrary, but provide instruction to the case rapporteur about how to improve the substance of the opinion in a variety of

---

[104] *Methods of Work of the Working Group*, Human Rights Council, A/HRC/36/38, July 13, 2017, at ¶ 5.
[105] *Id.*, at ¶ 17.

ways. They then provisionally adopt the opinion, with the agreed amendments to be added after the session by the case rapporteur, prior to it being finalized and published.

Sometimes, however, WGAD members have substantive questions that have not been sufficiently addressed by the written submissions. If a consensus emerges from discussions that further information is required from the government or the source, then it will defer consideration of the case to a subsequent session and will instruct the secretariat to obtain the additional information the WGAD requires.

More rarely, the draft opinion presented by the case rapporteur is contrary to the views of a significant number of other WGAD members. This can either be when a majority disagree with the outcome or the substance of the draft opinion. In such cases, there is substantial discussion among the WGAD members to reach a consensus. Sometimes, the case rapporteur is asked to substantially rework the opinion and the case is deferred for consideration to the next session.

C Timeframe for the Issuances of Opinions

Despite the increasing number of cases that the WGAD has been handling, it has become more efficient in processing individual cases, as measured by the timeframe between when a case is conveyed to a government and when the WGAD issues a case opinion:

THE WORKING GROUP HAS GOTTEN MORE EFFICIENT IN PROCESSING INDIVIDUAL CASES IN RECENT YEARS

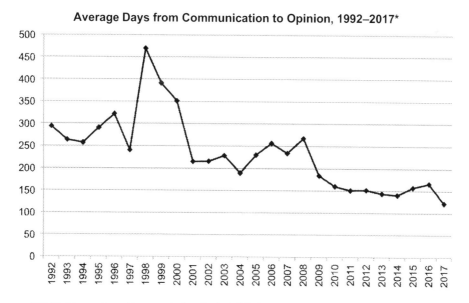

Average Days from Communication to Opinion, 1992–2017*

* This includes cases where opinions were actually rendered on individual cases; excludes opinions where date of communication not mentioned

Source: Author's analysis of case data from UN Working Group on Arbitrary Detention

Figure 9 Average days from communication to opinion

ANOTHER VIEW OF WORKING GROUP EFFICIENCY IN ISSUING OPINIONS

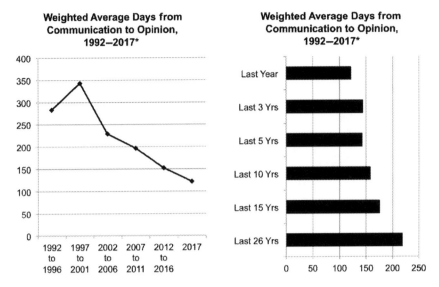

* This includes cases where opinions were actually rendered on individual cases; excludes small number of opinions where dates unmentioned

Source: Author's analysis of case data from UN Working Group on Arbitrary Detention

Figure 10 Another view of efficiency of Working Group processing cases

That said, when one looks at the countries that have the largest number of opinions, the range of average days to reach an opinion from the initial communication varies substantially:

CERTAIN COUNTRIES AMONG THOSE WITH MOST ISSUED OPINIONS TAKE LONGER TO REACH AN OPINION

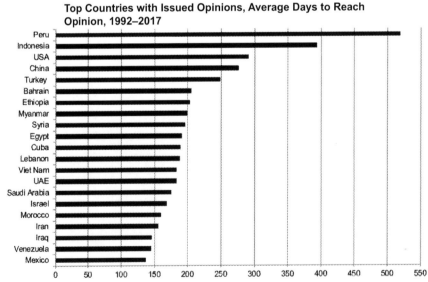

* This includes cases where opinions were actually rendered on individual cases; excludes small number of early opinions where dates unmentioned

Source: Author's analysis of case data from UN Working Group on Arbitrary Detention

Figure 11 Average days to reach opinion for top countries

VI Finalizing of the Opinion and Communication to the Government and Petitioner

At the conclusion of the WGAD session, its members return home with, in recent years, fifteen to twenty opinions they each need to finalize for publication. It is important to appreciate the WGAD's workload has been increasing in recent years:

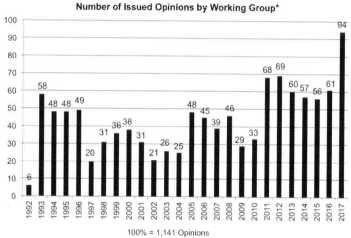

THE WORKING GROUP HAS BEEN HANDLING A SUBSTANTIAL NUMBER OF ADDITIONAL CASES IN RECENT YEARS

Number of Issued Opinions by Working Group*

100% = 1,141 Opinions

* This includes cases where opinions were actually rendered on individual cases; excludes opinions where date of communication not mentioned

Source: Author's analysis of case data from UN Working Group on Arbitrary Detention

Figure 12 Number of issued opinions, by year

In addition, it is also worth understanding from an analysis of the data the outcomes of WGAD, both across all its jurisprudence and where opinions have been adopted:

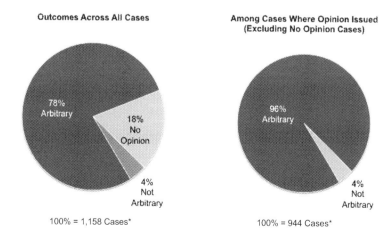

OUTCOME OF WORKING GROUP CASES, 1992–2017

Outcomes Across All Cases

78% Arbitrary
18% No Opinion
4% Not Arbitrary

100% = 1,158 Cases*

Among Cases Where Opinion Issued (Excluding No Opinion Cases)

96% Arbitrary
4% Not Arbitrary

100% = 944 Cases*

* A case can involve one or more individuals; includes all reported cases, regardless of whether an opinion was issued, excludes 42 cases where there were multiple findings for same detainee (e.g., on different periods of detention) or different detainees

Source: Author's analysis of case data from UN Working Group on Arbitrary Detention

Figure 13 Outcome of Working Group cases

After a session, WGAD staff will typically confirm with a source or government if asked whether an opinion has been adopted in a specific case, but they will not convey any further information. Based on the input received from other WGAD members, for each case the rapporteur needs to complete their drafting, editing, and proofing of each opinion.

On completion of each opinion, on a rolling basis, WGAD members send their final opinions to the secretariat for final proof and then communication and publication. It is important to appreciate, given the members are volunteer experts with other jobs, it can take weeks or even up to two months from the end of a WGAD session for opinions to be sent to governments and then to sources, though a one-month lag is average. Once completed, according to the Working Methods:

> The opinions rendered by the Working Group shall be transmitted to the Government concerned. Forty-eight hours after their transmittal, they shall be communicated to the source. An advance unedited version of the opinion will be published online once the source has been notified.[106]

In addition to being published online, the WGAD summarizes the opinions adopted in the prior year in its annual report.[107]

The quality of WGAD opinions has increased substantially in recent years, especially since the creation of its database, which allows for WGAD members to access and refer to prior opinions as persuasive authority. Nonetheless, enforcing WGAD opinions and their recommendations remains a serious challenge for petitioners. The mere publication of an opinion alone by the WGAD does not usually have a meaningful impact on a detainee's situation unless it is combined by the person's advocates with sustained political and public relations advocacy efforts. The opinions are also only rarely respected and deferred to by national judicial systems even though they are not infrequently presented by domestic counsel to petitioners in any ongoing legal proceedings.

At the same time, however, it is equally hard to overstate the value to the advocates for a detainee to be able to explain that the United Nations has found that person's detention arbitrary and in violation of international law. And for any detainee who is arbitrarily detained, in the author's experience, their greatest fear is that the world has forgotten them. To have the United Nations speak out on their behalf provides detainees with vindication, validation, and even protection from abuse, even if it does not immediately yield their release. And in the author's experience, prevailing before the WGAD has been of enormous value in ultimately having secured the freedom of countless clients.

VII Structure of Opinions

A *Opinion Number and Date Adopted*

The published opinions of the WGAD follow a traditional pattern, going back to its founding. The opinion heading lists the session number and dates of the session at which the opinion was adopted. It also provides an opinion number, year, and country, which

---

[106] *Id.*, at ¶ 18.
[107] *Id.*, at ¶19.

correspond to the chronological number of the opinion issued by the WGAD in that year and the adverse state in the proceeding, such as Opinion No. 49/2017 (Iran).

The very last line of every opinion provides the specific date of the WGAD's session when the opinion was formally adopted. It is important to understand that the date an opinion was published is found at the top of every opinion, but this is *not* the date the opinion was actually adopted.

B Preliminary Information

Opinions are presented in the form of a series of numbered paragraphs. In every opinion, in the first paragraph, the WGAD states:

> 1. The Working Group on Arbitrary Detention was established in resolution 1991/42 of the Commission on Human Rights, which extended and clarified the Working Group's mandate in its resolution 1997/50. Pursuant to General Assembly resolution 60/251 and Human Rights Council decision 1/102, the Council assumed the mandate of the Commission. The Council most recently extended the mandate of the Working Group for a three-year period in Council resolution 33/30 of 30 September 2016.[108]

In the second paragraph, the WGAD explains that in accordance with its Methods of Work it transmitted to the government of that country a communication regarding the detainee(s) on the specific date it was sent and then explains if the government responded to that communication. And in the third paragraph, the WGAD states that it regards a deprivation of liberty as arbitrary in the following cases, reprinting in full from the Methods of Work the five categories of its cases.

C Information from Source and Government

Having presented this preliminary information, the WGAD then discusses the allegations made by the source, and, if applicable, the response of the government, and the reply of the source. In recent jurisprudence, the WGAD has used headings to make it easier for the reader to follow the presentation of the opinion.

Thus, for example, in *Siamak Namazi and Mohammed Baquer Namazi v. Iran*,[109] the opinion included the following headings and quantity of numbered paragraphs of information after the preliminary information:

Submissions

Communication from the Source (two paragraphs)
Background (nine paragraphs)
Interrogations, Arrest, and Detention of Siamak Namazi (six paragraphs)
Arrest and Detention of Mohammed Baquer Namazi (ten paragraphs)
Trial and Appeal (seven paragraphs)
Current Conditions (four paragraphs)

---

[108] *See, e.g.,* Siamak Namazi and Mohammed Baquer Namazi v. Iran, Opinion No. 49/2017, Adopted Aug. 22, 2017, at ¶ 1 (Litigated by Author through Freedom Now).
[109] *Id.*

Categories of the Working Group (one paragraph)
Category II (one paragraph)
Category III (two paragraphs)
Response from the Government (two paragraphs)[110]

In explaining the submissions made by the parties, the WGAD is *not* yet rendering a judgment on the veracity of claims made by either side but is rather recounting what each has presented and how they responded to each other.

D Discussion and Disposition

Under the heading "Discussion," the WGAD then presents its detailed legal analysis. In *Siamak Namazi and Mohammed Baquer Namazi v. Iran*, this took sixteen numbered paragraphs. The WGAD then presents its conclusion under the heading "Disposition." The presentation of a case's disposition follows a formulaic approach across the WGAD's jurisprudence. It states "[i]n light of the foregoing, the Working Group renders the following opinion": In a case where the deprivation of liberty is found to be arbitrary, it specifically enumerates the provisions of the UDHR and ICCPR that were found to have been violated, concludes that the detention is arbitrary, and then lists the specific legal categories the cases were found to fall within. Thus, in this case, the WGAD stated:

> The deprivation of liberty of Mr. Siamak Namazi and Mr. Mohammed Baquer Namazi, being in contravention of articles 9, 10, and 11 of the Universal Declaration of Human Rights and of articles 9, 10, 14, and 26 of the International Covenant on Civil and Political Rights, is arbitrary and falls within categories III and IV.[111]

It is worth noting that in these cases specifically, the petitioner argued that the case fell within Categories II and III, but the WGAD concluded that the cases fell within Categories III and V. This had no material impact on the overall outcome, which was the rendering of the opinion that both Namazis were being held arbitrarily and in violation of international law. But it is worth noting to highlight another important point – that the WGAD can review the submissions by parties and can either agree, in whole or in part, with the arguments made by either side. And it can also on its own accord render legal conclusions that had not actually been argued by either side as well.

In this particular case, the author had argued that Siamak Namazi, who was a dual US-Iranian citizen, was being imprisoned in part in violation of his right to freedom of association under Category II, as the Government argued he was working with a hostile government because he had been affiliated with the National Endowment for Democracy, Woodrow Wilson Center for Scholars, and World Economic Forum. All three are independent NGOs, but the Government had asserted these were front groups for US spy organizations. But the WGAD read the same evidence, in light of its own experience with numerous dual national cases in Iran, as evincing a discriminatory intent against the Namazis, which it found primarily to be on the basis of their being dual nationals with the United States, which was a declared enemy of Iran. As a result, it viewed the case as

---

[110] The Government did not respond, but if it had there would have been an additional heading with numbered paragraphs entitled "Further Information from Source."

[111] *Id.*, at ¶ 55.

falling within Category V. But given that detainees can be classified as being arbitrarily detained under multiple categories, the WGAD could have just as easily also found violations under Category II and V (in addition to Category III).[112]

E Recommendations to Government

Although appearing in the latter part of the opinion under the disposition of the case, it is worth separately highlighting that on rendering an opinion of arbitrary detention, the WGAD makes specific recommendations to the government in the case.

In most cases, the WGAD uses similar language to present its first recommendation. As in the Namazis' cases, it says:

> Consequent upon the opinion rendered, the Working Group requests the Government to take the steps necessary to remedy the situation of Mr. Siamak Namazi and Mr. Mohammed Baquer Namazi without delay and bring it into conformity with the standards and principles set forth in the international norms on detention, including the Universal Declaration of Human Rights and the International Covenant on Civil and Political Rights.[113]

Although in all cases that the author has submitted to the WGAD a request has been made for it to urge the government to immediately release the detainee, the WGAD has only made this recommendation infrequently, consistent with its broader jurisprudence. This may generally be a reasonable approach to typical cases, given that in situations of deprivation of liberty where the violations are less severe, a government could take a range of remedial measures to bring their actions into compliance with its obligations under international law.

That said, however, no guidance is provided in the Methods of Work as to what recommendations may be made to a government if the WGAD determines that a deprivation of liberty is arbitrary and in violation of international law. They merely state that the WGAD "shall render an opinion to that effect and make recommendations to the Government."[114] And, unfortunately for petitioners, there has been no guidance as to what criteria the WGAD should consider when it decides whether to ask a government to remedy an arbitrary detention rather than release the detainee.

In the Namazis' case, the WGAD did recommend their release: "The Working Group considers that, taking into account all the circumstances of the case, the appropriate remedy would be to release Mr. Siamak Namazi and Mr. Mohammed Baquer Namazi immediately . . . ."[115]

But had not been intuitively obvious from the outside how the WGAD makes this critical decision in its opinions – and this decision matters enormously from the perspective of advocates for detainees wanting support for their urging a government to release a detainee after prevailing before the WGAD rather than seeing them subject to a new trial in systems that have already proven the difficulty of providing the detainee due process and the rule of law.

---

[112] *Id.*, at ¶¶ 42–43.
[113] *Id.*, at ¶ 56.
[114] *Methods of Work of the Working Group*, Human Rights Council, A/HRC/36/38, July 13, 2017, at ¶ 17(d).
[115] Siamak Namazi and Mohammed Baquer Namazi, at ¶ 57.

In *Ola Yusuf al-Qaradawi and Hossam al-Din Khalaf* v. *Egypt*,[116] the petitioners were a husband and wife who had been held in harsh prison conditions for close to a year without charge or trial. Unlike in the Namazis' case, the Government provided a detailed response, which was thoroughly examined by the WGAD and responded to by the petitioners. The WGAD's opinion was exceptionally well written and unsparing in its criticism of the Government for a wide array of violations of their rights. And the WGAD's disposition of the case showed virtually every relevant provision of the UDHR and ICCPR had been violated:

> The deprivation of liberty of Ola Yusuf al-Qaradawi and Hosam al-Din Khalaf, being in contravention of articles 2, 3, 5, 6, 7, 8, 9, 10, 11, 12, 13, and 25 of the Universal Declaration of Human Rights, of articles 2, 7, 9, 10, 12, 14, 16, 17, and 26 of the International Covenant on Civil and Political Rights, and of Article 16(7) of the International Convention on the Protection of the Rights of All Migrant Workers and Members of Their Families, is arbitrary and falls within Categories I, III and V.[117]

Unlike in the Namazis' case, here the WGAD also found a Category I violation even *after* considering the Government's response, demonstrating there was simply no legal basis for the detention of al-Qaradawi and Khalaf. Although the advanced edited opinion of the WGAD did not include a call for their immediate release, it was amended a short time later to include this provision. And the WGAD now has, as a matter of practice, adopted a standard set of recommendations published with all cases where a detention is found arbitrary, which includes a call for the immediate release of those detained.

F Referrals to Other Relevant UN Special Procedures

Under Section VII of its Methods of Work, the WGAD discusses how it coordinates its activities with other human rights mechanisms. As it considers and adopts individual opinions, the WGAD actively considers under Paragraph 33(a) whether based on the presented facts there are other UN Special Procedures whose mandates also cover the situation and might appropriately respond. Specifically, the Methods of Work states:

> If the Working Group, while examining allegations of violations of human rights, considers that the allegations could be more appropriately dealt with by another working group or special rapporteur, it will refer the allegations to the relevant working group or special rapporteur within whose competence they fall, for appropriate action.[118]

In adopting opinions, the WGAD specifically explains in the disposition section any specific referrals that it has made in relation to that individual case. For example, in the Namazis' case, the WGAD stated:

---

[116] Ola Yusuf al-Qaradawi & Hossam al-Din Khalaf v. Egypt, WGAD Opinion No. 26/2018, Adopted Apr. 23, 2018, at ¶ 77.
[117] *Id.*, at ¶ 82.
[118] *Methods of Work of the Working Group*, Human Rights Council, A/HRC/36/38, July 13, 2017, at ¶ 33(a).

In accordance with paragraph 33(a) of its methods of work, the Working Group refers the present case to the Special Rapporteur on the situation of human rights in the Islamic Republic of Iran.[119]

And in al-Qaradawi and Khalaf's case, the WGAD stated:

In accordance with paragraph 33(a) of its methods of work, the Working Group refers the present case to the Special Rapporteur on torture and cruel, inhuman or degrading treatment or punishment and the Special Rapporteur on the promotion and protection of human rights and fundamental freedoms while countering terrorism, for appropriate action.[120]

G Follow-Up Procedure

Shortly after its founding, the WGAD first noted a need "to ensure follow-up to the recommendations made in the Group's decision."[121] It proposed "the Commission on Human Rights should recommend to the Government that it report those measures to the Working Group within a period of four months following notification of the decision."[122] The UNCHR responded by requesting the WGAD "to make all suggestions and recommendations for better fulfillment of its task, particularly in regard to ways and means of ensuring the follow-up to its decisions, in cooperation with Governments."[123]

In December 1994, the WGAD specifically recommended a follow-up mechanism:

[A] Government which has been the subject of a Working Group decision deeming a detention to be arbitrary should be requested to inform the Working Group, within four months from the date of transmittal of the decision, of the measures adopted in compliance with the Group's recommendations. For the time being, it is suggested that this procedure should be applied only in cases in which the prisoner has not been released. Should the Government fail to abide by the Group's recommendations, the Group might proceed to recommend to the Commission on Human Rights that it should request that Government to report to the Commission on the matter, in accordance with the modalities deemed most appropriate by the Commission.[124]

This proposal, however, received a hostile response from some of the UNCHR's member states. The Government of Egypt, for instance, suggested the WGAD focus instead on "develop[ing] its dialogue and cooperation with Governments instead of seeking to impose counter-productive measures against them."[125] The UNCHR did not adopt a proposal at that time.

---

[119] Siamak Namazi and Mohammed Baquer Namazi, at ¶ 58.
[120] Ola Al-Qaradawi and Hossam Khalaf, at ¶ 85.
[121] *Report of the Working Group on Arbitrary Detention*, Commission on Human Rights, E/CN.4/1993/24, Jan. 12, 1993, at ¶ 42(b).
[122] *Id.*, at ¶ 43(d).
[123] Resolution 1993/36 (Arbitrary Detention), Commission on Human Rights, E/CN.4/1993/36, Mar. 5, 1993, at ¶ 18.
[124] *Report of the Working Group on Arbitrary Detention*, Commission on Human Rights, E/CN.4/1995/31, Dec. 21, 1994, at ¶ 56(c).
[125] *Id.*, at ¶ 56.

Nonetheless, this was an important issue that the author and many others discussed over years with WGAD members and staff, but in light of its highly limited resources, there was further resistance to developing a follow-up procedure. In 2011, the WGAD adopted what were then referred to as its Revised Methods of Work.[126] Among its innovations was the launch of a new follow-up process, which has grown in efficiency since its inclusion of this important request in the Methods of Work:

> Governments, sources and other parties should inform the Working Group of the follow-up action taken on the recommendations made by the Working Group in its opinion. This will enable the Working Group to keep the Human Rights Council informed of the progress made and of any difficulties encountered in implementing the recommendations, as well as of any failure to take action.[127]

In 2016, the HRC adopted Resolution 33/30, which extended the WGAD's mandate for another three years. This resolution included two references to the importance of follow-up. Specifically, the HRC requested states "to inform the Working Group of the steps they have taken [to remedy the situation of persons arbitrarily deprived of their liberty" and encouraged all states to "cooperate with the Working Group."[128]

Practically, to implement this provision of its Methods of Work, the WGAD now includes as the last section of its opinions, after the disposition of the case, specific instructions regarding the follow-up procedure. A typical follow-up procedure section can be seen in *Ola Yusuf al-Qaradawi and Hossam al-Din Khalaf* v. *Egypt*:

> 86. In accordance with paragraph 20 of its methods of work, the Working Group requests the source and the Government to provide it with information on action taken in follow-up to the recommendations made in the present opinion, including:
>
> (a) Whether Ms. al-Qaradawi and Mr. Khalaf have been released and, if so, on what date;
> (b) Whether compensation or other reparations have been made to Ms. al-Qaradawi and Mr. Khalaf;
> (c) Whether an investigation has been conducted into the violation of the rights of Ms. al-Qaradawi and Mr. Khalaf and, if so, the outcome of the investigation;
> (d) Whether any legislative amendments or changes in practice have been made to harmonize the laws and practices of Egypt with its international obligations in line with the present opinion;
> (e) Whether any other action has been taken to implement the present opinion.
>
> 87. The Government is invited to inform the Working Group of any difficulties it may have encountered in implementing the recommendations made in the present opinion and whether further technical assistance is required, for example, through a visit by the Working Group.
>
> 88. The Working Group requests the source and the Government to provide the above information within six months of the date of the transmission of the present opinion. However, the Working Group reserves the right to take its own action in follow-up to the

---

[126] *Report of the Working Group on Arbitrary Detention*, Human Rights Council, A/HRC/16/47, Adopted Jan. 19, 2011, at Annex (Revised Methods of Work of the Working Group).

[127] *Methods of Work of the Working Group*, Human Rights Council, A/HRC/36/38, July 13, 2017, at ¶ 20.

[128] Resolution 33/30 (Arbitrary Detention), Human Rights Council, A/HRC/RES/33/30, Adopted Sept. 30, 2016, at ¶¶ 3, 7.

opinion if new concerns in relation to the case are brought to its attention. Such action would enable the Working Group to inform the Human Rights Council of progress made in implementing its recommendations, as well as any failure to take action.

89. The Working Group requests the Government to disseminate through all available means the present opinion among all stakeholders.

90. The Working Group recalls that the Human Rights Council has encouraged all States to cooperate with the Working Group and requested them to take account of its views and, where necessary, to take appropriate steps to remedy the situation of persons arbitrarily deprived of their liberty, and to inform the Working Group of the steps they have taken.[129]

To coordinate its efforts, the WGAD later added to its Methods of Work the election of a Vice-Chair explicitly charged with being its focal point for follow up on all actions taken by the Working Group.[130] Since its founding, the WGAD has incorporated into its annual reports specific information it had received regarding the releases of detainees that were the subject of its prior opinions. Over its history, the WGAD has reported 1,636 releases across 379 of its opinions:

WORKING GROUP REPORTING OF RELEASES OF DETAINEES, BY NUMBER OF RELATED OPINIONS, 1992–2018

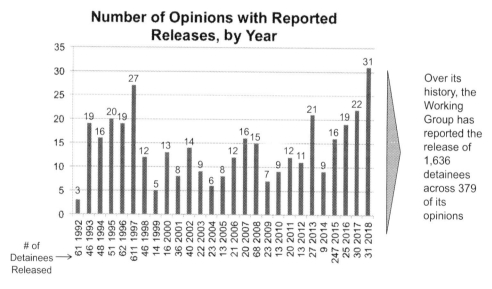

Over its history, the Working Group has reported the release of 1,636 detainees across 379 of its opinions

Source: Annual reports of the UN Working Group on Arbitrary Detention

Figure 14 Working Group reporting of releases of detainees that were subjects of its opinions

---

[129] Ola Al-Qaradawi and Hossam Khalaf, at ¶¶ 86–90.
[130] Id., at ¶ 3(c).

VIII Appeals of Opinions

Under its Methods of Work, the WGAD may review previously decided opinions either *proprio motu*, at its own initiation, or at the request of the government or source. The Methods of Work state in the pertinent part:

> In exceptional circumstances, the Working Group may *proprio motu* reconsider its opinions if it becomes aware of new facts that, if known at the time of the decision, would have led the Working Group to a different outcome. The Working Group may also reconsider its opinions at the request of the Government concerned or the source under the following conditions:
>
> (a) If the facts on which the request is based are considered by the Working Group to be entirely new and such as to have caused the Working Group to alter its decision had it been aware of them;
>
> (b) If the facts had not been known or had not been accessible to the party originating the request;
>
> (c) In a case where the request comes from a Government, on condition that the latter has observed the time limit for reply . . . .[131]

While opinions of the WGAD may technically be appealed, it has never in its history granted an appeal or modified its opinion:

APPEALS OF OPINIONS OF THE WORKING GROUP ON ARBITRARY DETENTION, 1992–2018

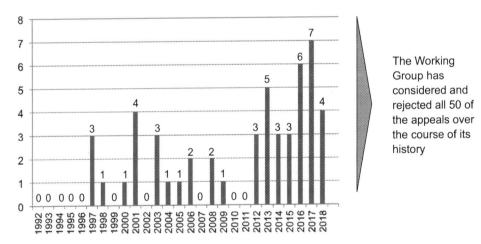

Source: Annual reports of the UN Working Group on Arbitrary Detention

Figure 15 Appeals of Working Group opinions

---

[131] *Methods of Work of the Working Group*, Human Rights Council, A/HRC/36/38, July 13, 2017, at ¶ 21.

While it is possible that no appeal meeting its criteria has ever been submitted, there are also reasonable due process questions that can be asked by both governments and sources about the fairness of having the very same experts who adjudicated a case being the same people that hear the appeal of the original opinion. Such an approach appears contrary to the WGAD's own jurisprudence. In *Youssef Mahmoud Chaabane* v. *Lebanon*, the WGAD found an appeal provided in that case was not an "effective remedy,"[132] in part because it was considered by judges who had been involved in the first trial and who would be unlikely to overturn a conviction they themselves handed down.[133] Of course, the WGAD is a quasi-judicial body and is not subject to the requirements of the ICCPR. But the WGAD may wish to consider in the future creating some kind of independent appellate review function. For example, under its Methods of Work, the WGAD "can appoint at any time a rapporteur on specific issues of interest."[134]

In response to appeals, the WGAD considers them individually, sends a letter to the appellant explaining the outcome of the appeal in relation to the criteria provided for in the Methods of Work, and then reports on the outcome of the appeal in its annual report. More recently, the WGAD has taken to listing the appeals presented by opinion number in its annual report and then reporting collectively "[a]fter carefully and closely examining the requests for review, the Working Group decided to maintain its opinions on the basis that none of the requests met criteria outlined in paragraph 21 of its methods of work."[135]

IX Follow-Up on Opinions

As noted earlier, as a matter of practice, the WGAD now includes in its opinions specific instructions on its follow-up procedure, requesting both the government and the source to provide it with updated information on the status of the detainee within six months after the opinion was adopted.

In addition, as a matter of course, the WGAD will also send a letter to the government and the source requesting any new information that they may have to report. This was the correspondence from the WGAD in *Siamak Namazi and Mohammed Baquer Namazi* v. *Iran*:

UN Letterhead
Working Group on Arbitrary Detention

17 April 2018

Dear Mr. Genser,
I wish to refer to the deprivation of liberty of Siamak Namazi and Mohammad Baquer Namazi, which you submitted for consideration of the Working Group on Arbitrary Detention and resulted in the adoption of Opinion No. 49/2017.

---

[132] Youssef Mahmoud Chaabane v. Lebanon, WGAD Opinion No. 10/2007, Adopted May 11, 2006, at ¶ 17.
[133] *Id.*, at ¶ 17; Anwar Ibrahim v. Malaysia, WGAD Opinion No. 22/2015, Adopted Sept. 1, 2015, at ¶ 31 (recognizing the significance of evident bias in judges at the appeals instance).
[134] Methods of Work, at ¶ 3(f).
[135] *Report of the Working Group on Arbitrary Detention*, Human Rights Council, A/HRC/33/50, July 11, 2016.

As you are aware, in this Opinion, the Working Group requested that it be informed within six months on the progress made with respect to its recommendations. Therefore, we would be grateful if you could inform the Working Group:

(a) Whether Mr. Siamak Namazi and Mr. Mohammed Baquer Namazi have been released and, if so, on what date;

(b) Whether compensation or other reparations have been made to Mr. Siamak Namazi and Mr. Mohammed Baquer Namazi;

(c) Whether any investigation has been conducted into the violation of the rights of Mr. Siamak Namazi and Mr. Mohammed Baquer Namazi;

(d) Whether any legislative amendments or changes in practice have been made to harmonise the Government's laws and practices with its international obligations in line with this Opinion;

(e) Whether any other action has been taken to implement the Opinion.

In addition, please inform the Working Group if any retaliatory action is alleged to have been taken against any of the subjects of the Opinion, their families or associates.

The Working Group would appreciate if you could provide the above information at your earliest convenience, and before 17 May 2018. This will enable the Working Group to keep the Human Rights Council informed of the progress made in implementing its recommendations.

> Yours sincerely,
> [Signature]
> Lucie Viersma
> Secretary
> Working Group on Arbitrary Detention

In addition to following up on prior opinions, the WGAD presents any material new information learned from this correspondence in its next annual report.

X Reprisals

In its most recent annual report, the WGAD for the first time noted with "grave concern" that it has regularly been receiving information about reprisals suffered by those who have been the subject of an urgent appeal, opinion, or follow-up procedure. It said that these reprisals have included "placement in solitary confinement, harsh prison conditions, threats and harassment against the individual and/or his or her family members, and accusatory articles in the pro-government media."[136] And it named six individuals who were subjects of six different opinions as those about whom it had received allegations of reprisals in the prior year.[137]

---

[136] *Report of the Working Group on Arbitrary Detention*, Human Rights Council, A/HRC/39/45, July 2, 2018, at ¶ 27.

[137] Id., at ¶¶ 28–29.

As a response to this disturbing trend, the WGAD appointed one of its members as the "Focal Point on Reprisals," it cited to Resolutions 12/2 and 24/24 of the HRC reminding all governments to refrain from all reprisals, and when such referrals have not already been made, the WGAD now sends reported cases to the Assistant Secretary-General for Human Rights, who is leading efforts at the United Nations to end intimidation and reprisals against those cooperating on human rights.[138]

---

[138] *Id.*, at ¶¶ 27, 30.

Part III. Case Jurisprudence

Between 1992 through 2017, the WGAD adopted a total of 1,200 cases brought by sources against 128 countries. Not surprisingly, a smaller number of countries constituted a substantial percentage of cases brought to the WGAD:

A SMALL NUMBER OF COUNTRIES REPRESENT MAJORITY OF CASES BROUGHT TO THE WORKING GROUP

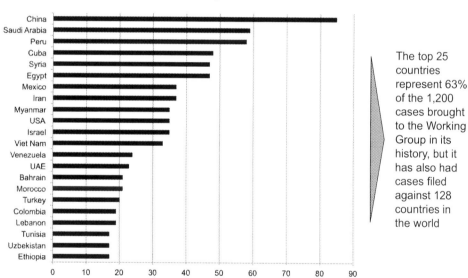

Top Countries, 1992–2017, by Number of Cases*

The top 25 countries represent 63% of the 1,200 cases brought to the Working Group in its history, but it has also had cases filed against 128 countries in the world

* A case can involve one or more individuals; includes all reported cases, including where no opinion adopted
Source: Author's analysis of case data from UN Working Group on Arbitrary Detention

Figure 16 Top twenty-five countries comprise majority of cases

This view is similar, when looking at cases brought to the WGAD in the last decade:

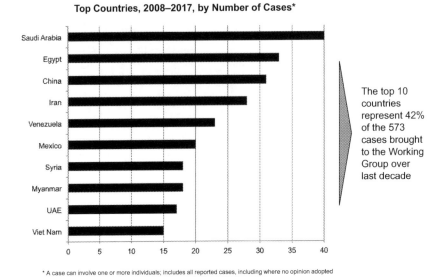

Figure 17 Top ten countries with cases brought to Working Group in last decade

An analysis of the cases considered shows almost half of the cases came from the Asia-Pacific Group and about 20 percent each coming from the Africa Group and the Latin America and the Caribbean Group:

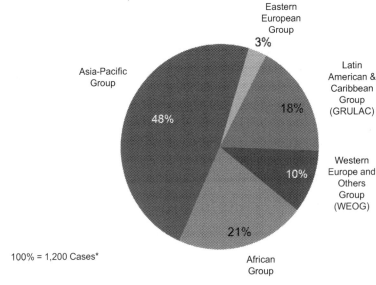

Figure 18 Distribution of cases by region

On cases for which the WGAD found a deprivation of liberty arbitrary, its decisions were roughly split evenly between opinions where it found a violation under one category of cases as compared to those where it found a violation under multiple categories:

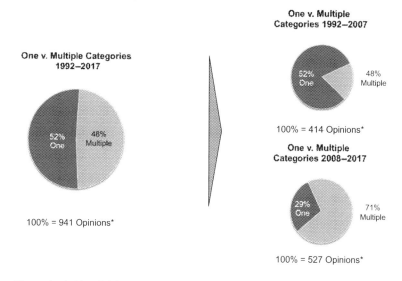

AMONG OPINIONS WITH FINDING OF ARBITRARY DETENTION, BASED ON ONE OR MULTIPLE CATEGORIES OF CASES

Figure 19 Basis of finding of arbitrary detention, one or multiple categories of cases

Across all cases in which a deprivation of liberty was found arbitrary, Category II and III violations were most common, with Category I violations also regularly appearing:

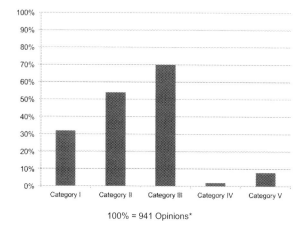

AMONG OPINIONS WITH FINDING OF ARBITRARY DETENTION, ON WHAT BASIS WAS CASE DECIDED, 1992–2017

Figure 20 Basis of finding of arbitrary detention, across case categories

Where issued opinions found cases decided on the basis of one category, 50 percent were found arbitrary under Category III, 38 percent under Category II, 11 percent under Category I, and 1 percent under Category IV. There were no opinions where a detention was found arbitrary exclusively under Category V.

OPINIONS WHERE ARBITRARY DETENTION FOUND ON BASIS OF ONE CATEGORY ONLY, 1992–2017

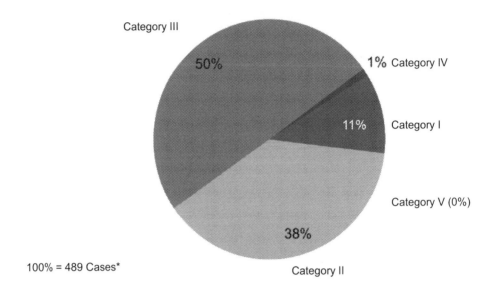

Category III

50%

1% Category IV

11% Category I

Category V (0%)

38%

100% = 489 Cases*

Category II

* As among issued opinions with finding of arbitrary detention; excludes opinions where no category specified
Source: Author's analysis of case data from UN Working Group on Arbitrary Detention

Figure 21 Basis of finding of arbitrary detention where opinion based on one category

4 Category I

No Legal Basis for Detention

According to the WGAD's Basic Principles and Guidelines, domestic law must authorize any and all restrictions on liberty.[1] The WGAD will categorize a case as arbitrary under Category I "[w]hen it is clearly impossible to invoke any legal basis justifying the deprivation of liberty, as when a person is kept in detention after the completion of his or her sentence or despite an amnesty law applicable to him or her."[2] Category I cases typically center on the right to not be deprived of one's liberty except on such grounds established by law, the right to not be held guilty for any criminal offense on account of an act or omission which did not constitute a criminal offense when it was committed, the right not to be tried twice for the same crime, situations where the detainee was granted amnesty but was not released, and in extraordinary rendition cases where prisoners are abducted and transferred across international borders outside of a lawful extradition hearing.

In its jurisprudence, most cases decided by the WGAD are primarily grounded in violations of other fundamental or due process rights and will sometimes also have Category I elements to them. But to understand the way these cases have been approached by the WGAD, it is useful to focus on the reasoning in cases where Category I violations are the primary or only justification for the WGAD determining a person's detention to be arbitrary and in violation of international law.

I No Penalty without Law

The principle of *nulla poena sine lege* (no penalty without law) grounds many Category I cases. Where the government simply cannot put forward any domestic legal basis for detention, the WGAD will find the detention arbitrary. Related situations occur when the alleged act was committed before that act was considered a crime.

Article 15(1) of the ICCPR states:

No one shall be held guilty of any criminal offence on account of any act or omission which did not constitute a criminal offence, under national or international law, at the

---

[1] *Basic Principles and Guidelines on the Remedies and Procedures on the Rights of Persons Deprived of Their Liberty to Bring Proceedings before a Court*, Working Group on Arbitrary Detention, Human Rights Council, A/HRC/30/27 (Annex), July 6, 2015, at ¶ 49.

[2] *Methods of Work of the Working Group on Arbitrary Detention*, Human Rights Council, A/HRC/36/38 (Annex), July 13, 2017, at ¶ 8(a).

time when it was committed. Nor shall a heavier penalty be imposed than the one that was applicable at the time when the criminal offence was committed. If, subsequent to the commission of the offence, provision is made by law for the imposition of the lighter penalty, the offender shall benefit thereby.[3]

And Article 11(2) of the UDHR provides:

No one shall be held guilty of any penal offence on account of any act or omission which did not constitute a penal offence, under national or international law, at the time when it was committed. Nor shall a heavier penalty be imposed than the one that was applicable at the time the penal offence was committed.[4]

Regional human rights treaties also apply to this kind of situation. Article 7(2) of the *African Charter on Human and Peoples' Rights* (ACHPR), Article 9 of the *American Convention on Human Rights* (ACHR) (titled "Freedom from Ex Post Facto Laws"), and Article 7(1) of the *European Convention on Human Rights* (ECHR) (titled "No Penalty without Law") echo the ICCPR and UDHR provisions. Speaking specifically of the ICCPR, ECHR, and ACHR, Shahram Dana states: "[a]ll three of these conventions codify the provision in an article separate from other procedural guarantees in criminal law, indicating 'its special significance for criminal trials . . . as well as for legal certainty in general.'"[5]

When the UDHR was adopted in 1948, the right to be free from penalty where no law exists and from *ex post facto* laws had already enjoyed wide international support. During debate of Article 11(2), Yugoslavian delegate Ljuba Radevanovic observed: "The *nulla poena sine lege* principle was almost universal in national law" at the time the Nuremburg Trials were held.[6] In Europe, the basis for this principle and its codification within the ECHR in 1950 emanated from the *Declaration of the Rights of Man and of the Citizen*, a product of the French Revolution in 1789.[7] Moreover, in addition to the prohibition against retroactivity, leading commentators consider the *nulla poena sine lege* principle to incorporate three distinct subparts: that the law be written (*lex scripta*), certain and predictable (*lex certa*), and that prohibition by analogy be forbidden (*lex stricta*).[8]

The WGAD's analysis in these kinds of situation is illustrated in its handling of the opinion regarding Shin Sook Ja's detention in the Democratic Republic of Korea (DPRK or North Korea).[9] Shin Sook Ja, a national of South Korea, left her country to work in

---

[3] *International Covenant on Civil and Political Rights*, G.A. Res. 2200A (XXI), 21 U.N. GAOR Supp. (No. 16), at 52, U.N. Doc. A/6316 (1966), 999 U.N.T.S. 171, *entered into force* Mar. 23, 1976, at Art. 9(1) (ICCPR).

[4] Universal Declaration of Human Rights, G.A. Res. 217A (III), U.N. Doc. A/810 (1948), at art. 11(2).

[5] Shahram Dana, *Beyond Retroactivity to Realizing Justice: A Theory on the Principles of Legality in International Criminal Law Sentencing*, 99(4) JOURNAL OF CRIMINAL LAW & CRIMINOLOGY 868 (2009).

[6] JOHANNES MORSINK, THE UNIVERSAL DECLARATION OF HUMAN RIGHTS: ORIGINS, DRAFTING, AND INTENT 58 (University of Pennsylvania Press, 2010).

[7] Article 8 states, "The law should establish only penalties that are strictly and evidently necessary, and no one can be punished but under a law established and promulgated before the offense and legally applied." GABRIEL HALLEVY, A MODERN TREATISE ON THE PRINCIPLES OF LEGALITY IN CRIMINAL LAW 69 (Springer Science & Business Media, 2010).

[8] Dana, at 869.

[9] Shin Sook Ja, et al. v. Democratic People's Republic of Korea, WGAD Opinion No. 4/2012, Adopted May 2, 2012.

Germany in 1970.[10] In 1972, Shin met and married Oh Kil Nam, also a national of South Korea who was studying economics at the University of Tübingen.[11] They had two daughters, Oh Hae Won and Oh Hyu Won.[12] At the time, Oh was an outspoken critic of the South Korean government.[13] In the 1980s Shin became ill with hepatitis.[14] The couple attracted the attention of North Korean agents who saw an opportunity.[15] They offered Oh an important job working as an economist for the North Korean government, and promised that his wife would receive first-class free medical care to treat her hepatitis.[16] Shin was strongly opposed to the idea, but eventually her husband persuaded her.[17] Not long after entering the DPRK, Oh realized he had made a terrible mistake. DPRK officials drove Shin's family to a guesthouse on a military base, where soldiers guarded them.[18] Shin never received medical treatment; instead, Oh and Shin were indoctrinated on the teachings of North Korean leader Kim Il-sung.[19]

Oh was eventually ordered to go to Germany to recruit more South Koreans to move to the DPRK, just as he had been recruited.[20] Shin persuaded her husband to disobey his orders and attempt to escape.[21] To ensure Oh's loyalty, Shin and her daughters were detained.[22] En route to Germany, Oh managed to escape DPRK control by writing on a piece of paper "Help Me" and explaining to immigration officials in Copenhagen that his passport was forged.[23]

In response, Shin and their two daughters, then aged nine and eleven, were imprisoned in the Yodok concentration camp (Kwan-li-so No. 15) in 1987.[24] The only grounds for detention were because her husband had not returned to the DPRK.[25] Isang, the one who had originally recruited Oh, informed him that his family was being detained to prevent them from returning to South Korea and because of Oh's betrayal to the DPRK.[26]

The DPRK responded to the WGAD petition only by stating that Shin had died and that their daughters, Oh Hae Won and Oh Kyu Won, "strongly refuse to deal with Mr. Oh and ask him not to bother them anymore."[27] The DPRK did not, however, provide any legal provisions justifying their detention.[28] Because the DPRK did not provide any legal provisions justifying Shin's detention, the WGAD held, "The source has put

---

[10] Id.

[11] Id.

[12] Evan Ramstad, S. Koreans Protest North's Prison Camps, WALL STREET JOURNAL, Aug. 20, 2011.

[13] Blaine Harden, A Family and a Conscience, Destroyed by North Korea's Cruelty, WASHINGTON POST, Feb. 22, 2010.

[14] Id.

[15] Robin Banerji, The Terrible Price of a Korean Defection, BBC NEWS, Apr. 25, 2012.

[16] Id.

[17] Id.

[18] Id.

[19] Id.

[20] Id.

[21] Kim Moon-soo, Time Ripe to Push for Rights in North Korea, SYDNEY MORNING HERALD, Jan. 2, 2012.

[22] Shin Sook Ja, et al., at ¶ 8.

[23] Banerji; Harden.

[24] Id.

[25] Shin Sook Ja, et al., at ¶ 8.

[26] Id., at ¶ 9.

[27] Id., at ¶ 19.

[28] Id.

forward a prima facie case that Shin Sook Ja, Oh Hae Won and Oh Kyu Won have been held in detention for many years, without any legal basis justifying their deprivation of liberty."[29] The WGAD found the detention to be in contravention of Article 11 of the UDHR, which guarantees both a right to the presumption of innocence and that no one be punished for something that is not a penal offense under national law.[30]

In a more recent case, *Waleed Abulkhair v. Saudi Arabia*, the WGAD cited to the *Max Planck Encyclopedia of International Law* to explain in further detail the fundamental guarantee of *nulla poena sine lege*. These include:

(a) the principle of non-retroactivity (*nullum crimen, nulla poena sine lege praevia*);
(b) the prohibition against analogy (*nullum crimen, nulla poena sine lege stricta*);
(c) the principle of certainty (*nullum crimen, nulla poena sine lege certa*); and
(d) the prohibition against uncodified, unwritten, or judge-made criminal provisions (*nullum crimen, nulla poena sine lege scripta*).[31]

Together, this means an act is only punishable by law if when committed it was the object of a "valid, sufficiently precise, written criminal law to which a sufficiently certain sanction was attached."[32]

The WGAD further explained that in its view the principle of legality also requires the substance of penal law be "due and appropriate in a democratic society that respects human dignity and rights (*nullum crimen, nulla poena sine lege apta*)."[33] And that it must, at a minimum, also satisfy:

(a) the principle of necessity (*nullum crimen, nulla poena sine necessitate*);
(b) the prerequisite of injustice (*nullum crimen, nulla poena sine injuria*); and
(c) the principle of guilt (*nullum crimen, nulla poena sine culpa*).[34]

Without these, a detention flouts the principle of legality and has no legal basis.

The material facts that give rise to Category I violations often also imply Category III fair trial rights violations as well.[35] The WGAD has in some cases, however, not felt the need to address both types of violation if doing so would be repetitive. In *Hung Linh Nguyen v. Viet Nam*, for example, the WGAD found a Category I violation based on the failure of the authorities to provide the detainee with an arrest warrant or any basis for his detention, and equally for the failure to bring him promptly before a judge and to have a decision rendered without undue delay.[36] The WGAD did not, however, discuss the facts separately as a Category III violation because of violations of fair trial rights.[37]

---

[29] *Id.*, at ¶ 20.
[30] *Id.*, at ¶ 27.
[31] Waleed Abulkhair v. Saudi Arabia, WGAD Opinion No. 10/2018, Adopted Apr. 19, 2018, at ¶ 50.
[32] *Id.*, at ¶ 50.
[33] *Id.*, at ¶ 53.
[34] *Id.*
[35] Mario Francisco Tadic Astorga v. Bolivia, WGAD Opinion No. 28/2014, Adopted Aug. 28, 2014, at ¶¶ 46–48.
[36] Hung Linh Nguyen v. Viet Nam, WGAD Opinion No. 46/2015, Adopted Dec. 3, 2015, at ¶¶ 27, 31.
[37] *Id.*, at ¶ 35.

There are numerous cases with different fact patterns where the WGAD has found detentions arbitrary because individuals were held without any basis in law. These include, as further variations of the application of the concept, the following categories of cases:

A Arrested without Warrant and Held without Charge

The WGAD has articulated that Article 9(2) of the ICCPR "has two elements: information about the reasons for arrest must be provided immediately upon arrest, and there must be prompt information about the charges provided thereafter."[38] "Prompt information" does not mean immediately subsequent to the arrest.[39] However, in *Mohamed Serra v. Egypt*, the WGAD found a detention arbitrary when thirty-six hours passed after arrest before information about the charges were provided to the detainee.[40] Other cases of this kind include:

- *Bertrand Mamour v. Central African Republic*. The detainee was arrested by the Presidential Security Unit without a warrant and had been held for three months incommunicado. The Government failed to respond to a request for information and the WGAD found he was held without any basis in law.[41]
- *Zeinab Jalalian v. Iran*. The detainee was not informed of the charges that led to her arrest, no arrest warrant was presented, and no court made an assessment of the lawfulness, necessity, and proportionality of the detention.[42]
- *Gloria Anwuri v. Nigeria*. In this case, a sister of a businessman suspected of having financed a failed coup d'état was arrested and detained for almost two years without charge or trial. She was also deprived of her right to challenge the legality of her detention.[43]
- *Jaweed Al-Ghussain v. Palestinian Authority*. Here, a Jordanian citizen who owed a debt to the Government was arrested without a warrant, held without charge, and provided no process of legal review for more than four months.[44]
- *Hussain Khaled Albuluwy v. Saudi Arabia*. In this case, a group of seven different people were detained without charge or trial in different circumstances.[45]
- *Nguyen Viet Dung v. Viet Nam*. In this case concerning an environmental and democratic rights activist, the WGAD explained the determination of lawfulness includes a comparative analysis to determine whether the domestic legislation authorizing detention is consistent with international human rights law requirements.[46]

---

[38] Mohamed Serria v. Egypt, WGAD Opinion No. 30/2017, Adopted Apr. 26, 2017, at ¶ 58.

[39] *Id.*, at ¶ 59.

[40] *Id.*

[41] Bertrand Mamour v. Central African Republic, WGAD Opinion No. 15/2007, Adopted Sept. 13, 2007, at ¶ 10.

[42] Zeinab Jalalian v. Iran, WGAD Opinion No. 1/2016, Adopted Apr. 18, 2016, at ¶ 34.

[43] Gloria Anwuri v. Nigeria, WGAD Decision No. 20/1993, Adopted Apr. 30, 1993, at ¶ 9.

[44] Jaweed Al-Ghussain v. Palestinian Authority, WGAD Opinion No. 31/2001, Adopted Dec. 4, 2001, at ¶ 13.

[45] Hussain Khaled Albuluwy v. Saudi Arabia, WGAD Opinion No. 9/2007, Adopted May 10, 2007, at ¶ 19.

[46] Nguyen Viet Dung v. Viet Nam, WGAD Opinion No. 45/2015, Adopted Dec. 3, 2015, at ¶¶ 14–15.

B Arrested and Detained by Government Agency without Legal Authority

In *Émile Bisimwa Muhirhi* v. *Democratic Republic of Congo*, an individual was detained by the country's national security agency, which intervened in a dispute between two private parties.[47] The WGAD found that the agency's role in effecting the detention was an abuse of authority and in excess of mandate, noting no legal document authorized the officers to take the detainee into custody.[48]

C Charges Changed without Explanation

In *Jose Marcos Mavungo* v. *Angola*, the WGAD found there was no lawful basis for detaining a human rights activist attempting to draw attention to the lack of transparency in the management of public resources after the charges against him were changed without explanation and prompt disclosure from sedition to rebellion.[49] In a different twist on the same theme, the detainee in *Tashi Wangchuk* v. *China* was charged two months after arrest and was informed that the charges would likely be changed.[50] The WGAD found a Category I violation for both the initial delay and the subsequent extended limbo the detainee endured regarding the state of his charges.[51]

D Detained under Vague Law

In *Hassan Zafar Arif* v. *Pakistan*, the detainee was imprisoned for listening to a speech made by a prominent figure in the Muttahida Qaumi movement, which according to Pakistani authorities made him a facilitator of the speech in question. He was detained under the Maintenance of Public Order Ordinance, a law authorizing detention unassociated with any criminal charge. The WGAD found the law was "extremely vague and lacks the requisite degree of precision and legal certainty [which] ... leads to deprivation of liberty which is unreasonable or unnecessary."[52] The WGAD in general finds Category I violations for criminal charges that "might allow an excessively broad interpretation of its provisions due to their vagueness, thus resulting in unjustified and arbitrary criminalization" of the legitimate exercise of certain rights (often, freedom of expression).[53]

E Detained after Release Order

In *Teudo Mordán Gerónimo* v. *Dominican Republic*, the detainee was arrested and charged with being a guerilla and inciting peasants to overthrow the Government. According to the source, the Criminal Court of Appeal granted a writ of *habeas corpus*,

---

[47] Émile Bisimwa Muhirhi v. Democratic Republic of Congo, WGAD Opinion No. 25/2015, Adopted Sept. 3, 2015, at ¶ 27.

[48] *Id.*

[49] Jose Marcos Mavungo v. Angola, WGAD Opinion No. 47/2015, Adopted Dec. 3, 2015, at ¶ 5.

[50] Tashi Wangchuck v. China, WGAD Opinion No. 69/2017, Adopted Nov. 20, 2017, at ¶ 26.

[51] *Id.*

[52] Hassan Zafar Arif v. Pakistan, WGAD Opinion No. 8/2017, Adopted Apr. 19, 2017, at ¶ 36.

[53] Musallam Mohamed Hamad al-Barrak v. Kuwait, WGAD Opinion No. 20/2017, Adopted Apr. 24, 2017, at ¶ 35.

which was later confirmed by the Supreme Court. Subsequently, the Attorney General ordered the detainee's release. Having not received a response from the Government, the WGAD found the detainee was continuing to be held by the National Police, without any legal grounds, in violation of the Supreme Court order.[54]

F Detained beyond Expiration of Sentence

The WGAD has consistently found a violation under Category I where a government detains a person beyond the expiration of their sentence. There are various ways in which this had occurred:

- *Bahareh Hedayat* v. *Iran*. A women's rights activist continued to be held after she had served the entirety of her initial five-year sentence.[55] The WGAD found a Category I violation since the decision to continue her detention was contrary to the five-year statute of limitations for the crime and violated provisions of the Iranian Penal Code.[56]
- *Mohamed Hassan Aboussedra* v. *Libya*. In this case, the detainee was held in secret detention for almost two years after the Appeals Court had ordered his release.[57]
- *Hanevy Ould Dahah* v. *Mauritania*. The detainee was convicted and sentenced to six months in prison for "offending public decency" after publishing a critical article about a politician online. Despite having been held four months after the expiration of his sentence, he remained imprisoned. The WGAD found "[t]he continued detention of this person, without legal basis in domestic law, is arbitrary."[58]
- *Driss Achebrak, et al.* v. *Morocco*. In one of its earliest cases, the WGAD determined that a group of nineteen soldiers who had been convicted of involvement in an attempt on the life of the King of Morocco some twenty years prior and were reportedly being held incommunicado in an unofficial prison, had been held beyond their sentences. The WGAD found insufficient a general response from the Government that the cases of soldiers followed that event "had been settled" and "all soldiers who had been imprisoned had been released."[59]
- *Fateh Jamus, et al.* v. *Syria*. Here, two men were detained for ten years in pretrial detention before being charged, convicted, and sentenced to fifteen years in prison for national security offenses. With credit for time served and having then served an additional five years in prison, they were then held for three more years until their ultimate release. Beyond numerous violations of their right to a fair trial, the WGAD also concluded that the additional three-year term of imprisonment "manifestly cannot be justified on any legal basis."[60]

In a twist on the same theme, when the WGAD visited Bahrain, it reported that under its Code of Criminal Procedure anyone sentenced to pay a fine could be imprisoned for

---

[54] Teudo Mordán Gerónimo v. Dominican Republic, Opinion No. 8/1993, Adopted Apr. 29, 1993, at ¶ 5(f).

[55] Bahareh Hadayat v. Islamic Republic of Iran, WGAD Opinion No. 2/2016, Adopted Apr. 19, 2016, at ¶ 35.

[56] Id.

[57] Mohamed Hassan Aboussedra v. Libya, WGAD Opinion No. 16/2007, Adopted Sept. 14, 2007, at ¶ 10.

[58] Hanevy Ould Dahah v. Mauritania, WGAD Opinion No. 18/2010, Adopted Aug. 31, 2010, at ¶ 16.

[59] Driss Achebrak v. Morocco, WGAD Decision No. 38/1992, Adopted Session No. 4, at ¶ 10(a).

[60] Fateh Jamus and Issam Dimashqi v. Syria, WGAD Opinion No. 21/2000, Adopted Sept. 14, 2000, at ¶ 16.

up to one year to compel performance.[61] In addition, during its visit to Iran, the WGAD found that despite having completed their terms of imprisonment, some people were kept in prison for years because they were unable to pay the fine and/or damages and interest emanating from their criminal conviction.[62]

G Detained for Extra-Legal "Rehabilitation"

In its country mission to Indonesia, prior to the independence of East Timor, the WGAD visited the local headquarters of the Indonesia intelligence service known as *Rumah Merah* or Red House. It explained that the Government had, until recently, used the facility as a detention center for East Timorese rebels. Government officials explained that rebels apprehended by the military would be "guided and investigated," and if they had committed crimes, they would be handed over to the police with a report and subsequently charged with crimes.[63] But if not, then they would be kept at *Rumah Merah* for a period of between one to three months for "rehabilitation." The WGAD was shown the interrogation and discharge forms for a Timorese man who had been apprehended and investigated on suspicion of links with a local rebel group but neither document mentioned any legal provision under which he might have been justifiably arrested and charged.[64] The WGAD concluded:

> It follows from these observations that, firstly, this method is geared more towards incitement to denunciation than to rehabilitation and that, secondly, the detention of these individuals who have never been charged under the Indonesian Criminal Code nor tried, is manifestly devoid of any legal basis … The Working Group therefore considers that such detention for "rehabilitation purposes" must be deemed to constitute arbitrary detention within the meaning of Category I of its methods of work.[65]

H Detained on General Charges of Threat to National Security

No lawful basis for detention was found in the case of *Nestora Salgado Garcia* v. *Mexico*, concerning a dual national of the United States and Mexico working for the rights of indigenous groups.[66] The detainee was taken into custody by Mexican security forces under the pretext of national security, denied access to consular services despite her presenting her United States passport, and, later on, she was charged with specific crimes.[67] This combination of oversights on the part of Mexican authorities rendered the case a Category I violation.[68]

---

[61] *Report of the Working Group on Arbitrary Detention: Mission to Bahrain*, Commission on Human Rights, E/CN.4/2002/77/Add.2, Mar. 5, 2002, at ¶ 92.

[62] *Report of the Working Group on Arbitrary Detention: Mission to Iran*, Commission on Human Rights, E/CN.4/2004/3/Add.2, June 27, 2003, at ¶ 58.

[63] *Report of the Working Group on Arbitrary Detention: Mission to Indonesia*, Commission on Human Rights, E/CN.4/2000/4/Add.2, Aug. 12, 1999, at ¶ 58.

[64] *Id.*, at ¶ 58.

[65] *Id.*, at ¶ 59.

[66] Nestora Salgado Garcia v. Mexico, WGAD Opinion No. 56/2015, Adopted Dec. 4, 2015, at ¶ 4.

[67] *Id.*, at ¶¶ 37–40.

[68] *Id.*, at ¶ 40.

I Detained under Law Not Authorizing Detention

Laws not regarding detention cannot be the lawful basis for arresting or holding a detainee. In *Laçin Akhmadjanov v. Afghanistan and the United States*, an Uzbek national was detained by the United States at the Bagram Theatre Internment Facility in Afghanistan. The ground for detention given by the United States was the Authorization for Use of Military Force, which grants the President of the United States power over military operations. The WGAD found this general domestic law did not provide legal authority for detaining anyone without further cause.[69] This conclusion about the law was reaffirmed in *Abdul Fatah and Sa'id Jamaluddin v. Afghanistan and the United States.*[70]

J Detained across an Extradition When Maximum Sentence Exceeded

In *Hassine Bettaibi v. United Arab Emirates*, the detainee was a dual French and Tunisian national who was extradited from Algeria to the UAE in relation to a prior conviction and six-month sentence for issuing a bad check for approximately $200,000. He complained to the WGAD that he should have been given credit in the UAE for the three months he spent in detention in Algeria awaiting extradition. The WGAD agreed and although the UAE did not respond to the WGAD's communication, it found that detaining him beyond six months was arbitrary "because it is clearly impossible to invoke any legal basis justifying it."[71]

K Detained after Incomplete Extradition Request

In *Sylvestre Ningaba, et al. v. Zaire*, the three detainees were Burundian military officers detained in Zaire and accused of involvement with the assassination of President Melchior Ndadaye of Burundi in October 1993. Under an extradition treaty between the countries, the Government applied for their extradition but failed to complete the process within the required three-month timeframe. Despite an order for their release from the Attorney General's office, only one was freed, while the remaining two continued to be detained and were ultimately extradited to Burundi more than a year later. The WGAD determined their detention between the expiration of the three-month period and their extradition was arbitrary and could not "be linked to any legal basis other than mere 'reason of the state,'" citing to a report of the UN Special Rapporteur on the Situation of Human Rights in Zaire.[72]

L Detained after Illegal Border Crossing after Order for Repatriation

In *Hachimuddin Sheikh, et al. v. Bangladesh*, the detainees and their minor grandson from India were visiting family in Bangladesh, where they were arrested, pled guilty, and

---

[69] Laçin Akhmadjanov v. Afghanistan & the United States, WGAD Opinion No. 53/2016, Adopted Nov. 23, 2016, at ¶ 44.
[70] Abdul Fatah and Sa'id Jamaluddin v. Afghanistan and the United States, WGAD Opinion No. 56/2016, Adopted Nov. 24, 2016, at ¶ 40.
[71] Hassane Bettaibi v. United Arab Emirates, WGAD Opinion No. 61/2012, Adopted Nov. 21, 2012, at ¶ 13.
[72] Sylvestre Ningaba, et al. v. Zaire, WGAD Opinion No. 7/1996, Adopted May 26, 1996, at ¶ 7.

served two months in prison for not possessing passports with required entry visas. Despite having completed their sentence and there being an order for their repatriation from a judge, more than a year later they continued to be held in prison in Bangladesh. Although the Government acknowledged receipt of the communication, it did not provide a detailed response. In determining the detention to be arbitrary, the WGAD noted various procedural violations of Bangladeshi law as well as a failure of implementation of the court order to repatriate the detainees. It also noted with special concern the detention of the minor child, which it explained was in violation of Bangladesh's obligations under Article 37 of the *Convention on the Rights of the Child*, which says that state parties should not deprive minors of their liberty and that detention should only be a matter of last resort.[73]

M Detained Post-Acquittal on Unspecified New Charges

In *Wael Aly Ahmed Aly v. Egypt*, the detainee was arrested for taking part in the protests in Tahrir Square following former President Hosni Mubarak's resignation. He was charged but later acquitted of violence and vandalism in a military court. Despite that, he was then transferred to a new prison and told he was being charged with "belonging to a banned organization." The detainee insisted he was not a member of the Muslim Brotherhood but rather a member of the National Democratic Party. In its response, the Government failed to explain why a year after his acquittal the detainee had not been released nor did it refer to new charges against him. The WGAD found both Category I and III violations.[74]

N Detained in Psychiatric Hospital without Due Process

In *Cao Maobing v. China*, the detainee's family reported he was involuntarily committed to a psychiatric hospital after conducting an interview with a journalist abroad about his labor organizing at his factory. Since then, he had been detained incommunicado. The hospital claimed in a written report he was "suffering from paranoid delusions" that caused "his attempt to disturb social order."[75] The Government said claims from the detainee's family that he had been exercising his rights to freedom of expression and association were "utter nonsense."[76] As a prerequisite to deciding this case, the WGAD determined for the first time that "forcing an individual against his will to stay in [a psychiatric institution] may be compared to deprivation of liberty provided it is carried out in closed premises which the person is not allowed to leave."[77]

   In rendering its opinion, the WGAD began by observing that the allegations of the detainee and response of the Government were basically contradictory. The WGAD observed, however, that the Government did not "provide specific information to convince the Working Group of the existence of sufficient safeguards against arbitrary detention of [political opponents] for alleged mental illness ... [including] legal

---

[73] Hachimuddin Sheikh, et al. v. Bangladesh, WGAD Opinion No. 63/2012, Adopted Nov. 21, 2012, at ¶ 23.

[74] Wael Aly Ahmed Aly v. Egypt, WGAD Opinion No. 1/2012, Adopted Apr. 30, 2012, at ¶ 27.

[75] Cao Maobing v. China, WGAD Opinion No. 1/2002, Adopted June 18, 2002, at ¶ 6.

[76] *Id.*, at ¶ 6.

[77] *Id.*, at ¶ 8.

provisions governing admission to and the holding of people with mental disorders in psychiatric hospitals, the system of monitoring the admission and stay in such institutions by an independent body … to prevent abuse, and the remedies available to psychiatric patients and their families to obtain review of continued detention."[78]

Psychiatric detentions are discussed in much greater detail in Chapter 2 on Deliberation No. 7 and in Chapter 6 (VI)(B).

O Detained for Conscientious Objection When Detention Not Valid Penalty

Although usually these cases are viewed as violations of Articles 18 of the ICCPR and UDHR as matters of thought, conscience, and religion, in *Frank Yair Estrada Marin, et al.* v. *Colombia*, four different individuals were forcibly conscripted into the Colombian military. According to the Government, conscientious objection "cannot be invoked unless it is expressly provided for in law … [s]ince the possibility of its application is not provided for in law and the current circumstances under which it has to be recognized are not laid down in current legislation, the authorities cannot acknowledge it or apply it."[79] In reaching its decision here, however, the WGAD focused on the fact that under Colombian law, penalties for those who do not report for military service are exclusively of a pecuniary nature and take the form of fines. It concluded that "[i]n no case are arrest, detention, and enrollment in the army against one's expressly declared will authorized."[80] As a result, it concluded that these actions by the Government had no basis in law.

Conscientious objection is discussed in greater detail in Chapter 5 (I)(C)(1).

P Detained in Violation of Parliamentary Immunity

There is no legal basis for arresting a lawmaker with immunity that has not been withdrawn in accordance with a process established by law. Parliamentary immunity cases are rare, but where "the legal order requires the withdrawal of immunity as a precondition for depriving a person of liberty, that requirement must be observed."[81] The WGAD has supported parliamentary immunity as a measure to protect legislative processes from judicial abuses.[82] The arrest of a member of the Iraqi Council of Representatives for political reasons in *Ahmad Suleiman Jami Muhanna al-Alwani* v. *Iraq* was found to "amply justify the guarantee of parliamentary inviolability."[83] And in *Mohamed Ould Ghadde* v. *Mauritania*, the WGAD also found a Category I violation when a detained lawmaker had not been stripped of parliamentary immunity.[84] But in *Milagro Amalia Ángela Sala* v. *Argentina*, the failure of the Government to properly remove a parliamentarian's immunity was found to be a violation of her rights under

---

[78] *Id.*, at ¶ 9.
[79] Frank Yair Estrada Marin, et al. v. Colombia, WGAD Opinion No. 8/2008, Adopted May 8, 2008, at ¶ 9.
[80] *Id.*, at ¶ 22.
[81] Ahmad Suleiman Jami Muhanna al-Alwani v. Iraq, WGAD Opinion No. 36/2017, Adopted Apr. 28, 2017, at ¶ 81.
[82] *Id.*, at ¶ 81.
[83] *Id.*, at ¶ 83.
[84] Mohamed Ould Ghadde v. Mauritania, WGAD Opinion No. 33/2018, Adopted Apr. 25, 2018, at ¶ 55.

Category III, rather than under Category I.[85] Undoubtedly, the detention of a parliamentarian without the lawful removal of their immunity could fall within either Category I or Category III.

Q Detained by Non-State Actor Attributed to State

In *Timchenko, et al. v. Nigeria*, a group of sailors were detained on a ship by Lonestar Drilling Company, which claimed to hold them against a debt of $17 million for cargo lost en route to Nigeria. Their passports were seized and they were not permitted to return home. The Nigerian Federal High Court ordered local authorities to bring the sailors before the court. But the Nigerian Port Authority refused to follow the court order. Although a non-state actor was responsible for the detention, the WGAD found this did not absolve the Government of its responsibility, when it continued to "knowingly tolerate this illegal situation and, further, refuse to carry out the court injunctions" requiring the release of the sailors.[86] The WGAD therefore was able to rule that this detention had no legal basis and the Government was responsible for their ongoing detention.

Where the non-state actor is funded or on the payroll of a government, the WGAD will render their decision as usual, as if the government in question has carried out the detention.[87] However, where the government has outlawed the non-state actor, the case is considered a hostage-taking or kidnapping and falls outside the competence of the WGAD.[88]

II Ex Post Facto Laws

Articles 15(1) of the ICCPR and 11(2) of the UDHR encompass both when a detainee is being punished for acts that do not constitute an offense under domestic law and when relevant domestic law was codified only after commission of the offense. Some early *ex post facto* cases were brought under Category III, but recent opinions have classified these cases as violations under Category I.[89]

On May 17, 2010, the Government of Venezuela amended a law giving the exclusive right to buy and sell foreign currency to the Central Bank of Venezuela.[90] The law was amended to include transactions involving bonds.[91] The detainee, Hernán José Sifontes Tovar, was the Executive President of a brokerage firm known as Econoinvest Case de Bolsa, C.A. (Econoinvest).[92] Prior to the amendment, Tovar and other

---

[85] Milagro Amalia Ángela Sala v. Argentina, WGAD Opinion No. 31/2016, Adopted Aug. 24, 2016, at ¶ 114.

[86] Volodymyr Timchenko, et al. v. Nigeria, WGAD Opinion No. 30/1999, Adopted Nov. 30, 1999, at ¶ 18(b).

[87] Abdu Ahmed Abdel Salam v. Libya, WGAD Opinion No. 39/2018, Adopted Apr. 26, 2018, at ¶¶ 31–32.

[88] Olga Rodas, et al. v. Colombia, WGAD Opinion No. 25/1999, Adopted Nov. 26, 1999, at ¶ 5.

[89] Eleuterio Zárate Luján v. Peru, WGAD Opinion No. 11/2000, Adopted May 17, 2000, at ¶ 8 (finding that retroactive application of a law rendered the detention arbitrary under Category III, unlike subsequent cases).

[90] Hernán José Sifontes Tovar et al. v. Venezuela, WGAD Opinion No. 65/2011, Adopted Nov. 23, 2011, at ¶ 14.

[91] *Id.* The original text stated, "The Central Bank of Venezuela shall have exclusive competence to buy and sell foreign currency of any amount through authorized foreign exchange dealers." The law was later amended to say "The Central Bank of Venezuela shall have the exclusive competence to buy and sell foreign currency of any amount, in cash or bonds."

[92] Hernán José Sifontes Tovar, et al., at ¶¶ 4, 28, 29.

members at Econoinvest bought and sold securities known as TICC bonds (*Títulos de Interés y Capital Cubiertos*), which were issued by the Government and denominated in US dollars.[93] Tovar and other employees[94] of Econoinvest were arrested without a warrant on May 24, 2010, for their buying and selling of TICC bonds prior to the May 17 amendment.[95] They were eventually charged with illegal currency trading and criminal association.[96]

The WGAD found the detention to violate "the right that 'No one shall be held guilty of any penal offence on account of any act or omission which did not constitute a penal offence, under national or international law, at the time when it was committed'" as guaranteed by Article 11(2) of the ICCPR and Article 15 of the UDHR.[97] In making its decision, the WGAD noted that "nearly all brokerage firms" were involved in the trading of TICC bonds prior to the change in law.[98] The WGAD also observed "[t]he activities of brokerage firms were always closely supervised by the authorities of the Bolivarian Republic of Venezuela. The Act on Illegal Foreign Exchange Transactions of 2007 clearly states that 'Bond transactions shall be excluded [from the aforementioned restrictions].'"[99] In addition, the WGAD observed "[f]rom the moment the amendment was introduced, Econoinvest ceased to carry out the transactions that had become illegal."[100] Lastly, the WGAD observed "the legality of the transactions carried out prior to the amendment of the law was expressly acknowledged in a memorandum sent by the Director-General of the Legal Office of the Ministry of the Economy and Finance on 15 July 2010."[101] The WGAD concluded "[t]he fact that ... the charges refer to acts committed before they were considered offences by law shows that there was no legal basis for the detention, which was therefore arbitrary under category I."[102]

In *Waleed Abulkhair* v. *Saudi Arabia*, the detainee was also prosecuted under an *ex post facto* law. Abulkhair was arrested for alleged violations of the Anti-Cyber Crime Law in connection with his human rights work and criticism of the Government's persecution of dissenters. But after his trial began in 2013, he was convicted under the Penal Law for Crimes of Terrorism and Its Financing, which did not come into force until early 2014.[103] The WGAD considered that "a law that was not in force at the time of the commission of the impugned acts cannot serve as the legal basis for detention or imprisonment as punishment for the said acts."[104] For support, they cited UDHR Article 11(2), which reaffirms the principle of *nullum crimen sine lege* (no crime without law).

---

[93] *Id.*, at ¶ 12.

[94] *Id.*, ¶¶ 4, 28, 29 (stating "Hernán José Sifontes Tovar ... was the Executive President ... Ernesto Enrique Rangel Aguilera ... was the Deputy Director ... and Juan Carlos Carvallo Villegas ... was the Sales Director.")

[95] Hernán José Sifontes Tovar, et al., at ¶ 4.

[96] *Id.*, at ¶30.

[97] *Id.*, at ¶ 34.

[98] *Id.*, at ¶ 31.

[99] *Id.*

[100] *Id.*, at ¶ 32.

[101] *Id.*, at ¶ 33.

[102] *Id.*, at ¶ 36.

[103] Waleed Abulkhair v. Saudi Arabia, WGAD Opinion No. 10/2018, Adopted Apr. 19, 2018, at ¶ 41.

[104] *Id.*, at ¶ 42.

III *Ne Bis In Idem* or Double Jeopardy

The Latin *ne bis in idem* translates as "not twice in the same [thing]" and is a legal doctrine that says no legal action can be instituted twice for the same cause of action. Although the concept originated in Roman Civil Law, it is equivalent to the prohibition against double jeopardy found in common law jurisdictions. Ordinarily, the WGAD would determine a violation of this principle to be a Category III case because it is contrary to Article 14(7) of the ICCPR, which states that "[n]o one shall be liable to be tried or punished again for an offence for which he has already been finally convicted or acquitted in accordance with the law and penal procedure of each country."

At the same time, however, a conviction obtained in violation of this prohibition also has no foundation in law and is also consequently a Category I case. For the purposes of the detainee, the finding of a violation under either Category I or III is sufficient to determine a detention to be arbitrary and in violation of international law, so where a country is a party to the ICCPR, the WGAD will generally find a violation under Category III.

But in *Mohammed Salim* v. *Pakistan*, where the country was not a party to the ICCPR, the WGAD appropriately characterized such a violation under Category I. In this case, the detainee was a minor child who was arrested with adults for alleged involvement in the murder of three police officers. He was sentenced to death in a military court but the following month acquitted on appeal. A month after that, the military court in which he had been convicted and then acquitted was abolished and declared unconstitutional, with convictions and sentences handed down but not yet implemented declared null and void. With these developments, a few months later Salim was rearrested, charged with the same offense, and detained. At the time of this case, he was awaiting trial. The WGAD determined that Salim had been "rearrested by police on the same charges as those in respect of which he had been acquitted, this being contrary to the *non bis in idem* rule set forth in Article 13 of the Constitution and a general principle of law."[105] It further observed this was also in violation of the UN Standard Minimum Rules for the Administration of Juvenile Justice.[106]

IV Detention after Amnesty

International law has little to say about any right to amnesty. Scholarly articles focus primarily on the duty to prosecute and the trend of states to grant amnesty for heinous international crimes as part of truth and reconciliation processes.[107] The ICCPR only states "[a]nyone sentenced to death shall have the right to seek pardon or commutation of the sentence. Amnesty, pardon or commutation of the sentence of death may be granted in all cases."[108] The UDHR does not mention amnesty. Rule 159 of the International Committee of the Red Cross's report on customary international humanitarianism also mentions amnesty in the context of armed conflicts:

---

[105] Mohammed Salim v. Pakistan, WGAD Opinion No. 6/2000, Adopted May 17, 2000, at ¶ 8.

[106] *Id.*

[107] *See, e.g.* Max Pensky, *Amnesty on Trial: Impunity, Accountability, and the Norms of International Law*, 1 Ethics & Global Policy 1 (2008) (Nov. 2018), www.binghamton.edu/philosophy/people/docs/pensky-amnesty-on-trial.pdf.

[108] ICCPR, at Art. 6(4).

At the end of hostilities, the authorities in power must endeavor to grant the broadest possible amnesty to persons who have participated in a non-international armed conflict, or those deprived of their liberty for reasons related to the armed conflict, with the exception of persons suspected of, accused of or sentenced for war crimes.[109]

Arbitrary detention cases that involve the failure to release a detainee after a grant of amnesty are exceedingly rare. The WGAD has handled the situation only one time in *Janie Model v. United Arab Emirates*.[110] Janie Model, a British citizen, was arrested in November 1999 in Dubai and eventually found guilty of credit card fraud.[111] He was granted amnesty in December 2003.[112] However, he was later informed that he would not be released until he paid a fine of 94,000 dirhams (US$25,000).[113] In its reply to the WGAD's communication, the UAE stated "[t]his person was included in the amnesty decree issued by His Highness Sheikh Mohammed Bin Rashid Al Maktum, the Crown Prince of Dubai and Minister of Defence … However, his release was suspended because he was implicated in a civil case."[114]

The WGAD began its analysis by clarifying that a grant of amnesty *can* be made contingent on discharging an ancillary pecuniary obligation imposed by the sentencing court for the offense for which the individual is being detained.[115] The WGAD also explained that an individual can be prevented from leaving a country until a civil law debt is paid or when pending civil litigation exists.[116] In Model's situation, however, it said "[t]he only ground for excluding Mr. Model from the amnesty was his alleged implication in a civil case, which apparently had nothing to do with his criminal conviction."[117] Furthermore "the Government did not invoke any legal basis explaining how and why involvement in a civil case could hinder someone's release from prison after being amnestied."[118] For these reasons the WGAD held "[t]he deprivation of liberty of Janie Model subsequent to the date he should have been released after being amnestied is arbitrary, being in contravention of article 9 of the [UDHR], and falls within category I."[119]

In *Mohammad Hossein Rafiee Hanood v. Iran*, the detainee was eligible for amnesty by operation of law, but it was not applied to him.[120] Under Article 10 of Iran's Amnesty Directive of March 2016, prisoners over the age of sixty-five who had served one-fifth or more of their sentence were entitled to early release. Rafiee, who was 71-years-old at the time of the WGAD opinion and had served over a year in jail, had earned his amnesty by law (other potentially arbitrary characteristics of his detention aside). Since

---

[109] Jean-Marie Henckaerts & Louise Doswald-Beck, Customary International Humanitarian Law, Vol. I: Rules (Cambridge University Press, 2005).

[110] Janie Model v. United Arab Emirates, WGAD Opinion No. 7/2004, Adopted May 27, 2004.

[111] *Id.*, at ¶ 5.

[112] *Id.*

[113] *Id.*

[114] *Id.*, at ¶ 6.

[115] *Id.*, at ¶ 8.

[116] *Id.*, at ¶ 9.

[117] *Id.*, at ¶ 8.

[118] *Id.*, at ¶ 8.

[119] *Id.*, at ¶ 10.

[120] Mohammad Hossein Rafiee Hanood v. Iran, WGAD Opinion No. 25/2016, Adopted Aug. 22, 2016, at ¶ 26.

he had not received it, the WGAD found his continued detention arbitrary under Category I.[121]

V Extraordinary Rendition

The practice of extraordinary rendition is the government-sponsored abduction and extrajudicial transfer of a person from one country to another, often to be interrogated in countries with less rigorous regulations for humane treatment of prisoners. In its 2007 Annual Report, the WGAD explains that "both human rights law and the anti-terror conventions adopted under the auspices of the United Nations enshrine a clear preference for extradition as the legal framework for such transfers. The practice of so-called 'renditions,' on the contrary, because it is aimed at avoiding all procedural safeguards, is not compatible with international law."[122]

Although often justified by governments as defensible and claimed to be legal in the name of national security, extraordinary rendition entails a broad range of due process violations found under Category III. Nevertheless, at the outset, the WGAD has determined that the actual rendition itself is first and foremost *ultra vires* and therefore beginning with the abduction is a Category I violation.

The case of *Zhiya Kassem Khammam al Hussain* v. *Saudi Arabia* presents a typical fact pattern in extraordinary renditions. The detainee, a citizen of Iraq residing in Kuwait, was taken by twenty members of the Kuwaiti State Security Agency and detained for two weeks before being sent by plane to Riyadh, Saudi Arabia. He was not given an arrest warrant, informed of reasons for his detention, or given the opportunity to challenge his transfer to Saudi Arabia. Since his arrival in Saudi Arabia, the detainee had been denied access to counsel, the ability to challenge the lawfulness of his detention, and access to family visits. In its response, the Government acknowledged the basic facts of the case but argued his prolonged detention was justified because he was involved in illegal fundraising that could be linked to groups threatening regional stability. In finding a violation of Article 9 of the UDHR under Category I, the WGAD cited to its prior annual report defining and condemning the practice of extraordinary renditions. It stated the WGAD "can only conclude that the detention of Mr. Al Hussain is devoid of any legal basis. The circumstance in itself already renders his detention contrary to applicable international norms and constitutes a violation of the right to liberty irrespective of the nature and motives of the accusations against him."[123]

In the similar case of *Walid Muhammad Shahir Muhammad al-Qadasi, et al.* v. *Yemen*, the three detainees were at various points in the custody of the United States before being transferred to Yemen. By the time their case was filed to the WGAD, some six months after their arrival in Yemen, the Government claimed it was still waiting to receive files from American authorities to transfer them to the prosecutor. The WGAD noted "with concern that the transfers of the three persons experienced before being detained in Yemen occurred outside the confines of any legal procedure, such as

---

[121] *Id.*

[122] *Report of the Working Group on Arbitrary Detention*, Human Rights Council, A/HRC/4/40, Jan. 7, 2007, at ¶ 2.

[123] Zhiya Kassem Khammam al Hussain v. Saudi Arabia, WGAD Opinion No. 19/2007, Adopted Nov. 22, 2007, at ¶ 20.

extradition, and do not allow the individuals access to counsel or to any judicial authority to contest the transfers."[124] It further noted "[n]o charges have been made by the Government against these three men. They have not been informed of any accusation against them, nor have been brought before any judicial authority. No legal procedure has been followed to accuse them. Their deprivation of liberty is, as such, devoid of any legal basis."[125]

The WGAD has also examined cases where governments abduct people from another sovereign state and bring them back to their own country. The most famous of these cases was *Humberto Alvarez Machain* v. *United States*. The detainee in this case had been charged with taking part in the kidnapping and murder of Drug Enforcement Administration (DEA) Special Agent Enrique Camarena Salazar in Mexico. He was, as described by the US Supreme Court, "abducted" to the United States by third parties directed by the DEA. The detainee complained that the United States had violated the extradition treaty between the US and Mexico.[126] Despite winning on these grounds in the Federal District Court and Ninth Circuit Court of Appeals, the US Supreme Court held that "forcible abduction does not prohibit ... trial in the United States court for violation of criminal law."[127] The detainee in this case was subsequently tried, acquitted, and then repatriated to Mexico more than two years after the abduction. Although the detainee had been released, the WGAD invoked its authority under its then Methods of Work that it "reserves the right to decide, on a case-by-case basis, whether or not the deprivation of liberty was arbitrary, notwithstanding the release of the person concerned."[128] The WGAD then examined the range of issues presented by this complex case and concluded that an "abduction" was contrary to the object and purpose of an extradition treaty and "like all conventions on the subject, is a comprehensive legal text which regulates the grounds and procedures for surrendering wanted persons and it details cases in which extradition can be denied. Obviously abduction is prohibited." It therefore concluded "[t]he deprivation of freedom, as a consequence of the arrest [in the United States], is therefore arbitrary."[129]

In a different context, *Mustafa Dirani* v. *Israel*, a Lebanese citizen and leader of a pro-Iranian militia was abducted from his home in Lebanon by Israeli commandos and taken back to Israel, where he was held incommunicado in administrative detention for six years. The detainee claimed this was to extract information about the whereabouts of an Israeli soldier, Ron Arad, who had been captured in Lebanon years earlier. Although the Government did not respond to its communication, the WGAD concluded that because he was only allowed legal representation more than four years after his abduction and had no recourse to challenge his detention over that time, his detention was "devoid of any legal basis."[130]

---

[124] Walid Muhammad Shahir Muhammad al-Qadasi, et al. v. Yemen, WGAD Opinion No. 47/2005, Adopted Nov. 30, 2005, at ¶ 19.

[125] *Id.*, at ¶ 20.

[126] Humberto Alvarez Machain v. United States of America, WGAD Decision No. 48/1993, Adopted Sept. 30, 1993, at ¶ 5(a).

[127] *Id.*, at ¶ 5(d).

[128] *Id.*, at ¶ 5(g).

[129] *Id.*, at ¶ 5(o).

[130] Mustafa Dirani v. Israel, WGAD Opinion No. 31/2000, Adopted Nov. 27, 2000, at ¶ 10.

The WGAD has also commented on the practice of extraordinary renditions more generally when visiting countries that regularly employ the practice. For example, in Equatorial Guinea, it reported it has received information about "the kidnapping by Government agents of nationals of Equatorial Guinea, who are taken from neighbouring countries to Malabo and held in secret detention there."[131] It further said that in some cases the Government has not even acknowledged these individuals were being detained, which meant they were technically missing. And it reported this was the case for four individuals – Juan Ondo Abaga, Felipe Esono Ntutumu, Florencio Ela Bibang, and Antimo Edu Nchama – who were unavailable to be interviewed by the WGAD on its visit to Black Beach military prison. Despite all four reportedly having refugee status in the countries where they were living, each was transferred to Equatorial Guinea on a military aircraft to Black Beach prison and had been detained without the benefit of any legal proceedings.[132]

[131] *Report of the Working Group on Arbitrary Detention: Mission to Equatorial Guinea*, Human Rights Council, A/HRC/7/4/Add.4, Feb. 18, 2008, at ¶ 69.

[132] *Id.*, at ¶ 70.

5   Category II

Violation of Fundamental Rights and Freedoms

According to the WGAD, Category II detentions arise under the following circumstances:

> When the deprivation of liberty results from the exercise of the rights or freedoms guaranteed by articles 7, 13-14, and 18-21 of the Universal Declaration of Human Rights and, insofar as States parties are concerned, by articles 12, 18-19, 21-22, and 25-27 of the International Covenant on Civil and Political Rights (category II).[1]

The fundamental rights and freedoms covered by this category include the right to equality under the law (UDHR Article 7 and ICCPR Article 26), freedom of movement (UDHR Article 13 and ICCPR Article 12), freedom to seek asylum from persecution (UDHR Article 14), freedom of religion (UDHR Article 18 and ICCPR Article 18), freedom of expression (UDHR Article 19 and ICCPR Article 19), freedom of assembly (UDHR Article 20 and ICCPR Article 21), freedom of association (UDHR Article 20 and ICCPR Article 22), freedom to participate in public affairs (UDHR Article 21 and ICCPR Article 25), and the right of minorities to enjoy their culture (ICCPR Article 27).

Most Category II cases relate to the freedoms of religion, expression, association, and assembly; fewer cases have been found arbitrary under Category II in relation to equal protection, freedom of movement, freedom to participate in public affairs, the right to seek asylum, and the rights of minority cultures. Each of these rights will be discussed specifically in the course of this chapter.

Violations of multiple rights may occur, and there are some areas in which the protections offered by these rights overlaps. Although the WGAD almost always confines itself to discussions of the rights enumerated specifically under the definition of Category II detentions, it will occasionally refer to non-enumerated rights. For example, it found a violation of Article 23 of the UDHR, which protects the right to work, where Venezuelan Judge María Lourdes Afiuni Mora had been harassed and detained because of a decision she had made in her professional role as a judge.[2] It also found that the detention of two doctors conducting HIV/AIDS prevention programs violated the right to education protected by Article 26 of the UDHR.[3] Finally, in several cases it has found violations

---

[1] *Methods of Work of the Working Group*, Human Rights Council, A/HRC/36/38, July 13, 2017, at ¶ 8.
[2] María Lourdes Afiuni Mora v. Venezuela, WGAD Opinion No. 20/2010, Adopted Sept. 1, 2010.
[3] Dr. Arash Alaei & Dr. Kamiar Alaei v. Iran, WGAD Opinion No. 6/2009, Adopted May 7, 2009.

of the right to one's privacy and reputation, including the enjoyment of the right to family life, enshrined in Article 17 of the ICCPR and Article 12 of the UDHR.[4]

In interpreting these rights, the WGAD relies on a variety of international human rights law sources. Particular weight is given to the interpretation of the Human Rights Committee (HR Committee), which is the treaty-monitoring body for the ICCPR. This includes the General Comments of the HR Committee, which are devoted to the interpretations of particular treaty provisions, as well as Views adopted by the HR Committee in individual cases considered under the *Optional Protocol to the ICCPR*. Additional sources include other UN Special Procedures,[5] declarations or resolutions from UN bodies,[6] and other international legal authorities.[7] The WGAD may also refer to other obligations and guidelines, which are relevant to a particular state.

At the request of the prior UN Commission for Human Rights (UNCHR), since 1996 the WGAD has only applied the ICCPR to states that are parties to it. Because of the small number of states that have still not ratified the ICCPR and the much richer commentary developed for these treaty rights, this chapter's discussion of international law focuses on applying the ICCPR. But significant differences between the ICCPR and UDHR will also be noted.

Evidentiary Considerations

Although the WGAD's general approach to evidence described earlier applies to Category II cases, when states violate fundamental rights and freedoms like those described here, they often cloak their persecution of a detainee behind pretextual charges. This raises special evidentiary issues because the WGAD regularly has to look behind charges to ascertain the real motives of the detaining government.

For example, the WGAD has said it requires more than a "simple deduction" that the exercise of fundamental human rights were the cause of an arrest or detention.[8] In *Omar Abdulrahman Ahmed Youssef Mabrouk* v. *Egypt and Kuwait*, the source believed that the detainee's arrest and imprisonment on charges that he had joined a "banned group" that

---

[4] Elie Dib Ghaled v. United Arab Emirates, WGAD Opinion No. 2/1998, Adopted May 13, 1998 (an indictment for fornication, where a marriage between a Muslim and Christian was considered invalid, was a violation of the right to privacy protected in Article 12); François Ayissi, et al. v. Cameroon, WGAD Opinion No. 22/2006, Adopted Aug. 31, 2006 (finding a violation of ICCPR Article 7 where Cameroon detained individuals under a law criminalizing homosexuality); María Lourdes Afiuni Mora v. Venezuela, WGAD Opinion No. 20/2010, Adopted Sept. 1, 2010 (finding a violation of UDHR Article 12 for unspecified reasons but likely because the detention interfered with the professional reputation of Judge Afiuni); Il Jo, et al. v. Democratic People's Republic of North Korea, WGAD Opinion No. 80/2017, Adopted Nov. 22, 2017, at ¶ 37 (finding that the detention of a North Korean citizen for accepting financial support from his South Korean sister violated the right to family life).

[5] Karmelo Landa Mendibe v. Spain, WGAD Opinion No. 17/2009, Adopted Sept. 4, 2009, at ¶ 45; Thulani Rudolf Maseko v. Swaziland, WGAD Opinion No. 6/2015, Adopted Apr. 22, 2015, at ¶ 28.

[6] Hassan Ahmed Hassan Al-Diqqi v. United Arab Emirates, WGAD Opinion No. 8/2009, Adopted Sept. 1, 2009, at ¶ 14 (citing to the UN General Assembly's Declaration on Human Rights Defenders); Mohamed bin Abdullah bin Ali Al-Abdulkareem v. Saudi Arabia, WGAD Opinion No. 43/2011, Adopted Sept. 2, 2011, at ¶ 14 (citing to Human Rights Council Resolution 12/16).

[7] For example, the International Court of Justice in Nasrin Sotoudeh v. Iran, WGAD Opinion No. 21/2011, Adopted May 5, 2011.

[8] Omar Abdulrahman Ahmed Youssef Mabrouk v. Egypt and Kuwait, WGAD Opinion No. 60/2016, Adopted Nov. 25, 2016, at ¶ 26.

committed "Internet-related crimes" were carried out in connection with the detainee's expression of political opinions through Facebook and participation in demonstrations.[9] However, the source admitted it was merely assuming the causal link between these activities and Mabrouk's arrest. The WGAD concluded this was merely one of multiple possible deductions – as such, they were not prepared to agree that Mabrouk's detention was arbitrary under Category II.[10] At the same time, however, the WGAD has also said that when individuals who are known human rights defenders are detained, their detention is subjected to a "particularly intense review."[11]

In *Nasrin Sotoudeh* v. *Iran*, a prominent Iranian human rights lawyer was sentenced to eleven years in prison based on charges of acting against national security and cooperating with a human rights body.[12] In addressing Sotoudeh's detention, the WGAD first identified the source's documentation of her extensive work as a human rights defender, noting her human rights advocacy and her work to represent those whose rights have been violated. It specifically referenced the *Declaration on Human Rights Defenders*, which ensures the right to make complaints regarding human rights violations and to provide qualified legal assistance in relation to the defense of human rights.[13]

The WGAD then found that the Government had not responded to the prima facie case presented by the source that Sotoudeh's detention was a result of the exercise of her fundamental rights and freedoms. As noted before, the Government cannot merely reference judgments or decisions; the WGAD rather requires "information that directly rebuts the claims that human rights guarantees have been violated."[14] The WGAD applied this approach to the detention of Sotoudeh, finding that the Government had failed to show that Sotoudeh was not detained for her work as a human rights defender and the exercise of her fundamental rights and freedoms.[15]

The same evidentiary approach was adopted in *Pierre-Claver Mbonimpa* v. *Burundi*, involving a Burundian human rights activist and founder of the Association for the Protection of Human Rights and Detained Persons. During a radio program in 2014, Mbonimpa publicly accused the youth wing of the ruling party of receiving weapons and military training in the eastern Democratic Republic of the Congo. A few days later, he was arrested and subsequently charged with inciting civil disobedience, spreading false rumors, and acts hostile to national security.[16] The source emphasized that the detention occurred in an environment of growing hostility toward human rights, in which other human rights defenders had been subject to sanctions.[17]

The Government did not respond to the communication. Accordingly, the WGAD began by reiterating the general evidentiary approach by which the burden of proof lies with the Government once a source makes prima facie allegations of an arbitrary

---

[9] *Id.*, at ¶ 9.

[10] *Id.*, at ¶ 26.

[11] Eskinder Nega v. Ethiopia, WGAD Opinion No. 62/2012, Adopted Nov. 21, 2012, at ¶ 39.

[12] Nasrin Sotoudeh v. Iran, WGAD Opinion No. 21/2011, Adopted May 5, 2011, at ¶ 5.

[13] *Id.*, at ¶ 29 (citing UN General Assembly, *Declaration on Human Rights Defenders*, A/RES/53/144, Mar. 8, 1999, at Art. 9(3)).

[14] *Id.*, at ¶ 31.

[15] Nasrin Sotoudeh, at ¶¶ 31–32.

[16] Pierre-Claver Mbonimpa v. Burundi, WGAD Opinion No. 33/2014, Adopted Aug. 28, 2014, at ¶¶ 3–6.

[17] *Pierre Claver Mbonimpa*, FOREIGN POLICY, 2015 (Nov. 2018),http://2015globalthinkers.foreignpolicy.com/#!advocates/detail/mbonimpa.

detention that violates international requirements.[18] It concluded that where there is "reliable prima facie information ... that a known human rights defender has been deprived of his liberty on questionable charges, where the conviction is not based on trustworthy evidence and where, in fact, the person has been punished for exercising his fundamental rights," the Government must provide the WGAD with specific information to justify the conviction.[19] As the Government failed to meet this burden, his detention was arbitrary.[20]

This evidentiary approach is also relevant where a human rights defender is convicted of an ordinary crime. A pretextual use of legitimate laws to improperly target activists is a recurring theme where the WGAD finds violations under Category II. For example, charges of extortion or assault have been brought against human rights defenders where the real basis for the detention is the exercise of fundamental rights and freedoms.[21] Likewise, a Chinese editor who published articles related to financial corruption and human rights activists was convicted on fraud charges. Finding that the detention was arbitrary and violated the editor's freedom of expression, the WGAD reiterated that where a human rights defender is detained for committing a regular crime, and there is a reliable allegation that the person is actually detained for exercising his rights, the Government has the burden of offering specific evidence in support of the conviction.[22]

Limitations and Derogations

Article 29 of the UDHR provides that the enumerated rights may be limited where necessary to protect the rights and freedoms of others, or to meet "the just requirements of morality, public order and the general welfare in a democratic society."[23] Under the ICCPR, limitations on the individual rights contain slight variations, and the text of the relevant Article should be relied on. Note, however, that these variations are often minor and the jurisprudence regarding limitations on one right may help to inform interpretations on another right. The WGAD's discussion of the limitations on the right to freedom of expression, for example, is especially well-developed and accordingly is a particularly rich source for guiding interpretations of identical limitation language contained in other rights.

Although the limitation provisions of the ICCPR vary, some key principles apply generally to their interpretation. The key guidelines for interpretation of these provisions are the *Siracusa Principles on the Limitation and Derogation Provisions in the International Covenant on Civil and Political Rights*, adopted in 1985 by the UN Economic and Social Council. These principles require strict interpretation of limitation provisions, and specify that interpretations should be made in light of the relevant right and so as not to jeopardize the core meaning of the right itself.[24] They also identify key elements of the

---

[18] Pierre-Claver Mbonimpa, at ¶ 20.

[19] *Id.*, at ¶¶ 20–21.

[20] *Id.*, at ¶ 27.

[21] Akzam Turgunov v. Uzbekistan, WGAD Opinion No. 53/2011, Adopted Nov. 17, 2011; Yorm Bopha v. Cambodia, WGAD Opinion No. 24/2013, Adopted Aug. 28, 2013.

[22] Wang Hanfei v. China, WGAD Opinion No. 21/2014, Adopted Aug. 25, 2014, at ¶ 30.

[23] UDHR, at Art. 29.

[24] UN Economic and Social Council, *Siracusa Principles on the Limitation and Derogation Provisions in the International Covenant on Civil and Political Rights*, E/CN.4/1985/4, Annex (1985), Principles 3–4, 7 (hereinafter Siracusa Principles).

limitation provisions – limitations must be necessary, which includes the element of proportionality, they must be provided for in the law, they must be applied with no more restrictive means than is necessary, and they should not be applied in an arbitrary manner.[25]

In addition to the limitation provisions contained in individual rights, the ICCPR provides that certain rights may be derogated from during times of public emergency, if specified procedures and guarantees are respected. The derogation provision of the ICCPR is contained in a separate article, rather than being specific to each right. Particular issues raised by the derogation of specific rights will also be addressed in the discussion on individual rights.

The WGAD has emphasized, in language drawn from the Council of Europe Commissioner for Human Rights, there is an "urgency of reverting to ordinary procedures and safeguards, by ending the state of emergency as soon as possible. Until then, the authorities should start rolling back the deviations from such procedures and safeguards as quickly as possible, through a nuanced, sector-by-sector and case-by-case approach."[26]

Article 4 of the ICCPR provides that if a public emergency that "threatens the life of the nation" is officially proclaimed, states may derogate from its obligations under the ICCPR, but only "to the extent strictly required by the exigencies of the situation."[27] This applies generally to the rights contained in the ICCPR; however, certain rights are non-derogable and must be fully respected even in times of emergency. Of the ICCPR rights specifically covered by Category II, only Article 18's right to freedom of religion is non-derogable. However, the HR Committee has noted that where a State may sufficiently respond to a threat based solely on the limitation provisions of derogable rights, the derogation provisions should not be relied on: for example, in instances of a mass demonstration that includes violent acts, the limitation provisions in Article 21 of the ICCPR are generally sufficient and derogation from the right would not be justified.[28]

States that rely on the derogation provisions of the ICCPR must meet a notice requirement, by which they must immediately inform other State parties to the ICCPR regarding which provisions have been derogated from and the rationale for such derogation. The HR Committee in *Silva, et al.* v. *Uruguay* noted that while the substantive right of states to derogate from specific rights is not dependent on the notification requirements, a failure to follow the procedure led the Committee to conclude that there was not a valid reason for the derogation.[29] The WGAD appears to have taken a similar approach, by which a failure to provide notice casts doubt on the legitimacy of detentions under supposed states of emergency. In *Peto Solomo, et al.* v. *Eritrea*, it emphasized Eritrea had neither formally proclaimed a state of emergency nor notified states parties to the ICCPR of any derogations from its provisions, before finding that the detention of eleven individuals who criticized the Government was arbitrary.[30]

---

[25] *Id.*, at Principles 5, 7, 10–11.

[26] Rebii Metin Görgeç v. Turkey, WGAD Opinion No. 1/2017, Adopted Apr. 19, 2017, at ¶ 55.

[27] ICCPR, at Art. 4(1).

[28] *General Comment No. 29*, Human Rights Committee, CCPR/C/21/Rev.1/Add.11 (2001), at ¶ 5.

[29] Silva, et al. v. Uruguay, Communication No. 34/1978, Human Rights Committee, CCPR/C/12/D/34/1978, Apr. 8, 1981, at ¶ 8.3.

[30] Peto Solomo, et al. v. Eritrea, WGAD Opinion No. 23/2007, Adopted Nov. 27, 2007, at ¶ 25.

Similarly, the WGAD has confirmed that even where notice of derogation from a particular right is given, this does not automatically extend to other rights. *Wa'ad al-Hidmy* v. *Israel* involved a Palestinian student detained for his involvement in demonstrations organized by a banned organization. Although Israel had declared a state of emergency and derogated from its Article 9 obligations, it had not specified derogation from any other right contained in the ICCPR. Because the youth was detained for the exercise of his right to freedom of opinion and expression by giving a public speech, Israel had improperly violated his right to freedom of expression without giving notice that it had derogated from its responsibility to protect this right.[31] Finally, the WGAD has expressed concern over emergency laws that remain in operation even after the Government has announced the termination of the derogations, as was the case where Sri Lanka informed the HR Committee of such termination but continued to enforce emergency regulations.[32]

Any permissible derogations must also follow the principles of necessity and proportionality.[33] The WGAD underscored these limitations in *Filep Jacob Semuel Karma* v. *Indonesia*, involving an individual arrested by Indonesia in connection with a peaceful flag-raising ceremony in support of independence for the Papua province. Indonesia had a number of emergency laws, some dating back several decades, which had never been abolished.[34] After raising concerns about these laws generally, the WGAD cited to General Comment No. 29 of the HR Committee to emphasize that all emergency laws must be necessary and proportionate.[35] It also referenced its own report on an earlier visit to Indonesia, which had criticized the emergency laws and recommended a set of guidelines to ensure domestic law was brought into compliance with Article 4 – a legal procedure for declaring a state of emergency, a listing of non-derogable rights, and measures to ensure proportionality is respected both in time and location. This latter element means that emergency laws should be limited to what is necessary in terms of duration and geographic zones covered, and renewal of the declared emergency should be subject to specific conditions. After raising concerns over the emergency laws, the WGAD found Karma had been detained arbitrarily, based on the exercise of his right to freedom of opinion and expression, assembly, and association.[36] And in its report on its country mission, it further emphasized that those arrested for flag raising were detained mostly for having peacefully exercised their beliefs.[37]

The element of proportionality, particularly important in the arbitrary detention context, was also addressed in *Wa'ad al-Hidmy* v. *Israel* regarding the Palestinian youth detained by Israel. The WGAD there noted that a two-year detention of a teenager, based solely on accusations that he participated in demonstrations by a banned organization, is disproportionate in relation to *any* public emergency. The WGAD concluded by noting that international humanitarian law cannot create "legal black holes" in which the

---

[31] Wa'ad al-Hidmy v. Israel, WGAD Opinion No. 9/2010, Adopted May 7, 2010, at ¶ 23.

[32] Gunasundaram Jayasundaram v. Sri Lanka, WGAD Opinion No. 38/2012, Adopted Aug. 31, 2012, at ¶ 29.

[33] General Comment No. 29, at ¶ 3–4; Siracusa Principles, at Principle 51.

[34] Report of the Working Group on Arbitrary Detention on Visit to Indonesia, Commission on Human Rights, E/CN.4/2000/4/Add.2, Aug. 12, 1999, at ¶¶ 41–49.

[35] General Comment No. 29, at ¶ 102.

[36] Filep Jacob Semuel Karma v. Indonesia, WGAD Opinion No. 48/2011, Adopted Sept. 2, 2011.

[37] Report of Working Group on the Mission to Indonesia, at ¶ 65.

protections of human rights law are suspended.[38] This case accordingly reflects the WGAD's response to many of the detentions in which states claim a state of emergency justifies a derogation – the states generally fail to show that a state of emergency that meets these requirements exists, which the WGAD either explicitly or implicitly recognizes before proceeding to apply the relevant provisions of the ICCPR and UDHR.[39]

I Freedom of Religion

What is frequently described as the right to freedom of religion is actually a much more comprehensive right, referred to in the ICCPR and UDHR as the "freedom of thought, conscience and religion," or later as "religion or belief." Freedom of religion should accordingly be understood to incorporate freedom of thought, conscience, religion, or belief.

Article 18 of the ICCPR explains:

1. Everyone shall have the right to freedom of thought, conscience and religion. This right shall include freedom to have or to adopt a religion or belief of his choice, and freedom, either individually or in community with others and in public or private, to manifest his religion or belief in worship, observance, practice and teaching.
2. No one shall be subject to coercion which would impair his freedom to have or to adopt a religion or belief of his choice.
3. Freedom to manifest one's religion or beliefs may be subject only to such limitations as are prescribed by law and are necessary to protect public safety, order, health, or morals or the fundamental rights and freedoms of others.
4. The States Parties to the present Covenant undertake to have respect for the liberty of parents and, when applicable, legal guardians to ensure the religious and moral education of their children in conformity with their own convictions.

And under the UDHR, more broadly:

Everyone has the right to freedom of thought, conscience and religion; this right includes freedom to change his religion or belief, and freedom, either alone or in community with others and in public or private, to manifest his religion or belief in teaching, practice, worship and observance.

Although Category II only references the rights protected by the ICCPR and UDHR, it should be noted that freedom of religion is also guaranteed in regional human rights treaties, including Article 8 of the *African Charter on Human and Peoples' Rights*, Article 12 of the *American Convention on Human Rights*, and Article 9 of the *European Convention on Human Rights*. Additional sources for interpreting the right, both of which have been cited in WGAD opinions, are the HR Committee's General Comment 22 and the *Declaration on the Elimination of All Forms of Intolerance and of Discrimination Based on Religion or Belief*.[40]

---

[38] Wa'ad al-Hidmy v. Israel, WGAD Opinion No. 9/2010, Adopted May 7, 2010, at ¶¶ 25–26.

[39] *See, e.g.*, Filep Jacob Semuel Karma v. Indonesia, WGAD Opinion No. 48/2011, Adopted Sept. 2, 2011; Gunasundaram Jayasundaram v. Sri Lanka, WGAD Opinion No. 38/2012, Adopted Aug. 31, 2012.

[40] Saeed Abedinigalangashi v. Iran, WGAD Opinion No. 18/2013, Adopted Aug. 26, 2013, at ¶ 25; Alimujiang Yimiti v. China, WGAD Opinion No. 29/2008, Adopted Sept. 26, 2008, at ¶ 15.

The right to freedom of religion was generally well established and widely recognized even at the time of the drafting of the UDHR and ICCPR. Indeed, Article 18 of the ICCPR did not occasion any reservations or declarations of interpretation from any states (with one legally insignificant exception).[41] Controversy over the scope of the right usually arises in the context of establishing when a government may permissibly limit the right. The freedom of religion is a non-derogable right, and cannot be suspended in times of emergency or otherwise, as is provided by Article 4 of the ICCPR and reflected in human rights law generally. In addition, the freedom to have a religion or belief is absolute; however, "(f)reedom to *manifest* one's religion or beliefs ..." is subject to certain permissible limitations as is articulated in ICCPR article 18(3).

This is an important distinction, as states often justify the detention of individuals based on religion or other belief as necessary for public safety, security, or other reasons. Accordingly, the following discussion will look first at what qualifies as the absolute right to freedom of religion, before turning to the manifestation of religion or belief and its permissible limitations. The section will end with a look at the WGAD's treatment of state targeting of individual groups through arbitrary detention or other means.

A *Freedom of Religion, Belief, Conscience, and Thought*

Religion, belief, conscience, and thought are recognized as having a special status due to the necessity of respect for the freedom of a person's inner life. Accordingly, this right is absolute. In discussing the importance of including freedom of thought in the language of the UDHR, Rene Cassin of France noted the "metaphysical significance" of freedom of thought, and its status as an "unconditional right." Even unexpressed inner thought, he noted, needed protection from indirect attacks by which states may seek to control or punish one's inner thoughts or beliefs.[42] Arbitrary detention provides a good example of just such an indirect attack, when it is used as a response to the exercise of this absolute right to freedom in one's inner thoughts and beliefs.

Because of this important observation, the right is interpreted broadly. Thought, conscience, religion, and belief are not defined in either the UDHR or ICCPR, or human rights law. They instead should be interpreted in a flexible and open manner. As General Comment 22 observes: "The right to freedom of thought, conscience and religion (which includes the freedom to hold beliefs) ... is far-reaching and profound; it encompasses freedom of thought on all matters, personal conviction and the commitment to religion or belief." Thus the right applies equally to traditional and institutional religions as well as newly established or informal ones.

Similarly, atheistic and nontheist beliefs are also protected.[43] The WGAD's jurisprudence reflects this breadth – it does not distinguish, for example, between older religions and beliefs or relatively newer ones such as Baha'i or Falun Gong. It should be noted, however, that where a detainee does not profess religious allegiance or professes religious

---

[41] Manfred Nowak, U.N. Covenant on Civil and Political Rights: CCPR Commentary 408 (N.P. Engel, 2nd ed., 2005) (noting Mexico's declaration of interpretation referenced the usual limitations on the right, which is likely already incorporated by ICCPR Article 18(3)).

[42] Commission on Human Rights, Third Session, Summary Record of the Sixtieth Meeting, E/CN.4/SR.60, June 4, 1948, at 10.

[43] General Comment No. 22, Human Rights Committee, HRI/GEN/1/Rev.1 (1994).

skepticism, the WGAD may find a violation of freedom of expression or other right instead, although this is discretionary and does not reflect an inability to find a freedom of religion violation in such cases.

Furthermore, attempts by the state to coerce an individual's religion, belief, thought, or conscience are prohibited.[44] This applies to all forms of coercion, both direct and indirect, including offering certain legal privileges based on religious affiliation.[45] This provision, when introduced, was understood to be linked to the right to change one's religion, which proved particularly controversial but nonetheless remains a protected right in modern human rights law.[46] Express inclusion of the right to change one's religion or belief under Article 18 was controversial during the drafting of both the UDHR and the ICCPR, and faced particular opposition from Islamic states concerned about conversion from Islam or missionary influences.[47] The UDHR ultimately kept the disputed language ("this right includes freedom to change his religion or belief"), but continuing opposition resulted in a compromise in the ICCPR, which only includes the freedom "to have or to adopt a religion or belief of his choice."[48]

Nonetheless, the HR Committee has repeatedly stressed that the right to change one's religion is absolute, including in General Comment 22, which interprets Article 18 to incorporate "the right to replace one's current religion or belief with another or to adopt atheistic views."[49]

Ultimately, the right should be understood to both protect an individual from state coercion and to protect the freedom to change one's religion. Although the WGAD has not needed to address the right to change one's religion explicitly, it has clearly condemned the use of arbitrary detention as a coercive measure infringing on freedom of religion. Thus the right to freedom of religion was violated where evangelical Christians were detained in Laos as a pretext for attempting to force the detainees to sign a renunciation of their beliefs.[50] The WGAD has also determined that the imposition of "re-education through labor" represented a coercive measure to undermine freedom of religion or belief.[51]

The broad scope of this right means that the WGAD does not necessarily need to delineate the line between religion, belief, thought, and conscience. This can be seen in the WGAD's opinions on Falun Gong, whose characterization as a religion is particularly politically and socially contentious. Falun Gong members themselves do not typically describe Falun Gong as a religion, given the lack of a clear structure, hierarchy, or even a deity.[52] The Chinese government refers to Falun Gong as a cult or

---

[44] ICCPR, at Art. 18(2).

[45] Id.

[46] Nowak, at 416.

[47] MARTIN SCHEININ, *Article 18*, THE UNIVERSAL DECLARATION OF HUMAN RIGHTS: A COMMON STANDARD OF ACHIEVEMENT 381 (Guðmundur S. Alfreðsson & Asbjørn Eide eds., Martinus Nijhoff, 1999); DAVID WEISSBRODT & CONNIE DE LA VEGA, INTERNATIONAL HUMAN RIGHTS: AN INTRODUCTION 97–98 (University of Pennsylvania Press, 2007).

[48] Id.

[49] SARAH JOSEPH & MELISSA CASTAN, THE INTERNATIONAL COVENANT ON CIVIL AND POLITICAL RIGHTS 504 (Oxford University Press, 2013); General Comment No. 22.

[50] Pa Tood, et al. v. Laos, WGAD Opinion No. 26/200, Adopted Sept. 14, 2000.

[51] Tang Xi Tao, et al. v. China, WGAD Opinion No. 5/2002, Adopted June 18, 2002.

[52] *China and Falun Gong*, Congressional Research Service, May 25, 2006, at 2.

sect (some critics outside of China do as well), rather than as a religion.[53] Characterizing Falun Gong as an institutional religion could also have important consequences for its status within China. Clearly how Falun Gong should be characterized raises multiple issues.

The question of Falun Gong's status arose specifically in *Qui Minghua* v. *China* regarding the detention of a Falun Gong practitioner. In 2004, her home was searched and various items seized, and she was taken into detention. She was told her arrest was related to her Falun Gong ties, but she was not provided with an arrest warrant, and was not given access to a lawyer. The Government, in its response, confirmed her arrest and ongoing detention, as well as the fact that her detention was based in the criminal law and her Falun Gong affiliation, but argued that her detention was justified.[54]

This opinion followed a number of prior opinions addressing the detention of either Falun Gong practitioners or those who made public comment about government policy regarding Falun Gong. In several of these opinions, the WGAD only found a violation of freedom of opinion and expression, without touching on freedom of religion.[55] Where Article 18 was invoked, the WGAD made reference generally to the right to religion and belief, with an emphasis on the lack of evidence showing that Falun Gong was a violent belief or the individual in questions held violent beliefs. In these opinions, the Government either did not respond to the communication or apparently did not address the question of whether Falun Gong was a religion.[56]

In Qiu's case, however, the Government responded specifically to address this question directly: "Falun Gong is not a religion but an anti-social, anti-scientific, misanthropic sect whose violent leanings are becoming daily more manifest." It then extended this claim to argue that Falun Gong represents a threat to public morals and safety, and has "repeatedly engaged in destructive activities of every kind."[57] This may be an argument for the detention being a permissible limitation on freedoms, but by claiming it is not a religion, the Government seems to be making a stronger claim that Falun Gong does not even fall under the rights protected by Article 18 in the first place. If this was indeed the argument, it would be an incorrect reading of the absolute nature of the freedom of belief, which the WGAD is quick to point out. The WGAD, referencing the guarantees of Article 18 of the UDHR, noted "to render an opinion in this case, the Working Group is not called upon to take a position on whether Falun Gong is a religion, a religious denomination, a sect, or a belief." It concluded by emphasizing that freedom of religion, thought, conscience, and belief are all protected as absolute rights.

---

[53] Craig S. Smith, *Rooting Out Falun Gong; China Makes War on Mysticism*, NEW YORK TIMES, Apr. 20, 2000,

[54] Qui Minghua v. China, WGAD Opinion No. 32/2005, Adopted Sept. 2, 2005.

[55] Yuhui Zhang v. China, WGAD Opinion No. 35/2000, Adopted Nov. 27, 2000; Li Chang, et al. v. China, WGAD Opinion No. 36/2000, Adopted Nov. 27, 2000; Huang Qi v. China, WGAD Opinion No. 15/2004, Adopted Sept. 15, 2004.

[56] Tang Xi Tao, et al. v. China, WGAD Opinion No. 5/2002, Adopted June 18, 2002; Chen Gang, et al. v. China, WGAD Opinion No. 7/2003, Adopted May 9, 2003; Li Ling & Pei Jilin v. China, WGAD Opinion No. 21/2003, Adopted Nov. 27, 2013.

[57] Qui Minghua v. China, WGAD Opinion No. 32/2005, Adopted Sept. 2, 2005, at ¶ 8.

B Manifestation of Religion or Belief

The distinction between the freedom of religion, thought, and conscience, and the *manifestation* of religion or belief is key for two reasons. First, it may be necessary to define precisely what qualifies as a legitimate manifestation of religion or belief to determine the scope of the right. Second, the manifestation of religion or belief may be limited and is not an absolute right.

Where personal beliefs can be defined broadly and without specific inquiry into what constitutes a religion, defining what is considered a legitimate manifestation of religion or belief may be necessary to determine what behaviors are covered by the right in the first place. A good example of this is in the HR Committee's view in *M.A.B., W.A.T. and J-A.Y.T. v. Canada*, where it found that "a belief consisting primarily or exclusively in the worship or distribution of a narcotic drug cannot be conceivably brought within the scope of article 18."[58] Although the HR Committee does not state this explicitly, presumably a detention based on a *belief* in either a spiritual quality to drug use, or in particular policies regarding drug use, would be arbitrary and a violation of one's rights. But drug use itself, when claimed as a religious practice, requires an inquiry into the boundary of religion and belief.

Although this raises several potentially fraught legal issues, the nature of the cases brought before the WGAD is such that they seldom must examine the precise border between protected religion practice and unprotected behavior. Even where governments argue that detained individuals pose a threat of some sort, these allegations are usually suspect or are pretextual. Accordingly, in such cases where the detentions are frequently found arbitrary, the WGAD usually finds that there is no evidence of such a threat, and it need not inquire into the boundaries of permissible religious practice. One exception to this approach, however, has been in the case of conscientious objectors, discussed in this chapter, where the WGAD has said that freedom of conscience may be considered a manifestation of religion or belief in certain circumstances.

Instead, determining what constitutes a manifestation of religion or belief is important for the WGAD for another reason – determining which category of cases that a detention falls under and, within category II, which fundamental rights and freedoms may be violated by a particular detention. Freedom to manifest one's religion is closely connected with the rights of freedom of opinion and expression, association, and assembly. Recognizing these connections and the potential overlap between these rights, the WGAD frequently defers to either the facts of the case or the preferences of the source in characterizing the rights, rather than establishing formalistic legal distinctions between the various rights.

Take, for example, its treatment of blasphemy cases. In *Abdul Kareem Nabil Suliman Amer v. Egypt*, an Egyptian blogger was charged with contempt of religion. In that case, the WGAD only found the Government in contravention of the right to freedom of opinion and expression, perhaps because the blogger was critical of religion and did not appear to consider himself religious. In another case, where the detainee denied having committed blasphemy, the WGAD did not find a Category II violation at all, but instead found a Category III violation. But in contrast, when blasphemy charges were brought

---

[58] M.A.B., W.A.T. & J-A.Y.T. v. Canada, Communication No. 570/1993, Human Rights Committee, CCPR/C/50/D/570/1993, Apr. 25, 1994.

against individuals belonging to a minority Islamic movement in Pakistan, an Article 18 violation was found instead.[59] Deference was made to the specific facts of the case and sources are able to characterize how the WGAD should view their alleged blasphemous conduct.

Such deference is made possible by an acceptance of a broad range of behavior as constituting manifestations of religion or belief. Although the scope of manifestations of religion or belief may be narrower than the absolute protection afforded interior thought, conscience, and belief, it nonetheless may cover a broad range of behaviors.

The *Declaration on the Elimination of All Forms of Intolerance and of Discrimination Based on Religion or Belief* outlines a non-exhaustive list, noting freedom of religion includes activities such as worship and religious assemblies; establishing charitable or humanitarian institutions; writing and dissemination of religious publications; instruction according to religion or belief; solicitation of donations; and communication with national and international communities.[60]

The WGAD has Category II violations where the detention was a response to many of these religious activities, but it has also gone further, finding violations of Article 18 where detainees had been involved in much more general forms of activism and social involvement. Thus Article 18 has been invoked where individuals engage in human rights or political advocacy as part of their affiliation with a religion institution, where religious leaders are engaged in such activities, or even where an individual is engaged in advocacy around freedom of religion issues.[61]

As a result, again, there is the potential for substantial overlap between freedom of religion and freedom of opinion and expression, and the WGAD's rational for choosing one over the other is not always well defined. This can be seen by comparing two opinions regarding the same person at different points in time. In *Thadeus Nguyen Van Ly v. Viet Nam*, the WGAD found that the detention of Father Thadeus Nguyen Van Ly, a Vietnamese priest who was well known for his human rights advocacy, violated his rights to freedom of religion, opinion, expression, and association when he was given eight years in prison for "spreading propaganda against the state." But this opinion contrasted with an earlier opinion by the WGAD regarding a prior detention of Father Ly's, where it only found a violation of freedom of opinion and expression when he had been sentenced to fifteen years in prison for "undermining national unity." The rationale for a finding of a violation of his right to freedom of religion violation in the later opinion

---

[59] Compare Abdul Kareem Nabil Suliman Amer v. Egypt, WGAD Opinion No. 35/2008, Adopted Nov. 20, 2008 and Ayub Masih v. Pakistan, WGAD Opinion No. 25/2001, Adopted Nov. 30, 2001 (Litigated by Author with Freedom Now), with Habibullah et al. v. Pakistan, WGAD Opinion No. 10/1996, Adopted May 23, 1996. Admittedly, in this last case, the facts as outlined in the opinion suggest the detained individuals were arrested merely for their faith, and not for expressing their faith, in which case article 19 would be inapplicable.

[60] *Declaration on the Elimination of All Forms of Intolerance and of Discrimination Based on Religion or Belief*, A/RES/36/55, art. 6(a)–(i), Nov. 25, 1981.

[61] *See, e.g.,* Tenzin Choewang, et al. v. China, WGAD Opinion No. 13/2003, Adopted Sept. 4, 2003; Mie Mie, et al. v. Myanmar, WGAD Opinion No. 12/2008, Adopted May 9, 2008; Thadeus Nguyen Van Ly v. Viet Nam, WGAD Opinion No. 6/2010, Adopted May 6, 2010 (Litigated by Author through Freedom Now).

but not the earlier one is not entirely clear, although his advocacy related to religious freedom in Viet Nam is noted in the second opinion.[62]

In *Gao Zhisheng v. China*, the WGAD found a violation of this courageous human rights lawyer's right to freedom of religion (and a range of fair trial rights), but it did not explain why it did not also find a violation of his right to freedom of opinion and expression, despite the fact that his detention resulted from his work as a human rights defender and his letters critical of the Government. Invoking Article 18 was not improper, given Gao's religious freedom advocacy, but excluding freedom of expression was an odd choice.[63]

Song Hyeok Kim v. Democratic People's Republic of Korea presented a more typical case of religious practitioners targeted for their activities promoting religion.[64] In North Korea, state authorities determined promoting Christianity was a threat to the dominant ideology of the state.[65] The WGAD noted that the detainee was targeted because of his material activity of bringing religious texts into the country.[66]

The WGAD's flexible use of the freedom of opinion and expression and religion likely reflects the fact that religious practitioners may view all or most of their actions as emanating from their religious convictions, and to this extent the WGAD's approach is a wise one. It also reflects the reality that many fundamental human rights overlap and are not neatly distinguishable, particularly when understood in the complex context of an individual's life.

However, such a broad reading of the boundaries of religious practice can result in inconsistencies, as described earlier. Furthermore, it may not be analytically coherent when governments successfully show that a detained individual was engaged in behavior that operates at the boundaries of legitimate religious or other practice, as with the case of narcotic use (noted in the HR Committee opinion just noted), or with conscientious objectors. The WGAD may accordingly be challenged to clarify its analysis in future cases, and this challenge should be kept in mind as the discussion turns to the scope of permissible limitations on the right to freedom of religion.

C Permissible Limitations

Article 18(3) of the ICCPR, although allowing limitations on the manifestation of religion or belief, requires that such limitations must be (a) prescribed by law and (b) necessary (c) to protect public safety, order, health, or morals or the fundamental rights and freedoms of others.[67] Governments arguing that a limitation on the right was proper frequently fail to show all of these requirements. Article 18(3) should furthermore be

---

[62] Thadeus Nguyen Van Ly v. Viet Nam, WGAD Opinion No. 20/2003, Adopted Nov. 27, 2003 (Litigated by Author through Freedom Now); Thadeus Nguyen Van Ly v. Viet Nam, WGAD Opinion No. 6/2010, Adopted May 6, 2010 (Litigated by Author through Freedom Now).

[63] Gao Zhisheng v. China, WGAD Opinion No. 26/2010, Adopted Nov. 19, 2010 (Litigated by Author through Freedom Now).

[64] Song Hyeok Kim v. Democratic People's Republic of Korea, WGAD Opinion No. 29/2015, Adopted Sept. 3, 2015, at ¶ 21.

[65] *Id.*, at ¶ 6.

[66] *Id.*, at ¶ 20.

[67] Irina Zaharchenko & Valida Jabrayliova v. Azerbaijan, WGAD Opinion No. 42/2015, Adopted Dec. 2, 2015, at ¶ 39.

"strictly interpreted."[68] Indeed, the WGAD has only once accepted a government argument for the application of Article 18(3), and a later opinion has called this into doubt. This can be seen in the context of conscientious objection, which provides a useful case study for examining the WGAD's treatment of Article 18(3).

1 Conscientious Objection

In *Halil Savda* v. *Turkey*, the detainee was tortured after being imprisoned in 1993. On his release, he was called to military service, which under Turkish law is mandatory for all men, without any exemption for reasons of conscience. He consistently refused to report to his unit and participate in military activities, claiming his prior torture and the dictates of his conscience would not allow him to serve as a soldier. He was accordingly determined to be a deserter and imprisoned on multiple occasions, during which he was reportedly subject to numerous instances of ill-treatment and torture.

The Government accepted that Savda was a genuine conscientious objector, but argued that "a right to conscientious objection has not yet been recognized as a human right under international law."[69] The WGAD found this conclusion to be mistaken, citing a HR Committee determination that South Korea's arrest of two conscientious objectors violated their right to freedom of religion. The HR Committee noted "while the right to manifest one's religion or belief does not as such imply the right to refuse all obligations imposed by law, it provides certain protection ... against being forced to act against genuinely-held religious belief."[70]

Concurring with this reasoning, the WGAD then examined Savda's detention in light of Article 18 of the ICCPR. It first found that "genuinely held beliefs of conscientious objection" constitute both "manifestations of one's religion" and "manifestations of conscience," as protected by Article 18(1) of the ICCPR. It then turned to whether the limitations on the right allowed in Article 18(3) applied, noting that while "restrictions on the exercise of the right to freedom of religion or belief in the context of conscientious objection might be justified, in other situations it might not."[71] Here, the Government had not provided any arguments for a lack of laws providing accommodation for conscientious objectors, or for the necessity of criminal prosecution of conscientious objectors, which would explain how such actions were necessary to protect the public interests described in Article 18(3). Accordingly, the WGAD found the detention did not reflect a permissible limitation on the right to manifest one's religion or conscience.

This opinion can be contrasted with a much earlier one adopted by the WGAD. In *Dimitrios Tsironic* v. *Greece*, the detention of a conscientious objector was determined not to be arbitrary. Although Greek law allowed a conscientious objector to participate in unarmed instead of armed military service, the detainee, a Jehovah's Witness, argued that any sort of military service whether armed or not was incompatible with his religious beliefs. Because no alternative civilian service was available, he was sentenced to four years in prison for his refusal to participate in military work. The WGAD determined that "it is difficult to conclude that military service or unarmed military service is per se

---

[68] General Comment No. 22, at ¶ 8.
[69] Halil Savda v. Turkey, WGAD Opinion No. 16/2008, Adopted May 9, 2008, at ¶ 35.
[70] Id.
[71] Id., at ¶35.

incompatible with the religious beliefs of Mr. Tsironic ... (b)eing a Jehovah's Witness does not confer on Mr. Tsironic a right to refuse on grounds of conscience to perform armed or unarmed military service."[72] The detention was accordingly found not to be arbitrary.

That said, however, in its country mission to Greece, the WGAD did observe that "conscientious objectors were frequently prosecuted," noting the case of Avraam Pouliasis, who had been convicted for objecting to compulsory military service in February 2012 and was sentenced to six months of imprisonment. By then, Greece had amended its laws to allow for alternative military service for conscientious objectors, but Pouliasis refused to perform this alternative service as well.[73] Similarly, on its country mission to Armenia, the WGAD reported that some eighty Jehovah's Witnesses had been arrested and imprisoned as conscientious objectors, noting alternative civil service, while established by law, was not functioning in practice.[74]

The WGAD's case in Greece may be distinguished from the later Turkey case on two different grounds. First, there may be a difference as to whether conscience objection is a manifestation of religious belief. In the Greece case, the WGAD appear comfortable inquiring into whether Tsironic's objections to military service are connected to his *religious* belief. This could be interpreted to mean that it did not think that conscientious objection can be conceived as falling under a manifestation of religion or belief. If that is a correct reading, the opinion on Savda may represent a broadening of the WGAD's understanding of what constitutes a manifestation of religion or belief, as they take care to note that his right to manifest his religion and his right to manifest his conscience are implicated. Alternatively, the different result between the two opinions could be read as a consequence of differences at the balancing stage. Greece did have some provisions for conscientious objectors already in place, allowing for unarmed military service, although not alternative civilian service. Turkey had no such provisions in place.

The opinion regarding Greece could therefore be understood to recognize that conscientious objection did constitute a manifestation of religion or belief, but given the availability of unarmed military service and the facts of the individual case, this was a permissible limitation, whereas in the Turkish case the balancing came out the other way.

In either analysis, the decision on Turkey reflects two important features of WGAD jurisprudence. First, it reflects a willingness of the WGAD to consider evolving human rights norms. General Comment 22, adopted a year after the opinion on the Greek conscientious objector, acknowledged that a growing number of states were placing conscientious objector provisions in their laws, and that while "The Covenant does not explicitly refer to a right to conscientious objection ... the Committee believes that such a right can be derived from article 18."[75] The WGAD may be evolving its jurisprudence in response to such developments in the HR Committee. Second, the decision underlies the burden placed on a government to justify any detentions it believes are a permissible

---

[72] Dimitrios Tsironic v. Greece, WGAD Opinion No. 34/1993, Adopted Sept. 29, 1993, at ¶ 6.

[73] *Report of the Working Group on Arbitrary Detention: Mission to Greece*, Human Rights Council, A/HRC/27/48/Add.2, June 30, 2014, at ¶ 108.

[74] *Report of the Working Group on Arbitrary Detention: Mission to Armenia*, Human Rights Council, A/HRC/16/47/Add.3, Feb. 17, 2011, at ¶ 68.

[75] General Comment No. 22, at ¶ 11.

limitation on the freedom of religion. The WGAD explicitly references the requirements of ICCPR Article 18(3), and Turkey's failure to establish them.

In assessing a government's attempts to establish the requirements outlined in Article 18(3), the WGAD is skeptical of arguments from governments that look pretextual or may be applied in a discriminatory or unjust manner. This is a recurring theme in cases where detained individuals are accused of terrorism or fomenting political unrest, which will be examined next.

2 Accusations of Terrorism and Religiously Motivated Violence

Despite the potentially significant government interest in guarding against terrorism or religiously motivated violence, the WGAD has made clear such an interest cannot be used as a sweeping excuse for targeting individuals because of their religious beliefs. It has particularly noted that while "since 11 September 2011 [sic], increased securitization of national laws, policies and regulations have led to closer collaboration among governments in the arrest, detention and deportation of individuals considered a threat to national security," this has led to "violations of certain fundamental human rights that protect the individual from arbitrary arrest and detention."[76]

Global concerns over terrorism and religiously motivated violence have both led to instances in which certain religious beliefs and violent ideologies are conflated and provided an easy pretext for governments wishing to silence dissidents or religious minorities. When allegations or charges are vague or ambiguous, and no specific criminal or violent acts described, the WGAD will consider this evidence that an individual was instead targeted for exercising a fundamental right or freedom such as religion. Thus detention based on an individual's "radical religious ideas," without further specification as to related activities that threatened the safety or stability of the country, was determined to be an arbitrary detention under Category II.[77] Similarly, where no evidence supported the linking of an Islamic religious preacher to terrorist attacks in Casablanca, the WGAD found that he was instead detained for exercising his freedoms of opinion and expression and religion.[78]

One opinion which exhibits this trend well is *Gaybullo Jalilov v. Uzbekistan*.[79] He was a religious freedom activist who monitored persecution of independent Muslims in Uzbekistan. He was tried, convicted, sentenced, and imprisoned on allegations of membership in a religious extremist group, and, as described by the Government "forming an organized criminal group with the goal of spreading religious extremism, and operating this group, whose main aim was to take over government control … ." According to the source, this sentence was based on a coerced confession and questionable witness testimony, which alleged Jalilov watched DVDs and participated in gatherings with religious extremist content.

In explaining Jalilov's detention to the WGAD, the Government argued his detention was a lawful limitation of Article 18(3), because he was "an active member of a religious

---

[76] Yahya Hussein Ahmad Shaqibel v. Saudi Arabia, WGAD Opinion No. 44/2013, Adopted Nov. 18, 2013, at ¶¶ 20–21.

[77] Mustapha Hamed Ahmed Chamia v. Egypt, WGAD Opinion No. 24/2007, Adopted Nov. 22, 2007, at ¶ 21.

[78] Mohamed Hassan Echerif el-Kettani v. Morocco, WGAD Opinion No. 35/2011, Adopted Sept. 1, 2013.

[79] Gaybullo Jalilov v. Uzbekistan, WGAD Opinion No. 4/2013, Adopted Apr. 30, 2013.

extremist group, whose main aim was to overthrow the current government." It further noted that Uzbekistan was a party to the *Shanghai Convention on Combating Terrorism, Separatism and Extremism*, which specifies that religious considerations should not be grounds for acquittal. This is a questionable use of this provision, given that Jalilov's sentence itself was suspect. But the reference does reveal how governments may use anti-terrorism instruments to justify arbitrary detentions. The Shanghai Convention, inciden-tally, is a regional instrument whose signatories also include Russia, China, Kyrgyzstan, Turkmenistan, and Kazakhstan, all of whom human rights groups have criticized for using anti-terrorism efforts as a means for suppressing internal dissent.

In its reply, the source argued that the Government had not identified the precise threat Jalilov posed to national security and the exception could not apply. The WGAD agreed that the lack of specificity was a problem: it noted the Government had provided no specific information to support the claim that Jalilov was linked to either an extremist organization or had called for violence. Instead, it determined the detention was based on his practice of his religion and his criticism of Government treatment of independent Muslims, in violation of his rights under Articles 18-19 of the ICCPR as well as a range of fair trial rights.

If there was evidence that Jalilov had been part of an extremist group, even barring the other abuses in his trial, would this be sufficient to justify his detention? In other words, is mere membership in a group with violent tendencies enough to justify a detention, or must more specific evidence of violent involvement be shown? The WGAD has not yet rendered an opinion on this question, and the answer may be highly fact dependent. But it is worth noting that this is another potential source of problematic pretextual targeting. The source reported Jalilov had been accused of membership in *Hizb ut-Tahrir*, a political Islamic movement that advocates for the establishment of an Islamic Caliphate but whose Uzbekistan branch expressly disavows violence. The Government nonetheless has a history of leveling accusations of terrorism against the group.[80] Imprisonment of members of a particular religion or a branch of a particular religion raises a particular set of concerns over religious discrimination and harassment, several of which the WGAD has wrestled with in the context of Category II detentions.

D Targeting of Religious Groups

Although the WGAD examines the detentions of individuals and accordingly the rights of those individuals, this discussion frequently is expanded into a discussion of the targeting of religious groups more generally. Targeting of groups is not unique to Category II detentions emanating from violations of the freedom of religion, but religious groups are a common target. Such cases raise some particular legal issues, including the status of minority religions under national law, instances of repeated or systematic discrimination, and the relationship between religious discrimination under Category V and Category II cases.

---

[80] *See generally* Emmanual Karagiannis, Political Islam in Uzbekistan: Hizb ut-Tahrir al-Islami, 58:2 Europe-Asia Studies, 261–280 (Mar. 2006).

1 Status of Religions in National Law

Neither the ICCPR nor UDHR forbid a state from recognizing a state or official religion. There is great diversity in national constitutional law as to the relations between religious and state structures.[81] However, the banning of certain religions or religious beliefs clearly is not permissible. Furthermore, where there is an official or state religion, this cannot justify an abridgement of the rights provided in Article 18, or discrimination against certain religious groups.[82] Given this concern with the targeting of those who do not follow official religious interpretations, the WGAD has easily found, with little discussion, violations of Article 18 of the ICCPR or UDHR where the detainee was accused of deviation from the Maliki Islamic rite in Morocco,[83] or of following alternate interpretations of Islam from the official one in Saudi Arabia.[84] A number of opinions have found arbitrary detentions of members of various banned or otherwise disapproved religious minorities. These include the Falun Gong in China, as described earlier, as well as the Unified Buddhist Church in Viet Nam,[85] Evangelical Christians in Laos,[86] members of the banned Al Arqam Islamic sect in Malaysia,[87] and the Baha'i in Iran.[88]

2 Repeated or Systematic Targeting of a Religious Group

The WGAD will not only examine targeting of a group, but will examine numerous attacks against a certain religious group over time, expressing particular concern where there are signs of repeated or continual targeting of a religious group. It will also place regular occurrences of arbitrary detention in a broader context, if necessary, recognizing a link with broader religious discrimination. A good example of the WGAD's treatment of a government regularly detaining members of a religious group are two opinions on Iran's treatment of the Baha'i. This faith, founded in Iran in the nineteenth century, emphasizes progressive divine revelation through various religions, and holds its founder to be the most recent manifestation of God.[89]

Because Islam holds Mohammed to be the final prophet, such views are considered heresy.[90] Accordingly there is "a pervasive view held within the Government that Baha'is represent a heretical sect with ties to foreign enemies."[91] The Baha'i faith is not an officially recognized religion in Iran, and there is a long history of discrimination and persecution of its members.

---

[81] Weissbrodt & De La Vega, at 99.

[82] General Comment No. 22.

[83] Mohamed Hassan Echerif el-Kettani.

[84] Yahya Hussein Ahmad Shaqibel v. Saudi Arabia, WGAD Opinion No. 44/2013, Adopted Nov. 18, 2013; Zakaria Mohamed Ali v. Saudi Arabia, WGAD Opinion No. 14/2014, Adopted Apr. 30, 2014.

[85] Phuc Tue Dang, et al. v. Viet Nam, WGAD Opinion No. 21/1997, Adopted Dec. 2, 1997; Thich Quang Do v. Viet Nam, WGAD Opinion No. 11/2001, Adopted Sept. 12, 2001.

[86] Pa Tood, et al. v. Laos, WGAD Opinion No. 26/2000, Adopted Sept. 14, 2000.

[87] Nasiruddin bin Ali, et al. v. Malaysia, WGAD Opinion No. 4/1997, Adopted May 15, 1997.

[88] Mahvash Sabet, et al. v. Iran, WGAD Opinion No. 34/2008, Adopted Nov. 20, 2008.

[89] *Baha'i at a Glance*, BBC (Nov. 2018), www.bbc.co.uk/religion/religions/bahai/ataglance/glance.shtml.

[90] A *Faith Denied: The Persecution of the Baha'is of Iran*, IRAN HUMAN RIGHTS DOCUMENTATION CENTER, Dec. 2006, at 4.

[91] *Report of the Special Rapporteur on the Situation of Human Rights in Iran*, Human Rights Council, A/HRC/25/61, Mar. 20, 2014.

In *Mahvash Sabet, et al. v. Iran*, seven Baha'i leaders were detained in Tehran.[92] Six were arrested at their homes in May 2008 by Ministry of Intelligence agents, and the seventh was summoned to the Ministry of Intelligence in March 2008. The source reported that no criminal charges had been brought against any of the individuals following their arrest, and the sole reason for the detention was their Baha'i faith and associated peaceful activities. The Government did not respond to the complaint. The WGAD noted that "the common element in these detentions is that all detainees are active leaders of the Baha'i community in Iran." Citing in full Article 18 of both the ICCPR and UDHR, the WGAD found the detention violated these articles, and was accordingly arbitrary.

Just four days after adopting this opinion, the WGAD adopted *Aziz Pourhamzeh, et al. v. Iran*, which dealt with an additional fourteen detained Baha'is, arrested or sentenced between 2005 and 2008.[93] Unlike the prior group of detainees, these individuals were primarily ordinary Baha'i community members – only one was reported to have had a coordinating role. All were either detained without being charged or found guilty of anti-Government or un-Islamic propaganda. Several had their homes or persons searched and Baha'i literature or other material seized. Iran did not respond to this complaint either (a fact about which the WGAD expressed particular frustration). Although the circumstances of detention vary slightly in this opinion, for the purposes of finding a Category II violation, the concerns of the WGAD and associated legal analysis are substantially the same. The WGAD again noted that freedom of religion is a fundamental right, that detentions were based solely on the practice of religious faith, and that accordingly the detentions were arbitrary under Category II.

Of particular note in these opinions is the WGAD's examination of the broader context of religious discrimination in which the detentions occurred, which it does in two ways. First, the WGAD expresses a concern with the ongoing and intensifying nature of arbitrary detention of Baha'i members. The treatment of the Baha'i in Iran was not new to the WGAD's experience – a report issued after a 2003 visit to Iran expressed "grave concern" that "followers of the Baha'i faith are continually persecuted," and criticized Iran's use of "revolving arrests" by which Baha'is were arrested, interrogated about their religious practices, and released.[94] In addition, the WGAD observed it had issued several urgent appeals to Iran related to the detention of Baha'is over the last decade. Such detentions also appeared to be becoming "more and more frequent": new information, received after the complaints in both the previously referenced opinions, described "a recent wave of arrests and imprisonments targeting members of the Baha'i community." Thus the WGAD was concerned both with the continuous nature of these arrests and future acceleration.

The second way in which WGAD contextualizes the individual detentions is by identifying forms of religious discrimination against the Baha'i not directly related to arbitrary detention. For example, it makes particular note of the fact that the Baha'i faith, unlike Armenian Christianity, Judaism, and Zoroastrianism, is not represented in the

[92] Mahvash Sabet, et al. v. Iran, WGAD Opinion No. 34/2008, Adopted Nov. 20, 2008.
[93] Aziz Pourhamzeh, et al. v. Iran, WGAD Opinion No. 39/2008, Adopted Nov. 24, 2008.
[94] *Report of the Working Group on Arbitrary Detention: Visit to Islamic Republic of Iran*, Commission on Human Rights, E/CN.4/2004/3/Add.2, June 22, 2003, at ¶¶ 45, 47.

Iranian Majlis and is not officially recognized.[95] Furthermore, the detentions are identi-fied as being "consistent with a pattern of harassment, intimidation, expulsions from universities, confiscation of property and even persecution." While such facts reflect concerns over political participation rights, or describe discrimination which assists in establishing violations of the freedom of religion, they do not directly speak to the arbitrary detentions of the individuals in the complaint. The WGAD quite reasonably recognizes that such detentions cannot be abstracted from more general discrimination.

Although the WGAD clearly criticizes Iran for its repeated and consistent arbitrary detention of Baha'is, it is more careful with describing such treatment as "systematic." The source in both opinions describes systematic mistreatment of the Baha'i. In *Mah-vash Sabet, et al. v. Iran*, the WGAD merely echoes the source's "serious concern about systematic discrimination and harassment of the Iranian Baha'is on the grounds of their religion," without going so far as to find systematic arbitrary detentions. In *Aziz Pour-hamzeh, et al. v. Iran*, it goes slightly further, observing that "arrest and detention of members of the Baha'i community in Iran appear to be more and more frequent and acquiring a systematic character." This careful wording likely reflects the potential implications of a WGAD finding of systematic arbitrary detentions. Under the Rome Statute of the International Criminal Court, "imprisonment or other severe deprivation of physical liberty in violation of fundamental rules of international law" may constitute a crime against humanity when widespread or systematic.[96] In annual reports and opinions issued after the ones discussed here, the WGAD expressly articulated this, noting that a widespread or systematic practice of detention can constitute a war crime or crime against humanity. Accordingly, the WGAD was likely already concerned about the implications of finding systematic arbitrary detentions by Iran.

3 Relationship to Category V

When the WGAD examines arbitrary detentions or other harassment of a religious group, as well as an individual, concerns over religious discrimination will likely be invoked. Because Category V specifically covers detentions that are "a violation of international law for reasons of discrimination based on . . . religion . . . political or other opinion . . . or other status," it is to be expected that where individuals are detained for reasons relating to their religious beliefs, the detention may fall under both Category II and Category V. It should be emphasized that the WGAD is not restricted from finding that an arbitrary detention falls within multiple categories, and the circumstances of a given case often dictate just such a finding.

The primary distinction to be drawn between the two categories is that whereas Category II applies when the detention results from the exercise of one's freedom of religion, category V applies to detentions that are themselves a form of religious discrimination. It is not entirely clear how meaningful a distinction is being made by the WGAD. In the case of Song Hyeok Kim, for example, the WGAD ruled both a Category II and V violation for the targeting of a Christian evangelist by North Korean

---

[95] Mahvash Sabet, et al. v. Iran, WGAD Opinion No. 34/2008, Adopted Nov. 20, 2008, ¶ 13.

[96] *Rome Statute of the International Criminal Court*, 2187 U.N.T.S. 90, *entered into force* July 1, 2002, at Art. 7(1)(e).

authorities, where the applicant's religious work itself constituted or was perceived as a threat to the dominant ideology of the state.[97]

Inasmuch as merely holding a particular belief can constitute an exercise of one's freedom of religion, presumably most detentions based on religious discrimination could also be characterized as detentions that are a response to the exercise of an individual's religions freedom. Indeed, prior to the introduction of Category V in 2011, references to religious discrimination are frequently incorporated into discussion of freedom of religion under Category II.

Category V was only introduced in 2011, so there are comparably fewer opinions that find that a detention falls both within Category II and Category V in relation to freedom of religion and belief. In *Saeed Abedinigalangashi v. Iran*, a Christian pastor with dual Iranian and American citizenship who was arrested while visiting relatives in Iran. The WGAD noted "the detention of persons solely because of the practice of their religious faith is a violation of the freedom of religion," and concluded that "Mr. Abedini has been deprived of his liberty for peacefully exercising the rights to freedom of religion, belief and association … ." The detention, accordingly, is a violation under Category II. The WGAD goes on to note that "in this case Mr. Abedini has been deprived of his liberty for being a practicing Christian, which amounts to discrimination based on religion," also being a violation of Category V.[98]

In contrast, consider *Mohamed Hassan Echerif el-Kettani v. Morocco*.[99] El-Kettani was an Imam who was accused of deviating from the Maliki Islamic rite in his sermons and detained on charges including unauthorized preaching, inciting jihad, and not blessing the King during his sermons. Despite the source invoking Category V, the WGAD only found the detention to fall within Categories II and III, without explaining its decision regarding Category V. However, one could surmise that this was because El-Kettani appeared to be targeted for the content of his religious sermons, rather than because of his particular religion. Thus although he appeared to be targeted for a particular religious belief, or religious interpretation, he did not face discrimination for his religious belief more generally (Islam). This could suggest that when a religious minority faces discrimination, there will be a Category V finding, but where an individual is detained for espousing a particular interpretation of a religion or belief, a Category II finding is more appropriate. Hopefully, as more opinions are issued under these categories, the precise relationship between detentions based on religious beliefs under Category II and under Category V will be articulated more precisely.

II Association

Under Article 22 of the ICCPR, freedom of association is provided as follows:

1. Everyone shall have the right to freedom of association with others, including the right to form and join trade unions for the protection of his interests.
2. No restrictions may be placed on the exercise of this right other than those which are prescribed by law and which are necessary in a democratic society in the

---

[97] Song Hyeok Kim v. Democratic People's Republic of Korea, WGAD Opinion No. 29/2015, Adopted Sept. 3, 2015, at ¶¶ 21–22.

[98] Saeed Abedinigalangash v. Iran, WGAD Opinion No. 2013/18, Adopted Aug. 24, 2013, at ¶ 27.

[99] Mohamed Hassan Echerif el-Kettani.

    interests of national security or public safety, public order (*ordre public*), the protection of public health or morals or the protection of the rights and freedoms of others. This article shall not prevent the imposition of lawful restrictions on members of the armed forces and of the police in their exercise of this right.

3. Nothing in this article shall authorize States Parties to the International Labour Organisation Convention of 1948 concerning Freedom of Association and Protection of the Right to Organize to take legislative measures which would prejudice, or to apply the law in such a manner as to prejudice, the guarantees provided for in that Convention.

Article 20 of the UDHR groups the rights to freedom of assembly and association together:

1. Everyone has the right to freedom of peaceful assembly and association.
2. No one may be compelled to belong to an association.

Freedom of association is guaranteed in regional human rights treaties as well, including Article 10 of the *African Charter on Human and Peoples' Rights*, Article 16 of the *American Convention for Human Rights*, and Article 11 of the *European Convention on Human Rights*. The International Labor Organization (ILO) has a committee on freedom of association, because of its special relevance to labor issues, and the United Nations has dedicated a Special Rapporteur to the Right of Freedom of Peaceful Assembly and Association. In addition to the interpretation of Article 22 by the HR Committee, these represent important sources for developing jurisprudence of this right.

A *Scope of the Right*

The kinds of associations covered by the right to freedom of association include the range of groups that individuals join in together for various purposes. A few particular classes of organizations covered by the right, however, are worth emphasizing because they are recurrent in the WGAD jurisprudence. First, human rights organizations are clearly covered by the right to freedom of association. The *Declaration on Human Rights Defenders* explains "the right, individually and in association with others," to promote and work toward the realization of human rights, as well as the right "(t)o form, join and participate in non-governmental organizations, associations or groups" for the purpose of promoting and protecting human rights.[100] The WGAD has similarly recognized that "belonging to a human rights organization ... is simply legitimate exercise" of, among other rights, the right to association.[101] The WGAD has accordingly found cases of arbitrary detention, based on the exercise of freedom of association, for detained members of a range of human rights organizations.[102] This frequently includes leaders

---

[100] *Declaration on Human Rights Defenders*, A/RES/53/144, Mar. 8, 1999, at Art. 1, 5.

[101] Afif Jamil Mazhar, et al. v. Syria, WGAD Opinion No. 10/1993, Adopted Apr. 29 1993, at ¶ 5(h).

[102] *See, e.g.*, Rubén Hoyos Ruiz, et al. v. Cuba, WGAD Opinion No. 26/1992, Adopted Session No. 4; Afif Jamil Mazhar, et al. v. Syria, WGAD Opinion No. 10/1993, Adopted Apr. 29 1993; Annakurban Amanklychev & Sapardurdy Khadzhied v. Turkmenistan, WGAD Opinion No. 15/2010, Adopted Aug. 31, 2010.

or founding members of these groups.[103] The protection also extends to association with clients or beneficiaries of a human rights organization.[104]

Detention based on a person's political associations is also improper. Like with human rights organizations, founding members or leaders of opposition political parties are similarly protected by the right, with the WGAD noting that "(t)o act as head of a political opposition movement … is simply lawful exercise of the rights to freedom of expression and opinion and to political association."[105] The WGAD saw a cluster of cases where members of political opposition parties were arbitrarily detained in the early years of its operations.[106] Many of these cases involved members of parties with an ideological perspective different than the current government who had been detained, such as Communist party members targeted in Syria and Sudan,[107] members of pro-democracy organizations in Cuba,[108] and members of pro-North Korea groups or groups supporting Korean reunification in South Korea.[109] The legacy of the Cold War may have contributed to this collection of association cases in the early 1990s, which have given way substantially to detentions based on associations with human rights groups. Nonetheless, the WGAD has continued to find arbitrary detentions based on political affiliation, such as the series of opinions on Burmese pro-democracy leader Aung San Suu Kyi.[110] Lastly, association with journalistic organizations also enjoys protection. In *Mahmoud Hussein Gomaa Ali v. Egypt* the WGAD noted that although the word "associations" normally refers to trade unions, NGOs, and private businesses "it is natural to include international broadcasters such as Al-Jazeera," and thus Ali "enjoys the right to choose freely to work for Al-Jazeera."[111]

Freedom of association incorporates not only the right to belong to an organization, but the right to meet in formal or informal gatherings. Here there is significant overlap between the right to privacy, the right to assembly, and the right to association. One

---

[103] Muhammed Abdullah al-Mas'ari & Abdullah al-Hamed v. Saudi Arabia, WGAD Opinion No. 60/1993, Adopted Dec. 9, 1993; Akzam Turgunov v. Uzbekistan, WGAD Opinion No. 53/2011, Adopted Nov. 17, 2011; Mazen Darwish, et al. v. Syria, WGAD Opinion No. 43/2013, Adopted Aug. 19, 2013.

[104] Ny Sokha, et al. v. Cambodia, WGAD Opinion No. 45/2016, Adopted Nov. 21, 2016, at ¶ 46.

[105] Yndamiro Restano Diaz v. Cuba, WGAD Opinion No. 12/1993, Apr. 29, 1993, ¶ 6(f); *see also* Pulat Akhunov v. Uzbekistan, WGAD Opinion No. 2/1994, May 17, 1994 (deputy chairman of the opposition Birlik movement targeted for political activities); Nguyen Dan Que v. Viet Nam, WGAD Opinion No. 14/1993, Apr. 30, 1993, at ¶ 10 (founding member of a Vietnamese political movement calling for a multi-party system detained, later case litigated by Author).

[106] *See, e.g.,* Vincent Chung v. Malaysia, WGAD Opinion No. 39/1992, Adopted Session No. 4 (supporter of the United Sabah Party, a legal political party, was detained arbitrarily); Fô Na Nsofa, et al. v. Guinea-Bissau, WGAD Opinion No. 5/1994, Adopted May 18, 1994;

[107] Riad Al Turk, et al. v. Syria, WGAD Opinion No. 6/1992, Adopted Session No. 4; Usama Ashur al-Askari, et al. v. Syria, WGAD Opinion No. 29/1995, Adopted Sept. 17, 1996; Mazim Shamsin and Firas Yunis v. Syria, WGAD Opinion No. 30/1996, Adopted Sept. 17, 1996; Mustafa al-Hussain, et al. v. Syria, WGAD Opinion No. 31/1996, Adopted Sept. 17, 1996; Mohamed Wahaba, et al. v. Sudan, WGAD Opinion No. 45/1993, Sept. 30, 1993.

[108] Aurea Feria Cano, et al. v. Cuba, WGAD Opinion No. 28/1992, Adopted Session No. 4; Yndamiro Restano Diaz v. Cuba, WGAD Opinion No. 12/1993, Apr. 29, 1993.

[109] Keun-Soo Hong v. South Korea, WGAD Opinion No. 47/1992, Adopted Dec. 9, 1992; Lee Jang-hyong, et al. v. South Korea, WGAD Opinion No. 1/1995, Adopted May 30, 1995.

[110] *See, e.g.,* Aung San Suu Kyi v. Myanmar, WGAD Opinion No. 2/2002, Adopted June 19, 2002; Aung San Suu Kyi v. Myanmar, WGAD Opinion No. 12/2010, Adopted May 7, 2010 (Litigated by Author through Freedom Now).

[111] Mahmoud Hussein Gomaa Ali v. Egypt, WGAD Opinion No. 83/2017, Adopted Nov. 22, 2017, at ¶ 74.

commentator has suggested that association can be distinguished from temporary demonstrations or purely private gatherings "when a gathering has been formed with the object of pursuing certain aims and has a degree of stability and thus some kind of institutional (though not formal) structure."[112] This may provide some context for drawing lines between the various rights, but it is important to remember that ultimately these activities are all generally protected under international human rights law. This may be why in several instances the WGAD describes Article 21 of the ICCPR, dealing with assembly, as constituting the "freedom of peaceful assembly and association,"[113] implying that freedom of assembly may also be understood to incorporate association.

Unlike the distinctions between freedom of assembly and association, however, the distinction between the right to privacy and the right to freedom of association is potentially more significant, given that some commentators have suggested that private gatherings do not constitute associations falling under the scope of Article 22 of the ICCPR.[114] Such gatherings would instead be covered under Article 17 of the ICCPR, which protects against "arbitrary or unlawful interference" with one's "privacy, family, home or correspondence," or through the nearly identical language in Article 12 of the UDHR. However, Category II does not list either of these articles as one of the enumerated rights within its scope. The WGAD has generally not been troubled by this distinction, and appears to interpret freedom of association to include private associations.[115] This even appears to extend to family associations, despite a HR Committee view related to a child custody dispute that suggests that family associations are not covered by Article 22 of the ICCPR.[116] In contrast, the WGAD has found in two opinions on North Korea that a practice of placing individuals in forced labor camps because of family ties under a "guilt by association system" was in violation of Article 20 of the UDHR.[117] The implication appears to be that whereas the distinction between private and public associations may be meaningful in other contexts, such as a child custody claim like that brought before the HR Committee, it has little bearing on whether an individual's detention is more or less arbitrary.

B Permissible Limitations and Derogations

From the language of Article 22(2) of the ICCPR, any restriction on freedom of association must be prescribed by law, for a legitimate interest, namely national security, public safety, public order, public health or morals, or the rights or freedoms of others,

---

[112] International Center for Not-for-Profit Law, Defending Civil Society, 14 Int'l J. Not-for-Profit L. 5, 40 (2012).

[113] Nasrin Sotoudeh v. Iran, WGAD Opinion No. 21/2011, Adopted May 5, 2011, at ¶ 30; see also Muhannad Al-Hassani v. Syria, WGAD Opinion No. 26/2011, Adopted Aug. 30, 2011.

[114] Nowak, at 498.

[115] Leonardo Miguel Bruzón Ávila, et al. v. Cuba, WGAD Opinion No. 17/2003, Adopted Sept. 5, 2003 (a detention resulting from a gathering that occurred in a private home was still a violation of freedom of association).

[116] P.S. v. Denmark, Communication No. 397/1990, Human Rights Committee, CCPR/C/45/D/297/1990, Aug. 18, 1992.

[117] Kim Im Bok, et al. v. Democratic People's Republic of Korea, WGAD Opinion No. 34/2013, Adopted Nov. 13, 2013; Choi Sang Soo, et al. v. Democratic People's Republic of Korea, WGAD Opinion No. 36/2013, Adopted Nov. 13, 2013 (although note that the WGAD, without explanation, does not find article 21 or 22 of the ICCPR).

and necessary in a democratic society to secure the legitimate interest. The WGAD has elaborated further to specify that legitimate concerns may arise where a right is practiced in such a way that there is a resort to violence in the exercise of the right, advocacy of national, racial, or religious hatred, or incitement to commit international crimes. In addition, it has noted that in placing limitations on the practice of rights, governments must respect the principle of proportionality and ensure that normal steps to preserve the rule of law have been taken.[118]

States may derogate from the right to freedom of association in certain states of emergency, provided they do so in accordance with the provisions of relevant human rights treaties.[119] As with other derogable rights, the principles of proportionality and necessity must govern any such derogation.[120] In regard to freedom of association, most jurisprudence has focused on permissible limitations, rather than instances where states claim a state of emergency exists. One notable exception is *Muhammad Munir Missouti, et al. v. Syria* on the detention of Communist party members in Syria, where martial law had been in force since 1963. The WGAD lamented the fact that "constitutional states of emergency tend to be used continually."[121] A later opinion on Syria similarly cited to the HR Committee to express concern over the use of state of emergency legislation to suppress human rights.[122] The following analysis, however, will focus on the boundaries of permissible limitations on the right to freedom of association in three areas where particular concerns over a State's limitation of the right may exist: regulations concerning registration, funding, and operations of an organization; trade unions; and criminal or terrorist organizations.

1 Organization Registration, Funding, and Ability to Operate

The HR Committee has determined that Article 22 of the ICCPR "extends to all activities of an organization" and applies not only to the right to form an organization but also "the right of such an organization freely to carry out its statutory activities."[123] States must accordingly offer positive protection to the civil society sphere.[124] Although the right to association is guaranteed even where an organization does not have legal status, organizations must also be allowed to seek legal personality, which is often necessary for their effective operation.[125] States can impose reasonable administrative requirements on organizations. For example, state regulations that require certain registration procedures from organizations, such as the submission of articles of association or financial information, may be permissible limitations of the right if they are in the interest of public

---

[118] ICCPR Art 22(2); Jigme Gyatso v. China, WGAD Opinion No. 8/2000, Adopted May 17, 2000, at ¶ 15.
[119] In particular, ICCPR Art 4.
[120] Filep Jacob Semuel Karma v. Indonesia, WGAD Opinion No. 48/2011, Adopted Sept. 2, 2011, at ¶ 21 (citing to the Human Rights Committee General Comment No. 29 on States of Emergency).
[121] Muhammad Munir Missouti, et al. v. Syria, WGAD Opinion No. 11/1993, Adopted Apr. 30, 1993, at ¶ 5(d).
[122] Muhannad Al-Hassani v. Syria, WGAD Opinion No. 26/2011, Adopted Aug. 30, 2011, at ¶ 25.
[123] Korneenko, et al. v. Belarus, Communication No. 1274/2004, Human Rights Committee, CCPR/C/88/D/1274/2004, Nov. 10, 2006, at ¶ 7.2.
[124] Nowak, at 498; Aleksandr Viktorovich Bialatski v. Belarus, WGAD Opinion No. 39/2012, Adopted Aug. 31, 2012, at ¶ 48 ("States are required to protect the establishment or activities of associations from interference by private parties.")
[125] International Center for Not-for-Profit Law, Defending Civil Society, 14 Int'l J. Not-for-Profit L. 5, 40 (2012).

order.[126] However, any registration requirements for NGOs must accordingly not be overly burdensome, improperly political or discriminatory, or expensive.[127]

The WGAD has consistently found violations of the right to freedom of association where organizations are denied official status for non-legitimate reasons and individuals are subsequently detained for participation in the illegal or unregistered organization. For example, detentions were found arbitrary where the Chinese government punished individuals for creating a social reform organization it found objectionable,[128] or where the Burmese government claimed a political opposition movement was unregistered and detained its founder.[129] Similarly, the WGAD found that imprisoning someone who established a human rights committee without registering the organization in Saudi Arabia was arbitrary because the obligation to seek authorization was neither lawful nor necessary to preserve the relevant public interests.[130]

Given that resources are necessary for organizations to operate, freedom of association includes the right to seek funds and other resources: access to external or foreign funding cannot be prohibited, fundraising capabilities should not be dependent on legal status, and burdensome constraints on an organization's ability to access funding should not be enacted.[131] The *Declaration on Human Rights Defenders* specifically outlines the right "individually and in association with others, to solicit, receive and utilize resources" so as to peacefully promote and protect human rights.[132] The WGAD has also found that the right to accept or collect funds for a human rights organization is protected by the right to freedom of association.[133] It particularly addressed this right in the context of a tax evasion charge brought by Belarus against a detained activist.

Aleksandr Bialatski is a Belarusian human rights activist, vice-president of the International Federation for Human Rights (FIDH), and Nobel Peace Prize nominee.[134] He was also chairman of the Viasna Centre for Human Rights, which was founded in 1996 after protests in Belarus to assist detained democracy activists, and he advocates for the development of civil society and respect for human rights in Belarus.[135] Because Viasna was deregistered by Belarusian authorities in 2003, it was not allowed to receive foreign funding through domestic bank accounts. In 2007, the HR Committee responded to a complaint brought by Bialatski and other members of Viasna and determined that the dissolution of Viasna was a violation of the freedom of association.

---

[126] Nowak, at 506–507.

[127] International Center for Not-for-Profit Law, *Defending Civil Society* (summarizing statements by the UN Special Rapporteur for Human Rights Defenders, European Court of Human Rights, Inter-American Commission on Human Rights, and others).

[128] Jin Haike and Zhang Honghai v. China, WGAD Opinion No. 32/2007, Adopted Nov. 28, 2007, ¶ 27.

[129] Ko Htin Kyaw v. Myanmar, WGAD Opinion No. 56/2013, Adopted Nov. 21, 2013, ¶ 8(a), 12–14.

[130] Sheikh Salman bin Fahd al-Awda, et al. v. Saudi Arabia, WGAD Opinion No. 48/1995, Adopted Dec. 1, 1995, at ¶ 8.

[131] *Report of the Special Rapporteur on the Rights to Freedom of Peaceful Assembly and of Association*, Human Rights Council, A/HRC/23/39, Apr. 24, 2013, at ¶17–20.

[132] *Declaration on Human Rights Defenders*, G.A. Res 53/144, A/RES/53/144, Mar. 8, 1999, at Annex, Art 13.

[133] Afif Jamil Mazhar, et al. v. Syria, WGAD Opinion No. 10/1993, Adopted Apr. 29, 1993, at ¶ 5(d-e); *see also* Kwon Young-Kil and Yang Kyu-hun v. South Korea, WGAD Opinion No. 25/1996, Adopted Sept. 18, 1996.

[134] *Biography: Aliaksandr Bialiatski*, FIDH (Nov. 2018), www.fidh.org/IMG/pdf/bio-ales_bialiatski-en.pdf.

[135] *About Viasna*, Viasna, June 24, 2002 (Nov. 2018), http://spring96.org/en/about.

It directed Belarus to re-register and compensate the organization.[136] Belarus did not comply and in August 2011, Bialatski was arrested and subsequently charged with tax evasion.[137]

The tax evasion case charged Bialatski with "concealment of profits on an especially large scale," a crime under the Criminal Code of Belarus, for failing to declare the existence of a private foreign bank account.[138] The Government argued that Bialatski's detention was based solely on the criminal offense of tax evasion, and suggested that the source "perversely interprets the situation . . . to give it a political hue."[139] In response, the source noted that because Viasna had been denied official registration, any financing for the organization necessarily had to be channeled through foreign bank accounts. Viasna was also forbidden from using foreign charitable contributions for human rights activities, meaning the Government had "thus cut off all possibilities for the organization to finance its human rights activities," in violation of Article 22 of the ICCPR.[140]

First, in finding Bialatski's detention arbitrary, the WGAD emphasized that given the context in which Viasna had been subject to harassment for its human rights activities, there was a heightened responsibility for the Government to engage in prompt, independent inquiry into any action against him: "When there are claims of human rights violations in this context, including a pattern of harassment," both domestic and international bodies "should apply the heightened standard of review of government action."[141] Where this heightened standard applies, domestic authorities have a duty to investigate promptly and independently, both institutionally and in practice. The need for this stricter review is particularly strengthened by critical findings by other international bodies regarding the dissolution of Viasna. But there was no evidence that the Government took the kind of independent and prompt review required by this heightened scrutiny. Thus while there "is no immunity for human rights defenders" against tax evasion charges, the Government action failed to appropriately protect human rights in this context.[142]

Second, if criminal liability is based on prior government action that violates human rights law, it will not be legally valid. Neither the domestic court judgments nor the Government's submission addressed the fact that the Viasna bank accounts were for fundraising purposes. In the absence of such information, the WGAD noted that criminal liability could not be based on prior government action, such as the deregistration of Viasna, which violated the right to freedom of association. Lacking government information to the contrary, the WGAD concluded this meant the criminal proceedings against Bialatski were also improper.[143]

Third, the criminal law provisions under which Bialatski was tried are not themselves human rights compliant, because the law fails to meet the Government's obligation to

---

[136] Belyatsky, et al v. Belarus, Communication No. 1296/2004, Human Rights Committee, CCPR/C/90/D/1296/2004, July 24, 2007, at ¶¶ 8–9.
[137] Aleksandr Viktorovich Bialatski v. Belarus, WGAD Opinion No. 39/2012, Adopted Aug. 31, 2012, at ¶¶ 4, 12.
[138] Id., at ¶ 4.
[139] Id., at ¶¶ 24, 26.
[140] Id., at ¶¶ 36–37.
[141] Id., at ¶ 45.
[142] Id., at ¶ 45.
[143] Id., at ¶ 47.

respect the right to freedom of association. The WGAD does not say the state must necessarily allow tax exemption for organizations like Viasna, but it notes that Article 22 imposes positive obligations on states to take "measures such as facilitating the tasks of associations by public funding or allowing tax exemptions" for foreign funding.[144] In an environment in which the Government has limited financial sources, the failure to provide tax exemption means a failure to protect the establishment or activities of civil society organizations. Furthermore, the WGAD noted, the Government has limited the financing activity of Viasna without meeting the requirements of Article 22(2) of the ICCPR that such limits must be lawful, imposed for a legitimate purpose, and necessary in a democratic society to achieve those purposes. Since the Government did not establish how de-registering Viasna or impairing its financing activities met these conditions, these were not proper limitations on the freedom of association. Bialatski's detention for pursuing these financing activities was therefore an arbitrary deprivation of his liberty.[145]

2 Trade Unions

Trade unions are associations like any other and their members are accordingly afforded the same association rights as members of any other organization. Some unique questions arise, however, in the context of what limitations states may place on trade unions, particularly to what extent general labor rights are incorporated into the freedom of association. Article 22(3) of the ICCPR explicitly specifies that those rights included in ILO Convention No. 87 are protected, which includes such rights as the right to organize, the rights of workers to join unions of their choosing, and the ability of unions to oversee their own internal administration.[146] Those labor rights not enumerated in ILO Convention No. 87 may be more contentious. For example, a controversial early HR Committee view found that a right to strike was not protected by Art 22(3) of the ICCPR, although more recent statements suggest a shift by the HR Committee on this issue.[147]

The WGAD has found the detention of individuals because of their trade union activity arbitrary on several occasions.[148] It has generally not been called on to make more difficult determinations regarding the appropriate boundaries of state regulation of labor unions. One early opinion, however, may shed some light on how the WGAD would approach laws that limit trade union activity in a manner that may violate freedom of association. *Kwon Young-Kil and Yang Kyu-hun* v. *South Korea* followed several years of organized labor disputes and protests and involved the detention of two labor leaders.

Kwon Young-kil and Yang Kyu-hun were the President and Vice-President, respectively, of the Korean Confederation of Trade Unions. The Korean Confederation of

---

[144] *Id.*, at ¶ 48.

[145] *Id.*, at ¶ 48–49.

[146] Freedom of Association and Protection of the Right to Organise Convention, July 9, 1948, 68 UNTS 17.

[147] J.B., et al. v. Canada, Communication No. 118/1982, Human Rights Committee, CCPR/C/28/D/118/1982, July 18, 1986; Joseph & Castan, at 661.

[148] *See, e.g.,* Noubir El Amaoui v. Morocco, WGAD Opinion No. 21/1993, Adopted Apr. 30, 1993; Orton Chirwa, et al. v. Malawi, WGAD Opinion No. 13/1993, Adopted Apr. 30, 1993; Atilay Aycin, et al. v. Turkey, WGAD Opinion No. 12/1996, Adopted May 23, 1996; Ulises González Moreno v. Cuba, WGAD Opinion No. 17/2013, Adopted Aug. 26, 2013.

Trade Unions was a new umbrella trade organization, which South Korean authorities considered illegal compared to the more pro-government and established Federation of Korean Trade Unions.[149] The two detainees were among a number of labor leaders arrested in the early 1990s, during a period of ongoing labor disputes in South Korea, many under charges of "third party intervention" in labor disputes.[150] "Third-party intervention" was when those with no immediate connection to a workplace were involved in a workplace dispute, and was interpreted by Korean authorities to include even advice to union members regarding their rights.[151] While South Korea had claimed such a law was necessary to protect the autonomy of labor unions, human rights groups argued the law had been used to silence activists and bring criminal charges against union leaders. Indeed, the ILO's Committee on Freedom of Association had already found that South Korea's ban on third-party intervention posed "a serious restriction on the free functioning of trade unions," and that detentions of trade union leaders for the exercise of their trade union rights violated freedom of association.[152] In response, South Korea was reportedly in the process of reconsidering the law, but in the meantime continued to charge and detain union leaders for third-party intervention.

The primary charges against Kwon and Yang centered on the third-party intervention charge, specifically Articles 12 and 13 of the Labour Dispute Adjustment Act, which prohibited strikes by public servants and unauthorized third party intervention in labor disputes.[153] Although there were more minor charges related to fundraising for the trade union and participating in demonstrations – both also potentially implicating human rights concerns – the primary charge remained that of third party intervention, particularly in relation to alleged instigation of illegal strikes. The Government appeared to acknowledge the shortcomings in the law, noting efforts to reform it following the recommendations of the ILO, but suggested that even under a revised law, Kwon's and Yang's actions would still have been improper, as their actions "went considerably beyond simple advice given to trade union members on their rights, since they instigated violent acts of dispute in violation of the criminal law and the relevant labour laws, which resulted in a serious threat to the public order."[154]

The WGAD filed Kwon's case following his release, but it found Yang's detention a violation under Category II, motivated by his exercise of freedom of expression, peaceful assembly, and association. It reaffirmed that the Labour Dispute Adjustment Act was not compliant with the ICCPR, and accordingly those detained under it were detained arbitrarily.[155] Unfortunately, the WGAD did not elaborate on this finding, perhaps because the Government itself had expressed intent to reform the law. This does appear, however, to be an expression of agreement with the findings of the ILO Committee on

---

[149] Amnesty International, ASA 25/10/96, Summary, Apr. 1996, Republic of Korea Update on Trade Union leaders.

[150] *South Korea: Labor Rights Violations under Democratic Rule*, Human Rights Watch, Nov. 1995.

[151] Kwon Young-Kil and Yang Kyu-hun v. South Korea, WGAD Opinion No. 25/1996, Adopted Sept. 18, 1996, at ¶ 5(a).

[152] *Report of the Committee on Freedom of Association*, Complaint against the Government of Korea, Case No. 1629, International Labour Organization, at ¶ 259 (1994).

[153] Kwon Young-Kil and Yang Kyu-hun v. South Korea, WGAD Opinion No. 25/1996, Adopted Sept. 18, 1996, at ¶ 6(a) (as reported in the Government's account).

[154] *Id.*, at ¶ 7.

[155] *Id.*, at ¶ 10

Freedom of Association, suggesting the WGAD may view that body as a source of authority for the status of the rights of trade unions.

The WGAD also clarified that whether Yang's actions threatened the public order, absent the third-party intervention provision, was speculative. It did acknowledge that it is feasible that organizing demonstrations or intervening in labor disputes could foreseeably result in harm to the public order. But in the given case, any potential harm posed by Yang's activities was insufficient to justify the restrictions placed on him. Thus the detention was arbitrary because the law governing the detention itself violated human rights standards. But even had the law been compliant with human rights standards, the WGAD said Yang's actions to organize demonstrations or become involved in a labor dispute did not pose sufficient risk of harm to justify a limitation of his freedom of association.[156]

3 Association with Terrorist or Criminal Organizations

Limitations may be placed on the right to association with terrorist or criminal organizations. The WGAD has acknowledged that criminalizing membership in a criminal group is a common means by which countries respond to organized crime and that the freedom of association does not preclude such legislation.[157] However, the WGAD has frequently found that laws or policies that criminalize membership in a group that is allegedly terrorist or violent violate, if applied arbitrarily, the right to freedom of association. Problems have arisen where a law is vague or overbroad, enforcement of a law or policy violates human rights standards, or an association is improperly labeled a criminal or terrorist organization.

Vague or overbroad laws or criminal charges may allow for detentions that are improperly based on an individual's right to freedom of association. In its mission to Turkey, the WGAD expressed concern over Turkey's overly broad definition of terrorism, as well as legislation in the country that allowed for terrorist charges even where the defendant had not committed a serious violent crime, noting how terrorist charges can be misused to restrict the right to expression, assembly, and association.[158]

Governments similarly cannot make vague reference to terrorist charges to justify detaining an individual. Where Bahrain failed to detail terrorist charges made against a detained human rights advocate, the WGAD questioned the true reasons for the detention, asking to which specific terrorist group the detainee belonged and what types of terrorist activities had he engaged in.[159]

Even where laws may not violate freedom of association as such, they may be enforced in a manner that does. In its mission to Honduras, the WGAD noted that a Honduran law that created an offense of "illicit association," criminalizing membership in violent youth gangs (*maras*), was not on its face incompatible with international human rights

---

[156] *Id.*, at ¶ 9.

[157] *Report of the Working Group on Arbitrary Detention: Mission to Honduras*, Human Rights Council, A/HRC/4/40/Add.4, Dec. 1, 2006, at ¶ 87.

[158] *Report of the Working Group on Arbitrary Detention: Mission to Turkey*, Human Rights Council, A/HRC/4/40/Add.5, Feb. 7, 2007, at Summary; Amer Jamil Jubran v. Jordan, WGAD Opinion No. 9/2016, Adopted Apr. 19, 2016, at ¶¶ 38–40, noting with concern the proliferation of anti-terrorism statutes to limit practice of arbitrary arrest and detention.

[159] Abdulhadi Abdulla Alkhawaja v. Bahrain, WGAD Opinion No. 6/2012, Adopted May 2, 2012, ¶ 42.

standards.[160] But the practical application of the Honduran law had raised concerns, as the use of tattoos to identify gang members meant tattooed individuals were permanently considered members of an "illicit association," even after they left the gang, and subject to arrest without warrant.[161] And the WGAD questioned whether a term of imprisonment of twelve to twenty years is "necessary in a democratic society for simple membership in a gang."[162]

Just as general terrorist or criminal laws may improperly infringe on freedom of association, so may the determination that a particular group is inherently criminal or violent. Where a group clearly has a peaceful human rights or political change agenda, it is often convenient for governments to label such groups as criminal or terrorist as a means of silencing dissent. In such cases, the WGAD will usually find evidence of criminal behavior lacking. Thus when China alleged that a political dissident and founder of an environmental organization was engaged in terrorist activities, the WGAD emphasized the lack of specific supporting evidence for this claim.[163] In particular, it questioned whether the ideology of the detainee's organization, described by the Government as "trying to paralyze the activity of Beijing by means of social worry and economic crisis," could be considered sufficient grounds for showing terrorist activity.[164] It was similarly skeptical where Viet Nam "seems to liken what is simply peaceful exercise of the rights of opinion, expression and association to 'activities to overthrow the Government.'"[165]

A more challenging legal question is presented when groups with ties to criminal elements or potentially violent or problematic ideologies may permissibly be banned or their members detained. The provisions of Articles 5 and 20 of the ICCPR, read with Article 22, suggest groups that aim to destroy the rights of others, disseminate propaganda for war, or advocate national, racial, or religious hatred that constitutes incitement to violence can be found illegal and precluded from operating.[166] In light of such provisions, the HR Committee found, for example, that laws that prohibited reorganizing the banned Italian fascist party were permissible as limitations on the freedom of association.[167]

However, these determinations are not always simple. This can clearly be seen in *Karmelo Landa Mendibe v. Spain*. Mendibe was a professor, Basque leader, and former member of the European Parliament, where he served as a representative of a political party, Herri Batasuna.[168] Herri Batasuna, known as Batasuna at the time of Mendibe's detention, was part of a Basque political coalition that arguably acted as the political wing of the Basque separatist group ETA, which used terrorist methods. Although Batasuna never explicitly supported terrorist tactics and no evidence suggested the group aided in terrorist attacks, the group also did not specifically condemn ETA's violent tactics. Given

---

[160] *Report of the Working Group on Arbitrary Detention: Mission to Honduras*, Human Rights Council, A/HRC/4/40/Add.4, Dec. 1, 2006, at ¶ 87.

[161] *Id.*, at ¶ 88.

[162] *Id.*, at ¶ 87.

[163] Feng Ming v. China, WGAD Opinion No. 43/2005, Adopted Nov. 29, 2005, at ¶ 21.

[164] *Id.* at ¶ 20.

[165] Nguyen Dan Que v. Viet Nam, WGAD Opinion No. 14/1993, Adopted Apr. 30, 1993, at ¶ 10.

[166] ICCPR, at Arts. 5, 20; Nowak, at 506–508.

[167] M.A. v. Italy, Communication No. 117/1981, Human Rights Committee, A/39/40, Sept. 21, 1984, at ¶ 13.3.

[168] Karmelo Landa Mendibe v. Spain, WGAD Opinion No. 17/2009, Adopted Sept. 4, 2009, at ¶ 5.

the likely overlap in membership between the two groups, Batasuna has faced particularized suspicion from the Government.[169] Indeed, Batasuna was declared illegal in Spain in 2003 due to its ETA ties (it remained legal in France, where it maintained a presence until dissolving in 2013).[170] Several of its leaders were subsequently detained or faced charges of belonging to a terrorist organization.[171] Mendibe was arrested in 2008 and accused of participating in the National Board of Batasuna.[172] Because this was the sole reason for his detention, a key question for the WGAD was whether the detention was in violation of his freedom to associate with a particular political party, here one with potential terrorist links.

First, the WGAD suggested that the banning of Batasuna itself may be troublesome under freedom of association and other freedoms guaranteed in the ICCPR, reaffirming anti-terrorism legislation must be lawful, necessary, and proportionate. Citing heavily to the work of the UN Special Rapporteur on the Promotion and Protection of Human Rights and Fundamental Freedoms While Countering Terrorism, the WGAD suggested the specific counter-terrorism legislation in this case was overbroad because it had also been used to limit the rights of civil society organizations such as political parties. The Special Rapporteur, on a mission to Spain, had commented specifically on Batasuna, expressing concern with sweeping bans on political parties that prohibit peaceful as well as non-peaceful elements. That said, in his report he did not make any determinations on the orientation of Batasuna itself.[173] The WGAD suggested that the broad ban on political parties and civil society groups did not appear necessary or proportionate.

Second, the WGAD stressed that association with a political party is protected under the right to freedom of association, even where that association is illegal: "(m)embership and leadership of a political party, legal or illegal, are legitimate acts and indisputable manifestations of freedom of expression and opinion and of the right of association."[174] The judgment of Spain's highest courts regarding the illegality of Batasuna was therefore not sufficient to permit a limitation on Mendibe's right to associate. Presumably, an individualized determination is instead needed. In assessing Mendibe's case, the WGAD noted that no role in "any criminal or terrorist act" had been alleged as grounds for his detention.[175] Mendibe had only been detained for exercising his right to associate with a political party, which is a protected right, and accordingly the WGAD found the detention a violation under Category II.

This analysis suggests that a sweeping determination of the danger posed by a specific group is insufficient to justify detention for association with such a group; rather, individualized evidence of criminal or violent activity is necessary. It is important to note, however, that this opinion is perhaps inconsistent with the WGAD's mission report on Honduras, where it suggested that a law that criminalized mere membership in a violent association was a permissible law.[176] The difference here appears to be based in

---

[169] *Batasuna Banned*, THE ECONOMIST, Aug. 29, 2002; *Profile: Batasuna*, BBC, Aug. 27, 2002.

[170] *Basque Party Linked to ETA Declares Its Own Dissolution*, THE GUARDIAN, Jan. 3, 2013.

[171] Victoria Burnett, *Basque Leaders Arrested in Spain*, NEW YORK TIMES, Oct. 6, 2007.

[172] Karmelo Landa Mendibe v. Spain, WGAD Opinion No. 17/2009, Adopted Sept. 4, 2009, at ¶ 50.

[173] *Report of the Special Rapporteur on the Promotion and Protection of Human Rights and Fundamental Freedoms While Countering Terrorism*, Human Rights Council, A/HRC/10/3/Add.2, Dec. 16, 2008, at ¶ 14.

[174] Karmelo Landa Mendibe v. Spain, WGAD Opinion No. 17/2009, Adopted Sept. 4, 2009, at ¶ 57.

[175] *Id.*, at ¶ 56.

[176] *Report of the Working Group on Arbitrary Detention: Mission to Honduras*, Human Rights Council, A/HRC/4/40/Add.4, Dec. 1, 2006, at ¶ 87.

the nature of the organization: association in purely criminal organizations, like gangs, needs to be distinguished from association in a political party, even if that party has violent ties.

III Assembly

The ICCPR separates the right to freedom of assembly and freedom of association into separate articles, with the right to assembly covered in Article 21:

> The right of peaceful assembly shall be recognized. No restrictions may be placed on the exercise of this right other than those imposed in conformity with the law and which are necessary in a democratic society in the interests of national security or public safety, public order (*ordre public*), the protection of public health or morals or the protection of the rights and freedoms of others.

Article 20(1) of the UDHR states simply:

> Everyone has the right to freedom of peaceful assembly or association.

Equivalent provisions are provided for in Article 11 of the *African Charter on Human and Peoples' Rights*, Article 15 of the *American Convention for Human Rights*, and Article 11 of the *European Convention on Human Rights*.

Because the UDHR combines assembly and association in the same article, when the WGAD finds a violation of Article 20 of the UDHR it is not always immediately clear whether they are referring to assembly, association, or both. Nonetheless, it is important to look at both rights distinctly, both because they are treated in separate articles in the ICCPR and because, despite potential overlap, the two rights do have slightly different features and content. However, the combination of the articles under the UDHR may account for a number of opinions where the WGAD finds a freedom of assembly violation, but only discusses freedom of association.[177]

There is also significant overlap between freedom of expression, association, and assembly: in almost all cases dealing with either assembly or association, a violation of freedom of expression also is found. Take, for example, Atilay Aycin, who was convicted and sentenced by a Turkish court on charges of spreading "separatist propaganda" following a speech expressing support for Kurdish independence.[178] The speech (freedom of expression) was made at a meeting in a public square (freedom of assembly), and Aycin was the general president of a trade union (freedom of association).[179]

A *Scope of the Right*

An assembly is any gathering of more than one person, covering the range of such meetings, whether in a closed room or in public, mobile or stationary, or with inclusive

---

[177] *See, e.g.*, Orton Chirwa, et al. v. Malawi, WGAD Opinion No. 13/1993, Adopted Apr. 30, 1993; Mohammad Shahadeh, et al. v. Syria, WGAD Opinion No. 6/2004, Adopted May 26, 2004.

[178] Atilay Aycin, et al. v. Turkey, WGAD Opinion No. 12/1995, Adopted May 23, 1996, at ¶ 5(a).

[179] *Id.*

or exclusive membership.[180] Both authorized and unauthorized assemblies fall within the scope of the right, as do spontaneous ones.[181] It is important to note that some kinds of assemblies fall under other rights: religious assemblies are covered by Article 18, private assemblies by Article 17, and assemblies of associations by Article 22.[182] The inference is that Article 21 is designed to address those assemblies not covered by these other rights, but the text of both the ICCPR and UDHR is all-encompassing and a particular assembly may conceivably be protected by multiple rights simultaneously.[183]

These distinctions have been reflected in the WGAD's jurisprudence. Thus "having a public meeting without violence" is a protected activity,[184] and a detention merely for participating in a demonstration, absent other charges or explanation, was arbitrary.[185] Activities protected under the right have included a speaking tour by the Vice President of the Burmese National League for Democracy,[186] gathering to discuss the creation of a political reform committee and publicizing such activities,[187] and participation in a peaceful flag-raising ceremony.[188] Detentions were similarly found arbitrary where they were the result of the organization of a funeral and other "unlawful assemblies" by South Korean activists,[189] holding unauthorized protests,[190] or "holding illegal meetings."[191]

The WGAD has on occasion taken a broad approach to interpreting freedom of assembly, finding violations of the right even where attendance at a particular assembly was not reported. For example, freedom of assembly was violated when members of the African National Congress were detained for voter education work in South Africa in the twilight of apartheid, perhaps because voter education meetings were understood to be incorporated into voter education work more generally.[192] In another case, freedom of assembly was violated where an individual who organized a demonstration, but ultimately did not attend the demonstration himself, was subsequently detained. The right accordingly covers both organizing an assembly and attending it.[193]

The text of both the ICCPR and UDHR protect only *peaceful* assembly. This explicitly places non-peaceful assemblies outside the scope of the right, creating a positive articulation of what is an essentially equivalent negative provision for the other rights, whose exercise may be limited when done in a violent manner.

Importantly, mere participation in demonstrations that have violent incidents does not necessarily impute a violent character to an individual's exercise of the right to assemble.

---

[180] Joseph & Castan, at 646 (noting the Human Rights Committee has said in Coleman v. Australia that freedom of assembly does not apply where someone acts alone).

[181] *Report of the Special Rapporteur on the Rights to Freedom of Peaceful Assembly and of Association*, Human Rights Council, May 21, 2012, A/HRC/20/27, ¶ 29.

[182] Joseph & Castan, at 646.

[183] *Id.*, at 645–646.

[184] Ryad Hamoud Al-Darrar v. Syria, WGAD Opinion No. 15/2006, Adopted May 12, 2006.

[185] Abdulhadi Abdulla Alkhawaja v. Bahrain, WGAD Opinion No. 6/2012, Adopted May 2, 2012, at ¶ 43.

[186] U Tin Oo v. Myanmar, WGAD Opinion No. 11/2005, Adopted May 26, 2005.

[187] Saud Mukhtar Al-Hashimi, et al. v. Saudi Arabia, WGAD Opinion No. 27/2007, Adopted Nov. 28, 2007.

[188] Filep Jacob Semuel Karma v. Indonesia, WGAD Opinion No. 48/2011, Adopted Sept. 2, 2011.

[189] Kim Sam-sok, et al. v. South Korea, WGAD Opinion No. 49/1995, Adopted Dec. 1, 1995, at ¶¶ 9–10.

[190] *See, e.g.*, Sekvan Aytu v. Turkey, WGAD Opinion No. 9/1993, Adopted Apr. 29, 1993.

[191] Femi Falana v. Nigeria, WGAD Opinion No. 22/1993, Adopted Apr. 30, 1993, at ¶ 4.

[192] Nathaniel Ngakantsi and Johannes Setlae v. South Africa, WGAD Opinion No. 15/1994, Adopted Sept. 28, 1994 (one detainee was arrested following a voter education meeting, but the WGAD refers to the voter education work engaged in more generally by both detainees as violating freedom of assembly).

[193] Jannes Hutahaen, et al. v. Indonesia, WGAD Opinion No. 18/1995, Adopted June 2, 1995.

Where the evidence showed Pierre Roger, a popular singer also known as Lapiro, attempted to calm demonstrators and acted to prevent riots in Cameroon, his involvement in those demonstrations was a protected exercise of the freedom of assembly.[194] Leaders of opposition movements or protests or any other individual involved in planning a demonstration or public assembly cannot be detained merely because attendees engage in violent conduct. Andrei Sannikov was an opposition electoral candidate in Belarus who encouraged protestors to demonstrate in Minsk. He gave a speech during which some individuals began breaking windows of a government building after which Sannikov was arrested.[195] The WGAD found that Sannikov was improperly detained and that his detention was a reaction to his status as an electoral candidate and participation in protests.[196]

Furthermore, the HR Committee has noted (and the WGAD has followed this approach) that the exercise of freedom of assembly may involve "a certain level of disruption to ordinary life" that does not rise to the level of violent activity.[197] That is, assemblies do not lose their legal protection for a certain level of disturbance. In *Can Thi Thieu v. Viet Nam*, the WGAD found that a protest that resulted in obstruction of traffic was not outside the scope of the right to freedom of assembly.[198] Furthermore, the Government failed to demonstrate why a subsequent twenty-month sentence was a response necessary and proportionate to a temporary traffic obstruction.[199]

The WGAD also requires sufficient evidence that a detained individual's exercise of his right to assembly was violent. In *Yao Fuxin v. China*, the detainee was a Chinese labor activist and former factory worker who assisted in organizing worker demonstrations as well as an independent corruption inquiry into company accounts after the closure of a steel factory in Liaoyang City. These activities took place in a context where economic troubles in China's industrial northeast in the 1990s and early 2000s resulted in the closure of factories and lay-offs of millions of workers.[200] The protests organized by Yao and others were reportedly attended by up to 30,000 people, many of whom were workers who had not been paid wages or pensions on the closure of local factories.[201] Shortly after Yao led demonstrations in front of local government offices, he was arrested near his home, held secretly in an unknown location, and eventually charged with "organizing illegal demonstrations" and "gathering a crowd to disrupt social order."[202]

The corruption allegations were apparently taken seriously by Liaoyang City officials, and the Government's response to the WGAD emphasized that multiple criminal cases, including one conviction, were in progress against corrupt officials. However, despite the acknowledged merit of Yao's cause, the Government maintained that his activities breached Chinese law and constituted the crime of organizing an unlawful assembly.

[194] Pierre Roger Lambo Sandjo (alias Lapiro) v. Cameroon, WGAD Opinion No. 32/2011, Adopted Sept. 1, 2011.

[195] Andrei Sannikov v. Belarus, WGAD Opinion No. 14/2012, Adopted May 4, 2012, at ¶¶ 3–4.

[196] *Id.*, at ¶ 40

[197] *Joint Report of the Special Rapporteur on the Rights to Freedom of Peaceful Assembly and of Association and the Special Rapporteur on Extrajudicial, Summary or Arbitrary Executions on the Proper Management of Assemblies*, Human Rights Council, A/HRC/31/66, Feb. 4, 2016, at ¶ 32; Can Thi Thieu v. Viet Nam, WGAD Opinion No. 79/2017, Adopted Nov. 22, 2017, at ¶ 56.

[198] Can Thi Thieu v. Viet Nam, WGAD Opinion No. 79/2017, Adopted Nov. 22, 2017, at ¶ 56.

[199] *Id.*, at ¶ 57.

[200] *Rustbelt Revival: Reforming the Northeast*, The Economist, June 16, 2012.

[201] *China Protest Leaders Go on Trial*, BBC, Jan. 15, 2003.

[202] Yao Fuxin v. China, WGAD Opinion No. 15/2002, Adopted Nov. 28, 2002, at ¶ 6.

In particular, it alleged that he took advantage of worker discontent to "plan, instigate and carry out a number of destructive activities," and engaged in violent conduct, including smashing public vehicles, disrupting government offices, and blocking traffic.[203] The source responded by emphasizing that there was no factual basis to support the allegations of violence attributed to Yao, whose actions had been peaceful.[204]

In weighing the dueling submissions, the WGAD emphasized that the decisive question was whether Yao exercised his right to peaceful assembly or rather was engaged in violent conduct. Given the contradictory claims regarding whether the detainee had engaged in violent acts, the failure of the Government to support its allegations with convincing evidence led the WGAD to conclude the detainee's actions could not be considered violent on a prima facie basis.[205] It observed that the kind of violent behavior that the Government attributed to Yao could have been recorded through a variety of means. But no evidence was presented to establish this record. The WGAD suggested acceptable documents would consist of "official records, witness statements in the criminal proceedings against Yao Fuxin, or court decisions pronounced against him." Without such documents, the WGAD was unwilling to make the assumption that Yao's conduct was violent. The implication of this analysis is that where violent behavior can be documented, the government has a duty to provide sufficient documentation to support claims that a detainee was engaged in violent acts instead of peaceful assembly.

It should be noted that even where a government attempts to provide evidence showing violent conduct, the WGAD will also inquire into the legitimacy of that evidence. Fernando de Araujo was an East Timorese student activist arrested in 1991 by Indonesian police, who had allegedly planted explosives in his residence. The original indictment in his case included charges related to his organization of a public demonstration, but made no mention of any explosives. Absent a specific response from the Government, the WGAD accepted that the fact that the indictment made no reference to the explosives, combined with a lack of any advocacy of violence in Mr. Araujo's activism, constituted evidence that the explosives were planted.[206]

B Limits to the Right

Per the language of the ICCPR, any limitation on the right to freedom of assembly must be imposed in conformity with the law and necessary in a democratic society to ensure a legitimate interest, meaning national security or public safety, public order, public health or morals, or protection of the rights and freedoms of others. The requirement of "necessary in a democratic society" incorporates the principle of proportionality and must correspond to a minimum democratic standard.[207] The WGAD has similarly determined that restrictions on the right to freedom of assembly must be "proportionate and justified."[208] As with the other rights, Article 29 of the UDHR governs limitations of the rights contained in the Universal Declaration.

---

[203] *Id.*, at ¶¶ 11, 12.
[204] *Id.*, at ¶ 13.
[205] Yao Fuxin v. China, WGAD Opinion No. 15/2002, Adopted Nov. 28, 2002, at ¶ 16.
[206] Fernando de Araujo v. Indonesia, WGAD Opinion No. 36/1993, Adopted Sept. 29, 1993, at ¶ 7.
[207] Nowak, at 491.
[208] 61 Individuals v. United Arab Emirates, WGAD Opinion No. 60/2013, Adopted Nov. 21, 2013, at ¶ 21.

Freedom of assembly is a derogable right, but as is always the case with derogable rights, during a state of emergency, human rights instruments must still be respected, as well as the principles of proportionality and necessity. The WGAD jurisprudence has not extensively discussed the freedom of assembly during states of emergency.

1 Laws and Regulations Limiting Freedom of Assembly

Where a law violates the right to freedom of assembly, detentions under that law will be arbitrary. Thus courts, to ensure a fair trial, must address laws that restrict the freedom of assembly when considering charges against those who were detained for exercising their freedom of assembly.[209] The primary opinion on freedom of assembly from the HR Committee is *Kivenmaa v. Finland*, which establishes the approach for evaluating notifications requirements for demonstrators. The HR Committee found that a require-ment that demonstrators notify police of an intended public protest six hours before was a permissible limitation under Article 21 of the ICCPR. However, a gathering of a few individuals at a public event where a banner was displayed did not constitute a demon-stration, and a requirement of pre-notification in that context would be an impermissible limitation on the right.[210] The Special Rapporteur on the Rights to Freedom of Peaceful Assembly and of Association has also given some guidance regarding permissible regula-tions on assemblies under human rights law, noting that while reasonable notification requirements may be permissible, the right to peaceful assembly should not be depend-ent on the issuance of a permit and spontaneous assemblies should be exempt from notification requirements.[211] Blanket bans on peaceful assembly are intrinsically dispro-portionate and prohibition of an assembly should be a measure of last resort.[212]

The WGAD has not generally found it necessary to explain in depth the scope of permissible regulations on assemblies. Several opinions have specified that provisions of various criminal codes violate the right to freedom of assembly, but with minimal explanation as to why.[213] The WGAD also decided that a detention under a blanket ban on assemblies was not justified and expressed concern regarding overly broad or vague laws that allow for inappropriately tailored limitations on the right to freedom of assembly.[214]

In addition, laws that define or interpret acts of peaceful assembly as violent or disruptive criminal conduct also violate the right to freedom of assembly. Thus, the WGAD determined that legislation that classified activities such as meeting with student

---

[209] Nabeel Abdulrasool Rajab v. Bahrain, WGAD Opinion No. 12/2013, Adopted May 3, 2013 (domestic courts should have addressed the legitimacy of a law banning public demonstrations).

[210] Kivenmaa v. Finland, Communication No. 412/1990, Human Rights Committee, CCPR/C/50/D/412/1990, Mar. 31, 1994, at ¶ 9.2.

[211] *Report of the Special Rapporteur on the Rights to Freedom of Peaceful Assembly and of Association*, General Assembly, A/68/299, Aug. 7, 2013, at ¶¶ 23–24.

[212] *Id.* at ¶ 25; *Report of the Special Rapporteur on the Rights to Freedom of Peaceful Assembly and of Association*, Human Rights Council, A/HRC/20/27, May 21, 2012, at ¶ 39.

[213] Ko Htin Kyaw v. Myanmar, WGAD Opinion No. 56/2013, Adopted Nov. 21, 2013, at ¶ 13; Nabeel Abdulrasool Rajab v. Bahrain, WGAD Opinion No. 12/2013, Adopted May 3, 2013, at ¶ 38.

[214] *Id.*, at ¶ 40; Afif Jamil Mazhar, et al. v. Syria, WGAD Opinion No. 10/1993, Adopted Apr. 29, 1993, at ¶ 5; Le Cong Dinh, et al. v. Viet Nam, WGAD Opinion No. 27/2012, Adopted Aug. 29, 2012, at ¶ 40 (explicitly referencing freedom of expression but extending the concern with overbroad criminal offences to freedom of assembly as well).

leaders or calling for student strikes to be "'counter-revolutionary propaganda and agitation', 'disturbing social order' and 'disturbing traffic'" is likely to be found to be inconsistent with international law.[215] Likewise, where separatist activities are punished under China's Penal Code, but a separatist activity is defined as even a peaceful demonstration, the Government violates the right to freedom of association.[216]

2 Police Responsibilities and Authority at Demonstrations

Police may interfere with certain assemblies when doing so is lawful, necessary, and to protect a legitimate interest, but the response must be proportionate. Article 21 of the ICCPR contains a slight wording variation from similar rights, in that limitations on the right must be "imposed in conformity with the law" rather than "provided" or "prescribed" by law.[217] In practice, the primary impact of this difference is that where police are granted a general authorization, they may determine that a particular demonstration is disturbing public order and interfere to break it up, provided the action has a basis in law.[218] However, this does *not* exempt police from the provisions regarding limitations of freedom of assembly protected by international law, and the principles of necessity and proportionality continue to apply. This has implications for use of force guidelines for police and the legality of certain crowd control measures, but for our purposes it is important primarily in terms of when police detention of protestors is appropriate.

Like other limitations of the right to freedom of assembly, police action must have authority under the law, be necessary in a democratic society, and protect an enumerated legitimate interest. Again, the principle of proportionality governs. Police must also differentiate between violent and non-violent protestors. During a visit to Argentina, the WGAD received conflicting reports regarding social protests by groups known as "*piqueteros*," or picketers, which involved blockading or occupying roads and occasionally resulted in violent clashes. It then expressed concern that protestors were detained regardless of whether their actions were peaceful or violent.[219] If a protestor resists arrest, this alone cannot justify a detention. Where an underlying arrest is based on criminal proceedings that were improperly initiated because of the detainee's exercise of his fundamental rights, charges such as resisting police officers or attempting to flee during arrest are also not valid.[220]

Governments should be particularly vigilant regarding policing and detention policies where mass arrests are made at large demonstrations. The WGAD has addressed such situations more extensively in its reports rather than individual opinions, perhaps because such mass detentions are often short-term and may be less likely to make their way to the WGAD as individual cases. Thus, the WGAD expressed concern over information received during a mission to Georgia, which suggested numerous procedural

---

[215] Chen Lantao v. China, WGAD Opinion No. 53/1993, Adopted Dec. 7, 1993, at ¶ 8.
[216] Ngawant Sandrol v. China, WGAD Opinion No. 28/2000, Adopted Sept. 14, 2000.
[217] *Compare* ICCPR, at Art. 21 *with* ICCPR, at Art. 19(3), 22(2).
[218] Nowak, at 489–490.
[219] *Report of the Working Group on Arbitrary Detention: Visit to Argentina*, Commission on Human Rights, E/CN.4/2004/3/Add.3, Dec. 23, 2003, at ¶¶ 49–50.
[220] Mohammad Salih Al Bajadi v. Saudi Arabia, WGAD Opinion No. 45/2013, Adopted Nov. 15, 2013, at ¶ 25.

irregularities in the detention of protestors in Tbilisi in May 2011.[221] Similarly, following protests surrounding the 2008 Armenian elections, it cited reports of mass detentions of opposition activists, which were not in conformity with international or national standards.[222]

During its visit to Argentina, the WGAD reported on the economic collapse of December 2001, which led to widespread protests, resulting in the blockading of roads, some of which were major highways, and the occupation of bridges, streets, railway, bus, underground stations, and public buildings.[223] These *piqueteros* were violating a law that makes illegal the disruption of transport. During its visit, the WGAD said the Government explained that the *piqueteros* were violent and infringed on other people's freedom of movement and transport and that some 3,000 were facing charges.[224] But representatives of the *piqueteros* movement explained to the WGAD that their actions were peaceful, that they took special care not to harm anyone, such as by letting ambulances through, and they did not demand payment or tolls. In response to these conflicting accounts, the WGAD stated:

> [U]nder international law, the right to peaceful assembly and the right to demonstrate peacefully must be recognized and guaranteed. No restrictions may be imposed on these rights other than those necessary in a democratic society, such as restrictions that are necessary in the interests of national security, public safety, public order, health or morals, or the protection of the rights and freedoms of others. The Working Group's concern arises from the complaints that it has received that the security forces usually make arrests and detain individuals during actions by *piqueteros* regardless of whether such actions are carried out in a peaceful or violent manner.[225]

Two WGAD opinions regarding detentions in Bahrain in 1995 have outlined some of the WGAD's particular expectations in situations of mass detentions of protestors. During this time of social unrest, the Government was routinely arresting protestors, reportedly including 200 secondary school pupils and children as young as twelve, in addition to large numbers of adult protestors.[226] Given the considerable number of detentions, the WGAD expressed disappointment that Bahrain had not provided details regarding the names, legal situation, or charges brought against those who were detained, tried, or released, or any information on the sentences of those brought to trial. This suggests that such documentation is a minimum for the responsibility of a Government who has detained a large number of protestors.[227]

Of course, police may improperly detain peaceful protestors on a smaller scale as well, as evidenced in *Léster Téllez Castro, et al. v. Cuba* and *Leonardo Miguel Bruzón Ávila,*

---

[221] *Report of the Working Group on Arbitrary Detention: Mission to Georgia*, Human Rights Council, A/HRC/19/57/Add.2, Jan. 27, 2012, at ¶¶ 69–77.

[222] *Report of the Working Group on Arbitrary Detention: Mission to Armenia*, Human Rights Council, A/HRC/16/47/Add.3, Feb. 17, 2011, at ¶¶ 55–58.

[223] *Report of the Working Group on Arbitrary Detention: Mission to Argentina*, Commission on Human Rights, E/CN.4/2004/3/Add.3, Dec. 23, 2003, at ¶ 49.

[224] *Id.*

[225] *Id.*, at ¶ 50.

[226] Hassan Ali Fadhel, et al. v. Bahrain, WGAD Opinion No. 21/1996, Adopted Sept. 17, 1996; Sadeq Abdulla Ebrahim, et al. v. Bahrain, WGAD Opinion No. 22/1996, Adopted Sept. 17, 1996.

[227] Sadeq Abdulla Ebrahim, et al., at ¶ 8.

et al. v. *Cuba*, which together address the detentions of several Cuban dissidents. Five of the detainees in the two opinions were arrested either for organizing protests or attending a meeting, and since the Government did not establish a justifiable reason for limiting their right to peacefully assemble, they represented fairly standard freedom of assembly Category II cases. The other three detainees, however, were arrested in relation to their role in protests outside a hospital and since heightened public interest concerns may be present at a medical facility, the opinions provide some unique context for determining the bounds of appropriate police interference with demonstrations.

Juan Carlos González Leyva, Léster Téllez Castro, and Carlos Brizuela Yera were arrested following a peaceful demonstration outside a hospital to which a journalist had been admitted after allegedly being beaten by police. Castro and Yera were also journalists and Leyva was a lawyer and the president of the Cuban Foundation for Human Rights. The source reported the protest was peaceful, consisting of prayer and chanting slogans, and that it did not block the hospital entrance.[228] It appears that some of the demonstrators, including those detained, sought treatment for the injured journalist and attempted to visit him in the hospital. The source also reported that all three had been held without any charges or a trial. In addition, Leyva, who is blind, was struck on the head during the arrest and did not receive necessary medical care while detained.

In contrast, the Government made extensive claims regarding disruption of medical services at the hospital, which it argued justified the arrests made by police. In regards to Castro and Yera, the Government alleged that the detainees caused serious disruptions to medical services at the hospital, their actions did not constitute a peaceful protest, and police intervention was necessary to protect the delivery of medical services.[229] It alleged that their actions "paralysed the public services of the hospital for over an hour," resulting in a frustration of the right to access medical services of the patients in the hospital.[230]

Similarly, the Government claimed that Leyva and others "went to the guardroom with the aim of engaging in disorderly conduct and fabricating a false image" of police misconduct toward the hospitalized journalist.[231] It specifically claimed that he "threatened and harassed" hospital staff and patients, that delivery of medical services was disrupted for almost two hours, and that as a result one patient took fright and suffered a heart attack, and emergency medical tests for children were delayed.[232] The response also argued that his injury during arrest was a result of self-harm, and that he hit his head against a metal door with the intent of blaming the injury on the police.

Despite the serious-sounding nature of the Government's claims, the WGAD dismissed them readily, finding all three detentions arbitrary. In evaluating the cases of Castro and Yera, it noted the Government and source agreed that the detention followed a protest across from the hospital, but that the Government had not shown evidence sufficient to refute the claim that it was a peaceful protest of police misconduct. Similarly, Leyva's actions had not been shown to be violent, and "the charges brought

---

[228] Leonardo Miguel Bruzón Ávila, et al. v. Cuba, WGAD Opinion No. 17/2003, Adopted Sept. 5, 2003, at ¶ 21.

[229] *Id.*, at ¶10–12; Léster Téllez Castro et al. v. Cuba, WGAD Opinion No. 16/2003, Adopted Sept. 5, 2003, at ¶ 7(a).

[230] Léster Téllez Castro, et al., at ¶ 7(a).

[231] Leonardo Miguel Bruzón Ávila, et al., at ¶ 11.

[232] *Id.*, at ¶¶ 12–13.

against him are ambiguous and have not clearly identified offences which could justify his detention."[233] Such analysis underscores the necessity of specific charges and documented proof where governments detain those exercising the right to peaceful assembly. Police cannot merely use the location of a protest to justify detention. Furthermore, the alleged reasons for the arrest of the individuals should be translated into justifiable criminal charges against the detainees, which did not occur here. The WGAD also noted that given the political nature of the protest, resisting arrest could have caused the disturbance at the hospital.[234] Because the arrest itself was improper, presumably, the disturbance was the fault of the officials effectuating the arrest rather than the detained individual. This emphasizes the positive responsibility of police to ensure basic human rights are respected.

3 The Arab Spring and Detention as a Political Tool to Suppress Demonstrations

Following and during the Arab Spring, which saw both peaceful and non-peaceful protests across the Arab region, many states resorted to detention of protestors to suppress political dissent or to attempt to control a deteriorating political situation. Several of these detentions eventually made their way to the WGAD, including the arbitrary detention of two prominent human rights activists who were arrested in Bahrain following their active participation in peaceful protests,[235] and four individuals detained after participating in demonstrations organized by the Islamic Jordanian Youth Movement.[236] States that did not see a full-fledged Arab Spring movement also reacted to regional trends by responding harshly to protests, as evidenced by WGAD opinions on arbitrary detentions in the United Arab Emirates and Saudi Arabia.[237] These cases highlight the way in which detention can be used as a tool to silence or harass protestors advocating for political change, as evidenced best by the case of a Yemeni demonstrator in *Mohammad Muthana Al Ammari v. Yemen*.

Mohammed Muthana Al Ammari was a teacher and father of two who participated in anti-government demonstrations in 2011. In January of that year, he was threatened by political security agents with physical harm unless he ceased demonstrating, and then in March was detained for a half-day. Nonetheless, he continued to demonstrate throughout 2011, and in December, he was arrested. Several days later his picture appeared in a pro-government newspaper, which announced the arrest of "six al-Qaida terrorists" and quoted a government source who identified him as a dangerous militant. After a lengthy pretrial detention, Al Ammari was convicted and sentenced on charges of "participation in an armed gang in order to carry out a military attack." Despite serving his two-year sentence, he remained in detention at the time of the issuance of the WGAD opinion.[238]

---

[233] *Id.*, at ¶ 24.
[234] *Id.*, at ¶ 24.
[235] Nabeel Abdulrasool Rajab v. Bahrain, WGAD Opinion No. 12/2013, Adopted May 3, 2013; Abdulhadi Abdulla Alkhawaja v. Bahrain, WGAD Opinion No. 6/2012, Adopted May 2, 2012.
[236] Hisham Al Heysah, et al. v. Jordan, WGAD Opinion No. 53/2013, Adopted Nov. 21, 2013.
[237] Mohammad Salih Al Bajadi v. Saudi Arabia, WGAD Opinion No. 45/2013, Adopted Nov. 15, 2013; Abdullah Al Hadidi v. United Arab Emirates, WGAD Opinion No. 42/2013, Adopted Nov. 15, 2013; 61 Individuals v. United Arab Emirates, WGAD Opinion No. 60/2013, Adopted Nov. 21, 2013.
[238] Mohammad Muthana Al Ammari v. Yemen, WGAD Opinion No. 13/2014, Adopted Apr. 30, 2014.

Unfortunately, Al Ammari was not the only Yemeni detained following anti-government demonstrations. Human Rights Watch detailed multiple instances of demonstrators being detained without charge or disappearing, many of whom reported torture and ill-treatment.[239] The WGAD also addressed the detention of another Yemeni who participated in 2011 demonstrations.[240] Haytham al-Zaeetari was secretly detained in 2013 and the source reported he had not been informed of the charges against him nor had he been brought before a judicial body. With no response from the Government, the WGAD emphasized "that Mr. Al-Zaeetari is known to be a member of a group of young activists who organized peaceful demonstrations," and found his detention to be a direct result of his right to freedom of assembly, among other rights.[241]

Such a pattern suggested a problematic government policy and this concern was reflected in the WGAD's finding of a violation of Category II in Al Ammari's case. Noting his peaceful participation in demonstrations prior to his arrest, the WGAD expressed concern over the threats and half-day detention by which Al Ammari was targeted prior to his long-term detention. Such action "illustrates the pattern whereby anti-Government demonstrators are detained in an attempt to prevent them ... from exercising their right to assembly."[242] His detention was accordingly a clear instance of government use of arbitrary detention to control or prevent the free exercise of the right to assembly. Although addressing the individual case before it, the WGAD appeared concerned with the broader trends in Yemen, emphasizing "the detention of an individual has far-reaching adverse consequences for his or her family and community, and society at large."[243]

An additional trend that concerned the WGAD was evidenced by the terrorist allegations leveled against Al Ammari. It noted "the use of the pretext of securitization is an increasing trend in a number of jurisdictions" and has accordingly led to decreased protection for fundamental human rights.[244] Although this analysis spoke more to the finding of a Category III violation in this case, it nonetheless reflects a worrisome convergence between accusations of terrorist activity and the targeting of anti-government demonstrators. It also represented an additional political tool to target peaceful demonstrators, which when combined with the kind of pre-detention harassment seen in Al Ammari's case, represented a worrying trend of silencing peaceful dissenters who were using peaceful assembly as a means of voicing political or social discontent.

IV Opinion and Expression

The WGAD has said that the freedom of expression "constitutes one of the basic conditions of the development of every individual."[245] Yet the exercise of this right is also the basis for a large number of the detentions that the WGAD has determined were

---

[239] *Yemen: Detained, Tortured, and Disappeared*, Human Rights Watch, May 7, 2012.
[240] Haytham al-Zaeetari v. Yemen, WGAD Opinion No. 11/2014, Adopted Apr. 29, 2014.
[241] *Id.*, at ¶ 18
[242] Mohammad Muthana Al Ammari, at ¶ 23.
[243] *Id.*, at ¶ 26.
[244] *Id.*, at ¶ 19.
[245] *Report of the Working Group on Arbitrary Detention*, Commission on Human Rights, E/CN.4/2006/7, Dec. 12, 2005, at ¶ 45.

arbitrary under Category II.[246] Analysis of the right to freedom of expression is accordingly a rich source of the WGAD's Category II jurisprudence.

Under Article 19 of the ICCPR:

1. Everyone shall have the right to hold opinions without interference.
2. Everyone shall have the right to freedom of expression; this right shall include freedom to seek, receive and impart information and ideas of all kinds, regardless of frontiers, either orally, in writing or in print, in the form of art, or through any other media of his choice.
3. The exercise of the rights provided for in paragraph 2 of this article carries with its special duties and responsibilities. It may therefore be subject to certain restrictions, but these shall only be such as are provided by law and are necessary:
   (a) For respect of the rights or reputations of others;
   (b) For the protection of national security or of public order (*ordre public*), or of public health or morals.

And Article 19 of the UDHR also protects the freedom of opinion and expression:
Everyone has the right to freedom of opinion and expression; this right includes freedom to hold opinions without interference and to seek, receive and impart information and ideas through any media and regardless of frontiers.

The right is similarly protected in the regional human rights instruments, specifically Article 9 of the *African Charter on Human and Peoples' Rights*, Article 13 of the *American Convention on Human Rights*, and Article 10 of the *European Convention on Human Rights*. Note that the regional instruments do contain variations in their articulation of the right and permissible limitations on its exercise.

The ICCPR distinguishes between freedom of opinion, as an absolute right, and the right to express that opinion, which may be limited. The freedom of expression is also a derogable right, where the provisions of Article 4 of the ICCPR are applicable. As with other rights in the UDHR, the general limitation provision contained in Article 29 applies to Article 19 of the UDHR.

The HR Committee's General Comment 34 on Article 19 is a key source for interpreting the scope of and limitations to the right to freedom of opinion and expression. The various international experts on the right to freedom of expression – specifically, the UN Special Rapporteur on Freedom of Opinion and Expression, Organization for Security and Cooperation in Europe Representative on Freedom of the Media, Organization of American States (OAS) Special Rapporteur on Freedom of Expression, and ACHPR Special Rapporteur on Freedom of Expression and Access to Information – have also issued a series of joint resolutions commenting on specific features of the right. In addition to its extensive case jurisprudence, the WGAD has also frequently commented on the wide array of ways that states have restricted freedom of opinion and expression through its country missions.[247]

---

[246] *Report of the Working Group on Arbitrary Detention*, Commission on Human Rights, E/CN.4/1999/63, Dec. 18, 1998, at ¶ 45.

[247] See, e.g., *Report of the Working Group on Arbitrary Detention on Mission to Azerbaijan*, Human Rights Council, A/HRC/36/37/Add.1, Aug. 2, 2017, at ¶ 87 (concluding "The Working Group observes that human rights defenders, journalists, political and religious leaders continue to be regularly detained under criminal or administrative charges. These practices are contrary to the obligations of Azerbaijan under international human rights law.")

A Freedom of Opinion

Articles 19 of the ICCPR and UDHR guarantee "the right to hold opinions without interference." This includes opinions of all forms and without exceptions. The WGAD has stressed that individuals have the right to believe in erroneous opinions,[248] as well as politically unpopular or offensive ones.[249] Freedom of opinion, like Article 18's freedom of belief, is an absolute right. The freedom to hold opinions may be distinguished from the freedom of thought and belief protected by Article 18(1), but the rights overlap and the distinction is not always clear. Some commentators have suggested that the distinction lies between religious beliefs and more secular opinions, while Manfred Novak suggests that the freedom of thought leads to the development of opinions.[250] The distinction is not necessarily crucial, however, because both Article 18(1) and 19(1) are absolute rights.

Where someone is detained merely because of their opinion, a violation of Article 19 has occurred. General Comment 34 explains "the harassment, intimidation or stigmatization of a person, including arrest, detention, trial or imprisonment for reasons of the opinions they may hold," is a violation of Article 19(1) of the ICCPR, meaning that any detention of an individual solely because of their opinion is invalid.[251] However, identifying when someone has been targeted solely for an opinion is challenging, because presumably an opinion can only be identified once it is expressed. Laws that criminalize holding certain opinions would violate Article 19(1), so if one is detained under such a law, this would violate ICCPR Article 19(1) rather than 19(2).[252] Where no such law exists, however, distinguishing between detentions violating Articles 19(1) and 19(2) is more challenging.

This reality is reflected in the practice of the WGAD, which even when referencing the ICCPR seldom differentiates between freedom of opinion and expression, generally finding an Article 19 violation without specifying if the detention violates 19(1) or 19(2) of the ICCPR.[253] Nonetheless, in several cases the WGAD has made a general reference to Article 19, which appears to incorporate freedom of opinion specifically. A Jordanian lawyer and member of the Arab Socialist Baath Party was detained by Syria "only for his political views and opinions," and accordingly his detention violated ICCPR and UDHR Articles 18 and 19.[254] Elsewhere, the WGAD has emphasized the right to hold opinions without interference "even if they should contradict official Government policies."[255]

In *Anwar Ibrahim* v. *Malaysia*, the case of a former deputy Prime Minister of Malaysia and then-serving Leader of the Opposition and Member of Parliament barred from attending parliamentary sessions as a result of his ongoing detention, the WGAD found

---

[248] Tri Agus Susanto Siswowihardjo v. Indonesia, WGAD Opinion No. 42/1996, Adopted Dec. 3, 1996, at ¶ 8.

[249] Abdenacer Younes Meftah Al Rabassi v. Libya, WGAD Opinion No. 27/2005, Adopted Aug. 30, 2005, at ¶ 10.

[250] *Compare Report of the Special Rapporteur, Mr. Abid Hussain, Pursuant to Commission on Human Rights Resolution 1993/45*, Commission on Human Rights, E/CN.4/1995/32, Dec. 14, 1994, at ¶ 25, *with* Nowak, at 441.

[251] General Comment No. 34, Human Rights Committee, CCPR/C/GC/34 (2011), at ¶ 9.

[252] *Id.* ("It is incompatible with paragraph 1 to criminalize the holding of an opinion.")

[253] *See, e.g.,* Mohammed Abbou v. Tunisia, WGAD Opinion No. 41/2005, Adopted Nov. 28, 2005, at ¶ 30; Le Cong Dinh, et al. v. Viet Nam, WGAD Opinion No. 27/2012, Adopted Aug. 29, 2012, at ¶ 42.

[254] Mujalli Nasrawin v. Syria, WGAD Opinion No. 35/1993, Adopted Sept. 29, 1993.

[255] Sonam Gyalpo v. China, WGAD Opinion No. 33/2007, Adopted Nov. 30, 2007, at ¶ 16.

a joint violation of the twin freedoms of opinion and expression.[256] The WGAD took note of the pattern of persecution, including the fact that he had been targeted on politicized charges, to rule he had been targeted for his activities as a political opposition leader.[257] The WGAD applied a similar analysis in the case of Gloria Macapagal-Arroyo, the former President of the Philippines, noting that the Government's defiance of court rulings to lift travel bans against her, the removal of judges in her cases, the timing of charges against her, and statements by officials suggesting she was guilty prior to her indictment all evidenced that she was targeted for her political opinion.[258]

Membership or involvement in certain groups may also serve as an indication of an individual's opinion. This is an area of overlap between Article 19(1) and the freedom of association, although the distinction is important because only Article 19(1) is absolute. The WGAD has occasionally found violations of Article 19, with an emphasis on freedom of opinion, where detentions are based on membership in political parties. For example, in two early opinions dealing with the detention of Communist Party members in the Philippines, the WGAD emphasized that the individuals were targeted for their opinions, noting that they should not have been arrested for "holding beliefs which they are and were entitled to hold under universally accepted principles."[259] (The reference to "beliefs" rather than "opinions" appears to be a misstatement; the WGAD does not discuss Article 18 in this opinion). In both cases the WGAD appears to base its determination that the individuals in question were targeted because of their opinions on the fact that they were detained under a law outlawing the political party of which they were a member.[260] Other early cases similarly find an Article 19 violation, but do not specifically find a violation of the right to freedom of association, where members of particular political associations are detained.[261] It is not clear whether this was the WGAD rendering opinions with less precision in its earlier years or rather a recognition of overlap between Article 19(1) and Article 22. However, given the absolute nature of 19 (1), an elaboration of when it is applicable would be desirable.

In addition to scenarios where an individual is detained for having a particular opinion, attempts to coerce the opinions of detainees may constitute a violation of Article 19(1). The WGAD has dealt with this issue specifically in the context of so-called rehabilitation or reintegration measures.

One form of detention that is particularly linked to serious infringements on the right to freedom of opinion is measures of "rehabilitation through labor." The WGAD has said that measures that have an improper purpose of coercing opinion or belief are always arbitrary. Recognizing that "rehabilitation through labor" measures may have this improper purpose, the WGAD noted in its first report to the UNCHR that there was a

---

[256] Anwar Ibrahim v. Malaysia, WGAD Opinion No. 22/2015, Adopted Sept. 1, 2015, at ¶ 38 (Litigated by the Author through Perseus Strategies).

[257] Id., at ¶ 37.

[258] Gloria Macagpal-Arroyo, at ¶ 44.

[259] Reynaldo Bernardo, et al. v. The Philippines, WGAD Opinion No. 30/1993, Adopted Apr. 30, 1993, at ¶ 15; see also Roland Abiog and Antonio Cabardo v. Philippines, WGAD Opinion No. 1/1993, Adopted Apr. 30, 1993.

[260] Reynaldo Bernardo, et al., at ¶ 15; Roland Abiog & Antonio Cabardo, at ¶ 9.

[261] Bernard Benoît, et al. v. Haiti, WGAD Decision No. 25/1993, Adopted Apr. 30, 1993 (members of a group calling for a return of Aristide in Haiti); Tebira Indris Habani, et al. v. Sudan, WGAD Opinion No. 13/1996, Adopted May 23, 1996 (members of the Ansar Sect in Sudan).

need to determine whether sanctions of rehabilitation through labor "generally designed to encourage an individual to change or even renounce his opinions, using methods resembling coercion, constitute, by definition, arbitrary detention under Category II."[262] Deliberation No. 4 was subsequently adopted to address the legal issues surrounding rehabilitation through labor, as well as similar measures bearing labels such as rehabilitation, reintegration into society, or reform.[263]

Deliberation No. 4 determines that where "the main purpose of the measure is political and/or cultural rehabilitation through self-criticism," instead of merely occupational rehabilitation, the deprivation of freedom is inherently arbitrary. This should be determined in light of its "conformity with the international norms relating to freedom of opinion and of expression," determined by reference to the rights referenced in Category II.[264] Deliberation No. 4 focuses particularly on the freedom of religion and belief, but subsequent commentary by the WGAD has made it clear that this is not an exclusive focus. In a 1998 report on its visit to China, the WGAD emphasized categorically that re-education through labor should never be applied to persons exercising their fundamental freedoms.[265]

In practice, the WGAD has found instances of arbitrary detention where "rehabilitation through labor" or similar measures are imposed in relation to multiple rights listed under Category II, but in particular to Article 19's guarantee of freedom of expression. Citing to Deliberation No. 4, the WGAD found that even where a sentence of re-education through labor for Falun Gong members was a "more favourable measure" than a prison sentence, it still constituted an arbitrary detention imposed for the exercise of the freedom of conscience and religion and the freedom of opinion and expression.[266] The WGAD similarly relied on Deliberation No. 4 where a poet, religious leaders and laity, and other Chinese citizens received sentences of re-education through labor, this time finding violations of the freedom of expression and the freedom of assembly.[267] In other opinions, although neither Deliberation No. 4 nor freedom of opinion is discussed explicitly, the WGAD has found instances of arbitrary detention, based on Article 19 and other rights, for those subject to ideologically coercive forced labor in China and in the North Korean gulag system.[268]

On the other hand, on some occasions the WGAD has chosen not to find a Category II violation even where an ideological conversion system is part of an individual's detention. The clearest example of this approach was in *Lee Jang-hyong, et al. v. South Korea*, where the WGAD found a Category III violation but failed to find a Category II

---

[262] *Report of the Working Group on Arbitrary Detention*, Commission on Human Rights, E/CN/4/1992/20, Jan. 21, 1992, at ¶ 23(d).

[263] *Report of the Working Group on Arbitrary Detention*, Commission on Human Rights, E/CN.4/1993/24, Jan. 12, 1993, at Deliberation No. 4, Preamble.

[264] *Id.*

[265] *Report Submitted by the Working Group on Arbitrary Detention: Visit to the People's Republic of China*, Commission on Human Rights, E/CN.4/1998/44/Add.2, Dec. 22, 1997, at ¶ 95.

[266] Cheng Gang, et al. v. China, WGAD Opinion No. 7/2003, Adopted May 9, 2003, at ¶ 30.

[267] Zhou Lunyou, et al. v. China, WGAD Opinion No. 66/1993, Adopted Dec. 9, 1993.

[268] Zhang Yinan v. China, WGAD Opinion No. 24/2004, Adopted Nov. 26, 2004; Kim Im Bok, et al. v. Democratic People's Republic of Korea, WGAD Opinion No. 34/2013, Adopted Nov. 13, 2013; Choi Seong Jai, et al. v. Democratic People's Republic of Korea, WGAD Opinion No. 35/2013, Adopted Nov. 13, 2013; Choi Sang Soo, et al. v. Democratic People's Republic of Korea, WGAD Opinion No. 36/2013, Adopted Nov. 13, 2013.

violation regarding the detention of Kim Sun-myung. Kim had been imprisoned by South Korea since 1951 in conditions of "extreme isolation," and denied release on parole for a refusal to renounce Communist opinions, making him one of the longest-held political prisoners in the world.[269] Although the WGAD confirmed that his detention was arbitrary under Category III, on account of the unfairness of his trials in the 1950s, it did not find a Category II violation in his case.

This may be contrasted with the view of the HR Committee several years later, in a communication regarding the South Korean "ideological conversion system."[270] That case involved Yong-Joo Kang, who was held in solitary confinement for thirteen years for refusing to convert from a worldview deemed to be communist.[271] The HR Committee found South Korea's actions violated Article 18(1) and 19(1) of the ICCPR by applying a coercive system in a discriminatory fashion, with a view of altering the political view of the inmate.[272] Such a finding would seem to have been similarly applicable in *Lee Jang-hyong, et al.* v. *South Korea*, given Kim's ongoing detention was based on his continued holding of certain political opinions.

B Scope of Freedom of Expression

The right to freedom of expression encompasses all forms of communications and any sort of idea that may be transmitted between persons.[273] The WGAD has confirmed this approach in its own experience and the forms of expression for which individuals are arbitrarily detained is similarly broad, covering a full range of forms and manners of expression.[274] Unlike the right to freedom of assembly, which is only protected if it is peaceful, all forms of expression fall within the scope of the right. This means that even unpopular, scandalous, blasphemous, or potentially criminal speech falls within the *scope* of the right, although such speech may be limited according to Article 19(3) of the ICCPR and Article 29(2) of the UDHR. The WGAD reiterated this approach in *Su Changlan* v. *China*, the case of a former school teacher and popular rights activist advocating for expansion of women's rights to land tenure. The WGAD stated in this case, "the fact (the detainee's) conduct was criminalized under domestic law in China did not deprive of her rights under international law," referring to Article 19 of the ICCPR.[275]

The WGAD has particularly noted that freedom of expression extends to ideas "that offend or disturb the State or any other sector of the population."[276] For example, in *James Mawdsley* v. *Myanmar*, the WGAD concluded "[p]eaceful expression of

---

[269] Lee Jang-hyong, et al. v. South Korea, WGAD Opinion No. 1/1995, Adopted May 30, 1995, at ¶¶ 5(b)–6. For a more detailed account of the coercive measures used to attempt to sway Sun-myung's political views, see Nicolas D. Kristof, *Free in Seoul after 44 Years and Still Defiant*, NEW YORK TIMES, Aug. 20, 1995.

[270] Kang v. South Korea, Communication No. 278/1999, Human Rights Committee, CCPR/C/78/D/878/1999, July 15, 2003.

[271] *Id.*, at ¶ 3.2.

[272] *Id.*, at ¶ 7.2.

[273] General Comment No. 34, at ¶ 11.

[274] *Report of the Working Group on Arbitrary Detention*, Commission on Human Rights, E/CN.4/2007/7, Dec. 12, 2005, at ¶ 46.

[275] Su Changlan v. China, WGAD Opinion No. 39/2015, Adopted Dec. 2, 2015, at ¶ 22.

[276] *Id.*, at ¶ 46.

opposition to any regime cannot give rise to arbitrary arrest."[277] Even possessing materials on a certain subject matter may be considered a form of expression protected under Article 19.[278] The refusal to speak or express oneself in a certain way is also protected. The WGAD found instances of arbitrary detention where an Iraqi journalist was detained for refusing to write articles in support of the Kuwaiti invasion and where a Jordanian activist was arrested after refusing to sign a statement expressing opposition to political protests.[279]

In addition, expression need not be verbal or affirmative. Gestures are forms of expression and the WGAD has found actions such as raising a fist or attempting to unfurl a banner to constitute forms of expression.[280] There is, therefore, overlap between Article 21 rights and the Article 19 freedom of expression guarantee.[281] In *Maikel Giovanni Rondón Romero, et al.* v. *Venezuela*, a joint submission concerning the detention of 315 detained demonstrators, the WGAD considered that preventing the detainees from participating in demonstrations violated their right to freedom of expression.[282] The treatment of the case under Article 19 primarily highlights that the WGAD has taken an expansive reading of when expression can be said to have been manifested. In *Ko Mya Aye* v. *Myanmar*, the detainee dressed in white and encouraged others to do the same.[283] In *Hassan Zafar Arif* v. *Pakistan*, Article 19 included even the right to just listen to a speech (as opposed to actually delivering one, an obvious form of expression).[284]

The text of the ICCPR explicitly incorporates protection for expression through "any other media," and accordingly detentions have been found arbitrary by the WGAD where they are based on expression in the form of letters,[285] petitions,[286] publications,[287] cartoons,[288] interviews,[289] active citizenship trainings,[290] television appearances,[291] and video footage.[292] This extends to new forms of media, especially the Internet, as the WGAD has dedicated a Deliberation particularly to the challenge of detentions resulting from the use of the Internet. Deliberation No. 8 acknowledges the differences between expression through the Internet and more traditional means of communication, but insists that these differences do not alter the fundamental meaning of freedom of

---

[277] James Mawdsley v. Myanmar, WGAD Opinion No. 25/2000, Adopted Sept. 14, 2000, at ¶ 12 (Litigated By Author).

[278] Sonam Gyalpo v. China, WGAD Opinion No. 33/2007, Adopted Nov. 30, 2007, at ¶ 16.

[279] Aziz Al-Syed Jasim v. Iraq, WGAD Opinion No. 52/1993, Adopted Dec. 7, 1993, at ¶ 9.

[280] Li Hai v. China, WGAD Opinion No. 19/1999, Adopted Sept. 16, 1999; Wang Wanxing v. China, WGAD Opinion No. 20/2001, Adopted Nov. 28, 2001.

[281] Maikel Giovanni Rondón Romero, et al. v. Venezuela, WGAD Opinion No. 51/2014, Adopted Nov. 21, 2014, at ¶ 39.

[282] Id., at ¶¶ 35, 37.

[283] Ko Mya Aye v. Myanmar, WGAD Opinion No. 28/2010, Adopted Nov. 22, 2010, at ¶ 24 (Litigated by Author).

[284] Hassan Zafar Arif v. Pakistan, WGAD Opinion No. 8/2017, Adopted Apr. 19, 2017, at ¶¶ 27–29.

[285] Mahmoud Sherifo, et al. v. Eritrea, WGAD Opinion No. 3/2002, Adopted June 17, 2002; Ouyang Yi and Zhao Changqing v. China, WGAD Opinion No. 26/2003, Adopted Nov. 28, 2003.

[286] Ko Mya Aye, at ¶ 24.

[287] Pedro Alvarez Martinez v. Cuba, WGAD Opinion No. 16/1992, Adopted Session No. 4.

[288] Manouchehr Karimzadeh v. Iran, WGAD Opinion No. 28/1994, Adopted Sept. 29, 1994.

[289] Tashi Wangchuck v. China, WGAD Opinion No. 69/2017, Adopted Nov. 20, 2017, at ¶ 34.

[290] Adil Bakheit, et al v. Sudan, WGAD Opinion No. 34/2016, Adopted Aug. 25, 2016, at ¶ 36.

[291] Ahmed Belaichi v. Morocco, WGAD Opinion No. 3/1994, Adopted May 17, 1994.

[292] Ko Than Htun and Ko Tin Htay v. Myanmar, WGAD Opinion No. 7/2008, Adopted May 8, 2008.

expression – "the freedom to impart, receive and seek information via the Internet is protected under international law in the same way as any other form of expression of opinions, ideas, or convictions."[293] Thus, in addition to more traditional methods of expression, Article 19 of the ICCPR and Article 19 of the UDHR "protect peaceful political discourse and commentary on public affairs via the Internet, including the expression of ideas that may be regarded as offensive."[294]

Multiple WGAD opinions have found instances of arbitrary detention where the detention is based on use of the Internet.[295] This has expressly included detentions based on expression communicated through e-mail,[296] blogging,[297] Twitter,[298] and Facebook.[299] Any limitations on the right to freedom of expression on the Internet must also be in strict accordance with the same human rights standards that apply to any other form of expression.[300]

For example, in *Nguyen Dan Que v. Viet Nam*, the WGAD concluded the detainee was in fact imprisoned for having written statements criticizing the Government, expressing his views about the lack of freedom of information in Viet Nam, and sending out these statements through the Internet. As such, this was a peaceful exercise of his freedom of opinion and expression and a violation of Article 19 of the ICCPR.[301]

The WGAD is also wary of overbroad criminal provisions being used to target persons engaged in critical expression. In *Iván Fernández Depestre v. Cuba*, for example, a political activist engaged in commemorating the anniversary of the death of a prominent historical figure from Cuba's past was charged with "pre-criminal social dangerousness."[302] The WGAD accepted the source's allegations that a Category II violation had occurred because the detainee had been targeted for his political opinion and expression.[303] The WGAD noted that a criminal charge must be associated with a particular act, displaying cognizance of the fact that vague provisions, such as the one in this case, are often used as weapons to target critical expression that cuts against accepted social conventions.[304]

[293] *Report of the Working Group on Arbitrary Detention*, Human Rights Council, E/CN.4/2007/7, Dec. 12, 2005, at ¶ 38.

[294] Pongsak Sriboonpeng v. Thailand, WGAD Opinion No. 44/2016, Adopted Nov. 21, 2016, at ¶ 29.

[295] Zouhair Yahyaoui v. Tunisia, WGAD Opinion No. 15/2003, Adopted Sept. 5, 2003; Huang Qi v. China, WGAD Opinion No. 15/2004, Adopted Sept. 15, 2004; Imed Al Chibani v. Libya, WGAD Opinion No. 6/2011, Adopted May 3, 2011.

[296] Nguyen Dan Que v. Viet Nam, WGAD Opinion No. 19/2004, Adopted Sept. 16, 2004 (Litigated by Author through Freedom Now); Abdenacer Younes Meftah Al Rabassi v. Libya, WGAD Opinion No. 27/2005, Adopted Aug. 30, 2005.

[297] Abdul Kareem Nabil Suliman Amer v. Egypt, WGAD Opinion No. 35/2008, Adopted Nov. 20, 2008.

[298] Khalifa Rabia Jajdi v. United Arab Emirates, WGAD Opinion No. 12/2014, Adopted Dec. 19, 2013; Abdullah Al Hadidi v. United Arab Emirates, WGAD Opinion No. 42/2013, Adopted Nov. 15, 2013; Abdullah Fairouz Abdullah Abd al-Kareem v. Kuwait, WGAD Opinion No. 28/2015, Adopted Sept. 3, 2015, at ¶ 27.

[299] Mohamed bin Abdullah bin Ali Al-Abdulkareem v. Saudi Arabia, WGAD Opinion No. 43/2011, Adopted Sept. 2, 2011.

[300] *Report of the Working Group on Arbitrary Detention*, Commission on Human Rights, E/CN.4/2006/7, Dec. 12, 2005.

[301] Nguyen Dan Que v. Viet Nam, WGAD Opinion No. 19/2004, Adopted Sept. 16, 2004, at ¶ 16.

[302] Iván Fernández Depestre v. Cuba, WGAD Opinion No. 9/2014, Adopted Apr. 23, 2014, at ¶¶ 4–5.

[303] *Id.*, at ¶ 26.

[304] *Id.*, at ¶ 24.

In many cases, restrictions on journalists and others engaged in activities that constitute expression of opinion are targeted by policies or practices that result in multiple human rights violations.[305] In such cases, the WGAD has often focused primarily on Article 19 as providing the nexus or cause for the targeting.[306] In the heavily publicized case of Jason Rezaian, an Iranian-American journalist detained while reporting as the Tehran correspondent for the *Washington Post*, the WGAD noted that the Government had pursued a policy of targeting dissidents and journalists.[307] In the absence of a response from the Government to the source's assertions, the WGAD relied primarily on observations by UN Special Rapporteurs and statements made at the General Assembly calling attention to the "widespread and serious restrictions ... on the right to freedom of expression," in finding a Category II violation.[308] Fair trial rights violations in that case were considered to have followed from the initial reprisal for the detainee's activities as a journalist.[309]

Arbitrary detentions in response to speech related to human rights protection and advocacy have been a particular concern for the WGAD, which has found detentions to be arbitrary when based on speech such as appearing before a human rights committee,[310] disseminating information regarding human rights abuses,[311] activism on behalf of others,[312] calling attention to the need for transparency in public affairs,[313] telling others about one's own insecure situation,[314] announcing a hunger strike and calling for civil disobedience,[315] and informing the United Nations about human rights violations.[316] Attendance at a human rights seminar, which could conceivably fall under freedom of assembly, was also found to fall under freedom of expression by the WGAD.[317]

Such detentions, which are formally characterized as "reprisals" for human rights related speech, receive heightened scrutiny from the WGAD.[318] The context of the ways in which persons are taken into custody, the crimes with which they are charged, and the conduct of their subsequent trials could evidence a reprisal for holding or expressing a political opinion. In *Gerardo Ernesto Carrero Delgado, et al.* v. *Venezuela*, a case involving several students arrested as part of an operation to dislodge protestors camped before an office of the UN Development Programme, the WGAD noted the

---

[305] Alhagie Abdoulie Ceesay v. The Gambia, WGAD Opinion No. 50/2015, Adopted Dec. 4, 2015, at ¶ 22.

[306] Jason Rezaian v. Iran, WGAD Opinion No. 44/2015, Adopted Dec. 3, 2015, at ¶ 35.

[307] *Id.* at ¶ 32.

[308] *Id.*, at ¶ 33.

[309] *Id.*, at ¶¶ 34, 36.

[310] Karanwi Meschack, et al. v. Nigeria, WGAD Opinion No. 2/1996, Adopted May 22, 1996.

[311] Li Hai v. China, WGAD Opinion No. 19/1999, Adopted Sept. 16, 1999.

[312] Enrique Guerrero Aviña v. Mexico, WGAD Opinion No. 55/2015, Adopted Dec. 4, 2015, at ¶ 27.

[313] Pedro Celestino Canché Herrera v. Mexico, WGAD Opinion No. 18/2015, Adopted Apr. 28, 2015, at ¶ 25.

[314] Rebiya Kadeer v. China, WGAD Opinion No. 30/2000, Adopted Nov. 27, 2000.

[315] Khemais Ksila v. Tunisia, WGAD Opinion No. 5/1999, Adopted May 20, 1999.

[316] Dr. Tin Min Htut and U Nyi Pu v. Myanmar, WGAD Opinion No. 4/2010, Adopted on May 5, 2010, at ¶ 22.

[317] Ali Khassif Saïd Al Qarni v. Saudi Arabia, WGAD Opinion No. 41/2011, Adopted Sept. 2, 2011.

[318] Librado Jacinto Baños Rodriguez v. Mexico, WGAD Opinion No. 19/2015, Adopted Apr. 28, 2015, at ¶ 18; Ahmed Mansoor v. United Arab Emirates, WGAD Opinion No. 64/2011, Adopted Nov. 22, 2011, at ¶ 20; Abdolfattah Soltani v. Iran, WGAD Opinion No. 54/2012, Adopted Nov. 19, 2012, at ¶ 29.

flimsiness of the charges and lack of evidence brought against the students showed that they were targeted for protesting government policies rather than on the cited grounds of security.[319]

In *Sheikh Suliaman al-Rashudi and Others* v. *Saudi Arabia*, several prominent political dissenters, including blogger Raif Badawi, whose cause had been taken up by Amnesty International, were detained for their writing and activism.[320] The detainees were charged with offenses the WGAD described as "too broad and imprecise," including "breaking allegiance to the ruler," "inciting disorder by calling for demonstrations," "insulting religious symbols," and "harming the image of the state by dissemination false information to foreign groups."[321] These crimes, the WGAD observed, could be utilized to criminalize the exercise of the right to freedom of expression, and therefore violated international standards.[322] The WGAD, in finding a Category II violation also noted the chronology of actions by the Government against the detainees.[323] These actions had included the opening of investigations into the activities of the known dissenters,[324] confiscation of property and cessation of social media accounts,[325] confiscation of books, documents, and computers,[326] fines for online activity,[327] and bans on appearances in the media.[328]

In another prominent case in Myanmar, four members of the "88 Generation" student movement, Min Ko Naing, Min Zayar, Pyone Cho, and Kyaw Min Yu, were summarily tried, convicted, and sentenced to sixty-five years in prison each for their political activities. The WGAD reminded the Government about its obligations under international law saying it:

> [C]onsiders that nothing in the original submission indicates that the entirely non-violent activities of these four members of the "88 Generation" movement . . . would not be protected by Articles 19, 20, and 21 of the Universal Declaration of Human Rights, all of which are at the core of political rights in a free and democratic society. The Working Group has no reason to doubt that the harsh prison sentences all four defendants have received are in reprisal for their peaceful political activities and membership in opposition movements.[329]

The WGAD applies the heightened standard of review when human rights defenders are detained and when there is a possible violation of their right to freedom of expression.[330] It has also noted that detentions that are in response to the exercise of the freedom of

---

[319] Gerardo Ernesto Carrero Delgado, et al. v. Venezuela, WGAD Opinion No. 26/2015, Adopted Sep. 3, 2015, at ¶¶ 4–5, 49.

[320] Sheikh Suliaman al-Rashudi, et al. v. Saudi Arabia, WGAD Opinion No. 38/2015, Adopted Sep. 4, 2015.

[321] *Id.*, at ¶¶ 26, 73.

[322] *Id.*

[323] *Id.*, at ¶ 72.

[324] *Id.*, at ¶ 10.

[325] *Id.*, at ¶ 11.

[326] *Id.*, at ¶ 18.

[327] *Id.*, at ¶ 28.

[328] *Id.*

[329] Min Zayar (Aung Myin), et al. v. Myanmar, WGAD Opinion No. 43/2008, Adopted Nov. 25, 2008, at ¶ 22. (Litigated by Author).

[330] Dilmurod Saidov v. Uzbekistan, WGAD Opinion No. 67/2012, Adopted Nov. 23, 2012, at ¶ 57; Frédéric Bauma Winga v. Democratic Republic of Congo, WGAD Opinion No. 31/2015, Adopted Sep. 3, 2015, at ¶ 19.

opinion and expression require a "particularly vigilant review of the application of fair trial guarantees."[331] This heightened scrutiny has been a particular concern of the WGAD where forms of political expression are at stake. Finding the detention of a Belarusian opposition politician to be arbitrary, the WGAD noted his detention had occurred the day before elections were held. Since the exercise of rights, including the right to freedom of expression in the context of the political process, represents "the very core of these fundamental freedoms," the WGAD undertakes a particularly intensive review in such situations.[332] The WGAD has also linked such cases of targeting human rights defenders to the rights of equality before the law and equal protection of the law under Articles 2 and 7 of the UDHR.[333]

C Permissible Limitations and Derogations

The practice of the WGAD is that a detention acting as a restriction on the freedom of expression is only justified when it has "a legal basis in domestic law, is not at variance with international law and is necessary to ensure the respect of the rights or reputations of others, or for the protection of national security, public order, public health or morals, and is proportionate to the pursued legitimate aims."[334] These requirements are largely derived from the text of the ICCPR, which as it does with other rights requires that restrictions on the freedom of expression are lawful and necessary to attain a proper purpose, which means respect for the rights or reputations of others and for the protection of national security, public order, or public health and morals. Article 29 of the UDHR also applies to restrictions on the freedom of expression, requiring that they be lawful and for the sole purpose of protecting the rights and freedoms of others, or morality, public order, and the general welfare in a democratic society.

The requirement that restrictions be "provided by law" means that the detention must be in conformity with domestic laws and international law. The detention must be justified under a domestic law that is universally accessible, in force at the time it is applied, and not arbitrary or unreasonable.[335] Even if this is established, mere conformity with domestic law will not justify a violation of international human rights law.[336] Where the detention violates international law obligations, the WGAD has said it is not necessary for it to rule on whether domestic law was violated.[337] However, it will also comment on the legality of a detention under domestic law as it finds appropriate. For example, it noted that the arrest of Venezuelan opposition leader Leopoldo López by the armed forces instead of civilian authorities was not justified under Venezuela's

---

[331] Dr. Tin Min Htut and U Nyi Pu, at ¶ 21.

[332] Mikalai Statkevich v. Belarus, WGAD Opinion No. 13/2011, Adopted May 4, 2011, at ¶ 9.

[333] Adilur Rahman Khan v. Malaysia, WGAD Opinion No. 67/2017, Adopted Nov. 20, 2017, at ¶ 24.

[334] *Report of the Working Group on Arbitrary Detention*, Commission on Human Rights, E/CN.4/2007/7, Dec. 12, 2005, at ¶ 43.

[335] UN Economic and Social Council, *Siracusa Principles on the Limitation and Derogation Provisions in the International Covenant on Civil and Political Rights*, E/CN.4/1985/4, Annex (1985), Principles 15–17 (hereinafter Siracusa Principles).

[336] Abdulkarim Al Khodr v. Saudi Arabia, WGAD Opinion No. 46/2013, Adopted Nov. 18, 2013, at ¶ 21.

[337] Filep Jacob Semuel Karma v. Indonesia, WGAD Opinion No. 48/2011, Adopted Sept. 2, 2011, at ¶ 23.

Constitution, and considered this as a factor supporting a finding of a Category II violation.[338] The WGAD has also specified that psychiatric detention cannot be used to curtail a person's freedom of expression.[339]

Domestic laws must also be sufficiently precise to enable individuals to determine what forms of expression are permitted and which are not and cannot grant officials unfettered discretion to restrict freedom of expression.[340] This precludes overbroad criminal offenses from constituting a valid restriction on the right to freedom of expression, a fact that has been well-established in WGAD jurisprudence as well as several WGAD reports on country missions.[341] The principle of *nullem crimen sine lege certa* (no crime without law), intended to be a fundamental due process guarantee, is subject to frequent abuse in the context of freedom of expression.[342] Examples of vague criminal offenses include that of "enemy propaganda,"[343] "broadcasting false or exaggerated news which would affect the morale of the country,"[344] and "divisionism."[345] Of particular concern are criminal offenses that are vague enough to be used against both those who peacefully exercise their right to freedom of expression and those who engage in violence.[346] A detention is also unlawful if a law is misapplied – a pretextual use of laws unrelated to issues of freedom of expression so as to punish free speech is not proper.[347]

Like the requirement that restrictions must be provided by law, the necessity requirement is a strict standard. Restrictions must be "absolutely necessary in a democratic society."[348] If the legitimate purpose of the state can be achieved through a different means that do not violate freedom of expression, the necessity test cannot be met. The requirement of necessity also incorporates that of proportionality. A detention must be a proportionate response to the threat posed by the expression in question.[349] Proper respect for the principle of proportionality means that both the form of the expression and the means of its dissemination should be considered. For example, heightened weight is given to uninhibited expression during public debate about political figures.[350]

---

[338] Leopoldo López Mendoza v. Venezuela, WGAD Opinion No. 26/2014, Adopted Aug. 26, 2014, at ¶ 56 (Represented by Author, But WGAD Submission Pre-Dated Representation).

[339] Xing Shiku v. China, WGAD Opinion No. 8/2014, Adopted Apr. 23, 2014, at ¶ 41.

[340] General Comment No. 34, at ¶ 35, cited in Gulmira Imin v. China, WGAD Opinion No. 29/2012, Adopted Aug. 29, 2012, at ¶ 28.

[341] Eskinder Nega v. Ethiopia, WGAD Opinion No. 62/2012, Adopted Nov. 21, 2012, at ¶ 35; Gulmira Imin, at ¶ 27; Sagr Mohamed Al Balloushi v. Oman, WGAD Opinion No. 54/2014, Adopted Nov. 21, 2014, at ¶ 30; Talib Ahmad Al Mamari v. Oman, WGAD Opinion No. 53/2014, Adopted Nov. 21, 2014, at ¶ 40; *Report of the Working Group on Arbitrary Detention: Mission to Turkey*, Human Rights Council, A/HRC/4/40/Add.5, Feb. 7, 2007, at Summary; *Working Group on Arbitrary Detention: Visit to Viet Nam*, Commission on Human Rights, E/CN.4/1995/31/Add.4, Dec. 21, 1994 at ¶ 58.

[342] Concerning 10 Individuals Associated with the Newspaper Cumhuriyet v. Turkey, WGAD Opinion No. 41/2017, Adopted Apr. 28, 2017, at ¶ 98.

[343] Félix A. Bonne Carcasés, et al. v. Cuba, WGAD Opinion No. 1/1998, Adopted May 15, 1998, at ¶ 3(a).

[344] Husam 'Ali Mulhim, et al. v. Syria, WGAD Opinion No. 10/2008, Adopted May 9, 2008, at ¶ 25.

[345] Agnès Uwimana Nkusi & Saïdati Mukakibibi v. Rwanda, WGAD Opinion No. 25/2012, Adopted Aug. 29, 2012, at ¶ 55.

[346] Le Cong Dinh, et al. v. Viet Nam, WGAD Opinion No. 27/2012, Adopted Aug. 29, 2012, at ¶ 39 (citing to *Working Group on Arbitrary Detention: Visit to Viet Nam*, Commission on Human Rights, E/CN.4/1995/31/Add.4, Dec. 21, 1994, at ¶ 58).

[347] *See, e.g.*, Hilal Mammadov v. Azerbaijan, WGAD Opinion No. 59/2013, Adopted Nov. 22, 2013.

[348] Huang Qi v. China, WGAD Opinion No. 15/2004, Adopted Sept. 15, 2004, at ¶ 14.

[349] Siracusa Principles, at Principle 10(d).

[350] General Comment No. 34, at ¶ 34.

Any alleged threat posed by free expression should also be considered in light of the powers of the state. In finding that a criminal sentence was disproportionate for offenses such as damaging the state's reputation or weakening national morale, the WGAD considered "the broad lack of proportionality between the power and impact of the work and activities carried out by a single individual, who should attend daily his persona professional, artistic, social and political activities, and the power and impact of an entire State machinery, with its Executive, Legislative and Judicial organs and its armed forces, police and security agents."[351]

Finally, limitations on the right to free expression must be justified based on certain enumerated grounds. The ICCPR specifically provides that limitations must be necessary for respecting the rights or reputations of others, or protecting national security, the public order, or public health or morals. Where one of these grounds is invoked, the state must show "in specific and individualized fashion" the nature of the threat posed by the speech in question.[352] In addition, there must be a "direct and immediate connection" between this threat and the expression in question.[353] Some states have imposed limitations on opinions and expressions that constitute an insult to public officials. Under the UDHR, limitations may only be imposed if expression infringes on the rights and freedoms of others and are consistent with "just requirements of morality, public order and the general welfare in a democratic society." Furthermore, "limitations to freedom of expression should not be employed for silencing calls to promote other human rights."[354] In *Abdullah Fairouz Abdullah Abd al-Kareem* v. *Kuwait*, the detainee was charged for having used his Twitter account to insult or post objectionable material about the Emir of Kuwait.[355] The WGAD, relying on HR Committee jurisprudence, noted that public officials such as heads of state are legitimately subject to criticism and the mere fact that forms of expression are considered insulting to public figures is not sufficient for imposition of penalties.[356] The WGAD is deeply skeptical of laws that prohibit defamation of public officials, especially when patently used to criminalize political dissent.

National security and public order are limitations that are particularly abused by those in positions of power in an attempt to justify rights violations.[357] This has also been seen in cases brought to the WGAD as well and therefore these two limitations will be explored in depth later in the chapter. The discussion will then turn to recurring themes in the jurisprudence related to the right to freedom of expression, in which governments may rely on multiple limitations to justify a particular detention. Accordingly, limitations based on protecting the "rights of others" will be discussed particularly in sections on hate speech and blasphemy laws, but are also invoked in numerous other contexts. However, a key guideline when assessing the relative weight of the importance of freedom of expression as compared to conflicting protected rights is that deference should be given to the most fundamental rights.[358] Limitations of expression that protect the reputations

---

[351] Mohamad Kamal Al-Labouani v. Syria, WGAD Opinion No. 24/2008, Adopted Sept. 12, 2008, at ¶ 22.

[352] General Comment No. 34, at ¶ 35, quoted in Liu Xianbin v. China, WGAD Opinion No. 23/2011, Adopted Aug. 29, 2011, at ¶ 24.

[353] General Comment No. 34, at ¶ 35, cited in Gulmira Imin, at ¶ 28.

[354] Huang Wenxun, et al v. China, WGAD Opinion No. 5/2017, Adopted Apr. 19, 2017, at ¶ 46.

[355] Abdullah Fairouz Abdullah Abd al-Kareem, at ¶ 6.

[356] *Id.*, at ¶ 42.

[357] Joseph & Castan, at 623.

[358] Siracusa Principles, at Principle 36.

of others are primarily relevant in the context of defamation laws and are also explored later. The limitation for public health in practice has little relevance for restrictions on freedom of speech, except perhaps for justifying restrictions on health misinformation or advertisements for harmful substances, but this has not yet been addressed in WGAD jurisprudence.[359] Finally, the public morality limitation, which typically arises in cases related to pornography or blasphemy laws, has also not been extensively addressed by the WGAD in the expression context. Even in blasphemy cases, governments have not extensively relied on the "public morality" justification for upholding such laws.[360]

The right to freedom of expression may be derogated from in public emergencies under the strict requirements of Article 4 of the ICCPR. Most of the WGAD's Category II cases in which a government argues a state of emergency exists involve violations of Article 19 of the ICCPR, although the resulting analysis applies more generally. The WGAD has noted particular concern with the tendency of states to rely on emergency provisions when writers or journalists are detained. For example, the WGAD notes a recurrence of cases in which the Nigerian government relied on emergency procedures to target journalists and authors, usually imposing heavy prison sentences following secret military tribunals.[361] Similarly, Myanmar has a history of using emergency provisions to detain writers or journalists.[362] And in Egypt, relying on the observations of UN Special Procedures, the WGAD has expressed concern at the targeting and intimidation of journalists, which is so pervasive as to constitute a "systemic problem."[363]

1 National Security

In 2010, the UN Special Rapporteur on Freedom of Opinion and Expression, as well as the parallel special representatives from the regional human rights bodies, issued a joint declaration in which they identified abuse of national security and anti-terrorism laws as one of the key challenges to protecting freedom of expression over the next decade.[364] In the WGAD context, the national security limitation has been frequently abused by governments who detain individuals for exercising their right to freedom of expression. After exploring generally the nature of the national security limitation, this discussion will specifically examine its application in the context of incitement to terrorism as well as the sharing of state secrets.

National security should be invoked as a justification for limiting freedom of expression only where a state faces a serious political or military threat.[365] Such a threat is force or the threat of force that endangers the existence of the state itself, its territorial integrity, or its political independence.[366] Beyond this high standard, international law

---

[359] Nowak, at 466.

[360] Id.

[361] George Mbah and Mohammed Sule v. Nigeria, WGAD Opinion No. 38/1996, Adopted Dec. 3, 1996, at ¶ 6.

[362] Dr. Ma Thida, et al. v. Myanmar, WGAD Opinion No. 13/1994, Adopted Sept. 28, 1994, at ¶ 8.

[363] Abdullah Ahmed Mohammed Ismail Alfakharany and Others v. Egypt, WGAD Opinion No. 7/2016, Adopted Apr. 19, 2016, at ¶¶ 48–49.

[364] *Tenth Anniversary Joint Declaration: Ten Key Challenges to Freedom of Expression in the Next Decade*, International Mechanisms for Promoting Freedom of Expression, Feb. 2, 2010, at ¶ 8.

[365] Nowak, at 463.

[366] Siracusa Principles, at Principle 29.

does not precisely define what constitutes a threat to national security, but it should be precisely defined in national legal frameworks, in accordance with international law.[367] Safeguards against abuse must accompany any limitations placed on freedom of expression for national security reasons, and states should not rely pretextually on national security justifications.[368] The WGAD has taken particular note that unsubstantiated references to national security concerns are insufficient to show that a detention based on an exercise of freedom of expression meets the Article 19(3) requirements.[369]

Like any other limitation under Article 19(3), limitations based on a national security justification must follow strictly the requirements of necessity and proportionality. This means that a government must show a connection between the speech in question and any alleged threat to national security interests. The *Johannesburg Principles on National Security, Freedom of Expression and Access to Information*, an important set of standards for interpreting the national security limitation, articulated a specific test for this requirement: Governments must show: "(a) the expression is intended to incite imminent violence; (b) it is likely to incite such violence; and (c) there is a direct and immediate connection between the expression and the likelihood or occurrence of such violence."[370] Although the WGAD has not explicitly adopted this test, it has cited approvingly to the Johannesburg Principles as a guideline for interpreting the national security limitation.[371] It has also particularly stressed the necessity of showing a causal link, citing to the HR Committee's General Comment 34 statement that a "direct and immediate connection between the expression and the threat" must be shown where the national security exception is invoked.[372]

The WGAD's jurisprudence consistently establishes that peaceful political and social discourse cannot be restricted on the basis that it represents a threat to national security. For example, a Kurdish writer who published a book about the conditions of Kurdish prisons was detained by Turkey for "disseminating separatist propaganda," a detention the WGAD found to be based solely on the peaceful exercise of the right to freedom of expression.[373] Peaceful political opposition to the Libyan regime was also an insufficient basis for the detention of an activist who was charged with "plotting to overthrow the regime," which the WGAD noted was problematically vague.[374] Similarly, the WGAD urged the Gambia to reconsider its interpretation of the crime of "sedition" after it had been used to detain a radio manager for his journalistic activities.[375]

---

[367] *Global Principles on National Security and the Right to Information (Tschwane Principles)*, June 12, 2013, at Principle 2(c).

[368] Siracusa Principles, at Principle 31.

[369] Abdel Rahman al-Shaghouri v. Syria, WGAD Opinion No. 4/2005, Adopted May 24, 2005, at ¶ 13.

[370] *Report of the Special Rapporteur, Mr. Abid Hussain, Pursuant to Commission on Human Rights Resolution 1993/45*, Commission on Human Rights, E.CN.4/1996/39, at Annex, The Johannesburg Principles on National Security, Freedom of Expression, and Access to Information, Mar. 22, 1996, at Principle 6 (hereinafter Joahnnesburg Principles).

[371] Filep Jacob Semuel Karma v. Indonesia, WGAD Opinion No. 48/2011, Adopted Sept. 2, 2011, at ¶ 21.

[372] Agnès Uwimana Nkusi & Saïdati Mukakibibi v. Rwanda, WGAD Opinion No. 25/2012, Adopted Aug. 29, 2012 at ¶ 57.

[373] Edip Polat v. Turkey, WGAD Opinion No. 37/1994, Adopted Nov. 29, 1994, at ¶ 8.

[374] Rashid el-Orfia v. Libya, WGAD Opinion No. 30/1995, Adopted Sept. 14, 1995, at ¶ 6.

[375] Alhagie Abdoulie Ceesay v. The Gambia, WGAD Opinion No. 50/2015, Adopted Dec. 4, 2015, at ¶ 22.

This logic has also applied to how the WGAD has assessed the characterization of crimes against national security during its country missions. For example, during an early mission to Viet Nam, it was unsparing in expressing its concerns about Vietnamese law:

> [T]he characterizations of offences as crimes against national security ... draw no distinction on the grounds of the use or non-use of violence or of incitement or non-incitement to violence. The Working Group notes that the present wording [the relevant law] is so vague that it could result in penalties being imposed not only on persons using violence for political ends, but also on persons who have merely exercised their legitimate right to freedom of opinion or expression. However justified – or at least understandable – this assimilation of peaceful political action and violent action may be in a state of war, it nevertheless is becoming less and less compatible with the new policies laid down by the Government ... In this regard, the Working Group is concerned at the lack of progress in lifting de facto or de jure restrictions.[376]

Similar concerns were raised by the WGAD from its country mission to China, where it observed:

> The revised Criminal Law, in the context of the offences endangering national security, makes no attempt to establish standards to determine the quality of acts that might or could harm national security ... The Working Group also notes with concern that many of the offences are vague and imprecise, thereby jeopardizing the fundamental rights of those who wish to exercise their right to hold an opinion or exercise their freedoms of expression, the press, assembly and religion.[377]

In its follow-up visit to China, some seven years later, the WGAD reported: "There is no doubt ... progress has been made, but as far as the criminal law is concerned, the situation has unfortunately not evolved and the recommendations of the Working Group have not been put into effect ... [it] continues to receive individual communications confirming its concerns were well founded."[378]

The WGAD may also require that a nexus be explicitly made between a detainee's opinion or expression and violent activities. In Zeinab Jalalian v. Iran, a female activist involved in advocacy for the nonmilitant wing of the Kurdish Free Life Party (PJAK), a dissident group, was charged with conducting "propaganda activities."[379] It was further alleged that her activities attracted "many to the organization."[380] The WGAD, however, noted that the authorities had failed to provide evidence that the detainee was involved with the militant wing of the same organization or in violent activities.[381] Failure to establish this nexus resulted in a finding that the detainee's right to freedom of opinion and expression had been violated.[382]

---

[376] *Report of Working Group on Arbitrary Detention: Visit to Viet Nam*, Commission on Human Rights, E/CN.4/1995/31/Add.4, Dec. 21, 1994, at ¶¶ 58, 65.

[377] *Report of Working Group on Arbitrary Detention: Visit to People's Republic of China*, Commission on Human Rights, E/CN.4/1998/44/Add.2, Dec. 22, 1997, at ¶¶ 106–107.

[378] *Report of Working Group on Arbitrary Detention: Follow-Up Visit to People's Republic of China*, Commission on Human Rights, E/CN.4/2005/6/Add.2, Dec. 29, 2004, at ¶¶ 23–24.

[379] Zeinab Jalalian v. Iran, WGAD Opinion No. 1/2016, Adopted Apr. 18, 2016, at ¶ 35.

[380] *Id.*

[381] *Id.*

[382] *Id.*, at ¶¶ 35, 46.

Even speech calling for separatism cannot be punished under the national security limitation if the speech does not call for violence. For example, distributing leaflets at a demonstration or waving the flag of the disputed Sahrawi region in Morocco was not a sufficient justification for Morocco's detention of several youths.[383] The WGAD elaborated further on the protections afforded to peaceful pro-separatist speech in Dolma Kyab v. China. China had detained Kyab, the author of an unpublished book on Tibetan history, and convicted him of espionage and illegal border crossing. Without engaging in a discussion of whether or not the book did contain separatist sympathies, the WGAD emphasized that any separatist advocacy could not be considered a threat unless nonpeaceful means were embraced. Since there was no factual proof of advocacy of violence in the book, there was no justification for detaining Kyab, even though his viewpoints may have conflicted with official Government policy.[384]

Allegations that individuals are involved in violent resistance must be specifically shown, as a general reference by a government to an individual's support for violent groups is insufficient. Three journalists were detained by Ethiopia for their work with a newspaper that had alleged sympathies with the Oromo Liberation Front, an armed resistance group. The newspaper had published interviews with leaders of the militia and documented human rights abuses against those suspected of links with the Oromo Liberation Front. The WGAD noted that this was protected speech, and that no open support for the activities of the armed group had been proven.[385] Similarly, general assertions of violent conduct also meant that Indonesia had arbitrarily detained a member of a pro-independence East Timorese movement. The activist was responsible for producing campaign materials given to foreign tourists, but the Government alleged he was also responsible for logistical and financial support for the campaign, including armaments. Because no evidence was provided to support the Government's allegation, the WGAD found the detention arbitrary – the production of campaign material was protected speech.[386]

The distinction drawn by these cases between speech that is peaceful and speech that incites violence is not always easy to draw. In determining when peaceful speech in support of political causes becomes speech that may be restricted because of national security concerns, it is helpful to compare the WGAD's opinion in *Amin Mekki Medani, Farouk Abu Eissa and Farah Ibrahim Mohamed Alagar* v. *Sudan* with its reasoning in *Tek Nath Rizal* v. *Bhutan*, a rare opinion in which the WGAD accepted that a detention restricting freedom of expression was properly restricted on national security ground.

In *Amin Mekki Medani, Farouk Abu Eissa and Farah Ibrahim Mohamed Alagar* v. *Sudan*, the Government detained three men involved in political strategy negotiations among opposition groups in Sudan – a human rights lawyer, a leader of a political opposition coalition, and an independent conflict resolution expert. The three men had either signed or been involved in negotiations over the "Sudan Call," a political declaration that sought to end the various conflicts across Sudan and work for reforms in the country. Two other Sudanese political and armed opposition groups also signed

---

[383] Andala Cheikh Abilil, et al. v. Morocco, WGAD Opinion 39/1996, Adopted Dec.3, 1996, at ¶¶ 9–10.

[384] Dolma Kyab v. China, WGAD Opinion No. 36/2007, Adopted Nov. 30, 2007, at ¶¶ 14–15.

[385] Moti Biyya, et al. v. Ethiopia, WGAD Opinion No. 18/1999, Adopted Sept. 15, 1999, at ¶ 10.

[386] Francisco Miranda Branco, et al. v. Indonesia, WGAD Opinion No. 36/1996, Adopted Sept. 19, 1996, at ¶ 18.

the declaration.[387] Although the Government did not respond to the WGAD's communication, in a letter regarding the detainees it had argued that the Sudan Call constituted an alliance with a rebel group and the detentions were necessary to protect national security and to further investigations into the rebel group.[388]

The WGAD found that the Government had failed to rebut the submission of the source that the detentions were based on either signing or being present at the signing of a document calling for political reforms and an end to conflicts. It reiterated that the right to freedom of expression cannot be restricted merely to muzzle advocacy of democratic tenets or human rights, and found a Category II violation infringing on the right to freedom of expression.[389] The implications of this opinion were that merely negotiating, communicating, or signing a document alongside armed groups is not sufficient to establish that the individuals in question are inciting violence.

By contrast, *Tek Nath Rizal* v. *Bhutan* was a rare case in which the WGAD found that a detention was valid where the Government has invoked national security grounds as a basis for restricting free expression. Tek Nath Rizal was allegedly involved in the writing of a booklet that criticized a decree issued by the King of Bhutan. He was convicted of charges that included sowing communal discord and calling for violent rebellion.[390] The Government argued that Tek Nath Rizal was engaged in anti-national activities, including disinformation campaigns designed to sow discord within Bhutan and between Bhutan and India. Specifically, it argued that Tek Nath Rizal was inciting rebellion among the Southern Bhutanese and falsely accusing the Government of using the census to discriminate against Bhutanese of Nepalese descent. This contrasted with the narrative presented by human rights activists internationally, who argued that his advocacy had not embraced violence.[391] In weighing the evidence before it, the WGAD accepted the Government's characterization of Tek Nath Rizal's speech. It observed that the source appeared to have an incomplete understanding of Tek Nath Rizal's activities and had not given the WGAD a basis for questioning the conclusions of the Bhutanese High Court.[392]

In finding the detention not to be in contravention of Article 19 and not arbitrary, the WGAD first referenced the National Security Act of 1992, which criminalized "sowing communal discord" between the Northern and Southern Bhutanese. It then described specific actions undertaken by Tek Nath Rizal, which included organizing meetings, conspiring with others "to achieve his ends by violence and non-violent means," and authorizing fund collection through threats or the use of force. These actions provided sufficient evidence to justify his arrest, trial, conviction, and sentencing.[393] Unfortunately, the WGAD's analysis here is somewhat vague, as the reference to conspiracy to use violence could be interpreted broadly. A more specific reference to the speech that constituted incitement to violence would have been clearer. Nonetheless, standing in contrast to the other WGAD opinions, this opinion suggests that if a government can

---

[387] Amin Mekki Medani, et al. v. Sudan, WGAD Opinion No. 9/2015, Adopted Apr. 24, 2015, at ¶ 6.

[388] *Id.*, at ¶ 12.

[389] *Id.*, at ¶¶ 25–27.

[390] Tek Nath Rizal v. Bhutan, WGAD Opinion No. 48/1994, Adopted Dec. 1, 1994, at ¶¶ 13–14.

[391] Amnesty International, for example, declared him a prisoner of conscience. *Appeal for the Release of Tek Nath Rizal: Prisoner of Conscience*, Amnesty International, Mar. 1994.

[392] Tek Nath Rizal, at ¶¶ 16–18.

[393] *Id.*, at ¶ 18.

identify violent advocacy or violent actions on the part of the speaker, it may be able to justify a detention out of concerns for national security. But, as shown by the other case in Sudan, the government cannot merely characterize the speech as violent (such as characterizing the Sudan Call as an alliance with rebel groups) without identifying that the speech of the speaker advocates violence in some manner.

Incitement to Terrorism

Speech that incites terrorism, as a subset of speech that incites violence, may in theory be limited by governments. For example, UN Security Council Resolution 1624 specifically calls on states to prohibit incitement to terrorist acts.[394] However, the WGAD has noted that there is a gap between the principle of legitimately restricting incitement to violence and the reality of arbitrary detentions under anti-terrorism laws.[395] Accordingly, it is imperative that regulations of "incitement to terrorism" are still considered in light of the same legal analysis governing the national security limitation more generally. Furthermore, speech that does not directly incite terrorism should not be criminalized under anti-terrorism laws, meaning that vague offenses such as supporting extremism or glorifying terrorism are problematic.[396] Unfortunately, vague or overly broad anti-terror laws are regularly relied on by governments justifying detentions and the WGAD has expressed particular concern over such laws being used to target those exercising fundamental rights and freedoms.[397]

Overly vague anti-terrorism laws have been inappropriately applied to suppress speech beyond what is necessary or proportionate to protect national security. For example, charges of "advocating terrorism" were brought against an Algerian who called for peaceful political change on his Facebook page and shared videos about Arab revolutions. The WGAD emphasized the right to call for peaceful political change and found that domestic law was not consistent with Algeria's obligations under international law by allowing for loose definitions of terrorism-related offenses so as to target non–terrorism-related speech.[398] Similarly, in a report from its country mission to Peru, the WGAD noted that the offense of "advocating terrorism" had been misused to punish an individual who painted a hammer and sickle, which could not be considered advocating terrorism.[399] Such broad terrorism offenses, which often also incorporate suspensions of certain fair trial guarantees, may also be used by governments to facilitate arrest and detention of political opponents or others for the exercise of freedom of expression.

---

[394] UN Security Council Resolution 1624, S/RES/1624 (2005), at ¶ 1(1).

[395] *Report of the Working Group on Arbitrary Detention: Report on the Mission to Peru*, Commission on Human Rights, E/CN.4/1999/63/Add.2, Jan. 11, 1999, at ¶ 123.

[396] *Joint Declaration on Defamation of Religions, and Anti-Terrorism and Anti-Extremism Legislation*, International Mechanisms for Promoting Freedom of Expression, Dec. 9, 2008; General Comment No. 34, at ¶ 46.

[397] *Report of the Working Group on Arbitrary Detention*, Commission on Human Rights, E/CN.4/2005/6, Dec. 1, 2004, at ¶¶ 62–63.

[398] Saber Saidi v. Algeria, WGAD Opinion No. 49/2012, Adopted Nov. 16, 2012, ¶¶ 17–19.

[399] *Report of the Working Group on Arbitrary Detention: Report on the Mission to Peru*, Commission on Human Rights, E/CN.4/1999/63/Add.2, Jan. 11, 1999, at ¶ 123.

The WGAD reports instances of extended pretrial detention allowed by anti-terrorism laws, for example, being used as a tool to target indigenous leaders following land use conflicts.[400]

If charges or allegations related to terrorist acts are vague and a government does not provide specific information regarding the alleged criminal conduct, the WGAD will find that the detention is arbitrary.[401] This is especially the case if the evidence shows the detainee engaged in speech that was merely critical of the government or controversial.[402] Since no specific crimes were alleged, the WGAD found that a Jordanian theologian and writer who was charged with "conspiracy with the objective of committing acts of terrorism" was actually detained for expressing political opinions in interviews with journalists.[403] Alternatively, the charge itself may also reveal that individuals are targeted for expressing their opinions. The Egyptian government detained several individuals and accused them of being committed to "extremist ideas" that posed a threat to public security, but never charged them with a specific crime.[404] The WGAD found that without specification as to what crime holding "extremist ideas" constitutes, such vague accusations left the WGAD with no reason for any conclusion except that the detention was based on the exercise of free speech rights. This was confirmed by the fact that fifteen other individuals were released from detention after the Government determined they had moderated their views, suggesting the only reason for the detention was for expressing opinions at variance with the views of the Government.[405] Where detentions on terrorism charges are part of a pattern of free speech restrictions, the WGAD may look to the more general situational context to examine the chilling effect that anti-terrorism law have on free speech within a country. In *Eskinder Nega* v. *Ethiopia*, the detainee was a dissident journalist who was a well-known critic of the Government and had founded several publications that had been banned or closed by the Government. After multiple detentions, he was finally sentenced in 2012 on charges of treason and terrorism, based on anti-terrorism provisions in the criminal code. The presiding judge, in his verdict, concluded Nega's speech could be properly limited when "used to undermine security" and claimed he was attempting to incite violence.[406]

The WGAD begins by criticizing Ethiopia's reliance on terrorism charges generally, before finding that Nega's detention was arbitrary. Citing to the HR Committee, it expressed concern over vagueness of Ethiopia's anti-terrorism proclamation and the broad scope of provisions such as "encouragement of and inducement to terrorism through publication."[407] It then observed that Ethiopia's media law contained

---

[400] *Report of the Working Group on Arbitrary Detention*, Commission on Human Rights, E/CN.4/2005/6, Dec. 1, 2004, at ¶ 62–63.
[401] Suleyman b. Nasser b. Abdulla Al-Alouane v Saudi Arabia, WGAD Opinion No. 22/2008, Adopted Sept. 10, 2008, at ¶ 16 (a "sweeping assertion" by Saudi Arabia that the detention related to terrorism was insufficient); Dr. Said b. Mubarek b. Zair v. Saudi Arabia, WGAD Opinion No. 36/2008, Adopted Nov. 21, 2008, at ¶ 19.
[402] Befekadu Hailu and Others v. Ethiopia, WGAD Opinion No. 10/2016, Adopted Apr. 20, 2016, at ¶ 44.
[403] Issam Mohamed Tahar Al Barquaoui Al Uteibi v. Jordan, WGAD Opinion No. 18/2007, Adopted Nov. 22, 2007, at ¶¶ 16–17.
[404] Yasser Essayed Chaabane Al Dib and 19 Other Persons v. Egypt, WGAD Opinion No. 21/2007, Adopted Nov. 22, 2007, at ¶ 14.
[405] *Id.*, at ¶ 22.
[406] Eskinder Nega v. Ethiopia, WGAD Opinion No. 62/2012, Adopted Nov. 21, 2012, at ¶ 17.
[407] *Id.*, at ¶ 32.

concerning provisions regarding newspaper registration requirements and severe penalties for criminal defamation, which had been misapplied in the anti-terrorism context. Journalists had been charged and newspapers closed, and for the journalist in question, the terrorism law was used to suspend fair trial rights. In short, together, these laws were being used as a tool to suppress legitimate political dissent.[408]

State Secrets

States may have legitimate interests in keeping certain information secret on national security grounds, but laws regulating state secrets must identify clear criteria as to what may or may not constitute classified information.[409] They must also accord with the requirements of Article 19(3) of the ICCPR. Vague or overbroad references to the sharing of state secrets will not be a sufficient basis for justifying a detention. In the WGAD's jurisprudence, detentions that a government has sought to justify on state secrets grounds have been found to be arbitrary on multiple occasions because it had not given sufficient indications of the reasons for secrecy. For example, in a case in which a South Korean opposition party worker had been accused of sharing state secrets with North Korea, the WGAD found the detention arbitrary in the absence of information from the Government, which "specified the secret material in question or the reason for which it was considered to constitute a State secret."[410] Elsewhere, it has faulted governments for failing to describe the "nature of the alleged classified intelligence" or not providing specific information to explain accusations of distributing state secrets abroad.[411]

The WGAD has also required a sufficiently precise showing of any alleged sharing of state secrets. Merely maintaining contacts with North Korean intelligence services was insufficient by itself to justify detaining a South Korean writer under Article 19(3)'s national security limitation.[412] Similarly, the WGAD expressed doubt as to how sending articles to overseas publications could constitute the sharing of state secrets, particularly noting concern with China's criminalization of merely contacting certain individuals or institutions outside of China.[413] Collaboration with foreign journalists or activists is also insufficient to justify espionage charges, such as those brought against two Turkmen human rights defenders who were collaborating with foreign journalists.[414] In another opinion, the WGAD found that the detention of a Pakistani journalist for anti-state activities was in reality based on his contacts with a BBC team investigating corruption, noting that inappropriate military involvement in the civilian case was evidence that the journalist's exercise of his right to freedom of expression was being restricted.[415]

---

[408] *Id.*, at ¶¶ 35–36.

[409] *Joint Declaration on Access to Information and Secrecy Legislation*, International Mechanisms for Promoting Freedom of Expression, Dec. 6, 2004.

[410] Lee Kun-hee and Choi Chin-sup v. South Korea, WGAD Opinion No. 29/1994, Adopted Sept. 29, 1994, at ¶ 6.

[411] Abdolfattah Soltani v. Iran, WGAD Opinion No. 26/2006, Sept. 1, 2006; Zhao Yan v. China, WGAD Opinion No. 33/2005, Adopted Sept. 2, 2005, at ¶ 15.

[412] Hwang Suk-Yong v. South Korea, WGAD Opinion No. 30/1994, Adopted Sept. 29. 1994, at ¶ 10.

[413] Shi Tao v. China, WGAD Opinion No. 27/2006, Adopted Sept. 1, 2006, at ¶¶ 18–20.

[414] Annakurban Amanklychev & Sapardurdy Khadzhied v. Turkmenistan, WGAD Opinion No. 15/2010, Adopted Aug. 31, 2010.

[415] Najam Sethi v. Pakistan, WGAD Opinion 13/2000, Adopted May 17, 2007.

Certain kinds of information can never constitute a state secret and accordingly detentions based on the sharing of such information will be found arbitrary. The Johannesburg Principles require that disclosure of state secrets cannot be punished on national security grounds if either "(1) the disclosure does not actually harm and is not likely to harm a legitimate national security interest, or (2) the public interest in knowing the information outweighs the harm from disclosure."[416] Similarly, the HR Committee's General Comment 34 holds that treason laws, sedition laws, and state secrets laws should not be used to prosecute those who disseminate information of legitimate public interest that does not threaten national security.[417] Specifically, information in the public interest includes information on human rights violations, environmental degradation, corruption, and political criticism, among others.[418]

The WGAD has expressed particular concern with the misuse of state secret laws to justify the detention of human rights and environmental activists. It previously recommended that governments ensure that "any legislation concerning national or State security is in no case extended to cover information relating to the defence and protection of either the environment or human rights."[419] It underscored this point further in an opinion on the detention of a Chinese activist, noting that characterizing human rights information as state secrets would imply that bodies such as the UN High Commissioner for Human Rights were effectively custodians of large volumes of state secrets. In reality, international law encourages the collection and dissemination of information regarding the protection of human rights, which cannot be characterized as state secrets.[420]

A good example of an arbitrary detention based on alleged state secrets can be found in *Grigorii Pasko v. Russia*. Pasko was a journalist and former Russian navy commander who had published a series of articles raising environmental concerns over the improper disposal of submarine nuclear waste material. He was accused of spying and disclosing state secrets and tried before an *in camera* military court. News sources reported that this was part of a strategy to treat Pasko as a military officer disclosing secrets rather than as a journalist exposing environmental degradation, keeping the specific charges classified.[421]

In regard to the charges against Pasko, the WGAD found that his detention was a violation of his rights under Article 19 of the ICCPR, and that the accusations of disclosing state secrets had no basis beyond his speech related to environmental protection. The opinion places special emphasis on the nature of speech about the environment – because environmental protection is "an issue that knows no boundaries," free engagement in ecological criticism should be allowed as it is protected under international law.[422] The WGAD also noted that the Russian state secrets law itself specifically provided that information on environmental conditions cannot constitute a state secret, an appropriate provision that had not been respected in Pasko's case. Accordingly, Pasko's detention violated his right to freedom of expression.[423]

---

[416] Johannesburg Principles, at Principle 15.
[417] General Comment No. 34, at ¶ 30.
[418] *Id.*; Johannesburg Principles, at Principles 2(b), 7.
[419] *Report of the Working Group on Arbitrary Detention*, Commission on Human Rights, E/CN.4/2001/14, Dec. 20, 2000, at ¶ 90.
[420] Li Hai v. China, WGAD Opinion No. 19/1999, Adopted Sept. 16, 1999, at ¶¶ 10–11.
[421] Michael R. Gordon, *Reporter Finds Russia Has Not Outlived Secrecy*, NEW YORK TIMES, Jan. 31, 1999.
[422] Grigorii Pasko v. Russian Federation, WGAD Opinion No. 9/1999, Adopted May 20, 1999, at ¶ 7(a).
[423] *Id.*

2 Public Order

The Siracusa Principles define "public order" as "the sum of rules which ensure the functioning of society or the set of fundamental principles on which society is founded."[424] The concept of "public order" is accordingly broader than that of "national security," allowing for appropriate prohibitions on speech that incites violence, disorder, or mass panic, in addition to that which poses a threat to national security.[425] Because the phrase "public order" allows for potentially varied interpretations, any law that restricts expression on this ground must be strictly necessary as well as precisely defined and limited to specific times and circumstances.[426]

As with the national security limitation, limitations on free speech cannot be justified by merely referencing disturbances to public order, absent further documentation to show the restriction is necessary to preserve the interest of maintaining public order.[427] The offense of "creating a public disturbance," which Cuba had brought against several persons involved in a demonstration calling for the release of political prisoners, was "a vague accusation which does not warrant detention."[428] Similarly, a detention based on charges of "presentation to the public of writings likely to disturb the public order" improperly punished speech that was critical of public officials in Tunisia.[429] Commenting on a provision of the Chinese Criminal Law, which criminalized "other illegal operations that seriously disrupt market order," the WGAD noted that the vagueness of this provision allowed for prosecutions of the peaceful exercise of free expression, as was the case with the specific detention in question.[430]

Peaceful forms of activism may be subject to limited administrative regulation, but detention as a response to peaceful expression will generally be invalid. Albania's detention of activists who distributed pamphlets reading "Down with the United States" was arbitrary, since distributing leaflets in a nonviolent manner was merely a permitted exercise of the right to freedom of expression.[431] Similarly, imprisoning people for sending information through email to opposition groups and the media was found to be arbitrary as it could not be construed as undermining public order and stability.[432] Detention may also be a disproportionate response to peaceful activism even if the activists do not strictly adhere to administrative regulations. For example, the Indonesian government argued that participants in a nonviolent protest had failed to seek prior permission for the protest (as well as alleging national security concerns). The WGAD did not address whether such a regulation was proper, but did emphasize that the protest

---

[424] Siracusa Principles, at Principle 19.

[425] Joseph & Castan, at 617–618.

[426] Nowak, at 58; *Report of the Special Rapporteur, Mr. Abid Hussain, Pursuant to Commission on Human Rights Resolution 1993/45*, Commission on Human Rights, E/CN.4/1995/32, Dec. 14, 1994, at ¶ 53.

[427] Liu Xianbin v. China, WGAD Opinion No. 23/2011, Adopted Aug. 29, 2011, at ¶ 25.

[428] Daniel Azpillaga Lombard, et al. v. Cuba, WGAD Opinion No. 13/1992, Adopted Session No. 4, at ¶ 6(f).

[429] Mohammed Abbou v. Tunisia, WGAD Opinion No. 41/2005, Adopted Nov. 28, 2005.

[430] Wang Hanfei v. China, WGAD Opinion No. 21/2014, Adopted Aug. 25, 2014, at ¶¶ 25–27; Jiaxi Ding v. People's Republic of China, WGAD Opinion No. 3/2015, Adopted Apr. 20, 2015, at ¶ 20, noting the use of Article 291 of the Criminal Code, which specifies the crime of "gathering a crowd to disrupt the order of a public place," to arrest human rights activists; Yu Shiwen, at ¶ 27.

[431] Sulejman Rrahman Mekollari, et al. v. Albania, WGAD Opinion No. 20/1996, Adopted Sept. 16, 1996, at ¶ 7.

[432] Thagyi Maung Zeya and Sithu Zeya v. Myanmar, WGAD Opinion No. 25/2011, Adopted Aug. 30, 2011, at ¶ 29 (Litigated by Author through Perseus Strategies).

lasted less than five minutes and was nonviolent and accepted the source's argument that the sentences imposed were "severely disproportionate to their act of civil disobedience."[433]

A more difficult issue relates to forms of expression, which constitute incitement to civil disobedience. Because civil disobedience involves intentional calls for acts of protest that violate the law, this is a difficult area to distinguish between speech that may be legitimately limited and that which merely constitutes a call to peaceful activism. Vague references to incitement to civil disobedience will not be sufficient to justify a detention. The WGAD expressed concern that an arbitrary interpretation of a Burundian law criminalizing "inciting civil disobedience" can lead to a failure to respect fundamental rights and freedoms.[434] Elsewhere it has found that a charge of "inciting disobedience of the law" had not been sufficiently explained by the Bahraini government, where the source had alleged that the detention was in reality based on the detainee's human rights work.[435] Beyond this, the WGAD has not dealt extensively with the question of when calls for civil disobedience should or should not result in detention, but some more specific guidance is provided in *Khemais Ksila* v. *Tunisia*.

In *Khemais Ksila* v. *Tunisia*, the detainee was a human rights activist who was arrested following his publication of a proclamation announcing his intention to begin a hunger strike and making an appeal for civil disobedience. The Government argued that Ksila had engaged in defamation of public authorities, appeals to disobey the law, and calls to engage in rebellion and violence.[436] The WGAD noted that it had carefully read the proclamation in question, and it contained no call to violence and merely constituted an appeal for peaceful protest. The detention accordingly constituted an infringement of Article 19 of the ICCPR and UDHR, and was arbitrary under Category II.[437] Significantly, the WGAD suggested that Ksila's direct call for civil disobedience was not itself likely to constitute either incitement to violence or to provoke a disturbance of public order. It then added that the speech did not constitute an "incitement to citizens to break the law of the land," which implied that the WGAD was distinguishing between calls for peaceful civil disobedience and other calls for unlawful action.[438] Unfortunately, it did not elaborate on this distinction, and this remains an issue where greater commentary from the WGAD would be helpful. This opinion suggests, however, that whether or not the civil disobedience in question calls for violent action is a key distinguishing factor in determining whether a detention for speech that calls for disobedience to the law is proper.

Public speech, as well as speech at protests and in public fora, may be subject to certain limited regulations for the maintenance of public order, provided the Article 19 (3) requirements are met.[439] This is closely connected to the jurisprudence on freedom

---

[433] Johan Teterisa, et al. v. Indonesia, WGAD Opinion No. 41/2008, Adopted Nov. 25, 2008, at ¶¶ 11, 16, 62–63.

[434] Pierre-Claver Mbonimpa v. Burundi, WGAD Opinion No. 33/2014, Adopted Aug. 28, 2014, at ¶ 26.

[435] Mohammed Hassan Sedif and Abdul Aziz Moussa v. Bahrain, WGAD Opinion No. 34/2014, Adopted Aug. 28, 2014, at ¶¶ 27–29.

[436] Khemais Ksila v. Tunisia, WGAD Opinion No. 5/1999, Adopted May 20, 1999, at ¶ 8.

[437] *Id.*, at ¶¶ 13, 16.

[438] *Id.*, at ¶ 11.

[439] General Comment No. 34, at ¶ 31.

of assembly, which affirms that such regulations must be proportionate and narrowly tailored.[440] A government seeking to justify a detention based on alleged incitement to violence must specifically identify relevant language in that person's speech. Following labor-related riots in Indonesia, trade union leader Muchtar Pakpahan was charged with inciting workers to violence through speeches and written materials.[441] The WGAD noted that Pakpahan was in a different city during the riots, no specific act that could be considered incitement to violence could be attributed to him, and his writings, which allegedly encouraged criminality, had not been presented to the WGAD. His detention was therefore found to be arbitrary and a violation of his right to freedom of expression, assembly, and association.[442]

In a more recent case, *Alaa Ahmed Seif al Islam El Fattah* v. *Egypt*, the WGAD examined the emerging use of social media and state censorship of Internet sources. The detainee in that case was an Egyptian human rights defender who operated an award-winning blog aggregator.[443] He was arrested after being held responsible for organizing demonstrations against the authorities through the social media platform Twitter.[444] The WGAD found the use of Twitter and other social media websites to invite people to peaceably protest were activities protected by the right to freedom of opinion and expression.[445] Further, generally stated reasons of public order would not suffice to excuse authorities imposing restrictions on the use of the Internet to organize people to action.[446]

Similarly, unless a cause and effect relationship between the speech in question and any criminal behavior or violence is established, a restriction on that speech cannot be justified. This was evidenced by the case of Venezuelan opposition politician Leopoldo López, who was detained after he gave a speech at a peaceful demonstration. After the march had ended, armed groups attacked the protestors, resulting in two deaths.[447] The Government argued that López was to blame for the violence, as well as related property destruction and arson, because he "personally instigated hatred and violence . . . creating a tense, hostile situation."[448] The WGAD, however, noted that the Government had given no indication of how López's speech may have resulted in the violent acts or property damage. In addition, the property damage and deaths had occurred at the "fringes of the demonstration," and happened after the march had ended.[449] Since there was no evidence showing a cause and effect relationship between the speech and the violence that occurred, López's detention could not be justified by holding him responsible for the deaths or property damage.[450]

---

[440] *See, e.g.,* Nabeel Abdulrasool Rajab v. Bahrain, WGAD Opinion No. 12/2013, Adopted May 3, 2013, at ¶ 40; Afif Jamil Mazhar, et al. v. Syria, WGAD Opinion No. 10/1993, Adopted Apr. 29, 1993, at ¶ 5; Le Cong Dinh, et al. v. Viet Nam, WGAD Opinion No. 27/2012, Adopted Aug. 29, 2012, at ¶ 40.

[441] Jannes Hutahaen, et al. v. Indonesia, WGAD Opinion No. 18/1995, Adopted June 2, 1995, at ¶ 7.

[442] *Id.,* at ¶¶ 12–13.

[443] Alaa Ahmed Seif al Islam El Fattah v. Egypt, WGAD Opinion No. 6/2016, Adopted Apr. 19, 2016, at ¶ 4.

[444] *Id.,* at ¶ 22.

[445] *Id.,* at ¶ 48.

[446] *Id.*

[447] Leopoldo López Mendoza v. Venezuela, WGAD Opinion No. 26/2014, Adopted Aug. 26, 2014, at ¶¶ 47–49.

[448] *Id.,* at ¶ 33.

[449] *Id.,* at ¶¶ 52, 54.

[450] *Id.,* at ¶ 54.

Finally, one other area in which public order serves as a rationale for restricting freedom of expression is in regard to contempt of court proceedings. Such proceedings may be legitimate if both the proceedings and the penalty are warranted as a means of maintaining order in a court.[451] The WGAD may address abuse of contempt of court provisions under Category III rather than Category II, particularly where fair trial rights are at stake.[452] However, in *Thulani Rudolf Maseko v. Swaziland*, it found a violation under Category II, where Swaziland had arrested a lawyer on charges of "contempt of court." The arrest was related to an article written by the lawyer in which he criticized the same Chief Justice who subsequently issued the warrant for his arrest.[453] Citing to the UN Special Rapporteur on the Independence of Judges and Lawyers, the WGAD noted that lawyers have the right "to take part in public discussions of matters concerning the law and the administration of justice."[454] Contempt proceedings are not an appropriate mechanism for restricting such legitimate discourse on the state of the justice system, and the use of contempt of court laws in this instance was a violation of the right to freedom of expression.[455]

3 Hate Speech

Hate speech, as a category of speech that governments may restrict, presents some particular legal characteristics because human rights law places a positive obligation on governments to limit certain forms of hate speech. However, these obligations should not serve as a pretext for limiting protected speech; they are specifically circumscribed and criminal penalties may not always be an appropriate reaction. The WGAD seldom finds it necessary to engage with the more challenging legal questions in this area because almost all of the cases in which governments have alleged a detainee engaged in hate speech have been clear examples of an unjustified reliance on such provisions.

Article 20 of the ICCPR contains an explicit and mandatory restriction on the permissible exercise of freedom of expression:

1. Any propaganda for war shall be prohibited by law.
2. Any advocacy of national, racial or religious hatred that constitutes incitement to discrimination, hostility or violence shall be prohibited by law.

Discrimination provisions in the ICCPR and UDHR, which provide for equal protection under the law, may also impose obligations on states to limit certain discriminatory speech. The ICCPR requires that "the law shall prohibit any discrimination," while the UDHR guarantees the right to be protected from any incitement to discrimination that violates the Declaration.[456]

Two specific forms of hate speech have unique legal instruments. The *Convention on the Prevention and Punishment of the Crime of Genocide* provides that, when committed with the requisite intent, the act of "direct and public incitement to commit genocide"

---

[451] General Comment No. 34, at ¶¶ 31.
[452] *See, e.g.*, Ko Mya Aye v. Myanmar, WGAD Opinion No. 28/2010, Adopted Nov. 22, 2010.
[453] Thulani Rudolf Maseko v. Swaziland, WGAD Opinion No. 6/2015, Adopted Apr. 22, 2015, at ¶ 4.
[454] *Id.*, at ¶ 28.
[455] *Id.*, at ¶¶ 29–30.
[456] UDHR, at Art. 7; ICCPR, at Art. 26.

may constitute genocide under the Convention.[457] Not all hate speech rises to this level, however, and the jurisprudence on hate speech is distinct from the jurisprudence governing incitement to genocide under the Genocide Convention.[458] Incitement to racial hatred is prohibited by the *Convention on the Elimination of Racial Discrimination* (CERD), which requires States to make it a punishable offense to disseminate ideas based on racial hatred or any incitement to racial discrimination.[459] This is somewhat less speech-protective than the ICCPR, requiring the banning of mere dissemination of racist ideas even if they do not constitute incitement to discrimination, hostility, or violence. Thus while the CERD Committee decisions may provide useful guidance for interpreting the law related to hate speech in the context of arbitrary detention, the directly applicable treaty is the ICCPR and also the UDHR, which may provide greater free speech protection.

In fulfilling these obligations to limit hate speech, states must strike a careful balance between the rights to freedom of expression and the prohibition on hate speech, particularly to ensure hate speech provisions are not abused.[460] First, any restrictions on the right to freedom of expression under Article 20 of the ICCPR must still comply with the requirements of Article 19(3).[461] Second, Article 20 presents a "high threshold," as "incitement to hatred must refer to the most severe and deeply felt form of opprobrium."[462] Beyond the definition of hate speech provided in Article 20, there is not a precise universal definition for hate speech in international law. However, there are several factors for differentiating hate speech from merely offensive speech, such as the purpose of the speech, the content of the speech, the relevant context, and the relationship between the speaker and the subject of the speech.[463] Additional relevant factors include the veracity of the speech and the intent of the speaker.[464]

Hate speech regulations are generally justified because of the threat they pose to the rights or reputations of others. The "rights and reputations of others" may refer to the interests of a community as a whole, such as the interests of the Jewish community generally in being free from anti-Semitism.[465] Speech that promotes a positive sense of

---

[457] *Convention on the Prevention and Punishment of the Crime of Genocide*, G.A. Res. 260, (1948), 78 U.N.T.S. 277, *entered into force* Jan. 12, 1951, at Art. 3(c).

[458] Nahimana v. Prosecutor, Judgment, International Criminal Tribunal for Rwanda Appeals Chamber, Nov. 28, 2007, at ¶ 693.

[459] *International Convention on the Elimination of all Forms of Racial Discrimination*, G.A. Res. 2106 (XX) (1965), 660 U.N.T.S. 195, *entered info force* Jan. 4, 1969, at Art. 4.

[460] *Report of the Special Rapporteur on the Promotion and Protection of the Right to Freedom of Opinion and Expression, Mr. Abid Hussain, Submitted in Accordance with Commission Resolution 2001/47*, Commission on Human Rights, E/CN.4/2002/75, Jan. 30, 2002, at ¶ 66.

[461] General Comment No. 34, at ¶ 50.

[462] *Rabat Plan of Action on the Prohibition of Advocacy of National, Racial or Religious Hatred That Constitutes Incitement to Discrimination, Hostility or Violence: Conclusions and Recommendations Emanating from the Four Regional Expert Workshops Organised by OHCHR*, Adopted by Experts in Rabat, Morocco, Oct. 5, 2012, at ¶ 22.

[463] Navanethem Pillay, *Freedom of Speech and Incitement to Criminal Activity: A Delicate Balance*, 14 New England Journal of International and Comparative Law 203, 208 (2008).

[464] *Joint Statement on Racism and the Media*, International Mechanisms for Promoting Freedom of Expression, Feb. 27, 2001.

[465] Faurisson v. France, Communication No. 550/1993, Human Rights Committee, CCPR/C/58/D/550/1993, Nov. 8, 1996, at ¶ 9.6.

group identity should not be construed as hate speech.[466] Similarly, criminalizing speech only because it exacerbates social tensions is inappropriate, given that merely offensive speech is protected.[467] Resolving difficult social issues, such as cultural or religious tensions, should be achieved by engaging in open discourse about those differences, rather than suppressing expression of those differences.[468] Unfortunately, vague domestic legislation and jurisprudence has resulted in a pervasive abuse of hate speech laws to persecute minorities instead of prosecuting actual cases of incitement to hatred.[469] The UN Special Rapporteur on Freedom of Opinion and Expression has noted this is a particularly acute concern "where respect for human rights and the rule of law is weak and hate speech laws have been used in the past against those they were intended to protect."[470]

This unfortunate reality has been reflected in the WGAD jurisprudence, where almost all cases in which a government alleges hate speech in reality reflect permissible political, social, or human rights advocacy.[471] Sometimes the detainee is advocating for minority rights, such as when China argued that a critic of the Government's treatment of the Uyghur minority was inciting ethnic hatred,[472] or when Uzbekistan charged an advocate for religious freedom of independent Muslims with incitement of ethnic, racial, or religious hatred.[473] Elsewhere, hate speech-related charges are used against human rights advocates more generally – Viet Nam argued a journalist writing on human rights issues was "sowing racial hatred,"[474] and a Burundi peasant who spoke about land confiscation by public officials was accused of incitement to ethnic hatred.[475]

A closer look at one of these cases, when compared with the only case where the WGAD has found a detention for hate speech to be justified, highlights the differences between actual hate speech and an abuse of hate speech provisions. A permissible detention for hate speech can be seen in *Ahmed Khalaoui v. Tunisia*, involving an individual who was arrested in 1994 for distributing anti-Semitic leaflets. The source claimed the leaflets had been distributed peacefully as an exercise of the freedom of expression, but the Government replied that the leaflets "called for confrontation with all Jews" and a boycott of conferences where Jews were in attendance.[476] Khalaoui also specifically called for Tunisians to harass a particular Jewish community in Tunisia.[477]

---

[466] *The Camden Principles on Freedom of Expression and Equality*, Article 19, Apr. 2009, at Principle 12.1.iv.

[467] *Joint Declaration on Publication of Confidential Information, Openness of National and International Bodies, Free Expression and Cultural/Religious Tensions, and Impunity in the Case of Attacks against Journalists*, International Mechanisms for Promoting Freedom of Expression, Dec. 19, 2006.

[468] *Id.*

[469] Rabat Plan, at ¶ 11.

[470] *Report of the Special Rapporteur on the Promotion and Protection of the Right to Freedom of Opinion and Expression, Mr. Abid Hussain, Submitted in Accordance with Commission Resolution 2001/47*, Commission on Human Rights, E/CN.4/2002/75, Jan. 30, 2002, at ¶ 65.

[471] Hilal Mammadov v. Azerbaijan, WGAD Opinion No. 59/2013, Adopted Nov. 22, 2013; Gaybullo Jalilov v. Uzbekistan, WGAD Opinion No. 4/2013, Adopted Apr. 30, 2013; Emile Ruvyiro v. Burundi, WGAD Opinion No. 48/1992, Adopted Session No. 5.

[472] Ilham Tohti v. China, WGAD Opinion No. 3/2014, Adopted Apr. 22, 2014, at ¶ 18.

[473] Gaybullo Jalilov v. Uzbekistan, WGAD Opinion No. 4/2013, Adopted Apr. 30, 2013, at ¶ 8.

[474] Francis Xavier Dang Xuan Dieu, et al. v. Viet Nam, WGAD Opinion No. 26/2013, Adopted Aug. 29, 2013, at ¶ 45.

[475] Emile Ruvyiro v. Burundi, WGAD Opinion No. 48/1992, Adopted Session No. 5, at ¶ 5.

[476] Ahmed Khalaoui v. Tunisia, WGAD Opinion No. 12/1994, Adopted Sept. 28, 1994, at ¶¶ 5–6.

[477] *Id.*, at ¶ 6.

He was subsequently charged with "incitement of hatred between races, religions and peoples and for publication of leaflets liable to disturb public order," resulting ultimately in a sentence of two years imprisonment for incitement to racial hatred and eight months for the publication of the leaflets.[478] The source appears not to have replied to these specific accusations, instead merely reiterating that Khalaoui was a political prisoner.[479]

The WGAD, characterizing Khalaoui's expression as "violently anti-Semitic," accepted that his arrest was a legitimate exercise of permissible laws. It stressed that the relevant limitations on free exercise of expression in Tunisian law were proper, citing to both ICCPR Article 19(3) and Article 20, as well as a HR Committee view which found anti-Semitic speech to be a form of advocacy of racial hatred that states have an obligation to prohibit under Article 20.[480] Although the WGAD did not comment further on the characteristics of the speech that made it hate speech rather than merely offensive speech, such anti-Semitic language has features that clearly place it in the category of hate speech – it targeted a particular racial, ethnic, and religious group and called for discrimination and specific harassment of that group.[481]

This case stands in sharp contrast with *Hilal Mammadov v. Azerbaijan*, which highlights the potential for abuse of hate speech provisions to target minorities or minority activists. Hilal Mammadov was an advocate for the Talysh people, an ethnic minority in southern Azerbaijan. In addition to being an editor of a Talysh language newspaper, he attracted international attention after uploading a video to YouTube of a song sung in a traditional style at a wedding.[482] The refrain of the song, which referenced an anti-Putin Internet meme, became popular among anti-government protestors in Russia and Azerbaijan.[483] Subsequently, a Russian television crew attended a Talysh folk festival at the invitation of Mammadov.[484] Only a few days after the festival, Mammadov was arrested in relation to alleged heroin possession (the source claimed evidence had been planted), and then subsequently charged with and sentenced for treason and inciting national racial, social, and religious hatred.[485]

In addition to accusing Mammadov of treason and hostile activities endangering national security, the Government claimed he had "delivered speeches harming the trust and respect for the lifestyle, culture, traditions and history" of various Azeri populations, leading to "incitement of hostility among said groups." Similarly, as an editor, he published articles that constituted "incitation to national-religious conflict."[486] More specifically, the Government reported that Mammadov's activities "included instructions and tasks aimed at initiating nationalist propaganda and raising awareness of the Talysh

[478] *Id.*

[479] *Id.*, at ¶ 7.

[480] *Id.*, at ¶ 8; J.R.T. & the W.G. Party v. Canada, Communication No. 104/1981, Human Rights Committee, CCPR/C/OP/2, Apr. 6, 1983, at ¶ 8(b).

[481] The European Court of Human Rights has expressed particular concern with speech that is a "general and vehement attack on one ethnic group." Pavel Ivanov v. Russia, Application No. 35222/04, Decision on Admissibility, European Court of Human Rights, Feb. 20, 2007, at ¶ 1; *see also* Mark Anthony Norwood v. United Kingdom, Application No. 23131/03, Decision on Admissibility, European Court of Human Rights, Nov. 16, 2004.

[482] Hilal Mammadov v. Azerbaijan, WGAD Opinion No. 59/2013, Adopted Nov. 22, 2013, at ¶ 44.

[483] Petition to the UN Working Group on Arbitrary Detention, Freedom Now, Dec. 12, 2013.

[484] Hilal Mammadov, at ¶ 44.

[485] *Id.*, at ¶¶ 26–27.

[486] *Id.*, at ¶ 29.

problem."[487] The Government thus mixes descriptions of permissible speech – such as "raising awareness" or writing articles on Talysh issues – with accusations of incitement to hostility or ethnic conflict. This represents a conflation of raising awareness of minority issues, as well as showcasing a minority culture, with incitement to hatred.

The WGAD makes short work of such claims, recognizing that Mammadov's speech was a legitimate exercise of free expression under Article 19 of the ICCPR and that the Government fails to provide a satisfactory explanation for the charges of incitement to hatred.[488] Given that most WGAD opinions on the topic of hate speech are addressing abusive reliance by governments on hate speech laws, it has not needed to give much attention to situations where a detained individual has engaged in hate speech, but the detention may nonetheless violate Article 19(3). Specifically, it has not had to address the question of when a criminal penalty, as opposed to administrative or other sanctions, is a disproportionate response to certain forms of hate speech.

In the absence of WGAD jurisprudence on this issue, a potential source for further guidance is the *Rabat Plan of Action on the prohibition of advocacy of national, racial or religious hatred that constitutes incitement to discrimination, hostility or violence* (the "Rabat Plan"), which was adopted in 2012 following a series of expert workshops sponsored by OHCHR.[489] The Rabat Plan expressed particular concern that a "clear distinction" be made between expression that should be met with criminal sanctions as opposed to civil or administrative sanctions.[490] Criminal sanctions should be "last resort measures to be only applied in strictly justifiable situations."[491]

To determine what situations justify criminal sanctions, the Rabat Plan proposes a six-part threshold test, which draws heavily on the international jurisprudence generally for distinguishing between hate speech and merely offensive speech. This includes (1) context, (2) the position or standing of the speaker, (3) intent, which must be more than negligence or recklessness, (4) content or form of the speech, (5) extent of the speech, and (6) likelihood of inciting action, including imminence.[492] This test presents one potential framework should the issue of the proportionality of criminal sanctions for hate speech arise before the WGAD.

One particular form of hate speech which the WGAD has needed to address is that of genocide denial. This may also be restricted as a form of hate speech. The right to freedom of expression does not permit states to penalize the expression of opinions about historical facts, but a general prohibition of an incorrect interpretation of past events is permissible.[493] The HR Committee, in *Faurisson v. France*, found that France had not violated the requirements of Article 19(3) of the ICCPR due to its criminal conviction of an academic who argued against the existence of extermination gas chambers in the Nazi concentration camps. Because denials of the Holocaust are a principle vehicle for anti-Semitism in France, restricting such denials was a necessary means of protecting the

---

[487] *Id.*, at ¶ 39.
[488] *Id.*, at ¶ 66.
[489] Rabat Plan.
[490] *Id.*, at ¶ 19.
[491] *Id.*, at ¶ 22.
[492] *Id.*, at ¶ 22.
[493] General Comment No. 34, at ¶ 49.

rights of the French Jewish community.[494] Speech that falls just short of genocide denial, however, may be protected. The European Court of Human Rights found that France violated the right to freedom of expression of two men responsible for an article which praised a French World War II leader and failed to acknowledge his role in deporting Jews to the death camps. The conviction, while lawful and for a legitimate purpose, was not necessary because the reputation of this historical figure "does not belong to the category of clearly established historical facts – such as the Holocaust – whose negation or revision" would be removed from the protection of freedom of expression, and because no explicit denial of the Holocaust was expressed.[495]

Like hate speech laws generally, laws regulating genocide denial are subject to abuse. This is a clear concern of the WGAD in Agnès Uwimana Nkusi and Saïdati Mukakibibi v. Rwanda, which addresses Rwandan laws related to genocide denial and divisionism. The role of the press in justifying and inciting the 1994 Rwandan genocide is well known, and anti-genocide laws have an important role in Rwanda.[496] Laws restricting genocide ideology also have an important role in Rwanda. However, human rights groups have criticized the vague wording of the anti-genocide laws, as well as their misuse to target political opponents.[497] This reality is present in the detention of Nkusi and Mukakibibi, both Rwandan newspaper journalists arrested in July 2010. Mukakibibi's charges related to an article that criticized Rwandan President Paul Kagame, based on which she was convicted for endangering national security but acquitted on charges of divisionism. Nkusi was sentenced and fined for endangering national security, genocide denial, defamation of the President, and divisionism. The genocide denial charge was based on a specific sentence written by Nkusi, which states: "Rwandans lived for a long time with this hatred until they ended up killing each other after [former President] Kinani [Habyarimana]'s death."[498] The High Court held that this sentence violated Article 4 of the genocide law, which prohibits anyone from "publicly show[ing], by his or her words, writings, images, or by any other means, that he or she has negated the genocide committed, rudely minimized it or attempted to justify or approve its grounds or any person who will have hidden or destroyed its evidence."

Nkusi was also charged under the divisionism law, which prohibits speech that divides or sparks conflicts among people, or causes an uprising that could result in strife based on discrimination. This charge was based on two articles, one of which claimed that jobs were reserved for specific groups of people, and another that addressed conflicts between the Abanyiginya and Abega clans, including alleged favoritism of President Kagame for his own clan.[499] The High Court held that the divisionism law was violated because Nkusi's statements regarding inter-clan tensions were "intended to create conflicts."

---

[494] Faurisson v. France, Communication No. 550/1993, Human Rights Committee, CCPR/C/58/D/550/1993, Nov. 8, 1996, at ¶ 9.7.

[495] Case of Lehideux and Isorni v. France, Application No. 55/1997/839/1045, Judgment, European Court of Human Rights, Sept. 23, 1998, at ¶ 47.

[496] Prosecutor v. Nahimana, Judgment, International Criminal Tribunal for Rwanda, Nov. 28, 2007 (convicting members of the media for crimes against humanity for their role in the Rwandan genocide).

[497] *Rwanda: Submission for the Universal Periodic Review*, Human Rights Watch, Mar. 2015.

[498] Agnès Uwimana Nkusi & Saïdati Mukakibibi v. Rwanda, WGAD Opinion No. 25/2012, Adopted Aug. 29, 2012, at ¶ 16 (citing to the Rwandan High Court judgment).

[499] *Id.*, at ¶¶ 22–23.

After the original submission, the Rwandan Supreme Court cleared Nkusi of the genocide denial and divisionism charges (it upheld the defamation and endangering national security convictions, as well as the national security conviction of Mukakibibi, which the WGAD subsequently addressed at length). Nonetheless, the WGAD felt addressing these laws was important, and underscored that its mandate includes examining the conformity of national law with international standards. In regard to the divisionism charges, it reiterated the necessity of conforming to the requirements of Article 19(3). The WGAD then went on to cite to the UN Independent Expert on Minority Issues, who noted that the current wording of the genocide laws is "problematic and ill-defined" and that "implementation of the laws has gone considerably beyond the limits to freedom of expression" provided in ICCPR Article 20(2).[500] Commenting specifically on the genocide denial charge, the WGAD also expressed concern with charges brought under the genocide denial law that fail to sufficiently demonstrate intentionality.[501] This opinion accordingly represents a caution against genocide denial laws that do not strictly conform to Article 19(3) and are not carefully defined and specific, resulting in the punishment of speech that does not constitute hate speech and an improper silencing of discussion of past events.

4 Defamation Laws and Criticism of Public Figures

Freedom of expression is the only right in the ICCPR that may be limited to protect the "reputations of others" as well as the rights of others. The relationship between freedom of expression and reputational concerns is particularly relevant for the WGAD jurisprudence in two areas – in relation to defamation laws and where political figures are criticized. Defamation laws may be a legitimate means of protecting the reputation of individuals, but are prone to abuse, and the WGAD has said that violation of such laws should not be punished by detention, as such punishment is disproportionate.[502] Detentions under laws that criminalize criticism of public officials are similarly improper – concern for the "reputations of others" cannot serve as a justification for protecting the state or public officials from criticism.[503]

Defamation laws vary in national legislation, but a good general definition of defamation has been provided by the UN Special Rapporteur on Freedom of Opinion and Expression: "An intentional false communication that injures another person's reputation."[504] To prevent abuse, defamation laws should meet certain guidelines. First, defamation only applies to false statements – defamation laws should provide for the truth of a statement as a defense.[505] The HR Committee's General Comment 34 has further noted that statements which by their nature cannot be verified should not be the

---

[500] *Id.*, at ¶ 55.
[501] *Id.*, at ¶ 56.
[502] Abdul Kareem Nabil Suliman Amer v. Egypt, WGAD Opinion No. 35/2008, Adopted Nov. 20, 2008, at ¶ 36.
[503] Siracusa Principles, at Principle 37.
[504] *Report of the Special Rapporteur on the Promotion and Protection of the Right to Freedom of Opinion and Expression*, Commission on Human Rights, E/CN.4/2006/55, Dec. 30, 2005, at ¶ 45.
[505] Adonis v. Philippines, Communication No. 1815/2008, Human Rights Committee, CCPR/C/103/D/1815/2008/Rev.1, Oct. 26, 2011, at ¶ 7.9.

subject of defamation laws.[506] Opinion statements, then, should not be punished under defamation laws, as noted by the WGAD when finding that the detention of an Indonesian journalist charged with defaming then-President Soeharto was arbitrary. The journalist's right to express his opinion was protected, even if it was erroneous, because "the right to hold an opinion and expressing it freely is the core of the right to freedom of expression."[507] Finally, persons or groups of persons may be defamed, but not abstract concepts or institutions, such as the state or an ideology.[508] For example, a Tunisian activist who announced a hunger strike was accused of "defamation of the public order," a charge rejected by the WGAD, who noted that this is merely one of the "most traditional forms of peaceful protest."[509] The WGAD has also not adopted "defamation of religion" as a legitimate justification for limiting freedom of expression, as is discussed in the section on blasphemy.

Even if defamation laws are carefully drafted and appropriately applied, however, in the WGAD context, defamation charges alone cannot serve as a justification for a detention. Several human rights authorities have interpreted the proportionality requirement in Article 19(3) to mean that detention is always a disproportionate penalty for defamation offenses.[510] The WGAD has expressly adopted this view in multiple opinions. For example, it has cited to a detailed passage on defamation in the HR Committee's General Comment No. 34, which affirms that criminal law should only apply in "the most serious of cases" and that "imprisonment is never an appropriate penalty."[511] Another opinion expresses concurrence with the Special Rapporteur on the Right to Freedom of Opinion and Expression, who had said that "jail sentences and disproportionate fines should totally be excluded for offences such as defamation."[512] Similarly, in finding the detention of a blogger to be arbitrary, the WGAD expressed concern with the "severe penalties for criminal defamation" in Ethiopian law.[513]

Laws that criminalize criticism of public figures or institutions sometimes resemble defamation laws, but they do not always distinguish between true and false speech. Where they offer heightened protection for public figures as compared to other persons, they improperly limit the right to freedom of expression – public figures generally enjoy less protection from criticism because the value of free debate on matters of public interest is heightened.[514] The ability to criticize public officials, institutions, or national or religious symbols constitutes a core part of the right to freedom of expression, so laws

---

[506] General Comment No. 34, at ¶ 47.

[507] Tri Agus Susanto Siswowihardjo v. Indonesia, WGAD Opinion No. 42/1996, Adopted Dec. 3, 1996.

[508] *Report of the Special Rapporteur on the Promotion and Protection of the Right to Freedom of Opinion and Expression*, Human Rights Council, A/HRC/14/23, Apr. 20, 2010, at ¶ 84.

[509] Khemais Ksila v. Tunisia, WGAD Opinion No. 5/1999, Adopted May 20, 1999, at ¶ 11.

[510] *Joint Declaration on Freedom of Expression and the Administration of Justice, Commercialization of Freedom of Expression and Criminal Defamation*, International Mechanisms for Promoting Freedom of Expression, Dec. 10, 2002. Regional human rights courts have also found that criminal defamation laws are disproportionate. Lohé Issa Konaté v. The Republic of Burkina Faso, Application No. 004/2013, Judgment, African Court on Human and Peoples' Rights, Dec. 5, 2014; Herrera-Ulloa v. Costa Rica, Judgment, Inter-American Court of Human Rights, July 2, 2004.

[511] General Comment No. 34, at ¶ 47; Agnès Uwimana Nkusi & Saïdati Mukakibibi, at ¶ 59.

[512] Abdul Kareem Nabil Suliman Amer v. Egypt, WGAD Opinion No. 35/2008, Adopted Nov. 20, 2008, at ¶ 36.

[513] Eskinder Nega v. Ethiopia, WGAD Opinion No. 62/2012, Adopted on Nov. 21, 2012, at ¶ 32.

[514] General Comment No. 34, at ¶ 38.

that forbid such criticism cannot be justified merely by reference to local culture or values.[515] This means that so-called lèse-majesté laws, which criminalize insults to a monarch, as well as laws forbidding disrespect for authority, national symbols or flags, or to the honor of public officials, all are problematic under Article 19 of the ICCPR.[516]

The WGAD has found a number of detentions to be arbitrary that are based on charges of insulting or offending public officials or institutions, particularly in regard to those who are detained for insulting or criticizing heads of states and political leaders.[517] The WGAD addresses the problems with such laws in particular depth in *Somyot Prueksakasemsuk v. Thailand*, involving the Thai lèse-majesté law. Somyot Prueksaka-semsuk, a Thai activist, held a press conference to launch a campaign calling for a parliamentary review of the lèse majesté law in the Thai criminal code, which provides that "whoever defames, insults or threatens the King, the Queen, the Heir-apparent or the Regent shall be punished with imprisonment of three to fifteen years." Five days later, he was arrested and charged under the same law he was protesting in relation to two articles he had published. In response, the Government argued that defamation against the monarch was a graver offence than defamation against an ordinary person and deserved a more serious punishment. It also argued that the limitation on freedom of expression was justified not only by respect for the reputation of the monarch but also for protection of public health and morals.[518]

The WGAD rejected these arguments, first noting its general concern that the Thai law suppressed debate on public interests and created a chilling effect on freedom of expression. Furthermore, it cited to the UN High Commissioner for Human Rights, who found the criminal sanctions to be neither necessary nor proportionate. In the case of Prueksakasemsuk specifically, the WGAD noted that although public figures also enjoy the protection of their rights, they are not immune from criticism.[519] Both the launch of the campaign and the publication of articles critical of the monarchy constituted forms of protected expression, and Prueksakasemsuk's detention was arbitrary because it violated his rights under Article 19 of the ICCPR and UDHR. In a similar case from the same context, the WGAD decried the use of lèse-majesté laws in *Pornthip Munkong v. Thailand*, a case concerning the detention of an organizer of theatrical performances containing political messages.[520] The WGAD noted that the laws were being instrumen-talized to suppress debates on matters of public interest and suppress dissent.[521]

In addition to the monarchy, other government institutions are similarly not immune from criticism. On multiple occasions the WGAD has found detentions to be arbitrary

---

[515] *Joint Declaration on Universality and the Right to Freedom of Expression*, International Mechanisms for Promoting Freedom of Expression, May 6, 2014.

[516] General Comment No. 34, at ¶ 38; Patiwat Saraiyaem v. Thailand, WGAD Opinion No. 41/2014, Adopted Nov. 19, 2014, at ¶¶ 27, 29.

[517] Abdulkarim Al Khodr v. Saudi Arabia, WGAD Opinion No. 46/2013, Adopted Nov. 18, 2013 (law professor charged with "insulting the ruler"); Abdul Kareem Nabil Suliman Amer v Egypt, WGAD Opinion No. 35/2008, Adopted Nov. 20, 2008 (Egyptian blogger sentenced to prison for "insulting the President"); Tri Agus Susanto Siswowihardjo v. Indonesia, WGAD Opinion No. 42/1996, Adopted Dec. 3, 1996 (editor sentenced for publishing an interview critical of President Socharto).

[518] Somyot Prueksakasemsuk v. Thailand, WGAD Opinion No. 35/2012, Adopted Aug. 30, 2012, at ¶ 17.

[519] *Id.*, at ¶ 24 (citing to General Comment No. 34).

[520] Pornthip Munkong v. Thailand, WGAD Opinion No. 43/2015, Adopted Dec. 2, 2015, at ¶ 19–21.

[521] *Id.*, at ¶ 18.

when they serve as punishment for criticizing the military.[522] Some of these cases involve activists who are tried under vague laws for crimes such as insulting or demoralizing the military.[523] Others involve members of the military themselves: for example, where a former member of the Syrian military was detained for books he published that criticized the military, his detention was arbitrary under Category II.[524] The detention of a Mexican general who wrote an article calling for an ombudsman to be appointed for the army was also found to be arbitrary and based on the lawful exercise of his right to freedom of expression.[525]

The WGAD has also spoken more generally about the widespread use of these kinds of laws during their country missions. During its visit to Belarus, the WGAD explained that it had received extensive information about the arbitrary detention of persons exercising their rights to freedom of opinion and expression, peaceful assembly, and disseminating information in a peaceful manner. It reported that there were some people arrested and detained briefly, charged with administrative offense. And it said it learned about people charged with criminal offenses and then convicted and sentenced to longer periods of detention.[526] It expressed serious concern that a number of provisions of the penal code with such offenses as "libel against the President of the Republic," "insult to the President," and "libel against an official" are defined in "wide and imprecise terms and leave room for the criminalization of conduct protected by international law."[527] And it reported it had learned that at least three journalists had been convicted in 2001 and 2002 on criminal charges of allegedly slandering the President.[528]

The WGAD also spoke to this issue generally in Equatorial Guinea, where it found that about 100 people were detained on pretextual charges for exercising their civil and political rights:

> During its visit, the Working Group was able to ascertain that a number of detainees are in prison for exercising their political rights. These persons are generally accused of having committed crimes against the State or offences against the President of the Republic, as defined in the Spanish Criminal Code of the colonial era. Some of them are serving particularly long sentences, having been convicted by military courts without the guarantees of due process. In some cases detainees were tried summarily, without the right to appeal their sentences. Non-governmental sources informed the Working Group that about 100 individuals are currently in detention for offences relating to the exercise of political rights.[529]

---

[522] José Francisco Gallardo Rodrìguez v. Mexico, WGAD Opinion No. 28/1998, Adopted Dec. 3, 1998; Khalil Brayez v. Syria, WGAD Opinion No. 53/1992, Adopted Dec. 9, 1992; Maikel Nabil Sanad v. Egypt, WGAD Opinion No. 50/2011, Adopted Sept. 2, 2011; Ahmed Belaichi v. Morocco, WGAD Opinion No. 3/1994, Adopted May 17, 1994; Grigorii Pasko v. Russian Federation, WGAD Opinion No. 9/1999, Adopted May 20, 1999.

[523] Maikel Nabil Sanad v. Egypt, WGAD Opinion No. 50/2011, Adopted Sept. 2, 2011; Ahmed Belaichi v. Morocco, WGAD Opinion No. 3/1994, Adopted May 17, 1994.

[524] Khalil Brayez v. Syria, WGAD Opinion No. 53/1992, Adopted Dec. 9, 1992.

[525] José Francisco Gallardo Rodrìguez v. Mexico, WGAD Opinion No. 28/1998, Adopted Dec. 3, 1998.

[526] *Report of the Working Group on Arbitrary Detention: Mission to Belarus*, Commission on Human Rights, E/CN.4/2005/6/Add.3, Nov. 25, 2004, at ¶ 58.

[527] *Id.*, at ¶ 59.

[528] *Id.*

[529] *Report of the Working Group on Arbitrary Detention: Mission to Equatorial Guinea*, Human Rights Council, A/HRC/7/4/Add.4, Feb. 18, 2008, at ¶ 75.

Closely linked to the question of the reputational rights of public figures is that of their privacy rights. The protection of the right to privacy is articulated in nearly identical language in Article 17 of the ICCPR: "No one shall be subjected ... to attacks upon his honour and reputation. Everyone has the right to the protection of the law against such interference or attacks" and Article 12 of the UDHR.[530]

The WGAD's opinion in *Ko Than Htun and Ko Tin Htay* v. *Myanmar* suggests that the privacy rights of public figures, like their reputational rights, may be less rigorous where matters of public concern are at stake. Two Burmese citizens, Ko Than Htun and Ko Tin Htay, possessed politically focused videos that included footage of the wedding of the daughter of a prominent political and military figure, Senior General Than Shwe. The video interspersed the wedding footage with images of poverty throughout Myanmar. Both individuals were found guilty of violating the video censorship regulations and inciting public fear. The Government argued that the videos were presumed to "discredit and impair the dignity of the Government," that the videos had been produced without license, and that the detainees were sanctioned for seeking to incite unrest through dissemination of the video.[531]

The WGAD's opinion begins by emphasizing that while the publication of "uncomfortable film footage" might be disagreeable to the Government, it was nonetheless protected by Article 19 of the UDHR. The right protects opinions that criticize or upset public figures, particularly when related to political issues. Somewhat unusually, even though the Government did not raise this issue, the WGAD felt it was necessary to address whether the right to privacy of the bride or others in the video had been violated. It found that "there is no indication that the competing right to privacy is capable of limiting the non-violent exercise" of the right to freedom of expression, given that the video incorporated a political statement "contrasting the life style of a family member of Senior General Than Schwe with images of poverty."[532] The political messaging of the video and its focus on matters of general public concern outweigh the privacy concern in this case.

Note that the Government argued that the speech in question was an insult to it generally, rather than an individual. This was not an instance where a defamation law would be applicable: the speech was true and institutions cannot be defamed. However, governments may not always keep these categories precise, such as Tunisia's reliance on a sentence of "defamation of the public order."[533] Detentions targeting the right to freedom of expression under such laws will be arbitrary, both because the laws themselves are vague, and because whether the speech is defamatory or merely critical of a public figure, detention is an inappropriate response.

5 Restrictions on the Media

For the WGAD, "the use of arbitrary detention to restrict press freedom is a particularly invidious violation of civil and political rights."[534] This echoes the concerns of

---

[530] UDHR, at Art. 12; ICCPR, at Art. 17.

[531] Ko Than Htun and Ko Tin Htay v. Myanmar, WGAD Opinion No. 7/2008, Adopted May 8, 2008, at ¶¶ 13–14, 19–20.

[532] *Id.*, at ¶ 20.

[533] Khemais Ksila v. Tunisia, WGAD Opinion No. 5/1999, Adopted May 20, 1999.

[534] Chief Ebrima Manneh v. The Gambia, WGAD Opinion No. 14/2009, Adopted Sept. 3, 2009, at ¶ 25.

international experts, such as the UN Special Rapporteur for Freedom of Opinion and Expression, who have noted the alarmingly high number of journalists detained globally, and the use of criminal laws to suppress the free operation of the press and silence discussion of politically sensitive topics.[535] These concerns stem from a few areas in which media regulations are particularly abused. First, laws that regulate the media frequently fail to meet the requirements of Article 19(3) of the ICCPR. Second, criminal penalties are a disproportionate response to violations of media regulations. Finally, states may pretextually rely on laws unrelated to media regulation in an attempt to silence and control the press.

Some media regulation is permissible under international law, if drafted and executed in accordance with Article 19(3). Media laws must not be overly restrictive of speech, meaning burdensome licensing requirements or fees are inappropriate, and states should not have a monopoly over the media.[536] Furthermore, any penalization of journalists or media members solely for engaging in political criticism can never be a justifiable restriction under Article 19(3).[537] The WGAD will comment on domestic media laws that suppress the freedom of expression without strictly conforming to these requirements. For example, in examining the detention of an Ethiopian journalist, it cited to concerns expressed by the HR Committee over registration requirements for newspapers and other media regulations that had resulted in the closure of many newspapers and harassment of the media.[538] Elsewhere, in a case involving two Iranian journalists of Kurdish origin, the WGAD stated that the Iranian media law was not in conformity with the right to freedom of expression and emphasized that such laws must be "unambiguous, narrow and accompanied by adequate safeguards against abuse."[539] Detentions have also been found to be arbitrary by the WGAD when based on charges such as printing and distributing unlawful publications, violating registration requirements, and offenses against the press law.[540]

Even if media laws restrict the freedom of expression for a permissible purpose, criminal penalties for violations of such regulations will be disproportionate. The Human Rights Council (HRC), in Resolution 12/16, calls on states to refrain from the use of imprisonment as a punishment for media offenses, since this would be disproportionate to the gravity of the offence.[541] The WGAD's opinion in *Chief Ebrima Manneh v. The Gambia* supports this approach. Chief Ebrima Manneh was a Gambian reporter arrested and held incommunicado on unknown charges but reportedly in relation to his attempts to republish a BBC story that noted Gambian President Yahya Jammed had come to power through a coup.[542] The WGAD first determined that Manneh's detention was not provided by law and detaining a reporter who attempted to publish an article critical of

---

[535] *Report of the Special Rapportuer on the Promotion and Protection of the Right to Freedom of Opinion and Expression*, Human Rights Council, A/HRC/20/17, June 4, 2012 at ¶¶ 78–79.

[536] General Comment No. 34, at ¶¶ 39–40.

[537] *Id.*, at ¶ 42.

[538] Eskinder Nega v. Ethiopia, WGAD Opinion No. 62/2012, Adopted Nov. 21, 2012, at ¶ 32.

[539] Khosro Kordpour and Massoud Kordpour v. Iran, WGAD Opinion No. 52/2013 Adopted Nov. 20, 2013, at ¶ 17.

[540] Pedro Alvarez Martínez v. Cuba, WGAD Opinion No. 16/1992, Adopted Session No. 4; Arswendo Atmowiloto v. Indonesia, WGAD Opinion No. 16/1993, Adopted Apr. 30, 1993; Aye Tha Aung, et al. v. Myanmar, WGAD Opinion No. 13/2001, Adopted Sept. 12, 2001.

[541] *Resolution 12/16: Freedom of Opinion and Expression*, Human Rights Council, A/HRC/RES/12/16, Oct. 12, 2009, at ¶ 5(j).

[542] Chief Ebrima Manneh v. The Gambia, WGAD Opinion No. 14/2009, Adopted Sept. 3, 2009, at ¶ 9.

the Head of State was not necessary to protect national security or any reputational interest. Furthermore, even if censorship of the article itself had been justified, a three-year incommunicado detention "can certainly not be considered necessary" within the meaning of Article 19(3) of the ICCPR.[543]

Governments also target journalists for exercising their right to freedom of the press by pretextually relying on non-media related charges. For example, in *Syamak Pourzand v. Iran*, an Iranian journalist with a reputation for being critical of the Government was arrested and charged with sexual harassment. In the absence of information from the Government explaining the penal charges brought against the journalist and given that he was also charged with anti-Iranian propaganda and undermining state security, the WGAD had "serious doubts about the real nature of and the motivation for the charges," and found the detention to contravene Article 19 of the ICCPR and UDHR.[544] In analyzing similar cases, the WGAD has identified various factors that have cast doubt on the veracity of allegations brought against journalists. Problematic media laws or a pattern of media harassment will serve as evidence that the detention of a journalist on alternative charges is a pretext for punishing the exercise of free speech.[545] The timing of an arrest is also relevant if an arrest of a journalist closely follows the publication of an article that criticized the government; this is evidence of persecution for journalistic work.[546] Charges brought against an individual using his pen name also led to an inference that his arrest was related to his exercise of his right to freedom of expression – although here the detainee was a poet rather than a journalist.[547]

6 Detentions under Blasphemy Laws

Blasphemy laws vary by state, but may be generally understood as those laws that penalize speech or acts that are considered offensive or sacrilegious to a religious community. In the modern era, they are primarily relied on in select Islamic states, and in some countries have been used to target not only specific forms of blasphemous expression but also religious minorities more generally.[548] Blasphemy laws have been a subject of particular controversy in human rights law and the history of this controversy provides important context for the WGAD jurisprudence on the subject.

During the 2000s, a movement led by certain Islamic nations in the United Nations resulted in a series of resolutions by the HRC (and its predecessor, the UNCHR) condemning the "defamation of religions."[549] While such resolutions sought to address legitimate concerns over global anti-Islamic sentiment, human rights observers emphasized that the concept of defamation of religion could be used to suppress free expression

---

[543] *Id.*, at ¶ 25.

[544] Syamak Pourzand v. Iran, WGAD Opinion No. 8/2003, Adopted May 9, 2003, at ¶ 8.

[545] Moussa Kaka v. Niger, WGAD Opinion No. 7/2009, Adopted May 7, 2009, at ¶¶ 29–30.

[546] Isa Saharkhiz v. Iran, WGAD Opinion No. 8/2010, Adopted May 6, 2010, at ¶ 20(b).

[547] Saleh bin Awad bin Saleh Al-Hweiti v. Saudi Arabia, WGAD Opinion No. 30/2011, Adopted Aug. 30, 2011, at ¶ 16.

[548] Jeroen Temperman, *Blasphemy, Defamation of Religions and Human Rights Law*, 26(4) NETHERLANDS QUARTERLY OF HUMAN RIGHTS 517, 521 (2008).

[549] *See, e.g.*, Resolution 2000/84, *Defamation of Religions*, Commission on Human Rights, Apr. 26, 2000; Resolution 7/19, *Combating Defamation of Religions*, Human Rights Council, Mar. 27, 2008.

and justify the targeting of political or religious minorities.[550] Recognizing these concerns, after several years of debate on the issue, the HRC has made a definite shift away from the concept, instead referencing a reliance on the hate speech provisions of Article 20 of the ICCPR for any law that regulates speech that targets religion.[551] Specifically, Resolution 16/18 avoided reference to the term "defamation of religions" and focused instead on condemning religious hatred or incitement to violence or discrimination based on religion.[552] Importantly, in adopting General Comment 34, the HR Committee affirmed that blasphemy laws or other prohibitions on disrespecting religions are incompatible with the ICCPR "except in the specific circumstances envisaged in article 20, paragraph 2."[553]

Accordingly, international law currently applies the test under Article 20 of the ICCPR rather than a reference to "defamation of religion." Furthermore, any laws based on Article 20 cannot discriminate among religions or belief systems and cannot be used to punish criticism of religious leaders or commentary on certain religious doctrines.[554] While religious groups may have rights to be free from hate speech or discrimination under Article 20, the reference to protecting the "rights of others" in ICCPR Article 19(3) cannot be understood to protect a particular religion itself from criticism.[555]

Given the controversy over this issue, the WGAD has sometimes avoided judging the legitimacy of blasphemy laws if the detention may be found arbitrary on other grounds. Thus, as described in the introduction to this book, the WGAD avoided finding a Category II detention, either under Article 18 or 19 of the UDHR in the case of Ayub Masih, a Pakistani Christian accused of blasphemy. Instead, the concern with blasphemy was folded into the Category III due process analysis, with the WGAD questioning whether a fair trial could be feasible when charges of blasphemy against Islam could only be heard by Muslim judges.[556] Elsewhere, the WGAD has found that detentions were not proper under the relevant domestic law, avoiding the broader question of the legitimacy of the law itself: the detention of two journalists who criticized a certain interpretation of the Koran violated their right to freedom of expression, and did not fall under the Bangladeshi law provision criminalizing "insults to the religious feelings of the Muslim community of Bangladesh."[557] Finally, on some occasions a government has failed to respond to the complaint or offered sufficient evidence justifying its reliance on blasphemy charges, and the WGAD has found the detention arbitrary without referencing the legality of the blasphemy law more generally.[558]

---

[550] *Letter from Civil Society Organizations to State Representatives: 'Defamation of Religion' at the 13th Session of the United Nations Human Rights Council*, Mar. 11, 2010.

[551] *Lecture at the London School of Economics: Freedom of Expression and Incitement to Hatred in the Context of International Human Rights Law*, UN High Commissioner for Human Rights Navanethem Pillay, Feb. 15, 2013.

[552] *Resolution 16/18, Combating Intolerance, Negative Stereotyping and Stigmatization of, and Discrimination, Incitement to Violence and Violence against, Persons Based on Religion or Belief*, Human Rights Council, Mar. 24, 2011.

[553] General Comment No. 34, at ¶ 48.

[554] *Id.*, at ¶ 48.

[555] *Report of Special Rapporteur on Freedom of Religion or Belief*, Human Rights Council, A/HRC/2/3, Sept. 20, 2006, at ¶ 38.

[556] Ayub Masih v. Pakistan, WGAD Opinion No. 25/2001, Adopted Nov. 30, 2001, at ¶ 19.

[557] Toab Khan and Borhan Ahmed v. Bangladesh, WGAD Opinion No. 5/1995, Adopted May 30, 1995, at ¶ 6.

[558] Arash Sigarchi v. Iran, WGAD Opinion No. 19/2006, Adopted Aug. 30, 2006; Manouchehr Karimzadeh v. Iran, WGAD Opinion No. 28/1994, Adopted Sept. 29, 1994.

Despite expressing hesitancy in some opinions to speak as to the legality of specific blasphemy laws, recent opinions by the WGAD have explicitly rejected the concept of "defamation of religions" and embraced the Article 20 based approach seen in General Comment 34 for evaluating charges of blasphemy or offenses against religion. This can be seen in *Abdul Kareem Nabil Suliman Amer v. Egypt*, which involved an Egyptian blogger and student who was detained after writing on his blog about riots that had followed the screening of a play believed to be anti-Islamic. After his university filed a complaint with the Public Prosecutor, he was sentenced to one year in prison for insulting the President and three years for contempt of religion.[559] The Government argued that the charge of contempt for religion was justified as a permissible restriction of the right to freedom of expression, in this case to protect freedom of belief, avoid inciting hatred, and prevent discrimination based on religious grounds. It also stated that Egyptian law criminalized contempt for all religions equally, without favoritism toward one particular creed.[560]

Responding to these claims, the WGAD began by reiterating that it views the right to freedom of expression and freedom of religion as reinforcing, rather than contradictory, rights. Accordingly, while defamation of religions may offend others, it does not directly result in a violation of the right to freedom of religion.[561] The WGAD directly quoted the UN Special Rapporteur on Freedom of Religion or Belief to emphasize that the freedom of religion protects persons and communities, but does not protect "religions or beliefs per se." It then affirmed that blasphemy "should be decriminalized as an insult to religion," and rather statements that call for hatred, discrimination, or violence toward a particular group should be penalized, in "the spirit of article 20."[562] Amer's detention was accordingly arbitrary and based on his exercise of the right to freedom of expression. This opinion, published in 2008 in the midst of the "defamation of religions" controversy, takes a clear stance against the concept of "defamation of religions," and indicates the WGAD's agreement with more recent trends in the human rights jurisprudence, including using Article 20 as the appropriate vehicle for addressing speech that constitutes religious hatred.

In addition to rejecting "defamation of religions" or laws that criminalize insulting religion as a valid basis for detention, the WGAD has emphasized that laws which attempt to respond to religious hatred must meet the same requirements as other restrictions on free expression. A few years after issuing its opinion on Amer, the WGAD reaffirmed its rejection of overly broad blasphemy laws in *Jabeur Mejri v. Tunisia*. Jabeur Mejri was convicted by Tunisia of offending sacred values and disrupting public order as a result of a document he posted online which contained messages and images of the Prophet Muhammad that were considered offensive.[563] Finding the detention arbitrary, the WGAD emphasized that the requirements of Article 19(3) must be strictly followed when expression is restricted, even in regard to offenses against religion. Furthermore, it observed "the right and the freedom to criticize a religion cannot, of themselves,

---

[559] Abdul Kareem Nabil Suliman Amer v. Egypt, WGAD Opinion No. 35/2008, Adopted Nov. 20, 2008, at ¶ 25.

[560] *Id.*, at ¶ 27.

[561] *Id.*, at ¶ 38.

[562] *Id.*, at ¶ 39.

[563] Jabeur Mejri v. Tunisia, WGAD Opinion No. 29/2013, Adopted Aug. 30, 2013, at ¶ 15.

constitute a violation" of the right to freedom of expression. The Government's reliance on "overly vague" definitions was accordingly improper.[564] This opinion confirms the WGAD's stance that there is no special category of "defamation of religions" under human rights law, and while states may and should penalize acts of religious hatred under Article 20 of the ICCPR, such laws (as well as detentions made under them) should conform to the requirements of Article 19(3) of the ICCPR.[565]

V Participation in Public Affairs/Government

Article 25 of the ICCPR emphasizes that the right to political participation in public affairs cannot be restricted either because of distinctions on protected grounds – which include race, color, sex, language, religion, political or other opinion, national or social origin, property, birth, or other status – or that are otherwise unreasonable. It states specifically:

> Every citizen shall have the right and the opportunity, without any of the distinctions mentioned in article 2 and without unreasonable restrictions:
>
> (a) To take part in the conduct of public affairs, directly or through freely chosen representatives;
> (b) To vote and to be elected at genuine periodic elections which shall be by universal and equal suffrage and shall be held by secret ballot, guaranteeing the free expression of the will of the electors;
> (c) To have access, on general terms of equality, to public service in his country.

Article 21 of the UDHR explains:

> 1. Everyone has the right to take part in the government of his country, directly or through freely chosen representatives.
> 2. Everyone has the right of equal access to public service in his country.
> 3. The will of the people shall be the basis of the authority of government; this will shall be expressed in periodic and genuine elections which shall be by universal and equal suffrage and shall be held by secret vote or by equivalent free voting procedures.

A Scope of the Right

The scope of Article 25 is broad and activities that fall within the exercise of political power include, but are not limited to, legislative, executive, and administrative activities within the functioning of the state.[566] It also includes the process and conduct of government affairs related to policymaking and exercise of state power.[567] The HR Committee has clarified that Article 25 rights also protect the freedom to engage in political activity individually or by association with political groups, criticism of the government, publishing material containing political content, or engaging in meetings

---

[564] Id., at ¶¶ 17–18.
[565] For a full discussion of the relationship between Article 19 and 20 of the ICCPR, see the section on hate speech.
[566] ALEX CONTE & RICHARD BURCHILL, DEFINING CIVIL AND POLITICAL RIGHTS: THE JURISPRUDENCE OF THE UNITED NATIONS HUMAN RIGHTS COMMITTEE 99 (Ashgate, 2009).
[567] Joseph & Castan, at ¶ 22.09.

or debates concerning political affairs.[568] The language of Article 25(a) provides a general formulation of the right, while Articles 25(b) and (c) concern specific elements of the general right.[569] Citizenship, as referred to in the Article, refers to persons within a particular state party's jurisdiction.[570]

1 Taking Part in Public Affairs

The right protected under Article 25(a) seeks to ensure that citizens are provided the opportunity to participate in all areas of public administration and the formulation and implementation of policy at all relevant levels – local, regional, national, and international.[571] States must accordingly provide and outline the structure of authority within their territory and set appropriate means for participation by citizens in their respective constitutions.[572] Article 25(a) does not, however, stretch so far as to require direct participation, nor does it set an ideal form of representative governance to remain sensitive to localized needs or differences.[573] In *Marshall v. Canada*, the HR Committee recognized that the tasks of providing institutions or means of participation are to be decided by political representatives in accordance with the particular laws of the concerned state.[574] The appropriate analysis, according to the HR Committee, is for the Article 25(a) right to be interpreted in light of the legal and constitutional framework of the particular state and for the specific measures for political activity provided by relevant domestic law.[575]

The HR Committee clarified that Article 25(a) is an individual and not collective right.[576] In *Diergaardt v. Namibia*, it rejected the claim that termination of self-government of a minority group by a state party would violate a community-wide right to participate in government or public affairs.[577] The HR Committee noted that though the integration of a previously autonomous region would necessarily impact the constituent members' Article 25 right, the applicants could not show that their access to public service would be diminished within the post-merger sovereign state.[578] Participation in public affairs, however, may be affected indirectly through elected representatives.[579] The modes for ensuring direct participation in public affairs are outlined specifically in

---

[568] Conte & Burchill, at 109; Aduayom, et al. v. Togo, Communication No. 422-24/1990, Human Rights Committee, CCPR/C/57/D/422-424/1990, Aug. 19, 1996.

[569] Nowak, at 441; Joseph & Castan, at 650.

[570] Joseph & Castan, at 651.

[571] Conte & Burchill, at 99.

[572] General Comment No. 25, CCPR/C/21/Rev.1/Add.7 (1996), at ¶ 5.

[573] See M. J. BOSSYUT, GUIDE TO THE "TRAVAUX PREPERATOIRES" OF THE INTERNATIONAL COVENANT ON CIVIL & POLITICAL RIGHTS 470 (Martinus Nijhoff Publishers, 1987).

[574] Marshall v. Canada, Communication No. 205/1986, Human Rights Committee, CCPR/C/43/D/205/1986, Nov. 4, 1991, at ¶ 5.5.

[575] Conte & Burchill, at 99.

[576] Joseph & Castan, at 653.

[577] Diergaardt v Namibia, Communication No. 760/1997, Human Rights Committee, CCPR/C/69/D/760/1997, Sept. 6, 2000, at ¶ 10.8.

[578] Id.

[579] Joseph & Castan, at 654–655; General Comment No. 25, at ¶ 7.

Article 25(b) and (c) – that is, through elections or public service – but also includes participating in debate or dialogue on issues of political concern.[580]

Article 25 requires that state parties provide for types of political systems or structures of governance that are representative of constituent citizens.[581] Autocratic governments that by nature restrict representation or bar citizens from participating in political activities de facto violate Article 25(a).[582] The HR Committee has found that unreasonable restrictions on citizens' participation as candidates in election campaigns, or from making necessary preparations for candidacy, violates Article 25(a).[583]

2 Elections and Voter Participation

Article 25(b) relates to the regulation of elections and seeks to protect the free expression of citizens' electoral will. As General Comment 25 to the ICCPR states, domestic and constitutional law must provide for the process of election.[584] This is a positive right, requiring states to ensure that citizens are provided the process and ability to participate in elections, a duty that prohibits the setting of restrictive registration requirement or the coercion of voters.[585] In some cases, states may be required to provide requisite support for groups or citizens with special needs, such as impediments to movement, and to publish materials in multiple languages to facilitate participation from otherwise excluded voters.[586] In addition, the state should ensure that voters have a free choice of candidates, and avoid discriminatory classification that would unduly limit the choice of the electorate.[587] Elections nevertheless have reasonable limitations, such as age restrictions and term limits, subject to the distinctions between citizens required by Article 2 (1).[588] Restrictions cannot be discriminatory or impose wage, educational, or property requirements.[589] State parties may also not restrict participation in elections on the basis of membership in an opposition political party.[590]

3 Access to Public Service

Article 25(c) protects citizens' rights of access to public service on the basis of equality and without discrimination. Access to public service includes fair opportunity for employment in the public sector or policy-making institutions. To meet this obligation, state

---

[580] Id., at ¶ 8.

[581] General Comment No. 25, at ¶ 7.

[582] Nowak, at 441.

[583] Bwalya v. Zambia, Communication No. 314/1988, Human Rights Committee, CCPR/C/48/D/314/1988, July 14, 1993, at ¶ 6.6.

[584] General Comment No. 25, at ¶ 7.

[585] Id., at ¶ 12.

[586] Id.

[587] General Comment No. 25, at ¶ 15; Joseph & Castan, at 664; see also Bwalya v. Zambia, Communication No. 314/1988, Human Rights Committee, CCPR/C/48/D/314/1988, July 14, 1993 (finding a violation of Article 25 where a candidate for election was excluded demonstrably for his affiliation with a particular party).

[588] General Comment No. 25, at ¶ 6; see e.g., Debreczeny v. The Netherlands, Communication No. 500/1992, Human Rights Committee, CCPR/C/53/D/500/1992, Apr. 3, 1995.

[589] Conte & Burchill, at 101.

[590] General Comment No. 25, at ¶ 10.

parties must ensure that the processes and criteria for employment, participation, and employment are objectively fair and reasonable.[591] Article 2(1) of the ICCPR and non-discrimination principles prohibit unlawful exclusion of citizens, including on the basis of their political opinion.[592] As the drafting history of Article 25(c) explains, domination of public offices by majority groups is not permitted.[593] Once employed or serving in the public interest, state parties must insulate citizens from political pressure, in order to ensure that the right is capable of being exercised effectively.[594] Dismissal from public service employment may also violate Article 25(c) protections if the facts of the dismissal case show that discharge may have been for political reasons or otherwise unfair.[595]

B Interpretation of Participation in Government Affairs

In *Pham Hong Son* v. *Viet Nam*, the WGAD found a violation of Article 25 with the arrest of a longtime government critic on the basis that the stated reasons for the detainee's arrest failed to conform to international law principles.[596] In this case, the Government refused to discuss the operative facts that would substantiate the specific grounds for the detainee's arrest, which was effected shortly after his publication of articles titled, "What is democracy?" and "Hopeful signs for democracy in Vietnam," the latter of which he had directly transmitted to senior government officials.[597] His initial arrest was made on an accusation of espionage for allegedly collaborating with international political groups sympathetic to the cause of democracy in Viet Nam, and for the dissemination of material that the Government said falsely "distort[ed] the policy of the Party and State."[598]

After release from his initial arrest, Pham was prevented by police from meeting with other pro-democracy activists in the country or from participating in any political activity, and from accessing the Internet.[599] The WGAD did not specify any particular act as directly violating Article 25 though the aggregation of these events generally supported its opinion.[600] The WGAD emphasized the content of his activism and writing was indisputably related to public affairs, because it called specifically for "political openness."[601] Most significantly, however, the WGAD emphasized that even if domestic laws have been violated those laws must be consistent with a state's international law obligations. Therefore, the mere fact that an arrest and detention of an individual appears to be in accordance with domestic law is not sufficient to avoid an adverse finding before the WGAD.[602]

---

[591] Conte & Burchill, at 106.

[592] General Comment No. 25, at ¶ 23.

[593] Bossvut, at 476.

[594] Conte & Burchill, at 106.

[595] Munoz v. Peru, Communication No. 203/1986, Human Rights Committee, CCPR/C/34/D/203/1986, Nov. 4, 1988; *see also* Mazou v. Cameroon, Communication No. 630/1995, Human Rights Committee, CCPR/C/72/D/630/1995, July 26, 2001.

[596] Pham Hong Son v. Viet Nam, WGAD Opinion No. 13/2007, Adopted May 11, 2007, at ¶¶ 30–31 (Litigated by Author through Freedom Now).

[597] *Id.*, at ¶ 11.

[598] *Id.*, at ¶ 14.

[599] *Id.*, at ¶ 20.

[600] *Id.*, at ¶¶ 31–32.

[601] *Id.*, at ¶ 31.

[602] *Id.*, at ¶ 29.

To draw the necessary nexus between the detention and grounds of political partici-pation, the WGAD will generally examine the underlying proceedings or pretrial interrogation for evidence of political bias. *Frédéric Bamvuginyumvira* v. *Burundi* concerned a former Vice President of Burundi, who in the course of his campaigning for constitutional reform that would lead to greater equity in powerholding between rival ethnic groups was intercepted and detained by security forces.[603] The WGAD, in finding a Category II violation, noted that the court "hesitated in making their assessment and adopted contradictory approaches" – irregularities in the proceedings that evinced that the real reason for the detention was the detainee's role as leader of the political opposition.[604] In *Mahmoud Abdulrahman al-Jaidah* v. *United Arab Emirates*, the WGAD noted that the fact that the detainee had been interrogated about his political convictions and ties to the Muslim Brotherhood showed that his detention was politically motivated and violated the applicant's freedom of opinion and expression.[605]

In an opinion concerning several activists and a newspaper publisher affiliated with the minority Shan group in Burma, the WGAD distinguished between protected polit-ical activity and military activity that did not fall within protection of Article 21 of the UDHR. The detainees in this case had been arrested and detained under treason provisions in Myanmar law.[606] The specific circumstances in the case, including the participation of the detainees in a peace process between the Government and the Shan minority, the direct substantive opposition of the detainees to the content of the proposed political resolution between the negotiating political stakeholders, and the general context of unresolved constitutional development, provided conclusive evidence to the WGAD that the activities in which the applicants were involved were political and not military in nature.[607]

Significantly, the WGAD expounded on its earlier jurisprudence that the characteris-tics of domestic legislation, if not compatible with international law principles, would evidence a political motive on the part of the detaining government, and thus contribute to a finding of an Article 25 violation. The WGAD referenced the treason provisions under which the detainees had been held in Myanmar to explain categories of laws that would be considered violative of international law principles. Specifically, overly vague, overbroad and over-restrictive criminal laws, such as those that made it an offense to "bring or attempt to bring into hatred and contempt, to excite or attempt to excite disaffection towards the Government," provisions prohibiting formation of organizations to "affect or disrupt the operation of state machinery" or "to mention false facts" in context of publication, and "to establish, without prior registration, enterprises for

---

[603] Frédéric Bamvuginyumvira v. Burundi, WGAD Opinion No. 30/2015, Adopted Sep. 3, 2015, at ¶¶ 4–5.

[604] *Id.*, at ¶ 44.

[605] Mahmoud Abdulrahman al-Jaidah v. United Arab Emirates, WGAD Opinion No. 35/2015, Adopted Sept. 4, 2015, at ¶ 45.

[606] Hkun Htun Oo, et al. v. Myanmar, WGAD Opinion No. 26/2008, Adopted Sept. 12, 2009, at ¶¶ 10–11, 13–17; *see also* Tran Thi Thuy, et al. v. Viet Nam, WGAD Opinion No. 46/2011, Adopted Sept. 2, 2011, at ¶ 22 (providing note of guidance for the State party to ensure conformity of domestic legislation to international human rights law principles).

[607] Hkun Htun Oo, at ¶ 33.

printing and publishing," would fall into the class of cases the WGAD would consider in violation of Article 25 principles.[608]

The WGAD generally looks to the detainee's past and most recent activities to ascertain if they qualify as protected participation in government or public affairs, not merely to the stated grounds articulated by the government.[609] The detainee's prior activities, history and mode of participation, and content of political views are relevant to the WGAD analysis of the Article 25 claims, as it is when examining claims of violations of Article 19 on freedom of opinion and expression. In *Antonio José Ledezma Díaz v. Venezuela*, for instance, the WGAD noted the profile of the detainee as a lawyer and public management specialist, and his then-current role as the Mayor of Caracas, as well as his support for a call by the opposition party, of which he was a member, advocating a change in regime by constitutional means.[610] The WGAD drew the necessary link between the detention and his political participation, noting that he had been harassed specifically because of his affiliation with the opposition party.[611] This approach is consistent with the HR Committee jurisprudence, which provides that Article 25 should be read broadly to encompass the freedom to engage in political activity, to debate issues of public policy or affairs, and to criticize government by publication or speech.[612]

In the case of *Abdulhadi Abdulla Alkhawaja v. Bahrain*, the WGAD discussed at some length the detainee's extensive work for the Bahrain Center for Human Rights, the nonviolent nature of his activities, and that the content of his activist cause was to encourage greater participation by Bahraini citizens, and in particular the Shi'ite minority, in politics.[613] The WGAD also noted, though primarily for purposes of ascertaining whether the Government's allegations were grounded in fact, the immediately preceding activity that provided the direct cause for arrest. Here, the detainee was arrested shortly after his participation in political protests, in which he had featured prominently as a speaker encouraging demonstrations.[614] Similarly, in *Andrei Sannikov v. Belarus*, the WGAD referenced specific statements made in a press conference by President Alexander Lukashenko shortly after the detainee's arrest, in which he said that "revolutionary activities" or "silly, muddle-headed" democratic participation would not be tolerated.[615] The immediate context of the detention, therefore, often demonstrates to the WGAD that activities engaged in by the detainee fall squarely within the protections of Article 25.

The WGAD has followed the HR Committee rulings that direct participation in election-related activities, if found to be disrupted, would be in violation of Article

---

[608] *Id.*, at ¶ 34; *see also* Antonio José Rivero González v. Venezuela, WGAD Opinion No. 47/2013, Adopted Nov. 18, 2013, at ¶ 32 (noting the vague and unexplained legal provisions and charges under which the applicant was detained, as evidence of politically-motivated detention).

[609] *See e.g.*, Abdulhadi Abdulla Alkhawaja v. Bahrain, WGAD Opinion No. 6/2012, Adopted May 2, 2012, at ¶¶ 4–5, 8 (providing the various provisions under which the applicant was detained, including managing a terrorist organization, attempting to overthrow the government, and financing terrorist activity, as well as other stated reasons for his arrest).

[610] Antonio José Ledezma Díaz, at ¶¶ 4, 27.

[611] *Id.*, at ¶ 29.

[612] Aduayom, et al. v. Togo, Communication No. 422-24/1990, Human Rights Committee, CCPR/C/57/D/422-424/1990, Aug. 19, 1996, at ¶ 7.5; Conte & Burchill, at 109.

[613] Abdulhadi Abdulla Alkhawaja, at ¶¶ 17–19.

[614] *Id.*, at ¶ 16.

[615] Andrei Sannikov v. Belarus, WGAD Opinion No. 14/2012, Adopted May 4, 2012, at ¶ 28.

25 of the ICCPR or Article 21 of the UDHR. In a Category I case related to the WGAD's Article 25 jurisprudence, it found that a judge and chairperson of a prominent political party in Ethiopia was being held arbitrarily because she was targeted for her political engagement.[616] The WGAD has also found a clear Article 25 violation in the imprisonment of an election monitor who had refused to overlook an instance of electoral fraud.[617] And in a case involving a variety of civil society participants – journalists, activists, human rights defenders, labor union leaders, and writers – advocating for the Government to call a referendum on electoral and institutional reform, the WGAD found a clear violation of Article 21 of the UDHR.[618] The WGAD in these cases found clear violations without providing specific or elaborate rationale because the content of sources' submissions and activities of these detainees was demonstrably political, intended explicitly to reform political institutions.[619]

The WGAD has, however, imported from HR Committee guidance a broad interpretation to the right to take part in public affairs. In the Zeinab Jalalian case, the WGAD cited the HR Committee as providing that "participating in the conduct of public debate and dialogue with (their) representatives or through their capacity to organize themselves" was included within the scope of the right.[620] The WGAD found, accordingly and in that case, that advocating for the rights of Kurdish women fell within this interpretation of activity.[621] That her activism was linked to public affairs could also be evinced, the WGAD provided from the trial court's assessment that the detainee had "attempted to influence public opinion against the regime."[622]

Category II violations have also been found when a detention is imposed to prevent exercise of the right to political participation, rather than in response to it. In *Musallam Mohamed Hamad al-Barrak v. Kuwait*, the WGAD considered that the arrest and prosecution of the detainee was an effort to prevent him from running in parliamentary elections.[623] These actions were found to be a violation of Article 25 of the ICCPR. It is worth noting that the WGAD did not specify they believed the arrest was a response to his campaign – but rather that the prevention of his campaign as a motivation for imprisonment rendered his detention arbitrary.[624]

Typically, the WGAD has not felt it necessary to engage in extended discussion and analysis where detainees are current or previously elected representatives or public officials arrested while engaging in political activities. In an earlier case involving the overnight detention by police of several elected representatives, who were also members of the opposition National League for Democracy (NLD) party in Myanmar, the WGAD

---

[616] Birtukan Mideksa Deme v. Ethiopia, WGAD Opinion No. 28/2009, Adopted Nov. 25, 2009, at ¶ 36.

[617] See e.g., Giorgi Mshvenieradz v. Georgia, WGAD Opinion No. 2/2004, Adopted May 25, 2004, at ¶¶ 5–6 (noting in addition the efforts of the applicant to report the electoral fraud).

[618] Nelson Aguiar Ramirez and 78 Others v. Cuba, WGAD Opinion No. 9/2003, Adopted May 9, 2003, at ¶ 23.

[619] Id., at ¶ 17 (noting that the Varela Project, the name of the organization with which all detainees were affiliated, intended to advocate for their favored change through constitutional means, and with the intention to strengthen democratic participation).

[620] Zeinab Jalalian v. Iran, WGAD Opinion No. 1/2016, Adopted Apr. 18, 2016, at ¶ 36.

[621] Id.

[622] Id.

[623] Musallam Mohamed Hamad al-Barrak v. Kuwait, WGAD Opinion No. 20/2017, Adopted Apr. 24, 2017, at ¶ 47.

[624] Id.

noted a clear violation of Article 21 of the UDHR.[625] Similarly, the WGAD also found Article 25 of the ICCPR violated in a case concerning the detention of Andrei Sannikov, a former Deputy Foreign Minister of Belarus, a civil rights champion, and an electoral candidate at the time of his arrest. He was addressing protestors at the time of his arrest in a rally to oppose constitutional amendments that would cut substantive protection for human rights in the country.[626] And when the Government of Venezuela detained Antonio Gonzales, a former Venezuelan general and public official turned opposition leader, his detention was found to be arbitrary.[627] The WGAD accepted the source's allegations without extended discussion, since the detainee's activities clearly fell within Article 25 protection.[628] Similarly, there was no discussion explaining the violation of Article 25 in *Mohamed Nasheed* v. *The Maldives*.[629] Yet in finding Venezuelan political opposition leader Leopoldo López's detention arbitrary, in part on the basis of his prior illegal disqualification to run for political office, the WGAD only referenced Article 21 of the UDHR, but not Article 25 of the ICCPR. This appears to have been an error as Venezuela is a party to the ICCPR.[630]

C Permissible Limitations

ICCPR General Comment 25 provides circumstances under which states may reasonably limit the right to participation in government and public affairs. Requirements for permissible limitations mirror those detailed in the prior section regarding restrictions on the Article 19 right to freedom of opinion and expression – authorities must ensure that the limitations are lawful, reasonable, temporally limited, and proportionate to the identified threat to public order.[631] The WGAD demonstrated in *Ahmed Saad Douma Saad, et al.* v. *Egypt* that it would assess domestic legislation or policies authorizing controls on public demonstrations critically.[632] In that case, the detainees were participants in a peaceful demonstration and were arrested pursuant to a restrictive law, adopted shortly after the lifting of the state of emergency that had resulted in a military takeover.[633] The WGAD outlined the aforementioned requirements for permissible limitations to Article 21 rights, and ruled that the law placed impermissibly "broad restrictions" on the rights to peaceful assembly, expression, and participation in public affairs, and had been used as "a tool for cracking down on peaceful demonstrations."[634] Since the law failed to comply with the strict requirements for limitation permitted under human rights law, the detentions were found to be in clear violation of both Article 19 and 21 guarantees.[635]

---

[625] U Tun Win, et al. v. Myanmar, WGAD Opinion No. 3/1999, Adopted May 20, 1999, at ¶ 11.
[626] Andrei Sannikov, at ¶¶ 3, 41.
[627] Antonio José Rivero González, at ¶ 3.
[628] Id., at ¶¶ 30–31.
[629] Mohamed Nasheed v. The Maldives, WGAD Opinion No. 33/2015, Adopted Sept. 4, 2015 (Litigated by Author through Freedom Now with Co-Counsel Amal Clooney and Ben Emmerson QC).
[630] Leopoldo López Mendoza v. Venezuela, WGAD Opinion No. 26/2014, Adopted Aug. 26, 2014.
[631] Ahmed Saad Douma Saad, et al. v. Egypt, WGAD Opinion No. 49/2015, Adopted Dec. 3, 2015, at ¶ 38.
[632] Id.
[633] Id., at ¶ 11.
[634] Id., at ¶ 39.
[635] Id., at ¶ 40.

The most common defense made to the WGAD, if a respondent government admits to a limitation of the right, is that the detainee's activity is violent in nature. The WGAD will look behind the allegation to determine whether the assertion of violence is substantiated by the facts of the detainee's activity. In a case involving a student activist, detained for encouraging various forms of civil disobedience in Myanmar, the WGAD noted that the Government could not justify detention without alleging or showing that the detainee encouraged or participated in violent acts.[636] And in a different case in Myanmar, the WGAD also looked behind the allegations and laws under which detainees have been arrested to show that in truth political activities have been wrongly characterized as criminal.[637]

The WGAD has also held, however, that even peaceful political activities intended to effect self-autonomy or self-determination for particular member groups of a state party are protected by Article 25, even though many state parties would criminalize such advocacy as treason.[638] The peaceful nature of activities renders permissible almost any political activity, removing them from those that governments can lawfully restrict under Article 25.[639] In rejecting the Bahrain government's assertion that the activities of Abdulhadi Alkhawaja were violent and terroristic to justify restrictions on his Article 19 and 25 rights, the WGAD stressed the nonviolent nature of the detainee's work with the Bahrain Center for Human Rights.[640] The WGAD has made similar observations of the peaceful nature of detainees' participation in public affairs to rule against government assertions that they were involved in activities intended to stir dissent, discord, or public disturbance.[641]

The WGAD is also reflexively concerned about situations where the work and political ambition of detainees is in furtherance of democratic governance, social justice, or human rights. In the case of Cuban dissidents who launched the Varela Project, a constitutional means of strengthening democratic representation, the WGAD stressed how such activities fell squarely within those rights protected by international law.[642] In the case of a political activist detained in Myanmar, the WGAD noted the intent of the detainee's protests were intended to draw attention from the United Nations on a range of legitimate political concerns in the absence of effective means of holding the government accountable.[643]

---

[636] Ko Mya Aye v. Myanmar, WGAD Opinion No. 28/2010, Adopted Nov. 22, 2010 at ¶ 24 (noting the Government failed to refute the source's claims that Ko Mya Aye had only ever engaged in "non-violent" and "wholly peaceful" means of protest, which included petitions and encouraging citizens to write letters, dressing differently to call for attention to his plea, and initiating a prayer campaign).

[637] Min Zayar, et al., at ¶ 24 (noting in this case that the Government failed to detail which of the applicants' various actions could be categorized within the broad criminal regulations on "communicating with anti-organizations declared as terrorist groups," "acceptance of illegal money from foreign sources," and which types of groups would be considered unacceptable).

[638] Id.

[639] Nelson Aguiar Ramirez, at ¶ 23 (noting that the Government of Cuba had failed to demonstrate with evidence their assertion that the activities of the detainers were violent).

[640] Abdulhadi Abdulla Alkhawaja, at ¶ 18.

[641] See e.g., Matrouk bin Hais, et al. v. Saudi Arabia, WGAD Opinion No. 25/2004, Adopted Nov. 26, 2004, at ¶ 16.

[642] Nelson Aguiar Ramirez, at ¶ 17.

[643] Min Zayar (Aung Myin), et al. v. Myanmar, WGAD Opinion No. 43/2008, Adopted Nov. 25, 2008, at ¶¶ 5, 12 (Litigated by Author).

The cause of political engagement to advance social justice includes a wide gambit of activity. In a case concerning members of Viet Nam Reform Party, a group accused by the Government of trying to overthrow it by undemocratic means, the WGAD found that the detainees' international and domestic advocacy efforts and attending of political education seminars were nonviolent activities directed at improving social justice.[644] The Government had alleged that the organization was reactionary in political motive, engaged in conspiracy to overthrow state authorities, and that the detainees had traveled to Thailand to receive political and military training to further their radical purpose.[645] The WGAD opinion finding in favor of the detainees concluded that given the history of the organization's work, their political activities, even if transnational in geographical scope, were protected under Article 25.[646]

Cases in which the detainees' activities are consistent with international law and reflect widespread public sentiment are also likely to be viewed sympathetically by the WGAD. In the case of Cuban intellectuals mentioned earlier, the WGAD, as evidence of the democratic nature of the detainees' activities and reform proposals, mentioned the strong public support for their political agenda, evidenced by a petition signed by 11,000 Cuban citizens.[647] In another case, the WGAD described an activist's protest against a dramatic hike in fuel prices as "legitimate," because it fell within the protections of Article 21.[648]

Similarly, many detainees are arrested as reprisals for their political activities that fall within the protections of Article 25 of the ICCPR and Article 21 of the UDHR. This is evident from the WGAD's emphasis on the diligent actions of an election monitor who attempted to report electoral fraud to independent and international election monitors, and who was detained after a policeman discovered his activities to expose these manipulations.[649] Another case arose in the context of a detainee's regular employment as an independent Uzbek public defense lawyer. He was accused of extortion in the course of his representation of an indigent client attempting to recover property in a civil settlement.[650] The WGAD found that the detention charges were a pretext to prevent the detainee from his rights protection activities, including through an opposition political party, and his legal advocacy to uncover corruption by police officials.[651]

D Overlap with Article 19 Freedom of Expression

The right to participation in government and public affairs is tied closely to the freedom of movement and association rights enumerated in Articles 19 of the ICCPR and UDHR. In some instances, the restriction on Article 19 freedoms contributes to restrictions on and will appear concomitant to the Article 25 right to participation in government and public affairs. In the case of Pham Hong Son, the collective circumstance of surveillance, physical harassment by officials to prevent the detainee's participation in political

---

[644] Tran Thi Thuy, et al., at ¶¶ 11, 20.
[645] Id., at ¶ 6.
[646] Id., at ¶ 20.
[647] Nelson Aguiar Ramirez, at ¶ 17.
[648] Min Zayar, et al., at ¶ 5.
[649] Giorgi Mshvenieradz, at ¶¶ 5–7.
[650] Akzam Turgunov v. Uzbekistan, WGAD Opinion No. 53/2011, Adopted Nov. 17, 2011, at ¶ 25.
[651] Id., at ¶ 48.

meetings, and access to communication devices were material to both Article 19 and 25 violations under the ICCPR.[652] It is clear, however, that banning independent publication of opposition views of political content may violate both the detainee's freedom of expression and right to participate in government and public affairs.[653]

In the case of Birtukan Deme, an Ethiopian jurist and political leader, the WGAD explained the intersections between the right to freedoms of expression, association, and political participation. It concluded: "As the leader of a political party in a democratic society, she clearly enjoys the right to address her supporters at home or while visiting a foreign country. The deprivation of liberty . . . also constitutes a violation of her right to freedom of association and assembly and the right to take part in the conduct of public affairs."[654] The WGAD similarly severally found violations of the right to freedom of expression, the right to freedom of peaceful assembly and association, and the right to take part in public affairs in *Khalida Jarrar v. Israel*, concerning the detention of a member of the Palestinian Legislative Council.[655]

Considering Article 19 and Article 25 claims jointly has also permitted the WGAD to examine cases involving writers, intellectuals, artists, and academics. In such cases, detainees have been targeted by the government for opinions either of explicit political import or viewed by authorities as capable of inducing or contributing to political dissent.[656] Also protected by this analysis are journalists who report on issues of human rights, and disseminate their work to further a political agenda.[657] In the case of several professors engaged in political writing and meetings in Saudi Arabia, the WGAD found that "peaceful dialogue" could be considered peaceful action with the objective to bring about progress in society.[658] Such dialogue is protected jointly by ICCPR Articles 19 and 21(1).[659] It is also worth noting that although the writings of one detainee found to be held arbitrarily were directly political in nature and called for democratic change, the works of others found held arbitrarily were literary or artistic, but were found nonetheless to be imputed political content or purpose by both the government and the WGAD.[660]

In cases where the state was not party to the ICCPR, the WGAD finds in favor of detainees under UDHR Article 21, as they are unable to specify an ICCPR Article 25 violation.[661] In other cases, the WGAD has found Article 25 violations under the ICCPR without finding a concurrent Article 21 violation under the UDHR.[662] While such a violation also must implicitly exist, it is sufficient to find a violation of a state's treaty obligations. In opinions where the state is a party to the ICCPR, the WGAD has not

---

[652] Pham Hong Son, at ¶ 20.

[653] Hkun Htun Oo, et al., at ¶ 34 (listing illustrative publications that applicants had published and which the Government barred from dissemination and publication. These included regular bulletins on the activity of Shan activists critical of the proposed points of resolution in the ceasefire negotiations, and other general objections to the predominant narrative of the political conflict).

[654] Birtukan Mideksa Deme, at ¶ 34

[655] Khalida Jarrar v. Israel, WGAD Opinion No. 15/2016, Adopted Apr. 22, 2016, at ¶ 28.

[656] *See e.g.*, Matrouk bin Hais, et al., ¶ 12, 15 (specifying that the Government's stated reason for the detention was that the views expressed by the applicants "endangered public order.")

[657] Muhammad Kaboudvand v. Iran, WGAD Opinion No. 48/2012, Adopted Nov. 16, 2012, at ¶¶ 4, 26.

[658] Matrouk bin Hais, et al., at ¶ 16.

[659] *Id.*, at ¶¶ 16, 18.

[660] *Id.*, at ¶ 5.

[661] *See e.g.*, Abdulhadi Abdulla Alkhawaja, at ¶ 47; Min Zayar, et al., at ¶¶ 27–28.

[662] Giorgi Mshvenieradz, at ¶ 10.

usually explained under which subpart of Article 25 it is ruling, although the type of political activity involved in most such cases suggests that Article 25(a) is most commonly implicated. The WGAD did in one case find a violation of UDHR Article 21(3) in the case of Michel Atangana, a French-Cameroonian national overseeing a public works project.[663] The detainee was accused of embezzlement and the source alleged that the arrest was under pretext for his support of an opposition leader.[664] Rather than find an ICCPR Article 25(c) violation for the obstruction of his work as a public servant, the WGAD ruled on the basis of his political views and participation manifested through a third-party representative, which falls under Article 25(a).[665]

VI Freedom of Movement

Under Article 12 of the ICCPR:

1. Everyone lawfully within the territory of a State shall, within that territory, have the right to liberty of movement and freedom to choose his residence.
2. Everyone shall be free to leave any country, including his own.
3. The above-mentioned rights shall not be subject to any restrictions except those which are provided by law, are necessary to protect national security, public order (ordre public), public health or morals or the rights and freedoms of others, and are consistent with the other rights recognized in the present Covenant.
4. No one shall be arbitrarily deprived of the right to enter his own country.

And under Article 13 of the UDHR:

1. Everyone has the right to freedom of movement and residence within the borders of each state.
2. Everyone has the right to leave any country, including his own, and to return to his country.

Thus the text of the right to free movement specifically protects several forms of movement – the freedom of movement within one's own country, the freedom to leave any country, and the right to enter one's own country. Although the rights contained in ICCPR Article 12(1) and 12(2) may be limited, such limitations must meet standards similar to those governing the limitation of other rights in the ICCPR – they must be necessary to achieve the stated purposes, proportionate, and the least intrusive means available to obtain the relevant interest.[666] The HR Committee's jurisprudence has specifically addressed the interpretation of these limitations. For example, in *Karker and Karker v. France*, The Committee accepted that France's restriction of the free movement of an individual with known terrorist associations was justified on national security grounds, emphasizing that the necessity of such restrictions had been evaluated by domestic courts and that the individual in question was still allowed to reside in a relatively wide area.[667] By contrast, Belgium's restrictions on the freedom of movement of

---

[663] Michel Thierry Atangana v. Cameroon, Opinion No. 38/2013, Adopted Nov. 13, 2013, at ¶ 3 (Author served as counsel to Atangana on other matters but did not represent him in this case).

[664] *Id.*, at ¶¶ 7–8.

[665] *Id.*, at ¶ 25.

[666] General Comment No. 27, Human Rights Committee, CCPR/C/21/Rev.1/Add.9 (1999), at ¶ 13.

[667] Karker & Karker v. France, Human Rights Committee, Communication 833/1998, CCPR/C/70/D/833/1998, Oct. 26, 2000, at ¶ 9.2.

individuals placed under sanctions by the Security Council violated their right to free movement. Belgium had dismissed the criminal investigations against the individuals and itself requested their names be removed from the sanctions list so the restriction was no longer necessary to protect national security or public order.[668]

Where states restrict the freedom of movement of journalists or human rights activists so as to prevent travel abroad, there may be simultaneous violations of the right to freedom of expression as well as the freedom of movement.[669] Unfortunately, this is a means by which governments attempt to prevent such activists from maintaining international contacts or networks. In *Dolma Kyab* v. *China*, a writer and history teacher living in Tibet was found guilty of espionage and illegally crossing the border. The Government alleged he frequently traveled outside of China to meet with those affiliated with the Dalai Lama and to recruit members for separatist activities.[670] After establishing that the writer was merely peacefully exercising his rights to freedom of expression and association, the WGAD cited to Article 13(2) of the UDHR, and determined that crossing a state border should not be criminalized.[671] A similar concern was found in *Pierre-Claver Mbonimpa* v. *Burundi*, in which an internationally known Burundian human rights defender was arrested while preparing to board a flight to Kenya. The WGAD found a violation of his right to freedom of movement under both the ICCPR and UDHR.[672]

The WGAD has also addressed impermissible restrictions on movement within one's own country in two cases on minorities in Myanmar. Both cases involved ethnic Kachin herdsman, living in internal displacement camps due to ethnic violence, who were arrested in 2012 as they were traveling to work.[673] The WGAD noted that there was a history of alleged human rights abuses against the Kachin people, including restrictions on their freedom of movement.[674] Since the Government failed to respond to the allegations of human rights violations or establish that the individuals were not detained based on their minority status, the WGAD found the detentions arbitrary, specifically noting violations of Article 13 of the UDHR.[675] Although it did not specifically elaborate on its finding that Article 13 was violated, presumably this was linked to the fact that the herdsmen were internally displaced as well as the more general restrictions on free movement of Kachin people that the WGAD had noted.

Likewise, detention for exercising the right to return to one's own country is in violation of Article 13(2) of the UDHR. In *Shin Gambira* v. *Myanmar*, the detainee was a Buddhist monk sentenced to six months of hard labor for "illegally" returning to Myanmar, even though he was a Myanmar citizen.[676] The WGAD found this was an

---

[668] Nabil Sayadi & Patricia Vinck v. Belgium, Human Rights Committee, Communication 1472/2006, CCPR/C/94/D/1472/2006, Oct. 22, 2008, at ¶ 10.8.

[669] General Comment No. 34, Human Rights Committee, CCPR/C/GC/34 (2011), at ¶ 45.

[670] Dolma Kyab v. China, WGAD Opinion No. 36/2007, Adopted Nov. 30, 2007, at ¶ 10.

[671] Id., at ¶ 16.

[672] Pierre-Claver Mbonimpa v. Burundi, WGAD Opinion No. 33/2014, Adopted Aug. 28, 2014.

[673] Laphai Gam v. Myanmar, WGAD Opinion No. 50/2013, Adopted Nov. 19, 2013, at ¶¶ 4–5 (Litigated by Author through Perseus Strategies); La Ring v. Myanmar, WGAD Opinion No. 24/2014, Adopted Aug. 26, 2014, at ¶¶ 3–4 (Litigated by Author through Perseus Strategies).

[674] Laphai Gam, at ¶ 35.

[675] Id., at ¶ 41; La Ring, at ¶ 22.

[676] Shin Gambira v. Myanmar, WGAD Opinion No. 33/2016, Adopted Aug. 25, 2016, at ¶ 23.

impermissible restriction on his freedom of movement, and as such his detention was arbitrary under Category II.[677]

These cases represent the primary instances in which the WGAD has addressed freedom of movement in the Category II context. Given that detention inherently involves a restriction of the freedom of movement, this right is implicated in other categories in addition to Category II.[678] There may be some inconsistency in terms of when the WGAD finds that a detention that violates an individual's freedom of movement falls under Category II as opposed to other categories.

For example, in *Thich Huyen Quang v. Viet Nam*, in which a Buddhist monk was placed under house arrest, the WGAD found only a Category II detention, based on a breach of the rights to freedom of movement and freedom of religion. The finding of the Article 13 breach of the UDHR appeared to be based on the deprivation of free movement caused by the house arrest.[679] By contrast, in *Lloyd Tarumbwa, Fanny Tembo and Terry Musona v. Zimbabwe*, the WGAD only found Category I and III violations in regards to several individuals subjected to a forced protective police custody that interfered with their right to freedom of movement.[680] Likewise, the confiscation of a journalist's passport in *Mahmoud Hussein Gomaa Ali v. Egypt* was a violation of his freedom of movement that resulted in a Category I violation.[681] Despite this apparent inconsistency, in theory a distinction can be drawn between detentions that punish the freedom of movement (Category II) and those that themselves constitute an improper deprivation of the right to move freely, which does appear to be reflected in the few cases addressing this right in the WGAD jurisprudence, as described earlier.

VII Minority Cultures to Enjoy Culture

Article 27 of the ICCPR provides:

In those States in which ethnic, religious or linguistic minorities exist, persons belonging to such minorities shall not be denied the right, in community with the other members of their group, to enjoy their own culture, to profess and practise their own religion, or to use their own language.

The right contained in Article 27 is an individual right, although one that also exists in common with a community, which belongs to those who are members of a common cultural, religious, or linguistic group.[682] Whether or not one is a member of a minority is not determined by any formal recognition of minority status by the state, but rather by objective criteria.[683] The right is linked to minority status, in which respect it differs from the more general right of everyone to "freely participate in the cultural life of the community," which is protected in Article 27 of the UDHR. That said, the UDHR provision is not explicitly covered by Category II and the WGAD has not addressed it,

---

[677] *Id.*, at ¶ 24.

[678] *See, e.g.*, Imed Al Chibani v. Libya, WGAD Opinion No. 6/2011, Adopted May 3, 2011, at ¶¶ 16–17.

[679] Thich Huyen Quang v Viet Nam, WGAD Opinion No. 4/2001, Adopted May 17, 2001.

[680] Lloyd Tarumbwa, et al. v. Zimbabwe, WGAD Opinion No. 15/2009, Adopted Sept. 3, 2009.

[681] Mahmoud Hussein Gomaa Ali v. Egypt, WGAD Opinion No. 83/2017, Adopted Nov. 22, 2017, at ¶ 64.

[682] General Comment No. 23, Human Rights Committee, CCPR/C/23/Rev.1/Add.5 (1994), at ¶ 1.

[683] *Id.* at ¶ 5.2.

although as noted in the introduction to this chapter, the WGAD will on occasion discuss rights not enumerated formally in Category II.

Article 27 of the ICCPR does not contain a limitation clause. Some balancing of the interests of the minority against the interests of a government may nonetheless be permissible. The HR Committee has distinguished between measures that deny a person his right to enjoy his culture, and those that "have a certain limited impact on the way of life of persons belong to a minority," and do not necessarily violate Article 27.[684] This was in the context of determining the extent to which governments must protect minority access to land and natural resources, however, and it is harder to imagine how such a balancing would operate where individuals have been detained for their participation in cultural practices. Article 27 must also be exercised in a manner that is consistent with other fundamental human rights.[685] For example, General Comment 22 on the Equality of Rights between Men and Women suggests that the rights enjoyed by minorities under Article 27 cannot be used as a basis for depriving women of their rights under the ICCPR.[686] This suggests that recourse to Article 27 may not serve as a means of avoiding criminal penalties for certain harmful cultural or religious practices. However, the WGAD has not had to address the potentially complicated tensions between the full exercise of Article 27 and the protection of other fundamental human rights.

The WGAD has only found a Category II violation under Article 27 in a handful of cases.[687] Although it has not extensively discussed the rights of minority groups in these cases, three offer some insight into its treatment of the right. In *Francis Xavier Dang Xuan Dieu, et al.* v. *Viet Nam*, a number of Vietnamese Christians were detained for their involvement in various forms of social activism. The WGAD found the detentions to be a violation of Article 27, as well as the right to freedom of expression and religion and the right to participate in public affairs. In doing so, it noted two problematically vague domestic law provisions that were used against the activists. The first criminalized activities aimed at overthrowing the government and the second prohibited propaganda against the state. This later provision includes the crime of "making, storing and/or circulating documents and/or cultural products with contents against the State."[688] The WGAD also emphasized that all the detainees were members of faith-based organizations and religious denominations.[689] Although it does not explain what features of this case result in the finding of an Article 27 violation, the WGAD was likely concerned by the criminalization of "cultural products with contents against the State," particularly where the law is used to target a religious minority.

In *Johan Teterisa et al.* v. *Indonesia*, a group of dancers who performed a traditional Moluccan war dance during an official ceremony in Indonesia were detained for

---

[684] Lansman & Lansman v. Finland, Communication No. 1023/2001, Human Rights Committee, CCPR/C/83/D/1023/2001, Mar. 17, 2005, at ¶ 7.2.

[685] General Comment No. 23, at ¶ 8.

[686] *General Comment No. 28*, Human Rights Committee, CCPR/C/21/Rev.1/Add.10 (2000), at ¶ 34.

[687] Francis Xavier Dang Xuan Dieu, et al. v. Viet Nam, WGAD Opinion No. 26/2013, Adopted Aug. 29, 2013; Johan Teterisa, et al. v. Indonesia, WGAD Opinion No. 41/2008, Adopted Nov. 25, 2008; Pierre Claver Mbonimpa v. Burundi, WGAD Opinion No. 33/2014, Adopted Aug. 28, 2014.

[688] Francis Xavier Dang Xuan Dieu, at ¶ 56.

[689] *Id.*, at ¶ 59.

displaying the flag of the South Moluccan Republic, a self-proclaimed republic by members of a Moluccan separatist group.[690] The dance was intended as a peaceful protest, but the Government considered these actions to constitute a display of separatist symbols, an act of treason, and a national security threat.[691] Most of the WGAD's analysis treats the dance as a form of protected expression. The WGAD distinguished between peaceful nationalist assertions and non-peaceful ones and found the act of peaceful protest to be protected under human rights law. The detentions were accordingly arbitrary.[692] The specific breach of ICCPR Article 27 is not discussed, but presumably the key factor is the performance of the traditional dance as a form of cultural expression. In a similar opinion involving Indonesian Moluccan nationalists, in which specific forms of cultural expression were not involved, no violation of Article 27 is mentioned.[693] This suggests that advocacy on minority issues can therefore be distinguished from the right to practice one's culture. Although both are protected under human rights law, the first will generally be protected under Article 19's freedom of expression, rather than Article 27.

In *Bakri Mohammed Abdul Latif et al.* v. *Egypt*, the WGAD found violations of Article 27 rendering arbitrary the detention of Nubian minorities in Egypt who had been arrested for "violently" disrupting traffic during a protest.[694] The WGAD noted that their protest had neither involved violence nor incited violence.[695] A presidential decree had demarcated areas on the border of Egypt as military zones, prohibiting entry and thus denying the right of Nubians in Egypt to return to their ancestral lands. The ensuing protest by fourteen Nubian activists was a "legitimate exercise of the right to demonstrate against the repression of Nubian people" and thus fell under the protection of Article 27.[696] It is worth noting, in this case Article 27 protected not just enjoyment of culture, but actions protesting a violation of this right.

VIII Equal Protection

Under Article 26 of the ICCPR:

All persons are equal before the law and are entitled without any discrimination to the equal protection of the law. In this respect, the law shall prohibit any discrimination and guarantee to all persons equal and effective protection against discrimination on any ground such as race, colour, sex, language, religion, political or other opinion, national or social origin, property, birth or other status.

And under Article 7 of the UDHR:

All are equal before the law and are entitled without any discrimination to equal protection of the law. All are entitled to equal protection against any discrimination in violation of this Declaration and against any incitement to such discrimination.

---

[690] Johan Teterisa, et al. v. Indonesia, WGAD Opinion No. 41/2008, Adopted Nov. 25, 2008, at ¶ 6; *Indonesia Activist Gets Life Term*, BBC, Apr. 4, 2008.

[691] Johan Teterisa, et al., at ¶¶ 13, 16.

[692] *Id.*, at ¶¶ 16–18; 22.

[693] Carel Tahiya, et al. v. Indonesia, WGAD Opinion No. 11/1999, Adopted May 20, 1999.

[694] Bakri Mohammed Abdul Latif, et al. v. Egypt, WGAD Opinion No. 28/2018, Adopted Apr. 24, 2018, at ¶ 72.

[695] *Id.*

[696] *Id.*, at ¶ 67.

The requirement that all persons are protected equally by the law incorporates the prohibition of discrimination.[697] Accordingly, there is significant overlap between this aspect of Category II and Category V. In its jurisprudence since the creation of Category V, the WGAD has occasionally found violations of Article 26 and Article 7 of the ICCPR and UDHR, respectively, but found these violations to fall under Category V rather than under Category II.[698] Elsewhere, it has found detentions based on discriminatory grounds to be arbitrary under both Categories II and V, expressly linking these equal protection provisions to the Category II violation. For example, in finding that the detention of a Muslim leader by Myanmar was arbitrary, the WGAD noted that "the lack of legal status of the Rohingya Muslims communities restricts their movement within the country, thus violating international human rights standards and discriminating against them on the grounds of religious identity."[699] It found the detention to be arbitrary under both Category II and Category V, but linked the violation of Article 7 under the UDHR to Category II.[700]

Since there is a full chapter in the book on Category V, this section will merely provide a brief overview of cases in which the WGAD has found violations under Article 26 of the ICCPR and Article 7 of the UDHR, with a focus on opinions adopted before the development of Category V in 2011.

In general, the WGAD will find detentions based solely on a discriminatory motive to be invalid. For example, it rejected Sri Lanka's claims that an individual of Tamil ethnicity was supporting terrorism and found that in reality he was detained solely because he was a member of the Tamil ethnic group in violation of his right to equal protection under Article 26 of the ICCPR.[701] Elsewhere, the WGAD found that Niger had detained several individuals merely on account of their Tuareg ethnicity and political affiliation, given that there was no evidence that they had any connection to the Tuareg rebel movement.[702]

The WGAD more specifically addressed a state's failure to provide equal protection under the law in *Elie Dib Ghaled* v. *United Arab Emirates*. The detainee in that case was a Christian Lebanese national married to a Muslim woman from the United Arab Emirates. The Government arrested him for violation of *Shari'a* law because of his marriage to a Muslim woman without his conversion to Islam.[703] The Government argued that the provision of *Shari'a* law in question was not discriminatory, because it applied universally and did not distinguish among persons based on their nationality or religion. However, the WGAD observed that one of the rights provided in the UDHR is the right of adults to marry "without any limitation as to race, nationality or religion."[704] The Government's prosecution of Ghaled for an invalid marriage meant that his marriage was treated differently because of his religious beliefs compared to other marriages. The WGAD found that "the differentiation between the legal status of individuals and the application of different standards of legal protection for adults of

---

[697] *General Comment No. 18*, Human Rights Committee, HRI/GEN/1/Rev.1 (1994), at ¶ 1.
[698] Gaybullo Jalilov v. Uzbekistan, WGAD Opinion No. 4/2013, Adopted Apr. 30, 2013.
[699] Tun Aung v. Myanmar, WGAD Opinion No. 49/2013, Adopted Nov. 19, 2013, at ¶ 24.
[700] *Id.*, at ¶ 28.
[701] Gunasundaram Jayasundaram v. Sri Lanka, WGAD Opinion No. 30/2008, Sept. 12, 2008.
[702] Mohamed Moussa, et al. v. Niger, WGAD Opinion No. 39/1993, Adopted Sept. 29, 1993.
[703] Elie Dib Ghaled v. United Arab Emirates, WGAD Opinion No. 2/1998, Adopted May 13, 1998, at ¶ 5.
[704] *Id.*, at ¶ 10.

different religions who married of their own free will" is a violation of Article 7 of the UDHR.[705]

Discrimination on the basis of a person's "sex" will be inferred from gender-specific treatment or from the fact that the activities for which the detainee was held concerned women's rights or fair treatment of vulnerable gender-based social groups. In *Zeinab Jalalian* v. *Iran*, the WGAD specifically noted the import of gender-specific threats made by government officials to the detainee. Threats of rape and demanding that the detainee be tested to prove her virginity were taken as evidence that she had been detained on the basis of her sex.[706] The detainee in that case was a women's rights activist, specifically engaged in the extension of rights to Kurdish women.[707] The WGAD also noted in that case that the detainee received particularly harsh treatment and was the only female political prisoner in the country at the time to have been sentenced to life imprisonment.[708]

Of the remaining opinions in which the WGAD has found a violation of equal protection guarantees in the Category II context, several address the question of whether, and to what extent, discrimination based on sexual orientation is prohibited under human rights law. The WGAD has followed the approach of the HR Committee in *Toonen* v. *Australia*, which is to treat the reference to "sex" in Article 26 of the ICCPR as including discrimination based on sexual orientation. Laws that criminalize homosexuality are accordingly in violation of Article 26. The WGAD expressly adopted this position in *Yasser Mohamed Salah, et al.* v. *Egypt*, involving a number of individuals detained by Egypt either on charges of offense against religion or on charges of homosexuality, on the grounds that they were inciting social dissention.[709]

Following a discussion of *Toonen*, as well as related human rights authorities who suggest that the right to equal protection includes discrimination based on sexual orientation, the WGAD determined that the detentions were arbitrary as they violated Article 26 of the ICCPR. It also found that the detentions contravene the nondiscrimination provisions contained in ICCPR Article 2(1) and UDHR Article 2(1).[710] The WGAD does not explicitly note that the detentions in *Yasser Mohamed Salah et al.* v. *Egypt* were arbitrary under Category II, but in two subsequent opinions involving Egyptians detained on charges of homosexuality, the WGAD specifically found Category II violations under Article 26 of the ICCPR, confirming its approach in *Yasser Mohamed Salah et al.* v. *Egypt*.[711] It also found violations of Article 26 of the ICCPR in an opinion on detentions under a similar law in Cameroon.[712]

The WGAD also expressly aligned equal protection and sexual orientation in *Cornelius Fonya* v. *Cameroon*.[713] Citing *Toonen* once more as well as the protections of Article

---

[705] *Id.*, at ¶ 12.

[706] Zeinab Jalalian v. Iran, WGAD Opinion No. 1/2016, Adopted Apr. 18, 2016, at ¶ 37.

[707] *Id.*

[708] *Id.*

[709] Yasser Mohamed Salah, et al. v. Egypt, WGAD Opinion No. 7/2002, Adopted June 21, 2002, at ¶¶ 24–25, 28.

[710] *Id.*, at ¶ 28.

[711] Messrs. A, B, C, & D v. Egypt, WGAD Opinion No. 42/2008, Adopted Nov. 25, 2008; Anonymous v. Egypt, WGAD Opinion No. 25/2009, Adopted Nov. 24, 2009.

[712] François Ayissi, et al. v. Cameroon, WGAD Opinion No. 22/2006, Adopted Aug. 31, 2006.

[713] Cornelius Fonya v. Cameroon, WGAD Opinion No. 14/2017, Adopted Apr. 21, 2017.

26 of the ICCPR, the WGAD found that the trial and prosecution of a man for homosexuality was also a violation of Article 17, which provides equal protection of the law against interference with privacy, family, home, and correspondence.[714] This warranted a decision that his arrest was arbitrary under Category II, and concurrently under Category V for discrimination on the basis of sexual orientation.[715]

In a slightly different twist to equal protection in light of the prohibition of discrimination on the basis of "other status," in its country mission to South Africa, the WGAD criticized its mandatory minimum sentencing law, which disportionately punished criminals who had committed murder, aggravated rape, and aggravated assault. It reported that judges and lawyers were especially critical of this law on the basis of the principle of equality before law and equal protection, noting it only applied to certain categories of severe offenses and not others.[716]

IX Right to Seek Asylum

The right to seek asylum is contained in Article 14(1) of the UDHR:

Everyone has the right to seek and to enjoy in other countries asylum from persecution.

The Basic Principles and Guidelines on Remedies and Procedures on the Right of Persons Deprived of Their Liberty to Bring Proceedings Before a Court notes that because seeking asylum is a right protected by international law and is neither a criminal nor an unlawful act, it cannot be invoked as the basis for a detention or other penalty.[717] Additionally, WGAD jurisprudence has cited the Convention Relating to the Status of Refugees, as well as its protocol, in support of this right. The HR Committee, in its General Comment No. 35, has stated that asylum seekers who enter unlawfully may be briefly detained to "document their entry, record their claims and determine their identity if it is in doubt."[718] However, further detention during claim resolution is arbitrary without an individualized reason such as flight risk or danger to national security.[719] However, the Category II right to seek asylum is rarely invoked in arbitrary detention cases, especially now with the overlap with Category IV.

Detention in the course of immigration proceedings is not arbitrary per se, and the WGAD will not find a Category II violation on the detention of an asylum-seeker alone. However, this detention must be based on an individualized assessment of the asylum-seeker, and be reasonable, necessary, and proportionate in each circumstance.[720] Extensions of administrative detention must be reassessed on an individual basis.[721] Seeking

---

[714] *Id.*, at ¶ 47.

[715] *Id.*, at ¶ 50.

[716] *Report of the Working Group on Arbitrary Detention: Mission to South Africa*, Commission on Human Rights, E/CN.4/2006/7/Add.3, Dec. 29, 2005, at ¶ 64.

[717] *Basic Principles and Guidelines on the Remedies and Procedures on the Rights of Persons Deprived of Their Liberty to Bring Proceedings Before a Court*, Working Group on Arbitrary Detention, A/HRC/30/27 (Annex), July 6, 2015, at ¶ 116.

[718] General Comment No. 35, at ¶ 18.

[719] *Id.*

[720] Abdalrahman Hussein v. Australia, WGAD Opinion No. 28/2017, Adopted Apr. 25, 2017, at ¶ 33.

[721] *Id.*, at ¶ 33.

asylum may not be treated as a crime and migrants may not be criminally prosecuted for it.[722] The WGAD draws these principles from the HR Committee, which has explained:

> Asylum seekers who unlawfully enter a State party's territory may be detained for a brief initial period in order to document their entry, record their claims and determine their identity if it is in doubt. To detain them further while their claims are being resolved would be arbitrary in the absence of particular reasons specific to the individual, such as an individualized likelihood of absconding, a danger of crimes against others or a risk of acts against national security.[723]

Over its history, the WGAD has not infrequently examined the availability of the right to seek asylum on its country missions. As one illustration, on its visit to the United Kingdom, it examined and expressed a wide array of specific concerns about the country's asylum system. Specifically, it expressed concerns about the following issues:

- The legal regime under which asylum processing operates can sufficiently prolong restrictions on liberty to result in arbitrary detentions.
- Detentions are often based on the availability of space rather than the quality of an applicant's case.
- Upon detention, there is no immediate access to a court, no written explanation for a detention is provided, and there is no judicial oversight of detention.
- There are no written rules or procedures that codify the Government's obligations towards detainees and their rights.
- There is no requirement for an applicant to be brought before an asylum adjudicator in a specified time and no timeframes for appeals.
- Decisions to detain applicants are made by immigration officers that may not have sufficient training in refugee law and there is no effective remedy to challenge a decision before a court or before an independent review body.[724]

Most individual cases that invoke the right to asylum will involve fact patterns that now fall within Category IV. In *Abdalrahman Hussein* v. *Australia*, the detention of a Syrian asylum-seeker with a lapsed visa was contested in both categories. He had been led to believe no action was required to renew his visa, but the WGAD found no other explanation for his three-year detention, and he had never received an explanation for the delay in renewing his visa. The WGAD concluded that he had been detained as a result of exercising his right to seek asylum, in violation of Article 14(1) of the UDHR.[725] The three years he had been detained without being presented before a judge also led to a finding that his detention was arbitrary under Category IV.

In *Mohammad Naim Amiri* v. *Australia*, a very similar case, the WGAD brought its analysis of another Article 14(1) claim in line with the HR Committee's General Comment 35. In this instance, the detention of an Afghani asylum-seeker was found to be arbitrary because no individualized explanation was given to justify the need to

---

[722] Mi Sook Kang and Ho Seok Kim v. Democratic People's Republic of Korea and China, WGAD Opinion No. 81/2017, Adopted Nov. 22, 2017, at ¶ 25.

[723] General Comment No. 35, at ¶ 18.

[724] *Report of the Working Group on Arbitrary Detention: Mission to United Kingdom*, Commission on Human Rights, E/CN.4/1999/63/Add.3, Dec. 18, 1998, at ¶ 18.

[725] Abdalrahman Hussein v. Australia, WGAD Opinion No. 28/2017, Adopted Apr. 25, 2017, at ¶ 34.

detain him.[726] Furthermore, no alternatives to detention were examined. As a result, the WGAD concluded Amiri was being held for exercising his right to seek asylum. It also found his detention arbitrary under Category IV for the same reasons as Abdalrahman Hussein's.

Despite the significant overlap, a Category IV claim is not a prerequisite to a claim based on the right to seek asylum. *Mi Sook Kang and Ho Seok Kim v. Democratic People's Republic of Korea and China* involved two DPRK nationals, both of whom attempted to seek asylum by entering China. Mi Sook Kang was arrested in Yanji, China, and repatriated to the DPRK in accordance with several extradition agreements between China and the DPRK.[727] Ho Seok Kim was attempting to seek asylum in South Korea when he was arrested on the border between Mongolia and China.[728] The WGAD found that both China and the DPRK had violated Article 14(1) of the UDHR – China for arresting them when they attempted to seek asylum and the DPRK for their subsequent detention as criminals.[729] Interestingly, the WGAD also found a related Category I violation because seeking asylum is a fundamental right; the offense of "treason against the 'fatherland'" could not have applied.[730] This left the detention of Mi Sook Kang and Ho Seok Kim without any legal basis.

---

[726] Mohammad Naim Amiri v. Australia, WGAD Opinion No. 42/2017, Adopted Aug. 21, 2017, at ¶ 32.

[727] Mi Sook Kang and Ho Seok Kim v. Democratic People's Republic of Korea and China, WGAD Opinion No. 81/2017, Adopted Nov. 22, 2017, at ¶ 4.

[728] *Id.*, at ¶ 5.

[729] *Id.*, at ¶¶ 20, 26.

[730] *Id.*, at ¶ 25.

6   Category III

Violation of Rights of Due Process

According to the WGAD, Category III detentions arise under the following circumstances:

> When the total or partial non-observance of the international norms relating to the right to a fair trial, established in the Universal Declaration of Human Rights and in the relevant international instruments accepted by the States concerned, is of such gravity as to give the deprivation of liberty an arbitrary character (category III);[1]

I Arrest without a Warrant

Arrest without warrant is often given minimal attention in relation to arbitrary detention, forming as it often does the first of an extended line of procedural irregularities contributing to the overall arbitrariness of a detention. A typical case in the context of several other fair trial violations is *Majid Al Nassif v. Saudi Arabia*, concerning a political dissenter arrested without warrant by masked security officials for his writings and participation in peaceful protests.[2] Following this arrest, the detainee was kept in conditions of solitary confinement without any notification of charges for over three months before being sentenced.[3] In finding "flagrant" fair trial rights violations, the WGAD observed numerous violations had occurred, including denial of access to counsel, incommunicado detention, and excessive delay in trial, in addition to the failure of authorities to present a warrant at the time of arrest.[4]

Nonetheless, arrest without warrant is a frequent feature in many opinions of the WGAD and it recognizes that the initial arrest often forms the first part of a deprivation of liberty. It therefore is among the initial considerations by the WGAD regarding a potential arbitrary detention.[5] Generally, a written warrant is required for an arrest to be lawful and not arbitrary, with only a limited and narrowly defined number of exceptions permitted. These exceptions include arrests carried out when police observe

---

[1] *Methods of Work of the Working Group*, Human Rights Council, A/HRC/36/38, July 13, 2017, at ¶ 8.
[2] Majid Al Nassif v. Saudi Arabia, WGAD Opinion No. 13/2015, Adopted Apr. 27, 2015, at ¶ 3.
[3] *Id.*, at ¶ 22.
[4] *Id.*, at ¶¶ 21–25.
[5] *Basic Principles and Guidelines on the Remedies and Procedures on the Rights of Persons Deprived of Their Liberty to Bring Proceedings Before a Court*, Working Group on Arbitrary Detention, A/HRC/30/27 (Annex), July 6, 2015, at ¶ 9.

a suspect carrying out a crime (*in flagrante delicto*) and arrests carried out during a declared state of emergency.

While international law does not specify the precise form and necessary contents of an arrest warrant, considering relevant norms, standards, and jurisprudence, it is clear warrants must at least detail the identity of the person to be arrested; contain sufficient details as to the grounds for their arrest; and be issued by a person with the requisite authority to do so. Possession of the warrant is required at the time of arrest – a delay of even a few hours results in arrest without a warrant.[6]

The failure to comply with these requirements can render a detention arbitrary. Nonetheless, the most common facts presented to the WGAD relate to circumstances where no arrest warrant of any kind was presented. As such, this section will explain both when arrest warrants are necessary, and the available, but not fully developed, patchwork of standards governing the form and substance of such warrants.

A *Applicable Law and Standards*

The WGAD draws on the ICCPR, UDHR, and the guidance in the Body of Principles for the Protection of All Persons under Any Form of Detention or Imprisonment. In addition, the WGAD will at times look to the views of the Human Rights Committee (HR Committee) adopted under the *Optional Protocol to the ICCPR* in factually similar cases. And in April 2015, after broad consultation, the WGAD also published the *Basic Principles and Guidelines on Remedies and Procedures on the Right of Anyone Deprived of Their Liberty to Bring Proceedings before a Court*.[7]

It is crucial to bear in mind, however, that the WGAD looks not only to the lawfulness of detentions in various states, but, crucially, to whether they are of an arbitrary nature or not. Arbitrariness is a far broader notion than illegality. For example, an arrest and subsequent detention carried out in accordance with domestic laws may nevertheless be deemed arbitrary by the WGAD.[8] As will be illustrated in the discussion of a number of WGAD opinions in this section, domestic laws permitting arrest without warrant, even where purportedly within the permissible exceptions to the requirement of an arrest warrant, such as arrest *in flagrante delicto* or under emergency powers, have later been characterized as arbitrary by the WGAD where they were determined to have actually been exercised outside the limits of these exceptions.

Article 9 of the ICCPR is the foundation for the WGAD's Category III decisions, although the WGAD will also often refer to the similar, but far less detailed, principles on arrest and detention contained in Article 9 of the UDHR.[9] Both articles are concerned with the protection of the liberty and security of individuals, particularly when they are faced with deprivation of that liberty in the form of arrest and detention. To fully preserve this right, Article 9 of the ICCPR provides standards to be observed not only in the initial

---

[6] Luu Van Vinh v. Viet Nam, WGAD Opinion No. 35/2018, Adopted Apr. 26, 2018, at ¶ 26.

[7] Basic Principles and Guidelines.

[8] *Human Rights in the Administration of Justice: A Manual on Human Rights for Judges, Prosecutors, and Lawyers*, Office of the UN High Commissioner for Human Rights, 2003, at 165–166 (and this is also the case with other international bodies, such as the Human Rights Committee).

[9] To a far lesser extent, the WGAD will also refer to the general right to liberty set out in article 3 of the UDHR, but this is rarely seen in more recent opinions.

deprivation of liberty but for the entire duration of such deprivation. In full, Article 9 of the ICCPR reads:

1. Everyone has the right to liberty and security of person. No one shall be subjected to arbitrary arrest or detention. No one shall be deprived of his liberty except on such grounds and in accordance with such procedure as are established by law.
2. Anyone who is arrested shall be informed, at the time of arrest, of the reasons for his arrest and shall be promptly informed of any charges against him.
3. Anyone arrested or detained on a criminal charge shall be brought promptly before a judge or other officer authorized by law to exercise judicial power and shall be entitled to trial within a reasonable time or to release. It shall not be the general rule that persons awaiting trial shall be detained in custody, but release may be subject to guarantees to appear for trial, at any other stage of the judicial proceedings, and, should occasion arise, for execution of the judgement [*sic*].
4. Anyone who is deprived of his liberty by arrest or detention shall be entitled to take proceedings before a court, in order that that court may decide without delay on the lawfulness of his detention and order his release if the detention is not lawful.
5. Anyone who has been the victim of unlawful arrest or detention shall have an enforceable right to compensation.

Article 9 thus builds on the more general right set out in Article 9 of the UDHR to freedom from "arbitrary arrest, detention or exile." And, while Article 9 protects this right, it does not transform it into an absolute freedom. Article 9 of the ICCPR does not protect against any and all instances of detention; rather, it guarantees freedom from *arbitrary or unlawful* arrest or detention. Where an arrest and detention have a legitimate legal basis, conform to the necessary legal standards and procedures, and are not otherwise arbitrary, the detention will not be found to be arbitrary and in violation of Article 9.[10]

Narrowing the focus to the issue of arrest, Article 9(2) requires that an apprehended individual "be informed, at the time of arrest, of the reasons for his arrest." In WGAD jurisprudence, this leaves no room for delay – in *Edith Vilma Huamán Quispe v. Peru*, a five-hour postponement was a violation of 9(2).[11] The information provided must include both the legal and factual basis for the arrest.[12] Article 9(1) establishes that the given reasons, to survive the test for arbitrariness and unlawfulness, must find a basis in law, adhere to established legal procedures, and not be otherwise unjust. In most cases, save for some exceptions addressed later in this section, this means that there must be a warrant for a person's arrest, and the warrant must set out the legal grounds for their arrest. The WGAD has also, not surprisingly, found that mass arrests made without warrant do not meet the requirements of the ICCPR.[13]

---

[10] SARAH JOSEPH & MELISSA CASTAN, THE INTERNATIONAL COVENANT ON CIVIL AND POLITICAL RIGHTS 304 (Oxford University Press, 2013).

[11] Edith Vilma Huamán Quispe v. Peru, WGAD Opinion No. 57/2016, Adopted Nov. 25, 2016, at ¶ 108.

[12] Yon Alexander Goicoechea Lara v. Venezuela, WGAD Opinion No. 18/2017, Adopted Apr. 24, 2017, at ¶ 38.

[13] In its country mission to El Salvador, the WGAD noted that mass arrests were made, especially of young people suspected of being gang members. It also observed that in 2011, the National Civil Police made over 56,000 arrests of which only 7,200 were made on the basis of a warrant. *Report of the Working Group on Arbitrary Detention: Mission to El Salvador*, Human Rights Council, A/HRC/22/44/Add.2, Jan. 11, 2013, at ¶¶ 109–111.

Article 14 of the ICCPR supports such a reading, albeit limited exclusively to criminal charges, holding that every individual facing criminal charges has the right to "be informed promptly and in detail in a language which he understands of the nature and cause of the charge against him." The WGAD has taken the language of Article 14(3)(a) of the ICCPR (that detainees have a right to be informed of the charges "in a language which he understands") to mean that failing to provide a translation or translator when charging a detainee is a due process violation. The Body of Principles supports this interpretation, stating that a person who does not adequately understand the language used by authorities is entitled to receive information in a language they understand, by use of an interpreter if necessary.[14] This was the case in *Gaspar Matalaev v. Turkmenistan*, where an ethnic Kazakh was arrested and tried in a language he did not speak.[15] The WGAD found a concurrent violation of Article 14(3)(f), since his court proceedings had also been conducted in a language he did not speak, with no translator provided.[16]

The WGAD has interpreted Article 14 to include the requirement that every arrested individual is "promptly informed of the charges [against her] by means of an arrest warrant," thus affirming the essential role of arrest warrants in preserving due process rights.[17] The text of the ICCPR does not, however, provide any further guidance as to when an arrest is arbitrary or illegal. Therefore, the WGAD has been obliged to refer to the other sources mentioned earlier in this section to set the parameters as to when an arrest is or is not permissible within Category III. The WGAD has affirmed that providing detainees with full information of the reasons for their arrest and detention, and regarding the charges brought against them, is an essential component of fair trial rights. In *Aracely del Carmen Gutiérrez Mejía, et al.* v. *El Salvador*, a group of prisoners had been held for a prolonged period of time without knowledge of the sentences they had been given or their legal status.[18] In that case, the WGAD found both Category I and III violations, and directed the authorities to provide both the relevant and necessary information to the prisoners and to release those whom the courts had acquitted.[19]

An important source referred to by the WGAD is the *Body of Principles for the Protection of All Persons under Any Form of Detention or Imprisonment*. While it is not legally binding, the Body of Principles was adopted by the UN General Assembly just a few years before the WGAD was established, in line with the growing attention the United Nations had been giving to the issue of arbitrary detention since the mid-1980s.[20] As a result, the WGAD has repeatedly drawn on the Body of Principles to determine the standards by which an arrest or detention is arbitrary or otherwise unlawful. The Body of Principles define "arrest" as "the act of apprehending a person for the alleged commission of an offence or by the action of an authority," as well as requiring that arrests be carried out "strictly in accordance with the provisions of the law and by competent

---

[14] *Body of Principles for the Protection of Persons under Any Form of Detention or Imprisonment*, UNGA Res. 47/173, 43 U.N. GAOR Supp. (No. 49), A/43/49, at 298 (1988), at Principle 14.

[15] Gaspar Matalaev v. Turkmenistan, WGAD Opinion No. 4/2018, Adopted Apr. 17, 2018, at ¶ 74.

[16] *Id.*, at ¶ 69.

[17] *See, e.g.*, Lenard Odillo, et al. v. Malawi, WGAD Opinion No. 15/2012, May 4, 2012, at ¶ 52.

[18] Aracely del Carmen Gutiérrez Mejía, et al. v. El Salvador, WGAD Opinion No. 20/2014, Adopted May 1, 2014, at ¶¶ 3–7.

[19] *Id.*, at ¶¶ 22–23.

[20] *Fact Sheet No. 26, The Working Group on Arbitrary Detention*, Office of UN High Commissioner for Human Rights, at II.

officials or persons authorized for that purpose." The Body of Principles also reiterates Article 9's call for the arrested individual to be informed at the time of his arrest of the reasons therefore, and that the reasons for his arrest be recorded, along with other pertinent details, including the time of arrest and the identities of the officials involved.[21]

The WGAD's Basic Principles and Guidelines reiterate the right to be informed of reasons for arrest, and further elaborates:

> Persons deprived of their liberty shall be informed about their rights and obligations under law through appropriate and accessible means. Among procedural safeguards, this includes the right to be informed, in a language and a means, mode, or format that the detainee understands, of the reasons justifying the deprivation of liberty, the possible judicial avenue to challenge the arbitrariness and lawfulness of the deprivation of liberty and the right to bring proceedings before the court and to obtain without delay appropriate and accessible remedies.[22]

The Basic Principles and Guidelines also require that the factual and legal basis for the detention must be promptly disclosed to either the detainee or their representative without delay.[23] A proper disclosure includes a copy of the order to detain, a copy of the detainee's case file, and disclosure of any material the authorities possess relating to their deprivation of liberty.[24] Authorities must have a means of verifying that a person has actually been informed of the reasons for their detention, meaning documentation such as video or audio recordings, print records, or witnesses.[25]

The WGAD will also on occasion cite the views of the HR Committee in its opinions because it has a significant body of jurisprudence concerning fair trial rights guaranteed by Articles 9 and 14 of the ICCPR. Therefore the WGAD cites to the Committee's analysis when facing similar factual scenarios. There are also a number of regional standards governing arrest without warrant, such as Article 5(1) of the *European Convention on Human Rights*, which holds that deprivations of liberty must not be arbitrary.[26] Although it should be noted that such regional standards are not much relied on in this particular area of WGAD jurisprudence. But most important to understanding the WGAD's approach to Category III, however, is its own rather substantial collection of opinions. It is critical to appreciate, however, that none of the law and standards set out in this section mention warrants in their definition of arbitrary arrest. Instead, the WGAD has drawn on the relevant provisions of the ICCPR, UDHR, and Body of Principles to determine general criteria for assessing instances of arrest without a proper warrant in the cases that come before it. This has predictably resulted in the WGAD requiring that

---

[21] Body of Principles, at Principles 10 and 12 (while the latter details must be recorded, the principles do not require the apprehended individual to be *informed* of anything more than the reasons for her arrest).

[22] Basic Principles and Guidelines, ¶ 10.

[23] *Id.*, ¶ 56.

[24] *Id.*

[25] *Id.*, ¶ 58.

[26] *Human Rights in the Administration of Justice: A Manual on Human Rights for Judges, Prosecutors and Lawyers*, Office of the UN High Commissioner for Human Rights, at 163–169 (2003) (the European Convention is the most enumerated, but certainly not the only, regional human rights document to address issues of detention and deprivation of liberty).

apprehended individuals know the reasons for their arrest, and that such reasons be based in law, are not arbitrary, and are set out in a valid arrest warrant.[27]

Since it began issuing opinions, the WGAD has handled a wide variety of Category III cases, a vast number of which have involved arrest without warrant. The general rule applied by the WGAD, as stated earlier, is that arrest without warrant is only permissible when the arrest is *in flagrante delicto* or carried out under emergency powers that satisfy all other procedural safeguards. But there are diverse sets of fact patterns in which the WGAD has issued opinions as to whether an arrest without warrant amounts to an arbitrary arrest. These can be analyzed as being dependent on (1) whether and when the detainee was informed of the reasons for their arrest and the charges against them; (2) whether the government argued that the arrest without warrant could somehow be justified as coming within a permissible exception; or (3) whether there was in fact a warrant but it was not in accordance with international norms. Each of these types of cases have presented the WGAD with particular questions as to the arbitrariness of an arrest, and together help explain the contours of the right to be free of being arrested without a warrant.

B Cases of Arrest without a Warrant

1 Later Charged

For a state to arrest a person without a warrant has long been held to be a violation of Article 9 of the ICCPR and Article 9 of the UDHR. This conclusion has been maintained, even if the persons arrested were charged but later released, making it clear that arrest without warrant is a violation in and of itself,[28] even though it is often just the first in a string of violations of the right to a fair trial. However, there may be some instances in which arrest without warrant would not be a violation of the relevant international legal standards.[29] Noting that a group of arrests without warrant were arbitrary in "the circumstances alleged," the WGAD took a preliminary step in discerning the instances in which arrest without warrant may be permissible. The arrests in question had not only been made without warrants, but without indication that the persons arrested:

> had either committed or was actually committing or attempting to commit an offence … had personal knowledge indicating that the person to be arrested had committed the offence … [or] that any of the persons arrested was at the time of arrest in the process of committing an offence or had any personal knowledge of facts in respect of an offence which had been committed indicating his involvement in the commission of offences.[30]

Thus, the *in flagrante delicto* exception did not apply, nor had emergency powers been used, rendering the arrests without warrant arbitrary. The fact that charges were

---

[27] Fact Sheet No. 26, at II and IV B.
[28] *See, e.g.*, Reynaldo Bernardo, et al. v. The Philippines, WGAD Opinion No. 30/1993, Adopted Apr. 30, 1993, at ¶ 17.
[29] *Id.*, at ¶¶ 11, 17.
[30] *Id.*

subsequently brought against these individuals four months later did not negate the arbitrary nature of their arrests without warrants.[31]

For many WGAD opinions, the failure by a state to produce an arrest warrant is often the first of many due process violations. But the distinction between arbitrary and unlawful must be considered, as domestic law standards governing a permissible passing of time between arrest and the subsequent issuing of a warrant may be so inappropriate, unjust, or unreasonable as to be arbitrary by international standards, despite being lawful in the domestic jurisdiction.[32]

Even where a detainee is later charged, this does not preclude their arrest from being arbitrary. For example, in the case of four Mexican citizens arrested without warrants and later charged as members of a revolutionary army, the WGAD made clear that, distinct from the subsequent charging and further rights violations occurring later in the case, the arrest without warrant was, in and of itself, arbitrary.[33] And this remained unchanged by the later charges that were brought after the detainees had been tortured and held incommunicado – a clear suggestion that the charges were based on information coerced from the detainees post-arrest.

But the issue is less clear where a detainee is charged with a criminal offense within two to three days after the arrest and there is no patently obvious indication of foul play in the intervening time. In this regard there is a margin of error that appears to be allowed by states. The shortest delay between arresting an individual and informing them of the charges against them, which the HR Committee has found to violate Article 9(2), is a delay of seven days.[34] But a number of cases suggest that both the WGAD and the HR Committee have been unwilling to find an arrest arbitrary where charges are issued within a seventy-two hour period.

However, as the WGAD has not expressly recognized such an exception, it is essential to focus on defining what being "promptly informed" of charges, as required by Article 9 (1) of the ICCPR, should mean. The seven-day HR Committee rule establishes a guideline – the WGAD has ruled that a slightly longer period of nine days between being arrested and being informed of charges is not "prompt."[35] Additionally, as discussed earlier, WGAD also interprets Article 14 of the ICCPR as requiring that persons, once arrested, be "promptly" presented with an arrest warrant detailing the charges against them.[36]

In other circumstances, individuals arrested without warrants can have them issued after the arrest has taken place.[37] Generally, the post-arrest issuing of a warrant occurs

---

[31] Id.

[32] Human Rights in the Administration of Justice, at 165–166 (citing communications of the Human Rights Committee: Gridin v. Russian Federation, Communication No. 770/1997, Human Rights Committee, CCPR/C/69/D/770/1997, July 20, 2000; Mukong v. Cameroon, Communication No. 458/1991, Human Rights Committee, CCPR/C/51/D/458/1991, July 21, 1994.

[33] Jacobo Silva Nogales, et al. v. Mexico, WGAD Opinion No. 37/2000, Adopted Nov. 27, 2000, at ¶¶ 10–11.

[34] Human Rights in the Administration of Justice, at 181–182 (2003) (citing Grant v. Jamaica, Communication No. 597/1994, Human Rights Committee, CCPR/C/56/D/597/1994, Mar. 22, 1996, at ¶ 8.1); see also Joseph & Castan, at 323 (reiterating that seven days is the shortest delay between arrest and being informed of charges that has been found by the Human Rights Committee to have breached ICCPR, Article 9 (2)).

[35] Pongsak Sriboonpeng v. Thailand, WGAD Opinion No. 44/2016, Adopted Nov. 21, 2016, at ¶ 33.

[36] Lenard Odillo, et al. v. Malawi, WGAD Opinion No. 15/2012, Adopted May 4, 2012, at ¶ 52.

[37] Saleh Farag Dhaifullah, et al. v. United Arab Emirates, WGAD Opinion No. 56/2014, Adopted Nov. 21, 2014, at ¶ 34.

within the following scenarios: the person was arrested *in flagrante delicto*; domestic laws allow for seventy-two hours between arrest and the issuing of a warrant; the authorities simply are not following procedural requirements; reasons that would justify arrest only came to light after the individual had been arrested and detained for some time; or, and often in connection with the preceding reason, because the authorities are trying to give the arrest a "semblance of legality" by later backdating an arrest warrant.[38] Where it can be concluded with certainty that an arrest warrant was retroactively issued, the WGAD will hold such a warrant to be arbitrary.[39]

As the WGAD itself recognizes, however, it can prove impossible to determine conclusively whether a warrant was issued before or after arrest, particularly where the authorities backdate the warrant.[40] It is therefore important to set out any facts that might indicate that the authorities lacked the necessary grounds at the time of the arrest, because the WGAD may consider them in finding a detention arbitrary, as it did in *Antonio José Rivero González* v. *Venezuela*. In this opinion, it concluded that: "[although] it is not possible to determine whether the arrest warrant was issued before or after the deprivation of liberty; nevertheless it is reasonable to think that the warrant might have been ordered as a result of the very statements that the defendant was making at that moment [once arrested]."[41] Similarly, the HR Committee has held an arrest to be in violation of Article 9(1) where the warrant was issued more than three days after the individual was arrested without warrant.[42] However, in this latter case, the HR Committee based their determination on the fact that domestic law required warrants to be issued within seventy-two hours of arrest. Thus, it did not independently find a delay of three days to be in and of itself arbitrary, because it was simply holding the state to its own domestic law standards. The WGAD's examination of when the delay in issuing an arrest warrant becomes arbitrary is similarly unclear. In its opinion, the WGAD did not specifically address the Government's argument that, under its domestic laws, it was not required to possess an arrest warrant prior to the apprehension of an individual – so long as the individual is either arrested or released within seventy-two hours. Thus, despite finding the overall deprivation of liberty to be arbitrary, the WGAD did not set forth clear guidance as to whether the passage of seventy-two hours between the detainee's arrest without warrant and the subsequent issuing of such a warrant would be arbitrary or not.[43]

It is therefore necessary to detail in any petition to the WGAD, the actual, or suspected, reasons for the delayed issuing of a warrant or presentation of charges. The presence and timing of the warrant can be a persuasive indicator of whether the authorities had reasonable and lawful grounds for the arrest. Although there remains uncertainty about the first seventy-two hours after arrest, beyond that time, the

---

[38] Antonio José Rivero González v. Venezuela, WGAD Opinion No. 47/2013, Adopted Nov. 18, 2013, at ¶ 5.

[39] Jason Zachary Puracal v. Nicaragua, WGAD Opinion No. 10/2012, Adopted May 4, 2012, at ¶ 25 (Litigated by Author through Perseus Strategies) ("The Working Group notes that no valid arrest warrant was shown when Mr. Puracal was arrested since it was not issued until the day after his arrest.").

[40] Antonio José Rivero González v. Venezuela, WGAD Opinion No. 47/2013, Adopted Nov. 18, 2013.

[41] *Id.*, at ¶ 29.

[42] Human Rights in the Administration of Justice, at 165 (citing Gridin v. Russian Federation, Communication No. 770/1997, Human Rights Committee, CCPR/C/69/D/770/1997, July 20, 2000, at ¶ 8.1).

[43] Andrei Sannikov v. Belarus, WGAD Opinion No. 14/2012, Adopted May 4, 2012.

subsequent presentation of a warrant or bringing of charges will rarely, if ever, remedy the arbitrary nature of an arrest without warrant.

2 Never Charged

In contrast to the previous subsection, many individuals who are arrested without warrant continue to be detained without charge for even greater periods of time – sometimes for decades. Lengthier and more complex cases often come before the WGAD where a person is not only arrested without warrant but also then detained without charge. Many, in fact, remain detained without charge while their petitions are considered by the WGAD. One such example is the case of a Chinese restaurant manager arrested without warrant in the Maldives, who was then detained for a further fifteen years with neither the production of an arrest warrant nor concrete charges against him.[44] Cases where no warrant is ever issued and no charges ever brought are routinely found arbitrary, because this amounts to not only a failure to promptly inform a person of the reasons for their arrest and any charges against them[45] but also constitutes a wholesale denial of the right to challenge one's detention.[46]

An early opinion from the WGAD regarding a case in the Philippines demonstrated that an arrest without a warrant, regardless of a later charge, is usually found arbitrary. Among three detainees arrested without warrants, two later had charges brought against them, while the third had still not been charged by the time the WGAD considered the petition. The WGAD found that all three detainees were subjected to arbitrary detentions in violation of Articles 9 and 14 of the ICCPR,[47] regardless of the fact that charges were, at some point, introduced for two of the detainees.

3 In Flagrante Delicto

There are certain grounds on which arrest without warrant can be permissible, but the WGAD has made conscientious efforts to delimit such grounds narrowly. The first ground for arrest without warrant that remains usually uncontested arises where an individual is arrested *in flagrante delicto* – while in the act of committing a crime. In numerous opinions where an individual has been arrested without a warrant, the WGAD as a matter of process examines whether the individual was apprehended *in flagrante delicto*, because such an arrest may permissibly be carried out without a warrant.[48] The need to qualify that an arrest without warrant was not *in flagrante delicto* reflects the nonarbitrary nature of warrantless arrest where the apprehended individual has been caught in the act of committing a crime.

However, the WGAD has sought to be sure this exception is not interpreted and applied in an overbroad manner. In its report on a mission to Mexico in 2003, the WGAD emphasized that the concept of arrest *in flagrante delicto* is limited to instances

[44] Richard Wu Mei De v. Maldives, WGAD Opinion No. 04/2009, Adopted May 6, 2009, at ¶ 30.
[45] ICCPR, at Art. 9 (2).
[46] ICCPR, at Art. 9 (3) and (4).
[47] Dioscoro Pendor, et al. v. The Philippines, WGAD Opinion No. 27/1993, Adopted Apr. 30, 1993, at ¶ 10.
[48] *See, e.g.*, Ernest Bennett, et al. v. Haiti, WGAD Opinion No. 23/2000, Sept. 14, 2000, at ¶ 41.

in which a person is caught actually committing the offense. The WGAD noted that Mexico's domestic laws extended the concept of arrest *in flagrante delicto* to encompass arrests of persons found within seventy-two hours of their having committed an alleged offense, so long as there were signs or evidence indicating the person's involvement.[49] The WGAD concluded that this overbroad interpretation of catching a person in the act based on alleged signs or evidence should not fall within the exception because it is materially different, violates the presumption of innocence, and carries too great a risk of possible arbitrary detention.[50]

This domestic law in Mexico continued to receive ongoing attention by complaints made to the WGAD.[51] In *Tomintat Marx Yu and Zhu Wei Yi v. Mexico*, two men were arrested without warrant for appearing at the home of a relative after being notified by a third party that the house was being raided by law enforcement. One of the detainees was taken into custody at the scene and then arrested by federal investigators, while the second was allowed to leave the scene with his seven-year-old nephew, only to be arrested thirty-five days later in connection with the raid.[52] Mexican authorities claimed that both arrests were executed because the detainees were caught, *in flagrante delicto*, in possession of a large sum of foreign currency at the house. The WGAD would not accept the Government's characterization of the arrest as *in flagrante delicto*, primarily because the money was discovered at the house prior to the detainees' arrival. This meant that at no point in the course of the raid were they in physical possession of the money: "It was simply money found in the house of someone with whom both had only family ties."[53] The opinion also noted, regarding the second detainee, that the lapse of over one month between the act and the arrest was irreconcilable with claims that the detainee was apprehended *in flagrante delicto*.[54] To be caught in the act is interpreted literally by the WGAD, meaning that the passage of time is a determinative factor.

The WGAD has also identified another abuse of *in flagrante delicto* arrests where a government has delegated to private third parties the power to carry out arrests. In its country mission to Colombia, it explained:

> In some areas of the country, the authorities have delegated to private security company employees, as well as to mining and oil companies and other individuals, the powers to carry out arrests, which should always be restricted to public officials as a matter of State authority. It is untenable to argue that these powers stem from the obligation to detain anyone committing an offence *in flagrante delicto* in the absence of the security forces or when the number of security force personnel is limited. *Flagrante delicto* refers to specific cases limited in time and cannot be used to justify this practice, which simply conceals the State's failure to fulfil its basic responsibilities. The fact is that these calls on individuals to detain persons are perceived by their intended audience, as well as by all

---

[49] *Report of the Working Group on Arbitrary Detention on Its Visit to Mexico*, Commission on Human Rights, Dec. 17, 2002, E/CN.4/2003/8/Add.3 at ¶ 39.

[50] *Id.*

[51] Tomintat Marx Yu and Zhu Wei Yi v. Mexico, WGAD Opinion No. 61/2011, Adopted Nov. 22, 2011.

[52] *Id.*, at ¶ 48.

[53] *Id.*, at ¶ 31.

[54] *Id.* (there was a time lapse of thirty-five days between petitioner Tomintat Marx Yu allegedly being caught committing the act in question and his subsequent arrest for that alleged crime).

of Colombian society, as an incitation and a delegation of duties to deprive citizens of their liberty without any authority taking responsibility.[55]

Of course, there are arrests *in flagrante delicto* that are both lawful and not arbitrary. The WGAD has declined to find arbitrary such arrests where it has not been provided with any additional information from the detainee that would suggest it was arbitrary.[56] Thus, arrests that are truly *in flagrante delicto* are permissible so far as the other legal and procedural standards are respected. But, the definition of *in flagrante delicto* has been interpreted and applied narrowly by the WGAD, so that it can only permit arrests executed while the identified individual is still in the act of committing the crime, or immediately thereafter. An *in flagrante* arrest "should make clear to anyone the cause of the arrest [and]... authorities still need to make a formal notification of the charges one they have decided on a criminal course of action."[57]

4 "Inviting" Witnesses to Police Stations

The WGAD has commented generally on the practice in certain countries of the police "inviting" individuals to come to the station as witnesses. In Armenia, for example, the police widely employ this practice and then arrest these individuals on the argument that they are material witnesses and not suspects. Often the invitation to come to the station was purely pretextual and the practice often results in having the status of the witness altered to suspect during their time in custody, without any court ruling or legal counsel.[58] The WGAD explained that in this context "[a]rrests are often not a consequence of a preceding police investigation, rather people are detained in order to be investigated. This affects not only the rights to personal freedom, free trial and presumption of innocence, but also the right to the security of person."[59]

5 Emergency Powers

An increasingly argued ground for lawful and non-arbitrary arrest without warrant occurs where a state claims to be acting under emergency powers. The ICCPR allows for derogations from the Covenant in times of emergency, including from Article 9.[60] However, the ICCPR also sets a high threshold for what qualifies as a public emergency and limits all derogations to only go as far as is "strictly required by the exigencies of the situation."[61] Given increased concern among many states with regards to terrorism and national security, such "states of emergency" often become semi-permanent realities. The

---

[55] *Report of the Working Group on Arbitrary Detention: Mission to Colombia*, Human Rights Council, A/HRC/10/21/Add.3, Feb. 16, 2009, at ¶ 83.

[56] Manuel Flores, et al. v. The Philippines, WGAD Opinion No. 9/2002, Adopted Sept. 11, 2002 (minors arrested without warrant but the petition submitted on their behalf did not indicate that the arrest was not *in flagrante delicto* or otherwise arbitrary, resulting in the WGAD declining to declare the arrest arbitrary).

[57] Mahmoud Abdel Shakour Abou Zeid Attitallah v. Egypt, WGAD Opinion No. 41/2016, Adopted Aug. 26, 2016, at ¶ 26.

[58] *Report of the Working Group on Arbitrary Detention: Mission to Armenia*, Human Rights Council, A/HRC/16/47/Add.3, Feb. 17, 2011, at ¶ 59.

[59] *Id.*, at ¶ 60.

[60] ICCPR, at Art. 4 (1) & (2) (article 9 is not among those listed as non-derogable).

[61] ICCPR, Art. 4 (1).

impact of such extended emergencies as it relates to arrest and detention is that many states allow their military and other national security officials to arrest and detain persons without warrant, if it can be claimed that to do so is necessary in the "exigencies of the situation." Thus not only do states suspend many of the procedural safeguards that the ICCPR mandates concerning arrest and detention, but they do so for prolonged periods of time.

A series of such cases relating to emergency provisions have come to the WGAD concerning Sri Lanka. The Government had been engaged in internal armed conflict with the Liberation Tigers of Tamil Eelam (LTTE). In 2006, the Government enacted emergency regulations in light of the ongoing conflict. These domestic laws allowed military personnel to carry out normally law enforcement functions, such as arrests and detentions. The emergency regulations also provided immunity for actions taken under the law, which could include arrests without warrant. The presence of such overbroad national security laws, however, did not make them compatible with the requirements of the ICCPR. The WGAD has denounced these kinds of vague and sweeping powers, which apply broadly to issues of public security and terrorism.[62] Warrants are rarely issued for such arrests when carried out by military authorities under the auspices of emergency legislation, rather than through regular law enforcement channels. In *Gunasundaram Jayasundaram* v. *Sri Lanka*, an Irish citizen in Sri Lanka was "arrested without an arrest warrant on orders of the military authorities under Emergency Regulation No. 19(2), which resulted in his prolonged detention," in connection with allegations of "providing monetary and material support to the LTTE," which the WGAD determined to be "unsubstantiated."[63] Such "emergency" arrests without warrant tend to result in detentions carried out indefinitely with few procedural safeguards that would apply to nonemergency detentions. Requiring warrants for such arrests is not only obligatory under the applicable laws and principles described earlier but it also serves to try to guard against the arbitrary detentions that often follow. Such detentions will be discussed in a later section specifically pertaining to the arbitrary nature of administrative or preventative detentions, which have been a prominent concern for the WGAD.[64]

Both the WGAD and the HR Committee have been highly critical of the purported emergency grounds for arrest cited by states.[65] They have noted that the declaration of states of emergency has not been strictly limited to instances in which the "life of the nation is at risk,"[66] and thus many states have derogated from their ICCPR obligations in times when they have no right to do so. In particular, the two bodies have noted the negative impact of such emergency powers on the right to liberty of the person and

---

[62] Gunasundaram Jayasundaram v. Sri Lanka, WGAD Opinion No. 38/2012, Adopted Aug. 31, 2012, at ¶ 28 ("These provisions seek to severely limit the accountability of civilian and military authorities exercising emergency powers, provided that the action of the official took place in the course of discharging official duties. Further, the overly vague definitions of offences; sweeping powers of the military; arbitrary grounds for arrest and detention; erosion of fair trial and due process rights; and curtailing of fundamental freedoms endanger the life, liberty and security of the people. The Working Group is concerned that the immunity provisions may have far-reaching implications on those who are deprived of their liberty in that the violations of their human rights can be carried out with impunity by State authorities. Laws that give immunity to public functionaries and which are inimical to the human rights protection of those who are deprived of their liberty should therefore be amended.").

[63] *Id.*, at ¶ 32.

[64] *See, e.g., Report of the Working Group on Arbitrary Detention*, Human Rights Council, Jan. 18, 2010, A/ HRC/13/30, at ¶¶ 72–75.

[65] *Id.*

[66] *Id.*

guarantees of a fair trial as set forth in the ICCPR and the UDHR.[67] Thus, the WGAD has often found arrest without warrant to be arbitrary, even where the state in question claims that such arrests were lawful under emergency powers.[68]

The WGAD will therefore subject the state's claim to a test of necessity and proportionality, even where a state claims its derogations were part of anti-terrorism or other emergency efforts. Importantly, the invocation of emergency powers does not remove the arrest and detention from the WGAD's scrutiny, but it may, where properly applied, suffice to render lawful and nonarbitrary an arrest without warrant which would never be permissible outside of the emergency. Nevertheless, it remains important that the state has not exceeded what the exigencies of the emergency demand and has also otherwise preserved the detainee's rights.[69]

To strengthen protection against the misuse of emergency legislation, especially in contexts of terrorism, the WGAD has specified that the principle of legality requires that authorities guarantee those rights that are provided for or retained by the emergency legislation enacted.[70] In *Muhamadanwar Hajiteh v. Thailand*, for example, the WGAD found the authorities had failed to provide the detainee, arrested on charges of terrorism, with the fair trial rights specifically guaranteed under the Emergency Decree of 2005, and that this omission gave rise to a Category III violation.[71]

6 Lack of Effective Warrant

While most of the WGAD's opinions that comment on arrest warrants relate to their total absence, the issuance of a warrant itself is never sufficient to assure the rights of the detainee are respected. It is equally essential that the issuance of a warrant be valid, and this often fails to be the case. The WGAD has held that arrest without a *valid* warrant is arbitrary, making it necessary to determine when an arrest warrant is so defective as to render it invalid.[72] As early as 1993, the WGAD addressed the issuance of defective arrest warrants. There are a number of ways a warrant may be defective and therefore invalid for the purposes of conducting a lawful and nonarbitrary arrest.

In *Rafael G. Baylosis, et al. v. The Philippines*, a detainee had his arrest warrant declared to be "defective, disentitling the authorities to effect the arrest." In that case, one of three individuals detained was arrested subject to a warrant "issued with reference to another person."[73] The two individuals shared the same surname, but were not the same person. The arrest, although carried out with a warrant, was arbitrary because the warrant did not validate the arrest of the individual who was in fact apprehended. Another ground on which an arrest warrant can be declared invalid arises when a warrant is issued in

---

[67] *Id.*

[68] A number of examples come from Sri Lanka, in which the WGAD has found arrest and detention to be arbitrary despite emergency powers that, domestically at least, render it permissible: *see, e.g.*, Gunasundaram Jayasundaram v. Sri Lanka, WGAD Opinion No. 38/2012, Adopted Aug. 31, 2012; Santhathevan Ganesharatnam v. Sri Lanka, WGAD Opinion No. 9/2013, Adopted May 2, 2013.

[69] *Id.*, at ¶¶ 38–39.

[70] Muhamadanwar Hajiteh v. Thailand, WGAD Opinion No. 19/2014, Adopted May 1, 2014, at ¶ 25.

[71] *Id.*, at ¶¶ 25, 30.

[72] Rafael G. Baylosis, et al. v. The Philippines, WGAD Opinion No. 5/1993, Adopted Apr. 30, 1993, at ¶ 6. ("Arrest without a valid search warrant is deemed to be arbitrary. It is in violation of article 9 of the Universal Declaration of Human Rights and article 9 of the International Covenant on Civil and Political Rights.")

[73] *Id.*, at ¶¶ 8–9.

relation to an alleged crime without any evidentiary support to implicate the named individual in such an act. Such grounds were also evidenced in the same case. The second individual in the case was arrested and detained based on an arrest warrant for crimes of "unlawful manufacture, sale, acquisition, disposition or possession of firearms or ammunition or machinery, tool or instrument used or intended to be used in the manufacture of any firearm or ammunition." But the lack of any factual evidence connecting him to such acts rendered the arrest warrant invalid, according to the WGAD.[74]

Procedural defects regarding the issuance of an arrest warrant constitute another potential source of invalidity. The WGAD has not, to date, set out any exhaustive checklist of necessary elements of an arrest warrant. It is nevertheless clear from the applicable international law and the WGAD's opinions that a warrant must, at a minimum, include the individual's name and details as to the reasons for their arrest.[75] It can also be assumed that the warrant should be dated, given that the time lapse between warrant and arrest is often a determinative issue as to whether an arrest was arbitrary or not. Additionally, a legal body with the authority to issue such warrants must issue the warrant. In *Zeinab Jalalian v. Iran*, the WGAD specified that an arrest warrant must be issued in compliance with certain requisite procedural specifications.[76] These include mention of which officials are authorized to make the arrest, when an arrest warrant will be required, and where individuals will be detained.[77] The WGAD noted that the authorities had failed to rebut the claim that procedure had not been followed, and ruled that the officials who detained Jalalian did not have authority to arrest or detain her.[78]

The Body of Principles, which assists the WGAD in interpreting the parameters of Articles 9 and 14 of the ICCPR, sets out a number of standards to be adhered to in the arrest of an individual. In particular, the Body of Principles requires that an arrest be carried out only by "competent officials or persons authorized for that purpose."[79] This assessment is supported by the more general ICCPR requirement that all arrests be in accordance with procedures established by law.[80]

In *Thulani Rudolf Maseko v. Swaziland*, the detainee was a human rights lawyer detained on charges of contempt of court. The detainee was arrested under a warrant issued by the Chief Justice, whom he had criticized for taking action against a government inspector that had investigated members of the judiciary involved in the misuse of government vehicles. In finding the arrest warrant invalid, the WGAD observed the detainee was held because he criticized the very judge who issued the arrest warrant and was remanded to pretrial detention despite it not having been sought by the prosecution.[81]

A further potential source of invalidity of an arrest warrant arises where a person with the requisite authority issues the warrant, but the warrant itself is missing signs of official endorsement. Such a situation arose in the case of a French national placed in

---

[74] *Id.*, at ¶ 6; Olesya Vedj v. Moldova, WGAD Opinion No. 12/2015, Adopted Apr. 27, 2015, at ¶ 7.

[75] ICCPR, at Art. 9 (2); Rafael G. Baylosis, et al. v. The Philippines, WGAD Opinion No. 5/1993, Adopted Apr. 30, 1993.

[76] Zeinab Jalalian v. Iran, WGAD Opinion No. 1/2016, Adopted Apr. 18, 2016, at ¶ 32.

[77] *Id.*

[78] *Id.*

[79] Body of Principles, at Principle 2; *see also* Fact Sheet No. 26 (in which the Principles are listed in the Annex, alongside the relevant articles of the ICCPR and UDHR).

[80] ICCPR, at Art. 9 (1).

[81] Thulani Rudolf Maseko v. Swaziland, WGAD Opinion No. 6/2015, Adopted Apr. 22, 2015, at ¶ 32.

preventative detention in connection with counterterrorism efforts in France. In its recital of the information received from the parties, the WGAD noted the source's claim that the arrest warrant presented at the time of arrest, although issued by a rogatory commission headed by a French judge, bore neither a signature nor an official seal.[82] The Government claimed that no arrest warrant was issued until four days after the arrest.[83] Unfortunately, the WGAD offered no conclusion as to the actual condition of the arrest warrant and its validity, but did find that in their totality, "the alleged procedural defects mentioned by the source, many of which the Government disputed, were not of such gravity as to confer on the deprivation of liberty an arbitrary character."[84] It thus remains unclear whether an arrest warrant is rendered invalid for lack of a signature or other mark of official endorsement.

A final scenario to examine is the situation of "John Doe" warrants, which are warrants issued without reference to a particular individual. "John Doe" warrants are a clear example of arrest warrants so fundamentally defective as to always be invalid and thus an arbitrary basis for arrest with no grounding in law. In the words of the WGAD, the issuance of warrants lacking identification of any individual "entitles the authorities to arrest persons without first applying their minds as to their identity. Such a procedure cannot but be considered as arbitrary. The person concerned is neither identified nor are the reasons for his arrest known at the time of effecting it."[85] As such, the WGAD unequivocally finds John Doe warrants to be arbitrary and in violation of Article 9 of both the ICCPR and UDHR. The "unbridled and unfettered exercise of power" that such warrants vest in the arresting authorities undermines any hope of proper due process for the detainee.[86]

C Analysis of Arrest without a Warrant

The general rule emphasized in the WGAD's jurisprudence is that an arrest without warrant, unless *in flagrante delicto* or falling within a very narrowly construed set of emergency exceptions, is arbitrary. Early on in its jurisprudence, the WGAD established that "arresting persons without a warrant, not informing them of the reason for their arrest and not filing charges against them within a reasonable period of time would render the detention arbitrary."[87] However, there are many variations on the fact pattern of what happens to persons arrested without warrant. A more nuanced application of the general rule articulated under Article 9 of the ICCPR and UDHR was therefore required and has emerged from the WGAD's jurisprudence.

Nevertheless, arrests without warrant are usually only addressed in passing in opinions of the WGAD. Therefore, while it is crucial to emphasize arrests without warrant, the totality of the circumstances of the detention will be reviewed by the WGAD.[88] When

---

[82] Joseph Antoine Peraldi v. France, WGAD Opinion No. 40/2005, Adopted Nov. 28, 2005, at ¶ 5.
[83] *Id.*, at ¶ 9.
[84] *Id.*, at ¶ 25.
[85] Roland Abiog and Antonio Cabardo v. Philippines, WGAD Opinion No. 1/1993, Adopted Apr. 30, 1993, at ¶ 7.
[86] *Id.*
[87] *Id.*
[88] Di Dafeng, et al. v. China, WGAD Opinion 44/1993, Adopted Sept. 30, 1993, at ¶ 7 (The opinion makes clear that arrest without warrant alone suffices for the finding of an article 9 violation, and that any further procedural violations are not necessary for such a finding, but merely "further" the violation: "The arbitrary nature of their arrest without a warrant is a clear violation of article 9 of the Universal Declaration of

discussing an arrest without a warrant, it is important for a source to detail exactly why the arrest was arbitrary. This requires stating that the arrest was without warrant and not *in flagrante delicto* or under emergency powers. Furthermore, even where an arrest without warrant was *in flagrante delicto* or under emergency powers, it may nonetheless be deemed arbitrary if the source explains that such exceptions were not applied in conformity with the WGAD's narrow interpretations of them.

In WGAD jurisprudence, arrests without warrant are generally a precursor to a string of rights violations. The necessity of arrest warrants to ongoing procedural fairness during detention is particularly evident in relation to the right to challenge the lawfulness of a detention and to present a defense. In this regard, the WGAD has made it expressly clear that to deny a detainee's lawyer access to the arrest warrant is, in itself, a serious breach of the right to a defense.[89] Therefore, while often not the most egregious due process violation faced by detainees whose cases have been brought to the WGAD, the importance of a proper arrest warrant to guaranteeing the overall fairness and legality of detention should not be overlooked.

II Incommunicado Detention

> Secret and/or incommunicado detention constitutes the most heinous violation of the norm protecting the right to liberty of a human being under customary international law. The arbitrariness is inherent in these forms of deprivation of liberty as the individual is left outside the cloak of any legal protection.[90]

Incommunicado detention is generally understood to refer to deprivation of liberty in which "a detainee's communication with other human beings is either highly restricted or nonexistent."[91] However, there is no authoritative treaty-based definition of incommunicado detention. This results in different human rights bodies and commentators offering slight variations in definition.

Most, however, recognize that a detainee should at a minimum be able to communicate with his family and legal counsel.[92] Thus, denying a detainee contact with his family and legal counsel renders a detention incommunicado. But the repeated reference to contact with family and legal counsel is perhaps best understood as shorthand for determining whether or not a detainee has any real opportunity to challenge their detention and to access the legal safeguards accorded to them, both in terms of due process and protection against cruel, inhuman, or degrading treatment and torture. This

---

Human Rights and article 9 of the International Covenant on Civil and Political Rights. Their continued detention without charge or trial is a further violation of the same rights.")

[89] Antonio José Rivero González v. Venezuela, WGAD Opinion No. 47/2013, Adopted Nov. 18, 2013, at ¶ 30 (noting that it violated Art. 14 (3) (b), ICCPR, and Principles 11, 12, 15, 17, 18, 23, 25, 32 and 33 of the Body of Principles).

[90] *Report of the Working Group on Arbitrary Detention*, Human Rights Council, A/HRC/22/44, Dec. 24, 2012, at ¶ 60.

[91] *Reply to Questions Raised by Member States during the Interactive Dialogue at the 66th Session of the UN General Assembly*, Special Rapporteur on Torture and Other Cruel, Inhuman or Degrading Treatment or Punishment, Oct. 18, 2011, at 1.

[92] Human Rights in the Administration of Justice, at 210.

determination is crucial, because incommunicado detention alone for a limited period of time is not normally considered a prima facie violation of a detainee's rights.[93]

Nonetheless, after a country mission to Norway, the WGAD expressed its general concern at the frequent use of isolation in detention, both in remand and after sentencing. It noted that "when in remand during the ongoing investigation, defendants may find themselves in partial or complete isolation, ordered by the competent court at the request of the police and prosecutors. Total isolation entails being locked up in a cell without any contact with other prison inmates or the outside world (television, radio or newspapers), except for a lawyer."[94]

That said, incommunicado detention when it also excludes counsel is a concern because it places the detainee "outside the cloak of any legal protection."[95] Incommunicado detention, dependent on its duration and facts,[96] can facilitate a wide range of rights violations. The common characteristic linking incommunicado detention to the violation of detainees' rights is "the absence of any realistic possibility of being brought before a court to test the legality of the detention."[97]

By being denied access to legal counsel, their family, and even to judges and judicial hearings, detainees held incommunicado are barred from all potential avenues through which to challenge their detention. Another grave concern arising from incommunicado detention is that it may facilitate or even constitute torture or other cruel, inhuman, or degrading treatment.[98]

As with most human rights violations, incommunicado detention must be carried out by the state in some form. Often, this will mean that government authorities carry out the arrest and subsequent detention, but it will also suffice for the government to have acquiesced to the detention.[99] Another essential element of incommunicado detention is that it be prolonged. Being held incommunicado for a period of merely a few days immediately after arrest will rarely, if ever, constitute a due process violation. However,

---

[93] It should be noted, however, that this issue is not wholly settled, with some believing that incommunicado detention creates such a high risk of interference with a detainee's rights as to be per se prohibited in international law, while others hold that incommunicado detention is only a problem as of the time rights violations result therefrom. *See, e.g.*, Human Rights in the Administration of Justice, at 210 ("The practice of holding detainees incommunicado, that is to say, keeping them totally isolated from the outside world without even allowing them access to their family and lawyer, does not per se appear to be outlawed by international human rights law, although the Human Rights Committee has stated in its General Comment No. 20, on article 7 of the Covenant, that 'provisions should … be made against incommunicado detention'."); *cf.* NIGEL S. RODLEY WITH MATT POLLARD, THE TREATMENT OF PRISONERS UNDER INTERNATIONAL LAW 462 (3rd ed. Oxford University Press, 2009) (noting that the Human Rights Committee has stated that incommunicado detention may "'as such,' 'in itself' or 'per se'" constitute a violation of ICCPR article 9(3), but that the Human Rights Committee has only made this determination in cases of "somewhat longer duration.").

[94] *Report of the Working Group on Arbitrary Detention: Mission to Norway*, Human Rights Council, A/HRC/7/4/Add.2, Oct. 11, 2007, at ¶ 73.

[95] *Report of the Working Group on Arbitrary Detention*, Human Rights Council, A/HRC/22/44, Dec. 24, 2012, at ¶ 60.

[96] *General Comment No. 35*, Human Rights Committee, CCPR/C/GC/35 (2014), at ¶ 35.

[97] Reply to Questions, at 1 (citing Aksoy v. Turkey, 1996-VI, Eur. Ct. H.R. 68).

[98] *Report of the Working Group on Arbitrary Detention*, Human Rights Council, A/HRC/22/44, Dec. 24, 2012, at ¶ 60.

[99] *Joint Study on Global Practices in Relation to Secret Detention in the Context of Countering Terrorism*, Human Rights Council, A/HRC/13/42, Feb. 19, 2010, at ¶ 8.

very often detainees are held incommunicado in the early days of detention where the detaining authorities have no legal basis for the arrest. In such cases, advocates may wish to challenge the detention as arbitrary under Category I, even if it has not been of a sufficiently substantial duration to form a Category III violation.[100]

On the due process violations arising from incommunicado detention, the WGAD in its jurisprudence suggests there must be approximately two weeks of incommunicado detention before it may be deemed arbitrary.[101] Shorter periods of incommunicado detention are generally not considered arbitrary.[102] However, the WGAD has required certain safeguards to be met in order for incommunicado detention of a little over one week to avoid being arbitrary, suggesting that the determination is contextual, rather than merely a question of how much time has passed.

For example, in *Mikel Egibar Mitxelena* v. *Spain*, the WGAD found that Spain's incommunicado detention of a suspected terrorist for eight days post-arrest was not arbitrary. Drawing primarily on the *Body of Principles for the Protection of All Persons under Any Form of Detention or Imprisonment*, the WGAD discussion set out that incommunicado detention may be justified where:

- There are "exceptional needs … [or] exceptional circumstances" necessitating incommunicado detention for a "brief period." In the case at hand, this was satisfied by the terrorism charges brought against the detainee.
- Measures are taken to ensure the "physical and psychological protection of the person under arrest." Here, the Spanish High Court was found to have acted appropriately in ordering daily medical examinations of the detainee.
- Legal counsel of the detainee's choosing is made available both during trial and in preparation for trial. Here, the detainee did not request legal counsel of his own choosing to be present during his interrogation and was therefore provided with a court-appointed lawyer who was present throughout.[103]

Thus, incommunicado detention for a week or so is permissible so long as there are exceptional circumstances necessitating it, the detainee has access to legal counsel, and protective measures are taken regarding the detainee's physical and psychological

---

[100] It should also be noted that even where the incommunicado detention is prolonged, the WGAD will sometimes consider the case as a Category I violation without also classifying it as Category III; *see, e.g.,* Mohamed Hassan Aboussedra v. Libya, WGAD Opinion 16/2007, Adopted Sept. 14, 2007 (the WGAD found only a Category I violation, despite concluding that, "[Detainee] has been secretly detained ever since, neither being able to consult a lawyer, nor presented to any judicial authority, nor charged by the Government with any offence.")

[101] José Gabriel Pastor Vives, et al. v. Peru, WGAD Opinion No. 50/1993, Adopted Sept. 30, 1993, at ¶ 5 ("The Working Group considers … [t]hat contraventions of the rules of due process, such as holding persons incommunicado for periods of up to more than 15 days … make the deprivation of freedom, during the first 15 days, arbitrary.")

[102] This is not without controversy. The Office of the High Commissioner has noted that during these first hours of incommunicado detention, the risk of torture, ill-treatment, and enforced disappearance is particularly high, raising the question of whether even short periods of incommunicado detention should be permissible. Human Rights in the Administration of Justice, at 211.

[103] Mikel Egibar Mitxelena v. Spain, WGAD Opinion No. 26/1999, Adopted Nov. 29, 1999, at ¶¶ 10–11.

wellbeing.[104] In contrast, incommunicado detention that denies the detainee access to legal counsel, endangers their wellbeing, or continues beyond a few weeks is arbitrary.[105]

The distinctions between justified and arbitrary incommunicado detention are perhaps easier to understand when considering the rights that may be violated as a result of prolonged incommunicado detention.

The rights most commonly violated include: the right of access to counsel; the right to adequate time and facilities to prepare and present a defense; the right to a fair trial; the right to *habeas corpus*; and the right to freedom from torture and other cruel, inhuman, or degrading treatment or punishment.

Additionally, torture may also intersect with the right to a fair trial in that torture is often inflicted for the purpose of extracting false confessions, which will then be used against the detainee at trial. The incommunicado nature of a detention makes it far easier to carry out torture than it would be if there were legal counsel, family, and members of the judicial profession in regular contact with the detainee. However, it is crucial to remember that prolonged incommunicado detention not only facilitates but may itself constitute torture.[106] The more prolonged the incommunicado detention, and the more limited the detainee's communications with other persons, the more likely it is to constitute torture. As will be illustrated later, incommunicado detention as torture has been a particular concern for the WGAD and other human rights bodies in recent years, especially in the context of the War on Terror.

Sadly, many instances of incommunicado detention continue for years, with some even spanning decades.[107] And some instances of incommunicado detention are so severe as to rise to the level of secret detention and thus enforced disappearance. It is helpful to conceive of secret detention and enforced disappearance as incommunicado detention with additional aggravating factors, heightening the severity of the detainee's

---

[104] *Id.*, ¶¶ 10–11; *Cf.* Iván Andrés Bressan Anzorena and Marcelo Santiago Tello Ferreyra v. Argentina, WGAD Opinion No. 52/2011, Adopted Nov. 17, 2011 (noting an incommunicado detention of seven days was found to be too restrictive, but there were not exceptional circumstances justifying it, nor were measures taken to safeguard the rights of the detainee; other human rights bodies have also affirmed that access to legal counsel is a non-derogable minimum protection for detainees held *incommunicado*); *see also, Interim Report of the Special Rapporteur of the Human Rights Council on Torture and Other Cruel, Inhuman or Degrading Treatment or Punishment*, General Assembly, A/66/268, Aug. 5, 2011, at ¶ 99.

[105] Anwar al-Bunni, et al. v. Syria, WGAD Opinion No. 5/2008, Adopted May 8, 2008, at ¶¶ 30–31 (two months of incommunicado detention without access to legal counsel was held to be arbitrary and a violation under Category III).

[106] Joint Study on Global Practices, at 2–3 ("Prolonged incommunicado detention may facilitate the perpetration of torture and other cruel, inhuman or degrading treatment or punishment, and may in itself constitute such treatment."); *Resolution 8/8: Torture and Other Cruel, Inhuman or Degrading Treatment*, Human Rights Council, A/HRC/RES/8/8, June 18, 2008, at ¶ 7 (c) ("[Reminds States that] Prolonged incommunicado detention or detention in secret places may facilitate the perpetration of torture and other cruel, inhuman or degrading treatment or punishment and can in itself constitute a form of such treatment, and urges all States to respect the safeguards concerning the liberty, security and the dignity of the person."); *Report of the Working Group on Arbitrary Detention*, Human Rights Council, A/HRC/16/47, Jan. 19, 2011, at ¶ 54 ("Prolonged incommunicado detention may facilitate the perpetration of torture and other cruel, inhuman or degrading treatment or punishment, and may in itself constitute such treatment.") *See also, Torture and Other Cruel, Inhuman or Degrading Treatment or Punishment*, G.A. Res 61/153, General Assembly, A/RES/61/153, Feb. 14, 2007, at ¶ 12.

[107] *See, e.g.,* Shin Sook Ja, et al. v. People's Democratic Republic of Korea, WGAD Opinion No. 4/2012, Adopted May 2, 2012 (the family went at least two decades without any information as to the detainee's whereabouts).

situation. Despite the lack of direct contact with family, "[i]ncommunicado detention includes situations where a detainee's family is informed that the person is 'safe', [even if it is] without disclosure of the location or nature of the person's detention."[108]

In contrast, secret detention arises in situations of incommunicado detention where, "the detaining or otherwise competent authority denies, refuses to confirm or deny or actively conceals the fact that the person is deprived of his/her liberty hidden from the outside world, including, for example family, independent lawyers or non-governmental organizations, or refuses to provide or actively conceals information about the fate or whereabouts of the detainee."[109]

Thus, the relationship is that secret detention is de facto incommunicado detention, but incommunicado detention is not necessarily secret, unless it also possesses the additional elements set out earlier. The WGAD has said "[w]hether detention is secret or not is determined by its incommunicado character and by the fact that State authorities ... do not disclose the place of detention or information about the fate of the detainee."[110] These secret detentions also de facto constitute enforced disappearances. Enforced disappearances, which must also be carried out by the state or with its acquiescence, are defined by "[g]overnment refusal to disclose the fate or whereabouts of the persons concerned or a refusal to acknowledge the deprivation of their liberty, which places such persons outside the protection of the law."[111] Secret detention is therefore to be understood as constituting a more egregious form of incommunicado detention and is a de facto case of enforced disappearance.[112]

Secret detentions have become a serious concern in the post-9/11 world, where those detained in connection with terrorism allegations may be tortured or subjected to other cruel, inhuman, or degrading treatment in order to secure confessions or other information of potential value in combatting terrorism. Nonetheless, seemingly "lesser" cases of incommunicado detention remain a serious threat to the rights and wellbeing of detainees outside of the War on Terror.

Therefore, this section considers a range of scenarios of incommunicado detention, which implicate a wide array of international norms and standards. These standards will first be explored before mapping and analyzing their application by the WGAD.

A *Applicable Laws and Standards*

The range of rights implicated by incommunicado detention is particularly large. This is primarily due to the nature of incommunicado detention as a facilitator of rights violations.[113] As discussed previously, while incommunicado detention itself is generally not a prima facie violation of law, it often facilitates many other serious violations of fundamental rights, generally provided for in the ICCPR and the UDHR. Therefore, while neither the ICCPR nor the UDHR expressly prohibit prolonged incommunicado

---

[108] Joint Study on Global Practices, at ¶ 31.

[109] *Id.*, at ¶ 8.

[110] *Id.*, at ¶ 9.

[111] Kingkeo Phongsely v. Laos, WGAD Opinion No. 51/2011, Adopted Sept. 2, 2011, at ¶ 11.

[112] *Report of the Working Group on Arbitrary Detention*, Human Rights Council, A/HRC/16/47, Dec. 26, 2011, at ¶ 54 ("Every instance of secret detention is by definition incommunicado detention.")

[113] General Comment No. 35, at ¶¶ 35, 56.

detention, they can be understood to prohibit it by extension whenever incommunicado detention results in a violation of the rights international law protects.

In contrast, the *Body of Principles for the Protection of All Persons under Any Form of Detention or Imprisonment* expressly states that "communication of the detained or imprisoned person with the outside world, and in particular his family or counsel, shall not be denied for more than a matter of days."[114] Thus, the Body of Principles is unique among international standards for prohibiting incommunicado detention per se, as opposed to prohibiting the many procedural violations that result from incommunicado detention. The latter are also covered by the Body of Principles, resulting in WGAD finding all of the following Principles to be implicated in various cases of incommunicado detention:

- Principle 11 – right to be promptly and effectively heard by judicial or other authority; right to present a defense; right to legal counsel.
- Principle 15 – right to communicate with the outside world, particularly with family and legal counsel.
- Principle 16 – right to notify/require appropriate authority to notify family or other appropriate persons of arrest, detention, transfer, and location.
- Principle 17 – right to assistance of legal counsel.
- Principle 18 – right to communicate with legal counsel and adequate time and facilities for this to occur.
- Principle 19 – right to be visited and contacted by family and to communicate with the outside world.[115]

The WGAD has also looked to the *United Nations Standard Minimum Rules for the Treatment of Prisoners* (the "Nelson Mandela Rules") in specifying that the maximum permissible length of solitary confinement is fifteen days.[116] Although frequently cited by the WGAD in cases of incommunicado detention,[117] the Body of Principles and Standard Minimum Rules are persuasive authority but are not binding treaties like the ICCPR. It is therefore essential to look to the specific and more traditionally fundamental rights of the ICCPR that are violated by incommunicado detention. These rights are grouped thematically in the next subsections, along with reference to other international legal instruments that further support such rights.

---

[114] Body of Principles, at Principle 15; Riad Al Turk, et al. v. Syria, WGAD Opinion No. 6/1992, Adopted Session No. 4, at ¶5 (d) ("Furthermore, unduly prolonged incommunicado detention is an infringement of Principle 15 of the Body of Principles").

[115] Note that the Body of Principles, consistent with the jurisprudence and commentary of numerous UN human rights bodies, also makes provision for justified use of incommunicado detention for a period limited to a "matter of days," unless a longer period is justified by "exceptional needs of the investigation." Body of Principles, at Principle 15, 16(4) and 18(3).

[116] Nazanin Zaghari-Ratcliffe v. Iran, WGAD Opinion No. 28/2016, Adopted Aug. 23, 2016, at ¶ 51.

[117] See, e.g., Miguel Fernando Ruiz-Conejo Márquez v. Peru, WGAD Opinion No. 42/1993, Adopted Sept. 29, 1993, at ¶ 5 (c) (Principles 11 (1), 16, 17, and 18); Riad Al Turk, et al. v. Syria, WGAD Opinion No. 6/1992, Adopted Session No. 4, at ¶ 5 (d) (Principle 15); Francis Xavier Dang Xuan Dieu, et al. v. Viet Nam, WGAD Opinion No. 26/2013, Adopted Aug. 29, 2013 (Principles 15 and 19); Hugo Sánchez Ramírez v. Mexico, WGAD Opinion No. 33/2012, Adopted Aug. 30, 2012 (Principles 15 and 19). But the WGAD also notes that these Principles allow for certain brief periods of incommunicado detention in exceptional circumstances, see, e.g., Mikel Egibar Mitxelena, at ¶ 10 (Principles 15, 16 (4), and 18 (3)).

1 Right to a Fair Trial/*Habeas Corpus*

As with all Category III cases, Articles 9 and 14 of the ICCPR and Articles 9 and 10 of the UDHR form the central legal arguments against incommunicado detention. Article 9(3) of the ICCPR is violated wherever incommunicado detention "prevents prompt presentation before a judge."[118] This also violates Article 10(1) of the UDHR.[119] And Article 9(4) is violated where "[a detainee is] held incommunicado and thereby . . . 'effectively barred from challenging his arrest and detention.'"[120] Incommunicado detention violates Article 14 of the ICCPR, particularly 14(3)(b) and (d), where denying the detainee contact with counsel has left them unable to communicate and work with legal counsel in order to prepare and present a defense.[121]

Furthermore, where the incommunicado nature is of such severity, perhaps even amounting to secret detention, that the detainee is denied a trial or other access to judicial authorities, further elements of Article 14 are violated, such as 14(3)(c). All of these violations relate directly to the right to a fair trial, and by virtue of that overlap with the right to counsel and the right to prepare and present a defense.

However, for many detainees there is a need to appear in court and be afforded a public hearing to challenge the legality of detention even before trial.[122] This is particularly pertinent for those detained without legal basis or without information as to the grounds for their arrest. This right of all detainees to bring proceedings before a court to challenge the legality of the detention, known as *habeas corpus*, is non-derogable under treaty law and customary international law.[123] Article 9(4) of the ICCPR and Articles 8, 9, and 10 of the UDHR underpin detainees' *habeas corpus* rights.[124] While *habeas corpus* is closely related to the right to a fair trial, it is important to note that the WGAD holds that *habeas corpus* "should be regarded not as a mere element in the right to a fair trial but . . . as a personal right."[125] The WGAD therefore considers denial of *habeas corpus* to be sufficient in itself to render a detention arbitrary, as will be discussed in greater detail later.[126]

---

[118] General Comment No. 35, at ¶ 35.

[119] Human Rights in the Administration of Justice, at 210 (citing Peñarrieta, et al. v. Bolivia, Communication No. 176/1984, Human Rights Committee, CCPR/C/OP/2, Nov. 2, 1987, at ¶ 16).

[120] Human Rights in the Administration of Justice, at 198 (citing Ignacio Dermit Barbato, et al. v. Uruguay, Communication No. 84/1981, Human Rights Committee, CCPR/C/OP/2, Oct. 21, 1982, at ¶ 10).

[121] Anwar al-Bunni, et al., at ¶ 31.

[122] Saparmamed Nepeskuliev v. Turkmenistan, WGAD Opinion No. 40/2015, Adopted Dec. 2, 2015, at ¶ 39.

[123] *Report of the Working Group on Arbitrary Detention*, Human Rights Council, A/HRC/22/44, Dec. 24, 2012, at ¶¶ 42–43, 46.

[124] *Report of the Working Group on Arbitrary Detention*, Human Rights Council, A/HRC/19/57, Dec. 26, 2011 at ¶ 59 (further stating that "[s]imilarly, principle 32 of the Body of Principles for the Protection of All Persons under Any Form of Detention or Imprisonment provides that a detained person or his counsel 'shall be entitled at any time to take proceedings according to domestic law' for the same purposes. This is also the understanding of the Human Rights Committee in its General Comment No. 8, paragraph 1...").

[125] *Id.*, at ¶ 59 (citing *Report of the Working Group on Arbitrary Detention*, Commission on Human Rights, E/CN.4/2004/3, Dec. 15, 2003, at ¶ 62).

[126] Furthermore, the WGAD holds that exercising the right of *habeas corpus* should not be burdensome to the detainee – at least not so burdensome as the formal procedural requirements of trial. *Id.*, at ¶ 63 ("there may be no requirement of legal formalities that, if not complied with, might lead to the inadmissibility of the remedy. Any individual should therefore be able to apply for it in writing, orally, by telephone, fax, e-mail or any other means, without the need for prior authorization.")

2 Access to Counsel

Naturally, the right of access to counsel overlaps greatly with the right to a fair trial. Article 14(3)(b) and (d) of the ICCPR, discussed in the preceding section, form the core of a detainee's right to access counsel. Principles 11, 15, 17, and 18 of the Body of Principles further support this right, but the WGAD will generally find it suffices to rely on Article 14(3) of the ICCPR to show that denial of access to counsel renders a detention arbitrary under Category III.[127]

3 Freedom from Torture and Other Cruel, Inhuman, and Degrading Treatment

It is now widely acknowledged among UN human rights bodies that prolonged incommunicado detention is capable of facilitating and constituting torture.[128] The Human Rights Council (HRC) and the UN General Assembly have affirmed this understanding and the WGAD has repeatedly relied on this in its opinions and annual reports.[129] As stated by the prior Commission on Human Rights (UNCHR) in Resolution 2003/38, "prolonged incommunicado detention may facilitate the perpetration of torture and can in itself constitute a form of cruel, inhuman or degrading treatment."[130] A number of holders of the position of UN Special Rapporteur on Torture and Other

---

[127] *See, e.g.*, Chief Ebrima Manneh v. The Gambia, WGAD Opinion No. 14/2009, Adopted Sept. 3, 2009, at ¶ 22 ("Mr. Manneh has not had his day in court. He has not even been charged with a criminal offence. He has not been allowed access to a lawyer to prepare his defence. His detention in this case is thus in violation of article 14, paragraph 3 (a), (b), and (c), of the International Covenant on Civil and Political Rights, which require that everyone shall be informed promptly of the nature and cause of the charge against them, to have adequate time and facilities for the preparation of their defence and to communicate with counsel of their own choosing, as well as to be tried without undue delay. His detention falls within Category III of the categories of arbitrary detention developed by the Working Group.")

[128] It can even constitute torture or another form of ill-treatment of family members in certain circumstances. Joint Study on Global Practices, at 2–3 ("Prolonged incommunicado detention may facilitate the perpetration of torture and other cruel, inhuman or degrading treatment or punishment, and may in itself constitute such treatment. The suffering caused to family members of a secretly detained (namely, disappeared) person may also amount to torture or other form of ill-treatment, and at the same time violates the right to the protection of family life.")

[129] *Id.*, at 2–3 ("Prolonged incommunicado detention may facilitate the perpetration of torture and other cruel, inhuman or degrading treatment or punishment, and may in itself constitute such treatment."); *Resolution 8/8: Torture and Other Cruel, Inhuman or Degrading Treatment*, Human Rights Council, A/HRC/8/8, June 18, 2008, at ¶ 7(c) ("[Reminds States that] Prolonged incommunicado detention or detention in secret places may facilitate the perpetration of torture and other cruel, inhuman or degrading treatment or punishment and can in itself constitute a form of such treatment, and urges all States to respect the safeguards concerning the liberty, security and the dignity of the person."); *Report of the Working Group on Arbitrary Detention*, Human Rights Council, A/HRC/16/47, Dec. 26, 2011, at ¶ 54 ("Prolonged incommunicado detention may facilitate the perpetration of torture and other cruel, inhuman or degrading treatment or punishment, and may in itself constitute such treatment."); Husam 'Ali Mulhim, et al. v. Syria, WGAD Opinion No. 10/2008, Adopted May 9, 2008, at ¶ 30 ("The Working Group recalls that prolonged incommunicado detention or detention in secret places may facilitate the perpetration of torture and other cruel, inhuman or degrading treatment or punishment and can in itself constitute a form of such treatment." Citing to *Torture and Other Cruel, Inhuman or Degrading Treatment or Punishment*, G.A. Res 61/153, General Assembly, A/RES/61/153, Feb. 14, 2007, at ¶ 12); General Assembly, *Torture and Other Cruel, Inhuman or Degrading Treatment or Punishment*, G.A. Res 60/148, A/RES/60/148, Feb. 21, 2006; *General Comment No. 20*, Human Rights Committee, HRI/GEN/1/Rev.1 (1992), at ¶ 11.

[130] *Report of the Working Group on Arbitrary Detention*, Human Rights Council, A/HRC/4/40, Jan. 9, 2007, at ¶ 48, fn. 12.

Cruel, Inhuman or Degrading Treatment have recommended that states prohibit the practice of incommunicado detention precisely because of the "high risk of severe harm to the detainee posed by incommunicado detention."[131] Special Rapporteur Nigel Rodley even declared "incommunicado detention is the most important determining factor as to whether an individual is at risk of torture."[132] International law's prohibition of torture and cruel, inhuman, or degrading treatment or punishment continues to apply in instances of detention, with no lowering of the standards of protection.[133] In fact, detainees, in comparison to persons at liberty, receive additional protections against torture and ill treatment because it is recognized that detainees are more vulnerable to such violations.[134] And the volume of calls from UN human rights bodies to recognize the risk of torture resulting from incommunicado detention has become particularly hard to ignore post-9/11 and the ensuing counter-terrorism measures.[135]

4 Additional Rights

Article 10(1) of the ICCPR can be viewed as something of a catchall right for detainees. It protects detainees' right to "be treated with humanity and with respect for the inherent dignity of the human person." The HR Committee has repeatedly held that prolonged incommunicado detention violates this right,[136] even where the incommunicado detention lasted no more than two weeks.[137] In contrast, the WGAD does not frequently find an Article 10(1) violation to arise from incommunicado detention. And in the few cases featuring incommunicado detention where such a violation is found, it is unclear whether the WGAD finds the violation to arise from the incommunicado nature of the detention, or from other elements of the detention.[138] Therefore, while prolonged

---

[131] Reply to Questions, at 3.

[132] *Report by the Special Rapporteur on the Question of Torture*, General Assembly, A/54/426, Oct. 1, 1999, at ¶ 42.

[133] ICCPR; UDHR; *Convention against Torture and Other Cruel, Inhuman or Degrading Treatment or Punishment*, G.A. Res. 39/46, 39 U.N, GAOR Supp. (No. 51), at 197, A/39/51 (1984), 1465 U.N.T.S. 85, *entered into force* June 26, 1987.

[134] In addition, see Body of Principles, at Principle 6; and specifically CAT, at Arts. 10–11.

[135] *Report of the Working Group on Arbitrary Detention*, Commission on Human Rights, E/CN.4/2005/6, Dec. 1, 2004, at ¶ 76; *Report of the Working Group on Arbitrary Detention*, Human Rights Council, A/HRC/16/47, Dec. 26, 2011, at ¶ 54; Karmelo Landa Mendibe, at ¶ 46.

[136] Peñarrieta, et al. v. Bolivia, Communication No. 176/1984, Human Rights Committee, CCPR/C/OP/2, Nov. 2, 1987, at ¶ 16 ("The Human Rights Committee, acting under article 5, paragraph 4, of the Optional Protocol to the International Covenant on Civil and Political Rights, is of the view that the facts as found by the Committee disclose violations of the Covenant with respect to . . . Article 9, paragraph 3, and 10, paragraph 1, because they were not brought promptly before a judge, but were kept incommunicado for 44 days following their arrest.").

[137] Rodley, at 464 (noting that it "might in future be found to be violated by an even shorter period of incommunicado detention.")

[138] *See, e.g.,* Omar Shehada Abu-Shanab v. Kuwait, WGAD Opinion No. 59/1993, Adopted Dec. 9, 1993 (finding of Article 10 violation, but it is simply "in light of the above," which would logically seem to be related to the seemingly secret and thus incommunicado nature of the detention, but this is never explicitly stated by the WGAD, who never even use the words "secret" or "incommunicado" in the opinion); Luis Williams Polo Rivera v. Peru, WGAD Opinion No. 32/2010, Adopted Nov. 25, 2010 (finding of Article 10 violation, but again it is not clear whether it is specifically in relation to the incommunicado character of the detention, which receives little attention from the WGAD). This reading is further supported in Imed Al Chibani v. Libya, WGAD Opinion No. 6/2011, Adopted May 3, 2011; Hasna Ali Yahya Husayn, et al. v. Iraq, WGAD Opinion No. 59/2011, Adopted Nov. 21, 2011.

incommunicado detention may constitute an Article 10(1) violation, this will not be as much of a concern for the WGAD as whether it constitutes an ICCPR Article 9 or 14 violation.

Article 16 of the ICCPR and Article 6 of the UDHR protect the right to be recognized as a person before the law. Because incommunicado detention frequently places a detainee outside the protection of the law (given the various rights violations that may occur and the lack of access to judicial authorities to prevent them), the WGAD may find it to be a violation of these Articles. This is typically the case when incommunicado detention results in an inability of the detainee to contest their deprivation of liberty, such as in *Hatem al Darawsheh* v. *Jordan*.[139]

Where incommunicado detention rises to the level of secret detention and thus enforced disappearance, the *International Convention for the Protection of All Persons from Enforced Disappearance* (ICPPED) is also engaged. The ICPPED expressly prohibits secret detention, and details the detainee's right "to communicate with and be visited by his or her family, counsel or any other person of his or her choice, subject only to the conditions established by law, or, if he or she is a foreigner, to communicate with his or her consular authorities, in accordance with applicable international law."[140] Although not as widely ratified as the ICCPR, this treaty governs incommunicado detention when it takes on the additional qualities of secret detention and enforced disappearance, reflecting the grave danger detainees face in such situations.

B Cases of Incommunicado Detention

As the implicated rights and international standards reflect, incommunicado detention relates to a great many areas of concern for the WGAD. To show how these various rights are engaged in practice, it is worth examining the variety of fact patterns that have been presented to the WGAD in relation to prolonged incommunicado detention and how it has assessed these situations.

1 Later Given Contact

Many detainees who are held incommunicado do not remain subject to these restrictions on their communications for the entirety of their detention. Instead, many regain contact with their family and legal counsel some time later in their detention.[141] However, even where only the first ten to fifteen days of a detention are incommunicado, this may nevertheless render the detention arbitrary. In a case where Peruvian military personnel were arrested and detained incommunicado for approximately the first two weeks of the detention, the WGAD found the incommunicado period of detention to be, itself, arbitrary. The WGAD considered "[t]hat contraventions of the rules of due process, such as holding persons incommunicado for periods of up to more than 15 days, not specifying

---

[139] Hatem al Darawsheh v. Jordan, WGAD Opinion No. 46/2017, Adopted Aug. 22, 2017, at ¶ 23.

[140] *International Convention for the Protection of All Persons from Enforced Disappearance*, G.A. Res. 61/177, 2716 U.N.T.S. 3 (2006), *entered into force* Dec. 23, 2010, at Art. 17(1) and 17(2)(d).

[141] Jassim al-Hulaibi v. Bahrain, WGAD Opinion No. 22/2014, Adopted Aug. 25, 2014, at ¶ 22, where the detainee was permitted only ten minutes of access to his family after a month of incommunicado detention and after a total of three months had lapsed since his initial arrest without warrant.

the reasons for their detention, or inability to communicate with counsel during that period constitute violations of the rules of due process of law and that such contraventions make the deprivation of freedom, during the first 15 days, arbitrary."[142] Therefore, even where communications are later restored, the WGAD recognizes that the damage has already been incurred and will still declare the earlier period of incommunicado detention to be a Category III violation.

Unfortunately, governments are not always forthcoming in bringing an end to the incommunicado aspect of a detention. There have been numerous instances where the family of a detainee will have to intervene repeatedly before there will be an end to the incommunicado detention, allowing the detainee to finally avail of their right to communicate with their family. This may require a great deal of persistence from a detainee's family. In the case of *Mohamed Rahmouni v. Algeria*, approximately six months passed between the detainee's arrest and his mother finally discovering the location of her son's detention.[143] Once she had learned his true location, his mother then had to resort to submitting complaints to the Minister of Defense, the Minister of Justice, the Commander of the First Military Region of Blida, and the Prosecutor of the military court of Blida before she was granted the right to visit her son. Approximately ten months passed between Rahmouni's arrest and his mother's first visit.

Despite his mother's eventual ability to communicate with her son by visiting him in prison, the WGAD still considered the detention to be arbitrary given the prolonged period of incommunicado detention that preceded it. Granting of communication at a later stage does not remedy earlier periods of prolonged incommunicado detention. The incommunicado nature of Rahmouni's detention had already facilitated his solitary confinement, his inability to learn of the charges against him, and his denial of access to counsel and thus of means to challenge his detention. Furthermore, his later contact with his mother did not, despite her best efforts, result in Rahmouni being granted access to legal counsel.[144] Given the number and gravity of due process violations suffered by a detainee as a result of incommunicado detention, with effects that continue to harm the detainee's interests even after communication is granted, it is understandable that the WGAD will not consider the ending of incommunicado detention to remedy the period that has already been inflicted on the detainee.

Another issue that arose in Rahmouni's case was the contact was inadequate: "The military authorities then informed her that she could come back only one month later, although a sign at the entrance indicated that visits to the prisoners took place every 15 days. According to the source, this unjustified restriction of the right of access seriously affected the emotional condition of the prisoner and his mother."[145]

Similarly, in *Francis Xavier Dang Xuan Dieu v. Viet Nam*, after a period spent incommunicado, fifteen of the sixteen detainees were only able to meet with their family on one or two occasions. The source alleged that the lack of "consistent and adequate access to legal counsel and family members [at trial]" constituted a violation of due

---

[142] José Gabriel Pastor Vives, et al., at ¶ 5.
[143] Mohamed Rahmouni v. Algeria, WGAD Opinion No. 33/2008, Adopted Nov. 20, 2008, at ¶¶ 9–10.
[144] Sadly, even his mother's subsequent efforts to obtain authorization for legal counsel to visit Rahmouni were denied, despite her having obtained an official letter from the Ministry of Defense in support of such visits. *Id.*, at ¶¶ 10–12.
[145] *Id.*, at ¶ 10.

process rights.[146] While both cases resulted in a finding of Category III violations, the WGAD has not yet expressed a stance on what, if anything, should be considered the minimum acceptable amount of contact between a detainee and their family and counsel. While this is perhaps easier to answer in regard to counsel – the detainee needs, according to the ICCPR, "adequate time and facilities" to communicate with counsel and prepare a defense[147] – the WGAD has not had occasion to comment on denial of access to family alone being sufficient to render a detention arbitrary.

In *James Mawdsley* v. *Myanmar*, the detainee was a British-Australian national who had repeatedly gotten himself detained in Myanmar protesting its military junta.[148] On his third detention, he was summarily tried, convicted, and sentenced to seventeen years in solitary confinement for handing out pro-democracy leaflets. The detainee was held in incommunicado through his trial, which happened on the same day he was detained. The WGAD was unsparing in its criticism of the Government:

> The allegations, unrebutted, demonstrate the violation of all norms of fair play and justice. Mr. Mawdsley was not informed of the reasons for his arrest; he was detained incommunicado without legal advice or representation; his trial was a mockery of all legal principles applicable in jurisdictions where the rule of law prevails.[149]

In this particular case, the release of the WGAD opinion directly resulted in Mawdsley's release, just days after it was made public.[150]

Sadly, there are many cases in which family and legal counsel struggle to get any contact at all. In some cases, it can take a petition and subsequent issuance of a WGAD opinion before a detaining government will grant communication with family and legal counsel. This was the case in *Yang Jianli* v. *China*, where the detainee was arrested without a warrant for allegedly entering China illegally and being a spy for Taiwan.[151] Yang was denied family visits and both access to and assistance of legal counsel. The incommunicado nature of Yang's detention was particularly extreme. His wife, who traveled from the United States to China to try to locate her husband and secure legal counsel to assist him, was forced to leave China the same day and return to the United States without seeing or learning of her husband and his fate. Later, after two months of incommunicado detention, police authorities in China finally informed Yang's brother that he had been formally arrested.[152] However, despite his brother now having some confirmation of Yang's arrest, Yang remained in incommunicado detention until immediately after the WGAD had issued an opinion in his case and his family and international counsel publicized the decision.[153]

---

[146] Francis Xavier Dang Xuan Dieu, et al., at ¶ 69.

[147] ICCPR, at Art. 14(3)(b).

[148] James Mawdsley was the author's first case, which he took on as a law student.

[149] James Mawdsley v. Myanmar, WGAD Opinion No. 25/2000, Adopted Sept. 14, 2000 (Litigated By Author).

[150] The author met Mawdsley on his return home from prison on October 20, 2000, at Heathrow Airport in London, United Kingdom.

[151] Yang Jianli v. China, WGAD Opinion No. 2/2003, Adopted May 7, 2003 (Litigated by Author through Freedom Now).

[152] Id., at ¶ 18.

[153] Freedom Now, *Media Advisory: Supporters Mark One-Year Anniversary of Chinese Dissident Yang Jianli's Imprisonment with Candlelight Vigil*, Apr. 24, 2003.

The WGAD has also spoken about incommunicado detention more broadly on its country missions. For example, in Belarus, the WGAD noted that pretrial detention system, which had been inherited from the Soviet era, could last up to eighteen months. It expressed concern that the investigator determined the detention regime, who could impose any restrictions, including disallowing outside contacts. And from interviewing detainees, the WGAD reported detainees were not allowed visits until a preliminary investigation was closed and the case sent to court.[154] It expressed dismay to learn that pretrial detention conditions in Belarus were "much worse than those of convicted persons," including "overcrowding, harsh conditions with severe restrictions on visits and contacts with family, no phone calls, lack of activities, and sometimes, lack of adequate facilities."[155]

2 Never Given Contact

Despite the best efforts of families to gain contact with their detained relatives, sometimes governments will refuse to relent and maintain incommunicado imprisonment. During its country mission to Iran, the WGAD confronted "for the first time since its establishment," a "strategy of widespread use of solitary confinement [which it notes is also incommunicado detention] for its own sake and not for traditional disciplinary purposes ... in its truncated visit to ... Evin Prison."[156] It said this was "not a matter of a few punishment cells, as exist in all prisons, but what is a 'prison within a prison,' fitted out for the systematic, large-scale use of absolute solitary confinement, frequently for very long periods."[157] It concluded that this system is "arbitrary in nature and must be ended."[158] And noted in its conclusion:

> It appears to be an established fact that the specific use of this kind of detention has allowed the extraction of "confessions" followed by "public repentance" (on television); besides their degrading nature, such statements are manifestly inadmissible as evidence; furthermore, such absolute solitary confinement, when it is of long duration, can be likened to inhuman treatment within the meaning of the Convention against Torture. The Working Group has brought this matter to the attention of the competent Special Rapporteur, in that he is also a recipient of the standing invitation issued by the Iranian authorities.[159]

In *Gao Zhisheng* v. *China*, a Chinese human rights lawyer and longstanding critic of its Government was arrested and disappeared by Chinese authorities for more than a year-and-a-half. His family did not learn of his whereabouts until months after the WGAD released its opinion in support of his case. In examining his detention, the WGAD connected his enforced disappearance with the arbitrary nature of his detention, noting:

---

[154] *Report of the Working Group on Arbitrary Detention: Mission to Belarus*, Commission on Human Rights, E/CN.4/2005/6/Add.3, Nov. 25, 2004, at ¶ 48.

[155] *Id.*, at ¶ 49.

[156] *Report of the Working Group on Arbitrary Detention: Mission to Iran*, Commission on Human Rights, E/CN.4/2004/3/Add.2, June 27, 2003, at ¶ 54.

[157] *Id.*

[158] *Id.*

[159] *Id.*, at ¶ 55.

The Working Group considers that the Government . . . recognizes that Zhisheng Gao is in its hands since 4 February 2009 and since that date no charge has been communicated to Zhisheng Gao; he has been allowed no access to a lawyer; his family does not know about his fate and whereabouts, whether he has been tried or what is his current situation. This leads the Working Group to believe that, if he was tried, Zhisheng Gao has not benefitted from a fair trial, particularly given the fact that the only justification for his arrest . . . relies on strong convictions that he has expressed, the alleged grounds for a withdrawal of his licence and his criminal records.[160]

Several cases from North Korea of defectors either detained in their attempted flight or returned by neighboring states to North Korean authorities also highlighted the predicament of such detainees and their families.[161] There are limits to what the WGAD can achieve in these kinds of cases. This is exemplified in the extreme case of Shin Sook Ja and her two daughters, who were detained in 1987 after Shin's husband, Oh Kil Nam, defected from North Korea.[162] They are believed to have remained in detention ever since, but the Government has been unwilling to provide Oh with information concerning his family's fate. The little information given by the Government in response to the WGAD included claims that Shin died of a preexisting medical condition while in detention sometime between 1986 and 2012, and that his two daughters wanted no communication with him. However, Shin's alleged death remains unverified,[163] and there is nothing to support the claim that Oh's daughters have chosen not to contact him. Oh last received communications from his daughters in 1991 and has had no news of the location of his wife and daughters since the early 1990s. Despite the WGAD condemning the secret detention of Oh's family as being arbitrary in violation of both Categories I and III, it appears that no further information has been gained as to the fate of Oh's family.[164] Sadly, this case illustrates that while a WGAD opinion can sometimes facilitate an end to an incommunicado detention, such opinions can also be ignored.

3 Later Brought to Trial

Just as later contact with family and legal counsel does not remedy the violations brought about by a prior period of incommunicado detention, neither does the eventual bringing of a detainee to trial in any way remedy prior due process violations.[165] Even where the later trial is in line with due process requirements, its fairness may be irreparably damaged by the denial of due process during incommunicado detention pretrial. For example, the presence of defense lawyers during trial alone is not sufficient to comply

---

[160] Gao Zhisheng v. China, WGAD Opinion No. 26/2010, Adopted Nov. 19, 2010, at ¶ 19.

[161] Hyang Sil-kwon v. Democratic People's Republic of Korea, WGAD Opinion No. 32/2015, Adopted Sep. 3, 2015.

[162] Shin Sook Ja, et al. v. Democratic People's Republic of Korea, WGAD Opinion No. 4/2012, Adopted May 2, 2012.

[163] Id., at ¶¶ 15, 17. And some believe that she was alive at least a year before the Government claimed she had died. See, Evan Ramstad, North Korea Says Oh's Wife Is Dead, WALL STREET JOURNAL, May 8, 2012.

[164] Jori Finkel, Art Man of Alcatraz, NEW YORK TIMES, Sept. 18. 2014 (stating in Sept. 2014 that "Ms. Shin appears to have died in captivity, according to an information binder provided by For-Site," thus suggesting that no new or contradicting news regarding her fate has come to light.)

[165] Zeinab Jalalian, at ¶ 33 (preventing detainee from accessing counsel until eight months after her arrest prevented from exercising her Article 9 rights, notwithstanding that she was eventually permitted a trial).

with the standards of a fair trial. Due process demands that "the accused [also] be provided with adequate time and facilities for the preparation of their defence and to communicate with counsel, which includes being able to meet with their lawyers in private before the trial."[166] Incommunicado detention that prevents the detainee from meeting with counsel to prepare their defense before trial therefore undermines the fairness of any later trial. Incommunicado detention poses another threat to the fairness of any subsequent trial in cases where such detention facilitated false confessions through torture or ill treatment. Where such statements are introduced against the defendant at trial, the violations of due process experienced during incommunicado detention come directly into the courtroom and compromise the trial.[167]

In considering the case of the disappeared and detained Chinese human rights lawyer Gao Zhisheng, the WGAD, having received no response from the Government, was unable to establish whether or not Gao had been brought to trial. However, the WGAD declared that even if Gao had been tried, it could not have been a fair trial. This finding was based in part on the suspected political motivations for his detention and in part on the incommunicado nature of his detention. In particular, the WGAD noted that the fairness of any trial was compromised by Gao's lack of access to legal counsel and the Government's refusal to inform Gao's family as to his fate.[168] In contrast, the WGAD has recognized the need for some secrecy early on so as not to compromise the establishment of a case, finding "[s]ecrecy of inquiry proceedings in the early stages of the investigation" will not necessarily result in a violation of the fairness of a subsequent trial.[169] However, the WGAD notes that this secrecy should not be extended to due process deprivations by way of prolonged incommunicado detention.

4 Never Brought to Trial

As Gao Zhisheng's case illustrates, it can be hard to ascertain whether or not individuals in secret detention have been brought to trial. Not all persons detained incommunicado are eventually brought to trial. Some will be detained without ever having the chance to challenge their detention in court. This was the case for a Gambian citizen, Chief Ebrimah Manneh, who is now believed to have since died in secret detention.

Manneh, a senior reporter for Gambia's *Daily Observer*, was observed at his newspaper being arrested without warrant by the Gambian National Intelligence Agency in 2006 and then was detained incommunicado, without charge or trial.[170] However, when WGAD considered Manneh's case, he was believed to still be alive after three years of secret detention.[171] The WGAD's opinion found Manneh's detention to be a violation under Categories I, II, and III.[172] The WGAD affirmed that "secret detention of a person is in itself a violation of the right to a fair trial," and thus violates Article 14(1) of

---

[166] Husam 'Ali Mulhim, et al. v. Syria, WGAD Opinion No. 10/2008, Adopted May 9, 2008, at ¶ 31.

[167] *Id.*, at ¶¶ 7, 27, 29.

[168] Gao Zhisheng v. China, WGAD Opinion No. 26/2010, Adopted Nov. 19, 2010, at ¶ 19 (Litigated by the Author through Freedom Now).

[169] Hillary Boma Awul, et al. v. Sudan, WGAD Opinion No. 29/1999, Adopted Nov. 30, 1999, at ¶ 12 (Litigated, In Part, by the Author).

[170] Chief Ebrima Manneh v. The Gambia, WGAD Opinion No. 14/2009, Adopted Sept. 3, 2009.

[171] *Id.*, at ¶ 8.

[172] *Id.*, at ¶¶ 19–25.

the ICCPR.[173] In addition, Manneh's secret detention deprived him of "his day in court," and of his right to access a lawyer with whom to prepare his defense, violating Article 14 (3) of the ICCPR.[174] The WGAD said that the secret detention was arbitrary because "no access to counsel or relatives is granted, no judicial control over the deprivation of liberty is exercised, no charges known to exist in [domestic] legislation are laid against the detainee with a view to the conduct of a trial, in short, where no legal procedure established by law whatsoever is followed."[175] A closely related reason for such arbitrariness, also expressed by the WGAD, is the absence of any legal basis, which brings the issue under Category I, in addition to Category III.[176]

It is important to note that Manneh's detention would still have been arbitrary even if he had later been brought to trial. The fact that he was never brought to trial only deepens the arbitrary nature of the detention.[177] Additionally, there remains another way in which Manneh's incommunicado detention, specifically his secret detention, violated his rights: "The detention of Mr. Manneh under such circumstances outside the confines of the law for close to three years has also exposed him to the risk of torture, and other cruel, inhuman or degrading treatment."[178] It is the secret nature of Manneh's detention that placed him "outside the confines of the law," and created a risk of torture or other ill treatment. Such risks exist in any prolonged incommunicado detention, even where it did not rise to the level of secret detention.[179] The grave risk of torture arising from incommunicado detention is explored in the following section.

5 Facilitating Torture or Other Cruel, Inhuman, or Degrading Treatment

It is widely recognized among the UN's various human rights bodies that "the incommunicado regime, regardless of the legal safeguards for its application, facilitates the commission of acts of torture and ill-treatment."[180] The WGAD itself is in agreement with the HR Committee that "prolonged incommunicado detention may facilitate the perpetration of torture."[181] Moreover, these UN bodies further recognize that prolonged

---

[173] *Id.*, at ¶ 21.

[174] *Id.*, at ¶ 22.

[175] *Id.*, at ¶ 19.

[176] *Id.*, at ¶ 19 ("the Working Group has classified detention at a secret place as arbitrary detention in terms of Category I...").

[177] However, the WGAD does not always explain its approach and will instead merge both the prolonged incommunicado detention and the absence of trial into one finding of arbitrariness – as the cited case exemplifies. Nevertheless, it should be remembered that elsewhere WGAD jurisprudence shows both elements to render the detention arbitrary in their own right. Juan Ondo Abaga, et al. v. Equatorial Guinea, WGAD Opinion No. 2/2008, Adopted May 7, 2008, at ¶ 14 ("With regard to Mr. Esono Ntutumu, his detention incommunicado, without trial, for over three years from the time of his abduction in Nigeria or for almost three years since his deprivation of liberty at the hands of the Government of Equatorial Guinea, is a serious violation of the standards of due process, which gives the deprivation of liberty an arbitrary character.")

[178] Chief Ebrima Manneh, at ¶ 20.

[179] See following section on prolonged incommunicado detention facilitating torture and other cruel, inhuman, and degrading treatment or punishment.

[180] *Conclusions and Recommendations of the Committee against Torture: Spain*, Committee against Torture CAT/C/CR/29/3 (2002), at ¶10.

[181] *Report of the Working Group on Arbitrary Detention*, Commission on Human Rights, E/CN.4/2005/6, Dec. 1, 2004, at ¶ 76.

incommunicado detention "can in itself constitute a form of cruel, inhuman or degrading treatment."[182]

It is important to appreciate how prolonged incommunicado detention may facilitate torture or other cruel, inhuman, or degrading treatment or punishment, before considering in the next section how it may even constitute such treatment.

Incommunicado and especially secret detention facilitates torture and other ill treatment because it denies the detainees the legal safeguards and communication with the outside world that would normally dissuade or prevent the detaining powers from acting in such a way. As a result, detaining authorities are largely free to act with impunity and in contravention of legal protections. They are accountable to no one because the detainee is cut off from the outside world and unable to have anyone raise a specific alarm on their behalf, other than that they are being held incommunicado. The WGAD has unequivocally stated that it "notes that it is precisely when suspects cannot communicate with their families and lawyers that they are most likely to be tortured."[183]

During its visit to Nicaragua, the WGAD reported that it had met detainees in correctional institutions who had practically no communication with the outside world because they were being held far from where they lived, their relatives were unable or unwilling to visit them, or they had no money to pay for a lawyer.[184] These kinds of prisoners were described as "*Los Donados*," dumped as gifts on the prison system. The WGAD concluded:

> [T]his situation could also give rise to arbitrary detention, since these persons are incapable of exercising privileges to which they might be entitled, such as, for example, parole once they have served part of their sentence. The delegation noted that poverty, marginalization and lack of education impeded the exercise of the rights and powers accorded to them by law.[185]

In *Husam 'Ali Mulhim, et al.* v. *Syria*, seven detainees were held incommunicado for over eight months.[186] They were then convicted of "taking action or making a written statement or speech which could endanger the State," seemingly as a result of their lawful exercise of the right to freedom of expression.[187] Brought before a military tribunal, the seven civilian detainees all claimed to have been "ill-treated in order to obtain false confessions while held in incommunicado detention."[188] But despite their allegations of forced confessions, the court nevertheless admitted the forced confessions as evidence against them.[189] In its response to the WGAD, the Government denied, in general terms, the use of torture and ill treatment. However, the WGAD found this insufficient to function as a denial of the specific allegations of ill treatment conveyed by the source. Nonetheless, the WGAD did not have an admission of such ill treatment from the Government, so it was left to determine, to the best of its ability, the likely truthfulness of such allegations. And

---

[182] *Id.*

[183] Ali Aarrass v. Morocco, WGAD Opinion No. 25/2013, Adopted Aug. 28, 2013, at ¶ 30.

[184] *Report of the Working Group on Arbitrary Detention: Mission to Nicaragua*, Human Rights Council, A/HRC/4/40/Add.3, Nov. 9, 2006, at ¶ 84.

[185] *Id.*

[186] Husam 'Ali Mulhim, et al. v. Syria, WGAD Opinion No. 10/2008, Adopted May 9, 2008, at ¶ 5.

[187] *Id.*, at ¶¶ 9, 35.

[188] *Id.*, at ¶ 7.

[189] *Id.*

for this purpose the incommunicado nature of the detention became significant: "the fact that the defendants were held incommunicado without access to their families and lawyers for some months increased the probability of ill-treatment."[190]

There have been numerous further cases brought before the WGAD that have involved the use of torture and ill-treatment to extract forced confessions from detainees held incommunicado.[191] Additionally, there are a number of cases in which the WGAD has made explicit the connection between incommunicado detention and increased risk of torture and ill treatment.[192] Not only is torture a rights violation in and of itself[193] but it can also lead to false confessions being accepted into evidence against a detainee at trial, thus wholly eviscerating the right to a fair trial. This was the case in *Ali Aarrass v. Morocco*, wherein the detainee was convicted "based exclusively on the records of preliminary investigations drawn up in illegal circumstances while he was held in incommunicado detention."[194] Further illustrating the danger of incommunicado detention as a facilitator of torture, the source claimed that Aarrass was only arrested due to the false information coerced under torture from a prior detainee who himself had been held incommunicado.[195] Yet the increased risk of torture or ill treatment is not the only way in which prolonged incommunicado detention intersects with this rights violation, as is explained in the following subsection.

6 Itself Constituting Torture or Other Cruel, Inhuman, or Degrading Treatment

> The ill-treatment threshold may be reached when the period of incommunicado detention is prolonged and additional circumstances prevail.[196]

Not only does incommunicado detention facilitate torture; it can in fact *be* torture and other cruel, inhuman, or degrading treatment. The General Assembly has adopted a resolution to this effect, reminding all states that "prolonged incommunicado detention or detention in secret places may facilitate the perpetration of torture and other cruel, inhuman or degrading treatment or punishment and can in itself constitute a form of such treatment."[197] In light of this relationship between incommunicado detention and

---

[190] *Id.*, at ¶ 30.

[191] *See, e.g.*, Abdullah Sultan Sabihat Al Alili v. United Arab Emirates, WGAD Opinion No. 3/2008, Adopted May 7, 2008; Ali Aarrass at ¶¶ 23, 28; Lee Jang-hyong, et al. v. South Korea, WGAD Opinion No. 1/1995, Adopted May 30, 1995, at ¶ 6.

[192] *See, e.g.*, Chief Ebrima Manneh, at ¶ 20; Ali Aarrass, at ¶ 30.

[193] ICCPR, at Art. 7; CAT, at Art. 2.

[194] Ali Aarrass, at ¶ 24.

[195] Ali Aarrass, at ¶ 6 (the detainee maintained that he had been tortured so that he would implicate others).

[196] Joint Study on Global Practices, A/HRC/13/42, Feb. 19, 2010, at ¶ 32 (authored by representatives from the WGAD and the WGEID, along with the Special Rapporteur on Torture and Other Cruel, Inhuman or Degrading Treatment or Punishment, and the Special Rapporteur on the Promotion and Protection of Human Rights and Fundamental Freedoms While Countering Terrorism).

[197] *Torture and Other Cruel, Inhuman or Degrading Treatment or Punishment*, G.A. Res 61/153, General Assembly, A/RES/61/153, Feb. 14, 2007, at ¶ 12 (emphasis added). The WGAD relied on and cited directly to this resolution in Husam 'Ali Mulhim, et al. v. Syria, WGAD Opinion No. 10/2008, Adopted May 9, 2008, at fn. 27; *see also*, Human Rights Council, *Resolution 8/8: Torture and Other Cruel, Inhuman or Degrading Treatment*, A/HRC/RES/8/8, June 18, 2008, at ¶ 7 (c).

torture, it is essential to elucidate when prolonged incommunicado detention is no longer a mere facilitator of torture, but rises to the level of perpetrating that torture.

In a Joint Study, a number of UN human rights experts, including a WGAD representative, set the standard as follows: "The ill-treatment threshold may be reached when the period of incommunicado detention is prolonged and additional circumstances prevail."[198] As previously discussed, the definition of prolonged alone currently begins at the two-week threshold. This leaves the question of what constitutes "additional circumstances" that transform a period of prolonged incommunicado detention into an act of torture or other mistreatment.

Drawing on the jurisprudence of the WGAD and the HR Committee, two sets of additional circumstances can elevate prolonged incommunicado detention to the act of torture: isolation (also known as solitary confinement) and secret detention and enforced disappearance.

However, the Joint Study does not explicitly enumerate the potential "additional circumstances" so expressly; instead it merely gives examples of cases that have been determined to meet this requirement. Therefore, this list should not be presumed to be exhaustive, rather the two sets of "additional circumstances" form a consistently recurring feature where prolonged incommunicado detention is found to constitute torture. Nevertheless, it remains a persuasive guide as to the approach of the WGAD and the HR Committee on this point.

The first example given in the Joint Study is the case of *Polay* v. *Peru*, where the HR Committee found inhuman and degrading treatment to have been imposed over eight months of incommunicado detention, of which 23.5 hours of every day were spent in an unlit cell in freezing temperatures.[199] While it may at first appear that the freezing temperatures and constant bright light served to elevate the incommunicado detention to constituting torture, this is unlikely to be the case. First, the freezing temperatures and constant bright light are conditions that could occur in a detention that is not incommunicado; at most, they are facilitated by the incommunicado detention, rather than being an element of it. Second, it is the detainee's confinement to his cell for almost the entirety of each day that functions as a particularly egregious form of incommunicado detention. It suggests that not only was the detainee denied contact with family and legal counsel, but that he was also isolated from others within the prison.

This reading is supported by *El-Megreisi* v. *Libya*, the second case cited in the Joint Study. There, the HR Committee found that "Mohammed Bashir El-Megreisi, by being subjected to prolonged incommunicado detention in an unknown location, is the victim of torture and cruel and inhuman treatment . . . ."[200] Here, the additional circumstance of the prolonged incommunicado detention is that it rose to the level of secret detention – he was held at an unknown location. Furthermore, the Joint Study also recalled how the Inter-American Court of Human Rights found that "prolonged isolation and deprivation of communications are in themselves cruel and inhuman treatment, even if it is not

---

[198] Joint Study on Global Practices, at ¶ 32.
[199] Joint Study on Global Practices, at ¶ 32 (citing Polay v. Peru, Communication No 577/1994, Human Rights Committee, CCPR/C/61/D/577/1994, Nov. 6, 1997).
[200] El-Megreisi v. Libya, Communication No. 440/1990, Human Rights Committee, CCPR/C/50/D/440/1990, Mar. 23, 1994, at ¶ 5.4.

known what has actually happened during the prolonged isolation of the particular individual." The Inter-American Court was not describing a case of incommunicado detention, but one that involved isolation of the detainee – deprivation of contact not only from the outside world but also within the prison. Thus, isolation is undeniably one of the "additional circumstances" that sees prolonged incommunicado detention constitute torture.

Beyond the cases cited in the Joint Study, the WGAD affirmed the prolonged incommunicado detention plus "additional circumstances" approach in *Karmelo Landa Mendibe v. Spain*. The case concerned the detention of a university professor and politician who was accused of involvement with the ETA terrorist organization.[201] The source explained Mendibe was subjected to long periods of incommunicado detention. During one of these periods, Mendibe was allegedly forced to spend five days in solitary confinement, naked, in a dirty, cockroach-infested cell that was constantly illuminated with "a blinding white light."[202] He then went on to face additional periods of prolonged incommunicado detention, some of which featured further restrictions on his liberty, such as denial of access to the prison courtyard, or solitary confinement.[203] In considering the nature of Mendibe's detention, the WGAD took care to be very explicit that it was only when these facts were "considered together" that it could be found that Mendibe's right to a fair trial was impaired (specifically, the presumption of his innocence). The crucial point here is that the lack of investigation into the specific allegations of torture *and* the periods of prolonged incommunicado detention had to be considered in combination before they would "allow maintaining that the presumption of Landa's innocence was impaired."[204]

The HR Committee has a far greater number of cases on this issue, and it has also consistently supported the understanding of "additional circumstances" in this respect as amounting to either isolation or enforced disappearance (secret detention). Former Special Rapporteur on Torture Nigel Rodley identified a number of cases in which the HR Committee found instances of prolonged incommunicado detention to be torture or other cruel, inhuman, and degrading treatment or punishment.[205] In *El-Megreisi v. Libya*, the detainee's family was unable to trace him for approximately three years, thus rendering his detention not only incommunicado but also secret.[206] And the fact that the location of the detainee was unknown was explicitly stated by the HR Committee as a consideration in determining his incommunicado detention to constitute torture: "El-Megreisi, by being subjected to prolonged incommunicado detention *in an unknown location*, is the victim of torture and cruel and inhuman treatment, in violation of articles 7 and 10, paragraph 1, of the Covenant."[207]

---

[201] Karmelo Landa Mendibe, at ¶¶ 5, 9.
[202] *Id.*, at ¶ 13.
[203] *Id.*, at ¶ 16.
[204] *Id.*, at ¶ 44.
[205] Rodley, at 465.
[206] El-Megreisi, at ¶ 2.2.
[207] *Id.*, at ¶ 5.4.

Similarly, the cases of *El Alwani v. Libya*,[208] *El Hassy and El Hassy v. Libya*,[209] *Laureano Atachahua v. Peru*,[210] and *Kimouche v. Algeria*[211] all featured prolonged incommunicado detention in the form of enforced disappearance, and were found to violate the prohibition against torture and other cruel, inhuman, or degrading treatment or punishment. And, the cases of *Mukong v. Cameroon*[212] and *Aber v. Algeria*[213] both saw prolonged incommunicado detention featuring isolation also amount to such violations. While the WGAD is not bound to follow the views of the HR Committee, they remain a very useful guide as to how the WGAD may consider cases. And the HR Committee views are in line with the WGAD opinion in *Karmelo Landa Mendibe v. Spain*.

However, recent developments in international law suggest a movement toward understanding all instances of prolonged incommunicado detention without access to a court to constitute torture or other cruel, inhuman, or degrading treatment. That is to say, prolonged incommunicado detention absent additional circumstances such as isolation or enforced disappearance may nonetheless constitute cruel, inhuman, or degrading treatment and, as extended further over time, torture.

In the HR Committee's General Comment 35, it states: "Prolonged incommunicado detention violates article 9 *and would generally be regarded as a violation of article 7*."[214] Even in *Karmelo Landa Mendibe v. Spain*, the WGAD implied the emergence of this trend by concluding that "it is well known that international human rights law considers prolonged incommunicado detention as a form of torture or cruel and inhuman treatment."[215] Furthermore, the WGAD itself, in declaring that "there exist certain core minimum principles for the treatment of detainees, including the right not to be ill-treated, tortured or held incommunicado," suggested that incommunicado detention is

---

[208] El Alwani v. Libya, Communication No. 1295/2004, Human Rights Committee, CCPR/C/90/D/1295/2004, July 11, 2007, at ¶ 6.5 ("In the circumstances, the Committee concludes that *the disappearance* of the author's brother, preventing him from any contact with his family or the outside world, constitutes a violation of article 7 of the Covenant.")

[209] El Hassy & El Hassy v. Libya, Communication No. 1422/2005, Human Rights Committee, CCPR/C/91/D/1422/2005, Oct. 24, 2007, at ¶ 6.6 ("Any act leading to such *disappearance* constitutes a violation of many of the rights enshrined in the Covenant, including...the right not to be subjected to torture or to cruel, inhuman or degrading treatment or punishment (art. 7)... [*emphasis added*]").

[210] Laureano Atachahua v. Peru, Communication No. 540/1993, Human Rights Committee, CCPR/C/56/D/540/1993, Mar. 25, 1996, at ¶ 8.5. ("In the circumstances, the Committee concludes that *the abduction and disappearance* of the victim *and prevention of contact with her family and with the outside world* constitute cruel and inhuman treatment, in violation of article 7... [*emphasis added*]").

[211] Kimouche v. Algeria, Communication No. 1328/2004, Human Rights Committee, CCPR/C/90/D/1328/2004, July 10, 2007, at ¶ 7.6 (again, this is a disappearance, not merely incommunicado).

[212] Mukong v. Cameroon, Communication No. 458/1991, Human Rights Committee, CCPR/C/51/D/458/1991, July 21, 1994, at 9.4. ("In this context, the Committee recalls its General Comment 20[44] which recommends that States parties should make provision against incommunicado detention and notes *that total isolation of a detained or imprisoned person may amount to acts prohibited by article 7... [emphasis added]*").

[213] Aber v. Algeria, Communication No. 1439/2005, Human Rights Committee, CCPR/C/90/D/1439/2005, July 13, 2007, at ¶¶ 2.6, 7.3 (reading "in the circumstances" in paragraph 7.3 to include the isolation experienced by the detainee while incommunicado).

[214] General Comment No. 35, at ¶ 56 (emphasis added) (it is worth noting that the preceding sentence reiterated that arbitrary detention creates risks of torture and ill-treatment, and quite succinctly demonstrates the emerging shift in international law, from the facilitation to the actual constitution of torture).

[215] Karmelo Landa Mendibe, at ¶ 46.

its own form of torture or ill treatment by listing it as an alternative to, rather than a derivative or precursor of, such acts.[216]

Nonetheless, it remains good practice for advocates to detail specific acts and conditions within a period of prolonged incommunicado detention that, even in a non-incommunicado detention, would constitute torture or other mistreatment. Doing so helps to preserve the case for finding the detention arbitrary even if the incommunicado period was not sufficiently prolonged, and adds further gravity to the claim regardless.

It is lastly worth observing that it is not merely the detainee who may suffer torture or other ill treatment. Where the detention is not only incommunicado but also secret, it can be argued that the detainee's relatives are also being subjected to cruel, inhuman, or degrading treatment. This argument can be made where the withholding of information such as the location or more general fate of the detainee has caused the detainee's relatives serious distress and suffering.[217]

7 Incommunicado Detention – Emergency Powers and Terrorism

States may derogate from certain rights in times of "public emergency which threatens the life of the nation."[218] However, some rights remain non-derogable, such as the right to life and freedom from torture.[219] But Articles 9 and 14 of the ICCPR, those most commonly engaged under Category III, are not included within the Covenant's list of non-derogable rights. Yet, despite their lack of recognition as non-derogable rights by the Covenant itself, there is now a general consensus that "the main elements of articles 9 and 14 of the Covenant, namely the right to *habeas corpus*, the presumption of innocence and minimum fair trial guarantees, as well as the prohibition of unacknow-ledged detention, must be respected even in times of emergency, including armed conflict."[220] In fact, the WGAD is emphatic that *habeas corpus* is to be considered as a personal right, and thus non-derogable, even in times of emergency.[221]

Additionally, the right to be treated with humanity and dignity under Article 10(1) of the ICCPR has since been recognized as a non-derogable right.[222] As the previous subsections have shown, prolonged incommunicado detention is not generally con-sidered to be prohibited per se, and it is therefore not a right that could be classified as non-derogable. Yet prolonged incommunicado detention is prohibited wherever it

---

[216] Hasna Ali Yahya Husayn, et al. v. Iraq, WGAD Opinion No. 59/2011, Adopted Nov. 21, 2011, at ¶ 13.

[217] Joint Study on Global Practices, at ¶ 35.

[218] ICCPR, at Art. 4 (subject to certain conditions, such as proportionality, necessity, appropriateness and legitimacy).

[219] ICCPR, at Art. 4(2); General Comment No. 20, at ¶ 3 (affirming no derogation from Article 7, even in times of emergency).

[220] Joint Study on Global Practices at ¶ 47.

[221] *Report of the Working Group on Arbitrary Detention*, Human Rights Council, A/HRC/19/57, Dec. 26, 2011 at ¶ 63(h).

[222] *General Comment No. 29*, Human Rights Committee, CCPR/C/21/Rev.1/Add.11 (2001), at ¶13(a) ("All persons deprived of their liberty shall be treated with humanity and with respect for the inherent dignity of the human person. Although this right, prescribed in article 10 of the Covenant, is not separately mentioned in the list of non-derogable rights in article 4, paragraph 2, the Committee believes that here the Covenant expresses a norm of general international law not subject to derogation. This is supported by the reference to the inherent dignity of the human person in the preamble to the Covenant and by the close connection between articles 7 and 10.")

violates other norms and standards of international law. And, incommunicado detention, as has been illustrated, facilitates and may even constitute a number of rights violations that are not derogable – even in times of emergency – such as torture and *habeas corpus*. Therefore, both secret and prolonged incommunicado detention remain prohibited in times of emergency in just the same way as they would in times of nonemergency.

This is precisely because incommunicado detention tends to engage numerous other rights, most pertinently in the emergency context, the right of *habeas corpus*, of humane treatment, and of freedom from torture – all of which are non-derogable rights.[223] Thus, there is something of a role reversal in the emergency context. Whereas incommunicado detention is generally viewed as creating a risk of violating *habeas corpus* rights, in an emergency context the non-derogable nature of *habeas corpus* in fact functions as a safeguard against incommunicado detention. Both the WGAD and the HR Committee have issued a number of opinions and communications to this effect.[224] The right of *habeas corpus*, in the WGAD's consideration, has attained the status of a *jus cogens* peremptory norm – affording it the greatest possible protection in international law.[225] And this same reasoning holds true for torture and inhuman treatment. As a result, most international bodies would likely find prolonged incommunicado detention to be impermissible, even in times of emergency.[226]

Unfortunately, this legal status has not prevented states from repeatedly attempting to legitimize the use of prolonged incommunicado detention in times of emergency.

Despite the WGAD and HR Committee's unequivocal and repeated declarations of the continued prohibition of secret detention at all times and in all circumstances, "the practice of secret detention in the context of countering terrorism is widespread and has been reinvigorated by the 'global war on terror.'"[227] The WGAD has noted in its jurisprudence that charges of engaging in terrorist activity or financing terrorist groups has, in the present context, been used as prima facie justification for the use of prolonged incommunicado detention.[228]

The WGAD has also repeatedly expressed concerns that "states of emergency are a root cause of arbitrary detentions."[229] This is a particularly pressing concern post-9/11, with the WGAD in 2008 noting

> the continuing tendency towards deprivation of liberty by States abusing states of emergency or derogation, invoking special powers specific to states of emergency without formal declaration, having recourse to military, special or emergency courts,

---

[223] Nigel S. Rodley with Matt Pollard, The Treatment of Prisoners under International Law 487 (3rd ed. Oxford University Press, 2009).

[224] Joint Study on Global Practices, at ¶ 48. ("The Working Group on Arbitrary Detention, in its opinions No. 43/2006, 2/2009 and 3/2009, concurred with the view of the Human Rights Committee that the right to *habeas corpus* must prevail even in states of emergency. The Working Group similarly stated that the right not to be detained incommunicado over prolonged periods of time could not be derogated from, even where a threat to the life of the nation existed.")

[225] Rodley, at 488. *See also Report of the Special Rapporteur on Torture and Other Cruel, Inhuman or Degrading Treatment or Punishment*, Human Rights Council, A/HRC/25/60, Apr. 10, 2014, at ¶ 40 (noting that the prohibition against torture has also achieved *jus cogens* status).

[226] Rodley, at 488.

[227] Joint Study on Global Practices.

[228] Salim Alaradi, et al. v. United Arab Emirates, WGAD Opinion No. 51/2015, Adopted Dec. 4, 2015, at ¶ 57.

[229] Human Rights Council, *Report of the Working Group on Arbitrary Detention*, A/HRC/7/4, Jan. 10, 2008, at ¶ 64.

not observing the principle of proportionality between the severity of the measures taken and the situation concerned, and employing vague definitions of offences allegedly designed to protect State security and combat terrorism.[230]

Thus, for example, the WGAD on its trip to Turkey expressed serious concern about the "overly broad application of the term terrorism" and "severe limitations the Anti-Terror Act may put on freedom of expression, association, and assembly."[231]

The WGAD has further followed the jurisprudence of the European Court of Human Rights and other jurisdictions in holding the United States responsible for international law violations committed by its agents on foreign soil.[232] In complex circumstances such as in *Shawqi Ahmad Omar v. Iraq*, the WGAD bifurcated the detention of a captured terror suspect characterized as an "enemy combatant" by United States Forces in Iraq: it separately delineated the violations under the first detention by United States military personnel in Iraq and then under the subsequent period of his detention after his handover to Iraqi authorities.[233]

The WGAD has painstakingly reiterated the need for states to comply with the principles of proportionality, necessity, and legitimacy in such situations:

> Whatever the threat, under no circumstances may detention based on emergency legislation last indefinitely. The Working Group attaches particular importance to the existence of effective internal control mechanisms over the legality of detention. It considers the remedy of habeas corpus as one of the most effective means of preventing and combating arbitrary detention. It must not be suspended or rendered impracticable in states of emergency.[234]

Three WGAD opinions cited in the Joint Study go directly to the issue of preserving the right of *habeas corpus* in incommunicado or secret detentions carried out in the context of the War on Terror.[235] These opinions considered at length the somewhat unique claims to emergency derogations made by the United States. However, the WGAD approach to this claim to emergency derogations is in keeping with its general approach to claims of public emergency: prolonged incommunicado detention is rarely, if ever, justified. Prolonged incommunicado detention could only be justified in a time of emergency where the State authorities took such safeguards as to ensure no violation of non-derogable rights.[236] That is to say, the authorities would need to ensure that the incommunicado detention could not possibly feature torture, ill treatment, and denial of

---

[230] *Id.*, at ¶ 59.

[231] *Report of the Working Group on Arbitrary Detention: Mission to Turkey*, Human Rights Council, A/HRC/4/40/Add.5, Feb. 7, 2007, at ¶ 71. The WGAD also noted that it had found individuals accused of terrorism who have spent in some cases 7, 8, 10, and up to 13 years in detention without having been found guilty of an offense. *Id.*, at ¶ 74.

[232] Shawqi Ahmad Omar v. Iraq, WGAD Opinion No. 5/2015, Adopted Apr. 23, 2014, at ¶ 18.

[233] *Id.*, at ¶ 16.

[234] *Id.*, at ¶ 64.

[235] Ali Saleh Kahlah Al-Marri v. United States, WGAD Opinion No. 43/2006, Adopted Nov. 24, 2006; Mohammed Abdul Rahman Al-Shimrani v. United States, WGAD Opinion No. 2/2009, Adopted May 6, 2009; Sanad Ali Yislam Al-Kazimi v. United States, WGAD Opinion No. 3/2009, Adopted May 6, 2009.

[236] Yongyuth Boondee v. Thailand, WGAD Opinion No. 15/2015, Adopted Apr. 28, 2015, at ¶ 24 (restating HR Committee guidance that detention without external safeguards that extends beyond forty-eight hours should be prohibited even in circumstances of emergency).

habeas corpus. Therefore, only a relatively short period of incommunicado detention could be permitted, even where all the safeguards are present, because after a certain amount of time, incommunicado detention may itself come to constitute torture or ill-treatment, or to have denied timely *habeas corpus*, and thus result in breaches of non-derogable rights.[237]

Moreover, even where derogations are permitted because there is a "public emergency which threatens the life of the nation," derogations are still limited in that: "the State must have officially proclaimed a state of emergency; the derogation measures must be limited to those strictly required by the exigencies of the situation; they must not be inconsistent with other international obligations of the State; and they must not be discriminatory."[238] In other words: "derogation measures must be 'strictly required' by the emergency situation. This requirement of proportionality implies that derogations cannot be justified when the same aim could be achieved through less intrusive means."[239]

In *Ali Saleh Kahlah Al-Marri v. United States*, the WGAD issued an opinion concerning the detention of the first non-United States national to be held as an "enemy combatant" on United States soil.[240] Following his arrest, Al-Marri was held in incommunicado detention for over a year, including being denied even visits from the International Committee of the Red Cross.[241] The United States frequently kept detainees without charge both to extract intelligence or to prevent the detainee from being able to return to their alleged terrorist activities. In line with these aims, many such detainees held in the name of the War on Terror were denied their right of *habeas corpus*. The WGAD found this to be the case for Al-Marri:

When the moment for him to be able to challenge these charges was close,

when his "day in court" was finally approaching after a year and a half, the President designated him an "enemy combatant" and the criminal charges were dropped. Thus Mr. Al-Marri, who had been in custody of the United States government on United States territory for a year and a half, was transformed by executive decree from criminal defendant into a person apprehended in the course of an armed conflict, and thus indefinitely deprived of the right to challenge his detention and defend himself against the accusations leveled against him.[242]

The WGAD thus found Al-Marri's prolonged incommunicado detention to be arbitrary, in violation of the non-derogable right of *habeas corpus*.[243] The non-derogable nature of the right of *habeas corpus* was reiterated by the WGAD in two subsequent War

---

[237] Mikel Egibar Mitxelena, at ¶¶ 10–11 (eight days of incommunicado detention was deemed not arbitrary due to extensive safeguarding measures; see discussion in the introduction to this section).

[238] Joint Study on Global Practices, at ¶ 44.

[239] *Id.*

[240] Ali Saleh Kahlah Al-Marri, at ¶ 7.

[241] *Id.*, at ¶ 7.

[242] *Id.*, at ¶ 35.

[243] *Id.*, at ¶ 36. It is also worth noting that the United States, unlike the United Kingdom, never made any formal declaration of derogation from Article 9 in the context of the "war on terror," despite acting in ways wholly incompatible with Article 9. *See*, Alfred de Zayas, *Human Rights and Indefinite Detention*. 87 INT'L REV RED CROSS 875, 18 (2005).

on Terror cases of arbitrary prolonged incommunicado detention, including *Mohammed Abdul Rahman Al-Shimrani v. United States*[244] and *Sanad Ali Yislam Al-Kazimi v. United States*.[245]

Outside of the War on Terror context, the WGAD remains critical of states' attempts to use emergency powers to justify prolonged incommunicado detention. For example, in the case of *Islam Subhy Abd al-Latif Atiyah al-Maziny v. Egypt*, a doctor was arrested and detained incommunicado and without charge under Egypt's Emergency Act No. 162 of 1958.[246] By the time of al-Maziny's arrest, the cited emergency laws had been in effect, invoking derogations under Article 4 of the ICCPR, for over fifty years.[247] The WGAD considered Egypt's declared state of emergency to fall short of the ICCPR's requirements for derogation because, having continued for over fifty years and beyond the continuance of the cited threat to the nation, the derogations had not been strictly limited.[248] Moreover, the Government had not made any effort to show how al-Maziny's detention was in any way related to the exigencies of the alleged emergency. Thus al-Maziny's detention, including its prolonged periods spent incommunicado, was deemed arbitrary and in violation of Categories I and III.[249] Many similar opinions rejecting claims of derogations under emergency laws that had stood for decades have been issued by the WGAD concerning Sri Lanka.[250] In short, emergency situations rarely, if ever, justify prolonged incommunicado detention.

8 Incommunicado Detention – Military Courts

Another common challenge to the right to a fair trial in times of emergency is the use of military courts to try civilians.[251] Such occurrences tend to arise in times of emergency, although it is not uncommon for civilian detainees to be tried and sentenced by military courts outside of the public emergency context.[252] While the case of a civilian being brought before a military court is not restricted to cases of incommunicado detention, detainees who are not permitted contact with their family, legal counsel, or even with the civilian judicial system are at an enhanced risk of being relegated to a military court. And military courts are generally considered to fall short of international standards of fair trial.

The WGAD has found that "the trial of civilians by military tribunals usually has an adverse effect on the enjoyment of the right to liberty of person, the right to a fair and,

---

[244] Mohammed Abdul Rahman Al-Shimrani, at ¶ 33 ("It is relevant to note here that the United States has not derogated from substantive provisions of the International Covenant on Civil and Political Rights and thus remains bound by its provisions. Even if it had, the right to habeas corpus, although not explicitly enumerated in the catalogue contained in article 4 of the International Covenant on Civil and Political Rights, belongs to the non-derogable rights even in states of emergencies [footnote omitted].")

[245] Sanad Ali Yislam Al-Kazimi, at ¶ 36.

[246] Islam Subhy Abd al-Latif Atiyah al-Maziny v. Egypt, WGAD Opinion No. 20/2008, Adopted Sept. 10, 2008.

[247] *Id.*, at ¶ 15.

[248] *Id.*, at ¶¶ 20–21.

[249] *Id.*, at ¶ 25.

[250] *See, e.g.*, Uthayakumar Palani v. Sri Lanka, WGAD Opinion No. 50/2012, Adopted Nov. 19, 2012.

[251] Khalida Jarrar, at ¶ 29 (the WGAD noting that the detainee's status as a civilian rendered it improper for her to be tried by a military court that lacked the requisite impartiality and independence).

[252] *Report of the Working Group on Arbitrary Detention*, Human Rights Council, A/HRC/13/30, Jan. 18, 2010, at ¶ 70.

above all, prompt trial, the right to be brought before a judge without delay, to be released pending trial, to appeal against detention and to be tried in public by a legally established, independent, competent and impartial court, the right to a presumption of innocence, to equality of arms and to access to evidence, the right to a free and adequate defence, the right to be tried without delay, etc."[253] Thus, the trial of civilians by military courts should only happen in exceptional cases.[254] A thorough examination of the numerous Category III violations arising from the use of military courts is contained in Chapter 7(V). This subsection will therefore focus solely on the narrower intersection between incommunicado detention and the use of military courts.

As with the various other rights violations discussed in this section, incommunicado detention may serve to facilitate the trial of civilians by military courts. Conversely, military courts in some states may have a mandate to order prolonged incommunicado detention of civilians, preventing the detainee from challenging the legality of their detention and seeking redress. This was the case in *Ahmad Qatamesh v. Israel*.[255] Qatamesh was a writer and activist accused by Israel of orchestrating terrorist attacks as a member of the Popular Front for the Liberation of Palestine, both charges he denied. He was then detained incommunicado for twenty-three days, until he was brought before a military judge. Due to the incommunicado nature of his detention, Qatamesh had been unable to communicate with his legal counsel and thus to prepare his defense. The military judge at a closed session extended Qatamesh's detention by thirty days, despite him not having had counsel present to oppose the decision. During this extension period, Qatamesh was only allowed restricted access to counsel.[256]

This extended period of detention, which remained largely incommunicado, was permissible due to the military jurisdiction under which Qatamesh was tried.[257] Such military court-sanctioned incommunicado detention "denies the detainee access to any domestic procedure in court for a review . . . no avenue of redress, judicial or otherwise, to challenge the legality of the detention," and thus renders a detention arbitrary under Category III.[258] Furthermore, the denial of legal assistance is particularly damaging when a detainee is to appear before a military, rather than a civilian, court, because military courts generally lack additional due process safeguards owed to defendants, thus rendering the accused doubly vulnerable.[259] In short, the combination of incommunicado detention and the use of military courts to try civilians can easily result in violations of the right to a fair trial.

---

[253] *Id.*, at ¶ 66.

[254] *Id.*, at ¶ 69 ("i.e. limited to cases where the State party can show that resorting to such trials is necessary and justified by objective and serious reasons, and where with regard to the specific class of individuals and offences at issue the regular civilian courts are unable to undertake the trials[] (general comment No. 32, para. 22).")

[255] Ahmad Qatamesh v. Israel, WGAD Opinion No. 26/1993, Adopted Apr. 30, 1993, at ¶ 8.

[256] *Id.*, at ¶ 6.

[257] *Id.*, at ¶ 8.

[258] *Id.*, at ¶ 8.

[259] *See, e.g.*, Abdul Rahman v. Syria, WGAD Opinion No. 37/2011, Adopted Sept. 1, 2011, at ¶ 5 (noting that, in the case of Syria, the military court "does not satisfy due process guarantees.")

C Analysis of Incommunicado Detention

Prolonged incommunicado detention, while not strictly a per se violation of international law, is generally recognized as being a prohibited practice because of its facilitative role in breaches of due process, the right to a fair trial, and torture. In fact, prolonged incommunicado detention may even constitute torture or other cruel, inhuman, or degrading treatment or punishment. Over many years, the WGAD and HR Committees have found prolonged incommunicado detention impermissible and have expressed grave concern at the rising use of the practice in the context of the War on Terror. At its heart, however, incommunicado detention is a human rights concern because it takes the detainee away from the hard-fought- protections of international law and often leaves them without any means to appeal their deprivation of liberty. In its most egregious forms, such as secret detention and enforced disappearance, incommunicado detention facilitates unlawful killings with impunity and serves as a form of torture or ill-treatment of detainees. Prolonged incommunicado detention should always, therefore, be raised in a petition to the WGAD, functioning as it does to serve as a warning flag that a detainee has suffered serious violations of international law.

Short periods of incommunicado detention, however, are not themselves contrary to international laws and standards, especially where the detaining authorities can show they have upheld vigorous safeguards against due process violations and ill treatment.[260] The WGAD is nevertheless very keen to ensure any incommunicado detention occurs only when absolutely necessary and for a period of a week or so, at most. In the context of terrorism and public emergencies, the WGAD maintains these strict limitations on the use of incommunicado detention, and has shown consistent concern over the use of secret detentions. Fears of torture and ill treatment have come to the fore in the context of the systemic use of secret detention as part of the War on Terror." And the WGAD is joined by many other human rights bodies in denouncing the use of prolonged incommunicado detention at all times.

III Denial of Right to Trial or Release within Reasonable Time, Including the Right to *Habeas Corpus*

The dual rights of prompt presentation before a judge (*habeas corpus*) and trial or release within a reasonable time are enshrined in Article 9(3) of the ICCPR. The text reads:

> Anyone arrested or detained on a criminal charge shall be brought promptly before a judge or other officer authorized by law to exercise judicial power and shall be entitled to trial within a reasonable time or to release. It shall not be the general rule that persons awaiting trial shall be detained in custody, but release may be subject to guarantees to appear for trial, at any other stage of the judicial proceedings, and, should occasion arise, for execution of the judgement [*sic*].[261]

This provision relates to two periods of time: the time between the detainee's arrest and when they are brought before a judge and, if they are not released, the time between that initial hearing and the beginning of their trial. These spans of time may be elided if a

---

[260] Mikel Egibar Mitxelena.
[261] ICCPR, at Art. 9(3).

detainee is never brought before a judge or is only brought before one to begin their trial. The HR Committee has further articulated specific standards for these two periods in its General Comment No. 35. The WGAD has generally followed the HR Committee in its analysis of what is required regarding pretrial detention and hearings.

The *Basic Principles and Guidelines on Remedies and Procedures on the Right of Persons Deprived of Their Liberty to Bring Proceedings before a Court* provide extensive guidance on the specifics of this right. It applies to "any individual who is deprived of liberty in any situation by or on behalf of a governmental authority at any level, including detention by non-State actors" and "may be exercised by anyone regardless of race, colour, sex, property, birth, age, national, ethnic, or social origin," and several other statuses.[262] Furthermore, the right "applies from the moment of apprehension and ends with the release of the detainee or the final judgment," and cannot be suspended or restricted in times of war or public emergency.[263] National legal systems must guarantee this right.[264]

The Basic Principles and Guidelines also explain some concurrent requirements of the right to challenge a deprivation of liberty. Domestic procedure must allow challenges to be brought by family members or legal representatives of the detainee, regardless of whether they can prove the detainee had consented to the challenge.[265] The court must ensure the physical presence of the detainee, especially during their first hearing, and be permitted to communicate with the judge.[266] This is to guard against the abuse of detainees through torture or ill-treatment.[267]

To rule that the deprivation of liberty is lawful and nonarbitrary, the court must be satisfied that the detention followed grounds and procedures of national and international law.[268] The decision of the court must be published "without delay" in a manner that is "clear, precise, complete, and sufficient."[269] A detainee is entitled to challenge their detention periodically, after "an appropriate period of time."[270] There should be "no substantial waiting period" between an application and hearing, and no waiting period whatsoever if the application alleges torture or ill-treatment.[271]

The *Body of Principles for the Protection of All Persons under Any Form of Detention or Imprisonment* likewise provides extensive discussion on these rights. The relevant Principles are:

- Principle 11: No one shall be detained without an effective opportunity to be heard promptly before a judicial authority, who must be empowered to review as appropriate the continuing detention.
- Principle 32: Proceedings challenging a detention must be simple, expeditious, and bear no cost to the detained person.

---

[262] Basic Principles and Guidelines, at ¶¶ 3, 8.
[263] *Id.*, ¶¶ 11, 4
[264] *Id.*, ¶ 2.
[265] Basic Principles and Guidelines, at ¶ 16.
[266] *Id.*, ¶ 75.
[267] *Id.*, ¶ 75.
[268] *Id.*, ¶ 24.
[269] *Id.*, ¶ 53.
[270] *Id.*, ¶¶ 62–63.
[271] *Id.*, ¶ 64.

- Principle 36(2): Detention of a person pending trial must be carried out only for the purposes of the administration of justice (e.g. to prevent hindrance to the investigation).
- Principle 37: Anyone detained on a criminal charge must be brought before a judicial authority promptly after arrest to decide without delay on the lawfulness and necessity of their detention.
- Principle 38: Anyone detained on a criminal charge is entitled to trial or release within a reasonable time.[272]

A Right to Prompt Appearance before a Judge

In addition to the first sentence of ICCPR Article 9(3), without expressly mentioning it, Article 9(4) provides for the right to *habeas corpus*.[273] It reads:

> Anyone who is deprived of his liberty by arrest or detention shall be entitled to take proceedings before a court, in order that that court may decide without delay on the lawfulness of his detention and order his release if the detention is not lawful.[274]

This right is further protected by Principle 37 of the *Body of Principles for the Protection of all Persons under Any Form of Detention or Imprisonment*.[275] The WGAD frequently cites Principle 37, as well as Articles 9(3) and 9(4) of the ICCPR and General Comment 35 of the HR Committee.

According to the HR Committee, the term "court" can signify not only a regular court but also a special court, including an administrative, constitutional, or military court. Its decision must pertain only to the lawfulness of the detention.[276] The HR Committee has recognized that the definition of "prompt" might vary on a case-by-case basis.[277] As specified by the Body of Principles, the procedures must be simple, speedy, and free of charge if the detainee cannot afford to pay, and the detainee has the right to continuing review of the lawfulness of detention at reasonable intervals.[278] Furthermore, the state party must be the one to initiate the detainee's challenges – the WGAD does not consider the mere ability to challenge a detention sufficient.[279]

In general, the HR Committee has found forty-eight hours to be a sufficient period of time to transport the detainee and afford them a judicial hearing – any lengthier holdings

---

[272] Body of Principles.

[273] A writ requiring a person under arrest to be brought before a judge or into court, especially to secure the person's release unless lawful grounds are shown for their detention.

[274] International Covenant on Civil and Political Rights, art. 9(4).

[275] Body of Principles, at Principle 37 (Principle 37 reiterates that detainees shall "shall be brought before a judicial or other authority provided by law promptly" after arrest to "decide without delay upon the lawfulness and necessity of detention." It also provides that a detained person has a right to make a statement before this authority on the treatment they received in custody.)

[276] *But see* Vuolanne v. Finland, Communication No. 265/1987, Human Rights Committee, CCPR/C/35/D/265/1987, Apr. 7, 1989 (stating that review of detention of a soldier by a superior military officer does not satisfy Article 9(4)).

[277] General Comment No. 35, at ¶ 33.

[278] Body of Principles, at Principle 32(2), 11(3), and 39.

[279] Marcos Antonio Aguilar-Rodriguez v. United States, WGAD Opinion No. 72/2017, Adopted Nov. 21, 2017, at ¶ 64.

"must remain absolutely exceptional and be justified under the circumstances."[280] The WGAD also takes note of these specifications in its Deliberation No. 9: "The Human Rights Committee has consistently found violations of article 9, paragraph 3, of the Covenant in cases of delays of a 'few days' before the person is brought before a judge."[281] It adds that any extension of this period must be "based on adequate reasons setting out a detailed justification."[282]

The WGAD has also applied the right to be brought promptly before a judge in several cases. A period of months between arrest and presentation before a judge is an obvious violation of Articles 9(3) and 9(4). This was the case in *Kamal Foroughi v. Iran*, in which the detainee was imprisoned for over eighteen months before he finally saw a judge.[283] Similarly, in *Xing Qingxian and Tang Zhishun v. China*, an arrest in October 2015 and a presentation before a judge in May 2016 (a period of eight months) was an unacceptable delay,[284] as was a delay of three weeks in *Salah Eddine Bassir v. Morocco*.[285] A closer case was *Yara Sallam v. Egypt*, in which a human rights defender was charged with, *inter alia*, taking part in an unauthorized protest march, threatening public security, and destroying private property.[286] She was not brought before a judicial authority for eight days.[287] The WGAD found this period to be unacceptably long, and referenced the HR Committee's General Comment in saying that a delay of over forty-eight hours must remain exceptional and be justified by the particular circumstances.[288] Compliance with domestic law pertaining to pretrial or preventative detention is not a valid excuse for violations of this rule.[289] Where a detainee has been released, the WGAD may decline to consider whether a length of detention slightly longer than forty-eight hours violated the detainee's rights.[290]

The Body of Principles provides that the "judicial or other authority" before which the detainee is brought must be one established "under the law whose status and tenure should afford the strongest possible guarantees of competence, impartiality, and independence."[291] The WGAD has adopted this requirement. The detainee in *Hatem al Darawsheh v. Jordan* was brought before a public prosecutor who accused him of being a supporter of the Islamic state.[292] This was not considered "an independent judicial review of the legal basis" of his detention.[293] In *Xia Lin v. China*, this section of the Body of Principles was quoted directly, and the official responsible for prosecutions to whom the

---

[280] General Comment No. 35, at ¶ 33.

[281] Deliberation No. 9, at ¶ 66.

[282] *Id.*

[283] Kamal Foroughi v. Iran, WGAD Opinion No. 7/2017, Adopted Apr. 19, 2017, at ¶ 37.

[284] Xing Qingxian and Tang Zhishun v. China, WGAD Opinion No. 30/2016, Adopted Aug. 24, 2016, at ¶ 24.

[285] Salah Eddine Bassir v. Morocco, WGAD Opinion No. 11/2017, Adopted Apr. 20, 2017, at ¶ 46.

[286] Yara Sallam v. Egypt, WGAD Opinion No. 52/2015, Adopted Dec. 4, 2015, at ¶ 7.

[287] *Id.*, at ¶ 46.

[288] *Id.*

[289] Hassan Zafar Arif v. Pakistan, WGAD Opinion No. 8/2017, Adopted Apr. 19, 2017, at ¶ 33.

[290] Evan Mawarire v. Zimbabwe, WGAD Opinion No. 82/2017, Adopted Nov. 22, 2017, at ¶ 42 (declining to consider whether a detention of three days prior to being brought before a judge violated international law).

[291] Body of Principles, at Use of Terms.

[292] Hatem al Darawsheh v. Jordan, WGAD Opinion No. 46/2017, Adopted Aug. 22, 2017, at ¶ 20.

[293] *Id.*

detainee was presented was not considered to be a sufficient judicial authority to satisfy this requirement.[294]

In its follow-up visit to China, the WGAD briefly reviewed the conformity of the Chinese system of arrest and pretrial detention with international standards.[295] First, it criticized Chinese law, which allowed for a detainee to be held for up to seven days on the basis of a prosecutor's approval, saying that this was problematic because the decision is not prompt and is taken on the basis of the case file.[296] Second, it explained that this approach did not meet international standards: "The rationale behind the requirement that the person in custody shall be brought before a court or a judicial officer is that before taking a decision on his arrest, the suspect shall be given an opportunity to argue against this decision."[297] And finally, it expressed "doubts that the status of the procurator as regulated by Chinese law fulfills the requirement of an officer authorized by law to exercise judicial power."[298] It noted that "in the absence of any unambiguous provision stating that the individual procurators are independent in exercising their power to take decisions on pre-trial detention matters," they do not meet the requirements of Article 9 (3) of the ICCPR.[299]

Article 9(4) may also apply to asylum seekers in administrative detention who have not been afforded the ability to challenge the legality of their detention before a judge. One such case was in *Abdalrahman Hussein v. Australia*, where a Syrian asylum seeker was arrested after being reassured by authorities he did not need to take any action to renew his visa.[300] After a detention period of over three years, he had yet to see a judge. However, although the WGAD agreed this was a violation of his rights under ICCPR Article 9(4), it concluded his detention was more properly classified within Category IV (on rights of asylum seekers), not Category III (on rights of due process) of its Methods of Work. This approach was affirmed in *Mohammed Naim Amiri v. Australia*.[301]

B General Rule against Pretrial Detention

The ICCPR promotes a general rule against pretrial detention. Under Article 9(3), it says "[i]t shall not be the general rule that persons awaiting trial shall be detained in custody, but release may be subject to guarantees to appear for trial, at any other stage of the judicial proceedings, and, should occasion arise, for execution of the judgement [*sic*]." The HR Committee has interpreted this provision to require an individualized determination of whether less restrictive measures are available to ensure a criminal defendant's appearance at trial.[302] The HR Committee elaborates:

---

[294] Xia Lin v. China, WGAD Opinion No. 43/2016, Adopted Aug. 26, 2016, at ¶¶ 19–20.

[295] *Report of Working Group on Arbitrary Detention: Follow-Up Visit to People's Republic of China*, Commission on Human Rights, E/CN.4/2005/6/Add.2, Dec. 29, 2004, at ¶ 32.

[296] *Id.*, at ¶ 32(a).

[297] *Id.*, at ¶ 32(b).

[298] *Id.*, at ¶ 32(c).

[299] *Id.*,

[300] Abdalrahman Hussein v. Australia, WGAD Opinion No. 28/2017, Adopted Apr. 25, 2017, at ¶ 31.

[301] Mohammad Naim Amiri v. Australia, WGAD Opinion No. 42/2017, Adopted Aug. 21, 2017, at ¶ 42.

[302] General Comment No. 35, at ¶ 38.

Detention pending trial must be based on an individualized determination that it is reasonable and necessary taking into account all the circumstances, for such purposes as to prevent flight, interference with evidence or the recurrence of crime. The relevant factors should be specified in law and should not include vague and expansive standards such as "public security."[303]

If the pretrial detention period has reached or exceeded the longest sentence a person might receive for their charges, they must be released.[304] The presumption against pretrial detention is strongest in the case of juvenile defendants.[305]

A government cannot circumvent limits of pretrial detention by giving it another name. During its visit to Ecuador, for example, the WGAD learned about amendments to the Code of Criminal Procedure that required judges to order what is referred to as *detención en firme* of a suspect, without taking into account if the constitutionally established time limit for pretrial detention has elapsed.[306] As such rulings are not subject to appeal, detainees in this situation must remain in prison until conviction and sentencing, despite the Constitution limiting pretrial detention to no more than one year. In addressing this situation, the WGAD concluded:

> *Detención en firme* is actually a form of pretrial detention - the name that is used is immaterial - and that it establishes an indefinite period of detention that exceeds the limits established by the Constitution. It also undermines the discretionary power of judges to decide each separate case on its merits and specific characteristics and to take the measures that they deem to be the most appropriate, whether in the form of detention or alternative measures. Lastly, it affects the right of the accused to be presumed innocent until their guilt is proved.[307]

Similarly, the WGAD will evaluate on a case by case basis if a particular kind of detention, short of imprisonment in a detention facility, contravenes limits on pretrial detention under international law. In its visit to Mexico, the WGAD examined the decisions by judges, at the request of prosecutors, to issue a home-curfew order or order banning a person from leaving a specific geographical area. While acknowledging the law's intent was to avoid sending a criminal suspect to prison unnecessarily, it observed that in practice curfews have become a form of preventive detention, often enforced in a "curfew house" or hotel and where supervision is overseen by the prosecutor and not the court.[308] It further explained after visiting a curfew house that detainees are not subject to curfew in their homes but in a private establishment, which is similar to a prison in terms of security, armed guards, and surveillance. It therefore concluded that "this arrangement in fact amounts to a form of preventive detention of an arbitrary nature, given the lack of oversight by the courts and implementations of the measures in place that, while not actually secret, are 'discreet.'"[309]

---

[303] *Id.*

[304] *Id.*

[305] *Id.*

[306] *Report of the Working Group on Arbitrary Detention: Mission to Ecuador*, Human Rights Council, A/HRC/4/40/Add.2, Oct. 26, 2006, at ¶ 65.

[307] *Id.*, at ¶ 66.

[308] *Report of the Working Group on Arbitrary Detention: Mission to Mexico*, Commission on Human Rights, E/CN.4/2003/8/Add.3, Dec. 17, 2002, at ¶¶ 45–46.

[309] *Id.*, at ¶ 50.

In its case jurisprudence, the WGAD has adopted many of the HR Committee's rules limiting pretrial detention. In particular, it has several times reiterated that pretrial detention must be an individualized exception rather than a default mechanism. In *Gloria Macapagal-Arroyo v. the Philippines*, involving the arrest and detention of a former President of the Philippines, the WGAD reaffirmed "the principle that release must be the rule and provisional detention the exception."[310]

Again, in *Teymur Akhmedov v. Kazakhstan*, the WGAD asserted that pretrial detention "must be an exceptional measure and as such should be justified in each individual case and assessed by a competent, independent judge."[311] The WGAD further determined that no individualized judgment was made before the application of pretrial detention. The domestic court had provided no specific reasoning as to why detention was necessary for Akhmedov and did not consider other custodial measures. This failure to give individualized reasoning for continued detention also led the WGAD to find a breach of ICCPR Article 14, which entitled the detainee to specific reasons for the decision of the court.[312] Furthermore, the detainee had been suffering from cancer that required surgical treatment – a factor that greatly reduced flight risk and weighed heavily in favor of other custodial measures, but which was not taken into account by the domestic court. As a result, his detention was deemed arbitrary under Category III.[313] In *Kem Sokha v. Cambodia*, the WGAD noted that pretrial detention is likely also unnecessary for "high-profile political leader[s]" as well as the severely ill, given that their recognizability reduces their flight risk.[314]

This is not to say that all explanations, even if theoretically individualized, will be accepted by the WGAD as justifications for pretrial detention. The detainee in *Thiansutham Suthijitseranee v. Thailand* was not provided an explanation for the denial of his pretrial detention. The Bangkok Military Court denied him bail based on the severity of the punishment for his *lèse majesté* offense, and the fact that he was considered a flight risk.[315] The WGAD, consistent with the HR Committee, held that severity or length of a potential sentence is not a proper basis for reasoning that pretrial detention is required.[316] Furthermore, they were doubtful of the actual individuality of the determination, given that of the sixty-six individuals accused of *lèse-majesté* since 2014, sixty-two had been denied bail.[317] Between the improper basis of reasoning and the "near-blanket denial" of bail in similar cases, the WGAD ruled that the Government had not met its burden for demonstrating the necessity of pretrial detention for the detainee.[318] *Thiansutham* repeated an identical ruling handed down on the same day in *Sasiphimon Patomwong-fangam v. Thailand*.[319]

The WGAD has also expressed concern over government systems that entrench pretrial detention. During an early country mission to Viet Nam, the WGAD

---

[310] Gloria Macapagal-Arroyo v. The Philippines, WGAD Opinion No. 24/2015, Adopted Sept. 2, 2015, at ¶ 37.

[311] Teymur Akhmedov v. Kazakhstan, WGAD Opinion No. 62/2017, Adopted Aug. 25, 2017, at ¶ 41.

[312] *Id.*, at ¶ 45.

[313] *Id.*, at ¶ 46.

[314] Kem Sokha v. Cambodia, WGAD Opinion No. 9/2018, Adopted Apr. 19, 2018, at ¶ 51.

[315] Thiansutham Suthijitseranee v. Thailand, WGAD Opinion No. 56/2017, Adopted Aug. 24, 2017, at ¶ 9.

[316] *Id.*, at ¶ 68.

[317] *Id.*

[318] *Id.*

[319] *Id.*, at ¶¶ 67–68.

commented on pretrial detention centers run by provincial authorities in the country. It recounted Vietnamese authorities explaining their law "prohibited visits from any other persons, including relatives, in order to prevent outside contacts from interfering with the investigation by facilitates," declining to let the WGAD visit one of these centers.[320] In response, the WGAD "expressed its profound regret at the authorities' unyielding attitude, and hoped that such a visit would be permitted in the course of a subsequent mission, especially since this would provide evidence of the spirit of cooperation and give proof of the sincere efforts of the Vietnamese authorities to provide the transparency necessary to make such visits meaningful and productive."[321]

Another way a governmental system can perpetuate pretrial detention is by discriminating against certain classes of detainees. In visiting Canada, the WGAD observed that pretrial detention "disparately impacts on vulnerable groups, such as the poor, persons living with mental health problems, Aboriginal people, and racial minorities."[322] It noted that in evaluating whether an accused person would attend future court hearings that judges look at the accused's "roots in the community," which when applied to marginalized people is likely to lead to denial of bail.[323]

On its visit to Germany, the WGAD noted that there were a disproportionate number of foreigners in pretrial detention as "one of the deciding factors [in determining whether to grant bail] is whether the detainee has any links, including friends and family, to hold him or her in the city or country and hence prevent him or her from jumping pretrial bail or release."[324] It further explained, "[h]ere the judicial system works against foreigners, as it is easily argued that they have no ties to the city or country and may flee. Hence the large numbers of foreigners in pretrial detention."[325] In a follow-up visit to Germany, the Government claimed to the WGAD there were no data to support its prior conclusion.[326]

The WGAD made similar observations on its country mission to Italy, where it noted that foreigners were much more likely to be imprisoned awaiting trial than Italians. It noted that the statistics showed that 49 percent of Italians and 72 percent of foreigners were prisoners not serving a final sentence. And it understood that on conviction foreigners were much more likely to receive a prison sentence, much less likely to benefit from alternatives to imprisonment, and much more likely to be imprisoned for minor offenses. It concluded that the primary explanation for this unequal treatment was that the system of alternatives to imprisonment, both before and during trial and after conviction, was "to a large extent premised on the offender having a certain identity and place of residence, a family and social network, a job, roots in the community. A judge is much less likely to find that a migrant meets these requirements than an Italian."[327] In its

---

[320] *Report of Working Group on Arbitrary Detention: Visit to Viet Nam*, Commission on Human Rights, E/CN.4/1995/31/Add.4, Dec. 21, 1994, at ¶ 50.

[321] *Id.*, at ¶ 51.

[322] *Report of the Working Group on Arbitrary Detention: Mission to Canada*, Commission on Human Rights, E/CN.4/2006/7/Add.2, Dec. 5, 2005, at ¶ 63.

[323] *Id.*

[324] *Report of the Working Group on Arbitrary Detention: Mission to Germany*, Human Rights Council, A/HRC/19/57/Add.3, Feb. 23, 2012, at ¶¶ 43, 63.

[325] *Id.*

[326] *Report of the Workiing Group on Arbitrary Detention: Follow-Up Mission to Germany*, Human Rights Council, A/HRC/30/36/Add.1, at ¶ 13.

[327] *Report of the Working Group on Arbitrary Detention: Mission to Italy*, Human Rights Council, A/HRC/10/21/Add.5, Jan. 26, 2009, at ¶¶ 64–65.

follow-up visit to Italy, the WGAD reaffirmed the "need to monitor and remedy the disproportionate application of pretrial detention in the case of foreign nationals," observing that 35 percent of prisoners in Italy were foreigners, partly because of the high rate of drug arrests in a country that is a corridor for the narcotics trade.[328]

Excessive bail may also be considered an Article 9(3) violation, along with unreasonable impediments to bail. In *Hana Aghigian, et al.* v. *Iran*, twenty-four members of the Baha'i faith with no criminal histories were arrested in connection with their religion. The WGAD found bail amounts of $60,000 and $120,000 to be excessive, given that the detainees were not flight risks and posed no danger to their communities.[329] However, the WGAD neglected in this case to specify at what point bail becomes excessive, or suggest an appropriate amount of bail for a detainee with little flight or other risk. In *Stella Nyanzi* v. *Uganda*, a human rights defender was imprisoned for social media posts critical of President Museveni. She was denied bail based on a refusal to undergo a mental exam, a process normally reserved for those under allegations of crimes like rape.[330] The WGAD found this an impermissible violation of ICCPR Article 9(3). Bail is not considered a "realistic alternative to detention" for asylum-seekers, whose pretrial liberty may not be contingent on their ability to pay.[331]

However, governments may demonstrate the necessity for denial of bail and pretrial detention for a particular individual. The WGAD has reiterated the HR Committee's analysis that pretrial detention may be allowed when "based on an individualized determination that it is reasonable and necessary taking into account all the circumstances, for such purposes as to prevent flight, interference with evidence or the recurrence of crime and the relevant factors should be specified in law and should not include vague and expansive standards such as 'public security.'"[332] As such, pretrial detention may not be made mandatory for all accused of a particular offense.[333] The WGAD has interpreted Article 14 of the ICCPR to require "a reasoned, individualized judgment on the application of pretrial detention" when a judge deems pretrial detention necessary.[334]

For instance, denial of bail in *Aránzazu Zuleta Amuchástegui* v. *Spain* and the resultant pretrial detention was not arbitrary.[335] The judge had given "reasoned individual opinions" on the denial of bail and extension of pretrial detention.[336] The fact that other detainees had been released on bail did not suggest a general rule in favor of pretrial detention.[337] The WGAD therefore had no reason to believe the denial of bail was for any reason other than to secure the detainee's appearance in court.[338] In *Ronnen Hersovici* v. *Romania*, the appellate court replaced the detainee's pretrial detention with

---

[328] *Report of the Working Group on Arbitrary Detention: Follow-Up Mission to Italy*, Human Rights Council, A/HRC/30/36/Add.3, June 10, 2015, at ¶ 15.

[329] Hana Aghigian, et al v. Iran, WGAD Opinion No. 9/2017, Adopted Apr. 19, 2017, at ¶ 28.

[330] Stella Nyanzi v. Uganda, WGAD Opinion No. 57/2017, Adopted Aug. 24, 2017, at ¶ 61(e).

[331] Marcos Antonio Aguilar-Rodriguez v. United States, WGAD Opinion No. 72/2017, Adopted Nov. 21, 2017, at ¶ 59.

[332] Thiansutham Suthijitscrance v. Thailand, WGAD Opinion No. 56/2017, Adopted Aug. 24, 2017, at ¶ 67.

[333] Nguyen Dang Minh Man v. Viet Nam, WGAD Opinion No. 40/2016, Adopted Aug. 26, 2016, at ¶ 41.

[334] Teymur Akhmedov v. Kazakhstan, WGAD Opinion No. 62/2017, Adopted Aug. 25, 2017, at ¶ 45.

[335] Aránzazu Zuleta Amuchástegui v. Spain, WGAD Opinion No. 36/2015, Adopted Sept. 4, 2015, at ¶ 77.

[336] *Id.*, at ¶ 76.

[337] *Id.*

[338] *Id.*, at ¶ 77.

house arrest.[339] To the WGAD, this suggested an individual determination of his circumstances (which included medical treatment for depression and panic attacks), and as a result they were "unable to state with certainty" that the state had not met its obligation for an individualized determination and could not rule this pretrial deprivation of liberty to be arbitrary.[340]

Controversies over bail have very occasionally been relevant to Category V cases. In *María Laura Pace and Jorge Oscar Petrone v. Argentina*, a source attempted to argue that a detainee's bail, set higher than that of his co-defendants, constituted economic discrimination that rendered his detention arbitrary under Category V.[341] The WGAD was not convinced this rendered his detention arbitrary.[342] *Marcos Antonio Aguilar-Rodriguez v. United States* was a subsequent case that successfully argued economic discrimination via excessive bail.[343] This was perhaps due to more favorable facts: here, the detainee was an undocumented migrant and was one example in a pattern of the United States setting excessively high bail for persons detained during migration proceedings. The WGAD noted that this practice in general was discriminatory since it "disproportionately affects those of humble backgrounds."[344]

A government may not argue for pretrial detention on the basis of the seriousness of the alleged offense alone, rather than any risks of flight or evidence tampering.[345] This reasoning has been repeatedly used by Thai courts to authorize pretrial detention for *lèse majesté* offenders.[346] Furthermore, pretrial detention may not be mandatory when the accused is charged with a particular offense without regard for individual circumstances.[347]

In cases involving minors, permissible pretrial detention is even more exceptional. Article 37(b) of the *Convention on the Rights of the Child* (CRC) provides that "the arrest, detention or imprisonment of a child shall be in conformity with the law and shall be used only as a measure of last resort and for the shortest appropriate period of time." The WGAD has adhered to these provisions of the CRC, finding that pretrial detention of minors "should be a disposition of last resort and for the minimum necessary period and should be limited to exceptional cases."[348] For support, the WGAD has also relied on Rule 13 of the *United Nations Standard Minimum Rules for the Administration of Juvenile Justice*.[349]

---

[339] Ronnen Herscovici v. Romania, WGAD Opinion No. 17/2018, Adopted Apr. 20, 2018, at ¶ 32.

[340] *Id.*, at ¶ 38.

[341] María Laura Pace and Jorge Oscar Petrone v. Argentina, WGAD Opinion No. 73/2017, Adopted Nov. 27, 2017, at ¶¶ 12–13.

[342] *Id.*, at ¶ 57.

[343] *Id.*, at ¶ 67.

[344] Marcos Antonio Aguilar-Rodriguez v. United States, WGAD Opinion No. 72/2017, Adopted Nov. 21, 2017, at ¶ 67.

[345] Milagro Amalia Ángela Sala v. Argentina, WGAD Opinion No. 31/2016, Adopted Aug. 24, 2016, at ¶ 111.

[346] Thiansutham Suthijitseranee v. Thailand, WGAD Opinion No. 56/2017, Adopted Aug. 24, 2017, at ¶ 68.

[347] *Id.*, at ¶ 67.

[348] Concerning a Minor v. Saudi Arabia, WGAD Opinion No. 52/2016, Adopted Nov. 23, 2016, at ¶ 17.

[349] Concerning a Minor Whose Name is Known by the Working Group v. Israel, WGAD Opinion No. 3/2017, Adopted Apr. 19, 2017, at ¶ 34. Rule 13 provides that detention of juveniles should be "used only as a measure of last resort and for the shortest possible period of time," and replaced by alternative measures such as supervision in a family or educational setting wherever possible.

C Right to Trial or Release within a Reasonable Time

If a detainee is not released following their initial hearing, Articles 9(3) and 14(3)(c) of the ICCPR protect their right to a trial within reasonable time, or "without undue delay." The HR Committee has cautioned "any delay in bringing the case to trial has to be assessed in the circumstances of each case, taking into account the complexity of the case, the conduct of the accused during the proceeding and the manner in which the matter was dealt with by the executive and judicial authorities."[350] Acceptable reasons for longer periods of pretrial detention might include obstructions in the investigation of the alleged crime – however, staff and budgetary constraints are not considered valid reasons for delay.[351] The state party will need to substantiate the given reason with documentation showing why lengthy pretrial detention was required.[352] If delays continue, a judge must reconsider the necessity of pretrial detention.[353] Failure to present a detainee at hearings or to notify them of the decision is a violation of ICCPR Article 9(3).[354]

Certain conditions must be met in pretrial detention. In *Bakri Mohammed Abdul Latif v. Egypt*, the WGAD noted that Article 10(2)(a) of the ICCPR requires pretrial detainees to be held separately from convicted prisoners.[355] Additionally, those held in pretrial detention should not be held by the same authorities responsible for investigating their charges.[356]

WGAD jurisprudence follows the international norm that pretrial detention should be "as short as possible."[357] In most cases, pretrial detention periods are often unambiguously too long. For instance, in *Xia Lin v. China*, twenty months of pretrial detention without any reason given for delay was an unacceptable period.[358] The same was true for a pretrial detention period of eight months for a minor arrested in Israel, a violation that was aggravated by the detainee's young age.[359] The six-month, incommunicado pretrial detention in *Hung Linh Nguyen v. Viet Nam* was "a clear violation of the part of the well-established international law on detention."[360]

In accordance with the HR Committee admonition to limit delays in bringing cases to trial, the WGAD assesses the validity of extended pretrial detention according to the facts of an individual case. For instance, in *Nguyen Dang Minh Man v. Viet Nam*, numerous extension orders were filed for Minh Man's pretrial detention period, specifying that

---

[350] General Comment No. 35, at ¶ 37.

[351] *Id.*

[352] Lodkham Thammavong, et al. v. Laos, WGAD Opinion No. 61/2017, Adopted Sept. 15, 2017, at ¶ 32.

[353] General Comment No. 35, at ¶ 37; Mateusz Piskorski v. Poland, WGAD Opinion No. 18/2018, Adopted Apr. 20, 2018, at ¶ 50 (finding that although the petitioner's detention was under regular review every three months, the repeated renewals meant he was effectively detained indefinitely, and as such the courts must reconsider alternatives to detention).

[354] Elvis Arakaza v. Burundi, WGAD Opinion No. 54/2017, Adopted Aug. 24, 2017, at ¶ 54.

[355] Bakri Mohammed Abdul Latif, et al. v. Egypt, WGAD Opinion No. 28/2018, Adopted Apr. 24, 2018, at ¶ 85 (This right is supported by Principle 8 of the Body of Principles for the Protection of All Persons under Any Form of Detention or Imprisonment).

[356] *Id.*, at ¶ 86.

[357] Ny Sokha, et al. v. Cambodia, WGAD Opinion No. 45/2016, Adopted Nov. 21, 2016, at ¶ 51.

[358] Xia Lin v. China, WGAD Opinion No. 43/2016, Adopted Aug. 26, 2016, at ¶ 22.

[359] Concerning a Minor Whose Name is Known by the Working Group v. Israel, WGAD Opinion No. 3/2017, Adopted Apr. 19, 2017, at ¶ 34.

[360] Hung Linh Nguyen v. Viet Nam, WGAD Opinion No. 46/2015, Adopted Dec. 3, 2015, at ¶ 34.

these extensions were "necessary for the investigation."[361] The WGAD found it unsatisfactory that the presiding court did not reconsider less restrictive alternatives, such as bail, while giving these periodic extension orders.[362]

In *Xia Lin* v. *China*, the WGAD concurred with the source, when the Government did not challenge their assertion, that the reason for extended pretrial detention was the lack of evidence against the detainee, which obviously constituted an unacceptable reason for delaying trial and a violation of Article 9 of the ICCPR.[363] The arresting officials in *Nguyen Ngoc Nhu Quynh* v. *Viet Nam* stated that the detainee would be imprisoned for a year and a half pending investigation, making it clear from the time of her arrest that the authorities had no intention of respecting her ICCPR Article 9(3) right to trial within a reasonable time.[364] In *Alberto Javier Antonio March Game* v. *Ecuador*, the Government attempted to justify a pretrial detention of seventeen months by referring to the delay the detainee had caused by filing writs of *habeas corpus*.[365] The WGAD noted that observance of other human rights was not an acceptable basis for a violation of this one.

D Counting of Time in Pretrial Detention toward Final Sentence

A final issue relating to pretrial detention relates to how it should be accounted for if the detainee is subsequently convicted and sentenced to prison. The WGAD addressed this issue in relation to its visit to South Africa because its law did not require judges to deduct time spent in pretrial detention from a final sentence. In discussing this issue, the WGAD stressed "pre-sentencing custody is time actually served in detention, and often in harsher circumstances than the sentence will ultimately call for."[366] It also noted that in many countries, not only is this time accounted for, but because of the harder conditions, the time is often multiplied two or three times and deducted from the final sentence given. The WGAD concluded:

> Although the Universal Declaration of Human Rights and the International Covenant on Civil and Political Rights do not specifically emphasize the need to take into account time spent in pretrial detention for computation of the sentence, human rights doctrine (from the European Court of Human Rights, the United Nations Human Rights Committee, the Inter-American Human Rights Court and this Working Group) has concluded that the courts should take into account this period and credit their sentence accordingly. Some even add that not observing this principle could amount to a violation of article 14, paragraph 7, of the International Covenant on Civil and Political Rights, which declares that "no one shall be liable to be ... punished again for one offence for which he has already been convicted."[367]

---

[361] Nguyen Dang Minh Man v. Viet Nam, WGAD Opinion No. 40/2016, Adopted Aug. 26, 2016, at ¶ 41.

[362] *Id.*, at ¶ 41.

[363] Xia Lin v. China, WGAD Opinion No. 43/2016, Adopted Aug. 26, 2016, at ¶ 23.

[364] Nguyen Ngoc Nhu Quynh v. Viet Nam, WGAD Opinion No. 27/2017, Adopted Apr. 25, 2017, at ¶ 44.

[365] Alberto Javier Antonio March Game v. Ecuador, WGAD Opinion No. 6/2018, Adopted Apr. 28, 2018, at ¶ 61.

[366] *Report of the Working Group on Arbitrary Detention: Mission to South Africa*, Commission on Human Rights, E/CN.4/2006/7/Add.3, Dec. 29, 2005, at ¶ 72–73.

[367] *Id.*, at ¶ 74.

IV Denial of Right to a Fair Trial

A *Denial of Right to Competent, Independent, and Impartial Tribunal*

Article 14(1) of the ICCPR, detailing the various protections for a fair trial, requires that trials be adjudicated by an "independent and impartial tribunal." The relevant language appears in the second sentence of Article 14(1),[368] which reads:

> In the determination of any criminal charge against him, or of his rights and obligations in a suit at law, everyone shall be entitled to a fair and public hearing by a competent, independent and impartial tribunal established by law.

Article 10 of the UDHR provides similar language to denote that a minimum quality of adjudication is expected for the protection of a person's right on apprehension and presentation before a legally authorized judicial authority. It states in the pertinent part:

> Everyone is entitled in full equality to a fair and public hearing by an independent and impartial tribunal, in the determination of his rights and obligations and of any criminal charge against him.

Together with the necessity of a fair and public hearing, the "independent and impartial tribunal" requirement constitutes the core aspect of "due process of law."[369] Several characteristics of an "independent and impartial tribunal," and of what constitutes a "fair trial" are detailed in paragraph 3 of Article 14. This guarantee applies only to cases that concern either criminal charges or the rights and obligations of individuals in a "suit at law."[370] It is an institutional guarantee that prevents cases of these natures from being decided by political bodies or administrative authorities that may be otherwise designated.[371] Accordingly, the Body of Principles specifies that any form of detention shall be ordered by or subject to the effective control of a judicial or other body.[372] To that end, the Basic Principles and Guidelines of the WGAD specify that the reviewing court must be a different body from the one who ordered the detention, and highlights the procedure of selecting and appointing judges as a potential avenue for undermining the independence of a tribunal.[373]

The independence and impartiality requirement also ensures the quality of adjudication.[374] The HR Committee emphasized in *Bahamonde* v. *Equatorial Guinea* the critical nature of a tribunal's independence, finding a detention arbitrary in cases where the judiciary is indistinguishable from the executive, or if the executive branch has the

---

[368] General Comment No. 32, at ¶ 3, 15.

[369] Nowak, at 241.

[370] General Comment No. 32, at ¶ 15, adding that the obligation may extend to acts that are "criminal in nature" and include sanctions that, irrespective of their categorization by domestic law, must be considered penal in effect; General Comment No. 32, at ¶ 18, noting that the tribunal must, at least in one stage of proceedings, identify the relevant rights and obligations of the applicant.

[371] Nowak, at 244.

[372] Phan (Sandy) Phan-Gillis v. China, WGAD Opinion No. 12/2016, Adopted Apr. 20, 2016, at ¶ 19 (citing Principle 4).

[373] Basic Principles and Guidelines, at ¶¶ 51–52.

[374] Lauri Letimaja & Matti Pellonpaa, "Article 10," in GUDMUNDUR ALFREDSOON & ASBJORN EIDE, THE UNIVERSAL DECLARATION OF HUMAN RIGHTS: A COMMON STANDARD OF ACHIEVEMENT 223.

ability to control or direct the workings of the adjudicatory body.[375] Separation of powers or "clear demarcation" between the judiciary and executive branches is essential to Article 14 compliance.[376]

These procedural requirements are especially implicated in cases concerning juveniles subjected to detention. The WGAD issued an opinion to this effect in a case concerning two unnamed minor brothers taken from their home by Egyptian authorities and charged with participating in rioting and illegal demonstrations.[377] In its opinion, the WGAD referenced the guarantees provided by the *Convention on the Rights of the Child* to minors being detained – it noted that such detention must be lawful, rendered as a means of last resort, limited to the shortest appropriate period, and that the child deprived of liberty must be guaranteed access to counsel and the right to challenge the detention before a competent, independent, and impartial adjudicating authority.[378] In that case, however, the detainees were never presented before a judge. The fourteen- and fifteen-year-old brothers had been in detention for several months, in explicit violation of Egyptian domestic law on the rights of children.[379] Accordingly, the WGAD found a Category III violation, citing the general nonobservance of fair trial norms in international law.[380]

The nature of a court may also disqualify it from appropriately hearing the cases of minors. In *Concerning Three Minors v. Saudi Arabia*, the juvenile detainees did receive a trial from the Specialized Criminal Court of Saudi Arabia.[381] However, the WGAD ruled that it should not be trying minors, since "such a special court, specifically designed to deal with so-called terrorism cases, raises serious concerns about its lack of independence and due procedure."[382] The WGAD did not elaborate further on the point, although the application of the death sentence by the Specialized Criminal Court was of particular concern.

1 Definition of a Tribunal

General Comment 32 to the ICCPR defines a tribunal, as used in Article 14(1), as "a body, regardless of domination, that is established by law," which is "independent of executive and legislative branches of government or enjoys, in specific cases, judicial independence in deciding legal matters that are judicial in nature."[383] Generally, the term "tribunal" applies to domestic courts, both civil and criminal, but also to specially formed adjudicatory institutions that differ in some substantive way from the category of "courts."[384] The three characteristics cited – competence, impartiality, and

---

[375] Bahamonde v. Equatorial Guinea, Communication No. 468/1991, Human Rights Committee, CCPR/C/49/D/468/1991, Oct. 20, 1993, at ¶ 9.4; Joseph & Castan, at 404.

[376] *Id.*

[377] Concerning Two Minors Whose Names are Known by the Working Group v. Egypt, WGAD Opinion No. 53/2015, Adopted Dec. 4, 2015, at ¶¶ 4, 8.

[378] *Id.*, at ¶ 31.

[379] *Id.*, at ¶ 33.

[380] *Id.*, at ¶ 37.

[381] Concerning Three Minors v. Saudi Arabia, WGAD Opinion No. 61/2016, Adopted Nov. 25, 2016, at ¶ 52.

[382] *Id.*, at ¶ 59.

[383] General Comment No. 32, at ¶ 18.

[384] Nowak, at 244–245.

independence – are prerequisites that together provide an absolute right from which there can be no exemption.[385] To be compliant with Article 14(1), a government must demonstrate that the tribunal in question satisfied the three elements required by the text of Article 14(1).[386]

Failure of authorities to provide or allow access to a tribunal with these characteristics is considered a prima facie violation of Article 14(1) unless the state concerned can show that the limitations were based on domestic legislation, necessary to pursue legitimate and permissible aims, or derived from principles of international law, such as rules on immunities.[387] As an illustration of this principle, the WGAD found a violation of Article 14(1) in *Jian Qisheng, et al. v. China*, a case in which several youth activists were detained and sentenced to reeducation without being put on trial.[388] The WGAD concluded the absence of legal proceedings that satisfied Article 14(1) constituted a violation of right to fair trial of such gravity that it confers on the deprivation of liberty an arbitrary character.[389]

2 Procedural and Institutional Guarantees of Fairness and Equality

Article 14, as a whole, must also be read as providing procedural and institutional guarantees of fairness and equality, but it does not provide relief for errors made by a tribunal that is considered competent for the purposes of adjudication.[390] The duty to review facts and evidence lies with the state parties involved and a violation of Article 14 (1) will not be found unless the tribunal or court is shown to have rendered arbitrary judgment not in keeping with the obligations of independence and impartiality.[391] A further disqualification from the protection of a tribunal applies in cases where the detainee does not have a cause of action recognized by domestic law.[392] However, the right to adjudication by an "independent and impartial tribunal" cannot otherwise be limited and any criminal conviction otherwise rendered will be considered incompatible with Article 14(1).[393]

The institutional guarantee of trial by a "competent, independent and impartial tribunal" is closely linked to the procedural guarantees of the right to a fair trial.[394] In WGAD jurisprudence, it is common for sources to allege an Article 14(1) violation that

---

[385] General Comment No. 32, at ¶ 18; Gonzalez del Rio v. Peru, Communication No. 263/1987, Human Rights Committee, CCPR/C/40/D/263/1987, Oct. 28, 2002 at ¶ 5.2.

[386] Jaramani Najib Youcef v. Syria, WGAD Opinion No. 11/2003, Adopted Sept. 3, 2003, at ¶ 13.

[387] General Comment No. 32, at ¶ 18; Issam Hasan Ashqar v. Israel, WGAD Opinion No. 26/2007, Adopted Nov. 11, 2007, at ¶ 31; Ahmed Omar Einein, et al. v. Syria, WGAD Opinion No. 28/2008, Adopted Sept. 12, 2008, at ¶ 25; Dr. Said b. Mubarek b. Zair v. Saudi Arabia, WGAD Opinion No. 36/2008, Adopted Nov. 21, 2008, at ¶ 20.

[388] Jian Qisheng, et al. v. China, WGAD Opinion No. 19/1996, Adopted May 23, 1996, at ¶ 7.

[389] Id., at ¶ 7(b); Christopher Ngoyi Mutamba v. Democratic Republic of Congo, WGAD Opinion No. 37/2015, Adopted Sep. 4, 2015, ¶ 33.

[390] General Comment No. 32, at ¶ 26.

[391] Id.; Reidl-Riedenstein, et al. v. Germany, Communication No. 1188/2003, Human Rights Committee, CCPR/C/82/D/1188/2003, Nov. 2, 2004, at ¶ 7.3; Bondarenko v. Belarus, Communication No. 886/1999, Human Rights Committee, CCPR/C/77/D/886/1999, Apr. 3, 2003, at ¶ 9.3.

[392] General Comment No. 32, at ¶ 17.

[393] Id., at ¶ 18.

[394] Nowak, at 246.

implicates both institutional and procedural characteristics of the trial in question.[395] There is significant overlap, therefore, between cases in which sources allege violations of the right to public hearing and cases where the competency, independence, and impartiality of a tribunal is attacked. In *Ali Aref Bourhan* v. *Djibouti*, a case concerning several detainees accused of subversion, they alleged a general violation of procedural fair trial rights and added that the trial chaired by military judges violated the requirement of judicial independence.[396] The WGAD found a violation of Article 14(1), but did not distinguish between procedural and institutional violations.[397]

Other rulings have been even less specific where the WGAD has simply found a general violation of Article 14. This seems to be the approach if there are various Article 14 violations alleged by the source.[398] The trials in *George Mbah and Mohammed Sule* v. *Nigeria* violated various fair trial rights, including the rights to public hearing, access to counsel, and to present a defense. It was also held before a secret military tribunal.[399] The WGAD failed to explain precisely why it found the detention to be arbitrary. Instead, the WGAD found a general violation of Article 14.[400] There are, however, examples from WGAD jurisprudence in which the specific procedural violations are independent of the critique of the tribunal's independence and impartiality. In *Maikel Nabil Samad* v. *Egypt*, the WGAD criticized the shortcomings of military tribunals generally, but also specified the various procedural rights that had been violated in the detainee's specific instance.[401]

In addition to a focus on the independence and impartiality of military tribunals, the WGAD has also found general fair trial rights violations in the context of increasingly prevalent collaboration between government authorities and armed groups. In two cases concerning the conflict in Libya, *Messrs. Al Gaoud and Others* v. *Libya* and *Farida Ali Abdul Hamid and Salim Mohamed Musa* v. *Libya*, the WGAD noted the peculiar circumstances in the country. In both cases, armed groups acting in collaboration with the Government had held the detainees.[402] The WGAD found the failure of the government authorities to provide for a timely trial, access to counsel, and to generally rectify the nature of the detentions violated the detainees' right to fair trial.[403]

3 Competence of Tribunal

Competence refers to the jurisdiction of the court by law to adjudicate cases of the type brought before it in a detainee's case, and in the narrow context of Article 14(1), to rule on

---

[395] Erkin Musaev v. Uzbekistan, WGAD Opinion No. 14/2008, Adopted May 9, 2008, at ¶ 38.

[396] Ali Aref Bourhan v. Djibouti, WGAD Opinion No. 40/1993, Adopted Feb. 22, 1993, at ¶ 5.

[397] *Id.*, at ¶ 6.

[398] Mansur Muhammad Ahmad Rajih v. Yemen, WGAD Opinion No. 51/1993, Adopted Dec. 7, 1993, at ¶ 12 (a).

[399] George Mbah and Mohammed Sule v. Nigeria, WGAD Opinion No. 38/1996, Adopted Dec. 3, 1996, at ¶ 6.

[400] *Id.*, at ¶ 7.

[401] Maikel Nabil Samad v. Egypt, WGAD Opinion No. 50/2011, Adopted Sept. 2, 2011, at ¶¶ 16–17; Khalida Jarrar, at ¶ 29.

[402] Farida Ali Abdul Hamid and Salim Mohamed Musa v. Libya, WGAD Opinion No. 3/2016, Adopted Apr. 19, 2016, at ¶ 14; Messrs. Al Gaoud, Al Kadiki, and Others v. Libya, WGAD Opinion No. 4/2016, Adopted Apr. 19, 2016, at ¶ 36.

[403] Farida Ali Abdul Hamid and Salim Mohamed Musa, at ¶ 20; Messrs. Al Gaoud, Al Kadiki, and Others, at ¶ 43.

criminal charges or on rights and obligations in a "suit at law."[404] The requirement is different from the ordinary meaning of the word, which implies that the tribunal should be overseen by appropriately qualified judges.[405] Competency, along with the requirement that the tribunal be "established by law," bars the use by state parties of bodies established on an *ad hoc* or arbitrary basis by specific administrative acts.[406] It was specified during drafting of Article 14 that inclusion of the word "competent" was to emphasize that the trial be held in courts "whose jurisdiction had previously been established by law."[407]

During its country mission to Angola, the WGAD faced a situation where only 14 of 165 municipalities had courts and there was a serious shortage of qualified judges in the country. As a result, it learned that "traditional authorities" largely carried out the administration of justice at the provincial level. The WGAD noted, however, "they are not competent to order detention, a factor which adds to a large backlog of criminal cases."[408] It also expressed concern that it had received reliable information that "police officers frequently sit on the bench as assessors," which it said was a "serious violation of the right to a fair trial," especially when Angola's Constitution required criminal trials to be conducted by three judges.[409] Given the lack of judges overall, the WGAD concluded "it would be preferable that only one judge conduct the trial if this is the only way to avoid having authorities who obviously lack the necessary independence and impartiality (or the necessary qualifications) round out the composition of the criminal court."[410]

In regards to its jurisprudence, the WGAD explicitly confronted the competence requirement in *Channy Cheam* v. *Cambodia*, the case of a Cambodian opposition leader and parliamentarian accused of organizing an illegal anti-state militia group.[411] The detainee in the case was tried by a military court, despite his status as a civilian, which the authorities claimed domestic law explicitly permitted.[412] The WGAD found that the military court was not competent as required by Article 14(1) to try the detainee because later amendments had abrogated the law that permitted trial of civilians by military authorities.[413] The opinion also provided a broader policy rationale for the requirement of a "competent" tribunal, describing it a cornerstone of the right to a fair trial and highlighting that stable regulation of competence was essential to public "trust and confidence" in the judicial system.[414]

Similarly, when ruling on the competence of a civilian court, the WGAD will examine whether the tribunal in question had jurisdiction, either over the subject matter or territoriality. In *Vincenzo Scarano Spisso* v. *Venezuela*, the detainee was an elected

---

[404] Nowak, at 241.

[405] ALEX CONTE & RICHARD BURCHILL, DEFINING CIVIL AND POLITICAL RIGHTS: THE JURISPRUDENCE OF THE UNITED NATIONS HUMAN RIGHTS COMMITTEE 165 (2009).

[406] Nowak, at 245.

[407] M. J. BOSSYUT, GUIDE TO THE "TRAVAUX PRÉPARATOIRES" OF THE INTERNATIONAL COVENANT ON CIVIL AND POLITICAL RIGHTS 283 (1987), adding that the phrasing "pre-established by law" was considered but rejected.

[408] Report of the Working Group on Mission to Angola, at ¶ 83.

[409] *Id.*, at ¶ 84.

[410] *Id.*

[411] Channy Cheam v. Cambodia, WGAD Opinion No. 39/2005, Adopted Nov. 25, 2005, at ¶ 6.

[412] *Id.*, at ¶ 14.

[413] *Id.*, at ¶ 19.

[414] *Id.*, at ¶ 23.

mayor tried in a criminal proceeding before the Constitutional Chamber for contempt of court.[415] The WGAD noted that the Constitutional Chamber itself specified that competence to render convictions for contempt lay with ordinary criminal courts after the Public Prosecution Service levied such a charge.[416] The WGAD then specified that the appropriate and competent body to prosecute and try the accused, per the Code of Criminal Procedure, was the Public Prosecution Service.[417] A finding that the court adjudicating the case was not a "competent tribunal" was considered sufficient grounds for the WGAD to conclude that the Article 14 right to fair trial had been violated.[418]

Instances in which jurisdiction is asserted by a military court may provide grounds for detainees to challenge the detention for lack of competence. In *Abdejdjouad Ameur Al Abadi* v. *Egypt*, a civilian was detained for his political activity and convicted by a military tribunal, but later obtained a release order from the ordinary civilian court.[419] Following his release, the person was again detained by security agencies under an emergency law, tried before a military tribunal, and convicted.[420] The WGAD noted that the military failed to honor release orders issued by a competent civilian court and ruled that there was no basis for the detainee's re-arrest and trial.[421] By implication, the language of the WGAD in its opinion on Al Abadi's detention suggests that the military tribunal was not a "competent tribunal" for the case, given that ordinarily competent civilian courts existed in parallel.

States may not cite the designation of a tribunal as a military court to exempt themselves from Article 14(1) guarantees.[422] The HR Committee is generally critical of the trial of civilians by military courts and tribunals, out of concern for impartiality and equity, and requires additional safeguards to be provided for such instances.[423] The use of military courts compliant with Article 14(1) requirements is permitted, but only when justified by objective and serious reasons and if regular courts are unable to hold trials.[424] The WGAD has stated "one of the most serious causes of arbitrary detention is the existence of special courts, military or otherwise."[425] It most strongly expressed its repugnance of military tribunals to try civilians in *'Abla Sa'adat et al.* v. *Israel*, a case of several human rights activists held in administrative detention and later tried by a military court under exclusive military jurisdiction.[426] The WGAD referred to its foundational position on military justice too, which states:

> If some form of military justice is to continue to exist, it should observe four rules: (a) it should be incompetent to try civilians; (b) it should be incompetent to try military

[415] Vincenzo Scarano Spisso v. Venezuela, WGAD Opinion No. 1/2015, Adopted Apr. 20, 2015, at ¶¶ 25–26.
[416] *Id.*, at ¶ 30.
[417] *Id.*
[418] *Id.*, at ¶ 31.
[419] Abdeldjouad Mahmoud Ameur Al Abadi v. Egypt, WGAD Opinion No. 22/2007, Adopted Nov. 22, 2007, at ¶¶ 6, 10–11.
[420] *Id.*, at ¶ 29.
[421] *Id.*, at ¶ 30.
[422] General Comment No. 32, at ¶ 22.
[423] *Id.*; General Comment No. 32, at ¶ 11; *Concluding Observations on Chile*, Human Rights Committee, CCPR/C/79/Add.104, at ¶ 9; Joseph & Castan, at 408.
[424] Conte & Burchill, at 168–169.
[425] Juan Ondo Abaga, et al. v. Equitorial Guinea, WGAD Opinion No. 2/2008, Adopted May 7, 2008, at ¶ 10.
[426] Abla Sa'adat et al. v. Israel, WGAD Opinion No. 3/2004, Adopted May 25, 2004, at ¶¶ 27, 29.

personnel if the victims include civilians; (c) it should be incompetent to try civilians and military personnel in the event of rebellion, sedition or any offence that jeopardizes or involves risk of jeopardizing a democratic regime; and (d) it should be prohibited [from] imposing the death penalty under any circumstances.[427]

There are various examples where the WGAD has found trials by military courts in violation of Article 14, citing the failure of such bodies to provide procedures that safeguard the rights of the detainee.[428] This is consistent with the HR Committee's warning that "often the reason for the establishment of (military) courts is to enable exceptional procedures to be applied which do not comply with ordinary standards of justice."[429] In *Annimmo Bassey, et al. v. Nigeria*, the WGAD specified the reasons why the military court could not be considered compliant with Article 14(1), which included the secrecy of trial and failure to provide access to counsel.[430] The WGAD took a similar approach in *Lori Berenson v. Peru*, the case of an American charged with the crime of treason in Peru.[431] In *'Abdel Rahman al-Shaghouri v. Syria*, the WGAD accepted the source's argument that the Syrian Supreme State Security Court's severe restrictions on the right to obtain legal representation and absent process for appeal renders the Court "neither independent nor impartial."[432]

An evaluation of procedural compliance is therefore necessary to establishing that the institutional guarantee of "competent, independent and impartial" tribunals is violated.[433] The explicit barring by military courts of judicial review by regular civilian courts also suggests a lack of judicial independence, and has been used by the WGAD to find a violation of Article 14(1) institutional guarantees.[434] Even if an opportunity for review is provided, the absence of other procedural safeguards may still create a violation of an applicant's fair trial rights.[435] The WGAD in the cases of detainees at Guantanamo Bay, Cuba, has required that a "meaningful review process" be provided.[436] In *Juan Ondo Abaga v. Equatorial Guinea*, the WGAD illustrated an example of military jurisdiction that could be considered too expansive.[437] Irregular general compliance with *habeas corpus*, rights to counsel and to present a defense, and barred avenues for appeals

---

[427] *Id.*, at ¶ 28; *Report of the Working Group on Arbitrary Detention*, Commission on Human Rights, E/CN. 4/1999/63, at ¶ 80.

[428] Mohammad Shahadeh, et al. v. Syria, WGAD Opinion No. 6/2004, Adopted May 26, 2004, at ¶ 10; Haytham al-Maleh v. Syria, WGAD Opinion No. 27/2010, Adopted Nov. 22, 2010, at ¶ 31; Tuhama Mahmour Ma'ruf v. Syria, WGAD Opinion No. 39/2011, Adopted Sept. 1, 2011, at ¶ 14; Tal Al-Mallouhi v. Syria, WGAD Opinion No. 38/2011, Adopted Sept. 1, 2011, at ¶ 13.

[429] *General Comment No. 13*, Human Rights Committee (1984), at ¶ 4; Mohammed Amin Kamal, et al. v. Egypt, WGAD Opinion No. 57/2011, Adopted Nov. 17, 2011, at ¶ 17

[430] Annimmo Bassey, et al. v. Nigeria, WGAD Opinion No. 37/1996, Adopted Dec. 3, 1996, at ¶ 6.

[431] Lori Berenson v. Peru, at ¶ 6.

[432] Abdel Rahman al-Shaghouri v. Syria, WGAD Opinion No. 4/2005, Adopted May 24, 2005, at ¶ 14.

[433] Vicenzo Scarano Spisso, at ¶¶ 29–31, detailing the various procedural errors while finding that the Constitutional Court was not a competent tribunal for the case.

[434] U Tin Oo v. Myanmar, WGAD Opinion No. 11/2005, Adopted May 26, 2005, at ¶ 9; Suleymane Ramadhan v. Egypt, WGAD Opinion No. 18/2008, Adopted Sept. 9, 2008, at ¶ 17; Sayed Mohammed Abdullah Nimr, et al. v. Egypt, WGAD Opinion No. 11/2012, Adopted May 3, 2012, at ¶ 18; Ouda Seliman Tarabin v. Egypt, WGAD Opinion No. 12/2012, Adopted May 3, 2012, at ¶ 20.

[435] Sanad Ali Yislam Al-Kazimi v. United States, WGAD Opinion No. 3/2009, Adopted May 6, 2009, at ¶ 26.

[436] Mohammed Abdul Rahman Al-Shimrani v. United States, WGAD Opinion No. 2/2009, Adopted May 6, 2009, at ¶ 32.

[437] Juan Ondo Abaga, at ¶ 11.

make it likely that the WGAD will find the military tribunals to have violated fair trial principles in specific instances.[438]

The WGAD has explicitly dispelled the idea that the criteria for determining whether a trial is fair have exclusively to do with procedures rather than with the nature of the tribunal. This was the Government's argument in *Suleymane Ramadhan* v. *Egypt*.[439] The WGAD distinguished between the judicial attitudes of civilian and military judges, noting that the latter are bound to obedience whereas the duty of the civilian judge requires independence.[440] It observed the close control of the executive, which appoints judges and allocates cases to the military tribunals.[441] In another case concerning the same system, *Mohamed Khirat al-Shatar* v. *Egypt*, the WGAD ruled the Egypt military tribunal lacked the requisite independence, competence, and objectivity because the judges were subject to close control of higher military authorities and lack the qualifications expected of judges.[442]

As this jurisprudence shows, the WGAD's primary concern is that military courts answer directly to the executive and therefore lack the requisite independence demanded by Article 14(1).[443] Military control of the entire process – from arrest to detention, trial, and conviction – has also been argued by detainees to demonstrate a "structural bias."[444] The WGAD reiterated conclusively in *Hamdi Al Ta'mari and Mohamad Baran* v. *Israel* that "military tribunals are neither independent nor impartial," since judges are subject to military discipline and remain dependent on supervisors for promotions and appointments.[445] As a result, the WGAD has uniformly held that military tribunals cannot guarantee conditions of fair trial or due process.[446] The WGAD's opinion in *Haytham al-Maleh* v. *Syria* cites Principle 8 of the *Draft Principles Governing the Administration of Military Tribunals* for guidance, which provides that "the jurisdiction of military courts should be limited to offences of a strictly military nature committed by military personnel."[447] The jurisprudence of the WGAD makes it clear that it envisages the role of military courts, should they be permitted to exist, to be very limited and completely barred from trying civilians.[448] This includes also guaranteeing that retired military officers be tried as civilians, with the mandate of military courts being limited strictly to serving military personnel only.[449]

---

[438] *Id.*, at ¶ 13.

[439] Suleymane Ramadhan, at ¶ 10.

[440] *Id.*, at ¶ 13.

[441] *Id.*

[442] Mohamed Khirat al-Shatar, et al. v. Egypt, WGAD Opinion No. 27/2008, Adopted Sept. 12, 2008, at ¶ 84.

[443] Mohamed Rahmouni v. Algeria, WGAD Opinion No. 33/2008, Adopted Nov. 20, 2008, at ¶ 14.

[444] Sanad Ali Yislam Al-Kazimi, at ¶ 14.

[445] Hamdi Al Ta'mari and Mohamad Baran v. Israel, WGAD Opinion No. 5/2010, Adopted May 6, 2010, at ¶ 31; Ahmad Qatamesh v. Israel, WGAD Opinion No. 58/2012, Adopted Nov. 20, 2012.

[446] Mohammad Abu-Shalbak v. Palestinian Authority, WGAD Opinion No. 13/2010, Adopted May 7, 2010, at ¶ 17.

[447] Haytham al-Maleh, at ¶ 30.

[448] *Id.*, at 28; Khaled Mohamed Hamza Abbas v. Egypt, WGAD Opinion No. 35/2014, Adopted Aug. 28, 2014, at ¶ 17.

[449] Juan Carlos Nieto Quintero v. Venezuela, WGAD Opinion No. 29/2014, Adopted Aug. 28, 2014, at ¶ 18.

4 Independence of Tribunal

The features relevant to gauging the independence of a tribunal may include the procedure by which judges were appointed, the qualification and competency of judges, and an assessment of the various factors that may influence adjudicators, such as guarantees of security, tenure, transfer, promotion, and suspension, and protections from political interference.[450] The guarantee is also intended to ensure that judges remain immune from the influence of powerful social groups, including the media, and from threats by litigants or concerned groups.[451]

Independence is objectively strengthened by constitutional guarantees or clear rules, procedures, and criteria regarding judicial appointments and conduct.[452] In its visit to Belarus, the WGAD noted "with concern that the procedure relating to tenure, disciplinary matters, and dismissal of judges at all levels to do not comply with the principle of independence and impartiality of the judiciary."[453] It found the President made all appointments and that judges of the Constitutional Court and Supreme Court could be summarily dismissed by the President, without any safeguards.[454]

And in its country mission to Equatorial Guinea, the WGAD observed that the legal status of the judiciary did not sufficiently guarantee its independence and that, in practice, only lawyers who supported the political party of the Government were elected as judges and law officers.[455] Unclear allocation of powers between judges or courts at different levels of the domestic judiciary has also been found by the WGAD to violate the independence criteria for competent tribunals.[456]

The WGAD has also found that courts' failure to compel the prosecution to present their case in a timely manner could also suggest a lack of independence.[457] In that case, *Befekadu Hailu and Others v. Ethiopia*, prosecutors delayed proceedings, despite repeated authorization of the trial by the court, causing the accused to be detained for almost eighteenth months before they could be acquitted.[458]

The drafting history of Article 14(1) reveals the emphasis on judicial freedom, with earlier versions of the text reflecting an effort to emphasize that judges be subject only to the law.[459] Judges must be provided process and opportunity to contest a dismissal prior

---

[450] General Comment No. 32, at ¶ 18; Joseph & Castan, at 404, noting that the HR Committee has in several instances found violations of Article 14, e.g. immovability of judges only after ten years of work, selection of judges by popular vote for six-year terms, and the vested power of the President to remove judges without adequate oversight.

[451] Nowak, at 245; Joseph & Castan, at 405; *Concluding Observations on Brazil*, Human Rights Committee, CCPR/C/79/Add.66, at ¶ 11.

[452] General Comment No. 32, at ¶ 19; Concluding Comments on Slovakia (1997), Human Rights Committee, CCPR/C/79/Add.79, at ¶ 18; Joseph & Castan, at 405, note that the HR Committee seems to discourage the prevalent practice of appointing judges by nomination or selection by the executive, except without very strict guidelines

[453] *Report of the Working Group on Arbitrary Detention: Mission to Belarus*, Commission on Human Rights, E/CN.4/2005/6/Add.3, Nov. 25, 2004, at ¶ 44.

[454] Id.

[455] *Report of the Working Group on Arbitrary Detention: Mission to Equatorial Guinea*, Human Rights Council, A/HRC/7/4/Add.4, Feb. 18, 2008, at ¶¶ 59–60.

[456] Shamila (Delara) Darabi Haghighi v. Iran, WGAD Opinion No. 4/2008, Adopted May 7, 2008, at ¶ 42.

[457] Befekadu Hailu and Others v. Ethiopia, WGAD Opinion No. 10/2016, Adopted Apr. 20, 2016, at ¶ 49.

[458] Id.

[459] Bossyut, at 282.

to their end of term in office.[460] Dismissal without specified reason or for grounds other than serious misconduct or incompetence may suggest that the judiciary is not wholly immune from executive influence.[461] Even in cases where officials are accused of misconduct or corruption, all proper procedures must be followed before dismissal is considered properly effected.[462]

Tenure is not only encouraged but considered essential to judicial independence.[463] The absence of tenure was a prominent reason for the WGAD's finding of a violation of the institutional safeguards in *Ahmed Mansoor v. United Arab Emirates*.[464] Ensuring the requirement of tenure is fulfilled may require a judge-specific assessment. In *Nasser Bin Ghaith v. United Arab Emirates*, an Egyptian judge tried the detainee.[465] Although the Government's Emirati judges receive tenure, non-national judges rely on annual contract renewal, which leaves them vulnerable to pressure from the Government.[466] The WGAD thus found that the detainee did not receive a hearing from an independent (or impartial) tribunal in violation of Article 10 of the UDHR.[467]

In its assessment of a court's independence, the WGAD may refer to observations made by various UN Special Procedures and draw on its own expert observations. In *Mikhail Marnych v. Belarus*, the case of a former member of the Belarusian Parliament accused of disclosing state secrets, the WGAD substantiated its ruling by drawing from a report from the Special Rapporteur on the Independence of Judges and Lawyers, which remarked that judicial independence in the country was "systematically undermined" by executive control.[468] The WGAD noted the detention order came from the prosecutor without ratification by the courts, as was the general practice.[469] Finally, the WGAD commented on the procedures for tenure and selection of judges, remarking that the rules fell short of expected international standards.[470] These institutional features taken together were held to violate the applicant's Article 14 right to fair trial.[471]

Similarly, in *Aung San Suu Kyi v. Myanmar*, one of a series of cases regarding her infamous periods of house arrest, the WGAD borrowed from the Special Rapporteur's findings that the judiciary "is far from independent" and "under the direct control of the Government (in its current functioning)" in finding that the institutional requirements were not satisfied.[472] The WGAD, finding a specific Article 14(1) violation in *Antonio José Ledezma Díaz v. Venezuela*, noted that the judge indicting the detainee was a provisional appointee, capable of being removed at short notice, and that the prosecutors, too, were

---

[460] General Comment No. 32, at ¶ 20; Pastukhov v. Bulgaria, Human Rights Committee, Communication No. 814/1998, CCPR/C/78/D/814/1998, Aug. 5, 2003, at ¶ 7.3.

[461] General Comment No. 32, at ¶ 20.

[462] *Id.*; Mundyo Busyo, et al. v. Democratic Republic of Congo, Communication No. 933/2000, Human Rights Committee, CCPR/C/78/D/933/2000, July 31, 2003, at ¶ 5.2.

[463] Joseph & Castan, at 405.

[464] Ahmed Mansoor v. United Arab Emirates, WGAD Opinion No. 64/2011, Adopted Nov. 22, 2011, at ¶ 23.

[465] Nasser Bin Ghaith v. United Arab Emirates, WGAD Opinion No. 76/2017, Adopted Nov. 21, 2017, at ¶ 79.

[466] *Id.*

[467] *Id.*

[468] Mikhail Marnych v. Belarus, WGAD Opinion No. 37/2005, Adopted Sept. 2, 2005, at ¶ 12(b)(i).

[469] *Id.*, at ¶ 34.

[470] *Id.*, at ¶ 39.

[471] *Id.*, at ¶ 40.

[472] Aung San Suu Kyi v. Myanmar, WGAD Opinion No. 12/2010, Adopted May 7, 2010, at ¶ 31 (Litigated by Author through Freedomn Now).

temporary staff.[473] The WGAD took the opportunity to remark generally on the lack of independence and autonomy of judges and prosecutors in the country, and raised a point of caution regarding the overreach of military authorities into matters more properly entrusted to civilian control.[474]

The practice of "faceless judges," also provides serious cause to suspect the independence of the adjudicating tribunal. The WGAD explained its views in *Fidel Ernesto Santana Mejia, et al.* v. *Colombia*, a case in which four Dominican citizens were indicted by a secret judge for participating in guerrilla activities.[475] The WGAD said that in cases where the judge is accorded the privilege of keeping his identity confidential, out of concern for security or for other reasons, the authorities must take supplementary safeguards to ensure that the judge remains independent and impartial in that specific instance.[476] In other cases, the WGAD has considered the use of faceless judges as "contrary to the principle of independent and impartial courts."[477]

5 Impartiality of Tribunal

To be considered impartial within the meaning of Article 14(1) the judgment rendered must be objectively free of bias or prejudice toward either party and give the appearance of impartiality to a disinterested observer.[478] The condition of impartiality is incumbent on both judges and juries.[479] The involvement of a judge personally related to a party in the case is patently inconsistent with the requirement.[480] Additionally, in its *Concluding Observations on Sudan*, the HR Committee emphasized the need for a judiciary that is representative of the population it serves, with specific emphasis on the inclusion of religious minorities and women.[481] The drafters of Article 14(1), concerned that justice would be undermined by inequalities and social privilege, considered requiring that the tribunal be established according to "democratic principles," though this language was ultimately rejected.[482]

In testing for impartiality, the WGAD seems to take a case-specific approach, testing the various parts of the trial for evidence of bias. When a judge in *Aramais Avakyan* v. *Uzbekistan* neglected to intervene when the accused was carried into his hearing on a stretcher as a result of the torture he had endured, the WGAD considered this to be a breach of the right to an impartial trial.[483]

---

[473] Antonio José Ledezma Díaz v. Bolivarian Republic of Venezuela, WGAD Opinion No. 27/2015, Adopted Sept. 3, 2015, at ¶ 30.

[474] *Id.*, at ¶¶ 31–34.

[475] Fidel Ernesto Santana Mejia, et al. v. Colombia, WGAD Opinion No. 26/1994, Adopted Sept. 29, 1994, at ¶ 5 (b), (h).

[476] *Id.*, at ¶ 5(h).

[477] Edilberto Aguilar Mercedes v. Peru, WGAD Opinion No. 29/2000, Adopted Nov. 27, 2000, at ¶ 9.

[478] General Comment No. 32, at ¶ 21; Karttunen v. Finland, Communication No. 387/1989, Human Rights Committee, CCPR/C/46/D/387/1989, Oct. 23, 1992, at ¶ 7.2.

[479] Conte & Burchill, 168.

[480] Raúl Linares Amundaray v. Venezuela, WGAD Opinion No. 28/2012, Adopted Aug. 29, 2012, at ¶ 18.

[481] *Concluding Observations on Sudan*, Human Rights Committee, CCPR/C/79/Add.85, at ¶ 21; Joseph & Castan, at 405, commenting on the importance of a "pluralistic judiciary" and the representation of "diverse values" within the judiciary.

[482] Bossyut, at 282.

[483] Aramais Avakyan v. Uzbekistan, WGAD Opinion No. 29/2017, Adopted Apr. 26, 2017, at ¶ 65.

In *Mansur Muhammad Ahmad Rajih* v. *Yemen*, the WGAD ruled that the selective inclusion of testimonies and failure of the courts to detail grounds for inadmissibility of certain pleadings evinced an objective bias.[484] Interestingly, the WGAD, in the case, also looked at allegations of pretrial treatment in ruling that the trial was likely driven by "mala-fide intent."[485] The use of torture and other forms of physical abuse may strengthen detainees' Article 14(1) claims, when present alongside substantive institutional shortcomings. In *Julio Rondinel Cano* v. *Peru*, the WGAD found the impartiality requirement violated as a result of the detainee's trial being suspended for more than eighteen months, denial of bail, and the failure of authorities to designate a court to resume the trial.[486] By a similar assessment, the court's willingness to sentence the detainee in *Alan Phillip Gross* v. *Cuba* to fifteen years in prison after a trial lasting barely two days was found to have violated the requirement.[487] Sometimes, the bias of a judge or panel of judges can be astonishing. A panel of judges in the domestic proceeding examined by the WGAD in *Mohamed Nasheed* v. *The Maldives* rendered a judgment that actually said "Defence witnesses would not be able to refute the evidence submitted by the prosecution against Mohamed Nasheed and hence, it was decided not to call any defence witnesses to the court." This was one of numerous violations of the detainee's due process rights.[488]

In some cases, the WGAD has found the requirement of impartiality to have been breached without much guidance or explanatory discussion.[489] In *Jacobo Silva Nogales, et al.* v. *Mexico*, a case concerning several social activists detained and tried in prison, the WGAD ruled that the trials could not be considered impartial.[490] The WGAD presumably based its finding on the various procedural shortcomings of their trials, the most significant of which was the secret nature of the proceedings and the associated limitations set by the judge on participation by concerned relatives of the accused.[491] The WGAD noted that the trial "was not conducted with the safeguards of impartiality," but did not consider it necessary to enumerate what specific safeguards were not or may have been taken.[492] In *Wang Bingzhang, et al.* v. *China*, the WGAD made a similar ruling, relying on procedural shortcomings in the trial to find that the institutional safeguards were violated as a result.[493]

In *Boniface Muriuki Chuma, et al* v. *South Sudan*, however, the WGAD provided a more extensive analysis of the impartiality of a "committee" adjudicating on the fate of five private workers detained at a National Security Camp.[494] The initial case concerning

---

[484] Mansur Muhammad Ahmad Rajih, at ¶ 10.

[485] *Id.*

[486] Julio Rondinel Cano v. Peru, WGAD Opinion No. 21/1994, Adopted Sept. 29, 1994, at ¶ 7(j).

[487] Alan Gross v. Cuba, WGAD Opinion No. 69/2012, Adopted Nov. 23, 2012, at ¶ 30 (Litigated by Author through Perseus Strategies).

[488] Mohamed Nasheed v. The Maldives, WGAD Opinion No. 33/2015, Adopted Sept. 4, 2015 (Litigated by Author through Freedom Now with Co-Counsel Amal Clooney and Ben Emmerson QC).

[489] Ryad Hamoud Al-Darrar v. Syria, WGAD Opinion No. 15/2006, Adopted May 12, 2006, at ¶ 16; Kyaw Zaw Lwin a.k.a. Nyi Nyi Aung v. Myanmar, WGAD Opinion No. 23/2010, Adopted Sept. 2, 2010, at ¶ 19.

[490] Jacobo Silva Nogales, et al. v. Mexico, WGAD Opinion No. 37/2000, Adopted Nov. 27, 2000, at ¶ 12.

[491] *Id.*, at ¶ 8(iii).

[492] *Id.*, at ¶ 12.

[493] Wang Bingzhang, et al. v. China, WGAD Opinion No. 10/2003, Adopted May 9, 2003, at ¶ 27(e).

[494] Boniface Muriuki Chuma, et al. v. South Sudan, WGAD Opinion No. 18/2016, Adopted Apr. 27, 2016, at ¶¶ 6–7.

the culpability of the accused in cybertheft was to be heard by the High Court.[495] The accused, however, were subsequently informed that the Court had dismissed their case and a "committee" of unspecified nature and composition was now handling their case.[496] The WGAD expressed concern that the "committee" could override the judicial power of the High Court and exercise competence over all stages of the judicial process.[497] The WGAD noted that the entity referred to as the "committee" was of an "exceptional character" and in violation of the requirement of an impartial tribunal.[498]

6 Intersection between Independence and Impartiality

The WGAD's analysis of impartiality may overlap with its assessments of a tribunal's independence and competence. In *Abassi Madani and Ali Benhadj v. Algeria*, the detainees, known political dissenters, were sentenced by a tribunal established by writ of the military and security forces.[499] The WGAD in its opinion noted that the adjudicatory body remained hierarchically subordinate to security officials, and that the military authorities appointed the civilian judge.[500] This violated the guarantees of both independence and impartiality.[501] The WGAD also noted that the tribunal had no manifest jurisdiction and did not follow standard trial procedures.[502] This latter observation was taken as evidence that the trial was not impartial, though the WGAD may more accurately have specified that the tribunal was not sufficiently competent to try the detainees.[503] In *Adam al Natour v. Jordan*, the WGAD relied on observations from the HR Committee about specialty courts in Jordan (such as the State Security Court that tried the detainee) in finding a concurrent lack of independence and impartiality.[504] Similar "faceless" judges or courts have also prompted the WGAD to find a concurrent lack of impartiality and independence, although such courts are more often addressed under the right to a public hearing.[505]

Yet in other cases the WGAD has explicitly separated the independence and impartiality analyses. In *Mustapha Adib v. Morocco*, the detainee, a whistleblower in the Moroccan army, was put on trial before a military tribunal that ignored earlier orders on the same case made by a civilian court.[506] The WGAD in its assessment noted the various peculiar procedures that the military tribunal required in the detainee's case to highlight that the trial had not been impartial, as required by Article 14(1).[507] To gauge the tribunal's independence, the WGAD explicitly critiqued the structure of the institution, its appointment procedures, and its composition to find that "(the tribunal) was the type

---

[495] *Id.*, at ¶¶ 9, 25(iii).
[496] *Id.*
[497] *Id.*, at ¶¶ 26–27.
[498] *Id.*, at ¶ 27.
[499] Abassi Madani and Ali Benhadj v. Algeria, WGAD Opinion No. 28/2001, Adopted Dec. 3, 2001, at ¶¶ 7, 9.
[500] *Id.*, at ¶ 24.
[501] *Id.*
[502] *Id.*, at ¶ 20.
[503] *Id.*
[504] Adam al Natour v. Jordan, WGAD Opinion No. 39/2016, Adopted Aug. 26, 2016, at ¶ 27.
[505] Mekan Yagmyrov, et al. v. Turkmenistan, WGAD Opinion No. 70/2017, Adopted Nov. 20, 2017, at ¶ 69.
[506] Mustapha Adib v. Morocco, WGAD Opinion No. 27/2001, Adopted Dec. 3, 2001, at ¶ 12.
[507] *Id.*, at ¶ 19.

of court whose independence from the executive is often in doubt."[508] The impartiality finding, importantly, was based on different factors.

The identity or composition of the court and its relationship to the detainee may also be relevant for a finding of bias or partiality. *Grigorii Pasko* v. *Russia* concerned a detainee who was a naval officer and journalist accused of spying by publishing an article critiquing the Russian Navy's methods of disposing nuclear waste from retired submarines.[509] Naval authorities in a military court conducted his trial.[510] The WGAD found the trial could not be considered impartial since the detainee was tried by the same authorities he had criticized.[511]

In *Xing Qingxian and Tang Zhishun* v. *China*, the WGAD ruled, perhaps obviously, that the official responsible for prosecution cannot be an impartial or independent authority to try the case at hand.[512] In *Saddam Hussein al-Tikriti* v. *Iraq and United States*, the WGAD noted that the presiding judges of the tribunal formed to try the former Iraqi head of state had been changed several times due to political pressure, giving the appearance of bias against the detainee.[513] Additionally, the authorities' failure to verify the qualifications of judges and test for links to political parties contributed to the WGAD's finding that the tribunal could not be considered impartial and independent.[514] In *Mohammed Rashid Hassan Nasser al-Ajami* v. *Qatar*, the investigating judge went on to serve as the presiding judge in the subsequent criminal trial and could not be considered impartial.[515]

Similarly, the identity of the judges or jury in connection with the nature of the case may also yield either an appearance or objective evidence of impartiality. In *Ayub Masih* v. *Pakistan*, the detainee was a member of the Christian religious minority in his country, and was accused of passing blasphemous remarks about Islamic tenets.[516] The statute under which he was charged mandated a Muslim judge hear the case and that the burden of proof lay with the detainee to show that he had not made the offensive remarks.[517] The WGAD found, on the basis of the identity of the judge, the charged religious fervor surrounding the case, and assorted procedural violations, that the trial could not be considered impartial.[518] Similarly, in *Antonio Herreros Rodriguez et al.* v. *United States*, the WGAD ruled that conducting a jury trial in the midst of an emotionally charged climate of "bias and prejudice" against the accused may not be satisfactorily impartial.[519] The WGAD noted that influential groups had continually

---

[508] *Id.*

[509] Grigorii Pasko v. Russian Federation, WGAD Opinion No. 9/1999, Adopted May 20, 1999, at ¶ 5.

[510] *Id.*, at ¶ 6.

[511] *Id.*, at ¶ 7(b).

[512] Xing Qingxian and Tang Zhishun v. China, WGAD Opinion No. 30/2016, Adopted Aug. 24, 2016, at ¶ 24.

[513] Saddam Hussein al-Tikriti v. Iraq and United States, WGAD Opinion No. 31/2006, Adopted Sept. 1, 2006, at ¶ 23.

[514] *Id.*

[515] Mohammed Rashid Hassan Nasser al-Ajami v. Qatar, WGAD Opinion No. 48/2016, Adopted Nov. 22, 2016, at ¶ 55.

[516] Ayub Masih v. Pakistan, WGAD Opinion No. 25/2001, Adopted Nov. 30, 2001, at ¶¶ 7, 12 (Litigated by Author through Freedom Now).

[517] *Id.*, at ¶ 13.

[518] *Id.*, *at* ¶ 19.

[519] Antonio Herreros Rodriguez, et al. v. United States, WGAD Opinion No. 19/2005, Adopted May 27, 2005, at ¶ 28.

portrayed the accused as guilty throughout the controversy, and that this suggested a climate void of the required "objectivity and impartiality."[520]

It is also clear that the overlap between procedural fair trial cases and the institutional guarantee of a "competent, independent and impartial tribunal" has created some inconsistencies in the WGAD's jurisprudence. In *Nuka Soleiman v. Indonesia*, for instance, selective and unexplained inclusion of witness testimonies was evidence that the court was not independent.[521] In *Israel Arzate Meléndez v. Mexico*, holding the trial in the absence of the accused was interpreted as evidence of impartiality and lack of independence on the part of the tribunal.[522] In *Mansur Muhammad Ahmad Rajih v. Yemen*, however, the same procedural lapses were taken to show bias or partiality, a separate ground within the Article 14(1) institutional guarantee.[523] The opposite approach was taken in *Yong Hun Choi v. China*, the case of a Korean citizen apprehended in China, in which the WGAD ruled specific procedural issues in violation of fair trial rights, but did not take them to imply that the court did not meet the "competent, independent and impartial" requirement.[524] And the WGAD in *Abdolfattah Solani v. Iran* similarly critiqued the procedural behavior of the Revolutionary Courts in the country, but did not explicitly hold them in violation of the institutional requirements.[525]

The most demonstrative example of a case in which the WGAD treated an institutional guarantees case as a general fair trial rights case is *Abdullah Öcalan v. Turkey*, the matter of a Kurdish dissident tried first in military court and later by a civilian judge.[526] Of particular concern to the WGAD was that the civilian judge who took over the case from the military court was known to have participated as an observer while the detainee appeared before the military tribunal. The WGAD reasoned that the judge should have recused himself from the matter, since his earlier participation in the trial may have been at the behest of the political authorities and otherwise hints at personal bias.[527] The WGAD nevertheless refrained from mentioning the impartiality requirement, and ruled a general UDHR Article 10 fair trial violation.[528]

B Denial of Right to Presumption of Innocence

The fundamental right of an accused in a criminal trial to be presumed innocent under the law is enshrined in Article 14(2) of the ICCPR.[529] The inclusion of the right in a separate paragraph reflects its importance to the guarantee of fair trial.[530] The provision that outlines the right reads:

---

[520] *Id.*, at ¶¶ 28–29.
[521] Nuka Soleiman v. Indonesia, WGAD Opinion No. 31/1994, Adopted Sept. 29, 1994, at ¶ 5.
[522] Israel Arzate Meléndez v. Mexico, WGAD Opinion No. 67/2011, Adopted Nov. 24, 2011, at ¶ 31.
[523] Mansur Muhammad Ahmad Rajih, at ¶ 10.
[524] Yong Hun Choi v. China, WGAD Opinion No. 20/2005, Adopted May 27, 2005, at ¶¶ 18–23.
[525] Abdolfattah Soltani v. Iran, WGAD Opinion No. 26/2006, Adopted Sept. 1, 2006, at ¶ 16.
[526] Abdullah Öcalan v. Turkey, WGAD Opinion No. 35/1999, Adopted Dec. 2, 1999.
[527] *Id.*, at ¶ 12(a).
[528] *Id.*, at ¶ 14.
[529] Burchill & Conte, at 176, emphasizing that the right applies as stated to "criminal trials only."
[530] Bossyut, at 292, noting that during drafting, the right was considered "so important that it was thought advisable to express it in a separate paragraph."

Everyone charged with a criminal offence shall have the right to be presumed innocent until proved guilty according to law.

UDHR Article 11(1), which protects the same right, reads:

Everyone charged with a penal offence has the right to be presumed innocent until proved guilty according to law in a public trial at which he has had all the guarantees necessary for his defense.

Principle 36(1) of the Body of Principles reiterates this right in nearly the same way. More specifically tailored to the presumption of innocence, Principle 13 of the *Basic Principles and Guidelines on Remedies and Procedures on the Right of Persons Deprived of Their Liberty to Bring Proceedings before a Court* provides:

In every instance of detention, the burden of establishing the legal basis and the reasonableness, necessity and proportionality of the detention lies with the authorities responsible for the detention.[531]

The guarantee to the presumption of innocence imposes on the prosecution the burden to prove the charge and to ensure that the accused in trial has the benefit of doubt.[532] Notably, the right is available not only to defendants in trial but also to any person accused prior to filing of the criminal charge.[533] The court may presume no guilt until the charge has been proven beyond reasonable doubt.[534] The protection remains in place until a binding conviction is issued and after the final appeal opportunity.[535] The right must also be taken into consideration during interrogation and investigation relating to the trial of an accused.[536]

In Brazil, the WGAD focused on the excessive recourse to pretrial detention, stating that the "presumption of innocence enshrined by the Constitution seems to be a practice that has been abandoned by judges."[537] It further observed "the excessive recourse to pretrial detention contradicts basic rule of law principles and also has implications for detainees, who are exposed to threats against their life, physical integrity and health, and to abuses and ill- treatment by guards and police officers."[538] And it found that many pretrial detainees were found to be held in a security level inappropriate for the offences that they had allegedly committed. Others had been detained for far longer as pretrial detainees than they would have expected if actually sentenced.[539]

An excessive reliance of a country's criminal justice system on plea bargaining can also implicate violations of the presumption of innocence. During its country mission to

---

[531] Basic Principles and Guidelines, at ¶ 21.

[532] General Comment No. 32, at ¶ 30.

[533] Nowak, at 254.

[534] General Comment No. 32, at ¶ 30; General Comment No. 13, at ¶ 7; Bossyut, at 292, showing that the "beyond reasonable doubt" language was removed from the text of Article 14(2); Nowak, at 254, explains that though the rule by which guilt is presumed depends on domestic law provisions, the "beyond reasonable doubt" requirement can be applied as a recognized principle of law.

[535] Nowak, at 254.

[536] Burchill & Conte, at 176.

[537] *Report of the Working Group on Arbitrary Detention: Mission to Brazil*, Human Rights Council, A/HRC/27/48/Add.3, June 30, 2014, at ¶ 100.

[538] *Id.*, at ¶ 99.

[539] *Id.*

Georgia, the WGAD received an "overwhelming amount of information" that plea bargaining heavily favored the prosecution and that most defendants "resort to a guilty plea in order to avoid lengthy custodial sentences."[540] It expressed its concern that "the presumption of innocence and the right to a fair trial have been undermined in the plea-bargaining process, as was evident in many of the interviews conducted."

An undue delay of proceedings may also violate the right to the presumption of innocence.[541] But at the same time, a dramatically rapid arrest, trial, and conviction also provide clear evidence that "the result was pre-determined," violating the right as well.[542] The fact that an accused had been denied bail, or found liable in other civil proceedings, should not affect the court's presumption of innocence.[543] The HR Committee has also noted that expressing the presumption of innocence vaguely or in ambiguous terms or with limiting conditions can render the guarantee ineffective.[544] If the right is found to have been violated, authorities can provide remedy through the judicial process.[545]

Though denial of bail has in these cases evidenced a denial of the right to be presumed innocent, in at least one case the WGAD has used domestic courts' insistence against providing bail where individual circumstances would have warranted it to assert an independent Category III violation without subsuming it within Article 14(2). In that case, *Gloria Macapagal-Arroyo v. the Philippines*, the WGAD reaffirmed that Article 9(3) of the ICCPR clearly provides that a presumption of release on bail and not detention must be the rule.[546] The WGAD stated that the domestic court in the Arroyo case should also have considered less invasive measures than detention, including house arrest, given the risk of detention to the applicant's health.[547]

Convicting a detainee with a charge of pre-criminal intent or otherwise out of concern that the accused will commit a crime at some future time will violate the right to presumption of innocence.[548] This was the WGAD's opinion in *Ulises González Moreno v. Cuba*, the case of a trade union leader found guilty of "pre-criminal social dangerousness" by the police.[549] *Karmelo Landa Mendibe v. Spain* was a similar case, since the detainee was presumed to be involved in terrorist activities and included in a list of highly dangerous persons immediately after arrest and before his trial.[550] The WGAD found a violation of the presumption of innocence since the designation meant that the detainee

---

[540] *Report of the Working Group on Arbitrary Detention: Mission to Georgia*, Human Rights Council, A/HRC/19/57/Add.2, Jan. 27, 2012, at ¶ 58.

[541] Basilia Ucan Nah v. Mexico, WGAD Opinion No. 36/2011, Adopted Sept. 1, 2011, at ¶ 36 (noting that the applicant's trial was delayed for over three years).

[542] Mohamed Nasheed v. The Maldives, WGAD Opinion No. 33/2015, Adopted Sept. 4, 2015, at ¶ 103(i).

[543] General Comment No. 32, at ¶ 30; Cagas, Bustin & Astillero v. Philippines, Communication No. 788/1997, Human Rights Committee, CCPR/C/73/D/788/1997, Oct. 3, 2001 at ¶ 7.3.

[544] General Comment No. 13, at ¶ 7; Jorge Quintana and Carlos Ortega v. Cuba, WGAD Opinion No. 29/1992, Adopted Session No. 4 at ¶ 6(g).

[545] Burchill & Conte, at 177; Vargas-Machuca v. Peru, Communication No. 906/2000, Human Rights Committee, at ¶ 7.3, finding that offensive conduct of the government, in dismissing the applicant from his government post without adequate hearing, was remedied by prompt reinstatement.

[546] Gloria Macagpal-Arroyo, at ¶ 37.

[547] Id., at ¶ 38.

[548] Ulises González Moreno v. Cuba, WGAD Opinion No. 17/2013 Adopted Aug. 26, 2013, at ¶ 13.

[549] Id., at ¶¶ 7, 23.

[550] Karmelo Landa Mendibe v. Spain, WGAD Opinion No. 17/2009, Adopted Sept. 4, 2009, at ¶ 24.

was automatically subjected to the stricter regime of incarceration the authorities reserve for dangerous persons.[551]

As noted earlier, the WGAD has affirmed that the detention of persons prior to convictions should be "an exception rather than the rule."[552] Indefinite detention without criminal conviction is not permitted.[553] Holding a detainee in pretrial detention out of precaution and on charges that did not constitute criminal offenses may also violate the guarantee.[554] Excessively lengthy pretrial detention will also violate the right.[555] "Mere conformity" of the court decision to detain with domestic law will not in itself justify excessively lengthy pretrial detention.[556] In *Jamali Khan v. India*, a violation was found because, among other facts, the detainee was imprisoned in a high-security jail despite court orders granting his application for bail.[557] Similarly, in *Mohamed Rahmouni v. Algeria*, the WGAD agreed the detainee had been presumed guilty by authorities as demonstrated by the poor treatment afforded him.[558] The detainee was tried by a special military court, kept in solitary confinement for six months, and denied various procedural rights.[559] Similarly, detaining a person who has yet to be convicted in the same facilities as convicted criminals will violate the presumption of innocence. In *Stella Nyanzi v. Uganda*, detaining a human rights defender in "a maximum security prison with death row inmates, despite her status as an unconvicted person" was a violation of Article 11(1) of the UDHR.[560]

Both the judge and public authorities must not prejudge the outcome of a trial.[561] The judge must conduct the trial without the bias of having formed a prior opinion regarding the guilt of the accused.[562] A verbal attack from a judge in *Narges Mohammadi v. Iran*, calling the detainee "an agent of the West" with open hostility, was an obvious violation of the presumption of innocence.[563] In *Dr. Tin Min Htut and U Nyi Pu v. Myanmar*, the WGAD ruled that the tone of a cursory opinion that did not cite adequate justification for detention revealed the presiding judge had prejudged the guilt of the detainees.[564]

---

[551] *Id.*, at ¶ 58(d).

[552] Motiur Rahman Nizami, et al. v. Bangladesh, WGAD Opinion No. 66/2011, Adopted Nov. 23, 2011, at ¶ 39; Gen. Jamil Al Sayed, et al. v. Lebanon, WGAD Opinion No. 37/2007, Adopted Nov. 30, 2007, at ¶ 45; Orlando Quintero Paez v. Colombia, WGAD Opinion No. 58/1993, Adopted Dec. 9, 1993, at ¶ 5 (finding a violation where the detention exceeded the legally permissible duration for the charge).

[553] *Id.*

[554] Hernán José Sifontes Tovar, et al. v. Venezuela, WGAD Opinion No. 65/2011, Adopted Nov. 23, 2011, at ¶ 34.

[555] Marcos Michel Siervo Sabarsky v. Venezuela, WGAD Opinion No. 27/2011, Adopted Aug. 30, 2011, at ¶ 34 (finding a pretrial detention lasting for more than a year in violation of the right to presumption of innocence); Gen. Nouhou Thiam, et al. v. Guinea, WGAD Opinion No. 20/2015, Adopted Apr. 29, 2015, at ¶ 14 (finding pretrial detention lacked legal basis where applicants were held in pretrial detention for three extra years).

[556] Gloria Macapagal-ArroyoSept., at ¶ 37.

[557] Jamali Khan v. India, WGAD Opinion No. 3/2010, Adopted May 4, 2010, at ¶ 6.

[558] Mohamed Rahmouni v. Algeria, WGAD Opinion No. 33/2008, Adopted Nov. 20, 2008, at ¶ 20.

[559] *Id.*

[560] Stella Nyanzi v. Uganda, WGAD Opinion No. 57/2017, Adopted Aug. 24, 2017, at ¶ 61(e).

[561] General Comment No. 13, at ¶ 7; General Comment No. 32, at ¶ 30; Nowak, at 254, explaining that the term "public authorities" covers, in particular, ministers and other influential government officials.

[562] General Comment No. 32, at ¶ 30.

[563] Narges Mohammadi v. Iran, WGAD Opinion No. 48/2017, Adopted Aug. 22, 2017, at ¶ 47.

[564] Tin Min Htut and U Nyi Pu v. Myanmar, WGAD Opinion No. 4/2010, Adopted May 5, 2010, at ¶ 13.

Similarly, a forty-five-minute deliberation for a sentence of twenty years of detention in *Ngô Hào* v. *Viet Nam* suggested the detainee's guilt had been pre-determined prior to the trial.[565] In *Mustapha Adib* v. *Morocco*, the requirement that the detainee, a member of the military, dress as a civilian in a trial that could result in his dismissal from the military was, in addition to other limitations, considered a violation of his right to be presumed innocent.[566] Additionally, state media or judicial news coverage should not present detainees as guilty.[567]

Statements made by high-ranking officials against the accused can reveal impermissible prejudgment by authorities.[568] These can interfere with the accused's presumption of innocence.[569] For instance, a fatwa issued by clerics against the detainee in *Mohammed Shaikh Ould Mohammed Ould M. Mkhaitir* v. *Mauritania* was found to violate his right to a presumption of innocence by distorting the outcome of his trial.[570] An Attorney General's claim that a detainee in *Daniel García Rodríguez and Reyes Alpízar Ortiz* v. *Mexico* and his family were part of a criminal network was an unacceptable public statement made outside the judicial process.[571] The WGAD has even found a statement made by officials to the media that a person is "wanted on suspicion of terrorism" to compromise the presumption of innocence.[572]

The WGAD also follows the HR Committee's General Comment No. 32 on the right to equality before court and tribunals and a fair trial, which states that "defendants should not be presented to the court in a manner indicating that they may be dangerous criminals as this violates the presumption of innocence."[573] Imprisoning or shackling the accused before or during trial is prohibited, since such measures denote that the accused is a dangerous criminal.[574] In *Nguyen Dang Minh Man* v. *Viet Nam*, a large police presence at the detainee's trial was also found to be a violation of this rule.[575] A large deployment of police officers and soldiers to block areas near the courthouse during an appeal hearing violated the presumption of innocence in *Can Thi*

---

[565] Ngô Hào v. Viet Nam, WGAD Opinion No. 36/2018, Adopted Apr. 26, 2018, at ¶ 55.

[566] Mustapha Adib v. Morocco, WGAD Opinion No. 27/2001, Adopted Dec. 3, 2001, at ¶ 12.

[567] Siamak Namazi and Mohammed Baquer Namazi v. Iran, WGAD Opinion No. 49/2017, Adopted Sept. 22, 2017, at ¶ 49 (referring to a judicial news video in which "images of the arrest of Mr. Namazi were directly juxtaposed with an image of his United States passport and a 'montage of anti-American themed images'.")

[568] Joseph & Castan, at 426; Gridin v. Russian Federation, Communication No. 770/1997, Human Rights Committee, CCPR/C/69/D/770/1997, July 20, 2000, at ¶ 8.3.

[569] Biram Dah Abeid, et al. v. Mauritania, WGAD Opinion No. 36/2016, Aug. 25, 2016, at ¶ 34, finding the President's referral to the accused as "criminals who should be punished" interfered with their UDHR Article 11 and ICCPR Article 14(2) rights.

[570] Mohammed Shaikh Ould Mohammed Ould M. Mkhaitir v. Mauritania, WGAD Opinion No. 35/2017, Adopted Apr. 27, 2017, at ¶ 44.

[571] Daniel García Rodríguez and Reyes Alpízar Ortiz v. Mexico, WGAD Opinion No. 66/2017, Adopted Aug. 25, 2017, at ¶ 69.

[572] Ahmad Suleiman Jami Muhanna al-Alwani v. Iraq, WGAD Opinion No. 36/2017, Adopted Apr. 28, 2017, at ¶ 88(c).

[573] Nguyen Dang Minh Man v. Viet Nam, WGAD Opinion No. 40/2016, Adopted Aug. 26, 2016, at ¶ 41.

[574] General Comment No. 32, at ¶ 30; Hamdi Al Ta'mari and Mohamad Baran v. Israel, WGAD Opinion No. 5/2010, Adopted May 6, 2010, at ¶ 30, ruling a violation of the right to be presumed innocent on the basis of facts that included presentation of the applicant in handcuffs and administrative detention of significant duration.

[575] Nguyen Dang Minh Man, at ¶ 41.

Thieu v. Viet Nam.[576] Finally, the period of pretrial detention should not be taken as indicative of an accused's guilt.[577]

Courts found to apply special or less-intensive criteria for detentions based on assumptions of an accused's guilt clearly violate the right to be presumed innocent.[578] In *Hugo Sánchez Ramírez v. Mexico*, the WGAD noted the practice of Mexican authorities of designating poor and indigenous civilians as perpetrators of serious crimes to easily meet crime reduction aims.[579] It was found that judges in such cases used different criteria in trials for such persons, applying less rigorous examination of evidence and police statements.[580] Similarly, in *Luis Williams Polo Rivera v. Peru*, the court limited the fair trial rights of the detainee, arguing that the right to be presumed innocent could be set aside since statements by co-defendants conclusively incriminated him.[581] The WGAD, however, found a violation of the right based on the various denied fair trial guarantees, but did not explicitly state that the justification presented by the Government was not a valid excuse for limiting the right to be presumed innocent.[582]

Reversing the burden of proof to the accused by assuming the prosecution's statements as accurate will also normally result in violations of Article 14(2) of the ICCPR and Article 11(1) of the UDHR, as demonstrated by the WGAD ruling in *Agnès Uwimana Nkusi and Saïdati Mukakibibi v. Rwanda*.[583] The WGAD has found in several cases that requiring a detainee to produce evidence of their innocence violates the accused's right to be presumed innocent, since it reverses the appropriate burden of proof.[584] In at least one case, the WGAD has linked the right to the presumption of innocence to Article 14(3) rights, which require procedural fairness. In this case, *Yong Hun Choi v. China*, the WGAD found the right to be presumed innocent can be respected only if assistance to counsel is guaranteed not just to those who can afford it but on every occasion when the interest of justice so demands.[585] The WGAD also ruled in *Jacobo Silva Nogales, et al. v. Mexico* that the right to be presumed innocent was violated when authorities forced the detainees to incriminate themselves under torture.[586] In *Karim Wade v. Senegal*, however, the WGAD outlined an exception to this rule barring reversal of the burden of proof.[587] In that case, the detainee, a former advisor to the President of Senegal, was held and charged with illicit enrichment.[588] The WGAD noted, however, that the shifting of burden of proof was a common procedural method in money-laundering matters,

---

[576] Can Thi Thieu v. Viet Nam, WGAD Opinion No. 79/2017, Adopted Nov. 22, 2017, at ¶ 62.

[577] *Id.*

[578] Hugo Sánchez Ramírez v. Mexico, WGAD Opinion No. 33/2012, Adopted Aug. 30, 2012, at ¶ 40.

[579] *Id.*, at ¶ 16.

[580] *Id.*, at ¶ 18.

[581] Luis Williams Polo Rivera v. Peru, WGAD Opinion No. 32/2010, Adopted Nov. 25, 2010, at ¶ 17.

[582] *Id.*, at ¶¶ 33–34; Wang Bingzhang, et al. v. China, WGAD Opinion No. 10/2003, Adopted May 9, 2003, at ¶ 27(e).

[583] Agnès Uwimana Nkusi & Saïdati Mukakibibi v. Rwanda, WGAD Opinion No. 25/2012, Adopted Aug. 29, 2012, at ¶ 40.

[584] Basilia Ucan Nah, at ¶ 22; Abdullah Sultan Sabihat Al Alili v. United Arab Emirates, WGAD Opinion No. 3/2008, Adopted May 7, 2008, at ¶ 21.

[585] Yong Hun Choi v. China, WGAD Opinion No. 20/2005, Adopted May 27, 2005, at ¶ 20.

[586] Jacobo Silva Nogales, et al. v. Mexico, WGAD Opinion No. 37/2000, Adopted Nov. 27, 2000, at ¶ 12; Luis Alberto Cantoral Benavides v. Peru, WGAD Opinion No. 22/1994, Adopted Sept. 29, 1994, at ¶¶ 5(a), (e).

[587] Karim Wade v. Senegal, WGAD Opinion No. 4/2015, Adopted Apr. 20, 2015, at ¶ 44.

[588] *Id.*, at ¶¶ 3–4.

reflected in UN and African Union conventions signed by Senegal, and therefore did not violate the presumption of innocence requirement.[589]

Media coverage that affirms the accused's guilt, or portrays the accused in a way that undermines the presumption of innocence, must be avoided.[590] The government has a positive duty in this regard to ensure the presumption of innocence, since adverse media attention or lobbying by social groups may influence the attitude of judges toward the accused.[591] A violation of the right to presumption of innocence was found in *Francisco José Cortés Aguilar, et al. v. Bolivia*, where the Government used the detainee's arrest to further official propaganda.[592] In that case, the WGAD ruled the detention of a Colombian human rights lawyer was trumpeted as a significant victory in the authorities' crackdown on terrorist activity, thereby breaching the requirement that an accused should be presumed innocent before his conviction.[593] A similar violation occurred in *Yousif Abdul Salam Faraj Abhara v. Libya*, where confessions of several detainees obtained under torture were publicly broadcast on television and Facebook.[594]

C Denial of Right to Present a Defense

The text of Article 14(3) of the ICCPR includes the protection that the right to fair trial includes the entitlement of the accused to present and prepare a defense and to legal assistance that guarantees that the accused is represented at trial. This right is provided in paragraphs (b) and (d) of Article 14(3), which read:

> In the determination of any criminal charge against him, everyone shall be entitled to the following minimum guarantees, in full equality: (b) To have adequate time and facilities for the preparation of his defense and to communicate with counsel of his own choosing; [. . .] (d) To be tried in his presence, and to defend himself in person or through legal assistance of his own choosing; to be informed, if he does not have legal assistance, of this right; and to have legal assistance assigned to him, in any case where the interests of justice so require, and without payment by him in any such case if he does not have sufficient means to pay for it.[595]

The Basic Principles and Guidelines on Remedies and Procedures on the Right of Persons Deprived of Their Liberty to Bring Proceedings before a Court state in Guideline 8 that the right to legal assistance is to be afforded "without delay. . . immediately after the moment of deprivation of liberty and at the latest prior to any questioning by an authority."[596] The WGAD has supported this approach in its jurisprudence, finding a

---

[589] *Id.*, at ¶ 44.
[590] General Comment No. 32, at ¶ 30.
[591] Nowak, at 254.
[592] Francisco José Cortés Aguilar, et al. v. Bolivia, WGAD Opinion No. 12/2005, Adopted May 26, 2005, at ¶ 10.
[593] *Id.*, at ¶ 9.
[594] Yousif Abdul Salam Faraj Abhara v. Libya, WGAD Opinion 6/2017, Adopted Apr. 29, 2017, at ¶ 44.
[595] General Comment No. 13, at ¶ 11.
[596] Basic Principles and Guidelines, ¶ 67.

forty-eight-hour period without legal assistance unacceptable in *Maria Chin Abdullah v. Malaysia*, because this right applies "immediately after the moment of apprehension."[597] Likewise, a fifteen-hour delay in *Mahmoud Hussein Gomaa Ali v. Egypt* was an unacceptable breach of the right to legal assistance, since Egypt had provided no justification or explanation for its conduct.[598] The Basic Principles and Guidelines also provides that communication counsel shall be provided at no cost for detainees who are unable to afford it.[599] Confidentiality of communications with legal assistance must be respected.[600] Importantly, the Basic Principles and Guidelines also states that legal counsel must be free to carry out their duties free from fear of reprisal or harassment.[601]

Additionally, the Principles encompass the right to adequate facilities, which can be achieved by compliance with their specifications. Every detainee must be able to access materials related to their detention, including materials referenced by prosecution, security, or immigration authorities to justify the detention. To this end, detaining authorities must disclose all relevant materials to the judge, with any proposed restrictions on disclosure to the judge or the detainee being necessary and proportionate, with no less restrictive alternatives such as redacted summaries available.[602] If authorities refuse a disclosure and the court is not empowered to compel it, the detainee must be released.[603]

Article 14(3)(b) likewise guarantees that the accused has sufficient time to communicate with counsel and prepare their defense for trial.[604] These guarantees apply to all stages of the trial, and allow the accused to acquaint themselves with the charges and documentary evidence against them.[605] To determine what specific allowance satisfies the "adequate time" requirement, the tribunal must assess the circumstances and nature of the trial.[606] If the prejudicial effects of an alleged nondisclosure may be remedied by filing a procedural motion to obtain excluded evidence, it is incumbent on the counsel of the accused to request an adjournment of proceedings.[607] Adjournment may also be sought by counsel of the accused should they reasonably feel that the time allocated for preparation of defense is inadequate.[608] Courts that deny or fail to respond to requests for adjournment based on reasonable grounds may be found in violation of the "adequate time" requirement.[609]

---

[597] Maria Chin Abdullah v. Malaysia, WGAD Opinion No. 50/2017, Adopted Aug. 23, 2017, at ¶ 65.

[598] Mahmoud Hussein Gomaa Ali v. Egypt, WGAD Opinion No. 83/2017, Adopted Nov. 22, 2017, at ¶ 63.

[599] Basic Principles and Guidelines, at ¶ 13.

[600] *Id.*, ¶ 69.

[601] *Id.*, ¶ 15.

[602] *Id.*, ¶ 78, 81.

[603] *Id.*, ¶ 82.

[604] General Comment No. 32, at ¶ 32.

[605] Nowak, at 256; Conte & Burchill, at 182–183.

[606] *Id.*; General Comment No. 13, at ¶ 9; Marques de Morais v. Angola, Communication No. 1128/2002, Human Rights Committee, CCPR/C/83/D/1128/2002, Mar. 29, 2005, at ¶ 5.4; Smith v. Jamaica, Communication No. 282/1988, Human Rights Committee, CCPR/C/47/D/282/1988, Mar. 31, 1993, at ¶ 10.4.

[607] Conte & Burchill, at 183.

[608] General Comment No. 32, at ¶ 32; Sawyers, Mclean & Mclean v. Jamaica, Communication No. 256/1987, Human Rights Committee CCPR/C/41/D/226/1987, Apr. 11, 1991, at ¶ 13.6.

[609] Shi Tao v. China, WGAD Opinion No. 27/2006, Adopted Sept. 1, 2006, at ¶ 17.

1 Adequate Time

The WGAD has followed the HR Committee's approach of determining "adequate time" by taking a case-specific approach.[610] In *Alan Phillip Gross v. Cuba*, the case of a US government contractor charged with engaging in subversion, the WGAD found that a period of seven days was sufficient for the detainee to prepare and present a defense.[611] In *Mohammed Amin Kamal and Ahmed Jaber Othman v. Egypt*, the WGAD found that a time of six days between arrest and trial, during which the detainees were also subjected to physical abuse and solitary confinement, was inadequate.[612] *Luis Polo Rivera v. Peru* was a more straightforward case, since the detainee was only permitted ten minutes to present his defense.[613] The WGAD also found a violation in *Erkin Musaev v. Uzbekistan*, where the detainee was made aware of the charges one day before trial.[614] A period of two days of preparation for a charge that carried a potential term of life imprisonment was found insufficient in *Miguel Ruiz-Conejo Márquez v. Peru*.[615] But in a more complex case, *Mohamed Nasheed v. The Maldives*, the WGAD found the detainee was not provided adequate time to prepare in a proceeding from arrest to trial to conviction with a term of thirteen years' imprisonment in less than three weeks, with hearings taking place almost daily and into the evenings.[616] In a related case, *Mohamed Nazim v. the Maldives*, five days was insufficient to prepare a defense for a serious criminal charge that eventually carried an eleven-year sentence.[617] Clearer cases where the WGAD has found a specific Article 14(3)(b) violation involve denial to counsel that stretches for a year or more after the initial arrest, where access to counsel was not afforded at all,[618] or where access to counsel was denied after an acquittal while detention continued.[619] Additionally, the WGAD has disapproved of access to counsel being contingent on the detainee foregoing another right, such as family visits.[620] This amounts to an "ongoing denial of counsel," since detainees should not have to choose between legal assistance and family visits.[621]

2 Adequate Facilities

"Adequate facilities" refers to the availability to the accused of evidence and documents necessary for preparation of the accused's defense, including evidence that is exculpatory and materials that the prosecution plans to offer in court against the

---

[610] Su Su Nway v. Myanmar, WGAD Opinion No. 4/2006, Adopted May 9, 2006, at ¶ 4(a).

[611] Alan Gross v. Cuba, WGAD Opinion No. 69/2012, Adopted Nov. 23, 2012, at ¶ 54 (Case Litigated by Author through Perseus Strategies).

[612] Mohammed Amin Kamal, et al. v. Egypt, WGAD Opinion No. 57/2011, Adopted Nov. 17, 2011, at ¶¶ 8, 15.

[613] Luis Williams Polo Rivera v. Peru, WGAD Opinion No. 32/2010, Adopted Nov. 25, 2010, at ¶ 7.

[614] Erkin Musaev v. Uzbekistan, WGAD Opinion No. 14/2008, Adopted May 9, 2008, at ¶ 40.

[615] Miguel Fernando Ruiz-Conejo Márquez v. Peru, WGAD Opinion No. 42/1993, Adopted Sept. 29, 1993, at ¶¶ 5(a), (e).

[616] Mohamed Nasheed v. The Maldives, WGAD Opinion No. 33/2015, Adopted Sept. 4, 2015, at ¶¶ 35, 103.

[617] Mohamed Nazim v. The Maldives, WGAD Opinion No. 59/2016, Adopted Nov. 25, 2016, at ¶ 63.

[618] Nadeer Saleh Mohseen Saleh al-Yafei v. Yemen, WGAD Opinion No. 47/2014, Adopted Nov. 19, 2014, at ¶ 18; Tariq Saleh Saeed Abdullah Alamoodi v. Yemen, WGAD Opinion No. 42/2014, Adopted Nov. 19, 2014, at ¶¶ 18, 20; Tahir Ali Abdi Jama v. Saudi Arabia, WGAD Opinion No. 32/2014, Adopted Aug. 28, 2014, at ¶ 15.

[619] Laçin Akhmadjanov v. Afghanistan & The United States, WGAD Opinion No. 53/2016, Adopted Nov. 23, 2016, at ¶ 55.

[620] Ny Sokha, et al. v. Cambodia, WGAD Opinion No. 45/2016, Adopted Nov. 21, 2016, at ¶ 49.

[621] *Id.*, at ¶ 49.

accused.[622] In *Tran Thi Thuy, et al.* v. *Viet Nam*, the WGAD found a clear violation of this guarantee where counsel for the detainees were denied access to a copy of the indictment and other essential documents.[623] In addition, the barring of counsel from attending pretrial proceedings contributed to the finding that detainees were denied the right to prepare their defense.[624] In *Sheikh Ahmed Ali al-Salman* v. *Bahrain*, the WGAD found a specific violation of Article 14(3)(b), where the detainee's lawyers were denied access to his speeches, which were included in the evidence on record and were allegedly misrepresented by the prosecution to support a ruling against him.[625] The finding in this case formed part of a more expansive ruling that the detainee had been denied any meaningful opportunity to challenge the evidence provided by the prosecution.[626] The language of Article 14(3)(b) does not, however, give the accused the right to be furnished with all relevant documents.[627]

Insufficient time to consult with counsel may also result in a 14(3)(b) violation. The WGAD notably held in *Husam 'Ali Mulhim, et al.* v. *Syria* that the mere presence of defense lawyers at trial is not sufficient to comply with fair trial guarantees.[628] It noted that the detainees were not allowed to communicate with their lawyers in the pretrial stage and thus could not have had adequate time or facilities to prepare a defense.[629] The WGAD found a similar inadequacy and Article 14(3)(b) violation in *Kursat Çevik* v. *Turkey*, in which the detainee was only allowed to meet with his lawyer four times over the course of nine months,[630] and in *Concerning 10 Individuals Associated with the Newspaper Cumhuriyet* v. *Turkey*, where the detainees were only permitted to meet with their lawyers for one hour per week.[631] A violation was also found in *Mohammad Hossein Rafiee Hanood* v. *Iran*, where the detainee only had access to his counsel over the telephone and never in person.[632]

The right to adequate time and facilities may overlap with Article 14(3)(e), which enshrines the right to cross-examine witnesses, whose testimonies form part of the prosecution's case against the accused. In *Andrés Elias Gil Gutiérrez* v. *Colombia*, the WGAD found a violation from the fact that the detainee had been denied the opportunity to cross-examine any witnesses and additionally was not apprised of the charge presented against him.[633] Presumably, the WGAD reasoned that barred access to witnesses also adds to the denial of "adequate facilities" for preparation of defense.

---

[622] General Comment No. 32, at ¶ 33, defining "exculpatory material" as that which may help establish the innocence of the accused or which is otherwise of use to counsel of the accused; Nowak, at 256; Yasseen & Thomas v. Republic of Guyana, Communication No. 676/1996, Human Rights Committee, CCPR/C/62/D/676/1996, Mar. 31, 1998, at ¶ 7.10.

[623] Tran Thi Thuy, et al. v. Viet Nam, WGAD Opinion No. 46/2011, Adopted Sept. 2, 2011, at ¶ 12.

[624] *Id.*, at ¶ 23.

[625] Sheikh Ahmed Ali al-Salman v. Bahrain, WGAD Opinion No. 23/2015, Adopted Sep. 2, 2015, at ¶¶ 10, 37.

[626] *Id.*, at ¶ 36. The WGAD noted that the detainee had been barred from addressing the court, his lawyers were searched prior to being allowed entry to the courtroom, and challenges to the witnesses being presented by the prosecution were disregarded.

[627] O.F. v. Norway, Communication No. 158/1983, Human Rights Committee, CCPR/C/OP/2, Oct. 26, 1984, at ¶ 5.5.

[628] Husam 'Ali Mulhim, et al. v. Syria, WGAD Opinion No. 10/2008, Adopted May 9, 2008, at ¶ 31.

[629] *Id.*

[630] Kursat Çevik v. Turkey, WGAD Opinion No. 38/2017, Adopted Apr. 28, 2017, at ¶ 78.

[631] Concerning 10 Individuals Associated with the Newspaper Cumhuriyet v. Turkey, WGAD Opinion No. 41/2017, Adopted Apr. 28, 2017, at ¶ 83.

[632] Mohammad Hossein Rafiee Hanood v. Iran, WGAD Opinion No. 25/2016, Adopted Aug. 22, 2016, at ¶ 30.

[633] Andrés Elias Gil Gutiérrez v. Colombia, WGAD Opinion No. 19/2009, Adopted Nov. 19, 2009, at ¶ 11.

The nature of the evidence used at trial to charge an accused is also relevant. The "adequate facilities" guarantee requires that in case of a claim that evidence was obtained by torture in violation of Article 7, the circumstances by which the evidence was procured must be made available to the accused and counsel.[634] Use of such material without providing a detainee the opportunity to have the evidence retracted falls short of the standard expected.[635] In other instances, the WGAD has found that a lack of specific details in the charges brought against a detainee can frustrate the ability to present an appropriate defense.[636] In that case, the audio evidence used to substantiate the arrest of a journalist for anti-state activities was found to be produced illegally.[637] In *Antonio Herreros Rodriguez, et al.* v. *United States*, the declaration of all evidence as confidential placed numerous restrictions on defense lawyers to access the material.[638] The WGAD declared that limiting access to trial documents by such bureaucratic means in this case was incompatible with the detainee's right to prepare a defense.[639]

3 Access to Evidence

Access to counsel takes on a special importance in cases involving national security.[640] The WGAD takes an unsympathetic view in instances where a government bars the accused from accessing some evidence by citing concerns for national security. In the *Balyoz or "Sledgehammer" Cases* v. *Turkey*, the WGAD refuted the Government's arguments that such restrictions are legitimate by noting that no such exemption applies to material that is presented as evidence against an accused at trial.[641] Authorities may not, therefore, use the pretext of national security to deny a detainee access to evidence used by prosecution at trial or to potentially exculpatory material.[642] The HR Committee, however, seems to have taken the approach that the authorities and adjudicating tribunal bear a heavy burden to ensure that the accused is able to present an adequate defense and cross-examine witnesses if information is redacted or kept from disclosure due to national security concerns.[643] The use of "secret evidence," undisclosed to the accused, clearly violates the "adequate facilities" requirement in Article 14(3)(d).[644]

---

[634] General Comment No. 32, at ¶ 33; Nowak, at 256; Erkin Musaev, at ¶ 36.

[635] Muhammad Geloo v. Saudi Arabia, WGAD Opinion No. 44/2011, Adopted Sept. 2, 2011, at ¶ 16.

[636] Moussa Kaka v. Niger, WGAD Opinion No. 7/2009, Adopted May 7, 2009, at ¶ 27; Abdul Rahman b. Abedlaziz al Sudays v. Saudi Arabia, WGAD Opinion No. 6/2008, Adopted May 8, 2008, at ¶ 18; Francisco José Cortés Aguilar, et al. v. Bolivia, WGAD Opinion No. 12/2005, Adopted May 26, 2005, at ¶ 19, noting that the charges made were "formulated in a general and imprecise manner, without defining the specific acts that constituted the criminal offences concerned."

[637] *Id.*, at ¶ 28.

[638] Antonio Herreros Rodriguez, et al. v. United States, WGAD Opinion No. 19/2005, Adopted May 27, 2005, at ¶¶ 20–21.

[639] *Id.*, at ¶ 30.

[640] Nazanin Zaghari-Ratcliffe v. Iran, WGAD Opinion No. 28/2016, Adopted Sept. 21, 2016, at ¶ 50.

[641] Balyoz or Sledgehammer Cases v. Turkey, WGAD Opinion No. 6/2013, Adopted May 1, 2013, at ¶ 76 (Litigated by Author through Perseus Strategies).

[642] *Id.*

[643] Conte & Burchill, at 184; Ahani v. Canada, Communication No. 1051/2002, Human Rights Committee, CCPR/C/80/D/1051/2002, Mar. 29, 2004, at ¶ 10.5; Fidel Ernesto Santana Mejía v. Colombia, WGAD Opinion No. 26/1994, Adopted Sept. 29, 1994, at ¶ 5(f).

[644] Ahmad Qatamish v. Israel, WGAD Opinion No. 58/2012, Adopted Nov. 20, 2012; Khaled Jaradat v. Israel, WGAD Opinion No. 23/2001, Adopted Nov. 29, 2001, at ¶ 6.

This does not mean that the detainee's right to access evidence is absolute – the state may restrict evidence on rare occasions. But the WGAD's Basic Principles and Guidelines specify that a court may only restrict disclosure of information where it is necessary and proportionate and where there are no less restrictive alternatives available that could achieve the same security goal.[645] In *Haritos Mahmadali Rahmonovich Hayit v. Tajikistan*, the WGAD found a 14(3)(b) violation, as well as a violation of the right to equality of arms, where the state failed to demonstrate no alternatives to withholding evidence were available.[646] The WGAD suggested alternatives such as redacted summaries or copies for use only within restricted premises.[647] In *Mateusz Piskorski v. Poland*, the WGAD found a less restrictive measure – allowing counsel to access classified documents in restricted premises for a limited time, and requiring notes to be left behind – unacceptable, as the Government had not demonstrated why this was necessary and proportionate, nor had they shown that less restrictive means such as providing copies would have been unable to achieve the same results.[648]

4 Presence at Trial

The HR Committee has explained that Article 14(3)(d) provides three distinct guarantees: that the accused (1) must be present during the trial, (2) be allowed to defend themselves in person or through legal assistance of their own choosing, and (3) be assigned legal assistance if required and without regard for their ability to pay for the services.[649] These guarantees apply once a detainee has been charged with a crime or for a right that renders the trial a "suit at law."[650] Trials held in the absence of the accused are permitted, but only with the assent of the absent party and with appropriate safeguards to ensure that their rights are upheld according to international standards.[651] In the absence of such steps, the WGAD will find trial in the absence of an accused a violation of Article 14(3)(d).[652] The HR Committee has stated that strict observance of the right to present a defense is particularly important in instances where trials are held in absentia.[653] A violation of the accused's right to be tried in person may be remedied by entitlement to a retrial.[654]

The right to be present at the trial and to defend oneself is, therefore, described as a "primary, unrestricted" right, which the accused may forego.[655] In such a case, the accused must be informed of the scheduling and presented with a request to attend in a timely manner.[656] The WGAD found this duty unfulfilled in *Suleyman b. Nasser*

---

[645] Basic Principles and Guidelines, at ¶ 80.

[646] Haritos Mahmadali Rahmonovich Hayit v. Tajikistan, WGAD Opinion No. 2/2018, Adopted Apr. 17, 2018, at ¶ 71.

[647] Id.

[648] Mateusz Piskorski v. Poland, WGAD Opinion No. 18/2018, Adopted Apr. 20, 2018, at ¶ 53.

[649] Id., at ¶¶ 36–38.

[650] Joseph & Castan, at 437.

[651] Id., at ¶ 36.

[652] Abassi Madani and Ali Benhadj v. Algeria, WGAD Opinion No. 28/2001, Adopted Dec. 3, 2001, at ¶ 24(iii).

[653] General Comment No. 13, at ¶ 11.

[654] Conte & Burchill, at 173.

[655] Nowak, at 259; *Concluding Observations on Finland*, Human Rights Committee, at ¶ 15.

[656] General Comment No. 32, at ¶ 36; Burchill & Conte, at 173; Mbenge v. Zaire, Communication No. 16/1977, Human Rights Committee, CCPR/C/OP/2, Mar. 25, 1983, at ¶ 14.1; Maleki v. Italy, Communication No. 699/1996, Human Rights Committee, CCPR/C/66/D/699/1996 July 27, 1999, at ¶ 9.4.

b. Abdullah Al-Alouane v. *Saudi Arabia*, since authorities did not inform the detainee of any charges or of the date of trial, nor did they permit the applicant to appoint a lawyer.[657] Failure to inform a detainee of the basic details of their trial was also sufficient for a fair trial rights violation ruling in *Di Liu* v. *China*.[658] The WGAD has also repeatedly found violations where the court has not given a detainee the opportunity to make statements in their defense at trial or to take counsel for this purpose.[659]

5 Access to Counsel

The closely related right to legal assistance is detailed in Principles 17 and 18 of the Body of Principles. Following arrest, a detainee must be informed of his right to counsel and have counsel assigned to them if they are unable to afford it on their own.[660] The detainee is entitled to communicate with their counsel, and communications between them may not be used as evidence against the detainee.[661] Nor may they be within the hearing of a law enforcement official. For these consultations, the detainee is to be provided with adequate time and facilities.[662]

The guarantee under Article 14(3)(d) requires that the accused must be informed of their right to counsel and presented with the opportunity to appoint a lawyer of their choosing.[663] Denial of the opportunity for a detainee to choose their own counsel became an issue in *Alexandr Klykov* v. *Russia*, where the public defender assigned to the case acted against the interests and rights of his client, allegedly by attempting to shield officials who had mistreated the detainee from criminal liability.[664]

Similarly, it is seriously problematic for a country to not have sufficient lawyers to assist criminal defendants. In one of its earliest country missions to Bhutan, the WGAD:

> [N]oted the complete absence of a legal community, the existence of which is necessary for the functioning of any legal system. In this context the Group observed that the institution of "*Jabmi*", a substitute for a lawyer, was not sufficiently entrenched and institutionalized to enable the accused to use them to advantage.[665]

In its follow-up visit to Bhutan, the Government reported that the procedure of the Royal Court of Justice requires criminal defendants to be informed about the institution of

---

[657] Suleyman b. Nasser b. Abdullah Al-Alouane v. Saudi Arabia, WGAD Opinion No. 22/2008, Adopted Sept. 10, 2008, at ¶ 16; Abdul Rahman b. Abedlaziz al Sudays, at ¶ 18.

[658] Di Liu v. China, WGAD Opinion No. 25/2003, Adopted Nov. 28, 2013, at ¶ 7.

[659] Thadeus Nguyen Van Ly v. Viet Nam, WGAD Opinion No. 6/2010, Adopted May 6, 2010, at ¶ 24 (Litigated by Author Through Freedom Now).

[660] Body of Principles, at Principle 17(1).

[661] *Id.*, at Principle 18(5).

[662] *Id.*, at Principle 18(2).

[663] Nowak, at 258; Yong Hun Choi v. China, WGAD Opinion No. 20/2005, Adopted May 27, 2005, at ¶ 18; Mohammad Shahadeh, et al. v. Syria, WGAD Opinion No. 6/2004, Adopted May 26, 2004, at ¶ 10; Wang Bingzhang, et al. v. China, WGAD Opinion No. 10/2003, Adopted May 9, 2003, at ¶ 27(c); Ali-Akbar Saidi-Sirjani, et al. v. Iran, WGAD Opinion No. 14/1996, Adopted May 23, 1996, at ¶ 6(b).

[664] Alexandr Klykov v. Russian Federation, WGAD Opinion No. 14/2016, Adopted Apr. 21, 2016, at ¶¶ 66, 80–81 (noting also that the Committee against Torture had observed a preexisting and widespread failure of Russian authorities to ensure that detainees were permitted prompt and competent access to counsel).

[665] *Report of Working Group on Arbitrary Detention: Visit to Bhutan*, Commission on Human Rights, E/CN.4/1995/31/Add.3, Dec. 16, 1994, at ¶ 22.

Jabmi and that "the draft on civil and criminal court procedures has incorporated the *Jabmi* system more elaborately."[666] The Government added "To disseminate this information and create public awareness, and in keeping with the [WGAD's prior] recommendation, the Royal Court of Justice conducted a month-long training workshop on *Jabmi* [in February and March of 1996] that was attended by 72 *Jabmis*."

This was a similar concern in Senegal, where the WGAD noted that with a population of 11.3 million people, it only had 350 lawyers, of which 300 were based in Dakar. While the Government had set up a state-funded legal aid system, the WGAD expressed serious concern about its not operating efficiently yet and the impact of the lack of lawyers on pretrial detention, which averaged three years between charges being brought and verdicts.[667]

The WGAD observed on its country mission to Azerbaijan that it had received "abundant information related to the denial or obstruction of the right of accused or convicted persons to be legally represented and to communicate freely with their lawyer, in particular by the administration of some detention centres, especially those dealing with the most serious offences."[668] In that regard, it determined the situation may "be the result of either a low number of lawyers available to represent accused persons, the inability of lawyers to adequately advise individuals facing criminal justice or their possible lack of independence" but that this assessment was contrary to the view of the President of the Bar Association, who claimed that anyone arrested got proper legal assistance from one of the more 1,000 lawyers operating in the country.[669]

And on its country mission to El Salvador, the WGAD was even more specific about how the Government interfered with the right to access to counsel. In its report, it stated:

> 74. The Working Group noted that lawyers do not tend to come to police stations. The Group also received numerous reports that, both in detention centres and prisons, lawyers and public defenders are subjected to rigorous searches when entering and leaving the establishments. Those searches are performed by members of the Armed Forces who even check the notes taken by defence lawyers during their interviews with their clients.

> 75. These practices deter defence lawyers from visiting prisons and consequently seriously undermine the right to a defence. The situation for women lawyers is even worse because they are sometimes also subjected to an improper, intrusive and even humiliating search ...

---

[666] *Report of Working Group on Arbitrary Detention: Follow-Up Visit to Bhutan*, Commission on Human Rights, E/CN.4/1997/4/Add.3, June 13, 1996, at ¶ 25.

[667] *Report of the Working Group on Arbitrary Detention: Mission to Senegal*, Human Rights Council, A/HRC/13/30/Add.3, Mar. 23, 2010, at ¶ 55. In addition, the WGAD expressed similar concerns on its country mission to Angola, where it observed "[t]he right of access to a lawyer and a corresponding legal aid system, as guaranteed by the Constitution, exists only in theory ... due to a serious shortage of qualified defence lawyers, especially in the provinces, tribunals appoint [many others] as public defenders. In the view of the Working Group, the majority of these persons are not able to act in the interests of the accused. It would like to stress that this situation needs to be urgently addressed." *Report of the Working Group on Arbitrary Detention: Mission to Angola*, Human Rights Council, A/HRC/7/4/Add.4, Feb. 29, 2008, at ¶ 82.

[668] *Report of the Working Group on Arbitrary Detention on Mission to Azerbaijan*, Human Rights Council, A/HRC/36/37/Add.1, Aug. 2, 2017, at ¶¶ 60–61.

[669] *Id.*

128. The right to an effective defence has been undermined by the intrusive and even degrading measures to which defence lawyers and even public defenders and prosecutors and members of the Attorney General's Office and the Office of the Human Rights Advocate have been subjected by members of the Armed Forces responsible for controlling entry to prisons.[670]

It is also a serious concern when a country does not require access to counsel for criminal defendants under its own laws at all. In Morocco, the WGAD found that its "Constitution provides that a person in custody must benefit, as soon as possible, from legal assistance and the possibility of communicating with relatives, in conformity with the law. However, immediate and direct access to a lawyer from the outset of detention is neither guaranteed under existing statutory law or in practice."[671]

And the WGAD found a serious problem for access to counsel in Hungary, where defense lawyers assigned and paid by the Government received only $15 an hour, had to travel long distances to provide assistance to clients, and had serious challenges accessing case materials compared to prosecutors. It concluded that "[t]hese factors create a difficult environment in which effective legal assistance cannot be guaranteed, and the Working Group notes this as a contributor to the high number of those in pretrial detention."[672]

An accused may reject assistance by any counsel, unless the "interests of justice" mandate the presence of legal counsel.[673] Possible reasons for a tribunal to require the accused to be assisted by a lawyer may be that the nature of a case or charge demands professional representation or if the accused is intent on substantially obstructing the proper conduct of a trial, or to protect vulnerable witnesses from contact with the accused.[674] The HR Committee has warned that any restriction on the right of an accused to represent themselves should not be absolute, not be beyond what is strictly necessary to uphold interests of justice, and justified by an "objective and sufficiently serious purpose."[675]

The requirement for the provision of legal assistance to the accused requires a case-specific assessment.[676] That said, the WGAD has also explained its general concerns during country missions when it has observed the inadequacies of country systems for the appointment of legal aid. For example, after a country mission to Nepal, it observed:

> The free legal aid provided for by the Constitution ... is very infrequently given, either because potential beneficiaries are ill-informed or (and more especially) because of lack of funds. Officially appointed lawyers receive little, if any, remuneration. While the presence of counsel during custody is possible, the Working Group observed that it is not compulsory and noted instances where detainees had not received assistance from counsel for almost a year after their arrest.[677]

---

[670] Working Group Mission to El Salvador, at ¶¶ 74–75, 128.

[671] *Report of the Working Group on Arbitrary Detention: Mission to Morocco*, Human Rights Council, A/HRC/27/48/Add.5, Aug. 4, 2014, at ¶ 44.

[672] *Report of the Working Group on Arbitrary Detention: Mission to Hungary*, Human Rights Council, A/HRC/27/48/Add.4, July 3, 2014, ¶ 82.

[673] General Comment No. 32, at ¶ 37.

[674] *Id.*

[675] *Id.*; Correia de Matos v. Portugal, Communication No. 1123/2002, Human Rights Committee, CCPR/C/86/D/1123/2002, Mar. 28, 2006 at ¶¶ 7.4–7.5.

[676] O.F. v. Norway, at ¶ 3.4.

[677] *Report of Working Group on Arbitrary Detention: Visit to Nepal*, Commission on Human Rights, E/CN.4/1997/4/Add.2, Nov. 26, 1996, at ¶ 25.

On individual cases, it must be determined, from the nature of the charge or by an analysis of the accused's chances of success on appeal, whether legal assistance has to be assigned "in the interest of justice."[678] For instance, the detainee in *Hassan Zafar Arif v. Pakistan* could afford a lawyer, but was unable to secure one due to the political nature of his case. The WGAD ruled in this case that it was the duty of authorities to ensure he could secure legal representation.[679] Any counsel provided by the authorities must render effective representation of the accused.[680] An accused is not entitled to a choice of lawyer if he is unable to afford one and is thus being provided with legal aid.[681] Where there are allegations otherwise, the state is responsible for providing documentary evidence to show that a lawyer had been appointed, consulted with the detainee, was present during interrogations, and provided defense at trial.[682]

The accused may, however, at any time decide not to make use of the appointed counsel and instead defend themselves in person.[683] Providing an accused with legal assistance but denying them the option to represent themselves also violates the minimum guarantee.[684] Substantiating evidence is required, however, where the accused does choose to represent themselves. In *Lodkham Thammavong v. Laos*, the source alleged that the detainees were denied access to a lawyer, and believed it highly unlikely they were provided with legal aid.[685] The Government, however, stated that the three had elected to represent themselves. The WGAD sided with the source, saying that the burden of proof is on the Government to show that they chose freely to represent themselves.[686] In any case, self-representation still would have been inappropriate for these particular detainees, given the heavy penalties they were facing, including the death penalty.

Death penalty cases require that the accused be assisted effectively by counsel at all stages of the trial.[687] The WGAD has drawn on the HR Committee's guidance to reiterate that "it is axiomatic that the accused must be effectively assisted by a lawyer at all stages of proceedings in cases involving capital punishment."[688]

The HR Committee has instructed that a violation of Article 14(3)(d) shall be found if the authorities otherwise obstruct lawyers of an accused to fulfill their responsibilities

---

[678] General Comment No. 32, at ¶ 38; Nowak, at 260; Lindon v. Australia, Human Rights Committee, Communication No. 646/1995, at ¶ 6.5.

[679] Hassan Zafar Arif v. Pakistan, WGAD Opinion No. 8/2017, Adopted Apr. 19, 2017, at ¶ 39.

[680] General Comment No. 32, at ¶ 38; Concluding Observations on the United States of America (1995), Human Rights Committee, at ¶ 23.

[681] Joseph & Castan, at 439.

[682] Ahmad Ali Mekkaoui v, United Arab Emirates, WGAD Opinion No. 47/2017, Adopted Aug. 22, 2017, at ¶ 31.

[683] Nowak, at 260; Hill & Hill v. Spain, Communication No. 526/1993, Human Rights Committee, CCPR/C/59/D/526/1993, Apr. 2, 1997 at ¶ 14.2.

[684] Angel Estrella v. Uruguay, Communication No. 74/1980, Human Rights Committee, CCPR/C/OP/2, Mar. 29, 1983, at ¶ 8.6.

[685] Lodkham Thammavong et al. v. Laos, WGAD Opinion No. 61/2017, Adopted Sept. 15, 2017, at ¶ 35.

[686] Id.

[687] General Comment No. 32, at ¶ 38; Aliboeva v. Tajikistan, Human Rights Committee, Communication No. 985/2001, CCPR/C/85/D/985/2001, Oct. 18, 2005 at ¶ 6.4; Kelly v. Jamaica, Communication No. 253/1987, Human Rights Committee, CCPR/C/41/D/253/1987, Apr. 8, 1991 at ¶ 5.10.

[688] Saif Al-Islam Gaddafi v. Libya, WGAD Opinion No. 41/2013, Adopted Nov. 14, 2013, at ¶ 35.

effectively.[689] In *Hasna Ali Yahya Husayn* v. *Iraq*, the WGAD found a violation of Article 14 since the constant intimidation of the applicant's lawyer restricted her ability and time to prepare her defense.[690] Likewise, six prison transfers in a year hampered access to counsel and violated Article 14 in *Braulio Jatar* v. *Venezuela*.[691] In *Mohamed Nazim* v. *The Maldives*, the court's refusal to allow defense counsel to present rebuttal evidence on the fabrication of prosecution evidence amounted to a "failure to ensure fairness."[692] In *Dr. Mohamad Kamal Al-Labouani* v. *Syria*, too, the WGAD applied similar reasoning, noting that the detainee had been denied private contact with lawyers during trial.[693] The source in that case had also drawn attention to the arrest immediately after trial of the accused's lead counsel.[694] Failure of authorities to provide appropriate security to counsel may also result in a violation of the guarantees. In *Saddam Hussein al-Tikriti* v. *Iraq and United States*, the WGAD ruled that the assassination of two of the detainee's counsel undermined his right to defend himself at trial.[695]

States are generally not liable for the general behavior of appointed lawyers unless their conduct is "incompatible with the interests of justice."[696] Behavior that rises to this level may include withdrawal of appeals without consulting the client, failure to appear before the court, or absence during witness examination or hearings.[697] In *Ahmed Omar Einein, et al.* v. *Syria*, however, the WGAD found a violation due to the failure of authorities to inform appointed counsel of the dates of hearings.[698] As a result, hearings of the accused were postponed three times.[699] States must only act in good faith when assigning legal counsel to accused parties.[700]

The WGAD observed the court had violated the right in the case of Saddam Hussein by barring him from appointing counsel of his own choosing and instead assigning the case to unprepared lawyers arbitrarily selected from among those present at hearings.[701] The WGAD also found a violation in *Gerardo Bermúdez Sánchez* v. *Colombia*, where the failure of the court to appoint a replacement left the accused without representation for two months in the middle of trial.[702] This is not to say that states cannot bar a lawyer

---

[689] General Comment No. 32, at ¶ 38; Arutyunyan v. Uzbekistan, Communication No. 917/2000, Human Rights Committee, CCPR/C/80/D/917/2000, Mar. 29, 2004 at ¶ 6.3; Francisco José Cortés Aguilar, et al., at ¶¶ 16–17 (finding of violation due to intimidation and harassment of lawyers associated with applicant).

[690] Hasna Ali Yahya Husayn, et al. v. Iraq, WGAD Opinion No. 59/2011, Adopted Nov. 21, 2011, at ¶ 17.

[691] Braulio Jatar v. Venezuela, WGAD Opinion No. 37/2017, Adopted Apr. 28, 2017, at ¶ 59.

[692] Mohamed Nazim v. The Maldives, WGAD Opinion No. 59/2016, Adopted Nov. 25, 2016, at ¶ 57.

[693] Dr. Mohamad Kamal Al-Labouani v. Syria, WGAD Opinion No. 24/2008, Adopted Sept. 12, 2008, at ¶ 27.

[694] Id., at ¶ 10.

[695] Saddam Hussein al-TikritiSept., at ¶ 24.

[696] General Comment No. 32, at ¶ 32; Joseph & Castan, at 445, noting that professional incompetence in matters of trial strategy has not been recognized by the HR Committee as grounds for an Article 14(3)(d) violation; H.C. v. Jamaica, Communication No. 383/1989, Human Rights Committee, CCPR/C/45/D/383/1989, July 28, 1992 at ¶ 6.3.

[697] Joseph & Castan, at 444–445.

[698] Omar Einein, et al. v. Syria, WGAD Opinion No. 28/2008, Adopted Sept. 12, 2008, at ¶¶ 22–23.

[699] Id., at ¶ 22.

[700] Grant v. Jamaica, Communication No. 353/1988, Human Rights Committee, CCPR/C/50/D/353/1988, Mar. 31, 1994 at ¶ 6.3.

[701] Saddam Hussein al-Tikriti, at ¶ 12.

[702] Gerardo Bermúdez Sánchez v. Colombia, WGAD Opinion No. 1/1996 (Revised), Adopted May 22, 1996, at ¶ 22.

from proceedings for conduct that conflicts with the administration of justice, but this may not leave a defendant without legal counsel.[703]

Since Article 14(3) guarantees for preparation and presentation of a defense apply to all stages of a trial, interrogation conducted without the presence of counsel violates the provisions.[704] The WGAD, concurring with the opinion of the European Court of Human Rights, has stressed that an accused is in a "particularly vulnerable position when interrogated (and) this particular vulnerability can only be properly compensated for by the assistance of a lawyer."[705] Accordingly, the WGAD in *Saif Al-Islam Gaddafi v. Libya* found a gross violation of Article 14(3) owing to the deprivation of the detainee's right to legal assistance in a case involving capital punishment and his interrogation without the presence of counsel.[706]

Hostile interference or an atmosphere of outside influence may constructively bar a detainee's right to defense in a criminal trial.[707] In *Ayub Masih v. Pakistan*, the case of a Christian man charged with making blasphemous comments against Islam, the state religion, the WGAD found that an atmosphere of intimidation and hostility restricted the effectiveness of the detainee's defense.[708] The atmosphere could be gauged by the seriousness of threats made by religious extremists against the accused, as well as an incident in which the accuser shot and injured the accused in the court premises.[709] The WGAD therefore interpreted the serious deficiencies in procedure to have constructively violated the detainee's right to present an effective defense.[710]

Conditions of detention may be of such quality that it renders impossible the right of an accused to make their defense in the prescribed manner.[711] In the case of Saif Al-Islam Gaddafi, the WGAD stated that unfairness in the treatment of the accused may rupture the process to such an extent that "it makes it impossible to piece together the constituent elements of fair trial."[712] The treatment referenced by the WGAD in that case included detention for far longer than the legal maximum and denial either to counsel or to adequate facilities that would have allowed the applicant to prepare a defense.[713] Based on the same rationale, the WGAD has held that the administrative detention used by Israeli authorities to hold Palestinian civilians infringes on detainees' rights to fair trial, since it prevents the accused from being present at trial, to be informed of their right to counsel, and denies them adequate time and facilities for the preparation of a defense.[714] Similarly, the "deplorable conditions" of detention in *Rebii Metin Görgeç v. Turkey*, combined with the denial of medication for "very serious health conditions" of the

---

[703] Ahmed Mahloof v. The Maldives, WGAD Opinion 15/2017, Adopted Apr. 21, 2017, at ¶ 85.
[704] Hasna Ali Yahya Husayn, at ¶ 17.
[705] Saif Al-Islam Gaddafi, at ¶ 31.
[706] *Id.*, at ¶ 29–30.
[707] General Comment No. 32, at ¶ 25.
[708] Ayub Masih v. Pakistan, WGAD Opinion 25/2001, Adopted Nov. 30, 2001, at ¶ 19.
[709] *Id.*, at ¶¶ 8, 19.
[710] *Id.*, at ¶ 19.
[711] Saif Al-Islam Gaddafi, at ¶ 44.
[712] *Id.*
[713] *Id.*, at ¶ 43.
[714] Ahmad Qatamish; Khader Adnan Musa v. Israel, WGAD Opinion No. 3/2012, Adopted May 1, 2012, at ¶¶ 20–22; Hamdi Al Ta'mari and Mohamad Baran v. Israel, WGAD Opinion No. 5/2010, Adopted May 6, 2010, at ¶ 25; Khaled Jaradat, at ¶¶ 6–7, 11.

detainee, were considered by the WGAD to negatively affect the detainee's ability to defend himself, as well as his chance of a fair trial.[715]

In instances where various impediments are observed to the workings of defense counsel, the WGAD will find a joint violation of Articles 14(3)(b) and (d). In *Nguyen Hoang Quoc Hung v. Viet Nam*, for example, detainees were barred from speaking to their lawyers and having their counsel present at trial, and were not provided access to materials needed to prepare an effective defense.[716] The facts touched on guarantees relating to the preparation and presentation of the accused's defense.[717] A joint violation was also found in *Maikel Nabil Sanad v. Egypt*, where the detainee was subject to an expedited review by a military tribunal.[718] The unusual process barred the detainee's lawyers from participating in trial and limited his chances to confer with counsel to prepare an effective defense.[719] In *Shi Tao v. China*, a violation was found because authorities suspended the license of the defense counsel, barring him from representing his client.[720] The court then failed to inform the replacement counsel of the dates of the second trial, thereby preventing the detainee from presenting an effective defense.[721] Likewise, a joint violation was found in *Ahmad Suleiman Jami Muhanna al-Alwani v. Iraq* because the defense counsel had been arrested and interrogated for twelve hours while blindfolded.[722]

Finally, the WGAD may rely on periodic observations made by human rights organs regarding the compliance of particular judicial bodies with Article 14(3) guarantees. In *Mus'ab al-Hariri v. Syria*, the WGAD referred to the HR Committee's report on Syria to presume that Supreme State Security Court trials are generally marked by various hindrances to fair trial, including limitations on accessing case material and on the accused's Article 14(3)(d) right to communicate with counsel.[723] The WGAD refrained from finding a violation of the detainee's right to prepare a defense in that instance, basing its opinion on other fair trial rights frustrated by the Court.[724] Similarly, in *Shi Tao v. China*, the WGAD referenced its own general observations to reiterate that the rights of defense are severely curtailed for detainees charged with transmitting state secrets, a charge in itself so vague that it results in numerous abuses.[725]

D Denial of Right to Present and Cross-Examine Witnesses

Article 14(3)(e) of the ICCPR entitles the accused to cross-examine witnesses to the same degree as the witnesses presented against him. The text of the relevant subsection reads:

---

[715] Rebii Metin Görgeç v. Turkey, WGAD Opinion No. 1/2017, Adopted Apr. 19, 2017, at ¶ 51.
[716] Nguyen Hoang Quoc Hung, et al. v. Viet Nam, WGAD Opinion No. 42/2012, Adopted Nov. 14, 2012, at ¶ 30.
[717] Id.
[718] Maikel Nabil Sanad v. Egypt, WGAD Opinion No. 50/2011, Adopted Sept. 2, 2011, at ¶ 10.
[719] Id., at ¶ 17.
[720] Shi Tao, at ¶¶ 7, 21.
[721] Id., at ¶ 17.
[722] Ahmad Suleiman Jami Muhanna al-Alwani v. Iraq, WGAD Opinion No. 36/2017, Adopted Apr. 28, 2017, at ¶ 88(f).
[723] Mus'ab al-Hariri v. Syria, WGAD Opinion No. 1/2008, Adopted May 7, 2008, at ¶ 18.
[724] Id., at ¶¶ 19–20.
[725] Shi Tao, at ¶ 21.

In the determination of any criminal charge against him, everyone shall be entitled to the following minimum guarantees, in full equality: ... (e) To examine, or have examined, the witnesses against him and to obtain the attendance and examination of witnesses on his behalf under the same conditions as witnesses against him.[726]

This guarantee, as explained by the HR Committee, is essential to ensure an effective defense by the accused and accords to both parties in a trial the same legal powers with respect to the participation of witnesses.[727] The power is not without limitations and the accused may not require any and all witnesses to attend, but is rather a right to question and have admitted those witnesses relevant to their defense.[728] Domestic law may limit admissibility of evidence and provide rules for how courts assess evidence, but must permit the accused to have a fair opportunity to question and challenge witnesses presented against them.[729] The language "to examine or have examined" was added to permit for procedural and structural differences between various legal systems.[730]

Since the Article 14(3)(e) guarantee is derived from the principle of "equality of arms," it is essential that the parties in trial have parity of powers with respect to examining witnesses.[731] Unequal allocation of time between the parties for cross-examination may suffice for a finding that the proceedings violated Article 14(3)(e).[732] The WGAD has also found the principle was not respected where a misapplication of law deprived the accused of proper adversarial procedures, including the right to present a defense.[733] In *Maung Chan Thar Kyaw v. Myanmar*, the WGAD found the parity clearly violated where all 24 witnesses examined were government officers presented by the prosecution.[734] Similarly, the court in *Mustapha Adib v. Morocco* was found to violate the guarantee for admitting all witnesses forwarded by the prosecution but denying all requests for witnesses by the detainee.[735]

Strict control of proceedings that unfairly limits the right of accused to present or cross-examine witnesses will result in a finding of violated Article 14(3)(e) rights.[736] In *Mohamed Nasheed v. The Maldives*, the WGAD found a violation because the court refused to allow any of the proposed defense witnesses.[737] And in *Nuka Soleiman v. Indonesia*, the WGAD found a violation where the court had admitted only one of seventeen witness testimonies requested by the detainee.[738]

---

[726] General Comment No. 13, at ¶ 12.

[727] General Comment No. 32, at ¶ 39.

[728] *Id.*; Nowak, at 261; Conte & Burchill, at 189–190, warning that the language of Article 14(3)(g) does not give rise to an "absolute right to submit evidence at any time or in any manner"; Gordon v. Jamaica, Communication No. 237/1987, Human Rights Committee, CCPR/C/46D/237/1987, Nov. 5, 1992 at ¶ 6.3.

[729] General Comment No. 32, at ¶ 39.

[730] Nowak, at 261; Bossyut, at 301.

[731] Nowak, at 261; Jansen-Gielen v. The Netherlands, Communication No. 846/1999, Human Rights Committee, Apr. 3, 2001, CCPR/C/71/D/846/1999, at ¶ 8.2.

[732] Ahmed Mansoor v. United Arab Emirates, WGAD Opinion No. 64/2011, Adopted Nov. 22, 2011, at ¶ 23.

[733] M'hamed Benyamina & Mourad Ikhlef v. Algeria, WGAD Opinion No. 38/2006, Adopted Nov. 21, 2006, at ¶ 26.

[734] Maung Chan Thar Kyaw v. Myanmar, WGAD Opinion No. 16/2004, Adopted Sept. 15, 2004, at ¶¶ 7, 11.

[735] Mustapha Adib v. Morocco, WGAD Opinion No. 27/2001, Adopted Dec. 3, 2001, at ¶ 12.

[736] Nuka Soleiman v. Indonesia, WGAD Opinion No. 31/1994, Adopted Sept. 29, 1994, at ¶ 6.

[737] Mohamed Nasheed v. The Maldives, WGAD Opinion No. 33/2015, Adopted Sept. 4, 2015, at ¶ 103(iii).

[738] *Id.*, at ¶ 5.

Domestic courts may have their own particular rules for admissibility but cannot unfairly apply evidentiary rules to exclude the accused from cross-examining witnesses or testimonies material to the charge. In *Muhannad Al-Hassani v. Syria*, the detainee, a human rights defender charged with conducting anti-state activities, sought to admit a witness who could testify that the accused did not have the criminal intent required for a conviction under the charges.[739] The court, however, denied the request with the explanation that "the court alone was competent to interpret criminal intent," so the witness requested was not required for the trial.[740] The WGAD found the explanation insufficient to rebut the presumption of an Article 14(3)(e) violation.[741] Similarly, in *Aung San Suu Kyi v. Myanmar*, the court rejected three of the four defense witnesses on the grounds that the requests to include those testimonies were either aimed at "vexation or delay or for defeating the ends of justice," or "not important."[742] The WGAD found the justifications unsatisfactory and ruled a violation of Article 10 of the UDHR.[743]

Barring the accused or his counsel from cross-examining a key witness, especially one whose statement plays a decisive role in a conviction, will also violate Article 14(3)(e).[744] This was the WGAD's ruling in *Akzam Turganov v. Uzbekistan*, the case of a human rights defender convicted of extortion by an alleged victim.[745] During trial, the prosecution interrogated the principal witness, whereas lawyers for the accused were not allowed to cross-examine him at any stage during the trial.[746] The WGAD has also, however, found that allowing only the testimony of a single, biased witness is also insufficient to meet the standards of fair trial.[747] Furthermore, defendants must be able to examine these witnesses in person. Other forms of testimony, such as a poor-quality videoconference call in *Max Bogayev and Talgat Ayanov v. Kazakhstan*, may impede assessment of a witness's credibility, which undermines the right to defense.[748]

Denying an accused the opportunity to cross-examine the prosecution's witnesses also violates the right to examine a witness in trial.[749] It is incumbent on courts to permit independent witnesses not of the prosecution's choosing to be examined by the parties.[750] The WGAD has also held that reliance on the testimonies of absent witnesses, who owing to their absence could not be cross-examined, suggests that the testimony is tainted.[751]

---

[739] Muhannad Al-Hassani v. Syria, WGAD Opinion No. 26/2011, Adopted Aug. 30, 2011, at ¶ 10.

[740] *Id.*, at ¶ 30.

[741] *Id.*

[742] Aung San Suu Kyi v. Myanmar, WGAD Opinion No. 12/2010, Adopted May 7, 2010, at ¶¶ 22–23.

[743] *Id.*, at ¶ 37.

[744] Akzam Turganov v. Uzbekistan, WGAD Opinion No. 53/2011, Adopted Nov. 17, 2011, at ¶ 44; Sheikh Ahmed Ali al-Salman, at ¶¶ 21, 37, where the applicant was denied any meaningful opportunity to call into question the evidence presented by the witnesses for the prosecution.

[745] Akzam Turganov, at ¶¶ 3–5.

[746] *Id.*, at ¶ 43.

[747] Ayub Masih, at ¶ 19.

[748] Max Bokayev and Talgat Ayanov v. Kazakhstan, WGAD Opinion No. 16/2017, Adopted Apr. 21, 2017, at ¶ 59.

[749] Luis Williams Polo Rivera, at ¶ 7.

[750] U Ohn Than v. Myanmar, WGAD Opinion No. 44/2008, Adopted Nov. 26, 2008, at ¶ 18.

[751] Fernando de Araujo v. Indonesia, WGAD Opinion No. 36/1993, Adopted Sept. 29, 1993, at ¶ 9.

The court, where required for a fair trial, must also permit the presentation of expert verification and opinions.[752] The refusal of a court to appoint independent experts was particularly controversial in the *Balyoz or "Sledgehammer" Cases v. Turkey*, which involved the trial of over three hundred persons accused of plotting to overthrow the Turkish regime.[753] Key evidence used to substantiate the allegations against the accused was in unverified digital form.[754] The tribunal refused to consider several expert reports presented by the defense that refuted the authenticity of the digital evidence or to appoint its own expert to review the evidence, prompting the WGAD to rule a violation of fair trial standards.[755]

Failure by a tribunal to admit a necessary or relevant witness, or to make available material witness statements, will result in a violation of the minimum guarantee.[756] Courts can constructively violate the right, as in *Hkun Htun Oo, et al. v. Myanmar*, where the short notice of the summons issued left little time for the cross-examination of witnesses.[757] In the case of Saddam Hussein, the court was found to have violated Article 14(3)(e) when, after initially agreeing to admit the defense's witnesses, it interrupted proceedings and thus denied the detainee's lawyers from cross-examining those witnesses.[758] No violation will be found, however, where the absence of a relevant witness at trial can be ascribed to professional misjudgment by the accused's counsel.[759]

Interestingly, *Bakri Mohammed Abdul Latif v. Egypt* found a violation of 14(3)(e) when the Government withheld video evidence that might have exonerated fourteen protestors.[760] For contesting the demarcation of their lands as out-of-bounds military zones, Nubian activists were arrested and charged with "violently" disrupting traffic. Although they asserted their protest had been peaceful, the Government alleged otherwise. The detainees requested disclosure of closed-circuit security camera footage that they claimed would corroborate the nonviolent nature of their activities. The WGAD believed this was an "entirely plausible" assertion, since government buildings are often surveilled, and found that the Government ignoring this request amounted to "withholding of important evidence requested by defence" that amounted to a breach of 14(3)(e).[761] The WGAD offered no explanation, however, as to why this omission was in particular a violation of the right to present and cross-examine witnesses.

Trials of civilians by military tribunals are particularly suspect, since there is a high chance that the detainee's procedural rights will be limited.[762] The WGAD noted in the

---

[752] Fuenzalida v. Ecuador, Communication No. 480/1991, Human Rights Committee, CCPR/C/57/D/480/ 1991, July 12, 1996, at ¶ 9.5; U Ohn Than, at ¶ 13.

[753] Balyoz or Sledgehammer Cases, at ¶ 16.

[754] *Id.*, at ¶ 14.

[755] *Id.*, at ¶ 75.

[756] Peart & Peart v. Jamaica, Communication No. 482/1991, Human Rights Committee, CCPR/C/54/D/464/ 1991, July 19, 1995, at ¶ 11.5.

[757] Hkun Htun Oo, et al. v. Myanmar, WGAD Opinion No. 26/2008, Adopted May 12, 2008, at ¶ 27.

[758] Saddam Hussein al-Tikriti, at ¶¶ 16, 25.

[759] Joseph & Castan, at 447; Pratt & Morgan v. Jamaica, Communication No. 225/1987, Human Rights Committee, CCPR/C/35/D/225/1987, Apr. 6, 1989, at ¶ 13.2.

[760] Bakri Mohammed Abdul Latif, et al. v. Egypt, WGAD Opinion No. 28/2018, Adopted Apr. 24, 2018, at ¶ 82.

[761] *Id.*

[762] Tal Al-Mallouhi v. Syria, WGAD Opinion No. 38/2011, Adopted Sept. 1, 2011, at ¶ 12 (finding that the detainee had been denied the necessary facilities to prepare a defense).

case of Maikel Nabil Sanad that the procedures of military tribunals are "often irregular," and commonly restrict access to lawyers, ability to prepare a defense, and the right to cross-examine witnesses.[763] The WGAD has also held emergency procedures that enable trial of civilians by military courts to violate fair trial rights generally, including the specific right to defense.[764] The practice of holding trials before "faceless judges" falls within this category of trials, and includes restrictions incompatible with the right of the defense to cross-examine witnesses.[765] The WGAD explained its stance on the workings of faceless courts in several cases from Peru, including *Edilberto Aguilar Mercedes v. Peru*, noting that the working of such courts is rife with infringements of an applicant's due process rights.[766]

States must ensure the absence of any direct or indirect influence, intrusion, expression of hostility by the public or interest groups, or biases among judges and juries that can frustrate the accused's chance of fairly examining witnesses.[767] In *Su Su Nway v. Myanmar*, the WGAD ruled a violation based on the authorities' intimidation of witnesses that could have testified in the detainee's favor at trial.[768]

The case of *Mohamed Hassan el-Kettani v. Morocco*, a religious figure accused of inciting violence, demonstrated how an Article 14(3)(e) violation may precipitate a further violation of an accused's right to prepare and present a defense.[769] The first violation occurred when a request by the detainee's lawyers to subpoena necessary witnesses was rejected by the court.[770] On notice of the rejection, the lawyers withdrew from the case in protest.[771] In their stead the court appointed counsel but only gave the replacement a few hours to prepare the detainee's defense.[772] The WGAD noted these separate grounds for their finding of a general Article 14 fair trial right violation.[773] In the case of Hkun Htun Oo, the right to defense was found to have been violated as a result of the court's short-notice summons, which left the detainee no time to admit and cross-examine necessary witnesses.[774]

Where numerous procedural violations are evident, the WGAD sometimes finds a general violation of Article 14, rather than separate its analysis and list all the relevant

---

[763] Maikel Nabil Sanad, at ¶ 16.

[764] George Mbah and Mohammed Sule v. Nigeria, WGAD Opinion No. 38/1996, Adopted Dec. 3, 1996, at ¶ 6; Annimmo Bassey, et al. v. Nigeria, WGAD Opinion No. 37/1996, Adopted Dec. 3, 1996, at ¶ 6.

[765] General Comment No. 32, at ¶ 23; Gridin v. Russian Federation, Communication No. 770/1997, Human Rights Committee, CCPR/C/69/D/770/1997, July 20, 2000, at ¶ 8.2.

[766] Edilberto Aguilar Mercedes v. Peru, WGAD Opinion No. 29/2000, Adopted Nov. 27, 2000, at ¶ 9; Antero Gargurevich Oliva v. Peru, WGAD Opinion No. 22/1998, Adopted Dec. 3, 1998, at ¶ 6(c); Pablo Abraham Huamán Morales v. Peru, WGAD Opinion No. 23/1998, Adopted Dec. 3, 1998, at ¶ 6(d); Carlos Florentino Molero Coca v. Peru, WGAD Opinion No. 24/1998, Adopted Dec. 3, 1998, at ¶ 6(e); Margarita M. Chiquiure Silva v. Peru, WGAD Opinion No. 25/1998, Adopted Dec. 3, 1998, at ¶ 6(c); Lori Berenson v. Peru, at ¶ 6(c).

[767] General Comment No. 32, at ¶ 25.

[768] Su Su Nway, at ¶ 6.

[769] Mohamed Hassan Echerif el-Kettani v. Morocco, WGAD Opinion No. 35/2011, Adopted Sept. 1, 2013, at ¶¶ 3–4.

[770] Id., at ¶ 13.

[771] Id., at ¶ 26(f).

[772] Id., at ¶ 13.

[773] Id., at ¶ 27.

[774] Hkun Htun Oo, et al., at ¶ 27.

sub-provisions.[775] This was the WGAD's approach in *Annakurban Amanklychev and Sapadurdy Khadzhied v. Turkmenistan*, the facts of which clearly demonstrated that the right to present and prepare a defense, to cross-examine witnesses, and to be tried before an impartial tribunal were all violated by the authorities.[776] The WGAD ruled similarly in the case of *Mohammad Kamal Al-Labouani v. Syria*, noting that the various procedural violations, which included the court overlooking evidence presented by the accused and barring witness examination, represented a "flagrant case of denial of fair trial."[777] Objective limitations in the development of evidence with respect to witnesses, among several other procedural violations, also led the WGAD to find an Article 14 violation generally in the case of *Erkin Musaev v. Uzbekistan*.[778] Yet on heavily contested cases where the detainee and the government have presented detailed arguments regarding due process rights, the WGAD will adopt more detailed opinions, explaining its reasoning more substantially.[779]

E Denial of Right to Public Hearing

Article 14(1) of the ICCPR includes the protection that the right to fair trial generally requires a public hearing. It states in the pertinent part:

> In the determination of any criminal charge against him, or of his rights and obligations in a suit at law, everyone shall be entitled to a fair and public hearing by a competent, independent and impartial tribunal established by law.[780]

And under Article 10 of the UDHR:

> Everyone is entitled in full equality to a fair and public hearing . . . in the determination of his rights and obligations and of any criminal charge against him.

And in relation to the presumption of innocence, Article 11(1) of the UDHR adds:

> Everyone charged with a penal offence has the right to be presumed innocent until proved guilty according to law at a public trial . . . .

Principle 36 of the Body of Principles reiterates this right nearly word-for-word.

1 Scope of the Right to a Public Hearing

At the outset, it should be noted that the specific requirements for fairness in Article 14(1) of the ICCPR and Articles 10 and 11(1) of the UDHR are covered separately.[781] But this

---

[775] Gen. Olusegun Obasanjo, et al. v. Nigeria, WGAD Opinion No. 6/1996, Adopted May 23, 1996, at ¶ 6; Orton Chirwa, et al. v. Malawi, WGAD Opinion No. 13/1993, Adopted Apr. 30, 1993, at ¶ 12.

[776] Annakurban Amanklychev and Sapadurdy Khadzhied v. Turkmenistan, WGAD Opinion No. 15/2010, Adopted Aug. 31, 2010, at ¶¶ 25, 27.

[777] Mohamad Kamal Al-Labouani, at ¶ 27.

[778] Erkin Musaev, at ¶ 40.

[779] Mohamed Nasheed, at ¶ 103.

[780] General Comment No. 32, at ¶ 15, specifying that the language that provides for the right to a public hearing is contained in the second sentence of Article 14(1).

[781] General Comment No. 13, at ¶ 5.

requirement of a public hearing is a bulwark and guarantee of the visibility of due process violations in court proceedings, beyond those other protections provided for explicitly.[782]

The HR Committee in General Comment 13 has stressed that Article 14(1) applies equally to cases that involve either "criminal charge(s)" or "rights and obligations in a suit of law."[783] Recognizing, however, that the definition or interpretation of these terms may differ by legal context, the HR Committee requires detailed explanation of how the legal system of the State party concerned construes the concepts.[784] The term, "suit at law," extends the right to fair trial to cases beyond the otherwise limited category of criminal cases.[785]

In *Y.L. v. Canada*, the HR Committee specified that the determination of what the term, "suit at law," includes should be case-specific and sensitive to the "particular features" of each communication.[786] The HR Committee view in this case clarified that the concept of a "suit at law," or an acceptable equivalent for application of Article 14, is "based on the nature of the right in question rather than on the status of one of the parties."[787] It may also differ based on what types of forums the particular legal system generally provides for adjudication in the type of legal matter presented.[788] Though that case was decided on a separate legal issue, the majority opinion focused on the nature of the right and whether a similar claim would normally be subject to judicial supervision and control.[789] The minority opinion spoke more clearly on the matter, determining that the administrative tribunal that made the final domestic decision did not possess the requisite features of a court, and that the relationship of the applicant as a soldier against the state was a special one.[790] Commentators favor the more expansive view of the majority in *Y.L. v. Canada*, arguing that it protects against unduly restrictive interpretations that State parties may employ to escape Article 14 obligations.[791]

The clearest equation for what constitutes a "suit at law" sufficient for Article 14 protections is that private law rights, such as those in tort or contracts, are included, while public law rights are also included if subject to judicial review.[792] The HR Committee has ruled that decisions by professional regulatory bodies are not included in the Article 14(1) concepts.[793] Procedures concerning an applicant's dismissal from employment or determination of social security benefits, on the other hand, have been found to be "suits

---

[782] Joseph & Castan, at 279.

[783] General Comment No. 13, at ¶ 2.

[784] *Id.*

[785] Joseph & Castan, at 279, noting that the language Article 14(1) is particularly significant because it is the only instance in the Article where noncriminal proceedings are mentioned.

[786] *Y.L. v. Canada*, Communication No. 112/1981, Human Rights Committee, CCPR/C/OP/2, Apr. 8, 1986, at ¶ 9.2.

[787] *Id.*; Conte & Burchill, at 118–119.

[788] *Id.*, noting in particular the context of common law jurisdictions, where no distinctions are made between public and private law, and in which courts may hear matters both on appeal and as forums of first instance.

[789] Joseph & Castan, at 281.

[790] *Y.L. v. Canada*, at ¶ 3.

[791] Joseph & Castan, at 281.

[792] *Id.*, at 282.

[793] *J.L. v. Australia*, Communication No. 491/1992, Human Rights Committee, CCPR/C/45/D/491/1992, July 28, 1992.

at law" for purposes of Article 14(1) protection.[794] Additionally, immigration proceedings concerning deportation may be included in the concept of "suit at law," though the HR Committee has not explicitly stated this.[795] Regional courts have reasoned that a criminal charge for application of Article 14(1) protections is regarded to exist not at the time a formal charge is brought, but rather as soon as a suspicion of criminal activity has been levied on a person, and if their position changes as a result.[796]

The term, "public trial," as used in Article 14(1), however, does not guarantee an oral hearing open to attendance by members of the public.[797] The HR Committee has confirmed that appellate proceedings may proceed on the basis of written presentations, as long as those proceedings and any judgments are disclosed to the public.[798] Failure to provide judgments or records in written form has been held by the HR Committee to violate Article 14(1).[799] Criminal cases at the first instance, however, must be conducted orally.[800] It is not necessary that members of the public attend proceedings, but merely that the court concerned make information about the time and venue of proceedings available to the public, in addition to making arrangements for accommodation for attendees.[801] It is also not necessary, as the HR Committee determined in *Mahmoud v. The Slovak Republic*, that the judgment be declared publicly so long as the hearing satisfied the publicity requirement.[802] The court must provide provisions within reasonable limit, in light of the nature of the case, the amount of interest and attendance expected, and the duration of the proceedings.[803] Pretrial proceedings need not be made public.[804]

Even if public attendance is not required, the publicity requirement is not satisfied if the publicized information is controlled and filtered by the state. In *Wu Zeheng, et al v. China*, attention from the state-run media, albeit continuous, was not sufficient, especially given that in addition to the public, members of the legal defense team were not allowed access to the trial. The WGAD ruled that "such a failure to provide a public trial would add considerable weight to giving the deprivation of liberty of the petitioners . . . an arbitrary character."[805]

---

[794] Casanovas v. France, Communication No. 441/1990, Human Rights Committee, CCPR/C/51/D/441/1990, July 19, 1994; Pons v. Spain, Communication No. 454/1991, Human Rights Committee, CCPR/C/55/D/454/1991, Oct. 30, 1995, at ¶ 5.2.

[795] V.M.R.B v. Canada, Communication No. 236/1987, Human Rights Committee, CCPR/C/33/D/236/1987, July 19, 1988.

[796] Lehtimaja & Pellonpaa, at 236.

[797] Karttunen v. Finland, Communication No. 387/1989, Human Rights Committee, CCPR/C/46/D/387/1989, Oct. 23, 1992; Bossyut, at 279, noting that the proposal to include the language, "public trial," was added by the representative of the United States, but limited only to criminal trials.

[798] R.M. v. Finland, Communication No. 301/1988, Human Rights Committee, CCPR/C/35/D/301/1988, Mar. 23, 1989; Joseph & Castan, at 304.

[799] McGoldrick, at 419; Sala de Touron v. Uruguay, Communication No. 32/1978, Human Rights Committee, CCPR/C/12/D/32/1978, Mar. 31, 1981.

[800] Id.

[801] Van Meurs v. The Netherlands, Communication No. 215/1986, Human Rights Committee, CCPR/C/39/D/215/1986, July 13, 1990, at ¶ 6.1–6.2.

[802] Conte & Burchill, at 124; Mahmoud v. The Slovak Republic, Communication No. 935/2000, Human Rights Committee, CCPR/C/72/D/935/2000, July 23, 2001.

[803] Van Meurs, at ¶ 8.2.

[804] Conte & Burchill, at 124.

[805] Wu Zeheng, et al. v. China, WGAD Opinion No. 46/2016, Adopted Nov. 22, 2016, at ¶ 56 (Litigated by Author through Perseus Strategies).

In UDHR analysis, the fair trial provision in Article 10 includes two distinct guarantees: the first, which speaks to the judicial procedure – that is, "fair and public hearing," – and second, the quality of adjudication, denoted by the "independent and impartial tribunal" requirement.[806] The public policy interest for the publicity requirement is to ensure accountability and raise public confidence in the judicial process.[807] In *Kyaw Zaw Lwin a.k.a. Nyi Nyi Aung v. Myanmar*, the WGAD found:

> A judicial process in closed sessions, before a Special Court, without explicit reasons, on common criminal charges, did not appear consistent with the principles and norms contained in the Universal Declaration of Human Rights nor with the international human rights standards. Consequently, the Working Group considers that the detention of Kyaw Zaw Lwin is arbitrary and corresponds to category III of the categories applied by the Working Group.[808]

And in *Hkun Htun Oo, et al. v. Myanmar*, concerning the detentions of seven political dissidents, the WGAD seems to have found the fact of a trial being held at a prohibitive distance from where the offense was committed as a sufficient basis for a violation of the right to a public hearing.[809] The actions of Myanmar authorities provided, in practical terms, a constructive barring of public attendance by logistical means.[810]

The UDHR Article 11(1) right to a public trial "according to law" can be violated by a nonobservance of procedural domestic law. In *Mohammed Rashid Hassan Nasser al-Ajami v. Qatar*, the detainee was a poet arrested for his recitation of a poem that was perceived to challenge the Emir of Qatar. Al-Ajami received an *in camera* proceeding, despite there being no basis in Qatari law for this sort of trial. The WGAD found that this breach of domestic law in and of itself constituted a breach of the right to a trial "according to law," in addition to a violation of al-Ajami's right to a public trial.[811]

Discussions during the drafting of Article 14(1) of the ICCPR follow a similar concern, that publicity has been recognized in most countries as an effective safeguard against arbitrary action by courts.[812]

In WGAD jurisprudence, the closed nature of a trial is routinely used as evidence of the lack of independence and impartiality of the adjudicating tribunal.[813] In *U Ohn Than v. Myanmar*, the case of a public servant involved in a strike against government economic policy, the source alleged several fair trial violations to call into question the independence of the trial process.[814] The WGAD accepted that the closed session, barred access to legal counsel, and presentation of independent witnesses made for an

---

[806] Letimaja & Pellonpaa, at 223.

[807] *Id.*, at 230.

[808] Kyaw Zaw Lwin a.k.a. Nyi Nyi Aung v. Myanmar, WGAD Opinion No. 23/2010, Adopted Sept. 2, 2010, at ¶ 20 (Litigated By Author through Freedom Now).

[809] Hkun Htun Oo, et al. v. Myanmar, WGAD Opinion No. 26/2008, Adopted Sept. 12, 2009, at ¶ 27.

[810] *Id.*

[811] Mohammed Rashid Hassan Nasser al-Ajami v. Qatar, WGAD Opinion No. 48/2016, Adopted Nov. 22, 2016, at ¶ 56.

[812] Bossyut, at 284.

[813] Shamila (Delara) Darabi Haghighi v. Iran, WGAD Opinion No. 4/2008, Adopted May 7, 2008, at ¶ 39 (concerning a detainee who did not receive public hearings on two separate occasions of her trial); Gulgeldy Annaniyazov v. Turkmenistan, WGAD Opinion No. 22/2013, Adopted Aug. 27, 2013, at ¶ 18 (noting that an "independent and impartial court would have conducted a public hearing.")

[814] U Ohn Than v. Myanmar, WGAD Opinion No. 44/2008, Adopted Nov. 26, 2008, at ¶¶ 13–14.

unfair trial.[815] This was also the argument presented by the source in *Hasna Ali Yahya Husayn* v. *Iraq*, a case concerning the trial and treatment of the widow detained by American and Iraqi security forces.[816] The trial at issue in the claim of Article 14 violations had lasted merely ten minutes and in a closed session, following which the defendant was convicted for violations of an anti-terrorism law.[817] The detainee was convicted for her failure to inform state authorities of activities in which her husband was alleged to have been involved.[818] The WGAD ruled that the circumstances of the detainee's trial in totality violated her rights to a fair trial.

Nevertheless, the WGAD's analysis of the fair trial violation claim did not take a step-by-step approach. The WGAD did not discuss in any notable detail or at length whether the legal action constituted a criminal charge or "suit at law" that warranted Article 14 protection. The limited discussion of the charge was narrowly concerned with whether the type of charge levied had any merit or whether the domestic court reached a fair decision.[819] Nevertheless, the WGAD implied in its discussion that the detainee was wrongly convicted of a criminal charge.[820] Though the WGAD also noted that the charge levied would be punished with the death penalty, it is not clear whether the severity of the punishment influenced the WGAD treatment of the case as a criminal one.[821] The analytical problem presented by *Hasna Ali Yahya Husayn* is that the Article 14 analysis is not examined separately by its constituent parts. The discussion of the closed quality of a trial, therefore, is not made distinct from the general Article 14 violations. Perhaps because several features of the applicant's trial besides its closed nature violated the right to fair trial, the WGAD found a general violation of Article 14 rather than specifying an Article 14(1) violation.[822]

The blocking of trials from publicity directly contravenes the first guarantee of the Article 10 fair trial provisions. The WGAD generally analyzes together those facts that speak to either the fairness or the public nature of the trial. This was the approach the WGAD adopted in one of the WGAD's opinion in *Aung San Suu Kyi* v. *Myanmar*. The WGAD first discussed at length the various ways in which the Government intentionally blocked legal proceedings from public view, doing so despite requests from the defendant's lawyers.[823] Also recounted was the limited access given by the Government to select diplomats and journalists.[824] The trial, in addition to this partial transparency, was open to its limited audience for only a few hours on four total occasions.[825] What the WGAD described as a "largely closed trial" was held to violate the detainee's right to a fair and

---

[815] *Id.*, at ¶ 18.
[816] Hasna Ali Yahya Husayn v. Iraq, WGAD Opinion No. 59/2011, Adopted Nov. 21, 2011, at ¶ 8.
[817] *Id.*, at ¶ 7.
[818] *Id.* at ¶ 18.
[819] *Id.*, noting that "the charge . . . is vague; that being the spouse of an alleged terrorist does not automatically ascribe criminality to the person."
[820] *Id.*
[821] *Id.*
[822] *Id.*, at ¶¶ 17, 21(a).
[823] Aung San Suu Kyi v. Myanmar, WGAD Opinion No. 12/2010, Adopted May 7, 2010, at ¶ 20 (Litigated by Author through Freedom Now).
[824] *Id.*
[825] *Id.*

public hearing.[826] The publicity of the trial seems also to have been undermined by a large and deterrent military presence, and by censorship of media coverage of the trial.[827]

In some more recent cases, the WGAD has articulated specific violations of Article 14 (1). In one such case, *Tran Thi Thuy, et al. v. Viet Nam*, the WGAD discussed the lengths to which the Government went to prevent attendance at proceeding. The case concerned seven land-rights activists affiliated with a local opposition political group.[828] According to the source, the detainees underwent a one-day closed trial.[829] The Government allegedly harassed the family members and supporters of the defendants, intending to intimidate and thereby dissuade concerned members of the public from attending the proceedings.[830] Foreign diplomats were also denied access to the trial.[831] The WGAD found a violation of ICCPR Article 14(1) and UDHR fair trial provisions, noting "it is the public character of the hearing that protects an accused against the administration of justice without public scrutiny."[832] In *Akzam Turganov v. Uzbekistan*, the WGAD ruled an Article 14(1) violation on the basis that the detainee had been convicted following a closed hearing that lasted merely fifteen minutes in duration.[833] The WGAD spoke more on the import of the public hearing requirement, stating "it is the public character of the hearing that protects an accused against possible flaws in the administration of justice."[834] In *Can Thi Thieu v. Viet Nam*, the WGAD found an Article 14(1) violation where fifty individuals who attempted to attend a hearing were taken away to police stations, and were tortured until release after the hearing had concluded.[835] In *Amarais Avakyan v. Uzbekistan*, the presence of two permitted impartial observers did not prevent the trial from being "nevertheless effectively ... behind closed doors."[836]

On a number of occasions, the WGAD has felt the need to enumerate in specific ways how Article 14 protections for fair trial have been violated. In *Erkin Musaev v. Uzbekistan*, an employee of an international nongovernmental organization was arrested, charged, and detained for several years.[837] Over the course of his detention, the detainee underwent several trials, each of which contained due process irregularities.[838] In finding a violation of Article 14, the WGAD not only noted the specific particular instances in which fair trial rights were violated but also provided a list for explanation that included the absence of a public hearing.[839] In another case, involving multiple detainees accused of links to the Al-Qaeda network of organizations, *Ahmad Omar Einein, et al. v. Syria*, the WGAD again listed the right to public hearing as one of the international standards

---

[826] *Id.*, at ¶ 33.

[827] *Id.*, at ¶ 20–21.

[828] Tran Thi Thuy, et al. v. Viet Nam, WGAD Opinion No. 46/2011, Adopted Sept. 2, 2011, at ¶ 3.

[829] *Id.*, at ¶ 15.

[830] *Id.*, at ¶ 14.

[831] *Id.*

[832] *Id.*, at ¶ 24.

[833] Akzam Turganov v. Uzbekistan, WGAD Opinion No. 53/2011, Adopted Nov. 17, 2011, at ¶¶ 17, 45 (Litigated by Freedom Now).

[834] *Id.*

[835] Can Thi Thieu v. Viet Nam, WGAD Opinion No. 79/2017, Adopted Nov. 22, 2017, at ¶ 61.

[836] Aramais Avakyan v. Uzbekistan, WGAD Opinion No. 29/2017, Adopted Apr. 26, 2017, at ¶ 67.

[837] Erkin Musaev v. Uzbekistan, WGAD Opinion No. 14/2008, Adopted May 9, 2008, at ¶¶ 5, 11, 17.

[838] *Id.*, at ¶¶ 18, 34–35.

[839] *Id.*, at ¶¶ 40–41.

of fair trial violated.[840] This seems to be the practice in cases where the WGAD wants to stress the gravity of the offenses a government is responsible for committing.

In other fair trial jurisprudence, the WGAD has declined to specify a violation of the right to public hearing specifically, even when the facts clearly suggest one. In *Phuc Tue Dang* v. *Viet Nam*, for example, the WGAD noted that the reported facts of the detainee's case included that the trail had been held in a closed courtroom with access denied by authorities to members of the public. The WGAD found a general violation of Article 14 fair trial rights, but did not list the various ways in which the rights were violated.[841] Presumably, this is because recounting the facts that implicated the violations to the right were enough to rule in the detainee's favor. The absence of a detailed ruling requires some inference to be drawn from the facts of the case – the WGAD seems to have found that notwithstanding the trial was held *in camera*, failure to publicize the time of the trial to family or concerned members of public, and barring entry to those wishing to attend, were sufficient for a violation of a detainee's right to public hearing.[842]

The WGAD places great emphasis in the public hearing analysis on the barring of family members or other persons intimately interested in the case.[843] In *Thadeus Nguyen Van Ly* v. *Viet Nam*, the WGAD held as relevant the barring of any religious officials from the trial of a vocal political dissident who was an officer of the Roman Catholic Church in the country prior to his arrest.[844] An Article 14 violation was found notwithstanding that permission had been granted to a few diplomats and international journalists to observe the trial for part of the proceedings.[845] Limited access, circumscribed by the prosecuting government given only to hand-picked observers, does not suffice either, as one of the Aung San Suu Kyi opinions made clear.[846] Selective access to a hearing was also found insufficient and in violation of UDHR fair trial guarantees in *Zhou Yun Jun* v. *China*, a case involving a detained pro-democracy dissenter.[847] The Government had argued that the attendance of five relatives of the detainee satisfied the public hearing requirement.[848]

From opinions of other cases where the WGAD declined to specify a violation of the right to public hearing, the WGAD has been satisfied to enumerate the various facts that violate Article 14 generally.[849] In *U Pa Pa Lay* v. *Myanmar*, for example, the WGAD mentions that the detainee's trial was held in prison and without any witnesses among several other violations that showcase a violation of fair trial rights.[850] In *Fawaz Tello* v. *Syria*, too, the WGAD discussed the secrecy of the trials and barred access to family members, among other limitations on the trial, as conferring together arbitrary character to the detention.[851]

---

[840] Ahmad Omar Einein, et al. v. Syria, WGAD Opinion No. 28/2008, Adopted Sept. 12, 2008, at ¶ 23.

[841] Phuc Tue Dang, et al. v. Viet Nam, WGAD Opinion No. 21/1997, Adopted Dec. 2, 1997, at ¶ 6(d)(ii).

[842] *Id.*

[843] Gulgeldy Annaniyazov, at ¶ 16.

[844] Thadeus Nguyen Van Ly v. Viet Nam, WGAD Opinion No. 6/2010, Adopted May 6, 2010, at ¶ 12.

[845] *Id.*, at ¶ 12.

[846] Aung San Suu Kyi, at ¶ 21.

[847] Zhou Yun Jun v. China, WGAD Opinion No. 29/2011, Adopted Aug. 30, 2011, at ¶ 31.

[848] *Id.*, at ¶ 24; Gulgeldy Annaniyazov, at ¶ 16, ruling an Article 14 violation partly as consequence of the barring of relatives to attend the trial.

[849] Johan Teterisa, et al. v. Indonesia, WGAD Opinion No. 41/2008, Adopted Nov. 28, 2008, at ¶ 20.

[850] U Pa Pa Lay v. Myanmar, WGAD Opinion No. 38/2000, Adopted Nov. 28, 2000, at ¶ 9.

[851] Fawaz Tello, et al. v. Syria, WGAD Opinion No. 11/2002, Adopted Sept. 12, 2002, at ¶ 25(d).

Since, in a typical case, the right to public hearing will appear as one of several violated guarantees of Article 14, attempting to gauge whether a secret trial on its own will suffice for the WGAD to find a violation may be unnecessarily specific. Nevertheless, in *Zouhair Yahyaoui v. Tunisia*, the WGAD emphasized in clear language that a "public hearing and the right to have the necessary time and facilities to prepare a defense and communicate with counsel chosen by the defendant are fundamental guarantees, the violation of which makes the deprivation of liberty arbitrary."[852] In another case, the WGAD referred to the right to a public hearing as comprising the "minimal norms" of fair trial under the UDHR.[853]

2 Exceptions

It is important to recognize that states may derogate from their Article 14 obligations under the ICCPR.[854] Nevertheless, while limited exceptions permit states to bar public disclosure or attendance of trials, the H Committee has placed great emphasis on the centrality of fair trial rights to proper administration of justice.[855] The public may be excluded from attending proceedings for moral reasons, maintenance of public order, or in the interest of parties' private lives.[856] In sexual abuse cases, for example, states frequently apply the exclusion on request.[857] Adverse publicity may also be considered sufficiently prejudicial as to violate Article 14.[858] The degree of publicity restricted is linked to the general evaluation of fairness.[859] This makes the analysis difficult to separate at times, particularly in cases involving faceless judges, in which restriction of publicity is taken as evidence of the lack of fairness. Failure of a state to justify any exclusions made would result in a finding that Article 14(1) has been violated.[860]

Some exceptional rationale grounded in proven facts, therefore, is required for any limitations on public attendance to be permitted. In *Kyaw Zaw Lwin v. Myanmar*, the WGAD held that trial in closed sessions, before a specially convened court, on "common criminal charges" did not appear consistent with the public hearing provision.[861] In another case, *Muhammad Kaboudvand v. Iran*, the Government had sought to justify its use of a closed court to try the detainee by invoking Article 188 of the Iranian penal code, which allowed this procedure in the interest of public morals.[862] The case concerned a

---

[852] Zouhair Yahyaoui v. Tunisia, WGAD Opinion No. 15/2003, Adopted Sept. 5, 2003, at ¶ 24.

[853] Xu Wenli v. China, WGAD Opinion No. 23/2003, Adopted Nov. 27, 2003, at ¶ 15; Min Zayar (Aung Myin), et al. v. Myanmar, WGAD Opinion No. 43/2008, Adopted Nov. 25, 2008, at ¶ 25(b).

[854] DOMINIC McGOLDRICK, THE HUMAN RIGHTS COMMITTEE: ITS ROLE IN THE DEVELOPMENT OF THE INTERNATIONAL COVENANT ON CIVIL AND POLITICAL RIGHTS 396 (1991).

[855] Id.

[856] Gulgeldy Annaniyazov, at ¶ 16.

[857] Z.P. v. Canada, Communication No. 341/1988, Human Rights Committee, CCPR/C/41/D/341/1988, Apr. 11, 1988, at ¶ 4.6.

[858] McTaggart v. Jamaica, Communication No. 749/1997, Human Rights Committee, CCPR/C/62/D/749/1997, Mar. 31, 1988, at ¶ 8.4.

[859] Lehtimaja & Pellonpaa, at 230.

[860] McGoldrick, at 419; Angel Estrella v. Uruguay, Communication No. 74/1980, Human Rights Committee, CCPR/C/OP/2, Mar. 29, 1983; Gulgeldy Annaniyazov, at ¶ 16.

[861] Kyaw Zaw Lwin a.k.a. Nyi Nyi Aung v. Myanmar, WGAD Opinion No. 23/2010, Adopted Sept. 2, 2010, at ¶ 20.

[862] Muhammad Kaboudvand v. Iran, WGAD Opinion No. 48/2012, Adopted Nov. 16, 2012, at ¶ 21.

journalist and dissident writer who had publicly advocated for democracy in Iran.[863] Though the WGAD did not provide in the opinion what the specific concerns for public morality were, it nevertheless rejected the Government's argument.[864] The WGAD accepted, in light of the Government's failure to respond, the source's report that claims on public morality were invoked incorrectly in relation to the detainee's case.[865] Reliance on domestic laws that excuse public trials, therefore, may not suffice to escape a finding that Article 14 was violated, especially if found that the law was erroneously applied to the facts of the case.

Most rulings of a violation of the public trial guarantee occur in the context of military or other types of non-civilian courts. In several rulings, the WGAD did not elaborate on or even specify the specific features of the trial that violated this guarantee. It was sufficient for the WGAD in *Ali Ardalan, et al. v. Iran*, to merely note that proceedings before the Revolutionary Court violated the right to public trial.[866] It may reasonably be inferred that specific types of tribunals or contexts are more likely to block trials from public access and will be viewed with heightened suspicion. Unless permissibly limited, the presence of military or security personnel at trials may dissuade public attendance. The WGAD has ruled that such "strict control" of court premises and proceedings renders proceedings suspect.[867] In *Nuka Soleiman v. Indonesia*, the WGAD found that military presence may create an "atmosphere of intimidation," sufficient to violate the right to public trial.[868] Other forms of military trials, which indict detainees following hearings completely in secret, present easier facts for the WGAD to rule a violation of Article 14.[869] In a similar vein, in one of the Aung San Suu Kyi opinions, the WGAD quoted expert in-country observations that the judiciary was "far from independent and is under the direct control of the Government and the military."[870]

Cases in which detainees are sentenced by military tribunals almost always result in rulings of various Article 14 violations. This is not surprising – such mechanisms of justice often provide expedited procedures for opposition political activists or combatants.[871] In many instances, the trials are presided over exclusively by military personnel, and defendants can be grouped together without sufficient review of individual circumstances. In military tribunal cases, therefore, the right to public trial is only one of several tenets of the right to fair trial violated. The closed nature of the trial is generally emphasized but addressed only after a larger discussion of questions about the impartiality of judges, insufficiency of evidence to convict, and denial of access to counsel.[872] In cases involving military tribunals, therefore, the closed nature of the courtroom that is the

---

[863] *Id.*, at ¶ 4.

[864] *Id.*, at ¶ 21.

[865] *Id.*

[866] Ali Ardalan, et al. v. Iran, WGAD Opinion No. 1/1992, Adopted Session No. 4, at ¶ 4.

[867] Nuka Soleiman v. Indonesia, WGAD Opinion No. 31/1994, Adopted Sept. 29, 1994, at ¶ 6.

[868] *Id.*, at 5.

[869] Lori Berenson v. Peru, at ¶ 6(c); Hillary Boma Awul, et al. v. Sudan, WGAD Opinion No. 29/1999, Adopted Nov. 30, 1999, at ¶ 9 (Litigated, in Part, by the Author); Shi Tao v. China, WGAD Opinion No. 27/2006, Adopted Sept. 1, 2006, at ¶ 21.

[870] Aung San Suu Kyi, at ¶ 32.

[871] Tal Al-Mallouhi v. Syria, WGAD Opinion No. 38/2011, Adopted Sept. 1, 2011, at ¶ 13 (noting in the context of Syrian military trials and special jurisdiction provisions that the procedures of military courts of the kind involved in this case did not respect Article 14 fair trial guarantees)

[872] General Olusegun Obsanji, et al., v. Nigeria, WGAD Opinion No. 6/1996, Adopted May 23, 1996, at ¶ 6.

basis of the violation of right to public trial pleadings is an add-on to several other fair trial rights violations.

The WGAD may also, in particularly egregious cases such as those where the detainee was held without any trial, highlight the lack of public hearing as one of the several due process guarantees ignored. In *U Tin Oo v. Myanmar*, a prominent Burmese political activist was arrested without warrant or charge but still was subsequently kept in detention by security forces. The WGAD listed the failure of the Government to provide a public hearing and denying access to legal counsel as two prominent due process discrepancies in U Tin Oo's administrative detention, giving rise to a violation of Article 10 of the UDHR.[873] In a similar case, *Deeq Mohamed Bere, et al. v. Lebanon*, in which the detainees received no trial whatsoever, the WGAD specified that the detainees were not afforded the opportunity to be tried in a fair and public hearing, as required by UDHR Articles 10 and 11.[874]

3 Faceless Courts

Cases involving "faceless" or anonymous judges constitute a separate category of cases that violate Article 14 protections. The precedent for how the WGAD will address "faceless" courts or judges was set by anti-terror legislation in Peru, which established a system of trials in which defendants were not denied public trials but judges were allowed to cover their faces.[875] Civilian courts, including the Supreme Court, operated as a "faceless court" while the authorities conducted operations against the *Sendero Luminoso* (Shining Path).[876] The policy rationale for this extraordinary measure was to protect judges from identification by groups classified as terrorist organizations.[877] Though the WGAD acknowledged the Government's reasoning that states "must protect judges so they can act without fear of reprisals," it observed that the Government had failed to provide adequate safeguards to ensure fair trial rights in view of their using such exceptional measures for protection.[878] The WGAD made clear in *Elmer Salvador Gutierrez v. Peru* that a failure to provide alternative means for upholding fair trial protections would violate Article 14 requirements.[879]

In *Polay v. Peru*, the HR Committee stated in no uncertain terms that this system of faceless courts violated Article 14 rights to fair trial because the "very nature of the system of trial by faceless judges ... is predicated on the exclusion of the public from proceedings."[880] The facelessness of the judges makes the independence and impartiality of the adjudicatory body suspect, since the judges may be serving members of the armed forces or other biased individuals.[881] The HR Committee has also raised concerns that the

---

[873] U Tin Oo v. Myanmar, WGAD Opinion No. 11/2005, Adopted May 26, 2005, at ¶¶ 9, 12.

[874] Deeq Mohamed Bere, et al. v. Lebanon, WGAD Opinion 29/2009, Adopted Nov. 25, 2009, at ¶ 30.

[875] *Concluding Comments on Peru (1996)*, Human Rights Committee, CCPR/C/79/Add. 67, at ¶ 12.

[876] Margarita M. Chiquiure Silva v. Peru, WGAD Opinion No. 25/1998, Adopted Dec. 3, 1998, at ¶ 6(b); Carlos Florentino Molero Coca v. Peru, WGAD Opinion No. 24/1998, Adopted Dec. 3, 1998, at ¶ 6(a).

[877] Polay v. Peru, Communication No. 577/1994, Human Rights Committee, CCPR/C/61/D/577/1994, Nov. 6, 1997, at ¶ 2.2.

[878] Elmer Salvador Gutierrez Vasquez v. Peru, WGAD Opinion No. 17/2001, Adopted Sept. 14, 2001, at ¶ 11.

[879] *Id.*

[880] *Id.*, at ¶ 8.8.

[881] *Id.*

anonymous judges may not have received the desired level of legal training.[882] In addition, the HR Committee in Polay found the system to violate the Article 14(2) right to presumption of innocence.[883] The system established by the "faceless court" policies created several other problems for individuals detained during that period. In some cases, the WGAD observed that "faceless" military courts imposed different judgments for detainees who had previously been tried by ordinary courts.[884] The WGAD ruled such instances as contrary to the principle of the unity of the jurisdiction of courts.[885] These circumstances led the WGAD in *Cesar Sanabria Casanova v. Peru* to reiterate that deprivation of liberty following indictment by a "faceless court" is contrary to international rules of legal due process.[886]

Another feature that is commonly part of "faceless courts" is anonymous witnesses. This is only allowed if it is necessary for protection of the parties involved but also provided that protective measures do not prejudice the rights of the accused.[887] Generally, these cases concerned individuals apprehended by the National Anti-Terrorism Department on suspicion of belonging to the *Sendero Luminoso*.[888] The WGAD disposed of several cases from Peru in which detainees had been indicted by "faceless courts" in 1998, noting that "such trials . . . constitute such a serious violation of the rules of due process as to confer on the deprivation of liberty an arbitrary character."[889] In another case, the WGAD referred to the system of conducting trial by faceless courts as an "exceptional system of justice" that by its existence alone confers an arbitrary character to a detention.[890] These rulings were made on the basis of the Working Group's country mission to Peru to investigate the functioning of "faceless courts."[891]

F Evidentiary Challenges: Improper Evidence and Absence of Evidence

There is a range of evidentiary problems that may be presented to the WGAD, including confessions compelled through torture, evidence obtained through entrapment, and detentions based seemingly on a total lack of evidence. Different provisions may apply to different types of evidentiary problems. Generally, however, these issues violate the right to a fair trial in Article 14 of the ICCPR and Article 10 of the UDHR.

---

[882] Concluding Observations on Peru, ¶ 12.

[883] Polay, at ¶ 8.8.

[884] Elmer Salvador Gutierrez Vasquez, at ¶ 9.

[885] *Id.*

[886] Cesar Sanabria Casanova v. Peru, WGAD Opinion No. 9/2000, Adopted May 17, 2000, at ¶ 11.

[887] *Concluding Comments on Colombia* (1997), Human Rights Committee, CCPR/C/79/Add. 75, at ¶ 21; Joseph & Castan, at 306.

[888] Antero Gargurevich Oliva v. Peru, WGAD Opinion No. 22/1998, Adopted Dec. 3, 1998, at ¶ 6(a); Marco Antonio Sanchez Narvaez v. Peru, WGAD Opinion No. 27/2000, Adopted Sept. 14, 2000, at ¶ 11.

[889] Carlos Florentino Molero Coca, at ¶ 6(e).

[890] Mirtha Ira Bueno Hidalgo v. Peru, WGAD Opinion No. 10/2000, Adopted May 17, 2000, at ¶ 11.

[891] Pablo Abraham Huamán Morales v. Peru, WGAD Opinion No. 23/1998, Adopted Dec. 3, 1998, at ¶ 6(d); Edilberto Aguilar Mercedes v. Peru, WGAD Opinion No. 29/2000, Adopted Nov. 27, 2000, at ¶ 10.

1 Improper Evidence Obtained through Torture

The Article 14 right to fair trial includes protections for detainees against the use of evidence improperly obtained. In the UDHR, this guarantee is included within the general Article 10 right to fair trial. Article 14(3)(g) of the ICCPR provides:

> In the determination of any criminal charge against him, everyone shall be entitled to the following minimum guarantees, in full equality: ... (g) Not to be compelled to testify against himself or to confess guilt.

This provision states the detainee, following detention or arrest, may not be compelled to confess their guilt or to self-incriminate.[892] The HR Committee has clarified in both General Comment 13 and *Berry* v. *Jamaica* that this safeguard requires evidence produced to be free from "any direct physical or psychological pressure from the investigating authorities on the accused with a view to obtaining a confession of guilt."[893] Such forced confessions are not admissible as evidence in criminal trials.[894] The HR Committee provides that force, duress, or other methods that violate Articles 7 and 10(1) of the ICCPR – provisions on torture and inhuman treatment – are used at times to extract information and confessions from detained individuals.[895] The HR Committee, in its jurisprudence, has found that rape in certain cases may constitute torture. The WGAD has affirmed this is indeed the case for rape or the threat thereof during deprivations of liberty and has voiced the opinion that forbidding such acts has become a peremptory norm.[896] The relationship between the authority figures and the detainee being held for interrogation may also contribute to a circumstance that rises to the level of duress or force required for Article 14(3)(g) to apply.[897]

The HR Committee has also found violations of Article 14(3)(g) where such statements were extracted under threat of death or extensive beatings that would cause serious injury, thereby rendering inadmissible confessions or other incriminating documents signed by the accused.[898] The use of torture for such purpose is without exception a violation of Article 14(3)(g).[899] General Comment 32 provides that the use of torture to extract confessions is "unacceptable."[900] The Body of Principles reiterates that no detained

---

[892] General Comment No. 32, at ¶ 41; Bossyut, at 305, noting that an additional clause that would include in the forms of compulsion "inducement by reward or immunity" was removed from early drafts.

[893] Berry v. Jamaica, Communication No. 330/1988, Human Rights Committee, CCPR/C/50/D/330/1988, Apr. 7, 1994, at ¶ 11.7.

[894] Nowak, at 345.

[895] Conte & Burchill, at 178; General Comment 32, at ¶ 60 (discussing ill-treatment by authorities).

[896] Rasha Nemer Jaafar al-Husseini, et al v. Iraq, WGAD Opinion No. 33/2017, Adopted Apr. 27, 2017I, at ¶ 91.

[897] Nowak, at 346, discussing Sanchez Lopez v. Spain, Communication No. 777/1997, Human Rights Committee, CCPR/C/67/D/777/1997, Nov. 25, 1999, at ¶ 6.4 (where HR Committee held that requiring a person who violated traffic laws and was caught on camera to admit, on subsequent questioning, to his guilt did not fall within the scope of Article 14(3)(g) protection even though the admission would be extracted under pressure from authority figures).

[898] Burgos v. Uruguay, Communication No. 52/1979, Human Rights Committee, CCPR/13/D/52/1979, July 12, 1981, at ¶ 13; Kurbanov v. Tajikistan, Communication No. 1096/2002, Human Rights Committee, CCPR/C/79/D/1096/2002, Nov. 6, 2003, at ¶ 7.5.

[899] Sahadeo v. Ghana, Communication No. 728/1996, Human Rights Committee, CCPR/C/73/D/728/1996, Oct. 29, 1998, at ¶ 9 (an early and representative case of HR Committee jurisprudence on the subject).

[900] General Comment No. 32, at ¶ 41.

person may be subjected to torture, and no circumstance may be invoked as a justification for doing so.[901] The WGAD has followed this guidance. The Basic Principles and Guidelines state that evidence obtained as a result of torture may not be invoked in any proceedings, unless as evidence against a person who inflicted the torture or to demonstrate that such acts took place.[902] This was expressed in *Ramze Shihab Ahmed Zanoun al-Rifa'i v. Iraq*:

> The right not to be compelled to testify against oneself or to confess guilt and the right to have access to counsel and legal aid are not intended to protect only the interests of the individual but also the interests of society as a whole, and to build trust in and the effectiveness of the judicial process and the reliability of evidence.[903]

In *Rami al-Mrayat v. Egypt*, the WGAD stated that the prohibition of torture provides grounds "beyond and independent of fair trial guarantees for exclusion of confession evidence obtained without access to legal advice."[904] To emphasize the substantive violations perpetrated to extract confessions, adjudicating officers are provided authority to consider any allegations made of Article 14(3)(g) violations at any stage of trial.[905]

Similarly, the WGAD criticized Morocco after hearing from authorities that confessions alone are not sufficient for a conviction and that corroborating material evidence is necessary, but then learning "the minutes of the preliminary interview, as established by the police on the basis of confessions obtained under torture, are in practice rarely rejected by the trial court. Testimonies received indicate that many cases that are submitted to the courts are based solely on confessions by the accused, in the absence of material evidence."[906] It further concluded:

> The Moroccan criminal judicial system relies heavily on confessions as the main evidence to support conviction. Complaints received by the Working Group indicate the use of torture by State officials to obtain evidence or confessions during initial questioning, in particular in counter-terrorism or internal security cases. The Working Group wishes to emphasize that confessions made in the absence of a lawyer are not admissible as evidence in criminal proceedings; this applies in particular to confessions made during the time spent in police custody.[907]

The HR Committee has emphasized in its jurisprudence that state parties must also institute appropriate procedural safeguards, by incorporating stringent evidentiary standards to this effect into codes of procedure or through appropriate legislation.[908] Once a violation of Article 14(3)(g) is alleged, the burden shifts to the government to rebut the claim by proving that the information or confession was obtained without duress or by

---

[901] Body of Principles, at Principle 6.
[902] Basic Principles and Guidelines, ¶ 77.
[903] Ramze Shihab Ahmed Zanoun al-Rifa'i v. Iraq, WGAD Opinion No. 29/2016, Adopted Aug. 23, 2016, at ¶ 28.
[904] Rami al-Mrayat v. United Arab Emirates, WGAD Opinion No. 27/2013, Adopted Aug. 29, 2013, at ¶ 30.
[905] General Comment No. 32, at ¶ 15.
[906] Report of the Working Group on Mission to Morocco, at ¶ 31.
[907] Id., at ¶ 78.
[908] *Concluding Observations on Romania*, Human Rights Committee, CCPR/C/79/Add. 111 (1999), at ¶ 13; Kpatcha Gnassingbé, et al. v. Togo, WGAD Opinion No. 45/2014, Adopted Nov. 19, 2014, at ¶ 27.

otherwise unlawful means.[909] The HR Committee has ruled that having the parties who allege torture bear the burden of proof in establishing that the evidence was extracted in violation of Article 14(3)(g) is itself a violation of judicial safeguards.[910] Failure of a government to fulfill this burden or to otherwise ignore the allegation of extraction of evidence by torture may result in a finding on the point in favor of the detainee.[911] The WGAD has repeatedly emphasized that a government's silence in response to assertion of material claims, which includes Article 14(3) violations, will be considered implicit acknowledgment that it does not dispute the claim.[912]

The rights articulated in Article 14(3)(g) are further elaborated in the Body of Principles. Principle 21 accordingly protects a detainee from self-incrimination or compelled confessions. It reads: "It shall be prohibited to take undue advantage of the situation of a detained or imprisoned person for the purpose of compelling him to confess, to incriminate himself otherwise or to testify against any other person."[913] In addition to confessions procured through torture, the guarantee also bars authorities from using self-incriminating confessions to charge minors.[914] If the facts of such a case also evidence torture, the WGAD has also reinforced that the situation was aggravated by the fact that the victim is a child.[915]

The WGAD has provided that an allegation that this Principle has been violated implicates international law on the prohibition of torture and procedural standards that bar the use of evidence obtained under torture or the threat of torture.[916] Accordingly, the WGAD references Article 15 of the *Convention Against Torture* (CAT) to articulate the applicable procedural rule in international law, which prohibits states from admitting as evidence any statement procured by torture.[917] Article 15, however, does provide a narrow exception for cases involving a person accused of torture and only permitting evidence from torture to show that a statement was made.[918]

In *Soner Onder* v. *Turkey*, the case of a Turkish student detained for his participation in a political demonstration held by the banned Kurdish Workers' Party, the WGAD first considered the question of whether a detention ordered on the basis of evidence resulting from confessions procured by use of torture conferred on the detention an arbitrary character.[919] The WGAD answered this inquiry in the affirmative, noting the explicit prohibition in international law on the use of evidence extracted through torture and

---

[909] Joseph & Castan, at 450.

[910] Juan Garcia Cruz and Santiago Sanchez Silvestre v. Mexico, WGAD Opinion No. 21/2013, Adopted Aug. 27, 2013, at ¶ 15.

[911] Laphai Gam, at ¶¶ 34, 39, noting that the respondent Government ignored entirely the stated allegation that torture had been used, and noting with concern that the allegation finds support in the documented use of torture in similar circumstances by the Government of Myanmar.

[912] *Id.*, at ¶ 38; Yang Jianli, at ¶¶ 16–18.

[913] Body of Principles, at Principle 21.

[914] Concerning a Minor (Whose Name is Known to the WGAD) v. Bahrain, WGAD Opinion No. 27/2014, Adopted Aug. 27, 2014, at ¶ 30.

[915] *Id.*, at ¶ 27.

[916] Soner Onder v. Turkey, WGAD Opinion No. 38/1994, Adopted Dec. 1, 1994, at ¶ 12.

[917] Convention against Torture, at Art. 15.

[918] *Id.*

[919] Soner Onder, at ¶ 10.

specific evidence of its use in the case of the detainee.[920] This was a Category III violation, since the arbitrary character of the detention was caused by at least partial nonobservance of international norms on the right to fair trial. The WGAD specified that it would look for guidance in similar cases to General Comments issued by the HR Committee, reports of the UN Special Rapporteur on Torture, and Other Cruel, Inhuman, and Degrading Treatment or Punishment, and monitoring reports issued by the Committee against Torture, on the issue and the specific circumstance of the responding state.[921]

In this case, the WGAD noted that domestic Turkish law used a more lenient definition of torture than the CAT but that, regardless, the practice by which evidence was procured from the detainee did not meet the Article 15 of the CAT prohibition.[922] The Government had provided medical reports that showed that the means for procuring the evidence did not have the requisite motive required by Turkish domestic law.[923] The WGAD examined this evidence against the CAT standard, concluding – based on medical certificates, produced in court in compliance with domestic procedural stand-ards – that activities that qualified as torture were used on the detainee.[924] The WGAD has held on several separate occasions that pervasive use of torture to extract evidence nullifies the possibility that the right to fair trial was guaranteed to the detainee.[925]

Reports or observations from UN Special Procedures or other independent sources may be relied on to substantiate the claim of an Article 14(3)(g) violation.[926] This seems especially true for cases where the government did not explicitly deny the claim, and the WGAD finds it necessary to examine the general practice of using torture in the country.[927] In *Hillary Boma Awul, et al.* v. *Sudan*, a case concerning prominent religious leaders from Sudan, the report of the UN Special Rapporteur on Extrajudicial, Sum-mary, or Arbitrary execution provided both specific and general background on the practices and misconduct of the Government.[928] The Special Rapporteur in this case had joined in making an urgent appeal on behalf of the individuals.[929] Using the report as independent evidence corroborating the detainees' claim of torture, the WGAD found a violation of Article 14 generally.[930] Presumably, this encompassed the specific violation of Article 14(3)(g), which the detainees had also argued.[931]

Permitting admission of evidence from third parties extracted through torture also violates Article 14(3)(g). The WGAD articulated this standard in *Selahattin Simsek* v. *Turkey*, the case of a teacher accused of and detained for being part of the illegal Kurdish nationalist party.[932] The detainee was tortured while in police custody but was

---

[920] *Id.*, at ¶¶ 18–19; Assem Kakoun v. Lebanon, WGAD Opinion No. 17/2008, Adopted Sept. 9, 2008, at ¶¶ 12–13.

[921] Soner Onder, at ¶ 11.

[922] *Id.*, at ¶ 13.

[923] *Id.*, at ¶¶ 15, 17.

[924] *Id.*, at ¶¶ 17(a), (c).

[925] Laphai Gam, at ¶ 39.

[926] Israel Arzate Meléndez v. Mexico, WGAD Opinion No. 67/2011, Adopted Nov. 24, 2011, at ¶ 31.

[927] Hillary Boma Awul, et al. v. Sudan, WGAD Opinion No. 29/1999, Adopted Nov. 30, 1999, at ¶ 16.

[928] *Id.*, at ¶ 16.

[929] *Id.*, at ¶ 5.

[930] *Id.*, at ¶ 25(a).

[931] *Id.*, at ¶ 16(b).

[932] Selahattin Simsek v. Turkey, WGAD Opinion No. 34/1995, Adopted Sept. 14, 1995, at ¶ 8(a).

convicted on the basis of evidence procured from third-party detainees.[933] These co-defendants in detainee's case had been tortured separately, but chose to submit confessions incriminating Simsek to secure the protection of a "repentance law," which provided relief in the form of shorter sentences in exchange for incriminating participants in the same crime.[934] The WGAD, therefore, took a broad approach in ruling Article 14 (3)(g) violations bar any evidence procured under torture, and not just self-incriminating evidence from the detainee himself.[935] The torture suffered by the detainee was separately held to be an Article 7 of the ICCPR violation as well.[936]

Forced confession has also been found to undermine the rights of detainees under Article 11(1) of the UDHR. In *Mohammed Rashid Hassan Nasser al-Ajami v. Qatar*, the WGAD found that forced confession as a result of inhuman and degrading treatment compromised "guarantees necessary for [the detainee's] defense."[937] This was reiterated in *Mahmood Abdulredha Hassan al-Jazeeri v. Bahrain*, although there has been little further elaboration on this point.[938]

Failure of governments to instigate timely and appropriately robust proceedings to determine whether detainees' serious claims of having statements extracted by torture have also been the basis for WGAD rulings against the government.[939] A representative case of this kind was *Juan Garcia Cruz and Santiago Silvestre v. Mexico*, concerning two Mexicans. The detainees were arrested without warrant and indicted on the basis of confessions – to their participation in banned militant organizations – they alleged had been procured during their torture.[940] The two detainees, according to the source, had been arrested without prior warrant, and detained for six months, during which time they were allegedly tortured.[941] Some years after their release, they were arrested pursuant to a warrant and convicted based on statements they had made during their prior detention.[942] No investigation, the source asserted, was carried out by the authorities until the following year, at which time a closed inquiry was made and no findings issued by responsible authorities.[943] The statements on which the prosecution had relied, the WGAD concluded, was "inadmissible and could not serve as a basis for charges, let alone a conviction, under Articles 4 to 7 (and) 10 to 14, and in particular Article 15 of the CAT."[944]

The WGAD has ruled that verdicts subsequent to an initial conviction based on evidence extracted using torture can "never be considered as having been handed down following due process rules."[945] In *Erkin Musaev v. Uzbekistan*, an aid worker was convicted on the basis of a confession he signed after being beaten and drugged while

---

[933] *Id.*, at ¶ 6.

[934] *Id.*

[935] *Id.*, at ¶¶ 7–8(a).

[936] *Id.*, at ¶ 8(a).

[937] Mohammed Rashid Hassan Nasser al-Ajami v. Qatar, WGAD Opinion No. 48/2016, Nov. 22, 2016, at ¶ 52.

[938] Mahmood Abdulredha Hasan al-Jazeeri v. Bahrain, WGAD Opinion No. 55/2016, Adopted Nov. 24, 2016, at ¶ 25.

[939] Zeinab Jalalian, at ¶ 40.

[940] Juan Garcia Cruz and Santiago Sanchez Silvestre, at ¶¶ 3, 11, 41–42.

[941] *Id.*, at ¶ 8.

[942] *Id.*, at ¶¶ 11, 13.

[943] *Id.*, at ¶ 12.

[944] *Id.*

[945] Erkin Musaev v. Uzbekistan, WGAD Opinion No. 14/2008, Adopted May 9, 2008, at ¶ 39.

in detention.[946] He was convicted on separate grounds in two subsequent trials, even though he had refused to sign a confession to these later charges.[947] The authorities conducted no investigation, even after the detainee had specified a claim that the evidence should not have been permitted in the trial.[948] The WGAD ruled that use of the confession in the initial trial violated Article 14(3)(g).[949] Since the evidence had informed not just the initial conviction but all subsequent trials, the Article 14(3)(g) violation contributed to other fair trial violations that occurred in the entire collection of proceedings.[950]

In *Ali Aref Bourhan* v. *Djibouti*, concerning a prominent Djiboutian politician accused of plotting to overthrow the Government, the Security Tribunal of Djibouti refused to examine allegations of an Article 14(3)(g) violation notwithstanding testimony from doctors that the detainee had been tortured.[951] A further violation was the failure to summon those allegedly responsible for the torture and reliance on the mere assertion by the prosecution that torture had never been practiced in the country.[952] The admittance of statements procured through torture, for which there was physical evidence, among other due process discrepancies, was ruled a clear violation of Article 14.[953] The WGAD, however, and without explanation, found violations of Articles 14(1), (2), 3(d), and 3(e), but not the specific paragraph on self-incrimination, 3(g).[954] In a similar case, *Amer Jamil Jubran* v. *Jordan*, a State Security Court refused to accept motions submitted by defense counsel regarding the exculpation of evidence procured through torture and refused to permit counsel the right to question officers who had allegedly tortured the detainee.[955] On appeal, the Court of Cassation upheld the verdict without considering the testimony of the detainee relating his torture at the hands of authorities.[956]

Failure to consider allegations of torture from a criminal defendant also demonstrates a lack of independence of the judiciary. In *Abdelkader Belliraj* v. *Morocco*, the detainee was kept incommunicado and tortured for twenty-eight days, until he was forced to sign a confession that said he had been involved in the murders of six people.[957] This issue was raised multiple times in successive proceedings – first by the detainee and then by his defense counsel – but was never taken into consideration by any judge.[958] The WGAD found this an especially serious omission and said it demonstrated "a lack of independence on the part of the representatives of the judiciary."[959] At the very least, the WGAD said, an independent tribunal would have required an investigation into the truth of these allegations before proceeding.[960]

---

[946] *Id.*, at ¶¶ 8–9.
[947] *Id.*, at ¶ 14.
[948] *Id.*, at ¶ 36.
[949] *Id.*, at ¶ 39.
[950] *Id.*
[951] Ali Aref Bourhan v. Djibouti, WGAD Opinion No. 40/1993, Adopted Sept. 29, 1993, at ¶ 5.
[952] *Id.*, at ¶ 5.
[953] *Id.*, at ¶¶ 6–7.
[954] *Id.*, at ¶ 7.
[955] Amer Jamil Jubran, at ¶ 33.
[956] *Id.*, at ¶ 34.
[957] Abdelkader Belliraj v. Morocco, WGAD Opinion No. 27/2016, Adopted Aug. 23, 2016, at ¶¶ 7–8.
[958] *Id.*, at ¶ 42.
[959] *Id.*
[960] *Id.*

The WGAD has also elaborated on the specific obligations that states are required to comply with under these circumstances and under Article 14(3)(g) generally. It noted that the Government of Mexico took five years to initiate an investigation from the time allegations of torture were originally raised, noted the opaque nature of the investigation without any mechanism for public scrutiny or accountability, and described the final ruling, which stated the detainees had failed to make the allegations in the time allotted in law. This conclusion did not consider the delays on the part of the authorities.[961] Beyond refraining from use of such tainted evidence, the Government should have conducted a "comprehensive investigation with a view of punishing the perpetrators."[962] In addition, as part of its recommendations, the WGAD called on the Government to "expedite and broaden investigation ... to impose exemplary penalties on all those responsible, regardless of the hierarchical level of the officials who ordered or participated in the acts of torture and its subsequent concealment."[963]

Violation of proper evidentiary standards and use of baseless charges for detention often arise within a larger pattern of abuses of fair trial rights.[964] In most cases, therefore, the WGAD finds concurrent violations of multiple paragraphs of Article 14. In *Muhammad Osama Sayes v. Syria*, a case concerning the arrests and detention of several Syrian citizens suspected to be members of banned political organizations, the WGAD found a violation of Article 14.[965] The detainees had been denied access to family and lawyers, were held without being notified of the reasons for arrest, and had evidence extracted by use of torture.[966] These practices were legal under the procedural rules of the Syrian Supreme State Security Court, which the HR Committee in a separate opinion had declared in violation of Articles 14(1), (3), and (5).[967] The WGAD, though noting the HR Committee opinion, did not feel the need to elaborate which specific paragraphs of Article 14 were violated.[968] In a later case from Syria, the WGAD extensively discussed the forms of torture used to compel a detainee's self-incriminating statement and ruled that Article 14(3)(g) was violated.[969]

The WGAD in this case illustrated that part of its approach in examining an alleged violation of Article 14 may include examining the procedures of the court or judicial body responsible for an indictment. The WGAD referred back for precedent to its previous observations on how the procedural standards at the Syrian Supreme State Security Court fell short of international standards.[970] This broad inquiry into the judicial system

---

[961] Juan Garcia Cruz and Santiago Sanchez Silvestre, at ¶ 35.

[962] *Id.*

[963] *Id.*, at ¶ 43.

[964] Muhammed Osama Sayes v. Syria, WGAD Opinion No. 16/2006, Adopted May 12, 2006, at ¶ 28 (noting that the lack of a number of procedural guarantees collectively contributed to a finding of the "gravity of the violation of the right" as sufficient to lend the detention arbitrary character); Tagi al-Maidan v. Bahrain, WGAD Opinion No. 1/2014, Adopted Apr. 22, 2014, at ¶¶ 17, 23, noting that the interrogation during which torture was alleged to have been used occurred without counsel for the applicant being present, which feature constituted a separate violation of Article 14..

[965] Muhammed Osama Sayes, at ¶ 30.

[966] *Id.*, at ¶ 27.

[967] *Id.*, at ¶ 28.

[968] *Id.*, at ¶ 30.

[969] Mus'ab al-Hariri v. Syria, WGAD Opinion No. 1/2008, Adopted May 7, 2008, at ¶¶ 6, 21.

[970] Muhammed Osama Sayes, at ¶ 28; Fateh Jamus and Issam Dimashqi v. Syria, WGAD Opinion No. 21/2000, Adopted Sept. 14, 2000, at ¶¶ 14–15.

was in response to the source's allegation that the procedure of the Security Court in its entirety, and in its several specific parts, violated the fair trial rights of anyone who stood trial.[971] In the absence of a sufficient response by the Government to the allegations presented, the WGAD used the general record of the court in question as persuasive authority for its finding that a violation of the detainees' fair trial rights had occurred.[972] In the previous case involving the Security Court, a detainee suspected of links to a communist party complained of a political trial, which had precluded him from accessing several procedural guarantees protected by Article 14.[973] In this case, the WGAD specified the particular rights and paragraphs of Article 14 that had been violated.[974]

The WGAD seems to take a closer look at the general circumstances under which a trial took place if the government is unwilling to cooperate. In the case of Ali Aref Bourhan, the WGAD noted government officials comprised the adjudicating authority at the Security Tribunal that had indicted the detainee.[975] The standard that Article 14 sets, the WGAD noted in its discussion, is for a tribunal to be overseen by independent judges.[976] This approach of looking at the backdrop of the trial or detention in the absence of government cooperation is more robust than in earlier cases, where the WGAD merely accepted without further analysis the submissions by the source.[977] Finding rulings on the basis of a general pattern or the institutional rules of procedure for a judicial body is useful to set a precedent for other cases with the same forum or that arise from the same law.[978] In some of these cases, the WGAD has found a general violation of Article 14, even where extraction of evidence under torture was alleged as a separate claim.[979]

In other cases, the WGAD does not specify which specific guarantees of fair trial rights were violated but finds instead a general violation of Article 14. In *Munayar Hasanov v. Uzbekistan*, the case of an Uzbek citizen sympathetic to Islamist groups, the WGAD found a general Article 14 violation but did not articulate which facts corresponded to which particular paragraph of Article 14.[980] It focused discussion on the flimsiness of the evidence that supported the detainees' conviction; however, the WGAD was of the view that the threshold standard for evidentiary procedure had not been met.[981] In *Dmitri Pavlov v. Azerbaijan*, though, the WGAD concurred with a finding of the Appeals Chamber of the International Criminal Court that "where the breaches of the accused are such as to make it impossible for him/her to make his/her defense within the framework of his rights, no fair trial can take place ... Unfairness in the treatment of the suspect or the accused may rupture the process to an extent making it impossible to

---

[971] Muhammed Osama Sayes, at ¶ 27.

[972] *Id.*, at ¶¶ 28–29.

[973] Fateh Jamus and Issam Dimashqi, at ¶¶ 5–6.

[974] *Id.*, at ¶ 15.

[975] Ali Aref Bourhan, at ¶ 5.

[976] *Id.*

[977] Lee Jang-hyong, et al. v. South Korea, WGAD Opinion No. 1/1995, Adopted Aug. 23, 1994, at ¶¶ 6, 8.

[978] Maxilian Robert, et al. v. Sri Lanka, WGAD Opinion No. 8/2005, Adopted May 25, 2005, at ¶¶ 8–10, taking account of the procedural effects of the Prevention of Terrorism Act (PTA), and noting that the law should no longer have effect.

[979] Lee Jang-hyong, at ¶ 8(a).

[980] Munavar and Ismail Hasanov v. Uzbekistan, WGAD Opinion No. 1/2000, Adopted May 16, 2001.

[981] *Id.*, at ¶ 7, noting that the conviction was based "solely on the basis of leaflets found in (the detainee's) house," the possession of which he had denied.

piece together the constituent elements of a fair trial."[982] In the same case, the WGAD had also found an Article 7 violation.[983]

The WGAD has also found violation of fair trial rights absent CAT violations, though most cases on invalid evidence have involved use of torture. The WGAD has found fair trial rights violations where physical duress amounted to "ill-treatment, humiliation, and coercion."[984] No allegations of torture were presented to the WGAD in *Cesaitino Correla* v. *Indonesia*, a case involving twenty-one East Timorese men accused of participating in communal riots.[985] The source did nonetheless allege that the detainees were forced to self-incriminate or testify against one another, not mentioning if either physical force or threat were used.[986] The WGAD found a general violation under Article 10 of the UDHR given the Government failed to respond to its communication.[987] In another case, the WGAD found an Article 14 violation where evidence procured through wiretapping was used to charge a detained journalist.[988] What made this information inadmissible, according to the WGAD, was the illegal manner in which it was obtained.[989] In another case of this kind, the use of circumstantial evidence in the conviction of a former Lebanese military officer was found, among other fair trial discrepancies, to violate Article 14(3).[990]

Similarly, the WGAD has been willing to find Article 14(3)(g) violations based on the likelihood that a confession was compelled, rather than any actual allegations of torture or physical duress. In *Pongsak Sriboonpeng* v. *Thailand*, the detainee confessed to a *lèse majesté* offense during a televised, police-organized press conference after nine days of military interrogation. During this time, there were no allegations of CAT violations, but the detainee was kept without legal counsel or notice to his family that he had been arrested. On this basis, the WGAD believed it was "unlikely that [the detainee] was afforded the right not to be compelled to confess guilt, contrary to article 14(3)(g)" of the ICCPR.[991]

In some cases, but not as a matter of routine, the WGAD has specified violations of the fair trial provisions of the Body of Principles. In *Youssef and Ashaher Al-Rai* v. *Palestinian Authority*, a case concerning the trial of two Palestinian cousins accused of murder, the

---

[982] Dmitiri Pavlov, et al. v. Azerbaijan, WGAD Opinion No. 22/2011, Adopted Aug. 29, 2011, at ¶ 51, *citing* Judgement on the Appeal of Thomas Lubanga Dyilo against the Decision on the Defence Challenge to the Jurisdiction of the Court pursuant to article 19 (2) (a) of the Statute of Oct. 3, 2006, Case No. ICC-01/04-01/06 (OA 4), App. Ch., 14 December 2006, ¶ 39.

[983] Dmitiri Pavlov, at ¶ 49.

[984] Abdullah Sultan Sabihat Al Alili v. United Arab Emirates, WGAD Opinion No. 3/2008, Adopted May 7, 2008, at ¶ 20; Abdelsalam Abdallah Salim and Akbar Omar v. United Arab Emirates, WGAD Opinion No. 34/2011, Adopted Sept. 1, 2011, at ¶ 11, finding the resort to evidence obtained under threat of forcible return to a jurisdiction where the detainee would face being given the death penalty violated UDHR Article 10.

[985] Cesaitino Correla, et al. v. Indonesia, WGAD Opinion No. 5/1997, Adopted May 15, 1997, at ¶¶ 5–6.

[986] *Id.*, at ¶ 6.

[987] *Id.*, at ¶ 8(a).

[988] Grigorii Pasko v. Russian Federation, WGAD Opinion No. 92/1999, Adopted May 20, 1999, at ¶ 7(b).

[989] *Id.*

[990] Naji Azziz Harb v. Syria, WGAD Opinion No. 20/2000, Adopted Sept. 14, 2000, at ¶ 10; Shamila (Delara) Darabi Haghighi v. Iran, WGAD Opinion No. 4/2008, Adopted May 7, 2008 (finding an Article 14 violation for failure to consider that the court failed to note that the confession, on which conviction was based, was legally revoked).

[991] Pongsak Sriboonpeng v. Thailand, WGAD Opinion No. 44/2016, Adopted Nov. 21, 2016, at ¶ 34.

WGAD found violations of Principles 21 and 27 of the Body of Principles.[992] The collective weight of these two Principles is the same as Article 14(3)(g) of the ICCPR, since Principle 21 prohibits use of torture or force for self-incrimination and Principle 27 bars admissibility of evidence obtained through these means.[993] The conduct offensive to these two Principles in this case was the use of depositions obtained by force.[994] The WGAD ruled that these violations, including the failure to permit access to counsel, gave the detention arbitrary character.[995] It is not clear, however, whether the WGAD would find that the violation of evidentiary principles alone would be sufficient for a case to be placed in Category III.

The WGAD has provided even more robust opinions articulating the various sources for international norms on evidentiary standards. In *Rodolfo Flores and Teodoro Garcia v. Mexico*, two environmental activists detained by the military on various charges, the WGAD found a specific violation of Article 14(g).[996] The source had alleged and provided evidence that torture methods had been used to extract information from the detainees.[997] In support of its conclusion, the WGAD cited to the *Guidelines on the Role of Prosecutors*, relevant reporting from the HR Committee on compulsion to self-incriminate and General Comment 20 on use of torture, in addition to Article 14(3)(g) and Principle 21.1 of the Body of Principles.[998] Finally, in *Ali Mahdi Hasan Saeed, et al. v. Bahrain*, the WGAD cited to the comparable provisions on prohibition on torture in Article 37(a) of the *Convention on the Rights of the Child*, where one of the detainees was under the age of eighteen at the time of detention and ill-treatment.[999]

2 Improper Evidence Obtained through Entrapment

Cases of entrapment are extremely rare compared with cases involving torture and coerced confession. Although they do not have as specific a provision in the ICCPR to protect criminal defendants from being entrapped, such cases are generally described as violating the Article 14 right to a fair trial. In dealing with this evidentiary issue, the WGAD has drawn on cases from the European Court of Human Rights. In *Teixeira de Castro v. Portugal*, a detainee "tempted by the money," had accepted payment from

---

[992] Youssef Al-Rai and Ashaher Al-Rai v. Palestinian Authority, WGAD Opinion No. 14/1999, Adopted Sept. 15, 1999, at ¶ 10.

[993] Body of Principles, at Principles 21 & 27.

[994] Youssef Al-Rai and Ashaher Al-Rai, at ¶ 9.

[995] Id.

[996] Rodolfo Montiel Flores and Teodoro Cabrera Garcia v. Mexico, WGAD Opinion No. 18/2001, Adopted Sept. 14, 2001, at ¶¶ 4, 11.

[997] Id., at ¶ 9(a).

[998] Id., at ¶ 10 (quoting Guideline 16 of the Guidelines on the Role of Prosecutors: "When prosecutors come into possession of evidence against suspects that they know or believe on reasonable grounds was obtained through recourse to unlawful methods, which constitute a grave violation of the suspect's human rights, especially involving torture or cruel, inhuman or degrading treatment or punishment, or other abuses of human rights, they shall refuse to use such evidence against anyone other than those who used such methods, or inform the Court accordingly, and shall take all necessary steps to ensure that those responsible for using such methods are brought to justice.")

[999] Ali Mahdi Hasan Saeed, et al. v. Bahrain, WGAD Opinion No. 41/2015, Adopted Dec. 2, 2015, at ¶ 42.

undercover police officers to purchase heroin.[1000] *Vanyan* v. *Russia* declared a violation of the right to a fair trial where law enforcement officials go beyond "investigating the applicant's criminal activity in an essentially passive manner."[1001]

Denis Matveyev v. *Russia* was an unusual WGAD case where improper evidence was derived from entrapment. Police agents posing as recovering addicts asked Matveyev to purchase heroin, which he did from a source who was cooperating with police in exchange for her own release.[1002] On four occasions, he purchased a little over half a gram of heroin mixture from the police informant with money given to him by the agents and delivered the drugs back to them each time. The source mentioned that the detainee was aware of the difficulties of withdrawal, and bought a heroin mixture that an expert testified would have been strong enough to alleviate the effects of withdrawal without inducing a narcotic effect.[1003]

The WGAD, citing *Vanyan* v. *Russia*, found a violation of the right to a fair trial because police had not confined themselves to investigating Matveyev in an "essentially passive manner," but rather "incited the commission of the offense."[1004] No facts put forward suggested that the purchase would have taken place without the intervention of police agents.[1005] Nor did the prosecutor offer any evidence for unlawful actions beside those incited by law enforcement.[1006] Thus, the detainee's right to a fair trial had been breached and his detention was arbitrary under Category III. Additionally, the WGAD made a Category II finding because, in their view, "the Government employed 'entrapment' to punish Matveyev for his human rights activities."[1007]

3 Excessive Weight Given to One Kind of Evidence over Others

Beyond problems that arise when improper evidence is used by a domestic tribunal, the WGAD has also expressed more general concerns about the way that a country's judiciary has considered one kind of evidence to the detriment of other kinds of evidence. After its country mission to El Salvador, the WGAD explained it had:

> [N]oticed that great weight is attached to witness statements in court proceedings, to the detriment of other evidence, such as scientific, documentary or forensic evidence. The excessive weight given to witness statements stems from the lack of resources for obtaining other more concrete, substantial or conclusive evidence. This has resulted in the emergence of a special kind of witness, known as *testigos criteriados* (defendants or convicts who turn State's evidence), and of informers, who receive benefits, such as release from custody, withdrawal of the charges against them or a reduction in their sentence in exchange for testifying against others. This mechanism was introduced under the so-called "Anti-*Maras* Act" of 2004. Although the Act was declared unconstitutional, the use of these types of witnesses continues to this day.[1008]

[1000] Denis Matveyev v. Russian Federation, WGAD Opinion No. 8/2013, Adopted May 2, 2014, at ¶ 69.
[1001] *Id.*
[1002] *Id.* at ¶ 24.
[1003] *Id.* at ¶ 27(f).
[1004] *Id.* at ¶¶ 69–70.
[1005] *Id.*
[1006] *Id.* at ¶ 16.
[1007] *Id.* at ¶ 75.
[1008] Working Group Mission to El Salvador, at ¶ 6.

4 Absence of Evidence

The WGAD has noted that the failure to produce any evidence to back up claims, allegations, or legal grounds for a detention raises the strong possibility that it is arbitrary. Often the grounds for the detainee's arrest and detention are covers for political or other motives that justify indiscriminate targeting of vulnerable members of society or opposition political groups. The manner in which a detainee's arrest and subsequent trial is handled is likely to reveal multiple violations of fair trial rights as well. It is common in such cases to find that the confession extracted in violation of Article 14(3)(g) is the dispositive or only evidence used to convict a detainee.[1009]

Though the WGAD does not substitute itself for the role of a domestic fact-finder, it nonetheless requires a responding state to rebut allegations presented by a source. Absent the presentation of such evidence, a government may not be able to benefit from the general rule limiting the WGAD from acting as a fact-finder of first instance.[1010] Failure to provide more than limited "laconic" submissions on charges contributes to a conclusion that the fair trial rights of the detainee have been violated.[1011] Similarly, use of secret evidence that is not revealed at any point of the trial or detention can contribute to a finding that Article 14 rights were violated.[1012] Revelations that key prosecutorial evidence has been fabricated can also be the basis for finding a due process violation.[1013]

A lack of corroborative evidence considered for the detainee's conviction may also suggest that a detention was purely for political activities or expression. In *Chang Ui-gyn v. South Korea*, the case of a South Korean detainee arrested on suspicion of collaborating with dissident political parties, the WGAD spoke at length on the basis for the conviction, noting that the conviction seemed to be based solely on a confession extracted under torture.[1014] The WGAD also accepted, given the Government's failure to provide any evidence to the contrary, that the detainees were involved in political activism of various sorts.[1015] There was no "independent corroborative evidence" of the detainee's involvement in espionage, the charge on which his arrest was based, and the WGAD found violations of Articles 14, 19, and 21 of the ICCPR.[1016] Though the WGAD did not act as the domestic fact finder, it did note that the evidence was not of a quality that would fulfill Article 14 standards of fair trial rights.

A number of cases where evidence is not produced have been in the context of counter-terrorism cases or contexts such as states of emergencies, in which security agencies are given broad latitude to detain suspects. In *Laphai Gam v. Myanmar*, concerning an internally displaced member of the minority ethnic Kachin group, the WGAD noted the failure of the Government to substantiate the legal grounds for arrest it had alleged with valid evidence rendered the detainee's detention arbitrary.[1017] In its

[1009] Chang Ui-gyn, et al. v. South Korea, WGAD Opinion No. 28/1993, Adopted Apr. 30, 1993, at ¶ 6.
[1010] Laphai Gam, at ¶ 26.
[1011] Muhammed Osama Sayes, at ¶ 26.
[1012] Khaled Jaradat v. Israel, WGAD Opinion No. 23/2001, Adopted Nov. 29, 2001, at ¶ 7; Zeinab Jalalian, at ¶ 39 (noting that the reliance on undisclosed reports from intelligence services did not constitute sufficient evidence).
[1013] Mohamed Nazim v. The Maldives, WGAD Opinion No. 59/2016, Adopted Nov. 25, 2016, at ¶ 63.
[1014] Chang Ui-gyn, at ¶¶ 6–7.
[1015] Id., at ¶¶ 8, 10.
[1016] Id., at ¶¶ 10, 12.
[1017] Laphai Gam, at ¶¶ 28, 41.

response to the source, the Government had argued the detainee was arrested based on findings that he was responsible for several bomb explosions, which constituted violations of the Explosive Substance Act. He had also been identified as a member of a banned organization.[1018] The source had argued that the Government had produced no evidence whatsoever in support of these assertions and that this suggested the detainee had been detained as part of a campaign against religious and ethnic minorities in Myanmar.[1019] The WGAD took note of this failure to produce evidence in connection with other defects, including the use of a military court in the detainee's trial, to find that his right to a fair trial had been violated.[1020] The WGAD's reasoning directly undercut the Government's claim that a "responsible team" had determined the detainee's guilt.[1021] Permitting the Army to arrest, try, and adjudicate left "little room" for an impartial trial.[1022]

In these types of cases where charges are politically motivated, the WGAD usually finds a general violation of Article 14. The reason is that most political trials are characterized by multiple violations of the "fundamental guarantees stemming from the right to a fair trial."[1023] In the case of Francisco Aguilar, a Bolivian human rights defender, the WGAD noted the case was "formulated in a general and imprecise manner, without defining the specific acts that the criminal offences concerned."[1024] This conclusion was based on the information that the Government had merely drawn up "a long list of undefined acts and evidence of unclear relevance," which prevented effective counsel to the detainees.[1025] In such cases, the WGAD approach to combine various fair trial violations into a general ruling makes it difficult to ascertain how the WGAD would weigh the evidentiary failings specifically.

G Denial to Right of Appeal

The right to an appeal of a criminal conviction is outlined separately in Article 14 of the ICCPR as an important due process and fair trial protection.[1026] The relevant language appears in Article 14(5), which declares:

> Everyone convicted of a crime shall have the right to his conviction and sentence being reviewed by a higher tribunal according to law.

The HR Committee has instructed that the language "according to law," cannot be read expansively as leaving states full discretion to determine the quality of the review.[1027] Instead, the language allows a diversity of legal remedies that may fulfill the requirement

---

[1018] *Id.*, at ¶¶ 17–20.

[1019] *Id.*, at ¶¶ 23, 26–27.

[1020] *Id.*, at ¶ 37.

[1021] *Id.*, at ¶ 25.

[1022] *Id.*, at ¶ 37.

[1023] Francisco José Cortés Aguilar, et al. v. Bolivia, WGAD Opinion No. 12/2005, Adopted May 26, 2005, at ¶ 22.

[1024] *Id.*, at ¶ 19.

[1025] *Id.*, at ¶ 8.

[1026] Bossyut, at 310; Nowak, at 266, providing a general history of the Right to Appeal as a relatively recent development in human rights law.

[1027] General Comment No. 32, at ¶ 45.

to provide opportunity to appeal.[1028] But the quality of the review opportunity holds greater weight and the authorities are under no obligation to provide more than one instance of appeal.[1029] Article 14(5) imposes a substantive duty to review the facts, sufficiency of evidence, the law applied, and the nature of the charge.[1030] Merely reviewing the prior case for formal or legal components will not suffice.[1031] To meet the requirement, a court of higher instance must have assessed the evidence taken to support the previous finding of guilt on the criminal charge.[1032] The detainee, however, does not have a right to a hearing *de novo*.[1033]

States also may not deny the right to appeal by arguing that the offense for which the detainee was indicted was not sufficiently serious and thus does not constitute a "crime" for the purposes of Article 14(5) protection.[1034] The protection, however, does not apply to cases constituting "suits at law," or to constitutional motions.[1035] As with the other fair trial rights protections, the Article 14(5) right applies until criminal proceedings are terminated and despite conviction, acquittal, or discontinuance.[1036] Notably, the HR Committee has clarified that the right of appeal extends not only to the result of the trial at first instance but also to decisions by appeals courts that aggravate the sentence or overturn a prior acquittal.[1037] The right is effective and must be provided even if the detainee was tried and convicted by the highest ordinary criminal court.[1038] The WGAD

[1028] *Id.*, referencing Gomariz Valera v. Spain, Communication No. 1095/2002, Human Rights Committee, CCPR/C/84/D/1095/2002, July 22, 2005, at ¶¶ 7, 10.4. (explaining the "according to law" language as recognizing the "modalities" by which review may be conducted by a higher tribunal; Salgar de Montejo v. Colombia, Human Rights Committee, Communication No. 64/1979).

[1029] General Comment No. 32, at ¶ 45, citing Rouse v. Philippines, Communication No. 1089/2002, Human Rights Committee, CCPR/C/84/D/1089/2002, July 25, 2005, at ¶ 7.6.

[1030] Conte & Burchill, at 194; General Comment No. 32, at ¶ 48; Khalilov v. Tajikistan, Communication No. 973/2001, Human Rights Committee, CCPR/C/83/D/973/2001, Mar. 30, 2005, at ¶ 7.5; Aliboev v. Tajikistan, Communication No. 985/2001, Human Rights Committee, CCPR/C/85/D/985/2001, Oct. 18, 2005, at ¶ 6.5, requiring a review of the "nature of the case."

[1031] General Comment No. 32, at ¶ 48; Gómez Vázquez v. Spain, Communication No. 701/1996, Human Rights Committee, U.N. Doc. CCPR/C/69/D/701/1996, Aug. 11, 2000, at ¶ 11.1 (finding a violation where the case was reviewed only for compliance with procedural rules).

[1032] General Comment No. 32, at ¶ 48, noting that a full retrial or hearing is not required if this standard is met; Rolando v. Philippines, Communication No. 1110/2002, Human Rights Committee, CCPR/C/82/D/1110/2002, Nov. 3, 2004, at ¶ 4.5; Reid v. Jamaica, Communication No. 355/1989, Human Rights Committee, CCPR/C/51/D/355/1989, July 8, 1994, at ¶ 14.3; Juma v. Australia, Communication No. 984/2001, Human Rights Committee, CCPR/C/78/D/984/2001, July 28, 2002, at ¶ 7.5; Perez Escolar v. Spain, Communication No. 1156/2003, Human Rights Committee, CCPR/C/86/D/1156/2003, Mar. 28, 2006, at ¶ 9.3 (finding the review sufficiently detailed to meet the Article 14(5) requirement).

[1033] Joseph & Castan, at 453.

[1034] Nowak, at 267; General Comment No. 32, at ¶ 45, specifying that the guarantee is "not confined to the most serious offences"; Salgar de Montejo, at ¶¶ 10.4, 7.1, refusing the government's argument that Article 14(5) did not set a mandatory appeal standard for offenses not classified as ordinary crimes in domestic law.

[1035] General Comment No. 32, at ¶ 46; I.P. v. Finland, Human Rights Committee, Communication No. 450/1991, CCPR/C/48/D/450/1991, July 26, 1993, at ¶ 6.2 (ruling that matters regarding imposition of taxes fall outside the scope of Article 14 protection since they constitute "suits at law"); Douglas, Gentles & Kerr v. Jamaica, Communication No. 352/1989, Human Rights Committee, CCPR/C/49/D/352/1989, Oct. 19, 1993, at ¶ 11.2.

[1036] Nowak, at 244.

[1037] *Id.*, at 268; Conte & Burchill, at 193; General Comment No. 32, at ¶ 47.

[1038] Terrón v. Spain, Communication No. 1073/2002, Human Rights Committee, CCPR/C/82/D/1073/2002, Nov. 5, 2004, at ¶¶ 7.3–7.4.

previously applied this instruction, noting in *Daniel Omar Ceballos* v. *Venezuela* that the detainee's trial at the first instance by the Supreme Court, the highest in the country, did not leave him any possibility to appeal his conviction.[1039]

Where the charge is clearly identified and based on a crime listed in domestic law or the government specifies a criminal charge, the WGAD usually does not reiterate that the detainee is entitled to the right to appeal.[1040] In *Mohammed Zaki* v. *The Maldives*, involving several political dissenters, however, the Government claimed the charges were political in nature and therefore disqualified from the possibility of appeal.[1041] The detainees were nevertheless subjected to criminal proceedings and booked under relevant sections of the penal code.[1042] In the absence of available judicial mechanisms for review, the detainees resorted to sending letters to the President and Ministry of Defense asking for relief.[1043] The WGAD found a general due process violation based on the four-month delay before trial and the barring of appeal opportunities.[1044]

The detainee must also be afforded "effective access" to the appellate review opportunity.[1045] This requirement, outlined in HR Committee jurisprudence, includes providing the detainee access to all written judgments, sufficiently reasoned, for each instance of appeal within a reasonable time.[1046] The detainee must also be furnished with other relevant material relating to the case, including transcripts of the trial, under this requirement.[1047] This also includes being informed of reasons for continued detention, if a lower court has ordered their release.[1048] Failure to provide a written judgment damages the appeal prospects of the accused and is a violation of the right to appeal.[1049] Effective access must be provided to each instance of appeal provided for by the domestic law of the relevant state.[1050] The WGAD reviewed the appeals process on this basis in *Wissam Rafeedie and Majid Isma'il Al-Talahmeh* v. *Israel*.[1051] The detainees in that case had argued that although an appeals committee did exist, it consisted of a military judge and operated on rules that prevented them from effectively challenging their

---

[1039] Daniel Omar Ceballos v. Venezuela, WGAD Opinion No. 30/2014, Adopted Aug. 28, 2014, at ¶ 39; Mahmoud Abdulrahman al-Jaidah v. United Arab Emirates, WGAD Opinion No. 35/2015, Adopted Sept. 4, 2015, at ¶ 47.

[1040] Choi Sang Soo, et al. v. Democratic People's Republic of Korea, WGAD Opinion No. 36/2013, Adopted Nov. 13, 2013, at ¶ 14 (identifying the particular article of domestic law that lists treason as a crime); Thaer Kanawi Abed el Zahra el Rimahi v. Lebanon, WGAD Opinion No. 14/2011, Adopted May 5, 2011, ¶ 14.

[1041] Mohammed Zaki v. Maldives, WGAD Opinion No. 14/2003, Adopted Sept. 4, 2003, at ¶ 14.

[1042] *Id.*, at ¶ 9.

[1043] *Id.*, at ¶ 14; Saqar Abdelkader Al Chouitier v. Yemen, WGAD Opinion No. 9/2008, Adopted May 8, 2008, at ¶ 8 (where detainees were left with a similar extralegal route for relief in the absence of available review procedures).

[1044] Mohammed Zaki, at ¶ 20.

[1045] General Comment No. 32, at ¶ 45.

[1046] *Id.*, at ¶ 48; Henry v. Jamaica, Communication No. 230/1987, Human Rights Committee, CCPR/C/43/D/230/1987, Nov. 1, 1991, at ¶ 8.4, finding a violation of this standard in the applicant's case.

[1047] General Comment No. 32, at ¶ 49; Lumley v. Jamaica, Communication No. 662/1995, Human Rights Committee, CCPR/C/65/D/662/1995, Apr. 30, 1999, at ¶ 7.5.

[1048] Abdul Fatah and Sa'id Jamaluddin v. Afghanistan and The United States, WGAD Opinion No. 56/2016, Adopted Nov. 24, 2016, at ¶ 52.

[1049] Siamak Namazi and Mohammed Baquer Namazi v. Iran, WGAD Opinion No. 49/2017, Adopted Sept. 22, 2017, at ¶ 48 (Litigated by Author through Freedom Now).

[1050] Nowak, at 267–268; Conte & Burchill, at 195.

[1051] Wissam Rafeedie and Majid Isma'il Al-Talahmeh v. Israel, WGAD Opinion No. 17/1996, Adopted May 23, 1996.

detention.[1052] Evidence presented against the detainees would not be disclosed if deemed to endanger national security.[1053] The WGAD ruled that the structure and procedures available to the detainees could not be considered an "effective possibility to appeal" of their administrative detention.[1054]

The WGAD has since taken a somewhat different approach to assessing the effectiveness of a review. The demonstrative case in this regard is *Youssef Mahmoud Chaabane* v. *Lebanon*, where the WGAD found the available review was not an "effective remedy."[1055] The detainee had been denied review at a first instance because convictions of the Justice Council were not subject to appeal.[1056] After the law was amended to permit review, the detainee was granted the appeal but his conviction was upheld.[1057] The WGAD noted that the appeal was considered by judges who had been involved in the first trial and who would likely be reluctant to overturn the conviction.[1058] The appeals court also failed to adequately review the sufficiency of evidence and did not consider that the evidence had been extracted under torture.[1059] These characteristics of the court's composition and approach rendered the appeal ineffective and therefore in violation of Article 14(5).[1060]

In *Beatriz del Rosario Rivero Martínez* v. *Colombia*, the WGAD found the appellate courts rejection of the principle *no reformatio in peius* denied the detainee an adequate and effective appeal.[1061] The principle prevents appellate courts from putting the accused in a worse position post-appeal. As a result of appealing to the Court for the Execution of Penalties and Security Measures of Cartagena, the detainee had her sentence adjusted from 90 months to 112.[1062] The WGAD considered this a violation of Article 14 of the ICCPR.

The WGAD ruled in *Sanad Ali Yislam Al-Kazimi* v. *United States*, the case of a Guantanamo detainee, that the review must be "meaningful" and address the evidentiary and legal bases of the detention.[1063] The source had explained the detainee's case had been reviewed, but only to determine the necessity of further detention and whether he still presented a security threat to the United States.[1064] The review was conducted not by the federal courts but the Combatant Status Review Tribunal created by the Department of Defense.[1065] The WGAD accepted the source's argument that the procedures for

---

[1052] *Id.*, at ¶ 7.
[1053] *Id.* If reviewed, the evidence would be presented to the committee in the absence of the detainees and counsel; Hamdi Al Ta'mari and Mohamad Baran v. Israel, WGAD Opinion No. 5/2010, Adopted May 6, 2010, at ¶ 25 (stating that this measure rendered the appeal "illusory.")
[1054] Wissam Rafeedie and Majid Isma'il Al-Talahmeh, at ¶ 8.
[1055] Youssef Mahmoud Chaabane v. Lebanon, WGAD Opinion No. 10/2007, Adopted May 11, 2006, at ¶ 17.
[1056] *Id.*, at ¶ 7.
[1057] *Id.*, at ¶¶ 14, 17.
[1058] *Id.*, at ¶ 17; Anwar Ibrahim v. Malaysia, WGAD Opinion No. 22/2015, Adopted Sept. 1, 2015, at ¶ 31 (recognizing the significance of evident bias in judges at the appeals instance).
[1059] Youssef Mahmoud Chaabane, at ¶¶ 17, 19.
[1060] *Id.*, at ¶¶ 19, 21.
[1061] Beatriz del Rosario Rivero Martínez v. Colombia, WGAD Opinion No. 77/2017, Adopted Nov. 21, 2017, at ¶ 47.
[1062] *Id.*, at ¶¶ 21–22.
[1063] Sanad Ali Yislam Al-Kazimi v. United States, WGAD Opinion No. 3/2009, Adopted May 6, 2009, at ¶¶ 32, 35.
[1064] *Id.*, at ¶ 25.
[1065] *Id.*, at ¶¶ 8, 26.

review at the tribunal, which included the use of secret evidence and hearings and setting of limitations on the accused's participation, departed from standards of fair trial, and were therefore not adequately "meaningful."[1066]

Failure of authorities to hold appeal proceedings, where provided for and permitted by law, will also be held by the WGAD to violate the right to appeal.[1067] Denying detainees' requests to appeal sentences has been found to be a violation on various contexts, as has claiming that the detainee waived his right to appeal.[1068] In *Ali-Akbar Saidi-Sirjani, et al. v. Iran*, one of the detainees, a formerly high-ranking politician, was sentenced to life imprisonment in a truncated proceeding for engaging in espionage for the United States.[1069] He appealed the verdict but no judicial hearing took place.[1070] The detainee remained in detention for over a year.[1071] The WGAD found a general Article 14 violation but specified that the detainee had been deprived of his right to appeal.[1072] A violation was also found in *Bweendo Mulengela, et al. v. Zambia*, where the Constitution explicitly guaranteed the right to review detentions, but where courts were barred from questioning the decision of the Executive to order administrative detention for the preservation of public security.[1073]

Authorities must, according to further HR Committee guidance on the subject, ensure that the judicial or other body tasked with hearing the appeal be sufficiently empowered to review the case substantively.[1074] The WGAD, however, refrained from reiterating this requirement in an early case, *Sha'ban Rateb Jabarin v. Israel*.[1075] The source had argued that the only available forum for reviewing a detainee's detention, an Appeals Committee run by military forces, was severely restricted in its assessment of the underlying case.[1076] The WGAD noted the allegation that the rules of evidence and restriction of powers on the Appeals Committee rendered it an ineffective forum for appeal.[1077] The final assessment of the Article 14 violation, however, centered on the failure of authorities to bring the detainee to trial.[1078] Since no indictment took place after the detainee's arrest, the WGAD did not need to assess the sufficiency of the appeals opportunity in detail.[1079]

[1066] *Id.*, at ¶¶ 8, 35.

[1067] Bweendo Mulengela, et al. v. Zambia, WGAD Opinion No. 49/1993, Adopted Sept. 30, 1993, at ¶ 6.

[1068] Abdallah Hamoud Al-Twijri, et. al. v. Iraq, WGAD Opinion No. 43/2012, Adopted Nov. 14, 2012, at ¶¶ 9–11; Chen Kegui v. China, WGAD Opinion No. 2/2014, Adopted Apr. 22, 2014, at ¶¶ 33–34 (Litigated by Author through Freedom Now)(terming the rules precluding requests to appeal as "barriers to remedies"); Haytham al-Maleh v. Syria, WGAD Opinion No. 27/2010, Adopted Nov. 22, 2010, at ¶ 15; Albino Akol Akol, et al. v. Sudan, WGAD Opinion No. 37/1992, Adopted Session No. 4, at ¶ 5(a).

[1069] Ali-Akbar Saidi-Sirjani, et al. v. Iran, WGAD Opinion No. 14/1996, Adopted May 23, 1996, at ¶ 6(b).

[1070] *Id.*

[1071] *Id.*, at ¶ 7.

[1072] *Id.*, at ¶¶ 7, 8(b).

[1073] Bweendo Mulengela, et al., at ¶ 5(f).

[1074] Jason Zachary Puracal v. Nicaragua, WGAD Opinion No. 10/2012, Adopted May 4, 2012, ¶ 19 (questioning the efficacy of the system of appeals).

[1075] Sha'ban Rateb Jabarin v. Israel, WGAD Opinion No. 16/1994, Adopted Sept. 28, 1994, at ¶¶ 6, 13.

[1076] *Id.*, at ¶ 6.

[1077] *Id.*

[1078] *Id.*, at ¶ 13.

[1079] *Id.*, at ¶ 12.

In many instances, the WGAD has ruled on general circumstances where the detainee had no possibility for appeal.[1080] In three cases of North Korean detainees suspected of defection, for example, the WGAD assessed the various general practices of the authorities against similarly situated detainees to find a violation of the Article 14(5) requirement.[1081] The "total absence" of judicial remedies or appellate procedures at the detention camps used for defectors and the routine use of indefinite detention for persons were evidence of a clear violation of the right to appeal.[1082] That the defectors were all charged with treason, a codified crime in North Korean domestic law, qualified the applicants for protection under Article 14 (5).[1083] In *U Pa Pa Lay* v. *Myanmar*, the detainee was tried at the prison site, in secret, and handed a sentence that was deemed final.[1084] The WGAD noted that the preclusion from any appeal was one of various other glaring fair trial rights violations in the case.[1085] Frustrating the possibility of appeal, by changing or subverting the attendant rules governing appeals, was also found to violate the right in *Mohamed Nasheed* v. *The Maldives*.[1086]

Cases tried in military courts, in secret, or by other irregular judicial mechanism may per se violate a detainee's right to appeal.[1087] In three concurrent cases from Syria, the WGAD took the opportunity to reiterate its disapproval of military courts.[1088] The fact that cases adjudicated by military and other courts of exceptional jurisdiction could not be appealed was identified as a key failing that rendered such tribunals in breach of due process guarantees.[1089] Precedent for these rulings was set by early cases from Nigeria concerning the structural due process failures in trials conducted by military courts.[1090] The WGAD has separately pronounced that the procedures of the Supreme State Security Court and military tribunals in Syria fall short of international fair trial standards,

---

[1080]   U Ohn Than v. Myanmar, WGAD Opinion No. 44/2008, Adopted Nov. 26, 2008, at ¶ 18; Mohammad Shahadeh, et al. v. Syria, WGAD Opinion No. 6/2004, Adopted May 26, 2004, at ¶ 8; Phuc Tue Dang, et al. v. Viet Nam, WGAD Opinion No. 21/1997, Adopted Dec. 2, 1997, at ¶ 8; Haile-Mariam Dagne, et al. v. Ethiopia, WGAD Opinion No. 45/1992, Adopted Dec. 8, 1992, at ¶ 6; Oscar Pompilio Estrada Laguna and Norberto Monsalve Bedoya v. Panama, WGAD Opinion No. 16/2013, Adopted Aug. 26, 2013, at ¶ 7.

[1081]   Choi Sang Soo, et al., at ¶ 23; Choi Seong Jai, et al. v. Democratic People's Republic of Korea, WGAD Opinion No. 35/2013, Adopted Nov. 13, 2013, at ¶ 24; Kim Im Bok, et al. v. Democratic People's Republic of Korea, WGAD Opinion No. 34/2013, Adopted Nov. 13, 2013, at ¶ 22.

[1082]   Choi Sang Soo, et al., at ¶ 22; Choi Seong Jai, et al., at ¶ 23; Kim Im Bok, et al., at ¶ 21.

[1083]   Choi Sang Soo, et al., at ¶ 14; Choi Seong Jai, et al., at ¶¶ 7, 9; Kim Im Bok, et al., at ¶¶ 9, 12.

[1084]   U Pa Pa Lay v. Myanmar, WGAD Opinion No. 38/2000, Adopted Nov. 28, 2000, at ¶ 6.

[1085]   Id., at ¶ 9.

[1086]   Mohamed Nasheed v. The Maldives, WGAD Opinion No. 33/2015, Adopted Sept. 4, 2015, at ¶ 103.

[1087]   Jaramani Najib Youcef v. Syria, WGAD Opinion No. 11/2003, Adopted Sept. 3, 2003, at ¶¶ 7–8, 12 (noting that the secretive nature of the trial and its characteristics barring the applicant from appeal, if substantiated, would evidence a violation of Article 14 rights); Carlos Florentino Molero Coca v. Peru, WGAD Opinion No. 24/1998, Adopted Dec. 3, 1998, at ¶ 6(e) (noting that the decisions of faceless courts cannot be challenged); Lori Berenson v. Peru, at ¶ 6(c); Ouda Seliman Tarabin v. Egypt, WGAD Opinion No. 12/2012, Adopted May 3, 2012, at ¶ 20; Hamadi Jabali and Mohammed al-Nouri v. Tunisia, WGAD Opinion No. 51/1992, Adopted Session No. 5, at ¶ 6.

[1088]   Abdul Rahman v. Syria, WGAD Opinion No. 37/2011, Adopted Sept. 1, 2011, at ¶ 13; Tal Al-Mallouhi v. Syria, WGAD Opinion No. 38/2011, Adopted Sept. 1, 2011, at ¶ 13; Tuhama Mahmud Ma'ruf v. Syria, WGAD Opinion No. 39/2011, Adopted Sept. 1, 2011, at ¶ 14.

[1089]   Abdul Rahman, at ¶ 12; Tal Al-Mallouhi, at ¶ 12; Tuhama Mahmoud Ma'rouf, at ¶ 13; Mohamed Khirat al-Shatar, et al. v. Egypt, WGAD Opinion No. 27/2008, Adopted Sept. 12, 2008, at ¶ 85, noting that military courts were run as a parallel and separate justice system to regular courts.

[1090]   George Mbah and Mohammed Sule v. Nigeria, WGAD Opinion No. 38/1996, Adopted Dec. 3, 1996, at ¶ 6; Annimmo Bassey, et al. v. Nigeria, WGAD Opinion No. 37/1996, Adopted Dec. 3, 1996, at ¶ 6; Niran Malaolu v. Nigeria, WGAD Opinion No. 6/1999, Adopted May 20, 1999, at ¶ 9.

for reasons including barring the right of detainees to challenge the lawfulness of their detention.[1091] In two other materially similar cases from Syria, the court based specific Article 14(5) violations on the impossibility of appealing a judgment of this court.[1092]

The right to appeal takes on special importance in cases involving the death penalty.[1093] In that instance, denying a detainee's access to legal aid, or failing to inform the accused of the counsel's intention not to contest the charge, violates Article 14(5).[1094] In *Zeinab Jalalian v. Iran*, the WGAD took note of the death penalty context and stated that the detainee should have been provided access to counsel of her choosing for her appeal.[1095] However, this lapse was categorized as an Article 14(3)(b) and (d) violation.[1096] The right to appeal violation was based on the cursory nature of the judgments and the court's inadequate consideration of the factual, evidentiary, and legal basis of the conviction.[1097] The HR Committee has articulated that the failure to provide sufficient legal aid should properly be found a violation of both Article 14(3)(d) and 14(5).[1098]

The HR Committee has also instructed that undue delays in trial, a separate violation under Article 14(3)(c), may also impair the right to appeal.[1099] The WGAD has followed this approach, ruling in *Mohamed Abdullah Al Uteibi v. Saudi Arabia* that a six-month long detention without an opportunity for review violated the detainee's right to appeal.[1100] In that case, the detainee was not presented before a judge in the first instance until six months after his arrest.[1101] Additionally, the authorities disregarded the release order granted by the judge after the eventual trial.[1102] No further opportunity or procedure was provided to contest the legality of the detention.[1103] In an earlier case, however, *Hagos Atsheba, et al. v. Ethiopia*, the detainees, all with connections to political office, were held in prolonged detention for over two years without being brought to trial.[1104]

[1091] Ahmad Omar Einein, et al. v. Syria, WGAD Opinion No. 28/2008, Adopted Sept. 12, 2008, at ¶ 23; 'Abdel Rahman al-Shaghouri v. Syria, WGAD Opinion No. 4/2005, Adopted May 24, 2005, at ¶ 14, specifying the Article 14(5) failings of the SSSC; Nezar Rastanawi v. Syria, WGAD Opinion No. 23/2008, Adopted Sept. 12, 2008, at ¶ 8; Bassel Khartabil v. Syria, WGAD Opinion No. 5/2015, Adopted Apr. 21, 2015, at ¶ 25.

[1092] Husam 'Ali Mulhim, et al. v. Syria, WGAD Opinion No. 10/2008, Adopted May 9, 2008, at ¶¶ 10, 32; Mus'ab al-Hariri v. Syria, WGAD Opinion No. 1/2008, Adopted May 7, 2008, at ¶¶ 18, 20; Muhammad Osama Sayes, et al. v. Syria, WGAD Opinion No. 16/2006, Adopted May 12, 2006, at ¶ 28.

[1093] General Comment No. 32, at ¶ 51; Conte & Burchill, at 197–198.

[1094] General Comment No. 32, at ¶ 51; LaVende v. Trinidad and Tobago, Communication No. 554/1993, Human Rights Committee, CCPR/C/61/D/554/1993, Oct. 29, 1997, at ¶ 5.8; Smith & Stewart v. Jamaica, Communication No. 554/1993, Human Rights Committee, CCPR/C/65/D/668/1995, May 12, 1999, at ¶ 7.3; Gallimore v. Jamaica, Communication No. 680/1996, Human Rights Committee, CCPR/C/66/D/680/1996, Sept. 16, 1999, at ¶ 7.4.

[1095] Zeinab Jalalian v. Iran, WGAD Opinion No. 1/2016, Adopted Apr. 18, 2016, at ¶ 39.

[1096] *Id.*

[1097] *Id.*

[1098] General Comment No. 32, at ¶ 51.

[1099] Joseph & Castan, at 456; Conte & Burchill, at 197; General Comment No. 32, at ¶ 49, citing Kennedy v. Trinidad & Tobago, Communication No. 845/1998, Human Rights Committee, CCPR/C/74/D/845/1998, Mar. 26, 2002, at ¶ 3.2 (where the trials for appeal were delayed for between twenty-six and thirty-eight months in several instances).

[1100] Mohamed Abdullah Al Uteibi v. Saudi Arabia, WGAD Opinion No. 33/2011, Adopted Sept. 1, 2011, at ¶ 12; Thaer Kanawi Abed el Zahra el Rimahi, at ¶¶ 18–19.

[1101] Mohamed Abdullah Al Uteibi, at ¶ 12.

[1102] *Id.*

[1103] *Id.*, at ¶ 14.

[1104] Hagos Atsheba, et al. v. Ethiopia, WGAD Opinion No. 55/1993, Adopted Dec. 8, 1993, at ¶ 5(c).

The WGAD did not, in that instance, supplement the finding of an Article 14(3)(c) with an Article 14(5) ruling.[1105]

Undue delays in trial at the first instance or for appeal proceedings have featured in other cases. In *Thaer Kanawi el Rimahi* v. *Lebanon*, the case of an Iraqi refugee charged with the crime of illegally entering Lebanon, the detainee's trial was postponed for two months and rescheduled eleven times.[1106] The detainee continued to be held despite a criminal court's ruling that he had served the entirety of his sentence.[1107] The WGAD found a general fair trial violation, noting that the detainee had been held for a total of eleven months without being provided an opportunity to appeal.[1108] The WGAD ruled similarly in *Mohamed Nazim* v. *The Maldives*, finding that a five-month delay in hearing the appeal of a former politician was a due process violation.[1109] In *Christophe Désiré Bengono* v. *Cameroon*, the detainee encountered several hurdles in obtaining an appeal hearing, which was eventually heard over two years after he had filed a request for review.[1110] Excessively lengthy proceedings, both in the first instance and on appeal, may also be held to violate the right to appeal or fair trial rights generally.[1111]

Where several fair trial rights are violated, the WGAD has often found a general Article 14 violation instead of listing Article 14(5) as having been specifically violated.[1112] In the case of Mohamed Abdullah Al Uteibi, the case of a Saudi activist detained for over six months without charge, the WGAD stressed the violation of the detainee's right to a fair hearing before an independent tribunal, but subsumed the right to appeal assessment within a broad UDHR Article 10 violation ruling.[1113] Similarly, in *Sheikh Suliaman al-Rashudi, et al.* v. *Saudi Arabia*, the WGAD noted the barriers to appeal, which included higher courts' refusal to exercise jurisdiction over the detainees' case, but did not separate the analysis into its constituent parts.[1114] Notably, in *Assem Kakoun* v. *Lebanon*, where the source had specifically provided that the detainee's explicit request for review had been declared inadmissible by authorities, the WGAD also did not conduct a separate Article 14 (5) analysis.[1115] Again, this was presumably because the case displayed numerous due process violations, of which the right to appeal was only one ignored component.[1116]

In other cases, the WGAD has isolated the fair trial violations and found a specific violation of the right to appeal under Article 14(5).[1117] In *Husam 'Ali Mulhim* v. *Syria*, the case of several political dissenters, the court found the right to adequate time and

---

[1105] *Id.*, at ¶ 7.
[1106] Thaer Kanawi Abed el Zahra el Rimahi, at ¶¶ 4–6, 11.
[1107] *Id.*, at ¶ 8.
[1108] *Id.*, at ¶¶ 15, 18.
[1109] Mohamed Nazim v. The Maldives, WGAD Opinion No. 59/2016, Adopted Nov. 25, 2016, at ¶ 63.
[1110] Christophe Désiré Bengono v. Cameroon, WGAD Opinion No. 46/2014, Adopted Nov. 19, 2014, at ¶¶ 25–26.
[1111] Paul Eric Kingue v. Cameroon, WGAD Opinion No. 38/2014, Adopted Aug. 29, 2014, at ¶¶ 29–30.
[1112] Choi Sang Soo, et al., at ¶ 35; Mohammad Shahadeh, et al., at ¶ 12; Phuc Tue Dang, et al., at ¶ 10.
[1113] Mohamed Abdullah Al Uteibi, at ¶ 14.
[1114] Sheikh Suliaman al-Rashudi, et al. v. Saudi Arabia, WGAD Opinion No. 38/2015, Adopted Sept. 4, 2015, at ¶¶ 73–74, 80.
[1115] Assem Kakoun v. Lebanon, WGAD Opinion No. 17/2008, Adopted Sept. 9, 2008, at ¶¶ 7(c), 10.
[1116] *Id.*, at ¶ 10.
[1117] Mus'ab al-Hariri, at ¶ 20; Mbanza Judicaël, et al. v. Republic of Congo, WGAD Opinion No. 44/2014, Adopted Nov. 9, 2014, at ¶ 32; Saddam Hussein al-Tikriti v. United States, WGAD Opinion No. 46/2005, Adopted Nov. 30, 2005, at ¶ 33; Tariq Aziz v. Iraq and United States, WGAD Opinion No. 45/2005, Adopted Nov. 30, 2005, at ¶ 28.

facilities to prepare defense, protection against self-incrimination, and the right to appeal separately violated.[1118] The detailed examination of the particular due process violations was supported by prior observations about the shortcomings of the Security Court as a judicial body.[1119] In another case from Syria, *Naji Azziz Harb* v. *Syria*, a former army officer was sentenced to life imprisonment by a military tribunal entirely comprising military personnel.[1120] The WGAD separated the various fair trial violations in the case and especially noted the impossibility of appealing the decision of the tribunal, finding an Article 14(5) violation.[1121] The analytical approach to adjudicating right to appeal violations has, therefore, been inconsistent.

A specific Article 14(5) analysis was conducted and a violation found in *Djema'a el Seyed Suleymane Ramadhan* v. *Egypt*.[1122] The detainee in that case was a civilian suspected of membership in a terrorist organization and tried on a criminal charge by a military tribunal.[1123] The WGAD noted with concern that decisions of the military tribunals were not subject to any appeal nor had the authorities provided for a military appeals court as contemplated by a prior amendment of the Military Judgments Act.[1124] The structural and procedural barriers to a review of the conviction were found to have violated Article 14(5).[1125] Interestingly, the WGAD stated in its ruling that Article 14(5) gave the detainee the right to "have his conviction and sentence revised by a higher tribunal."[1126] HR Committee jurisprudence does not provide such an expansive reading and does not presuppose the result of a subsequent review. The scope of the WGAD's ruling may be limited, however, to cases involving very broad and vague charges of terrorism that were most likely politically motivated.[1127]

V Military Tribunals

Military tribunals are not prohibited by international law per se.[1128] However, the administration of justice through military tribunals has raised serious concerns in terms of "access to justice, impunity for past human rights abuses, the independence and

---

[1118] Husam 'Ali Mulhim, et al., at ¶¶ 31–32 (specifically finding violations of Article 14 paras. 3(b) and (g), and 5).

[1119] *Id.*, at ¶ 10.

[1120] Naji Azziz Harb v. Syria, WGAD Opinion No. 20/2000, Adopted Sept. 14, 2000, at ¶¶ 5–6.

[1121] *Id.*, at ¶ 10; Tarek Mostafa Marei and Abdel Karim Al Mustafa v. Lebanon, WGAD Opinion No. 48/2014, Adopted Nov. 19, 2014, at ¶ 17.

[1122] Djema'a el Seyed Suleymane Ramadhan v. Egypt, WGAD Opinion No. 18/2008, Adopted Sept. 9, 2008, at ¶ 22.

[1123] *Id.*, at ¶¶ 6–8.

[1124] *Id.*, at ¶¶ 14, 17; Concerning 12 Individuals v. Egypt, WGAD Opinion No. 10/2014, Adopted Apr. 24, 2014, at ¶ 18 (relying on a similar precedent and assessment of military courts in Egypt).

[1125] Djema'a el Seyed Suleymane Ramadhan, at ¶ 22.

[1126] *Id.*

[1127] *Id.*, at ¶ 17; Ali Mahdi Hasan Saeed, et al. v. Bahrain, WGAD Opinion No. 41/2015, Adopted Dec. 2, 2015, at fn. 3, referencing WGAD guidelines regarding the protections attendant to applicants arrested on terrorism charges.

[1128] *Report of the Special Rapporteur on the Independence of Judges and Lawyers*, Human Rights Council, A/61/384, Sept. 12, 2006, A/61/384, at ¶ 20 ("The trying of human rights violations by military tribunals is explicitly prohibited only in article 9 of the Inter-American Convention on Forced Disappearance of Persons, and article 16 of the Declaration on the Protection of All Persons from Enforced Disappearance.")

impartiality of military tribunals, and respect for the fair trial rights of the accused."[1129] In many countries, military tribunals try members of the armed forces for serious human rights violations or try civilians, in violation of applicable international principles.[1130] For over a decade, an important body of international jurisprudence on military tribunals has been developed based on general human rights norms relating to the administration of justice.[1131] The interpretation of the right to a fair trial has provided a foundation for the limitations on the trial of civilians by military tribunals.[1132] In recent years, several different human rights treaty bodies, UN Special Procedures, and regional human rights bodies have highlighted the challenges military tribunals pose to the enjoyment of human rights.[1133]

Treaty bodies have also addressed the issue of military justice. In its General Comment 13, the HR Committee declared "the provisions of article 14 apply to all courts and tribunals within the scope of that article whether ordinary or specialized."[1134] It pointed out the existence of military tribunals that try civilians and that often the reason for the establishment of military tribunals is to "enable exceptional procedures to be applied which do not comply with normal standards of justice."[1135] The HR Committee acknowledged that while the ICCPR does not prohibit such courts, trial of civilians by such courts should be "very exceptional and take under conditions which genuinely afford the full guarantees stipulated in article 14."[1136] In its General Comment 32, the HR Committee reiterated its concern for military tribunals. It noted that the trial of civilians by military tribunals must be "limited to cases where the State party can show that resorting to such trials is necessary and justified by objective and serious reasons, and where with regard to the specific class of individuals and offences at issue the regular civilian courts are unable to undertake the trials."[1137] In addition, the Committee against Torture and the Committee on the Rights of the Child has also noted "with concern the unbroken pattern of impunity and the continuous tendency to refer serious violations of human rights to the military justice system."[1138]

Many UN Special Procedures have also expressed their concerns about military tribunals. The UN Special Rapporteur on the Independence of Judges and Lawyers has addressed the question of the establishment and operation of military and special tribunals on multiple occasions.[1139] In 2013, the Special Rapporteur submitted a report on

---

[1129] *Report of the Special Rapporteur on the Independence of Judges and Lawyers*, Human Rights Council, A/68/285, Aug. 7, 2013.

[1130] *Report of the Special Rapporteur on the Independence of Judges and Lawyers*, Human Rights Council, A/61/384, Sept. 12, 2006, at ¶ 18.

[1131] *Id.*, at ¶ 20.

[1132] *Id.*

[1133] *Report of the Special Rapporteur on the Independence of Judges and Lawyers*, Human Rights Council, A/68/285, Aug. 7, 2013, at ¶ 19.

[1134] General Comment No. 13, *at* ¶ 4.

[1135] *Id.*

[1136] *Id.*

[1137] General Comment No. 32, at ¶ 22.

[1138] *Consideration of Reports Submitted by States Parties under Article 44 of the Convention*, Committee on the Rights of the Child, CRC/C/COL/CO/3, June 8, 2006, ¶ 44.

[1139] *See generally Report of the Special Rapporteur on the Independence of Judges and Lawyers*, Human Rights Council, A/HRC/8/4, May 13, 2008; *Report of the Special Rapporteur on the Independence of Judges and Lawyers*, Human Rights Council, A/HRC/11/41, Mar. 24, 2009; *Report of the Special Rapporteur on the Independence of Judges and Lawyers*, Human Rights Council, A/HRC/20/19, June 7, 2012; *Report of the*

the issue of military tribunals to consider their compliance with internationally recognized fair trial standards.[140] The report observed that military tribunals raise serious concerns in terms of access to justice, impunity for past human rights abuses, the independence and impartiality of military tribunals, and respect for the fair trial rights of the accused.[141]

The report emphasized that military tribunals must respect fair trial and the due process guarantees set out in Articles 9 and 14 of the ICCPR. It focused on four thematic areas, including (1) the independence and impartiality of military tribunals; (2) the personal jurisdiction of military tribunals, including the question of investigation and prosecution of civilians; (3) the subject-matter jurisdiction of military tribunals, including the question of investigation and prosecution of serious human rights violations allegedly perpetrated by military personnel; and (4) the application of fair trial guarantees in proceedings before military tribunals.[142]

Regarding the independence and impartiality of military tribunals, the report suggested that the independence of military tribunals be guaranteed at the highest level possible.[143] To do so, it recommended their independence and their inclusion within the general administration of justice system be guaranteed in the constitution or a fundamental law.[144] In addition, independence and the status of military judges should be protected through domestic legislation.[145]

In relation to the personal jurisdiction of military tribunals, the report noted that the jurisprudence of international law shows that there is a "strong trend against extending the criminal jurisdiction of military tribunals over civilians."[146] The report stated that the jurisdiction of military tribunals should be restricted to offences of a "strictly military nature committed by military personnel."[147] The reports suggested that the trial of civilians in military tribunals should be limited strictly to exceptional cases concerning civilians assimilated to military personnel by virtue of their function and/or geographical presence who have allegedly perpetrated an offence outside the territory of the State and where regular courts are unable to undertake the trial.[148]

With regard to the jurisdiction of military tribunals, the report recommended that military tribunals should be limited to criminal offences of a strictly military nature that

---

Special Rapporteur on the Independence of Judges and Lawyers, Human Rights Council, E/CN.4/2004/60, Dec. 31, 2003; *Report of the United Nations Development Fund for Women on the Elimination of Violence against Women*, United Nations Development Fund for Women, E/CN.4/2006/60, Dec. 20, 2005; Special Rapporteur on the independence of judges and lawyers, *Report of the Special Rapporteur on the independence of judges and lawyers*, A/61/384, Sept. 12, 2006; *Report of the Special Rapporteur on the Independence of Judges and Lawyers*, Human Rights Council, A/62/207, Aug. 6, 2007; *Report of the Special Rapporteur on the Independence of Judges and Lawyers*, Human Rights Council, A/63/271, Aug. 12, 2008; *Report of the Special Rapporteur on the Independence of Judges and Lawyers*, Human Rights Council, A/68/285, Aug. 7, 2013.

[140] *Report of the Special Rapporteur on the Independence of Judges and Lawyers*, Human Rights Council, A/68/285, Aug. 7, 2013, at ¶ 4.

[141] *Id.*, at ¶ 14.

[142] *Id.*, at ¶ 4.

[143] *Id.*, at ¶ 36.

[144] *Id.*, at ¶ 93.

[145] *Id.*, at ¶ 95.

[146] *Id.*, at ¶ 47.

[147] *Id.*, at ¶ 54, 100.

[148] *Id.*, at ¶ 102.

by "their own nature relate exclusively to legally protected interests of military order, such as desertion, insubordination or abandonment of post or command."[1149]

And regarding the application of fair trial guarantees, the report emphasized that military tribunals must apply the principles of international law relating to a fair trial, guaranteeing the right to defense, equality of arms, and right to appeal.[1150]

The prior UN Special Rapporteur of the Sub-Commission on the Promotion and Protection of Human Rights also made a significant contribution. In 2006, the Special Rapporteur elaborated a set of draft principles concerning the administration of justice through military tribunals, which was the culmination of an undertaking the Sub-Commission had engaged for several years.[1151] As will be explained in further detail, the principles aimed to establish a minimum system of universally applicable rules to regulate military justice.[1152] Other Special Rapporteurs have expressed similar concerns as well. The report of the UN Special Rapporteur on the Promotion and Protection of Human Rights and Fundamental Freedoms While Countering Terrorism expressed concerns over the use of military tribunals, and called for the limitation of their use to only trials of military personnel for acts committed in the course of military actions.[1153] The report also emphasized that the trial of civilians by military tribunals should take place only in limited exceptional circumstances "necessary and justified by objective and serious reasons."[1154] The UN Special Rapporteur on Extrajudicial, Summary or Arbitrary Executions has also highlighted that "as an empirical matter, subjecting allegations of human rights abuse to military jurisdiction often leads to impunity."[1155]

The WGAD has also developed a body of jurisprudence on military tribunals over its existence. The WGAD first expressed its concern over military tribunals in its annual report in 1993. Here, the WGAD noted that although military courts "do not seem to be strictly inconsistent with international rules," they are being used more frequently to try dissidents who are then denied the right to be heard by an independent and impartial tribunal, which is the "very essence of the human right to justice."[1156] Since then, the WGAD has repeatedly raised its concern over military tribunals, recognizing that "one of the most serious causes of arbitrary detention is precisely the existence of [military

---

[1149] *Id.*, at ¶ 98.

[1150] *Id.*, at ¶¶ 72, 107–10.

[1151] *Id.*, at ¶ 18 (noting that "beginning with the questionnaire drawn up by Mr. Louis Joinet for his report to the Sub-Commission at its fifty-third session (E/CN.4/Sub.2/2001/WG.1/CRP.3, annex), followed by his report to the fifty-fourth session (E/CN.4/Sub.2/2002/4), and the reports by Mr. Emmanuel Decaux to the fifty-fifth session (E/CN.4/Sub.2/2003/4), fifty-sixth session (E/CN.4/Sub.2/2004/7) and fifty-seventh session (E/CN.4/Sub.2/2005/9)."); *Issue of the Administration of Justice through Military Tribunals*, Special Rapporteur of the Sub-Commission on the Promotion and Protection of Human Rights, E/CN.4/2006/58, Jan. 13, 2006, at ¶ 5.

[1152] *Id.*, ¶ 10.

[1153] *Report of the Special Rapporteur on the Promotion and Protection of Human Rights and Fundamental Freedoms While Countering Terrorism*, Human Rights Council, A/63/223, Aug. 6, 2008, at ¶¶ 25–27.

[1154] *Id.*, at ¶ 28; *See also An Updated Framework Draft of Principles and Guidelines Concerning Human Rights and Terrorism*, Human Rights Council, A/HRC/Sub.1/58/30, Aug. 3, 2006, at ¶ 46.

[1155] *Report of the Special Rapporteur on Extrajudicial, Summary or Arbitrary Executions*, E/CN.4/2006/53, Mar. 8, 2006, at ¶ 37.

[1156] *Report of the Working Group on Arbitrary Detention*, Commission on Human Rights, E/CN.4/1993/24, Jan. 12, 1993, at ¶ 34.

tribunals], virtually none of which respects the guarantees of the right to a fair trial."[157] It has underscored that fair trial rights must be guaranteed by military tribunals, and that military tribunals generally do not meet those guarantees.[158] In *Mohamed Essayed Ali Rasslan v. Egypt*, the WGAD explained that the development of international law over the last fifteen years supports the consistent jurisprudence of the WGAD that the right to a fair trial under Article 14 of the ICCPR and Article 10 of the UDHR "excludes the criminal jurisdiction of military courts over civilians."[159]

To that end, the WGAD formulated its own rules regarding military justice, which first appeared in its report on the mission to Peru in 1999. In agreeing with the statement of the UN Special Rapporteur on the Independence of Judges and Lawyers that "international law is developing a consensus as to the need to restrict drastically, or even prohibit, this practice [abuse of military justice]," the WGAD recommended four rules that must be observed in military justice:

(a) It should be incompetent to try civilians; (b) It should be incompetent to try military personnel if the victims include civilians; (c) It should be incompetent to try civilians and military personnel in the event of rebellion, sedition or any offence that jeopardizes or involves risk of jeopardizing a democratic regime; and (d) It should be prohibited from imposing the death penalty under any circumstances.[160]

Later, an additional rule was added: "If civilians have also been indicted in a case, military tribunals should not try military personnel."[161] In the WGAD's *Basic Principles and Guidelines on Remedies and Procedures on the Right of Anyone Deprived of Their Liberty to Bring Proceedings before a Court*, the WGAD also stated that "[m]ilitary tribunals are not competent to review the arbitrariness and lawfulness of the detention of civilians. Military judges and military prosecutors do not meet the fundamental requirements of independence and impartiality."[162]

---

[157] *Report of the Working Group on Arbitrary Detention*, Commission on Human Rights, E/CN.4/2004/3, Dec. 15, 2003, at ¶ 67; *see also Report of the Working Group on Arbitrary Detention*, Commission on Human Rights, E/CN.4/1996/40, at ¶ 107.

[158] *Report of the Working Group on Arbitrary Detention*, Commission on Human Rights, E/CN.4/1994/27, Dec. 12, 1993, at ¶¶ 29, 34–35; *Report of the Working Group on Arbitrary Detention*, Commission on Human Rights, E/CN.4/1995/31, Dec. 21, 1994, at ¶ 44; *Report of the Working Group on Arbitrary Detention*, Commission on Human Rights, E/CN.4/1996/40, at ¶ 107; *Report of the Working Group on Arbitrary Detention*, Commission on Human Rights, E/CN.4/1999/63, Dec. 18, 1998, at ¶¶ 49, 79–80; *Report of the Working Group on Arbitrary Detention*, Commission on Human Rights, E/CN.4/2001/14, Dec. 20, 2000, at ¶ 36; *Report of the Working Group on Arbitrary Detention*, Commission on Human Rights, E/CN.4/2004/3, Dec. 15, 2003, at ¶¶ 58, 59, 67;

    Report of the Working Group on Arbitrary Detention, Human Rights Council, A/HRC/4/40, Jan. 9, 2007, at ¶ 6; *Report of the Working Group on Arbitrary Detention*, Human Rights Council, A/HRC/7/4, Jan. 10, 2008, at ¶¶ 63–66, 78, 82; *Report of the Working Group on Arbitrary Detention*, Human Rights Council, A/HRC/13/30, Jan. 18, 2010, at ¶¶ 66–71; *Report of the Working Group on Arbitrary Detention*, Human Rights Council, A/HRC/27/48, June 30, 2014, at ¶¶ 66–71.

[159] Concerning 12 Individuals v. Egypt, WGAD Opinion No. 10/2014, Adopted Apr. 24, 2014, at ¶ 23.

[160] *Report of the Working Group on Arbitrary Detention: Mission to Peru*, Commission on Human Rights, E/CN.4/1999/63/Add.2, Jan. 11, 1999, at ¶¶ 179–180.

[161] *Report of the Working Group on Arbitrary Detention*, Human Rights Council, A/HRC/27/48, June 30, 2014, at ¶ 69.

[162] Basic Principles and Guidelines, at ¶ 55.

Other regional human rights systems have also developed a jurisprudence prohibiting the use of military tribunals in trying civilians. The Inter-American system holds the position that the trying of civilians by military tribunals conflicts with the articles of the *American Convention on Human Rights*, which guarantee the right to be tried by an independent and impartial court and the right to a fair trial.[1163] The Inter-American Court of Human Rights has stated:

> In a democratic Government of Laws the penal military jurisdiction shall have a restrictive and exceptional scope and shall lead to the protection of special juridical interests, related to the functions assigned by law to the military forces. Consequently, civilians must be excluded from the military jurisdiction scope and only the military shall be judged by commission of crime or offences that by its own nature attempt against legally protected interests of military order.[1164]

The African Commission on Human and Peoples' Rights has also criticized the trial of civilians by military tribunals.[1165] It has interpreted Articles 7 and 26 of the *African Charter on Human and Peoples' Rights* on the right to a fair trial to prohibit military jurisdiction over civilians.[1166] Moreover, the reference to military tribunals found in the *Principles and Guidelines on the Right to a Fair Trial and Legal Assistance in Africa* adopted in 2003 not only prohibits the use of military courts to try civilians, but also stipulates that all civilians have a right not to be tried by such courts.[1167]

Although the European Court of Human Rights has not developed a significant body of jurisprudence regarding military justice,[1168] it has stated that the existence of any military jurisdiction should be subjected to careful scrutiny. It has held that civilians cannot be tried before military courts that are composed of military personnel.[1169] The Court also noted the

---

[1163] Concerning 12 Individuals, at ¶ 21; *Report of the Special Rapporteur on the Independence of Judges and Lawyers*, Human Rights Council, A/61/384, Sept. 12, 2006, at ¶ 26.

[1164] Concerning 12 Individuals, at ¶ 21; *see also* Durand and Ugarte v. Peru, Judgment, Inter-Am Ct. H.R. (Ser. C) No. 68, at ¶ 117 (Aug. 16, 2000); Cantoral-Benavides v. Peru, Judgment, Inter-Am Ct. H.R. (Ser. C) No. 69 (Aug. 18, 2000).

[1165] *Report of the Special Rapporteur on the Independence of Judges and Lawyers*, Commission on Human Rights, A/61/384, Sept. 12, 2006, at ¶ 29.; *see also* Civil Liberties Organisation, Legal Defence Centre, Legal Defence and Assistance Project v. Nigeria, African Commission on Human and Peoples' Rights, Comm. No. 218/98 (1998); Forum of Conscience v. Sierra Leone, African Commission on Human and Peoples' Rights, Comm. No. 223/98 (2000); Annette Pagnoulle (on behalf of Abdoulaye Mazou) vs. Cameroon, African Commission on Human and Peoples' Rights, Comm. No. 39/90, (1997); Constitutional Rights Project v. Nigeria, African Commission on Human and Peoples' Rights, Comm. No. 60/91 (1995).

[1166] Concerning 12 Individuals, at ¶ 20.

[1167] *Report of the Special Rapporteur on the Independence of Judges and Lawyers*, Human Rights Council, A/61/384, Sept. 12, 2006, at ¶ 29; *Report of the Special Rapporteur on the Independence of Judges and Lawyers*, Human Rights Council, A/68/285, Aug. 7, 2013, at ¶ 17.

[1168] *Report of the Special Rapporteur on the Independence of Judges and Lawyers*, Human Rights Council, A/61/384, Sept. 12, 2006, at ¶ 28.

[1169] Concerning 12 Individuals, at ¶ 22.; Ergin v. Turkey (No. 6), Application No. 47533/99, European Court of Human Rights, May 4, 2006, at ¶ 45.; *see also* Incal v. Turkey, Application No. 22678/93, European Court of Human Rights, June 9, 1998; Çiraklar v. Turkey, Application No. 70/1997/854/1061, European Court of Human Rights, Oct. 28, 1998; Gerger v. Turkey, Application No. 24919/94, European Court of Human Rights, July 8, 1999; Karatas v. Turkey, Application No. 23168/94, European Court of Human Rights, July 8, 1999.

"developments over the last decade at international level, which confirm[s] the existence of a trend towards excluding the criminal jurisdiction of military courts over civilians."[1170]

A *Applicable Laws and Standards*

There is no outright prohibition of military tribunals in international human rights treaties. However, the fair trial rights guaranteed under Article 14 of the ICCPR still apply to them as stated by the HR Committee in General Comment 32: "The provisions of article 14 apply to all courts and tribunals within the scope of that article whether ordinary or specialized, civilian or military."[1171] And when it comes to the trying of civilians in military tribunals, different human rights bodies share the same principle that they should not try civilians, except in very limited circumstances. The HR Committee emphasized:

> While the Covenant does not prohibit the trial of civilians in military or special courts, it requires that such trials are in full conformity with the requirements of article 14 and that its guarantees cannot be limited or modified because of the military or special character of the court concerned. Therefore, it is important to take all necessary measures to ensure that such trials take place under conditions which genuinely afford the full guarantees stipulated in article 14. Trials of civilians by military or special courts should be exceptional, i.e. limited to cases where the State party can show that resorting to such trials is necessary and justified by objective and serious reasons, and where with regard to the specific class of individuals and offences at issue the regular civilian courts are unable to undertake the trials.[1172]

Thus, military tribunals implicate a range of rights enshrined in the ICCPR and the UDHR, and other international human rights principles.

There are several different human rights sources that the WGAD draws from in its military tribunal cases. The WGAD relies mostly on the ICCPR and the UDHR in its opinions. Occasionally, the WGAD refers to the *Draft Principles Governing the Administration of Justice through Military Tribunals*, which have gained a wide acceptance in the international human rights world. As mentioned previously, the WGAD has even formulated its own rules regarding military tribunals.

The WGAD has consistently found military tribunals to violate Articles 9 and 14 of the ICCPR and Articles 9 and 10 of the UDHR. Both Articles 9 and 14 of the ICCPR guarantee a "series of specific rights" more specified than Articles 9 and 10 of the UDHR.[1173] The WGAD agreed with the HR Committee "that the provisions of article 14 of the International Covenant on Civil and Political Rights apply to all kinds of courts, whether ordinary or emergency courts." Thus "[u]ndoubtedly, the Covenant does not prohibit military courts, even when they try civilians, but conditions reveal no less clearly that trials of civilians by such courts must be exceptional and must be held under conditions of full respect for all the guarantees set out in article 14."[1174]

[1170] Concerning 12 Individuals, at ¶ 22.

[1171] General Comment No. 32, at ¶ 22.

[1172] *Id.*

[1173] *Id.*, at ¶ 2.

[1174] *Report of the Working Group on Arbitrary Detention*, Commission on Human Rights, E/CN.4/1994/27, Dec. 12, 1993, at ¶ 35.

The WGAD has found almost all the rights provided in Articles 9 and 14 of the ICCPR to be violated by military tribunals.[1175] In one of its reports, the WGAD stressed that "a court composed of a low-ranking soldier or other military personnel cannot be considered 'a competent, independent and impartial tribunal', as defined under international human rights law."[1176] Noting that military tribunals are "likely to produce an effect contrary to the enjoyment of the human rights and to a fair trial with due guarantees," the WGAD listed fair trial rights adversely affected by military tribunals, which overlap with the rights guaranteed in Articles 9 and 14 of the ICCPR.[1177] They include the rights:

- To liberty and security of person (ICCPR Article 9(1));
- To appeal against detention; to be brought promptly before an independent and impartial judge; to be brought to trial in the shortest possible time; to be released pending trial (ICCPR Article 9(3));
- To challenge the lawfulness of their detention (ICCPR Article 9(4));
- To a fair and prompt trial (ICCPR Article 14(1));
- To be tried in public by a legally established, independent, competent and impartial court (ICCPR Article 14(1);
- To a presumption of innocence (ICCPR Article 14(2);
- To be tried without undue delay (ICCPR Article 14(3)(c);
- To a free and adequate defence (ICCPR 14(3)(d);
- To equality of arms between prosecution and defence;
- To access to evidence submitted by the prosecution; and
- To other fundamental judicial guarantees of a fair trial.[1178]

In addition, the WGAD has found other rights in Articles 9 and 14 of the ICCPR to be violated by military tribunals in its opinions. These include the rights:

[1175] *See generally Report of the Special Rapporteur on the Independence of Judges and Lawyers*, Human Rights Council, A/HRC/8/4, May 13, 2008; *Report of the Special Rapporteur on the Independence of Judges and Lawyers*, Human Rights Council, A/HRC/11/41, Mar. 24, 2009; *Report of the Special Rapporteur on the Independence of Judges and Lawyers*, Human Rights Council, A/HRC/20/19, June 7, 2012; *Report of the Special Rapporteur on the Independence of Judges and Lawyers*, Commission on Human Rights, E/CN.4/2004/60, Dec. 31, 2003; *Report of the United Nations Development Fund for Women on the Elimination of Violence against Women*, United Nations Development Fund for Women, E/CN.4/2006/60, Dec. 20, 2005; *Report of the Special Rapporteur on the Independence of Judges and Lawyers*, Human Rights Council, A/61/384, Sept. 12, 2006; *Report of the Special Rapporteur on the Independence of Judges and Lawyers*, Human Rights Council, A/62/207, Aug. 6, 2007; *Report of the Special Rapporteur on the Independence of Judges and Lawyers*, Human Rights Council, A/63/271, Aug. 12, 2008; *Report of the Special Rapporteur on the Independence of Judges and Lawyers*, Human Rights Council, A/68/285, Aug. 7, 2013.

[1176] *Report of the Working Group on Arbitrary Detention*, Human Rights Council, A/HRC/27/48, June 30, 2014, at ¶ 68.

[1177] *Report of the Working Group on Arbitrary Detention*, Human Rights Council, A/HRC/13/30, Jan. 18, 2010, at ¶¶ 66–67; *Report of the Working Group on Arbitrary Detention*, Human Rights Council, A/HRC/27/48, June 30, 2014, at ¶ 68.

[1178] *Id.*

- To be informed, at the time of arrest, of the reasons for their arrest and shall be notified without delay of any charge brought against them (ICCPR Article 9(2));[1179]
- To have adequate time and facilities for the preparation of their defence and to communicate with counsel of their own choosing (ICCPR Article 14(3)(b));[1180]
- To examine witnesses (ICCPR Article 14(3)(e));[1181]
- To appeal (ICCPR Article 14(5));[1182]
- To be informed in detail of the nature and cause of the charges brought against them;[1183]
- Not to be compelled to testify against themselves or to confess guilt;[1184] against double jeopardy (ICCPR Article 14(7)).[1185]

This clearly shows that according to the WGAD, on a prima facie basis, military tribunals violate most of the rights enshrined in Articles 9 and 14 of the ICCPR and Articles 9 and 10 of the UDHR.

Aside from the ICCPR and the UDHR, there is another set of soft law principles that is applicable to military tribunals. In 2006, the Special Rapporteur of the Sub-Commission on the Promotion and Protection of Human Rights, Emmanuel Decaux, submitted a report to the Commission of Human Rights entitled *Draft Principles Governing the Administration of Justice through Military Tribunals*.[1186] The principles aimed to establish a minimum system of universally applicable rules to regulate military justice, with the idea that military justice must be "an integral part of the general judicial system."[1187] Developed in consultation with human rights experts, jurists, and military personnel from all parts of the word, the principles set out specific provisions relating to the establishment and functioning of military tribunals.[1188] Although the principles have not been adopted by the HRC nor endorsed by the General Assembly, the principles have gained a wide acceptance in the human rights world.[1189] Both the WGAD and the

---

[1179] Mohammed Ali Najem, et al. v. Lebanon, WGAD Opinion No. 57/2014, Adopted Nov. 21, 2014, at ¶ 25.

[1180] Maikel Nabil Sanad v. Egypt, WGAD Opinion No. 50/2011, Adopted Feb. 29, 2012, at ¶ 17.

[1181] Id.

[1182] Id.

[1183] Yacoub Hanna Shamoun v. Syria, WGAD Opinion No. 9/2012, Adopted May 3, 2012, at ¶ 21.

[1184] Djameleddine Laskri v. Algeria, WGAD Opinion No. 17/2014, Adopted Apr. 30, 2014, at ¶ 51.

[1185] Halil Savda v. Turkey, WGAD Opinion No. 16/2008, Adopted July 20, 2007, at ¶ 39; Mohamed Khirat al-Shatar, et al. v. Egypt, WGAD Opinion No. 27/2008, Adopted Sept. 12, 2008, at ¶ 78(c); Matan Kaminer, et al. v. Israel, WGAD Opinion No. 24/2003, Adopted Nov. 28, 2003, at ¶¶ 30–31.

[1186] *Issue of the Administration of Justice through Military Tribunals*, Special Rapporteur of the Sub-Commission on the Promotion and Protection of Human Rights, Commission on Human Rights, E/CN.4/2006/58, Jan. 13, 2006.

[1187] Id., at ¶ 10.

[1188] Id., at ¶ 9; *Report of the Special Rapporteur on the Independence of Judges and Lawyers*, Human Rights Council, A/68/285, Aug. 7, 2013, at ¶ 18.

[1189] Concerning 12 Individuals, at ¶ 19 (In its opinions, annual reports, and other documents in which it has addressed the issue, the Working Group has relied on the report on the issue of the administration of justice through military tribunals, which was submitted to the Commission on Human Rights in 2006); Eugene Fidell, *Military Justice and Its Reform*, Just Security, May 23, 2016; *see generally Report of the Special Rapporteur on the Independence of Judges and Lawyers*, Human Rights Council, A/68/285, Aug. 7, 2013 (making reference to the Principles throughout the report); *Report of the Special Rapporteur on the Independence of Judges and Lawyers*, Human Rights Council, A/68/285, Aug. 7, 2013, at ¶ 18 ("The principles have been positively cited in jurisprudence of the European Court of Human Rights," for example, in Ergin, at. ¶¶ 24, 45).

UN Special Rapporteur on the Independence of Judges and Lawyers have urged the HRC to adopt the principles on several instances.[1190]

In addition, the WGAD expressed its reliance on these principles by stating that, "[i]n its opinions, annual reports, and other documents in which it has addressed the issue [of military justice], the Working Group has relied on [the Draft Principles]."[1191]

Among the twenty principles that were formulated, the following principles require special attention:

- Principle 2: Respect for the standards of international law – Military tribunals must abide by international law guarantees of the right to a fair trial, even in times of emergency.
- Principle 5: Jurisdiction of military courts to try civilians – Military tribunals should have no jurisdiction to try civilians.
- Principle 8: Functional authority of military courts – The jurisdiction of military courts should be limited to offences of a strictly military nature committed by military personnel.
- Principle 10: Limitations on military secrecy – The rules that make it possible to invoke the secrecy of military information should not be diverted from their original purpose in order to obstruct the course of justice or to violate human rights. Military secrecy may not be invoked (a) where deprivation liberty is at issue, (b) to obstruct judicial process, (c) to deny judges and authorities access to documents, (d) to obstruct the publication of court sentences, (e) to obstruct the effective exercise of *habeas corpus*.
- Principle 12: Guarantee of *habeas corpus* – In all circumstances, military tribunals must respect *habeas corpus* rights.
- Principle 13: Right to a competent, independent and impartial tribunal – Military tribunals must be competent, independent and impartial at every stage of legal proceedings from initial investigation to trial.
- Principle 14: Public nature of hearings – Hearings must be public and the holding of sessions in camera should be exceptional and be authorized by a specific, well-grounded decision the legality of which is subject to review.
- Principle 15: Guarantee of the rights of the defence and the right to a just and fair trial – Military tribunals must ensure right to a defense and a fair trial. Military tribunals must offer the following guarantees: (a) the right to presumption of innocence, (b) the right to be informed promptly of the details of the offence and the rights and facilities necessary for their defense, (c) individual criminal responsibility, (d) the right to be tried without undue delay in their presence, (e) the right to defend themselves in person or through legal assistance of their choosing, (f) the privilege against self-incrimination, (g) the right to cross-examine witnesses, (h) not to use evidence obtained through torture, cruel, inhuman or degrading treatment, (i) no conviction on the strength of anonymous testimony or secret evidence, (j) the

---

[1190] *Report of the Working Group on Arbitrary Detention*, Human Rights Council, A/HRC/27/48, June 30, 2014, at ¶ 71, 92; *Report of the Special Rapporteur on the Independence of Judges and Lawyers*, Human Rights Council, A/68/285, Aug. 7, 2013, at ¶ 92.

[1191] Mr. Obaidullah v. United States, WGAD Opinion No. 10/2013, Adopted July 25, 2013, at ¶ 19.

right to appeal, (k) the right be informed of their rights to judicial and other remedies.

- Principle 17: Recourse procedures in the ordinary courts – The authority of military tribunals must be limited to ruling in first instance, and appeal should be brought before the civil courts.

Another set of applicable principles is the WGAD's own rules regarding military tribunals. The WGAD came up with its own minimum standards for military tribunals in 1999.[1192] In its 2014 annual report, the WGAD noted that military tribunals cannot be considered "a competent, independent and impartial tribunal."[1193] It emphasized that the use of military tribunals to try civilians is "in violation of International Covenant and customary international law as confirmed by the constant jurisprudence of the Working Group."[1194] The WGAD also noted that the intervention of a military judge "is likely to produce an effect contrary to the enjoyment of the human rights and to a fair trial with due guarantees."[1195] These minimum standards today are now:

(a) Military tribunals should only be competent to try military personnel for military offences;
(b) If civilians have also been indicted in a case, military tribunals should not try military personnel;
(c) Military courts should not try military personnel if any of the victims are civilians;
(d) Military tribunals should not be competent to consider cases of rebellion, the sedition or attacks against a democratic regime, since in those cases the victims are all citizens of the country concerned;
(e) Military tribunals should never be competent to impose the death penalty.[1196]

It also then explained more broadly how military justice can fall within each of the five legal categories of its cases:

(a) Category I: Military forces often stop and detain persons for a long time and military judges often order continuing detention in the absence of any legal basis;
(b) Category II: Many detainees brought before military courts have been detained simply for exercising a fundamental freedom, such as the freedom of opinion and expression, freedom of association, freedom of assembly or freedom of religion;

[1192] *Report of the Working Group on Arbitrary Detention: Report on the Mission to Peru*, E/CN.4/1999/63/ Add.2, Jan. 11, 1999, at ¶¶ 179–180. This version only had four principles, excluding (b) above, which was added in *Report of the Working Group on Arbitrary Detention*, Human Rights Council, A/HRC/27/48, June 30, 2014; *see also Report of the Working Group on Arbitrary Detention*, Commission on Human Rights, E/CN.4/1999/63, Dec. 18, 1998, at ¶ 80.

[1193] *Report of the Working Group on Arbitrary Detention*, Human Rights Council, A/HRC/27/48, June 30, 2014, at ¶ 68.

[1194] *Id.*

[1195] *Id.* ("The Working Group wishes to reiterate the human rights of accused persons, particularly their rights to be brought promptly before an independent and impartial judge; to be brought to trial in the shortest possible time; to be tried without undue delay; to challenge the lawfulness of their detention; to the presumption of innocence; to a public trial; to equality of arms between prosecution and defence; to access to evidence submitted by the prosecution; and other fundamental judicial guarantees of a fair trial.")

[1196] *Id.*, at ¶ 69.

(c) Category III: Military judges and military prosecutors often do not meet the fundamental requirements of independence and impartiality; military procedures applied by military courts often do not respect the basic guarantees for a fair trial;

(d) Category IV: Individuals brought before military courts are often migrants in an irregular situation, asylum seekers and refugees captured by military forces at borders, at sea and in airports;

(e) Category V: Many people brought before military courts are foreign nationals coming from a country considered hostile to the country.

B Cases of Military Tribunals

1 Military Personnel Tried by Military Tribunals

Military tribunals are not prohibited by international law and the WGAD does not totally ban the use of military tribunals. The WGAD highlighted that Article 14 of the ICCPR does not rule out trials before military courts as long as all fair trial standards set out therein are guaranteed.[1197] So the fair trial rights guaranteed in Article 14 of the ICCPR must apply to military personnel being tried by military tribunals. Therefore, the WGAD has found the use of military tribunals in violation of the ICCPR when military tribunals have failed to abide by the standards of fair trials.

In *Juan Ondo Abaga* v. *Equatorial Guinea*, the WGAD found that the guarantee of *habeas corpus*, the public nature of proceedings, the guarantee of the rights of the defense and the right to a just and fair trial, and the recourse procedures in the ordinary courts are applicable even to military personnel tried in military courts.[1198]

In *Grigorii Pasko* v. *Russia*, the WGAD ruled Pasko's deprivation of liberty to be arbitrary because the "proceedings before the military judicial organs violate[ed] the individual's right to a fair trial."[1199] Pasko was a commander in the Russian navy who was accused of spying and disclosing state secrets.[1200] Several trial defects were found by the WGAD. Pasko's trial was held *in camera* before a military court of the Russian Pacific fleet, his lawyers were stripped of their power of attorney, his request that the documents confiscated from him be examined in independent and impartial manner was denied by the investigating authorities, and evidence against Pasko included information obtained illegally by wire-tapping.[1201] The WGAD found that such flaws violate his right to a fair trial guaranteed in Articles 9 and 14 of ICCPR and Articles 9 and 10 of the UDHR.[1202]

And in *Mustapha Adib* v. *Morocco*, the WGAD found arbitrary the deprivation of liberty of Adib, a member of the military, because the military tribunal violated his right to a fair trial.[1203] Adib was sentenced by the Permanent Tribunal of the Royal Armed Forces to "two and a half years' imprisonment and to dismissal from the army" for

---

[1197] *Report of the Working Group on Arbitrary Detention*, Human Rights Council, A/HRC/7/4, Jan. 10, 2008, ¶ 66.

[1198] Juan Ondo Abaga, ¶ 13.

[1199] Grigorii Pasko v. Russian Federation, WGAD Opinion No. 09/1999, Adopted May 20, 1999, ¶ 7(b).

[1200] *Id.*, at ¶ 5–6.

[1201] *Id.*, at ¶ 7(b).

[1202] *Id.*

[1203] Mustapha Adib v. Morocco, WGAD Opinion No. 27/2001, Adopted Dec. 3, 2001.

violating military rules and contempt of the army.[1204] In that case, no preliminary hearing was held and he was ordered to appear in civilian dress.[1205] He was judged *in absentia* without his lawyers being present after "he had protested against the systematic rejection of his counsel's requests, particularly the request to call witnesses, and had called for a fair trial."[1206] The WGAD found that the military tribunal acted in a way "that cast doubts on its impartiality by infringing the presumption of innocence of the accused and by hindering his deference."[1207] It then found his deprivation of liberty arbitrary because his fair trial rights under Article 14(1) of the ICCPR were violated.[1208] The WGAD noted, however, that its conclusion is case specific, and "should not therefore be interpreted as a position of principle regarding the incompatibility of justice by military courts and the standards of fair trial."[1209] This statement supports the view that the WGAD, in principle, does not prohibit the use of military tribunals trying military personnel as long as they meet the fair trial standards guaranteed in international human rights law.

2 Civilians Tried by Military Tribunals

The WGAD takes the view that "in principle, military courts should not try civilians."[1210] In its report, the WGAD declared "[t]he trial of civilians or decisions placing civilians in preventive detention by military courts are in violation of the International Covenant and customary international law as confirmed by the constant jurisprudence of the Working Group."[1211] The WGAD's own minimum standard for military tribunals also states "military tribunals should only be competent to try military personnel for military offences."[1212] The WGAD's opinions also confirm this view. In *Sayed Mohammed Abdullah Nimr, et al. v. Egypt*, the WGAD stated that it "has consistently held the view that whatever the charges faced, civilians should not be tried by military courts, as such courts cannot be considered independent and impartial tribunals for civilians."[1213] It has also stated that "the constant jurisprudence of the Working Group that the right to a fair

---

[1204] *Id.*, at ¶ 11, 17.
[1205] *Id.*, at ¶ 18.
[1206] *Id.*
[1207] *Id.*, at ¶ 19.
[1208] *Id.*, at ¶ 20.
[1209] *Id.*, at ¶ 21.
[1210] Mohammed Amin Kamal, et al. v. Egypt, WGAD Opinion No. 57/2011, Adopted Nov. 17, 2011, at ¶ 18; Abdulhadi Abdulla Alkhawaja v. Bahrain, WGAD Opinion No. 6/2012, Adopted July 13, 2012, ¶ 45.
[1211] *Report of the Working Group on Arbitrary Detention*, Human Rights Council, A/HRC/27/48, June 30, 2014, at ¶ 66.; *See also Report of the Working Group on Arbitrary Detention*, Human Rights Council, A/HRC/13/30, Jan. 18, 2010, at ¶ 66 ("the Working Group wishes to reiterate that the trial of civilians by military tribunals usually has an adverse effect on the enjoyment of the right to liberty of person, the right to a fair trial, to appeal against detention and to be tried in public by a legally established, independent, competent and impartial court, the right to a presumption of innocence, to equality of arms and to access to evidence, the right to a free and adequate defence, etc.").
[1212] *Report of the Working Group on Arbitrary Detention*, Human Rights Council, A/HRC/27/48, June 30, 2014, ¶ 68.
[1213] Sayed Mohammed Abdullah Nimr, et al. v. Egypt, WGAD Opinion No. 11/2012, Adopted July 17, 2012, at ¶ 18.

trial under article 10 of the Universal Declaration of Human Rights and article 14 of the Covenant excludes the criminal jurisdiction of military courts over civilians."[1214]

The WGAD, however, does not rule out the possibility that the trial of civilians by military tribunals might be allowed in very limited and exceptional circumstances, although it has never issued such an opinion. The WGAD noted "that article 14 of the ICCPR does not rule out trials before military courts as long as all fair trial standards set out in article 14 are guaranteed." However, it is of the opinion that "states must provide objective and serious justification for trying civilians before military courts. Such trials may only be conducted if civilian courts are unable to deal with a specific class of individuals or offences. Trials of civilians before military or special courts must be the exception. Governments must provide objective and serious justification for trying civilians before military courts. Such trials may only be conducted if civilian courts are unable to deal with a specific class of individuals or offences."[1215]

Nonetheless, the WGAD has never found any trial of civilians by military tribunals to fall under such exceptional circumstances. In *Abdeldjouad Mahmoud Ameur Al Abadi* v. *Egypt*, the WGAD held that merely stating a civilian committed crimes of military nature is not an exceptional circumstance that warrants a military jurisdiction. Al Abadi, a civilian, was tried by military tribunals. Regarding his trial "the Government solely pointed out that Mr. Al Abadi has committed offences of a military character but it has not specified in what consisted those offences nor the facts which gave place to such qualification."[1216] Thus, the WGAD found that the Government had not provided any explanation to justify his trial by a military tribunal, and found the trial in violation of Article 14 of the ICCPR.[1217]

In *Juan Ondo Abaga* v. *Equatorial Guinea*, the WGAD held that linking civilians to military personnel in the commission of an alleged crime does not justify military jurisdiction. In the case, military personnel and civilians were tried before a military tribunal on the charges of acts against national security, rebellion, treason, and attempting to overthrow the Government based on their alleged participation in the attempted coup.[1218] They were tried *in absentia*.[1219] The WGAD observed that the crimes that they were charged with "are typically classified as political offenses, and, in the present case, they were allegedly committed by civilians in conjunction with military personnel."[1220] Noting the principles that civilians should not be tried by military tribunals and that the fair trial rights must be guaranteed for military personnel tried by

---

[1214] Concerning 12 Individuals, at ¶ 23; *see also* Haytham al-Maleh v. Syria, WGAD Opinion No. 27/2010, Adopted Nov. 22, 2010, at ¶ 30 ("Pursuant to principle No. 5 of the Draft Principles Governing the Administration of Justice through Military Tribunals (E/CN.4/2006/58), military courts should, in principle, have no jurisdiction to try civilians. In all circumstances, the State shall ensure that civilians accused of a criminal offence of any nature are tried by civilian courts. Principle No. 8 adds that "the jurisdiction of military courts should be limited to offences of a strictly military nature committed by military personnel.")

[1215] *Report of the Working Group on Arbitrary Detention*, Human Rights Council, A/HRC/7/4, Jan. 10, 2008, at ¶ 66.

[1216] Abdeldjouad Mahmoud Ameur Al Abadi v. Egypt, WGAD Opinion No. 22/2007, Adopted Nov. 22, 2007, at ¶ 27.

[1217] *Id.*

[1218] Juan Ondo Abaga, 2008, at ¶ 5.

[1219] *Id.*, at ¶ 6.

[1220] *Id.*, at ¶ 8.

military tribunals, the WGAD found these principles were "totally disregarded in the trial conducted against" the detainees.[1221] When the WGAD has found that civilians are improperly tried by military tribunals, to remedy the situation, it has called for the immediate release of the civilians or trial before an independent and impartial tribunal with all the guarantees of due process, human rights, and the norms of international law.[1222]

3 Civilians Tried by Military Tribunals in Times of Emergency

The WGAD has held that claims of emergency cannot justify the use of military tribunals to try civilians. The WGAD has raised its concern "over deprivation of liberty occurring during states of emergency and over recourse to military, special or emergency courts, especially in the context of countering terrorism."[1223] Noting the frequency of arbitrary detentions occurring during states of emergency, the WGAD stressed that they must be "imposed in strict compliance with the principle of proportionality," and that the measures "including the suspension of and restrictions on derogable fundamental rights and freedoms must pursue a legitimate goal." In *Djema'a al Seyed Suleymane Ramadhan v. Egypt*, the WGAD ruled the Government's declaration of a state of emergency illegitimate because it failed to meet the requirements of the ICCPR. The WGAD observed that a justified emergency order requires "an exceptional situation of 'public emergency'," which "'threatens the life of the nation.'"[1224] Egypt's emergency order was made in 1981 when President Anwar Sadat was assassinated and had continued since then.[1225] The WGAD found that although it was possible to consider the assassination "a situation of public emergency which could threaten the life of the nation, this argument seems to be less valid today."[1226] It declared then that the state of emergency is "clearly affecting the rights of persons whom objectively did not have links to that crime."[1227]

The WGAD noted that military jurisdiction over civilians during states of emergency "inevitably touches upon the right to fair trial guarantees" in Article 14 of the ICCPR and Article 10 of the UDHR.[1228] The WGAD noted that, in addition to non-derogable rights in Article 4(2) of the ICCPR, certain customary international law rights such as *habeas corpus* rights are non-derogable during states of emergency and applicable to non-party states of the ICCPR as well. The WGAD therefore holds the view that fundamental requirements of fair trial must be respected during a state of emergency.[1229]

In *'Abla Sa'adat, et al. v. Israel*, the WGAD found administrative detention and military tribunal hearing of two civilians were not justified by claims of emergency. In

---

[1221] *Id.*

[1222] Mohammad Abu-Shalbak v. Palestinia Authority, WGAD Opinion No. 13/2010, Adopted May 7, 2010, at ¶ 25.

[1223] *Report of the Working Group on Arbitrary Detention*, Human Rights Council, A/HRC/7/4, Jan. 10, 2008, at ¶ 78.

[1224] Djema'a al Seyed Suleymane Ramadhan v. Egypt, WGAD Opinion No. 18/2008, Adopted Sept. 9, 2008, at ¶ 19.

[1225] *Id.*, at ¶¶ 20–21.

[1226] *Id.*, at ¶ 21.

[1227] *Id.*

[1228] *Report of the Working Group on Arbitrary Detention*, Human Rights Council, A/HRC/7/4, Jan. 10, 2008, at ¶ 65.

[1229] Abdeldjouad Mahmoud Ameur Al Abadi v. Egypt, WGAD Opinion No. 22/2007, Adopted Nov. 22, 2007, at ¶ 31; *General Comment No. 29*, Human Rights Committee, CCPR/C/21/Rev.1/Add.11 (2001).

that case, two women were arrested by the Government for their alleged involvement with Hamas. After being administratively detained, they were charged with criminal offenses by a military court. The WGAD found that even in the state of emergency and the state's reservation to Article 9 of the ICCPR, "international human rights standards on protecting the right of liberty would still apply in its territory."[1230] The WGAD explained that even in the state of emergency, a state has to maintain certain fundamental aspects of the right to liberty "which are considered necessary for the protection of non-derogable rights or which are non-derogable under the State's other international obligations." It further explained:

> These include the requirements that the grounds and procedures for the detention be prescribed by law, the right to be informed of the reasons of the detention, prompt access to legal counsel and family, an impartial trial by an independent tribunal, and prescribed limits upon the length of prolonged detention. These protections are also considered to include appropriate and effective judicial review mechanisms to supervise detentions promptly upon arrest or detention and at reasonable intervals when detention is extended.[1231]

The WGAD concluded that most of these requirements were not met – the civilians were tried by a military court not independent from the executive branch, had to confront difficulties in legal counseling, and had a total lack of information regarding their charges.[1232]

4 Military Tribunals Displacing Ordinary Courts

The WGAD has ruled in multiple cases regarding situations where special courts replaced military tribunals. Although now abolished,[1233] the Supreme State Security Court was a special court of Syria, created under 1963 emergency legislation.[1234] Initially, the emergency law authorized the referral of offenses against the security of the state and public order to military courts.[1235] In 1968, however, Legislative Decree No. 47 replaced the exceptional military courts with the Security Court.[1236] It had jurisdiction over "all persons, civilian or military, whatever their rank or immunity."[1237] It inherited the exceptional military court jurisdiction as well as the authority to look at "all other cases referred to it by the martial law governor."[1238] Legislative Decree No. 47 also exempted the Security Court from the rules of procedure followed by regular Syrian courts.[1239] And it did not allow appeal of its decisions and was accountable only to the Minister of the

---

[1230] Abla Sa'adat et al. v. Israel, WGAD Opinion No. 3/2004, Adopted May 25, 2004, at ¶ 31.

[1231] *Id.*, at ¶ 33.

[1232] *Id.*, at ¶ 34.

[1233] *Syrian Decrees on Ending State of Emergency, Abolishing SSSC, Regulating Right to Peaceful Demonstration*, SYRIAN ARAB NEWS AGENCY, Apr. 21, 2011.

[1234] Human Rights Watch, Far from Justice: Syria's Supreme State Security Court 10 (2009).

[1235] *Id.*

[1236] *Id.*

[1237] *Id.*

[1238] *Id.*

[1239] *Id.*

Interior.[1240] The Security Court was used by the Syrian authorities to prosecute those of whom they did not approve.[1241]

The WGAD found the Security Court to violate Articles 9 and 14 of the ICCPR and Articles 9 and 10 of the UDHR on numerous occasions.[1242] In particular, the WGAD found the Security Court to violate: (1) The right to a fair and public hearing before a competent, independent, and impartial tribunal; (2) The right to be informed promptly and in detail of the nature and cause of the charges against them; (3) The right of everyone to challenge the lawfulness of their detention before an independent and impartial court; (4) The right to have adequate time and facilities for the preparation of their defense and to communicate with legal counsel of their own choosing; (5) The right to defend themselves in person or through legal assistance; (6) The right to be tried without undue delay; (7) The obligation on the State to investigate allegations of torture and not to use coerced confessions as evidence; and (8) The right to have their conviction and sentence reviewed by a higher tribunal.[1243]

5 Military Tribunals and the War on Terror/Guantanamo Bay

On several occasions, the WGAD has addressed the issues regarding detentions in the War on Terror and the issues regarding the United States prison at Guantanamo Bay, Cuba. The WGAD has raised its concern "over deprivation of liberty occurring during states of emergency and over recourse to military, special or emergency courts, especially in the context of countering terrorism."[1244] In its 2008 annual report, the WGAD promulgated a list of principles applicable to deprivation of liberty of persons accused of acts of terrorism in conformity with Articles 9 and 14 of the ICCPR and Articles 9 and 10 of the UDHR:

(a) Terrorist activities carried out by individuals shall be considered as punishable criminal offences, which shall be sanctioned by applying current and relevant criminal and penal procedure laws according to the different legal systems;
(b) Resort to administrative detention against suspects of such criminal activities is inadmissible;
(c) The detention of persons who are suspected of terrorist activities shall be accompanied by concrete charges;
(d) The persons detained under charges of terrorist acts shall be immediately informed of them, and shall be brought before a competent judicial authority, as soon as possible, and no later than within a reasonable time period;
(e) The persons detained under charges of terrorist activities shall enjoy the effective right to *habeas corpus* following their detention;

[1240] *Id.*
[1241] *Id.*, at 1.
[1242] *See, e.g.*, WGAD Opinion No. 39/2011; WGAD Opinion No. 38/2011; WGAD Opinion No. 37/2011; WGAD Opinion No. 28/2008; WGAD Opinion No. 7/2005; WGAD Opinion No. 4/2005.
[1243] Ahmed Omar Einein, et al. v. Syria, WGAD Opinion No. 28/2008, Adopted Sept. 12, 2008, at ¶ 23.
[1244] *Report of the Working Group on Arbitrary Detention*, Human Rights Council, A/HRC/7/4, Jan. 10, 2008, at ¶ 78.

(f) The exercise of the right to *habeas corpus* does not impede on the obligation of the law enforcement authority responsible for the decision for detention or maintaining the detention, to present the detained person before a competent and independent judicial authority within a reasonable time period. Such person shall be brought before a competent and independent judicial authority, which then evaluates the accusations, the basis of the deprivation of liberty, and the continuation of the judicial process;

(g) In the development of judgments against them, the persons accused of having engaged in terrorist activities shall have a right to enjoy the necessary guarantees of a fair trial, access to legal counsel and representation, as well as the ability to present exculpatory evidence and arguments under the same conditions as the prosecution, all of which should take place in an adversarial process;

(h) The persons convicted by a court of having carried out terrorist activities shall have the right to appeal against their sentences.[1245]

Also in the Basic Principles and Guidelines on Remedies and Procedures on the Right of Anyone Deprived of Their Liberty to Bring Proceedings before a Court, the WGAD included a guideline regarding those suspected to have engaged in terrorist activities:

(a) They shall be immediately informed of the charges against them, and be brought before a competent and independent judicial authority as soon as possible, within a reasonable period of time;

(b) They shall enjoy the effective right to judicial determination of the arbitrariness and lawfulness of their detention;

(c) The exercise of the right to judicial oversight of their detention shall not impede the obligation of the law enforcement authority responsible for the decision to detain or to maintain the detention to present suspects before a competent and independent judicial authority within a reasonable period of time. Such persons shall be brought before the judicial authority, which will then evaluate the accusations, the basis of the deprivation of liberty and the continuation of the judicial process;

(d) In the proceedings against them, suspects shall have a right to enjoy the necessary guarantees of a fair trial, access to legal counsel and the ability to present exculpatory evidence and arguments under the same conditions as the prosecution, all of which should take place in an adversarial process.[1246]

As such, the WGAD demanded that fair trial rights be guaranteed in counter-terrorism situations. It was in this context that the WGAD has found Guantanamo Bay's Combatant Status Review Tribunals and the Administrative Board Review to be inadequate "to satisfy the right to a fair and independent trial as these are military tribunals of a summary nature."[1247]

[1245] *Report of the Working Group on Arbitrary Detention*, Human Rights Council, A/HRC/10/21, Feb. 16, 2009, at ¶¶ 53–54.

[1246] Basic Principles and Guidelines, at Guideline 17.

[1247] Mohammed Abdul Rahman Al-Shimrani v. United States, WGAD Opinion No. 2/2009, Adopted May 6, 2009, at ¶ 35.

In May 2013, the WGAD published a joint statement with the Inter-American Commission on Human Rights (IACHR), the UN Special Rapporteur on Torture, and Other Cruel, Inhuman or Degrading Treatment or Punishment, the UN Special Rapporteur on Human Rights While Countering Terrorism, and the UN Special Rapporteur on the Right of Everyone to the Enjoyment of the Highest Attainable Standard of Physical and Mental Health, which called for the end to the indefinite detention of individuals being detained at Guantanamo Bay.[1248]

The report called on the United States "to respect and guarantee the life, health and personal integrity of detainees at the Guantanamo Naval Base" in the context of the then hunger strike; adopt measures to end "the indefinite detention of persons; provide for their release or prosecution, in accordance with due process and the principles and standards of international human rights law; allow for independent monitoring by international human rights bodies; and close the detention center at the Guantanamo Naval Base."[1249] In particular, the report specifically urged the United States to:

(a) adopt all legislative, administrative, judicial, and any other types of measures necessary to prosecute, with full respect for the right to due process, the individuals being held at Guantánamo Naval Base or, where appropriate, to provide for their immediate release or transfer to a third country, in accordance with international law;

(b) expedite the process of release and transfer of those detainees who have been certified for release by the Government itself;

(c) conduct a serious, independent, and impartial investigation into the acts of forced feeding of inmates on hunger strike and the alleged violence being used in those procedures;

(d) allow the IACHR and the United Nations Human Rights Council mechanisms, such as the Working Group and the UN Special Rapporteurs, to conduct monitoring visits to the Guantánamo detention center under conditions in which they can freely move about the installations and meet freely and privately with the prisoners; and (e) take concrete, decisive steps toward closing the detention center at the Guantánamo Naval Base once and for all.[1250]

This was not the first time the WGAD had addressed detentions in Guantanamo Bay. In 2006, the WGAD published a report on the situation of detainees there jointly with the UN Special Rapporteur on the Independence of Judges and Lawyers, the UN Special Rapporteur on Torture and Other Cruel, Inhuman or Degrading Treatment or Punishment, the UN Special Rapporteur on Freedom of Religion or Belief, and the UN Special Rapporteur on the Right of Everyone to the Enjoyment of the Highest Attainable Standard of Physical and Mental Health. The report declared that "[i]nternational human rights law is applicable to the analysis of the situation of detainees in

---

[1248] *Inter-American Commission on Human Rights, UN Working Group on Arbitrary Detention, UN Special Rapporteur on Torture, UN Special Rapporteur on Human Rights and Counter-Terrorism, and UN Special Rapporteur on Health Reiterate Need to End the Indefinite Detention of Individuals at Guatánamo Naval Base in Light of Current Human Rights Crisis,* May 1, 2013.

[1249] *Id.*

[1250] *Id.*

Guantanamo Bay."[1251] The report observed that situations of armed conflict, including situations of occupation, imply the full applicability of relevant provisions of international humanitarian law and of international human rights law, with the exception of guarantees derogated from, provided such derogations have been declared in accordance with Article 4 of the ICCPR by a state.[1252] The report found that, according to Article 9 of the ICCPR, the detainees at Guantanamo Bay were entitled to challenge their detention and to obtain release if detention is found to lack a proper legal basis.[1253] Also, the report found it was a violation of Article 14 of the ICCPR for the United States to be the judge, prosecutor, and defense counsel for the detainees at Guantanamo Bay.[1254] And the report then urged the Government to bring the detainees to trial according to Articles 9 and 14 of the ICCPR or release them without further delay and to close the facilities.[1255]

Before that, in its 2002 annual report, the WGAD published a "Legal Opinion Regarding the Deprivation of Liberty of Persons Detained in Guantanamo Bay," which adopted the approach that the application of international humanitarian law to an international or non-international armed conflict does not exclude the application of human rights law. It explained that the two bodies of law are complementary and not mutually exclusive. In the case of a conflict between the provisions of the two legal regimes with regard to a specific situation, the *lex specialis* will have to be identified and applied.[1256] In the WGAD's 2006 annual report, "it responded to the United States Government submissions to the Working Group's Opinion No. 29/2006 (United States of America)." The Government had referred to the US Supreme Court judgment in *Hamdan v. Rumsfeld*, asserting that the law of armed conflicts governed the armed conflict with Al-Qaida. In its 2006 annual report, as in its 2005 annual report, the WGAD pointed out that "the application of international humanitarian law … does not exclude the application of international human rights law."[1257]

The WGAD has also issued several opinions finding detentions at Guantanamo Bay to be arbitrary. For example, in *Obaidullah v. United States of America*, the detainee was held for three months at Bagram Air Base in Afghanistan after a raid in his home, where he was allegedly not informed of the reasons for his detention and was coerced into making false statements and tortured.[1258] After being transferred to Guantanamo Bay, the source alleged he had been subject to torture and inhuman treatment, and had been detained since then. He was not informed of the reason for his detention nor charged and it was reported that he was detained based on a tip from an unknown source that he was associated with al-Qaeda.[1259] From 2004 to 2007, he appeared before a military Combatant Status Review Tribunal (CSRT) and Administrative Review Boards, which held that

---

[1251] *Report of the Working Group on Arbitrary Detention*, Commission on Human Rights, E/CN.4/2006/120, Feb. 27, 2006, at ¶ 83.

[1252] *Id.*; Mr. Obaidullah v. United States, WGAD Opinion No. 10/2013, Adopted July 25, 2013, at ¶ 29.

[1253] *Report of the Working Group on Arbitrary Detention*, Commission on Human Rights, E/CN.4/2006/120, Feb. 27, 2006, ¶ 84.

[1254] *Id.*, at ¶ 85.

[1255] *Id.*, at ¶¶ 95–96.

[1256] *Report of the Working Group on Arbitrary Detention*, Commission on Human Rights, E/CN.4/2003/8, Dec. 16, 2002, at ¶ 64; Abdul Jaber al-Kubaisi v. Iraq and United States, WGAD Opinon No. 44/2005, Adopted Nov. 30, 2005, at ¶ 13.

[1257] Mr. Obaidullah v. United States, WGAD Opinion No. 10/2013, Adopted July 25, 2013, at ¶ 28.

[1258] *Id.*, at ¶ 3.

[1259] *Id.*, at ¶ 4.

he should remain in detention despite his denial of any connection with Al-Qaeda.[1260] The source argued that the hearings did not guarantee basic procedural protections. In 2008, Obaidullah filed a *habeas corpus* proceeding in the US District Court for the District of Columbia, which was denied in 2010.[1261] His appeal was also denied in 2012.[1262]

In its discussion, the WGAD referred to its joint statement that found the continued detention of detainees at Guantanamo Bay constitutes a violation of international law.[1263] Noting that the United States has not derogated from the ICCPR and that the application of international humanitarian law could not exclude application of human rights law, the WGAD referred to its previous opinions and reports to find that "the obligations of the United States under international human rights law extend to persons detained at Guantanamo Bay."[1264] However, even if the United States had derogated from the ICCPR, the WGAD found "customary international law on arbitrary detention would apply, and in this case it does so as peremptory norm (*jus cogens*) of international law."[1265] Also noting its previous statement that the struggle against international terrorism cannot be characterized as armed conflict under contemporary international law, the WGAD found Obaidullah's detention to even contravene international humanitarian law because there was no concrete evidence of his belligerent activity or direct participation in hostilities.[1266] The WGAD ruled his detention arbitrary. With regards to Category III, the WGAD found violations of Articles 9 and 14 of the ICCPR because he was not provided with the reasons for his detention, not promptly brought before a judicial authority for review of his detention, and not provided with legal counsel within a reasonable time.[1267]

In 2017, the WGAD's opinion in *Ammar al-Baluchi* v. *United States* addressed several of the continuing problems with detention at Guantanamo, fitting some frequent rights violations into the WGAD's five categories.

First, the WGAD considered that the Authorization to Use Military Force was not a legal basis for detention unless the United States could prove an armed conflict existed as of September 11, 2001, and the detainee had been a part of the hostilities.[1268] The WGAD did not consider itself competent to answer this question, but found that because his hearings before the CSRT did not fulfill his right to be brought promptly before a judge, there was still no legal basis for his detention.[1269] Under the US Supreme Court decision in *Boumediene* v. *Bush,* CSRT hearings were not considered an acceptable substitute for habeas proceedings.[1270] Thus, al-Baluchi's detention was arbitrary under Category I, having no legal basis.

[1260] *Id.,* at ¶¶ 5–7.
[1261] *Id.,* at ¶¶ 8–9
[1262] *Id.,* at ¶ 10.
[1263] *Id.,* at ¶ 24.
[1264] *Id.,* at ¶ 31.
[1265] *Id.,* at ¶ 32.
[1266] *Id.,* at ¶ 33.
[1267] *Id.,* at ¶ 39.
[1268] Ammar al-Baluchi v. United States, WGAD Opinion No. 89/2017, Adopted Nov. 24, 2017, at ¶ 41.
[1269] *Id.,* at ¶ 46.
[1270] *Id.*

Second, the WGAD found assorted due process violations related to the nature of Guantanamo detention and CSRT proceedings. These included lack of access to evidence due to overclassification, prolonged (verging on indefinite) pretrial detention, and a presupposition of guilt due to the CSRT classification as an enemy combatant.[1271] In a more unusual violation, the WGAD found that information that had been denied to al-Baluchi's lawyers regarding his torture at CIA black sites had been provided to the director of the film *Zero Dark Thirty*. The film later portrayed a character clearly based on al-Baluchi being tortured and confessing information that later enables the location of Osama bin Laden. The WGAD found this to be another violation of the presumption of innocence.[1272]

Finally, the WGAD made a Category V finding that al-Baluchi had been the victim of discrimination based on his status as a foreign national (like Obaidullah), as well as his religious beliefs as a Muslim.[1273]

6 Denial of Appeal to Civilian Courts from Military Tribunals

Military tribunals must allow appeal to a higher court. Article 14(5) of the ICCPR provides "[e]veryone convicted of a crime shall have the right to his conviction and sentence being reviewed by a higher tribunal according to law." The WGAD has found on several occasions that military tribunals that do not allow appeal of their decision violate a detainee's right to appeal.[1274] In *Djema'a al Seyed Suleymane Ramadhan v. Egypt*, the detainee was arrested and detained without warrant in Egypt on allegations of being a member of a terrorist organization.[1275] He was prosecuted in a military court and sentenced to life in prison.[1276] Egyptian law "did not contemplate judicial appeal to a higher court, neither civilian nor military."[1277] The WGAD noted that although Egypt has recently amended the law to establish a military appeals court, the detainee "did not have the opportunity to lodge an appeal before a higher court."[1278] The WGAD then found his right to appeal, under Article 14(5) of the ICCPR, had been denied.[1279]

7 Secret and Faceless Proceedings in Military Tribunals

The WGAD condemns secret and faceless proceedings in military tribunals. Article 14(1) of the ICCPR provides that "everyone shall be entitled to a fair and public hearing by a competent, independent and impartial tribunal established by law." The WGAD has held that secret and faceless military trials cannot be justified when the trial procedures do not guarantee detainees their right to fair trial.

[1271] *Id.*, at ¶¶ 51, 54, 55.
[1272] *Id.*, at ¶ 51.
[1273] *Id.*, at ¶ 62.
[1274] Djema'a al Seyed Suleymane Ramadhan v. Egypt, WGAD Opinion No. 18/2008, Adopted Sept. 9, 2008; Mohamed Khirat al-Shatar, et al. v. Egypt, WGAD Opinion No. 27/2008, Adopted Sept. 12, 2008.
[1275] *Id.*, at ¶ 4.
[1276] *Id.*, at ¶ 6.
[1277] *Id.*
[1278] *Id.*, at ¶ 14.
[1279] *Id.*, at ¶ 22.

In *Lori Berenson* v. *Peru*, an American citizen in Peru was arrested and sentenced by a secret military court to life in prison for the crime of treason.[1280] The WGAD found that secret trials "with minimum defence guarantees" constituted a violation of her right to due process.[1281] In *George Mbah et al.* v. *Nigeria*, a magazine editor was tried by secret military tribunal and sentenced to life imprisonment for "publishing materials which could obstruct the work of the coup plotters tribunal" and for "misleading the public."[1282] The WGAD held that the trial violated fair trial guarantees because the detainees did not have the right to be informed in detail of the charges brought against them, to be defended by a counsel of their own choice, to dispose of sufficient time to prepare their defense, or to appeal against their conviction and sentence.[1283]

8 Minors Tried by Military Tribunal

The WGAD has previously found due process violations in the trial of minors by military tribunals. Minors are entitled to a "further layer of protection" than adults, and their fair trial guarantees are non-derogable rights.[1284] In *Messrs. Hamdi Al Ta'mari, et al.* v. *Israel*, the WGAD made clear that minors are to be protected and that military tribunals are not the right forum to adjudicate the cases of minors. In that case, two minors were detained under a series of administrative detentions without charge, which were confirmed by the Military Administrative Detention Court, and accused of membership in Islamic Jihad on the basis of secret information.[1285] The WGAD found that "critical ingredients of the right to a fair trial" were absent in the case. It explained that the claim of "absolute necessity" according to Article 42 of the *Geneva Convention relative to the Protection of Civilian Persons in Time of War* (Fourth Geneva Convention) and Article 4 of the ICCPR was not satisfied.[1286] Then the WGAD noted that the minors were denied their "right to a fair trial guaranteed by article 40, paragraph 2(b) of the Convention on the Rights of the Child."[1287] The WGAD observed that although Articles 9 and 14 of the ICCPR may be derogated from "under limited circumstances," "no such derogation is permitted pursuant to the [CRC]."[1288]

In *Mohammed Amin Kamal et al.* v. *Egypt*, two minors were arrested for breach of curfew in Cairo and sentenced to five years in prison by a military court.[1289] In relation to the detention of minors, the WGAD found the Government in breach of Articles 37(b), 37(d), and 40(4) of the *Convention on the Rights of the Child*, because they were "arrested, brought to trial and sentenced without having sufficient time to prepare their defense or to confer with a lawyer, and without their families being informed."[1290] The

---

[1280] Lori Berenson v. Peru.

[1281] *Id.*, at ¶ 6(c).

[1282] George Mbah and Mohammed Sule v. Nigeria, WGAD Opinion No. 38/1996, Adopted Dec. 3, 1996, at ¶ 5(a).

[1283] *Id.*, at ¶ 7.

[1284] Messrs. Hamdi Al Ta'mari, et al. v. Israel, WGAD Opinion No. 5/2010, Adopted May 6, 2010, at ¶¶ 28–29.

[1285] *Id.*, at ¶¶ 7, 9, 37–38.

[1286] *Id.*, at ¶ 29.

[1287] *Id.*, at ¶ 30.

[1288] *Id.*

[1289] Mohammed Amin Kamal, et al. v. Egypt, WGAD Opinion No. 57/2011, Adopted Nov. 17, 2011, at ¶ 4.

[1290] *Id.*, at ¶ 15; Convention on the Rights of the Child, at Art. 37(b): "No child shall be deprived of his or her liberty unlawfully or arbitrarily. The arrest, detention or imprisonment of a child shall be in conformity

WGAD "emphasized the need for distinct treatment of minors and adults, in particular as far as rules of procedure are concerned."[1291] The WGAD has stated that an exceptionally high standard of "promptness" applies in the case of minors, and that they must be brought before a judge not longer than forty-eight hours after their arrest, unless in exceptional cases.[1292] Minor or juvenile detainees must be physically present at the hearing to ensure an adequate inquiry into the treatment they received in custody.[1293]

C Analysis of Trials by Military Tribunal

The WGAD has consistently held that military tribunals should only try military personnel for military offenses and that the safeguards that apply to all courts should also apply to military tribunals. It has also held that military tribunals should not try civilians. And even where a military tribunal restricts its jurisdiction in line with the recommendations of human rights bodies, these standards are often harder for military tribunals to observe – such as the impartiality of military judges and defense lawyers or the right to have a public hearing. There does not seem to be much enthusiasm for the HRC or the General Assembly to adopt the draft principles on military tribunals developed by the prior UN Special Rapporteur of the Sub-Commission on the Promotion and Protection of Human Rights given democracies and autocracies alike are engaged in fighting terrorism, but they nevertheless continue to permeate the jurisprudence on the question of military tribunals. In short, military tribunals should adhere to the same standards and implement the same safeguards as all ordinary courts and it is especially important that they do so given their predisposition to violate such standards. Therefore, advocates should be wary of military tribunals and the likelihood that they will deny a person their full due process protections.

VI Administrative Detentions

A Debtor's Prison

Under Article 11 of the ICCPR: "[n]o one shall be imprisoned merely on the ground of inability to fulfill a contractual obligation." This provision effectively outlaws the use by countries of imprisonment to compel individuals to pay their debts, but in practice debtor's prison exists around the world. While these kinds of cases have not individually

---

with the law and shall be used only as a measure of last resort and for the shortest appropriate period of time."; Convention on the Rights of the Child, Art. 37(d): "Every child deprived of his or her liberty shall have the right to prompt access to legal and other appropriate assistance, as well as the right to challenge the legality of the deprivation of his or her liberty before a court or other competent, independent and impartial authority, and to a prompt decision on any such action."; Convention on the Rights of the Child, Art. 40(4): "A variety of dispositions, such as care, guidance and supervision orders; counselling; probation; foster care; education and vocational training programmes and other alternatives to institutional care shall be available to ensure that children are dealt with in a manner appropriate to their well-being and proportionate both to their circumstances and the offence."

[1291] Mohammed Amin Kamal, et al., at ¶ 18.
[1292] Concerning a Minor (Whose Named Is Known to the Working Group) v. Egypt, WGAD Opinion No. 14/2015, Adopted Apr. 27, 2015, at ¶ 28.
[1293] Id.

been addressed in the WGAD's jurisprudence, it has expressed concerns about these practices during country missions.

For example, on its visit to Bahrain, the WGAD reported that imprisonment for debt is particularly common, noting detainees include those who could not pay a fine imposed by a court, those in pretrial detention who could not afford to post bail, and those held in connection with private debts.[1294] In relation to private debts, it reported that Bahrain's Code of Civil Procedure allowed for a creditor who made a daily payment to the state of about $120 to imprison a recalcitrant debtor for up to three months to compel him to pay his debt. It specifically recommended that "as regards imprisonment for contractual debt, the Government should arrange to have the laws permitting incarceration for failure to pay civil debts repealed," in accordance with the requirement of Article 11 of the ICCPR.[1295]

During its visit to Nicaragua, the WGAD learned about "enforcement by committal" under its civil law, which provides power to a judge to order a person's detention if they have violated a contract and then fail to surrender an item provided as a loan guarantee or asset kept on deposit. In such circumstances, a person may be detained for up to a year.[1296] The WGAD observed that Nicaragua's Constitution says that no one can be detained for bad debts, but this does not limit the power of the judiciary to take action for a person's failure to pay spousal and child support. In addressing this situation, the WGAD said:

> [It] believes that a clear distinction should be made between the civil obligation to pay a debt resulting from a maintenance obligation and the offence of abandoning a family; just as a distinction should be drawn between the civil obligation to pay a debt and the offence of fraudulently disposing of an item handed over as a pledge or deposit. The acts leading to civil and criminal consequences may be the same but the legal provisions governing them differ substantially.[1297]

Brazil is another country where a person can be imprisoned for their failure to pay child support. In a high-profile case, a former Real Madrid soccer player, Roberto Carlos, was sentenced to three months in prison for failing to pay £15,000 in child support.[1298] These kinds of laws can also operate with perverse effect. The author represents a client, Christopher Brann of Houston, Texas, whose then-wife, Marcelle Guimaraes, and in-laws Carlos and Jemima Guimaraes abducted his son Nico to Brazil in June 2013. Despite the United States and Brazil agreeing Brann's son had been abducted, the judiciary in Brazil has refused for more than five years to comply with its obligations under the *Hague Convention on the Civil Aspects of International Child Abduction* and return Nico to Texas to determine all rights of custody. This enabled Brann's ex-wife to secure an order of arrest against him for $50,000 in back child support, which practically requires him to finance his own son's abduction. Even with his ex–in-laws having been

[1294] *Report of the Working Group on Arbitrary Detention: Mission to Bahrain*, Commission on Human Rights, E/CN.4/2002/77/Add.2, Mar. 5, 2002, at ¶¶ 92–93.

[1295] *Id.*, at ¶ 113.

[1296] *Report of the Working Group on Arbitrary Detention: Mission to Nicaragua*, Human Rights Council, A/HRC/4/40/Add.3, Nov. 9, 2006, at ¶ 95.

[1297] *Id.*, at ¶ 95.

[1298] *Rob's Jail Time*, THE SUN, Aug. 24, 2017.

convicted in Houston, Texas, of international parental child abduction,[1299] Brann cannot return to Brazil to visit his son or he will be arrested and imprisoned.

During its visit to the United States, the WGAD expressed serious concern about the detentions of indigent people who had been detained for their failure to pay court-ordered fines and fees. In finding these detentions to be neither necessary nor proportionate, it observed:

> The practice was referred to as "debtors' prison", as it involved incarcerating people who could not pay minor fines or traffic tickets without determining their ability to pay and without offering alternative measures, such as community service, a reduced payment or a reasonable payment schedule. For example, in 2014, more than 560,000 municipal cases in Texas were closed when the defendant served time in prison in exchange for the city forgiving the unpaid fines.[1300]

B Psychiatric, Disability, and Drug User Detentions

As noted earlier, the WGAD previously adopted Deliberation No. 7, which focuses exclusively on the practice of psychiatric detentions. There are only a very small number of cases in its jurisprudence involving psychiatric detentions, but the WGAD has offered further comment on psychiatric and disability detentions in the context of its country missions that it has conducted.

1 Psychiatric and Disability

In Azerbaijan, the WGAD observed its domestic law allowed for the deprivation of liberty based on disability, involuntary hospitalization, and forced institutionalization, including of children and adults with intellectual and psychosocial disabilities. It expressed grave concern about these practices, noting:

> [M]any patients in psychiatric institutions were held against their will. Even those who might have voluntarily entered the facilities could not leave freely. The Working Group did not receive any information on the establishment of an independent monitoring system for such facilities that would ensure that all places where people with intellectual and psychosocial disability are held for involuntary treatment are regularly visited to guarantee the proper implementation of the safeguards.[1301]

In traveling to Germany, the WGAD learned about the practice of *Sicherungsverwahrungl*, which describes the situation of detainees who have served their criminal sentences but are subsequently detained in preventative detention. Such circumstances are sometimes foreseen in advance by courts or later, after a detainee is deemed to represent a "danger to society."[1302] It reported that it had learned these kinds of detentions were also

---

[1299] *Brazilian Grandparents Convicted in High-Profile Kidnapping Case*, ABC News, May 25, 2018.
[1300] *Report of the Working Group on Arbitrary Detention on Visit to the United States of America*, Human Rights Council, A/HRC/36/37, July 17, 2017, at ¶ 57.
[1301] Report of the Working Group on Mission to Azerbaijan, ¶¶ 31, 46.
[1302] *Report of the Working Group on Arbitrary Detention: Mission to Germany*, Human Rights Council, A/HRC/19/57/Add.3, Feb. 23, 2012, at ¶ 28.

being used in cases of "social disorder," where the requirements under German law had not been met, such as the case of a woman who had completed a medium-length sentence and was continuing to be held despite a lack of specific procedures that could be initiated to secure her release.

In December 2009, the European Court of Human Rights had issued a judgment challenging the domestic consensus in Germany, which found that post-sentence preventative detention must be classified as a "penalty" under the *European Convention on Human Rights*. Yet despite that decision, the practice persisted. The WGAD concluded "[t]his is a fundamental rights issue that should not depend on European or international supervision to be set right."[1303]

By the time of the WGAD's follow-up visit to Germany, 252 people remained in post-conviction preventive detention, down from more than 500 during the prior visit. In addition, the WGAD reported the entire system was "undergoing a major reform" because of a series of European Court judgments.[1304] The Government explained that a new law was implementing the "distance requirement," which "is the difference in treatment between preventive detainees and prisoners serving sentences."[1305] It said that this new approach was "freedom-oriented and therapy-based" with a goal to "enable those in preventive detention to be released as early as possible by reducing the risk they pose."[1306]

During its visit to Malta, the WGAD expressed concern about the involuntary detention of the potentially mentally ill. It learned admission to closed wards at Mount Carmel Hospital was compulsory for an observation period of up to twenty-eight days if two registered doctors made a recommendation for admission, supported by an application by the nearest relative or a mental welfare officer. The WGAD noted with concern there was no right of appeal in the event of a compulsory admission for what it described as a "prolonged period" of twenty-eight days.[1307] In its follow-up visit to Malta, the WGAD examined the role of the Board of Visitors for Detained Persons, which it said should be protected by law, given authority to request changes in detention conditions, and should have its mandate extended to the mental hospital, as it is a key location where individuals are being deprived of their liberty.[1308]

Similarly, the WGAD was very concerned about the practice of psychiatric detention in Mauritania, where there was no legal basis for the involuntary detention of a person suffering from a psychiatric disorder. In the absence of a legal framework, mental hospitals "delegate" responsibility for a detention to a family member, who must remain with the patient at the hospital. The WGAD explained that there was no provision for a judicial appeal to allow a patient to challenge their committal to a psychiatric institution,

---

[1303] *Id.*, at ¶ 34.

[1304] *Report of the Working Group on Arbitrary Detention: Follow-Up Mission to Germany*, Human Rights Council, A/HRC/30/36/Add.1, July 10, 2015, at ¶ 19.

[1305] *Id.*, at ¶ 20.

[1306] *Id.*

[1307] *Report of the Working Group on Arbitrary Detention: Mission to Malta*, Human Rights Council, A/HRC/13/30/Add.2, Jan. 18, 2010, at ¶¶ 67–68.

[1308] *Report of the Working Group on Arbitrary Detention: Follow-Up Mission to Malta*, Human Rights Council, A/HRC/33/50/Add.1, Oct. 7, 2016, at ¶¶ 60–61.

and it stated that "a legal framework for involuntary internment in institutions providing psychiatric treatment needs to be adopted."[1309]

In New Zealand, the WGAD found that people with mental illness or intellectual disabilities could also be detained for purposes of mandatory care and treatment. It found that although "the trigger for detention is not mental illness but rather the risk of harm to self or others, the Working Group noted that the criteria for determining the risk are not clear and that the Act allows medical practitioners a wide margin of discretion to determine whether a person should undergo compulsory assessment and treatment."[1310]

During its visit to Norway, the WGAD learned about its system of preventive detention, which was aimed at "protecting society from serious and violent offenders when there is a high risk of repeated offence, so that an ordinary fixed prison term with subsequent unconditional release is considered to be insufficient to protect society at large."[1311] It observed that among the seventy-seven prisoners, their characteristics include "a low level of education, no social network, psychiatric disorder and/or poor social skills, but also their vulnerability to assault or abuse by others" and that they spend on average ten years in preventive detention.[1312]

While the courts in Norway oversee its system of preventive detention, it expressed serious concern that:

> Preventive detention could, in the extreme, amount to indefinite detention . . . A related matter is the lack of certainty about the date of release, if any, for prisoners necessarily attached to a system of preventive detention with a minimum and a maximum period of time to be served in prison, if the maximum term can be prolonged potentially indefinitely . . . even if the courts ultimately decide on the release, stay or extension of the maximum term, the judiciary has to rely on the assessment and information provided by the correctional services authorities. It also appears to be difficult for the prisoners concerned to have decisions to their detriment reversed on appeal.[1313]

In Turkey, the WGAD explained that civil courts had jurisdiction to assign to institutions individuals who "harm their own family and surroundings."[1314] It explained that it wished to see two specific improvements to Turkey's system for institutionalizing the mentally ill:

> Firstly, the law should provide more detail both on the substantive criteria and the procedural safeguards for involuntary commitment to mental health institutions, including an automatic periodic review of the necessity of deprivation of liberty. Secondly, in practice in many cases there is no judicial decision providing a legal basis for the assignment.[1315]

[1309] *Report of the Working Group on Arbitrary Detention: Mission to Mauritania*, Human Rights Council, A/HRC/10/21/Add.2, Nov. 21, 2008, at ¶¶ 69–71.

[1310] *Report of the Working Group on Arbitrary Detention: Mission to New Zealand*, Human Rights Council, A/HRC/30/36/Add.2, July 6, 2015, at ¶ 78.

[1311] Report of Working Group on Mission to Norway, at ¶ 80.

[1312] *Id.*

[1313] *Id.*, at ¶ 82.

[1314] *Report of the Working Group on Arbitrary Detention: Mission to Turkey*, Human Rights Council, A/HRC/4/40/Add.5, Feb. 7, 2007, at ¶ 92.

[1315] *Id.*, at ¶ 93.

During its visit to the United States, the WGAD identified a disturbing trend involving the use of civil laws to confine pregnant women suspected of substance abuse. It observed that five states, Minnesota, Oklahoma, North Dakota, South Dakota, and Wisconsin, all allow these practices. And it explained that women in this context have been placed in residential treatment facilities "without sound medical evidence they are drug dependent or that the health of their fetus has been jeopardized, thus removing them from their homes, families, and employment."[1316] It further observed that the civil proceedings to commit pregnant women are often closed, lack meaningful standards, and provide few procedural protections, and may even take place without the mother having legal representation. The WGAD concluded "This form of deprivation of liberty is gendered and discriminatory in its reach and application, as pregnancy, combined with the presumption of drug or other substance abuse, is the determining factor for involuntary treatment."[1317]

And in Ukraine, the WGAD expressed serious concern about its administrative law criminalizing "vagrancy." The term "vagrant" is not defined by law but its purpose is to "combat socially inadequate behavior" and there are special detention facilities for vagrants, which reportedly operate with inhuman conditions. In practice, the law is applied to anyone who cannot produce an identity document when stopped by police. Those detained can be held in an administrative detention for up to thirty days, without the involvement of a court of law.[1318] The WGAD concluded this practice violates Article 9(4) of the ICCPR, which requires detainees to be able to challenge the legality of their detention in court. It also expressed serious concern about reports it had received that this period of detention was used by law enforcement officials to extract coerced confessions on criminal charges. At the time of its visit, the WGAD understood amendments to the relevant law were being considered to require a court order for detention no later than seventy-two hours after the arrest.[1319]

2 Drug Users

As noted earlier, in its 2015 annual report, the WGAD observed both from country missions and communications that it had received information that drug control laws and policies have triggered arbitrary detentions. Although it did not formally adopt a deliberation, the WGAD then described its concerns in substantial detail, both putting countries on notice about these issues and signaling to potential sources that this is an area of new focus.[1320]

In examining the situation in Brazil, the WGAD observed that the "excessive use of detention as a punitive measure for drug users raises questions regarding fundamental human rights."[1321] It expressed serious concern about how police reportedly target drug

---

[1316] *Id.*, at ¶¶ 72–73.

[1317] *Id.*, at ¶ 74.

[1318] *Report of the Working Group on Arbitrary Detention: Mission to Ukraine*, Human Rights Council, A/HRC/10/21/Add.4, Feb. 9, 2009, at ¶¶ 62–63.

[1319] *Id.*, at ¶ 64.

[1320] *Report of the Working Group on Arbitrary Detention*, Human Rights Council, A/HRC/30/436, July 15, 2015, at ¶¶ 57–62.

[1321] *Report of the Working Group on Arbitrary Detention: Mission to Brazil*, Human Rights Council, A/HRC/27/48/Add.3, June 30, 2014, at ¶ 112.

users to arrest them and have often carried out arrests indiscriminately. And it found that periodic reviews by the judiciary are often not carried out once a drug user has been detained. It concluded:

> The Working Group considers that, in all cases, drug addicts should be held in compulsory confinement only by judicial order and consent has been sought, if the person has refused medical treatment and undergone a medical examination. It should be applied for only short periods of time, and only when the drug addict is considered a threat to society.[1322]

C Other Administrative Offenses

In many countries around the world, the WGAD has observed the practice of detaining individuals on minor administrative offenses, which are often used as a pretext to infringe on fundamental rights and freedoms. Given the relatively short detention periods for detainees imprisoned for these kinds of minor administrative offenses, the WGAD has not had occasion to consider such detentions in its case jurisprudence. But it has repeatedly addressed these kinds of administrative detentions when conducting country missions.

During its visit to Armenia, the WGAD examined the aftermath of the country's presidential election on February 19, 2008, where public demonstrations were held against the election results. Mass arrests and detentions occurred and 10 people were killed and 200 injured. More than 5,000 people were arrested for several hours and 110 opposition activists were charged and tried for such offenses as "mass disorders," "possession of weapons," "resisting arrest," and "usurpation of State authority." In commenting on these events, the WGAD emphasized the importance of the right to freedom of opinion and expression and rights to peaceful assembly and association. It said the Government has an important role "in ensuring that these rights are protected in conformity with the Constitution, prescribed national laws and international laws and standards on human rights. It would also like to see an improvement in the situation of those who wish to exercise these rights, particularly during significant milestones such as governmental elections."[1323]

In Argentina, the WGAD reported on the powers of police in some parts of the country to detain individuals on violations of specific laws that are more administrative rather than criminal and which should be punished by a caution or a fine. For example, in Buenos Aires, the Urban Coexistence Code allowed police to take action against behavior or acts considered "contrary to public morality and decency." It reported that transsexuals, transvestites, and prostitutes (despite prostitution not being illegal) were often punished for such misdemeanors.[1324] In its response to this conduct, which was perhaps less open-minded because it was fifteen years ago but nonetheless reached the right conclusion, it observed:

[1322] *Id.*, at ¶ 119.

[1323] Report of the Working Group on Mission to Armenia, at ¶¶ 55, 58.

[1324] *Report of the Working Group on Arbitrary Detention: Mission to Argentina*, Commission on Human Rights, E/CN.4/2004/3/Add.3, Dec. 23, 2003, at ¶ 51.

The Working Group does not deny that the behaviour of certain individuals, whether or not they belong to sexual minorities, may at times be provocative or offend against public morality. However, Argentine legislation does not appear to define sufficiently clearly which behaviour it wishes to prohibit or punish, or the limits of such behaviour. This lack of clarity gives police officers a large amount of discretion, which often leads to arbitrary enforcement of the law. It has been alleged that it is not so much the act itself that they are targeting but individuals, because of their appearance or clothes or the threat that they might pose. In this context, the outcome is usually arbitrary detention.[1325]

In Azerbaijan, the WGAD found the administrative offenses of "hooliganism" and "refusal to obey public authorities" were overbroad and that penalties imposed under these offenses were often disproportionate. It explained:

The Working Group considers that there should be legal clarity as to what constitutes incriminating acts; proportionality between the offences and the related sentences; and strict separation between law enforcement agents and the prosecution authorities. Also, the principle of contradiction in criminal justice, whereby the accused person is provided with effective legal assistance and representation throughout the process, must be fully respected, including in cases of administrative offences.[1326]

In Colombia, the WGAD reported that its National Police were "continuing its practice of carrying out round-ups or raids in big cities, justifying the practice as a preventative measure. Communities of sexual minorities complained of being detained frequently because of their appearance or clothes. Beggars, the destitute, vagrants, people who look suspicious, and even street vendors, whose goods are confiscated, are also detained."[1327] It also expressed concern that although the military in Colombia do not legally have detention powers, it acted as police in isolated rural areas and conflict zones outside the reach of the National Police. And it specifically criticized the military's "mass detentions of young persons with a view to checking their military status. Those who are deemed to have failed to register, to respond to being called up or to have performed military service are taken to the barracks for forced recruitment."[1328] The WGAD criticized a similar practice of the armed forces making arrests and detentions despite not having the legal powers to do so in Equatorial Guinea. The WGAD explained the military "often set up road checkpoints, especially at the entrance to cities, and demand payment of a sum of money for passage. Those who refuse to pay these illegal charges are often beaten and arrested."[1329]

After its visit to Georgia, the WGAD expressed its serious concern about the mass arrests and detentions of about 150 people that were a response to anti-government protests in Tbilisi on May 26, 2011. It reported having interviewed many of the detainees who had been placed in administrative detention because of their involvement in the protests. They reported to the WGAD members that they had been arrested for offenses

---

[1325] *Id.*, at ¶ 52.
[1326] Report of the Working Group on Mission to Azerbaijan, at ¶ 51.
[1327] *Report of the Working Group on Arbitrary Detention: Mission to Colombia*, Human Rights Council, A/HRC/10/21/Add.3, Feb. 16, 2009, at ¶¶ 56, 59.
[1328] *Id.*, at ¶ 66.
[1329] Report of the Working Group on Mission to Equatorial Guinea, at ¶ 67.

such as swearing and resisting arrest by the police, and the Government acknowledged seventy-five protesters were fined and ninety-nine detained for up to two months for "hooliganism" and "resistance to the police" under the Administrative Offences Code.[1330]

The WGAD also commented on practices in Hungary, where there were a wide range of misdemeanors punishable with confinement and that the country's domestic laws allowed judges to change a fine or community service to confinement without hearing from the offender if the fine was not paid or work was not completed. Among specific laws of concern to the WGAD was one that criminalizes homelessness by stating that living on public premises and storing personal property on public premises constitutes a petty offense for which a violator may be fined or confined.[1331] In addition, the WGAD said it had interviewed detainees who were serving time for having not worn a seatbelt, having broken a bicycle light, jaywalking, and walking across a street under the influence of alcohol.[1332] It found that a common reason fines were not paid was financial limitations. In examining this system of misdemeanors, the WGAD concluded:

> It seemed that an automatic conversion of a fine to confinement took place without the offender being in court to challenge the confinement. This automatic system of conversion concerns the Working Group, as a person should be able to challenge any deprivation of liberty in light of one's own and unique circumstance, for instance where family or financial situations can be explained to a judicial authority to shed light on the inability to pay a fine. This situation is aggravated by the fact that only a particular section of the population is unfairly disadvantaged: those who are poor or who may not have the means to provide financial assurance against confinement . . . The principle of proportionality should be applied in these situations and, importantly, alternative measures to confinement such as community work should be utilized.[1333]

In Malaysia, the WGAD reported that four specific preventative laws – the Internal Security Act, Emergency Ordinance, Special Preventive Measure Act, and Restricted Residence Act – establish investigative detention to prevent a suspect from fleeing, destroying evidence, or committing a future crime. They also interfere with the right to a fair trial and restrict detainees' access to counsel. In relation to these laws, the WGAD concluded:

> These preventive laws allow State institutions, particularly the police and the Office of the Attorney General, to elude the normal penal procedure for common crimes and offences. It also gives the Minister for Home Affairs excessive powers to keep people in detention indefinitely. The Emergency Ordinance is used for this purpose in particular. In the detention centres reserved for detainees under these laws, the Working Group found people charged with common offences who should in principle be treated under the regular penal procedure.[1334]

[1330] Report of the Working Group on Mission to Georgia, at ¶¶ 69–70.
[1331] Report of the Working Group on Mission to Hungary, at ¶¶ 110–111.
[1332] *Id.*, at ¶ 112.
[1333] *Id.*, at ¶¶ 113–114.
[1334] *Report of the Working Group on Arbitrary Detention: Mission to Malaysia*, Human Rights Council, A/HRC/16/47/Add.3, Feb. 8, 2011, at ¶ 28.

The situation examined by the WGAD in Mauritania provided an opportunity to look at a legal system "formally founded on the rules and standards of sharia," which it noted had "shortcomings in respect of international principles and standards, particularly with regard to the importance of proof and the prohibition of sex-based discrimination."[1335] For example, the WGAD said it had heard persistent allegations that sharia rules of adultery were being used to exert pressure on women who had been sexually abused or raped, where the accused often threatened to denounce them for adultery, thereby leaving women "doubly victimized."[1336] The WGAD also expressed concern about the provision of sharia law that criminalized "public offences against Islamic morals and decency," which was an overbroad and vague statute. It reported that it understood that this law had been used to prosecute individuals for the possession and sale of alcohol. And it expressed serious concern about the prosecution of a woman under this statute who had been sentenced to two years in prison for the possession of a condom, which was interpreted as a public attack on Islamic morals and decency.[1337]

VII Mass Detentions

In *Kang Min-ho, et al.* v. *Democratic People's Republic of Korea*, the WGAD addressed the detentions of three individuals imprisoned in *Kwan-li-so* Camps 14 and 15 for the actions of family members that had fled or defected from North Korea. Two of the detainees, a mother and son, had been detained for accepting money from a relative, a prominent dissident-turned-journalist and defector to South Korea. The third detainee had been imprisoned with his entire family for over forty years for his brother's defection during the Korean War. He and his youngest son had been tortured for the escape attempts of his wife and eldest son, which resulted in the breaking of both his legs. In reflection on the estimated 150,000–200,000 political prisoners detained in six prisons across North Korea for similar guilt-by-association offenses, the WGAD extended its analysis of these detentions beyond the three detainees:

> The Working Group recalls … that under certain circumstances, widespread or systematic imprisonment or other severe deprivation of liberty in violation of fundamental rules of international law, might constitute crimes against humanity. The current case makes it necessary to reaffirm this. The duty to comply with international human rights that are peremptory and *erga omnes* norms such as the prohibition of arbitrary detention, lies with all bodies and representatives of the State, and on all individuals … The Working Group reminds the Democratic People's Republic of Korea of its duties to comply with international human rights obligations, not to detain arbitrarily, to release persons who are arbitrarily detained, and to provide compensation to them.[1338]

This DPRK case is one of several in which the WGAD has commented on situations of mass detentions. Mass detentions are not necessarily an issue in cases that involve

---

[1335] Report of Working Group on Mission to Mauritania, at ¶ 75.
[1336] *Id.*, at ¶ 76.
[1337] *Id.*, at ¶ 77.
[1338] Kang Min-ho, et al. v. Democratic People's Republic of Korea, WGAD Opinion No. 47/2012, Adopted Nov. 15, 2012, at ¶ 19, 22 (Litigated by Author through Perseus Strategies).

multiple detainees. For the purposes of this analysis, "mass detention" is defined as the large-scale imprisonment of people for similar reasons or collective crimes, where each detention is typically not given individual consideration. Mass detentions are particularly important in their own right under international law because they can, if conducted in a particular manner, be properly analyzed as crimes against humanity.[1339] Beyond its work on individual cases, the WGAD has also issued Deliberation No. 4 on Rehabilitation through Labour,[1340] Deliberation No. 7 on Psychiatric Detentions,[1341] and an opinion on drug policies and arbitrary detention,[1342] which each speak to broader systems the WGAD has concluded perpetuate arbitrary detentions.

Often, mass detention cases are brought to the WGAD by naming several of the detainees being held in a specific place or for a specific reason shared by the much larger number of individuals. Although it relies on information from the petition to decide the specified cases, the WGAD will also look to comments from UN sources and other independent international reporting to substantiate allegations that arbitrary detentions are occurring on a large scale. Drawing from these sources, the WGAD will typically comment on the mass detention as a whole. The DPRK case is a clear example of this reasoning process – having heard information from the source regarding three individuals and having reviewed other reporting on the general situation of political prisoner camps in North Korea from the General Assembly, HRC, UN Special Procedures, and treaty bodies, the WGAD issued an opinion denouncing not just the imprisonment of the three detainees, but of the hundreds of thousands of suspected arbitrary detentions in the DPRK.

A *Inferring Broader Violations from Individual Cases and Context*

The WGAD's handling of detentions at Camp Liberty and Camp Ashraf in Iraq mirrored how it handled the DPRK prison camps. Camp Ashraf was a twenty-five-year-old settlement in Iraq by 3,400 members of an Iranian opposition organization who enjoyed "protected persons" status under the Fourth Geneva Convention while the Coalition Forces were present in Iraq.[1343] However, under the United States–Iraq Status of Forces Agreement, control of Camp Ashraf was transferred to the Government of Iraq in 2009 and, subsequently, conditions deteriorated for the residents. The first WGAD case

---

[1339] Under Article 7(1)(e) of the Rome Statute, which established the International Criminal Court, one of the crimes against humanity is: "Imprisonment or other severe deprivation of physical liberty in violation of fundamental rules of international law." *Rome Statute of the International Criminal* Court, UN General Assembly, July 17, 1998, *entered into force* July 1, 2002. To qualify as crimes against humanity, such imprisonments must be committed "as part of a widespread or systematic attack directed against a civilian population, with knowledge of the attack. Rome Statute, at Art. 7(1).

[1340] *Report of the Working Group on Arbitrary Detention*, Commission on Human Rights, E/CN.4/1993/24, Jan. 12, 1993.

[1341] *Report of the Working Group on Arbitrary Detention*, Commission on Human Rights, E/CN.4/2005/6, Dec. 1, 2004.

[1342] *Report of the Working Group on Arbitrary Detention*, Human Rights Council, A/HRC/30/436, July 15, 2015, at ¶¶ 57–62.

[1343] Jalil Gholamzadeh Golmarzi Hossein, et al. v. Iraq, WGAD Opinion No. 11/2010, Adopted May 7, 2010, at ¶ 9.

concerning Camp Ashraf was brought after an unprovoked attack by Iraqi police in 2009, which resulted in the arbitrary detention of thirty-seven residents.[1344] The Government continually blocked the flow of food and medicine to Ashraf and, after a second unprovoked attack in 2011, announced its intent to close Camp Ashraf and send its residents back to Iran.[1345]

After the second attack and with United Nations intervention, the Government agreed to transfer Camp Ashraf residents to Camp Liberty, where their refugee status could be determined and voluntary resettlement in third countries could begin. However, conditions in Camp Liberty were far below international standards, and the transferred residents were neither permitted to receive visitors, access counsel, nor leave the Camp, in violation of their rights as asylum-seekers.[1346] Furthermore, the private lives of residents were under constant surveillance, and between the lack of privacy, headcounts, and police presence, Camp Liberty was practically a prison, though no resident had been tried or convicted for a crime.[1347]

The first Camp Liberty case, *Hossein Dadkhah, et al. v. Iraq*, was brought on behalf of ten detainees who formerly resided at Camp Ashraf.[1348] Though 10 people was just a fraction of the 400 transferred from Camp Liberty at that point, the conditions were common to all residents. With no rebuttal from the Government and having already been familiarized with the situation in their prior opinion on Camp Ashraf, the WGAD found that "there is no legal justification for holding the above-mentioned persons and other individuals in Camp Liberty," since they were asylum-seekers under international law and had not been tried or convicted for any crime.[1349]

In *Mehdi Abedi, et al. v. Iraq*, the WGAD was asked to "extend its prior opinion regarding the detention of 10 residents of Camp Liberty (opinion No. 16/2012) to all the residents of Camp Liberty and Camp Ashraf, *in toto*, as their situation is either identical to or fundamentally the same as that addressed in the opinion."[1350] *Mehdi Abedi* was brought on behalf of ten Ashraf and ten Liberty residents. However, being familiar with the situation in the Camps from its prior cases and other UN interventions, the WGAD extended their ruling beyond the petitioners to hold that all "residents of both Camp Liberty and Camp Ashraf are effectively deprived of their liberty without any legal justification."[1351]

After the coup attempt in Turkey in July 2016, the WGAD handled a number of individual cases of arbitrary detention but also spoke more broadly about the country's widely known patterns and practices of arbitrary detention.[1352] For example, it noted with concern "the apparently widespread practice in Turkey of 'guilt by association' and echoe[d] the concerns raised by the Council of Europe Commissioner for Human Rights in that respect, where such practices as arresting family members of suspects and seizing

---

[1344] *Id.*, at ¶ 16.
[1345] Mehdi Abedi, et al. v. Iraq, WGAD Opinion 32/2012, Adopted Aug. 30, 2012, at ¶ 4.
[1346] *Id.* at ¶ 6.
[1347] Hossein Dadkhah, et al. v. Iraq, WGAD Opinion No. 16/2012, Adopted May 4, 2012, at ¶ 5.
[1348] *Id.*
[1349] *Id.*, at ¶¶ 15, 17.
[1350] Mehdi Abedi, et al., at ¶ 21 (Litigated by Author through Perseus Strategies).
[1351] *Id.*, at ¶ 31.
[1352] Rebii Metin Görgeç v. Turkey, WGAD Opinion No. 1/2017, Adopted Apr. 19, 2017, at ¶¶ 59–60 (Litigated by Author through Perseus Strategies).

their passports appear to have become a common occurrence."[1353] And the WGAD indicated that it was "aware that a large number of individuals have been arrested" and reminded the Government to "adhere to its human rights obligations, including the fundamental elements of due process, even under the declared emergency situation."[1354]

B Inferring Broader Violations from Repetition of Fact Patterns

The WGAD may also choose to rule on mass detentions where it sees a repetitive series of related individual cases. For instance, Australia has been involved in a series of individual cases relating to its detention policies for migrants and asylum-seekers. Each WGAD session in 2017 had a case relating to a migrant detained by Australia, and there have already been two similar opinions issued in the first cases of 2018.[1355] The deprivations of liberty of each of these detainees was found arbitrary in violation of international law. Although each of these instances considered specific detainees and the facts of their case, the repetition of similar and ongoing violations of due process and arbitrary grounds for detention has led the WGAD to render an opinion on the situation of migrants in Australia generally when cases are brought within this fact pattern.

Reza Raeesi v. Australia and Papua New Guinea was one such case, involving an Iranian national who sought asylum in Australia from persecution based on his sexual orientation.[1356] The WGAD began by examining the individual circumstances of his initial arrest in Australia and his eventual detention in the Manus Regional Processing Center in Papua New Guinea, including details specific to Raeesi such as his poor health, depression, and potential prison sentence for homosexuality if he were to be resettled in Papua New Guinea. Turning to reports from the UN High Commissioner for Refugees, the WGAD considered the situation at the detention facility in Papua New Guinea failed to meet international standards of protection for migrants and asylum-seekers.[1357] Additionally, it examined recommendations from the Committee against Torture, which addressed the harsh and inadequate conditions in offshore processing centers.[1358] Thus, in its disposition of the case, the WGAD concluded not only that Raeesi's detention was arbitrary, but that "The conclusions reached by the Working Group in the present opinion, including those on the remedies ... apply to other persons finding themselves in similar situations in centres on Manus Island and other places of detention outside Australian territory."[1359]

More recent WGAD opinions related to such detentions in Australia have addressed the opinion from the High Court of Australia in *Al-Kateb* v. *Godwin*. The effect of *Al-*

[1353] *Id.*

[1354] *Id.*

[1355] Abdalrahman Hussein v. Australia, WGAD Opinion No. 28/2017, Adopted Apr. 25, 2017; Mohammad Naim Amiri v. Australia, WGAD Opinion No. 42/2017, Adopted Aug. 21, 2017; Said Imasi v. Australia, WGAD Opinion No. 71/2017, Adopted Nov. 21, 2017; William Yekrop v. Australia, WGAD Opinion No. 20/2018, Adopted Apr. 20, 2018; Ghasem Hamedani v. Australia, WGAD Opinion No. 21/2018, Adopted Apr. 20, 2018.

[1356] Reza Raeesi v. Australia and Papua New Guinea, WGAD Opinion No. 52/2014, Adopted Nov. 21, 2014, at ¶¶ 6–8.

[1357] *Id.*, at ¶¶ 28, 32.

[1358] *Id.*, at ¶¶ 37–38.

[1359] *Id.*, at ¶ 50.

Kateb v. *Godwin* was to deny noncitizens a path to challenging administrative detention in Australia. This has been a point of contention in several WGAD cases.[1360] In each, after giving consideration to the initial circumstances of each petitioner, the WGAD will typically reference the HR Committee decision in *F.J., et al* v. *Australia*, which found that noncitizens had no effective remedy against an ongoing detention. Repeatedly, the WGAD has held that *Al-Kateb* v. *Godwin* creates a "situation [that] is discriminatory" in contradiction of Articles 16 and 26 of the ICCPR.[1361] Thus, although each case in this series is brought for an individual detainee for the consideration of an individual case, the WGAD has noted the repetition of similar fact patterns and, in combination with reports from international bodies, uses these specific cases to comment on recurring violations on a larger scale.

The series of WGAD cases relating to detainees of the United States at Guantanamo Bay, Cuba, provides a similar, high-profile example of how the Working Group may translate a series of individual decisions into rulings on situations of mass detention. As the line of Guantanamo cases progressed, WGAD opinions on individual cases began to include general condemnations of detention at Guantanamo Bay and relevant practices. For instance, several cases consider any hearing before the Combatant Status Review Tribunal to be insufficient for a fair trial, calling it a "military tribunal of a summary nature."[1362] In *Ammar al-Baluchi* v. *United States*, the most recent WGAD case to deal with detention in Guantanamo, the WGAD summarizes a long line of cases and legal opinions to conclude that "the Working Group's jurisprudence has consistently determined that prolonged and indefinite detention at Guantánamo Bay is arbitrary."[1363]

Having received "many communications alleging the arbitrary character of detention measures applied in the United States as part of its investigations into the terrorist acts of 11 September 2001," the WGAD also issued a report unrelated to any particular case condemning detention in Guantanamo.[1364] And the WGAD in 2006 issued a joint report with four UN Special Procedures finding, among other things, that the United States was obligated to extend international human rights to all persons detained at Guantanamo.[1365] The joint report also found that for all Guantanamo detainees the right to challenge the legality of detention "is currently being violated, and the continuing

---

[1360] Abdalrahman Hussein v. Australia, WGAD Opinion No. 28/2017, Adopted Apr. 25, 2017, at ¶ 39; Mohammad Naim Amiri v. Australia, WGAD Opinion No. 42/2017, Adopted Aug. 21, 2017, at ¶ 44; Said Imasi v. Australia, WGAD Opinion No. 71/2017, Adopted Nov. 21, 2017, at ¶ 55; William Yekrop v. Australia, WGAD Opinion No. 20/2018, Adopted Apr. 20, 2018, at ¶ 68; Ghasem Hamedani v. Australia, WGAD Opinion No. 21/2018, Adopted Apr. 20, 2018, at ¶ 78.

[1361] William Yekrop v. Australia, WGAD Opinion No. 20/2018, Adopted Apr. 20, 2018, at ¶ 67.

[1362] Ammar al-Baluchi v. United States, WGAD Opinion No. 89/2017, Adopted Nov. 24, 2017, at ¶ 46 (citing opinions 50/2014, 10/2013, and 2/2009).

[1363] *Id.*, at ¶ 37(d).

[1364] *Report of the Working Group on Arbitrary Detention*, Commission on Human Rights, E/CN.4/2003/8, Dec. 16, 2002, at ¶ 61 (a legal opinion on Guantanamo issued by the Working Group not in connection with a particular case).

[1365] *Situation of Detainees at Guantanamo Bay: Report of the Chairperson-Rapporteur of the Working Group on Arbitrary Detention, Special Rapporteur on the Independence of Judges and Lawyers, Special Rapporteur on Torture and Other Cruel, Inhuman or Degrading Treatment or Punishment, Special Rapporteur on Freedom of Religion or Belief, and the Special Rapporteur on the Right of Everyone to the Enjoyment of the Highest Attainable Standard of Physical and Mental Health*, Commission on Human Rights, E/CN.4/2006/120, Feb. 27, 2006, at ¶¶ 10–11.

detention of all persons held at Guantánamo Bay amounts to arbitrary detention in violation of article 9 of ICCPR."[1366]

C Examining Situations of Large Cohort of Detainees Together

The *Balyoz or "Sledgehammer" Cases* involved 250 current and former Turkish military officers detained in 2003 for an alleged plot to provoke hostilities with a third country in order to justify a military takeover.[1367] Three indictments, issued between July 2010 and September 2011, resulted in the arrest and detentions of a total of 365 individuals.[1368] The 250 Sledgehammer detainees represented in the WGAD case were victims of broad due process violations, including lengthy pretrial detentions, withholding of evidence, and violations of attorney–client confidentiality.[1369] Additionally, the allegations of involvement in the coup were put forward against the defendants as a group.[1370]

Unlike the instances mentioned previously, the author, who was representing the defendants in the Sledgehammer case, named each of the detainees rather than bringing the cases of a few individuals in connection with reports of the broader injustice. Due to the treatment of the defendants as a collective in the domestic proceedings, the WGAD found it appropriate to address all 250 detentions in one opinion.[1371] It did so by broad considerations of the due process and other violations that had been alleged and applied to all the detainees. The WGAD considered that the Government had not shown the necessity for the lengthy pretrial detention for of the 250 detainees, nor had it sufficiently disputed the allegations of procedural irregularities.[1372] In light of this, the WGAD was willing to rule in a mass opinion that the detention of all 250 Sledgehammer defendants was arbitrary under Category III.

VIII Extraditions

Separate and distinct from cases of extraordinary rendition, which occur outside any legal framework, there is the distinct case of individuals detained pending legal resolution of a claim by a third country to extradite such people for alleged crimes. Under international law, extradition cases are procedural processes that do not constitute the detention of a person based on "criminal charges" falling within the full range of the protections of Article 14 of the ICCPR. Nevertheless, numerous protections of the ICCPR still apply. In *Ronald Everett* v. *Spain*, the Human Rights Committee heard a complaint of a British citizen who alleged he had been wrongly extradited to the United Kingdom. The Committee's analysis in this case serves as a guide for applying the ICCPR to extraditions:

> Recalling its earlier case law the Committee considers that although the Covenant does not require that extradition procedures be judicial in nature, extradition as such does not fall outside the protection of the Covenant. On the contrary, several provisions,

---

[1366] *Id.*, at ¶ 84.
[1367] Balyoz or Sledgehammer Cases v. Turkey, WGAD Opinion No. 6/2013, Adopted May 1, 2013, at ¶ 4.
[1368] *Id.*, at ¶ 6.
[1369] *Id.*, at ¶¶ 23, 25, 27.
[1370] *Id.*, at ¶ 72.
[1371] *Id.*
[1372] *Id.* at ¶¶ 74–75.

including articles 6, 7, 9, and 13, are necessarily applicable in relation to extradition. Particularly, in cases where, as the current one, the judiciary is involved in deciding about extradition, it must respect the principles of impartiality, fairness, and equality, as enshrined in article 14, paragraph 1, and also reflected in article 13 of the Covenant. Nevertheless, the Committee considers that even when decided by a court the consideration of an extradition request does not amount to the determination of a criminal charge in the meaning of article 14.[1373]

By analogy, this question has also been examined by the European Court of Human Rights in applying the *European Convention on Human Rights*. In *Quinn* v. *France*, the European Court examined the extended detention of an American who was ultimately extradited to Switzerland under the *European Convention on Extradition*.[1374] In examining the case against France, the European Court concluded that the applicant had been held "in detention with a view to extradition ... [for a period of] ... one year, eleven months, and six days" before the extradition was carried out. It noted that the applicant's detention with a view to extradition was "unusually long." It concluded:

> It is clear from the wording ... of Article 5(1)(f) [regarding the presumed lawfulness of detentions pending deportation] that deprivation of liberty under this sub-paragraph will be justified only for as long as the extradition proceedings are being conducted. It follows that if such proceedings are not being prosecuted with due diligence, the detention will cease to be justified under Article 5(1)(f). The Court notes that, at the different stages of the extradition proceedings, there were delays of sufficient length to render the total duration of those proceedings excessive.[1375]

In its annual report in 2000, the WGAD addressed the arbitrary deprivation of liberty that can emanate from the diverse and inconsistent systems of states for responding to requests for extradition:

> The Working Group notes that issues concerning the extradition of individuals raise questions related to deprivation of liberty. In the absence of an international convention on extradition issues, disparate extradition procedures applicable in varying jurisdictions make the liberty of individuals subject to municipal laws. A large number of domestic procedures do not provide for a maximum period of detention within which extradition procedures must be completed. Lack of uniformity subjects individuals facing extradition proceedings to deprivation of liberty in varying degrees, depending on the applicable domestic procedure. Yet another aspect relates to the period of deprivation of liberty pending extradition not being included in the sentence, upon extradition and subsequent conviction in the requesting State. The Working Group observes that these and other related aspects will be considered by it in a future deliberation, in an attempt to bring about uniformity and rationality in matters relating to deprivation of liberty of persons pending extradition or extradited persons.[1376]

[1373] Everett v. Spain, Communication No. 961/2000, Human Rights Committee, CCPR/C/81/D/961/2000, July 9, 2004.

[1374] Quinn v. France, Application No. 18580/91, Judgment, European Court of Human Rights, Mar. 22, 1995.

[1375] *Id.*, at ¶ 48.

[1376] *Report of the Working Group on Arbitrary Detention*, Commission on Human Rights, E/CN.4/2001/14, Dec. 20, 2000, at ¶ 81.

Coming from its observations, the WGAD specifically advised states to set a maximum period for detentions pending extraditions and that states receiving extradited individuals count as time served detentions pending extraditions.[1377] Because by their nature extraditions involve a sending and receiving country, improperly implemented extradition procedures may create a shared responsibility for an arbitrary detention if both states' actions contribute to a violation of human rights.[1378]

It is important to reaffirm extraditions are administrative and not criminal proceedings. Although the WGAD has not consistently acted in this manner, sometimes treating detainees held pending extradition as having the rights of criminal defendants, it has allowed some deviations from proper procedure to be permitted as long as there is proper judicial oversight and a presumption against pre-extradition detention.

For instance, in *Mukhtar Ablyazov* v. *France*, the WGAD did not consider it consequential that the detainee was not provided with interpretation service and was not permitted to call and question witnesses or examine certain pieces of evidence during his extradition hearing.[1379] When the detainee had the full assistance of his lawyers, the absence of translators was not a violation of enough gravity to render his detention arbitrary. Furthermore, although Ablyazov was technically correct in claiming the right to examine witnesses and evidence, the WGAD held that these rights "would have greater bearing on the consideration of the merits of the case" than on an extradition hearing.[1380] As such, the violation of these rights was not "of sufficient consequence" to justify a finding of arbitrary detention.[1381]

However, the defendant in an extradition case still has rights that extraditing countries must respect. As mentioned earlier, unnecessary or extended pretrial detention is a common abuse of due process rights in extradition cases. Since extradition is an administrative and not criminal proceeding, the general rule against pretrial detention is particularly strong.[1382] This does not mean detention is impermissible where a suspect has a likelihood of compromising evidence or attempting to evade justice.[1383] However, in cases like Ablyazov's, the length of the proceedings may offset the justification for detention. Although the WGAD agreed with the Government of France that, if released, Ablyazov would have the means of jeopardizing evidence against him, this did not justify a three-year detention for an administrative proceeding, especially given that no alternatives such as judicial supervision had been considered.[1384] Additionally, the WGAD found the three-year delay to be a violation of Ablyazov's right to a trial within a reasonable time or to release.[1385]

This right to a prompt hearing appears in multiple extradition cases. That said, however, WGAD jurisprudence on the subject is somewhat contradictory. While Ablyazov's administrative detention was found to be too long, the WGAD did

[1377] *Id.*, at ¶¶ 95–96.
[1378] Abdullah Ahmed Mohammed Ismail Alfakharany, et al v. Egypt, WGAD Opinion No. 7/2016, Adopted Apr. 19, 2016, at ¶ 54.
[1379] Mukhtar Ablyazov v. France, WGAD Opinion No. 49/2016, Adopted Nov. 23, 2016.
[1380] *Id.*
[1381] *Id.*
[1382] *Id.*, at ¶ 72.
[1383] *Id.*
[1384] *Id.*
[1385] *Id.*, at ¶ 67.

acknowledge that part of the delay was due to "numerous legal challenges filed" by the detainee.[1386] This contribution to the length of the proceedings did not preclude a finding of arbitrary detention.

However, the WGAD came to the opposition conclusion in *Marco Pasini Beltrán and Carlos Cabal Peniche* v. *Australia*.[1387] In that case, the detainees were two Mexican nationals who had been detained in Australia for two-and-a-half years pending extradition, in the same manner as convicted persons. Their abnormally long detentions were a "result of the fact that they have availed themselves of all the guarantees to a fair trial provided for by law and have instituted all the proceedings for which Australian law provides in their situation."[1388] However, unlike in Ablyazov's case, the WGAD found this to mean that the length of detention "could not be attributed to the Government of Australia," and thus the detention of Beltrán and Peniche was not arbitrary.[1389]

Because Beltrán and Peniche's case was decided several years prior to Ablyazov's, the latter may be more instructive for new WGAD cases that involve the intersection of extradition hearings and the right to a speedy trial. *Julian Assange* v. *Sweden and the United Kingdom* dealt with this overlap as well, although this was a highly unusual case and its conclusions were contested even within the WGAD itself. Assessing the 550-day period during which the defendant lived under bail conditions while exercising every avenue to appeal his extradition, the WGAD had "no choice but to query what has hindered judicial management of any kind from occurring in a reasonable manner for such an extended period of time."[1390] This analysis may apply when the WGAD deals with the prompt trial requirements in extradition cases where the defendant is living under bail conditions. However, because the WGAD is only competent to rule on deprivations of liberty, not restrictions of liberty, this holding may not hold in future cases.

Although the WGAD has repeatedly disclaimed that it will not substitute itself for a domestic fact finder, extradition law appears to be one area in which the WGAD occasionally examines and interprets domestic law. In one early case, *John Samboma, et al* v. *Namibia*, the WGAD declined to comment on the allegation that the extraditions in question had not been executed according to proper domestic procedure.[1391] But in Assange's case, the WGAD interpreted amendments to United Kingdom extradition legislation to mean that, had the detainee's case been tried a few years later, his extradition would not have been approved.[1392] This interpretation was included in the list of elements that rendered his detention arbitrary.[1393] Similarly, in *Carlos Federico Guardo* v. *Argentina*, the WGAD examined Argentina's Act No. 24767 on International Cooperation in Criminal Matters, which requires extradition requests to be denied unless the requesting state guarantees that time served in Argentina pending the

---

[1386] *Id.*

[1387] Marco Pasini Beltrán and Carlos Cabal Peniche v. Australia, WGAD Opinion No. 15/2001, Adopted Sept. 13, 2001, at ¶ 24.

[1388] *Id.*, at ¶ 23.

[1389] *Id.*, at ¶¶ 23–24.

[1390] Julian Assange v. Sweden and United Kingdom, WGAD Opinion No. 54/2015, Adopted Dec. 4, 2015, at ¶ 80.

[1391] John Samboma, et al v. Namibia, WGAD Opinion No. 48/2005, Adopted Nov. 30, 2005, at ¶ 10.

[1392] Julian Assange, at ¶ 91.

[1393] *Id.*

extradition will be credited toward any sentence later received after extradition.[1394] In Guardo's case, Argentina was the requesting state but the WGAD nonetheless interpreted Act. No. 24767 to apply to both inbound and outbound extraditions, finding "Argentina cannot act contrary to the rules it applies itself when considering extradition requests from other States."[1395]

Extradition cases also call on the WGAD to interpret and apply international law, which falls within their mandate. This may include bilateral extradition treaties or larger, multilateral conventions. For instance, the WGAD held the abduction of the detainee in *Humberto Alvarez-Machain* v. *United States* to constitute a violation of the US–Mexico Extradition Treaty.[1396] Although the treaty did not explicitly prohibit abduction as a means of extradition, the WGAD reasoned that "this is implicitly prohibited when the subject matter - cooperation in the struggle against crime by surrendering offenders – is regulated in all dimensions by the treaty in question."[1397] In *Muhammad Yusuf and Ali Yasin Ahmed* v. *Djibouti, Sweden, and United States*, two Swedish citizens were arrested in Djibouti and transported to the United States. The WGAD assessed and agreed with the Swedish Constitutional Affairs Committee's interpretation of the *Vienna Convention on Consular Relations*, finding that the detainee's extradition did not bring Sweden's consular duties to an end, and that "foreign authorities may have a duty to intervene with diplomatic means" where a deprivation of liberty violates the law.[1398]

Where transfers from one state to another are too irregular or informal, they fall under the category of extraordinary rendition, not extradition.[1399] In particular, extraditions undertaken in the name of counterterrorism often tend to possess informal or irregular qualities that deprive a detention of the legal basis extradition may offer.[1400] The exact line between extradition and extraordinary rendition is unclear in WGAD jurisprudence – the term "extradition" may still be used in certain cases where the transport of a detainee possesses irregular qualities, like in *Muhammad Yusuf and Ali Yasin Ahmed* v. *Djibouti, Sweden, and United States*. The WGAD has nonetheless issued a recommendation against all forms of extraordinary rendition, and in its jurisprudence, detention resulting from extraordinary rendition is arbitrary under Category I.[1401]

[1394] Carlos Federico Guardo v. Argentina, WGAD Opinion No. 47/2011, Adopted Sept. 2, 2011, at ¶ 28.

[1395] *Id.*

[1396] Humberto Alvarez Machain v. United States, WGAD Opinion No. 48/1993, Adopted Sept. 30, 1993, at ¶ 5(n).

[1397] *Id.*

[1398] Muhammad Yusuf and Ali Yasin Ahmed v. Djibouti, Sweden, and United States, WGAD Opinion No. 57/2013, Adopted Nov. 21, 2013, at ¶ 68.

[1399] Amine Mohammed al-Bakry v. Afghanistan and United States, WGAD Opinion No. 11/2007, Adopted May 11, 2007, at ¶ 15.

[1400] Muhammad Yusuf and Ali Yasin Ahmed (involving the probably irregular extradition of two Swedish nationals); Amine Mohammed al-Bakry v. Afghanistan and United States, WGAD Opinion No. 11/2007, Adopted May 11, 2007 (involving the abduction of a businessman for his affiliation with a family member of Osama bin Laden); Ibn al-Shaykh al-Libi, et al v. United States, WGAD Opinion No. 29/2006, Adopted Sept. 1, 2006, at ¶ 11 (discussing irregular transport in counter-terrorism cases generally).

[1401] *Report of the Working Group on Arbitrary Detention*, Human Rights Council, A/HRC/4/40, Jan. 9, 2007, at ¶ 50.

IX Disproportionate or Excessive Sentencing

Although the WGAD has not had occasion to evaluate disproportionate or excessive sentencing in the context of its case jurisprudence, there is a substantial body of international law focused on promoting the use of noncustodial measures as an alternative to imprisonment. It has also commented on the general issue in the context of country missions. Under the *Standard Minimum Rules for Non-Custodial Measures* (Tokyo Rules), as well as regional standards from the Americas, Africa, and Europe, countries should develop noncustodial measures in order to provide greater flexibility to make sentences proportional to the nature and gravity of the offense and reduce the use of imprisonment.[1402] The development of these kinds of guidelines and standards emanated from the increasing use in recent decades of such measures as excessively long sentences that result from life without parole sentences, recidivist statutes (e.g. three strikes statutes), consecutive sentences, and mandatory minimum sentences.

Under the Tokyo Rules, the personality and background of the offender as well as the protection of society should be considered, to avoid the unnecessary use of imprisonment.[1403]

The introduction, definition, and application of noncustodial measures must be prescribed by law. And the imposition of a noncustodial measure must be based on an assessment of established criteria regarding the nature and gravity of the offense and the personality and background of the offender, the purposes of sentencing, and the rights of victims. The sentencing authority must be able to exercise discretion, but with full accountability and in accordance with the rule of law.[1404]

The Tokyo Rules also provide a detailed list of potential alternatives to detention:

> Sentencing authorities may dispose of cases in the following ways:
> (a) verbal sanctions, such as admonition, reprimand and warning;
> (b) conditional discharge;
> (c) status penalties;
> (d) economic sanctions and monetary penalties, such as fines and day fines;
> (e) confiscation or an expropriation order;
> (f) restitution to the victim or a compensation order;
> (g) suspended or deferred sentence;
> (h) probation and judicial supervision;
> (i) a community service order;
> (j) referral to an attendance center;
> (k) house arrest;
> (l) any other mode of non-institutional treatment; or
> (m) some combination of the measures listed above.[1405]

The WGAD looked at the general issue of disproportionate or excessive sentencing during its country mission to Georgia. It noted that since the country adopted a zero tolerance policy in 2004, the number of criminal convictions with custodial sentences

---

[1402] *UN Standard Minimum Rules for Non-custodial Masures*, Resolution 45/110, General Assembly, Dec. 14, 1990 (Tokyo Rules), at Rule 1.5.

[1403] *Id.*, at Rule 2.3.

[1404] *Id.*, at Rule 3.1–3.3.

[1405] *Id.*, at Rule 8.2.

increased rapidly and when combined with high rates of plea bargaining resulted in an estimated acquittal rate of 0.1 percent.[1406] While this has drastically reduced crime in Georgia, the WGAD observed it had led to lengthy and harsh sentences for both criminal and administrative offenses, which were disproportionate with the crimes committed.[1407]

Similarly, in Iran, the WGAD found from its interviews with both political and ordinary prisoners that the length of sentences was disproportionate with the seriousness of the offense and that there were manifest disparities from one court to another.[1408]

The WGAD examined the law on mandatory minimum sentencing in South Africa. It specifically focused on the high rate of incarceration coming from the Government responding to public pressure and the media to address the high rate of criminality in the country.[1409] But the WGAD observed that the "harsh and long sentences … and mandatory minimum sentences" applicable to murder, aggravated rape, and aggravated assault has led not only to "a worrisome number of persons in detention serving long sentences compared to the gravity of the crime committed, but has also led to an alarming rate of overcrowding in detention facilities."[1410] It reported that this law was heavily criticized by judges and lawyers in South Africa as "restricting the discretionary power of judges in giving an appropriate sentence that would take into account the circumstances of each case and the character of the accused."[1411]

X Juvenile Justice

In cases involving juvenile detainees, several treaties and United Nations guidelines apply, especially regarding standards to minimize deprivations of liberty. The *Convention on the Rights of the Child* (CRC) provides:

> No child shall be deprived of his or her liberty unlawfully or arbitrarily. The arrest, detention or imprisonment of a child shall be in conformity with the law and shall be used only as a measure of last resort and for the shortest appropriate period of time.[1412]

This principle has been reaffirmed in the *United Nations Rules for the Protection of Juveniles Deprived of Their Liberty* (sections 1 and 2) as well as the *United Nations Standard Minimum Rules for the Administration of Juvenile Justice* (sections 13.1, 18.2, and 19.1).[1413] Additionally, the CRC states:

> Every child deprived of his or her liberty shall have the right to prompt access to legal and other appropriate assistance, as well as the right to challenge the legality of the deprivation of his or her liberty before a court or other competent, independent and impartial authority, and to a prompt decision on any such action.[1414]

[1406] Report of the Working Group on Mission to Georgia, at ¶ 38.

[1407] *Id.*, at ¶ 59.

[1408] Report of the Working Group on Mission to Iran, at ¶ 58.

[1409] Report of the Working Group on Mission to South Africa, at ¶ 62.

[1410] *Id.*, at ¶ 63.

[1411] *Id.*, at ¶ 64.

[1412] Convention on the Rights of the Child, at Art. 37(b).

[1413] Concerning a Minor (Whose Named Is Known to the Working Group) v. Egypt, WGAD Opinion No. 14/2015, Adopted Apr. 27, 2015, at ¶ 27.

[1414] Convention on the Rights of the Child, at Art. 37(d).

International law on the rights of juvenile detainees runs parallel to the rights of adult offenders in many ways. The Standard Minimum Rules provides that "basic procedural safeguards," such as the presumption of innocence, the right to counsel, the right to examine witnesses, and the right to appeal, all still apply to juvenile defendants.[1415] However, the application of such rights may be held to stricter standards for minor defendants. For instance, while the HR Committee has found that the right to a "prompt" hearing for adult detainees is fulfilled if undertaken within forty-eight hours after their arrest, this period is shortened to twenty-four hours for juvenile detainees.[1416] Pretrial detention of juveniles "should be avoided," but where necessary the pretrial period should elapse "in an especially speedy fashion."[1417]

The CRC establishes that the best interests of the minor remain a priority at all times.[1418] As such, juvenile detainees enjoy certain rights that separate them from adult defendants. This encompasses the right to be tried in a juvenile justice system[1419] and the right to be housed separately from adult detainees both before and after conviction.[1420] The detainee also has the right to have their parents or guardians informed of the arrest immediately after it happens, and to have them present at subsequent proceedings so long as their presence is not deemed to be against the best interest of the detainee.[1421] During all stages of the arrest, detention, or trial, the age and capabilities of the juvenile detainee are to be kept in mind to inform the discretion of the authorities involved.[1422]

In its jurisprudence as well as during country missions, the WGAD has observed the special rights and standards applicable to juvenile detainees. Country visit reports frequently include recommendations for the government to improve access to or efficiency within their juvenile justice system. For instance, on its mission to the United States, the WGAD expressed support for the recent Supreme Court decisions abolishing mandatory life sentences for certain juvenile offenders, while reminding authorities that the practice of certain states in trying persons as young as fourteen as adult offenders is incompatible with international law.[1423] The WGAD examines not only a country's standing domestic law on juvenile detainees, but also how these laws are put into practice. Its mission report on Azerbaijan noted that although the country had adopted juvenile justice standards largely compliant with international law, the delegation could not find an appreciable difference between the treatment of adult and juvenile detainees.[1424]

[1415] United Nations Standard Minimum Rules for the Administration of Juvenile Justice, at Rule 7.1.

[1416] General Comment No, 35, at ¶ 33.

[1417] *Id.*, at ¶ 37.

[1418] *Report of the Working Group on Arbitrary Detention: Mission to El Salvador*, Human Rights Council, A/HRC/22/44/Add.2, Jan. 11, 2013, at ¶ 78.

[1419] Concerning a Minor Whose Name Is Known to the Working Group v. Israel, WGAD Opinion No. 13/2016, Adopted Apr. 21, 2016, at ¶ 22.

[1420] *Report of the Working Group on Arbitrary Detention: Mission to the United States of America*, Human Rights Council, A/HRC/36/37/Add.2, July 17, 2017, at ¶ 67.

[1421] United Nations Standard Minimum Rules for the Administration of Juvenile Justice, at Rules 7.1, 10.1, & 15.2.

[1422] *Id.*, at Rule 6.1.

[1423] *Report of the Working Group on Arbitrary Detention: Mission to the United States of America*, Human Rights Council, A/HRC/36/37/Add.2, July 17, 2017, at ¶¶ 66–67.

[1424] *Report of the Working Group on Arbitrary Detention: Mission to Azerbaijan*, Human Rights Council, A/HRC/36/37/Add.1, Aug. 2, 2017, at ¶ 70.

Where the standards applicable to juvenile detainees are violated, the WGAD will find such detentions to be arbitrary. For instance, in *Concerning a Minor Whose Name Is Known by the Working Group* v. *Egypt*, a seventeen-year-old student was detained for four months in the Transfer Department of the Alexandria Security Directorate, a facility that housed adult detainees.[1425] Although the Government argued that he was held separate from adult detainees, the WGAD nevertheless found this to be an irregular detention violating the minor's rights because he was not housed in an available juvenile custody facility.[1426] Furthermore, the length of this detention violated his right to a fair trial. In *Concerning a Minor Whose Name Is Known by the Working Group* v. *Israel*, trial by a military tribunal violated the sixteen-year-old detainee's due process rights to be tried by a juvenile justice system.[1427] His detention was therefore found to be arbitrary under Category III. The WGAD has noted a pattern of cases involving Palestinian minors detained by Israel and denied their full procedural rights.[1428]

The violation of rights specific to juvenile detainees is often accompanied by treatment that would similarly violate the rights of adults. The WGAD handles such cases in a manner similar to the cases of adult detainees, but will note where juvenile status results in a breach of a supplemental international standard. In another case involving Israel, a detained twelve-year-old was denied legal assistance and forced to sign a confession stating that he had a knife on his person at the time of arrest. The WGAD noted the denial of legal assistance breached not only Article 37(d) of the CRC, but Article 14(3)(b) of the ICCPR (which guarantees legal assistance to all detainees regardless of age).[1429] Likewise, the coerced confession violated Articles 40(2)(b)(i) and (iv) of the CRC, as well as Article 14(2) of the ICCPR.[1430] And failure to notify the detainee's family of his arrest was a violation of Rules 7 and 10 of the United Nations Standard Minimum *Rules* (applicable to juvenile detainees), as well as Principle 19 of the *Body of Principles for the Protection of All Persons under Any Form of Detention or Imprisonment* (applicable to all detainees).[1431] Thus, although a government will be found responsible for general violations of international law regardless, the juvenile status of the detainee may mean there are additional violations of international law implicated in a minor's detention.

XI Unusual Case: *Julian Assange* v. *Sweden and the United Kingdom*

The WGAD addressed the definitional qualities of detention, stretching the outer boundaries of its jurisprudence, in the unusual case of *Julian Assange* v. *Sweden and the United Kingdom*.[1432] The highly publicized and controversial opinion, found to be a

---

[1425] Concerning a Minor (Whose Named Is Known to the Working Group) v. Egypt, WGAD Opinion No. 14/2015, Adopted Apr. 27, 2015, at ¶¶ 25–26.

[1426] *Id.*

[1427] Concerning a Minor Whose Name Is Known to the Working Group v. Israel, WGAD Opinion No. 13/2016, Adopted Apr. 21, 2016, at ¶ 22.

[1428] Concerning a Minor Whose Name Is Known by the Working Group v. Israel, WGAD Opinion No. 3/2017, Adopted Apr. 19, 2017, at ¶ 37.

[1429] *Id.*, at ¶ 31.

[1430] *Id.*, at ¶ 33.

[1431] *Id.*, at ¶ 32.

[1432] Julian Assange v. Sweden and United Kingdom, WGAD Opinion No. 54/2015, Adopted Dec. 4, 2015, at ¶ 86 (In addition to a dissenting opinion by WGAD member Vladimir Tochilovsky, WGAD member Leigh Toomey had to recuse herself from considering the case because she was Australian, like Assange).

deprivation of liberty under Category III, concerned the publisher and journalist who had obtained and disclosed confidential documents and material belonging to several states, including diplomatic cables.[1433] On Assange's "leak" of this material, he became the object of criminal charges by the United States, the primary target of his disclosure. Simultaneously, he became subject to a European arrest warrant issued by Sweden for unrelated criminal charges in that country.[1434] He was subsequently detained by the United Kingdom but, fearing he would be extradited to the United States, sought refuge in the Embassy of Ecuador in London.[1435] After years of residence in the Embassy, he filed a petition to the WGAD against Sweden and the United Kingdom claiming that his residence at the Embassy was involuntary and amounted to detention. The two respondent countries contested this assertion, and addressed several other points relating to asylum, due process, extradition, and conditions of bail. In a lengthy decision, which produced the first of only two dissenting opinions in WGAD history, Assange's ongoing residence in the Embassy of Ecuador was found to be an arbitrary detention.[1436]

A Timeline of the Case

On August 20, 2010, two women identified as SW and AA came forward to police to file complaints against Julian Assange that would later become the basis of an arrest warrant specifying one count of rape, two counts of sexual molestation, and one count of unlawful coercion. Assange, initially cooperating with the investigation, was interviewed ten days later, but subsequently left Sweden for the United Kingdom on September 27. On November 18, the Stockholm District Court found he should be arrested. His appeal was denied the next week and, on November 26, Swedish prosecutor Marianne Ny signed a European Arrest Warrant specifying the four charges listed previously in this section. The European Arrest Warrant would allow the United Kingdom to pursue his arrest and eventual extradition to Sweden.

On December 7, 2010, Assange surrendered himself to UK authorities. He was taken to Wandsworth prison and, at his own request, placed in a cell by himself. After ten days, he was granted bail by the UK Administrative Court, with several conditions. He would be electronically monitored and required to check in with police daily. Additionally, he was required to remain in his place of residence (the bail address) from 10 pm to 8 am daily. Accepting these conditions, Assange continued to challenge his extradition to Sweden. He remained under these bail conditions for a total of 550 days.

On June 14, 2012, a UK Supreme Court decision closed Assange's last avenue for domestic relief. With extradition to Sweden imminent and his concern about a subsequent potential extradition to the United States from there, on June 19, Assange entered the Embassy of Ecuador in breach of his bail conditions, where he asked for and received protection from the Government of Ecuador. Within a month, Ecuador notified the United Kingdom that it had granted Assange diplomatic asylum. UK authorities instituted a surveillance and monitoring regime around the Embassy.

[1433] *Id.*, at ¶ 4.
[1434] *Id.*, at ¶ 7.
[1435] *Id.*, at ¶¶ 10–12, 86.
[1436] *Id.*, at ¶ 92.

Two years later, the United Kingdom amended its Extradition Act 2003 to bar extradition where the person in question had not been charged with crimes. However, section 12(A)(1) of the amended law also specified that the bar does not apply if the domestic law of the country requesting extradition requires the person be present to be charged and their absence is the sole reason a charge has yet to be filed. This was a point of discussion in Assange's petition to the WGAD, which was filed in September 2014.

The WGAD opinion, adopted on December 4, 2015, unleashed a tidal wave of international criticism when it was announced in February 2016.[1437] Several UK officials disparaged the UN for its "factually upside down" ruling.[1438] Assange, who had claimed he would surrender himself if the WGAD ruled against him, called the decision a "victory of historic importance."[1439] The majority opinion was supported by four of the five WGAD members, with Ukrainian member Vladimir Tochilovsky authoring the only dissenting opinion in the WGAD's jurisprudence. Although the practical situation of Assange remained unchanged, the opinion lent him credibility in his fight to avoid extradition.

By the time the WGAD opinion was released, three of the four charges on Assange's European Arrest Warrant had lapsed. The fourth and most serious charge is due to expire in 2020. In early 2018, the Embassy of Ecuador cut his Internet connections, computers, and phones, and when Ecuador President Lenin Moreno traveled to London in July 2018, it was reported that Ecuador and the United Kingdom were close to finalizing a deal where Ecuador would withdraw its diplomatic asylum from Assange and he would be expelled from the Embassy, which later happened in April 2019.[1440]

B Assange's Complaint to the WGAD

The Petition filed with the WGAD made two general arguments – that Assange had in fact been deprived of his liberty against his will and that this deprivation was arbitrary and illegal. The majority of the Petition is dedicated to proving the second point, encompassing the issues of asylum, extradition, violations of criminal procedure, and the revision of the United Kingdom Extradition Act 2003.[1441]

1 Assange Was Deprived of Liberty against His Will

The first section of the Petition focused on proving that the unusual conditions of his situation in the Embassy amounted to deprivation. The section briefly noted his stay in Wandsworth prison and his 550 days under bail conditions (which the petition describes as house arrest).[1442] Mostly, the Petition focused on his current circumstances, describing his situation in the Embassy as "confined to . . . an area of 30m2, [where] he has no access

---

[1437] David Barrett, *Julian Assange: UN Ridiculed After Its Experts Rule Wikileaks Founder "Detained" in Embassy*, THE TELEGRAPH, Feb. 5, 2016.

[1438] *Id.*

[1439] *Id.*

[1440] Glenn Greenwald, *Ecuador Will Immediately Withdraw Asylum for Julian Assange and Hand Him over to the UK, What Comes Next?* THE INTERCEPT, July 21, 2018.

[1441] The petition is available at (Nov. 2018) justice4assange.com/IMG/pdf/assange-wgad.pdf.

[1442] Petition to the Working Group on Arbitrary Detention, Julian Assange v. Sweden and the United Kingdom (Undated), at fn. 16.

to fresh air or sunlight, his communications are restricted and often interfered with, he does not have access to adequate medical facilities, [and] he is subjected to a continuous and pervasive form of round the clock surveillance ... in a constant state of legal and procedural insecurity."[1443]

a Assange Claims He Has Been Deprived of Liberty

The Petition's first task was to convince the WGAD that Assange's residence in the Embassy amounted to a deprivation of liberty. Assange reminded the WGAD that in assessing deprivation it focuses on "effect, rather than form."[1444] For support, the Petition cites WGAD Deliberation Nos. 1 and 5 (the use of Deliberation No. 5 will be the first of many points to borrow from WGAD jurisprudence regarding more traditional political asylum seekers and to apply the findings to Assange's diplomatic asylum). Deliberation No. 5 on the situation regarding immigrants and asylum-seekers explains that places of custody may include different spaces that go by a variety of names.[1445] Deliberation No. 1 clarifies the definition of house arrest, specifying "house arrest may be compared to deprivation of liberty provided that it is carried out in closed premises which the person is not allowed to leave."[1446] Assange's confinement, according to the Petition, is an obvious fit for the WGAD's definition of deprivation of liberty. He is confined to closed premises (the Embassy) under intrusive and constant surveillance, and "it is no more accurate to claim that Mr. Assange is 'allowed to leave' then it would be to accurate to claim that a prisoner is free to attempt to escape from prison."[1447]

b Confinement to the Embassy Is Not Volitional

Having alleged that his confinement in the Embassy amounts to a deprivation of liberty, the Petition sets out to demonstrate that Assange's circumstances are not of his own making. Drawing once again on jurisprudence created for traditional asylum-seekers, the Petition cites the UNHCR principle that forcing a person to choose between confine-ment and exercise of their right to seek or enjoy asylum constitutes detention.[1448] Forcing a choice is a violation of ICCPR Article 9, which protects both liberty *and* security of person.[1449]

Several WGAD and ECtHR opinions with similar holding are cited as cases analogous to Assange's circumstances. In *Mustafa Abdi v. United Kingdom*, the WGAD found an asylum-seeker's detention arbitrary when he was being indefinitely detained until he signed a letter agreeing to return to Somalia.[1450] The WGAD rejected the contention that Abdi's detention was volitional because he had chosen detention over deportation to a combat zone. In the same case, the ECtHR agreed that the existence of an option to leave the United Kingdom and face persecution elsewhere is not a "trump card" that

---

[1443] Petition to the Working Group on Arbitrary Detention, at ¶ 2.
[1444] *Id.*, at ¶ 27.
[1445] *Id.*, at ¶ 30.
[1446] *Id.*, at ¶ 34.
[1447] *Id.*, at ¶ 34.
[1448] *Id.*, at ¶ 38.
[1449] *Id.*, at ¶ 37.
[1450] *Mustafa Abdi v. United Kingdom*, WGAD Opinion 45/2006, Adopted Nov. 24, 2006, at ¶ 19.

justifies indefinite detention.[1451] Other ECtHR cases confirm that deprivation of liberty is not conditional because asylum seekers are free to leave the country (*Amuur v. France*), or because an applicant refuses to cooperate with a deportation that could end their detention (*Mikolenko v. Estonia*).[1452]

The Petition argued that the arbitrariness of Assange's detention is even more pronounced than in the cited cases, because he had already been granted what the Petition claims as "asylum."[1453] Like Mustafa Abdi, Assange was presented with a "non-choice" to either remain in detention or risk persecution in another country. The United Kingdom and Sweden cannot therefore claim that his detention is voluntary. The Petition pointed out that his confinement in the Embassy had already exceeded the length of detention in some of the cited ECtHR cases.[1454]

2 Assange's Deprivation of Liberty Is Arbitrary

The main focus of the Petition offers four factors contributing to the arbitrary nature of Assange's alleged detention in the Ecuadorian Embassy. The first was the failure of Sweden and the United Kingdom to acknowledge his asylum and guarantee *non-refoulement* (which the Petition associates with Category II and IV). Second are the "disproportionate" actions of the Swedish prosecutor (Category I and III). Next is the indefinite nature of his detention and lack of judicial review (Categories I, III, and IV). And finally, the Petition cites the absence of acceptable minimum conditions for prolonged detention (Category III).

a Assange Has Been Denied the Full Benefits of Asylum

Nearly a third of the Petition is dedicated to describing how Assange had been arbitrarily deprived of his liberty for the exercise of his right to seek asylum. Under Article 19(2) of the UDHR, no person may be extradited to a state where they face a serious risk of death, torture, or other inhuman and degrading treatment. Assange contended that the fate of his Wikileaks source Chelsea Manning (who endured eleven months in solitary confinement), coupled with Sweden's and the United Kingdom's histories of being complicit in US mistreatment of detainees, demonstrated his serious risk of *refoulement* to the United States.[1455] The likelihood of mistreatment should Assange be extradited to the United States, the Petition asserted, imposed on all states a duty to prevent Assange's *refoulement* – asylum being one possible protective measure.[1456] The United Kingdom and

---

[1451] Abdi v. United Kingdom, Application No. 27770/08, Judgment, European Court of Human Rights, Oct. 4, 2013, at ¶¶ 65–75.

[1452] Amuur v. France, Application No. 19776/92, Judgment, European Court of Human Rights, June 25, 1996; Mikolenko v. Estonia, Application No. 10664/05, European Court of Human Rights, Oct. 8, 2009, at ¶¶ 65, 68.

[1453] Petition to the Working Group on Arbitrary Detention, at ¶ 47. The Petition also points out that because Assange has already been formally granted "asylum," it is "neither necessary nor appropriate" for the WGAD to reexamine the basis for the decision to grant it (i.e. the real likelihood that Assange will face persecution or harm if extradited). *Id.*

[1454] *Id.*, at ¶ 48.

[1455] *Id.*, at ¶¶ 57, 76–81.

[1456] *Id.*, at ¶ 58.

Sweden, both signatories to the Refugee Convention, were in violation of their duty to provide assurances Assange will not be extradited to a country where he might face inhuman or degrading treatment.[1457]

The Petition also addressed the validity of diplomatic asylum under international law (although it claimed this was not the only basis for asylum Ecuador asserted), contending that Sweden and the United Kingdom were obligated to respect it under customary international law.[1458] The United Kingdom itself, the Petition contended, has previously granted diplomatic asylum on humanitarian grounds, as have numerous other states (eight Latin American and six European embassies during the Spanish Civil War, several embassies in China for North Korean defectors, etc.)[1459] Furthermore, this duty to respect diplomatic asylum includes an obligation to grant safe passage from the territorial state.[1460] The Petition claimed this has been expressed in the *OAS Treaty on Asylum and Political Refuge* of 1939 and the *Caracas Convention on Diplomatic Asylum* of 1954, both of which have been ratified by over a dozen Latin American countries and Haiti.[1461] Thus, the Petition declares that customary international law includes the right to diplomatic asylum, which must be respected by Sweden and the United Kingdom.

Lastly, the Petition contends that even if the United Kingdom and Sweden do not consider themselves obliged to recognize diplomatic asylum, they violated a host of Assange's rights in how they treated him, including:

- The right to the presumption of innocence.
- The right not to be detained for an unreasonable length of time.
- The right to present a defense.
- The right to appropriate premises, where he may receive medical treatment and family visits.
- The right to receive confidential legal advice.
- The right to fresh air, sunlight, and outside exercise.

The Petition does not offer analysis discussing how each of these rights had been violated.

b Acts by the Swedish Prosecutor Resulted in Cumulatively Harsh and Disproportionate Deprivation

The Petition alleges that the Swedish prosecutor's decision to issue a European Arrest Warrant rather than interview Assange outside of Sweden was a disproportionate act that violated several of his rights under the ICCPR. Assange had offered the alternatives of an interview via video link, an interview on Embassy premises, a written statement, or an in-person interview in Sweden with assurances made regarding *non-refoulement* to the United States, all of which were denied without an explanation of the considerations made.[1462] This refusal is "grossly disproportionate and unreasonable," argued the

---

[1457] *Id.*, at ¶ 81.
[1458] *Id.*, at ¶ 86.
[1459] *Id.*, at ¶¶ 87–88.
[1460] *Id.*, at ¶ 91.
[1461] *Id.*, at ¶¶ 92–93.
[1462] *Id.*, at ¶¶ 96, 101.

Petition, given that Swedish prosecutors "routinely" interview suspects abroad, and that any hypothetical inconveniences to the prosecutor "pale into insignificance" next to Assange's risk of *refoulement*.[1463]

The refusal implicated Assange's right to a speedy resolution of his case, since the investigation is stalled without his testimony.[1464] Additionally, it compromised his right to present a defense and has resulted in a lengthy pretrial detention that, by virtue of its being longer than the maximum sentence he might face, is incompatible with the presumption of innocence.[1465] These due process violations, the Petition alleged, rendered his detention arbitrary under Category III. Additionally, the Petition asserted that Sweden's refusal to consider this confinement in calculating a sentence could result in Assange serving time twice for the same conduct. This exposes him to a "likely" double jeopardy violation and detention with no legal basis, which he claims could create a violation under Category I.[1466]

c Detention Is Indefinite and Lacks Judicial Review

By refusing to recognize Assange's confinement in the Embassy, the Petition says, the United Kingdom and Sweden have denied him any means of seeking judicial review that could resolve the current situation.[1467] Furthermore, he claimed the legal basis of UK surveillance of the Embassy has never been disclosed to him and as such he is unable to contest its necessity and proportionality.[1468] Having been denied the ability to contest these measures in a court of law, the Petition claims Assange is "effectively in a legal vacuum … and is residing in prolonged state of uncertainty."[1469] The Petition claimed this rendered his deprivation of liberty arbitrary under Categories I, III, and IV.[1470]

d Ecuadorian Embassy Does Not Meet Minimum Conditions of Detention

Briefly, the Petition points out that the Embassy is neither a house nor a detention center and is, as such, unequipped to deal with a long-term resident.[1471] The lack of access to medical facilities increases the risk that, were his health to deteriorate, he may be at risk of serious consequences. He is also to receive other minimum entitlements such as the one hour outside per day required by Article 21(1) of the Nelson Mandela Rules, or private communication with his lawyers or family.[1472]

[1463] *Id.*, at ¶¶ 101, 103–104.
[1464] *Id.*, ¶ 105.
[1465] *Id.*, ¶¶ 105–109.
[1466] *Id.*, at ¶ 113.
[1467] *Id.*, at ¶ 114.
[1468] *Id.*, at ¶¶ 115–116.
[1469] *Id.*, at ¶ 123.
[1470] *Id.*, at ¶ 51(a.iii).
[1471] *Id.*, at ¶ 126.
[1472] *Id.*, at ¶¶ 128–130.

C Government Responses to Assange's Petition

After Assange's Petition was received by the WGAD, a three-and-a-half-page summary of the allegations was transmitted to the Governments of Sweden and the United Kingdom on September 16, 2014.[1473] Both Governments responded shortly thereafter, with Sweden responding on November 3 and the United Kingdom on November 13.

1 Response from the Government of Sweden

The Government emphasized four points in its reply – that Assange did not face a risk of *refoulement* to the United States, that Sweden is not obliged to recognize his diplomatic asylum, that Assange's residence in the Embassy is not a deprivation of liberty, and that Sweden was complying with its obligations under international law.

a Petitioner's Assertions Regarding Asylum Are Incorrect

Sweden had two main points regarding the claims of Ecuador to have granted asylum to Assange. First, Assange had no real risk of *refoulement*. The Government emphasized that it had received no requests for Assange's extradition to a third country. If any requests were received, they would undergo a "thorough examination" of the particular circumstances. The Swedish Extradition for Criminal Offences Act restricts the Government from extradition unless a comparable act is punishable in Sweden, the death penalty will not be imposed, and (in the case of a person unwilling to be extradited) the Supreme Court has issued a supporting opinion. As such any discussion of risk of *refoulement* to the United States resulting from extradition to Sweden was purely hypothetical.[1474] The pursuit of Sweden's European Arrest Warrant was an entirely different matter from pursuing *refoulement* to a third state.[1475]

Second, the Government contended that no international legal instrument or obligation requires it to recognize the diplomatic asylum granted to Assange.[1476] As confirmed by the International Court of Justice, international law generally does not recognize the right to diplomatic asylum. Although Ecuador is a party to the *Convention on Diplomatic Asylum*, Sweden reminded the WGAD this was a regional instrument and had no application to Sweden as a non-party.[1477] Furthermore, in international instruments on the subject, including the *Convention on Diplomatic Asylum*, the right to seek and enjoy asylum does not apply when invoked for protection from an ordinary, nonpolitical crime. The Government contended crimes for which Assange was to be extradited (rape, sexual molestation, and unlawful coercion) all fell squarely within the nonpolitical crime exception.[1478]

[1473] The author was able to view a copy of the WGAD's communication to the states by one of the parties to the case.

[1474] *Id.*, at ¶ 23.

[1475] *Id.*, at ¶ 21.

[1476] *Id.*, at ¶ 26.

[1477] *Id.*

[1478] *Id.*, at ¶ 27.

b The Swedish Criminal Investigation Has Not Violated Assange's Rights

To counter the Petition's allegations of fair trial rights, the Government asserted that Assange in fact does have all the formal rights of a criminal defendant. Swedish criminal procedure, which is compatible with the *European Convention on Human Rights*, entitles a suspect to examine all materials relevant to an allegation, and only after the suspect declares no further investigative measures are required does the prosecutor issue an indictment.[1479] Sweden emphasized that the prosecutor is still in the preliminary stage of the investigation.

The prosecutor's refusal to use alternative methods to question Assange without extraditing him to Sweden is not a decision over which the Government has power. According to the Government, it may not interfere with a case being handled by the Swedish public authority.[1480] The prosecutor overseeing the preliminary investigation has the sole discretion to determine that the suspect's presence is necessary. In this case the prosecutor, who has the best knowledge of the investigation and is in the best position to determine necessity, decided that Assange's presence is necessary taking into account all considerations, including the interests of the victims.[1481] Once Assange is returned to Sweden, a decision to detain or release him there is in the hands of the Stockholm District Court to decide after a new hearing.

c Assange Is Not Detained and Resides in the Ecuadorian Embassy Voluntarily

In relation to the Petition's first argument, the Government maintained that Assange cannot be regarded as deprived of liberty because he has chosen voluntarily to reside in the Embassy.[1482] Because Swedish authorities cannot control his decision to remain in the Embassy, there exists no causal link between the European Arrest Warrant and Assange's current situation.[1483] For support, the Government cites two cases in which the WGAD implies the necessity for a causal connection between the detainee's exercise of fundamental rights and their subsequent detention.[1484] It reiterated that Assange is free to leave the Embassy at any time.[1485]

2 Response from the Government of the United Kingdom

In its brief reply, the United Kingdom pointed out that Assange was granted *diplomatic asylum* and *not* political asylum under the 1954 *Convention on Diplomatic Asylum*. The United Kingdom is not a party to the 1954 Convention, does not recognize diplomatic asylum, and thus does not acknowledge any legal obligations arising from grants thereof.[1486] Furthermore, the United Kingdom considers the use of the Embassy to

---

[1479] *Id.*, at ¶ 32.
[1480] *Id.*, at ¶ 35.
[1481] *Id.*
[1482] Julian Assange v. Sweden and the United Kingdom, WGAD Opinion No. 54/2015, Adopted Dec. 4, 2015, at ¶ 30.
[1483] *Id.*, at ¶ 30.
[1484] *Id.* (citing Saqar Abdelkader Al Chouitier v. Yemen, WGAD Opinion No. 9/2008, Adopted May 8, 2008, at ¶ 21; Hossein Mossavi, et al. v. Iran, WGAD Opinion No. 30/2012, Adopted Aug. 29, 2012, at ¶ 26).
[1485] *Id.*
[1486] *Id.*, at ¶ 41.

enable Assange to avoid arrest for serious sexual offenses is a serious breach of Ecuador's obligations under the *Vienna Convention on Diplomatic Relations*, to which both Ecuador and the United Kingdom are state parties.[1487]

D WGAD *Opinion*

The opinion of the WGAD finding the detention of Julian Assange a violation under Category III was released in 2016 to widespread criticism. It requested the Governments of the United Kingdom and Sweden ensure Assange's safety and freedom of movement and accord him an enforceable right to compensation in accordance with Article 9(5) of the ICCPR.[1488]

1 Assange's Current and Previous Situations Were Deprivations of Liberty

The WGAD went beyond Assange's claim that his confinement to the Embassy was an arbitrary deprivation of liberty to assert that it was actually a "prolongation of the already continued deprivation of liberty" that began with Assange's ten days in Wandsworth Prison and continued through his 550 days under bail conditions.[1489] The initial ten days in isolation, the WGAD said, was of the type that left a detainee "outside the cloak of any legal protection, including access to legal assistance," in spite of the fact that Assange had access to both lawyers and courts and had been isolated by his own request.[1490] The 550 days under bail conditions, during which Assange was filing appeals against his extradition, led the WGAD to "query what has hindered judicial management of any kind from occurring in a reasonable manner for such an extended period of time."[1491] The "various forms of harsh restrictions" such as monitoring by electronic tag, reporting to police, and a nightly curfew continued the deprivation of liberty in the form of house arrest. Finally, his confinement and surveillance in the Embassy constituted arbitrary detention as noted in Deliberation No. 9 "in breach of the principles of reasonableness, necessity and proportionality."[1492] Without much analysis of whether or why these situations constituted detention in the first place, the WGAD found Assange had not been guaranteed his fair trial rights during each of these three periods of time.

2 Procedural Defects Related to the Charges in Sweden Render Detention Arbitrary

A main concern of the WGAD was that the only basis for Assange's detention appeared to be an arrest warrant based on allegations, and not a formal indictment.[1493] In the course of criminal administration, the WGAD said, there had been a "substantial failure to exercise due diligence" in a number of ways.[1494] Despite expressing a willingness to

---

[1487] *Id.*, at ¶ 42.
[1488] David Barrett, *Julian Assange: UN Ridiculed After Its Experts Rule Wikileaks Founder "Detained" in Embassy*, THE TELEGRAPH, Feb. 5, 2016.
[1489] Julian Assange, at ¶ 83.
[1490] *Id.*, at ¶ 79.
[1491] *Id.*, at ¶ 80.
[1492] *Id.*, at ¶ 83.
[1493] *Id.*, at ¶ 86.
[1494] *Id.*, at ¶ 90.

participate in the investigation, Assange remained after five years without any predictable judicial process and with the Swedish prosecutor failing to exercise compliance with the rule of proportionality. Consequentially, his situation had become "excessive and unnecessary," meaning that from a "temporal perspective" his current position was worse than if he had simply appeared in Sweden for questioning. Furthermore, the WGAD believed that the granting of asylum from Ecuador should have received more consideration in determinations, rather than sweeping judgment. Lastly, the WGAD mentioned that the "state of indefinite procrastination" to which these elements contribute does not serve the interests of the victims concerned.[1495]

These failures had contributed to a series of violations that rendered Assange's detention arbitrary. First, his lack of opportunity to access exculpatory evidence and inability to provide a statement to the prosecutor had denied him the opportunity to defend himself. Second, the duration of his detention was incompatible with the presumption of innocence. Third, the lack of judicial review or remedy for a "prolonged confinement and the highly intrusive surveillance" was inappropriate. Furthermore, the facilities in which he was detained lacked the necessary medical equipment required for places of detention, leading to the possibility that anything more than a mild illness could put Assange's health at risk. Finally, the changes to the United Kingdom's Extradition Act were decidedly not retroactive and would not benefit Assange in his fight against extradition. The WGAD did not elaborate on exactly how this rendered his detention arbitrary, other than that it was likely to continue his detention. In light of these factors, the WGAD determined the detention of Assange in the Embassy was arbitrary under Category III.

3 Individual Dissenting Opinion of Working Group Member Vladimir Tochilovsky

In only one of two dissenting opinions to ever be issued by a Working Group Member, Tochilovsky pointed out that Assange had been using the Embassy to avoid arrest, and that "fugitives are often self-confined within the places where they evade arrest and detention."[1496] Premises of self-confinement in areas where arrest warrants are not recognized cannot constitute detention for the purposes of the Working Group's analysis.

Furthermore, the house arrest of Assange in 2011 and 2012 was a *restriction* of liberty rather than a deprivation of liberty under the WGAD's own definitions, since Assange was permitted to leave the residence daily. Restrictions of liberty are outside the WGAD's competence. As such, issues related to "fugitives' self-confinement, such as asylum and extradition," fall outside the WGAD mandate. Assange's complaint, Tochilovsky concluded, would be more appropriately considered by an appropriate UN treaty body or the ECtHR.

E Unusual Approach to WGAD Opinion

The highly political nature of Assange's activities ensured that any WGAD opinion would provoke a strong reaction. But beyond the inevitable criticism for any major decision related to the national security interests of several important countries, the

---

[1495] *Id.*
[1496] *Id.*, at Annex, ¶ 3.

WGAD's appeared flawed in a range of ways, including misapplications of international law, the creation of unprecedented rights, and the rendering of opinions that fell outside of its mandate.

1 Acting Contrary to the Methods of Work and Prior Deliberation

In deciding Assange's case the WGAD appeared to act contrary to its Methods of Work and its mandate from the HRC. First, the WGAD only conveyed to Sweden and the United Kingdom a three-page summary of Assange's lengthy Petition. Fact Sheet No. 26 on the Working Group on Arbitrary Detention states "The Group attaches great importance to the adversarial character of its procedure." However, a true adversarial procedure requires that each party should have knowledge of the arguments being put forward by the opposing party, in order to be able to present contrary arguments and evidence. Thus, the WGAD should have either restricted its analysis to the arguments it shared with the United Kingdom or provided them with a much more detailed summary of the Petition. This appeared particularly unfair as in its opinion, the WGAD rendered conclusions of law based on facts and legal arguments presented in the Petition, which the Governments had never seen or had the opportunity to dispute.

Second, it was very surprising to see the WGAD characterize Assange's 550-day period of bail as a "house arrest." Consider the following excerpt from the opinion:

> That initial deprivation of liberty then continued in the form of house arrest for some 550 days. This again was not contested by any of the two States. During this prolonged period of house arrest, Mr. Assange had been subjected to various forms of harsh restrictions, including monitoring using an electric tag, an obligation to report to the police every day and *a ban on being outside of his place of residence at night*. In this regard, the Working Group has no choice but to query what has prohibited the unfolding of judicial management of any kind in a reasonable manner from occurring for such extended period of time.[1497]

Yet the WGAD's claim this was a house arrest was conclusory. Under its own Deliberation No. 1, the definition of house arrest is very clear:

> [H]ouse arrest may be compared to deprivation of liberty *provided that it is carried out in closed premises which the person is not allowed to leave*. In all <u>other</u> situations, it will devolve on the Working Group to decide, on a case-by-case basis, whether the case in question constitutes a form of detention, and if so, whether it has an arbitrary character.[1498]

In its opinion, the WGAD acknowledged implicitly Assange could be out of his home every day and was only restricted from leaving at night. Yet this is incompatible with its definition that for him to be under house arrest he had to be on closed premises and not allowed to leave. While the WGAD had the authority to ascertain if the restrictions of bail placed on him resulted in an arbitrary deprivation of liberty for this time period, it did not appear to have discretion under its own definition to describe this as house arrest.[1499]

[1497] *Id.*, at ¶ 87 (emphasis added).
[1498] *Report of the Working Group on Arbitrary Detention*, Commission on Human Rights, E/CN.4/1993/24, Jan. 12, 1993, ¶ 19 (emphasis added).
[1499] Julian Assange, at ¶ 80.

Finally, the WGAD had found that the 2014 Amendments to the United Kingdom's Extradition Act would have resulted in a rejection of Sweden's extradition request.[1500] This was an unusual conclusion for the WGAD to make as it was interpreting British law and appeared to be substituting itself for a domestic fact finder. In addition, the WGAD assumed that the benefits of the 2014 Amendments should be applied retroactively to Assange's extradition case, which concluded with a final judgment from the UK Supreme Court in 2012. This faulty assumption flowed from the WGAD appearing throughout the opinion to fail to realize that an extradition is not a criminal proceeding but rather a civil proceeding. As such, there is no requirement under international law that changes in procedure on already decided civil proceedings be applied retroactively.

2 Imputing Nonexistent Rights to Defendants in Extradition Proceedings

In *Ronald Everett* v. *Spain*, the HR Committee found that "even when decided by a court the consideration of an extradition request does not amount to the determination of a criminal charge."[1501] However, in the Assange case the WGAD appeared to bootstrap alleged violations of Assange's rights as a criminal defendant in Sweden to mean a UK civil extradition proceeding would need to meet all the requirements of Article 14 of the ICCPR. And ordinarily, the WGAD examines detentions to determine if they are conducted in accordance with the relevant international legal standards. But rather than determining if Sweden and the United Kingdom had acted in compliance with the *European Convention on Human Rights*, which in fact allows detentions pending extraditions, the WGAD instead looked at claims regarding Sweden's domestic legal justification and process for issuing the European Arrest Warrant to determine Assange's detention was arbitrary. It appeared that Assange's only real complaint to the WGAD regarding his UK extradition proceeding is that he did not prevail, which is not a valid basis for finding it breached its obligations under international law.

3 Requiring Countries to Honor Diplomatic Asylum

In its opinion, the WGAD states: "Despite the fact that the Republic of Ecuador has granted him asylum in August 2012, his newly acquired status has not been recognized by neither Sweden nor the UK."[1502] In this simple statement, the WGAD appears to have equated diplomatic asylum with the more traditional territorial or political asylum, which a country grants to a person within their borders.

Yet in *Colombia* v. *Peru*, the ICJ found that a grant of diplomatic asylum "involves a derogation from the sovereignty of that State" because it "constitutes an intervention in matters which are exclusively within the competence of that State."[1503] The drafters of the *Vienna Convention on Diplomatic Relations* clearly refused a request to add diplomatic asylum, despite the urging of some Latin American countries. And that treaty emphasizes in Article 41(3) that "[t]he premises of the mission must not be used in any

---

[1500] *Id.*, at ¶ 91(e).
[1501] Everett v. Spain, Communication No. 961/2000, Human Rights Committee, CCPR/C/81/D/961/2000, July 9, 2004.
[1502] Julian Assange, at ¶ 88.
[1503] Colombia v. Peru, Merits, Judgment, International Court of Justice, ICJ Rep. 266, Nov. 20, 1950.

manner incompatible with the functions of the mission as laid down in the present Convention . . . ."[1504] It is unclear why the WGAD failed to examine Ecuador's violation of the Vienna Convention or the ICJ precedent emphasizing that the granting of diplomatic asylum interferes with state sovereignty.

4 Incentivizing Breaches of Domestic and International Law

The most fundamental problem with the WGAD's opinion, however, is it endorses two clear breaches of law by third parties and then holds Sweden and the United Kingdom responsible for the consequences of those independent decisions they could not control. First, Assange violated the law by breaking his conditions of bail and entering the Embassy. And second, Ecuador breached international law by offering him diplomatic asylum in their Embassy, misusing their premises under the *Vienna Convention on Diplomatic Relations*.

The legal doctrine of *ex turpi causa non oritur action* (from a dishonorable cause an action does not arise) stands for the proposition that a plaintiff will be unable to pursue a legal remedy if it arises in connection with his own illegal act. Yet the WGAD rewarded Assange for his decision to jump bail and then excused Ecuador's flagrant violation of international law, giving diplomatic asylum a status it simply does not have. There is no other case in the WGAD's jurisprudence that encourages detainees and states to breach their obligations under domestic and international law.

F Rejection of Appeal

In 2016, the WGAD considered an appeal submitted by Sweden and the United Kingdom to the original opinion. In a conclusory manner, the WGAD dismissed the appeal along with others presented during that year, stating: "After examining the requests for review, the Working Group decided to maintain its opinions on the basis that none of the requests met the criteria outlined . . . [in] its methods of work."[1505]

[1504] *Vienna Convention on Diplomatic Relations*, 500 UNTS 95, Apr. 18, 1961, *entered into force* Apr. 24, 1964.
[1505] *Report of the Working Group on Arbitrary Detention*, Human Rights Council, A/HRC/36/37, July 19, 2017, at ¶ 28.

7 Category IV

Violation of Rights of Asylum Seekers

I Applicable Law and Standards

As added by the WGAD to its Methods of Work in 2011, Category IV detentions are cases that present with the following facts:

> When asylum seekers, immigrants or refugees are subjected to prolonged administrative custody without the possibility of administrative or judicial review or remedy.[1]

Though recognized as a separate category in the Methods of Work, administrative detention for refugees and asylum seekers were originally noted as a concerning practice and added to the mandate of the WGAD by Resolution 1997/50 of the Commission on Human Rights (UNCHR).[2]

In subsequent engagement with the UNCHR, the WGAD issued in its original Deliberation No. 5 the following observations about the specific protections for refugees and asylum seekers that must be provided to them: Specifically, applicants for asylum denied entry at the border must be (1) informed in clear terms and in their own language of the reasons for refusal of status; (2) provided the possibility to contact concerned persons, including lawyers and relatives; (3) if arrested, brought before a judicial authority for resolution of dispute promptly; (4) registered with their signature and all details of detention and release from custody; and (5) if placed in administrative detention, informed of all applicable disciplinary rules and guarantees of rights.[3]

In the same deliberation, the WGAD noted the following applicable guarantees concerning the detention of migrants and refugees: that (1) decisions to detain must be taken by an empowered and responsible authority in accordance with the law; (2) the detention may not be unlimited in duration but specifically limited to a maximum duration; (3) detainees must be formally notified of the decision to detain, and of the

---

[1] *Methods of Work of the Working Group*, Human Rights Council, A/HRC/36/38, July 13, 2017, at ¶ 8(d). A refugee is defined as a person who has a "well-founded fear of being persecuted for reasons of race, religion, nationality, membership of a particular social group or political opinion, is outside the country of his nationality and is unable or, owing to such fear, is unwilling to avail himself of the protection of that country; or who, not having a nationality and being outside the country of his former habitual residence as a result of such events, is unable or, owing to such fear, is unwilling to return to it." Convention relating to the Status of Refugees (1951), Article 1(A)(2).

[2] Resolution 1997/50, Commission on Human Rights, E.CN.4/1997/50, Apr. 15, 1997, at ¶ 4.

[3] *Deliberation No. 5 on Situation Regarding Immigrants and Asylum-Seekers* in *Report of the Working Group on Arbitrary Detention*, Commission on Human Rights, E/CN.4/2000/4, Dec. 28, 1999, at Principles 1–5.

details for remedies; (4) asylum seekers in facilities must be separate from those housing persons detained under criminal law; and (5) UNHCR and other responsible international bodies must be allowed access to the detained.[4] The *Body of Principles for the Protection of All Persons under Any Form of Detention or Imprisonment* also confers on authorities the duty to promptly inform detainees with refugee status of their right to communicate with a representative of the responsible international protection agency.[5]

In 2018, the WGAD undertook to revise Deliberation No. 5, as it was "concerned by the rising prevalence of deprivation of liberty of immigrants and asylum-seekers in recent years, recognizing the need to consolidate the developments in its own jurisprudence."[6] The revised Deliberation No. 5 on the deprivation of liberty of migrants expanded the scope of concerned persons beyond simply "immigrants and asylum-seekers." In the now-current Revised Deliberation, the term "migrant" is defined to mean:

> Any person who is moving or has moved across an international border away from his or her habitual place of residence, regardless of: (a) the person's legal status; (b) whether the movement is voluntary or involuntary; (c) the cause of the movement; or (d) the duration of stay. The term shall be taken to include asylum seekers, refugees, and stateless persons.[7]

The ten principles in the original deliberation were greatly expanded on to create eleven sections encompassing the right to seek asylum, the exceptionality and standards of migrant detention, and the rights to be observed in migrant proceedings. The WGAD emphasized that these apply to states regardless of factors such as an influx of large numbers of migrants.[8]

The *Basic Principles and Guidelines on Remedies and Procedures on the Right of Persons Deprived of Their Liberty to Bring Proceedings before a Court* also specifically addresses measures for non-nationals including migrants, asylum-seekers, refugees, and stateless persons. Principle 21 emphasizes that migrants still retain the right to be informed of the reasons for their arrest (with translation provided, if necessary), bring proceedings challenging their detention, appear before a judge, and be provided with prompt and effective legal assistance.[9] Detention of children based on their migration status or their parents' status is always prohibited.[10]

II Limitations and Exclusions

It must be noted the Human Rights Committee (HR Committee) recognizes that the detention of asylum seekers is not absolutely prohibited or always arbitrary, but must be

---

[4] *Id.*, Principles 6–10.

[5] *Body of Principles for the Protection of Persons under Any Form of Detention or Imprisonment*, UNGA Res. 47/173, 43 U.N. GAOR Supp. (No. 49), A/43/49, at 298 (1988), at Principle 16(2).

[6] *Revised Deliberation No. 5 on the Deprivation of Liberty of Migrants*, Feb. 7, 2018, at ¶ 3 (Advanced Edited Version has been published, but without a UN document number).

[7] Revised Deliberation No. 5, at ¶ 6.

[8] *Id.*

[9] *Basic Principles and Guidelines on the Remedies and Procedures on the Rights of Persons Deprived of Their Liberty to Bring Proceedings before a Court*, Working Group on Arbitrary Detention, A/HRC/30/27 (Annex), July 6, 2015, ¶¶ 42–43.

[10] *Id.*, at ¶¶ 46, 114.

justified as reasonable, necessary, and proportional in connection with the peculiar circumstances of the particular case.[11] Reasons for such temporary measures may include determining the identity of the applicant or when time is required to properly document and register their entry.[12] The WGAD has further specified that locations where asylum seekers and other protected classes of migrants may be detained include places of custody in border areas, premises under the authority of the police or prison administrators, on board vehicles for transport of migrants, in transit zones, or other ad hoc detention centers.[13]

The WGAD addressed the issue of mandatory detentions in its country mission to the United States. From its visit, it observed the following:

> [N]on-United States citizens who have been convicted of certain criminal offences and non-United States citizens deemed to be a national security risk are subject to mandatory detention … Under expedited removal, non-United States citizens, including asylum seekers, "whose inadmissibility is being considered" or who have a prior removal order are subject to mandatory detention pending further immigration proceedings. [An estimated] 352,850 people are detained each year across the United States pending the outcome of their immigration proceedings [which] costs United States taxpayers approximately $2 billion annually.[14]

In assessing how the United States has handled irregular migrants, it concluded:

> The Working Group is of the view that the mandatory detention of immigrants, especially asylum seekers, is contrary to international human rights and refugee rights standards. Furthermore, it recalls that individuals held in immigration detention shall be brought promptly before a judicial authority empowered to order their release or to vary the conditions of release. If detention is ordered, it should be subject to regular, periodic reviews to ensure that it is reasonable, necessary, proportional and lawful, and that alternatives to detention are considered.[15]

In Malta, the WGAD noted that its Immigration Act imposed detention indiscriminately on all migrants in irregular situations and that because there was no time limit to detentions, the detention period is potentially indefinite. It also criticized Malta's policies because detention of irregular migrants is not ordered or reviewed by a court of law, but rather by an administrative Immigration Appeals Board, which functions outside the judiciary. And it noted that "the legal remedies theoretically available to challenge the

---

[11] Guy S. Goodwin-Gill & Jane McAdam, The Refugee in International Law 462 (Oxford University Press, 2007), noting that the prohibition against arbitrary detention in human rights law is stronger protection than what the Refugee Convention provides; General Comment No. 35, Human Rights Committee, CCPR/C/GC/35 (2014), at ¶ 18; Alex Conte & Richard Burchill, Defining Civil and Political Rights: The Jurisprudence of the United Nations Human Rights Committee 101 (Ashgate, 2009); C v. Australia, Communication No. 900/1999, Human Rights Committee, CCPR/C/76/D/900/1999, Oct. 28, 2002, at ¶ 8.2.

[12] Goodwin-Gill & McAdam, at 464; General Comment No. 35, at ¶ 18; Bakhtiyari & Bakhtiyari v. Australia, Communication No. 1069/2002, Human Rights Committee, CCPR/C/79/D/1069/2002, Oct. 29, 2003, at ¶¶ 9.2–9.3.

[13] Revised Deliberation No. 5.

[14] Report of the Working Group on Arbitrary Detention on Visit to the United States, Human Rights Council, A/HRC/36/37, July 17, 2017, at ¶ 24.

[15] Id., at ¶ 26.

necessity and legality of detention before courts of law cannot be considered as effective in practice because of a lack of access to legal aid."[16]

The WGAD was similarly critical of Greece from its country mission where it expressed serious concern about its migration policies and its Operation Xenios Zeus, which led to the widespread detention of migrants across the country, many of whom had lived and worked in Greece for years. It observed that the detainees that it met had little or no information in a language they could understand about the reasons for their detention, its duration, or their right to challenge their detention and deportation. The WGAD concluded that it "deeply regrets the policy [sic] of systematically detaining all irregular migrants detected entering the territory of Greece, including families and unaccompanied children, as well as the sweep operations and subsequent detentions in the context of operation Xenios Zeus."[17]

III Extension of Protections to Other Class of Migrants, Including Stateless People

The WGAD has extended these protections to other classes of migrants, such as those in irregular situations or persons found to be stateless. In *Raul Garcia* v. *Barbados*, the detainee was a Cuban national denied repatriation to Cuba due to his prolonged absence from the country. He lost residence status in the United States and was also barred from entering Colombia, where he had last lived and engaged in criminal activity.[18] He was arrested, tried, convicted, and sentenced to twenty years in prison in Barbados on drug-related charges and had served his full sentence.[19] But due to his unusual citizenship status, he was being held in close confinement, under constant guard, and his movement and communications were severely restricted.[20] The WGAD, finding a violation of Category IV, concluded that his continued detention, which was equivalent to the detention of a criminal, was no longer a proportional measure for a person in the detainee's circumstances, whether he was classified as an irregular migrant or a stateless person.[21]

The case of *Said Imasi* v. *Australia* provided "an extreme example of statelessness as that of someone with no known birth date, birth place or family origins."[22] The inability of government authorities to establish his identity with certainty led to his being imprisoned for almost eight years.[23] The WGAD remarked this was a "considerable period of time that should have been more than sufficient." While acknowledging the probable impossibility of establishing his identity posed a significant challenge to

---

[16] *Report of the Working Group on Arbitrary Detention: Mission to Malta*, Human Rights Council, A/HRC/13/30/Add.2, Jan. 18, 2010, at ¶¶ 36–37, 62–63.

[17] *Report of the Working Group on Arbitrary Detention: Mission to Greece*, Human Rights Council, A/HRC/27/48/Add.2, June 30, 2014, at ¶¶ 64–65.

[18] Raul Garcia v. Barbados, WGAD Opinion No. 2/2013, Adopted Apr. 30, 2013, at ¶¶ 13–14.

[19] *Id.*, at ¶ 21.

[20] *Id.*, at ¶ 10.

[21] *Id.*, at ¶¶ 22, 24.

[22] Said Imasi v. Australia, WGAD Opinion No. 71/2017, Adopted Nov. 21, 2017, at ¶ 49.

[23] *Id.*, at ¶¶ 41, 47.

authorities, the WGAD refused to accept this situation as a justification for Imasi's ongoing detention.[24] The WGAD found his detention arbitrary under Category IV and additional violations of his right to take his case before a court.

IV Detention Not Justified by Inability of State to Carry out Deportation

In *Michael Mvogo v. Canada*, the WGAD ruled that the "inability of a State party to carry out the expulsion of an individual does not justify detention beyond the shortest period of time or where there are alternatives to detention, and under no circumstances indefinite detention."[25] In that case, the detainee was a citizen of Cameroon who had been held for over seven years, owing both to confusion about his origins and the failure of authorities in his home country to cooperate in establishing his status.[26] The WGAD ruled in favor of the detainee, despite his apparent attempts to obscure his identity and delay his deportation.[27] The opinion stated that notwithstanding the detainee's actions, detention must be necessary and proportionate, and effected only after alternatives have been adequately considered and exhausted.[28] The detainee in this case had not been afforded a chance to present witnesses in his defense, had been held in a detention facility for a prolonged period of time, and prevented from attending reviews of his administrative status.[29]

V Detention of Foreigners Pending Removal on National Security Grounds

In its country mission to Canada, the WGAD examined extensively the issue of "security certificates" under Canadian law. A security certificate is a mechanism by which the Government can detain and deport foreign nationals from Canada. Under this system, the Government can issue a certificate for a noncitizen who it suspects has violated human rights, is part of organized crime, or is perceived to be a threat to national security. Subjects of a certificate are inadmissible to Canada and subject to a removal order.[30]

The WGAD said it was "gravely concerned about the following elements, which undermine the security certificate detainee's rights to a fair hearing, to challenge evidence used against them, not to incriminate themselves, and to judicial review of detention."[31] It then proceeded to list a number of specific concerns. These included:

- It only applies to non-Canadian citizens.
- If the person certified is not a legal permanent resident of Canada, then detention is mandatory.

---

[24] Said Imasi v. Australia, WGAD Opinion No. 71/2017, Adopted Nov. 21, 2017, at ¶ 49.
[25] Michael Mvogo v. Canada, WGAD Opinion No. 15/2014, Adopted Nov. 21, 2017, at ¶ 23.
[26] *Id.*, at ¶ 2
[27] *Id.*, at ¶¶ 8–10.
[28] *Id.*, at ¶ 24.
[29] *Id.*, at ¶¶ 15–16.
[30] *What Is a Security Certificate?* Public Safety Canada, Dec. 1, 2015.
[31] *Report of the Working Group on Arbitrary Detention: Mission to Canada*, Commission on Human Rights, E/CN.4/2006/7/Add.2, Dec. 5, 2005, at ¶ 84.

- There is no limit to the length of a security certificate detention; among the four detained in Canada at that time, they had been held from four to six years.
- The only way to end the detention is deportation, but the four men in custody, all Arab Muslims, argue they would be at substantial risk of torture if deported.
- The evidence that resulted in the issuance of the security certificate is secret; the detainee and their lawyer only get a summary of the evidence, making it difficult to effectively challenge allegations made against the detainee.
- The Federal Court with the power to review them does not have jurisdiction to determine if it was justified; it can only assess the "reasonableness" of the Government's allegations.
- If a determination is made by a court that a security certificate is reasonable, its decision is final and unappealable, removal is ordered, and the detainee cannot apply for refugee protection.[32]

The WGAD concluded by emphasizing that it was especially troubled by the delay with which noncitizens under a security certificate can challenge their detention. Despite Article 9(4) of the ICCPR requiring that "anyone who is deprived of his liberty by arrest or detention shall be entitled to take proceedings before a court, in order that the court may decide without delay on the lawfulness of his detention and order his release if the detention is not lawful," it observed that in the case of Mahmoud Jaballah, one of the four men detained under a security certificate, he had been held without criminal charges for five years and only given the chance to challenge his detention once.[33]

VI Detention Cannot Be Used by States as a Deterrent

The WGAD has emphasized that detention cannot be used as a dissuasive measure but only as a last resort and for the shortest possible period of time.[34] It is not permissible, for example, to house asylum seekers in overcrowded facilities or in conditions that pose a risk to their mental and physical health.[35] Authorities must also provide alternatives to administrative detention.[36] Accordingly, they must put in place strict limits on the length of detention and provide judicial oversight of detentions through legislation or by administrative means.[37] Because asylum-seekers' alternatives to detention should not depend on their ability to pay for them, the WGAD does not consider bail a "realistic alternative to detention."[38]

When private companies have day-to-day operational control of detention facilities, it raises suspicion of inadequate state protection.[39] However, even where humane standards

---

[32] *Id.*

[33] *Id.*, at ¶ 85.

[34] Mohammad Khairallah Hamid Ali v. Lebanon, WGAD Opinion No. 56/2011, Adopted Nov. 17, 2011, at ¶¶ 12, 13; Deliberation No. 5, at Principle 7.

[35] Reza Racesi v. Australia and Papua New Guinea, WGAD Opinion No. 52/2014, Adopted Nov. 21, 2014, at ¶ 24; Sayed Abdellatif, et al. v. Australia, WGAD Opinion No. 8/2015, Adopted Apr. 24, 2015, at ¶ 25.

[36] Mehdi Abedi, et al. v. Iraq, WGAD Opinion No. 32/2012, Adopted Aug. 30, 2012, at ¶ 34 (Litigated by Author through Perseus Strategies).

[37] Mohammad Khairullah Hamid Ali, at ¶ 14.

[38] Marcos Antonio Aguilar-Rodriguez v. United States, WGAD Opinion No. 72/2017, Adopted Nov. 21, 2017, at ¶ 59.

[39] Sayed Abdellatif, et al., at ¶ 25; Reza Racesi, at ¶ 25.

of treatment are prescribed, detention can still exceed the legal limit. In *Mohammad Khairullah Hamid Ali v. Lebanon*, the detainee's imprisonment exceeded the forty-eight-hour period of detention before the detained is to be presented before a judge permitted by the relevant articles of the Lebanese Criminal Code.[40]

VII State Justifications for the Detention of Refugees, Asylum Seekers, and Migrants

Refugees may only be detained with the proper authorization by a competent and legally qualified authority. As a practical matter, a detainee can establish their refugee status by providing evidence of a refugee certificate provided either by UNHCR or state authorities.[41] Unregistered migrants may, however, provide other forms of proof to the WGAD that they were seeking refuge in the country of detention.[42] Once a decision has been taken as to the detainee's status, the conditions of detention must meet the principle of proportionality and not be excessive in light of the facts and circumstances of their case. This rule is especially emphasized in cases of asylum seekers, since no crime has been committed in the majority of cases and permissible grounds for detention are generally thin.[43]

That said, the HR Committee has conceded that detention for a period longer than that strictly necessary for processing an application may be justified if the asylum seekers pose a threat to national security, based on an individualized assessment.[44] However, authorities must provide opportunities for review of detention to the applicant.[45] Once a person has been investigated and deemed eligible for protection, no further detention is justified.

In *Sayed Abdellatif, et al. v. Australia*, the detainees were an Egyptian citizen and his family who were held for having entered Australia by unlawful means and without proper authorization.[46] The family was initially determined to have prima facie claims to protection, but their status determination proceedings were halted while Australian authorities investigated an international warrant for the applicant's arrest, issued by the Egyptian government in connection with the mass trial of political dissidents.[47] Though the detainee was later cleared for entry and found not to pose a security risk to Australia, he continued to be detained apart from his family.[48] The WGAD found the authorities failed to take the necessary procedural and administrative steps to process the detainee's release and status determination, resulting in prolonged detention, and in effect penalizing the detainee's wife and children in the process.[49] It is evident from this case the WGAD will not hesitate to scrutinize authorities' claims that the principle of

---

[40] Mohammad Khairullah Hamid Ali, at ¶ 6.
[41] Jawad Kazem Mhabes Mohammed Al Jabouri v. Lebanon, WGAD Opinion No. 55/2011, Adopted Nov. 17, 2011, at ¶ 16.
[42] Adnam El Hadj v. Spain, WGAD Opinion No. 37/2012, Adopted Aug. 30, 2012, at ¶ 13.
[43] Michael Mvogo, at ¶ 24.
[44] General Comment No. 35, at ¶ 18.
[45] Sayed Abdellatif, et al., at ¶ 24.
[46] Id., at ¶ 5.
[47] Id., at ¶¶ 7–8.
[48] Id., at ¶ 10.
[49] Id., at ¶ 29.

proportionality was considered in official decision-making and adequately addressed. A proper assessment must be done on a case-by-case basis, taking into account factors that may render the applicant particularly vulnerable to harm.[50]

The facts that may give rise to a finding of a Category IV violation often overlap significantly with evidence of a Category III violation of the Article 14(3)(c) right to be tried without undue delay.[51] The WGAD has at various times, for example, classified cases involving refugees in Lebanon as one category or the other or both.

In *Thaer Kanawi Abed el Zahra el Rimahi v. Lebanon*, over an eleven-month detention period, the fact the detainee's trial had been cancelled no fewer than eleven times was together considered to have given rise to both Category III and IV violations.[52] The WGAD did not consider it necessary to separate the analysis by category. But in the case of eighty-seven persons detained in a Palestinian refugee camp by Lebanese authorities, the WGAD declined to find a Category IV violation, instead finding the extended delays and due process failures as exclusively a series of Category III violations.[53] In that case, *Mohammed Ali Najem and Others v. Lebanon*, the grave due process abuses included a delay of almost six years between the initial detentions and the first opportunity for the detainees to have their claims heard.[54] The WGAD did, however, reiterate its concern for the treatment of refugees and asylum seekers in the country, citing its previous opinions on Lebanon.[55] But in the case of *Mohammad Khairullah Hamid Ali v. Lebanon*, however, the WGAD did not specify a Category III violation despite finding the practices of the authorities contrary to ICCPR Articles 9 and 14.[56] Presumably, this was because the allegations centered specifically on the detainee's rights as a refugee and his detention, and not on the nature of the trials.[57]

VIII State Failures to Provide Opportunity for Judicial or Administrative Review

The WGAD will also find violations when there are inadequate legislative protections for refugees, asylum seekers, and migrants, such as limiting or providing no opportunity for judicial or administrative review.[58]

Speaking generally as one illustration of WGAD concerns, during its visit to Germany, the WGAD expressed concern about the country's "fast track" procedure at Frankfurt Airport, an accelerated process for asylum applicants from countries considered to be safe states or origin. It is intended to make possible a quick decision on easy cases, which the Federal Office for Migrants and Refugees decides within two days. The WGAD expressed its concern about the procedure because "if the application for political asylum

---

[50] *Id.*, at ¶ 26 (discussing the effect of detention on asylum-seekers' children).

[51] Thaer Kanawi Abed el Zahra el Rimahi v. Lebanon, WGAD Opinion No. 14/2011, Adopted May 5, 2011, at ¶¶ 19–20.

[52] *Id.*, at ¶¶ 6, 15.

[53] Mohammed Ali Najem, et al. v. Lebanon, WGAD Opinion No. 57/2014, Adopted Nov. 21, 2014, at ¶ 36.

[54] *Id.*, at ¶¶ 10, 31.

[55] *Id.*, at ¶ 35.

[56] Mohammad Khairullah Hamid Ali, at ¶ 17(a).

[57] *Id.*, at ¶ 10.

[58] Reza Racesi, at ¶ 30 (noting that there was "no adequate regulatory framework of detention; no adequate process by which the necessity of detention of an individual was made reviewable; no clearly defined process in place to consider claims for refugee status, although such a process is imminent; and no time limit on the duration of detention.")

is rejected, the applicant has only three days to appeal to the Administrative Court. This period seems to be insufficient to allow the applicant to prepare her or his appeal."[59] In its follow-up visit to Germany, the WGAD reported on a landmark decision of the German Federal Constitutional Court, which found that "the restriction of movement and liberty at these facilities does not constitution detention [because] there is the option to leave by plane."[60] It criticized this judgment as problematic and inconsistent with judgments against Germany before the European Court of Human Rights because asylum seekers cannot easily just return home, and those who arrive in Frankfurt would need proper documentation and financial means to purchase a plane ticket.[61] Although the WGAD concluded the fast track procedure remains problematic "as it emphasizes speediness and shortened deadlines for legal remedies," it also noted that in 2013, only 48 decisions were taken, with 972 applications made in Germany airports and 127,023 asylum applications made in Germany in total.[62]

In *Jawad Kazem Mhabes Mohammed Al Jabouri* v. *Lebanon*, the case of an Iraqi national with valid refugee status in Lebanon who was arrested on a criminal charge, the WGAD specified that the specific feature of the detention that resulted in a Category IV violation was the authorities' failure to present the detainee any opportunity to argue against or challenge a deportation order.[63] Violations of fair trial rights were also found on the basis of the same period of detention, but because he remained in prison despite having served his initial sentence.[64] A clearer case for the WGAD was *Adnam El Hadj* v. *Spain*, in which a Moroccan migrant was deported the same day as his arrest, without being afforded an opportunity to challenge his detention.[65] According to the source, the detainee was found to have caused a disturbance while in custody, prompting authorities to accelerate the deportation process impermissibly.[66]

The authorities' failure to provide detainees with an opportunity to challenge the lawfulness of their detention before a court or administrative proceeding will per se render a detention prolonged in violation of Category IV regardless of whether the detainee is eventually served with an expulsion or deportation order. Although violations of fair trial rights typically render a detention arbitrary under Category III, the WGAD will often instead find a Category IV violation, even when the source brings the claim under Category III. For instance, in *Mohammad Naim Amiri* v. *Australia*, the source alleged that Amiri's inability to challenge his detention breached Article 9(4) of the ICCPR and rendered it arbitrary under Category III.[67] However, the WGAD found a Category IV violation instead. The WGAD provided little explanation for making the distinction in that case or in a similar case, *Abdalrahman Hussein* v. *Australia*.[68]

---

[59] Report of Working Group on Mission to Germany, at ¶ 53.

[60] *Report of the Working Group on Arbitrary Detention: Follow-Up Mission to Germany*, Human Rights Council, A/HRC/30/36/Add.1, July 10, 2015, at ¶ 64.

[61] *Id.*

[62] *Id.*, at ¶ 65.

[63] Jawad Kazem Mhabes Mohammed Al Jabouri, at ¶ 23.

[64] *Id.*

[65] Adnam El Hadj, at ¶¶ 13, 19.

[66] *Id.*, at ¶ 13.

[67] Mohammad Naim Amiri v. Australia, WGAD Opinion No. 42/2017, Adopted Aug. 21, 2017, at ¶¶ 40–42.

[68] Abdalrahman Hussein v. Australia, WGAD Opinion No. 28/2017, Adopted Apr. 25, 2017.

A combination of factors, such as delays in refugee status determination, lack of clarity to detainees about the process and duration of their detention, and inhuman conditions, will also result in a Category IV violation.[69] The WGAD observed in *Abbas Shadar Zaber al-Lami* v. *Lebanon* that such restrictions leave the detainee "defenseless, with no possibility of seeking a judicial remedy or benefiting from the safeguards to which persons deprived of their liberty are entitled under international law."[70] When reviews are afforded, they should be substantive in quality, not limited only to basic standards of review such as challenging the reasonableness of detention, but extend to the detainee their right to access lawyers and to refute the legality of detention.[71] Barriers to access to justice such as requiring detainees to pay for legal services for representation before a tribunal tasked with determining refugee status violate basic protection principles.[72]

The WGAD has also referred to particular states' "disturbing tendency" to use administrative custody for refugees, asylum seekers, and migrants.[73] Citing three prior cases originating in Lebanon, the WGAD reprimanded the Government in *Jawad Kazem Al Jabouri* for placing the protected class of persons in an "irregular situation" by holding them in administrative custody.[74] An observation to this effect may also be made on the basis of findings made during WGAD country missions.[75] When such prohibited treatment of refugees, asylum seekers, and migrants is routine policy, it creates a practical presumption against a government's cited reasons for detention.

IX State Failure to Honor Valid Refugee or Lawful Immigration Status

The WGAD will consider if authorities have disregarded a detainee's valid refugee or lawful immigration status when determining if a Category IV violation has occurred.[76] In the *Thaer Kanawi Abed el Zahra el Rimahi* v. *Lebanon*, the WGAD referred to the detainee's having been issued a refugee certificate number by UNHCR to underscore the validity of the detainee's status under international law and right to reside within the territory of Lebanon.[77] The authorities had charged the detainee in the case with unlawful entry and residence.[78] This charge, that the detainee in question entered the country without proper authorization, is the most commonly cited reason for initial arrest and detention in cases concerning refugees.[79] This determination is contrary to international law regulating refugee status and presents a prima facie violation of Article 9 of the ICCPR's requirement that any detention decision to detain be grounded in

---

[69] Reza Racesi, at ¶ 34.

[70] Abbas Shadar Zabed al-Lami v. Lebanon, WGAD Opinion No. 12/2011, Adopted May 4, 2011, at ¶ 16.

[71] Reza Racesi, at ¶¶ 23, 47.

[72] *Id.*, at ¶ 27.

[73] Jawad Kazem Mhabes Mohammed Al Jabouri, at ¶ 25; Abbas Shadar Zabed al-Lami, at ¶ 17; Mohammad Khairullah Hamid Ali, at ¶ 16.

[74] Jawad Kazem Mhabes Mohammed Al Jabouri, at ¶ 25.

[75] Reza Racesi, at ¶¶ 24–25.

[76] Abbas Shadar Zabed al-Lami, at ¶ 17; Hossein Dadkhah, et al. v. Iraq, WGAD Opinion No. 16/2012, Adopted May 4, 2012, at ¶ 15.

[77] Thaer Kanawi Abed el Zahra el Rimahi, at ¶ 4.

[78] *Id.*

[79] Abbas Shadar Zabed al-Lami, at ¶ 9.

procedures established by law.[80] Accordingly, in this case the WGAD also found a
Category I violation in addition to a Category IV violation.[81]

X Detentions of Migrants by States in Prisons or by Police

Detaining a refugee, asylum seeker, or migrant in a prison or by police violates both
international law and the WGAD's revised Deliberation No. 5. Even in the absence of
other aggravating factors, such as prolonged detention or ill-treatment, the comingling
of persons held under criminal law and migrants will be sufficient for the WGAD to
find a violation under Category IV.[82] The detention of migrants in prison also frequently prevents detainees' access to counsel or communication with relatives. The
WGAD criticized this general practice in Azerbaijan noting "asylum seekers whose
status had not yet been settled were placed in the facility together with convicts who
had served their sentence and were awaiting their voluntary return to their country of
origin."[83]

In *Abbas Shadar Zabed al-Lami* v. *Lebanon*, regarding an Iraqi refugee detained by
Lebanese police in prison, the WGAD added that because the detainee had been held in
improper facilities, he was unable to have access to representation as required by law.[84] In
that instance, the WGAD need not have qualified the emphasis on detention by police
authorities with the observation that the detention was also affected without court
authorization.[85]

Regardless of judicial instruction, the treatment of refugees, asylum seekers, and
migrants as criminals runs contrary to international law. This prohibition was best
illustrated by the WGAD in *Hossein Dadkhah, et al.* v. *Iraq*, a case involving ten Iranian
asylum seekers among thousands detained at Camp Liberty, a former United States
military base in Iraq. As described by the source, the detainees were kept in substandard
living conditions, assigned cells, prevented from contacting relatives or lawyers, constantly surveyed, and subject to disciplinary rules akin to those employed in prisons.[86]
The source labeled these conditions "inhumane and appalling."[87] The WGAD recognized the situation was equivalent to their being detained as if they were criminals and
therefore was unjustified given the protected status of the applicants as asylum seekers.[88]
The WGAD reaffirmed this finding in a subsequent case, *Mehdi Abedi, et al.* v. *Iraq*,
featuring the larger group of Iranian applicants detained by Iraqi authorities at two military
bases despite their later formal classification by the UNHCR as asylum seekers.[89] The

---

[80] *Id.*, at ¶¶ 11, 16–17.
[81] *Id.*, at ¶ 19.
[82] Abbas Shadar Zabed al-Lami, at ¶ 15.
[83] *Report of the Working Group on Arbitrary Detention on Mission to Azerbaijan*, Human Rights Council, A/
HRC/36/37/Add.1, Aug. 2, 2017, at ¶ 29.
[84] Abbas Shadar Zabed al-Lami, at ¶ 15.
[85] *Id.*
[86] Hossein Dadkhah, et al., at ¶¶ 4–8.
[87] *Id.*, at ¶ 7.
[88] *Id.*, at ¶¶ 15–17.
[89] Mehdi Abedi, et al., at ¶¶ 30, 36.

WGAD accepted the source's argument that the offensive conditions at these bases were "either identical or fundamentally the same" as those in the Hossein Dadkhah case.[90]

As the cases from Iraq demonstrate, isolating detainees from contact with the outside world, and in particular relatives and legal counsel, indicates an asylum seeker is being put in punitive detention rather than being housed prior to final determination of their refugee status. In the *Mehdi Abedi* case, the WGAD specified that the prohibition on detainees leaving the camp, depriving them of visits from family, friends, and concerned supporters, and blocking the means for them to communicate freely with the outside world were unlawful restrictions on a protected class of persons.[91] Appropriate and permissible alternatives to confining detention centers may include procedures for regular reporting to concerned authorities, possibility of release on bail, alternative housing in open centers or designated places without unreasonable confinement.[92] The WGAD has warned, however, that such measures must not become, in effect, alternatives to justified release.[93]

XI Detentions of Migrants by States in Private Detention Facilities

Although the issue of privatization of immigrant detention has not been seen in its jurisprudence, the WGAD has expressed serious concern about the outsourcing to private companies by states of immigration-related detention, noting in its country mission to the United States that it was "one of the elements that facilitated the significant expansion of immigration-related custody."[94]

The WGAD found from its interviews with detainees in private facilities in the United States there were serious concerns both about the conditions of their detention and their treatment throughout the immigration detention process. This included concerns about "substandard conditions at the moment of apprehension, the poor quality of food and drinking water, the limits imposed on recreation time and access to medical services, the lack of books and information in languages other than English, and the practice of solitary confinement."[95] In addition, the WGAD observed that "private companies did not require the same level of expertise of its employees and did not provide the same level of employee training as government-run facilities."[96]

XII Detentions of Children

The WGAD expressed that it was "deeply disturbed" to learn during its country mission to the United States about the detention of unaccompanied child immigrants. It reported "According to information received in March 2017, the Department of Homeland Security was reportedly considering separating children from parents caught crossing the border, in an attempt to deter illegal immigration from Mexico."[97] It further

---

[90] *Id.*, at ¶¶ 20, 31.
[91] *Id.*, at ¶¶ 31, 34.
[92] Reza Racesi, at ¶ 24.
[93] *Id.*
[94] Working Group Visit to the United States, at ¶ 33.
[95] *Id.*, at ¶ 34.
[96] *Id.*, at ¶ 35.
[97] *Id.*, at ¶ 41.

explained "The best interests of the child is to be a primary consideration in all actions concerning children. Accordingly, the deprivation of liberty of children by the United States authorities should be consistent with the best interests of the child, which means it should be prohibited."[98] The WGAD's cogent observations from July 2017 were prescient; in the summer of 2018, the Trump Administration faced a public outcry over a slightly different issue regarding its practices of separating and detaining the minor children of migrants entering the United States illegally.[99]

XIII Status of Refugees and Asylum Seekers Who Return Home

In seeking to refute an allegation of a Category IV violation resulting from a detainee's arrest, a government may point to the fact that a refugee or asylum-seeker left the country "voluntarily" after a certain period but later returned.[100] In such cases, the WGAD has looked to the facts surrounding the detainee's decision to return to their home country.[101] Should the WGAD find an applicant's departure was impacted by the circumstances of an arbitrary and unjustified deprivation of liberty, it has rejected the government's argument, finding a Category IV violation.[102] Significantly, the WGAD has only found it necessary to find that the decision was a consequence of the arbitrary detention.[103]

XIV Refugees and Asylum Seekers Who Threaten National Security or Commit Serious Crimes

The WGAD has conceded that there is one permissible exception to the prohibition of constructive expulsion or *refoulement*: when a refugee is regarded a danger to the security of the host country or if he or she has committed a particularly serious crime.[104] Even where the authorities had not claimed the exception, the WGAD previously issued an opinion on whether the grounds cited for a detainee's arrest met the standard for the exception to apply.[105] That said, illegal entry or remaining in a territory without proper authorization does not amount to a crime of sufficient severity.[106] In all cases, authorities must also take into consideration individual circumstances that might put a detainee in particular risk by prolonged detention, such as identification as homosexual, bisexual, transgender, or intersex.[107]

---

[98] *Id.*, at ¶ 42.
[99] *See, e.g.*, *Senate Panel Skewers Trump Officials over Migrant Family Separations*, WASHINGTON POST, July 31, 2018.
[100] Thaer Kanawi Abed el Zahra el Rimahi, at ¶ 15.
[101] *Id.*
[102] *Id.*, at ¶ 17.
[103] *Id.*; Goodwin-Gill & McAdam, at 201.
[104] Abbas Shadar Zabed al-Lami, at ¶ 13.
[105] *Id.*, at ¶ 14.
[106] *Id.*
[107] Reza Raeesi, at ¶ 35.

XV State Diversion of Asylum Seekers to Third Countries

The WGAD has focused recently on regional arrangements, mostly used by countries receiving large numbers of refugees, which divert asylum seekers to third countries for administrative processing and detention, collectively violating several principles of protection for asylum seekers.[108] In *Reza Raeesi v. Australia and Papua New Guinea*, the WGAD examined this practice in detail. The detainee in that case was an Iranian citizen facing a risk of persecution on the basis of his sexual orientation, for which he potentially faced the death sentence in his home country. He was diverted while journeying to Australia to detention facilities in Papua New Guinea against his express wishes and under duress.[109] The detainee was informed, according to the source, that the only possibility for him if he were found to qualify for refugee status, was permanent resettlement in Papua New Guinea and not in Australia.[110] This would have exposed the detainee to additional persecution, since homosexuality is a crime punishable by law in Papua New Guinea.[111] Furthermore, the conditions in which the detainee was kept were heavily surveilled, subject to heavy-handed disciplinary tactics, not limited to a proscribed period, and prevented him from receiving necessary medical care.[112]

The WGAD, in its extensive discussion of the case, conceded that such arrangements were not per se unlawful, though it gave the impression that the receiving country was clearly seeking to circumvent its obligations under international law.[113] Australian authorities had claimed the policy of diverting asylum seekers to a third-country detention center to await processing was proportional with its policy objective of preventing migrants from circumventing regular migration channels.[114] The WGAD, however, found that the proportionality principle requires detention to be the last possible resort, used only after exhausting alternatives to the measure.[115] It further determined the practical result of the policy in this case was to place an asylum seeker in a condition of irregular migration, effectively criminalizing asylum seekers, a policy that exceeded the cited legitimate interest of insulating territories from excessive migration flows.[116]

In addition, the WGAD then detailed the following features of the policy as actually implemented that violated the detainee's right to be free from an arbitrary deprivation of his liberty: choice, conditions, and arrangements of detention facilities, inadequate framework for review of the decision to detain, protracted period of detention, denial of access to family and counsel, and a failure by authorities to undertake an initial assessment of the proportionality of their decision to detain the asylum seeker.[117] In this

---

[108] *Id.*, at ¶ 22; HURST HANNUM, GUIDE TO INTERNATIONAL HUMAN RIGHTS PRACTICE 261 (Transnational Publishers, 2004), (summarizing contemporary policy developments and abuse of the "safe third country" provision in international refugee law); Goodwin-Gill & McAdam, at 371–372 (categorizing such practices as interception measures).

[109] *Reza Raeesi*, at ¶¶ 4–6.

[110] *Id.*, at ¶ 6.

[111] *Id.*, at ¶ 8.

[112] *Id.*, at ¶¶ 10–12, 24.

[113] *Id.*, at ¶¶ 22, 50 (explicitly extending the protections and reasoning provided in the Reza Raeesi case to any persons placed in similar circumstances, in offshore processing centers in Nauru and Papua New Guinea following their redirection by Australian authorities).

[114] *Id.*, at ¶ 12.

[115] *Id.*, at ¶ 22.

[116] *Id.*

[117] *Id.*, at ¶¶ 25–32.

case, the decision to detain was automatic and in execution of an indiscriminate and mandated policy, rather than allowing for checks of proportionality to be conducted with sensitivity to the particulars of each case.[118]

To foreclose the possibility of a receiving country fully outsourcing its responsibilities to protect asylum seekers, the WGAD specified that administering countries retain their obligations under international law even when a detainee is detained outside its territory in offshore processing centers.[119] In *Ghasem Hamedani* v. *Australia*, for example, the WGAD explained that although Papua New Guinea authorities currently exercised exclusive effective control over the detainee, the decision to detain and transfer him had been made on Australian soil by Australian authorities.[120] Thus, the WGAD "reject [ed] any submissions that the responsibility of the Australian authorities is not implicated" in Hamedani's detention.[121] As such, the transfer of their detainee to a third country did not shield the Australian government from being held responsible for his ongoing detention. This retention of state responsibility is also reflected in the WGAD's Revised Deliberation No. 5.[122]

---

[118] *Id.*, at ¶ 25; Sayed Abdellatif, et al., at ¶ 25 (restating this finding).
[119] Reza Raeesi, at ¶¶ 38, 41, relying on a determination made by UNHCR to this effect.
[120] Ghasem Hamedani v. Australia, WGAD Opinion No. 21/2018, Adopted Apr. 20, 2018, at ¶¶ 58–59.
[121] *Id.*, at ¶¶ 59.
[122] Revised Deliberation No. 5, at ¶ 9.

8 Category V

Discrimination on Protected Grounds

Category V includes within the WGAD mandate cases that can be classified as the following:

> When the deprivation of liberty constitutes a violation of the international law for reasons of discrimination based on birth, national, ethnic or social origin, language, religion, economic condition, political or other opinion, gender, sexual orientation, disability or other status, that aims towards or can result in ignoring the equality of human rights.[1]

Category V was added as a new category of legal cases involving the deprivation of liberty by the WGAD in 2011. The category is based on the principle of nondiscrimination, essential to human rights protection and from which derogation is strictly limited.[2] Article 26 of the ICCPR serves as a general right of nondiscrimination to which the WGAD must refer.[3] Category V may be seen as a supplemental guarantee meant to protect particularly at-risk populations. The key element in the categorization is the "for reasons of" language, which requires a cognizable nexus between the deprivation of liberty and the reason for that punitive action. The Human Rights Committee (HR Committee), however, recognizes that a practice need not be explicitly or intentionally discriminatory to be censured; implicit, accidental, or having a discriminatory effect would also be found in violation of anti-discrimination principles.[4] The WGAD may recognize discrimination on the basis of more than one listed ground simultaneously.[5]

---

[1] *Methods of Work of the Working Group*, Human Rights Council, A/HRC/36/38, July 13, 2017, at ¶ 8(e).

[2] Sarah Joseph & Melissa Castan, The International Covenant on Civil and Political Rights: Cases, Materials, and Commentary 914 (Oxford University Press, 2004); Alex Conte & Richard Burchill, Defining Civil and Political Rights: The Jurisprudence of the United Nations Human Rights Committee 161 (2009), characterizing the prohibition of discrimination as a "pervasive theme" of ICCPR, as illustrated by inclusion in Articles 2(1), 3, 4(1), 20, 23, 24, 25, and 26.

[3] *General Comment No. 18*, Human Rights Committee (1989), at ¶ 1; Broeks v. The Netherlands, Communication No. 172/1984, Human Rights Committee, CCPR/C/OP/2/196, Apr. 9, 1987, at ¶ 12.3.

[4] Conte & Burchill, at 165; Simunek, et al. v. The Czech Republic, Communication No. 516/1992, Human Rights Committee, CCPR/C/54/D/516/1992, July 31, 1995, at ¶ 11.7 (stating that discriminatory effect without intention of legislation will be dispositive for a finding in favor of an applicant).

[5] Laphai Gam v. Myanmar, WGAD Opinion No. 50/2013, Adopted Nov. 19, 2013, at ¶¶ 35, 41 (finding discrimination for an applicant belonging to both a minority ethnic and religious group); Zeinab Jalalian v. Iran, WGAD Opinion No. 1/2016, Adopted Apr. 18, 2016, at ¶¶ 37–38 (finding discrimination on the joint bases of sex, political opinion, and national or social origin); Francis Xavier Dang Xuan Dieu, et al. v. Viet Nam, WGAD Opinion No. 26/2013, Adopted Aug. 29, 2013, at ¶¶ 58–60 (concerning the detention of

In 2017, the WGAD provided further explanation in its annual report about how it assesses if a source has demonstrated a prima facie case of deprivation of liberty on discriminatory grounds. Specifically, the WGAD takes into account a number of factors, including whether:

(a) The deprivation of liberty was part of a pattern of persecution against the detained person (e.g. a person was targeted on multiple occasions through previous detention, acts of violence or threats);

(b) Other persons with similarly distinguishing characteristics have also been persecuted (e.g. several members of a particular ethnic group are detained for no apparent reason, other than their ethnicity);

(c) The authorities have made statements to, or conducted themselves toward, the detained person in a manner that indicates a discriminatory attitude (e.g. female detainees threatened with rape or forced to undergo virginity testing, or a detainee is held in worse conditions or for a longer period than other detainees in similar circumstances);

(d) The context suggests that the authorities have detained a person on discriminatory grounds or to prevent them from exercising their human rights (e.g. political leaders detained after expressing their political opinions or detained for offences that disqualify them from holding political office);

(e) The alleged conduct for which the person is detained is only a criminal offence for members of his or her group (e.g. criminalization of consensual same-sex conduct between adults).[6]

Authorities may escape censure if they can show that the measure taken by authorities justifiably differentiated between groups of people, and if the criteria for the grouping was reasonable and objective, and had a legitimate purpose.[7] Justifications recognized as objective and reasonable include measures for the protection of health and safety, fulfillment of duties to provide social services such as public education, and in limited instances the protection of public morals and keeping of public order.[8] Governments seeking to defend the detention of persons as necessary by law and policy must provide a valid rationale connecting the measure to the permissible grounds for differentiation.[9]

I Birth

In *Ola Yusuf al-Qaradawi and Hossam al-Din Khalaf* v. *Egypt*, the daughter and son-in-law of Sheikh Yusuf al-Qaradawi, who has been described as having inspired the Muslim

---

human rights activists whose work related to their membership in faith-based organizations and religious denominations).

[6] *Report of the Working Group on Arbitrary Detention*, Human Rights Council, A/HRC/36/37, July 19, 2017, at ¶ 48.

[7] *Id.*, at 174–175; General Comment No. 18, at ¶¶ 10, 13 (providing that differentiation intended to correct past discrimination is based on a justifiable reason and is therefore permitted).

[8] Conte & Burchill, at 178 (specifying that the HR Committee looks for "objective and reasonable criteria that is compatible with the objectives of the Covenant, namely the protection of public order and human dignity.")

[9] Irina Zaharchenko & Valida Jabrayliova v. Azerbaijan, WGAD Opinion No. 42/2015, Adopted Dec. 2, 2015, at ¶¶ 39, 41.

Brotherhood and was an outspoken critic of Egyptian President Abdel Fattah el-Sisi, were detained on vague claims of connections to the Muslim Brotherhood. Egypt had also imposed sanctions against Sheikh al-Qaradawi and numerous members of his family.[10] The lack of detail in the accusations led the WGAD to conclude that al-Qaradawi and Khalaf had been detained because of their family ties with Sheikh al-Qaradawi.[11] This was "discrimination based on birth and family relations," and rendered their detention arbitrary as "no one should be deprived of liberty for the crimes, real or not, committed by their family member by birth or marriage in a free, democratic society."[12]

II National, Ethnic, or Social Origin

National, ethnic, or social origin may also be the basis of an arbitrary detention. However, the WGAD must be able to "establish with the requisite degree of certainty... [targeting] on the basis of nationality" – unsubstantiated allegations of discrimination are not enough for a Category V finding.[13] However, the WGAD also may be prepared to infer discrimination on the basis of nationality when "no other reason can be invoked to justify" the detention (such as if there has been no response from the government).[14] The WGAD has examined detentions based on national, ethnic, or social origins both in its country missions and in individual cases in its jurisprudence.

In New Zealand, the WGAD observed 51.4 percent of the prison population was indigenous Maori, while they comprised only 15 percent of the general population. In examining this situation, it said:

> The Working Group is concerned at the overrepresentation of Maori and Pacific Islanders in the criminal justice system. The Working Group found indications of bias at all levels of the criminal justice process: the investigative stage, with searches and apprehension; police or court bail; extended custody in remand; all aspects of prosecution and the court process, including sentencing; and the parole process, including the sanctions for breach of parole conditions.[15]

From its trip to Nicaragua, the WGAD reported on the situation of indigenous groups and those of African descent who live on the Caribbean coastal region of the country and who have been excluded from its political life and economic development, subject to a neglect "which sometimes borders on racism."[16] While the WGAD said that the conditions at a prison there were poor but understandable, it also described the situation with 104 men detained in the four cell-blocks of the police station. It said there were bunks for

[10] Ola Yusuf al-Qaradawi & Hossam al-Din Khalaf v. Egypt, WGAD Opinion No. 26/2018, Adopted Apr. 23, 2018, at ¶ 77 (Litigated by Author through Perseus Strategies).

[11] Id., at ¶ 79.

[12] Id.

[13] Abdul Fatah and Sa'id Jamaluddin v. Afghanistan and the United States, WGAD Opinion No. 56/2016, Adopted Nov. 24, 2016, at ¶ 54.

[14] Id., at ¶ 36.

[15] Report of the Working Group on Arbitrary Detention: Mission to New Zealand, Human Rights Council, A/HRC/30/36/Add.2, July 6, 2015, at ¶¶ 54, 92.

[16] Report of the Working Group on Arbitrary Detention: Mission to Nicaragua, Human Rights Council, A/HRC/4/40/Add.3, Nov. 9, 2006, at ¶ 89.

only three detainees in each cell, with the rest sleeping on the floor or in hammocks hung from the ceiling, and the cells were "filthy, dark and damp, without ventilation."[17]

In Morocco, the WGAD said it has received "numerous complaints indicating a pattern of excessive use of force in repressing demonstrations and in arresting protestors or persons suspected of participating in demonstrations calling for self-determination of the Sahrawi population."[18]

And in Hungary, the WGAD observed that the "Roma are more often subjected to police stop and search operations, which increases the likelihood that they will end up in the criminal justice system. It has also been pointed out that, because Roma are often amongst the poorest members of society, they are more likely to need to rely on officially appointed defence counsel, who are poorly paid and tend to be less active in defending their clients."[19]

With respect to individual cases, the WGAD accepted the allegation of discrimination from the source regarding a Palestinian minor as undisputed (since Israel had neglected to respond). In light of the historical discrimination against Palestinians by the Government, it concluded there was a violation of Category V.[20] The WGAD has relied on a "pattern" of documented discrimination against Palestinians by the Government in multiple cases.[21]

Two cases from Myanmar, of detainees Brang Yung and La Ring, aptly illustrated the vulnerability of persons belonging to ethnic groups that are politically mobilized and active in calling for greater recognition within a country.[22] In both cases, the detainees, ethnic Kachin, were arrested, tortured, and forced to falsely confess an affiliation with the Kachin Independence Army.[23] Noting the tension between ethnic communities and the state in Myanmar, and the authorities' specific military operations against ethnic Kachins, the WGAD found Category V violations based on discrimination on the basis of the detainees' ethnic origin.[24] The WGAD will also take into consideration the general treatment in the concerned country of similarly situated applicants or the groups they can be classified within to determine discriminatory state practice.[25] In the Brang Yung, for example, the WGAD cited the findings of the Special Rapporteur on the Situation of Human Rights in Myanmar to place the applicant's particular treatment in a larger context of discriminatory practice against the Kachin ethnic group.[26] In a third case

---

[17] *Id.*, at ¶ 90.

[18] *Report of the Working Group on Arbitrary Detention: Mission to Morocco*, Human Rights Council, A/HRC/27/48/Add.5, Aug. 4, 2014, ¶ 64.

[19] *Report of the Working Group on Arbitrary Detention: Mission to Hungary*, Human Rights Council, A/HRC/27/48/Add.4, July 3, 2014, at ¶ 120.

[20] *Id.*, at ¶ 38.

[21] Omar Nazzal v. Israel, WGAD Opinion No. 21/2017, Adopted Apr. 24, 2017, at ¶¶ 36–37; Ali Abdul Rahman Mahmoud Jaradat v. Israel, WGAD Opinion No. 44/2017, Adopted Aug. 21, 2017, at ¶ 38.

[22] Brang Yung v. Myanmar, WGAD Opinion No. 6/2014, Adopted Apr. 23, 2014, at ¶ 3 (Litigated by Author); La Ring v. Myanmar, WGAD Opinion No. 24/2014, Adopted Aug. 26, 2014, at ¶ 3 (Litigated by Author).

[23] Brang Yung, at ¶ 7; La Ring, at ¶ 5.

[24] Brang Yung, at ¶¶ 17–18, 22; La Ring, at ¶¶ 16–17, 22(c).

[25] Irina Zaharchenko and Valida Jabrayliova, at ¶ 22 (drawing attention to the authorities' longstanding policy of targeting Jehovah's Witnesses for distributing literature or otherwise promoting their faith); Saeed Abedinigalangashi, at ¶ 24 (citing concerns of the Special Rapporteur on the situation of human rights in the Islamic Republic of Iran regarding the treatment of religious minorities).

[26] Brang Yung, at ¶ 19; Tun Aung, at ¶ 21–22 (noting a similar observation from the Special Rapporteur about the treatment of Rohingya Muslims in Myanmar).

involving a Kachin applicant, *Laphai Gam* v. *Myanmar*, the WGAD supplemented the ethnic discrimination claim with the finding that he had also been subjected to discriminatory treatment for his Christian faith.[27]

In other instances, particularly in cases of indigenous persons working for the human rights of their communities, the WGAD has considered reprisals for reasons of human rights work as synonymous with discrimination on the basis of indigenous identity.[28] This was the ruling in *Librado Jacinto Baños Rodriguez* v. *Mexico*, involving a detainee of Afro-indigenous descent actively involved in the rights of other Afro-descendants and indigenous peoples in the region.[29] A decisive factor in the WGAD ruling was its recognition of Mexican indigenous communities as particularly vulnerable groups.[30] An identical ruling was made in *Pedro Celestino Canché Herrera* v. *Mexico*, an adjoining case of a Mayan water rights activist.[31] In another case, however, the WGAD observed that discrimination on the basis of the detainee's indigenous identity occurred.[32] No Category V violation was found though, perhaps because the source had not included the charge of discrimination in its communication.[33]

As a matter of application, the WGAD has held that the jurisdiction and responsibilities of states extend beyond their immediate borders, and equally apply to their acts and those of their agents abroad, and especially where the state is holding persons in detention.[34] The detainee in *Obaidullah* v. *United States* was an ethnic Pashtun taken into custody from Afghanistan and transferred first to Bagram base and later to the Guantanamo Bay detention facility in connection with terror-related charges.[35] Though there was no conviction or concrete evidence that the detainee had participated in belligerent activities, he continued to be detained at the facility for over ten years.[36] In that case, and in *Mustafa al Hawsawi* v. *United States*, the Government argued that the detention served the legitimate purpose of preventing a combatant from engaging in violence against the United States.[37] The WGAD found discrimination on the basis of nationality in both instances, presumably because the detainees would not otherwise have been subjected to such prolonged detention.[38]

---

[27] Laphai Gam v. Myanmar, WGAD Opinion No. 50/2013, Adopted Nov. 19, 2013, at ¶ 35. The religious discrimination finding was substantiated by evidence that the applicant was forced to stand in crucifixion position, a punishment meted out to him specifically because of his Christian faith.

[28] Pedro Celestino Canché Herrera v. Mexico, WGAD Opinion No. 18/2015, Adopted Apr. 28, 2015, at ¶¶ 24–25.

[29] Librado Jacinto Baños Rodriguez v. Mexico, WGAD Opinion No. 19/2015, Adopted Apr. 28, 2015, at ¶¶ 3, 18–19.

[30] *Id.*, at ¶ 16.

[31] Pedro Celestino Canché Herrera, at ¶ 26.

[32] Damian Gallardo Martinez v. Mexico, WGAD Opinion No. 23/2014, Adopted Aug. 26, 2014, at ¶ 22.

[33] *Id.*, at ¶¶ 20, 28. The opinion focused instead on the activities of the applicant as a defender of the human rights of indigenous communities in the country.

[34] Mr. Obaidullah v. United States, WGAD Opinion No. 10/2013, Adopted May 3, 2013, at ¶¶ 29–31 (citing *Report on the Situation of Detainees at Guantanamo Bay*, Working Group on Arbitrary Detention, E/CN.4/2006/120, Feb. 27, 2006, at ¶ 11; Mustafa al Hawsawi v. United States and Cuba, WGAD Opinion No. 50/2014, Adopted Nov. 20, 2014, at ¶ 65.

[35] Obaidullah, at ¶¶ 3–4.

[36] *Id.*, at ¶¶ 16–17, 21.

[37] *Id.*, at ¶ 33; Mustafa al Hawsawi, at ¶ 68.

[38] Obaidullah, at ¶ 42; Mustafa al Hawsawi, at ¶ 82.

The WGAD has also examined cases of discrimination against dual nationals. In *Siamak Namazi and Mohammed Baquer Namazi v. Iran*, a father and son who were dual US and Iranian citizens were both convicted and sentenced to ten years' imprisonment for "collaborating with a hostile government," referencing the United States.[39] The WGAD found that the source had established a prima facie case that "the arrest and detention of the Namazis were motivated by a discriminatory factor, namely, their status as dual Iranian-US nationals and their links with various organisations located outside of Iran."[40] In its analysis, as noted earlier as its general approach to Category V, the WGAD discussed how other persons with similarly distinguishing characteristics have also been persecuted. It observed it had "made findings of arbitrary detention with respect to several cases involving dual nationals in Iran."[41] And it also noted that the Special Rapporteur on the Situation of Human Rights in the Islamic Republic of Iran "has referred in a recent report to the detention of dual nationals."[42] This led the WGAD to find a violation under Category V, in addition to a wide array of fair trial violations under Category III.

In *Nazanin Zaghari-Ratcliffe v. Iran*, the detainee had been arrested, in part, on the basis of her dual Iranian-British national status (and the distrust this status engendered in the authorities). The WGAD concluded she was "targeted on the basis of her 'national or social origin' as a dual national."[43] A similar case was decided in *Kamal Foroughi v. Iran*, in which another Iranian-British dual national was targeted on the basis of his dual national status.[44] The WGAD found several factors supporting this conclusion, including the lack of evidence for espionage at his trial for national security offenses, his lack of previous criminal records or suspicious behavior, and Iranian officials' insistence that he speak only Farsi when communicating with his family.[45]

The national or ethnic origin language has also been broadly interpreted by the WGAD to include racial discrimination.[46] The applicant in *Adnam El Hadj v. Spain* was a Moroccan migrant detained, held, and duly deported by Spanish authorities following a racially charged altercation with police officers.[47] The WGAD took note of the offensive insults, noting their racial content, and interpreted it as evidence of a demonstrated discriminatory intent.[48] In ruling a Category V violation, the WGAD reminded that discrimination on the basis of nationality, ethnic, or social origin disregards the "essential equality of all persons," and therefore reflects a core value.[49] It is to be noted, however, that the Adnam El Hadj case presented conclusive evidence of racial discrimination in authorities' attitude toward migrants. It is as yet unclear how the

---

[39] Siamak Namazi and Mohammed Baquer Namazi v. Iran, WGAD Opinion No. 49/2017, Adopted Sept. 22, 2017 (Litigated by Author through Freedom Now).

[40] *Id.*, at ¶ 43.

[41] *Id.*, at ¶ 44.

[42] *Id.* (citing *Report of the Special Rapporteur on the Situation of Human Rights in Iran*, A/71/418, Sept. 30, 2016, at ¶¶ 36–38).

[43] Nazanin Zaghari-Ratcliffe v. Iran, WGAD Opinion No. 28/2016, Adopted Sept. 21, 2016, at ¶ 49.

[44] Kamal Foroughi v. Iran, WGAD Opinion No. 7/2017, Adopted Apr. 19, 2017, at ¶ 39.

[45] *Id.*, at ¶ 40.

[46] Policies intended to control migration, however, are not per se discriminatory, since based on reasons considered justifiable, such as concerns for public safety and need to control irregular migration flows. Reza Raeesi, at ¶ 22.

[47] Adnam El Hadj v. Spain, WGAD Opinion No. 37/2012, Adopted Aug. 30, 2012, at ¶¶ 3–4.

[48] *Id.*, at ¶ 13.

[49] *Id.*, at ¶ 19.

WGAD will analyze harder cases, where discrimination is implicit in authorities' attitudes or where embedded in the policies under which persons are detained. The WGAD has, however, reached behind exclusionary statutes to highlight discriminatory effect or intent. In *Gunasundaram Jayasundaram* v. *Sri Lanka*, the WGAD noted that anti-terrorism laws targeting the LTTE group effectively put persons of Tamil origin at serious risk of detention and harm.[50] Relying on human rights reporting from the region, the WGAD found that a Category V discrimination against the detainee for reasons of his ethnic origin.[51]

III Language

In *Marcos Antonio Aguilar-Rodriguez* v. *United States*, the WGAD found a Category V based on his membership in a linguistic minority.[52] The detainee was a Salvadorian national who attempted to leave the gang he had joined as a minor and was eventually forced to leave the country. He was detained in Arizona several years later. His detention was considered discriminatory, in part, because he was required to defend himself without a translator or legal assistance and limited access to Spanish legal materials, which disadvantaged him as a member of a linguistic minority (that is, a Spanish-speaker).[53]

IV Religion

Category V cases involving detention for reasons of a person's religion have been analyzed similarly to political opinion cases. Minority religions in a state hostile to dissenting religious opinions will be given particular consideration.[54] In *Song Hyeong Kim* v. *Democratic People's Republic of Korea*, the detainee was alleged to have been targeted because of his interest in and subsequent promotion of Christianity in the country.[55] In the absence of a substantive reply from the authorities, and noting that the spread of Christianity is considered a threat to the state by authorities, the WGAD found the detainee's Article 18 right to freedom of religion violated.[56] Since the detention was motivated by the detainee's minority religious convictions, the case was classified in both Category II and V.[57] A clear case of religious discrimination was *Saeed Abedinigalangashi* v. *Iran*, concerning a pastor charged with harm to national security by holding Christian services in private residences.[58] The explicitly religious content of the charge,

---

[50] Gunasundaram Jayasundaram v. Sri Lanka, WGAD Opinion No. 38/2012, Adopted Aug. 31, 2012, at ¶ 31.
[51] *Id.*, at ¶¶ 30, 34.
[52] Marcos Antonio Aguilar-Rodriguez v. United States, WGAD Opinion No. 72/2017, Adopted Nov. 21, 2017, at ¶ 66.
[53] *Id.*, at ¶ 66.
[54] Saeed Abedinigalangashi v. Iran, WGAD Opinion No. 18/2013, Adopted Aug. 26, 2013, at ¶ 20; Tun Aung v. Myanmar, WGAD Opinion No. 49/2013, Adopted Nov. 19, 2013, at ¶¶ 24, 28.
[55] Song Hyeok Kim v. Democratic People's Republic of Korea, WGAD Opinion No. 29/2015, Adopted Sept. 3, 2015, at ¶ 4.
[56] *Id.*, at ¶¶ 5, 11.
[57] *Id.*, at ¶¶ 20–21.
[58] Saeed Abedinigalangashi, at ¶ 7; Tun Aung, at ¶ 21 (presenting a similar case for the WGAD, where the applicant was an active and moderately inclined Muslim community leader in Myanmar).

and the fact that the authorities contravened the constitutionally protected rights of a religious minority, resulted in a Category V religious discrimination finding.[59]

Well-documented patterns of arbitrary arrest and detention of members of a religious community on the basis of their faith can lead the WGAD to a Category V finding.[60] In *Hana Aghigian et al. v. Iran*, the frequent imprisonment of members of the Baha'i faith for their religious beliefs supported a Category V finding in the case of twenty-four individuals arrested for faith-related activities.[61] Further supporting this finding was the religious tone of the vaguely worded charges that included, among others, "spreading corruption on Earth."[62] In *Teymur Akhmedov v. Kazakhstan*, the WGAD once again relied on a pattern of discrimination (against Jehovah's Witnesses), as well as the simultaneous search of other premises owned by members of the same religion and the seizure of artifacts to infer that the detainee's arrest had a discriminatory motive.[63]

A less obvious case of religious discrimination concerned another Jehovah's Witness who had refused military service in *Daniil Islamov v. Tajikistan*.[64] As he had been deprived of his liberty and was being held in a military camp for being a conscientious objector, his detention was found arbitrary under Category I (no legal basis). However, the source also alleged that by detaining Islamov for a religious objection to military service, the military was "attempting to coerce him into abandoning his religion," and that therefore his detention should be found arbitrary under Category V.[65] With little explanation, the WGAD noted that Islamov had "been a victim of discrimination on the basis of his religious belief," although there the source had not alleged any particular facts to indicate a Jehovah's Witness would be treated differently from a nonreligious conscientious objector.[66] The WGAD made a concurrent Category II finding since it was "without doubt that Mr. Islamov's fate derives directly from his religious expression as a Jehovah's Witness."[67]

In *Nizar Bou Nassar Eddine v. Lebanon*, the WGAD rejected a claim of religious discrimination. The detainee was a member of the Druze faith and an internal security officer who had been arrested after a local Druze leader spoke out against corruption and scandals emerging that involved the internal security force.[68] The source alleged that although Eddine had been arrested in connection with corruption scandals with no proven connection to him, several other officers who were of the same religion as the Minister of the Interior and had been connected with suspicious funds remained free. Despite this, the WGAD rejected his claim of religious discrimination, saying it lacked evidence required for a better assessment of Eddine's situation in the "global context" of Lebanon.[69] Eddine's detention was still found to be arbitrary under Categories I and III.

---

[59] *Id.*, at ¶¶ 17, 28.
[60] Hana Aghigian, et al v. Iran, WGAD Opinion No. 9/2017, Adopted Apr. 19, 2017, at ¶ 23.
[61] *Id.*
[62] *Id.*
[63] Teymur Akhmedov v. Kazakhstan, WGAD Opinion No. 62/2017, Adopted Aug. 25, 2017, at ¶ 49.
[64] Daniil Islamov v. Tajikistan, WGAD Opinion No. 43/2017, Adopted Aug. 21, 2017, at ¶ 36.
[65] *Id.*
[66] *Id.*
[67] *Id.*, at ¶ 34.
[68] Nizar Bou Nassar Eddine v. Lebanon, WGAD Opinion No. 52/2017, Adopted Aug. 23, 2017, at ¶ 30.
[69] *Id.*

The WGAD has been particularly cognizant of the use of anti-terrorism statutes or charges to target religious dissenters.[70] It reiterated this concern in *Gaybullo Jalilov v. Uzbekistan*, concerning a Muslim human rights activist compiling information on the targeting of independent Muslims in the country.[71] The detainee had been charged with membership in a religious extremist group intending to overthrow the Government of the country.[72] The charges were based specifically on evidence of the applicant's participation in religious gatherings and on statements from the detainee himself regarding his independent practice of Islam.[73] The Government's failure to provide any specific evidence of the alleged link to terrorist groups suggested to the WGAD that the charge was a pretext to target the applicant for his religious beliefs and for his advocacy on behalf of other Muslims.[74] No substantive distinction was made between the Category II and V assessments.[75]

Where the government attempts to justify the measure taken or indicates that the detention was affected to implement a policy, the WGAD may briefly discuss the reasonableness or rationale of the measure. In *Irina Zaharchenko and Valida Jabrayliova v. Azerbaijan*, the case of two Jehovah's Witnesses, the Government defended the detention as lawful and justified by the detainees' failure to obtain appropriate authorization for publicly distributing religious literature.[76] A second reason for authorities' concern with the Jehovah's Witnesses was due to members' refusal to serve in the military.[77] The WGAD noted that the authorities had failed to explain how barring the applicants from distributing religious texts was detrimental to society and therefore justified as a valid measure to safeguard public morals.[78] The WGAD did not, however, find it necessary to rule the policy of requiring prior authorization for religious activity as discriminatory, though it reiterated that limitations to the freedom of religion must be strictly limited.[79] It also did not concern itself with the task of labeling the targeting of Jehovah's Witnesses through conscientious objector cases as evidence of general and widespread discrimination.[80]

And in *Wu Zeheng, et al. v. China*, the WGAD found the detainees' imprisonment arbitrary under Category V, because "the discrimination against them and the persecution experienced by the owners of businesses affiliated with their religion is based on their being part of a protected class, i.e., their religious beliefs and association."[81]

---

[70] *Report of the Working Group on Arbitrary Detention*, Commission on Human Rights, E/CN.4/2004/3, Dec. 15, 2003, at ¶ 63; Francis Xavier Dang Xuan Dieu, et al., at ¶¶ 23, 59.

[71] Gaybullo Jalilov v. Uzbekistan, WGAD Opinion No. 4/2013, Adopted Apr. 30, 2013, at ¶¶ 4, 69.

[72] *Id.*, at ¶ 70.

[73] *Id.*, at ¶¶ 7, 12, 23.

[74] *Id.*, at ¶¶ 71–73.

[75] *Id.*, at ¶¶ 75–76, 81.

[76] Irina Zaharchenko and Valida Jabrayliova, at ¶¶ 24–26.

[77] *Id.*, at ¶¶ 28, 33.

[78] *Id.*, at ¶ 41.

[79] *Id.*, at ¶ 39.

[80] *Id.*, at ¶ 42 (noting that this discussion was "irrelevant" to the circumstances of the applicants in the case).

[81] Wu Zeheng, et al. v. China, WGAD Opinion No. 46/2016, Adopted Nov. 22, 2016, at ¶ 63 (Litigated by Author through Perseus Strategies).

V Economic Condition

In *Marcos Antonio Aguilar-Rodriguez* v. *United States*, discussed earlier, the WGAD found a Category V violation also on the basis of his economic status.[82] The detainee was imprisoned in Arizona. His bail was set at $6,000, an amount he could not afford, and on appeal was increased to $20,000. The WGAD noted a pattern in the United States of setting bail unrealistically high so that persons detained for immigration proceedings are unable to afford an alternative to detention, and remarked that this practice was discriminatory since it "disproportionately affects those of humble backgrounds."[83]

VI Political Opinion

The relationship between Category II freedom of expression or opinion cases and Category V claims based on discrimination for reasons of political opinion has been examined briefly earlier in this book. In general, there is a "strong presumption" that deprivation of liberty based on the exercise of fundamental political rights will also constitute discrimination based on political views.[84] Such cases often involve current or former elected officials – positions of which the WGAD will take note, since they "necessarily attract respect."[85] The principal case demonstrating the lack of clarity in WGAD analysis on the topic is *Mohamed Nasheed* v. *The Maldives*. The detainee in that case was a prominent politician and environmentalist, who served as the President of Maldives before being forced to resign, and was subsequently arrested and detained on a charge of terrorism.[86] The source alleged both a Category II violation of the applicant's freedom of expression and opinion and a Category V violation for discrimination on the basis of his political opinion.[87] The feature considered discriminatory by the source was the reason provided by the authorities for the detainee's arrest, alleging that it was a pretext for targeting a prominent political opponent.[88] The Government centered on the effect of the detention, arguing that he continued to make political statements after his arrest.[89]

The WGAD, however, found that the detention both "resulted from" the detainee's exercise of right to political expression, and was targeted "on the basis" of his political opinion.[90] Though the distinction made was slight, it nevertheless suggests that the requirement for a finding of a Category V violation is that the reason for detention was the detainee's political opinion. A Category II violation may, however, occur merely

---

[82] Marcos Antonio Aguilar-Rodriguez v. United States, WGAD Opinion No. 72/2017, Adopted Nov. 21, 2017, at ¶ 66.

[83] *Id.*, at ¶ 67.

[84] Thirumurugan Gandhi v. India, WGAD Opinion No. 88/2017, Adopted Nov. 23, 2017, at ¶ 43.

[85] Ahmed Mahloof v. The Maldives, WGAD Opinion 15/2017, Adopted Apr. 21, 2017, at ¶ 93.

[86] Mohamed Nasheed v. The Maldives, WGAD Opinion No. 33/2015, Adopted Sept. 4, 2015, at ¶¶ 4, 8 (Litigated by Author through Freedom Now and Co-counsel Ben Emmerson QC and Amal Clooney).

[87] *Id.*, at ¶ 25.

[88] *Id.*, at ¶ 88.

[89] *Id.*, at ¶ 53.

[90] *Id.*, at ¶¶ 98–99, 110. The WGAD did not feel it necessary to separate its substantive analysis of the Category II and V claims, nor did it expand on its analytical approach to such cases. This is in contrast with the language of Francis Xavier Dang Xuan Dieu, et al. v. Viet Nam, at ¶¶ 24, 71, where the source's allegation that discrimination was "on the basis" of the applicants' political opinion provided the basis for both Category II and V claims, the WGAD failing to draw a substantive distinction.

when the right to political opinion is curtailed, whatever the reason for the detention may be. This, however, does not appear to conform to the HR Committee's jurisprudential approach, which considers a discriminatory effect sufficient and does not require an analysis of the explicit intention behind the measure taken by authorities. The Nasheed ruling, and the WGAD's increased willingness to consider Category V violations in connection with Category II allegations, will likely lead to more and similar findings in cases of activists targeted by authorities for their dissident views.

The WGAD seemed to draw a greater distinction between the Category II and V analyses in *Gloria Macapagal-Arroyo v. Philippines*, the case concerning a former President of the Philippines and then-sitting member of the House of Representatives.[91] The detainee had been arrested and detained in connection with ongoing charges of plunder and corruption, allegations the source claimed were politically motivated.[92] The source had alleged that the intent of the authorities was to disqualify the former President from the political scene.[93] The WGAD centered its Category II assessment on the fact that, as a result of the ongoing detention, the applicant was "effectively barred" from serving in her elected role and official capacity.[94] The acts that together evidenced discrimination on the basis of political opinion were listed separately, and included the removal of judges in the corruption cases, the timing of the charges, and comments by public officials insinuating her guilt before the conclusion of the trials.[95]

A clear case of demonstrated targeting for reasons of political opinion would bear similarity to *Andargachew Tsige v. Ethiopia and Yemen*, which concerned the detention of an Ethiopian political activist previously charged with engaging in terrorist activity.[96] The WGAD noted that the detainee had been arrested and charged immediately following the Ethiopian parliamentary elections, during which he had participated actively to promote Ginbot 7, an opposition party of which he was a founder.[97] The timing, as noted in the Gloria Arroyo case, was highly suggestive of a discriminatory intent.[98] As a result, it ruled that the detention in the first instance by Ethiopian authorities fell within Category II and V.[99] WGAD jurisprudence on the subject, therefore, suggests that evidence of a politically motivated charge or intent to subvert opposing political opinions will be sufficient for a Category V ruling.[100] The WGAD has also willing to infer discrimination on the basis of political opinion in contexts involving widespread political imprisonment or the history between the government and detainee in question.[101]

---

[91] Gloria Macapagal-Arroyo v. The Philippines, WGAD Opinion No. 24/2015, Adopted Sept. 2, 2015, at ¶ 3.

[92] *Id.*, at ¶¶ 4, 14.

[93] *Id.*, at ¶ 14.

[94] *Id.*, at ¶ 43.

[95] *Id.*

[96] Andargachew Tsige v. Ethiopia and Yemen, WGAD Opinion No. 2/2015, Adopted Apr. 20, 2015, at ¶ 4.

[97] *Id.*, at ¶¶ 4, 21.

[98] Gloria Macapagal-Arroyo, at ¶ 43; Francis Xavier Dang Xuan Dieu, et al., at ¶ 60 (noting that the arrests were made proximate to the trial of a prominent human rights activist).

[99] Andargachew Tsige, at ¶ 26.

[100] Francis Xavier Dang Xuan Dieu, et al., at ¶ 67 (noting the erroneous characterization of the applicants' lawful, pro-democracy political opinions as terrorism-inclined. The applicants in this case were journalists, human rights activists, and writers all affiliated with religious organizations.)

[101] Tsegon Gyal v. China, WGAD Opinion No. 4/2017, Adopted Apr. 19, 2017, at ¶ 25.

In another case, *Khalida Jarrar v. Israel*, concerning an elected member of the Palestinian Legislative Council, the WGAD focused its discrimination finding on "political opinion" and not on nationality or ethnic origin.[102] This approach was informed by evidence that the Israeli authorities specifically charged her for her affiliation and active involvement with an illegal organization, including for her activities as a political representative.[103] The WGAD noted that her activism was related to the mistreatment of Palestinians, but notably did not find it necessary to find an additional ground for discrimination.[104] The WGAD did, however, find detention based on Palestinian origin in an earlier case of a child detained for "stone throwing."[105] In that case, the WGAD took into account the history of abuses inflicted by Israeli military forces on Palestinian children in contravention of the *Convention on the Rights of the Child*.[106] The WGAD considered the dispositive ground to be the Palestinian identity of the detainee, and did not impute a political intent onto the crime of "stone throwing."[107]

In a minority of cases, the WGAD has ruled only a Category V violation without also classifying the case in Category II.[108] In *Salem Lani, et al. v. Tunisia*, the WGAD acknowledged that the detainees were targeted for exercising their right to freedom of expression, but declined to perform a Category II analysis.[109] The detainees in that case were arrested for their affiliation with an illegal political movement, and immediately following their participation in a demonstration.[110] The source had not alleged a Category II violation, choosing instead to characterize the detention as discrimination on the basis of the detainee's "political opinion," likely to preempt the Government's argument that the party had been banned for justifiable reasons.[111] Finding in favor of the detainees, the WGAD noted that "there is every indication that (their) membership of the *Ennahda* party is at the very root of the proceedings against them" and without which the applicants would not have been found culpable of the crimes alleged.[112] Both discriminatory intent and effect, the opinion suggests, existed. The Salem Lani case indicates that the casting of Category II claims as a Category V allegation achieves a materially similar aim.

Where a government denies that the detention resulted from discrimination on the basis of political opinion, they must provide evidence with sufficient specificity to prove otherwise. In *Maria Chin Abdullah v. Malaysia*, the Malaysian government argued that the detainee had been arrested not for her political beliefs or activity as a human rights defender, but under section 124(C) of the Penal Code for documents found in her office

---

[102] Khalida Jarrar at ¶ 18. Notably, the source had only alleged discrimination on the "political opinion" ground; however, the Mexico indigenous rights cases demonstrate that the WGAD has found discrimination on a ground not specified in the complaint of its own initiative.

[103] *Id.*, at ¶ 6.

[104] *Id.*, at ¶ 28.

[105] Concerning a Minor Whose Name Is Known to the Working Group v. Israel, WGAD Opinion No. 13/2016, Adopted Apr. 21, 2016, at ¶ 29.

[106] *Id.*, at ¶¶ 26–28.

[107] *Id.*, at ¶ 29.

[108] Mustafa al Hawsawi, at ¶ 87 (concerning the case of a Guantanamo Bay detainee whose activities were not described as a Category II claim).

[109] Salem Lani, et al. v. Tunisia, WGAD Opinion No. 39/2014, Adopted Nov. 18, 2014, at ¶¶ 33, 35.

[110] *Id.*, at ¶¶ 4–5, 26.

[111] *Id.*, at ¶ 26.

[112] *Id.*, at ¶ 33.

that signaled a threat to parliamentary democracy.[113] The WGAD rejected this contention, saying that the Government had submitted no evidence indicating they ever had any reason to believe Abdullah had or had planned to engage in activity that threatened parliamentary democracy.[114] As a result, they accepted the source's characterization of the arrest as one based on Abdullah's political beliefs. Opinions without political content may have in WGAD jurisprudence also been protected on the principle of anti-discrimination and Category V.

Rasha Nemer Jaafar al-Husseini v. *Iraq* was an unusual use of Category V, regarding the mass arrest of the staff and their family members of a former Iraqi Vice President in retaliation for his flight to Kurdistan.[115] Although there was no allegation that the detainees themselves were being persecuted on the basis of their own political opinions, detention on the basis of their affiliation with the former Vice President was found to be arbitrary under Category V, for "discrimination based on political or other opinion aimed at and resulting in ignoring the quality of human beings."[116] Thus, it appears the WGAD was willing to find detention arbitrary when enacted on the basis of the political opinions of a third party. It also emphasized that collective punishment and guilt by association are unacceptable practices, and that "individual criminal responsibility is one of the most fundamental tenets of modern law."[117]

The al-Husseini case would seem to stand for the proposition that actual membership in a political movement is not required for the WGAD to find a Category V violation. However, the WGAD declined to rule that the arrest of eighteen people in *Assem Adawy et al.* v. *Egypt*, on various charges such as "belonging to a banned group," "spreading false news," and "incitement to demonstrate," fell under Category V.[118] Despite the fact that the WGAD found fifteen of the eighteen detainees had been arrested for exercising their freedom of expression, and the source's allegation that the eighteen had been arrested "on the mere suspicion of 'belonging to a political movement,'" the WGAD did not believe they had enough information for a finding of discrimination.[119] They did not clarify whether this lack of information was regarding the "mere suspicion" motive for arrest, or the activities of the detainees. It may be that an arrest based on suspected political opinion is not always an acceptable basis for a Category V finding.

VII Other Opinion

Ma Chunling v. *China* concerned the detention of a practitioner and exponent of Falun Gong, a spiritual and meditative practice considered disruptive to social order by the concerned authorities.[120] Evidence that suggested discrimination included police raids on material she owned on the subject, the content of the interrogations to which she was subject, and the general practice of Chinese authorities of persecuting members of the

---

[113] Maria Chin Abdullah v. Malaysia, WGAD Opinion No. 50/2017, Adopted Aug. 23, 2017, at ¶ 72.

[114] *Id.*, at ¶ 73.

[115] Rasha Nemer Jaafar al-Husseini, et al v. Iraq, WGAD Opinion No. 33/2017, Adopted Apr. 27, 2017, at ¶¶ 31–32.

[116] *Id.*, at ¶ 101.

[117] *Id.*, at ¶ 98.

[118] Assem Adawy, et al. v. Egypt, WGAD Opinion No. 78/2017, Adopted Nov. 22, 2017, at ¶ 72.

[119] *Id.*, at ¶ 55.

[120] Ma Chunling v. China, WGAD Opinion No. 4/2014, Adopted Apr. 22, 2014, at ¶¶ 4, 14.

Falun Gong association.[121] Significantly, the WGAD did not classify the practice or adherence to Falun Gong as a religious conviction and instead connected it with a general Article 19 violation of freedom of opinion and expression.[122] Since the ruling did not specifically mention which ground of Category V was invoked, the discrimination is presumed to be a recognized and protected "other," non-political opinion.[123]

VIII Gender

Gender discrimination is notably recognized as its own ground for a Category V violation. The WGAD ruled on this ground in *Zeinab Jalalian v. Iran*, the case of a Kurdish applicant who actively advocated for women's rights and social causes targeted toward young women in Iraq and Iran.[124] The facts of her detention that evidenced sex discrimination included the nature of her activities, in particular that she was traveling to lecture female high school students in Iran on women's rights when she was first arrested, and the treatment she received while in detention.[125] The applicant was threatened, among other things, with rape and virginity testing.[126] At the time, she was the only female prisoner in Iran sentenced to life imprisonment.[127] Finally, her identity as a Kurdish woman specifically led to the discriminatory treatment she suffered at the hands of Iranian authorities.[128] A Category II violation was also found on the basis of the effect on the applicant's expression, namely her advocacy for social and political reform that would benefit women in society.[129]

IX Sexual Orientation

Discrimination on the basis of sexual orientation is also grounds for a Category V finding, although sources rarely make such allegations. One example is *Cornelius Fonya v. Cameroon*, in which the detainee claimed he was denied equal protection of the law and prosecuted on the basis of his sexual orientation. Cameroon denied this was the case, and told the WGAD they had prosecuted Fonya because his partner was allegedly a minor. However, the relevant court documents directly contradicted this claim, as charges listed did not include the ones Cameroon had specified to the WGAD.[130] In finding a Category V violation, the WGAD also castigated Cameroon for their criminalization of homosexuality, reiterating that detention on the basis of sexual orientation is always arbitrary.[131] The WGAD also found a

[121] *Id.*, at ¶¶ 6–8, 20.
[122] *Id.*, at ¶¶ 22–23.
[123] *Id.*, at ¶ 24.
[124] *Zeinab Jalalian*, at ¶ 4.
[125] *Id.*, at ¶ 37.
[126] *Id.*, at ¶¶ 15, 27.
[127] *Id.*, at ¶ 37.
[128] *Id.*
[129] *Id.*, at ¶ 38.
[130] *Cornelius Fonya v. Cameroon*, WGAD Opinion No. 14/2017, Adopted Apr. 21, 2017, at ¶ 45.
[131] *Id.*, at ¶ 51.

concurrent violation of Category II, claiming that Fonya had not received equal protection of the law as a result of this persecution.[132]

X Disability

The arbitrariness of detention on the basis of disability is emphasized in multiple paragraphs of the WGAD's Basic Principles and Guidelines (and is the only Category V status to receive such attention).[133] A straightforward case of discrimination on the basis of physical disability is *Zaheer Seepersad v. Trinidad and Tobago*, in which a detainee with physical disabilities was confined to a psychiatric facility for an initial period of two months, and a second stretch of sixteen days.[134] This was in spite of the fact that he did not suffer from any mental illness, and the doctor who issued his certificate of confinement had never examined him personally.[135] The WGAD repeated the fact that psychiatric detention is still a deprivation of liberty, and as such due process of law must be followed when imposing it.[136] Furthermore, Seepersad's confinement "was made purely on the basis of his physical impairments," and was therefore discriminatory, bringing his case under Category V.[137]

The WGAD follows the HR Committee approach to disability by including within the ambit of this listed ground mental or intellectual disabilities. The demonstrative case in this regard is *A v. New Zealand*, in which the applicant suffered from longstanding mental health issues, had been housed in preventive detention for a prolonged period, and charged with sexual offenses after a change in criminal law amended culpability rules for persons with mental disability.[138] The WGAD ruled that holding the detainee for a too-prolonged time, after he had fulfilled his sentence, for fear he may reoffend, and without provision of rehabilitative services, was discriminatory and punitive practice based on the applicant's disability.[139] Though governments may have justifiable reasons for detaining disabled persons, this must be based on a careful review and the detained cannot be treated as a convicted prisoner in punitive circumstances.[140]

In *N v. Japan*, the WGAD ruled that the detainee was being imprisoned on the basis of his psychiatric disorder, discrimination which rendered his detention arbitrary under Category V.[141] Although he had been arrested in the act of stealing a soda from a barbecue house, and the WGAD accepted that the police may have been correctly arresting him in flagrante delicto, the subsequent nine months of detention after being transferred to Tokyo Metropolitan Matsuzawa Hospital were arbitrary.[142] As there was no evidence that N had been violent or dangerous to himself or others at the time of his

---

[132] *Id.*, at ¶ 50.
[133] Basic Principles and Guidelines, at ¶¶ 38, 103.
[134] Zaheer Seepersad v. Trinidad and Tobago, WGAD Opinion No. 68/2017, Adopted Nov. 20, 2017, at ¶ 21.
[135] *Id.*, at ¶¶ 24–25.
[136] *Id.*, at ¶ 26.
[137] *Id.*, at ¶ 33.
[138] A v. New Zealand, WGAD Opinion No. 21/2015, Adopted Apr. 29, 2015, at ¶¶ 5–10.
[139] *Id.*, at ¶ 24, 27 (instructing specifically that the conditions for holding the applicant, a disabled person no longer serving his sentence, must differ from those for convicted prisoners).
[140] *Id.*, at ¶ 26.
[141] Mr. N. v. Japan, WGAD Opinion No. 8/2018, Adopted May 23, 2018, at ¶ 44.
[142] *Id.*, at ¶ 42.

arrest, and his transfer to the hospital had no connection to his initial arrest, his detention could have only been on the basis of his disorder.[143]

XI Other Status

The HR Committee has provided some guidance on the interpretation of the "other status" language, which acts as a bar from foreclosing detainees discriminated on an unlisted ground from protection. The HR Committee requires that detainees belong to an "identifiably distinct category" that puts them at risk of discrimination.[144] There has not been guidance, however, on what quality or characteristic will render a group sufficiently identifiable and distinct.[145] The presence of a shared identifying characteristic that is immutable and cannot be concealed or changed, however, would likely meet the requirement for protection.[146]

A Citizenship

The WGAD has found Category V violations on the basis of citizenship status, both when there is discrimination on the basis of one citizenship or on the basis of a detainee being a dual national.

Citizenship status is not specifically mentioned in the text of Category V, but the WGAD has included it under the aegis of "any other status." In two very similar cases, *Abdalrahman Hussein v. Australia* and *Mohammed Naim Amiri v. Australia*, the WGAD examined the detentions of two asylum seekers who, under the High Court of Australia ruling in *Al-Kateb v. Godwin*, were unable to challenge their detentions.[147] *Al-Kateb v. Godwin* ruled that while Australian citizens were able to challenge their administrative detention in court, noncitizens were not. Thus, the WGAD found that the effective lack of remedy for non-citizens in both cases not only violated Articles 16 and 26 of the ICCPR but rendered their detention arbitrary under Category V.[148]

B Family Status

Although the WGAD has not yet issued an opinion under Category V regarding a case of an arbitrary detention emanating from discrimination on the basis of family status, it is only a matter of time before this happens because particularly repressive governments often target the family members of dissidents for persecution and even arbitrary detention.

An especially high-profile example of this kind of discrimination was presented in *Chen Kegui v. China*. Chen was the nephew of the renowned Chinese barefoot lawyer

---

[143] *Id.*, at ¶ 46.
[144] B.d.B, et al. v. The Netherlands, Communication No. 273/1989, Human Rights Committee, A/44/40, Mar. 30, 1989, at ¶ 6.7.
[145] Conte & Burchill, at 172.
[146] *Id.*, at 173 (noting that sex and gender discrimination would meet this requirement, even if not separately provided for).
[147] Abdalrahman Hussein v. Australia, WGAD Opinion No. 28/2017, Adopted Apr. 25, 2017, at ¶ 38; Mohammad Naim Amiri v. Australia, WGAD Opinion No. 42/2017, Adopted Aug. 21, 2017, at ¶ 43.
[148] Abdalrahman Hussein v. Australia, at ¶ 40; Mohammad Naim Amiri v. Australia, at ¶ 45.

Chen Guangcheng, who was the subject of a highly publicized escape from house arrest to the United States Embassy in Beijing in April 2012. After this occurred, local party officials and hired thugs entered the homes of Chen Guangcheng's extended family attacking whomever they found. Chen Kegui was beaten but used a kitchen knife to defend himself. He was later forced to confess to the charge of attempted murder and summarily tried, convicted, and sentenced to three years imprisonment. Having also considered a less than detailed response from the Government, the WGAD found there were "major obstacles to the holding of a fair trial" and that his deprivation of liberty was arbitrary and in violation of Category III.[149]

Additionally, in *Rebii Metin Görgeç v. Turkey*, the WGAD noted the arrest and detention of the wife of the detainee, observing they were both similarly mistreated. It noted with concern the "apparently widespread treatment in Turkey of 'guilt by association'" where family members of suspects were themselves regularly targeted.[150] And it quoted from the Council of Europe Commissioner for Human Rights, who had said "any measure treating family members of a suspect also as potential suspects should not exist in a democratic society, even during a state of emergency."[151]

C Human Rights Defenders

Human rights defenders have assumed a special status within Category V, as they have in Category II (fundamental rights). Within Category II, the WGAD has applied the fundamental right of equal protection of the law to detained human rights defenders, stating that "references to 'political or other opinion' and 'other status' in article 26 of the Covenant include a person's status as a human rights defender."[152] In determining whether someone is a human rights defender, the WGAD often references the *Declaration on Human Rights Defenders*, and takes note of international recognition individuals have received for their human rights work.[153] However, it is important to note that international prominence is not a prerequisite to being considered a human rights defender – the Declaration specifies that every person has the right to promote the protection and realization of human rights at both the national and international level.[154] The WGAD has similarly reiterated that the human rights protections are extended to all, regardless of one's status as an activist.[155]

The WGAD has expanded on this reasoning to address human rights defenders under Category V as an "other status" on which discrimination renders a detention arbitrary. Initially thrown together with political opinion in cases like *Max Bokayev and Talgat*

---

[149] Chen Kegui v. China, WGAD Opinion No. 2/2014, Adopted Apr. 22, 2014 (Litigated by Author through Freedom Now with Co-Counsel Chen Guangcheng).

[150] Rebii Metin Görgeç v. Turkey, WGAD Opinion No. 1/2017, Adopted Apr. 19, 2017, at ¶ 59 (Litigated by Author through Perseus Strategies).

[151] *Id.*, at ¶ 60.

[152] Ny Sokha, et al. v. Cambodia, WGAD Opinion No. 45/2016, Adopted Nov. 21, 2016, at ¶ 44.

[153] Ahmed Mansoor v. United Arab Emirates, WGAD Opinion No. 64/2011, Adopted Nov. 22, 2011, at ¶ 18; Abdolfattah Soltani v. Iran, WGAD Opinion No. 54/2012, Adopted Nov. 19, 2012, at ¶¶ 29–30; Pierre-Claver Mbonimpa, at ¶¶ 24–25.

[154] *Declaration on Human Rights Defenders*, General Assembly, A/RES/53/144, Mar. 8, 1999, at Art. 1.

[155] Nelson Aguiar Ramirez and 78 Others v. Cuba, WGAD Opinion No. 9/2003, Adopted May 9, 2003.

Ayanov v. *Kazakhstan*,[156] many recent Category V cases reference human rights defender as a standalone status. For instance, in *Nguyen Van Dai* v. *Viet Nam* (concerning a human rights defender who conducted community training on legal rights), the WGAD found that his detention was "part of a pattern of persecution for his activities as a human rights defender."[157] In *Narges Mohammadi* v. *Iran*, the WGAD combined the Category II and V analyses to rule that because human rights defender status was protected by Article 26 of the ICCPR, discriminatory arrests based on this status fall under Category V.[158]

D Whistleblowers

In *Paulo Jenaro Diez Gargari* v. *Mexico*, the detainee uncovered cost discrepancies in a government toll road project and requested clarification from the state. This set off a "pattern of harassment," culminating in an arrest for a firearm that had been allegedly planted in the detainee's car. The WGAD found he had been "singled out and subjected to political persecution for his work and the work of his employer." Although it neglected to specify the exact status on which the discrimination was based, the WGAD nevertheless found a Category V violation based on these facts.[159] Practically, this was discrimination against the detainee on the basis of his status as a whistleblower.

---

[156] Max Bokayev and Talgat Ayanov v. Kazakhstan, WGAD Opinion No. 16/2017, Adopted Apr. 21, 2017, at ¶ 56.

[157] Nguyen Van Dai v. Viet Nam, WGAD Opinion No. 26/2017, Adopted Apr. 25, 2017, at ¶ 57.

[158] Narges Mohammadi v. Iran, WGAD Opinion No. 48/2017, Adopted Aug. 22, 2017, at ¶ 50.

[159] Paulo Jenaro Diez Gargari v. Mexico, WGAD Opinion No. 58/2016, Adopted Nov. 25, 2016, at ¶ 20.

9   Detention Not Arbitrary

This chapter examines cases where the WGAD has declined to find the deprivation of liberty of a detainee arbitrary, either by rejecting the source's allegations on the merits, noting that the application failed to comply with the procedures explained in its Methods of Work, or for other reasons. Under its Methods of Work, the WGAD makes a case-specific determination of the arbitrariness of any detention.[1] They present the WGAD with the following options, outside of finding the detention arbitrary as alleged: file the case without an opinion on the nature of detention in cases where a detainee has been released; classify the case as pending until further information is produced; or refer the matter to a more appropriate rapporteur, independent expert, or working group.[2]

I Government's Response Successfully Rebuts Source's Claims or Corroborated by the Record

A detention will be found lawful and not arbitrary if the government's response successfully rebuts the source's claims or is corroborated by other records.[3] The WGAD found the detention lawful in *Mohamed El Ghanam v. Switzerland*, the case of a former military officer detained on three separate occasions and alleged to have been deprived of fair trial rights.[4] This opinion was substantiated by the source's acknowledgment of the lawfulness of detention in its comments on the government's response and by court records showing the detainee did have access to counsel.[5] In *Khaled Kaddar v. Morocco*, the WGAD commented on the specific nature of the Government's responses to vague allegations by the source.[6] The Government's response, deemed sufficient by the WGAD, covered both the particular reasons for arrest, detailed the proceedings at trial, and provided a detailed list of the protections afforded to the detainee at every stage of detention.[7] The WGAD ruled on a softer standard in *Amer Haddara, et al. v. Australia*,

---

[1] *Methods of Work of the Working Group*, Human Rights Council, A/HRC/36/38, July 13, 2017, at ¶ 17; Joseph Antoine Peraldi v. France, WGAD Opinion No. 40/2005, Adopted Nov. 28, 2005, at ¶ 21
[2] Methods of Work, at ¶¶ 17(a), 17(c), and 33(a).
[3] Mahmadruzi Iskandarov v. Tajikistan, WGAD Opinion No. 39/2006, Adopted Nov. 21, 2006, at ¶¶ 17–18.
[4] Mohamed El Ghanem v. Switzerland, WGAD Opinion No. 13/2013, Adopted Aug. 26, 2013, at ¶¶ 4, 15.
[5] *Id.*, at ¶ 30; Oscar Eliecer Paña Navarro, et al. v. Colombia, WGAD Opinion No. 41/1995, Adopted Nov. 30, 1995, at ¶ 5.
[6] Khaled Kaddar v. Morocco, WGAD Opinion No. 68/2012, Adopted Nov. 23, 2012, at ¶ 26.
[7] *Id.*, at ¶¶ 12–24.

taking as sufficient the mere fact that domestic courts had given "serious consideration" to the detainees' arguments.[8]

The standard for what is sufficient for the presentation of a rebuttal of the source's claims can be deduced from other similarly decided cases. In cases where fair trial rights are alleged to have been violated, the government can provide the particulars of trials and appeals, including showing the presence of counsel, opportunity for review, and compliance of proceedings with applicable rules of procedure.[9] In *Severino Puentes Sosa* v. *United States*, the Government enumerated and substantiated the legal and factual bases for denying parole to the detainee and therefore his detention was found to not be arbitrary.[10] In *Antonio José Garcés Loor* v. *Ecuador*, the Government successfully demonstrated that no "substantial procedural formalities" were omitted in the detainee's case.[11] In *Syed Asad Humayun* v. *Saudi Arabia*, the WGAD accepted the claim by the Government that alleged due process lapses, which were viewed at that stage to not have been serious, could still be corrected in the course of proceedings.[12] If the source alleges the detainee is being held in violation of fundamental rights and freedoms, the government may rebut the claim if credible information can be presented detailing the arrest warrant or charges filed against the detainee or by revealing the information on which the decision to detain was made.[13]

II Government Has Complied with International Law

The WGAD has also found, on weighing the particular facts and circumstances of individual cases, that governments have complied with the requirements of international law.[14] For example, in *Paul Ikobonga Lopo* v. *United Kingdom*, the WGAD ruled that the detainee had been provided sufficient opportunities to challenge the administrative detention, the use of which lengthened his detention, and that the refusal of bail in his case had a clear legal basis.[15] In another immigration case, *Vatcharee Pronsivakulchai*

---

[8] Amer Haddara, et al. v. Australia, WGAD Opinion No. 7/2007, Adopted May 9, 2007, at ¶ 26 (noting in that case, however, that the applicants were charged of serious crimes and implied that this merited exceptional treatment. The WGAD nevertheless highlighted its concern that conditions for persons charged with terrorism were severely restrictive).

[9] Dechen Wangmon v. Bhutan, WGAD Opinion No. 40/2011, Adopted Sep. 1, 2011, at ¶ 15; Fouad Lakel v. Algeria, WGAD Opinion No. 28/2007, Adopted Nov. 27, 2007, at ¶ 24; Walid Lamine Tahar Samaali v. Tunisia, WGAD Opinion No. 36/2005, Adopted Sep. 2, 2005, at ¶¶ 14-16; Leonard Peltier v. United States, WGAD Opinion No. 15/2005, Adopted May 26, 2005, at ¶ 10.

[10] Severino Puentes Sosa v. United States, WGAD Opinion No. 31/1999, Adopted Dec. 1, 1999, at ¶¶ 12–17; Georges Ibrahim Abdallah v. France, WGAD Opinion No. 23/2013, Adopted Aug. 28, 2013, at ¶ 26 (regarding denial of parole).

[11] Antonio José Garcés Loor v. Ecuador, WGAD Opinion No. 12/2007, Adopted May 11, 2007, at ¶ 14.

[12] Syed Asad Humayun v. Saudi Arabia, WGAD Opinion No. 44/2006, Adopted Nov. 22, 2006, at ¶ 13; Saddam Hussein al-Tikriti v. Iraq and United States, WGAD Opinion No. 46/2005, Adopted Nov. 30, 2005, at ¶ 37 (ruling that it would be "premature" to rule a violation where ongoing proceedings provided an opportunity to correct due process lapses; in that case, however, the allegations were well-substantiated and the WGAD filed the case as pending).

[13] *Id.*, at ¶¶ 11–12 (government highlighting that the arrest was for engaging in illegal businesses with an unfriendly country rather than for exercise of his right to expression); Tek Nath Rizal v. Bhutan, WGAD Opinion No. 48/1994, Adopted Dec. 1, 1994, at ¶ 18.

[14] Aïcha Dhaouadi, et al. v. Tunisia, WGAD Opinion No. 5/1996, Adopted May 23, 1996, at ¶ 7.

[15] Paul Ikobonga Lopo v. United Kingdom, WGAD Opinion No. 13/2006, Adopted May 11, 2006, at ¶¶ 29–30.

v. *United States*, the WGAD noted the prolonged imprisonment of the detainee was not because of violations of international law by the authorities but rather as a result of her legitimate exercise of challenging the denial of her asylum application through domestic legal proceedings.[16] And in *Mohammed Abdillahi God, et al. v. Djibouti*, the WGAD found the domestic legislation authorizing the detention complied with international norms and that the detainee had both counsel and the opportunity to challenge his detention.[17]

III Exception to Prohibition against Detention Applies

The government may also prevail in cases where it can show that an exception to the prohibition against detention applied.[18] In *Prince Edward Bilbao Pingol, et al. v. The Philippines*, the separation of minors from their parents was ruled lawful since it was based on a determination of likelihood of abuse or neglect that complied with the *Convention on the Rights of the Child*.[19] In addition, the detainees had been placed in an appropriate facility and judicial methods of review of custody were available, though never engaged by the parents.[20] As in this case, the government must show that it complied with and provided the safeguards required by the applicable instrument in the circumstances. In *Viktoria Maligina v. Latvia*, where the detainee was alleged to have been tried after an unduly prolonged time in custody, the WGAD accepted that the seriousness of the crime justified the unusually long duration of pretrial detention.[21] In *Kwon Young-Hil and Yang Kyu-Hun v. South Korea*, however, the Government argued but failed in showing that the detention of a labor activist was justified for reasons of safeguarding public order.[22]

IV Narrow Exception Allowing Preventative Detention When Danger to Community

The WGAD may, in narrow cases, find preventative detention to be justified. In *Gary Maui Isherwood v. New Zealand*, a number of factors strongly in favor of the Government allowed the WGAD to make a very narrow holding permitting the continued detention of a repeat violent sex offender who had served his complete sentence.[23] These factors included the gravity of Isherwood's offense, the likelihood of his committing similar crimes, the unavailability of less restrictive measures, his failure to participate in

---

[16] Vatcharee Pronsivakulchai v. United States, WGAD Opinion No. 35/2007, Adopted Nov. 30, 2006, at ¶ 29; Marco Pasini Beltrán and Carlos Cabal Peniche v. Australia, WGAD Opinion No.15/2001, Adopted Sep. 13, 2001, at ¶ 23.

[17] Mohammed Abdillahi God, et al. v. Djibouti, WGAD Opinion No. 14/2002, Adopted Sep. 13, 2002, at ¶¶ 17–18.

[18] Ahmed Khalaoui v. Tunisia, WGAD Opinion No. 12/1994, Adopted Sept. 28, 1994, at ¶¶ 8–9.

[19] Prince Edward Bilbao Pingol, et al. v. The Philippines, WGAD Opinion No. 5/2012, Adopted May 2, 2012, at ¶ 31.

[20] *Id.*, at ¶¶ 32–33.

[21] Viktoria Maligina v. Latvia, WGAD Opinion No. 6/2005, Adopted May 25, 2005, at ¶ 9; Oscar Eliecer Paña Navarro, et al., at ¶ 5(d).

[22] Kwon Young-Hil and Yang Kyu-Hun v. South Korea, WGAD Opinion No. 25/1996, Adopted Sep. 17, 1996, at ¶¶ 7, 12.

[23] Gary Maui Isherwood v. New Zealand, WGAD Opinion No. 32/2016, Adopted Oct. 7, 2016, at ¶ 63.

rehabilitation efforts, and the regular review of his situation by the New Zealand Parole Board that would guard against the possibility of his detention becoming indefinite.[24]

The WGAD also took into account that his right to liberty was counterbalanced by the public's right to safety and security.[25] They emphasized, however, that "the present case should not be understood as diminishing the right to liberty and that each case must be considered in its own context."[26] *Isherwood* stands in contrast to a prior opinion, *A v. New Zealand*, where a man with severe intellectual disabilities was placed in preventative detention with no plan for his rehabilitation.[27] The WGAD also acknowledged that a minority opinion of the Human Rights Committee (HR Committee) expressed the view that preventative detention, since not based on past acts but the likelihood of future ones, is always per se arbitrary.[28] However, the WGAD ruled consistently with the HR Committee majority, and found that because Isherwood's preventative detention was "genuinely aimed at [his] rehabilitation and reintegration into society," it was not arbitrary.[29]

The WGAD may provide opinions ruling the lawfulness of detention, even in the absence of a comment from the source on the government's rebuttal.[30] As in *Shokrukh Sabirov v. Switzerland*, the case of an Uzbek citizen held on criminal charges, the WGAD may take this approach if it finds itself in a position to decide on the case even without further information from the source.[31] Presumably, the WGAD found the Government's reply sufficient in its detail and content to defeat the original claims.

In another case, *Abdurasul Khudoynazarov v. Uzbekistan*, however, specific rebuttal by the Government was not alone considered sufficient to find the detention lawful.[32] The WGAD noted that the information provided by the Government and source were contradictory on most aspects, and that absent further response from the source, it did not have enough information to pronounce final judgment.[33] The WGAD has also reserved the right to make specific recommendations to the Government even if it found the detention to have not been arbitrary.[34] For instance, in *Pedro Katunda Kambangu v. Lithuania*, the WGAD, despite not finding the detainee's deprivation of liberty in this case arbitrary, nonetheless encouraged the authorities to curb the policy of holding asylum-seekers and migrants indefinitely.[35]

---

[24] *Id.*, at ¶¶ 45, 51, 58, and 60.

[25] *Id.*, at ¶ 50.

[26] *Id.*, at ¶ 54.

[27] *Id.*, at ¶ 55.

[28] *Id.*, at ¶ 62.

[29] *Id.*, at ¶ 63.

[30] Shokhrukh Sabirov v. Switzerland, WGAD Opinion No. 64/2012, Adopted Nov. 22, 2012, at ¶ 13; Konstantinos Georgiou v. Australia, WGAD Opinion No. 25/2007, Adopted Nov. 27, 2007, at ¶ 31; Antonio José Garcés Loor, at ¶ 22; Waynebourne Clive Anthony Bridgewater v. United States, WGAD Opinion No. 2/2001, Adopted May 16, 2001, at ¶¶ 11–12.

[31] Shokhrukh Sabirov, at ¶ 13.

[32] Abdurasul Khudoynazarov v. Uzbekistan, WGAD Opinion No. 34/2012, Adopted Aug. 30, 2012, at ¶¶ 21, 23.

[33] *Id.*, at ¶ 23. The distinguishing feature between this case and *Sahirov* seems to be the "serious difference" between the allegations of the source and the content of the government's response; Kang Jung Sok and Ko Sang Mun v. Democratic People's Republic of Korea, WGAD Opinion No. 29/1995, Adopted Sep. 13, 1995, at ¶ 7.

[34] Methods of Work, at ¶ 17(b).

[35] Pedro Katunda Kambangu v. Lithuania, WGAD Opinion No. 24/2000, Adopted Sept. 14, 2000, at ¶¶ 21–22.

V WGAD Asked to Substitute Itself for Domestic Fact Finder

The WGAD will refuse to find a detention arbitrary when it is asked to substitute itself for a domestic fact finder.[36] As it has explained repeatedly, the WGAD is not a domestic appellate court hearing a case on appeal to evaluate the quality of judgment and review the evidence at the court of first instance.[37] The WGAD reminded the source of this limitation in *Raúl Hernández Abundio v. Mexico*, where it declined to assess if the domestic trial court properly assessed the evidence.[38] In *Olivier Acuña Barba v. Mexico*, the WGAD similarly determined it fell outside its mandate to consider if the domestic court judgment fit the evidence on file.[39] And in *Sidi Fall v. Mauritania*, the WGAD declined to find a violation on the basis of the alleged failure of domestic courts to comply with its rules of procedure.[40] Violations of domestic rules alone, the WGAD explained, did not necessarily amount to a fair trial violation under international law sufficient to render the detention arbitrary.[41]

VI Failure by Source to Properly Argue a Case

Failures by a source to provide sufficient evidence or to assert a violation of international law can result in a finding that a detention is not arbitrary.[42] In *Ziad Abi-Saleh and Jean-Pierre Daccache v. Lebanon*, the WGAD noted that the source, while alleging a violation of international law for use of confession extracted by torture, failed to provide the requisite evidence the torture "actually did take place."[43] And in *Ronnen Hersovici v. Romania*, the source did not provide sufficient information about the decision to place the detainee under house arrest for the WGAD to "state with certainty" that there had been no individualized evaluation of his circumstances.[44] Even absent a successful rebuttal by a government, a source's failure to supply adequate evidence to support an allegation can result in it being rejected.[45] In *Fouad Lakel v. Algeria*, the WGAD noted it

---

[36] Tariq Aziz v. Iraq and United States, WGAD Opinion No. 45/2005, Adopted Nov. 30, 2005, at ¶ 24 (noting that it was not competent to rule on the international humanitarian law aspects of the case); Manuel Flores, et al. v. The Philippines, WGAD Opinion No. 9/2002, Adopted Sep. 11, 2002, at ¶ 11; Olga Rodas, et al. v. Colombia, WGAD Opinion No. 25/1999, Adopted Nov. 26, 1999, at ¶ 5.

[37] Daisuke Mori v. Japan, WGAD Opinion No. 42/2006, Adopted Nov. 21, 2006, at ¶ 33; George Atkinson v. United Arab Emirates, WGAD Opinion No. 16/2002, Adopted Nov. 29, 2002, at ¶ 18; Joseph Antoine Peraldi, at ¶ 22 (explaining that its role is limited to assessing compliance of governments with the relevant rules of international law).

[38] Raúl Hernández Abundio v. Mexico, WGAD Opinion No. 33/2010, Adopted Nov. 25, 2010, at ¶ 11.

[39] Olivier Acuña Barba, at ¶ 16.

[40] Sidi Fall v. Mauritania, WGAD Opinion No. 10/2002, Adopted Sep. 11, 2002, at ¶ 24.

[41] *Id.*, at ¶ 23.

[42] Aleksander Klishin, et al. v. India, WGAD Opinion No. 7/1999, Adopted May 20, 1999, at ¶¶ 11–12; Leonard Peltier, at ¶¶ 8–9; Chinniah Atputharajah and 12 Others v. Sri Lanka, WGAD Opinion No. 21/2001, Adopted Nov. 28, 2001, at ¶ 24(b); Shin Sook Ja, et al. v. Democratic People's Republic of Korea, WGAD Opinion No. 2/1995, adopted May 30, 1995, at ¶ 7.

[43] Ziad Abi-Saleh and Jean-Pierre Daccache v. Lebanon, WGAD Opinion No. 41/1996, Adopted Dec. 3, 1996, at ¶ 8.

[44] Ronnen Herscovici v. Romania, WGAD Opinion No. 17/2018, Adopted Apr. 20, 2018, at ¶ 38.

[45] Olivier Acuña Barba v. Mexico, WGAD Opinion No. 25/2008, Adopted Sep. 10, 2008, at ¶ 19; Salaheddine Bennia, et al. v. Algeria, WGAD Opinion No. 10/2006, Adopted May 11, 2006, at ¶ 9; Mohammad Ahmad El-Khalili v. Iraq, WGAD Opinion No. 4/1995, Adopted May 30, 1995, at ¶ 8.

could not pronounce judgment on apparent mistreatment or torture since the source had failed to make a claim on this point.[46]

VII Failure by Source to Reply to Government's Response

The WGAD will also find in the government's favor if the source fails to adequately refute assertions made in a response by authorities that contradict the original allegations.[47] Where the source fails to repudiate the specific evidence provided by the government on reply, the WGAD will base its opinion on the unchallenged evidence.[48]

VIII Source Contradicts Itself in Reply to Government's Response

The WGAD will also decline to find in a detainee's favor if the source offers material statements that substantially contradict the original claim.[49] In *Ziyuan Ren* v. *China*, the source lodged a complaint against the Government regarding a detainee who was charged with attempting to subvert state authority by publishing a booklet with anti-government sentiments and establishing an organization whose mission was to overthrow the Government.[50] The source alleged a specific violation of the detainee's right to freedom of expression and opinion.[51] However, following the Government's response, the source amended its assertion, now acknowledging the detainee's booklet was never published and arguing the prosecution failed to prove that the offensive organization actually existed.[52] The WGAD found the information provided by the source to be contradictory, noting there was insufficient evidence for it to determine if the detainee's activities were protected by international law.[53]

IX Case Does Not Fall within WGAD's Categories of Arbitrary Deprivation of Liberty

The WGAD may also decide that a detention is not arbitrary by concluding from its own assessment of the facts that the case does not fall within its categories of cases or that the circumstances were not of sufficient gravity to render the detention arbitrary.[54] In *Álvaro Robles Sibaja* v. *Mexico*, the detainee was alleged to have been imprisoned for a time longer than required by domestic law.[55] The WGAD examined the concerned domestic

---

[46] Fouad Lakel, at ¶ 26; Wilfredo Estanislao Saavedra Marreros v. Peru, WGAD Opinion No. 7/1992, Adopted Session No. 4, at ¶ 6(l).

[47] Svetlana Bakhmina v. Russian Federation, WGAD Opinion No. 28/2005, Adopted Aug. 31, 2005, at ¶ 26.

[48] Fouad Lakel, at ¶ 24–25; Azihar Salim v. Maldives, WGAD Opinion No. 11/2004, Adopted May 27, 2004, at ¶ 13.

[49] Syed Asad Humayun, at ¶ 12.

[50] Ziyuan Ren v. China, WGAD Opinion No. 55/2014, Adopted Nov. 21, 2014, at ¶ 6.

[51] *Id.*, at ¶ 11.

[52] *Id.*, at ¶ 27.

[53] *Id.*, at ¶ 28.

[54] Joseph Antoine Peraldi, at ¶ 23 (finding that the trial was not unduly delayed, given the nature of charges); Svetlana Bakhmina, at ¶ 25; Igor Sutyagin v. Russian Federation, WGAD Opinion No. 14/2001, Adopted Sep. 12, 2001, at ¶ 8; Dimitrios Tsironic v. Greece, WGAD Opinion No. 34/1993, Adopted Sep. 29, 1993, at ¶ 6.

[55] Álvaro Robles Sibaja v. Mexico, WGAD Opinion No. 23/2009, Adopted Nov. 22, 2009, at ¶ 5.

rules and found, on the basis of its own reading of the law, that the detention could not be considered arbitrary under any category.[56] The source in *Orlando Alberto Ramirez v. Colombia* had argued the detainee's right to present a defense had been restricted by the domestic court's refusal to allow it to submit supplemental statements or allow for expert testimony to contradict the incriminating evidence.[57] The WGAD found that the right to a defense could not be interpreted as "an absolute right to have all kinds of tests performed," and found the defense had sufficient opportunity to put on its case.[58] The WGAD has also held that the right to defense is not violated by the widely employed practice of holding initial inquires in secret to further preliminary investigations.[59]

In a case involving a minor detained twice by Malaysia, the WGAD reaffirmed that certain violations of the right to a fair trial do not carry such gravity as to render a detention arbitrary.[60] The WGAD had identified the minor's first detention as arbitrary, since he had not been informed of the reasons for his arrest, had not been afforded legal assistance, and was subjected to a practice known as "chain remand" (where individuals are re-arrested by different police officers and held under new remand orders once the initial period has elapsed).[61] But the source also alleged his second detention was also arbitrary, arguing it was unfair that he had been charged with two adults and tried in the Magistrate's Court rather than a special court for children. However, the WGAD noted that although he should have been charged by a juvenile court "the procedures applied by the court and the sentence imposed ... appear to have taken into account the best interests of the minor in accordance with the Convention on the Rights of the Child."[62] As such, the WGAD concluded that his case in the Magistrate's Court did "not amount to a violation of the right to fair trial of such gravity as to render the minor's pretrial detention arbitrary," although in other circumstances trial of a minor in an ordinary court may result in unacceptable violations.[63]

Interestingly, in this case, the opinion was issued despite the WGAD having already concluded that he was not actually being detained in relation to his conviction in the Magistrate's Court. The source had reported that after his conviction the minor was required to wear an electronic monitor, report to police regularly, and obtain written approval before leaving his locality. The WGAD considered its jurisprudential definition of house arrest, which requires "closed premises which the person is not allowed to leave." Although the reporting conditions were restrictive, the minor was not detained in closed premises and was free to come and go. Thus, the WGAD did not consider the minor to be detained.[64] But in accordance with its Working Methods, it nonetheless issued its opinion on the case.

---

[56] *Id.*, at ¶¶ 8–9.
[57] Orlando Alberto Ramirez v. Colombia, WGAD Opinion No. 20/2004, Adopted Nov. 23, 2004, at ¶¶ 11–12.
[58] *Id.*, at ¶ 35; Topchubek Turgunaliev and Timur Stamkulov v. Kyrgyzstan, WGAD Opinion No. 7/1997, Adopted May 15, 1997, at ¶ 9(d) (finding that the trial complied with all relevant international standards for fair trial).
[59] Mikel Egibar Mitxelena v. Spain, WGAD Opinion No. 26/1999, Adopted Nov. 29, 1999, at ¶ 12.
[60] Concerning a Minor Whose Name Is Known to the Working Group v. Malaysia, WGAD Opinion No. 37/2018, Apr. 26, 2018, at ¶ 43.
[61] *Id.*, at ¶¶ 30, 32, 40.
[62] *Id.*, at ¶ 43.
[63] *Id.*
[64] *Id.*, at ¶ 25.

X Detainee Released, Case Filed, but Detention Not Arbitrary

If the detainee has been released, the case will be filed under subsection 17(a) of the Methods of Work.[65] For instance, the WGAD filed without comment the case of twelve North Korean defectors who had been detained by South Korea pending examination of their eligibility for protection. It noted that as of the filing the twelve women had been released and were living as ordinary citizens in South Korea with no physical restrictions.[66] However, the WGAD in some instances may comment on aspects of the case that remain unresolved notwithstanding the detainee's release.[67]

The WGAD may also explain that there were apparent violations of particular rights and clarify what would have constituted lawful conduct in such a situation, without finding for the detainee on any grounds.[68] In *Yuri Korepanov* v. *Uzbekistan*, for example, after filing the case the WGAD explained its concerns about several state practices that appeared to violate standards of due process and liberty of movement.[69] After filing the case in *Michael Moungar* v. *United Kingdom* because the detainee had already been deported, the WGAD said it considered pre-deportation administrative detention in violation of fair trial rights.[70] But the WGAD may refrain from making such observations if the government has, on its own initiative, recognized the need for reform.[71]

Sometimes the WGAD will decide that, notwithstanding the detainee's release and its filing the case, prior detention was not arbitrary. In *William Agyegyam* v. *United Kingdom*, the WGAD found the Government complied with all the relevant legal and procedural guarantees required by international law.[72] The detainee in that case was a Ghanaian citizen who had overstayed his visa and was to be deported to Ghana.[73] He claimed asylum but the application was reviewed and rejected by the appropriate authorities.[74] The WGAD outlined the various stages of his proceedings before

---

[65] Methods of Work of the Working Group, at ¶ 17(a); Abdel Razak al-Mansuri v. Libya, WGAD Opinion No. 8/2006, Adopted May 11, 2006, at ¶ 5 (reminding that this rule grounded in the "paramount objective of the WGAD to obtain the release of persons from detention"); Tawfiq Ahmad Ali Al Sabary v. Saudi Arabia, WGAD Opinion No. 18/2014, Adopted May 1, 2014, at ¶¶ 11–12; Jacob Ostreicher v. Bolivia, WGAD Opinion No. 7/2014, Adopted Apr. 23, 2014, at ¶¶ 19–20; Mohamed Amiri Salimou v. Comoros, WGAD Opinion No. 15/2013, Adopted Aug. 26, 2013, at ¶ 15; Edison Palomino Banguero v. Colombia, WGAD Opinion No. 30/2010, Adopted Nov. 25, 2010, at ¶¶ 9–10.

[66] Concerning 12 Female Defectors of the DPRK v. South Korea, WGAD Opinion No. 13/2017, Adopted Apr. 20, 2017, at ¶ 36.

[67] Abdumavlon Abdurakhmonov v. Uzbekistan, WGAD Opinion No. 40/2013, Adopted Nov. 14, 2013, at ¶ 12, noting that the reasons for the initial arrest remain unclear; Chee Siok Chin v. Singapore, WGAD Opinion No. 10/2010, Adopted May 7, 2010, at ¶ 29 (observing that the domestic law challenged in the instance must conform to international law standards).

[68] Yuri Korepanov v. Uzbekistan, WGAD Opinion No. 30/2013, Adopted Aug. 30, 2013, at ¶¶ 24–26.

[69] Id., at ¶¶ 27–28; Mohammad Abu Alkhair v. Palestinian Authority, WGAD Opinion No. 22/2009, Adopted Nov. 20, 2009, at ¶ 16(a) (finding due process violations notwithstanding eventual release in similar case).

[70] Michael Moungar v. United Kingdom, WGAD Opinion No. 19/2008, Adopted Sep. 10, 2008, at ¶¶ 22–23; Wang Shimai, et al. v. Australia, WGAD Opinion No. 23/2005, Adopted Aug. 29, 2005, at ¶ 5 (recalling previously observed concerns about "potentially indeterminate" administrative detention for migrants).

[71] Ratna Sarumpaet, et al. v. Indonesia, WGAD Opinion No. 21/1998, Adopted Sep. 17, 1998, at ¶ 12; Kwon Young-Hil and Yang Kyu-Hun, at ¶ 11.

[72] William Agyegyam v. United Kingdom, WGAD Opinion No. 28/1999, Adopted Dec. 1, 1999, at ¶ 9.

[73] Id., at ¶ 5.

[74] Id., at ¶ 7.

immigration authorities and found the detainee was not unfairly deprived of any fair trial protections.[75] In most cases, however, the WGAD has filed cases of released detainees without judging the nature of the detention.[76]

In cases involving a group of detainees, the WGAD will differentiate between the circumstances of the different individuals – filing without prejudging the detention of one subclass and providing an opinion on the others.[77] The WGAD employed this analytical approach in *Mohamed Khirat Al-Shatar and 25 others v. Egypt* to distinguish the circumstances of detainees since acquitted and released with those convicted and arbitrarily detained.[78] In *Chen Gang, et al. v. China*, concerning a group of detainees targeted for practicing Falun Gong, the WGAD found Category II violations for unreleased detainees but filed the cases with regard to those no longer in custody.[79] Similarly, in *Salaheddine Bennia, et al. v. Algeria*, the WGAD filed the cases with respect to released detainees while deciding that the allegation regarding the remaining applicant was insufficiently substantiated.[80] Where necessary, the WGAD has also separated distinct periods of detention, and provided its analysis by the information available about each.[81] In *José Gabriel Pastor Vives, et al. v. Peru*, for example, the WGAD found that detention up to a particular date was arbitrary while noting that it did not have sufficient information to rule on the later period.[82] In other cases, where a detainee was released but then rearrested while the WGAD's determination was pending, the case will be filed but a communication will be sent to the government with regards to the new allegations.[83]

XI Case Pending, Issuance of Opinion Deferred

Under its Methods of Work, the WGAD will designate a case as pending a final adjudication should it deem the information provided by the source or government inadequate to support the issuance of an opinion.[84] To be reading for the adoption of an opinion, the

---

[75] *Id.*, at ¶¶ 7, 9.

[76] Ikechukwu Joseph Ojike v. Romania, WGAD Opinion No. 7/2013, Adopted May 1, 2013, at ¶ 14; Kim Young Hwan, et al. v. China, WGAD Opinion No. 51/2012, Adopted Nov. 19, 2012, at ¶ 20; Mubashar Ahmad, et al. v. Pakistan, WGAD Opinion No. 7/2010, Adopted May 6, 2010, at ¶ 4; Abul Kashem Palash v. Bangladesh, WGAD Opinion No. 38/2007, Adopted Nov. 30, 2007, at ¶ 4; Wu Hao v. China, WGAD Opinion No. 41/2006, Adopted Nov. 21, 2006, at ¶ 4.

[77] Mohamed Khirat al-Shatar, et al. v. Egypt, WGAD Opinion No. 27/2008, Adopted Sep. 12, 2008, at ¶ 86; Abla Sa'adat, et al. v. Israel, WGAD Opinion No. 3/2004, Adopted May 25, 2004, at ¶ 35; Aye Tha Aung, et al. v. Myanmar, WGAD Opinion No. 13/2001, Adopted Sept. 12, 2001, at ¶ 13.

[78] Mohamed Khirat Al-Shatar, at ¶ 80; Muhammad Radzi bin Abdu Razak, et al. v. Malaysia, WGAD Opinion No. 10/2004, Adopted May 28, 2004, at ¶ 13 (producing a similarly distinguishing ruling).

[79] Chen Gang, et al. v. China, WGAD Opinion No. 7/2003, Adopted May 9, 2003, at ¶ 33; Francisco Miranda Branco, et al. v. Indonesia, WGAD Opinion No. 36/1996, Adopted Sept. 19, 1996, at ¶ 21.

[80] Salaheddine Bennia, et al., at ¶¶ 8–9; Tariq Aziz, at ¶ 34(b); S. Sellathurai, et al. v. Sri Lanka, WGAD Opinion No. 1/1996, Adopted May 23, 1996, at ¶ 11; Luis Rolo Huamán Morales, et al. v. Peru, WGAD Opinion No. 42/1995, Adopted Nov. 30, 1995, at ¶ 4.

[81] José Gabriel Pastor Vives, et al. v. Peru, WGAD Opinion No. 50/1993, Adopted Sep. 30, 1993, at ¶¶ 5(c), 6(a).

[82] *Id.*, at ¶ 6(a).

[83] José Daniel Ferrer García v. Cuba, WGAD Opinion No. 13/2012, Adopted May 4, 2012, at ¶¶ 15–16.

[84] Methods of Work, at ¶ 17(c); Arsen Klinchaev, et al. v. Ukraine, WGAD Opinion No. 5/2016, Adopted Apr. 19, 2016, at ¶ 26; Lucía Agüero Romero, et al. v. Paraguay, Adopted Aug. 30, 2013, at ¶¶ 34-35; Joseph Kalimbiro Ciusi v. Burundi, WGAD Opinion No. 14/2013, Adopted Aug. 26, 2013, at ¶¶ 83–86; Pastor Gong Shengliang v. China, WGAD Opinion No. 21/2008, Adopted Sep. 10, 2008, at ¶ 30.

information provided must be "sufficiently precise and concordant."[85] The WGAD has generally held a case as pending where the source has failed to clarify material gaps in information that the government's reply suggests are relevant to a final ruling.[86]

In *Marco Antonio de Santiago de Rios* v. *Mexico*, the WGAD considered that the incidents, as described, seemed to lack the requisite severity and did not clearly fall into any applicable category.[87] The source in that case had originally alleged that the detainee had been tortured while arbitrarily detained, but failed to provide accompanying details following the Government's rebuttal of the claims.[88] The WGAD may also enumerate specific questions that the source has failed to answer as it did in *Olexander Oshchepkov* v. *Ukraine*, where it provisionally filed the case.[89] Relevant information may include, but is not limited to, specifying the applicable legislation under which the charge was brought, exceptions that may apply to the case, or updates on judicial proceedings.[90] WGAD country missions, where possible or planned, may also supply any identified gaps in information.[91]

The WGAD left the case pending in *Loknath Acharya* v. *Bhutan and India* due to the extremely limited information available regarding the arrest and detention of a Bhutanese refugee and human rights activist.[92] Although the WGAD was not in a position to conclude his detention fell into any of the five categories, it was unusually directive in trying to give the source a second chance. It invited the source to submit "further information, including affidavits or statements from witnesses, any official documents sent to or from the Governments of Bhutan and India, or any other information that would clarify the circumstances of Acharya's deprivation of liberty."[93] This request for primary evidence is unusual given the WGAD has repeatedly said it will not act as a domestic fact-finder.

This same provision of the Methods of Work has also been referenced in different situations.[94] For example, the WGAD may designate a case as pending if there remains an unresolved discrepancy, inconsistencies, or "serious differences" between the

---

[85] Nurdan Baysahan, et al. v. Turkey, WGAD Opinion No. 20/1998, Adopted Sep. 17, 1998, at ¶ 9; Avni Klinaku, et al. v. Federal Republic of Yugoslavia, WGAD Opinion No. 15/1998, Adopted Sep. 16, 1998, at ¶ 9.

[86] Olexander Oshchepkov v. Ukraine, WGAD Opinion No. 18/2009, Adopted Nov. 19, 2009, at ¶¶ 13–15; Issam Mohammed Saleh al Adwan v. Kuwait, WGAD Opinion No. 3/1997, Adopted May 14, 1997, at ¶ 7; Ghassam Attamleh v. Israel, WGAD Opinion No. 16/1996, Adopted May 23, 1996, at ¶ 6.

[87] Marco Antonio de Santiago de Rios v. Mexico, WGAD Opinion No. 58/2013, Adopted Nov. 22, 2013, at ¶ 18.

[88] *Id.*, at ¶ 17.

[89] Olexander Oshchepkov, at ¶¶ 13, 16; Francisco Caraballo v. Colombia, WGAD Opinion No. 16/2001, Adopted Sep. 13, 2001, at ¶ 15.

[90] Francisco José Cortés Aguilar, et al. v. Bolivia, WGAD Opinion No. 13/2004, Adopted Sept. 15, 2004, at ¶ 21; Lorenzo Páez Núñez v. Cuba, WGAD Opinion No. 18/1998, Adopted Sep. 17, 1998, at ¶ 12.

[91] Sybila Arredondo Guevara v. Peru, WGAD Opinion No. 43/1996, Adopted Dec. 3, 1996, at ¶¶ 7–9 (leaving a final ruling pending until it had conducted a pre-planned visit to Peru to assess the issue of faceless courts); Lori Berenson v. Peru, WGAD Opinion No. 45/1996, Adopted Dec. 3, 1996, at ¶ 5(d); Marìa Elena Loayza Tamayo v. Peru, WGAD Opinion No. 46/1996, Adopted Dec. 3, 1996, at ¶ 5(f); Xanana Gusmao v. Indonesia, WGAD Opinion No. 34/1994, Adopted Sep. 30, 1994, at ¶¶ 12–14.

[92] Loknath Acharya v. Bhutan and India, WGAD Opinion No. 2/2017, Adopted Apr. 19, 2017, at ¶ 21.

[93] *Id.*, at ¶ 24.

[94] Tenzin Choewang, et al. v. China, WGAD Opinion No. 13/2003, Adopted Sept. 4, 2003, at ¶ 24 (serving as an example where the WGAD filed the case given that the whereabouts of one applicant remained unexplained by the government).

information submitted by both parties.[95] In *Alexandr Rafalskiy* v. *Ukraine*, the source and Government referred to different dates for the same instance of detention.[96] Since this information was relevant to the case, given that the detainee was alleged to have been tortured during this period, the WGAD decided to classify the case as pending until the Government submitted further information about the location of the detention.[97] The WGAD may also keep a case pending if, for example, there remains an opportunity for the alleged violation to be corrected. In *Saddam Hussein al-Tikriti* v. *Iraq and United States*, the case of the former Iraqi president, the WGAD decided to remain apprised of further developments in the course of ongoing criminal proceedings to determine if the apparent and concerning procedural flaws persisted.[98] Finally, the WGAD may opt to designate a case as pending if a detainee's whereabouts have not been established and it is unclear whether they have been released or remain in custody.[99]

The WGAD detailed its approach to assessing conflicting information provided by both sides in a communication in *José Daniel Ferrer García* v. *Cuba*.[100] The WGAD explained that opinions are formulated by way of an adversarial system of argumentation, in which both sides provide "credible, reliable and trustworthy information and properly substantiated arguments."[101] By contrast, if the source's allegations and the government's claims in response are vague or contain disparaging remarks about the circumstances of the case rather than specific and detailed responses, the WGAD cannot distill material and sufficient information for a final ruling.[102] In this case, the WGAD reprimanded the source for failing to provide evidence for its allegations and the Government for using its opportunity for a response to accuse the source of slander and acting in bad faith.[103] In *Raúl Hernández Abundio* v. *Mexico*, reliance by the source on witnesses of dubious credibility was ruled insufficient information to support a ruling in favor of the detainee.[104] If for any reason the source communicates its intent to withdraw the case from consideration, the WGAD will file the matter definitively.

In the alternative, the WGAD may choose to file the case under Paragraph 10(f) of its Methods of Work, if it is presented by incomplete or inadequate information by the source, or if the source fails to respond to a request for further information. This provision says that a communication should include "all elements presented by the source that aim to inform the Working Group on the full status of the reported situation . . . ." It then says

---

[95] Alexandr Rafalskiy v. Ukraine, WGAD Opinion No. 16/2009, Adopted Sep. 4, 2009, at ¶ 26; Pastor Gong Shengliang, at ¶ 31; Andrei Ivantoc v. Moldova, WGAD Opinion No. 8/2004, Adopted May 27, 2004, at ¶¶ 16–17; Margarita M. Chuquiure Silva v. Peru, WGAD Opinion No. 34/1996, Adopted Sep. 17, 1996, at ¶ 5(e).

[96] *Id.*

[97] *Id.*, at ¶¶ 27–28.

[98] Saddam Hussein al-Tikriti, at ¶ 37; Aleksandr Nikitin v. Russian Federation, WGAD Opinion No. 14/1997, Adopted Sep. 18, 1997 (finding the WGAD waiting until the trial had been completed so that it could rule on the basis of compiled and final information).

[99] Tenzin Choewang, et al., at ¶ 24; Edward Anton Amaradas, et al. v. Sri Lanka, WGAD Opinion No. 24/2001, Adopted Nov. 29, 2001, at ¶ 10(a); Jampa Ngodrup, et al. v. China, WGAD Opinion No. 65/1993, Adopted Dec. 9, 1993, at ¶¶ 7(ii), 11(b).

[100] José Daniel Ferrer García v. Cuba, WGAD Opinion No. 24/2012, Adopted Aug. 28, 2012, at ¶¶ 20–23.

[101] *Id.*, at ¶ 23.

[102] *Id.*, at ¶ 21(noting that the government in that case characterized the source's allegations as "false and slanderous.")

[103] *Id.*, at ¶¶ 21–22.

[104] Raúl Hernández Abundio, at ¶ 12.

"[a]n absence of information or an absence of a response by the source may lead the Working Group to terminate its consideration of the case."[105]

The WGAD made use of this option in *Olesya Vedj* v. *Moldova*, noting that the detainee had not alleged any violation that would fall into one of the listed categories of detention.[106] The primary allegation in that case was that the detainee had been arrested without sufficient evidence of her involvement in the crime, the assessment of which the WGAD considers outside its mandate.[107] In an adjoining case, *Nikolai Tsipovic* v. *Moldova*, the WGAD similarly filed the case after the source failed to respond to the Government's explanation that the pretrial detention was permitted by domestic law rules on crimes considered particularly serious.[108] In both instances, further detail or clarification would not have changed the WGAD's assessment that the alleged violations would not fall within any of the listed categories.[109] In cases of this kind, therefore, filing the case according to paragraph 10(f) of the Working Methods is preferred to leaving the final determination pending until further, clarifying information is presented.[110]

XII Case Referred to Other UN Special Procedure

Under its Methods of Work, the WGAD can refer the case to another competent and more relevant rapporteur, independent expert, or working group should it find that that body can more appropriately rule on the case.[111] It can also work jointly with another human rights body if the facts of the case fall within the ambit of both.[112]

In *Kingkeo Phongsely* v. *Laos*, the WGAD referred the case of a Laotian activist to the Working Group on Enforced or Involuntary Disappearances.[113] In that case it noted the detainee's continued detention was an "enforced disappearance": she was deprived of her liberty against her will by officials of or supported by the Government and her fate thereafter not disclosed or acknowledged by authorities.[114] Similarly, in *Aránzazu Zulueta Amuchástegui* v. *Spain*, the WGAD observed the conditions of the detainee's detention, which included solitary confinement, and referred the case on its own initiative to the Special Rapporteur on Torture and Other Cruel, Inhuman and Degrading Treatment.[115] The WGAD will also abstain from providing an opinion if it is discovered that the more competent forum is already considering the case.[116]

---

[105] Methods of Work, at ¶ 10(f).

[106] Olesya Vedj v. Moldova, WGAD Opinion No. 12/2015, Adopted Apr. 27, 2015, at ¶ 12.

[107] *Id.*, at ¶ 11.

[108] Nikolai Tsipovic v. Moldova, WGAD Opinion No. 11/2015, Adopted Apr. 27, 2015, at ¶¶ 4, 8.

[109] *Id.*, at ¶ 9; Olesya Vedj, at ¶ 12.

[110] Djuro Kljaic v. Serbia, WGAD Opinion No. 48/2015, Adopted Dec. 3, 2015, at ¶ 19.

[111] Methods of Work, at ¶ 33(a); Sybila Arredondo Guevara, WGAD Opinion No. 4/2000, Adopted May 16, 2000, at ¶ 10, for an earlier case of this kind; Luis Enrique Quinto Facho v. Peru, WGAD Opinion No. 25/1994, Adopted Sep. 29, 1994, at ¶ 6(b).

[112] Methods of Work, at ¶ 33(b).

[113] Kingkeo Phongsely v. Laos, WGAD Opinion No. 51/2011, Adopted Sept. 2, 2011, at ¶ 12.

[114] *Id.*, at ¶ 11. The WGAD employed the definition used by the Working Group on Enforced or Involuntary Disappearances that it thought more appropriately placed to pronounce judgment on the case.

[115] Aránzazu Zulucta Amuchástegui v. Spain, WGAD Opinion No. 36/2015, Adopted Sep. 4, 2015, at ¶ 72.

[116] Shafiq Abd Al-Wahab v. Palestinian Authority, WGAD Opinion No. 16/1998, Adopted Sep. 16, 1998, at ¶¶ 4–5 (referring the case to the Working Group on Enforced or Involuntary Disappearances on discovering the history of the case).

Part IV. Additional Case Studies

10 *Mohamed Nasheed v. The Maldives*

I Introduction

A *Background*

Mohamed Nasheed is a Maldivian environmental activist, renowned journalist, and politician who served as the first democratically elected President of the Maldives from 2008 to 2012. Nasheed made a name for himself as a dissident journalist, regularly reporting on human rights abuses in the Maldives and challenging the authoritarian administration of former President Maumoon Gayoom (1978–2008).[1]

As a result of his activism, the Government has repeatedly targeted Nasheed. From 1991 to 2005, he was arrested at least ten times.[2] In a prior opinion from the mid-1990s, the WGAD found that Nasheed had been arbitrarily detained because of his dissenting political opinion.[3]

In 2003, Nasheed helped establish the Maldivian Democratic Party (MDP), an opposition political party. Five years later, in the country's first-ever multi-party presidential election, Nasheed ran for President on the MDP ticket and won with 54 percent of the popular vote. Under his leadership, the Maldives embarked on significant pro-democracy and human rights reforms. He was also a major climate change activist.[4]

However, Nasheed's reforms were cut short in February 2012 after a coup in which he was forced to resign under threat of violence against him and domestic unrest caused by his political opponents. One of these opponents was Abdulla Yameen, the half-brother of former President Maumoon Gayoom, who would go on to replace Nasheed as president from 2013 to present. Yameen sought to overturn many of Nasheed's reforms and returned the country to even more severe authoritarian rule than that of his half-brother, who later actually broke with Yameen and joined forces with Nasheed to try and restore democracy to the Maldives.[5]

---

[1] Petition to the Working Group on Arbitrary Detention, Freedom Now, Apr. 30, 2015, at 9–12 (Litigated by Author through Freedom Now with Co-Counsel Amal Clooney and Ben Emmerson QC) [hereinafter Nasheed Petition].

[2] Olivia Lang, *'Anni' Heralds New Era in Maldives*, BBC News, Oct. 29, 2018.

[3] Mohamed Nasheed and Mohamed Shafeeq v. The Maldives, WGAD Opinion No. 36/1995, Adopted Nov. 24, 1995.

[4] Nasheed Petition, at 11–12.

[5] *Id.*, at 7 and Mark Lynas, *Mohamed Nasheed's Overthrow is a Blow to the Maldives and Democracy*, THE GUARDIAN, Feb. 22, 2012.

B The Facts of Mohamed Nasheed's Case

1 Underlying Allegations

Almost immediately after his resignation, Nasheed became the target of politically motivated legal proceedings. In November 2012, as the 2013 presidential campaign was heating up, the Government charged Nasheed with the crime of "illegal detention" for his alleged role in the January 2012 arrest and detention of the Chief Judge of the Maldivian Criminal Court, Abdulla Mohamed. The crime of illegal detention carried a maximum sentence of three years' imprisonment.[6]

Nasheed repeatedly and categorically denied the allegations as being fabricated by the Government in an overtly political attempt to silence him and derail his chances of being re-elected. Although Nasheed had ordered the investigation of Judge Abdulla for judicial misconduct, it was the Maldives National Defense Force (MNDF) that was exclusively responsible for the judge's detention. There was no evidence Nasheed ever instructed anybody orally or in writing to arrest or detain Judge Abdulla. The Supreme Court of the Maldives also concurred in this assessment when it attributed the detention of Judge Mohamad to the MNDF, not Nasheed.[7]

In July 2013, the ongoing criminal proceedings against Nasheed were terminated. While Nasheed went on to garner a strong showing of popular support during the 2013 presidential elections, he narrowly lost to Yameen. Despite the election date being arbitrarily postponed on several occasions by the Supreme Court and numerous other irregularities during the voting process, Nasheed accepted the defeat, publicly acknowledging "democracy is a process."[8]

The case against Nasheed remained dormant for about two years after Nasheed's electoral loss. Once the Government realized that Nasheed continued to pose a political threat to Yameen, however, it renewed its campaign against him. On February 16, 2015, the Government dropped the illegal detention charge against Nasheed. But just six days later, in contravention of Maldivian law, the Government replaced the prior charges with new, trumped-up terrorism charges based on the same underlying facts as the 2012 illegal detention case.[9] Specifically, the Government charged Nasheed with "the act or intention of kidnapping or abduction of person(s) or of taking hostage(s)."[10] This charge carried a minimum sentence of ten years.[11]

2 Arrest and Trial

Nasheed was not informed of the charges against him until he was arrested later that same day, on February 22, 2015, pursuant to a defective arrest warrant. Just a day later, on February 23, 2015, the trial against Nasheed commenced.[12]

---

[6] Nasheed Petition, at 12.
[7] *Id.*, at 13–14.
[8] *Id.*, at 14.
[9] *Id.*, at 15.
[10] Prevention of Terrorism Act 1990, No. 10/1990, at § 2(b).
[11] *Id.*, at § 6(b).
[12] Nasheed Petition, at 15–16.

The trial lasted a mere twenty days and was replete with serious violations of domestic and international fair trial rights.[13] For example, Nasheed was physically manhandled by police and then refused adequate medical care, prevented from having access to his lawyers, and denied the opportunity to cross-examine or present his own witnesses.[14] Moreover, the judges handling the case were clearly biased against Nasheed and should have recused themselves, because they were friends and close colleagues of Judge Abdulla, who had provided evidence against Nasheed in the prior illegal arrest case.[15]

The Court's denial of Nasheed's rights was so severe that on March 8, 2015, Nasheed's lawyers were forced to withdraw from the case under the belief that if they continued to represent him they would be violating the applicable rules of professional responsibility requiring counsel to provide an adequate defense. The Court continued on with the trial despite Nasheed's repeated requests to obtain new legal counsel.[16]

After having been denied the opportunity to prepare or present his case, Nasheed was summarily convicted and sentenced to thirteen years in prison on March 13, 2015, based solely on the evidence provided by the Government. This occurred less than three weeks after Nasheed was first arrested and charged.[17]

Nasheed was subsequently placed in solitary confinement until April 27, 2015. He was then arbitrarily transferred into a "maximum security" prison and placed in a cell especially constructed for him next to the prison garbage dump. Throughout his detention, Nasheed was often denied the opportunity to speak to his family and counsel.[18]

On Nasheed's conviction, the Parliament also passed an unconstitutional law banning all prisoners from being members of political parties, which was clearly aimed at preventing Nasheed from leading the MDP. Having been sentenced for terrorism-related crimes, Nasheed was also disqualified from running for political office for the length of his detention plus three additional years.[19]

II Petition to Working Group on Arbitrary Detention

A *The Lead Up to the Petition and Its Submission*

For the domestic proceedings, Nasheed already had an extremely qualified team of Maldivian lawyers working literally around-the-clock in his defense. Their primary focus after his conviction was lodging an appeal, which would be similarly fraught with illegal acts and procedural irregularities by the Government.[20]

In order to elevate his case to the international stage, however, Nasheed decided to hire international counsel to engage with the United Nations, foreign governments, and the international media. On April 7, 2015, his international legal team was announced. It

---

[13] *Id.*, at 45.
[14] *Id.*, at 27, 54.
[15] *Id.*, at 38.
[16] *Id.*, at 43.
[17] *Id.*, at 27.
[18] *Id.*, at 52–53.
[19] *Id.*, at 18.
[20] *Id.*, at 18–19.

consisted of the author, Ben Emmerson QC, a barrister at Matrix Chambers, and Amal Clooney, a barrister at Doughty Street Chambers.[21]

The first task for the international legal team was drafting a petition to the WGAD. At a press conference at the National Press Club in Washington, DC, on April 30, 2015, the author and Clooney announced, alongside Nasheed's wife, Laila Ali, that the petition to the WGAD had been filed.[22]

Included in the Petition was a Request for Urgent Action based on serious concerns about his mistreatment by Maldivian officials. Additionally, there were concerns about Nasheed's existing health conditions, which were exacerbated by inappropriate detention conditions and a lack of adequate medical treatment. Given these circumstances, there was credible reason to believe that Nasheed's health was at risk and every effort should be taken to act quickly to prevent any irreversible harm.[23]

As will be discussed in detail in this chapter, the 55-page, 292-footnote Petition (note, this was prior to the Methods of Work being changed to limit submissions to twenty pages) alleged that the arrest, trial, conviction, and imprisonment of Nasheed constituted an arbitrary deprivation of liberty under Categories I, II, III, and V of the WGAD's categories of cases. Although some of the Government's violations of domestic and international law fell under more than one of these categories, the Petition noted them only in the most relevant category. In particular, the Petition emphasized violations of the rights guaranteed by the *International Covenant on Civil and Political Rights* (ICCPR), to which the Maldives is a state party.[24]

B Category I: Arbitrary Detention

The Petition first alleged that the arbitrary detention of Nasheed was a violation under Category I because there was no legal basis justifying his detention.[25] Specifically, the Petition pointed to two examples supporting this allegation: First, Nasheed was charged under a facially vague anti-terrorism law and second, the Government presented no evidence that Nasheed committed the alleged act of which he was accused, which even if proven, would not satisfy the elements of the charged crime of "terrorism."

The definition of terrorism in the Prevention of Terrorism Act under which Nasheed was charged was contrary to well-established international standards requiring precision in how criminal statutes were drafted. In support of its arguments, the Petition cited to past WGAD precedent that expressed concern about anti-terrorism laws containing an "extremely vague and broad definition of terrorism," because they "bring within their fold the innocent and the suspect alike and thereby increase the risk of arbitrary detention."[26] The Petition also noted that the Human Rights Committee (HR Committee) had

---

[21] Press Release, *President Mohamed Nasheed Announces International Legal Team*, Perseus Strategies, Apr. 7, 2015.

[22] Media Advisory, *Fighting for the Release of Imprisoned Former Maldives President Nasheed Mohamed*, Apr. 30, 2015.

[23] Nasheed Petition, at 3–4.

[24] *Id.*, at 19.

[25] *Revised Fact Sheet No. 26: The Working Group on Arbitrary Detention*, Office of the UN High Commissioner for Human Rights, at pt. IV(B) [hereinafter Fact Sheet No. 26].

[26] *Question of The Human Rights of all Persons Subjected to any Form of Detention or Imprisonment*, Working Group on Arbitrary Detention, E/CN.4/1995/31, Dec. 21, 1994, at ¶ 25(d).

previously found that charging individuals under vague anti-terrorism laws might constitute violations of Articles 9 and 15 of the ICCPR, which guarantee the right to liberty and the principle of legality, respectively.[27]

Among other things, the provision of the Prevention of Terrorism Act that Nasheed was charged with relied on vague concepts such as "terror tactics" and a "political motive," as well as a broad definition of "aiding and abetting" liability. This is particularly concerning since the provision also criminalizes the "intent" to commit allegedly terrorist-like actions.[28] Moreover, the arrest warrant under which Nasheed was arrested generically referred to "terrorism" and did not specify the criminal conduct for which Nasheed was detained. As Nasheed noted during trial, at no point did the Government "fully explain the charges raised against me."[29] Under WGAD and HR Committee precedent, this is a strong showing that there was no legal basis for detaining Nasheed.

In addition, the Petition argued that the Government did not provide evidence that Nasheed ordered the arrest of Judge Abdulla and that even if he did, this action would not have constituted "terrorism" under the law. The Petition cited to a prior opinion of the WGAD that found that two individuals were arbitrarily detained under Category I because they were not informed of the concrete charges against them or the reasons for their detention and no evidence was presented substantiating the alleged crime "except for a vague reference to suspicions of terrorism."[30]

While Nasheed was charged with the "terrorist" act of "kidnapping or abduction of persons or of taking hostage(s)" for allegedly arresting Judge Abdulla, the Government failed to provide any evidence that Nasheed ordered the judge's arrest. In fact, as previously mentioned, there was direct evidence refuting that claim in the form of a Maldivian Supreme Court decision assigning responsibility for the arrest and detention of Judge Abdulla to the MNDF. Moreover, even if Nasheed were involved, the Government failed to provide evidence that the arrest of Judge Abdulla was an act of terrorism under the anti-terrorism law that Nasheed was charged with. There was no evidence supporting the Government's allegations that the arrest of Judge Abdulla, which was conducted in accordance with the law and under suspicions that the judge posed a risk to public safety, constituted an abduction, kidnapping, or taking of hostages under Maldivian law. As a result, there was no factual or legal basis to charge Nasheed with an act of terrorism.[31]

C Category II: Arbitrary Detention

The Petition also alleged that the arbitrary detention of Nasheed was a violation under Category II because he was detained simply for exercising his substantive fundamental rights and freedoms under international law.[32] In particular, the Petition argued that he

---

[27] *Concluding Observations: Ethiopia*, Human Rights Committee, CCPR/C/ETH/CO/1, Aug. 19, 2011, at ¶ 15.

[28] Nasheed Petition, at 20.

[29] Closing Statement Prepared by President Nasheed (Nov. 2018), http://raeesnasheed.com/archives/25236.

[30] Chérif Al Karoui and Hichem Matri v. Kingdom of Saudi Arabia, WGAD Opinion No. 45/2011, Feb. 29, 2012, ¶¶ 11, 55.

[31] Nasheed Petition, at 20–22.

[32] Fact Sheet No. 26, at pt. IV(B).

was detained because he was exercising the following substantive rights under the ICCPR:

- Article 19: "Everyone shall have the right to hold opinions without interference ... [and] [e]veryone shall have the right to freedom of expression ... [that] shall include freedom to seek, receive, and impart information and ideas of all kinds ... "
- Article 22(1): "Everyone shall have the right to freedom of association with others ... "
- Article 25: "Every citizen shall have the right and the opportunity ... [t]o take part in the conduct of public affairs, directly or through freely chosen representatives ... [t]o vote and to be elected at genuine periodic elections ... [and] [t]o have access, on general terms of equality, to public service in his country."[33]

1 Right to Freedom of Opinion and Expression

The Petition argued the Government detained Nasheed as punishment for him exercising his right to freedom of opinion and expression, which is guaranteed by Article 19 of the ICCPR. In support of its arguments, the Petition cited to the HR Committee, which had previously noted that this right is particularly important to members of political opposition groups, like Nasheed, and includes "the right of individuals to criticize or openly and publicly evaluate their Governments without fear of interference or punishment."[34]

The Petition noted several examples of public criticisms Nasheed had made against the Government immediately prior to his arrest and then emphasized how the international community had repeatedly found that the Government's continued persecution of Nasheed was a pretext to curtail his right to freedom of opinion and expression as a frequent public critic of the Government.[35] For instance, the United States Government expressed concern about the arbitrariness of Nasheed's detention, specifically the Government's attempts to curtail his right to free speech and peaceful protest.[36] Critically, in the prior opinion regarding Nasheed's 1995 detention, the WGAD itself noted that the Government's detention of Nasheed was "solely motivated by the will to suppress [his] critical voice" and was therefore "arbitrary since [Nasheed] merely exercised [his] right to freedom of opinion and expression."[37]

While the Petition noted that the right to freedom of opinion and expression is not absolute, it argued that in this particular case the Government had no justification under international law to limit Nasheed's speech.[38]

---

[33] *International Covenant on Civil and Political Rights*, G.A. Res 2200A (XXI), 21 U.N. GAOR Supp. (No. 16), at 52, U.N. Doc. A/6316 (1966), 999 U.N.T.S. 171, entered into force Mar. 23, 1976, at Art. 19, 22, 25 [hereinafter ICCPR].

[34] Marques de Morais v. Angola, Communication No. 1128/2002, Human Rights Committee, CCPR/C/83/D/1128/2002, Mar. 29, 2005, at ¶ 6.7.

[35] Nasheed Petition, at 23–27.

[36] *Statement on Trial of Former President Nasheed in the Maldives*, US Department of State, Mar. 13, 2015.

[37] WGAD Decision No. 36/1995, at ¶ 7.

[38] Nasheed Petition, at 23–27.

2 Right to Freedom of Association

The Petition argued that the Government detained Nasheed as punishment for him exercising his right to freedom of association, which is guaranteed by both Maldivian law[39] and Article 22(1) of the ICCPR.

The Petition's argument was largely similar to the one it made with regards to the right to freedom of opinion and expression, except it further emphasized how Nasheed was specifically detained because he was the leader of the MDP, the most popular opposition political party in the Maldives. According to the Petition, this was particularly obvious by the actions the Government took following Nasheed's conviction. Merely two weeks after Nasheed was convicted, the Government adopted a new law stripping people serving prison sentences of their political party membership, which *de facto* prohibited Nasheed from continuing to serve as leader of the MDP. While this was not directly applicable to the WGAD's examination of whether Nasheed's detention was in response to the exercise of his right to freedom of association, it was relevant to show the Government was engaged in a campaign to discredit his image, suppress his involvement in national politics, and silence his voice.[40]

3 Right to Freedom of Political Participation

The Petition argued that the Government detained Nasheed as punishment for him exercising his right to freedom of political participation, which is guaranteed by Article 25 of the ICCPR. In particular, it emphasized how the Government timed the original charges against Nasheed to coincide with his 2013 presidential campaign and how it then trumped up the charges against Nasheed when it saw he remained politically popular despite the accusations he faced. Moreover, the *de facto* effect of convicting Nasheed of trumped-up terrorism charges was that he was disqualified from running for political office for the length of his detention plus three additional years.[41]

D Category III: Arbitrary Detention

The Petition also alleged that the arbitrary detention of Nasheed was a violation under Category III gross abuses of his fair trial rights.[42] To support this claim, the Petition cited numerous independent international observers who had raised concerns about how Nasheed was charged, arrested, tried, convicted, and detained in a mere twenty days. These included the UN High Commissioner for Human Rights, who called the trial against Nasheed "a rushed process that appears to contravene the Maldives' own laws,"[43] as well as the UN Special Rapporteur on the Independence of Judges and Lawyers, who denounced the Government's "lack of respect for the most basic principles of fair trial

---

[39] CONSTITUTION OF THE REPUBLIC OF MALDIVES (2008), at Art. 30(a).
[40] Nasheed Petition, at 27–28.
[41] *Id.*, at 28–31.
[42] Fact Sheet No. 26, at pt. IV(B).
[43] *Conduct of Trial of Maldives Ex-President Raises Serious Concerns – Zeid*, Office of the UN High Commissioner for Human Rights, Mar. 18, 2015.

and due process during ... Nasheed's criminal proceedings," as "simply unacceptable in any democratic society."[44]

In particular, the Petition claimed that the following due process violations under the ICCPR were so egregious that Nasheed's conviction and detention was arbitrary without even considering the lack of substantive merit or evidentiary support of the Government's claim:

- Article 7: "No one shall be subjected to torture or to cruel, inhuman, or degrading treatment or punishment."
- Article 9(1): "Everyone has the right to liberty and security of person. No one shall be subjected to arbitrary arrest or detention. No one shall be deprived of his liberty except on such grounds and in accordance with such procedure as are established by law."
- Article 14(1): "All persons shall be equal before the courts and tribunals."
- Article 14(1): "[E]veryone shall be entitled to ... a competent, independent, and impartial tribunal established by law."
- Article 14(1): "Everyone shall be entitled to a ... public hearing"
- Article 14(2): "[T]he right to be presumed innocent until proved guilty according to the law."
- Articles 14(3)(b) and 14(3)(d): "[T]o communicate with counsel of his own choosing ... [and] [t]o be tried in his presence and to defend himself in person or through legal assistance of his own choosing."
- Articles 14(3)(b) and 14(3)(e): "To have adequate time and facilities for the preparation of his defence ... [and] to examine, or have examined, the witnesses against him and to obtain the attendance and examination of witnesses on his behalf under the same conditions as witnesses against him."
- Article 14(5): "[T]he right to his conviction and sentence being reviewed by a higher tribunal according to law."[45]

1 Right to Freedom from Cruel, Inhuman, or Degrading Treatment or Punishment

The Petition argued that the Government denied Nasheed the right to be free from cruel, inhuman, or degrading treatment or punishment as guaranteed by Article 7 of the ICCPR. To support its arguments, the Petition cited to other international instruments that note that solitary confinement, deprivation of medical care, and grossly disproportionate sentences, all of which are conditions that Nasheed faced, were violations of international law and could even constitute torture in certain instances.[46]

On multiple occasions and in contravention of Maldivian law,[47] the Government subjected Nasheed to solitary confinement, a "harsh measure" that the UN Special Rapporteur on Torture and Other Cruel, Inhuman or Degrading Treatment or Punishment said could cause "severe mental pain ... [and] amount to torture or cruel inhuman

---

[44] *Maldives: "No Democracy is Possible without Fair and Independent Justice," UN Rights Expert*, Office of the UN High Commissioner for Human Rights, Mar. 19, 2015.

[45] ICCPR, at art. 7, 9, 14.

[46] Nasheed Petition, at 52–53.

[47] Constitution of the Maldives, at Art. 54.

or degrading treatment ... when used as a punishment, during pretrial detention, [or] indefinitely ... "[48] After Nasheed's arrest, the Government transferred him to three different locations and had subjected him to approximately six weeks of 24/7 solitary confinement by the time the Petition was filed.[49] The most recent cell that Nasheed had been moved to was infested with pests, unreasonably small, and had been specially designated for him because of its unsanitary living conditions next to the prison garbage dump. Throughout his time in solitary confinement, Nasheed was allowed to receive only limited visits and his family was regularly denied the right to visit him, despite the Government having previously said they would not be denied.[50]

The Government's cruel, inhuman, and degrading use of solitary confinement against Nasheed was exacerbated by its repeated refusal to provide Nasheed with proper medical care. He faced several physical injuries after police officers used excessive force to drag him into the courtroom on the first day of trial after he tried to speak to the media. Rather than provide him with medical care for injuries its own public officials caused, the Government refused to allow an independent medical doctor who had been sent on behalf of the Maldives Human Rights Commission to examine Nasheed. At the time the Petition was filed, the extent of Nasheed's injuries was still unknown because the Government refused to allow x-rays to be taken.[51]

Additionally, the Petition also noted that the sentence that Nasheed was given amounted to cruel, inhuman, or degrading punishment because it was grossly disproportionate. It referred to a previous WGAD opinion that expressed grave concern over the disproportionality of prison sentences. In that opinion, the WGAD found that a detention could be considered arbitrary if it was based on a prison sentence of "excessive length."[52] This would clearly apply in this case since Nasheed was sentenced to over a decade in prison for only allegedly ordering the arrest and detention of Judge Abdulla. The Petition also referenced a previous European Court of Human Rights (ECtHR) case that found that severe minimum statutory sentences could themselves also be "grossly disproportionate" when they do not permit the sentencing judge to consider mitigating factors including a defendant's lower level of culpability.[53] This would also clearly apply here since the minimum sentence under the anti-terrorism law that Nasheed was charged with was ten years and the law applies the same sentencing regime to a wide variety of offenses of different gravity. Thus, under past WGAD and ECtHR precedent, both Nasheed's individual thirteen-year sentence and the fact that he was deliberately charged under an anti-terrorism law with a strict minimum statutory sentence should be reason to consider that Nasheed faced cruel, inhuman, or degrading punishment.[54]

---

[48] UN *Special Rapporteur on Torture Calls for Prohibition of Solitary Confinement*, Office of the UN High Commissioner for Human Rights, Oct. 18, 2011.

[49] See Email from Petitioner to Sharof Azizov, Working Group on Arbitrary Detention, Office of the UN High Commissioner for Human Rights, May 11, 2015 [hereinafter May 11, 2015 Email from Petitioner].

[50] Nasheed Petition, at 52–53.

[51] Id.

[52] Muhammad Kaboudvand v. Iran, WGAD Opinion No. 48/2012, Adopted Nov. 16, 2012, at ¶ 19.

[53] Soering v. United Kingdom, Application No. 14038/88, European Court of Human Rights, July 7, 1989, at ¶ 104.

[54] Nasheed Petition, at 50.

2 Right to not Be Subjected to Arbitrary Arrest

The Petition argued that the Government denied Nasheed the right to be free from arbitrary arrest as guaranteed by Article 9(1) of the ICCPR. In support of its arguments, the Petition cited to a previous WGAD opinion, in which it concluded that an arrest must be carried out in strict accordance with domestic law, and that at the bare minimum an "arrest without a valid search warrant is illegal, [and] contrary to international standards."[55] Under this standard, Nasheed's arrest was highly irregular and arbitrary because, though a warrant was presented, it was invalid in three ways under Maldivian law.

First, the arrest warrant was issued contrary to Maldivian law because it was issued at the request of the Prosecutor General. Under Maldivian law,[56] the Prosecutor General does not have the power or authority to request an arrest warrant from courts, as this responsibility typically falls only to a criminal investigatory agency like the police.[57]

Second, the arrest warrant was issued contrary to Maldivian law[58] because it was missing critical pieces of key information. The period of detention, the place where Nasheed should be detained, and the time and date when he should be brought to trial were all missing from the original warrant pursuant to which Nasheed was detained. The Court then realized this mistake and to cover up its error issued a second arrest warrant that included this information.[59]

Third, the arrest warrant was issued contrary to Maldivian law[60] because it justified Nasheed's detention without reasonable and probable grounds. The arrest warrant ordered Nasheed to be arrested because he was "likely to abscond to avoid facing terrorism charges."[61] The Petition noted this lacked any reasonable and probable basis because Nasheed had never absconded from Court and he had personally told the Prosecutor General of his intention to appeal in Court. In the over twenty instances that Nasheed had been arbitrarily arrested in the Maldives, not once did he choose to flee the country rather than face the alleged charges against him head on.[62]

Although Nasheed raised all of these procedural irregularities to the Court, it refused to provide a hearing on the sufficiency or legality of the arrest warrant.[63]

3 Right to Equality before the Law

The Petition argued that the Government denied Nasheed the right to be treated equal before the law as guaranteed by Article 14(1) of the ICCPR. In support of its arguments, the Petition cited to the HR Committee, which had previously explained that this right

---

[55] Baylosis, et. al v. The Phillipines, WGAD Opinion No. 5/1993, Apr. 30, 1993, at ¶ 6.
[56] Prosecutor General's Act of 2008, No. 9/2008, at § 15(b).
[57] Nasheed Petition, at 33.
[58] Constitution of the Maldives, at art. 45.
[59] Nasheed Petition, at 33–34.
[60] Constitution of the Maldives, at art. 46.
[61] *Former President Arrested Under Anti-Terrorism Law*, THE GUARDIAN, Feb. 22, 2015.
[62] Nasheed Petition, at 34.
[63] *Id.*

ensures that "the same procedural rights are ... provided to all the parties ... [without] actual disadvantage or other unfairness to the defendant."[64]

The most flagrant violation of this right noted by the Petition was that Nasheed was prevented from presenting any defense witnesses and from cross-examining the prosecution witnesses.[65] In fact, the Court determined, without hearing any of Nasheed's witnesses, that they "would not be able to refute the evidence submitted by the prosecution," and therefore should not be called.[66]

4 Right to a Fair Hearing by an Independent and Impartial Tribunal

The Petition argued that the Government denied Nasheed the right to an independent and impartial tribunal as guaranteed by Article 14(1) of the ICCPR. The Petition emphasized that the WGAD called the right to an independent and impartial tribunal one of the most integral aspects of due process.[67]

The Petition provided several examples of how the Government failed to provide Nasheed a fair hearing by an independent and impartial tribunal. This was manifested in four major ways: (1) the process through which the terrorism charges were filed against Nasheed was unconstitutional; (2) the entire proceeding against Nasheed was politically motivated; (3) many of the actors involved in the judicial process against Nasheed had conflicts of interest; and (4) the Court rendered a verdict wholly contrary to the evidence presented.

First, the process through which the terrorism charges were filed against Nasheed by the Prosecutor General was unconstitutional under Maldivian law and the Court failed to rectify this wrongdoing, which provides strong evidence that the Court was not acting independently. The Prosecutor General does not have the authority to withdraw charges against an individual and then replace them with new charges based on the same set of facts, but this is precisely what was done to Nasheed. Even though the Court knew this, it dismissed the argument without discussion.[68]

Second, the timing of the charges against Nasheed and the unjustifiable haste of the proceedings against him provided a strong indication that all Government actors involved in the case, including the Court, were politically pressured to convict Nasheed. As previously noted, the original arbitrary detention charges against Nasheed were filed to coincide with his 2013 presidential campaign, and the trumped-up terrorism charges against Nasheed were filed shortly after a key coalition partner of Yameen's withdrew from the governing coalition and changed to Nasheed's opposition coalition. In light of the timing of the charges and investigation against Nasheed, many of the decisions made by the judiciary, which were unjustified, unprecedented, and highly prejudicial, clearly seemed to be politically motivated. Among other things, this included conducting the trial in a hasty manner, where Nasheed was denied the opportunity to seek bail, forced to

---

[64] *General Comment No. 32 on Article 14: Right to Equality before Courts and Tribunals and to a Fair Trial*, Human Rights Committee, CCPR/C/GC/32 (2007), at ¶ 13.

[65] Nasheed Petition, at 34–35.

[66] *Synopsis of The Case Report of Proceedings Re: Prosecutor General v. Mohamed Nasheed*, Report No. 145-A/2015/87, Criminal Court of Malé, Republic of Maldives, Mar. 29, 2015, at ¶ 17.

[67] *See, e.g.*, Abdallah Hamoud Al-Twijri, et al. v. Iraq, WGAD Opinion No. 43/2012, Adopted Nov. 14, 2012, at ¶ 46.7.

[68] Nasheed Petition, at 36.

attend evening hearings almost every day with little opportunity to prepare his defense, and restricted to a ten-day period to appeal his conviction.[69]

Third, the serious conflicts of interest shared by many of the actors involved in the judicial proceedings against Nasheed provide additional evidence that he was not provided a fair hearing by an independent and impartial tribunal. The Prosecutor General that filed the charges against Nasheed and two of the three presiding judges in Nasheed's case were present at the time of Judge Abdulla's arrest, which should have been sufficient reason in and of itself for all of them to recuse themselves. In fact, there was even further evidence of the judges' lack of impartiality because the judges submitted witness testimony to the prosecution that was relied on to convict Nasheed, and both referred to Judge Abdulla as their "boss" and a "close friend." Nevertheless, despite this substantial evidence of a clear conflict of interest, the judges denied a recusal request submitted by Nasheed after only twenty minutes of deliberation.[70]

Fourth, in convicting Nasheed of ordering the arrest and detention of the Judge, the Court rendered a verdict wholly contrary to that which an independent and impartial tribunal would have reached based on the evidence available. None of the prosecution witnesses, including Judge Abdulla himself, provided any direct or indirect evidence that Nasheed ordered Judge Abdulla's arrest or detention. And, the only other evidence at trial that implicated Nasheed was based solely on impermissible double hearsay.[71]

5 Right to a Public Trial

The Petition argued that the Government denied Nasheed the right to a public trial as guaranteed by Article 14(1) of the ICCPR.

The Petition explained several examples of the Government's serious disregard for trying Nasheed through a public, transparent process. Contrary to Maldivian law,[72] little notice of the date and time of the trial proceedings was provided to the public. Even when notice was provided, the Court removed several courtroom seats during Nasheed's proceedings so that only a maximum of forty people could attend and, oftentimes, outright denied access to all outside observers. Furthermore, the Court refused requests by both international and domestic human rights groups to monitor the trial proceedings. Without justification, the Court also explicitly denied Nasheed a hearing on the legality of his arrest warrant because it did not want the hearing to be made public as would have been required by law.[73]

6 Right to Presumption of Innocence

The Petition argued that the Government denied Nasheed the right to be presumed innocent as guaranteed by Article 14(2) of the ICCPR. The Petition cited to the HR Committee, which had stated this provision unambiguously guarantees "no guilt can be

---

[69] *Id.*, at 37.
[70] *Id.*, at 38–39.
[71] *Id.*, at 39–40.
[72] Constitution of the Maldives, at Art. 42(a)–42(b).
[73] Nasheed Petition, at 48.

presumed until the charge has been proved beyond a reasonable doubt."[74] The HR Committee has also stated that it is "a duty for all public authorities to refrain from prejudging the outcome of a trial."[75]

Several examples of how the Government had prejudged Nasheed's guilt were noted in the Petition. In particular, it again referenced the fact that the length between Nasheed being arrested and sentenced was a mere twenty days. If a full trial on the facts had occurred it should have taken substantially longer, particularly given the complex nature of terrorism cases and the seriousness of the alleged charges.[76] This was a sentiment echoed by international actors, such as the UN Special Rapporteur on the Independence of Judges and Lawyers, who stated that "the speed of the proceedings combined with the lack of fairness in the procedures lead me to believe the outcome of the trial [against Nasheed] may have been pre-determined."[77]

Further evidence that even the Court itself failed to grant Nasheed the presumption of innocence, in contravention of Maldivian law,[78] is clear from statements made inside and outside the courtroom by the presiding judges. The three-judge panel that convicted Nasheed explicitly admitted that they took Nasheed's past "criminal record" into account to determine his guilt, despite the fact that this "criminal record" was only evidence of past persecution by the Government and had no relevance to the charges Nasheed was currently facing. Additionally, one of the judges tweeted that Nasheed should not be presumed innocent, but instead needs to prove his innocence. This claim not only lacked legal basis, but was particularly outrageous because the Court repeatedly refused to provide Nasheed with the time and adequate resources to present a defense.[79]

7 Right to Access Counsel

The Petition argued that the Government denied Nasheed the right to access counsel as guaranteed by Articles 14(3)(b) and 14(3)(d) of the ICCPR.

From the very first day of proceedings, the Government repeatedly denied Nasheed the opportunity to consult meaningfully with his counsel. His lawyers were denied access to the courtroom during Nasheed's first hearing because the Government claimed that they were required to register with the court two days prior to the hearing, which was a requirement that was impossible to comply with since Nasheed was arbitrarily arrested a day before his first hearing. Contrary to Maldivian law,[80] Nasheed's lawyers were on another occasion not only denied adequate time to prepare his defense but also prevented from consulting with Nasheed and forced to sit in a physically separate location from him. And, on yet another occasion, Nasheed's counsel was arbitrarily and

---

[74] Sarah Joseph & Melissa Castan, The International Covenant on Civil and Political Rights: Cases, Materials, and Commentary 308 (Oxford University Press, 2004).

[75] Id.

[76] Nasheed Petition, at 41–42.

[77] Maldives: "No Democracy is Possible Without Fair and Independent Justice," UN Rights Expert, Office of the UN High Commissioner for Human Rights, Mar. 19, 2015.

[78] Constitution of the Maldives, at Art. 51(h).

[79] Nasheed Petition, at 41–42.

[80] Constitution of the Maldives, at art. 48(b).

unreasonably limited to speaking for only ten minutes even though the prosecution did not face any such limit.[81]

Ultimately, the Government went a step further and outright denied Nasheed legal representation. By effectively making it impossible for Nasheed's lawyers to adequately represent him during the trial, as described earlier in this section, the Government caused Nasheed's lawyers to withdraw from the case. Thereafter, the Government refused Nasheed's requests to obtain new counsel of his own choosing, as well as Nasheed's request to have a court-appointed counsel assigned to represent him. This resulted in the court continuing to hold hearings, including Nasheed's conviction and sentencing, without the presence of defense lawyers. Rather than admit its own errors, in the case summary the Court inexplicably blamed these conditions on Nasheed even though all the facts prove that the Court consistently obstructed the lawyers' ability to defend Nasheed and, therefore, created the conditions that led to Nasheed being left without his original counsel.[82]

8 Right to Prepare an Adequate Defense, Call Witnesses, and Examine Evidence

The Petition argued that the Government denied Nasheed the rights to prepare an adequate defense and call and examine witnesses and evidence as guaranteed by Articles 14(3)(b) and 14(3)(e) of the ICCPR.

First, the Petition focused on how Nasheed was denied adequate time to prepare a defense. Although the HR Committee has noted that adequate time depends on the particular circumstances of each case, it has also stated that at a minimum it must include the right to "act diligently and fearlessly in pursuing all available defenses."[83] Nasheed's lawyers were prevented from acting diligently from the very first hearing that took place one day after Nasheed was arrested, which prevented Nasheed or his lawyers from reviewing the charges and preparing a response. Contrary to Maldivian law, Nasheed was also only given two days to prepare for the second hearing instead of the standard ten days, which is something that occurred in other instances in the mere twenty days that his trial lasted. In fact, as previously mentioned, the lack of adequate time to prepare a defense was one of the primary reasons Nasheed's original counsel was forced to withdraw from the case.[84]

Second, the Petition discussed how Nasheed was denied full access to the evidence against him. For example, in one instance the Government claimed they had a CD containing video and audio recordings of Nasheed ordering Judge Abdulla's arrest, but the CD was not provided to Nasheed's lawyers until the day it was to be shown in Court. This occurred repeatedly throughout Nasheed's trial. And, even when they did receive the evidence, as with the CD, it was corrupted and missing a substantial amount of files

---

[81] Nasheed Petition, at 42–43.
[82] *Id.*
[83] *General Comment No. 13: Article 14 (Administration of Justice) Equality before the Courts and the Right to a Fair and Public Hearing by an Independent Court Established by Law*, Human Rights Committee, HRI/GEN/1/Rev.1, Apr. 13, 1984 at ¶ 11.
[84] Nasheed Petition, at 45.

and did not include any kind of statement or confession that Nasheed ordered Judge Abdulla's arrest as the Government claimed.[85]

Third, the Petition also discussed how Nasheed was prevented from adequately cross-examining Government witnesses, as well as from presenting his own witnesses. Although Nasheed sought to call four witnesses, the Court claimed that they "would not be able to refute the evidence submitted by the prosecution" and refused to call them. This amounted to the Court erroneously assuming Nasheed was guilty before hearing any evidence to the contrary. In fact, the bias of the Court against Nasheed was made clear when it severely curtailed the limited opportunity Nasheed had to examine the Government's witnesses. Not only did the Court improperly remove witness names from the witnesses list in an attempt to undermine the defense but it also prohibited Nasheed's counsel from questioning the credibility of any of the prosecution witnesses.[86]

Additionally, the Petition also referenced two sets of actions taken by the Court that exemplified the utter bias shown against Nasheed with regards to these due process provisions. The first was that Nasheed was consistently denied the right to challenge the improper conduct of the Court because it ignored or dismissed all of Nasheed's requests without much, if any, discussion. The second was that while denying Nasheed's requests to call witnesses, the Court took it on itself to independently call Judge Abdulla as a witness and then relied on that improper evidence to implicate Nasheed.[87]

9 Right to Make a Timely Appeal

The Petition argued that the Government denied Nasheed the right to make a timely appeal of his conviction as guaranteed by Article 14(5) of the ICCPR.

Up until 2015, defendants had up to ninety days to file an appeal under Maldivian law, but immediately prior to Nasheed's arrest the Supreme Court amended the law so that defendants only had ten days to do so. This was an extra-constitutional decision by the Supreme Court. And when Nasheed nevertheless attempted to adhere to the new requirements and informed the Court of his intention to appeal, he was prevented from doing so because the Court failed to provide him with a trial record until after the ten-day appeals deadline had already expired.[88] As the HR Committee has previously recognized, a written trial record is necessary for the effective exercise of the right to appeal.[89] By severely limiting the time in which Nasheed could file an appeal and then making it substantively impossible for Nasheed to meet that unreasonable deadline in the first place, the Government stripped him of his right to make a time appeal, which effectively exhausted Nasheed's domestic remedies to overturn his conviction.

---

[85] *Id.*, at 45–46.
[86] *Id.*
[87] *Id.*
[88] *Id.*, at 48–50.
[89] *See, e.g.*, Van Hulst v. Netherlands, Communication No. 903/1999, Human Rights Committee, CCPR/C/82/D/903/1999, Nov. 1, 1999, at ¶ 6.4.

E Category V: Arbitrary Detention

Finally, the Petition alleged that the arbitrary detention of Nasheed was a violation under Category V because it occurred for reasons of discrimination based on Nasheed's political opinion.[90] However, since there was limited Working Group jurisprudence at the time of submission, and because the argument overlapped significantly with those under Category II, this section merely summarized the claim that Nasheed was politically persecuted.[91]

III Government Response to the Petition

A The Lead Up to the Response and Its Submission

The Government of the Maldives received communication of the submission of the Petition to the WGAD on May 12, 2015.[92] In response to mounting international criticism, the Government publicly hired the London-based consultancy firm Omnia Strategy, founded by Cherie Blair, the wife of former UK Prime Minister Tony Blair, for a reported £420,000.[93] In addition to drafting the Government's Response to the WGAD, Omnia Strategy was tasked with advising the Government on developing a "broader strategy for democracy consolidation." The Government claimed that its choice to hire Omnia Strategy, "underscores the Government's commitment to strengthen democratic institutions of the State and to promote a culture of respect for human rights in the Maldives, adhering to international norms."[94]

Over the next two months, the Government fully engaged in the WGAD process, with its counsel carrying out a two-week "research mission" to evaluate evidence of abuses presented in the Petition. On June 27, 2015, Minister of Foreign Affairs Dunya Maumoon held a press conference with Omnia Strategy in which the Government asserted that the "research mission" revealed that the claims made in the Petition were "baseless."[95] Two days later, the Government sent a letter to the President of the Human Rights Council (HRC) reiterating that Nasheed was afforded an independent and impartial tribunal and that his sentencing was not politically motivated.[96] Finally, on July 10, 2015, the Government submitted its over 100-page, 48-annex Response to the WGAD (again, this was before the Methods of Work were amended to limit submissions to the WGAD to twenty pages).[97]

The morning that its Response was submitted, the Government held another public press conference in which it discussed the major arguments made. In short, the

---

[90] Fact Sheet No. 26, at pt. IV(B).

[91] Nasheed Petition, at 53.

[92] Mohamed Nasheed v. The Maldives, WGAD Opinion No. 33/2015, Adopted Sept. 4, 2015, at 1.

[93] Joint Press Release, MINISTRY OF FOREIGN AFFAIRS AND ATTORNEY GENERAL'S OFFICE, June 17, 2015; Philip Sherwell, *Cherie Blair's Firm Investigated Allegations £10,000 Maldives Payment Came Via Interpol Fugitive*, THE TELEGRAPH, Feb. 19, 2016.

[94] Joint Press Release.

[95] *Omnia Strategy Helping Government Respond to UN Working Group on Arbitrary Detention*, MINIVAN NEWS, June 27, 2015.

[96] Mohamed Nasheed, at ¶ 65.

[97] Reply to the Response of the Government of the Maldives on Behalf of Nasheed, Perseus Strategies, Apr. 11. 2013, at 3.

Government's argument was that (1) Nasheed was "properly charged ... for an extremely serious offense," (2) the Petition "to the [WGAD] seeks to divert the attention from [that] offense," and (3) although there may have been some due process irregularities throughout Nasheed's trial, none "were so serious, either individually or collectively, so as to render ... [his] detention arbitrary."[98] In addition to these general statements, the Response made two procedural arguments and addressed the merits of some of the Category I, II, III, and V violations raised in the Petition.

B Arguments Regarding Procedure

The Response from the Government first argued that there were two major procedural reasons why the WGAD could not reach the merits of the international law violations noted in the Petition:

- Domestic remedies had not been exhausted.
- There was a conflict of interest within Nasheed's legal team.

The next sections discuss the Government's arguments relative to each of these points.

1 Exhaustion of Domestic Remedies

The Response argued that the WGAD must deem the case inadmissible because domestic remedies had not yet been exhausted. Specifically, the Response noted that Nasheed had a right to appeal. Despite the Petition's claim that the Court made it impossible for Nasheed to appeal on time, the Response noted that there were domestic provisions that would allow Nasheed to still file an appeal. According to the Government, a defendant can extend his period to appeal in instances when the Court causes a delay. Nasheed could also file an appeal out of time and then justify the reason for it being filed out of time.[99]

2 Conflict of Interest within Nasheed's Legal Team

The Response argued that the WGAD must deem the case inadmissible because there was a conflict of interest created by the fact that one of the members of Nasheed's legal team, Ben Emmerson, was a UN Special Rapporteur. Specifically, the Response argued that the independence of the WGAD is placed in jeopardy by the fact that Emmerson, who was involved in the submission of the Petition, was part of the same UN Special Procedures system as the WGAD. According to the WGAD's Opinion, the Response claimed that it did not matter that Emmerson was not a member of the WGAD, because the mere fact that he had a UN human rights mandate meant that he "must withdraw [from the case], and that the [Petition] is comprimised entirely and must be dismissed on this basis."[100]

---

[98] Press Conference, *The Government of Maldives Submits Its Response to UN Working Group in the Case Filed by Former President Nasheed*, GENEVA PRESS CLUB, July 10, 2015 [hereafter Government Press Conference].

[99] *Id.*; Mohamed Nasheed, at ¶ 63.

[100] *Id.*, at ¶ 52.

C Arguments Regarding Category I Violations

After making these broader procedural arguments, the Response turned to addressing the specific categories of human rights violations alleged in the Petition. With regards to the Category I violation, the Response argued that Nasheed was "convicted by a Maldivian Court in accordance with Maldivian law," and that, therefore, the WGAD was precluded from hearing his case under Category I. The Response was acting under the assumption that Category I violations cannot be addressed by the WGAD when a domestic court acting in accordance with domestic law convicts an individual.[101]

The Response did not substantively address the Petition's Category I arguments regarding the vagueness of the anti-terrorism law and the charge that an arrest and detention by the military did not constitute "terrorism." Instead, it stated that the WGAD should not consider these issues, because it would not be within the WGAD's jurisdiction to determine whether or not the terrorism charge is rightly characterized under domestic law. It also stated that Nasheed's alleged crime of kidnapping would similarly constitute an offense under terrorism legislation in other respected international judicial systems.[102]

D Arguments Regarding Category II and V Violations

With regards to the Category II and V violations, the Response argued that there was no evidence that the terrorism charge against Nasheed was politically motivated. The Response emphasized that Nasheed was allowed to actively participate in politics throughout the period of the original detention charges and in the period leading up to the conviction on the terrorism charges. Since "[t]he case against ... Nasheed is specifically related to allegations of an individual criminal act, and not to the exercise of his ... freedom of opinion and expression, association, and political participation ... no evidence [exists] of discrimination on the basis of political opinion."[103]

E Arguments Regarding Category III Violations

With regards to the Category III violations, the Response sought to address the merits of many of the alleged ICCPR violations noted in the Petition.

1 Right to Freedom from Cruel, Inhuman, or Degrading Treatment or Punishment

The Response denied that the Government had violated Nasheed's right to freedom from cruel, inhuman, or degrading treatment or punishment. In particular, it asserted that Nasheed was never the "subject of ill-treatment" by attempting to refute the Petition's assertions that he was held in solitary confinement and denied medical care after being the victim of excessive force by the Government.[104]

---

[101] *Id.*, at ¶ 53.
[102] *Id.*
[103] Mohamed Nasheed, at ¶ 53.
[104] *Id.*, at ¶ 64.

The Response argued that, from the Government's perspective, Nasheed was never held in solitary confinement. The Government admitted that it separated Nasheed from other prisoners, but claimed that it did so only to protect Nasheed's safety amid "security concerns" due to him being a former president.[105] And, in any case, it noted that under "exceptional circumstances" international law permits the Government to hold detainees in incommunicado detention for a matter of days.[106] It also made the blanket claim that the facilities Nasheed was held in "far exceed minimum standards."[107]

The Government also disputed the Petition's characterization of Nasheed's injuries and alleged lack of access to medical care. Although it admitted that the Government had used physical force to bring Nasheed into trial, it said that the force was not "excessive" and that Nasheed had been "warned not to speak to the media outside the court."[108] It further justified the physical force used by citing to a Police Integrity Commission review that found that it was proportionate to the situation. And, even if Nasheed did receive injuries from that encounter, the Response emphasized that the Government eventually provided him with some medical care, just not the one of his own choosing.[109]

The Response did not substantively address the Petition's claim that the gross disproportionality of Nasheed's sentence rendered his detention cruel, inhuman, or degrading punishment.

2 Right to not Be Subjected to Arbitrary Arrest

The Response denied that the Government had violated Nasheed's right to not be subjected to arbitrary arrest. Without rebuking the specifics of the Petition's allegations, the Response merely stated that the "initiation of the terrorism charges ... was the result of a detailed investigation" and that the "warrant was lawfully sought and issued, and clearly set out the charges."[110]

Aside from these blanket statements, the Government addressed only one of the three reasons noted by the Petition as to why Nasheed's detention was arbitrary: that there was no reasonable and probable basis for detaining Nasheed and denying him bail. The Government noted that the terrorism charge related to a non-bailable offense. Additionally, it alleged that Nasheed had attempted to flee from judicial proceedings on two previous occasions and that, as a former president, he had "the means and the wherewithal to abscond."[111]

3 Right to Equality before the Law

The Response denied that the Government had violated Nasheed's right to equality before the law. It recognized that "[t]he law cannot be applied selectively," but argued

[105] *Id.*
[106] *Id.*, at ¶ 55.
[107] *Id.*, at ¶ 64.
[108] *Id.*
[109] *Id.*
[110] *Id.*, at ¶ 56.
[111] *Id.*, at ¶ 57.

that it was Nasheed's legal team, not the Government, that was doing so by failing to recognize that Nasheed had been properly convicted in accordance with Maldivian law.[112] It said that Nasheed was consistently "interfering with an independent judiciary and circumventing the rule of law."[113]

4 Right to a Fair Hearing by an Independent and Impartial Tribunal

The Response denied that the Government had violated Nasheed's right to a fair hearing by an independent and impartial tribunal. It only focused on one of the four major arguments made by the Petition concerning this provision: the conflict of interest of the public officials handling the trial. The Response first clarified that the Prosecutor General recused himself from the trial after filing the charges against Nasheed. It then argued that it was irrelevant that two of the presiding judges witnessed the arrest of Judge Abdulla, because they were still not privy in advance to the investigation against Nasheed or to the evidence that the prosecution would present to the Court.[114]

The Response did not substantively address the Petition's claims that Nasheed was charged through an unconstitutional process, that he faced a politically motivated judicial process, and that the verdict rendered by the Court was wholly contrary to the evidence presented.

5 Right to a Public Trial

The Response denied that the Government had violated Nasheed's right to a public trial. It not only justified hearings being held in the evenings as a necessary security measure but also emphasized that on certain occasions members of the public were allowed to observe the proceedings, including human rights organizations like the Bar Human Rights Committee of England (BHRC).[115]

6 Right to Presumption of Innocence

The Response denied that the Government had violated Nasheed's right to the presumption of innocence. Without elaborating further, the Response said it was appropriate for the Court to have taken Nasheed's previous convictions into account in sentencing him on the terrorism charges. It also claimed that none of the statements made by the presiding judges were sufficient to "reverse the burden of proof in violation of the presumption of innocence."[116]

7 Right to Access Counsel

The Response denied that the Government had violated Nasheed's right to access counsel. It noted that Nasheed was originally able to choose a counsel of his own choice

[112] Government Press Conference.
[113] *Id.*
[114] Mohamed Nasheed, at ¶ 61.
[115] *Id.*, at ¶ 62.
[116] *Id.*, at ¶ 60.

and that detailed logs of the facilities indicate that he was able to meet with them on an almost daily basis, even after they chose to withdraw from the case.[117] This is also one of the provisions in which the Government argued that even if there were some violations of Nasheed's due process rights, it "was not of sufficient importance to nullify the proceedings."[118]

8 Right to Prepare an Adequate Defense, Call Witnesses, and Examine Evidence

The Response denied that the Government had violated Nasheed's rights to adequate time to prepare a defense, call witnesses, and examine evidence.

In relation to the right to adequate time to prepare a defense, the Response rejected the argument that twentydays for Nasheed's trial was unjustly hasty. In particular, the Response justified the near daily hearings by arguing that Nasheed knew about the facts of the case against him for over a year in advance because the materials used as the basis of the terrorism charge were the same as those that had been used as the basis for the previous 2012 charge against him. Unlike the Petition, the Response disagreed with the claim that the change in the nature of the legal charge against Nasheed mattered in determining whether Nasheed should have been given more time to prepare a defense.[119]

In relation to both the right to call witnesses and the right to examine evidence, the Response reiterated that the Court had inherent discretion to hear relevant evidence and to refuse to hear witnesses. The Response argued that it was more important to note that Nasheed was given the right to ask the Court to examine evidence and call witnesses, even if all his attempts were refused. It also again placed the blame in large part on Nasheed for failing to specify what issues the proposed defense witnesses would give evidence on.[120]

9 Right to Make a Timely Appeal

The Response denied that the Government had violated Nasheed's right to make a timely appeal. The Government essentially repeated the same arguments it made in the exhaustion of domestic remedies section concerning Nasheed's ability to file an out of time appeal. Moreover, the Response placed the blame on Nasheed rather than the Court for missing the ten-day appeal time window. It claimed that Nasheed delayed the appeals process by initially refusing to sign the trial record he received, without referencing the fact that the trial record provided by the Court was incomplete.[121]

F Additional Updates Provided by the Government

Following the submission of its Response, the Government of the Maldives continued to defend its actions before the international community, which included communicating updates on Nasheed's situation to the WGAD. On August 19, 2015, the Government sent

---

[117] Government Press Conference.
[118] Mohamed Nasheed, at ¶ 58.
[119] Id.
[120] Id., at ¶ 59.
[121] Id., at ¶ 63.

a letter to the WGAD informing them of two major updates: (1) the Prosecutor General had filed an appeal on behalf of Nasheed that included many of the matters raised by the Petition to the WGAD; and (2) Nasheed had been temporarily moved to house arrest for medical examination. The Government claimed that these two actions were "evidence- . . . [of] its commitment to the fundamental rights of its citizens."[122]

IV Reply to the Government's Response

Per the WGAD's Methods of Work, Perseus Strategies filed a 44-page, 263-footnote Reply to the Government's Response on August 19, 2015.[123] The Reply criticized several of the counterarguments made by the Government, but in particular attacked its overall credibility: "[T]he Government of the Maldives is asking the WGAD to disbelieve not only what Nasheed says, but also what every international organization, third-party government, and NGO that has looked at this case has concluded."[124] In further support of this argument, the Reply noted four aspects of the Response that undermined the Government's credibility.

First, the Reply argued that "despite a [Response] of over 100 pages, the Government does not even attempt to refute the evidence of violations of international law."[125] Instead, "the length of the [R]esponse is an attempt to divert attention from the case by telling a much broader and irrelevant story . . . and presenting a negative view of Nasheed's term as President."[126]

Second, the Reply argued that the Response was asking the WGAD to substitute itself as a domestic fact-finder by arguing that Nasheed was actually guilty of the crimes of which he had been charged. While the Reply made clear again its belief that the Government did not provide any evidence that Nasheed ordered or was involved in Judge Abdulla's arrest, it emphasized that determining Nasheed's guilt was "outside the scope of the WGAD's review," which is only "to determine whether or not a person is detained arbitrarily and in violation of international law."[127]

Third, the Reply argued that the majority of the Response relied on blanket statements devoid of concrete evidence. The Response "simply dismisses, without cogent explanation or convincing proof to the contrary, the evidence – confirmed by independent experts – that the prosecution of Nasheed was politically motivated."[128] On the contrary, the Reply argues that the fact that "the [Maldives'] chief prosecutor announced an intention to appeal the conviction that he himself secured" was evidence that even Maldivian authorities recognized the severity of the violations of international law associated with Nasheed's prosecution.[129]

Fourth, the Reply argued that there were several examples of "demonstrably deceptive claims" made by the Government in its Response.[130]

---

[122] *Id.*, at ¶¶ 67–69.
[123] *Id.*, ¶ 70.
[124] Reply to the Government of the Maldives, at 3.
[125] *Id.*
[126] *Id.*, at 4.
[127] *Id.*, at 3.
[128] *Id.*, at 4.
[129] *Id.*, at 3.
[130] *Id.*, at 4.

And finally, the Reply argued that for all the "lip service to human rights and fundamental freedoms" in the Response, "the Government shows scant regard for international human rights law standards."[131] The Reply notes that the Response justified the Government's practice of incommunicado detention, suggested that a judge can "forget" his biases, dismisses the importance of defense counsel being present in court, and diminished the importance of the presumption of innocence.[132]

The following provides further detail on the specific arguments the Reply made to the WGAD in response to the procedural and substantive defenses the Government offered as justification for Nasheed's detention.

A Addressing the Response's Arguments Regarding Procedure

1 Exhaustion of Domestic Remedies

The Reply argued that, contrary to the Government's assertions, the Petition was properly brought before the WGAD, regardless of whether domestic remedies had been exhausted. Although exhaustion of domestic remedies is a requirement for cases brought before the HR Committee and other international human rights mechanisms, this standard is not applicable to the WGAD. According to the Reply, "all of the governing documents for the WGAD reinforce that there is no requirement that local remedies be exhausted," including Fact Sheet No. 26, the WGAD's [then] Revised Methods of Work.[133] Even the WGAD itself has stated that it is necessary that it not be held to the requirement of waiting for exhaustion of domestic remedies because "under its mandate a rapid response is required" to address situations of wrongly detained persons.[134] Therefore, the Reply argued that it does not matter if Nasheed's case had subsequently been appealed domestically.

2 Conflict of Interest within Nasheed's legal team

The Reply also argued that, contrary to the Government's assertions, the presence of a UN Special Rapporteur (Emmerson) within Nasheed's legal team did not pose a conflict of interest for the WGAD. According to the Reply, it is an "outlandish conclusion" to suggest that a Special Rapporteur is prohibited "from maintaining a legal practice focusing on human rights or making an independent submission, in his personal capacity, to another one of the UN Special Procedures [the WGAD]."[135] It emphasized that there are no relevant international standards or codes of conduct that suggest that this is the case, and that if there is some individual allegation of impropriety against Emmerson it would be an issue to raise as a complaint to officials within the HRC, not the WGAD, "whose independence and impartiality is not in question."[136]

---

[131] Id.
[132] Id., at 4–5.
[133] Id., at 41.
[134] Mohamed Dihani v. Morocco, WGAD Opinion No. 19/2013, Adopted Aug. 27, 2013, at ¶ 28.
[135] Reply to the Government of the Maldives, at 42.
[136] Id., at 43.

B Addressing the Response's Arguments Regarding the Merits of the Category I Violations

The Reply reiterated that Nasheed's detention lacked legal basis under Category I because the allegation against Nasheed did not properly constitute an offense under the vague anti-terrorism law under which Nasheed was charged and there was no evidence he carried out the alleged offense in the first place.[137]

The Reply also addressed the two justifications offered by the Government as to why no Category I violations occurred: (1) the argument made by the Response that anti-terrorism laws in other developed legal systems are similarly vague; and (2) the argument made by the Response that the mere fact that Nasheed was charged and convicted under appropriate domestic law meant there was a legal basis for his detention.[138]

In response to the first argument, the Reply remarked that the Government's argument was insufficient because, unlike the other anti-terrorism laws the Response referred to, the law under which Nasheed was charged lacked both an *actus reus* and *mens rea* element. Moreover, at the time that the original 2012 charges against Nasheed were brought, it was acknowledged that ordering Judge Abdulla's arrest did not meet the plain language definition of terrorism under the statute.[139]

In response to the second argument, the Reply emphasized that it was not sufficient for the Government to make conclusory claims that Nasheed had been properly charged under domestic law, but that it "must show" that this is the case, which it did not.[140] Again, by simply pointing to what was presented at Court, "the Government presented no evidence [to the WGAD] that Nasheed ordered the arrest of Judge Abdulla, which is the key issue in the case. Neither the indictment nor the judgment spells out what he allegedly did. What did he order? Who did he issue the order to? When? How?"[141]

C Addressing the Response's Arguments Regarding the Merits of the Category II and V Violations

The Reply reiterated that Nasheed's detention was a patently clear politically motivated attempt to interfere with Nasheed's rights to freedom of opinion and expression, association, and political participation, rendering his detention arbitrary under Categories II and V.[142]

The Reply also addressed the purported justifications offered by the Government in its Response. It noted that the Government was incorrect in stating that a "crime charged must necessarily relate to the exercise of protected fundamental rights."[143] As the WGAD has consistently noted, it looks "behind criminal charges to see if they were, in fact, used as a pretext to limit the exercise of fundamental rights."[144] In this regard, "[a] broad range of independent and international voices . . . support [Nasheed's] claim that the terrorism

---

[137] *Id.*, at 37–40.
[138] *Id.*
[139] *Id.*, at 38.
[140] *Id.*, at 40.
[141] *Id.*, at 29.
[142] *Id.*, at 29–37.
[143] *Id.*, at 29.
[144] *Id.*; *see, e.g.*, Peng Ming v. China, WGAD Opinion No. 43/2005, Adopted Nov. 29 2005.

charge was simply a pretext for his prosecution,"[145] and "the Government's mere blanket details and spurious historical claims do not constitute evidence sufficient in any way to contradict [this]. . . "[146]

D Addressing the Response's Arguments Regarding the Merits of the Category III Violations

The Reply also elaborated on the majority of the due process violations noted in the initial Petition that rendered Nasheed's detention arbitrary under Category III.

1 Right to Equality before the Law

The Reply reiterated that the Government failed to dispute that Nasheed was selectively targeted and that he was not allowed to present any witnesses, which is a flagrant violation of Article 14(1) of the ICCPR.[147]

2 Right to a Fair Hearing by an Independent and Impartial Tribunal

The Reply reiterated that the Government failed to dispute the majority of the violations to the right to a fair hearing by an independent and impartial tribunal under Article 14(1) of the ICCPR noted in the initial Petition. In particular, the unconstitutional process through which the terrorism charges were filed, the politically motivated nature of the proceedings, and the rendering of a verdict against Nasheed wholly contrary to the evidence were allegations not rebutted by the Government, so the Reply asked the WGAD to accept them as fact.[148]

In terms of the allegations that there were clear conflicts of interest by the Prosecutor General and the judges, which the Response also did directly address, the Reply argued that the Government made "significant and deliberate understatement[s]" or "untrue" statements of the involvement of these actors in the case.[149] For example, contrary to what the Government had claimed, the Prosecutor General did not recuse himself from the trial. Although the prosecution team claimed that the Prosecutor General would recuse himself if needed, he never did. Similarly, the Reply emphasizes that "the Government omits to mention that the two judges were not only present at the time of Judge Abdulla's arrest, but they filed witness complaints that were used as evidence in the proceedings against Nasheed . . . "[150] The Response then cites to WGAD jurisprudence that confirms that these conditions give rise to bias and warrant the recusal of the affected actors.[151]

---

[145] *Id.*, at 32.
[146] *Id.*
[147] *Id.*, at 14–15.
[148] *Id.*, at 9–14.
[149] *Id.*, at 11.
[150] *Id.*
[151] *Id.*

3 Right to a Public Trial

The Reply reiterated that the Government violated Nasheed's right to a public trial under Article 14(1) of the ICCPR. In its Response, the Government cites to the presence of some human rights organizations at the trial, like the BHRC, as evidence that substantial portions of the trial were open to the public. However, the Government ignores the report published by the BHRC itself, which noted that the BHRC says it was arbitrarily excluded from the proceedings on one occasion and concluded that "the right to a public hearing cannot properly be said to have been adequately guaranteed in this case . . . given the failure by the court to provide adequate facilities for the attendance of interested members of the public."[152] Even if most of the hearings were technically open to the public, there is still a violation of Nasheed's right to a public trial because the Government failed to provide a "legitimate basis" for the "unduly limited number of individuals who were able to attend proceedings . . . and the exclusion of independent trial monitors from court on more than one occasion."[153]

The Reply also rejected the Government's assertion that the hearings had to be held at night for security reasons. It referred to night hearings as a further blatant attempt to "restrict[] the openness of proceedings to the general public."[154]

4 Right to Presumption of Innocence

The Reply reiterated that the Government violated Nasheed's presumption of innocence under Article 14(2) of the ICCPR by improperly taking Nasheed's past convictions into account when convicting him. Although the Government argues that it is allowed to do so, it "misses the point"[155] because it ignores and fails to "dispute the independent determinations that . . . [these] prior convictions were arbitrary."[156] A government cannot take past convictions into account "when it is established that they are the result of political persecutions."[157] In support of this position, the Reply cited to the HR Committee, which had previously found that the "improper use of previous convictions . . . can violate the presumption of innocence."[158]

5 Right to Access Counsel

The Reply reiterated that the Government violated Nasheed's right to access counsel under Articles 14(3)(b) and 14(3)(d) of the ICCPR. Even though Nasheed was initially able to choose his own counsel, the mere fact that "four out of the ten trial hearings took place without counsel being present," including important hearings like those where bail was discussed and where prosecution evidence was presented, makes it "simply not

[152] Blinne Ní Ghrálaigh, *Trial Observation Report: Prosecution of Mohamed Nasheed, Former President of the Republic of the Maldives*, BAR HUMAN RIGHTS COMM. OF ENGLAND & WALES, Apr. 2015, at 42–43.
[153] *Id.*, at 25.
[154] *Id.*, at 25–26.
[155] *Id.*, at 9.
[156] *Id.*, at 8–9.
[157] *Id.*, at 9.
[158] *See, e.g.*, Koreba v. Belarus, Communication No. 1390/2005, Human Rights Committee, CCPR/C/ 100/ D/1390/2005, Oct. 25, 2010.

possible [for the Government] to argue that the right to counsel was not violated."[159] While the Government "formally stated" that Nasheed could appoint new counsel once his original counsel withdrew, "he was only given 24 hours ... to do so and this made it practically impossible for him to secure new representation," since he was held in prison and had "no way to reach new counsel overnight ... "[160] According to the Reply, the Court just continued with the trial rather than provide more time for Nasheed to get new counsel.[161]

Moreover, even assuming for the sake of argument that the failure to appoint counsel was solely attributable to Nasheed, "this would not relieve the Government of its responsibility to ensure adequate and effective representation by counsel."[162] The HR Committee has previously made clear that the right to access counsel is an obligation incumbent on the state.[163]

6 Right to Prepare an Adequate Defense, Call Witnesses, and Examine Evidence

The Reply reiterated that the Government violated Nasheed's rights to prepare an adequate defense, call witnesses, and examine evidence under Articles 14(3)(b) and 14 (3)(e) of the ICCPR. It also rejected each of the justifications offered by the Government in its Response.[164]

First, the Reply rejected the Government's contention that Nasheed had adequate time to prepare his defense because the evidence used against him was identical to that used in the previous trial against him in 2012. In rebutting this argument, the Reply first noted that the evidence against Nasheed in the 2015 trial was not actually identical, as at least twenty-one documents were entirely new and not relied on in the 2012 trial. Even if the evidence was identical, the Government still failed to provide reasonable time for Nasheed to prepare his defense because the legal basis of the 2015 charges was different than that of the 2012 charges.[165] Under the ICCPR, the right to prepare an adequate defense runs "from the moment the person has been made aware of the charges against him, not merely of the available evidence," which means that additional time must be provided under international law each time a new charge is brought.[166] Providing only one night for Nasheed and his counsel to review more than 1,000 pages of documents, regardless of whether the majority of those documents had been available since the 2012 charges, was not adequate time.[167]

Second, the Reply focused on how the Government did not dispute the arguments made in the Petition regarding the refusal of providing access to evidence. The

[159] Reply to the Government of the Maldives, at 20.
[160] Id., at 24.
[161] Id., at 23–24.
[162] Id., at 24.
[163] See, e.g., Borisenko v. Hungary, Communication No. 852/1999, Human Rights Committee, CCPR/C/75/ D/852/1999, Oct. 14, 2002, at ¶ 7.5.
[164] Reply to the Government of the Maldives, at 15–23.
[165] Id., at 17.
[166] Id.
[167] Id., at 19.

Government disputed neither the fact that the Court refused the request for an adjournment nor the fact that the Court did not disclose video and audio evidence.[168]

Third, the Reply rejected the Government's contention that it was the defense's fault that Nasheed was unable to present witnesses because they did not provide information on what each witness would discuss. In fact, there can be no suggestion that this is the case because the Court itself noted in detail in its Judgment what each "[defense] witness was going to give testimony about in terms that confirmed their relevance to the charges in the case."[169] Moreover, the Government cannot justify that the Court had inherent discretion to limit the right to cross-examine prosecution witnesses because international human rights organizations have emphasized that defendants should have an opportunity to challenge "any aspect of the witness' statement or testimony ... including his or her credibility."[170] Exceptions can be made in exceptional circumstances, but no such circumstances existed in Nasheed's trial.[171]

7 Right to Make a Timely Appeal

The Reply reiterated that the Government's Response never "rebutted the claim" that Nasheed was denied the right to make a timely appeal under Article 14(5), since the justifications the Government offered were based on "incorrect and erroneous material."[172]

Specifically, the Reply disputed the Government's assertions that Maldivian law provided procedures by which Nasheed could extend his appeal deadline or file an out of time appeal, calling these statements "willful misrepresentations of the law in the Maldives."[173]

V The WGAD's Opinion

The WGAD considered Nasheed's case and issued Opinion No. 33/2015 on October 2, 2015.[174] After "extensive submissions" by both the Government and Nasheed's legal team, the WGAD ultimately and in dramatic fashion rejected the Government's counterarguments.[175]

The WGAD accepted that Nasheed's conviction and detention were arbitrary under all four categories argued in the Petition: that there was no legal basis (Category I); that it resulted from the exercise of his rights of freedom of opinion and expression, association, and political participation (Category II); that there were serious due process violations (Category III); and that he was targeted on the basis of his "political opinion" (Category V). The WGAD found that the Government's actions constituted violations of all the

---

[168] *Id.*
[169] *Id.*, at 21.
[170] *Id.*, at 23.
[171] *Id.*
[172] *Id.*, at 28.
[173] *Id.*, at 26.
[174] Mohamed Nasheed, at ¶ 1.
[175] *Id.*, at ¶ 110.

ICCPR articles cited in the Petition, except Article 7 of the ICCPR regarding the use of cruel, inhuman, or unusual punishment.[176]

The WGAD requested that the Government of the Maldives "take the necessary steps to remedy the situation of Mr. Nasheed without delay and bring it into conformity with the [international] standards and principles," which must include the right to political life under Article 25 of the ICCPR.[177] It urged the Government to "release Mr. Nasheed immediately and accord him an enforceable right to compensation."[178]

The next sections provide further detail on what the WGAD's Opinion stated about each of the procedural arguments and due process violations raised in the case.

A *The Government of the Maldives' Procedural Arguments Were Invalid*

1 Exhaustion of Domestic Remedies

The WGAD agreed with the argument made in the Petition regarding the exhaustion of domestic remedies: "[a]s the [WGAD] has previously made clear in its jurisprudence, there is no requirement that domestic remedies be first exhausted."[179]

2 Conflict of Interest within Nasheed's Legal Team

The WGAD agreed with the argument made in the Petition regarding the alleged conflict of interest in Nasheed's legal team: "Given that the [WGAD] has adopted this Opinion by consensus among its five independent members ... no reasonable person could conclude that its independence is compromised by the fact that one of the four [members of Nasheed's legal team] is a Special Rapporteur."[180]

B *The Government of the Maldives' Detention of Nasheed was Arbitrary under Category I*

The Opinion stated, in agreement with the Petition, that Nasheed's detention was arbitrary under Category I because it was "clearly impossible [for the Government] to invoke any legal basis justifying the deprivation of liberty of Mr. Nasheed."[181] The WGAD rejected the Government's contention that there was a legal basis for Nasheed's detention since he was convicted by a domestic court.[182]

The WGAD found that "[i]n simply producing a list of witnesses and evidence in its [R]esponse ... the Government ... failed to rebut the assertion ... that there was no evidence produced at the trial that Mr. Nasheed had ordered Judge Abdulla's arrest."[183] The WGAD also agreed that the Government did not show how the alleged criminal act would have constituted the charged crime: "The [WGAD] considers that the

---

[176] *Id.*
[177] *Id.*, at ¶ 111.
[178] *Id.*, at ¶ 112.
[179] *Id.*, at ¶ 108.
[180] *Id.*, at ¶ 109.
[181] *Id.*, at ¶ 95.
[182] *Id.*, at ¶ 94
[183] *Id.*

Government has not explained how the arrest of Judge Abdulla, which was carried out by the MNDF under an order given by a third party, could constitute terrorism [by Nasheed.]"[184]

C The Government of the Maldives' Detention of Nasheed was Arbitrary under Category II and V

The Opinion stated, in agreement with the Petition, that Nasheed's detention was arbitrary under Category II because it "resulted from the exercise of his right as a political opposition leader to express views contrary to the Government, to associate with his own and other political parties, and to participate in the public life in the Maldives."[185] In other words, the WGAD agreed that the Government had violated Nasheed's rights to freedom of opinion and expression (Article 19), association (Article 22(1)), and political participation (Article 25).[186]

The WGAD pointed to four major factors that, taken together, strongly suggested that Nasheed's conviction was politically motivated. The first was the history of political proceedings brought against Nasheed, including his 1994 detention. The second was the sudden way in which the charges against Nasheed were reinstituted after the Government lost a key coalition partner to Nasheed's political party. The third was the timing of the Government's ban on prisoners being members of political parties merely two weeks after Nasheed was convicted. And the fourth was the fact that the actual effect of the conviction was that Nasheed would be unable to participate in the 2018 elections against Yameen.[187]

D The Government of the Maldives' Detention of Nasheed was Arbitrary under Category III

The Opinion stated, in agreement with the Petition, that Nasheed's detention was arbitrary under Category III because "there were several serious due process violations which, taken together, demonstrate that Mr. Nasheed did not receive a fair trial."[188] Without going into detail, the WGAD found that the Government had violated Nasheed's rights to: not be subjected to arbitrary arrest (Article 9(1)), equality before the law (Article 14(1)), an independent and impartial tribunal (Article 14(1)), a public trial (Article 14(1)), presumption of innocence (Article 14(2)), access counsel (Articles 14(3)(b) and 14(3)(d)), prepare an adequate defense and call witnesses and examine evidence (Articles 14(3)(b) and 14(3)(e)), and make a timely appeal (Article 14(5)).[189]

Although the WGAD did not find that the Government violated Nasheed's right to freedom from being subjected to torture or to cruel, inhuman, or degrading treatment or punishment under Article 7, as the Petition alleged, it expressed serious concern about Nasheed's "physical and psychological integrity" and the conditions under which he had

---

[184] *Id.*
[185] *Id.*, at ¶ 97.
[186] *Id.*, at ¶ 98.
[187] *Id.*, at ¶ 97.
[188] *Id.*, at ¶ 103.
[189] *Id.*, ¶ 104–5.

been treated.[190] In particular, it reminded the Government that the abolition or restriction of solitary confinement as punishment "should be undertaken and encouraged."[191] The WGAD, however, felt it did "not need to refer the matter to the relevant Special Rapporteur for follow up action,"[192] because Nasheed "recently received medical attention while under house arrest, and was recently visited by a delegation from the OHCHR."[193]

In rejecting the Government's Category III counterarguments, the WGAD placed substantial weight on the observations of other international human rights organizations. In particular, it cited statements by other UN bodies, such as an Office of the United Nations High Commissioner for Human Rights press briefing that called Nasheed's trial "vastly unfair... [i]n the absence of an adequate criminal code, evidence law, and criminal procedures,"[194] as well as previous UN reports documenting a history of "reactivation of old cases to arrest opposition members ... "[195] The WGAD strongly emphasized that "[w]hile this information from multiple sources does not bind [it], it is difficult for the Government to credibly contend that Mr. Nasheed's trial met international standards despite [this] overwhelming evidence to the contrary."[196]

VI Resolution

The WGAD's conclusion that Nasheed was arbitrarily detained in violation of international law was a significant blow to the Government, particularly given its high-profile counsel, extensive engagement in the WGAD's proceedings, and its repeated, public denials of having violated Nasheed's most basic human rights. The Opinion secured significant international support, particularly from the United States and Europe, and helped shine a light on the Maldives' deteriorating human rights situation.

In the months following the Opinion, Nasheed's international legal team continued to place substantial political and public relations pressure on the Government. For instance, the author with his co-counsel published multiple op-eds urging the international community to demand Nasheed's release amid his worsening medical condition,[197] released reports requesting that foreign governments impose targeted sanctions on serious human rights abusers in the Maldives,[198] and led an effort to get the US Senate

---

[190] *Id.*, ¶ 106.

[191] *Id.*, ¶ 107.

[192] *Id.*

[193] *Id.*

[194] *Id.*, ¶ 100.

[195] *Id.*, ¶ 101.

[196] *Id.*, ¶ 102.

[197] *See, e.g.*, Jared Genser & Amal Clooney, *The Maldives in Meltdown*, FOREIGN POLICY, Oct. 20, 2015; Jared Genser & Julia Kuperminc, *A Human-Rights Crisis Wracks Paradise*, THE WALL STREET JOURNAL, Dec. 16, 2015; Jared Genser, *In the Maldives, the First Democratically Elected President is Imprisoned While Islamic State Fighters Go Free*, THE WASHINGTON POST, Jan. 17, 2016.

[198] *Moving from Condemnation to Action: The Case for the United States to Impose Targeted Financial Sanctions and Travel Bans on Serious Human Rights Abusers in the Maldives*, Freedom Now, Jan. 11, 2016; *see also Moving from Condemnation to Action: The Case for the European Union to Impose Restrictive Measures on Serious Human Rights Abusers in the Maldives*, Perseus Strategies, Feb. 26, 2018.

to unanimously adopt a resolution asking the Government of the Maldives for Nasheed's freedom.[199]

As a direct result of this burgeoning international pressure, the Government reversed its original position and allowed Nasheed to travel to the United Kingdom in January 2016 for medical leave.[200] At the time, Nasheed suffered from a major spinal injury that had been exacerbated by lack of adequate medical care, and multiple doctors had recommended that he undergo microsurgery on his spine, a procedure that was not available in the Maldives.[201]

After the Government denied his request to have his medical leave extended, and amid clear signs that the Government would place him back in prison as soon as he returned to the Maldives, Nasheed requested asylum in the United Kingdom. In May 2016, Nasheed was granted "political refugee status" by the British government.[202]

But Nasheed's struggles against the Government did not end there, as he continued to fight to have his political rights restored in order to return to the Maldives and challenge President Yameen in the 2018 presidential elections. In October 2016, the author through Perseus Strategies filed a complaint with the HR Committee asking that his rights to run in the country's presidential elections be restored, arguing that his disqualification from running for office emanated from an arbitrary detention and was, therefore, equally arbitrary.[203] After extensive engagement by the Government and responding to its reply, on April 4, 2018, the HR Committee adopted a view agreeing with Nasheed:

> [T]he Committee also observes that the judicial proceedings in which the author was finally sentenced and convicted on charges of terrorism were politically motivated, had serious flaws and violated the right to fair trial ... Accordingly, the Committee considers that, in the circumstances of the author's case, the restrictions of his right to stand for office, as result of the said conviction and sentence, are arbitrary. In light of the foregoing, the Committee considers that the author's rights under article 25 of the Covenant have been violated by the State party.[204]

The HR Committee then specifically urged the Government "to provide an effective and enforceable remedy to Nasheed," such as "restor[ing] his right to stand for office, including the office of President."[205]

On February 1, 2018, the Maldivian Supreme Court ordered that Nasheed and eight other political prisoners be given a retrial and have their current sentences overturned after finding that "prosecutors and judges had been influenced to conduct politically motivated investigations." This ruling sparked brief hope that Nasheed would be able to return to the Maldives and run for office.[206] However, the Government refused to

---

[199] Press Release, *The United States Senate Unanimously Adopts Resolution Urging Injustice of His Conviction without Due Process be Resolved in Strong Rebuke to Maldives Government Demand that Former President Mohamed Nasheed Return to Prison*, Perseus Strategies, Apr. 7, 2016.

[200] Brett Garling, *The Island President Released from Prison to the UK*, Huffington Post, Feb. 1, 2016.

[201] A Human-Rights Crisis Wracks Paradise.

[202] *Nasheed Granted Political Asylum in UK*, Maldives Independent, May 23, 2016.

[203] *Ex-Prez Mohamed Nasheed Knocks UN's Door to Get His Political Rights Restored Before 2018 Presidential Elections*, Focus Maldives, Oct. 8, 2016.

[204] Nasheed v. The Maldives, Communication Nos. 2270/2013 and 2851/2016, Human Rights Committee, CCPR/C/122/D/2851/2016, Apr. 4, 2018, ¶ 8.7.

[205] *Id.*, at ¶¶ 10–11.

[206] *Maldives Court Orders Release and Retrial of Ex-President Mohamed Nasheed*, DW News, Feb. 2, 2018.

comply with either of the rulings by the HR Committee and the country's own Supreme Court. In fact, the Government arrested two of the Supreme Court judges that ordered Nasheed to be released for their decision.[207]

Nasheed remained in exile and continues to be deprived of his political rights. On June 29, 2018, he was forced to concede that he would be practically unable to run in the Maldives' 2018 presidential elections because of the illegal actions taken by the Yameen government.[208] Nasheed's longtime friend and co-founder of the MDP Ibrahim Mohamed Solih was nominated to run for President and on September 23, 2018, Solih beat Yameen in a landslide, with 58 percent of the vote to Yameen's 42 percent.[209] On November 2, President Nasheed returned to The Maldives after two years in exile and was greeted by tens of thousands of supporters, after the Supreme Court suspended his conviction and agreed to review it.[210] And on November 17, President Solih was inaugurated, restoring democracy to The Maldives.

---

[207] Aaquib Khan, *Mohamed Nasheed on the Maldives Crisis*, THE DIPLOMAT, Mar. 28, 2018.

[208] Tweet by Former Maldivian President Mohamed Nasheed (@MohamedNasheed), TWITTER, June 29, 2018, 1:18 am (Nov. 2018), https://twitter.com/MohamedNasheed/status/1012611245147611136.

[209] *Maldives Election: Opposition Defeats China-Backed Abdulla Yameen*, BBC, Sept. 24, 2018.

[210] *The Exiled Ex-President of The Maldives Has Returned in the Wake of His Rival's Election Loss*, ASSOCIATED PRESS, Nov. 2, 2018.

11 *"Balyoz" or Sledgehammer Cases* v. *Turkey*

I Introduction

A *Background*

Since the Republic of Turkey's founding in 1923, its military has been the guarantor of the country's secular values. In accordance with this perceived role, the military has organized several coups, the results of which have been a strained relationship with the country's Islamist civilian governments. The first coup occurred in 1960 with the arrest and execution of then Prime Minister Adnan Menderes by Turkish generals. In 1980, the Turkish military rewrote the constitution to grant itself increased political power. And a coup in 1997, known as the "postmodern" coup, targeted Islamist influence in Turkish society, including the Fethullah Gülen Movement.[1]

The persistent power struggle between Turkey's secular military and Islamist civilian governments came to a head following the rise to power in 2002 of the Justice and Development Party (AKP), headed by Prime Minister Recep Tayyip Erdogan. At the time, the AKP was allied with the Fethullah Gülen Movement (Gülenists). As the ruling party, the AKP faced accusations of exerting authoritarian tendencies for its disregard for due process of law, particularly for its opponents in the armed forces.[2]

One manifestation of this tendency was the *Ergenekon* investigation, launched in 2007 following the AKP's reelection, after Turkish police were anonymously informed of a plot to destabilize the Government and uncovered a crate of grenades in Istanbul. The Government alleged that "Ergenekon" was a clandestine organization responsible for every act of political violence in Turkey in the past thirty years. Although the *Ergenekon* investigation was initially viewed as a welcome effort at uprooting Turkey's national security state, it increasingly became apparent by 2011 that there was a severe lack of due process in the legal investigation. For example, the only evidence tying the over 300 individuals accused with involvement in *Ergenekon* consisted of digital materials and audio recordings that were later shown to be either fraudulent or immaterial. In fact, the only common characteristic among the accused was their political opposition to the AKP and Gülenists.[3]

---

[1] Sledgehammer Petition to the Working Group on Arbitrary Detention, Perseus Strategies, Sept. 12, 2012, at 5.

[2] *Id.*, at 6–7.

[3] *Id.*; Gareth Jenkins, The Ergenekon Releases and Prospects for the Rule of Law in Turkey, THE TURKEY ANALYST, Mar. 12, 2014.

It was in this context of politically motivated prosecutions by the Government, and historic tension between the Turkish armed forces and the civilian governments, that the "Balyoz" or Sledgehammer cases arose.

B The Facts of the "Balyoz" or Sledgehammer Cases

1 Underlying Allegations

On January 21, 2010, *Taraf*, a prominent Turkish newspaper, published an article by reporter Mehmet Baransu detailing an alleged 2003 coup plot to overthrow the Government, code-named "Sledgehammer." Baransu, who was known at *Taraf* for his anti-military exposés, had been anonymously provided with purported coup plans and other documents that alleged substantial numbers of Turkish military officers were directly targeting Erdogan and the AKP. The alleged coup plans included – provoking instability through a military confrontation with Greece; bombing mosques; taking over hospitals and pharmacies; and jailing journalists and politicians. As claimed in the documents, the ultimate goal of the alleged coup was to replace the AKP with a predetermined list of government officials that was acceptable to the military.[4]

In total, the materials provided to Baransu consisted of 2,229 pages of documents, 19 data CDs, and multiple audio recordings. Most of that evidence was extraneous to the alleged coup plot, including the majority of the CDs and about 1,077 document pages that dated back to 1980–1984.[5] Of the materials remaining, supposedly relevant evidence used to substantiate the alleged coup plot, the most important were ten audio recordings and two CDs: CD #11 and CD #17.

The audio recordings were from an actual Turkish military seminar attended by 162 officers in March 2003. The seminar was a training exercise for strengthening military response to hypothetical threats, including a potential Islamist uprising. Although the voice recordings of the seminar were genuine, no evidence substantiated the Government's claim that the seminar was a "dress rehearsal" for a coup. Critically, none of the audio recordings contain mention of the alleged code-name of the coup, *Sledgehammer*, nor did they directly or indirectly reference the crimes or plots alleged. Additionally, reports from observers who monitored the event noted that it was nothing but a typical training exercise.[6]

CD #17 consisted of twenty-two Microsoft Word documents and four Microsoft PowerPoint documents containing the purported core coup materials. CD #11 consisted of approximately 152 relevant files, including all the files found in CD #17. The files on both CDs were unsigned digital documents dated 2002–2003.[7]

There were many issues with the allegedly incriminating files on CD #11 and CD #17 that pointed to the evidence not being authentic. For example, even though the Government claimed that these incriminating files were genuine military documents, a military report concluded that there were no traces of this information on military computers.[8] The CD files were also replete with other errors, such as misspellings of

---

[4] Sledgehammer Petition, at 8.
[5] *Id.*, at 9.
[6] *Id.*, at 8–11.
[7] *Id.*, at 10.
[8] *Id.*, at 25.

officers' names, incorrect military formatting, misstated military ranks, and allegations that officers were present within Turkey on certain dates when there was clear evidence they were not.[9]

In fact, substantial anachronisms throughout the files strongly indicated that the incriminating evidence in the CDs, purportedly last saved in 2002 and 2003, had been forged using a computer that was manually backdated. According to reports by independent forensic experts, approximately sixty-seven Word and Excel documents in CD #11 and CD #17 contained the font "Calibri," a font that did not exist until the 2007 version of Microsoft Office was released in mid-2006. Similarly, at least nine PowerPoint CD files contained references to particular types of XML schemas that did not exist until the 2007 version of Microsoft Office. Additionally, scores of files contained references to names of organizations that existed only after 2002 and 2003. For example, the evidence identifies a list of newspapers that were not established until after 2003, and contains a list of employees at a Turkish military contractor with names of employees who did not begin working there until 2007.[10]

Further anonymous tips in December 2010 and April 2011 led to the collection of additional alleged evidence that prosecutors claim they discovered at the Gölcük Naval Command Base and the home of a retired air force Colonel. This new evidence consisted of a detached hard drive and a thumb drive, which largely contained files identical to those found in CD #11. As with the materials used to substantiate the first round of indictments, there was strong evidence they were forged. Independent forensic experts concluded that the detached hard drive was copied from a computer whose system clock was set back to reflect an earlier time than when it was created and that the thumb drive contained multiple files that could not have been created from 2002 to 2003.[11]

2 Arrests and Trial

On July 6, 2010, a few months after the publication of the *Taraf* article, the Government issued a first round of indictments against 195 Turkish military officers, charged with attempting to overthrow the Government. The primary evidence used to substantiate these indictments were the audio recordings along with CD #11 and CD #17.[12]

Two more rounds of indictments followed over the next year. On June 16, 2011, a second set of indictments charged twenty-eight more individuals. On November 23, 2011, a third set of indictments charged another 143 individuals. These latter two rounds of indictments were based on the evidence collected at the Gölcük Naval Command Base and the retired air force Colonel's home. All of these Defendants were charged with attempting to overthrow the Government.[13]

Meanwhile, the trial commenced on December 16, 2010, at the Istanbul 10th High Criminal Court. The Government proceeded to trial despite being aware of the clear

[9] *Id.*, at 15–17; Dani Rodrik, *Ergenekon and Sledgehammer: Building or Undermining the Rule of Law?* 10 TURKISH POLICY QUARTERLY 99, 101–6 (2011).

[10] Sledgehammer Petition, at 14–17.

[11] *Id.*, at 11–12.

[12] *Id.*, at 2.

[13] *Id.*, at 11–12.

lack of concrete evidence not only substantiating the coup plot but also individually tying the accused military officers to the alleged crime.[14]

By September 2012, there were a total of 365 defendants accused of involvement in the *Sledgehammer* Coup Plot: 363 serving and retired military officers and two civilians.[15] Of these military officers, approximately 250 were arrested and detained for various periods throughout the trial.[16] These officers were detained for periods ranging from fifteen to twenty-three months, and dozens were detained for up to four months pretrial detention.[17]

II Petition to Working Group on Arbitrary Detention

A *The Lead Up to the Petition*

As with the prior *Ergenekon* investigation, the *Sledgehammer* trial was marred from the outset with systemic due process violations, of which the aforementioned arbitrary arrests and detentions were but one component. As will be discussed in depth, the due process violations included the Court denying defendants equal access to witnesses, allowing illegally obtained evidence to be admitted, and failing to adhere to its own procedural requirements.[18]

There was substantial pushback against these violations within Turkey by the defendants' lawyers. On March 26, 2012, the defense lawyers staged a walk out due to unfairness in the legal proceedings. Shortly thereafter, on April 6, 2012, the Istanbul Bar Association presented a letter to the Court in support of the defense lawyers, requesting that a fair trial be held. On April 16, 2012, the defense lawyers also attempted to file a complaint with the Turkish Supreme Board of Judges and Prosecutors claiming their right to defense and a fair trial had been violated. These efforts were ultimately to no avail. On August 6, 2012, the Court again ruled that the arbitrary detention of the defendants would continue.

As it became increasingly apparent that no legal redress was available within Turkey to ensure that the defendants would receive a fair trial, family members of the 250 detainees founded an NGO called *Vardiya Bizde* to advocate for their release. The author was contacted by *Vardiya Bizde* in June 2012 to represent the detainees.

B *Submission of Petition: Category III Arbitrary Detention*

On September 12, 2012, Perseus Strategies filed a 33-page, 142-footnote Petition to the WGAD (this was before the twenty-page limit for submissions) documenting the Government's brazen violations of international law and Turkish law. The Petition was submitted approximately nine days before the Trial concluded on September 21, 2012. The Petition explained that the arbitrary deprivation of liberty fell within Category III

---

[14] *Id.*, at 2.
[15] *Id.*
[16] *Id.*, at 9, 11–12.
[17] *Id.*, at 29.
[18] *Id.*, at 23–27.

because of serious fair trial violations.[19] In particular, the Petition argued that the following violations of Article 14 of the ICCPR rendered the detention arbitrary:[20]

- Article 14(2): "[T]he right to be presumed innocent until proved guilty according to law."
- Article 14(3)(b): "To have adequate time and facilities for the preparation of his defense and to communicate with counsel of his own choosing."
- Article 14(3)(c): "To be tried without undue delay."
- Article 14(3)(e): "To examine, or have examined, the witnesses against him and to obtain the attendance and examination of witnesses on his behalf under the same conditions as witnesses against him."[21]

Ultimately, the Petition requested that the WGAD take two measures in response to these alleged due process violations. The first was to "[d]etermine [that] the Government of Turkey is holding the Defendants in contravention of its international obligations." The second was to "[u]rge the immediate release of the Defendants and an enforceable right of compensation for their arbitrary detention."[22]

1 Right to Presumption of Innocence

The Petition argued that throughout the *Sledgehammer* trial, the Government did not treat the detainees as innocent until proven guilty as guaranteed by Article 14(2) of the ICCPR. The Petition cited to the Human Rights Committee (HR Committee), which had stated that this provision unambiguously guarantees that "no guilt can be presumed until the charge has been proved beyond a reasonable doubt."[23] The HR Committee had also stated that it is "a duty for all public authorities to refrain from prejudging the outcome of a trial."[24]

The Petition provided several examples depicting how the Government shifted the burden of proof to the detainees to prove their innocence. This was manifested in two major ways – the Government failed to provide allegedly incriminating and exculpatory evidence to the detainees in a timely fashion and the Court ignored its own procedural requirements for evaluating evidence.

First, in violation of Turkish law,[25] prosecutors failed to share information with the detainees in a timely manner, placing a heavy burden on them to prove their innocence. For instance, the first round of detainees indicted were not provided access to any of the documents allegedly implicating them in the investigation until after the trial had already commenced. The detainees did not receive access to forensic images of the primary

---

[19] *Revised Fact Sheet No. 26: The Working Group on Arbitrary Detention*, Office of the UN High Commissioner for Human Rights, at pt. IV(B) [hereinafter Fact Sheet No. 26].

[20] *Id.*, at 22–32.

[21] International Covenant on Civil and Political Rights, G.A. Res 2200A (XXI), 21 U.N. GAOR Supp. (No. 16), at 52, U.N. Doc. A/6316 (1966), 999 U.N.T.S. 171, *entered into force* Mar. 23, 1976, at Art. 14(2)–14(3) [hereinafter ICCPR].

[22] Sledgehammer Petition, at 4.

[23] Sarah Joseph & Melissa Castan, The International Covenant on Civil and Political Rights: Cases, Materials, and Commentary 308 (Oxford University Press, 2004).

[24] *Id.*

[25] Turkish Criminal Procedure Code (2005), at Art. 160, Art. 170(5).

evidence against them, CD #11 and CD #17, until twenty-two months after the prosecution received the CDs. And, they also were not provided access to forensic images of the additional evidence collected at the Naval Command Base until thirteen months after they were seized.[26]

Moreover, evidence that pointed toward exonerating the detainees was either distorted or not included in the indictments despite being known to prosecutors. Not a single one of the numerous anachronisms, errors, and other inconsistencies indicating the fraudulent nature of the incriminating evidence was mentioned in the indictment. In fact, communications showing that the prosecutors were aware of these inconsistencies were placed in storage, where the defense lawyers had no access to them. The military report that concluded that there were no traces of the allegedly incriminating information in CDs #11 and #17 in military computers was also not included in the indictment and only shared with the defense after fifteen months. Other statements by employees of the 1st Army stating that they did not recognize or remember the incriminating CDs were distorted to seem like they corroborated the authenticity of the evidence.[27]

Second, the Court bypassed several procedural requirements meant to ensure that an accused can present a full and proper defense, which strongly suggested that the Court presumed that the detainees were guilty. Although Turkish law[28] requires that evidence obtained illegally or otherwise invalid be ruled inadmissible and defendants be afforded the opportunity to respond to the documents, neither of these requirements were met. For example, the Court allowed prosecutors to issue a final statement on March 29, 2012, that relied on illegally recorded evidence. Additionally, the unsigned documents that were never authenticated or traced to military computers were allowed to be admitted as the central focus of the prosecution's case. And the Court bypassed the stage where the detainees should have had a right to examine and challenge the validity and admissibility of the proffered evidence. Instead, the Court claimed that examining the validity and admissibility of the evidence would "not make any concrete contribution" to the trial.[29]

Additionally, the Petition noted two other individual instances showing a violation of the right to presumption of innocence. On August 4, 2012, the Turkish Supreme Military Council, headed at the time by then Prime Minister Erdogan, forcibly retired thirty-four generals and admirals who were defendants in the *Sledgehammer* trial. As noted by a Turkish journalist, "[T]hese commanders, who may be innocent, should not have been forced to retire. It seems odd and little more than an excuse to reshape the military." And when some detainees made "so-called defamatory" statements related to the forged evidence and how the Court had denied them their right to challenge it, the Government issued new indictments against them.[30]

2 Right to Attorney–Client Confidentiality

The Petition argued that the Government denied the detainees the right to have confidentiality in communications with their lawyers without restrictions, pressures, or

---

[26] Sledgehammer Petition, at 2.
[27] Id., at 25.
[28] Turkish Criminal Procedure Code, at Art. 206(2)(a), Art. 209–216.
[29] Sledgehammer Petition, at 26–27.
[30] Id., at 20, 23–24.

undue interference as guaranteed by Article 14(3)(b) of the ICCPR. In support of its arguments, the Petition cited a prior opinion of the WGAD that highlighted the importance of this provision by noting the ability of defendants to "have private meetings with their lawyer" is one of many "critical procedural safeguards" against arbitrary detention.[31] The Petition also referenced Turkish law that also contains a similar attorney–client provision to that of the ICCPR.[32]

The Petition discussed one dramatic way that illustrated how this right was violated. On June 13, 2011, the Court installed microphones on the ceilings of the court room to record conversations, including those between the detainees and their attorneys, which effectively prevented confidential communication between them going forward through the trial.[33]

3 Right to Trial without Undue Delay

The Petition argued that the Government denied the detainees the right to be tried without undue delay as required by Article 14(3)(c). In support of its arguments, the Petition cited to the HR Committee, which had previously said that "a delay of twenty-three months or more between arrest and conviction at first instance, and/or between the conclusion of an appeal, [are] prima facie breaches [of] article 14(3)(c)."[34] The Petition also cited to a previous WGAD opinion, in which it considered the "continued detention of persons in custody for more than two years after deprivation of liberty" as "serious."[35] It also noted the WGAD's opinion "that a person shall be brought without delay before a judge requires promptness not only at the initial moment of detention, but at all subsequent stages."[36]

By those standards, the continued detention of the detainees was, at least in some instances, a prima facie showing of undue delay. During the *Sledgehammer* trial, approximately 21 of the detainees had been imprisoned for up to 23 months, 142 for 19 months, and 87 for up to 15 months. As mentioned previously, dozens of the detainees were also held in pretrial detention for up to four and a half months. Contrary to Turkish law[37], the Court did not provide an opportunity for bail during this period. In all instances, the Court ruled that the detention would continue and denied the detainees a right to contest the detention at trial.[38]

The Government also did not provide any justification for why a delay would be necessary. In support of this argument, the Petition cited to a previous WGAD opinion that stated "[p]reventive detention must not be the general rule."[39] The Petition also cited to the HR Committee, which has noted that a deprivation of liberty cannot be justified when it is manifestly disproportionate, unjust, or unpredictable.[40] The Petition

---

[31] Sa'dun Sheikhu, et al., v. Syria, WGAD Opinion No. 27/2009, Adopted Nov. 24, 2009.
[32] Turkish Criminal Procedure Code, at Art. 154.
[33] Sledgehammer Petition, at 31–32.
[34] Joseph & Castan, at 314.
[35] Alfredo Raymundo Chaves, et al., v. Peru, Decision No. 43/1995, Adopted Nov. 30, 1995.
[36] Id.
[37] Turkish Criminal Procedure Code, at Art. 101, Art. 108.
[38] Sledgehammer Petition, at 28–31.
[39] Alfredo Raymundo Chaves, et al.
[40] Sledgehammer Petition, at 29.

noted that this was consistent with domestic law, which stated that preventive detention "must not only be lawful but reasonable in all the circumstances . . . [as well as] necessary in all the circumstances, for example to prevent flight, interference with evidence or the recurrence of crime."[41]

The Government failed to justify the repeated instances of undue delay associated with the detainees' continued detention at every stage of the trial. Therefore, the Petition argued that their detention was unjust and disproportionate because there was no justification, as there was no evidence suggesting that the detainees presented a potential flight risk or that they were likely to be involved in the recurrence of any of their alleged crimes. In fact, the Court acted against Turkish law by offering no reasoned explanation at all as to why the detainees could not be released, instead only providing vague overgeneralizations that lacked legal grounding.[42] In addition, the Petition argued the imprisonment of the 250 detainees was also disproportionate because several other defendants in the *Sledgehammer* trial were tried while free, despite the fact that all defendants had similar factual circumstances and were charged with similar crimes.[43]

4 Right to Examine Evidence and Call Witnesses

Finally, the Petition argued that the Government denied the detainees the equal opportunity it gave to the prosecution to call witnesses and examine evidence, both of which are rights guaranteed by Article 14(3)(e) of the ICCPR. Throughout the trial, it was patently obvious that the detainees did not have equal access to the Court in either of these two regards. With regards to the right to call witnesses, which is also protected by Turkish law,[44] detainees were repeatedly denied their requests to call two key witnesses that the prosecution failed to question. One of the witnesses was the former Commander of Land Forces, who was credited in the indictment with preventing the alleged coup. The other was a senior military officer at the time of the 2003 workshop who was often credited in media reports with halting the coup preparations. Yet despite the purported roles these individuals played in "preventing" the alleged coup, the Court deemed their testimony "unnecessary." On January 20, 2012, the Court postponed the decision on hearing the witnesses until after the completion of the defenses. Two months later, on March 29, 2012, it denied the request to hear the witnesses outright, and reaffirmed that decision on April 19, 2012.[45]

With regards to the right to examine evidence, the Court allowed prosecutors to handpick their own experts, while simultaneously denying the detainees' request for a court-appointed independent expert. Contrary to Turkish law, which mandates forensic findings be issued by a court-appointed expert,[46] the Court admitted forensic reports made by a specific expert from the Scientific and Technological Research Council of Turkey (TÜBITAK) that had been selected by prosecutors. The expert was not even

[41] Van Alphen v. The Netherlands, Communication No. 305/1998, Human Rights Committee, CCPR/C/39/D/305/1998, July 23, 1990.
[42] Turkish Criminal Procedure Code, at Art. 101, Art. 108.
[43] Sledgehammer Petition, at 29.
[44] Turkish Criminal Procedure Code, at Art. 177.
[45] Sledgehammer Petition, at 27–28.
[46] Turkish Criminal Procedure Code, at Art. 64.

sworn in before the Court until two years after completing his forensic report. Moreover, as with the request for witnesses, the Court repeatedly rejected the detainees' reasonable request to appoint an independent expert, given the highly suspect nature of the incriminating evidence. Despite the fact that reports by independent forensic experts in the United States, Germany, and Turkey all concurred that the incriminating evidence was forged because it was created after 2003, the Court claimed, as previously mentioned, that additional, independently issued forensic reports would "not make any concrete contribution" to the trial.[47]

III Government Response to the Petition

The Government of Turkey received communication of the submission of the Petition to the WGAD on September 12, 2012.[48] Per the WGAD's Methods of Work, the Government was given a sixty-day timeframe in which to respond to the allegations made in the initial Petition.[49] Although the WGAD allows governments to request a one-month extension, they must do so within the initial sixty-day timeframe, which in this case expired on November 12, 2012.

A *Serious Procedural Irregularities in Government's Response*

On November 15, 2012, three days *after* the initial timeframe had expired, the Government requested an extension. Despite the Government's delay, the WGAD granted a one-month extension during its working session, citing the complexity of the case. On December 12, 2012, the Government submitted its official Response, which the WGAD then sent a summary of to Perseus Strategies on January 10, 2013.[50]

After submitting its Response, the Government once again displayed serious disregard for the WGAD's procedural requirements when it submitted additional documentation several months late. In March 2013, the Government submitted twelve DVDs and one CD to the WGAD for consideration.[51] And on April 22, 2013,[52] Perseus Strategies was informed by the WGAD that the Government had again submitted additional materials in the form of a new CD containing a document titled "reasoned verdict" of approximately 1,500 pages in length, which had been issued by the Court on January 7, 2013.[53] The submission of these additional documents more than three months after the Government's initial Response dramatically contravened the WGAD's Methods of Work.[54]

---

[47] Sledgehammer Petition, at 27–28.
[48] Balyoz or Sledgehammer Cases v. Turkey, WGAD Opinion No. 6/2013, Adopted May 1, 2013 (Litigated by Author through Perseus Strategies).
[49] *Id.*
[50] *Id.*
[51] Reply to the Response of the Government of the Republic of Turkey on Behalf of the Defendants in the Sledgehammer Trial, Perseus Strategies, Apr. 11, 2013, at ¶ 3.
[52] Email from Mr. Miguel de la Lama, Secretary, Working Group on Arbitrary Detention, United Nations High Commissioners for Human Rights, Apr. 22, 2013.
[53] *Id.*
[54] *Id.*

While these materials could have been submitted as part of the Government's Response, or shortly thereafter, the Government instead waited to submit it all mere days before the session during which the WGAD was set to consider the Petition. Moreover, the materials should have been inconsequential to the WGAD's consideration of the case because the majority of it was pasted from the indictments used to charge the detainees (as discussed in detail later).

B Arguments Regarding Procedure

The Response from the Government primarily argued that there were several procedural reasons why the WGAD could not reach the merits of the international law violations noted in the Petition:

- Domestic remedies had not been exhausted.
- The WGAD does not substitute itself as domestic fact finder.
- There was already a European Court of Human Rights (ECtHR) case on identical or parallel issues.
- Article 14 of the ICCPR does not apply until final judgment.

The next sections discuss the Government's arguments relative to each of these points, drawn from how it was characterized in the WGAD's Opinion.

1 Exhaustion of Domestic Remedies

The Response argued that the WGAD must deem the case inadmissible because domestic remedies had not yet been exhausted. Specifically, it noted that the detainees had a right to appeal before the Turkish Constitutional Court. It also noted that there was a newly employed mechanism within the country through which the detainees could claim that their fundamental human rights were violated. The Response regarded it to be a "well-established principle of customary international law" that detainees cannot allege violations of their rights before any international authority unless first giving "national authorities the opportunity to rule on the question."[55]

2 Substitution of Working Group as Domestic Fact Finder

The Response argued that the WGAD must deem the case inadmissible because it cannot act as a domestic fact finder. Specifically, it argued that the detainees were asking the WGAD to decide the merits of the digital evidence used to implicate the detainees and to find that it was forged. The Response emphasized that it was "not within [the WGAD's] mandate to . . . to evaluate the facts and evidence in the case, nor . . . [to act as] a substitute for national courts of appeals."[56]

---

[55] Balyoz or Sledgehammer Cases, at ¶ 58.
[56] Id., at ¶ 47.

3 Preclusion Due to Similar ECtHR Case

The Response also argued that the WGAD must also deem the case inadmissible because some of the detainees had submitted a similar petition to the ECtHR. The basis of the Government's argument was the (faulty) assumption that the WGAD operated under the same admissibility procedures as the ECtHR – that it is precluded from reviewing alleged violations of international law in a petition if the exact same violations have been submitted before another international tribunal.[57]

4 ICCPR Article 14 Applies Only after Final Judgment

The final procedural argument raised by the Government in its Response was the claim that Article 14 of the ICCPR did not apply until after a final judgment is issued. Since the initial Petition was submitted about two weeks before a final judgment had been rendered in the trial, the Response argued that the WGAD should dismiss all the Article 14 violations noted in the Petition.

The Response argued that "nobody could be really sure about the value of the evidence until the end of the trial and the judicial process," so only "detention after trial may fall within the mandate of the [WGAD]." Accordingly, the Response emphasized that only certain claims – those related to ICCPR Article 9 – fell within the WGAD's scope in this particular case.[58]

C Arguments Regarding the Merits of the Due Process Violations

Although the Response denied the WGAD's jurisdiction to address the primary ICCPR provisions noted in the Petition, it nevertheless indirectly addressed the merits of some, but not all, of the alleged Article 14 violations, specifically:

- Article 14(2): Presumption of innocence.
- Article 14(3)(c): Trial without undue delay.

Neither the right to attorney–client confidentiality under Article 14(3)(b) nor the right to examine evidence and call witnesses under Article 14(3)(e) were directly or indirectly referenced in the Response.

1 Right to Presumption of Innocence

Without explicitly mentioning Article 14(2), the Response denied that the Government had violated the right to presumption of innocence. The Response stated "that [the Government] respects the presumption of innocence ... and accords primary import-ance to this principle."[59] The Response likewise argued that the Government "relies on concrete facts and elements of proof," and that an "independent and impartial court" conducted the trial.[60]

---

[57] *Id.*, at ¶ 49.
[58] *Id.*, at ¶ 46.
[59] *Id.*
[60] *Id.*, at ¶ 52.

Aside from these blanket denials, the Government addressed only one of the numerous examples of violations noted in the Petition regarding the presumption of innocence – the right to be provided exculpatory evidence in a timely fashion. The Government acknowledged that it restricted detainees' access to the allegedly incriminating evidence, but in its Response argued that it was justified for two reasons – to protect its national security interests and to preserve the confidentiality of the investigation. The Response did not provide further elaboration. Furthermore, the Government justified withholding the evidence by citing to ECtHR case law, which it claimed does not provide defendants with the right of access to all elements of the case at the initial phase of the investigation.[61]

2 Right to Trial without Undue Delay

Without explicitly referencing Article 14(3)(c), the Response denied that the Government had violated the right to a trial without undue delay. It argued that the Government complied with its domestic law and that "the provisional detention of the defendants was justified in this case, under the international instruments ratified by Turkey."[62]

The Response did not contest the periods of detention noted in the Petition, but provided a number of arguments justifying the length of detention. First, the Response argued that detention is justified if there are "plausible reasons to suspect a person of having committed a crime."[63] In particular, it argued that there were plausible reasons in this case given the evidence collected, the nature of the alleged crime, and Turkey's sociopolitical context. Second, the Response pointed to the complexity of the case and the possibility that the detainees could exert undue pressure on witnesses as further reasons for the lengthy detention. Third, the Response noted that the conditions of detention were monitored at regular intervals. Finally, the Response argued that under ECtHR case law the continued detention of the detainees for twenty-three months or less was not a prima facie showing of undue delay.[64]

D New References to Article 9 of the ICCPR

The Response argued that it had complied with other Article 9 provisions that were not explicitly identified in the initial Petition to the WGAD. The Government alleged in its Response that its adherence to these provisions demonstrated that the detainees' imprisonment was not arbitrary under ICCPR Article 9(1):

- Article 9(2): "Anyone who is arrested shall be informed, at the time of arrest, of the reasons for his arrest and shall be promptly informed of any charges against him."
- Article 9(4): "Anyone who is deprived of his liberty by arrest or detention shall be entitled to take proceedings before a court, in order that that court may decide without delay on the lawfulness of his detention and order his release if the detention is not lawful."

[61] Id.
[62] Id., at ¶ 50.
[63] Id.
[64] Id., ¶¶ 50–54.

1 Right to Be Informed of Charges

The Response argued that the Government informed the detainees of the charges against them within the shortest time limits guaranteed by Article 9(2). Critically, the Government did not contest that it failed to provide detainees with access to much of the allegedly incriminating materials until after the commencement of the trial.[65]

2 Right to Proceedings before a Court

The Response argued that the Government provided the detainees with the right to contest their arbitrary detention before a court as guaranteed by Article 9(4). In particular, the Response noted that the detainees had the ability to be represented by a lawyer of their own choosing, that petitioners had the opportunity to object against the orders for their detention, and that the detainees had an opportunity to contest their restricted access to all of the elements in the files. Critically, as previously mentioned, the Government did not directly contest the Petition's arguments regarding the numerous instances of undue delay, including lack of bail, which is a guarantee also referenced within Article 9(4).[66]

IV Reply to the Government's Response

Per the WGAD's Methods of Work, Perseus Strategies filed a detailed Reply to the Government's Response on April 11, 2013. Before addressing the arguments raised in the Response, the Reply addressed the serious procedural irregularities exhibited by the Government in its submission of materials to the WGAD.

A *Addressing the Serious Procedural Irregularities in the Government's Response*

First, the Reply noted that the Government requested an extension three days late and that the WGAD accepted this late extension, in contravention of its own Methods of Work. The Reply noted that although Turkey was within its right to request an extension, it should not have been allowed to submit a late extension request because the effect of doing so "delayed the issuance of an opinion on the case from November 2012 to May 2013. This ... materially damaged [petitioners] who were hoping for an opinion to be issued [in November 2012]."[67] The Reply argued that "[u]nder these circumstances, we do not believe it would be fair to [petitioners] – the 250 detained individuals on whose behalf we are working – for the [WGAD] to accept the Turkish Government's Response after it patently failed to respect the clear deadlines provided by the Working Group."[68]

Second, the Reply criticized the Government's submission of additional materials in the form of CDs and DVDs in March 2013, at least three months after it submitted its Response. The Reply argued that the materials should not be considered because they were submitted late in contravention of the Methods of Work. The Reply also made two

---

[65] Balyoz or Sledgehammer Cases, at ¶ 55.
[66] Id.
[67] Reply to the Government of Turkey, at 3.
[68] Id.

further arguments as to why this late submission was nothing but a "flagrant attempt to delay these proceedings" and "bury the [WGAD] in the details of the domestic court case."[69] The first argument was that these materials were ones that could have easily been furnished as part of the Government's initial Response. The second was that the WGAD has no need to examine primary evidence relating to the underlying charges and that these materials did not relate to violations of international law. Thus, the Reply considered it "puzzling why the Turkish Government provided [these materials] to the [WGAD] given that it knows determining the veracity of this evidence is outside the [WGAD]'s mandate."[70]

As previously mentioned, a few weeks after Perseus Strategies submitted its Reply it was informed that the Government had again submitted additional materials to the WGAD. In subsequent correspondence with the WGAD in late-April, the author reiterated his concerns over the Government's serious disregard of the Methods of Work: "[We] do not believe a review of these additional materials, whether intensely or at a high-level will change the outcome of the case in any way. As we stated in our Reply ... we believe the only point at issue in this case is whether the Government of Turkey provided the defendants their due process rights ... " The author again emphasized that the late submission of the additional materials should not further delay the WGAD's Opinion and that "justice delayed is justice denied."[71]

Ultimately, the Reply emphasized that while "we understand, encourage, and are eminently grateful that the [WGAD] seeks to engage with Governments on cases of arbitrary detention," the WGAD should not deviate from its own, "explicitly well-defined and unambiguous" rules in doing so.[72]

B Addressing the Responses' Arguments Regarding Procedure

After addressing the procedural irregularities in the Response, the Reply turned to the major procedural points made by the Government to support its argument that consideration of the Petition should not fall within the WGAD's jurisdiction. The Reply addressed the arguments relating to: (1) the exhaustion of domestic remedies; (2) the substitution of WGAD as a domestic fact finder; and (3) potential preclusion as a result of a similar ECtHR case.

1 Exhaustion of Domestic Remedies

The Reply argued that, contrary to the Government's assertions, the Petition was properly before the WGAD, regardless of whether domestic remedies had been exhausted. Although exhaustion of domestic remedies is a requirement for cases brought before the ECtHR, this standard is not applicable to the WGAD. According to the Reply, it is necessary for the WGAD to take this position "so that a wrongly detained defendant can

---

[69] Id.
[70] Id., at 6.
[71] Apr. 22 Email from Petitioner.
[72] Reply to the Government of Turkey, at 3.

prove his/her arbitrary detention and be released, rather than spending years in incarceration as his/her case makes its way through several rounds of appeal."[73]

2 Substitution of Working Group as Domestic Fact Finder

The Reply agreed that the WGAD cannot act as a domestic fact finder, but argued that the detainees were not asking the WGAD to operate outside its mandate. Contrary to the Government's assertions, the initial Petition only asked the WGAD "to determine whether the rights to a fair trial and due process guaranteed by international law have been respected."[74]

To this effect, the Reply emphasized that the initial Petition "brought the assertions of forged evidence to the [WGAD] so that it can understand why the failure of the Turkish Court to consider the authenticity of this evidence is of such crucial importance."[75] It added that "it is not necessary for the [WGAD] to view the contents of the DVDs/CD" to determine that failure to provide detainees with an opportunity to challenge these "demonstrably fabricated" materials "constitutes a due process violation per se."[76]

3 Preclusion Due to Similar ECtHR Case

The Reply argued that, contrary to the Government's assertions, the WGAD was not precluded from considering the Petition because of the existence of a similar ECtHR case. To support its argument, the Reply cited to the Methods of Work, which stated that it will preclude itself only if the case has been previously submitted to another treaty body and "the person and facts involved [in the cases] are the same."[77]

First, the Reply noted that the ECtHR was not a treaty body, but a court. On this fact alone, the WGAD would not be precluded from hearing a case previously before the ECtHR.[78]

However, the Reply went on to argue that even if this were not the case, the WGAD would still not be precluded from hearing this case because neither the people nor the facts involved in the case before the WGAD were the same as those before the ECtHR. The case before the ECtHR only involved one individual, General Cetin Dogan, while the case before the WGAD involved 250 detainees.[79]

Additionally, the case before the ECtHR covered a distinct set of procedural violations than those raised in the Petition. Since the ECtHR, unlike the WGAD, is limited to hearing issues for which domestic remedies have been exhausted, the issues raised before the ECtHR were much narrower. For example, the following issues were raised in the initial ECtHR submission, but not the WGAD Petition: the specific length of General Dogan's individual detention; General Dogan's health problems; General Dogan's individual petitions to Turkish courts calling for his release; and the failure of the

---

[73] *Id.*, at 4.
[74] *Id.*, at 6.
[75] *Id.*
[76] *Id.*
[77] Fact Sheet No. 26, at pt. VII(A).
[78] Reply to the Government of Turkey, at 5.
[79] *Id.*

prosecutor to communicate an opinion regarding the case to General Dogan. Moreover, the ECtHR limited itself to examining only "the alleged breach of *habeas corpus* principles with a special emphasis on the violation of equality of arms when deciding on the legality of his detention." The Reply emphasized that none of these specific issues were brought before the WGAD.[80]

C Addressing the Responses' Arguments Regarding the Merits of the Due Process Violations

Finally, the Reply addressed the arguments made in the Response regarding the merits of the alleged violations of ICCPR and other due process abuses articulated in the Petition. It first emphasized that in its Response, the Government dedicated literally "only a few paragraphs in response to the due process violations raised in our Petition."[81] In fact, the Government failed to dispute or refute the majority of allegations of due process violations. And when the Government did address them, it offered only conclusory statements to the effect that "all the fundamental guarantees of the right to a fair trial ... have been met in this case."[82]

Moreover, the Reply noted that since the submission of the initial Petition, other international organizations had independently confirmed the due process violations. Most importantly, the European Commission stated that there were substantial due process concerns throughout every phase of the *Sledgehammer* trial, including "lengthy pre-trial detention," "excessively long and catch-all indictments," and problems with "the judiciary accept[ing] mainly evidence collected by the police only, or supplied by secret witnesses."[83] Perseus Strategies also briefed three reputable international NGOs, Freedom House, Reporters Without Borders, and the Project on Middle East and Democracy, who then wrote a letter to President Obama discussing their concern with the due process violations in the *Sledgehammer* Trial: "[h]undreds of military officers ... [were] arrested and charged through trials dogged by allegations of fabricated evidence used by the prosecution."[84]

As will be discussed later, the Reply also reiterated and elaborated on each of the due process violations noted in the initial Petition: (1) presumption of innocence; (2) attorney–client confidentiality; (3) trial without undue delay; and (4) right to call and examine witnesses. Given the Government failed to refute the facts regarding these due process violations, the Reply urged the WGAD to consider the detainees' description of the facts as accurate in accordance with its standard practice, which is to say that undisputed facts should be accepted as truth. The Reply also asked that the WGAD, as it has in previous instances, consider that the undisputed evidence presented in the Petition was also corroborated by reputable independent observers.[85]

---

[80] *Id.*

[81] *Id.*, at 8.

[82] *Id.*

[83] *Turkey 2012 Progress Report*, European Commission, Oct. 10, 2012, at 7.

[84] *Obama Must Speak Out on Hostile Climate for Free Speech in Turkey*, Freedom House et al., Jan. 10, 2013.

[85] Reply to the Government of Turkey, at 8.

1 Right to Presumption of Innocence

The Reply reiterated that the Government did not dispute in its Response the multiple instances raised in the Petition showing the detainees' right to be presumed innocent as guaranteed by Article 14(2) of the ICCPR was violated. These instances included the Government's forced retirement of Turkish officers, the Court's issuance of additional indictments against the Defendants for "defamatory" statements, the Court's restriction of access to exculpatory evidence, and the Court's disregard for its own procedural requirements.

The Reply also addressed the purported justifications offered by the Government in its Response. It noted that in addressing presumption of innocence, the Government "simply states in a conclusory manner, without further explanation, that '[the Government of Turkey] respects the presumption of innocence of the Petitioners and accords primary importance to this principle.'" Furthermore, the Reply argues that the Government's justification that the detainees were restricted access to exculpatory evidence for "national security" and "confidentiality" concerns was immaterial because Turkish law dictates without exception that prosecutors must "present evidence that implicates as well as that which exculpates." Moreover, the Reply noted that to give effect to other ICCPR protections afforded to defendants, such as Article 14(3)(a), it "necessarily requires the accused to have access to all the information being used to justify an indictment against him/her."

2 Right to Attorney–Client Confidentiality

The Reply reiterated that the Government did not dispute in its Response that it placed microphones on the ceiling of the courtroom to record conversations between detainees and their counsel, which is a violation of attorney–client confidentiality as guaranteed by Article 14(3)(b) of the ICCPR.[86]

3 Right to Trial without Undue Delay

The Reply reiterated that the preventative and pretrial detention of the detainees for up to twenty-three months was excessive, that the Court never provided legal justifications for its decisions affirming the continued detention, and that the detention could not be legal because it was "manifestly disproportionate, unjust, [and] unpredictable." The Reply notes that the Government in its Response never disputes the facts of the detainees' imprisonment.[87]

The Reply also addressed the primary justification offered by the Government as to why the continued detention was not a violation of detainees' right to trial without undue delay: that the ECtHR did not consider twenty-three months to be a showing of undue delay. The Reply pointed out that only past decisions by the HR Committee and the WGAD are pertinent and that in those decisions these bodies have found that continued detention of the kind exhibited in this case violates the right to trial without undue delay. As a result, "[w]hile the Turkish Government defends these long detention periods of the

---

[86] *Id.*, at 13.
[87] *Id.*, at 12.

Defendants by citing to cases where the [ECtHR] allegedly sanctioned detention period of several years, these cases are irrelevant ... before the [WGAD]" because they are not binding.[88]

4 Right to Examine Evidence and Call Witnesses

The Reply reiterated that the Government did not dispute in its Response that it prevented the Defendants from calling witnesses and appointing independent experts to examine the incriminating evidence against them, as guaranteed by Article 14(3)(e) of the ICCPR.[89]

V The WGAD's Opinion

Although the WGAD was non-responsive with regards to the serious procedural concerns raised by Perseus Strategies regarding the Government's deliberate attempts to delay the proceedings, the WGAD did not further delay the issuance of its Opinion of the *Sledgehammer* case as had been feared. The WGAD considered the case and issued Opinion No. 6/2013 on July 5, 2013.[90]

Overall, the WGAD strongly agreed with the petitioners that the Government did not contest the alleged due process violations. The Opinion noted "the Government does not avail itself of the opportunity of offering an explanation of the various allegations in relation to due process violations either by acknowledging that these have indeed taken place ... or by rebutting or otherwise disputing them."[91] As a result, it noted the WGAD "must base its opinion on the case [on the facts] as provided by the [petitioners]," in the initial Petition and Reply.[92]

The WGAD did take "duly into account" the procedural arguments and other justifications provided by the Government, but rejected them.[93] It unequivocally stated that "[t]he deprivation of liberty of the 250 detained defendants in the ... Sledgehammer cases is arbitrary, in contravention of articles 9 and 14 of the [ICCPR] ... [and] falls within category III" of the WGAD's arbitrary detention cases.[94] The WGAD requested "the Government of Turkey to remedy the situation of these 250 persons in accordance with [international law]."[95] It also urged the Government to provide an adequate remedy, such as an enforceable right to compensation as guaranteed by Article 9(5) of the ICCPR.

The next section contains further detail on what the WGAD's Opinion stated about each of the procedural arguments and due process violations raised in the case.

---

[88] *Id.*, at 11.
[89] *Id.*, at 9.
[90] Balyoz or Sledgehammer Cases.
[91] *Id.*, at ¶ 73.
[92] *Id.*
[93] *Id.*
[94] *Id.*, at ¶ 79.
[95] *Id.*, at ¶ 80.

A *The Government of Turkey's Procedural Arguments Were Invalid*

1 Exhaustion of Domestic Remedies

The WGAD agreed with the petitioners that it is not bound by any rule requiring domestic remedies to be exhausted to deliver an opinion on a case. The WGAD "does not follow such doctrines in the same way as domestic courts or certain other international courts, tribunals or other human rights."[96] The WGAD emphasized that only by disregarding whether domestic remedies have been exhausted is it "able to fulfill its mandate to consider cases . . . of violations of the right of the accused to be tried within a reasonable time or to be released."[97]

2 Preclusion Due to Similar ECtHR Case

The WGAD also agreed with the petitioners that it is not precluded from hearing the case "on the sole ground that an identical or the same application is pending before the [ECtHR]."[98] The WGAD emphasized that it "does not have the same admissibility criteria as the European Court . . . [because] the European Court will primarily review compliance with the European Convention on Human Rights, and the [WGAD] with the ICCPR and customary international law."[99]

B *The Government of Turkey Violated the Due Process Rights Guaranteed by the ICCPR and Held the Petitioners in Violation of Its International Obligations*

1 Right to Presumption of Innocence

The WGAD did not per se find that the Government violated the Defendants' presumption of innocence as guaranteed by Article 14(2) of the ICCPR. However, the Opinion found that the two major due process violations noted in the initial Petition under Article 14(2) – the restricted access to exculpatory evidence and the Court ignoring its own procedural requirements – constituted violations of other ICCPR articles. In this sense, the Opinion agreed with the substance of the arguments made in the initial Petition and rejected the arguments made by the Government in its Response.

Specifically, the Opinion found that the restricted access to exculpatory evidence constituted a violation under Article 14(3)(b) because it prevented the petitioners from having adequate time for the preparation of their defense. The WGAD disagreed with the Government's assertions that restricting the petitioners' access to investigation files were legitimate under international law because it was justified by national security interests and confidentiality needs. The WGAD emphatically noted that such pretexts would be legitimate only "in regard to the material which is not used then as evidence against the accused at trial and is not of exculpatory nature." Since the materials the petitioners were restricted from having access to in a timely manner were the key evidence raised by the prosecution at trial and other potentially exculpatory evidence,

---

[96] *Id.*, at ¶ 69.
[97] *Id.*
[98] *Id.*, at ¶ 71.
[99] *Id.*

the Opinion found that the Government was not justified in violating the petitioners' due process rights.[100]

With regards to the issue of the Turkish Court's disregard for its own procedural requirements, the initial Petition had argued that this was a violation of both the right to presumption of innocence under Article 14(2) and the right to call witnesses and examine evidence under Article 14(3)(e). The Opinion found that it was a violation of the latter, but not the former, as will be discussed further next.

2 Right to Attorney–Client Confidentiality

The Opinion stated, in agreement with the Petition, that the Government violated the petitioners' right to attorney–client confidentiality as guaranteed by Article 14(3)(b). The Opinion specifically emphasized that "[t]he Government did not rebut the allegation that microphones placed throughout the courtroom enabled the Government to listen to confidential attorney-client communications during the trial."[101]

3 Right to Trial without Undue Delay

The Opinion stated, in agreement with the Petition, that the Government violated the petitioners' right to a trial without undue delay. However, the WGAD found that this right was better guaranteed in the present case by Article 9(3), rather than Article 14(3)(c) as alleged in the initial Petition. Article 9(3) states in the pertinent part: "Anyone arrested or detained on a criminal charge shall be brought promptly before a judge ... and shall be entitled to trial within a reasonable time or to release. It shall not be the general rule that persons awaiting trial shall be detained in custody."

The WGAD first acknowledged that whether the right to a trial without undue delay has been violated is a question that "depends on the circumstances and complexity of each case and, where appropriate, on the use of remedies and of the right periodically to contest the accused's continued preventive detention."[102] The WGAD then went on to explain that "[t]he Government has not shown that the defendants had effective remedies ... [and] the Government has not shown that the courts provided periodic decisions stating the legal and factual grounds the continued detention of the defendants."[103] This, along with the fact that there was no justification for not having a bail opportunity and that there was no proportionality argument made, provided "sufficient grounds" for the WGAD to conclude that the Government had violated the petitioners' right to a trial without undue delay.[104]

4 Right to Call Witnesses and Examine Evidence

The Opinion stated, in agreement with the petitioners, that the Government violated the Defendants' right to call witnesses and examine evidence as guaranteed by Article 14(3)(e).

[100] Id., at ¶ 78.
[101] Id.
[102] Balyoz or Sledgehammer Cases, at ¶ 74.
[103] Id.
[104] Id.

The WGAD noted that the Government "did not dispute [Petitioners'] allegations about procedural irregularities in the first phase of the trial . . . for evaluating the authenticity of evidence or that they refused to consider three expert reports . . . refuting the authenticity of the digital evidence." Further, the WGAD noted that the Response did not dispute that the petitioners were prohibited from calling two key witnesses and appointing their own independent forensic expert.[105]

VI Resolution

As previously mentioned, on September 21, 2012, the Turkish Court convicted 323 of the original 365 defendants for attempting to overthrow the Government. All of the 250 detainees represented by Perseus Strategies to the WGAD were among those convicted and given sentences ranging from sixteen to twenty years. While the defendants were awaiting their appeals process and an opinion by the WGAD, they continued to remain arbitrarily detained in violation of international law.[106]

The situation changed, however, after the WGAD issued its Opinion in July 2013. The Opinion garnered significant international support, particularly from the United States, the European Union, and international civil society groups. This created substantial political and public relations pressure on the Government to release the *Sledgehammer* defendants.[107]

In addition to the WGAD's Opinion, one other event made a major contribution to the eventual release of the *Sledgehammer* defendants: the AKP's break with the Gülenists. The rift between the former political allies culminated in an outright power struggle by December 2013, which saw the Gülenists accusing the AKP of corruption and the AKP accusing the Gülenists of creating a "parallel state."[108] The Gülenists were seen as having orchestrated the *Sledgehammer* trial, so once the rift between the AKP and the Gülenists occurred, no incentive remained for Prime Minister Erdogan to continue the detention of the *Sledgehammer* defendants. As the author noted, even though Erdogan was clearly "complicit" and "on the same page" as the Gülenists throughout the *Sledgehammer* trial,[109] by 2014 he was denouncing the entire process as a sham carried out by the Gülenists using illegal wiretaps, forged evidence, and media disinformation.[110]

By early 2014, it became clear that the release of the detainees was imminent, as the Government shifted away from defending the *Sledgehammer* process to discrediting it. In March 2014, the Turkish Parliament abolished the special courts used to try the military

---

[105] *Id.*
[106] Reply to the Government of Turkey, at 1–2.
[107] Dani Rodrik, *The Plot against the Generals*, June 2014, at 29–30.
[108] Tim Arango, *Tainted Trials against Army Now Haunt Turk's Leader*, INTERNATIONAL NEW YORK TIMES, Feb. 18, 2014.
[109] *Id.*
[110] Rodrik, at 30.

officers during the *Sledgehammer* trial. Then, on June 18, 2014, Turkey's Constitutional Court issued a ruling that the rights of the *Sledgehammer* defendants had been violated. A day later, on June 19, 2014, Turkey's Supreme Court finally ordered the release and retrial of all the *Sledgehammer* defendants whose convictions had not already been overturned, acknowledging that "[their] rights had been violated."[111]

---

[111] Ceylan Yeginsu, *Turkish Officers Convicted in 2012 Coup Case Are Released*, NEW YORK TIMES, June 19, 2014.

12 *Aung San Suu Kyi* v. *Myanmar*

I Introduction

Imprisoned under house arrest for fifteen years over a twenty-one-year period, from 1989 to 2010, the Burmese pro-democracy leader and human rights activist Aung San Suu Kyi became one of the world's most prominent political prisoners and the face of the Myanmar opposition movement. In 1991, she was awarded the Nobel Peace "for her non-violent struggle for democracy and human rights."[1] Over the course of her imprisonment, Aung San Suu Kyi was the subject of six WGAD opinions. The author was hired by her family to serve as her international counsel from mid-2006 until her release on November 13, 2010. He worked with Aung San Suu Kyi's local counsel, U Nyan Win and U Kyi Win, along with countless others globally, to utilize the latter three opinions, in combination with political and public relations advocacy efforts, to advance efforts to secure her freedom and that of other political prisoners from the military junta. Under house arrest, Aung San Suu Kyi was denied access to virtually everyone from the outside world other than her doctor, domestic lawyer, occasional diplomat friendly to the military junta, and Liaison Minister for the then-junta U Aung Kyi.

For cases such as Aung San Suu Kyi's, where the detention of a prisoner is intimately tied in with the future of the country, WGAD opinions are less valuable tools by themselves. Nevertheless, to express her appreciation to the WGAD for its relentless engagement on her situation, Aung San Suu Kyi provided a video message for its twentieth anniversary in 2011, where she said: "We would like to thank the Working Group for all that it has done for political prisoners in Burma of whom I was one until last year … For political prisoners, the knowledge that there are people outside in the free world who care for us and who are working for our release means a great deal."[2] Such comments reaffirm that in addition to the legitimacy provided to a detainee's case, WGAD opinions are deeply meaningful to the arbitrarily detained themselves.

This chapter will begin with a summary of the political history of Myanmar as well as Aung San Suu Kyi's role in the country's political situation. It will then examine the six cases of Aung San Suu Kyi before the WGAD. And finally it will connect how these last three opinions were incorporated into the international campaign to secure her freedom.

---

[1] *Aung San Suu Kyi Facts* (Aug. 2018), www.nobelprize.org/nobel_prizes/peace/laureates/1991/kyi-facts.html.
[2] *Aung San Suu Kyi on Arbitrary Detention*, Nov. 17, 2011 (Aug. 2018), www.youtube.com/watch?v=gO0d7blW3ls.

A Background

In January 1948, Burma[3] received independence from the British Government, which had colonized the country since 1885. Only three years prior, in March 1945, Burma was liberated from the Japanese occupation of World War II. Figuring prominently in these events was General Aung San of the Anti-Fascist People's Freedom League, who led the movement against Japanese occupation and played a major role in the negotiations between the Burmese independence movement and the British. Widely considered Burma's founding father, Aung San was assassinated before Burma was formally granted independence.[4] He was, of course, Aung San Suu Kyi's father.

From 1948 to 1962, Burma operated as a representative democracy complete with a constitution that established a bicameral legislature led by the prime minister and cabinet. The newly independent Burma was an ethnically diverse country that established semi-autonomous states for the country's various non-Burmese minority groups, including the Shan, Kachin, Kayin, Kaya, and Chin. During this period, however, internal tensions along political, social, and ethnic lines threatened the stability of the country.[5]

In 1958, Prime Minister U Nu asked the military, led by General Ne Win, to reestablish order in the country. The military government lasted two years and after an election in 1960, civilian rule under U Nu was restored. However, in 1962, Ne Win led a military coup and overthrew the government. He abolished the constitution and created an ultra-nationalist military government.[6] Establishing a platform of the "Burmese Way to Socialism," Ne Win expelled many foreign nationals, nationalized private business, including the media, and implemented an isolationist foreign policy that disconnected Burma from the rest of the world. In 1974, a new constitution was adopted that established Burma as a one-party state led by the Burma Socialist Program Party (BSPP), with a unicameral legislature. During this time, Burma became one of the poorest countries in the world.[7]

After twenty-five years of BSPP rule, the Burmese economy collapsed in 1987. Food prices soared and rice shortages appeared throughout the country.[8] To stabilize the economy, the Government demonetized the currency; however, doing so cause many

---

[3] In Burmese language, the country is known as either Bama, its spoken name, or Myanma, its written name. The country was referred to as Burma from as early as the late 1700s through its independence in 1948. Even after a military junta overthrew the country's democratically elected government in 1962, it continued to be referred to as Burma. In 1989, after enormous domestic turmoil and a massacre of thousands of unarmed protesters on August 8, 1988, the military junta unilaterally changed the country's name to Myanmar. Aung San Suu Kyi and the Burmese democracy movement kept referring to the country as Burma. After taking office in April 2016, Aung San Suu Kyi clarified that foreigners were free to use either name "because there is nothing in the constitution of our country that says you must use any term in particular." *What's in a Name? Not Much According to Aung San Suu Kyi, Who Tells Diplomats They Can Use Myanmar or Burma*, ASSOCIATED PRESS, Apr. 23, 2016. Thus, the country will be referred to as Burma when it was referred to that way and to Myanmar thereafter.

[4] *Background Note: Burma*, US Department of State, Dec. 2004 (Nov. 2018), www.state.gov/r/pa/ei/bgn/35910.htm; *Myanmar: History*, WORLD ENCYCLOPEDIA (6th ed. 2005).

[5] *Id.*

[6] *Id.*

[7] *Id.*; Mark Tallentire, *The Burma Road to Ruin*, THE GUARDIAN, Sept. 18, 2018.

[8] John V. Dennis, *A Review of National Social Policies: Myanmar* (1999) (hereinafter Dennis Report).

people to lose their savings.[9] In response, nonviolent protests broke out in the capital city of Rangoon. The protests were led by students and Buddhist monks, who called for a reform of the government and change in the regime. The demonstrations grew in size as the general public, along with civil servants and members of the armed forces, joined the students and monks. The Government responded to these protests with lethal force and on August 8, 1988, military forces killed thousands of protesters.[10]

The 8/8/88 Massacre came to define the political movement and led to its renaming as the 8888 uprising. In response to the massacre, a group of military leaders staged a coup and took over the Government. These military rulers declared martial law, thus abolishing the constitution, and established a new military junta entitled the State Law and Order Restoration Council (SLORC). The SLORC continued to quell the protests through violent measures and thus, as a result of state repression, thousands more died.[11] In 1989, as noted earlier, the military junta unilaterally changed the country's name to Myanmar.

During the 8888 Uprising, Aung San Suu Kyi gave her first political speech and emerged as a leader of the opposition, organized around the political party, the National League of Democracy (NLD), which she co-founded. As a result of her growing popularity and thus threat to the SLORC, the military junta placed Aung San Suu Kyi under house arrest in 1989. A few months later, the SLORC declared the scheduling of multiparty democratic elections in an attempt to mitigate the 8888 uprising. On May 27, 1990, parliamentary general elections occurred in Burma for the first time in thirty years.[12] Though Aung San Suu Kyi remained under house arrest and was barred from being a candidate, her NLD party won over 80 percent of parliamentary seats. The NLD landslide victory surprised the SLORC military junta, which delayed the transition of power and prevented the newly elected parliament from being seated.[13] The SLORC argued that any attempt to convene parliament to form a government would be only a "parallel government" because the SLORC remained the "legal government."[14]

The SLORC never allowed the new parliament to meet. Even after the election, the SLORC refused to acknowledge the validity of the results, forced many elected MPs and party members into exile, and arbitrarily detained political activists and NLD party members, including Aung San Suu Kyi and the NLD party chairman, General U Tin Oo.[15] Over twenty elected MPs died while in prison.[16] The UN General Assembly

---

[9] Bertil Lintner, Outrage: Burma's Struggle for Democracy 192 (White Lotus Books, 1990); Alan Berlow, *Notes on a Fascist Disneyland: Behind Burma's Enchanting Façade, a Police State Tightens the Screws*, Los Angeles Times, May 20, 1990.

[10] Background Note; Myanmar: History.

[11] *Id.*

[12] *Id.*; Dennis Report.

[13] Terry McCarthy and Yuli Ismartono, *Opposition Vote Leaves Burma's Rulers Stunned*, The Independent, June 15, 1990.

[14] On July 13, 1990, Maj. Gen. Khin Nyunt at the 100th SLORC Press Conference stated: "[i]f a political party convenes a parliament and forms a government according to its own wishes, then such a government can only be a parallel government. If that happens, the SLORC Government, which is a legal government, will not look on with folded arms."

[15] Roger Matthews, *Burmese Troops Stand By to Crush Demonstrations: Second Anniversary of Brutal Suppression of Democracy Movement*, Financial Times, Sept. 18, 1990.

[16] Moe Aye, *Uphill Battle of the NLD*, The Irrawaddy, May 2018.

unanimously condemned the Government for its refusal to recognize its democratically elected parliament.[17]

For years after the 1990 elections, tensions flared between the opposition movement and the military junta running the Government. When out of house arrest, Aung San Suu Kyi was active in the pro-democracy movement and refused to remain silent. Throughout her advocacy, she received countless death threats and multiple attacks on her life. A year after the end of her second period of house arrest, pro-government supporters attacked Aung San Suu Kyi and her supporters at a rally, killing seventy NLD members. The Depayin Massacre led to Aung San Suu Kyi's third and final house arrest.[18]

Four years later, national protests began anew in August 2007 after the military junta removed fuel subsidies as a way to mitigate economic depression. The protests, led again by students and monks, were labeled the Saffron Revolution and were again met with a violent response from the state. International condemnation was widespread, with many countries levying sanctions on the Government. The UN Security Council also adopted a presidential statement on the situation in Burma urging the early release of Aung San Suu Kyi and political prisoners, tripartite dialogue between the junta, NLD, and ethnic groups, and open access for humanitarian relief to the conflict zones.[19]

These tensions lasted years and led to a renewed international focus on the human rights situation in Myanmar. The renewed international pressure paired with the declining economic and political situation made way for the slow process of a democratic transition in Burma, which resulted in Aung San Suu Kyi being released on November 13, 2010, after spending fifteen of the previous twenty-one years under house arrest.[20] Myanmar would not see free and fair multiparty elections until 2012, when Aung San Suu Kyi and the NLD would go on to win thirty-five of the forty-five available seats in a

---

[17] Background Note; Myanmar: History.

[18] Peter Popham, *"They Were screaming: Die, Die, Die!": The Dramatic Inside Story of Aung San Suu Kyi's Darkest Hour*, THE INDEPENDENT, Oct. 16, 2011.

[19] *Statement by the President of the Security Council – The Situation in Myanmar*, Security Council, Oct. 11, 2007. The first case that the author brought on his own to the WGAD was regarding James Mawdsley, a British-Australian national given a seventeen-year prison sentence in Burma for handing out pro-democracy leaflets. James Mawdsley v. Myanmar, WGAD Opinion No. 25/2000, Adopted Sept. 14, 2000. The author remained deeply engaged in the situation in Burma after his graduation from law school in 2001. In 2005, he led a team of a dozen lawyers and staff at his global law firm commissioned by Archbishop Desmond M. Tutu and former Czech Republic President Václav Havel to produce a detailed report arguing for the Security Council to engage in the situation in Myanmar. *Threat to the Peace: A Call for the UN Security Council to Act in Burma*, DLA Piper Rudnick Gray Cary, Sept. 20, 2005. With extensive advocacy and strong support from the NLD, this led to the Security Council in a contested vote placing the situation in Myanmar on its permanent agenda. *Security Council, In Procedural Action, Votes to Include Human Rights Situation in Myanmar on Its Agenda*, Security Council, SC/8832, 5526th Meeting, Sept. 15, 2006. The Security Council later rejected a resolution advanced by the United States and United Kingdom because of vetoes by China and the Russian Federation. *Security Council Fails to Adopt Draft Resolution on Myanmar, Owing to Negative Votes By China, Russian Federation*, Security Council, SC/8939, 5619th Meeting, Jan. 12, 2007. But the substance of that draft resolution was the foundation for the October 2007 resolution adopted in response to the junta's violent response to the Saffron Revolution. It was the author's work with Archbishop Tutu and President Havel that led Aung San Suu Kyi's family to learn about his efforts and to ask him subsequently to represent her pro bono.

[20] *2007 Uprising in Burma*, Burma Campaign UK (Aug. 2018), http://burmacampaign.org.uk/about-burma/2007-uprising-in-burma/.

by-election in its national Parliament.[21] In 2015, the NLD won an absolute majority in the legislature, 348 of the 664 seats in the two houses, ensuring that their candidate of choice would be president. Notably Aung San Suu Kyi has been constitutionally barred from the presidency because of a provision specifically designed to ban her from the office. And thus, her close friend and ally Htin Kyaw was tapped to become Myanmar's President.[22] Today Burma is a fledgling democracy and Aung San Suu Kyi serves as its de facto head of state in the roles of State Counsellor, which is similar to a Prime Minister, Minister of the President's Office, and Minister of Foreign Affairs.

B *The Facts of Aung San Suu Kyi's Case*

1 First House Arrest (1989–1995)

On July 20, 1989, Aung San Suu Kyi was detained under house arrest for the first time. She had been a leader in the pro-democracy movement in Burma and had co-founded the National League for Democracy in 1988. During this time period, she called repeatedly for nonviolent resistance against the martial law imposed by the Burmese government. In 1990, after the NLD swept the parliamentary elections, Aung San Suu Kyi was considered the most likely candidate for Prime Minister; however, the Government never accepted the election and ultimately invalidated it. During this first detention, Aung San Suu Kyi was almost completely isolated from the outside world and under the constant watch of armed guards. The Government never publicly charged Aung San Suu Kyi but defended her detention by saying she was trying to create divisions between the Burmese armed forces and the people of Burma.

According to the Government, Aung San Suu Kyi was held under the administrative detention provisions of the 1975 State Protection Law. The WGAD described the provisions of the Act as "allow[ing] for restrictions to be imposed on the fundamental rights of a citizen if he or she has performed, or is performing, or is believed to be performing, an act endangering State sovereignty and security" for a maximum period of five years.[23] During her detention, which lasted until 1995, the WGAD issued its first Opinion on Aung San Suu Kyi where it classified her house arrest as arbitrary and in violation of international law. Two years into her detention, Aung San Suu Kyi received the Nobel Peace Prize, which her two sons had to accept on her behalf as the Government refused to let her attend the ceremony.

2 Second House Arrest (2000–2002)

Aung San Suu Kyi was arrested and placed under house arrest again five years later on September 22, 2000. Though she was not formally charged or tried, she was arrested after having attempted to board a train to Mandalay, which her counsel believed violated an alleged travel ban that prevented her from leaving Rangoon. During this time period, the WGAD issued a second Opinion describing her house arrest as being arbitrary and in

[21] Esmer Golluoglu, *Aung San Suu Kyi Hails "New Era" for Burma after Landslide Victory*, THE GUARDIAN, Feb. 4, 2012.

[22] *Suu Kyi's National League for Democracy Wins Majority in Myanmar*, BBC NEWS, Nov. 13, 2015. In March 2018, Win Myint became the President of Myanmar.

[23] Aung San Suu Kyi v. Myanmar, WGAD Opinion No. 2/2002, Adopted June 19, 2002, at ¶ 6.

violation of international law. On May 6, 2002, after UN-led negotiations with the government, Aung San Suu Kyi was released from house arrest.

3 Third House Arrest (2003–2010)

A year later, on May 31, 2003, Aung San Suu Kyi was arrested again and sent to Insein Prison, and later a military guest house, without charges or trial. She was not allowed access to her lawyers or relatives; however, a few independent observers were able to visit her. Aung San Suu Kyi was arrested after violence orchestrated by a government-sponsored mob broke out at one of her rallies, resulting in at least seventy deaths of NLD members. In response to enquiries from the WGAD in 2003, the Government argued that it was detaining Aung San Suu Kyi for her own safety. And again, the WGAD issued its third Opinion on Aung San Suu Kyi's case, finding this new period of detention arbitrary and in violation of international law.

Aung San Suu Kyi was ultimately transferred back to her home for continued detention. On May 24, 2006, Ibrahim Gambari, UN Special Envoy of the Secretary-General on the situation in Myanmar, was able to visit Aung San Suu Kyi and publicly called for her release.[24] Three days later, on May 27, 2006, the Burmese authorities extended Aung San Suu Kyi's house arrest for another year.

Also, during this time, Major General and National Police Chief Khin Yi told a regional police forces conference that "the release of Ms. Suu Kyi would likely have little effect on the country's political stability and that there would not be rallies and riots if Ms. Suu Kyi was released since public support for her has fallen."[25] Such comments undermined the Government's arguments that Aung San Suu Kyi posed a threat to the State. In response to the extension of her house arrest, the WGAD issued its fourth Opinion on her case, finding this extension to be in violation of international law. In defending the extension, the Government changed its position from house arrest as a form of protection for Aung San Suu Kyi to arguing that she conducted a campaign to discredit the Government with "the intention of harming the integrity of the Union and solidarity of the national races" and thus represent a threat to the state.[26] On May 28, 2008, the Government renewed Aung San Suu Kyi's detention for another year without providing any reason. Still she had not been formally charged with having committed any crimes and received no trial. The WGAD, in its fifth Opinion on Aung San Suu Kyi's case, identified this extension of house arrest as not only in violation of international law but Burmese law as well because it exceeded the five-year maximum detention sentence as set by the 1975 State Protection Law.

On May 3, 2009, six years into Aung San Suu Kyi's third extended period of house arrest, James Yettaw, an American citizen, covertly swam across the lake in Aung San Suu Kyi's backyard and was able to gain access to her home. Yettaw had made a similar attempt on November 30, 2008; however, at that time, Aung San Suu Kyi refused to see

---

[24] After being denied repeatedly to visit Aung San Suu Kyi again by the Burmese government, the previous UN Special Envoy, Razali Ismail, resigned from his post in January 2006. *United Nations' Burma Envoy Quits*, BBC NEWS, Jan. 8, 2006.

[25] Aung San Suu Kyi v. Myanmar, WGAD Opinion No. 2/2007, Adopted May 8, 2007 (Litigated by Author through Freedom Now).

[26] *Id.*, at ¶ 13.

him, and he left. This time, however, because Yettaw was suffering from asthma and leg cramps, Aung San Suu Kyi provided him temporary shelter. Beyond a quick logistical exchange of information, she did not engage with Yettaw and remained upstairs as he recovered. Aung San Suu Kyi did not report Yettaw's presence to authorities this trip because she had planned to inform her doctor, Dr. Tin Myo Win, on his next visit scheduled for May 7, 2009, as she did not want the guards on duty to get in trouble for Yettaw's intrusion. When Yettaw intruded in 2008, Aung San Suu Kyi had informed authorities through Dr. Tin Myo Win with no repercussion. This time, however, Yettaw was able to leave on May 5, 2009, but was caught by security forces and questioned. In a later released video, Yettaw shared that he had asked to take a photo with Aung San Suu Kyi and she refused. In the video, he is heard saying "She looks frightened and I am sorry about this."[27]

On May 14, 2009, Aung San Suu Kyi was taken to Insein Prison in Rangoon and, because of Yettaw's intrusion, charged with breaching the terms of her house arrest and, thus, violating Article 22 of the 1975 State Protection law.[28] Aung San Suu Kyi's trial took place in a courtroom inside Insein Prison and lasted from May 18 to August 11, 2009. During that time period, she was only allowed intermittent access to her lawyers, who were faced with reprisals for their involvement in her case.[29] The defense put forward five witnesses, but three were rejected by the Court. But the Court approved all twenty-three of the prosecution's witnesses and ultimately fourteen testified. On May 25, 2009, a week into the trial, the prosecution cancelled its remaining witnesses, forcing Aung San Suu Kyi to testify the next day, without any contact with her lawyers. She was not able to meet with her lawyers until after the witness testimony had concluded on May 30, 2009. On August 11, 2009, Aung San Suu Kyi was sentenced to three years of hard labor, which was then commuted to an eighteen-month extension of her house arrest.[30]

Throughout her trial, Aung San Suu Kyi's legal team requested a public trial, which was rejected by the court. The trial was open to select diplomats and domestic journalists on four occasions for a limited number of hours. The Government closely monitored these court observers and instructed the domestic journalists to follow closely the official court reports. In July 2009, UN Secretary General Ban Ki-moon visited Burma, but was not able to meet with Aung San Suu Kyi. On October 2, 2009, an appellate court rejected Aung San Suu Kyi's appeal. The WGAD, in its sixth Opinion on Aung San Suu Kyi's case, found no legal basis for the charges against Aung San Suu Kyi and serious procedural flaws in the 2009 trial, finding her detention arbitrary and in violation of international law. After serving the eighteen-month extension of her house arrest, Aung San Suu Kyi was finally released on November 12, 2010.

---

[27] Aung San Suu Kyi v. Myanmar, WGAD Opinion No. 12/2010, Adopted May 7, 2010, at ¶ 12 (Litigated by Author through Freedom Now).

[28] Article 22 states "any person against whom action is taken, who opposes, resists, or disobeys any order passed under this Law shall be liable to imprisonment for a period of three years to five years, or a fine of up to 5,000 kyats, or both." State Protection Law, Pyithu Hluttaw Law No. 3 (1975).

[29] One lawyer had his law license revoked and another lawyer's wife was fired from her government job.

[30] Aung San Suu Kyi v. Myanmar, WGAD Opinion No. 12/2010, Adopted May 7, 2010, at ¶¶ 16–23.

II Petitions to Working Group on Arbitrary Detention and Its Opinions

Over the course of her fifteen years of imprisonment, Aung San Suu Kyi's counsel submitted six different petitions to the WGAD. The Petitions were submitted either at the start of a new period of house arrest or when a house arrest was extended. The Government only responded to the first four Petitions, providing different arguments to justify her detention. The WGAD ruled in favor of Aung San Suu Kyi in all six Petitions and set an important precedent on how it can issue multiple opinions relating to one person when they are the subject of constant persecution from a government.[31]

A *Opinion No. 8/1992*

The first Petition was submitted after Aung San Suu Kyi's first house arrest starting on July 20, 1989. Her lawyers at the time accused the Government of arbitrarily imprisoning Aung San Suu Kyi because of her status as a leader in the Burmese pro-democracy movement and for her "peaceful exercise of [her] rights to freedom of expression and assembly, rights which are guaranteed under articles 19 and 20 of the Universal Declaration of Human Rights."[32] The Government's response, as summarized by the WGAD, cited the 1975 State Protection Law and argued that Aung San Suu Kyi, through her speeches on nonviolence and peaceful resistance, "created situations that endangered the State; she tried to cause division between the Tatmadaw (armed forces) and the people, and engaged in activities (inciting) hatred of the people towards the Tatmadaw."[33] The Government also noted that under 1975 State Protection Law, formal arrest is not required and the suspension of certain rights and restriction of movement and outside contacts can be imposed.[34]

In its analysis, the WGAD observed that while the Government confirmed it had placed Aung San Suu Kyi under house arrest for her critical comments about its actions, it had not alleged she had resorted to violence, incited violence, or threatened in any way the public order. As such, the WGAD found that it "appears that the measure applied to [her] is based solely on the fact that [she] had freely and peacefully exercised [her] rights to freedom of opinion, expression and association, rights that are guaranteed under articles 19 and 20 of the Universal Declaration of Human Rights and articles 19 and 21

---

[31] Notably, for individuals who are repeatedly targeted by a government, the WGAD may revisit the detention of the subject of a prior opinion and consider issuing a new opinion regarding a new period of detention. But this is decided as a matter of the WGAD's discretion. In Gao Zhisheng v. China, the WGAD concluded that the government's disappearance of a prominent human rights lawyer constituted a "clear non-observance of the international norms relating to the right to a fair trial." Gao Zhisheng v. China, WGAD Opinion No. 26/2010, Adopted Nov. 19, 2010 (Litigated by Author through Freedom Now). In December 2011, the Government sent Gao back to prison, reimposing a previously suspended three-year prison term for inciting subversion, despite having disappeared him for twenty months at the time that decision was made. In January 2012, the author submitted a new petition to the WGAD. In two subsequent sessions, the WGAD considered if it should make a new communication to the Government, in light of it having already sent a follow-up letter to the Government asking for an update on the case. On December 3, 2012, the Secretary to the WGAD wrote to the author reporting "The Working Group decided not to submit the case on Gao Zhisheng and to wait for the response from the Government to its follow up letter."

[32] Aung San Suu Kyi and U Nu v. Myanmar, WGAD Opinion No. 8/1992, Adopted Session No. 4, at ¶ 7.

[33] *Id.*, at ¶ 9.

[34] *Id.*, at ¶ 11.

of the International Covenant on Civil and Political Rights."[35] Furthermore, the WGAD found that holding Aung San Suu Kyi under house arrest "without charge or trial" and without access to her counsel, denied her the capacity to "challenge [her] deprivation of liberty before a court" and thus, "[i]t therefore appears that articles 9, 10 and 11 of the Universal Declaration of Human Rights and articles 9 and 14 of the International Covenant on Civil and Political Rights have been violated."[36] Given the violations found by the WGAD, it concluded Aung San Suu Kyi's detention was arbitrary under Categories II and III of its Methods of Work.

B Opinion No. 2/2002

The second Petition was submitted in relation to Aung San Suu Kyi's second house arrest starting on September 22, 2000. Her lawyers argued that her travel ban and house arrest were a result of her exercising the rights and freedoms relating to movement, expression, assembly, and participation in public life as guaranteed by Articles 13, 19, 20, and 21 of the UDHR. Additionally, her lawyers argued that her being placed under house arrest without charges or trial violated her due process rights guaranteed by Articles 8, 9, 10, and 11 of the UDHR. They also noted that she was denied any access to visiting dignitaries, except for the then-UN Special Rapporteur on the Situation of Human Rights in Myanmar and a European Union delegation.[37] The Government, in its response, denied that Aung San Suu Kyi was under arbitrary detention, as she has been allowed visits from foreign dignitaries, who said she was in good health, and to participate in meetings of the NLD. It did not contest that she was under house arrest imposed by military authorities nor that she was never charged with any crime.[38]

The WGAD began its analysis making clear that though the Government may not believe Aung San Suu Kyi's house arrest to be considered arbitrary detention, "house arrest may be compared to deprivation of liberty provided that it is carried out in closed premises which the person is not allowed to leave."[39] As such, the WGAD found that Aung San Suu Kyi's house arrest, both previous and current, amounted to arbitrary detention. The WGAD also noted that it did not consider there to be a legal basis upon which Aung San Suu Kyi was detained. And it further observed the Government did not contest that Aung San Suu Kyi was imprisoned without charge or trial. Given these factors, the WGAD delivered a very similar opinion to its prior opinion on the case, affirming that Aung San Suu Kyi is being deprived of her liberty, in violation of Articles 9, 10, 19, and 20 of the UDHR, and thus finding detention to be an arbitrary deprivation of liberty under Categories II and III.[40]

---

[35] *Id.*, at ¶ 14.
[36] *Id.*, at ¶ 16 (This was back in the early years of the WGAD, when it would apply provisions of the ICCPR, even if a country was not a party to the treaty).
[37] Aung San Suu Kyi v. Myanmar, WGAD Opinion No. 2/2002, Adopted June 19, 2002, at ¶¶ 5–10.
[38] *Id.*, at ¶¶ 11–12.
[39] *Id.*, at ¶ 13.
[40] *Id.*, at ¶¶ 14–17.

C Opinion No. 9/2004

The third Petition to the WGAD was submitted after Aung San Suu Kyi's third house arrest, which followed the Depayin Massacre, on May 31, 2003. In that Petition, which was submitted with an urgent action appeal, Aung San Suu Kyi's lawyers noted that after the massacre she was originally detained in Insein Prison and then moved to a military guest house. During this time, she was held in detention without charge and with no access to relatives or lawyers. Only certain independent observers were able to visit her. In the Petition, Aung San Suu Kyi's lawyers explained she was again being held under the 1975 State Protection Law, which as summarized previously, allows for detention, up to five years, without charge or trial if a person is deemed a threat to the state.[41]

The Government responded in three different communications. The first two responded to two of the WGAD's urgent appeals and the third was a formal response to the Petition itself. In its responses, the Government argued that Aung San Suu Kyi had not been arrested but "had only been taken into protective custody for her own safety" after the Depayin Massacre.[42] The Government commented that such precautions were necessary for Aung San Suu Kyi's safety and then explained how it had helped facilitate her work as the General Secretary of the NLD over the past year "by granting her status of distinguished person."[43] The Government explained such privileges had to be curbed in the wake of the Depayin Massacre because "as a result of the activities of [Aung San Suu Kyi's] supporters and members of the party, unlawful and violent acts had recently taken place, causing disturbances which endangered the process of national reconciliation."[44] The Government noted that Aung San Suu Kyi had been visited by the Special Representative of the United Nations Secretary-General and the Special Rapporteur of the Commission on Human Rights as well as members of her party. And she had been given medical care when needed.[45] Lastly, the Government commented that while it could have initiated legal action against her under domestic legislation, it had chosen "to adopt a magnanimous attitude and is providing her protection in her own interests."[46] Lawyers for Aung San Suu Kyi rejected the Government's claims, arguing that she was being held in alleged protective custody against her will and that no protective custody persists for a year. They also noted that the telephone line to her residence had been disconnected and further alleged that she was only being detained because of her role as leader of the opposition.[47]

The WGAD began its analysis by noting the two previous opinions on Aung San Suu Kyi's case and commented that her present situation is akin to her previous arbitrary detentions, where she was held without charges or trial and subject to restrictions of whom she communicates with in the outside world. The WGAD considered the Government's argument – that Aung San Suu Kyi was in detention for her own benefit and protection and to also prevent further incidents of any kind – was in violation of

---

[41] Aung San Suu Kyi v. Myanmar, WGAD Opinion No. 9/2004, Adopted May 28, 2004, at ¶¶ 5–7.
[42] Id., at ¶ 9.
[43] Id., at ¶ 10.
[44] Id.
[45] Id., at ¶¶ 8–11.
[46] Id., at ¶ 12.
[47] Id., at ¶ 13.

Article 9 of the UDHR.[48] And as such, it ruled this current detention was arbitrary under Category I. This was the first time that the WGAD applied Category I to Aung San Suu Kyi's case and it seemed that this application came as a result of the Government's arguments trying to justify her detention.[49] The WGAD did not invoke Categories II or III in this Opinion, perhaps because both Categories had been applied in the previous two decisions, which the WGAD mentioned in the beginning of this Opinion.

D *Opinion No. 2/2007*

The fourth Petition for Aung San Suu Kyi's case was submitted after the Government extended her house arrest for another year on May 27, 2006. Her lawyers, who now included the author, repeated the facts of her detention, which was in its fourth year, and added several new arguments. The Petition noted serious concern for Aung San Suu Kyi's health as she had only infrequent access to her medical doctors. It observed that Ibrahim Gambari, the Special Envoy of the Secretary-General on the situation in Myanmar, was able to visit her on May 24, 2006, and then called for her release. It commented that she continued to have no opportunity for legal redress. And it reaffirmed that Aung San Suu Kyi was being imprisoned for her pro-democracy advocacy and status as the leader of the opposition.[50] The Petition argued there was no legal justification for her detention and that "no controlling body, acting in good faith, would find or believe that she is a potential danger to the State."[51] It also cited comments from May 23, 2006, by Major General Khin Yi at a regional police conference, where he stated that "the release of Ms. Suu Kyi would likely have little effect on the country's political stability and that there would not be rallies and riots if Ms. Suu Kyi was released since public support for her has fallen."[52]

In its response, the Government recounted the events of 2003 and argued that Aung San Suu Kyi "carried out activities detrimental to the peace and tranquility of the livelihood of the local community."[53] Specifically, the Government claimed she "delivered speeches to discredit the Government to impair the dignity thereof and also conducted campaigning with the intention of harming the integrity of the Union and solidarity of the national races."[54] Thus, as opposed to arguing that Aung San Suu Kyi was under house arrest for her own safety, the Government was now arguing that she was under house arrest because of the threat she posed to the state. In its response, the Government cited multiple domestic laws that allowed for an individual to be detained without trial in order "to safeguard the State against the dangers of those desiring to cause subversive acts."[55]

In its analysis, the WGAD noted that this Opinion was the fourth on Aung San Suu Kyi's case and that "the basic facts in the previous opinions and the present

[48] *Id.*, at ¶¶ 14–15.
[49] *Id.*, at ¶ 16.
[50] Aung San Suu Kyi v. Myanmar, WGAD Opinion No. 2/2007, Adopted May 8, 2007, at ¶¶ 4–8 (Litigated by Author through Freedom Now).
[51] *Id.*, at ¶ 10.
[52] *Id.*, at ¶ 9.
[53] *Id.*, at ¶ 13.
[54] *Id.*
[55] *Id.*, at ¶¶ 13–15.

communication are either identical or very similar."[56] It highlighted that Aung San Suu Kyi was being prevented from participation in the political life of her country and that her detention, in addition to detrimental psychological and health effects, is "tantamount to deprivation of liberty . . . and aimed to prevent her to exercise her right to freedom of opinion and expression."[57] Additionally, the WGAD commented that these restraints placed on her prevented a fair judicial process, as noted by the Government in its justification of house arrest without trial. The WGAD labeled as "unsubstantiated" the Government's accusations of Aung San Suu Kyi's actions as detrimental to the peace and tranquility of the State and the WGAD also noted that the Government itself did not assert that Aung San Suu Kyi ever resorted to violence.[58] The WGAD further commented that "the obvious unwillingness of the Government to comply with the Working Group's Opinions and recommendations to put an end to the house arrest of Ms. Suu Kyi is particularly worrying."[59] And the WGAD found the extension of Aung San Suu Kyi's house arrest to be in violation of Articles 9, 10, and 19 of the UDHR and arbitrary under Categories II and III of its Methods of Work.[60] The Opinion of this case was significant in that it demonstrated that the WGAD can consider the extension of the same detention as grounds for a new opinion.

E Opinion No. 46/2008

The fifth Petition to the WGAD on Aung San Suu Kyi's case was submitted after her house arrest was extended for the second time on May 28, 2008. The Petition argued that with the expiration of her house arrest detention order, the applicability of the corresponding WGAD Opinion expired as well. This premise was again accepted by the WGAD. According to the Petition, the Government extended her house arrest under the provisions of the 1975 State Protection Law; however, this extension was in violation of domestic law, as the 1975 State Protection Law only allowed for house arrest up to five years. Similar to the previous extension, the Petition noted that the Government still had not charged Aung San Suu Kyi with any crime nor initiated Court proceedings. Her lawyers also noted that her condition had not improved since their prior submission. Aung San Suu Kyi still did not have regular access to her lawyers or relatives and, beyond select, government-approved diplomats, the only people to visit her regularly were her doctor and the person to deliver her food.[61] The Government did not respond to the WGAD's communication on the Petition.[62]

In its analysis, the WGAD acknowledged that the five-year detention period permitted by the 1975 State Protection Law had passed, and thus "the most recent extension on 28 May 2008 amounts to a prima facie violation of the Union of Myanmar's own laws."[63] While the WGAD explained there was a vague definition of when a detention begins in

---

[56] *Id.*, at ¶ 17.
[57] *Id.*
[58] *Id.*
[59] *Id.*, at ¶ 18.
[60] *Id.*
[61] Aung San Suu Kyi v. Myanmar, WGAD Opinion No. 46/2008, Adopted Nov. 28, 2008, at ¶¶ 4-10 (Litigated by Author through Freedom Now).
[62] *Id.*, at ¶ 11.
[63] *Id.*, at ¶ 12.

the 1975 State Protection Law – it could be when a person is arrested or when the order of arrest is made – it also acknowledged that "it would be inconsistent with basic principles of rule of law for a detention to begin only when an order is issued under this law and not when a person's liberty or freedom of movement is restricted."[64] And thus, following this interpretation, the WGAD found that:

> The renewal of Ms. Aung San Suu Kyi's placement under house arrest is arbitrary as it violates the rights and fundamental freedoms established in the Universal Declaration of Human Rights, the Body of Principles for the Protection of All Persons under Any Form of Detention or Imprisonment, and the Standard Minimum Rules for the Treatment of Prisoners, falling under categories I, II and, III of the categories applicable to the cases submitted to the Working Group on Arbitrary Detention.[65]

In this Opinion, similar to the previous opinions, the WGAD cited the violation of Articles 9, 10, and 19 of the UDHR as well as Myanmar domestic law as the grounds of its ruling.[66] Additionally, this was the first Opinion where the WGAD found violations of Categories I, II, and III in the same Opinion. It also acknowledged for the first time that it had decided to "transmit this Opinion to the Special Adviser of the Secretary-General, Mr. Ibrahim Gambari, as well as to the Special Rapporteur on the situation of Human Rights in Myanmar, Mr. Tomás Ojea Quintana, for their consideration."[67]

F Opinion No. 12/2010

The sixth and final Petition submitted to the WGAD on Aung San Suu Kyi's case related to the final eighteen-month extension of Aung San Suu Kyi's third extended period of house arrest. The Government extended this third extended period for a third time on August 11, 2009, accusing her of violating the conditions of her house arrest after John Yettaw's intrusion. The Petition described the events relating to Yettaw's intrusion and the due process violations associated with the subsequent trial. It argued that Aung San Suu Kyi should not be liable for any of Yettaw's actions and that she had responded in a way that was consistent with similar past events.[68] The Government did not respond to the WGAD's communication on this Petition.[69]

In its analysis, the WGAD emphasized the Government was charging Aung San Suu Kyi for violating a house arrest that the WGAD "repeatedly found lacking legal basis."[70] As such, the WGAD noted "no charges can flow from the violation of the terms of this previous house arrest order."[71] In considering the intrusion of John Yettaw, the WGAD found there was no evidence that Aung San Suu Kyi knew or welcomed Yettaw and that she had taken reasonable measures to minimize contact with him. Furthermore,

---

[64] *Id.*, at ¶ 14.
[65] *Id.*, at ¶ 15.
[66] *Id.*, at ¶ 16.
[67] *Id.*
[68] *Aung San Suu Kyi v. Myanmar*, WGAD Opinion No. 12/2010, Adopted May 7, 2010, at ¶¶ 6–24 (Litigated by Author through Freedom Now).
[69] *Id.*, at ¶ 25.
[70] *Id.*, at ¶ 26.
[71] *Id.*

the WGAD noted that there was no way that Aung San Suu Kyi could have prevented his intrusion. The WGAD also considered expert reports at the United Nations, which had declared the judiciary as neither independent from the Government nor impartial. The WGAD considered the myriad of abuses in Aung San Suu Kyi's trial and found the Government in violation of international norms and law relating to the right to a fair trial as enshrined in in Article 10 of the UDHR, Principles 15, 17(2), 18, and 19 of the *Body of Principles for the Protection of All Persons under Any Form of Detention or Imprisonment*, and Article 37 of the *Standard Minimum Rules for the Treatment of Prisoners*.[72]

Additionally, the WGAD noted Aung San Suu Kyi's inability to access her counsel and consistent medical care and found the Government to be violating the right to access medical care enshrined in Principle 24 of the Body of Principles and Articles 24 and 25 of the Standard Minimum Rules. The WGAD ultimately found the Government in violation of Articles 9, 10, 19, and 20 of the UDHR.[73] And thus, citing again Categories I, II, and III in the same Opinion, the WGAD found her continued detention arbitrary and in violation of international law.[74]

Aung San Suu Kyi was ultimately released after the eighteen-month house arrest extension ended on November 13, 2010. Given her international prominence and strong support of her own people, Aung San Suu Kyi was considered an existential threat to the Government. It is therefore not surprising the six opinions of the WGAD alone were insufficient to secure her release from these three periods of extended house arrest. Nonetheless, her being the only imprisoned Nobel Peace Prize Laureate at the time, combined with these opinions and sustained political and public relations advocacy, made her the most famous political prisoner in the world. It was central to maintaining pressure on the Government that it be held to account by the WGAD every time it extended her illegal house arrest.

III Campaign to Secure Aung San Suu Kyi's Freedom

Given the extraordinary threat that Aung San Suu Kyi posed to the Government, securing her freedom took much more than prevailing in numerous opinions before the WGAD. For cases of prominent political figures, WGAD opinions are just one component of the overall strategy to secure their release. WGAD opinions in the case of political prisoners legitimize the claims of arbitrary detention, and multiple opinions serve as updates that can re-energize international attention on the prisoner. In cases like Aung San Suu Kyi's, the advocacy related to her case required developing a strategy that maximized the impact of each WGAD opinion to maintain pressure on the military junta of Burma. This section highlights key elements of the broader efforts that resulted in her freedom, such as international engagement, bilateral engagement, and the media, which all combined with the efforts of countless others globally pushing for her freedom and that of Myanmar's thousands of political prisoners.

---

[72] *Id.*, at ¶¶ 27–33.
[73] *Id.*, at ¶¶ 26–36.
[74] *Id.*, at ¶ 37.

A *International Engagement*

Under military dictatorship, Myanmar became the focus of much international attention. By the time the author joined Aung San Suu Kyi's legal team as international counsel in 2006, there had already been three WGAD opinions in her favor. Though the legal team would ultimately submit three more cases to the WGAD to maximize pressure on the Government, the opinions of the Working Group had to be paired with other international advocacy efforts, such as the aforementioned initiative at the Security Council. Obtaining an opinion from the WGAD gives a political prisoner's case legitimacy, as the global community appreciates the significance of having a UN body find a prisoner's detention to be an arbitrary deprivation of liberty in violation of international law. It also provides independent validation of the legitimacy of the detainee's claims.

On the highest profile political prisoner cases, it can be extremely effective to mobilize luminaries to assist, such as Nobel Peace Prize Laureates and former presidents and prime ministers. At times, they can even be utilized as impartial negotiators with connections to former ally states. As noted earlier, Archbishop Tutu and President Havel worked to get the situation of Myanmar on the Security Council's agenda, even though ultimately it resulted in a vetoed resolution in January 2007.[75]

In May 2007, a few months after the vetoed resolution and prior to the Saffron Revolution, the author, along with these dignitaries and former Norwegian Prime Minister Kjell Magne Bondevik, organized a letter to Burmese junta leader General Than Shwe from fifty-nine former heads of state calling for the release of "the world's only imprisoned Nobel Peace Prize Laureate."[76] Months later, when the Saffron Revolution happened in August 2007 and the Government gunned down monks and journalists in the streets, China and Russia stood aside and allowed the Security Council to issue a Presidential Statement with a roadmap to address the future of international engagement on Burma, which included a call for the "early release" of Aung San Suu Kyi and other political prisoners.[77]

In December 2008, the author helped organize a letter from 112 former heads of state from more than 50 countries to UN Secretary-General Ban Ki-moon urging him to travel to Myanmar to press for the release of Aung San Suu Kyi and other political prisoners.[78] Immediately after the letter was sent, Bondevik spoke to the Secretary-General, who within days had organized a discussion in New York for the countries that were a part of the "Group of Friends of Myanmar" caucus. The letter put enormous pressure on Ban Ki-moon to travel there. He visited Myanmar in July 2009 and although he was not allowed to visit Aung San Suu Kyi, this engagement at the international level created new

---

[75] Security Council Fails to Adopt Draft Resolution on Myanmar.

[76] *59 Former Heads of State Call for Burma to Release World's Only Imprisoned Nobel Peace Prize Laureate*, May 15, 2007, *available at* www.freedom-now.org/wp-content/uploads/2010/09/Suu-Kyi-Letter-from-59-Former-Heads-of-State-5.15.07.pdf (last accessed Aug. 2018).

[77] Statement by the President of the Security Council – The Situation in Myanmar.

[78] *Letter from 112 Former Presidents and Prime Ministers Sent to UN Secretary-General Urging Him to Press for Release of All Political Prisoners in Burma by the End of 2008*, Dec. 3, 2008 (Aug. 2018), www.freedom-now.org/wp-content/uploads/2010/09/Suu-Kyi-Letter-from-112-Former-Presidents-and-Prime-Ministers-12.3.08.pdf.

pressure for the Government and its allies and further emboldened other international actors. In 2009, the Security Council would issue two further press statements expressing concern for Aung San Suu Kyi.[79]

B Bilateral Pressure

In addition to the multilateral pressure, the author, along with other members of Aung San Suu Kyi's legal team, worked to increase bilateral pressure on the Government through like-minded governments. In the United States, effective advocacy from rights groups, especially the Institute for Asian Democracy and US Campaign for Burma, directed at President George W. Bush not only increased sanctions substantially but resulted in First Lady Laura Bush personally taking up the cause of restoring democracy to Myanmar.[80] President Barack Obama renewed these sanctions and his National Security Council, working with the author, secured a public statement from President Obama calling for the release of Aung San Suu Kyi, which was timed to the issuance of the most recent WGAD opinion in 2009.[81] Additional efforts that year included an April 4, 2009, public letter from seventeen Members of Congress to US Secretary of State Hillary Clinton, urging her to press for the release of Aung San Suu Kyi, which she did publicly on May 14, 2009.[82] And on April 14, 2009, twelve members of the US Senate Women's Caucus wrote a public letter to Secretary-General Ban Ki-Moon urging him to exert more international political pressure on Burma's military junta.[83]

Similar initiatives were undertaken in the United Kingdom, which as a result of its colonial history had deep connections to different aspects of Burmese society. As a result of the relentless efforts of Burma Campaign UK, the United Kingdom, working with the European Union, first issued sanctions against Myanmar in 1996. However, in 2007 and 2009 they renewed these sanctions, citing Aung San Suu Kyi's house arrest extension as a reason for the 2009 extension.[84] These sanctions and declarations had the impact of increasing pressure on the Government while also emboldening human rights activists in the country by reminding them that members of the international community recognized their struggle and were working to support them however possible.

And beyond the special focus on the United States and United Kingdom, the author traveled the world, often with Burmese activists, to advocate for the freedom of Aung San Suu Kyi and Myanmar's political prisoners. Over the five years the author worked on her behalf, he traveled to many countries to meet with government officials, civil society groups, and journalists, including Australia, Austria, Belgium, China, Czech Republic,

---

[79] *Security Council Press Statement on Myanmar*, Security Council, SC/9662, May 22, 2009; *Security Council Press Statement on Myanmar*, Security Council, SC/9731, Aug. 13, 2009.

[80] David E. Sanger and Steven Lee Myers, US *Steps up Confrontation with Myanmar*, THE NEW YORK TIMES, Sep. 29, 2007.

[81] *Statement on the Detention of Aung San Suu Kyi in Burma*, May 26, 2009 (Aug. 2018), www.presidency .ucsb.edu/ws/index.php?pid=86182.

[82] *Letter to Secretary Clinton from Members of US Congress*, Apr. 3, 2009 (Aug. 2018) www.freedom-now.org/wp-content/uploads/2010/09/Suu-Kyi-Letter-from-Members-of-the-US-Congress-4.3.09.pdf; *Myanmar Democracy Leader Facing Trial after American's Swim*, CNN, May 17, 2009.

[83] *Senate Women's Caucus on Burma Calls on UN Secretary General Ban Ki-moon to Exert More International Political Pressure on Burma's Military Junta*, Apr. 14, 2009 (Aug. 2018), www.freedom-now.org/wp-content/uploads/2010/09/Suu-Kyi-Letter-from-US-Senate-Womens-Caucus-4.9.09.pdf.

[84] *Who Maintain Sanctions on Burma?* BBC NEWS, Oct. 18, 2010.

Estonia, France, Germany, Greece, Italy, Jordan, Latvia, Japan, Malaysia, Portugal, South Korea, South Africa, Spain, Switzerland, The Philippines, and Thailand, among others.

C Media and Opinion Editorials

To maximize pressure on the Government, multilateral and bilateral diplomatic efforts and the work of civil society groups had to be paired with a focused media strategy. The press was critical to maintaining international pressure on the Government, as under the spotlight of the global community, it had clearly felt pressured to restrain its actions. Over the five years that the author served as international counsel to Aung San Suu Kyi, he was interviewed by more than 500 television, print, and radio journalists, including many interviews with Voice of America, Radio Free Asia, and BBC Burmese Service, all of which broadcast inside Myanmar in Burmese. While some of the news coverage was driven by events, such as when the American John Yettaw swam to Aung San Suu Kyi's home and broke in, every opportunity was taken to break news. For example, each time the WGAD found that Aung San Suu Kyi was being held in violation of international law, a press release was sent out, which generated news coverage.[85]

In addition to publishing press releases to generate media coverage tied with current developments, the author sought to influence global public opinion and press for action through a relentless series of twenty-eight opinion editorials (opeds) in key newspapers at critical moments over the five years he served as her international counsel.[86] The opinion pieces were all crafted to fit the intended audience and what specific actions should be taken and by whom.

---

[85] See, e.g., *Detention of Aung San Suu Kyi in Burma Illegal, Says UN*, THE GUARDIAN, Mar. 24, 2009.

[86] See Jared Genser: *Now We Must All Stand With The Lady*, THE TIMES (London), Nov. 15, 2010; *No More Charades*, LOS ANGELES TIMES, Oct. 25, 2010; *No More Charades*, LOS ANGELES TIMES, Oct. 25, 2010; *Dialog Uten Resultater* (Dialogue Without Results), VERDENS GANG (Oslo), Apr. 27, 2010; *Pressuring the Burmese Junta*, INTERNATIONAL HERALD TRIBUNE, Aug. 13, 2009; *The Burmese Junta Still Fears Suu Kyi*, WALL STREET JOURNAL, May 18, 2009 (reprinted in WALL STREET JOURNAL ASIA); *More UN Action for Myanmar*, THE KOREA TIMES, Dec. 17, 2008 (reprinted in SOUTH CHINA MORNING POST); *Free Aung San Suu Kyi*, THE AGE (Melbourne), Oct. 24, 2008 (also reprinted in BRISBANE TIMES, WAToday (Perth), and THE KOREA TIMES); *A Roadmap for Democracy in Burma*, FAR EASTERN ECONOMIC REVIEW, July 25, 2008; *The US Must Do More for Burma*, HUFFINGTON POST, June 18, 2008; *RI Running Out of Time to Play Key Role in Myanmar*, JAKARTA POST, June 12, 2008; *How Long Must the Burmese Wait?*, INTERNATIONAL HERALD TRIBUNE, May 29, 2008; *Burma's Next Wave of Dying*, BOSTON GLOBE, May 21, 2008; *SA Again Turns Its Back on the Burmese*, BUSINESS DAY (Johannesburg), May 13, 2008; *The Lie After the Storm*, FAR EASTERN ECONOMIC REVIEW, May 2008; *How to Deal with Burma*, WALL STREET JOURNAL ASIA, Feb. 1, 2008; *Fresh Start Needed to Deal With Junta*, SYDNEY MORNING HERALD, Dec. 10, 2007; *America Must Do More to End Myanmar Misery*, BALTIMORE SUN, Oct. 26, 2007; *A New Strategy for Burma*, BOSTON GLOBE, Oct. 5, 2007; *Gordon Brown's Strange Silence on Burma*, THE INDEPENDENT (UK), Aug. 27, 2007; *Prisoner in Myanmar: The Lady and The Junta*, INTERNATIONAL HERALD TRIBUNE, June 2, 2007; *Slovakia Can Help*, SME (Bratislava, Slovakia), May 16, 2007; *Estonia Needs to Advocate for Freedom in Burma*, EESTI PAEVALEHT (Tallinn, Estonia), Apr. 10, 2007; *Latvia Can Help Bring Freedom to Burma*, DIENA (Riga), Feb. 5, 2007; *SA Should Return the Favour*, THE STAR (Johannesburg), Jan. 17, 2006; *Do the Right Thing*, WALL STREET JOURNAL ASIA, May 31, 2006; *The Drum Beats Louder for UN Action on Burma*, THE NATION (Bangkok), May 10, 2006; *A Path to Peace in Burma*, FAR EASTERN ECONOMIC REVIEW, Dec. 2005; *Myanmar: A Job for the Security Council*, INTERNATIONAL HERALD TRIBUNE, Sept. 20, 2005.

For example, right after Aung San Suu Kyi was released, an oped in *the Times* (London) highlighted how the international community can best support her and the pro-democracy movement once she is out of jail.[87] An oped in the *Wall Street Journal* encouraged members of the United Nations to take action on the deteriorating human rights situation in Myanmar.[88] Other opeds were tailored toward how specific governments could best utilize their historic relationships with Myanmar or their status in the region in order to free Aung San Suu Kyi. For example, an oped in the *Jakarta Post* identified how the Indonesian president, as the leader of a regional power, could help influence the human rights situation in Myanmar.[89] Another piece in *The Age* (Melbourne) pressed the Australian government to act in support of Aung San Suu Kyi.[90] And an oped in *The Star* (Johannesburg) made a more historical argument, citing how the then-democratic Government of Myanmar sought to sanction apartheid South Africa until the Burmese government became a military junta, and the now-democratic South African government should return the favor and stand up for human rights in Myanmar.[91] And opeds were even published in countries in the local languages that may not on the surface seem relevant to Myanmar, such as in Slovakia,[92] because it was a member of the Security Council, or in Latvia and Estonia because they were members of the European Union and as former Soviet-occupied countries their people should support having the EU sanction Myanmar.[93] Other opeds targeted specific leaders, such as in the United Kingdom, when Prime Minister Gordon Brown identified Aung San Suu Kyi as one of his heroes, but had not been taking specific actions to help on her case.[94]

Ultimately, these opinion pieces had to educate readers about Myanmar, summarize Aung San Suu Kyi's case, and then advocate for specific actions to be undertaken by governments or multilateral institutions. A strong oped, published at the right time and in the right publication, can have an important effect.

IV Conclusion

As the then most prominent political prisoner in the world and existential threat to the military junta in Myanmar, securing Aung San Suu Kyi's release required mobilizing global action not only on her behalf but for the greater cause of restoring democracy for the some 50 million people of her country. Given the enormity of that challenge and the general view held worldwide that she was clearly a political prisoner, it is not surprising that the series of six WGAD opinions on her case spanning more than fifteen years were not the top focus of the international community. Nonetheless, they played an important role in providing independent legal validation of her arbitrary detention and they helped mobilize strategic political and public relations efforts globally to sustain specific pressure

---

[87] *Now We Must All Stand with The Lady.*
[88] *Do the Right Thing.*
[89] *RI Running Out of Time to Play Key Role in Myanmar.*
[90] *Free Aung San Suu Kyi.*
[91] *SA Should Return the Favour.*
[92] *Slovakia Can Help.*
[93] *Estonia Needs to Advocate for Freedom in Burma; Latvia Can Help Bring Freedom to Burma.*
[94] *Gordon Brown's Strange Silence on Burma.*

on the Government regarding her case. Aung San Suu Kyi herself recognized how important WGAD opinions are to prisoners, saying the work of the WGAD "is invaluable to so many people." And, according to her, the support from the WGAD "is what strengthens us throughout years of isolation. This is what makes us believe it is worthwhile to stand up for one's convictions, for one's free conscience."[95]

---

[95] *Aung San Suu Kyi on Arbitrary Detention*, Nov. 17, 2011 (Aug. 2018), www.youtube.com/watch?v= gOod7blW3ls.

13 *Mukhtar Ablyazov v. France*

I Introduction

A Background

Since its independence from the Soviet Union in 1991, Kazakhstan has been led by President Nursultan Nazarbayev, a Soviet-era politician who has remained in the position by concentrating all political power in his office.[1] No election in the post-Soviet republic has ever met international standards; in March 2015, Nazarbayev won reelection with 95 percent of the vote in a snap election widely panned by the international community.[2] Beyond the complete absence of free and fair elections, the current Government prohibits citizens from enjoying their rights to freedom of expression, assembly, association, and religion. In the past few years, there have been major crackdowns on newspapers, which are the only source of independent news in the country, and many of the country's prisons are filled with detainees serving sentences for peacefully assembling without a permit. Of particular concern to many states and international organizations is the pervasive use of torture in state-run detention centers.

B Facts of the Case

1 Underlying Allegations

One well-known opponent of the present Kazakh regime is Mukhtar Ablyazov, an entrepreneur and former government minister. Ablyazov rose to political prominence as Chairman of the Supervisory Board of the state-owned Kazakhstan Electricity Grid Operating Company (KEGOC). Due to his success at KEGOC, Ablyazov was then appointed Minister of Energy, Industry and Trade of the Republic of Kazakhstan in 1998 and served in this post until 1999, when the Kazakhstan government was dissolved. Disillusioned by Nazarbayev's corruption and protectionist economic policies, Ablyazov refused to take office in Nazarbayev's new government and returned to the private sector.[3]

---

[1] *Country Reports on Human Rights Practices for 2014*, US DEPARTMENT OF STATE, 2014.
[2] Bruce Panner, *Kazakhstan's Long Term President to Run in Snap Election – Again*, THE GUARDIAN, Mar. 11, 2015.
[3] Petition to the Working Group on Arbitrary Detention, Perseus Strategies, Jan. 12, 2016, at 10.

531

In November 2001, Ablyazov co-founded the Democratic Choice of Kazakhstan, an opposition political movement calling for economic liberalization and the decentralization of political power through democratic reform. As one of the most outspoken leaders of the movement,[4] Ablyazov was arrested in 2002 on charges of abuse of office and financial crimes allegedly committed while chair of the KEGOC, and he was sentenced to six years in prison with no right of appeal. While he was in prison, Ablyazov was subjected to severe physical and psychological torture and ill-treatment. International observers considered the trial to be politically motivated and in violation of international legal standards.[5]

In May 2003, after having served ten months of a six-year sentence, Ablyazov was released on a pardon from Nazarbayev – but only on the condition, agreed to under duress, that he cease his political activities.[6] Once he was released from prison, Ablyazov moved to Russia and resumed business activities there, while also maintaining his political activities by funding opposition groups and independent media.[7]

In 2005, Nazarbayev personally called Ablyazov back to Kazakhstan and asked him to take the reins at BTA Bank, where he would serve as its chair. Ablyazov had previously been an owner of the bank, but lost control of the bank and his other business holdings during his wrongful imprisonment in 2002. Though Ablyazov took the position, he believed that Nazarbayev's true motive was to bring him under the regime's control. BTA Bank grew under Ablyazov's leadership, and was named "The Best Bank in Central Asia" by *Euromoney* financial magazine in 2007.[8]

With Ablyazov having made the bank increasingly successful, the regime sought to wrest control away from him. Nazarbayev personally demanded that 50 percent of the bank's shares be transferred to his representatives, which Ablyazov refused.[9] Consequently, Nazarbayev ordered the Government to nationalize the bank in February 2009.[10] The nationalization was authorized by a secret decree that was never provided to BTA Bank or its shareholders and whose property was effectively confiscated by the nationalization. Ablyazov was dismissed from his role and, fearing further persecution, sought refuge in the United Kingdom.

After Ablyazov departed Kazakhstan, the Government brought charges against him for alleged financial misconduct, and officials in Ukraine and Russia also initiated criminal proceedings against Ablyazov, according to an independent NGO, "acting as proxies of the government of Kazakhstan."[11] There was substantial evidence of Kazakhstan's illegal influence on the Russian and Ukrainian proceedings against Ablyazov; for

---

[4] Barbara Junisbai & Azamat Junisbai, *The Democratic Choice of Kazakhstan: A Case Study in Economic Liberalization, Intraelite Cleavage, and Political Opposition*, 13 Demokratizatsiya 380 (2005).

[5] *Concern in Europe and Central Asia, Jul. – December 2002*, Amnesty Int'l 40, EUR 01/002/2003, July 2003 (Nov. 2018), www.amnesty.org/en/documents/eur01/002/2003/en/ [hereinafter July 2003 Amnesty Statement].

[6] Daisy Sindelar, *How Far Will Nazarbayev Go to Take Down Mukhtar Ablyazov?* Radio Free Europe/Radio Liberty, June 7, 2013 [hereinafter How Far Will Nazarbayev Go].

[7] Elliot Blair Smith, *Kazakhstan's Bank Lending Frozen in Subprime Squeeze*, Bloomberg, Dec. 20, 2007.

[8] Awards, BTA Bank (Nov. 2018), http://bta.kz/en/about/awards/.

[9] Igor Savchenko, *Report: Analysis of Documents in the Case of Ablyazov*, Open Dialog Foundation, Sept. 11, 2015, at s. 1 [hereinafter Open Dialog Foundation Report].

[10] *Id.*

[11] Open Letter from Thor Halvorssen, President, Human Rights Foundation, and Garry Kasparov, Chairman, Human Rights Foundation, to Christiane Taubira, Minister of Justice, France, Jan. 2, 2014 [hereinafter Open Letter from Human Rights Foundation].

example, communications between the Ukrainian investigator and the Kazakhstan Prosecutor's Office demonstrated that the Ukrainian investigator was given orders on how to conduct the investigation – and on what decision to reach.[12] And as revealed in documents published by whistleblowers on a Wikileaks-style website (documents that Kazakhstan has conceded to be authentic), the Russian proceedings were similarly driven by the Nazarbayev regime.

Recognizing the politically motivated persecution behind the criminal proceedings driven by Kazakhstan, the United Kingdom granted Ablyazov political asylum in July 2011 after having thoroughly considered his asylum application over a two-year period.[13] During Ablyazov's stay in the United Kingdom from 2009 to 2012, intelligence and police officials sought to protect him: in January 2011, he was issued an "Osman warning" by the London Metropolitan Police, informing him of a real and immediate risk of politically motivated kidnapping or physical harm. Against the backdrop of the Osman warning, which was based upon reliable British intelligence, and after receiving other credible death threats, Ablyazov fled the United Kingdom to continental Europe in February 2012.[14]

2 Arrest and Detention

After arriving in continental Europe, Ablyazov concealed his location for fear of again being targeted by Kazakhstan agents. However, private detectives working for Kazakhstan located Ablyazov in France and alerted BTA Bank's French lawyers of his presence. One of BTA's lawyers then directly contacted the prosecutor in Aix-en-Provence to ask her to proceed with Ablyazov's arrest. On July 31, 2013, French police arrested Ablyazov, acting pursuant to an INTERPOL Red Notice issued by Ukraine, even though they had neither a domestic judicial warrant for his arrest nor an extradition request. Furthermore, while the Red Notice was based on a purported arrest warrant issued by a Kiev court on September 24, 2010, it was later revealed the Kiev court had issued a detention order that was misrepresented as an arrest warrant by Ukraine to INTERPOL. The Red Notice was never made public, nor has a copy ever been provided to Ablyazov. Members of the European Parliament have since referred to the existence of this Red Notice for Ablyazov's arrest as "a compelling case of misuse of the INTERPOL system in the persecution of members of the Kazakh political opposition."[15]

Following Ablyazov's arrest, an initial hearing was held in Aix-en-Provence on August 1, 2013. There it was decided that Ablyazov would be held in custody until the court could consider the request for his extradition. It was not until August 14, 2013, that Ukraine even formally requested Ablyazov's extradition. However, the documents were in French and Ukrainian, languages Ablyazov does not understand, and he was not

[12] Open Dialog Foundation Report, at s. 1.

[13] Simon Goodley, *Mukhtar Ablyazov Exiled Kazakh Businessman Granted Asylum in UK*, THE GUARDIAN, July 12, 2011.

[14] *UN Human Rights Experts Urge Italy to Seek Return of Illegally Deported Kazakh Mother and Daughter*, Office of the UN High Commissioner for Human Rights, July 18, 2013.

[15] Open Letter from Ana Gomes, Member of the European Parliament, and Marju Lauristin, Member of the European Parliament, to Federica Mogherini, High Representative of the European Union for Foreign Affairs and Security Policy, Vice-President of the European Commission.

provided a Russian translation until October 17, 2013. A second extradition request, from Russia, was received by France on August 27, 2013, and formally notified to Ablyazov on November 5, 2013.[16]

The requests for extradition were first heard in Aix-en-Provence on December 12, 2013, with decisions issued on January 9, 2014, in favor of extradition with priority to Russia. On appeal to the French Court of Cassation, however, due to egregious procedural violations committed by the Aix-en-Provence Court, the Court of Cassation annulled the decision and transferred the two case files to be reconsidered by a court in Lyon.[17] After two hearings in Lyon to review the extradition requests, on September 25 and October 17, 2014, the Court issued decisions in favor of extradition, again with priority to Russia. The Court of Cassation once again took up Ablyazov's case on appeal, but on March 4, 2015, the Court refused to annul the Lyon Court's decisions in favor of extradition after determining merely that that Court had not committed any procedural errors. On September 17, 2015, despite numerous appeals made by internationally respected NGOs such as Human Rights Watch and Amnesty International, French Prime Minister Manuel Valls signed a decree ordering Ablyazov's extradition to Russia.[18] Ablyazov appealed to the *Conseil d'État* – France's supreme administrative court – to block the order, and enlisted the assistance of Perseus Strategies to prepare a complaint against France to the WGAD.

II Petition to Working Group on Arbitrary Detention

On January 12, 2016, Perseus Strategies filed a 56-page, 151-footnote Petition (the Petition) with the WGAD, asserting that the continued detention in France of Ablyazov constituted an arbitrary deprivation of his liberty[19] under Categories I and III, as set forth by the WGAD's categories of cases. Under Category I, the Petition argued that there was no legal basis for Ablyazov's detention due to the excessive length of detention pending an extradition and the request's political nature. Under Category III, the Petition asserted:

- The Government failed to provide Ablyazov with a timely explanation of the reason for his arrest.
- The Government failed to act within a reasonable time and without undue delay.
- The Government failed to provide Ablyazov an independent and impartial tribunal.
- The Government interfered with Ablyazov's access to and representation by counsel.

---

[16] Alessandra Prentice & Jean-Francois Rosnoblet, *Russia Asks France to Extradite Kazakh Oligarch Ablyazov*, REUTERS, Aug. 21, 2013.

[17] Petition to the Working Group on Arbitrary Detention, Perseus Strategies, Jan. 12, 2016, at 15.

[18] *Id.*, at 16.

[19] An arbitrary deprivation of liberty is defined as any "depriv[ation] of liberty except on such grounds and in accordance with such procedures as are established by law." International Covenant on Civil and Political Rights, G.A. Res 2200A (XXI), 21 U.N. GAOR Supp. (No. 16), at 52, U.N. Doc. A/6316 (1966), 999 U.N.T.S. 171, *entered into force* Mar. 23, 1976, at Art. 9(1) [hereinafter ICCPR]. Such a deprivation of liberty is specifically prohibited by international law. *Id.* "No one shall be subjected to arbitrary arrest, detention or exile." Universal Declaration of Human Rights, G.A. Res. 217A (III), U.N. Doc. A/810, at art. 9 (1948) [hereinafter Universal Declaration]. "Arrest, detention or imprisonment shall only be carried out strictly in accordance with the provisions of the law." Body of Principles for the Protection of Persons under Any Form of Detention or Imprisonment, at Principle 2, G.A. Res. 47/173, Principle 2, 43 U.N. GAOR Supp. (No. 49) at 298, U.N. Doc. A/43/49 (1988) [hereinafter Body of Principles].

- The Government interfered with the right to prepare a defense, call, and examine witnesses, and withheld key evidence.
- The Government failed to provide Ablyazov with a competent translator.

As France has ratified[20] the *International Covenant on Civil and Political Rights* (ICCPR), the Petition cited to its relevant articles, as well as to the *Universal Declaration of Human Rights* (UDHR) and the *Body of Principles for the Protection of All Persons under Any Form of Detention or Imprisonment.*[21] In addition, the Petition cited to the *European Convention on Extradition* because it is applicable to this case and because France, Russia, and Ukraine had all ratified the Convention.

The Petition related exclusively to the ongoing arbitrary detention of Ablyazov in France and not in any respect to the potential risk of torture, unfair trial, or other human rights violations that might have resulted if an extradition to Russia, Ukraine, or Kazakhstan were actually carried out. This was done to preserve Ablyazov's right to bring a case to the European Court of Human Rights on the basis of irremediable harm due to torture and other fundamental human rights violations, as well as in respect of deficiencies in France's handling of his extradition proceedings unrelated to his prolonged and arbitrary detention.[22]

Ultimately, the Petition requested that the WGAD issue an Opinion "finding Ablyazov's ongoing detention to be in violation of France's obligations under the relevant provisions of the ICCPR and UDHR." The Petition also asked the WGAD to call for Ablyazov's immediate release, to request that "France investigate and hold to account all those responsible for his unlawful arrest and detention," and to request that "France award Ablyazov compensation for the harm caused by being deprived of his liberty."[23]

A *Procedural Note Regarding Treatment of Extradition under ICCPR*

With regards to the ICCPR, it is important to understand at the outset the unusual way in which extradition cases are treated. While numerous protections of the ICCPR apply in extradition cases, these cases are procedural and are not "criminal charges"; therefore, many protections under Article 14 are not triggered. To explain the nuances of applying the ICCPR to extradition cases, the Petition cited *Ronald Everett* v. *Spain*, where the Human Rights Committee (HR Committee) heard a complaint of a British citizen who alleged he had been wrongly extradited to the United Kingdom. The HR Committee concluded that while extraditions do not fall outside the protection of the Covenant, and indeed receive the protection of Articles 6, 7, 9, and 13, the consideration of an extradition request "does not amount to the determination of a criminal charge in the meaning of Article 14."[24]

---

[20] *Status of Ratification of the Principal International Human Rights Treaties*, Mar. 18, 2015 (Nov. 2018), http://indicators.ohchr.org.
[21] UN Basic Principles and Guidelines, Summary.
[22] Petition to the Working Group on Arbitrary Detention, at 4.
[23] *Id.*
[24] Everett v. Spain, Communication No. 961/2000, Human Rights Committee, CCPR/C/81/D/961/2000, July 9, 2004.

B *Category I Arbitrary Detention*

Under Category I, the Petition argued that there was no legal basis for Ablyazov's detention due to the excessive length of detention pending extradition that violated international law and the political motivations of the extradition request.

1 Violation of France's Obligations under the European Convention on Human Rights

The Petition explained the ongoing detention of Ablyazov violated France's obligations under the *European Convention on Human Rights* (ECHR). To support this argument, the Petition cited *Quinn* v. *France*, in which the European Court of Human Rights (ECtHR) concluded that extradition proceedings that are not conducted with due diligence violate Article 5(1)(f) of the ECHR regarding the presumed lawfulness of detentions pending deportation.[25]

At the time of the Petition's submission, Ablyazov had been detained in France with a view to extradition for two years, five months, and twelve days. In *Quinn*, the ECtHR found a shorter delay of one year, eleven months, and six days in length pending an extradition was too long. The Petition highlighted numerous examples of unjustifiable extended delays on the part of the Government, which will be discussed in greater detail later. The Petition particularly cited the procedural errors that plagued the extradition proceedings in Aix-en-Provence, noting that after the Court of Cassation annulled the Aix-en-Provence decisions and remanded the case to a new court in Lyon, Ablyazov, at no fault of his own, was forced to restart his extradition proceedings after more than eight months in detention.[26]

2 Political Motivations of the Extradition Request

The Petition further demonstrated that the detention lacked a legal basis because the extradition request was invalid under the *European Covenant on Extradition*. Specifically, politically motivated requests are invalid under the treaty.[27] The Petition provided extensive evidence of such political motivations.

First, there was substantial evidence that Ukraine and Russia acted as proxies for the Kazakhstan Government in a concerted and manufactured campaign against Ablyazov. To illustrate this, the Petition detailed Ablyazov's politically turbulent relationship with Nazarbayev and the Kazakhstan regime, including his 2002 imprisonment and torture, his 2003 conditional pardon, and his 2009 dismissal from BTA Bank and subsequent flight from Kazakhstan.

Ablyazov's defense provided such evidence to the Lyon Court that the charges in Ukraine and Russia were fabrications and misrepresentations engineered by Kazakhstan for political purposes in processes replete with corruption and human rights abuses. However, the court simply ignored or brushed off such substantial documentary evidence without further inquiry and omitted from its judgment any substantive analysis of

---

[25] Application No. 18580/91, Judgment, Mar. 22, 1995.
[26] Petition to the Working Group on Arbitrary Detention, at 22.
[27] European Convention on Extradition, *entered into force* Apr. 18, 1960, at Arts. 3(1) and 3(2).

Ablyazov's claims that the Ukrainian and Russian extradition requests were politically motivated. Citing *Yang Jianli* v. *China*, the Petition notes that while the objective of the WGAD is not to act as a domestic fact-finder, the WGAD is properly situated to assess whether the international norms and standards have been observed in proceedings during which an individual is deprived of their liberty. Thus, the Petition asked the WGAD to evaluate the evidence of the politically motivated extradition request for the narrow purpose of demonstrating that the Lyon Court's failure to hear, consider, and provide a substantive response in its judgment to these claims rendered Ablyazov's detention as lacking a legal basis.[28]

Second, the Petition contextualized Ablyazov's persecution within a broader examination of the Kazakhstan Government's desire to silence political opposition. Indeed, its persecution of political opponents was not limited to Ablyazov; at the time of the Petition's submission, no less than nine European countries either refused extraditions or granted asylum or similar protection to ten of Ablyazov's co-accused associates (business associates and political allies) and family members.[29] Kazakhstan's persecution of political opponents is so well-documented that numerous international organizations and political figures argued that the case against Ablyazov was politically motivated, including Amnesty International,[30] the International Federation for Human Rights,[31] Ukrainian Helsinki Human Rights Union,[32] and members of the European Parliament.[33]

C Category III Violations

1 Right to Timely Explanation of Reason for Arrest or Details of Charge

The Petition argued that France's failure to provide Ablyazov with a timely explanation of the reason for his arrests and the details of his charges in a language he understood amounted to a violation of Article 9(2) of the ICCPR. Although Ablyazov was arrested by French police on July 31, 2013, he was not informed of the reasons for his arrest in a language he understood until October 17, 2013. Ukraine also withheld a copy of the purported arrest warrant, which was cited in the INTERPOL Red Notice, until December 4, 2013, which was 126 days after his arrest. Therefore, to arrest Ablyazov, French authorities wrongly relied upon a document that Ukraine had asserted in its INTERPOL Red Notice to be an arrest warrant, but which in fact was not. This was discovered by Ablyazov when he was finally provided a copy of the document 126 days after his arrest.[34]

---

[28] Petition to the Working Group on Arbitrary Detention, at 23–25.

[29] *Id.*, at 27.

[30] *France: Stop Extradition of Kazakhstani Opposition Activist at Risk of Torture*, AMNESTY INTERNATIONAL, Oct. 24, 2014.

[31] Open Letter from Karim Lahidji, President, International Federation for Human Rights (FIDH); Pierre Tartakowsky, President, French Human Rights League (LDH); and Roza Akylbekova, Director, Kazakhstan International Bureau for Human Rights (KIBHR), to Manuel Valls, then French Minister of the Interior, and Laurent Fabius, French Minister of Foreign Affairs, Sept. 5, 2013 (Nov. 2018), https://www.fidh.org/en/region/europe-central-asia/kazakhstan/kazakhstan-open-letter-to-mr-valls-and-mr-fabius-concerning-the-potential-13908.

[32] Letter from Ukrainian Helsinki Human Rights Union to the President, Prime Minister, Minister of the Interior, Minister of Justice, and Foreign Minister of France, Sept. 25, 2014.

[33] Open Letter from Kosma Zlotowski, Member of the European Parliament, to Christiane Taubira, French Minister of Justice, Oct. 30, 2014.

[34] Petition to the Working Group on Arbitrary Detention, at 33.

Similarly, the Russian extradition request was only provided to Ablyazov on November 5, 2013, 98 days after his arrest, and his French counsel did not receive a comprehensible French translation until September 3, 2014, more than a year after his arrest.[35] In both cases, French judicial authorities deemed that the procedurally flawed circumstances of his arrest had no bearing on his ongoing detention.

In prior opinions, the WGAD has found that the failure to inform a detainee of the charges against him for much shorter periods of time constituted a violation of Article 9 (2). For example, the Petition cited *Saqar Abdelkader Al Chouitier v. Yemen*, where the WGAD found that holding a person for fifty-two days without having been informed of the charges against him constituted a violation of Article 9.[36]

2 Right to Proceedings without Undue Delay

The Petition claimed that the French proceedings were unduly delayed, in violation of ICCPR Article 9(4). At the time of the Petition's submission, Ablyazov had been detained in France for over two years and five months, with his case on appeal to the *Conseil d'État*. The Petition asserted that the delay was attributed to French authorities and judicial officers, who acted without requisite diligence and therefore unlawfully and unnecessarily prolonged the proceedings. The Petition specifically noted the procedural errors in the Aix-en-Provence Court that led to an annulled decision by the Court of Cassation and the nineteen-day delay between the issuance of the French extradition decree on September 17, 2015, and its delivery to Ablyazov on October 6, 2015.[37]

3 Right to an Independent and Impartial Tribunal

Recalling that *Ronald Everett v. Spain* affirmed ICCPR protections for individuals in extradition proceedings, the Petition further argued that Ablyazov was not provided with an independent and impartial tribunal, as required by ICCPR Article 14(1). The Petition provided evidence that the French judiciary was not acting of its own accord, but was rather influenced by political pressures, and therefore was not fair, impartial, or independent. The Petition also confirmed that international organizations and political figures repeatedly challenged the independence and impartiality of the French judiciary in Ablyazov's case, including Amnesty International[38] and the Human Rights Foundation.[39]

a Interference of Kazakhstan

First, French authorities maintained inappropriately close relationships with representatives of Kazakhstan, Ukraine, and Russia, demonstrating a clear bias in the French judicial establishment in favor of validating the outcome of the Ablyazov proceedings and glossing over whatever shortcuts or detours were taken to achieve that result.

---

[35] *Id.*, at 34.
[36] Saqar Abdelkader Al Chouitier v. Yemen, WGAD Opinion No. 9/2008, Adopted May 8, 2008, at ¶¶ 19, 22.
[37] Petition to the Working Group on Arbitrary Detention, at 35.
[38] *France: Ensure Safety of Kazakhstani Opposition Figure*, AMNESTY INTERNATIONAL, Aug. 1, 2013 (Nov. 2018), www.amnesty.org/en/latest/news/2013/08/france-ensure-safety-kazakhstani-opposition-figure/.
[39] Open Letter from Human Rights Foundation.

Of particular concern was the relationship between the prosecutor charged with matters of extradition in Aix-en-Provence and a French lawyer representing BTA Bank. The two personally exchanged multiple emails, spoke on the phone, and saw one another at Ablyazov's extradition hearings. Additionally, BTA Bank's counsel secretly provided information and documents to the prosecutor, which were not included in the public record or shared with the defense. The prosecutor had also secretly provided documents to the judges who were to decide on the extradition, which had been given to her by individuals acting for Ukraine, Russia, and Kazakhstan. The documents contained severe inaccuracies and misinformation.[40]

b Interference of Ukraine

The Petition notes another incident where French lawyers representing Ukraine submitted an eighteen-page brief to the court, despite not being entitled under French law, as a non-party to the proceedings, to file any brief or equivalent document. The brief was provided to Ablyazov's defense less than an hour before the deadline for written submissions.[41] This was a problem for two reasons: the Court was in possession of an illegally submitted non-party brief, and Ablyazov's defense was unable to timely prepare and submit a point-by-point written response. As it did many times, the Court rejected a challenge to this brief by Ablyazov's counsel and relied on the illegally submitted brief in its decision in favor of extradition.

Furthermore, on the same day, a second set of documents was also provided to the Aix-en-Provence prosecutor in secret by a French lawyer representing Ukraine.[42] This secretly submitted documentation was never put into the court record and therefore the defense never had an opportunity to oppose the arguments therein.

c Interference of Russia

In addition to the prosecutor's close relationship with representatives of Kazakhstan and Ukraine, she was also communicating with a Russian representative during the Aix-en-Provence proceedings. At the December 12, 2013, hearing, a Russia-provided document was given to the prosecutor, who without disclosing to Ablyazov provided a copy to the judges hearing the extradition case, and the judges copied certain wording *verbatim* into its decision.[43]

Additionally, Russia's French translation of its extradition request was so poor that the documents were ruled to be "ambiguous and indecipherable" in a report by an expert in jurilinguistics. The initial unintelligible French translation had already been relied on by the court in Aix-en-Provence in rendering its decision on January 9, 2014, in favor of extradition to Russia. The court ignored the matter and moved forward with the extradition proceedings, presumably confident to do so because the Court had secretly been

---

[40] Petition to the Working Group on Arbitrary Detention, at 38.
[41] *Id.*, at 39.
[42] *Id.*, at 40.
[43] *Id.*

provided additional documents in a language it could understand, without providing those documents to Ablyazov's defense.[44]

Extradition requests under the *European Convention on Extradition* are routinely rejected when a requesting state fails to provide a translation of sufficient quality. The Lyon Court acknowledged that the translation was unacceptable.[45] However, rather than rejecting the request or requiring Russia to provide an improved translation, the Lyon Court ordered that France step in to prepare a new French translation of Russia's extradition file, commissioning French court-certified translators paid for by the French Ministry of Justice.[46]

The impact was twofold: first, the Aix-en-Provence Court forced Ablyazov's defense to use a French translation of the extradition file that was incomprehensible, indicating a malicious level of bias against Ablyazov; second, the Court forced Ablyazov to rack up extended time in detention, since his lawyers did not receive a comprehensible French translation of the extradition file until September 3, 2014, that is, nine months and twenty-one days after the initial, incomprehensible translation was provided to them on November 5, 2013.

d Rushed Proceedings

Despite dramatic delays by the French judicial system, the Aix-en-Provence proceedings were limited to one day – December 12, 2013. The vast majority of the day was filled with long recitations of allegations against Ablyazov and citations of foreign law, replete with inaccuracies and facts taken out of context.[47] When it was finally Ablyazov's turn to present his defense, it was already evening, and he was provided only twenty minutes for his concluding remarks. During those twenty minutes, the judges appeared inattentive, chatting among themselves and telling Ablyazov, at one point, to "hurry up," violating the principles of impartiality and the equality of arms.

4 Right to Have Access to and Representation by Counsel

The Petition argued that Ablyazov was also denied adequate access to and representation by legal counsel of his choosing, contravening Articles 9(4) and 14(1) of the ICCPR; Article 6(3)(c) of the ECHR was also cited, as it elaborates further on ICCPR rights. Ablyazov asked on multiple occasions to allow his family's lawyer, Peter Sahlas, to make oral arguments in his defense. Sahlas was best-positioned to assist Ablyazov and counter misleading and false declarations made by a Russian prosecutor during the Russian extradition request proceedings due to Sahlas's experience with Russian law and language and his deep familiarity with the complex multi-jurisdictional issues faced by Ablyazov since 2009. The Court refused to allow Sahlas to appear, despite the head of the Lyon Bar having written to the presiding judge at the Lyon Court, informing them that the Bar encouraged the Court to allow Sahlas to participate in the proceedings for "the good administration of justice" and "the effective exercise of rights to a defense" under

---

[44] *Id.*, at 41.
[45] *Id.*, at 42.
[46] *Id.*, at 43.
[47] *Id.*

the ECHR and the ICCPR.[48] The Court instead relied on the misleading and false declarations made by the Russian prosecutor, who, as Russia is not a party to the proceedings, should not have been permitted to engage in the proceedings, to order Ablyazov's extradition to Russia.

When Ablyazov's lawyers attempted to visit him in custody, they were arbitrarily turned away on multiple occasions and refused to meet with counsel visiting Ablyazov.[49] When counsel was allowed to meet with Ablyazov, the rules imposed by the French authorities for visiting Ablyazov in prison made it practically impossible to mount an effective defense. These included limitations on the number of hours lawyers could spend with Ablyazov and the type of materials they could have access to in the prison.[50] Given the circumstances – the limited visiting hours that were often cut short, a significant language barrier, the logistics for lawyers to get to the prison, and the sheer complexity of the case – Ablyazov was not afforded adequate time to consult with his counsel while in detention.

These challenges were exacerbated by the fact that Ablyazov encountered numerous barriers to accessing case files. From November 27 to December 8, 2014, while preparing for his Court of Cassation hearing, Ablyazov was transferred twice: first from a prison in Corbas, near Lyon, to a prison in the Paris region, then back to a different prison in the Lyon region, in Villefranche-sur-Saône. His case materials and personal effects were left behind in the Corbas prison. When Ablyazov arrived in Villefranche-sur-Saône on December 8, he had still not received the Russian translation of the Lyon Court decisions nor had he received his case materials.[51]

During his three extradition hearings, Ablyazov was set apart from his lawyers in the courtroom. During many hearings, the small size of the courtroom did not permit him to have confidential discussions with his lawyers.[52]

5 Right to Prepare a Defense, Call and Examine Witnesses, and Access Key Evidence

The Petition argued that the French judiciary further violated Articles 9(4) and 14(1) of the ICCPR by denying Ablyazov adequate time to present his defense, access to evidence and adequate time to prepare a defense, and opportunity to produce his own evidence and witnesses. As noted, the Aix-en-Provence proceedings were crammed into one day, allowing Ablyazov only twenty minutes to address the Court.[53] The Lyon Court was hardly an improvement. Despite Ablyazov having made written submissions to the Court in advance of the hearing to expedite and facilitate a number of preliminary procedural matters, many of these issues were only dealt with on the morning of September 25, 2014. The Court then intended to hear the rest of the proceedings the same day, including a request from Ablyazov for conditional release, and both Ukraine's and Russia's extradition requests.[54] The Court only allowed for a second day of hearings after it became

---

[48] *Id.*, at 45–46.
[49] *Id.*, at 47.
[50] *Id.*, at 48.
[51] *Id.*, at 47.
[52] *Id.*, at 49.
[53] *Id.*, at 50–51.
[54] *Id.*, at 51.

apparent that a second day would in fact be necessary, but in light of the complex nature of the case and serious deficiencies in the requesting countries' requests, Ablyazov's time to present a defense was ultimately limited.

As discussed previously, Ablyazov and his counsel were not given access to evidence introduced to the Court. Furthermore, some of the evidence was introduced improperly by non-parties and done secretly to conceal the obvious misconduct. Additionally, when documents were provided, they were often given shortly before hearings, or were incomprehensible machine-generated translations, making it practically impossible for Ablyazov's counsel to review them effectively and to prepare a defense.

Ablyazov was also not allowed to call any witnesses to his defense throughout the proceedings. Five witnesses were present at the Lyon hearing on September 25, 2014, and six witnesses were present at the Lyon hearing on October 17, 2014. All were properly registered with the court, and intended to provide independent testimony about their assessment of the political nature of the charges against Ablyazov. While the defense considered this testimony absolutely essential for the Lyon Court to understand and to assess the political and human rights implications of the case, the court arbitrarily refused to hear any witnesses.[55] Although Ablyazov is not a criminal defendant as described under Article 14(3)(e) of the ICCPR, the Petition argued that the failure of the Lyon Court to allow Ablyazov's witnesses to testify was nonetheless a clear breach of its requirement to act fairly in extradition proceedings as required by the standards articulated in *Ronald Everett* v. *Spain*,[56] particularly given both Ukraine and Russia were allowed to present lengthy arguments of their own on top of those of the French prosecutor.

Finally, the Petition noted that Ablyazov and his lawyers were consistently denied the right to contest and remedy the improper conduct of the judiciary as numerous requests, petitions, appeals, and complaints related to due process abuses were summarily ignored or dismissed.[57]

6 Right to Have a Competent Translator

The Petition cited to the UN Basic Principles and Guidelines, which stipulate that in addition to the right to be informed of the reasons justifying detention, available judicial remedies, and the content of court decisions, such information must be conveyed in a language and a means, mode, or format that the detainee understands,[58] and if necessary, a non-national must be provided with the free assistance of an interpreter.[59]

The Petition argued that the French courts failed to respect this right, and thus compromised the fairness of the proceedings. Ablyazov's defense made motions well in advance of the hearings, proposing to have simultaneous interpretation equipment temporarily set up in the courtroom for use by court-approved interpreters, but the motions were denied, despite the fact that the hearings were conducted in French, a

---

[55] *Id.*, at 53.
[56] Everett v. Spain.
[57] Petition to the Working Group on Arbitrary Detention, Perseus Strategies, at 54.
[58] UN Basic Principles and Guidelines, at Principle 7, ¶ 10.
[59] *Id.*, at Principle 21, ¶ 42.

language that Ablyazov does not understand. On at least one occasion, he was placed in a glass booth. Although he was provided with two interpreters, it was difficult to hear inside the booth as the microphones in the booth were not functioning. The lack of simultaneous interpretation equipment meant that less than 5 percent of the courtroom proceedings were actually interpreted into Russian for Ablyazov.[60]

Apart from the inadequate interpretation facilities provided during the hearings, the Petition argued that France also failed to provide comprehensible and timely Russian translations at several other key points in Ablyazov's proceedings. There was no interpreter present at the time of Ablyazov's arrest, meaning that Ablyazov was not informed in a timely manner of the reasons for his arrest. Subsequently, Ablyazov did not receive a Russian translation of the Ukrainian extradition request for nearly seven weeks after his detention had begun. Similarly, there were significant delays in providing Ablyazov with Russian translations of the French court decisions against him. Most egregiously, Russian translations of the Court's decisions were not even provided to Ablyazov or his legal team prior to the appeals deadline.[61]

III Government Responses to the Petition

A Serious Procedural Irregularities

After submission of the Petition to the WGAD on January 13, 2016, the author experienced unusually grave administrative delays on the part of the WGAD. The author received confirmation of the WGAD's receipt of the Petition on January 28, 2016. If the communication were timely conveyed to the French government, it would have been given a sixty-day timeframe in which to respond to the allegations made in the initial Petition or request a one-month extension. A response from the Government in this time span would have made the case ripe for the adoption of an opinion during the WGAD's April 2016 session. However, the WGAD did not confirm that the communication had been conveyed to the Government until May 23, 2016, right up against the timeframe where the case could be ready to be considered during WGAD's August 2016 session. In the nearly four-month period between the submission and its communication to the Government, the author asked officials of the WGAD at least sixteen times, via phone, email, and in-person, if the Petition had been conveyed to France. Numerous justifications and obfuscations were provided, including confusion over whom the case had been assigned to on its staff, statements noting that "many cases reach [the Working Group] every day and similarly deserve urgent action and attention," and ignoring the author's correspondence altogether.

Knowing that with the original delays, the case could not be considered during its April 2016 session, the author stressed to WGAD its communication had to be sent out by May 23, 2016, for consideration in the August 2016 session. As the deadline approached, the author was told that the WGAD could not expect France to respond

---

[60] Petition to the Working Group on Arbitrary Detention, at 55.
[61] Id.

to a communication sent in a working language other than their own. The author promptly countered that the UN Correspondence Manual only requires that the source submit materials in one of the working languages of the WGAD, not a particular language. The administrative delays were so egregious that the author raised specific concerns to WGAD members, higher-level staff at the Office of the High Commissioner for Human Rights, and the head of the Special Procedures Branch of OHCHR.

The WGAD confirmed that the Petition was conveyed to the Government on May 23, 2016. Incredibly, it noted in its correspondence with the author that the communication was also sent to the Governments of Russia, Ukraine, and Kazakhstan "for their information and comments." This was despite the fact that the Petition was lodged solely against France and the entire legal analysis of the complaint focused exclusively on France's alleged violations of international law in French domestic proceedings. As was emphasized in the Petition, Russia, Ukraine, and Kazakhstan were not parties to the extradition proceedings between Ablyazov and France. The WGAD's Methods of Work then only envisage communications being sent to Governments against whom complaints were lodged.[62] In requesting a formal review of this unusual decision via email, the author noted the lack of legal justification for conveying the communications to three non-parties, which lacked any competence to provide relevant information to the WGAD regarding whether or not France acted in accordance with its obligations under its own and international law. Despite the author's objection, the WGAD allowed Russia, Ukraine, and Kazakhstan to submit governmental responses for the WGAD's consideration. The submission of the case to Kazakhstan was especially problematic given Ablyazov had been granted political asylum in the United Kingdom because of his well-founded fear of persecution by the Kazakhstan Government. This communication, intentionally and with no concern about the consequence, provided a government that had been found to be persecuting Ablyazov with important information about his situation in France.

After the communication was conveyed to the four governments, the author experienced additional procedural irregularities. The author's further emails that requested the status of responses from the four governments were met with confusion over who was responsible for replying, delayed responses, and silence. Although the case should have been considered in August 2016, in September the author was informed its consideration had been deferred to the WGAD's November 2016 session without explanation.

B *Response from the Government of France*

Recalling that governmental responses to WGAD communications remain confidential and are treated with the utmost discretion, the discussion of these responses is limited to how they are described in the WGAD's Opinion. After receiving the communication, the Government of France submitted a ninety-page response to the communication on July 25, 2016. However, the deadline for France to submit a governmental response was July

---

[62] *Methods of Work of the Working Group on Arbitrary Detention*, A/HRC/33/66, July 12, 2016, at ¶ 15.

19, 2016, and because the Government did not justify the delay or request an extension, the WGAD did not consider the response as having been transmitted within the required time.

C Responses from the Governments of Ukraine and Kazakhstan

Despite the fact that the Governments of Ukraine and Kazakhstan were not qualified to comment on the French extradition proceedings at hand, as the two governments even admitted in their responses, the WGAD allowed all these governments to submit responses to the communication.

On August 31, 2016, the Government of Ukraine submitted a twenty-six-page Response that admitted that it could not speak to the nature of the French proceedings. Ukraine provided this response after an extended deadline of August 19, 2016; nevertheless, the WGAD accepted this response for its consideration.

On July 19, 2016, the Government of Kazakhstan submitted a ninety-four-page Response with a 10,000-page appendix that was largely irrelevant to the complaints against the French proceedings. On August 19, 2016, Kazakhstan also submitted a three-page addendum accompanied by 1,369 pages of enclosures that was similarly irrelevant to the French proceedings.

Again, the Governments of Ukraine and Kazakhstan did not possess the competence to provide insight into the extradition proceedings between Ablyazov and the Government of France. Regardless, the WGAD decided to assess, in their words, the "huge quantity of information" received from the two governments.

IV Replies to the Governments' Responses

A Reply to the Government of France

On August 19, 2016, Perseus Strategies submitted a twenty-nine-page Reply to the Response from the Government of France. The Reply reiterated the numerous due process abuses of the French proceedings, and noted that if the Government does not adequately rebut the claims made in the original complaint, then the WGAD must accept the source's claims as facts for a determination.

B Replies to the Governments of Ukraine and Kazakhstan

Because the Governments of Ukraine and Kazakhstan were not parties to the French extradition proceedings, there was no reason to substantively engage with the extraordinarily long Responses of the two governments. Perseus Strategies submitted brief Replies to the Government of Ukraine on November 16, 2016, and to the Government of Kazakhstan on August 19, 2016. Perseus Strategies also submitted a brief reply to Kazakhstan's addendum on August 21, 2016. These replies asked the WGAD to disregard the responses of the two governments, as they were not qualified to comment on the French proceedings, which were at the heart of the WGAD complaint.

V The WGAD's Opinion

The WGAD issued Opinion No. 49/2016 on December 7, 2016.[63] While finding that Ablyazov's detention was arbitrary under Category III, the Opinion was remarkably brief at twelve pages, considering the volume of evidence submitted and the Opinion's conclusion that this was a "highly complex case."[64] Upon further examination, despite noting that Ablyazov's "credibility and the reliability of the information are not, in essence, in doubt," it appeared that the WGAD summarily dismissed Ablyazov's complaints without even a cursory analysis of their substance.[65] And despite the concerns of irregularities raised by Perseus Strategies, the WGAD felt it necessary to convey the complaint to and gather information from Russia, Ukraine, and Kazakhstan "to fully understand the circumstances that led to [Ablyazov's] detention and the allegation that he is being persecuted."[66]

Further detail on what the WGAD's Opinion stated about each of the violations raised in the case follows.

A *Ablyazov's Detention Was Not without Legal Basis*

The WGAD did not address the argument that the blatant political motivations of the extradition request rendered the request legally invalid under the *European Convention on Extradition*. The WGAD also did not analyze the unjustifiable extended delays on the part of the Government in relation to a Category I violation.

B *Ablyazov's Detention Was Found Narrowly to Be Arbitrary under Category III*

1 Timely Explanation of Reason for Arrest or Details of Charge

The WGAD rejected the claim that Ablyazov was denied timely notification of the reasons for his arrest and detention and of the charges against him.[67] The Opinion affirmatively cited the INTERPOL notice that had been issued at the time of arrest, despite that INTERPOL notice not being founded on an actual arrest warrant. The WGAD also noted that France stated that Ablyazov's detention was confirmed the day after arrest by a judge. The WGAD quickly concluded that it "can thus be inferred that Mr. Ablyazov was made aware of the reasons for his arrest," despite Ablyazov not being informed of the reasons for his arrest in a language he understood until seventy-eight days after his arrest. Without justification, the WGAD concluded that this delay did not lead to the violation of any rights.

It is also notable that the Opinion cited information contained in the Government's Response, despite the Opinion's acknowledgment that the Government's Response was not submitted within the required time.

---

[63] *Mukhtar Ablyazov v. France*, WGAD Opinion No. 49/2016, Adopted Nov. 23, 2016 (Litigated by Author through Perseus Strategies).

[64] *Mukhtar Ablyazov*, at ¶ 54.

[65] *Mukhtar Ablyazov*, at ¶ 64.

[66] *Mukhtar Ablyazov*, at ¶ 62.

[67] *Mukhtar Ablyazov*, at ¶ 66.

2 Failure to Act within a Reasonable Time and without Undue Delay

The WGAD agreed with the argument that the Government violated Ablyazov's right to proceedings without undue delay.[68] The WGAD noted that the "numerous legal challenges filed by Mr. Ablyazov may have contributed to the duration of his detention" and stated that the Government had justified the rejection for conditional release because Ablyazov "would have the means of jeopardizing the evidence against him and evading justice." Nevertheless, the WGAD cited the recent Court of Cassation ruling that found that the French proceedings in connection with the extradition request by Ukraine were excessively long, as Ablyazov's detention surpassed three years. The WGAD thus concluded that Ablyazov had been denied a prompt hearing, in violation of ICCPR Articles 9(4) and 14(3)(c) under Category III.

3 Failure to Provide Ablyazov an Independent and Impartial Tribunal

Despite the vast amount of evidence provided to demonstrate the lack of impartiality within the French judicial system, the WGAD states that this evidence amounts to "insinuations" that the WGAD was "unable to corroborate for want of sufficient evidence."[69]

4 Interference with Ablyazov's Access to and Representation by Counsel

In the span of two sentences, the WGAD rejected the extensive evidence that his right to counsel was violated, citing a lack of "objective evidence."[70]

5 Interference with the Right to Prepare a Defense, Call and Examine Witnesses, and Access Key Evidence

The WGAD rejected the argument that French authorities limited his ability to call and question witnesses and withheld key pieces of evidence.[71] The WGAD noted that these rights have a greater bearing on the consideration of the merits of the case, which the extradition procedure is not competent to determine. Thus, the WGAD found that a violation of either of these aspects would not be of "sufficient consequence" to find Ablyazov's detention arbitrary.

6 Failure to Provide Ablyazov with a Competent Translator

The WGAD also rejected the argument that the French authorities failed to provide him with necessary interpretation services at his proceedings.[72] The Opinion notes that especially in light of the fact that Ablyazov "always had the counsel of his lawyers" (which he did not), such a violation would not be of "sufficient consequence" to find Ablyazov's detention arbitrary.

---

[68] *Id.*, at ¶ 67.
[69] *Id.*
[70] Mukhtar Ablyazov, at ¶ 69.
[71] *Id.*, at ¶ 71.
[72] *Id.*, at ¶ 70.

VI Resolution

As previously mentioned, during the WGAD proceedings, Ablyazov challenged the decree ordering his extradition to Russia on appeal to the *Conseil d'État*, France's supreme administrative tribunal. Action from the United Nations on his case came at the very last possible moment where it could impact his extradition and the decision before that body; had it come any later, these actions could have happened after his extradition to Russia where the consequences on his life and safety could have been permanent and irreversible.

Specifically, on December 8, 2016, the UN Special Rapporteur on Torture, Nils Melzer, issued a statement urging the Government of France not to extradite Ablyazov because there were serious grounds to believe he was at risk of being subjected to torture.[73] The very next morning, the WGAD issued its own opinion, which was urgently conveyed to the *Conseil d'État*. Immediately thereafter, it cancelled Ablyazov's extradition decree, finding that the extradition request was politically motivated and that Kazakhstan attempted to influence Russian and Ukrainian authorities to lobby for the extradition of Ablyazov.[74] It was the first time in French history that an extradition decree was cancelled because an extradition would cause an individual's situation to be aggravated due to political persecution. Ablyazov was released from French custody and currently resides in Paris, where he now has political asylum. The Government of Kazakhstan continues to pursue Ablyazov's associates and their families.

The author has never received a clear explanation about why this case had so many procedural and substantive irregularities in how it was handled by the WGAD, but thankfully *Mukhtar Ablyazov* v. *France* was highly atypical of its generally strong and professional engagement on individual cases.

---

[73] *UN Rapporteur Urges France Not to Extradite Kazakh Dissident Tycoon to Russia*, RFE/RL, Dec. 8, 2016.
[74] Mukhtar Ablyazov v. Government of France, *Conseil d'État*, No. 394399, 400239, Dec. 9, 2016.

14 *Yang Jianli* v. *China*

I Introduction

A *Background*

At the time of his arrest in April 2002, Yang Jianli was a thirty-nine- year-old scholar and democracy activist, who was well known for his efforts to promote democracy in China. Born a Chinese citizen, Yang had resided in the United States since 1986. He holds doctoral degrees in mathematics from the University of California at Berkeley and in political economy and government from Harvard University's John F. Kennedy School of Government.[1] Yang was the founder and president of the Foundation for China 21st Century, through which he promoted the cause of democracy in China.

In 1989, while a graduate student resident in the United States, Yang traveled to China to provide support to Chinese students in Beijing then actively involved in pro-democracy activism. The Chinese government responded with force to the student demonstrations, as a result of which many Chinese were injured and killed. In the aftermath of the Tiananmen Square massacre, hundreds of protesters were arrested. Many, such as Yang, were forced to flee the country.

Since 1989, Yang had to reside in the United States. It was commonly known he was one of among approximately fifty expatriate Chinese dissidents who had been "black-listed" by the Chinese government, making their return to China impossible. The Chinese government never formally acknowledged this blacklist.

Notwithstanding this informal prohibition, Yang returned to China on April 19, 2002, to observe labor unrest in northeastern China. He was detained by Chinese authorities shortly thereafter.[2]

B *The Facts of the Case*

On April 26, 2002, authorities of the Kunming City Public Security Bureau detained Yang Jianli at the airport in Kunming, China, and brought him to a hotel near the local

---

[1] The author met Yang while they were both students at Harvard University in Fall 1997 and together they were part of a core group that planned the protests against then Chinese President Jiang Zemin's visit in Nov. 1997. It was Yang, in part, who inspired the author to go to law school to become a human rights lawyer.

[2] Petition to the Working Group on Arbitrary Detention, Freedom Now, Dec. 9, 2002, at 2–3.

airport. Yang spoke by telephone with his wife who was at their home in Brookline, Massachusetts, at that time. Yang informed his wife, Christina Fu, that he had been detained and was being held in a hotel room guarded by Chinese police officers. Communication was cut off the next day.

When Fu, who was also a US citizen, traveled from the United States to China to secure legal representation for Yang on May 23, 2002, she was forcibly expelled by Chinese authorities the same day. Also that month, Yang's brother sought to find him but the police, State Security, and the Foreign Ministry would not even confirm his detention.

In late June, the police in Linyi, Shandong Province, called Yang's brother by telephone and told him that Yang had been arrested. They did not provide him with any information about his arrest or even the charges. The following month, the Foreign Ministry informed the US Embassy in Beijing by letter that Yang had been arrested on June 21, 2002. It said the Beijing Public Security Bureau was detaining him and a copy of the formal detention notice would soon be issued.[3]

As of the date of the filing to the WGAD, which was in December 2002, it had been 225 days since Yang's arrest and no detention notice had been provided to Yang's family in China or abroad. But by that stage, given Yang's prominence in the Chinese democracy movement, he secured support from many United States Senators, Members of Congress, and other dignitaries who have expressed deep concern to the Chinese about his ongoing incommunicado detention.[4]

II Petition to Working Group on Arbitrary Detention

A *The Lead Up to the Petition*

On December 9, 2002, the author, through Freedom Now, filed a Petition to the WGAD. As Yang had been detained for more than seven months incommunicado and he was a high-profile critic of the Chinese government, the Petition invoked the WGAD's urgent action procedure. And in also requesting the WGAD adopt an opinion on his case through its regular procedure, the Petition asserted Yang's detention was an arbitrary deprivation of liberty under Category III, in violation of his rights to a fair trial. Under Category III, the Petition asserted:

- The Chinese Government violated Yang's right to be informed of the charges against him and detained him beyond the time limit for a warrant to be issued.
- The Chinese Government denied Yang all access to counsel.
- The Chinese Government was holding Yang incommunicado, violating his right to be brought promptly before a judge and to be tried within a reasonable period of time or be released.

---

[3] *Id.*, at 4.
[4] This included seven US Senators, thirty US Members of Congress, Archbishop Desmond Tutu, President Lawrence Summers of Harvard University, thirty-four Faculty of Harvard University, and many others.

As China had signed but not ratified the *International Covenant on Civil and Political Rights*,[5] the Petition cited to its relevant articles, as well as to the *Universal Declaration on Human Rights* and *Body of Principles for the Protection of All Persons under Any Form of Detention or Imprisonment*.

B Request for Urgent Action

In making its request invoking the urgent action procedure, the Petition explained Yang had been detained incommunicado by Chinese authorities for more than seven months. The Chinese government had refused to allow members of Yang's family to visit him or to arrange to provide him with legal counsel. Nor had the Chinese government presented formal charges against him. In light of these facts, Yang's longstanding involvement in China's pro-democracy movement, and his being a "blacklisted" dissident, the Petition expressed serious concern that his life or health could be in serious danger.

C Submission of Petition: Category III Arbitrary Detention

1 Right to Notification of Charges

In its treatment of Yang, Chinese authorities violated numerous provisions of its Criminal Procedure Law. Specifically, it had failed to notify his employer or family that he had been detained, held him for more than thirty-seven days in detention without the issuance of an arrest warrant, and failed to inform him of the charges that he was facing.[6]

The Petition used these examples of China flouting its own law to reinforce how it was also proactively violating the ICCPR. Article 9(2) of the ICCPR requires "[a]nyone who is arrested shall be informed, at the time of arrest, of the reasons for his arrest and shall be promptly informed of any charges against him." And under Principle 13 of the Body of Principles: "[a]ny person shall, at the moment of his arrest and at the commencement of detention or imprisonment, or promptly thereafter, be provided … with information on and an explanation of his rights and how to avail himself of such rights." And under Principle 12: "(1) There shall be duly recorded: (a) the reasons for the arrest; (b) the time of the arrest … (c) the identity of the law enforcement officials concerned … (2) Such records shall be communicated to the detained person … in the form prescribed by law."

2 Right to Access to Counsel

By holding Yang incommunicado, Chinese authorities were violating his right under Chinese law to select and meet a lawyer, immediately after his first interrogation, and this right is not contingent on approval by authorities unless a case involves "state secrets." Although Chinese authorities were claiming he had a right to counsel, and Yang's brother was told to see him and arrange counsel, he must first present a copy of Yang's detention notice to the Beijing Public Security Bureau. As noted previously, Chinese

---

[5] As a signatory, China is bound to not make any affirmative violations of the ICCPR as this would undermine the object and purpose of a treaty. But having not ratified the treaty, China is not required to immediately bring its domestic law into compliance with its obligations under the ICCPR.

[6] Petition to the Working Group on Arbitrary Detention, at 5–8.

authorities never provided Yang's family with the notice, thereby making it impossible for them to have access to him or arrange a lawyer.

Again, these violations of Chinese law were used to reinforce the way in which Yang's rights were being violated under the ICCPR. The Petition explained that "Article 14(1) of the ICCPR guarantees anyone accused of a criminal charge 'adequate time and facilities for the preparation of his defense and to communicate with counsel of his own choosing.'"[7]

3 Right to *Habeas Corpus*

The Petition explained that Article 9(4) of the ICCPR entitles any person who has been arrested or detained for whatever reason to challenge the lawfulness of his detention in a court without delay. This right stems from the Anglo-American legal principle of *habeas corpus* and exists regardless of whether deprivation of liberty is unlawful. On its face, the Human Rights Committee has stated that incommunicado detention renders a *habeas corpus* action impossible, thereby violating Article 9(4). Therefore, the Chinese government's detention of Yang also violated Article 9(4) of the ICCPR.

4 Right to Trial or Release in Reasonable Time

The Petition explained that under Article 9(3) of the ICCPR, anyone who is detained on a criminal charge "shall be entitled to trial within a reasonable time or to release." As of the time of the filing of the Petition, Yang had been in detention for more than seven months. Accordingly, the Chinese government was violating Article 9(3) of the ICCPR and Principle 11 of the Body of Principles.

III Government Response to the Petition And Reply to Response

The Government of China was sent the communication of the Petition by the WGAD on January 27, 2003.[8] The Government's response to the communication, which was then provided by the WGAD to the author, was less than one page. As summarized later in the WGAD's Opinion, the Government's Response was the following:

> [T]he Government stated that Yang Jianli was apprehended by the Chinese public security authorities in April 2002 for unlawfully entering the country on another person's passport. On 21 June 2002, after obtaining due approval from the Beijing city procurator's office, he was taken into custody by the Beijing public security authorities on suspicion that his activities were in breach of the provisions of article 322 of the Chinese Criminal Code, relating to the offence of illegally crossing the State frontier, and, in accordance with due legal process, his relatives living in the country were notified. In the course of the investigation into Mr. Yang's case, the judicial authorities ascertained that he might also have committed other offences and his case is currently still under investigation, in accordance with the law.[9]

---

[7] *Id.*, at 9.
[8] *Yang Jianli* v. *China*, WGAD Opinion No. 2/2003, Adopted July 5, 2013.
[9] *Id.*, at ¶ 14.

In the Opinion, the WGAD also restated the Government's strong generalized assertions in its Response as to its legal system and its compliance with its own and international law. The Government stated "China has set in place comprehensive domestic legislation to safeguard human rights. Under the Chinese Constitution, citizens enjoy freedom of speech, of the press, of assembly and of association and other extensive freedoms, and the Constitution stipulates that no citizen may be arrested except with the approval or by decision of the procurator's office and that arrests may only be made by the public security authorities." It further stated that "the Chinese Criminal Code and the Chinese Code of Criminal Procedure, together with the Police Act and other statutes, all contain strict provisions" for the prevention of torture.[10]

Without providing specific rebuttals to the facts as presented in the Petition, the Government also offered conclusory statements about how Yang was treated in full accordance with his rights under Chinese and international law stating:

> Yang Jianli was taken into custody solely because he was suspected of having breached Chinese law. In the case in question, the Chinese public security authorities have acted in strict accordance with due legal process; the lawful rights of the person concerned have been fully protected. The action taken against Yang Jianli does not constitute an instance of arbitrary detention.[11]

In the Reply to the Response, it was noted that China failed to deny most of the specific charges that had been presented in the Petition and had also been corroborated by reputable international observers, which were repeated in summary form. It was therefore then requested that all of these charges be admitted as fact, in keeping with the WGAD's consistent practice, citing to its prior opinion in *Wang Wanxing v. China*.[12]

In addition, the Reply responded directly to the Government's assertion he was taken into custody under Article 322 of the Chinese Criminal Code, which relates to illegal border crossing. It pointed out that this law says that if a person is convicted of the offense and the "circumstances are serious," that the sentence can be "not more than one year of fixed-term imprisonment."[13]

The Reply to the Response was filed with the WGAD on April 28, 2003, which was more than one year after Yang was taken into custody on April 26, 2002. Thus, the Reply explained, even if Yang were later to be found guilty of this charge, he had already been detained for more than the maximum term of imprisonment.

---

[10] *Id.*, at ¶ 15.

[11] *Id.*

[12] In this opinion, the WGAD stated "[a]gainst the detailed allegations of the source that the detention of Wang Wanxing was politically motivated . . . the Government did not submit any evidence or arguments to the contrary . . . Since the Government failed to adduce convincing arguments or evidence to refute the allegations of the source, the Working Group cannot but conclude that . . . the detention of Wang Wanxing . . . is arbitrary." Wang Wanxing v. China, Opinion No. 20/2001, Adopted June 18, 2002, at ¶¶ 14–16.

[13] Reply to the Government's Response to the Working Group on Arbitrary Detention, Freedom Now, Apr. 28, 2003, at 4.

IV The WGAD's Opinion

On May 7, 2003, the WGAD adopted its Opinion No. 2/2003 on *Yang Jianli v. China*.[14]

A *Preliminary Observations on the Government's Response and Approach to the Evidence*

Although the WGAD welcomed receiving a response to its communication, in its Opinion it "regret[ed], however, that the Government has not addressed all the important issues raised by the source." Nonetheless, in accordance with its approach to evidence in individual cases, the WGAD said it "believes that it is in a position to render an opinion on the facts and circumstances of the case, in the context of the allegations made and the response of the Government thereto."[15]

In addition, the WGAD decided to restate how it approaches the question of evidence in individual cases:

> Bearing in mind that the criminal procedure in the case of Yang Jianli is ongoing, the Working Group points out that its task is not to evaluate facts and evidence in a particular case; this would be tantamount to replacing the national courts, which falls outside the Working Group's remit. The Working Group is called upon to assess whether the international norms and standards have been observed in the criminal procedure during which Yang Jianli has been and is being deprived of his liberty.[16]

B *Legal Analysis*

As context for its legal analysis, the WGAD observed that the Government had not contested the allegations put forward in the Petition that Yang's brother was only informally told about his arrest and that the failure to provide a written detention notice was in violation of Chinese law requiring notice be provided within twenty-four hours. It observed that the Government had not invoked any of the exceptions to justify its failure to provide notice. The Government did not contest that the failure to provide written notice to Yang's family deprived them of the ability to retain counsel for him. And it did not deny that despite Chinese law limiting warrantless detention to thirty-seven days that Yang had not been released.[17] The WGAD said it "cannot but conclude that to keep Yang Jianli in detention for more than two months without an arrest warrant and without enabling his family to hire a lawyer to defend him constitute an infringement of the basic international norms relating to the right to a fair trial."[18]

In light of this rather abbreviated analysis, which was likely much shorter than it otherwise would have been if the Government had sought to refute the factual allegations with specificity, the WGAD concluded:

---

[14] Yang Jianli v. China, Opinion No. 2/2003, Adopted May 5, 2013.
[15] *Id.*, at ¶ 4.
[16] *Id.*
[17] *Id.*, at ¶ 18.
[18] *Id.*

The failure to observe Yang Jianli's right to a fair trial is of such gravity as to give his deprivation of liberty an arbitrary character. Therefore, his arrest and detention are arbitrary, being in contravention of article 9 of the Universal Declaration of Human Rights and of article 9 of the International Covenant on Civil and Political Rights, and falls within category III of the categories applicable to the consideration of cases submitted to the Working Group.[19]

V Resolution[20]

Shortly after Yang's detention, at the urging of the author acting on his behalf, members of the international community began inquiring about his ongoing detention.[21] In May 2002, members of the US House and Senate sent letters to the Chinese Ambassador to the United States, expressing concern about Yang's detention, seeking information about his health and safety, and asking for his immediate release.[22] In June, members of Congress sent further requests seeking formal notice of charges on which he was being held. And in August of that year, US Senators urged then Chinese President Jiang Zemin to remedy Yang's situation and provide him with due process rights.[23]

On June 4, 2003, the author officially released the WGAD's opinion at a press conference with Yang's wife and several members of Congress. This publicity marked a turning point in the ability to pressure China to resolve the case. Previously, due to Yang's illegal entry into China, many US lawmakers were hesitant to press for his release directly and did no more than inquire about his treatment and call for respect of due process. As a result of the WGAD opinion, that same month, members of the US Congress increased their pressure on China to release Yang. The House "unanimously passed a resolution condemning China and calling for Yang's release," and a similar resolution unanimously passed in the Senate. Three members of the European Parliament also sent letters to Chinese President Hu Jintao, expressing concern for Yang and urging China to release him.[24]

In June 2003, over a year after his initial detention, the City of Beijing Bureau of National Security issued an opinion recommending Yang's prosecution for illegal

---

[19] *Id.*

[20] This section of the case study is drawn substantially from a law review article published previously by the author. Jared Genser & Margaret Winterkorn-Meikle, *The Intersection of Politics and International Law: The United Nations Working Group on Arbitrary Detention in Theory and in Practice*, 39 COLUMBIA HUMAN RIGHTS LAW REVIEW 101–169 (2008).

[21] The first co-author, in representing Yang Jianli, requested that members of Congress make these inquiries. Letter from Tom Lantos, Co-Chair, Cong. Human Rights Caucus, Frank Wolf, Co-Chair, Cong. Human Rights Caucus, Barney Frank, Member, Cong. Human Rights Caucus, Chris Smith, Member, Cong. Human Rights Caucus, to Yang Jiechi, Chinese Ambassador to the United States, May 8, 2002.

[22] Letter from the US Senate to the Honorable Yang Jiechi, Chinese Ambassador to the United States, May 22, 2002; *see also* Letter from US Congress to the Honorable Yang Jiechi, Chinese Ambassador to the United States, May 8, 2002 (requesting that the People's Republic of China apply humanitarian considerations to Yang).

[23] Letter from the US Senate Comm. on Foreign Affairs to His Excellency Jiang Zemin, President, People's Republic of China, Aug. 13, 2002.

[24] *Congress Condemns China for Detaining Massachusetts Activist*, ASSOCIATED PRESS, June 25, 2003.

entry into the country and suspected espionage.[25] Yang's trial consisted of a one-day closed meeting of the court on August 4, 2003. As evidence of the espionage, the Government cited Yang's "confession," materials from the National Department of State Security, and applications Yang submitted to the "Chinese Youth Development Foundation," a group on whose behalf Yang allegedly accepted assignments from a Taiwanese espionage agency in the United States. As evidence of the crime of illegal entry, the Government cited Yang's confession, his American re-entry permit, a friend's passport, a forged identification card, an entry card, and several witnesses' testimony.[26]

The international call for Yang's release continued and intensified following his trial. Members of Congress and the media urged President Bush to raise the issue of Yang's detention during a meeting in the United States with President Hu in December 2003.[27] Yang's family petitioned the Chinese government to release Yang in March 2004. The media reported that prison guards were allegedly abusing Yang on account of his complaint that he had not received a verdict following his trial in August 2003.[28] Sixty-six members of Congress signed a letter to China's president "expressing outrage over the treatment of US-based dissident Yang Jianli."[29] The Chinese Foreign Ministry spokesman issued a statement in response, labeling the letter "an interference in the judicial process of China."

The Second Intermediate People's Court of Beijing finally handed down Yang's five-year sentence on May 13, 2004, nearly a year following his in-court hearing on August 4, 2003. The court stated that Yang was being punished for illegally crossing the border into China and engaging in espionage.[30]

Yang's sentence prompted sharp criticism from US lawmakers, who called the sentence unjustified and urged Beijing to release him, again invoking the WGAD opinion.[31] In October 2004, members of the US House and Senate again petitioned

[25] City of Beijing Bureau of National Security Opinion Recommending Prosecution, 2003 Beijing Bureau of National Security Prosecution #3, June 4, 2003.

[26] The court later noted that during the trial, per the prosecutor's request, the court postponed the hearing so as to allow additional investigation. According to the judgment issued on May 4, 2004, the court twice postponed the trial date, citing complexity and severity of the case as reasons for the continuation. The trial resumed on May 13, 2004, when the judgment of the court was issued. Penal Judgment of the Second Intermediate People's Court of Beijing, ICP2 No. 1224, May 13, 2004.

[27] John Pomfret, *Bush Asked to Press China on Jailed Activist*, WASHINGTON POST, Oct. 17, 2003; Lolita Baldor, *Bush Urged to Ask Chinese Premier to Release Jailed Activist*, ASSOCIATED PRESS, Dec. 5, 2003.

[28] *See, e.g., US Queries China over Alleged Mistreatment of Dissident in Prison*, AGENCE FRANCE PRESS, Apr. 20, 2004 (further describing allegations of abuse of Yang Jianli and US efforts to obtain further information); Lolita Baldor, *State Department Rebukes China for Treatment of Jailed Activist*, ASSOCIATED PRESS, Apr. 20, 2004 (explaining how Jianli "was kept in handcuffs in solitary confinement and denied exercise and reading materials after he began a small protest of his involvement.")

[29] Elaine Kurtenbach, *US Officials Await Response from China on Protest over Jailed Activist*, ASSOCIATED PRESS, Apr. 27, 2004.

[30] Penal Judgment of the Second Intermediate People's Court of Beijing, ICP2 No. 1224, May 13, 2004.

[31] *US Lawmakers Criticize China for Jailing US-Based Dissident*, VOICE OF AMERICA, May 13, 2004; *see also US Lawmakers Condemn Sentencing of Leading Chinese Dissident*, AGENCE FRANCE PRESSE, May 13, 2004 (quoting various Members of Congress and their reactions to Yang's sentencing).

President Hu for Yang's parole.[32] Nevertheless, despite strong international pressure, China refused to grant parole.[33]

In prison, Yang's health declined sharply. In January 2005, after Yang had suffered a stroke in prison, the US Congress again petitioned the Chinese government to release him, this time urging that he be released on medical parole. On the third anniversary of Yang's detention, Congress marked Yang's struggle by holding a press conference; one member even condemned the Chinese government's actions as "barbari[c]."[34] Two months later, on June 15, 2005, the US Senate sent another letter to President Hu urging him to grant Yang medical parole, stressing the hard conditions of his imprisonment, and reaffirming that the United Nations found him to be held in violation of international law. The letter pointed out the hypocrisy in Yang's treatment in light of a human rights report released by the Chinese government in 2005, which declared that China was making special efforts to combat human rights abuses against individuals in custody.[35]

In April 2006, nearly four years after Yang's initial detention, 119 Members of Congress urged President Bush to raise Yang's case with President Hu.[36] During Hu's visit to the United States, the press noted that "[p]rotestors followed Hu everywhere, waiting at street corners along his route." It is estimated that the US Embassy brought Yang's case to "Beijing's attention more than 60 times."[37]

Yang was finally released on April 27, 2007, after serving his full five-year sentence, despite having been eligible for parole since late 2004. Although Yang served his full sentence, it is important to note the effect the international pressure had on his detention. Within days of the public release of the WGAD's opinion, Yang received access to counsel. Yang's trial was also likely held in response to the many criticisms of his detention and demands for his release. Significantly, given that the conviction rate for political crimes in China is virtually 100 percent, the fact that Yang received the minimum five-year sentence rather than the death penalty or life in prison was in all likelihood another important result of constant international pressure on the Chinese government.

---

[32] On Oct. 6, 2004, eighty-five members of Congress sent a letter to Chinese President Hu Jintao on Yang Jianli's behalf. Letter from Members of US House of Representatives to His Excellency Hu Jintao, President, People's Republic of China, Oct. 6, 2004. A similar letter was sent on the same day by twenty-one US Senators. Letter from Members of US Senate to His Excellency Hu Jintao, President, People's Republic of China, Oct. 6, 2004.

[33] *US Lawmakers Petition Chinese Leader to Grant Dissident Parole*, AGENCE FRANCE PRESSE, Oct. 6, 2004.

[34] *US Slams China's Detention of Yang*, AGENCE FRANCE PRESS, Apr. 27, 2005.

[35] Letter from the US Senate to His Excellency Hu Jintao, President, People's Republic of China, June 15, 2005.

[36] *119 US Lawmakers Urge Bush to Raise Chinese Dissident's Case*, AGENCE FRANCE PRESSE, Apr. 10, 2006.

[37] *Protests Dog China's Hu Wherever He Goes*, AGENCE FRANCE PRESSE, Apr. 19, 2006.

Table of Authorities

APPENDICES

Required Legal Materials

Appendix 1. Methods of Work of the Working Group on Arbitrary Detention*

<table>
<tr><td>United Nations</td><td>A/HRC/36/38</td></tr>
</table>

 **General Assembly**	Distr.: General 13 July 2017 Original: English

Human Rights Council
Thirty-sixth session
Agenda item 3
Promotion and protection of all human rights, civil, political, economic, social and cultural rights, including the right to development

I. Introduction

1. The methods of work take account of the specific features of the terms of reference of the Working Group on Arbitrary Detention under Commission on Human Rights resolutions 1991/42, 1992/28, 1993/36, 1994/32, 1995/59, 1996/28, 1997/50, 1998/41, 1999/37, 2000/36, 2001/40, 2002/42, 2003/31 and 2004/39, as well as Human Rights Council resolutions 6/4, 10/9, 15/18, 24/7 and 33/30. In resolution 1991/42, the Commission gave the Working Group the task not only of informing the Commission by means of a comprehensive report, but also of investigating cases of deprivation of liberty imposed arbitrarily.

---

* The present methods of work supersede those contained in document A/HRC/33/66.

GE.17-11805(E)

Please recycle

II. Functioning of the Working Group

2. The Working Group was established by the Commission on Human Rights in its resolution 1991/42. The initial mandate of the Working Group was renewed by the Commission and the Human Rights Council. The Council assumed the mandate of the Commission in its decision 1/102, and it renewed the Working Group's mandate in its resolutions 6/4, 15/18, 24/7 and 33/30. The Working Group's mandate is considered for renewal every three years.

3. The Working Group is organized internally as follows:

(a) The Working Group shall elect, at its spring session, a Chair-Rapporteur and two Vice-Chairs for a term of one year, taking due account of the need for rotation among the geographical regions and the gender balance, among other considerations. They shall take office at the end of the same session. Each officer can be re-elected;

(b) The Chair-Rapporteur shall perform the functions conferred upon him or her by the resolution that creates or renews the mandate of the Working Group, the methods of work and the decisions of the Working Group. The Chair-Rapporteur shall represent the Working Group before the Human Rights Council, States and other relevant stakeholders. She or he shall chair the sessions of the Working Group;

(c) One of the Vice-Chairs shall be the Working Group's focal point for individual complaints; the other shall be the focal point for follow-up on all actions taken by the Working Group;

(d) In the exercise of their functions, the Chair-Rapporteur and the Vice-Chairs shall remain under the authority of the Working Group. In the absence of the Chair-Rapporteur, one of the Vice-Chairs shall temporarily assume the assigned functions of the Chair-Rapporteur as required by the circumstances;

(e) Each of these three officers shall report fully to the Working Group at the beginning of each session on activities they have undertaken during the inter-sessional period, and on any activity undertaken during a session without the other members of the Working Group;

(f) The Working Group can appoint at any time a rapporteur on specific issues of interest.

4. The Working Group meets at least three times a year, for at least five to eight working days, generally in Geneva.

5. When the case under consideration or the country visit concerns a country of which one of the members of the Working Group is a national, or in other situations where there may be a conflict of interest, that member shall not participate in the discussion of the case, in the visit or in the preparation of the report on the visit.

6. During the course of its deliberations, when dealing with individual cases or situations, the Working Group renders opinions, which are listed in the annual report it submits to the Human Rights Council. The opinions of the Working Group are the result of consensus; where consensus is not reached, the view of a majority of the members of the Working Group is adopted as the view of the Working Group.

III. Implementation of the mandate of the Working Group

7. The mandate of the Working Group is to investigate cases of deprivation of liberty imposed arbitrarily. In the discharge of its mandate, the Working Group refers to the

relevant international standards set forth in the Universal Declaration of Human Rights, as well as to the relevant international instruments accepted by the States concerned, in particular the International Covenant on Civil and Political Rights, the Convention relating to the Status of Refugees of 1951 and the Protocol relating to the Status of Refugees of 1967, the International Convention on the Elimination of All Forms of Racial Discrimination and, when appropriate, any other relevant standards, including the following:

(a) The Convention on the Rights of the Child;

(b) The Convention against Torture and Other Cruel, Inhuman or Degrading Treatment or Punishment;

(c) The International Convention on the Protection of the Rights of All Migrant Workers and Members of Their Families;

(d) The Convention on the Rights of Persons with Disabilities;

(e) The Body of Principles for the Protection of All Persons under Any Form of Detention or Imprisonment;

(f) The United Nations Standard Minimum Rules for the Treatment of Prisoners (the Nelson Mandela Rules);

(g) The United Nations Rules for the Protection of Juveniles Deprived of their Liberty;

(h) The United Nations Standard Minimum Rules for the Administration of Juvenile Justice (the Beijing Rules);

(i) The United Nations Basic Principles and Guidelines on Remedies and Procedures on the Right of Anyone Deprived of Their Liberty to Bring Proceedings Before a Court.

8. As a general rule, in dealing with situations of arbitrary deprivation of liberty within the meaning of paragraph 15 of resolution 1997/50, the Working Group shall refer, in the discharge of its mandate, to the following five legal categories:

(a) When it is clearly impossible to invoke any legal basis justifying the deprivation of liberty, as when a person is kept in detention after the completion of his or her sentence or despite an amnesty law applicable to him or her (category I);

(b) When the deprivation of liberty results from the exercise of the rights or freedoms guaranteed by articles 7, 13-14 and 18-21 of the Universal Declaration of Human Rights and, insofar as States parties are concerned, by articles 12, 18-19, 21-22 and 25-27 of the International Covenant on Civil and Political Rights (category II);

(c) When the total or partial non-observance of the international norms relating to the right to a fair trial, established in the Universal Declaration of Human Rights and in the relevant international instruments accepted by the States concerned, is of such gravity as to give the deprivation of liberty an arbitrary character (category III);

(d) When asylum seekers, immigrants or refugees are subjected to prolonged administrative custody without the possibility of administrative or judicial review or remedy (category IV);

(e) When the deprivation of liberty constitutes a violation of international law on the grounds of discrimination based on birth, national, ethnic or social origin, language, religion, economic condition, political or other opinion, gender, sexual orientation, disability, or any other status, that aims towards or can result in ignoring the equality of human beings (category V).

IV. Submission and consideration of communications

A. Submission of communications to the Working Group

9. Communications shall be submitted in writing and addressed to the secretariat, giving the family name, first name and address of the sender and (optionally) his or her telephone, telex and telefax numbers or e-mail address.

10. As far as possible, each case shall form the subject of a presentation indicating the circumstances of the arrest or detention and the family name, first name and any other information making it possible to identify the person detained, as well as the latter's legal status, particularly:

(a) The date and place of the arrest or detention or of any other form of deprivation of liberty and the identity of those presumed to have carried it out, together with any other information shedding light on the circumstances in which the person was deprived of liberty;

(b) The reasons given by the authorities for the arrest, detention or deprivation of liberty;

(c) The legislation applied in the case;

(d) The action taken, including investigatory action or the exercise of internal remedies, by the administrative and judicial authorities, as well as the steps taken at the international or regional levels, and the results of such action or the reasons why such measures were ineffective or were not taken;

(e) An account of the reasons why the deprivation of liberty is deemed arbitrary;

(f) A report of all elements presented by the source that aim to inform the Working Group on the full status of the reported situation, such as the beginning of a trial; the granting of provisional or definitive release; and changes of incarceration conditions or venue or of any other similar circumstances. An absence of information or an absence of a response by the source may lead the Working Group to terminate its consideration of the case.

11. In order to facilitate the Working Group's work, it is hoped that communications will be submitted using the model questionnaire available from the Working Group's secretariat. Communications shall not exceed 20 pages and any additional material, including annexes, exceeding that limit may not be taken into account by the Working Group.

12. Communications addressed to the Working Group may be received from the individuals concerned, their families or their representatives. Such communications may also be transmitted by Governments and intergovernmental and non-governmental organizations as well as by national institutions for the promotion and protection of human rights. In dealing with communications, the Working Group will give consideration to articles 9, 10 and 14 of the Code of Conduct for Special Procedures Mandate-Holders of the Human Rights Council.

13. In accordance with the provisions of paragraph 4 of Human Rights Commission resolution 1993/36, the Working Group may, on its own initiative, take up cases that might constitute arbitrary deprivation of liberty.

14. When the Working Group is not in session, the Chair-Rapporteur, or in his or her absence the Vice-Chairs (see para. 3 (c) and (d) above), may decide to bring the case to the attention of the Government.

B. *Consideration of communications*

15. In the interest of ensuring mutual cooperation, communications shall be brought to the attention of the Government and the reply of the latter shall be brought to the attention of the source of the communication for its further comments. They shall be transmitted by the Chair-Rapporteur of the Working Group or, if she or he is not available, by the Vice-Chairs (see para. 3 (c) and (d) above). In the case of Governments, the letter shall be transmitted through the Permanent Representative to the United Nations Office at Geneva. In the letter the Working Group shall request the Government to reply within 60 days, during which appropriate inquiries may be carried out by the Government so as to furnish the Working Group with the fullest possible information. In the letter the Working Group shall also inform the Government that the Working Group is authorized to render an opinion determining whether the reported deprivation of liberty was arbitrary or not. Replies shall not exceed 20 pages and any additional material, including annexes, exceeding that limit may not be taken into account by the Working Group. If a reply is not received from the Government within the time limit, the Working Group may render an opinion on the basis of the information submitted by the source.

16. If the Government desires an extension of the time limit, it shall inform the Working Group of the reasons for requesting one, so that it may be granted a further period of a maximum of one month in which to reply. Even if no reply has been received upon expiry of the time limit set, the Working Group may render an opinion on the basis of all the information it has obtained.

C. *Action taken on communications*

17. In the light of the information obtained, the Working Group shall take one of the following measures:

(a) If the person has been released, for whatever reason, following the referral of the case to the Working Group, the case is filed. The Working Group reserves the right to render an opinion, on a case-by-case basis, whether or not the deprivation of liberty was arbitrary, notwithstanding the release of the person concerned;

(b) If the Working Group considers that the case is not one of arbitrary detention, it shall render an opinion to that effect. The Working Group can also make recommendations in this case if it considers it necessary;

(c) If the Working Group considers that further information is required from the Government or from the source, it may keep the case pending until that information is received;

(d) If the Working Group considers that the arbitrary nature of the detention is established, it shall render an opinion to that effect and make recommendations to the Government.

18. The opinions rendered by the Working Group shall be transmitted to the Government concerned. Forty-eight hours after their transmittal, they shall be communicated to the source. An advance unedited version of the opinion will be published online once the source has been notified.

19. The opinions rendered by the Working Group shall be brought to the attention of the Human Rights Council in its annual report.

20. Governments, sources and other parties should inform the Working Group of the follow-up action taken on the recommendations made by the Working Group in its opinion. This will enable the Working Group to keep the Human Rights Council informed of the progress made and of any difficulties encountered in implementing the recommendations, as well as of any failure to take action.

D. Procedure for review of opinions

21. In exceptional circumstances, the Working Group may *proprio motu* reconsider its opinions if it becomes aware of new facts that, if known at the time of the decision, would have led the Working Group to a different outcome. The Working Group may also reconsider its opinions at the request of the Government concerned or the source under the following conditions:

(a) If the facts on which the request is based are considered by the Working Group to be entirely new and such as to have caused the Working Group to alter its decision had it been aware of them;

(b) If the facts had not been known or had not been accessible to the party originating the request;

(c) In a case where the request comes from a Government, on condition that the latter has observed the time limit for reply referred to in paragraphs 15-16 above;

V. Urgent action procedure

22. A procedure known as "urgent action" may be resorted to in the following cases:

(a) In cases in which there are sufficiently reliable allegations that a person is being arbitrarily deprived of his or her liberty and that the continuation of such deprivation constitutes a serious threat to that person's health, physical or psychological integrity or even to his or her life;

(b) In cases in which, even when no such threat is alleged to exist, there are particular circumstances that warrant an urgent action.

23. After having transmitted an urgent appeal to the Government, the Working Group may transmit the case through its regular procedure in order to render an opinion on whether the deprivation of liberty was arbitrary or not. Such appeals, which are of a purely humanitarian nature, in no way prejudge any opinion the Working Group may render. The Government is required to respond separately for the urgent action procedure and the regular procedure.

24. The Chair-Rapporteur, or in his or her absence the Vice-Chairs (see para. 3 (c) and (d) above), shall transmit the appeal by the most rapid means to the Minister for Foreign Affairs through the Permanent Mission of the country concerned.

VI. Country visits

25. For the purposes of completing its task, the Working Group frequently pays visits on official mission. The visits are prepared in collaboration with the Government, the United Nations agencies in the field and civil society representatives. The visits are an opportunity

for the Working Group to engage in direct dialogue with the Government concerned and with representatives of civil society, with the aim of better understanding the situation of deprivation of liberty in the country and the underlying reasons for arbitrary detention. An important part of these missions are visits to detention centres, including penitentiaries, prisons, police stations, detention centres for migrants and psychiatric hospitals.

26. When the Working Group receives an invitation from a Government to conduct a country visit, it responds by inviting the Permanent Representative of the State to the United Nations Office at Geneva to a meeting to determine the dates and terms of the visit. The secretariat of the Working Group initiates a dialogue with the parties involved in the visit with a view to taking all practical measures to facilitate the mission. The preparation for the visit is conducted in close cooperation with diplomatic authorities of the host country and United Nations agencies.

27. The Government must assure the Working Group that, during the visit, the Working Group will have the opportunity to conduct meetings with the highest authorities of the branches of the State (political, administrative, legislative and judicial authorities), that it will be able to visit penitentiaries, prisons, police stations, immigration detention centres, military prisons, detention centres for juveniles and psychiatric hospitals and that it will be able to meet with all the authorities and officials who affect the personal liberty of persons subjected to the jurisdiction of the host State. The Working Group shall also conduct meetings with international bodies and agencies as well as with non-governmental organizations, lawyers, bar associations and other professional associations of interest, national human rights institutions, diplomatic and consular representatives and religious authorities. Absolute confidentiality shall be guaranteed during the interviews between the Working Group and persons deprived of their liberty. The Government shall guarantee there will be no reprisals against persons interviewed by the Working Group.

28. The Working Group shall conduct at least two visits per year, and its delegation will be composed of at least two of its members.

29. At the end of its visit, the Working Group shall submit a preliminary statement to the Government, informing it about its preliminary findings. It shall inform the public of its findings by means of a press conference after debriefing the Government.

30. A report shall be prepared by the Working Group, and once adopted it shall be communicated to the Government of the country visited with a view to gathering its observations on factual and legal errors. The final report shall take into consideration the observations of the Government. It shall be published as an addendum to the annual report.

31. During the visit, members of the Working Group shall respect the legislation of the host country.

32. Two years after its visit, the Working Group shall request the Government to present a report on the implementation of the recommendations formulated in the mission report. All of the stakeholders involved in the visit shall be informed during the follow-up procedure and shall submit their observations. If necessary, the Working Group shall request a follow-up visit to the country concerned.

VII. Coordination with other human rights mechanisms

33. In order to strengthen the good coordination that already exists between the various United Nations bodies working in the field of human rights (see Commission on Human Rights resolution 1997/50, para. 1 (b)), the Working Group takes action as follows:

(a) If the Working Group, while examining allegations of violations of human rights, considers that the allegations could be more appropriately dealt with by another working group or special rapporteur, it will refer the allegations to the relevant working group or special rapporteur within whose competence they fall, for appropriate action;

(b) If the Working Group receives allegations of violations of human rights that fall within its competence as well as within the competence of another thematic mechanism, it may consider taking appropriate action jointly with the working group or special rapporteur concerned;

(c) If communications concerning a country for which the Human Rights Council has appointed a special rapporteur, or another appropriate mechanism with reference to that country, are referred to the Working Group, the latter, in consultation with the rapporteur or the person responsible, shall decide on the action to be taken;

(d) If a communication addressed to the Working Group is concerned with a situation that has already been referred to another body, action shall be taken as follows:

(i) If the function of the body to which the matter has been referred is to deal with the general development of human rights within its area of competence (e.g. most of the special rapporteurs, representatives of the Secretary-General, independent experts), the Working Group shall retain competence to deal with the matter;

(ii) However, if the body to which the matter has already been referred has the function of dealing with individual cases (e.g. the Human Rights Committee and other treaty bodies), the Working Group shall transmit the case to that other body if the person and facts involved are the same.

34. The Working Group shall not make visits to countries for which the Human Rights Council has already appointed a country rapporteur or another appropriate mechanism with reference to that country, unless the special rapporteur or the person responsible considers the visit by the Working Group to be useful.

Appendix 2. Model Questionnaire to be Completed by Persons Alleging Arbitrary Arrest or Detention[1]

Copyright © 2018 United Nations. Reprinted with the permission of the United Nations.

I. IDENTITY

1. Family name: . . . .
2. First name: . . . .
3. Sex: (Male) (Female)
4. Birth date or age (at the time of detention): . . . .
5. Nationality/Nationalities:
6. (a) Identity document (if any): . . . .
   (b) Issued by: . . . .
   (c) On (date): . . . .
   (d) No.: . . . .
7. Profession and/or activity (if believed to be relevant to the arrest/detention):
   . . . .
8. Address of usual residence:
   . . . .
   . . . .

II. Arrest[2]

1. Date of arrest:
2. Place of arrest (as detailed as possible):
   . . . .
   . . . .
   . . . .
   . . . .
   . . . .

---

[1] *This questionnaire should be addressed to the Working Group on Arbitrary Detention. Office of the High Commissioner for Human Rights, United Nations Office at Geneva, 8-14 avenue de la Paix, 1211 Geneva 10, Switzerland, fax No.(41) (0) 22 917.90.06, E-mail: wgad@ohchr.org; and, urgent-action@ohchr.org. A separate questionnaire must be completed for each case of alleged arbitrary arrest or detention. As far as possible, all details requested should be given. Nevertheless, failure to do so will not necessarily result in inadmissibility of the communication.*

[2] For the purpose of this questionnaire, "arrest" refers to the initial act of apprehending a person.

"Detention" means and includes any deprivation of liberty before, during and after trial. In some cases, only section II or III may be applicable. Nonetheless, whenever possible, both sections should be completed.

3. Forces who carried out the arrest or are believed to have carried it out:

....

....

....

4. Did they show a warrant or other decision by a public authority?
   (Yes)........ (No).........

5. Authority who issued the warrant or decision:

....

....

....

6. Reasons for the arrest imputed by the authorities:

....

....

....

....

....

7. Legal basis for the arrest including relevant legislation applied (if known):

....

....

III. Detention
   1. Date of detention:
   2. Duration of detention (if not known, probable duration):

....

   3. Forces holding the detainee under custody:

....

....

....

   4. Places of detention (indicate any transfer and present place of detention):

....

....

....

   5. Authorities that ordered the detention:

....

....

....

   6. Reasons for the detention imputed by the authorities:

....

....

....

....

....

   7. Legal basis for the detention including relevant legislation applied (if known):

....

....

....

....

IV. Describe the circumstances of the arrest.

V. Indicate reasons why you consider the arrest and/or detention to be arbitrary[3]. Specifically provide details on whether:

(i) The basis for the deprivation of liberty is authorized by the Constitution or the domestic law?

(ii) The reason the individual has been deprived of liberty is a result of the exercise of his or her rights or freedoms guaranteed by articles 7, 13, 14, 18, 19, 20 and 21 of the Universal Declaration of Human Rights and, insofar as States parties are concerned, by articles 12, 18, 19, 21, 22, 25, 26 and 27 of the International Covenant on Civil and Political Rights?

(iii) The international norms relating the right to a fair trial have been totally or partially observed, specifically, articles 9 and 10 of the Universal Declaration of Human Rights and, insofar as States parties are concerned, by articles 9 and 14 of the International Covenant on Civil and Political Rights?

(iv) In the case of an asylum seeker, migrant or refugee who has been subjected to prolonged administrative custody, if he or she has been guaranteed the possibility of administrative or judicial review or remedy?

(v) The individual has been deprived of his or her liberty for reasons of discrimination based on birth; national, ethnic or social origin; language; religion; economic condition; political or other opinion; gender; sexual orientation; or disability or other status which aims towards or can result in ignoring the equality of human rights?

. . . .
. . . .
. . . .
. . . .
. . . .
. . . .
. . . .
. . . .

VI. Indicate internal steps, including domestic remedies, taken especially with the legal and administrative authorities, particularly for the purpose of establishing the detention and, as appropriate, their results or the reasons why such steps or remedies were ineffective or why they were not taken.[4]

. . . .
. . . .
. . . .
. . . .
. . . .

---

[3] Copies of documents that prove the arbitrary nature of the arrest or detention, or help to understand the specific circumstances of the case, as well as any other relevant information, may also be attached to this questionnaire.

[4] Note that the Methods of Work of the Working Group do not require exhaustion of all available domestic remedies for the communication to be admissible for consideration by the Working Group.

VII. Full name, postal and electronic addresses of the person(s) submitting the information (telephone and fax number, if possible).[5]

....

....

....

....

....

....

Date: .... Signature: ....

---

[5] If a case is submitted to the Working Group by anyone other than the victim or his family, such a person or organization should indicate authorization by the victim or his family to act on their behalf. If, however the authorization is not readily available, the Working Group reserves the right to proceed without the authorization. All details concerning the person(s) submitting the information to the Working Group, and any authorization provided by the victim or his family, will be kept confidential.

Appendix 3. UN Basic Principles and Guidelines on Remedies and Procedures on the Right of Anyone Deprived of Their Liberty to Bring Proceedings Before a Court

United Nations

A/HRC/30/37

General Assembly

Distr.: General
6 July 2015

Original: English

Thirtieth session
Agenda item 3
**Promotion and protection of all human rights,
civil, political, economic, social and cultural rights,
including the right to development**

REPORT OF THE WORKING GROUP ON ARBITRARY DETENTION

UNITED NATIONS BASIC PRINCIPLES AND GUIDELINES ON REMEDIES
AND PROCEDURES ON THE RIGHT OF ANYONE DEPRIVED OF THEIR
LIBERTY TO BRING PROCEEDINGS BEFORE A COURT

Summary

The present report is submitted pursuant to Human Rights Council resolution 20/16, in which the Council requested the Working Group on Arbitrary Detention to present to the Council before the end of 2015 draft basic principles and guidelines on remedies and procedures on the right of anyone deprived of his or her liberty by arrest or detention to bring proceedings before a court in order that the court may decide without delay on the lawfulness of his or her detention and order his or her release if the detention is not lawful. The United Nations Basic Principles and Guidelines on Remedies and Procedures on the Right of Anyone Deprived of Their Liberty to Bring Proceedings Before a Court annexed to the present report are based on international law, standards and recognized good practice, and are intended to provide States with guidance on fulfilling, in compliance with international law, their obligation to avoid the arbitrary deprivation of liberty.

1. The right of anyone deprived of his or her liberty to bring proceedings before a court, in order that the court may decide without delay on the lawfulness of his or her detention and obtain appropriate remedies upon a successful challenge, is widely recognized in international and regional human rights instruments, the jurisprudence of the International Court of Justice and of international human rights mechanisms, including in the reports and country visits of treaty bodies and special procedure mandate holders, regional human rights mechanisms, in the domestic law of States and the jurisprudence of national courts.

2. The right to challenge the lawfulness of detention before a court is a self-standing human right, the absence of which constitutes a human rights violation. It is a judicial remedy designed to protect personal freedom and physical integrity against arbitrary arrest, detention, including secret detention, exile, forced disappearance or risk of torture and other cruel, inhuman or degrading treatment or punishment. It is also a means of determining the whereabouts and state of health of detainees and of identifying the authority ordering or carrying out the deprivation of liberty.

3. This judicial remedy is essential to preserve legality in a democratic society. The effective exercise of this fundamental safeguard of personal liberty in all situations of deprivation of liberty, without delay and without exception, resulting in appropriate remedies and reparations, including an entitlement to release upon a successful challenge, must be guaranteed by the State. Numerous international and regional human rights bodies and instruments have articulated a strong position on the non-derogability in any circumstance of the right to bring such proceedings before a court. The Working Group on Arbitrary Detention urges all States to incorporate this position into their national laws. In practice, the absence of inclusive and robust national legal frameworks to ensure the effective exercise of the right to bring proceedings before a court has resulted in a protection gap for persons deprived of their liberty.

4. In this light, the Human Rights Council, in its resolution 20/16, requested the Working Group to present to the Council draft basic principles and guidelines on remedies and procedures on the right of anyone deprived of his or her liberty by arrest or detention to bring proceedings before a court in order that the court may decide without delay on the lawfulness of his or her detention and order his or her release if the detention is not lawful. The Working Group has complied closely with the request of the Council, that it seek the views of States, relevant United Nations agencies, intergovernmental organizations, treaty bodies and, in particular, the Human Rights Committee, other special procedures, national human rights institutions, non-governmental organizations and other stakeholders. In 2013, the Working Group distributed a questionnaire to stakeholders in which it requested details on the right to bring such proceedings in their respective legal framework.

5. The Working Group submitted to the Human Rights Council, at its twenty-seventh session, a thematic report on the international, regional and national legal frameworks on the right to challenge the lawfulness and arbitrariness of detention before court (A/HRC/27/47). In the report, the Working Group documented general practice accepted as law, and further best practices in applying the requirements of international law. States and other stakeholders continued to make submissions up until the final

session, when the document was adopted, adding to the materials available to the Working Group.

6. On 1 and 2 September 2014, the Working Group convened a global consultation in Geneva to bring together experts to elaborate on the scope and content of the right to bring proceedings before a court and to receive without delay appropriate remedies, and to allow stakeholders to contribute to the development of the Basic Principles and Guidelines (see annex). The background paper drew on the thematic report submitted to the Council (A/HRC/27/47) to set out the substantive and procedural obligations of States to ensure the meaningful exercise of the right to bring proceedings before a court and current State practice in implementing each of the obligations, highlighting several examples of good practice.

7. The Basic Principles and Guidelines, drawn from international standards and recognized good practice, are aimed at providing States with guidance on the fundamental principles on which the laws and procedures regulating the right to bring proceedings before a court should be based, and on the elements required for its effective exercise.

8. In the present Basic Principles and Guidelines, the terms "everyone", "anyone" or "any person" denote every human being without discrimination based on race, colour, sex, property, birth, age, national, ethnic or social origin, language, religion, economic condition, political or other opinion, sexual orientation or gender identity, disability or other status, and any ground that aims at or may result in undermining the enjoyment of human rights on a basis of equality. It includes, but is not limited to, girls and boys, soldiers, persons with disabilities, including psychosocial and intellectual disabilities, lesbian, gay, bisexual, transgender and intersex persons, non-nationals, including migrants regardless of their migration status, refugees and asylum seekers, internally displaced persons, stateless persons and trafficked persons and persons at risk of being trafficked, persons accused or convicted of a crime, persons who have or are suspected to have engaged in the preparation, commission or instigation of acts of terrorism, drug users, persons with dementia, human rights defenders and activists, older persons, persons living with HIV/AIDS and other serious communicable or chronic diseases, indigenous peoples, sex workers and minorities based on national or ethnic, cultural, religious and linguistic identity.

9. Deprivation of personal liberty is without free consent. For the purposes of the present Basic Principles and Guidelines, the term "deprivation of liberty" covers the period from the initial moment of apprehension until arrest, pretrial and post-trial detention periods. This includes placing individuals in temporary custody in protective detention or in international or transit zones in stations, ports and airports, house arrest, rehabilitation through labour, retention in recognized and non-recognized centres for non-nationals, including migrants regardless of their migration status, refugees and asylum seekers, and internally displaced persons, gathering centres, hospitals, psychiatric or other medical facilities or any other facilities where they remain under constant surveillance, given that may not only amount to restrictions to personal freedom of movement but also constitute the de facto deprivation of liberty. It also includes detention during armed conflicts and emergency situations, administrative detention for security reasons, and the detention of individuals considered civilian internees under international humanitarian law.

10. In the present Basic Principles and Guidelines, deprivation of liberty is regarded as "arbitrary" in the following cases:

(a) When it is clearly impossible to invoke any legal basis to justify the deprivation of liberty (such as when a person is kept in detention after the completion of his or her sentence, or despite an amnesty law applicable to the detainee, or when a person detained as a prisoner of war, is kept in detention after the cessation of effective hostilities);

(b) When the deprivation of liberty results from the exercise of the rights or freedoms guaranteed by articles 7, 13, 14, 18, 19, 20 and 21 of the Universal Declaration of Human Rights and, insofar as States parties are concerned, by articles 12, 18, 19, 21, 22, 25, 26 and 27 of the International Covenant on Civil and Political Rights;

(c) When the total or partial non-observance of the international norms relating to the right to a fair trial, established in the Universal Declaration of Human Rights and in the relevant international instruments accepted by the State concerned, is of such gravity as to give the deprivation of liberty an arbitrary character;

(d) When asylum seekers, immigrants or refugees are subjected to prolonged administrative custody without the possibility of administrative or judicial review or remedy;

(e) When the deprivation of liberty constitutes a violation of international law for reasons of discrimination based on birth, national, ethnic or social origin, language, religion, economic condition, political or other opinion, gender, sexual orientation, disability or other status, and which is aimed at or may result in ignoring the equality of human rights.

11. In deliberation No. 9 concerning the definition and scope of arbitrary deprivation of liberty under customary international law (see A/HRC/22/44, paras. 37-75), the Working Group restated its constant jurisprudence on the prohibition of all forms of arbitrary deprivation of liberty, and demonstrated that it is general practice accepted as law, constituting customary international law and a peremptory norm (*jus cogens*). In its annual report for 2013 (A/HRC/27/48), the Working Group restated that the prohibition of arbitrariness in the deprivation of liberty requires a strict review of the lawfulness, necessity and proportionality of any measure depriving anyone of their liberty; this standard of review is applicable at all stages of legal proceedings. In the interactive dialogue held at the twenty-second session of the Council, States gave general support for the conclusions of the deliberation. The present Basic Principles and Guidelines adopt the criteria laid out by the International Court of Justice in its judgement of 20 July 2012 concerning Questions relating to the Obligation to Prosecute or Extradite (*Belgium v. Senegal*) when confirming the status of the prohibition of torture as a peremptory norm (*jus cogens*). The prohibition of arbitrary detention is supported by the widespread international practice and on the *opinio juris* of States. It appears in numerous international instruments of universal application and has been introduced into the domestic law of almost all States. Lastly, arbitrary detention is regularly denounced within national and international forums.

12. For the purposes of the present Basic Principles and Guidelines, deprivation of liberty is regarded as "unlawful" when it is not on such grounds and in accordance with

procedures established by law. It refers to both detention that violates domestic law and detention that is incompatible with the Universal Declaration of Human Rights, general principles of international law, customary international law, international humanitarian law, as well as with the relevant international human rights instruments accepted by the States concerned. It also includes detention that may have been lawful at its inception but has become unlawful because the individual has served the entire sentence of imprisonment, following the expiry of the period for which the person was remanded into custody or because the circumstances that initially justified the detention have changed.

13. States employ different models to regulate the exercise of the right to bring proceedings before a court to challenge the arbitrariness and lawfulness of detention and to obtain appropriate remedies without delay. Although no specific model is endorsed in the principles and guidelines, States are encouraged to guarantee this right in law and in practice.

14. The Basic Principles and Guidelines are based on the recognition that States should take a series of measures to establish and/or to reinforce the procedural safeguards provided to persons deprived of their liberty.

15. The Working Group recalls the Preamble to the Charter of the United Nations, which refers to the determination of the peoples of the United Nations "to establish conditions under which justice and respect for the obligations arising from treaties and other sources of international law can be maintained". One of the purposes of the United Nations is "to maintain international peace and security" and, to that end, "to take effective collective measures for the prevention and removal of threats to the peace, and for the suppression of acts of aggression or other breaches of the peace, and to bring about by peaceful means, and in conformity with the principles of justice and international law, adjustment or settlement of international disputes or situations which might lead to a breach of the peace". Furthermore, according to Article 2 of the Charter, "all Members shall give the United Nations every assistance in any action it takes in accordance with the present Charter". The Working Group recalls the reaffirmation in numerous Security Council resolutions, including in resolution 2170 (2014), of the duty of Member States to comply with all their obligations under international law, in particular international human rights, refugee and international humanitarian law, underscoring also that effective counter-terrorism measures and respect for human rights, fundamental freedoms and the rule of law are complementary and mutually reinforcing.

16. Recognizing that certain groups are more vulnerable when deprived of their liberty, the Basic Principles and Guidelines provide specific provisions for women and girls, children, persons with disabilities and non-nationals, including migrants regardless of their migration status, refugees, asylum seekers and stateless persons.

17. The scope of the Basic Principles and Guidelines is distinct from the right of anyone arrested or detained on a criminal charge to be brought promptly before a judge or other judicial authority and tried within a reasonable time or be released.

18. Nothing in the present Basic Principles and Guidelines should be interpreted as providing a lesser degree of protection than that provided under existing national laws and regulations and international and regional human rights conventions or covenants applicable to the liberty and security of person.

ANNEX

BASIC PRINCIPLES AND GUIDELINES ON REMEDIES AND
PROCEDURES ON THE RIGHT OF PERSONS DEPRIVED OF THEIR
LIBERTY TO BRING PROCEEDINGS BEFORE A COURT

I. Principles

Principle 1   Right to be free from arbitrary or unlawful deprivation of liberty

1. Recognizing that everyone has the right to be free from arbitrary or unlawful deprivation of liberty, everyone is guaranteed the right to take proceedings before a court in order that that court may decide on the arbitrariness or lawfulness of the detention, and to obtain without delay appropriate and accessible remedies.

Principle 2   Responsibilities of the State and others

2. National legal systems at the highest possible level, including, where applicable, in the Constitution, must guarantee the right to take proceedings before a court to challenge the arbitrariness and lawfulness of detention and to receive without delay appropriate and accessible remedies. A comprehensive set of applicable procedures shall be enacted to ensure that the right is accessible and effective, including the provision of procedural and reasonable accommodation, for all persons in all situations of deprivation of liberty. The human and financial resources necessary shall be allocated to the administration of the justice system. The right to bring such proceedings before a court must also be protected in private relationships such that the duties apply to international organizations and, under certain circumstances, to non-State actors.

Principle 3   Scope of application

3. Any individual who is deprived of liberty in any situation by or on behalf of a governmental authority at any level, including detention by non-State actors that is authorized by domestic law, has the right to take proceedings before a court in the State's jurisdiction to challenge the arbitrariness and lawfulness of his or her deprivation of liberty and to receive without delay appropriate and accessible remedies. Exerting authority over any form of detention will constitute the effective control over the detention and make the detainee subject to the State's jurisdiction. Involvement in detention will give the State the duty to ensure the detainee's right to bring proceedings before a court.

Principle 4   Non-derogability

4. The right to bring proceedings before a court to challenge the arbitrariness and lawfulness of detention and to obtain without delay appropriate and accessible remedies is not derogable under international law.

5. The right is not to be suspended, rendered impracticable, restricted or abolished under any circumstances, even in times of war, armed conflict or public emergency that threatens the life of the nation and the existence of which is officially proclaimed.

6. The international law review of measures to accommodate practical constraints in the application of some procedural elements of the right to bring proceedings will depend upon the character, intensity, pervasiveness and particular context of the emergency and upon the corresponding proportionality and reasonableness of the derogation. Such measures must not, in their adoption, represent any abuse of power nor have the effect of negating the existence of the right to bring such proceedings before a court.

7. Any such practical measures in the application of the right to bring proceedings before a court to challenge the detention are permitted only to the extent and for the period of time strictly required by the exigencies of the situation, provided that such measures are consistent with the State's other obligations under international law, including provisions of international humanitarian law relating to the deprivation of liberty, and are non-discriminatory.

Principle 5   Non-discrimination

8. The right to bring proceedings before a court to challenge the arbitrariness and lawfulness of detention and to receive without delay appropriate and accessible remedies may be exercised by anyone regardless of race, colour, sex, property, birth, age, national, ethnic or social origin, language, religion, economic condition, political or other opinion, sexual orientation or gender identity, asylum seekingor migration status, or disability or any other status.

Principle 6   The court as reviewing body

9. A court shall review the arbitrariness and lawfulness of the deprivation of liberty. It shall be established by law and bear the full characteristics of a competent, independent and impartial judicial authority capable of exercising recognizable judicial powers, including the power to order immediate release if the detention is found to be arbitrary or unlawful.

Principle 7   Right to be informed

10. Persons deprived of their liberty shall be informed about their rights and obligations under law through appropriate and accessible means. Among other procedural safeguards, this includes the right to be informed, in a language and a means, mode or format that the detainee understands, of the reasons justifying the deprivation of liberty, the possible judicial avenue to challenge the arbitrariness and lawfulness of the deprivation of liberty and the right to bring proceedings before the court and to obtain without delay appropriate and accessible remedies.

Principle 8   Time frame for bringing proceedings before a court

11. The right to bring proceedings before a court without delay to challenge the arbitrariness and lawfulness of the deprivation of liberty and to obtain without delay appropriate and accessible remedies applies from the moment of apprehension and ends with the release of the detainee or the final judgement, depending on the circumstances.

The right to claim remedies after release may not be rendered ineffective by any statute of limitations.

Principle 9   *Assistance by legal counsel and access to legal aid*

12. Persons deprived of their liberty shall have the right to legal assistance by counsel of their choice, at any time during their detention, including immediately after the moment of apprehension. Upon apprehension, all persons shall be promptly informed of this right.

13. Assistance by legal counsel in the proceedings shall be at no cost for a detained person without adequate means or for the individual bringing proceedings before a court on the detainee's behalf. In such cases, effective legal aid shall be provided promptly at all stages of the deprivation of liberty; this includes, but is not limited to, the detainee's unhindered access to legal counsel provided by the legal aid regime.

14. Persons deprived of their liberty shall be accorded adequate time and facilities to prepare their case, including through disclosure of information in accordance with the present Basic Principles and Guidelines, and to freely communicate with legal counsel of their choice.

15. Legal counsel shall be able to carry out their functions effectively and independently, free from fear of reprisal, interference, intimidation, hindrance or harassment. Authorities shall respect the privacy and confidentiality of legal counsel-detainee communications.

Principle 10   *Persons able to bring proceedings before a court*

16. Procedures shall allow anyone to bring proceedings before a court to challenge the arbitrariness and lawfulness of the deprivation of liberty and to obtain without delay appropriate and accessible remedies, including the detainee, his or her legal representative, family members or other interested parties, whether or not they have proof of the consent of the detainee.

17. No restrictions may be imposed on the detainee's ability to contact his or her legal representative, family members or other interested parties.

Principle 11   *Appearance of the detainee before the court*

18. The court should guarantee the physical presence of the detainee before it, especially for the first hearing of the challenge to the arbitrariness and lawfulness of the deprivation of liberty and every time that the person deprived of liberty requests to appear physically before the court.

Principle 12   *Equality before the courts*

19. The proceedings shall be fair and effective in practice, and the parties to the proceedings in question shall be ensured the right to equal access to present their full case, and equality of arms, and be treated without any discrimination before the courts.

20. Every individual deprived of liberty shall be guaranteed the right to have access to all material related to the detention or presented to the court by State authorities to

preserve the equality of arms. The requirement that the same procedural rights be provided to all parties is subject only to distinctions that are based on the law and can be justified on objective, reasonable grounds not entailing actual disadvantage or other unfairness to the detained person.

Principle 13   Burden of proof

21. In every instance of detention, the burden of establishing the legal basis and the reasonableness, necessity and proportionality of the detention lies with the authorities responsible for the detention.

Principle 14   Standard of review

22. No restriction may be imposed on the court's authority to review the factual and legal basis of the arbitrariness and lawfulness of the deprivation of liberty.

23. The court shall consider all available evidence that has a bearing on the arbitrariness and lawfulness of detention, namely, the grounds justifying the detention, and its necessity and proportionality to the aim sought in view of the individual circumstances of the detainee, and not merely its reasonableness or other lower standards of review.

24. In order to determine that a case of deprivation of liberty is non-arbitrary and lawful, the court shall be satisfied that the detention was carried out on grounds and according to procedures prescribed by national law and that are in accordance with international standards, and that, in particular, it was and remains non-arbitrary and lawful under both national and international law.

Principle 15   Remedies and reparations

25. Any person arbitrarily or unlawfully detained is guaranteed access to effective remedies and reparations capable of providing restitution, compensation, rehabilitation, satisfaction and guarantees of non-repetition. Reparations should be adequate, effective and prompt. States shall undertake prompt, effective and impartial investigations wherever there is reasonable ground to believe that detention has been arbitrary. The duty applies in any territory under a State's jurisdiction or wherever the State exercises effective control, or otherwise as the result of its actions or omissions of its servants. The right to reparation cannot be rendered ineffective by amnesties, immunities, statutes of limitations or other defence of the State.

26. Where a court determines that the deprivation of liberty is arbitrary or unlawful, it shall order a conditional or unconditional release from detention. Relevant authorities shall give immediate effect to any order for release.

Principle 16   Exercise of the right to bring proceedings before a court in situations of armed conflict, public danger or other emergency threatening the independence or security of a State

27. All detained persons in a situation of armed conflict as properly characterized under international humanitarian law, or in other circumstances of public danger or other emergency that threatens the independence or security of a State, are guaranteed

the exercise of the right to bring proceedings before a court to challenge the arbitrariness and lawfulness of the deprivation of liberty and to receive without delay appropriate and accessible remedies. This right and corresponding procedural guarantees complement and mutually strengthen the rules of international humanitarian law.

28. Domestic legislative frameworks should not allow for any restriction on the safeguards of persons deprived of their liberty concerning the right to bring proceedings before a court under counter-terrorism measures, emergency legislation or drug-related policies.

29. A State that detains a person in a situation of armed conflict as properly character-ized under international humanitarian law, or in other circumstances of public danger or other emergency that threatens the independence or security of a State, has by definition that person within its effective control, and thus within its jurisdiction, and shall therefore guarantee the exercise of the right of the detainee to bring proceedings before a court to challenge the arbitrariness or lawfulness of the deprivation of liberty and to receive without delay appropriate and accessible remedies. Reconsideration, appeal or periodic review of decisions to intern or place in assigned residence alien civilians in the territory of a party to an international armed conflict, or civilians in an occupied territory, shall comply with the present Basic Principles and Guidelines, including Basic Principle 6 on the court as reviewing body.

30. Prisoners of war should be entitled to bring proceedings before a court to challenge the arbitrariness and lawfulness of the deprivation of liberty and to receive without delay appropriate and accessible remedies, where the detainee (a) challenges his or her status as a prisoner of war; (b) claims to be entitled to repatriation or transfer to a neutral State if seriously injured or ill; or (c) claims not to have been released or repatriated without delay following the cessation of active hostilities.

31. Administrative detention or internment in the context of a non-international armed conflict may only be permitted in times of public emergency threatening the life of the nation and the existence of which is officially proclaimed. Any consequent deviation from procedural elements of the right to bring proceedings before a court to challenge the arbitrariness and lawfulness of the deprivation of liberty and to receive without delay appropriate and accessible remedies must be in conformity with the present Basic Principles and Guidelines, including on the principles of non-derogability, the right to be informed and the court as reviewing body, and the guidelines on equality of arms and burden of proof.

32. During armed conflict, the deprivation of the liberty of children must only be a measure of last resort and for the shortest period of time. Basic legal safeguards must be provided in all circumstances, including for children deprived of liberty for their protec-tion or rehabilitation, particularly if detained by military or security services. Safeguards include the right to legal assistance and a periodic review of the legality of the deprivation of their liberty by a court. The child has the right to have the deprivation of liberty acknowledged by the authorities and to communicate with relatives and friends.

Principle 17   Specific obligations to guarantee access to the right to bring proceedings before a court

33. The adoption of specific measures are required under international law to ensure meaningful access to the right to bring proceedings before a court to challenge the

arbitrariness and lawfulness of detention and to receive without delay appropriate and accessible remedies by certain groups of detainees. This includes – but is not limited to children – women (in particular pregnant and breastfeeding women), older persons, persons detained in solitary confinement or other forms of incommunicado detention of restricted regimes of confinement, persons with disabilities, including psychosocial and intellectual disabilities, persons living with HIV/AIDS and other serious communicable or contagious diseases, persons with dementia, drug users, indigenous persons, sex workers, lesbian, gay, bisexual, transgender and intersex persons, minorities as based on national or ethnic, cultural, religious or linguistic identity, non-nationals, including migrants regardless of their migration status, asylum seekers and refugees, internally displaced persons, stateless persons and trafficked persons or persons at risk of being trafficked.

Principle 18   *Specific measures for children*

34. Children may only be deprived of their liberty as a measure of last resort and for the shortest possible period of time. The right of the child to have his or her best interests taken as a primary consideration shall be paramount in any decision-making and action taken in relation to children deprived of their liberty.

35. The exercise of the right to challenge the arbitrariness and lawfulness of the detention of children shall be prioritized and accessible, age-appropriate, multidisciplinary, effective and responsive to the specific legal and social needs of children.

36. The authorities overseeing the detention of children shall *ex officio* request courts to review the arbitrariness and lawfulness of their detention. This does not exclude the right of any child deprived of his or her liberty to bring such proceedings before a court in his or her own name or, if it is in his or her best interests, through a representative or an appropriate body.

Principle 19   *Specific measures for women and girls*

37. Appropriate and tailored measures shall be taken into account in the provision of accessibility and reasonable accommodation to ensure the ability of women and girls to exercise their right to bring proceedings before a court to challenge the arbitrariness and lawfulness of detention and to receive without delay appropriate and accessible remedies. This includes introducing an active policy of incorporating a gender equality perspective into all policies, laws, procedures, programmes and practices relating to the deprivation of liberty to ensure equal and fair access to justice.

Principle 20   *Specific measures for persons with disabilities*

38. Courts, while reviewing the arbitrariness and lawfulness of the deprivation of liberty of persons with disabilities, shall comply with the State's obligation to prohibit involuntary committal or internment on the grounds of the existence of an impairment or perceived impairment, particularly on the basis of psychosocial or intellectual

disability or perceived psychosocial or intellectual disability, as well as with their obligation to design and implement de-institutionalization strategies based on the human rights model of disability. The review must include the possibility of appeal.

39. The deprivation of liberty of a person with a disability, including physical, mental, intellectual or sensory impairments, is required to be in conformity with the law, including international law, offering the same substantive and procedural guarantees available to others and consistent with the right to humane treatment and the inherent dignity of the person.

40. Persons with disabilities are entitled to be treated on an equal basis with others, and not to be discriminated against on the basis of disability. Protection from violence, abuse and ill-treatment of any kind must be ensured.

41. Persons with disabilities are entitled to request individualized and appropriate accommodations and support, if needed, to exercise the right to challenge the arbitrariness and lawfulness of their detention in accessible ways.

Principle 21   Specific measures for non-nationals, including migrants regardless of their migration status, asylum seekers, refugees and stateless persons

42. Non-nationals, including migrants regardless of their status, asylum seekers, refugees and stateless persons, in any situation of deprivation of liberty shall be informed of the reasons for their detention and their rights in connection with the detention order. This includes the right to bring proceedings before a court to challenge the arbitrariness and lawfulness and the necessity and proportionality of their detention, and to receive without delay appropriate and accessible remedies. It also includes the right of the above-mentioned persons to legal assistance in accordance with the basic requirement of prompt and effective provision of legal assistance, in a language that they use and in a means, mode or format they understand, and the right to the free assistance of an interpreter if they cannot understand or speak the language used in court.

43. Irrespective of the body responsible for their detention order, administrative or other, such non-nationals shall be guaranteed access to a court of law empowered to order immediate release or able to vary the conditions of release. They shall promptly be brought before a judicial authority before which they should have access to automatic, regular periodic reviews of their detention to ensure that it remains necessary, proportional, lawful and non-arbitrary. This does not exclude their right to bring proceedings before a court to challenge the lawfulness or arbitrariness of their detention.

44. Proceedings of challenges to decisions regarding immigration detention must be suspensive to avoid expulsion prior to the case-by-case examination of migrants in administrative detention, regardless of their status.

45. The deprivation of liberty as a penalty or punitive sanction in the area of immigration control is prohibited.

46. The deprivation of liberty of an unaccompanied or separated migrant or of an asylum-seeking, refugee or stateless child is prohibited. Detaining children because of their parents' migration status will always violate the principle of the best interests of the child and constitutes a violation of the rights of the child.

II. Guidelines

Guideline 1   Scope of application

47. The right to bring proceedings before a court to challenge the arbitrariness and lawfulness of detention and to receive without delay appropriate and accessible remedies is applicable:

(a) To all situations of deprivation of liberty, including not only to detention for purposes of criminal proceedings but also to situations of detention under administrative and other fields of law, including military detention, security detention, detention under counter-terrorism measures, involuntary confinement in medical or psychiatric facilities, migration detention, detention for extradition, arbitrary arrests, house arrest, solitary confinement, detention for vagrancy or drug addiction, and detention of children for educational purposes;

(b) Irrespective of the place of detention or the legal terminology used in the legislation. Any form of deprivation of liberty on any ground must be subject to effective oversight and control by the judiciary.

Guideline 2   Prescription in national law

48. A strict legality requirement is applicable to both the form of the legal basis and the procedure for its adoption. The legal framework that establishes the process to challenge the arbitrariness and lawfulness of detention shall have a sufficient degree of precision, be drafted in clear and unambiguous language, be realistically accessible and ensure that the exact meaning of the relevant provisions and the consequences of its application are foreseeable to a degree reasonable for the circumstances.

49. Any restriction on liberty must be authorized in national legislation. Depending on the national legal system, restrictions may be based on the Constitution or in the common law. Legislative acts are to be drafted in accordance with the procedural provisions of the Constitution.

Guideline 3   Non-derogability

50. In times of public emergency threatening the life of the nation and the existence of which is officially proclaimed, States may take measures to accommodate practical constraints in the application of some procedural elements of the right to bring proceedings before a court to challenge the arbitrariness and lawfulness of detention and to obtain without delay appropriate and accessible remedies only to the extent strictly required by the exigencies of the situation, provided that:

(a) The court's authority to decide without delay on the arbitrariness and lawfulness of detention, and to order immediate release if the detention is not lawful, is not itself diminished;

(b) The duty of relevant authorities to give immediate effect to an order for release is not diminished;

(c) Such measures are prescribed by law, necessary in the exigencies of the situation (including by virtue of the fact that less restrictive measures would be insufficient to achieve the same purpose), proportionate and non-discriminatory;

(d) Such measures apply temporarily, only for as long as the exigencies of the situation require, and are accompanied by mechanisms to review periodically their continued necessity and proportionality;

(e) Such measures are consistent with ensuring fair, effective and adversarial proceedings;

(f) Such measures are not otherwise inconsistent with international law.

Guideline 4   Characteristics of the court and procedural guidelines for review of the detention

51. The court reviewing the arbitrariness and lawfulness of the detention must be a different body from the one that ordered the detention.

52. The competence, independence and impartiality of such a court should not be undermined by procedures or rules pertaining to the selection and appointment of judges.

53. In undertaking the review of the detention, the court has the authority:

(a) To consider the application as a matter of urgency. Adjudication of the case, including time for preparation of the hearing, should take place as expeditiously as possible, and should not be delayed because of insufficiency of evidence. Delays attributable to the detainee or his or her legal representative do not count as judicial delay;

(b) To ensure the presence of the detainee regardless of whether he or she has asked to appear;

(c) To order immediate release if the detention is found to be arbitrary or unlawful. Any court order of release shall be respected and immediately implemented by the State authorities;

(d) To render and publicize its decision on the arbitrariness and lawfulness of the detention without delay and within established deadlines. In addition to being reasoned and particularized, the court's decision should be clear, precise, complete and sufficient, the contents of which should be made understood in a language and a means, mode or format that the detainee understands. In the event of an unsuccessful challenge, the court, in its decision, must provide reasons for why the individual should remain in detention in the light of the principle that liberty should be the rule and detention the exception. If further restrictions on the liberty of the individual are under consideration, such consideration shall be dealt with in compliance with the principles of international law;

(e) To take measures against the State authorities in control of the detention where the deprivation of liberty is determined to be arbitrary or unlawful and/or the treatment during the deprivation of liberty was found to be abusive.

54. For certain forms of detention, States may, exceptionally, enact legislation regulating proceedings before a specialized tribunal. Such a tribunal:

(a) Must be established by law affording all guarantees of competence, impartiality and the enjoyment of judicial independence in deciding legal matters in proceedings that are judicial in nature;

(b) May only be considered legitimate and legally valid if reasonable and objective criteria justify its existence, that is, there exists a special legal condition and/or vulnerability of the person that requires specific protection by a specialized tribunal. The right to equality before the law and to equal protection of the law without any discrimination does not make all differences of treatment discriminatory. Differentiation based on reasonable and objective criteria does not amount to prohibited discrimination.

55. Military tribunals are not competent to review the arbitrariness and lawfulness of the detention of civilians. Military judges and military prosecutors do not meet the fundamental requirements of independence and impartiality.

Guideline 5   Right to be informed

56. The factual and legal basis for the detention shall be disclosed to the detainee and/or his or her representative without delay so as to provide adequate time to prepare the challenge. Disclosure includes a copy of the detention order, access to and a copy of the case file, in addition to the disclosure of any material in the possession of the authorities or to which they may gain access relating to the reasons for the deprivation of liberty.

57. In any facility where persons are deprived of their liberty, the detaining authorities must inform detainees of their entitlement to bring proceedings and to receive a reasoned and individualized decision without delay, including on how to commence the procedure and potential consequences of voluntarily waiving those rights. Such information should be provided in a manner that is gender- and culture-sensitive and corresponds to the needs of specific groups, including illiterate persons, minorities, persons with disabilities, older persons, indigenous peoples, non-nationals, including migrants regardless of their migration status, refugees, asylum seekers, stateless persons and children. The information shall be provided in a language and a means, mode or format that is accessible and that the said persons understand, taking into account augmentative and alternative means of communications for persons with a mental or physical impairment. In the case of children, information must be provided in a manner appropriate to their age and maturity.

58. Means of verification that a person has actually been informed shall be established. These means may include documentation of the person having been informed by way of printed record, audiotape, videotape or witnesses.

59. The above-mentioned information should also be widely published and made accessible to the general public and to geographically isolated groups and groups marginalized as a result of discriminatory practices. Use should be made of radio and television programmes, regional and local newspapers, the Internet and other means, in particular following any changes to the law or specific issues affecting a community.

Guideline 6   Registers and record-keeping

60. To ensure the accuracy and completeness of registers and adequate case management, and to ensure that State authorities know at all times who is held in their custody or detention facilities, including prisons and any other place of deprivation of liberty:

   (a) All records must contain the following minimum information, disaggregated by sex and age of the detainee:
      (i)   The identity of the person;
      (ii) The date, time and place where the person was deprived of liberty, and the identity of the authority that deprived the person of liberty;
      (iii) The authority that ordered the deprivation of liberty and the grounds for it;
      (iv) The authority responsible for supervising the deprivation of liberty;
      (v)   The place of deprivation of liberty, the date and time of admission to the place of deprivation of liberty, and the authority responsible for the place of deprivation of liberty;
      (vi) Relevant information on the detainee's state of health;
      (vii) In the event of death of the detainee during the deprivation of liberty, the circumstances and cause of death and the destination of the remains;
      (viii) The date and time of release or transfer to another place of detention, the destination and the authority responsible for the transfer;
   (b) Known procedures must be in place to safeguard against unauthorized access or modification of any information contained in the register and/or records of persons deprived of liberty;
   (c) The registers and/or records of persons deprived of liberty shall be made promptly available, upon request, to any judicial or other competent authority or institution authorized for that purpose by the law;
   (d) Known procedures must be in place to release immediately a detainee upon discovery that he or she is continuing to be detained despite having completed serving a sentence or detention order;
   (e) In the event of non-compliance with such requirements, sanctions against the State authorities responsible are necessary.

Guideline 7   Time frame for bringing proceedings before a court

61. To ensure that an individual is not be deprived of his or her liberty without being given an effective opportunity to be heard without delay by a court of law, no substantial waiting period shall exist before a detainee can bring a first challenge to the arbitrariness and lawfulness of detention. Authorities shall facilitate the detainee's right to bring proceedings before a court and immediate access to legal counsel to prepare the detainee's case.

62. Given that circumstances can change and lead to the possibility that a previous legal justification for a detention is no longer applicable, detainees should have the right to challenge their detention periodically.

63. After a court has held that the circumstances justify the detention, the individual is entitled to take proceedings again on similar grounds after an appropriate period of time has passed, depending on the nature of the relevant circumstances.

64. There shall be no substantial waiting period between each application and no waiting period in cases of alleged torture or other ill-treatment, or risk of such treatment, or incommunicado detention, or where the life, health or legal situation of the detainee may be irreversibly damaged.

65. The initiation of the challenge multiple times does not relieve authorities of the obligation to ensure the regular, periodic judicial or other review of the necessity and proportionality of continuing detention, nor exclude the possibility of periodic review by the court *proprio motu.*

66. Where a decision upholding the arbitrariness and lawfulness of detention is subject to appeal in accordance with national legislation, it should be adjudicated upon expeditiously. Any appeals by the State are to be filed within legally defined limits and circumstances.

Guideline 8   *Assistance by legal counsel and access to legal aid*

67. Access shall be provided without delay to legal counsel immediately after the moment of deprivation of liberty and at the latest prior to any questioning by an authority, and thereafter throughout the period of detention. This includes providing detainees with the means to contact legal counsel of their choice.

68. Effective legal aid shall be provided promptly after the time of apprehension in order to ensure that the unaffordable cost of legal counsel does not present a barrier to individuals deprived of their liberty, or his or her representative, without adequate means to bring proceedings before a court.

69. Respect for the confidentiality of communications, including meetings, correspondence, telephone calls and other forms of communications, with legal counsel are to be ensured. Such communications may be held in the sight of officials provided that they are conducted out of their hearing. In the event that confidentiality is broken, any information obtained shall be considered inadmissible as evidence.

70. Access to legal counsel should not be unlawfully or unreasonably restricted. If access to legal counsel is delayed or denied, or detained persons are not adequately informed of their right to assistance by legal counsel in a timely manner, a range of remedies shall be available in accordance with the present Basic Principles and Guidelines.

71. Where the services of legal counsel are not available, every effort shall be made to ensure that services available from suitably qualified legal assistance providers are accessible to detainees under conditions that guarantee the full respect of the rights of detainees as set out in international law and standards.

Guideline 9   *Persons able to bring proceedings before a court*

72. A wider group of individuals with a legitimate interest in the case may bring proceedings before a court, including family members, caregivers or legal guardian of the detainee, State authorities independent of the detaining authority, the ombudsman or national human rights institution, non-governmental organizations, the employer or co-workers.

73. When proceedings are initiated by a person other than the detainee, the court shall make every effort to discover the detained person's will and preferences, and accommodate and support the detained person in participating effectively on his or her own behalf.

74. An informal, cost-free and simplified process to bring such proceedings before a court shall be ensured.

Guideline 10   Appearance before the court

75. To ensure the effectiveness and fairness of proceedings and to strengthen the protection of detainees from other violations, such as torture or other ill-treatment, a court should guarantee the physical presence of the detainee before it, in particular for the first hearing of the challenge to the arbitrariness and lawfulness of the deprivation of liberty and every time that the person deprived of liberty requests to appear physically before the court. This shall be ensured through implementation of the following measures:

(a) Any person deprived of his or her liberty, and not only persons charged with a criminal offence, shall enjoy the right to appear promptly before a court in order to challenge the deprivation of liberty and the conditions of detention, including acts of torture and ill-treatment;

(b) The court shall ensure that the detainee may communicate with the judge without the presence of any official involved in his or her deprivation of liberty;

(c) State authorities having control over the detainee who fail in their obligation to produce without unreasonable delay the detained person before the court, on demand of that person or by court order, should be sanctioned as a matter of criminal and administrative law.

Guideline 11   Equality of arms

76. To ensure that the procedure is guided by the adversarial principle and equality of arms, the following conditions shall be guaranteed in all proceedings, whether of a criminal or non-criminal nature:

(a) Full and complete access by detainees and their legal counsel to the material related to the detention or presented to the court, as well as a complete copy of them;

(b) The ability of detainees to challenge any documents relating to their case file, including all the arguments and material elements adduced by the authorities, including the prosecution, the security apparatus and the immigration authorities, to justify the detention, which may be determinative in establishing the arbitrariness and lawfulness of his or her detention.

Guideline 12   Admissibility of evidence obtained by torture or other prohibited treatment

77. Any statement established to have been made or any other evidence obtained as a result of torture or other cruel, inhuman or degrading treatment shall not be invoked as

evidence in any proceedings, except against a person accused of torture or other prohibited treatment as evidence that the statement was made or that other such acts took place.

Guideline 13   Disclosure of information

78. The detaining authority shall provide all relevant information to the judge, the detainee and/or his or her lawyer. Disclosure is to include exculpatory information, which includes not only information that establishes an accused person's innocence but also other information that could assist the detainee, for example, in arguing that his or her detention is not lawful or that the reasons for his or her detention no longer apply.

79. Sanctions, including criminal penalties, shall be imposed on officials who withhold or refuse to disclose information relevant to the proceedings or who otherwise delay or obstruct proceedings.

80. The disclosure of information may be restricted only if the court concludes that:

(a) A restriction on disclosure is demonstrated to be necessary to pursue a legitimate aim, such as protecting national security, respecting the rights or reputation of another individual or protecting public order, health or morals, as long as such restrictions are non-discriminatory and consistent with relevant standards of international law;

(b) It has been demonstrated that less restrictive measures would be unable to achieve the same result, such as providing redacted summaries of information that clearly point to the factual basis for the detention.

81. Any proposed restriction on the disclosure of information is to be proportionate. An assessment of proportionality requires a balance between how well the non-disclosure protects the legitimate aims being pursued and the negative impact that this will have on the ability of the person to respond to the case or to pursue a challenge to the arbitrariness and lawfulness of detention. If a less restrictive measure is able to achieve the legitimate aim, the more restrictive measure is to be refused.

82. If the authorities refuse to make the disclosure and the court does not have the authority to compel such a disclosure, the court must order the release of the person detained.

Guideline 14   Burden of proof

83. The State authorities shall establish before the court that:

(a) The legal basis for the detention in question is in conformity with international standards;

(b) The detention is justified in accordance with the principles of necessity, reasonableness and proportionality;

(c) Other less intrusive means of achieving the same objectives have been considered in the individual case.

84. The burden of proof must be met in a manner that is known in detail to the detainee, complete with supporting evidence, including those who are defendants in security-related cases.

Guideline 15   *Standard of review*

85. When reviewing the arbitrariness and lawfulness of the detention, the court is empowered:

(a) To examine and act on the elements of inappropriateness, injustice, lawfulness, legality, predictability, and due process of law, and on basic principles of reasonableness, proportionality and necessity. Such an examination will take into account details such as age, gender and marginalized groups;

(b) To consider whether the detention remains justified or whether release is warranted in the light of all the changing circumstances of the detained individual's case, including health, family life, protection claims or other attempts to regularize one's status;

(c) To consider and make a pronouncement on whether alternatives to detention have been considered, including non-custodial alternatives to detention in accordance with the United Nations Standard Minimum Rules for Non-custodial Measures (the Tokyo Rules) and the United Nations Rules on the Treatment of Women Prisoners and Non-custodial Measures for Women Offenders (the Bangkok Rules);

(d) To take into account any orders of detention made subsequent to the commencement of court proceedings and prior to the rendering of the court's decision.

86. When assessing whether the measures taken are in compliance with international standards, the prohibition of particular grounds of detention or forms of detention are to be complied with, and the needs of specific persons affected and any vulnerability are to be taken into consideration, given that the arbitrariness and unlawfulness of detention may include the unsuitability of detention for the persons in question.

Guideline 16   *Remedies and reparations*

87. Judicial orders of release must be executed as soon as they become operative, as continued detention would be considered arbitrary.

88. A copy of the decision finding the detention arbitrary or unlawful is to be transmitted to the person concerned, with notification of the procedures for obtaining reparations. The person has the right to full compensation for material harm, elimination of the consequences of material harm and restoration of all rights that were either denied or infringed.

89. In the event of a detainee's death, the right to compensation in accordance with established procedures falls to the detainee's heirs.

90. The enforceable right to receive compensation for anyone determined to have been arbitrarily or unlawfully detained and for any harm suffered by the person as a result of unlawful deprivation of liberty, irrespective of whether the detaining authorities were responsible for such harm, shall be regulated by comprehensive legislation. Compensation shall also be made available to persons subjected to criminal charges that were subsequently dropped.

91. Compensation out of the public treasury of the State, federal entity or municipality for material damage suffered by a victim of arbitrary of unlawful detention may include earnings, pensions, social benefits and other monies lost as a result of the criminal

prosecution; any property of the victim that was seized or otherwise appropriated by the State on the basis of a conviction or court ruling; compensation for lack of health care, rehabilitation, and accessible and reasonable accommodation in the place of detention; fines and trial costs borne by the victim as a result of the enforcement of the conviction; the victim's legal costs; and other costs.

92. Victims of arbitrary or unlawful detention shall, in accordance with the Basic Principles and Guidelines on the Right to a Remedy and Reparation for Victims of Gross Violations of International Human Rights Law and Serious Violations of International Humanitarian Law, also have an enforceable right before the competent domestic authority to prompt and adequate:

   (a) Restitution;
   (b) Rehabilitation;
   (c) Satisfaction;
   (d) Guarantees of non-repetition.

Guideline 17   Exercise of the right to bring proceedings before a court in situations of armed conflict, public danger or other emergency threatening the independence or security of a State

93. Where persons who have or are suspected to have engaged in the preparation, commission or instigation of acts of terrorism are deprived of their liberty:

(a) They shall be immediately informed of the charges against them, and be brought before a competent and independent judicial authority as soon as possible, within a reasonable period of time;

(b) They shall enjoy the effective right to judicial determination of the arbitrariness and lawfulness of their detention;

(c) The exercise of the right to judicial oversight of their detention shall not impede the obligation of the law enforcement authority responsible for the decision to detain or to maintain the detention to present suspects before a competent and independent judicial authority within a reasonable period of time. Such persons shall be brought before the judicial authority, which will then evaluate the accusations, the basis of the deprivation of liberty and the continuation of the judicial process;

(d) In the proceedings against them, suspects shall have a right to enjoy the necessary guarantees of a fair trial, access to legal counsel and the ability to present exculpatory evidence and arguments under the same conditions as the prosecution, all of which should take place in an adversarial process.

94. Where civilians are detained in relation to an international armed conflict, the following conditions are to be ensured:

(a) Reconsideration of a decision to intern or to place in assigned residence alien civilians in the territory of a party to an international armed conflict, or civilians in an occupied territory, or appeal in the case of internment or assigned residence, must be undertaken "as soon as possible" or "with the least possible delay". While the meaning of these expressions must be determined on a case-by-case basis, any delay in bringing a person before the court or administrative board must not exceed a few days and must be proportional in the particular context;

(b) Although the particular procedures for reconsideration or appeal are to be determined by the detaining or occupying Power, such proceedings must always be undertaken by a court or administrative board that offers the necessary guarantees of independence and impartiality, and the processes of which include and respect fundamental procedural safeguards;

(c) Where decisions to intern or to place a civilian in assigned residence are maintained in accordance with the latter proceedings, internment or residential assignment must be periodically reviewed, at least twice a year. Such a review is to be undertaken by a court or administrative board that offers the necessary guarantees of independence and impartiality, and the processes of which include and respect fundamental procedural safeguards;

95. The right of persons detained as prisoners of war to bring proceedings before court without to delay to challenge the arbitrariness and lawfulness of their detention and to receive appropriate and accessible remedy is to be respected, in order to:

(a) Determine whether a person falls within the category of prisoner of war;

(b) Act as a check to ensure that a seriously injured or ill prisoner of war is repatriated or transferred to a neutral State;

(c) Act as a check to ensure that prisoners of war are released and repatriated without delay after the cessation of active hostilities.

96. With regard to detention in relation to a non-international armed conflict:

(a) Administrative detention or internment may only be permitted in the exceptional circumstance where a public emergency is invoked to justify such detention. In such a case, the detaining State must show that:

    (i) The emergency has risen to a level justifying derogation;

    (ii) Administrative detention is required on the basis of the grounds and procedures prescribed by law of the State in which the detention occurs and is consistent with international law;

    (iii) The administrative detention of the person is necessary, proportionate and non-discriminatory, and the threat posed by that individual cannot be addressed by alternative measures short of administrative detention;

(b) A person subject to administrative detention has the right to bring proceedings before a court that offers the necessary guarantees of independence and impartiality, and the processes of which include and respect fundamental procedural safeguards, including disclosure of the reasons for the detention and the right to defend oneself, including by means of legal counsel;

(c) Where a decision to detain a person subject to administrative detention is maintained, the necessity of the detention must be periodically reviewed by a court or administrative board that offers the necessary guarantees of independence and impartiality, and the processes of which include and respect fundamental procedural safeguards;

(d) Where an internment regime is established, it shall be consistent with international human rights law and international humanitarian law applicable to non-international armed conflict to allow full compliance with the right to bring proceedings before a court.

Guideline 18   *Specific measures for children*

97. Diversion and alternative measures to the deprivation of liberty, where appropriate, are to be used and given priority. The right to legal and other appropriate assistance is to be ensured so that deprivation of liberty is a measure of last resort and only applied for the shortest appropriate period of time.

98. A safe, child-sensitive environment should be established for children deprived of their liberty. Detained children should be treated with dignity and respect, and in a manner that takes into account any element leading to vulnerability, in particular with regard to girls, younger children, children with disabilities, non-nationals, including migrants regardless of their migration status, refugees and asylum-seeking children, stateless children, trafficked children or children at risk of being trafficked, children from minority, ethnic or indigenous groups and lesbian, gay, bisexual, transgender or intersex children.

99. Effective mechanisms shall be in place to verify the age of persons deprived of their liberty. Assessments are to be conducted in a scientific, safe, child- and gender-sensitive and fair manner, avoiding any risk of violation of the physical and psychological integrity of the child, and giving due respect to human dignity. Prior to the outcome of an assessment, individuals should be accorded the benefit of the doubt such that they are treated as a child. In the event of remaining uncertainty following the outcome of an assessment such that there is a possibility that the individual is a child, she or he should be treated as a child.

100. To ensure that children have prompt and effective access to an independent and child-sensitive process to bring proceedings before a court to challenge the arbitrariness and lawfulness of their detention and to receive without delay appropriate and accessible remedies, the following specific measures shall be enacted:

(a) All legislation, policies and practices related to children deprived of liberty and their right to bring proceedings before a court are guided by the right of the child to have his or her best interests taken as a primary consideration;

(b) Legal or other appropriate assistance, including interpretation, is provided to children deprived of liberty free of charge in all proceedings;

(c) Children who are deprived of their liberty for any reason are able to contact their parents or guardians immediately and are able to consult freely and in full confidentiality with them. It is prohibited to interview such a child in the absence of his or her legal counsel, and parent or guardian, when available;

(d) Information on rights is to be provided in a manner appropriate for the child's age and maturity, in a language and a means, mode or format that the child can understand and in a manner that is gender- and culture-sensitive. The said information should in addition be provided to parents, guardians or caregivers of the child;

(e) Any child deprived of his or her liberty has the right to bring a complaint in his or her own name or, if it is in his or her best interests, through a representative or an appropriate body. Children are to be allowed to be heard either directly or through a representative or an appropriate body in any proceedings. Wherever possible, children should have the opportunity to be heard directly. If children choose to be heard through a representative, steps are to be taken to ensure that their views are transmitted correctly to the competent body and that the representative is aware that he or she represents exclusively the interests of the child;

(f) National laws should stipulate measures aimed at the prevention of ill-treatment or intimidation of a child who brings or has brought such a complaint, and should provide for sanctions against persons in violation of such laws;

(g) The child has the right to have the matter determined in the presence of his or her parents or legal guardian, unless such an arrangement is not considered to be in the best interests of the child. In cases of conflict of interest, courts and relevant complaint mechanisms should be empowered to exclude parents and/or legal representatives from proceedings and to appoint an ad hoc legal guardian to represent a child's interests;

(h) Each case from the outset is to be handled expeditiously, without any unnecessary delay. Decisions are to be rendered as soon as possible, and no later than two weeks after a challenge has been made;

(i) The privacy and personal data of a child who is or who has been involved in judicial or non-judicial proceedings and other interventions should be protected at all stages, and such protection should be guaranteed by law. This generally implies that no information or personal data may be made available or published by the competent authorities that could reveal or indirectly enable the disclosure of the child's identity, including images of the child, detailed descriptions of the child or the child's family, names or addresses of the child's family members and audio and video records.

Guideline 19 *Specific measures for women and girls*

101. Applicable and appropriate measures shall be taken to provide accessibility and reasonable accommodation ensuring the right of all women and girls to equal and fair access of the right to bring proceedings before a court to challenge the arbitrariness and lawfulness of detention and to receive without delay appropriate and accessible remedies. These measures include:

(a) Introducing an active policy of incorporating a gender equality perspective into all policies, laws, procedures, programmes and practices that are designed to protect the rights and specific status and distinct needs of women and girls who are subject to the deprivation of their liberty;

(b) Taking active steps to ensure that, where possible, persons who possess education, training, skills and experience in the gender-specific needs and rights of women are available to provide legal aid, advice and court support services in all legal proceedings to female detainees.

102. The practice of keeping girls and women in detention for the purpose of protecting them from risks of serious violence (protective custody) should be eliminated. Alternative measures are to ensure the protection of women and girls without jeopardizing their liberty.

Guideline 20   Specific measures for persons with disabilities

103. The involuntary committal or internment of persons on the grounds of the existence of an impairment or perceived impairment, particularly on the basis of psychosocial or intellectual disability or perceived psychosocial or intellectual disability, is prohibited. States shall take all necessary legislative, administrative and judicial measures to prevent and remedy involuntary committals or internments based on disability.

104. Where a person with a disability is deprived of his or her liberty through any process, that person is, on an equal basis with others, entitled to guarantees in accordance with international human rights law, necessarily including the right to liberty and security of person, reasonable accommodation and humane treatment in accordance with the objectives and principles of the highest standards of international law pertaining to the rights of persons with disabilities.

105. A mechanism complete with due process of law guarantees shall be established to review cases of placement in any situation of deprivation of liberty without specific, free and informed consent. Such reviews are to include the possibility of appeal.

106. Measures shall be taken to ensure accessibility and the provision of reasonable accommodation to persons with disabilities in their place of deprivation of liberty, including the following guarantees:

(a) Persons with a physical, mental, psychosocial, intellectual or sensory disability deprived of their liberty are to be treated with humanity and respect, and in a manner that takes into account their needs by the provision of reasonable accommodation in order to facilitate their effective procedural performance;

(b) All health and support services, including all mental health-care services, are to be provided based on the free and informed consent of the person concerned. The denial of legal capacity of persons with disabilities and detention in institutions against their will, without their consent or with the consent of a substituted decision-maker constitutes arbitrary deprivation of liberty in violation of international law. Perceived or actual deficits in mental capacity, namely, the decision-making skills of a person that naturally vary from one to another, may not be used as justification for denying legal capacity, understood as the ability to hold rights and duties (legal standing) and to exercise those rights and duties (legal agency);

(c) Persons with disabilities are to have access to, on an equal basis with other persons subject to detention, the physical environment, information and communications, and other facilities provided by the detaining authority. Accordingly, all relevant measures are to be taken, including the identification and removal of obstacles and barriers to access so that persons with disabilities who are deprived of their liberty may live independently and participate fully in all aspects of daily life in their place of deprivation of liberty;

(d) Accessibility should also take into account the gender and age of persons with disabilities, and equal access should be provided regardless of the type of impairment, legal status, social condition, gender and age of the detainee;

(e) Persons with disabilities shall be provided with legal or other appropriate support, including interpretation and peer support mechanisms, so that individuals receiving services in mental health facilities or residential facilities of any kind may be informed about their rights and remedies under domestic and international law, including those contained in the present Basic Principles and Guidelines, and organizations may act on behalf of those detained against their will.

107. The following measures shall be taken to ensure procedural accommodation and the provision of accessibility and reasonable accommodation for the exercise of the substantive rights of access to justice and equal recognition before the law:

(a) Persons with disabilities shall be informed about, and provided access to, promptly and as required, appropriate support to exercise their legal capacity with respect to proceedings related to the detention and in the detention setting itself. Support in the exercise of legal capacity is to respect the rights, will and preferences of persons with disabilities and should never amount to substituted decision-making;

(b) Persons with psychosocial disabilities are to be given the opportunity to stand trial promptly, with support and accommodations as may be needed, rather than declaring such persons incompetent;

(c) Persons with disabilities are to have access, on an equal basis with other persons subject to detention, to buildings in which law enforcement agencies and the judiciary are located. Jurisdictional entities must ensure that their services include information and communication that is accessible to persons with disabilities. Appropriate measures shall be taken to provide signage in Braille and in easy to read and understand forms of live assistance and intermediaries, including guides, readers and professional sign language interpreters, to facilitate accessibility to communication in the facilities of jurisdictional entities;

(d) Individuals who are currently detained in a psychiatric hospital or similar institution and/or subjected to forced treatment, or who may be so detained or forcibly treated in the future, must be informed about ways in which they may effectively and promptly secure their release, including injunctive relief;

(e) Injunctive relief should consist in an order requiring the facility to release the person immediately and/or to cease immediately any forced treatment and any systemic measures, such as those requiring mental health facilities to unlock their doors and to inform persons of their right to leave, and establishing a public authority to provide for access to housing, means of subsistence and other forms of economic and social support in order to facilitate de-institutionalization and the right to live independently and be included in the community. Such assistance programmes should not be centred on the provision of mental health services or treatment, but free or affordable community-based services, including alternatives that are free from medical diagnosis and interventions. Access to medications and assistance in withdrawing from medications should be made available for those who so decide;

(f) Persons with disabilities are provided with compensation, as well as other forms of reparations, in the case of arbitrary or unlawful deprivation of liberty. The said compensation is also to take into account the damage caused by lack of accessibility, denial of reasonable accommodation or lack of health care and rehabilitation that have affected persons with a disability deprived of liberty.

Guideline 21   Specific measures for non-nationals, including migrants regardless of their migration status, asylum seekers, refugees and stateless persons

108. Any restrictions on the liberty of non-nationals, including migrants regardless of their migration status, asylum seekers, refugees and stateless persons, is to be a measure of last resort, necessary and proportionate, and imposed only where less restrictive alternatives have been considered and been found to be inadequate to meet legitimate purposes.

109. All individuals who find themselves in the territory or subject to the State's jurisdiction shall be guaranteed effective and free access to the courts of law. This includes the right:

(a) To be informed orally and in writing of the reasons for detention, and on the rights of persons in detention, including the right to challenge the arbitrariness and lawfulness of detention, in a language, means, mode or format that the person detained understands. This may require the provision of information through qualified interpreters and translators at no cost to the detainee and the publicizing of information, including through posters and television monitors in places of detention;

(b) To bring proceedings, either personally or through a representative, before a court to challenge the necessity, proportionality, arbitrariness and lawfulness of detention and to receive without delay appropriate and accessible remedies;

(c) To contact, and be contacted by, any interested parties that might be able to address their needs and to provide them with relevant information or legal assistance, including providing facilities to meet with such persons. This is particularly important where migrant detention facilities are located in remote locations far from population centres. In such situations, mobile courts and video conferencing may be used to gain accessibility to a court of law but do not preclude the right of a detained person to appear in person before a judge.

110. The monitoring of all places of immigration detention and public reporting by relevant United Nations agencies, regional and international human rights mechanisms, national human rights institutions, non-governmental organizations and consular officials (conditional upon request by persons in immigration detention) shall be permitted to ensure that the exercise of the right to bring proceedings before court to challenge the lawfulness and arbitrariness of detention and to receive appropriate remedies is accessible and effective.

111. Decisions regarding the detention of non-nationals are to take into account also the effect of the detention on the physical and mental health of the said persons. When physical and mental security cannot be guaranteed in detention, authorities should provide alternatives to detention.

112. All decisions and actions taken in relation to non-nationals below the age of 18, whether accompanied or unaccompanied, shall be guided by the right of the child to have his or her best interests taken as a primary consideration, and shall accord with the specific protections afforded to children in the present Basic Principles and Guidelines.

113. National legislative frameworks and migration policies shall reflect that the detention of children because of their or their parent's migration status always constitutes a violation of the rights of the child, and contravenes the right of the child to have his or her best interests taken as a primary consideration.

114. Unaccompanied children who are non-nationals shall be informed about their legal status to ensure that they fully understand their situation. Public defence services and/or guardians made available to children are to be adequately trained to work with children, particularly taking into account the extreme vulnerability and need for care, and are to speak a language they understand. Children who are non-nationals should not be placed in detention centres or shelters for migrants, but in non-custodial community-based alternatives to detention, where they may receive all services necessary for their protection, such as adequate nutrition, access to quality education and leisure, care, physical and psychological medical care and security. Special attention should be given to family reunification.

115. In the case of migrants in an irregular situation, the scope of the judicial review should not be confined to a formal assessment of the migrant's current migration status, but also include the possibility of release if detention is determined to be unnecessary, disproportionate, unlawful or arbitrary.

116. In the case of asylum seekers, the scope of judicial review should recognize that there is a right to seek asylum under international law and that, given that it is neither an unlawful nor a criminal act, it cannot be invoked as grounds for their detention. Asylum seekers and refugees are to be protected from penalization for their illegal entry or stay in accordance with international refugee law, including through the use of detention.

Guideline 22   *Implementation measures*

117. Legislative, administrative, judicial and other measures, including through the development of common law principles, shall be adopted to give effect to the present Basic Principles and Guidelines to ensure that the rights and obligations contained in them are always guaranteed in law and practice, including in the event of a public emergency threatening the life of the nation and the existence of which has been officially proclaimed.

118. The above-mentioned measures shall include a review of existing legislative, administrative and other provisions to assess compatibility with the present Basic Principles and Guidelines. The country visits of the Working Group on Arbitrary Detention present an opportunity to engage in direct dialogue with the Government of the State in question and with representatives of civil society with the aim of assisting in the implementation of the principles and guidelines.

119. For the proper implementation of these guarantees, States are encouraged to promote appropriate training for those working in the field of the administration of justice, including police and prison staff. This measure also includes providing training to judges, tribunal and legal officers on how to apply customary international law and rules from the International Convention on Civil and Political Rights, as well as relevant international standards. The Working Group on Arbitrary Detention stands ready to assist in fulfilling this duty of States.

120. Legislation shall be enacted to consider a crime any act or omission that impedes or restricts the right of anyone deprived of his or her liberty to bring proceedings before a court to challenge the arbitrariness and lawfulness of detention and to receive without delay appropriate and accessible remedies.

121. Violations of the rights enshrined in the present Basic Principles and Guidelines shall be investigated, prosecuted and punished.

122. The present Basic Principles and Guidelines shall be widely disseminated, including to justice sector actors, the community and to national human rights institutions, national preventative mechanisms, statutory oversight authorities and other institutions or organizations with a mandate to provide accountability, oversight or inspections to places of deprivation of liberty. Accessible formats for the mentioned dissemination must also be considered. The Office of the High Commissioner is respectfully requested to further the dissemination of the Basic Principles and Guidelines.

Index

Printed in the United States
By Bookmasters